D1285002

Contents

Preface   2

Initiating the Marketing Process   3
Creating Customer Relationships and Value through Marketing   4
Developing Successful Organizational and Marketing Strategies   24
Appendix: Building an Effective Marketing Plan   50
Understanding the Marketing Environment, Ethical Behavior, and Social Responsibility   64

Understanding Buyers and Markets   89
Understanding Consumer Behavior   90
Understanding Organizations as Customers   118
Understanding and Reaching Global Consumers and Markets   138

Targeting Marketing Opportunities   165
Marketing Research: From Customer Insights to Actions   166
Market Segmentation, Targeting, and Positioning   194

Satisfying Marketing Opportunities   219
Developing New Products and Services   220
Managing Successful Products, Services, and Brands   250
Pricing Products and Services   280
Managing Marketing Channels and Supply Chains   306
Retailing and Wholesaling   332
Integrated Marketing Communications and Direct Marketing   358
Advertising, Sales Promotion, and Public Relations   382
Using Social Media to Connect with Consumers   410
Personal Selling and Sales Management   436
Implementing Interactive and Multichannel Marketing   460
Appendix: Planning a Career in Marketing   483
Company/Product Index   496
Subject Index   502
Endsheets   528
Glossary   530
Name Index   537

Online Supplements   543

Connect Online Access for Marketing: The Core, Sixth Edition   544
Access Code for the Online Supplements   545

Course MARKETING: THE CORE
SIXTH EDITION
ROGER KERIN & STEVEN HARTLEY

http://create.mheducation.com

ISBN-10: 1308880987   ISBN-13: 9781308880983

Credits

Preface: *Chapter from Marketing: The Core, Sixth Edition by Kerin, Hartley, 2016*   2

Initiating the Marketing Process   3

Creating Customer Relationships and Value through Marketing: *Chapter 1 from Marketing: The Core, Sixth Edition by Kerin, Hartley, 2016*   4

Developing Successful Organizational and Marketing Strategies: *Chapter 2 from Marketing: The Core, Sixth Edition by Kerin, Hartley, 2016*   24

Appendix: Building an Effective Marketing Plan: *Chapter A from Marketing: The Core, Sixth Edition by Kerin, Hartley, 2016*   50

Understanding the Marketing Environment, Ethical Behavior, and Social Responsibility: *Chapter 3 from Marketing: The Core, Sixth Edition by Kerin, Hartley, 2016*   64

Understanding Buyers and Markets   89

Understanding Consumer Behavior: *Chapter 4 from Marketing: The Core, Sixth Edition by Kerin, Hartley, 2016*   90

Understanding Organizations as Customers: *Chapter 5 from Marketing: The Core, Sixth Edition by Kerin, Hartley, 2016*   118

Understanding and Reaching Global Consumers and Markets: *Chapter 6 from Marketing: The Core, Sixth Edition by Kerin, Hartley, 2016*   138

Targeting Marketing Opportunities   165

Marketing Research: From Customer Insights to Actions: *Chapter 7 from Marketing: The Core, Sixth Edition by Kerin, Hartley, 2016*   166

Market Segmentation, Targeting, and Positioning: *Chapter 8 from Marketing: The Core, Sixth Edition by Kerin, Hartley, 2016*   194

Satisfying Marketing Opportunities   219

Developing New Products and Services: *Chapter 9 from Marketing: The Core, Sixth Edition by Kerin, Hartley, 2016*   220

Managing Successful Products, Services, and Brands: *Chapter 10 from Marketing: The Core, Sixth Edition by Kerin, Hartley, 2016*   250

Pricing Products and Services: *Chapter 11 from Marketing: The Core, Sixth Edition by Kerin, Hartley, 2016*   280

Managing Marketing Channels and Supply Chains: *Chapter 12 from Marketing: The Core, Sixth Edition by Kerin, Hartley, 2016*   306

Retailing and Wholesaling: *Chapter 13 from Marketing: The Core, Sixth Edition by Kerin, Hartley, 2016*   332

Integrated Marketing Communications and Direct Marketing: *Chapter 14 from Marketing: The Core, Sixth Edition by Kerin, Hartley, 2016*   358

Advertising, Sales Promotion, and Public Relations: *Chapter 15 from Marketing: The Core, Sixth Edition by Kerin, Hartley, 2016* 382

Using Social Media to Connect with Consumers: *Chapter 16 from Marketing: The Core, Sixth Edition by Kerin, Hartley, 2016* 410

Personal Selling and Sales Management: *Chapter 17 from Marketing: The Core, Sixth Edition by Kerin, Hartley, 2016* 436

Implementing Interactive and Multichannel Marketing: *Chapter 18 from Marketing: The Core, Sixth Edition by Kerin, Hartley, 2016* 460

Appendix: Planning a Career in Marketing: *Chapter B from Marketing: The Core, Sixth Edition by Kerin, Hartley, 2016* 483

Company/Product Index: *Chapter from Marketing: The Core, Sixth Edition by Kerin, Hartley, 2016* 496

Subject Index: *Chapter from Marketing: The Core, Sixth Edition by Kerin, Hartley, 2016* 502

Endsheets: *Chapter from Marketing: The Core, Sixth Edition by Kerin, Hartley, 2016* 528

Glossary: *Chapter from Marketing: The Core, Sixth Edition by Kerin, Hartley, 2016* 530

Name Index: *Chapter from Marketing: The Core, Sixth Edition by Kerin, Hartley, 2016* 537

Online Supplements 543

Connect Online Access for Marketing: The Core, Sixth Edition: *Media by Kerin* 544

Access Code for the Online Supplements 545

PREFACE

Marketing: The Core utilizes a unique, innovative, and effective pedagogical approach developed by the authors through the integration of their combined classroom, college, and university experiences. The elements of this approach have been the foundation for each edition of *Marketing: The Core* and serve as the core of the text and its supplements as they evolve and adapt to changes in student learning styles, the growth of the marketing discipline, and the development of new instructional technologies. The distinctive features of the approach are illustrated below:

High-Engagement Style
Easy-to-read, high-involvement, interactive writing style that engages students through active learning techniques.

Rigorous Framework
A pedagogy based on the use of learning objectives, learning reviews, learning objectives reviews, and supportive student supplements.

Personalized Marketing
A vivid and accurate description of businesses, marketing professionals, and entrepreneurs—through cases, exercises, and testimonials—that allows students to personalize marketing and identify possible career interests.

Marketing: The Core 6/e Pedagogical Approach

Traditional and Contemporary Coverage
Comprehensive and integrated coverage of traditional and contemporary marketing concepts.

Integrated Technology
The use of powerful technical resources and learning solutions, such as Connect, LearnSmart, SmartBook, www.kerinmarketing.com, and Video links.

Marketing Decision Making
The use of extended examples, cases, and videos involving people making marketing decisions.

The goal of the 6th edition of *Marketing: The Core* is to create an exceptional experience for today's students and instructors of marketing. The development of *Marketing: The Core* was based on a rigorous process of assessment, and the outcome of the process is a text and package of learning tools that are based on *engagement*, *leadership*, and *innovation* in marketing education.

Initiating the Marketing Process

1

Creating Customer Relationships and Value through Marketing

LEARNING OBJECTIVES

After reading this chapter you should be able to:

 LO 1-1 Define marketing and identify the two primary goals of marketing.

 LO 1-2 Explain how marketing discovers and satisfies consumer needs.

 LO 1-3 Distinguish between marketing mix factors and environmental forces.

 LO 1-4 Explain how organizations build strong customer relationships and customer value through marketing.

LAUNCHING A *NEW* BILLION-DOLLAR FOOD CATEGORY—IN JUST SEVEN YEARS!

Thousands of newly launched consumer products quietly fail every year. How could an entirely new food category skyrocket to success? The answer: Look at Chobani® Greek Yogurt!

In 2005, Turkish immigrant Hamdi Ulukaya opened his mail in New Berlin, New York, and saw an ad that said, "Fully equipped yogurt factory for sale." He bought the plant (built in 1885), painted the walls, hired a yogurt master from Turkey, and turned his attention to the task of developing high-quality Greek yogurt. He named it Chobani, which means "shepherd" in Turkish.[1]

Developing Chobani's Unique Greek Yogurt

Hamdi Ulukaya is not fond of American-style yogurt. He says, "In Turkey we eat strained yogurt, which is rich and creamy, at every meal." The straining process removes much of the liquid whey while leaving behind more protein than the unstrained American yogurts. "I was very picky. It took us 18 months to get the recipe right. But in 2007, we had it. I knew I had only one shot, and it had to be perfect," says Ulukaya.[2]

Reaching Customers

From the very beginning, Ulukaya and team pushed for distribution in major grocery chains and in their main dairy cases, *not* confined to the specialty or health food sections of these chains or in smaller, niche stores. The reason was that he was convinced that typical Americans would really like Greek yogurt if they tried it. Ulukaya's conviction paid off, and today Chobani has over a billion dollars a year in sales.

Chobani had little money for traditional advertising in 2007, so it relied on one happy customer telling another about this new Chobani Greek Yogurt. But Chobani increased its public awareness significantly through sponsoring the 2012 and 2014 U.S. Olympic and Paralympic Teams.

A plan to send 5,000 cups of its Chobani Greek Yogurt to the 2014 Sochi Winter Olympics hit a roadblock, however, when Russian authorities said it failed to meet their customs rules. So Chobani sent the 5,000 cups to food banks in New York and New Jersey. This donation reflects Chobani's commitment to charitable activities—giving 10 percent of its profits to support people and organizations working for positive, long-lasting change.

Chobani introduced its "Simply 100 Greek Yogurt" in December 2013—a 100-calorie, 5.3-ounce cup that is smaller than its original

Video 1-1
**Chobani 2014
Super Bowl Ad**
kerin.tv/cr6e/v1-1

6-ounce cups.[3] Then its 2014 Super Bowl "yogurt bear" commercial proved a hit. It featured a sales clerk ducking behind the counter while the disruptive bear tries to buy a cup of Chobani Greek Yogurt.

Just over six years from launch, Chobani boasts over 800,000 Facebook fans and has single-handedly created the new food category of "Greek yogurt." The company's YouTube channel features "Just Add Good" recipes to show customers how to use its tasty products in meals and desserts. It also interacts with consumers through a half-dozen other social media sites such as Twitter and Instagram, acknowledging everyone who mentions the brand.

Chobani, Marketing, and You

By 2014, Chobani had about 38 percent of the U.S. Greek yogurt market and about 19 percent of the entire U.S. yogurt market. Will Hamdi Ulukaya and his Chobani Greek Yogurt continue this fantastic success—especially with the appearance of competing Greek yogurts from Yoplait, Dannon, and PepsiCo?[4] For Ulukaya, one key factor will be how well Chobani uses marketing—the subject of this book.

WHAT IS MARKETING?

The good news is that you are already a marketing expert! You perform many marketing activities and make marketing-related decisions every day. For example, would you sell more LG 55-inch 3D OLED HD Smart TVs at $9,999 or $999 each? You answered $999, right? So your experience in shopping gives you some expertise in marketing. As a consumer, you've been involved in thousands of marketing decisions, but mostly on the buying and not the selling side.

Are you a marketing expert? If so, what would you pay for this cutting-edge TV?

The bad news is that good marketing isn't always easy. That's why every year thousands of new products fail in the marketplace and then quietly slide into oblivion.

Marketing and Your Career

Marketing affects all individuals, all organizations, all industries, and all countries. This book seeks to teach you marketing concepts, often by having you actually "do marketing"—by putting you in the shoes of a marketing manager facing actual marketing decisions. The book also shows marketing's many applications and how it affects our lives. This knowledge should make you a better consumer and enable you to be a more informed citizen, and Appendix B is intended to help you in your career planning.

Perhaps your future will involve doing sales and marketing for a large organization. Working for a well-known company—Apple, Ford, Facebook, or General Mills—can be personally satisfying and financially rewarding, and you may gain special respect from your friends.

Small businesses also offer marketing careers. Small businesses are the source of the majority of new U.S. jobs. So you might become your own boss by being an entrepreneur and starting your own business.

In February 2004, a 19-year-old college sophomore from Harvard University started his own small web service business from his dorm room. He billed it as "an online

The chief executive officer of the world's largest social media company started it as a 19-year-old college sophomore.

directory that connects people through social networks at colleges." That student, of course, was Mark Zuckerberg.[5] The success of the Facebook launch defies comprehension. Zuckerberg's Thefacebook.com website signed up 900 Harvard students in the four days after it appeared in early 2004. By the second week, there were almost 5,000 members. Unlike Facebook, not every Internet start-up reaches over a billion users a few years after its launch. In fact, more than half of all new businesses fail within five years of their start-up.

Marketing: Delivering Benefits to the Organization, Its Stakeholders, and Society

LO 1-1 Define marketing and identify the two primary goals of marketing.

marketing
The activity for creating and delivering offerings that benefit the organization, its stakeholders, and society.

The American Marketing Association represents marketing professionals. Combining its 2004 and 2007 definitions, "**marketing** is the activity for creating, communicating, delivering, and exchanging offerings that benefit its customers, the organization, its stakeholders, and society at large."[6] This definition shows that marketing is far more than simply advertising or personal selling. It stresses the need to deliver genuine benefits in the goods, services, and ideas marketed to customers. The organization doing the marketing, the stakeholders affected (such as customers, employees, suppliers, and shareholders), and society should all benefit.

To serve both buyers and sellers, marketing seeks (1) to discover the needs and wants of prospective customers and (2) to satisfy them. These prospective customers

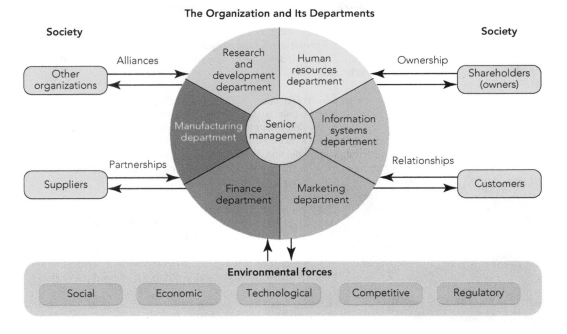

The Organization and Its Departments

FIGURE 1–1
A marketing department relates to many people, organizations, and forces. Note that the marketing department both *shapes* and *is shaped by* its relationship with these internal and external groups.

exchange
The trade of things of value between a buyer and a seller so that each is better off.

include both individuals, buying for themselves and their households, and organizations, buying for their own use (such as manufacturers) or for resale (such as wholesalers and retailers). The key to achieving these two objectives is the idea of **exchange**, which is the trade of things of value between a buyer and a seller so that each is better off after the trade.[7]

The Diverse Elements Influencing Marketing Actions

Although an organization's marketing activity focuses on assessing and satisfying consumer needs, countless other people, groups, and forces interact to shape the nature of its actions (see Figure 1–1). Foremost is the organization itself, whose mission and objectives determine what business it is in and what goals it seeks. Within the organization, management is responsible for establishing these goals. The marketing department works closely with other departments and employees to help provide the customer-satisfying products required for the organization to survive and prosper.

Figure 1–1 also shows the key people, groups, and forces outside the organization that influence its marketing activities. The marketing department is responsible for facilitating relationships, partnerships, and alliances with the organization's customers, its shareholders (or often representatives of nonprofit organizations), its suppliers, and other organizations. Environmental forces involving social, economic, technological, competitive, and regulatory considerations also shape an organization's marketing actions. Finally, an organization's marketing decisions are affected by and, in turn, often have an important impact on society as a whole.

The organization must strike a balance among the sometimes differing interests of these groups. For example, it is not possible to simultaneously provide the lowest-priced and highest-quality products to customers and pay the highest prices to suppliers, the highest wages to employees, and the maximum dividends to shareholders.

What Is Needed for Marketing to Occur

For marketing to occur, at least four factors are required: (1) two or more parties (individuals or organizations) with unsatisfied needs, (2) a desire and ability on their part to have their needs satisfied, (3) a way for the parties to communicate, and (4) something to exchange.

Two or More Parties with Unsatisfied Needs   Suppose you've developed an unmet need—a desire for a late-night dinner after studying for an exam—but you don't yet know that Domino's Pizza has a location in your area. Also unknown to you is that Domino's recently introduced its tasty Handmade Pan Pizza, just waiting to be ordered, handmade, and delivered. This is an example of two parties with unmet needs: you, desiring a meal, and your local Domino's Pizza owner, needing someone to buy a Handmade Pan Pizza.

Marketing doesn't happen in a vacuum. The text describes the four factors needed to buy a product like a Domino's Handmade Pan Pizza.

Desire and Ability to Satisfy These Needs   Both you and the Domino's Pizza owner want to satisfy these unmet needs. Furthermore, you have the money to buy the Domino's Handmade Pan Pizza and the time to order it online or over the telephone. The Domino's owner has not only the desire to sell its Handmade Pan Pizza but also the ability to do so since the pizza is easily made and delivered to (or picked up by) you.

A Way for the Parties to Communicate   The marketing transaction of purchasing a Domino's Handmade Pan Pizza will never occur unless you know the product exists and its location (street/web address and/or phone number). Similarly, the Domino's Pizza owner won't sell the Handmade Pan Pizza unless there's a market of potential buyers nearby. When you receive a coupon in the mail or drive by the Domino's store location, this communication barrier between you (the buyer) and the Domino's Pizza owner (the seller) is overcome.

Something to Exchange   Marketing occurs when the transaction takes place and both the buyer and seller exchange something of value. In this case, you exchange your money ($7.99) for the Domino's Handmade Pan Pizza. Both you and the Domino's Pizza owner have gained and also given up something, but you are both better off because each of you has satisfied the other's unmet needs. You have the opportunity to eat a Domino's Handmade Pan Pizza to satisfy your hunger, but you gave up some money to do so; the Domino's Pizza owner gave up the Handmade Pan Pizza but received money, which will help the owner remain in business. The ethical and legal foundations of this exchange process are central to marketing and are discussed in Chapter 4.

> **learning review**
>
> 1-1. What is marketing?
>
> 1-2. Marketing focuses on _____ and _____ consumer needs.
>
> 1-3. What four factors are needed for marketing to occur?

HOW MARKETING DISCOVERS AND SATISFIES CONSUMER NEEDS

 LO 1-2 Explain how marketing discovers and satisfies consumer needs.

Discovering and satisfying consumer needs in order to develop and offer successful products is so important to understanding marketing that we look at each of these two steps in detail next. Let's start by asking you to analyze the three products below.

For these three products, identify (1) what benefits the product provides buyers and (2) what factors or "showstoppers" might doom the product in the marketplace. Answers are discussed in the text.

Vanilla-mint-flavored toothpaste in an aerosol container

An e-commerce site with financial benefits for users.

A T-shirt with an upbeat "Life Is Good" message

Discovering Consumer Needs

The first objective in marketing is discovering the needs of prospective customers. But these prospective customers may not always know or be able to describe what they need and want. When Apple built its first Apple II personal computer and started a new industry, consumers didn't really know what the benefits would be and had to be educated about how to use personal computers. In contrast, 3M listened to ideas from hundreds of students about how they study and take notes and then put several of these ideas into its Post-it® Flag Highlighters, discussed later in the chapter. This is where effective marketing research, the topic of Chapter 7, can help.

The Challenge: Meeting Consumer Needs with New Products

New-product experts generally estimate that up to 94 percent of the more than 40,000 new consumer products (food, beverage, health, beauty, and other household and pet products) introduced in the United States annually "don't succeed in the long run."[8] Robert M. McMath, who has studied more than 110,000 of these new-product launches, has two key suggestions: (1) focus on what the customer benefit is, and (2) learn from past mistakes.[9]

The solution to preventing product failures seems embarrassingly obvious. First, find out what consumers need and want. Second, produce what they need and want, and don't produce what they don't need and want. The three products shown above illustrate just how difficult it is to achieve new-product success, a topic covered in more detail in Chapter 9.

Without reading further, think about the potential benefits to customers and possible "showstoppers"—factors that might doom the product—for each of the three products pictured. Some of the products may come out of your past, and others may be on your horizon. Here's a quick analysis of the three products:

- *Dr. Care Toothpaste.* After extensive research, Dr. Care family toothpaste in its aerosol container was introduced more than two decades ago. The vanilla-mint-flavored product's benefits were advertised as being easy to use and sanitary. Pretend for a minute that you are five years old and left alone in the bathroom to brush your teeth using your Dr. Care toothpaste. Hmm! Apparently, surprised parents were not enthusiastic about the bathroom wall paintings sprayed by their future Rembrandts—a showstopper that doomed this creative product.[10]

- *StuffDOT®.* This recent startup is a social e-commerce site that seeks to change the way consumers interact with online retailers by sharing the value people create with their online activity. This is possible because Internet retailers like Amazon and Target.com make small payments to the owners of websites that

Video 1-2
StuffDOT
Strategies
kerin.tv/cr6e/v1-2

refer shoppers to their products. These payments are a big and growing business, generating a projected $4.5 billion by 2016.[11] StuffDOT's founders believe that consumers deserve to share in those payments, so they have developed a platform that enables users to earn a fair share of the revenue that they generate by sharing links and shopping online. A potential showstopper: StuffDOT offers its members the chance to earn cash back on the purchases they make online. But will consumers understand the benefits of StuffDOT well enough to change their shopping habits in order to take advantage of the opportunity?

• *Life Is Good*® T-shirts. In 1989, brothers Bert and John Jacobs put their artwork on T-shirts that they tried to sell mostly at colleges and street fairs around Boston and up and down the East Coast. By 1994 they had exactly $78 in their bank account. That year they discussed how people seemed worn down by the constant negative information from the media. They decided to put the "Life Is Good" message on their T-shirts to stress the good in the world, which led to today's success.[12] Do you own one of their T-shirts? The potential showstopper is their finding ways to keep ahead of the hundreds of firms in the apparel business that might try a copycat strategy.

Firms spend billions of dollars every year on marketing and technical research to avoid new-product failure—the fate that befell Dr. Care Toothpaste. So meeting the needs of consumers is a daily marketing challenge for firms like StuffDOT and Life Is Good, whose underlying strategies and experiences we'll explore further later in the book.

Studying late at night for an exam and being hungry, you decide to microwave a Hot Pockets Bacon Cheddar Cheese Melt sandwich. Is this a need or want? The text discusses the role of marketing in influencing decisions like this.

Consumer Needs and Consumer Wants   Should marketing try to satisfy consumer needs or consumer wants? Marketing tries to do both. Heated debates rage over this question, fueled by the definitions of needs and wants and the amount of freedom given to prospective customers to make their own buying decisions.

A *need* occurs when a person feels deprived of basic necessities such as food, clothing, and shelter. A *want* is a need that is shaped by a person's knowledge, culture, and personality. So if you feel hungry, you have developed a basic need and desire to eat something. Let's say you then want to eat an apple or a Hot Pockets Bacon Cheddar Cheese Melt microwave sandwich because, based on your past experience, you know these will satisfy your hunger need. Effective marketing, in the form of creating an awareness of good products at convenient locations, can clearly shape a person's wants.

Certainly, marketing tries to influence what we buy. A question then arises: At what point do we want government and society to step in to protect consumers? Most consumers would say they want government to protect us from harmful drugs and unsafe cars but not from candy bars and soft drinks. To protect college students, should government restrict their use of credit cards? Such questions have no clear-cut answers, which is why legal and ethical issues are central to marketing. Because even psychologists and economists still debate the exact meanings of *need* and *want*, we shall use the terms interchangeably throughout the book.

As shown in the left side of Figure 1–2, discovering needs involves looking carefully at prospective customers, whether they are children buying M&Ms candy, college students buying Chobani Greek Yogurt, or firms buying Xerox color copiers. A principal activity of a firm's marketing department is to scrutinize its consumers to understand what they need and want and the forces that shape those needs and wants.

market
People with both the desire and the ability to buy a specific offering.

What a Market Is   Potential consumers make up a **market**, which is people with both the desire and the ability to buy a specific offering. All markets ultimately are people. Even when we say a firm bought a Xerox copier, we mean one or several people in the firm decided to buy it. People who are aware of their unmet needs may

FIGURE 1–2
Marketing seeks first to discover consumer needs through extensive research. It then seeks to satisfy those needs by successfully implementing a marketing program possessing the right combination of the marketing mix—the four Ps.

have the desire to buy the product, but that alone isn't sufficient. People must also have the ability to buy, such as the authority, time, and money. People may even "buy" an idea that results in an action, such as having their blood pressure checked annually or turning down their thermostat to save energy.

Satisfying Consumer Needs

target market
One or more specific groups of potential consumers toward which an organization directs its marketing program.

Marketing doesn't stop with the discovery of consumer needs. Because the organization obviously can't satisfy all consumer needs, it must concentrate its efforts on certain needs of a specific group of potential consumers. This is the **target market**—one or more specific groups of potential consumers toward which an organization directs its marketing program.

LO 1-3   Distinguish between marketing mix factors and environmental forces.

The Four Ps: Controllable Marketing Mix Factors   Having selected its target market consumers, the firm must take steps to satisfy their needs, as shown in the right side of Figure 1–2. Someone in the organization's marketing department, often the marketing manager, must develop a complete marketing program to reach consumers by using a combination of four elements, often called "the four Ps"—a useful shorthand reference to them first published by Professor E. Jerome McCarthy:[13]

- *Product.* A good, service, or idea to satisfy the consumer's needs.
- *Price.* What is exchanged for the product.
- *Promotion.* A means of communication between the seller and buyer.
- *Place.* A means of getting the product to the consumer.

marketing mix
The controllable factors—product, price, promotion, and place—that the marketing manager can use to solve a marketing problem.

We'll define each of the four Ps more carefully later in the book, but for now it's important to remember that they are the elements of the **marketing mix**. These four elements are the controllable factors—product, price, promotion, and place—that can be used by the marketing manager to solve a marketing problem. For example, when a company puts a product on sale, it is changing one element of the marketing mix—namely, the price. The marketing mix elements are called *controllable factors* because they are under the control of the marketing department in an organization.

customer value proposition
A cluster of benefits that an organization promises customers to satisfy their needs.

Designing an effective marketing mix also conveys to potential buyers a clear **customer value proposition**, which is a cluster of benefits that an organization promises customers to satisfy their needs. For example, Walmart's customer value proposition can be described as "everyday low prices for a broad range of products that are always in stock in convenient locations." Michelin's customer value proposition can be summed up as "providing safety-conscious parents greater security in tires at a premium price."[14]

The Uncontrollable, Environmental Forces   While marketers can control their marketing mix factors, there are forces that are mostly beyond their control (see Figure 1–1). These are the **environmental forces** that affect a marketing decision, which consist of social, economic, technological, competitive, and regulatory forces. Examples are what consumers themselves want and need, changing technology, the state of the economy in terms of whether it is expanding or contracting, actions that competitors take, and government restrictions. Covered in detail in Chapter 3, these five forces may serve as accelerators or brakes on marketing, sometimes expanding an organization's marketing opportunities and at other times restricting them.

Traditionally, many marketing executives have treated these environmental forces as rigid, absolute constraints that are entirely outside their influence. However, recent studies and marketing successes have shown that a forward-looking, action-oriented firm can often affect some environmental forces by achieving technological or competitive breakthroughs, such as Apple's iPhone or Chobani's Greek Yogurt.

> **environmental forces**
> The uncontrollable social, economic, technological, competitive, and regulatory forces that affect the results of a marketing decision.

THE MARKETING PROGRAM: HOW CUSTOMER RELATIONSHIPS ARE BUILT

>
> **LO 1-4**   Explain how organizations build strong customer relationships and customer value through marketing.

An organization's marketing program connects it with its customers. To clarify this link, we will first discuss the critically important concepts of customer value, customer relationships, and relationship marketing. Then we will illustrate these concepts using 3M's marketing program for its new Post-it® Flag Highlighter products.

Relationship Marketing: Easy to Understand, Hard to Do

Intense competition in today's fast-paced global markets has prompted many successful U.S. firms to focus on "customer value." Gaining loyal customers by providing unique value is the essence of successful marketing. What is new is a more careful attempt at understanding how a firm's customers perceive value and then actually creating and delivering that value to them. **Customer value** is the unique combination of benefits received by targeted buyers that includes quality, convenience, on-time delivery, and both before-sale and after-sale service at a specific price. Firms now actually try to place a dollar value on the purchases of loyal, satisfied customers during their lifetimes. For example, loyal Kleenex customers average 6.7 boxes a year, about $994 over 60 years in today's dollars.[15]

> **customer value**
> Buyers' benefits, including quality, convenience, on-time delivery, and before- and after-sale service at a specific price.

Research suggests that firms cannot succeed by being all things to all people. Instead, firms seek to build long-term relationships with customers by providing unique value to them. Many successful firms deliver outstanding customer value with one of three value strategies: best price, best product, or best service.[16]

With the intense competition among U.S. businesses, being seen as "best" is admittedly difficult. Still, successful firms like U.S. Bank (whose ad is shown), Target, and Starbucks have achieved great results as reflected in the mission, vision, and values statements they stress and live by:[17]

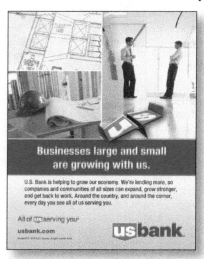

U.S. Bank provides customer value using a very specific approach. For its strategy, see the text.

- Best service: U.S. Bank. The brand-line in the U.S. Bank ad—"All of US serving you®"—reinforces its commitment to best-in-class customer service, while providing a complete array of financial products and services.
- Best price: Target. It uses the Target brand promise of "Expect More, Pay Less®" to "make Target the preferred shopping destination for our guests by delivering outstanding value."
- Best product: Starbucks. Starbucks seeks "to inspire and nurture the human spirit—one person, one cup and one neighborhood at a time," stressing quality coffee and ethics in the process.

Remaining among the "best" is a continuing challenge for today's businesses.

Apple uses relationship marketing concepts with its iMac—tailoring the product to the taste of an individual customer and delivering it quickly.

relationship marketing
Linking the organization to its individual customers, employees, suppliers, and other partners for their mutual long-term benefit.

marketing program
A plan that integrates the marketing mix to provide a good, service, or idea to prospective buyers.

market segments
Relatively homogeneous groups of prospective buyers that (1) have common needs and (2) will respond similarly to a marketing action.

A firm achieves meaningful customer relationships by creating connections with its customers through careful coordination of the product, its price, the way it's promoted, and how it's placed.

The hallmark of developing and maintaining effective customer relationships is today called **relationship marketing**, which links the organization to its individual customers, employees, suppliers, and other partners for their mutual long-term benefit. Relationship marketing involves a personal, ongoing relationship between the organization and its individual customers that begins before and continues after the sale.[18]

Huge manufacturers find this rigorous standard of relationship marketing difficult to achieve. Today's information technology, along with cutting-edge manufacturing and marketing processes, has led to tailoring products or services to the tastes of individual customers in high volumes at a relatively low cost. So you can place an Internet order for an Apple iMac and have it delivered in four or five days—in a configuration tailored to your unique wants. But with today's Internet purchases, you will probably have difficulty achieving the same personal, tender-loving-care connection that you once had with your neighborhood computer store, bookstore, or other local retailer.

The Marketing Program and Market Segments

Effective relationship marketing strategies help marketing managers discover what prospective customers need and convert these ideas into marketable products (see Figure 1–3). These concepts must then be converted into a tangible **marketing program**—a plan that integrates the marketing mix to provide a good, service, or idea to prospective buyers. Ideally, they can be formed into **market segments**, which are relatively homogeneous groups of prospective buyers that (1) have common needs and (2) will respond similarly to a marketing action. This action might be a product feature, a promotion, or a price. As shown in Figure 1–3, in an effective organization this process is continuous: Consumer needs trigger product concepts that are translated into actual products that stimulate further discovery of consumer needs.

learning review

1-4. An organization can't satisfy the needs of all consumers, so it must focus on one or more subgroups, which are its _____.

1-5. What are the four marketing mix elements that make up the organization's marketing program?

1-6. What are environmental forces?

3M's Strategy and Marketing Program to Help Students Study

"How do college students *really* study?" asked David Windorski, a 3M inventor of Post-it® brand products, when thinking about adding a new item to the Post-it® line.[19]

To answer this question, Windorski worked with a team of four college students. Their task was to observe and question dozens of students about their study behavior, such as how they used their textbooks, took notes, wrote term papers, and reviewed for exams. Often, they watched students highlight a passage and then mark the page with a Post-it® Note or Post-it® Flag. Windorski realized he could pair an existing Post-it® product with a highlighter—merging the functions of two products into one to help students study!

3M's initial product line of Post-it® Flag Highlighters and Post-it® Flag Pens includes variations in color and line widths.

Moving from Ideas to a Marketable Highlighter Product

After working on 15 or 20 wood and clay models, Windorski concluded he had to build a highlighter product that would dispense Post-it® Flags because the Post-it® Notes were simply too large to put inside the barrel of a highlighter.

Hundreds of the initial highlighter prototypes with Post-it® Flags inside were produced and given to students—and also office workers—to get their reactions. This research showed users wanted a convenient, reliable cover to protect the Post-it® Flags in the highlighter. So Windorski's rotating cover for the Post-it® Flag Highlighter was born.

Adding the Post-it® Flag Pen

Most of David Windorski's initial design energies had gone into his Post-it® Flag Highlighter research and development. But Windorski also considered other related products. Many people in offices need immediate access to Post-it® Flags while writing with pens. Students are a potential market for this product, too, but probably a smaller market segment than office workers.

A Marketing Program for the Post-it® Flag Highlighter and Pen

After several years of research, development, and production engineering, 3M introduced its new products. Figure 1–3 outlines the strategies for each of the four marketing mix elements in 3M's program to market its Post-it® Flag Highlighters and Post-it® Flag Pens. Although similar, we can compare the marketing program for each of the two products:

* *Post-it® Flag Highlighter.* The target market shown in the orange column in Figure 1–3 is mainly college students, so 3M's initial challenge was to build student awareness of a product that they didn't know existed. The company used

FIGURE 1–3
Marketing programs for the launch of two Post-it® brand products targeted at two target market segments.

MARKETING PROGRAM ACTION TO REACH:

MARKETING MIX ELEMENT	COLLEGE STUDENT MARKET SEGMENT	OFFICE WORKER MARKET SEGMENT	RATIONALE FOR MARKETING PROGRAM ACTION
Product strategy	Offer Post-it® Flag Highlighter to help college students in their studying	Offer Post-it® Flag Pen to help office workers in their day-to-day work activities	Listen carefully to the needs and wants of potential customer segments to use 3M technology to introduce a useful, innovative product
Price strategy	Seek retail price of about $3.99 to $4.99 for a single Post-it® Flag Highlighter or $5.99 to $7.99 for a three-pack	Seek retail price of about $3.99 to $4.99 for a single Post-it® Flag Pen; wholesale prices are lower	Set prices that provide genuine value to the customer segment being targeted
Promotion strategy	Run limited promotion with a TV ad and some ads in college newspapers and then rely on student word-of-mouth messages	Run limited promotion among distributors to get them to stock the product	Increase awareness among potential users who have never heard of this new, innovative 3M product
Place strategy	Distribute Post-it® Flag Highlighters through college bookstores, office supply stores, and mass merchandisers	Distribute Post-it® Flag Pens through office wholesalers and retailers as well as mass merchandisers	Make it easy for prospective buyers to buy at convenient retail outlets (both products) or to get at work (Post-it® Flag Pens only)

a mix of print ads in college newspapers and a TV ad and then relied on word-of-mouth advertising—students telling their friends about how great the product is. Gaining distribution in college bookstores was also critical. Plus, 3M charged a price to distributors that it hoped would give a reasonable bookstore price to students and an acceptable profit to distributors and 3M.

- *Post-it® Flag Pen.* The primary target market shown in the green column in Figure 1–3 is people working in offices. The Post-it® Flag Pens are mainly business products—bought by the purchasing department in an organization and stocked as office supplies for employees to use. So the marketing program for Post-it® Flag Pens emphasizes gaining distribution in outlets used by an organization's purchasing department.

How well did these new 3M products do in the marketplace? They have done so well that 3M bestowed a prestigious award on David Windorski and his team. And in what must be considered any inventor's dream come true, Oprah Winfrey flew Windorski to Chicago to appear on her TV show and thank him in person. She told Windorski and her audience about the Post-it® Flag Highlighter: "David, I know you never thought this would happen when you were in your 3M lab . . . but I want you to take a bow before America for the invention of this . . . (highlighter). It's the most incredible invention," she said.[20]

Welcome to the third generation of Post-it® Flag Highlighters: the 3-in-1 Post-it® Flag Pen and Highlighter. The cap contains the Post-it® flags.

Video 1-3
3M Post-it® Flag Highlighters Ad
kerin.tv/cr6e/v1-3

Extending the Product Line The success of these two products has also led Windorski to design a second generation of Post-it® Flag Highlighters and Pens *without* the rotating cover to make it easier to insert replacement flags. The new tapered design is also easier for students to hold and use.

The success of the second generation of Post-it® Flag Highlighters, in turn, has spawned a family of related products. One is a line of Post-it® Flag Pens with yellow, pink, or blue inks, available individually or in a three-pack.

Is it too much trouble when you're studying to grab for a 3M Post-it® Flag, then a highlighter, and then your pen? You're in luck! New to the family of 3M products is the latest generation of David Windorski's innovations: A 3-in-1 combination that has a highlighter on one end, a pen on the other, and 3M Post-it® Flags in the removable cap, as shown in the photo. In addition, 3M recently introduced two more products to its Post-it® Flag Highlighter line: a Post-it® Flag + Gel Pen and a Post-it® Flag + Permanent Marker. Each includes a comfortable grip, up to four different colors, and 50 flags.

HOW MARKETING BECAME SO IMPORTANT

To understand why marketing is a driving force in the modern global economy, let us look at (1) the evolution of the market orientation, (2) ethics and social responsibility in marketing, and (3) the breadth and depth of marketing activities.

Evolution of the Market Orientation

Marketing became the motivating force among many American firms in the 1950s, which led to the **marketing concept**—the idea that an organization should (1) strive to satisfy the needs of consumers while also (2) trying to achieve the organization's goals. General Electric probably launched the marketing concept and its focus on consumers when its 1952 annual report stated: "The concept introduces . . . marketing . . . at the beginning rather than the end of the production cycle and integrates marketing into each phase of the business."[21]

Firms such as General Electric, Marriott, and Facebook have achieved great success by putting huge effort into implementing the marketing concept, giving their firms what has been called a *market orientation*. An organization that has a

marketing concept
The idea that an organization should strive to satisfy the needs of consumers while also trying to achieve the organization's goals.

market orientation
Focusing organizational efforts to collect and use information about customers' needs to create customer value.

market orientation focuses its efforts on (1) continuously collecting information about customers' needs, (2) sharing this information across departments, and (3) using it to create customer value.[22]

Starting in the 1980s, American businesses have stressed closer relationships with customers. This has led to business–customer relationships through social media websites such as Facebook, Twitter, and YouTube, among others.

An important outgrowth of this focus on the customer is the recent attention placed on *customer relationship management (CRM),* the process of identifying prospective buyers, understanding them intimately, and developing favorable long-term perceptions of the organization and its offerings so that buyers will choose them in the marketplace.[23] This process requires the involvement and commitment of managers and employees throughout the organization[24] and a growing application of information, communication, and Internet technology, as will be described throughout this book.

Fortune magazine recently named Trader Joe's its "hottest retailer." This reflects the company's focus on providing a great customer experience, as described in the text.

The foundation of customer relationship management is really *customer experience,* which is the internal response that customers have to all aspects of an organization and its offering. This internal response includes both the direct and indirect contacts of the customer with the company. Direct contacts include the customer's contacts with the seller through buying, using, and obtaining service. Indirect contacts most often involve unplanned "touches" with the company through word-of-mouth comments from other customers, reviewers, and news reports. In terms of outstanding customer experience, Trader Joe's is high on the list and was recently named "America's hottest retailer" by *Fortune* magazine.[25]

What makes the customer experience and loyalty of shoppers at Trader Joe's unique? The reasons include:

- Setting low prices, made possible by offering its own brands rather than well-known national ones.
- Offering unusual, affordable products not available from other retailers, like the Thai lime-and-chili cashews.
- Providing rare employee "engagement" to help customers, like actually walking them to where the roasted chestnuts are—rather than saying "aisle five."

This commitment to providing a *real* customer experience, rather than just paying lip service to it, is what gives Trader Joe's its *Fortune* rating.

The disconnect between what companies *think they are providing* versus what customers *say they are receiving* shows how important customer experience is. In a recent survey of 362 companies, only 8 percent of customers described the experience they received as being "superior," but 80 percent of the companies believed they were supplying a "superior" customer experience.[26]

Ethics and Social Responsibility: Balancing Interests of Groups

Today, the standards of marketing practice have shifted from an emphasis on producers' interests to consumers' interests. Organizations increasingly consider the social and environmental consequences of their actions for all parties.

Ethics   Many marketing issues are not specifically addressed by existing laws and regulations. Should information about a firm's customers be sold to other organizations? Should consumers be on their own to assess the safety of a product? These questions raise difficult ethical issues. Many companies, industries, and professional associations have developed codes of ethics to assist managers.

societal marketing concept
The view that organizations should discover and satisfy the needs of consumers in a way that also provides for society's well-being.

Social Responsibility

While many ethical issues involve only the buyer and seller, others involve society as a whole. A manufacturer dumping toxic wastes into streams has an impact on the environment and society. This example illustrates the issue of social responsibility, the idea that individuals and organizations are accountable to a larger society. The well-being of society at large should also be recognized in an organization's marketing decisions. In fact, some marketing experts stress the **societal marketing concept**, the view that an organization should discover and satisfy the needs of its consumers in a way that also provides for society's well-being.[27] For example, 3M turned fibrous strands of the spiky leaves of Mexico's agave plant into environment-friendly Scotchbrite® Greener Clean "non-scratch scrub sponges" for use in the kitchen.[28]

Marketing art museums: An exotic Louvre in Abu Dhabi . . .

Video 1-4
Hermitage Tour
kerin.tv/cr6e/v1-4

product
A good, service, or idea consisting of a bundle of tangible and intangible attributes that satisfies consumers' needs and is received in exchange for money or something else of value.

. . . and a virtual tour of Russia's Hermitage.

The Breadth and Depth of Marketing

Marketing today affects every person and organization. To understand this, let's analyze (1) who markets, (2) what is marketed, (3) who buys and uses what is marketed, (4) who benefits from these marketing activities, and (5) how consumers benefit.

Who Markets?

Every organization markets. It's obvious that business firms involved in manufacturing (Heinz), retailing (Trader Joe's), and providing services (Marriott) market their offerings. And nonprofit organizations such as your local hospital or college, places (cities, states, countries), and even special causes (Race for the Cure) also engage in marketing. Finally, individuals such as political candidates often use marketing to gain voter attention and preference.

What Is Marketed?

Goods, services, and ideas are marketed. *Goods* are physical objects, such as toothpaste, cameras, or computers, that satisfy consumer needs. *Services* are intangible items such as airline trips, financial advice, or art museums. *Ideas* are thoughts about concepts, actions, or causes.

In this book, goods, services, and ideas are all considered "products" that are marketed. So a **product** is a good, service, or idea consisting of a bundle of tangible and intangible attributes that satisfies consumers' needs and is received in exchange for money or something else of value.

Services like those offered by art museums, hospitals, and sports teams are relying more heavily on effective marketing. For example, financial pressures have caused art museums to innovate to market their unique services—the viewing of works of art by visitors—to increase revenues. This often involves levels of rare creativity unthinkable several decades ago.

This creativity ranges from establishing a global brand identity by launching overseas museums to offering sit-at-home video tours. France's Louvre, home to the *Mona Lisa* painting, is developing a new satellite museum in Abu Dhabi housed in an architecturally space-age building.[29] Russia's world-class 1,000-room State Hermitage Museum wanted to find a way to market itself to potential first-time visitors. So it partnered with IBM to let you take a "virtual tour" of its exhibits while watching on your iPad and relaxing.

Ideas are most often marketed by nonprofit organizations or the government. So the Nature Conservancy markets the cause of protecting the environment. Charities market the idea that it's worthwhile for you to donate your time or money. The Peace Corps markets to recruit qualified volunteers. And state governments in Arizona and Florida market taking a warm, sunny winter vacation in their states.

ultimate consumers
The people who use the products and services purchased for a household.

organizational buyers
Manufacturers, wholesalers, retailers, and government agencies that buy products and services for their own use or for resale.

Who Buys and Uses What Is Marketed?   Both individuals and organizations buy and use products that are marketed. **Ultimate consumers** are the people—whether 80 years or eight months old—who use the products and services purchased for a household. In contrast, **organizational buyers** are those manufacturers, wholesalers, retailers, and government agencies that buy products and services for their own use or for resale. Although the terms *consumers, buyers,* and *customers* are sometimes used for both ultimate consumers and organizations, there is no consistency on this. In this book you will be able to tell from the example whether the buyers are ultimate consumers, organizations, or both.

Who Benefits?   In our free-enterprise society, there are three specific groups that benefit from effective marketing: consumers who buy, organizations that sell, and society as a whole. True competition between products and services in the marketplace ensures that consumers can find value from the best products, the lowest prices, or exceptional service. Providing choices leads to the consumer satisfaction and quality of life that we expect from our economic system.

Organizations that provide need-satisfying products with effective marketing programs—for example, Target, IBM, and Avon—have blossomed. But competition creates problems for ineffective competitors, including the hundreds of dot-com businesses, such as Pets.com, that failed over a decade ago.

Finally, effective marketing benefits society.[30] It enhances competition, which both improves the quality of products and services and lowers their prices. This makes countries more competitive in world markets and provides jobs and a higher standard of living for their citizens.

utility
The benefits or customer value received by users of the product.

How Do Consumers Benefit?   Marketing creates **utility**, the benefits or customer value received by users of the product. This utility is the result of the marketing exchange process and the way society benefits from marketing. There are four different utilities: form, place, time, and possession. The production of the product or service constitutes *form utility. Place utility* means having the offering available where consumers need it, whereas *time utility* means having it available when needed. *Possession utility* is the value of making an item easy to purchase through the provision of credit cards or financial arrangements. Marketing creates its utilities by bridging space (place utility) and hours (time utility) to provide products (form utility) for consumers to own and use (possession utility).

> **learning review**
>
> **1-7.** What are the two key characteristics of the marketing concept?
>
> **1-8.** What is the difference between ultimate consumers and organizational buyers?

LEARNING OBJECTIVES REVIEW

LO 1-1 *Define marketing and identify the two primary goals of marketing.*

Marketing is an organizational function and a set of processes for creating, communicating, and delivering value to customers and for managing customer relationships in ways that benefit the organization and its stakeholders. This definition relates to two primary goals of marketing: (*a*) discovering the needs of prospective customers and (*b*) satisfying them.

LO 1-2 *Explain how marketing discovers and satisfies consumer needs.*

The first objective in marketing is discovering the needs and wants of consumers who are prospective buyers and customers. A need occurs when a person feels deprived of basic necessities such as food, clothing, and shelter. A want is a need that is shaped by a person's knowledge, culture, and personality. The second objective in marketing is satisfying the needs of targeted consumers. Because an organization obviously can't satisfy all consumer needs, it must concentrate its efforts on certain needs of a specific group of potential consumers or target market—one or more specific groups of potential consumers toward which an organization directs its marketing program. Finally, the organization develops a set of marketing actions in the form of a unique marketing program to reach them.

LO 1-3 *Distinguish between marketing mix factors and environmental forces.*

Four elements in a marketing program designed to satisfy customer needs are product, price, promotion, and place. These elements are called the marketing mix, the four Ps, or the marketer's controllable variables. Environmental forces, also called uncontrollable variables, are largely beyond the organi-zation's control. These include social, economic, technological, competitive, and regulatory forces.

LO 1-4 *Explain how organizations build strong customer relationships and customer value through marketing.*

The essence of successful marketing is to provide sufficient value to gain loyal, long-term customers. Customer value is the unique combination of benefits received by targeted buyers that usually includes quality, price, convenience, on-time delivery, and both before-sale and after-sale service. Marketers do this by using one of three value strategies: best price, best product, or best service.

LEARNING REVIEW ANSWERS

1-1 **What is marketing?**
Answer: Marketing is the activity for creating, communicating, delivering, and exchanging offerings that benefit customers, the organization, its stakeholders, and society at large.

1-2 **Marketing focuses on _____ and _____ consumer needs.**
Answer: discovering; satisfying

1-3 **What four factors are needed for marketing to occur?**
Answer: The four factors are: (1) two or more parties (individuals or organizations) with unsatisfied needs; (2) a desire and ability on their part to have their needs satisfied; (3) a way for the parties to communicate; and (4) something to exchange.

1-4 **An organization can't satisfy the needs of all consumers, so it must focus on one or more subgroups, which are its _____.**
Answer: target market

1-5 **What are the four marketing mix elements that make up the organization's marketing program?**
Answer: product, price, promotion, place

1-6 **What are environmental forces?**
Answer: Environmental forces are the uncontrollable forces that affect a marketing decision. They consist of social, economic, technological, competitive, and regulatory forces.

1-7 **What are the two key characteristics of the marketing concept?**
Answer: An organization should (1) strive to satisfy the needs of consumers while also (2) trying to achieve the organization's goals.

1-8 **What is the difference between ultimate consumers and organizational buyers?**
Answer: Ultimate consumers are the people who use the products and services purchased for a household. Organizational buyers are those manufacturers, wholesalers, retailers, and government agencies that buy products and services for their own use or for resale.

FOCUSING ON KEY TERMS

customer value p. 10
customer value proposition p. 9
environmental forces p. 10
exchange p. 5
market p. 8
market orientation p. 14

market segments p. 11
marketing p. 4
marketing concept p. 13
marketing mix p. 9
marketing program p. 11
organizational buyers p. 16

product p. 15
relationship marketing p. 11
societal marketing concept p. 15
target market p. 9
ultimate consumers p. 16
utility p. 16

APPLYING MARKETING KNOWLEDGE

1 What consumer wants (or benefits) are met by the following products or services? (*a*) 3M Post-it® Flag Highlighter, (*b*) Nike running shoes, (*c*) Hertz Rent-A-Car, and (*d*) television home shopping programs.

2 Each of the four products, services, or programs in question 1 has substitutes. Respective examples are (*a*) a Bic™ highlighter, (*b*) regular tennis shoes, (*c*) taking a bus, and (*d*) a department store. What consumer benefits might these substitutes have in each case that some consumers might value more highly than those mentioned in question 1?

3 What are the characteristics (e.g., age, income, education) of the target market customers for the following products or services? (*a*) *National Geographic* magazine, (*b*) Chobani Greek Yogurt, (*c*) New York Giants football team, and (*d*) Facebook.

4   A college in a metropolitan area wishes to increase its evening-school offerings of business-related courses such as marketing, accounting, finance, and management. Who are the target market customers (students) for these courses?

5   What actions involving the four marketing mix elements might be used to reach the target market in question 4?

6   What environmental forces (uncontrollable variables) must the college in question 4 consider in designing its marketing program?

7   Does a firm have the right to "create" wants and try to persuade consumers to buy goods and services they didn't know about earlier? What are examples of "good" and "bad" want creation? Who should decide what is good and what is bad?

BUILDING YOUR MARKETING PLAN

If your instructor assigns a marketing plan for your class, don't make a face and complain about the work—for two special reasons. First, you will get insights into trying to actually "do marketing" that often go beyond what you can get by simply reading the textbook. Second, thousands of graduating students every year get their first job by showing prospective employers a "portfolio" of samples of their written work from college—often a marketing plan if they have one. This can work for you.

This "Building Your Marketing Plan" section at the end of each chapter suggests ways to improve and focus your marketing plan. You will use the sample marketing plan in Appendix A (following Chapter 2) as a guide, and this section after each chapter will help you apply those Appendix A ideas to your own marketing plan.

The first step in writing a good marketing plan is to have a business or product that enthuses you and for which you can get detailed information, so you can avoid glittering generalities. We offer these additional bits of advice in selecting a topic:

- *Do* pick a topic that has personal interest for you—a family business; a business, product, or service you or a friend might want to launch; or a student organization that needs marketing help.
- *Do not* pick a topic that is so large it can't be covered adequately or so abstract it will lack specifics.

1   Now to get you started on your marketing plan, list four or five possible topics and compare these with the criteria your instructor suggests and those shown above. Think hard, because your decision will be with you all term and may influence the quality of the resulting marketing plan you show to a prospective employer.

2   When you have selected your marketing plan topic, whether the plan is for an actual business, a possible business, or a student organization, write the "company description" in your plan, as shown in Appendix A (following Chapter 2).

VIDEO CASE 1   Chobani®: Making *Greek Yogurt* a Household Name

Video 1-5
Chobani
Video Case
kerin.tv/cr6e/v1-5

"Everybody should be able to enjoy a pure, simple cup of yogurt. And that's what Chobani is," says Hamdi Ulukaya, founder and chief executive officer of Chobani, Inc., in summarizing his vision for the company. As the winner of the 2013 Ernst & Young World Entrepreneur of the Year award, his words and success story carry great credibility.

THE IDEA

Hamdi Ulukaya came to the United States in 1994 to learn English and study business. Ulukaya had no real experience in the yogurt business. He grew up on his family's dairy farm in eastern Turkey eating the thick, tangy yogurt of his homeland. In his view, American yogurt was too thin, too sweet, and too fake.

So he decided to produce what is known as "Greek yogurt"—an authentic strained version like he ate as a child that has a thick texture, high protein content, and with little or no fat. With his five-person team, Ulukaya worked 18 months to perfect the recipe for Chobani Greek Yogurt.

Chobani's new-product launch in 2007 focused on the classic "4Ps" elements of marketing mix actions: product, price, place, and promotion.

PRODUCT STRATEGY

The product strategy for the Chobani brand focused on the separate elements of (1) the product itself and (2) its packaging.

The Chobani product strategy stresses its authentic straining process that removes excess liquid whey, resulting in a thicker, creamier yogurt. Chobani uses three pounds of milk to make one pound of Chobani Greek Yogurt. Some other features that make Chobani Greek Yogurt *"nothing but good,"* to quote its tagline:

* Higher in protein than regular yogurt.
* Made with real fruit and only natural ingredients.
* Preservative-free.
* No artificial flavors or artificial sweeteners.
* Contains five live and active cultures, including three probiotics.

Then, and still today, Ulukaya obsesses about Chobani's packaging of the original cups. In 2007, Ulukaya concluded that *not any cup* would do. He insisted on a European-style cup with a circular opening *exactly* 95 millimeters across—a shorter, wider cup more visible on retailer's shelves. Also, Ulukaya chose shrink-on plastic sleeves that adhere to the cup and offer eye-popping colors.

"With our packaging people would say, 'You're making it all look different and why are you doing that?'" says Kyle O'Brien, executive vice president of sales. "If people pay attention to our cups, we know we have won them, because what's inside the cup is different from anything else on the shelf."

PRICE STRATEGY

To keep control of their product, Ulukaya and O'Brien approached retailers directly rather than going through distributors. Prices were set high enough to recover Chobani's costs and give reasonable margins to retailers but not so high that future rivals could undercut its price. Today, prices remain at about $1.29 for a single-serve cup.

PLACE STRATEGY

Ulukaya's decision to get Chobani Greek Yogurt into the conventional yogurt aisle of traditional supermarkets—not on specialty shelves or in health food stores—proved to be sheer genius. Today Chobani sees its Greek Yogurt widely distributed in both conventional and mass supermarkets, club stores, and natural food stores. On the horizon: growing distribution in convenience and drug stores, as well as schools. Chobani is also educating food service directors at schools across the United States about Greek yogurt's health benefits for schoolkids.

The Chobani growth staggers imagination. From the company's first order of 200 cases in 2007, its 2014 sales have grown to over 2 million cases per week. To increase capacity, in 2012 Chobani opened a nearly one million square foot plant in Idaho—the largest yogurt manufacturing facility in the world.

PROMOTION STRATEGY

In its early years Chobani had no money for traditional advertising, so it relied on word-of-mouth recommendation from enthusiastic customers. It has now run successful national advertising campaigns, including sponsorship of the 2012 and 2014 U.S. Olympic and Paralympic Teams.

"Social media has been important to Chobani, which has embraced a high-touch model that emphasizes positive communication with its customers," says Sujean Lee, head of corporate affairs. Today, Chobani's Customer Loyalty Team receives about 7,000 customer e-mails and phone calls a month and makes return phone calls to most of them. Consumers also get a handwritten note. Chobani launched its "Go Real Chobani" campaign in 2013 to highlight that it is a *real* company making *real* products and engaging consumers through *real* conversations.

Besides Facebook (www.Facebook.com/Chobani), the company interacts with its consumers through Twitter, Pinterest, Instagram, Foursquare, and other social media platforms. Chobani Kitchen (www.chobanikitchen.com) is an online resource with recipes, videos, and tips on how to use its Greek yogurt in favorite recipes.

Chobani stresses new product innovation. "Today we offer our Chobani Greek Yogurt in single-serve and multi-serve sizes, while expanding our authentic strained Greek yogurt to new occasions and forms," says Joshua Dean, vice president of brand advertising. Its recent new-product offerings include:

* Chobani Bite®—3.5-ounce 4-packs to reach the new "indulgent" segment of Chobani customers—those wanting a healthy afternoon or evening snack. Sample flavor: Raspberry with Dark Chocolate Chips.

- Chobani Champions® Tubes—made for kids, the 2.25-ounce tubes offer low-fat, blended Chobani flavors with fruit in grab-and-go packaging. Sample flavor: Jammin' Strawberry.
- Chobani Flip™ (photo, previous page)—a 5.3-ounce, two-compartment package that lets consumers bend or "flip" mix-ins like granola or hazelnuts into the Chobani Greek Yogurt compartment. Sample flavor: Almond Coco Loco, a coconut low-fat yogurt paired with dark chocolate and sliced toasted almonds.

How do you test ideas for new Greek yogurt flavors? In Chobani's case, it opened what it calls a "first-of-its-kind Mediterranean yogurt bar"—called Chobani SoHo—in a trendy New York City neighborhood. Here, customers can try new yogurt creations—leading to potential new flavors or products in the future.

Hmmm! Ready to schedule a visit to New York City and Chobani SoHo, and perhaps influence what Chobani customers will be buying in the future?

WHERE TO NOW?

A community foundation, international operations, and a unique test-market boutique in New York City (photo, above) give a peek at Chobani's future.

Chobani gives 10 percent of all profits to its Shepherd's Gift Foundation to support people and organizations working for positive, long-lasting change. The name comes from the "spirit of a shepherd," an expression in Turkey used to describe people who give without expecting anything in return.

International markets provide a growth opportunity. Already sold internationally in Australia, Chobani opened its international headquarters office in 2013. Other countries have far greater annual per capita consumption than that for U.S. consumers, so Chobani is assessing new international markets.

Questions

1 From the information about Chobani in the case and at the start of the chapter, (*a*) whom did Hamdi Ulukaya identify as the target for his first cups of Greek yogurt and (*b*) what was his initial "4Ps" marketing strategy?

2 (*a*) What marketing actions would you expect the companies selling Yoplait, Dannon, and PepsiCo yogurts to take in response to Chobani's appearance and (*b*) how might Chobani respond?

3 What are (*a*) the advantages and (*b*) the disadvantages of Chobani's Customer Loyalty Team that handles communication with customers—from phone calls and e-mails to Facebook and Twitter messages?

4 As Chobani seeks to build its brand, it opened a unique retail store in New York City: Chobani SoHo. Why did Chobani do this?

5 (*a*) What criteria might Chobani use when it seeks markets in new countries and (*b*) what three or four countries meet these criteria?

Chapter Notes

1. Dave Fusaro, "Chobani Selected as *Food Processing* 2012 Processor of the Year," *Food Processing*, December 5, 2012; see http://www.foodprocessing.com/articles/2012/processor-of-the-year.html.
2. Meghan Walsh, "Chobani Takes Gold in the Yogurt Aisle," *Bloomberg Businessweek*, July 31, 2012; see http://www.businessweek.com/articles/2012-07-31/chobani-takes-gold-in-the-yogurt-aisle.
3. Keri Gans, "Chobani Releases New 100-Calorie Greek Yogurt," *Shape Magazine*, December 10, 2013; see http://www.shape.com/blogs/weight-loss-coach/chobani-releases-new-greek-yogurt.
4. Gillian Tan, Annie Gasparro, and Telis Demos, "Chobani Considers Strategic Options," *The Wall Street Journal*, March 12, 2014, p. B2; Bryan Gruley, "How a Turkish Immigrant Made a Billion Dollars in Eight Years Selling . . . Yogurt," *Bloomberg Businessweek*, January 31, 2013, pp. 60–64; and Sarah Nassauer, "The Greek Yogurt Culture War," *The Wall Street Journal*, September 4, 2013, pp. D1, D3.
5. Lev Grossman, "2010 Person of the Year: Mark Zuckerberg," *Time*, December 27, 2010–January 3, 2011, pp. 44–75; and Ben Mezrich, *The Accidental Billionaire* (New York: Anchor Books, 2009), pp. 92–150.
6. To compare the 2004 and 2007 American Marketing Association (AMA) definitions of "marketing," see Lisa M. Keefe, "Marketing Defined," *Marketing News*, January 15, 2008, pp. 28–29. The 2007 AMA approved definition is: "Marketing is the activity, set of institutions, and processes for creating, communicating, delivering, and exchanging offerings that have value for customers, clients, partners, and society at large."
7. Richard P. Bagozzi, "Marketing as Exchange," *Journal of Marketing*, October 1975, pp. 32–39.
8. Productscan® Online database of new products, from *Marketing Intelligence Service*, December 17, 2003. See www.productscan.com. [NOTE: Now known as Datamonitor's Product Launch Analytics.]

9. Robert M. McMath and Thom Forbes, *What Were They Thinking?* (New York: Times Business, 1998), pp. 3–22; see also http://www.gfkamerica.com/practice_areas/gfk_innovation/newproductworks/index.en.html.

10. Ibid.

11. Affiliate Marketing—The Direct and Indirect Value that Affiliates Deliver to Advertisers," prepared by Forrester Consulting for Rakuten LinkShare, June 2012, p. 4. See http://m.www.linksynergy.com/share/pdf/2012_various/forrester_rakuten_linkShare_062612.pdf

12. Dinah Eng, "Life Is Good in the T-Shirt Business," *Fortune*, May 19, 2014, pp. 39–42.

13. Jerome McCarthy, *Basic Marketing: A Managerial Approach* (Homewood, IL: Richard D. Irwin, 1960).

14. Roger A. Kerin and Robert A. Peterson, *Strategic Marketing Problems: Cases and Comments*, 13th ed. (Upper Saddle River, NJ: Prentice-Hall, 2013), Ch. 1.

15. V. Kumar, *Managing Customers for Profit* (Upper Saddle River, NJ: Pearson Education, 2008); and "What's a Loyal Customer Worth?" *Fortune*, December 11, 1995, p. 182.

16. Michael Treacy and Fred D. Wiersema, *The Discipline of Market Leaders* (Reading, MA: Addison-Wesley, 1995).

17. Target and Starbucks corporate websites; and personal interview with Jennifer Neuman, U.S. Bank Corporation.

18. Robert W. Palmatier, Rajiv P. Dant, Dhruv Grewal, and Kenneth R. Evans, "Factors Influencing the Effectiveness of Relationship Marketing: A Meta-Analysis," *Journal of Relationship Marketing*, October 2006, pp. 136–53.

19. The 3M Post-it® Flag Highlighter and 3M Post-it® Flag Pen examples are based on a series of interviews and meetings with 3M inventor and researcher David Windorski from 2004 to 2011.

20. See www.oprah.com for January 15, 2008; and "Post-it® Flags Co-Sponsors Oprah's Live Web Event," *3M Stemwinder*, March 4–17, 2008, p. 3.

21. *Annual Report* (New York: General Electric Company, 1952), p. 21.

22. John C. Narver, Stanley F. Slater, and Brian Tietje, "Creating a Market Orientation," *Journal of Market Focused Management*, no. 2 (1998), pp. 241–55.

23. The definition of customer relationship management is adapted from Rajendra K. Srivastava, Tasadduq A. Shervani, and Liam Fahey, "Marketing, Business Processes, and Shareholder Value: An Embedded View of Marketing Activities and the Discipline of Marketing," *Journal of Marketing*, special issue (1999), pp. 168–79.

24. Gary F. Gebhardt, Gregory S. Carpenter, and John F. Sherry Jr., "Creating a Market Orientation: A Longitudinal, Multifirm, Grounded Analysis of Cultural Transformation," *Journal of Marketing*, October 2006, pp. 37–55.

25. Beth Kowitt, "Inside Trader Joe's," *Fortune*, September 6, 2010, p. 87.

26. Christopher Meyer and Andre Schwager, "Understanding Customer Experience," *Harvard Business Review*, February 2007, pp. 117–26.

27. Philip Kotler and Sidney J. Levy, "Broadening the Concept of Marketing," *Journal of Marketing*, January 1969, pp. 10–15; and Jim Rendon, "When Nations Need a Little Marketing," *The New York Times*, November 23, 2003, p. BU6.

28. Dee DePass, "From Agave to a 'Green Scrubby,'" *Star Tribune*, September 22, 2013, p. D4.

29. "Temples of Delight," *The Economist*, December 21, 2013, pp. 3–10; Peter Gumbel, "Louvre, Inc.," *Time*, August 11, 2008, pp. 51–52; and Stella Wai-Art Law, *A Branding Context: The Guggenheim and the Louvre* (Columbus, OH: The Ohio State University, M.A. Thesis, 2008).

30. William L. Wilkie and Elizabeth S. Moore, "Marketing's Relationship to Society," Chapter 1 in *Handbook of Marketing*, ed. Barton Weitz and Robin Wensley (London: Sage Publications, 2006), pp. 9–38.

Chobani, Inc.: This case was written by William Rudelius, based on personal interviews with Chobani executives Joshua Dean, Sujean Lee, and Kyle O'Brien. Other sources include "The Chobani Story," MEDIA@CHOBANI.COM, 2013; Megan Durisin, "Chobani CEO: Our Success Has Nothing to Do with Yogurt," *Business Retail Insider*, May 3, 2013, p. 1; and Sarah E. Needleman, "Old Factory, Snap Decision Spawn Greek Yogurt Craze," *The Wall Street Journal*, June 21, 2012, pp. B1, B2.

Credits

2 Developing Successful Organizational and Marketing Strategies

LEARNING OBJECTIVES

After reading this chapter you should be able to:

LO 2-1 Describe three kinds of organizations and the three levels of strategy in them.

LO 2-2 Describe core values, mission, organizational culture, business, and goals.

LO 2-3 Explain why managers use marketing dashboards and marketing metrics.

LO 2-4 Discuss how an organization assesses where it is now and where it seeks to be.

LO 2-5 Explain the three steps of the planning phase of the strategic marketing process.

LO 2-6 Describe the four components of the implementation phase of the strategic marketing process.

LO 2-7 Discuss how managers identify and act on deviations from plans.

STARTING A BUSINESS BY GETTING AN "A" IN AN ICE CREAM-MAKING COURSE!

Ben & Jerry's started in 1978 when longtime friends Ben Cohen and Jerry Greenfield headed north to Vermont to start an ice cream parlor in a renovated gas station. Buoyed with enthusiasm, $12,000 in borrowed and saved money, and ideas from a $5 Penn State correspondence course in ice cream making, Ben and Jerry were off scooping.[1]

The two founding entrepreneurs of Ben & Jerry's have successfully implemented some highly creative organizational and marketing strategies over the years. These include:

- *Caring Dairy.* Their milk and cream are bought from a cooperative that guarantees its supplies are bovine growth hormone free.

- *PartnerShops.* Their "social entrepreneurship" PartnerShop programs enable community-based nonprofit organizations to own and operate Scoop Shops that help employ at-risk youth and young adults to better their lives.

- *B-Corp Certified.* Their social mission has earned them "B-Corp" certification. This is a designation from B-Lab, a nonprofit organization whose purpose is to "use the power of business to solve social and environmental problems" in order to positively impact the community and environment within which the organization operates.[2]

As you can see, Ben & Jerry's Homemade Holdings, Inc., links its mission statement to social causes designed to improve humanity by marketing delicious products with creatively funky names.

Today, Ben & Jerry's is owned by Unilever, which is the market leader in the global ice cream industry—one that is expected to reach $68 billion by 2015.[3] While customers love Ben & Jerry's rich premium ice cream, many buy its products to support its social mission. As a testament to its success, Ben & Jerry's has over 7 million fans on Facebook—the most of any premium ice cream marketer!

Chapter 2 describes how organizations set goals to provide an overall direction to their organizational and marketing strategies. The marketing department of an organization converts these strategies into plans that must be implemented and then evaluated so deviations can be exploited or corrected based on the marketing environment.

TODAY'S ORGANIZATIONS

LO 2-1 Describe three kinds of organizations and the three levels of strategy in them.

In studying today's visionary organizations, it is important to recognize (1) the kinds of organizations that exist, (2) what strategy is, and (3) how this strategy relates to the three levels of structure found in many large organizations.

Kinds of Organizations

An *organization* is a legal entity that consists of people who share a common mission. This motivates them to develop *offerings* (goods, services, or ideas) that create value for both the organization and its customers by satisfying their needs and wants.[4] Today's organizations are of three types: (1) for-profit organizations, (2) nonprofit organizations, and (3) government agencies.

A *for-profit organization,* often called a *business firm,* is a privately owned organization such as Target, Nike, or Cree that serves its customers to earn a profit so that it can survive. **Profit** is the money left after a for-profit organization subtracts its total expenses from its total revenues and is the reward for the risk it undertakes in marketing its offerings.

profit
The reward to a for-profit organization for the risk it undertakes in marketing its offerings.

Making Responsible Decisions

Using Social Entrepreneurship to Help People

What do Teach For America and SightLife have in common?

The answer: They are "social entrepreneurs" that are actively practicing—you guessed it!—social entrepreneurship. In a nutshell, social entrepreneurship applies innovative approaches to organize, create, and manage a venture to solve the practical needs of society. These usually are nonprofit organizations and focus on issues facing people who lack the financial or political means to solve their own problems. Let's look at the two social entrepreneurs mentioned above, models of creative nonprofit organizations.

TEACHFORAMERICA

Teach For America works in partnership with communities to expand educational opportunity for children facing the challenges of poverty. Founded in 1990, Teach For America recruits and develops a diverse corps of outstanding individuals of all academic disciplines to commit two years to teach in high-need schools and become lifelong leaders in the movement to end educational inequity. Today, 11,000

corps members are teaching in 48 urban and rural regions across the country, while 32,000 alumni work across sectors to ensure that all children have access to an excellent education.

SightLife® The World Through New Eyes™

The mission of SightLife is incredibly clear and specific: "To end cornea blindness." Cornea blindness, affecting 10 million people globally, can be cured by transplanting a donated, healthy cornea to replace a diseased one. Seattle-based SightLife finds cornea donors and prepares the tissues for surgery. SightLife works with eye surgeons and health organizations in about 30 countries. In 2012, SightLife provided almost 14,000 corneas for transplant—improving the lives of their recipients.

Cree is an example of a for-profit organization. Its Cree® LED light bulb replaces the traditional incandescent bulb, is 84 percent more energy efficient, and lasts for 25,000 hours.

Video 2-1
Cree® LED Bulb Ad
kerin.tv/cr6e/v2-1

In contrast, a *nonprofit organization* is a nongovernmental organization that serves its customers but does not have profit as an organizational goal. Instead, its goals may be operational efficiency or client satisfaction. Regardless, it also must receive sufficient funds above its expenses to continue operations. Social entrepreneurs like Teach For America and SightLife, described in the Making Responsible Decisions box, seek to solve the practical needs of society and are usually structured as nonprofit organizations.[5] For simplicity in the rest of the book, the terms *firm, company,* and *organization* are used interchangeably to cover both for-profit and nonprofit organizations.

Lastly, a *government agency* is a federal, state, county, or city unit that provides a specific service to its constituents. For example, the Census Bureau, a unit of the U.S. Department of Commerce, is a federal government agency that provides population and economic data.

Organizations that develop similar offerings create an *industry*, such as the computer industry or the automobile industry.[6] As a result, organizations make strategic decisions that reflect the dynamics of the industry to create a compelling and sustainable advantage for their offerings relative to those of competitors to achieve a superior level of performance.[7] Much of an organization's marketing strategy is having a clear understanding of the industry within which it competes.

What Is Strategy?

An organization has limited human, financial, technological, and other resources available to produce and market its offerings—it can't be all things to all people! Every organization must develop strategies to help focus and direct its efforts to accomplish

strategy
An organization's long-term course of action that delivers a unique customer experience while achieving its goals.

its goals. However, the definition of strategy has been the subject of debate among management and marketing theorists. For our purpose, **strategy** is an organization's long-term course of action designed to deliver a unique customer experience while achieving its goals.[8] All organizations set a strategic direction. And marketing helps to both set this direction and move the organization there.

The Structure of Today's Organizations

Large organizations are extremely complex. They usually consist of three organizational levels whose strategies are linked to marketing, as shown in Figure 2–1.

Corporate Level   The *corporate level* is where top management directs overall strategy for the entire organization. "Top management" usually means the board of directors and senior management officers with a variety of skills and experiences that are invaluable in establishing the organization's overall strategy.

The president or chief executive officer (CEO) is the highest ranking officer in the organization and is usually a member of its board of directors. This person must possess leadership skills ranging from overseeing the organization's daily operations to spearheading strategy planning efforts that may determine its very survival.

In recent years, many large firms have changed the title of the head of marketing from vice president of marketing to chief marketing officer (CMO). These CMOs have an increasingly important role in top management because of their ability to think strategically. Most bring multi-industry backgrounds, cross-functional management expertise, analytical skills, and intuitive marketing insights to their job. These CMOs are increasingly called upon to be their organizations' "visionaries for the future" by staying in touch with consumers' needs and wants.[9]

Strategic Business Unit Level   Some multimarket, multiproduct firms, such as Prada and Johnson & Johnson, manage a portfolio or group of businesses. Each group is a *strategic business unit (SBU)*, which is a subsidiary, division, or unit of an organization that markets a set of related offerings to a clearly defined target market.

FIGURE 2–1
The board of directors oversees the three levels of strategy in organizations: corporate, strategic business unit, and functional.

Prada manages a portfolio or group of businesses—including perfume, leather goods, and luggage—each of which may be viewed as a strategic business unit (SBU).

At the *strategic business unit level*, managers set a more focused direction for their unit to exploit value-creating opportunities. For less complex firms with a single business focus, such as Ben & Jerry's, the corporate and business unit levels may merge.

Functional Level   Each strategic business unit has a *functional level*, where groups of specialists actually create value for the organization. The term *department* generally refers to these specialized functions such as marketing and finance (see Figure 2–1). At the functional level, the organization's strategic direction becomes its most specific. Just as there is a hierarchy of levels within an organization, there is a hierarchy of strategic directions set by managers at each level.

A key role of the marketing department is to look outward by listening to customers, developing offerings, implementing marketing program actions, and then evaluating whether those actions are achieving the organization's goals. When developing marketing programs for new or improved offerings, an organization's senior management may form *cross-functional teams*. These consist of a small number of people from different departments who are mutually accountable to accomplish a task or a common set of performance goals. Sometimes these teams will have outside suppliers or customers, to assist them.

> **learning review**
>
> 2-1. What is the difference between a for-profit and a nonprofit organization?
>
> 2-2. What are examples of a functional level in an organization?

STRATEGY IN VISIONARY ORGANIZATIONS

 Describe core values, mission, organizational culture, business, and goals.

To be successful, today's organizations must be forward-looking. They must anticipate future events and then respond quickly and effectively to those events. A visionary organization must specify its foundation (why does it exist?), set a direction (what will it do?), and formulate strategies (how will it do it?), as shown in Figure 2–2.[10]

Organizational Foundation: Why Does It Exist?

An organization's foundation is its philosophical reason for being—why it exists. Successful visionary organizations use this foundation to guide and inspire their employees through three elements: core values, mission, and organizational culture.

core values
The fundamental, passionate, and enduring principles that guide an organization.

Core Values   An organization's **core values** are the fundamental, passionate, and enduring principles that guide its conduct over time. A firm's founders or senior management develop these core values, which are consistent with their essential beliefs and character.[11] They capture the firm's heart and soul and serve to inspire and motivate its *stakeholders*—employees, shareholders, board of directors, suppliers,

FIGURE 2–2
Today's visionary organizations use key elements to (1) establish a foundation and (2) set a direction using (3) strategies that enable them to develop and market their products successfully.

mission
A statement or vision of an organization's function in society.

distributors, creditors, unions, government, local communities, and customers. Core values also are timeless and guide the organization's conduct. To be effective, an organization's core values must be communicated to and supported by its top management and employees; if not, they are just hollow words.[12]

Mission By understanding its core values, an organization can take steps to define its **mission**, a statement of the organization's function in society that often identifies its customers, markets, products, and technologies. Often used interchangeably with *vision*, a *mission statement* should be clear, concise, meaningful, inspirational, and long-term.[13]

Medtronic is a world leader in producing heart pacemakers and other electrical stimulation devices to treat diabetes, Parkinson's disease, and chronic back pain.[14] Medtronic almost died in infancy when it was trying to raise start-up capital. A world-renowned consulting company surveyed doctors and "concluded there was no foreseeable market for pacemakers."[15] Earl Bakken, its founder, wrote this mission statement for Medtronic when it was launched a half century ago and which today remains virtually unchanged:

> To contribute to human welfare by application of biomedical engineering in the research, design, manufacture, and sale of instruments or appliances that alleviate pain, restore health, and extend life.

This statement exhibits the qualities of a good mission: a clear, challenging, and compelling picture of an envisioned future.[16]

Recently, many organizations have added a social element to their mission statements to reflect an ideal that is morally right and worthwhile. This is what Ben & Jerry's social mission statement shows in the chapter opener. Stakeholders, particularly customers, employees, and now society, are asking organizations to be exceptional citizens by providing long-term value while solving society's problems.

Organizational Culture An organization must connect with all of its stakeholders. Thus, an important corporate-level marketing function is communicating its core values and mission to them. Medtronic presents every new employee with a medallion depicting a "rising figure" on one side and the company's mission statement on the other. And each December, several patients describe to a large employee holiday celebration how Medtronic devices have changed their lives. These activities send clear messages to employees and other stakeholders about Medtronic's **organizational culture**—the set of values, ideas, attitudes, and norms of behavior that is learned and shared among the members of an organization.

organizational culture
The set of values, ideas, attitudes, and behavioral norms that is learned and shared among the members of an organization.

Organizational Direction: What Will It Do?

As shown in Figure 2–2, the organization's foundation enables it to set a direction in terms of (1) the "business" it is in and (2) its specific goals.

business
The underlying industry or market sector of an organization's offering.

Business A **business** describes the clear, broad, underlying industry or market sector of an organization's offering. To help define its business, an organization looks at the set of organizations that sell similar offerings—those that are in direct competition with each other—such as "the ice cream business." It can then begin to answer the questions, "What do we do?" or "What business are we in?"

Professor Theodore Levitt saw that 20th century American railroads defined their business too narrowly, proclaiming, "We are in the railroad business!" This myopic focus caused them to lose sight of who their customers were and what they needed. So railroads failed to develop strategies to compete with airlines, barges, pipelines, and trucks. As a result, many railroads merged or went bankrupt. Railroads should have realized they were in "the transportation business."[17]

In the first half of the 20th century, what "business" did railroad executives believe they were in? The text reveals their disastrous error.

With today's increased global competition, many organizations are rethinking their *business model*, the strategies an organization develops to provide value to the customers it serves. Technological innovation is often the trigger for this business model change. American newspapers are looking for a new business model as former subscribers now get their news online. Bookstore retailer Barnes & Noble, too, is rethinking its *business model* as e-book readers like Amazon's Kindle and Apple's iPad have gained widespread popularity.

Rovio Entertainment Ltd., the Finnish developer of the Angry Birds video games, is redefining the business it is in. Taking a lesson from Theodore Levitt, Rovio sees itself as being an "entertainment company," *not* a "gaming company." Time will tell whether the Angry Birds brand and image that works so well with its video games will carry over to amusement parks, clothing, toys, soda, candy, and movies![18]

Video 2-2
Angry Birds
kerin.tv/cr6e/v2-2

goals (objectives)
Statements of an accomplishment of a task to be achieved, often by a specific time.

market share
Ratio of a firm's sales to the total sales of all firms in the industry.

Goals **Goals** or **objectives** (terms used interchangeably in this book) are statements of an accomplishment of a task to be achieved, often by a specific time. Goals convert an organization's mission and business into long- and short-term performance targets. Business firms can pursue several different types of goals:

- *Profit.* Most firms seek to maximize profits—to get as high a financial return on their investments (ROI) as possible.
- *Sales* (dollars or units). If profits are acceptable, a firm may elect to maintain or increase its sales even though profits may not be maximized.
- *Market share.* **Market share** is the ratio of sales revenue of the firm to the total sales revenue of all firms in the industry, including the firm itself.
- *Quality.* A firm may offer the highest quality, as Medtronic does with its implantable medical devices.
- *Customer satisfaction.* Customers are the reason the organization exists, so their perceptions and actions are of vital importance. Satisfaction can be measured with surveys or by the number of customer complaints.
- *Employee welfare.* A firm may recognize the critical importance of its employees by stating its goal of providing them with good employment opportunities and working conditions.
- *Social responsibility.* Firms may seek to balance the conflicting goals of stakeholders to promote their overall welfare, even at the expense of profits.

Nonprofit organizations (such as museums and hospitals) also have goals, such as to serve consumers as efficiently as possible. Similarly, government agencies set goals that seek to serve the public good.

Organizational Strategies: How Will It Do It?

Rovio, the maker of Angry Birds, is altering its business model to include stuffed animals, which requires entirely new organizational strategies.

As shown in Figure 2–2, the organizational foundation sets the "why" of organizations and the organizational direction sets the "what." To convert these into actual results, the organizational strategies are concerned with the "how." These organizational strategies vary in at least two ways, depending on (1) a strategy's level in the organization and (2) the offerings an organization provides to its customers.

Variation by Level   Moving down the levels in an organization involves creating increasingly specific, detailed strategies and plans. So, at the corporate level, top managers may struggle with writing a meaningful mission statement; while at the functional level, the issue is who makes tomorrow's sales call.

Variation by Product   Organizational strategies also vary by the organization's products. The strategy will be far different when marketing a very tangible physical good (a Medtronic heart pacemaker), a service (a Southwest Airlines flight), or an idea (a donation to the American Red Cross). This is Rovio's challenge as it tries to extend its new business model of becoming an "entertainment company" to encompass stuffed toys, amusement parks, and movies.

Most organizations develop a marketing plan as a part of their strategic marketing planning efforts. A **marketing plan** is a road map for the marketing actions of an organization for a specified future time period, such as one year or five years. The planning phase of the strategic marketing process (discussed later) usually results in a marketing plan that directs the marketing actions of an organization. Appendix A at the end of this chapter provides guidelines for writing a marketing plan.

marketing plan
A road map for the marketing activities of an organization for a specified future time period.

> **learning review**
>
> 2-3. What is the meaning of an organization's mission?
>
> 2-4. What is the difference between an organization's business and its goals?

Tracking Strategic Performance with Marketing Dashboards

LO 2-3 Explain why managers use marketing dashboards and marketing metrics.

Although marketing managers can set strategic directions for their organizations, how do they know if they are making progress in getting there? One answer is to measure performance by using marketing dashboards.

Car Dashboards and Marketing Dashboards   A **marketing dashboard** is the visual computer display of the essential information related to achieving a marketing objective.[19] Often, active hyperlinks provide further detail. An example is when a chief marketing officer (CMO) wants to see daily what the effect of a new TV advertising campaign is on a product's sales.[20]

The idea of a marketing dashboard really comes from the display of information found on a car's dashboard. On a car's dashboard, we glance at the fuel gauge and take action when our gas is getting low. With a marketing dashboard, a marketing manager glances at a graph or table and makes a decision whether to take action or to analyze the problem further.

marketing dashboard
The visual computer display of essential marketing information.

Dashboards, Metrics, and Plans   The marketing dashboard of Sonatica, a hypothetical hardware and software firm, appears in Figure 2–3 on the next page. It shows graphic displays of key performance indicators linked to its product lines. Each display in a marketing dashboard shows a **marketing metric**, which is a measure of the quantitative value or trend of a marketing action or result.[21] Choosing

marketing metric
A measure of the value or trend of a marketing action or result.

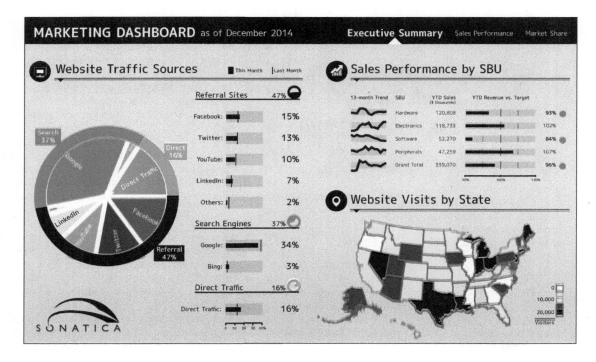

FIGURE 2–3
An effective marketing dashboard, like this one from Sonatica, a hypothetical hardware and software firm, helps managers assess a business situation at a glance.

which marketing metrics to display is critical for a busy manager, who can be overwhelmed with irrelevant data.[22]

Today's marketers use *data visualization,* which presents information about an organization's marketing metrics graphically so marketers can quickly (1) spot deviations from plans during the evaluation phase and (2) take corrective actions.[23] This book uses data visualization in many figures to highlight in color key points described in the text. The Sonatica marketing dashboard in Figure 2–3 uses data visualization tools like a pie chart, a line or bar chart, and a map to show how parts of its business are performing as of December 2014:

- *Website Traffic Sources.* The color-coded perimeter of the pie chart shows the three main sources of website traffic (referral sites at 47 percent, search engines at 37 percent, and direct traffic at 16 percent). These three colors link to those of the circles in the column of website traffic sources. Of the 47 percent of traffic coming from referral sites, the horizontal *bullet graphs* to the right show that Sonatica's Facebook visits comprise 15 percent of total website traffic, up from a month ago (as shown by the vertical line).
- *Sales Performance by SBU.* The *spark lines* (the wavy lines in the far left column) show the 13-month trends of Sonatica's strategic business units (SBUs). For example, the trends in electronics and peripherals are generally up, causing their sales to exceed their YTD (year to date) targets. Conversely, both software and hardware sales failed to meet YTD targets, a problem quickly noted by a marketing manager seeing the red "warning" circles in their rows at the far right. This suggests that immediate corrective actions are needed for the software and hardware SBUs.
- *Website Visits by State.* The U.S. map shows that the darker the state, the greater the number of website visits for the current month. For example, Texas has close to 20,000 visits per month, while Illinois has none.

Using Marketing Dashboards
How Well Is Ben & Jerry's Doing?

As the marketing manager for Ben & Jerry's, you need to assess how it is doing within the United States in the super-premium ice cream market in which it competes. For this, you choose two marketing metrics: dollar sales and dollar market share.

Your Challenge   Scanner data from checkout counters in supermarkets and other retailers show the total industry sales of super-premium ice cream were $1.25 billion in 2014. Internal company data show you that Ben & Jerry's sold 50 million units at an average price of $5.00 per unit in 2014. A "unit" in super-premium ice cream is one pint.

Your Findings   Dollar sales and dollar market share can be calculated for 2014 using simple formulas and displayed on the Ben & Jerry's marketing dashboard as follows:

$$\text{Dollar sales}(\$) = \text{Average price} \times \text{Quantity sold}$$
$$= \$5.00 \times 50 \text{ million units}$$
$$= \$250 \text{ million}$$

$$\text{Dollar market share}(\%) = \frac{\text{Ben \& Jerry's sales (\$)}}{\text{Total industry sales (\$)}}$$
$$= \frac{\$250 \text{ million}}{\$1.25 \text{ billion}}$$
$$= 0.20 \text{ or } 20\%$$

Your dashboard displays show that from 2013 to 2014 dollar sales increased from $240 million to $250 million and that dollar market share grew from 18.4 to 20.0 percent.

Ben & Jerry's Dollar Sales

Ben & Jerry's Dollar Market Share

Your Action   The results need to be compared with the goals established for these metrics. In addition, they should be compared with previous years' results to see if the trends are increasing, flat, or decreasing. This will lead to marketing actions.

The Ben & Jerry's dashboard in the Using Marketing Dashboards box shows how the two widely used marketing metrics of dollar sales and dollar market share can help the company assess its growth performance from 2013 to 2014. The Using Marketing Dashboard boxes in later chapters highlight other key marketing metrics and how they can lead to marketing actions.

SETTING STRATEGIC DIRECTIONS

LO 2-4 Discuss how an organization assesses where it is now and where it seeks to be.

To set a strategic direction, an organization needs to answer two difficult questions: (1) Where are we now? and (2) Where do we want to go?

A Look Around: Where Are We Now?

Asking an organization where it is at the present time involves identifying its competencies, customers, and competitors.

Competencies   Senior managers must ask the question: What do we do best? The answer involves an assessment of the organization's core *competencies*, which are its special capabilities—the skills, technologies, and resources—that distinguish it from other organizations and provide customer value. Exploiting these competencies can lead to success.

Video 2-3
Medtronic
kerin.tv/cr6e/v2-3

Medtronic's competencies include world-class technology, training, and service that respond to life-threatening medical needs. *Bloomberg Businessweek* magazine has called Medtronic "the standard setter for quality."[24] Competencies should be distinctive enough to provide a *competitive advantage*, a unique strength relative to competitors that provides superior returns, often based on quality, time, cost, or innovation.[25]

Customers   Ben & Jerry's customers are ice cream and frozen yogurt eaters who have different preferences (form, flavor, health, and convenience). Medtronic's pacemaker customers include cardiologists and heart surgeons who serve patients that need this type of device. Lands' End communicates a remarkable commitment to its customers and its product quality with these unconditional words:

Guaranteed. Period.®

The Lands' End website points out that this guarantee has always been an unconditional one. It reads: "If you're not satisfied with any item, simply return it to us at any time for an exchange or refund of its purchase price." But to get the message across more clearly to its customers, it created the two-word guarantee. The point is that Lands' End's strategy must provide genuine value to customers to ensure that they have a satisfying experience.

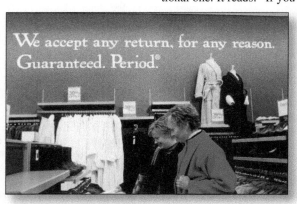

Lands' End's unconditional guarantee for its products highlights its focus on customers.

Competitors   In today's global marketplace, the distinctions among competitors are increasingly blurred. Lands' End started as a catalog retailer. But today, Lands' End competes with not only other clothing catalog retailers but also traditional department stores, mass merchandisers, and specialty shops. Even well-known clothing brands such as Liz Claiborne now have their own chain stores. Although only some of the clothing in any of these stores directly competes with Lands' End offerings, all of these retailers have websites to sell their offerings over the Internet. This means there's a lot of competition out there.

Growth Strategies: Where Do We Want to Go?

Knowing where the organization is at the present time enables managers to set a direction for the firm and allocate resources to move in that direction. Business portfolio analysis and diversification analysis aid managers with these decisions.

Business Portfolio Analysis   Successful organizations have a portfolio or range of offerings (products and services) that possess different growth rates and market shares within the industry in which they operate. The Boston Consulting Group (BCG), an internationally known management consulting firm, has developed **business portfolio analysis**. It is a technique that managers use to quantify performance measures and growth targets to analyze their firms' strategic business units (SBUs) as though they were a collection of separate investments.[26] The purpose of this tool is to determine which SBU or offering generates cash and which one requires cash to fund the organization's growth opportunities.

business portfolio analysis
A technique that managers use to quantify performance measures and growth targets of their firms' strategic business units.

Let's assume you are filling the shoes of Apple CEO Tim Cook. Based on your knowledge of Apple products, you are currently conducting a quick analysis of four

FIGURE 2–4
Boston Consulting Group (BCG) business portfolio analysis for four of Apple's consumer-related SBUs. The red arrow indicates typical movement of a product through the matrix.

What can Apple expect in future growth of sales revenues from its Mac Pro/ iMac/MacBook products...

... or its iPad/iPad mini tablet devices?

major Apple SBUs through 2016. We will introduce you to using business portfolio analysis as we look at the possible future of four Apple SBUs.

The BCG business portfolio analysis requires an organization to locate the position of each of its SBUs on a growth-share matrix (see Figure 2–4). The vertical axis is the *market growth rate*, which is the annual rate of growth of the SBU's industry. The horizontal axis is the *relative market share*, defined as the sales of the SBU divided by the sales of the largest firm in the industry. A relative market share of 10× (at the left end of the scale) means that the SBU has 10 times the share of its largest competitor, whereas a share of 0.1× (at the right end of the scale) means it has only 10 percent of the share of its largest competitor.

The BCG has given specific names and descriptions to the four resulting quadrants in its growth-share matrix based on the amount of cash they generate for or require from the organization:

1. *Question marks* are SBUs with a low share of high-growth markets. They require large injections of cash just to maintain their market share, much less increase it. The name implies management's dilemma for these SBUs: choosing the right ones to invest in and phasing out the rest.
2. *Stars* are SBUs with a high share of high-growth markets that may need extra cash to finance their own rapid future growth. When their growth slows, they are likely to become cash cows.
3. *Cash cows* are SBUs that generate large amounts of cash, far more than they can use. They have dominant shares of slow-growth markets and provide cash to cover the organization's overhead and to invest in other SBUs.
4. *Dogs* are SBUs with low shares of slow-growth markets. Although they may generate enough cash to sustain themselves, they may not become real winners for the organization. Dropping SBUs that are dogs may be required if they consume more cash than they generate, except when relationships with other SBUs, competitive considerations, or potential strategic alliances exist.[27]

An organization's SBUs often start as question marks and go counterclockwise around Figure 2–4 to become stars, then cash cows, and finally dogs—as shown by the red arrow in the center of Figure 2–4. Because an organization has limited influence on the market growth rate, its main objective is to try to change its relative dollar or unit market share. To do this, management decides what strategic role each SBU should have in the future and either injects cash into or removes cash from it.

Using the BCG business portfolio analysis framework, Figure 2–4 shows that the Apple picture might look this way from 2013 to 2016 for its four strategic business units:[28]

1. *iPhone* (smartphones). Apple launched its revolutionary iPhone smartphone in 2007. iPhone unit sales skyrocketed but have since leveled off. By 2017, the smartphone market is expected to grow at an annual rate of 13 percent due to falling prices. Apple's iPhone had a 15 percent share of the global smartphone market in 2013—second to Samsung, whose share was 41 percent. Apple's iPhone is a *question mark* and may remain so for the next few years as it introduces new, compelling models such as the iPhone 6.[29]

2. *iPad/iPad mini* (tablet devices). Launched in 2010, iPad unit sales reached an astonishing 40 percent market share by 2013—leading both Samsung's Galaxy (18 percent) and Amazon's Kindle (4 percent). Global tablet unit sales are expected to more than double by 2016 as consumers switch from desktop and laptop PCs to tablet devices, with Apple still the market share leader. As these products mature, Apple's iPad/iPad mini SBU that is now a *star* may move toward being a *cash cow* as its growth begins to subside after 2016.[30]

3. *iPod* (MP3 music players). Apple entered the MP3 player market with its iPod device in 2001. Today, Apple sells four iPod product lines (classic, nano, shuffle, and touch). By 2013, Apple had a 70 percent share of this market! However, global MP3 music player unit sales are falling and are expected to decline further by 2016 because smartphones will continue to replace MP3 devices. For Apple, its iPod SBU is a *cash cow* (high market share in a low-growth market) and is likely to remain one for the near future.[31]

4. *iMac/Mac Pro/MacBook* (Apple's desktop and laptop personal computers or PCs). By mid-2013, Apple offered three lines of desktops (Mac Pro, iMac, and Mac mini) and two lines of laptops (MacBook Pro and MacBook Air). Global PC unit sales have declined in recent years due to the growth of tablet devices. Although Apple has slightly increased its global market share, by 2016, global PC unit sales are expected to fall dramatically due to the explosion in tablet device sales. As a result, Apple's Mac PC SBU appears to be moving toward being a *dog*.[32]

So, how did you—as Tim Cook—rank the growth opportunity for each of Apple's four SBUs for the future? In terms of priority, perhaps Apple will "milk" the cash generated from the iMac/Mac Pro/MacBook PC SBU [4] and iPod MP3 player SBU [3] to fund the investments needed to exploit the growth opportunities projected for the iPhone smartphone SBU [1] and the iPad/iPad mini tablet devices SBU [2]. Is Apple concerned? With its history of pulling exotic new-product "rabbits out of its hat," let's wait and see!

The primary strength of business portfolio analysis lies in forcing a firm to place each of its SBUs in the growth-share matrix, which in turn suggests which SBUs will be cash producers and cash users in the future. Weaknesses of this analysis arise from the difficulty in (1) getting the needed information and (2) incorporating competitive data into business portfolio analysis.[33]

How can Ben & Jerry's develop new products and social responsibility programs that contribute to its mission? The text describes how the strategic marketing process and its SWOT analysis can help.

diversification analysis
A technique a firm uses to search for growth opportunities from among current and new products and markets.

Diversification Analysis **Diversification analysis** is a technique that helps a firm search for growth opportunities from among current and new markets as well as current and new products.[34] For any market, there is both a current product (what the firm now sells) and a new product (what the firm might sell in the future). And for any product there is both a current market (the firm's existing customers) and a new market (the firm's potential customers). As Ben & Jerry's seeks to increase sales revenues, it considers all four market-product strategies shown in Figure 2–5:

- *Market penetration* is a marketing strategy to increase sales of current products in current markets, such as selling more Ben & Jerry's Bonnaroo Buzz Fair

FIGURE 2–5
Four market-product strategies: alternative ways to expand sales revenues for Ben & Jerry's using diversification analysis.

MARKETS	PRODUCTS	
	Current	**New**
Current	**Market penetration** Selling more Ben & Jerry's super-premium ice cream to Americans	**Product development** Selling a new product such as children's clothing under the Ben & Jerry's brand to Americans
New	**Market development** Selling Ben & Jerry's super-premium ice cream to Brazilians for the first time	**Diversification** Selling a new product such as children's clothing under the Ben & Jerry's brand to Brazilians for the first time

Video 2-4
B&J's Bonnaroo Buzz Ad
kerin.tv/cr6e/v2-4

Trade–sourced ice cream to U.S. consumers. There is no change in either the basic product line or the markets served. Increased sales are generated by selling either more ice cream (through better promotion or distribution) *or* the same amount of ice cream at a higher price to its current customers.

- *Market development* is a marketing strategy to sell current products to new markets. For Ben & Jerry's, Brazil is an attractive new market. There is good news and bad news for this strategy: As household incomes of Brazilians increase, consumers can buy more ice cream; however, the Ben & Jerry's brand may be unknown to Brazilian consumers.
- *Product development* is a marketing strategy of selling new products to current markets. Ben & Jerry's could leverage its brand by selling children's clothing in the United States. This strategy is risky because Americans may not see the company's expertise in ice cream as extending to children's clothing.
- *Diversification* is a marketing strategy of developing new products and selling them in new markets. This is a potentially high-risk strategy for Ben & Jerry's if it decides to try to sell Ben & Jerry's branded clothing in Brazil. Why? Because the firm has neither previous production nor marketing experience from which to draw in marketing clothing to Brazilian consumers.

learning review

2-5. What is the difference between a marketing dashboard and a marketing metric?

2-6. What is business portfolio analysis?

2-7. Explain the four market-product strategies in diversification analysis.

THE STRATEGIC MARKETING PROCESS

LO 2-5
Explain the three steps of the planning phase of the strategic marketing process.

strategic marketing process
An approach whereby an organization allocates its marketing mix resources to reach its target markets.

After an organization assesses where it is and where it wants to go, other questions emerge, such as:

1. How do we allocate our resources to get where we want to go?
2. How do we convert our plans into actions?
3. How do our results compare with our plans, and do deviations require new plans?

To answer these questions, an organization uses the **strategic marketing process**, whereby an organization allocates its marketing mix resources to reach its target markets. This process is divided into three phases: planning, implementation, and evaluation, as shown in Figure 2–6 on the next page.

CHAPTER 2   Developing Successful Organizational and Marketing Strategies

35

situation analysis
Taking stock of where a firm or product has been recently, where it is now, and where it is headed.

SWOT analysis
An acronym describing an organization's appraisal of its internal strengths and weaknesses and its external opportunities and threats.

The Planning Phase of the Strategic Marketing Process

Figure 2–6 shows the three steps in the planning phase of the strategic marketing process: (1) situation (SWOT) analysis, (2) market-product focus and goal setting, and (3) the marketing program.

Step 1: Situation (SWOT) Analysis   The essence of **situation analysis** is taking stock of where the firm or product has been recently, where it is now, and where it is headed in terms of the organization's marketing plans and the external forces and trends affecting it. An effective summary of a situation analysis is a **SWOT analysis**, an acronym describing an organization's appraisal of its internal **S**trengths and **W**eaknesses and its external **O**pportunities and **T**hreats.

The SWOT analysis is based on an exhaustive study of four areas that form the foundation upon which the firm builds its marketing program:

- Identify trends in the organization's industry.
- Analyze the organization's competitors.
- Assess the organization itself.
- Research the organization's present and prospective customers.

Assume you are responsible for doing the SWOT analysis for Ben & Jerry's shown in Figure 2–7. The SWOT table has four cells formed by the combination of internal versus external factors (the rows) and favorable versus unfavorable factors (the columns) that identify Ben & Jerry's strengths, weaknesses, opportunities, and threats.

The task is to translate the results of the SWOT analysis into specific marketing actions that will help the firm grow. The ultimate goal is to identify the *critical* strategy-related factors that impact the firm and then build on vital strengths, correct glaring weaknesses, exploit significant opportunities, and avoid disaster-laden threats.

The Ben & Jerry's SWOT analysis in Figure 2–7 can be the basis for these kinds of specific marketing actions. An action in each of the four cells might be:

- *Build on a strength.* Find specific efficiencies in distribution with parent-company Unilever's existing ice cream brands.

FIGURE 2–7
Ben & Jerry's: A SWOT analysis to keep it growing. The picture painted in this SWOT analysis is the basis for management actions.

LOCATION OF FACTOR	TYPE OF FACTOR	
	Favorable	Unfavorable
Internal	**Strengths** • Prestigious, well-known brand name among U.S. consumers • Complements Unilever's other ice cream brands • Recognized for its social mission, values, and actions	**Weaknesses** • B&J's social responsibility actions could reduce focus • Experienced managers needed to help growth • Modest sales growth and profits in recent years
External	**Opportunities** • Growing demand for quality ice cream in overseas markets • Increasing U.S. demand for Greek-style yogurt • Many U.S. firms successfully use product and brand extensions	**Threats** • B&J customers read nutritional labels and are concerned with sugary and fatty desserts • Competes with General Mills and Nestlé brands • Increasing competition in international markets

- *Correct a weakness.* Recruit experienced managers from other consumer product firms to help stimulate growth.
- *Exploit an opportunity.* Develop new product lines of low-fat, low-carb frozen Greek-style yogurt flavors to respond to changes in consumer tastes.
- *Avoid a disaster-laden threat.* Focus on less risky international markets, such as Brazil and Argentina.

Step 2: Market-Product Focus and Goal Setting   Determining which products will be directed toward which customers (step 2 of the planning phase in Figure 2–6) is essential for developing an effective marketing program (step 3). This decision is often based on **market segmentation**, which involves aggregating prospective buyers into groups, or segments, that (1) have common needs and (2) will respond similarly to a marketing action. This enables an organization to focus specific marketing programs on its target market segments.

In the case of Medtronic, executives researched a potential new market in Asia by talking extensively with doctors in India and China. Medtronic discovered that these doctors wanted an affordable pacemaker that was reliable and easy to implant. So Medtronic developed and marketed a new product, the Champion™ pacemaker, directed at satisfying their needs.

Goal setting involves specifying measurable marketing objectives to be achieved. For example, the goal may be to introduce Medtronic's Champion™ pacemaker in emerging markets, starting in Asia. Let's examine Medtronic's five-year plan to reach the "affordable and reliable" pacemaker segment that results in its marketing program:[35]

- *Set marketing and product goals.* Chances of new-product success are increased by specifying both market and product goals. Based on their market research, Medtronic executives set the following goal: Market the Chinese-produced Champion™ pacemaker to Asian markets within three years.
- *Select target markets.* The Champion™ pacemaker will be targeted at cardiologists and heart surgery clinics in India, China, and other Asian countries.
- *Find points of difference.* **Points of difference** are those characteristics of a product that make it superior to competitive substitutes. Just as a competitive advantage is a unique strength of an entire organization compared to its competitors, points of difference are unique characteristics of one of its products that make it superior to competitive products it faces in the marketplace. For the Champion™ pacemaker, the key points of difference are its high quality, long life, reliability, ease of use, and low cost.

market segmentation
The aggregating of potential buyers into groups that have common needs and will respond similarly to a marketing action.

points of difference
Those characteristics of a product that make it superior to competitive substitutes.

• *Position the product.* The pacemaker will be "positioned" in cardiologists' and patients' minds as a medical device that is high quality and reliable with a long, nine-year life. The name Champion was selected after testing acceptable names among doctors in India, China, Pakistan, Singapore, and Malaysia.

So step 2 in the planning phase of the strategic marketing process—deciding which products will be directed toward which customers—is the foundation for step 3, developing the marketing program.

Step 3: Marketing Program   Activities in step 2 tell the marketing manager which customers to target and which customer needs the firm's product offerings can satisfy—the *who* and *what* aspects of the strategic marketing process. The *how* aspect—step 3 in the planning phase—involves developing the program's marketing mix (the four Ps) and its budget. Figure 2–8 shows that each marketing mix element is combined to provide a cohesive marketing program. The five-year marketing plan for Medtronic's Champion™ pacemaker includes these marketing mix actions:

• *Product strategy.* Offer a Champion brand heart pacemaker with only those features needed by Asian patients.
• *Price strategy.* Manufacture the Champion to control costs so that it can be priced below $1,000 (in U.S. dollars)—an affordable price for Asian markets.
• *Promotion strategy.* Introduce the Champion at medical conventions across Asia to demonstrate its many beneficial features.
• *Place (distribution) strategy.* Search out, utilize, and train reputable medical device distributors across Asia to call on cardiologists and medical clinics.

Putting this marketing program into effect requires that the firm commit time and money to it in the form of a sales forecast (see Chapter 7) and budget that must be approved by top management.

FIGURE 2–8
The four Ps elements of the marketing mix must be blended to produce a cohesive marketing program.

learning review

2-8. What are the three steps of the planning phase of the strategic marketing process?

2-9. What are points of difference and why are they important?

The Implementation Phase of the Strategic Marketing Process

LO 2-6 Describe the four components of the implementation phase of the strategic marketing process.

As shown in Figure 2–6, the result of the hours spent in the planning phase of the strategic marketing process is the firm's marketing plan. Implementation, the second phase of the strategic marketing process, involves carrying out the marketing plan that emerges from the planning phase. If the firm cannot execute the marketing plan—in the implementation phase—the planning phase wasted time and resources.

There are four components of the implementation phase: (1) obtaining resources, (2) designing the marketing organization, (3) defining precise tasks, responsibilities, and deadlines, and (4) actually executing the marketing program designed in the planning phase.

Obtaining Resources A key task in the implementation phase of the strategic marketing process is finding adequate human and financial resources to execute the marketing program successfully. Small business owners often obtain funds from savings, family, friends, and bank loans. Marketing managers in existing organizations obtain these resources by getting top management to divert profits from BCG stars or cash cows.

Designing the Marketing Organization A marketing program needs a marketing organization to implement it. Figure 2–9 shows the organization chart of a typical manufacturing firm, giving some details of the marketing department's structure. Four managers of marketing activities are shown to report to the vice president of marketing or chief marketing officer (CMO). Several regional sales managers and an international sales manager may report to the manager of sales. The product or brand managers and their subordinates help plan, implement, and evaluate the marketing plans for their offerings. However, the entire marketing organization is responsible for converting these marketing plans into realistic marketing actions.

Defining Precise Tasks, Responsibilities, and Deadlines Successful implementation requires team members know the tasks for which they are responsible and the deadlines for completing them. To implement the thousands of tasks on a new aircraft design, Lockheed Martin typically holds weekly program meetings. The outcome of each of these meetings is an *action item list*, an aid to implementing a marketing plan consisting of four columns: (1) the task, (2) the person responsible for completing that task,

FIGURE 2–9
Organization of a typical manufacturing firm, showing a breakdown of the marketing department.

(3) the date to finish the task, and (4) what is to be delivered. Within hours of completing a program meeting, the action item list is circulated to those attending. This then serves as the starting agenda for the next meeting. Meeting minutes are viewed as secondary and backward-looking. Action item lists are forward-looking, clarify the targets, and put strong pressure on people to achieve their designated tasks by the deadline.

Suppose, for example, that you and two friends undertake a term project on the problem, "How can the college increase attendance at its performing arts concerts?" The instructor says the term project must involve a mail survey of a sample of students, and the written report with the survey results must be submitted by the end of the 11-week quarter. To begin, you identify all the project tasks and then estimate the time required to complete each one. To complete it in 11 weeks, your team must plan which activities can be done concurrently (at the same time) to save time.

Scheduling activities can be done efficiently with a *Gantt chart*, which is a graph of a program schedule. Figure 2–10 shows a Gantt chart—invented by Henry L. Gantt— used to schedule the class project, demonstrating how the concurrent work on several tasks enables the students to finish the project on time. Software programs such as Microsoft Project simplify the task of developing a program schedule or Gantt chart.

The key to all scheduling techniques is to distinguish tasks that *must* be done sequentially from those that *can* be done concurrently. For example, Tasks 1 and 2 that are shaded yellow in Figure 2–10 *must* be done sequentially. This is because in order to type and copy the final questionnaire before mailing (Task 2), the student *must* have a final draft of the questionnaire (Task 1). In contrast, Tasks 6 and 7 that are shaded blue *can* be done concurrently. So writing the final report (Task 7) *can* be started before tabulating the questions (Task 6) is completed. This overlap speeds up project completion.

Executing the Marketing Program Marketing plans are meaningless without effective execution of those plans. This requires attention to detail for both marketing strategies and marketing tactics. A **marketing strategy** is the means by which a marketing goal is to be achieved, usually characterized by a specified target market and a marketing program to reach it. The term implies both the end sought (target market) and the means or actions to achieve it (marketing program).

To implement a marketing program successfully, hundreds of detailed decisions are often required to develop the actions that comprise a marketing program for an offering. These actions, called **marketing tactics**, are detailed day-to-day operational marketing actions for each element of the marketing mix that contribute to the overall success of marketing strategies. Writing ads and setting prices for new product lines are examples of marketing tactics.

marketing strategy
The means by which a marketing goal is to be achieved.

marketing tactics
Detailed day-to-day operational decisions essential to the overall success of marketing strategies.

FIGURE 2–10
This Gantt chart shows how three students (A, B, and C) can schedule tasks to complete a term project on time. Software programs, such as Microsoft Project, simplify the task of developing a program schedule or Gantt chart.

Task description	Students involved in task	Week of quarter 1 2 3 4 5 6 7 8 9 10 11
1. Construct, test on friends, and complete a final draft of a questionnaire	A	
2. Type and copy the final questionnaire	C	
3. Randomly select the names of 200 students from the school directory	A	
4. Address and stamp envelopes; mail questionnaires	C	
5. Collect returned questionnaires	B	
6. Tabulate and analyze data from returned questionnaires	B	
7. Write final report	A, B, C	
8. Type and submit final report	C	

KEY: ▲ Planned completion date ▢ Planned period of work Current date
▲ Actual completion date ▢ Actual period of work

FIGURE 2–11
The evaluation phase of the strategic marketing process requires that the organization compare actual results with goals to identify and act on deviations to fill in its "planning gap." The text describes how Apple is working to fill in its planning gap.

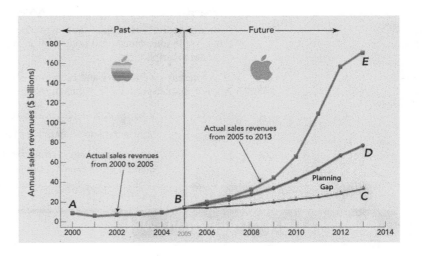

LO 2-7 Discuss how managers identify and act on deviations from plans.

The Evaluation Phase of the Strategic Marketing Process

The evaluation phase of the strategic marketing process seeks to keep the marketing program moving in the direction set for it (see Figure 2–6). Accomplishing this requires the marketing manager to (1) compare the results of the marketing program with the goals in the written plans to identify deviations and (2) act on these deviations—exploiting positive deviations and correcting negative ones.

Comparing Results with Plans to Identify Deviations   At the end of its fiscal year, which is September 30, Apple begins the evaluation phase of its strategic marketing process. Suppose you are on an Apple task force in late 2005 that is responsible for making plans through 2013. You observe that extending the 2000–2005 trend of Apple's recent sales revenues (line AB in Figure 2–11) to 2013 along line BC shows an annual growth in sales revenue unacceptable to Apple's management.

Looking at potential new products in the Apple pipeline, your task force set an aggressive annual sales growth target of 25 percent per year—the line BD in Figure 2–11. This would give sales revenues of $34 billion in 2009 and $78 billion in 2013.

This reveals a gray wedge-shaped gap DBC in the figure. Planners call this the *planning gap*, the difference between the projection of the path to reach a new sales revenue goal (line BD) and the projection of the path of a plan already in place (line BC). The ultimate purpose of the firm's marketing program is to "fill in" this planning gap—in the case of your Apple task force, to move its future sales revenue line from the slow-growth line BC up to the more challenging target of line BD.

The essence of evaluation involves comparing actual results with goals set. To reach aggressive growth targets in sales revenues, firms like Apple continuously look for a new Boston Consulting Group SBU or product *cash cow* or *star*—like the Apple Watch introduced in September 2014.

Acting on Deviations   When evaluation shows that actual performance differs from expectations, managers need to take immediate marketing actions—exploiting positive deviations and correcting negative ones. Comparing the explosion in Apple's actual sales revenues from 2006 to 2013 (line BE in Figure 2–11) to its target sales revenues (line BD) shows Apple's rare, world-class ability to both generate and anticipate consumer demand and commercialize new technologies for its revolutionary offerings. Let's consider some of its marketing actions:

- *Exploiting a positive deviation.* Favorable customer reactions to Apple's iPhone (2007) and its iPad (2010) enable it to sell the products globally and to introduce improved versions and models, such as the iPad mini (2012).

- *Correcting a negative deviation.* As Apple's desktop PCs became dated, it moved aggressively to replace them with new iMacs (2012) and Mac Pro (2013). Also, Apple introduced an iPhone mini in 2013 to spur sales in China, a huge market for smartphones.

Apple has several *stars* and *cash cows* to fill in its planning gap. We shall explore Apple's market-product strategies in more detail later in Chapters 8 and 9.

---

learning review

2-10. What is the implementation phase of the strategic marketing process?

2-11. How do the goals set for a marketing program in the planning phase relate to the evaluation phase of the strategic marketing process?

LEARNING OBJECTIVES REVIEW

LO 2-1 *Describe three kinds of organizations and the three levels of strategy in them.*

An organization is a legal entity that consists of people who share a common mission. It develops offerings (goods, services, or ideas) that create value for both the organization and its customers by satisfying their needs and wants. Today's organizations are of three types: for-profit organizations, nonprofit organizations, and government agencies. A for-profit organization serves its customers to earn a profit so that it can survive. A nonprofit organization is a nongovernmental organization that serves its customers but does not have profit as an organizational goal. Instead, its goals may be operational efficiency or client satisfaction. A government agency is a federal, state, county, or city unit that provides a specific service to its constituents. Most large for-profit and nonprofit organizations are divided into three levels of strategy: (*a*) the corporate level, where top management directs overall strategy for the entire organization; (*b*) the strategic business unit level, where managers set a more specific strategic direction for their businesses to exploit value-creating opportunities; and (*c*) the functional level, where groups of specialists actually create value for the organization.

LO 2-2 *Describe core values, mission, organizational culture, business, and goals.*

Organizations exist to accomplish something for someone. Core values are the organization's fundamental, passionate, and enduring principles that guide its conduct over time. The organization's mission is a statement of its function in society, often identifying its customers, markets, products, and technologies. Organizational culture is a set of values, ideas, attitudes, and norms of behavior that is learned and shared among the members of an organization. To answer the question, "What business are we in?" an organization defines its "business"—the clear, broad, underlying industry category or market sector of its offering. Finally, the organization's goals (or objectives) are statements of an accomplishment of a task to be achieved, often by a specific time.

LO 2-3 *Explain why managers use marketing dashboards and marketing metrics.*

Marketing managers use marketing dashboards to visually display on a single computer screen the essential information required to make a decision to take an action or further analyze a problem. This information consists of key performance measures of a product category, such as sales or market share, and is known as a marketing metric, which is a measure of the quantitative value or trend of a marketing activity or result. Most organizations tie their marketing metrics to the quantitative objectives established in their marketing plan, which is a road map for the marketing activities of an organization for a specified future time period, such as one year or five years.

LO 2-4 *Discuss how an organization assesses where it is now and where it seeks to be.*

Managers of an organization ask two key questions to set a strategic direction. The first question, "Where are we now?" requires an organization to (*a*) reevaluate its competencies to ensure that its special capabilities still provide a competitive advantage; (*b*) assess its present and prospective customers to ensure they have a satisfying customer experience—the central goal of marketing today; and (*c*) analyze its current and potential competitors from a global perspective to determine whether it needs to redefine its business. The second question, "Where do we want to go?" requires an organization to set a specific direction and allocate resources to move it in that direction. Business portfolio and diversification analyses help an organization do this. Managers use business portfolio analysis to assess the organization's strategic business units (SBUs), product lines, or individual products as though they were a collection of separate investments (*cash cows*, *stars*, *question marks*, and *dogs*) to determine the amount of cash each should receive. Diversification analysis is a tool that helps managers use one or a combination of four strategies to increase revenues: market penetration; market development; product development; and diversification.

LO 2-5 *Explain the three steps of the planning phase of the strategic marketing process.*

An organization uses the strategic marketing process to allocate its marketing mix resources to reach its target markets. This process is divided into three phases: planning, implementation, and evaluation. The planning phase consists of (*a*) a situation (SWOT) analysis, which involves taking stock of where the firm or product has been recently, where it is now, and where it is headed and focuses on the organization's internal factors (strengths and weaknesses) and the external forces and trends affecting it (opportunities and threats); (*b*) a market-product focus through market segmentation (grouping buyers into segments with common needs and similar responses to marketing programs) and goal setting, which in part requires creating points of difference (those characteristics of a product that make it superior to competitive substitutes); and (*c*) a marketing program that specifies the budget and actions (marketing strategies and tactics) for each marketing mix element.

LO 2-6 *Describe the four components of the implementation phase of the strategic marketing process.*

The implementation phase of the strategic marketing process carries out the marketing plan that emerges from the planning phase. It has four key components: (*a*) obtaining resources; (*b*) designing the marketing organization to perform product management,

marketing research, sales, and advertising and promotion activities; (*c*) developing schedules to identify the tasks that need to be done and the time, the people responsible, and the deadlines for each task—often with an action item list and Gantt chart; and (*d*) executing the marketing strategies, and the associated marketing tactics that contribute to the firm's overall success.

LO 2-7 *Discuss how managers identify and act on deviations from plans.*

The evaluation phase of the strategic marketing process seeks to keep the marketing program moving in the direction that was established in the marketing plan. This requires the marketing manager to compare the results from the marketing program with the marketing plan's goals to (*a*) identify deviations or "planning gaps" and (*b*) take corrective actions to exploit positive deviations or correct negative ones.

LEARNING REVIEW ANSWERS

2-1 What is the difference between a for-profit and a non-profit organization?

Answer: A for-profit organization is a privately owned organization that serves its customers to earn a profit so that it can survive. A nonprofit organization is a nongovernmental organization that serves its customers but does not have profit as an organizational goal. Instead, its goals may be operational efficiency or client satisfaction.

2-2 What are examples of a functional level in an organization?

Answer: The functional level in an organization is where groups of specialists from the marketing, finance, manufacturing/operations, accounting, information systems, research & development, and/or human resources departments focus on a specific strategic direction to create value for the organization.

2-3 What is the meaning of an organization's mission?

Answer: A mission is a clear, concise, meaningful, inspirational, and long-term statement of the organization's function in society, often identifying its customers, markets, products, and technologies. It is often used interchangeably with *vision*.

2-4 What is the difference between an organization's business and its goals?

Answer: An organization's business describes the clear, broad, underlying industry or market sector of an organization's offering. An organization's goals (or objectives) are statements of an accomplishment of a task to be achieved, often by a specific time.

2-5 What is the difference between a marketing dashboard and a marketing metric?

Answer: A marketing dashboard is the visual computer display of the essential information related to achieving a marketing objective. Each variable displayed in a marketing dashboard is a marketing metric, which is a measure of the quantitative value or trend of a marketing action or result.

2-6 What is business portfolio analysis?

Answer: Business portfolio analysis is a technique that managers use to quantify performance measures and growth targets to analyze their firms' strategic business units (SBUs) as though they were a collection of separate

investments. The purpose of this tool is to determine which SBU or offering generates cash and which one requires cash to fund the organization's growth opportunities.

2-7 Explain the four market-product strategies in diversification analysis.

Answer: The four market-product strategies in diversification analysis are: (1) Market penetration, which is a marketing strategy to increase sales of current products in current markets. There is no change in either the basic product line or the markets served. (2) Market development, which is a marketing strategy to sell current products to new markets. (3) Product development, which is a marketing strategy of selling new products to current markets. (4) Diversification, which is a marketing strategy of developing new products and selling them in new markets.

2-8 What are the three steps of the planning phase of the strategic marketing process?

Answer: The three steps of the planning phase of the strategic marketing process are: (1) Situation analysis, which involves taking stock of where the firm or product has been recently, where it is now, and where it is headed in terms of the organization's marketing plans and the external forces and trends affecting it. (2) Market-product focus and goal setting, which determines what products an organization will offer to which customers. (3) Marketing program, which is where an organization develops the marketing mix elements and budget for each offering.

2-9 What are points of difference and why are they important?

Answer: Points of difference are those characteristics of a product that make it superior to competitive substitutes— offerings the organization faces in the marketplace. They are important factors in the success or failure of a new product.

2-10 What is the implementation phase of the strategic marketing process?

Answer: The implementation phase carries out the marketing plan that emerges from the planning phase and consists of: (1) obtaining resources; (2) designing the marketing organization; (3) defining precise tasks, responsibilities, and deadlines; and (4) executing the marketing program designed in the planning phase.

2-11 **How do the goals set for a marketing program in the planning phase relate to the evaluation phase of the strategic marketing process?**
Answer: The planning phase goals or objectives are used as the benchmarks with which the actual performance results are compared in the evaluation phase to identify deviations from the written marketing plans and then exploit positive ones or correct negative ones.

FOCUSING ON KEY TERMS

business p. 28
business portfolio analysis p. 32
core values p. 26
diversification analysis p. 34
goals (objectives) p. 28
market segmentation p. 37
market share p. 28

marketing dashboard p. 29
marketing metric p. 29
marketing plan p. 29
marketing strategy p. 40
marketing tactics p. 40
mission p. 27
objectives (goals) p. 28

organizational culture p. 27
points of difference p. 37
profit p. 23
situation analysis p. 36
strategic marketing process p. 35
strategy p. 25
SWOT analysis p. 36

APPLYING MARKETING KNOWLEDGE

1 (a) Using Medtronic as an example, explain how a mission statement gives it a strategic direction. (b) Create a mission statement for your own career.

2 What competencies best describe (a) your college or university and (b) your favorite restaurant?

3 Compare the advantages and disadvantages of Ben & Jerry's attempting to expand sales revenues by using (a) a product development strategy or (b) a market development strategy.

4 Select one strength, one weakness, one opportunity, and one threat from the Ben & Jerry's SWOT analysis shown in Figure 2–7. Suggest an action that a B&J marketing manager might take to address each factor.

5 What is the main result of each of the three phases of the strategic marketing process? (a) planning, (b) implementation, and (c) evaluation.

6 Parts of Tasks 5 and 6 in Figure 2–10 are done both concurrently and sequentially. (a) How can this be? (b) How does it help the students meet the term paper deadline? (c) What is the main advantage of scheduling tasks concurrently rather than sequentially?

7 The goal-setting step in the planning phase of the strategic marketing process sets quantified objectives for use in the evaluation phase. What does a manager do if measured results fail to meet objectives? Exceed objectives?

BUILDING YOUR MARKETING PLAN

1 Read Appendix A, "Building an Effective Marketing Plan." Then write a 600-word executive summary for the Paradise Kitchens marketing plan using the numbered headings shown in the plan. When you have completed the draft of your own marketing plan, write a 600-word executive summary to go in the front of your own marketing plan.

2 Using Chapter 2 and Appendix A as guides, focus your marketing plan by (a) writing your mission statement in 25 words or less, (b) listing three nonfinancial goals and three financial goals, (c) writing your competitive advantage in 35 words or less, and (d) creating a SWOT analysis table.

3 Draw a simple organization chart for your organization.

VIDEO CASE 2   IBM: Using Strategy to Build a "Smarter Planet"

Video 2-5
IBM Video Case
kerin.tv/cr6e/v2-5

"'Smarter Planet' is not an advertising campaign, it's not even a marketing campaign, it is a business strategy," explains Ann Rubin, vice president of advertising at IBM.
The "Smarter Planet" strategy is based on the idea that the next major revolution in the global marketplace will be the instrumentation and integration of the world's processes and infrastructures, generating unprecedented amounts of data. The data captured and analyzed in industries such as banking, energy, health care, and retailing will allow IBM to help businesses be more efficient, productive, and responsive.

THE COMPANY

Founded in 1911, IBM has a history of innovation and focus on customers. The blue covers on its computers, blue letters in the IBM logo, and dark blue suits worn by IBM salespeople led to the now popular company nickname, "Big Blue." Today, it has over 430,000 employees in more than 170 countries. *Forbes* magazine ranks IBM as the fourth most valuable brand in the world. The company is a leading developer of new business technologies, receiving more than 5,000 patents each year. Some of its well-known inventions include the automated teller machine (ATM), the hard disk drive, the magnetic stripe card, relational databases, and the Universal Product Code (UPC). In addition, IBM recently gained attention for its artificial intelligence program called Watson, which challenged two *Jeopardy!* game show champions and won! According to Virginia Rometty, the current CEO of IBM, "IBM is an innovation company."

VALUES, MISSION, AND STRATEGY

Recently, IBM initiated a project to facilitate online discussions of key business issues among 50,000 employees to identify common themes and perspectives. According to Sam Palmisano, former CEO of IBM, "We needed to affirm IBM's reason for being, what sets the company apart, and what should drive our actions as individual IBMers." The results were three underlying values of IBM's business practices: (1) dedication to every client's success, (2) innovation that matters—for our company and for the world, and (3) trust and personal responsibility in all relationships. These values now come to life at IBM in its "policies, procedures, and daily operations," explains Palmisano.

IBM's core values also help to define its mission, or its general function in society. In clear, concise, inspirational language, IBM's mission statement is:

- At IBM, we strive to lead in the invention, development and manufacture of the industry's most advanced information technologies, including computer systems, software, storage systems, and microelectronics.
- We translate these advanced technologies into value for our customers through our professional solutions, services, and consulting businesses worldwide.

The mission, and the values it represents, helps define the organizational culture at IBM. Executives, managers, and all employees create the culture through the strategies they select and the detailed plans for accomplishing them.

IBM's strategies are based on its assessment of fundamental changes in the business environment. First, IBM sees global changes such as fewer trade barriers, the growth of developing economies, and increasing access to the World Wide Web. These changes necessitate a new type of corporation that IBM calls the "globally integrated enterprise." Second, IBM foresees a new model of computing that includes computational capability in phones, cameras, cars, and other appliances and allows economic, social, and physical systems to be connected. This connectivity creates a "smarter planet." Finally, IBM predicts a growing demand for custom-made technological solutions that help organizations measure and achieve specific outcomes.

As a result, IBM began to shift from commodity-based businesses such as PCs and hard disk drives, to "customizable" businesses such as software and services. The change in IBM was so substantial that it has described its plan in a document called the *2015 Road Map*. The Map describes four strategic opportunities: (1) growth markets such as China, India, Brazil, and Africa, (2) business analytics and optimization, (3) cloud and smarter computing, and (4) the connected, "smarter" planet. These opportunities suggest a strategy that delivers value through business and IT innovation to selected industries with an integrated enterprise. The overarching strategy that highlights IBM's capabilities is called "Building a Smarter Planet."

BUILDING A SMARTER PLANET

The Smarter Planet initiative is designed for clients who value IBM's industry and process expertise, systems integration capability, and research capacity. A smarter planet, while global by definition, happens on the industry level. It is driven by forward-thinking organizations that share a common outlook: They see change as an opportunity, and they act on possibilities, not just react to problems.

John Kennedy, vice president of marketing, explains, "'A Smarter Planet' actually surfaced from observing what was happening in our clients. They were looking to take the vast amount of data that was being generated inside their companies and looking to better understand it." To IBM "smart" solutions have three characteristics. They are instrumented, they are intelligent, and they are interconnected. Millions of digital devices, now connected through the Internet, produce data that can be turned into knowledge through advanced computational power. IBM believes that this knowledge can help reduce costs, cut waste, improve efficiency, and increase productivity for companies, industries, and cities.

Since introducing the Smarter Planet strategy, IBM has collaborated with more than 600 organizations around the globe. The success of the strategy is evident in the broad range of industries where "smart" solutions are being implemented. They include banking; communications; electronics, automotive and aerospace; energy and utilities; government; health care; insurance; oil and gas; retailing; and transportation. Each industry has reported a variety of applications.

In a study of 439 cities, for example, smart solutions such as ramp metering, signal coordination, and accident management reduced travel delays by more than 700,000 annually, saving each city $15 million. A study by the U.S. Department of Energy found that consumers with smart electric meters cut their power usage and saved 10 percent on their power bills. Retailers who implemented smart systems to analyze buying behavior, merchandise assortment, and demand were able to cut supply chain costs by 30 percent, reduce inventory levels by 25 percent, and increase sales by 10 percent.

THE BUILDING A SMARTER PLANET MARKETING PLAN

Marketing and communications professionals at IBM have developed the marketing plan for IBM's "Smarter Planet" strategy. The general goal is to describe the company's view of the next era of information technology and its impact on business and society. The execution of the plan includes messaging from IBM leaders, an advertising campaign, an Internet presence, and public relations communications. In addition, IBM measures and tracks the performance of the marketing activities.

The importance of the Smarter Planet strategy was first communicated through a message from the top. Palmisano prepared a "Letter from the Chairman" for the annual report. His message was a powerful statement. Smarter Planet, according to Palmisano, "is not a metaphor. It describes the infusion of intelligence into the way the world actually works."

IBM also used a print and television advertising campaign to add detail to the general message. The ads focused on the ability to improve the world now, with IBM's help. "I think what's different about Smarter Planet," says Ann Rubin, "is that it was not inward facing, it was looking out at what the world needed. We felt like we could go out there and influence the world for the better."

IBM recently celebrated its 100th anniversary! Its record of success is testimony to the resilience of a business model that encourages long-term strategies that can say "Welcome to a Smarter Planet."

Questions

1 What is IBM's "Smarter Planet" business strategy? How does this strategy relate to IBM's mission and values?
2 Conduct a SWOT analysis for IBM's Smarter Planet initiative. What are the relevant trends to consider for the next three to five years?
3 How can IBM communicate its strategy to companies, cities, and governments?
4 What are the benefits of the Smarter Planet initiative to (a) society and (b) IBM?
5 How should IBM measure the results of the Smarter Planet strategy?

Chapter Notes

1. Information obtained from selected web pages and press releases from the Ben & Jerry's website, www.benjerry.com; and "Ice Cream History Revealed! What Was Ben & Jerry's First Ice Cream Flavor?" *BusinessWire,* November 15, 2011, http://www.business-wire.com/news/home/20111115007275/en/Ice-Cream-History-Revealed!-Ben-Jerry's-Ice-.
2. Joe Van Brussel, "Ben & Jerry's Become B-Corp Certified, Adds Credibility to Impact Investing Movement," *Huffington Post: Business,* October 23, 2012; see http://www.huffingtonpost.com/2012/10/23/ben-and-jerrys-b-corp-impact-investing_n_2005315.
3. "Ice Cream: Global Industry Guide," *Datamonitor,* April 27, 2010, press release posted at MarketResearch.com; see http://www.marketresearch.com/MarketLine-v3883/Ice-cream-Global-Guide-6509861.
4. Roger Kerin and Robert Peterson, *Strategic Marketing Problems: Cases and Comments,* 13th ed. (Upper Saddle River, NJ: Prentice Hall, 2013), p. 140.
5. See http://www.teachforamerica.org; and Wendy Kaufman, "Ex-Starbucks Exec Helps Develop Global Eye Banks," *National Public Radio,* March 8, 2011.
6. For a discussion on how industries are defined and offerings are classified, see the following: the American Marketing Association

website, which provides one definition of an industry (www.marketingpower.com/mg-dictionary-view1509.php) and the Census Bureau's Economic Classification Policy Committee Issues Paper #1 (www.census.gov/epcd/naics/issues1), which aggregates industries in the NAICS (www.census.gov/epcd/www/naicsdev.htm) from a "production-oriented" view.
7. W. Chan Kim and Reneé Mauborgne, "Blue Ocean Strategy: From Theory to Practice," *California Management Review* 47, no. 3 (*Spring 2005*), p. 105; and Michael E. Porter, "What Is Strategy?" *Harvard Business Review* OnPoint Article, November–December 1996, p. 2.
8. The definition of *strategy* reflects thoughts appearing in Porter, "What Is Strategy?" pp. 4, 8; a condensed definition of strategy is found on the American Marketing Association website: www.marketingpower.com; and Gerry Johnson, Kevan Scholes, and Richard Wittington, *Exploring Corporate Strategy* (Upper Saddle River, NJ: Prentice Hall, 2005), p. 10.
9. George S. Day and Robert Malcolm, "The CMO and the Future of Marketing," *Marketing Management,* Spring 2012, pp. 34–43; Christine Moorman, "Ten Trends from The CMO Survey™," *Marketing Management,* Fall 2012, pp. 15–17; John Kador, "The View from Marketing: How to Get the Most from Your CMO," *Chief Executive,*

July/August 2011, pp. 60–61; Jessica Shambora, "Wanted: Fearless Marketing Execs," *Fortune*, April 15, 2011, p. 27; Roger A. Kerin, "Strategic Marketing and the CMO," *Journal of Marketing*, October 2005, pp. 12–13; and The CMO Council: Biographies of Selected Advisory Board Members. See www.cmocouncil.org/advisory-board.php.

10. Taken in part from Jim Collins and Jerry I. Porras, *Built to Last: Successful Habits of Visionary Companies* (New York: HarperCollins Publishers, 2002), p. 54.

11. Ibid., p. 73; and Patrick M. Lencioni, "Make Your Values Mean Something," *Harvard Business Review*, July 2002, p. 6.

12. Catherine M. Dalton, "When Organizational Values Are Mere Rhetoric," *Business Horizons* 49 (September–October 2006), p. 345.

13. Collins and Porras, *Built to Last*, pp. 94–95; and Tom Krattenmaker, "Write a Mission Statement That Your Company Is Willing to Live," *Harvard Management Communication Letter*, March 2002, pp. 3–4.

14. James Walsh, "U.S. Patient Gets Vitamin-Sized Medtronic Pacemaker," *Star Tribune*, February 21, 2014, pp. D1, D6.

15. Tom Holloran, "Remarks to Medtronic Employees at the Celebration of the 50th Anniversary of Earl Bakken's Invention of the Wearable Pacemaker," December 6, 2007; and Janet Moore, "An Enduring Mission," *Star Tribune*, December 27, 2010, pp. D1, D2.

16. Collins and Porras, *Built to Last*, pp. 219–233.

17. Theodore Levitt, "Marketing Myopia," *Harvard Business Review*, July–August 1960, pp. 45–56.

18. John McDermott, "With 'Angry Birds Star Wars,' Rovio Has Another Gaming, Merchandise Hit on Its Hands," *Advertising Age*, November 13, 2012. See http://adage.com/article/digital/angry-birds-star-wars-rovio-gaming-merchandise-hit-hands/238280.

19. The definition is adapted from Stephen Few, *Information Dashboard Design: The Effective Visual Communication of Data* (Sebastopol, CA: O'Reilly Media, Inc., 2006), pp. 2–46.

20. Koen Pauwels, et al., *Dashboards & Marketing: Why, What, How and What Research Is Needed?* (Hanover, NH: Tuck School, Dartmouth, May 2008).

21. Mark Jeffery, *Data-Driven Marketing: The 15 Metrics Everyone in Marketing Should Know* (Hoboken, NJ: John Wiley & Sons, Inc., 2010), Chapter 1; Paul W. Farris, Neil T. Bendle, Phillip E. Pfeifer, and David J. Reibstein, *Marketing Metrics*, 2nd ed. (Upper Saddle River, NJ: Wharton School Publishing, 2010).

22. Art Weinstein and Shane Smith, "Game Plan," *Marketing Management*, Fall 2012, pp. 24–31; Alexander Chiang, "Special Interview with Stephen Few, Dashboard and Data Visualization Expert," *Marketing Dashboard*, July 14, 2011; and Stephen Few, *Now You See It* (Oakland, CA: Analytics Press, 2009), Chapters 1–3.

23. The now-classic reference on effective graphic presentation is Edward R. Tufte, *The Visual Display of Quantitative Information*, 2nd ed. (Cheshire, CT: Graphics Press, 2001); see also Few, *Information Dashboard Design*, Chapters 3–5.

24. Michael Arndt, "High-Tech and Handcrafted," *Businessweek*, July 5, 2004, pp. 86–87.

25. Kerin and Peterson, *Strategic Marketing Problems*, pp. 2–3; and Derek F. Abell, *Defining the Business* (Englewood Cliffs, NJ: Prentice Hall, 1980), p. 18.

26. Adapted from *The Experience Curve Reviewed, IV: The Growth Share Matrix of the Product Portfolio* (Boston: The Boston Consulting Group, 1973). See also https://www.bcgperspectives.com/content/classics/strategy_the_product_portfolio (registration and login required for access).

27. Roger A. Kerin, Vijay Mahajan, and P. Rajan Varadarajan, *Contemporary Perspectives on Strategic Marketing Planning* (Boston: Allyn & Bacon, 1990), p. 52.

28. See the Apple press release library at http://www.apple.com/pr/library.

29. "Gartner: Apple Falls Below 20% in Smartphone Market Share," *MacDailyNews*, May 14, 2013. See http://macdailynews.com/2013/05/14/gartner-apple-falls-below-20-in-smartphone-market-share; Ingrid Lunden, "IDC: Android OEMs Shipped 162M Smartphones in Q1, More Than 4X Apple's Rate; Windows Phone Now in (Distant) Third," *Tech Crunch*, May 16, 2013. See http://techcrunch.com/2013/05/16/idc-android-oems-shipped-162m-smartphones-in-q1-more-than-4x-apples-rate-windows-phone-now-a-distant-third/.

30. Larry Magid, "Apple's Tablets Selling Well but Market Share Slips While Samsung Grows," *Forbes*, May 1, 2013. See http://www.forbes.com/sites/larrymagid/2013/05/01/apples-tablet-market-share-slips-and-samsung-grows; Lisa Rapaport, "Tablet Sales to More Than Double by 2016," *SFGate*, December 5, 2012. See http://www.sfgate.com/technology/article/Tablet-sales-to-more-than-double-by-2016-4094671.php.

31. "iPod Still Has 70% of MP3 Player Market," *MacTech*. See http://www.mactech.com/2012/07/24/ipod-still-has-70-mp3-player-market; Zak Islam, "Smartphones Heavily Decrease Sales of iPod, MP3 Players," *Tom's Hardware*, December 31, 2012. See http://www.tomshardware.com/news/Smartphones-iPod-MP3-Players-Sales,20062.html.

32. "May PC Shipments Reflect Slow Second Quarter, According to IDC," IDC press release, June 28, 2013. See http://www.idc.com/getdoc.jsp?containerId=prUS24202913.

33. Strengths and weaknesses of the BCG technique are based on Derek F. Abell and John S. Hammond, *Strategic Market Planning: Problem and Analytic Approaches* (Englewood Cliffs, NJ: Prentice Hall, 1979); Yoram Wind, Vijay Mahajan, and Donald Swire, "An Empirical Comparison of Standardized Portfolio Models," *Journal of Marketing*, Spring 1983, pp. 89–99; and J. Scott Armstrong and Roderick J. Brodie, "Effects of Portfolio Planning Methods on Decision Making: Experimental Results," *International Journal of Research in Marketing*, Winter 1994, pp. 73–84.

34. H. Igor Ansoff, "Strategies for Diversification," *Harvard Business Review*, September–October 1957, pp. 113–24.

35. Geoff Colvin, "How to Fix a Great American Business," *Fortune*, November 12, 2012, pp. 96–100; and Linda Swenson and Kenneth E. Goodpaster, *Medtronic in China (A)* (Minneapolis, MN: University of St. Thomas, 1999), pp. 4–5.

IBM: This case was written by Steven Hartley. Sources: Jessi Hempel, "IBM's Super Second Act," *Fortune*, March 21, 2011, pp. 114–24; Jessi Hempel, "IBM's Massive Bet on Watson," *Fortune*, October 7, 2013, pp. 81–88; Kurt Badenhausen, "The World's Most Valuable Brands," *Forbes*, August 30, 2010, p. 34; Jeffrey M. O'Brien, "IBM's Grand Plan to Save the Planet," *Fortune*, May 4, 2009, pp. 84–91; *IBM 2009 Annual Report*; *IBM 2010 Annual Report*; Samuel J. Palmisano, "Our Values at Work on Being an IBMer," IBM website, see http://www.ibm.com/ibm/values/us.

Credits

P. 23, Rex Features via AP Images; P. 24, Teach For America logos are trademarks or registered trademarks of Teach For America, Inc.; P. 24, Courtesy SightLife; P. 24, Used with permission; Courtesy Cree, Inc.; P. 26, Imaginechina via AP Images; P. 28, Digital Vision; P. 29, Juho Kuva/Bloomberg/Getty Images; P. 30, Courtesy Roger A. Kerin, Steven W. Hartley, William Rudelius; P. 32, ©Rick Armstrong; P. 33, ©duckycards/iStockphoto LP; P. 33, ©Eddisonphotos/iStockphoto LP; P. 33, ©Cesare Ferrari/iStockphoto LP; P. 33, Flickr Editorial/Getty Images; P. 33, flickr Editorial/Getty Images; P. 33, ©Saturated/iStockphoto LP; P. 34, ©M. Hruby; P. 41, Photo by Mickey Pfleger/Time & Life Pictures/Getty Images; P. 41, Photographer: Jerome Favre/Bloomberg via Getty Images; P. 44, Courtesy IBM Corporation; P. 45, Courtesy IBM Corporation.

APPENDIX A

BUILDING AN EFFECTIVE MARKETING PLAN

"If you have a real product with a distinctive point of difference that satisfies the needs of customers, you may have a winner," says Arthur R. Kydd, who has helped launch more than 60 start-up firms. "And you get a real feel for this in a well-written marketing or business plan," he explains.[1]

This appendix (1) describes what marketing and business plans are, including the purposes and guidelines in writing effective plans, and (2) provides a sample marketing plan.

MARKETING PLANS AND BUSINESS PLANS

After explaining the meanings, purposes, and audiences of marketing plans and business plans, this section describes some writing guidelines for them and what external funders often look for in successful plans.

Meanings, Purposes, and Audiences

A *marketing plan* is a road map for the marketing actions of an organization for a specified future time period, such as one year or five years.[2] No single "generic" marketing plan applies to all organizations and all situations. Rather, the specific format for a marketing plan for an organization depends on the following:

- *The target audience and purpose.* Elements included in a particular marketing plan depend heavily on (1) who the audience is and (2) what its purpose is. A marketing plan for an internal audience seeks to point the direction for future marketing activities and is sent to all individuals in the organization who must implement the plan or who will be affected by it. If the plan is directed to an external audience, such as friends, banks, venture capitalists, or crowdfunding sources like Kickstarter for the purpose of raising capital, it has the additional function of being an important sales document. So it contains elements such as the strategic plan/focus, organization, structure, and biographies of key personnel that would rarely appear in an internal marketing

plan. The elements of a marketing plan for each of these two audiences are compared in Figure A–1.

- *The kind and complexity of the organization.* A neighborhood restaurant has a less detailed marketing plan than Medtronic, which serves international markets. The restaurant's plan would be relatively simple and directed at serving customers in a local market. In Medtronic's case, because there is a hierarchy of marketing plans, various levels of detail would be used—such as the entire organization, the strategic business unit, or the product/product line.
- *The industry.* Both the restaurant serving a local market and Medtronic, selling heart pacemakers globally, analyze competition. However, their geographic scopes are far different, as are the complexities of their offerings and, hence, the time periods likely to be covered by their plans. A one-year marketing plan may be adequate for the restaurant, but Medtronic may need a five-year planning horizon because product development cycles for complex, new medical devices may be many years.

In contrast to a marketing plan, a **business plan** is a road map for the entire organization for a specified future period of time, such as one year or five years.[3] A key difference between a marketing plan and a business plan is that the business plan contains details on the research and development (R&D)/operations/manufacturing activities of the organization. Even for a manufacturing business, the marketing plan is probably 60 or 70 percent of the entire business plan. For firms like a small restaurant or an auto repair shop, their marketing and business plans are virtually identical. The elements of a business plan typically targeted at internal and external audiences appear in the two right-hand columns in Figure A–1.

The Most-Asked Questions by Outside Audiences

Lenders and prospective investors reading a business or marketing plan that is used to seek new capital are

Element of the plan	Marketing plan		Business plan	
	For internal audience (to direct the firm)	For external audience (to raise capital)	For internal audience (to direct the firm)	For external audience (to raise capital)
1. Executive summary	✓	✓	✓	✓
2. Description of company		✓		✓
3. Strategic plan/focus		✓		✓
4. Situation analysis	✓	✓	✓	✓
5. Market-product focus	✓	✓	✓	✓
6. Marketing program strategy and tactics	✓	✓	✓	✓
7. R&D and operations program			✓	✓
8. Financial projections	✓	✓	✓	✓
9. Organization structure		✓		✓
10. Implementation plan	✓	✓	✓	✓
11. Evaluation	✓		✓	
Appendix A: Biographies of key personnel		✓		✓
Appendix B, etc.: Details on other topics	✓	✓	✓	✓

FIGURE A–1
Elements in typical marketing and business plans targeted at different audiences.

probably the toughest audiences to satisfy. Their most-asked questions include the following:

1. Is the business or marketing idea valid?
2. Is there something unique or distinctive about the product or service that separates it from substitutes and competitors?
3. Is there a clear market for the product or service?
4. Are the financial projections realistic and healthy?
5. Are the key management and technical personnel capable, and do they have a track record in the industry within which they must compete?
6. Does the plan clearly describe how those providing capital will get their money back and make a profit?

Rhonda Abrams, author of books on writing business plans, observes, "Although you may spend five months preparing your plan, the cold, hard fact is that an investor or lender can dismiss it in less than five minutes. If you don't make a positive impression in those critical first five minutes, your plan will be rejected."[4] While her comments apply to plans seeking to raise capital, the first five questions listed above apply equally well to plans prepared for internal audiences.

Writing and Style Suggestions

There are no magic one-size-fits-all guidelines for writing successful marketing and business plans. Still, the following writing and style guidelines generally apply:[5]

- Use a direct, professional writing style. Use appropriate business terms without jargon. Present and future tenses with active voice ("I will write an effective marketing plan") are generally better than past tense and passive voice ("An effective marketing plan was written by me").
- Be positive and specific to convey potential success. At the same time, avoid superlatives ("terrific," "wonderful"). Specifics are better than glittering generalities.
- Use numbers for impact, justifying projections with reasonable quantitative assumptions, where possible.
- Use bullet points for succinctness and emphasis. As with the list you are reading, bullets enable key points to be highlighted effectively.

- Use A-level (the first level) and B-level (the second level) headings under the numbered section headings to help readers make easy transitions from one topic to another. This also forces the writer to organize the plan more carefully.
- Use visuals where appropriate. Photos, illustrations, graphs, and charts enable massive amounts of information to be presented succinctly.
- Shoot for a plan 15 to 35 pages in length, not including financial projections and appendices. An uncomplicated small business may require only 15 pages, while a high-technology start-up may require more than 35 pages.
- Use care in layout, design, and presentation. Use 11- or 12-point type (you are now reading 10.5-point type) in the text. Use a serif type (with "feet," like that you are reading now) in the text because it is easier to read, and sans serif (without "feet") in graphs and charts like Figure A–1. A bound report with a nice cover and a clear title page adds professionalism.

These guidelines are used, where possible, in the sample marketing plan that follows.

SAMPLE FIVE-YEAR MARKETING PLAN FOR PARADISE KITCHENS, INC.

To help interpret the marketing plan for Paradise Kitchens, Inc., that follows, we will describe the company and suggest some guidelines for interpreting the plan.[6]

Background on Paradise Kitchens, Inc.

Randall and Leah Peters have over 40 years of food industry experience for General Foods and Pillsbury with a number of diverse responsibilities. With these backgrounds and their savings, they co-founded Paradise Kitchens, Inc., to produce and market a new line of high-quality frozen chili products.

Interpreting the Marketing Plan

The marketing plan on the next pages, based on an actual Paradise Kitchens plan, is directed at an external audience (see Figure A–1). For simplicity, let us assume it is early 2015, the Peters have company data through 2014, and they are developing a five-year marketing plan through 2019. Some details and dates have been altered, but the basic logic of the plan has been kept.

Notes in the margins next to the Paradise Kitchens plan fall into two categories:

1. *Substantive notes* are in blue boxes. These notes explain the significance of an element in the marketing plan and are keyed to chapter references in this textbook.
2. *Writing style, format, and layout notes* are in red boxes and explain the editorial or visual rationale for the element.

A word of encouragement: Writing an effective marketing plan is hard but also challenging and satisfying work. Dozens of the authors' students have used effective marketing plans they wrote for class in their interviewing portfolio to show prospective employers what they could do and to help them get their first job.

Appendix Notes

1. Personal interview with Arthur R. Kydd, St. Croix Management Group.
2. A guide to writing marketing plans is William A. Cohen, *The Marketing Plan,* 5th ed. (New York: Wiley and Sons, 2006).
3. Examples of guides to writing business plans include Rhonda Abrams, *Business Plan in a Day,* 3rd ed. (Palo Alto, CA: The Planning Shop, a Division of Rhonda, Inc., 2013); Rhonda Abrams, *Successful Business Plan Secrets & Strategies,* 5th ed. (Palo Alto, CA: The Planning Shop, a Division of Rhonda, Inc., 2010); and Joseph A. Covello and Brian J. Hazelgren, *The Complete Book of Business Plans,* 2nd ed. (Naperville, IL: Sourcebooks, 2006).
4. Abrams, *Successful Business Plan Secrets & Strategies,* ch. 4.
5. Some of these points are adapted from Abrams, *Successful Business Plan Secrets & Strategies,* chs. 1–3; others were adapted from William Rudelius, *Guidelines for Technical Report Writing* (Minneapolis: University of Minnesota, undated). See also William Strunk, Jr., and E.B. White, *The Elements of Style,* 4th ed. (Needham Heights, MA: Allyn & Bacon, 2000).
6. Personal interviews with Randall F. and Leah E. Peters, Paradise Kitchens, Inc.

Color-Coding Legend

Blue boxes explain significance of marketing plan elements.

Red boxes give writing style, format, and layout guidelines.

The Table of Contents provides quick access to the topics in the plan, usually organized by section and subsection headings.

Seen by many experts as the single most important element in the plan, the two-page Executive Summary "sells" the plan to readers through its clarity and brevity. For space reasons, it is not shown here, but the Building Your Marketing Plan exercise at the end of Chapter 2 asks the reader to write an Executive Summary for this plan.

The Company Description highlights the recent history and recent successes of the organization.

The Strategic Focus and Plan sets the strategic direction for the entire organization, a direction with which proposed actions of the marketing plan must be consistent. This section is not included in all marketing plans. See Chapter 2.

The qualitative Mission statement focuses the activities of Paradise Kitchens for the stakeholder groups to be served. See Chapter 2.

FIVE-YEAR MARKETING PLAN
Paradise Kitchens,® Inc.

Table of Contents

1. Executive Summary

2. Company Description

Paradise Kitchens,® Inc., was started by co-founders Randall F. Peters and Leah E. Peters to develop and market Howlin' Coyote® Chili, a unique line of single serve and microwavable Southwestern/Mexican style frozen chili products. The Howlin' Coyote line of chili was first introduced into the Minneapolis–St. Paul market and expanded to Denver two years later and Phoenix two years after that.

To the Company's knowledge, Howlin' Coyote is the only premium-quality, authentic Southwestern/Mexican style, frozen chili sold in U.S. grocery stores. Its high quality has gained fast, widespread acceptance in its targeted markets. In fact, same-store sales doubled in the last year for which data are available. The Company believes the Howlin' Coyote brand can be extended to other categories of Southwestern/Mexican food products, such as tacos, enchiladas, and burritos.

Paradise Kitchens believes its high-quality, high-price strategy has proven successful. This marketing plan outlines how the Company will extend its geographic coverage from 3 markets to 20 markets by the year 2019.

3. Strategic Focus and Plan

This section covers three aspects of corporate strategy that influence the marketing plan: (1) the mission, (2) goals, and (3) core competency/sustainable competitive advantage of Paradise Kitchens.

Mission

The mission of Paradise Kitchens is to market lines of high-quality Southwestern/Mexican food products at premium prices that satisfy consumers in this fast-growing food segment while providing challenging career opportunities for employees and above-average returns to stockholders.

The Goals section sets both the nonfinancial and financial targets—where possible in quantitative terms—against which the company's performance will be measured. See Chapter 2.

Goals

For the coming five years Paradise Kitchens seeks to achieve the following goals:

- Nonfinancial goals
    1. To retain its present image as the highest-quality line of Southwestern/Mexican products in the food categories in which it competes.
    2. To enter 17 new metropolitan markets.
    3. To achieve national distribution in two convenience store or supermarket chains by 2015 and five by 2016.
    4. To add a new product line every third year.
    5. To be among the top five chili lines—regardless of packaging (frozen or canned)—in one-third of the metro markets in which it competes by 2016 and two-thirds by 2018.
- Financial goals
    1. To obtain a real (inflation-adjusted) growth in earnings per share of 8 percent per year over time.
    2. To obtain a return on equity of at least 20 percent.
    3. To have a public stock offering by the year 2016.

Lists use parallel construction to improve readability—in this case a series of infinitives starting with "To . . ."

Core Competency and Sustainable Competitive Advantage

In terms of core competency, Paradise Kitchens seeks to achieve a unique ability to (1) provide distinctive, high-quality chilies and related products using Southwestern/Mexican recipes that appeal to and excite contemporary tastes for these products and (2) deliver these products to the customer's table using effective manufacturing and distribution systems that maintain the Company's quality standards.

Photos or sample ads can illustrate key points effectively, even if they are not in color as they appear here.

To translate these core competencies into a sustainable competitive advantage, the Company will work closely with key suppliers and distributors to build the relationships and alliances necessary to satisfy the high taste standards of our customers.

To help achieve national distribution through chains, Paradise Kitchens introduced this point-of-purchase ad that adheres statically to the glass door of the freezer case.

A brief caption on photos and sample ads ties them to the text and highlights their reason for being included.

To improve readability, each numbered section usually starts on a new page. (This is not done in this plan to save space.)

The Situation Analysis is a snapshot to answer the question, "Where are we now?" See Chapter 2.

The SWOT analysis identifies strengths, weaknesses, opportunities, and threats to provide a solid foundation, which is the springboard to identify subsequent actions in the marketing plan. See Chapter 2.

Each long table, graph, or photo is given a figure number and title. It then appears as soon as possible after the first reference in the text, accommodating necessary page breaks. This avoids breaking long tables like this one in the middle. Short tables or graphs are often inserted in the text without figure numbers because they don't cause serious problems with page breaks.

Effective tables seek to summarize a large amount of information in a short amount of space.

4. Situation Analysis

This situation analysis starts with a snapshot of the current environment in which Paradise Kitchens finds itself by providing a brief SWOT (strengths, weaknesses, opportunities, threats) analysis. After this overview, the analysis probes ever-finer levels of detail: industry, competitors, company, and consumers.

SWOT Analysis

Figure 1 shows the internal and external factors affecting the market opportunities for Paradise Kitchens. Stated briefly, this SWOT analysis highlights the great strides taken by the company since its products first appeared on grocers' shelves.

Figure 1. SWOT Analysis for Paradise Kitchens

Internal Factors	Strengths	Weaknesses
Management	Experienced and entrepreneurial management and board	Small size can restrict options
Offerings	Unique, high-quality, high-price products	Many lower-quality, lower-price competitors
Marketing	Distribution in three markets with excellent consumer acceptance	No national awareness or distribution; restricted shelf space in the freezer section
Personnel	Good workforce, though small; little turnover	Big gap if key employee leaves
Finance	Excellent growth in sales revenues	Limited resources may restrict growth opportunities when compared to giant competitors
Manufacturing	Sole supplier ensures high quality	Lack economies of scale of huge competitors
R&D	Continuing efforts to ensure quality in delivered products	Lack of canning and microwavable food processing expertise

External Factors	Opportunities	Threats
Consumer/Social	Upscale market, likely to be stable; Southwestern/Mexican food category is fast-growing segment due to growth in Hispanic American population and desire for spicier foods	Premium price may limit access to mass markets; consumers value a strong brand name
Competitive	Distinctive name and packaging in its markets	Not patentable; competitors can attempt to duplicate product; others better able to pay slotting fees
Technological	Technical breakthroughs enable smaller food producers to achieve many economies available to large competitors	Competitors have gained economies in canning and microwavable food processing
Economic	Consumer income is high; convenience important to U.S. households	More households "eating out," and bringing prepared take-out into home
Legal/Regulatory	High U.S. Food & Drug Administration standards eliminate fly-by-night competitors	Mergers among large competitors being approved by government

The text discussion of Figure 1 (the SWOT Analysis table) elaborates on its more important elements. This "walks" the reader through the information from the vantage point of the plan's writer.

The Industry Analysis section provides the backdrop for the subsequent, more detailed analysis of competition, the company, and the company's customers. Without an in-depth understanding of the industry, the remaining analysis may be misdirected. See Chapter 2.

Sales of Mexican entrees are significant and provide a variety of future opportunities for Paradise Kitchens.

Even though relatively brief, this in-depth treatment of sales of Mexican foods in the U.S. demonstrates to the plan's readers the company's understanding of the industry within which it competes.

The Competitor Analysis section demonstrates that the company has a realistic understanding of its major chili competitors and their marketing strategies. Again, a realistic assessment gives confidence that subsequent marketing actions in the plan rest on a solid foundation. See Chapters 2, 3, 7, and 8.

In the Company's favor internally are its strengths: an experienced management team and board of directors, excellent acceptance of its product line in the three metropolitan markets within which it competes, and a strong manufacturing and distribution system to serve these limited markets. Favorable external factors (opportunities) include the increasing appeal of Southwestern/Mexican foods, the strength of the upscale market for the Company's products, and food-processing technological breakthroughs that make it easier for smaller food producers to compete.

Among unfavorable factors, the main weakness is the limited size of Paradise Kitchens relative to its competitors in terms of the depth of the management team, the available financial resources, and the national awareness and distribution of product lines. Threats include the danger that the Company's premium prices may limit access to mass markets and competition from the "eating-out" and "take-out" markets.

Industry Analysis: Trends in Frozen and Mexican Foods

Frozen Foods. According to *Grocery Headquarters*, consumers are flocking to the frozen food section of grocery retailers. The reasons: hectic lifestyles demanding increased convenience and an abundance of new, tastier, and nutritious products. By 2013, total sales of frozen food in supermarkets, drugstores, and mass merchandisers, such as Target and Costco (excluding Walmart), were over $35 billion. Prepared frozen meals, which are defined as meals or entrees that are frozen and require minimal preparation, accounted for about one-quarter of the total frozen food market.

Sales of Mexican entrees were over $650 million in 2013. Heavy consumers of frozen meals, those who eat five or more meals every two weeks, tend to be kids, teens, and adults 35–44 years old.

Mexican Foods. Currently, Mexican foods such as burritos, enchiladas, and tacos are used in two-thirds of American households. These trends reflect a generally more favorable attitude on the part of all Americans toward spicy foods that include red chili peppers. The growing Hispanic population in the United States, over 50 million and about $1.2 trillion in purchasing power in 2013, partly explains the increasing demand for Mexican food. This Hispanic purchasing power is projected to be over $1.5 trillion by 2016.

Competitor Analysis: The Chili Market

The chili market represents over $500 million in annual sales. On average, consumers buy five to six servings annually, according to the NPD Group. The products fall primarily into two groups: canned chili (75 percent of sales) and dry chili (25 percent of sales).

This page uses a "block" style and does *not* indent each paragraph, although an extra space separates each paragraph. Compare this page with the opposite page, which has indented paragraphs. Most readers find that indented paragraphs in marketing plans and long reports are easier to follow.

The Company Analysis provides details of the company's strengths and marketing strategies that will enable it to achieve the mission and goals identified earlier. See Chapters 2 and 7.

The "A heading" for this section ("4. Situation Analysis," which appears on p. 53) identifies the major section of the plan. The "B heading" of Customer Analysis has a more dominant typeface and position than the lower-level "C heading" of Customer Characteristics. These headings introduce the reader to the sequence and level of topics covered within each major "A level" section. The organization of this textbook uses this kind of structure and headings.

Satisfying customers and providing genuine value to them is why organizations exist in a market economy. This section addresses the questions "Who are the customers for Paradise Kitchens's products?" See Chapters 4, 5, 6, 7, and 8.

Bluntly put, the major disadvantage of the segment's dominant product, canned chili, is that it does not taste very good. A taste test described in an issue of *Consumer Reports* magazine ranked 26 canned chili products "poor" to "fair" in overall sensory quality. The study concluded, "Chili doesn't have to be hot to be good. But really good chili, hot or mild, doesn't come out of a can."

Company Analysis

The husband-and-wife team that co-founded Paradise Kitchens, Inc., has 44 years of experience between them in the food-processing business. Both have played key roles in the management of the Pillsbury Company. They are being advised by a highly seasoned group of business professionals, who have extensive understanding of the requirements for new-product development.

The Company now uses a single outside producer with which it works closely to maintain the consistently high quality required in its products. The greater volume has increased production efficiencies, resulting in a steady decrease in the cost of goods sold.

Customer Analysis

In terms of customer analysis, this section describes (1) the characteristics of customers expected to buy Howlin' Coyote products and (2) health and nutrition concerns of Americans today.

Customer Characteristics.   Demographically, chili products in general are purchased by consumers representing a broad range of socioeconomic backgrounds. Howlin' Coyote chili is purchased chiefly by consumers who have achieved higher levels of education and whose income is $50,000 and higher. These consumers represent 50 percent of canned and dry mix chili users.

The household buying Howlin' Coyote has one to three people in it. Among married couples, Howlin' Coyote is predominantly bought by households in which both spouses work. While women are a majority of the buyers, single men represent a significant segment.

Because the chili offers a quick way to make a tasty meal, the product's biggest users tend to be those most pressed for time. Howlin' Coyote's premium pricing also means that its purchasers are skewed toward the higher end of the income range. Buyers range in age from 25 to 54 years old and often live in the western United States where spicy foods are more readily eaten.

The five Howlin' Coyote entrees offer a quick, tasty meal with high-quality ingredients.

This section demonstrates the company's insights into a major trend that has a potentially large impact.

Health and Nutrition Concerns. Coverage of food issues in the U.S. media is often erratic and occasionally alarmist. Because Americans are concerned about their diets, studies from organizations of widely varying credibility frequently receive significant attention from the major news organizations. For instance, a study of fat levels of movie popcorn was reported in all the major media. Similarly, studies on the healthfulness of Mexican food have received prominent play in print and broadcast reports. The high caloric levels of much Mexican and Southwestern-style food have been widely reported and often exaggerated. Some Mexican frozen-food competitors, such as Don Miguel, Mission Foods, Ruiz Foods, and José Olé, plan to offer or have recently offered more "carb-friendly" and "fat-friendly" products in response to this concern.

Howlin' Coyote is already lower in calories, fat, and sodium than its competitors, and those qualities are not currently being stressed in its promotions. Instead, in the space and time available for promotions, Howlin' Coyote's taste, convenience, and flexibility are stressed.

The size of headings should give a professional look to the report and not overwhelm the reader. These two headings are too large.

5. Market-Product Focus

This section describes the five-year marketing and product objectives for Paradise Kitchens and the target markets, points of difference, and positioning of its lines of Howlin' Coyote chilies.

Marketing and Product Objectives

Howlin' Coyote's marketing intent is to take full advantage of its brand potential while building a base from which other revenue sources can be mined—both in and out of the retail grocery business. These are detailed in four areas below:

As noted in Chapters 2, 9, and 10, the chances of success for a new product significantly increase if objectives are set for the product itself and if target market segments are identified for it. Diversification analysis, discussed in Chapter 2, helps identify the market segments to target. This section makes these explicit for Paradise Kitchens. The objectives also serve as the planned targets against which marketing activities are measured in program implementation and evaluation.

- *Current markets.* Current markets will be grown by expanding brand and flavor distribution at the retail level. In addition, same-store sales will be grown by increasing consumer awareness and repeat purchases, thereby leading to the more efficient broker/warehouse distribution channel.

- *New markets.* By the end of Year 5, the chili, salsa, burrito, and enchilada business will be expanded to a total of 20 metropolitan areas, which represent 53 percent of the 38 major U.S. metropolitan markets. This will represent 70 percent of U.S. food store sales.

- *Food service.* Food service sales will include chili products and smothering sauces. Sales are expected to reach $693,000 by the end of Year 3 and $1.5 million by the end of Year 5.

- *New products.* Howlin' Coyote's brand presence will be expanded at the retail

> A heading should be spaced closer to the text that follows (and that it describes) than the preceding section to avoid confusion for the reader. This rule is not followed for the Target Markets heading, which now unfortunately appears to "float" between the preceding and following paragraphs.

> This section identifies the specific niches or target markets toward which the company's products are directed. When appropriate and when space permits, this section often includes a market-product grid. See Chapter 8.

> An organization cannot grow by offering only "me-too products." The greatest single factor in a new product's failure is the lack of significant "points of difference" that set it apart from competitors' substitutes. This section makes these points of difference explicit. See Chapter 9.

> A positioning strategy helps communicate the unique points of difference of a company's products to prospective customers in a simple, clear way. This section describes this positioning. See Chapters 8 and 9.

level through the addition of new products in the frozen-foods section. This will be accomplished through new-product concept screening in Year 1 to identify new potential products. These products will be brought to market in Years 2 and 3.

To help buyers see the many different uses for Howlin' Coyote chili, recipes are even printed on the *inside* of the packages.

Target Markets

The primary target market for Howlin' Coyote products is households with one to three people, where often both adults work, and with individual income typically above $50,000 per year. These households contain more experienced, adventurous consumers of Southwestern/Mexican food and want premium quality products.

Points of Difference

The "points of difference"—characteristics that make Howlin' Coyote chilies unique relative to competitors—fall into three important areas:

- *Unique taste and convenience.* No known competitor offers a high-quality, "authentic" frozen chili in a range of flavors. And no existing chili has the same combination of quick preparation and home-style taste that Howlin' Coyote does.
- *Taste trends.* The American palate is increasingly intrigued by hot spices. In response to this trend, Howlin' Coyote brands offer more "kick" than most other prepared chilies.
- *Premium packaging.* Howlin' Coyote's packaging graphics convey the unique, high-quality product contained inside and the product's nontraditional positioning.

Positioning

In the past, chili products have been either convenient or tasty, but not both. Howlin' Coyote pairs these two desirable characteristics to obtain a positioning in consumers' minds as very high-quality "authentic Southwestern/Mexican tasting" chilies that can be prepared easily and quickly.

Everything that has gone before in the marketing plan sets the stage for the marketing mix actions—the four Ps—covered in the marketing program. See Chapters 9 through 18.

This section describes in detail three key elements of the company's product strategy: the product line, its quality and how this is achieved, and its "cutting edge" packaging. See Chapters 9 and 10.

This Price Strategy section makes the company's price point very clear, along with its price position relative to potential substitutes. When appropriate and when space permits, this section might contain a break-even analysis. See Chapter 11.

This "introductory overview" sentence tells the reader the topics covered in the section—in this case in-store demonstrations, recipes, and cents-off coupons. While this sentence may be omitted in short memos or plans, it helps readers see where the text is leading. These sentences are used throughout this plan. This textbook also generally uses these introductory overview sentences to aid your comprehension.

6. Marketing Program

The four marketing mix elements of the Howlin' Coyote chili marketing program are detailed below. Note that "chile" is the vegetable and "chili" is the dish.

Product Strategy

After first summarizing the product line, this section describes Howlin Coyote's approach to product quality and packaging.

Product Line. Howlin' Coyote chili, retailing for $3.99 for an 11-ounce serving, is available in five flavors: Green Chile Chili, Red Chile Chili, Beef and Black Bean Chili, Chicken Chunk Chili, and Mean Bean Chili.

Unique Product Quality. The flavoring systems of the Howlin' Coyote chilies are proprietary. The products' tastiness is due to extra care lavished upon the ingredients during production. The ingredients used are of unusually high quality. Meats are low-fat cuts and are fresh, not frozen, to preserve cell structure and moistness. Chilies are fire-roasted for fresher taste. Tomatoes and vegetables are of select quality. No preservatives or artificial flavors are used.

Packaging. Reflecting the "cutting edge" marketing strategy of its producers, Howlin' Coyote bucks conventional wisdom in its packaging. It specifically avoids placing predictable photographs of the product on its containers. Instead, Howlin' Coyote's package shows a Southwestern motif that communicates the product's out-of-the-ordinary positioning. As noted earlier, both women and men represent significant segments of actual purchasers of Howlin' Coyote Chili. The Southwestern motif on the packaging is deliberately designed to appeal to both women and men.

The Southwestern motif makes Howlin' Coyote's packages stand out in a supermarket's freezer case.

Price Strategy

At a $3.99 retail price for an 11-ounce package, Howlin' Coyote chili is priced comparably to the other frozen offerings but higher than the canned and dried chili varieties. However, the significant taste advantages it has over canned chilies and the convenience advantages over dried chilies justify this pricing strategy. This retail price also provides adequate margins for wholesalers and retailers in Howlin' Coyote's channel of distribution.

Promotion Strategy

Key promotion programs feature in-store demonstrations, recipes, and cents-off coupons.

Elements of the Promotion Strategy are highlighted in terms of the three key promotional activities the company is emphasizing: in-store demonstrations, recipes, and cents-off coupons. For space reasons, the company's online strategies are not shown in the plan. See Chapters 14, 15, and 16.

Another bulleted list adds many details for the reader, including methods of gaining customer awareness, trial, and repeat purchases as Howlin' Coyote enters new metropolitan areas.

The Place Strategy is described here in terms of both (1) the present method and (2) the new one to be used when the increased sales volume makes it feasible. See Chapters 12 and 13.

All the marketing mix decisions covered in the just-described marketing program have both revenue and expense effects. These are summarized in this section of the marketing plan.

Note that this section contains no introductory overview sentence. While the sentence is not essential, many readers prefer to see it to avoid the abrupt start with Past Sales Revenues.

In-Store Demonstrations. In-store demonstrations enable consumers to try Howlin' Coyote products and discover their unique qualities. Demos will be conducted regularly in all markets to increase awareness and trial purchases.

Recipes. Because the products' flexibility of use is a key selling point, recipes are offered to consumers to stimulate use. The recipes are given at all in-store demonstrations, on the back of packages, through a mail-in recipe book offer, and in coupons sent by direct-mail or freestanding inserts.

Cents-Off Coupons. To generate trial and repeat purchase of Howlin' Coyote products, coupons are distributed in four ways:

- *In Sunday newspaper inserts*. These inserts are widely read and help generate awareness.
- *In-pack coupons*. Each box of Howlin' Coyote chili will contain coupons for $1 off two more packages of the chili. These coupons will be included for the first three months the product is shipped to a new market. Doing so encourages repeat purchases by new users.
- *Direct-mail chili coupons*. Those households that fit the Howlin' Coyote demographics described previously will be mailed coupons.
- *In-store demonstrations*. Coupons will be passed out at in-store demonstrations to give an additional incentive to purchase.

Place (Distribution) Strategy

Howlin' Coyote is distributed in its present markets through a food distributor. The distributor buys the product, warehouses it, and then resells and delivers it to grocery retailers on a store-by-store basis. As sales grow, we will shift to a more efficient system using a broker who sells the products to retail chains and grocery wholesalers.

Sunday newspaper inserts encourage consumer trial and provide recipes to show how Howlin' Coyote chili can be used in summer meals.

7. Financial Data and Projections

Past Sales Revenues

Historically, Howlin' Coyote has had a steady increase in sales revenues since its introduction in 2006. In 2010, sales jumped spectacularly, due largely to new

The graph shows more clearly the dramatic growth of sales revenue than data in a table would do.

The Five-Year Projections section starts with the judgment forecast of cases sold and the resulting net sales. Gross profit and then operating profit—critical for the company's survival—are projected. An actual plan often contains many pages of computer-generated spreadsheet projections, usually shown in an appendix to the plan.

Because this table is very short, it is woven into the text, rather than given a figure number and a title.

Because the plan proposes to enter 17 new metropolitan markets in the coming five years (for a total of 20), it is not possible to simply extrapolate the trend in Figure 2. Instead, management's judgment must be used. Methods of making sales forecasts—including the "lost horse" technique used here—are discussed in Chapter 7.

The Organization of Paradise Kitchens appears here. It reflects the bare-bones organizational structure of successful small businesses. Often a more elaborate marketing plan will show the new positions expected to be added as the firm grows.

promotion strategies. Sales have continued to rise, but at a less dramatic rate. Sales revenues appear in Figure 2.

Five-Year Projections

Five-year financial projections for Paradise Kitchens appear below. These projections reflect the continuing growth in the number of cases sold (with eight packages of Howlin' Coyote chili per case).

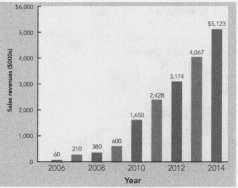

Figure 2.   Sales Revenues for Paradise Kitchens, Inc.

		Projections (000s)				
Financial Element	Actual 2014	Year 1 2015	Year 2 2016	Year 3 2017	Year 4 2018	Year 5 2019
Cases sold (000s)	353	684	889	1,249	1,499	1,799
Net sales ($000s)	$5,123	$9,913	$12,884	$18,111	$21,733	$26,080
Gross profit ($000s)	$2,545	$4,820	$6,527	$8,831	$10,597	$12,717
Operating profit ($000s)	$339	$985	$2,906	$2,805	$3,366	$4,039

8. Organization

Paradise Kitchens's present organization appears in Figure 3. It shows the four people reporting to the President. Below this level are both the full-time and part-time employees of the Company.

Figure 3.   The Paradise Kitchens Organization

At present, Paradise Kitchens operates with full-time employees in only essential positions. It now augments its full-time staff with key advisors, consultants, and subcontractors. As the firm grows, people with special expertise will be added to the staff.

9. Implementation Plan

The Implementation Plan shows how the company will turn its plan into results. Charts are often used to set deadlines and assign responsibilities for the many tactical marketing decisions needed to enter a new market.

Introducing Howlin' Coyote chilies to 17 new metropolitan markets is a complex task and requires that creative promotional activities gain consumer awareness and initial trial. Counting the three existing metropolitan markets in which Paradise Kitchens competes, by 2019 it will be in 20 metropolitan markets or 53 percent of the top 38 U.S. metropolitan markets. The anticipated rollout schedule to enter these metropolitan markets appears in Figure 4.

Figure 4.   Rollout Schedule to Enter New U.S. Markets

Year	New Markets Added Each Year	Cumulative Markets	Cumulative Percentage of 38 Major U.S. Markets
Last (2014)	2	5	16
Year 1 (2015)	3	8	21
Year 2 (2016)	4	12	29
Year 3 (2017)	2	14	37
Year 4 (2018)	3	17	45
Year 5 (2019)	3	20	53

The essence of Evaluation is comparing actual sales with the targeted values set in the plan and taking appropriate actions. Note that the section briefly describes a contingency plan for alternative actions, depending on how successful the entry into a new market turns out to be.

The diverse regional tastes in chili will be monitored carefully to assess whether minor modifications may be required in the chili recipes. As the rollout to new metropolitan areas continues, Paradise Kitchens will assess manufacturing and distribution trade-offs. This is important in determining whether to start new production with selected high-quality regional contract packers.

10. Evaluation

Monthly sales targets in cases have been set for Howlin' Coyote chili for each metropolitan area. Actual case sales will be compared with these targets and tactical marketing programs modified to reflect the unique sets of factors in each metropolitan area.

Various appendices may appear at the end of the plan, depending on the plan's purpose and audience. For example, résumés of key personnel or detailed financial spreadsheets often appear in appendices. For space reasons these are not shown here.

Appendix A. Biographical Sketches of Key Personnel

Appendix B. Detailed Financial Projections

Credits

3

Understanding the Marketing Environment, Ethical Behavior, and Social Responsibility

LEARNING OBJECTIVES

After reading this chapter you should be able to:

 LO 3-1 Explain the purpose of environmental scanning.

 LO 3-2 Describe social forces such as demographics and culture.

 LO 3-3 Discuss how economic forces affect marketing.

 LO 3-4 Describe how technological changes can affect marketing.

 LO 3-5 Discuss the forms of competition that exist in a market.

 LO 3-6 Explain how regulatory forces ensure competition and protect producers and consumers.

 LO 3-7 Identify factors that influence ethical and unethical marketing decisions.

 LO 3-8 Describe the different concepts of social responsibility.

HOW DO YOU ATTRACT 1 BILLION CUSTOMERS? MOVE FAST AND BREAK THINGS!

In just nine years since he started Facebook from his Harvard dorm room, Mark Zuckerberg has one-seventh of the world's population as customers.

How did Facebook grow so quickly? Zuckerberg's management mantra "move fast and break things" was perfectly matched with a rapidly changing marketing environment! Let's take a look at how environmental forces influenced Facebook and where Facebook is headed in the future.

Facebook and the Influence of Environmental Forces

There are many forces that influenced Facebook:

- *Social forces* changed as almost every aspect of our society moved toward transparency. People wanted tools for obtaining information, offering opinions, and interacting with friends, and they began sharing more and more information about themselves.

- *Economic forces* also influenced the demand for Facebook as the cost of wireless connectivity, Internet service, and smartphones rapidly declined and made social networking affordable for consumers around the world.

- *Technological advances* in data storage, server speed, and software integration made Facebook fast and convenient. Its megadata centers in Oregon, North Carolina, and Sweden offered increasingly efficient energy and heat management.

- *Competitive forces* by companies such as MySpace encouraged rapid expansion. Today, Google and Facebook are becoming fierce competitors for the role of society's depository of information.

- *Legal and regulatory forces* also influenced the development of Facebook. The company obtained rights to the name, developed privacy guidelines, and adapted to many Securities and Exchange Commission regulations when it became a publicly traded company.

Zuckerberg's rapid response to changes in the environment and his willingness to "break" old things by trying new things resulted in a unique social network that quickly connected the world.

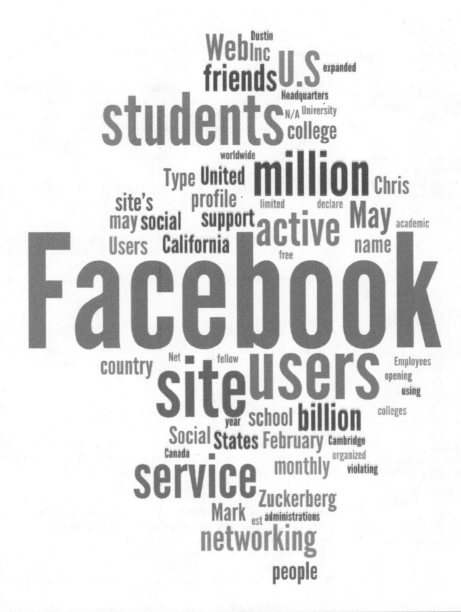

Facebook in the Future

Facebook is likely to respond to many changes in the future also. As people post more information about themselves, for example, Facebook will become more predictive about individual preferences. The future Facebook is also likely to include expansion into other countries where Internet service is just becoming available. Finally, Facebook will become increasingly mobile as smartphones grow in popularity.[1]

Many businesses operate in environments where important forces change. Anticipating and responding to changes often means the difference between marketing success and failure. This chapter describes how the marketing environment has changed in the past and how it is likely to change in the future.

ENVIRONMENTAL SCANNING

LO 3-1 Explain the purpose of environmental scanning.

environmental scanning
The process of acquiring information on events outside the organization to identify and interpret potential trends.

Changes in the marketing environment are a source of opportunities and threats to be managed. The process of continually acquiring information on events occurring outside the organization to identify and interpret potential trends is called **environmental scanning**. Environmental trends typically arise from five sources: social, economic, technological, competitive, and regulatory forces. As shown in Figure 3–1 and described later in this chapter, these forces affect the marketing activities of a firm in numerous ways.

An Environmental Scan of Today's Marketplace

What trends might affect marketing in the future? A firm conducting an environmental scan of the marketplace might uncover key trends such as the way consumers are changing how they use media, the increasing impact of new technologies such as robots, and the growth of online privacy advocacy and regulation.[2] These trends affect consumers and the organizations that serve them. Trends such as these are described in the following discussion of the five environmental forces.

SOCIAL FORCES

LO 3-2 Describe social forces such as demographics and culture.

social forces
The demographic characteristics and the culture of the population.

demographics
Description of a population according to characteristics such as age, gender, ethnicity, income, and occupation.

The **social forces** of the environment include the demographic characteristics of the population and its culture. Changes in these forces can have a dramatic impact on marketing strategy.

Demographics

Describing a population according to selected characteristics such as age, gender, ethnicity, income, and occupation is referred to as **demographics**. Three key demographic characteristics include a population profile, a description of generational cohorts, and a description of racial and ethnic diversity.

The Population at a Glance   The most recent estimates indicate there are 7.1 billion people in the world today, and the population is likely to grow to 9.6 billion by 2050. While this growth has led to the term *population explosion*, the increases have not occurred worldwide; they are primarily in the developing countries of Africa, Asia, and Latin America. In fact, India is predicted to have the world's largest population in 2050 with 1.69 billion people, and China will be a close second with 1.31 billion people. World population projections show that the proportion of the world's population in more developed countries such as the United States, Japan, Australia, and those in Europe is declining.[3]

Studies of the demographic characteristics of the U.S. population suggest several important trends. Generally, the population is becoming larger, older, and more diverse. The U.S. Census Bureau estimates that the current population of the United States is 316 million people. If current trends in life expectancy, birthrates, and immigration continue, by 2030 the U.S. population will exceed 358 million people.[4]

baby boomers
The generation of children born between 1946 and 1964.

Generation X
The generation of people born between 1965 and 1976.

Generational Cohorts   A major reason for the graying of America is that the 76 million **baby boomers**—the generation of children born between 1946 and 1964—are growing older. Baby boomers are retiring at a rate of 10,000 every 24 hours, and they will all be 65 or older by 2030.[5]

The baby boom cohort is followed by **Generation X**, which includes the 50 million people born between 1965 and 1976. This period is also known as the *baby bust*, because during this time the number of children born each year was declining. This is a generation of consumers who are self-reliant, supportive of racial and ethnic diversity,

FIGURE 3–1
Environmental forces affect the organization, as well as its suppliers and customers.

and better educated than any previous generation. They also have become the largest segment of business travelers.[6]

The generational cohort labeled **Generation Y**, or *millennials*, includes the 72 million Americans born between 1977 and 1994. This was a period of increasing births, which resulted from baby boomers having children, and it is often referred to as the *echo-boom* or *baby boomlet*. Generation Y exerts influence on music, sports, computers, video games, and all forms of communication and networking. The Making Responsible Decisions box on the next page describes how millennials' interest in sustainability is influencing colleges, graduate schools, and employers.[7]

Generation Y
The 72 million Americans born between 1977 and 1994.

Racial and Ethnic Diversity   A notable trend is the changing racial and ethnic composition of the U.S. population. Approximately one in three U.S. residents belongs to the following racial or ethnic groups: African American, Native American or Alaska Native, Asian American, or Native Hawaiian or Pacific Islander. While the growing size of these groups has been identified through new Census data, their economic

Which generational cohorts are these three advertisers trying to reach?

Making Responsible Decisions

Millennials Are Going to Change the World!

Millennials are determined to make a difference in the world and, by doing so, make the world a better place. They are idealistic and eager to get started, particularly when it comes to environmental sustainability, which millennials believe is part of what it means to be socially responsible. The group includes students in college and graduate school and many early career employees. In different ways each group is making its voice heard.

There are approximately 17 million undergraduate millennials who expect sustainable campus communities that include LEED (Leadership in Energy and Environmental Design)-certified housing, campus transit systems, and recycling programs. They view themselves as part of the "ecoRenaissance" movement. Graduate students are looking for programs with sustainability electives, case studies, and potential for involvement with organizations such as Net Impact (www.netimpact.org), a nonprofit for students who want to create "positive social and

NET IMPACT

Video 3-1
Net Impact
kerin.tv/cr6e/v3-1

environmental change in the workplace and the world." Early career employees want "green" jobs such as social responsibility officer, environmental consultant, and sustainability database specialist at companies that are eco-conscious and advocate good citizenship.

Sara Hochman is a typical example. She was interested in environmental issues in college, and her first job was as an environmental consultant. To make a bigger impact on her clients, she decided she needed to "beef up" her business skills, so she enrolled in graduate school at the University of Chicago where she could take an elective on renewable energy and join the Energy Club. Similarly, a recent college graduate joined the Peace Corps because, she said, "I want to be part of something bigger than just me-me-me."

Have you made similar choices or decisions based on your interest and concern about sustainability? What will the world look like after the millennials have made their changes? It is difficult to predict. As experts Peter Leyden and Ruy Teixeira advise, however, we should, "Hang on for the ride!"

---

impact on the marketplace is also very noticeable. By 2015, Hispanics, African Americans, and Asian Americans will spend $1.3 trillion, $1.1 trillion, and $880 billion each year, respectively. To adapt to this new marketplace, many companies are developing **multicultural marketing** programs, which are combinations of the marketing mix that reflect the unique attitudes, ancestry, communication preferences, and lifestyles of different races and ethnic groups.[8]

multicultural marketing
Marketing programs that reflect unique aspects of different races.

Culture

culture
The set of values, ideas, and attitudes that is learned and shared among the members of a group.

A second social force, **culture**, incorporates the set of values, ideas, and attitudes that are learned and shared among the members of a group. Because many of the elements of culture influence consumer buying patterns, monitoring national and global cultural trends is important for marketing. Cross-cultural analysis needed for global marketing is discussed in Chapter 6.

Culture also includes values that may differ over time and between countries. During the 1970s, a list of values in the United States included achievement, work, efficiency, and material comfort. Today, commonly held values include personal control, continuous change, equality, individualism, self-help, competition, future orientation, and action. These values are useful in understanding most current behaviors of U.S. consumers, particularly when they are compared to values in other countries. Contrasting values outside the United States, for example, include belief in fate, the importance of tradition, the importance of rank and status, a focus on group welfare, and acceptance of birthright.

An increasingly important value for consumers in the United States and around the globe is sustainability and preserving the environment. Concern for the environment is one reason consumers are buying hybrid gas-electric automobiles, such as the Toyota Prius, the Chevy Volt, and the Ford C-MAX. Companies are also changing their business practices to respond to trends in consumer values. Coca-Cola has been working on alleviating global water scarcity, Facebook has committed to reducing the carbon footprint of its data centers by 25 percent by 2015, and Wal-Mart Stores, Inc., has set ambitious goals to cut energy use by buying more local products, reducing packaging, and switching to renewable power. Recent research also indicates that consumers are committed to brands with a strong link to social action.[9]

---

learning review

3-1. Describe three generational cohorts.

3-2. Why are many companies developing multicultural marketing programs?

3-3. How are important values such as sustainability reflected in the marketplace today?

ECONOMIC FORCES

Discuss how economic forces affect marketing.

economy
Pertains to the income, expenditures, and resources that affect the cost of running a business or household.

The second component of the environmental scan, the **economy**, pertains to the income, expenditures, and resources that affect the cost of running a business and household. We'll consider two aspects of these economic forces: a macroeconomic view of the marketplace and a microeconomic perspective of consumer income.

Macroeconomic Conditions

Of particular concern at the macroeconomic level is the performance of the economy based on indicators such as GDP (gross domestic product), unemployment, and price changes (inflation or deflation). In an inflationary economy, the cost to produce and buy products and services escalates as prices increase. From a marketing standpoint, if prices rise faster than consumer incomes, the number of items consumers can buy decreases. This relationship is evident in the cost of a college education. The College Board reports that since 2000 college tuition and fees have increased 146 percent (from $3,508 to $8,655) while family incomes have increased less than 19 percent. The share of family income required to pay for tuition at public four-year colleges has risen from 8 percent in 2000 to 17 percent today.[10]

Periods of declining economic activity are referred to as recessions. During recessions, businesses decrease production, unemployment rises, and many consumers have less money to spend. The U.S. economy experienced recessions from 1973–75, 1981–82, 1990–91, and in 2001. Most recently, a recessionary period began in 2007 and ended in 2009, becoming the longest in recent history.[11]

Consumer Income

The microeconomic trends in terms of consumer income are also important issues for marketers. Having a product that meets the needs of consumers may be of little value if they are unable to purchase it. A consumer's ability to buy is related to income, which consists of gross, disposable, and discretionary components.

Gross Income   The total amount of money made in one year by a person, household, or family unit is referred to as *gross income* (or "money income" at the Census Bureau). While the typical U.S. household earned only about $8,700 of income in 1970, it earned about $51,017 in 2012. When gross income is adjusted for inflation, however, income of that typical U.S. household was relatively stable. In fact, inflation-adjusted income has varied between only $45,146 and $54,489 since 1970. Approximately 54 percent of U.S. households have an annual income between $25,000 and $99,999.[12] Are you from a typical household?

Disposable Income   The second income component, *disposable income*, is the money a consumer has left after paying taxes to use for necessities such as food, housing, clothing, and transportation. Thus, if taxes rise or fall faster than income, consumers are likely to have more or less disposable income. Similarly, dramatic changes in the prices of products can require spending adjustments. In recent years, for example, as the price of gasoline increased, consumers found themselves adjusting their spending in other categories. In addition, the decline in home prices has had a psychological impact on consumers, who tend to spend more when they feel their net worth is rising and postpone purchases when it declines. During a recessionary period, spending, debt, and use of credit all decline. The recent downturn has led many consumers to switch from premium brands to lower-priced brands.[13]

Discretionary Income   The third component of income is *discretionary income*, the money that remains after paying for taxes and necessities. Discretionary income is used for luxury items such as a Cunard cruise. An obvious problem in defining discretionary versus disposable income is determining what is a luxury and what is a necessity.

The Department of Labor monitors consumer expenditures through its annual Consumer Expenditure Survey. In 2011, consumers spent about 13 percent of their income on food, 34 percent on housing, and 4 percent on clothes. While an additional 24 percent is often spent on transportation and health care, the remainder is generally viewed as discretionary. The percentage of income spent on food and housing typically declines as income increases, which can provide an increase in discretionary income. Discretionary expenditures also can be increased by reducing savings. The Bureau of Labor Statistics observed that during the 1990s and early 2000s the savings rate declined to zero. That trend was reversed in 2008 when the government issued stimulus checks designed to improve the economy and, instead of spending the money, consumers saved it. Recent data on consumer expenditures indicate that the savings rate is now approximately 3.7 percent.[14]

As consumers' discretionary income increases, so does the opportunity to indulge in the luxurious leisure travel marketed by Cunard.

Cunard Cruise Line
www.cunard.com

TECHNOLOGICAL FORCES

 LO 3-4 Describe how technological changes can affect marketing.

technology
Inventions or innovations from applied science or engineering research.

Our society is in a period of dramatic technological change. **Technology**, the third environmental force, refers to inventions or innovations from applied science or engineering research. Each new wave of technological innovation can replace existing products and companies. Do you recognize the items pictured below and what they may replace?

Technology of Tomorrow

Technological change is the result of research, so it is difficult to predict. Some of the most dramatic technological changes occurring now, however, include the following:

- Connectivity will grow to include all customers, machines, vehicles, appliances, and mobile devices to create the "Internet of Things."
- Computers will develop all five senses to create intelligent data collection and personalized predictive capabilities.
- Green technologies such as smart grid electricity services, online energy management, and consumer-generated energy (e.g., home wind turbines) will gain widespread acceptance among American consumers.
- 3D technologies will move from movie theaters and televisions to many new and useful applications.

Some of these trends in technology are already being realized in today's marketplace. Vail Ski Resort, for example, uses sensors in ski passes to track skiers and to monitor how many vertical feet they cover in a day. The phone app MindMeld uses speech recognition to listen to your phone calls and pull up search data related to your conversations. Bloomingdale's is trying virtual dressing rooms that use 3D technology to allow shoppers to try different clothes, colors, and accessories. Other technologies such as Skype's television cameras, Chevy's electric cars, and Fitbit's biometric wristbands are likely to replace or become substitutes for existing products and services such as telephones, gasoline-powered vehicles, and traditional medical equipment.[15]

Technological change leads to new products. What products might be replaced by these innovations?

Technology's Impact on Customer Value

Advances in technology have important effects on marketing. First, the cost of technology is plummeting, causing the customer value assessment of technology-based products to focus on other dimensions such as quality, service, and relationships. *PC Magazine* (www.pcmag.com) publishes an article titled, "The Best Free Software," each year to tell readers about companies that give their software away, with the expectation that advertising or upgrade purchases will generate revenue. A similar approach is used by many U.S. mobile phone vendors, who charge little for the telephone if the purchase leads to a long-term telephone service contract.[16]

Technology also provides value through the development of new products. More than 3,000 companies recently unveiled 20,000 new products at the Consumer Electronics Show held in Las Vegas. New products included Samsung's phones with a flexible screen, transparent 3D televisions by Hisense, and driverless vehicle technologies from Audi and Lexus. Similarly, *Better Homes and Gardens* magazine announced 63 best new product award winners in four categories: beauty, food and beverage, health and personal care, and household. Some of the winners included Taste Nirvana's coconut water, the Nestlé Crunch Girl Scout Thin Mint candy bar, and Tide's single-dose laundry detergent pods.[17]

Technology can also change existing products and the ways they are produced. Many companies are using technological developments to recycle products through the manufacturing cycle several times. The National Association for PET Container Resources, for example, estimates that 29 percent of all plastic bottles are now recycled, usually to make polyester fibers that are spun into everything from sweaters to upholstery.

marketspace
An information- and communication-based electronic exchange environment occupied by digitized offerings.

The transformative power of technology may be best illustrated by the rapid growth of the **marketspace**, an information- and communication-based electronic exchange environment mostly occupied by sophisticated computer and telecommunication technologies and digitized offerings. Any activity that uses some form of electronic communication in the inventory, exchange, advertisement, distribution, and payment of products and services is often called *electronic commerce*. Network technologies are now used for everything from filing expense reports, to monitoring daily sales, to sharing information with employees, to communicating instantly with suppliers.

COMPETITIVE FORCES

competition
Alternative firms that could provide a product to satisfy a specific market's needs.

The fourth component of the environmental scan, **competition**, refers to the alternative firms that could provide a product to satisfy a specific market's needs. There are various forms of competition, and each company must consider its present and potential competitors in designing its marketing strategy.

Alternative Forms of Competition

LO 3-5 Discuss the forms of competition that exist in a market.

Four basic forms of competition form a continuum from pure competition to monopolistic competition to oligopoly to pure monopoly.

At one end of the continuum is *pure competition*, in which there are many sellers and they each have a similar product. Companies that deal in commodities common to agribusiness (for example, wheat, rice, and grain) often are in a pure competition position in which distribution (in the sense of shipping products) is important but other elements of marketing have little impact.

In the second point on the continuum, *monopolistic competition*, many sellers compete with substitutable products within a price range. For example, if the price of coffee rises too much, consumers may switch to tea. Coupons or sales are frequently used marketing tactics.

Oligopoly, a common industry structure, occurs when a few companies control the majority of industry sales. The wireless telephone industry, for example, is dominated by Verizon, AT&T, Sprint, and T-Mobile, which have 117, 107, 55, and 34 million subscribers, respectively. Similarly, the entertainment industry in the United States is dominated by Viacom, Disney, and Time Warner, and the major firms in the U.S. defense contractor industry are Boeing, Northrop Grumman, and Lockheed Martin. Critics of oligopolies suggest that because there are few sellers, price competition among firms is not desirable because it leads to reduced profits for all producers.[18]

The final point on the continuum, *pure monopoly*, occurs when only one firm sells the product. Monopolies are common for producers of products and services considered essential to a community: water, electricity, and cable service. Typically, marketing plays a small role in a monopolistic setting because it is regulated by the state or federal government. Government control usually seeks to ensure price protection for the buyer. Concern that Microsoft's 86 percent share of the PC operating system market was a monopoly led to lawsuits and consent decrees from the U.S. Justice Department and investigations and fines from the European Union. A recent Federal Trade Commission investigation of Google found that although the company's market share of the online search market exceeds 70 percent, it had not harmed competition in the marketplace. An investigation by the European Union, however, is still in progress.[19]

Small Businesses as Competitors

While large companies provide familiar examples of the forms and components of competition, small businesses make up the majority of the competitive landscape for most businesses. Consider that there are approximately 28 million small businesses in the United States, which employ half of all private sector employees. In addition, small businesses generate 64 percent of all new jobs and 44 percent of the gross domestic product (GDP). Research has shown a strong correlation between national economic growth and the level of new small business activity in previous years.[20]

---

learning review

3-4. What is the difference between a consumer's disposable and discretionary income?

3-5. How does technology impact customer value?

3-6. In pure competition there are a _____ number of sellers.

REGULATORY FORCES

LO 3-6 Explain how regulatory forces ensure competition and protect producers and consumers.

For any organization, the marketing and broader business decisions are constrained, directed, and influenced by regulatory forces. **Regulation** consists of restrictions state and federal laws place on business with regard to the conduct of its activities. Regulation exists to protect companies as well as consumers. Much of the regulation from the federal and state levels is the result of an active political process and has been passed to ensure competition and fair business practices. For consumers, the focus of legislation is to protect them from unfair trade practices and ensure their safety.

regulation
Restrictions that state and federal laws place on business.

Protecting Competition

Major federal legislation has been passed to encourage competition, which is deemed desirable because it permits the consumer to determine which competitor will succeed and which will fail. The first such law was the *Sherman Antitrust Act* (1890). Lobbying by farmers in the Midwest against fixed railroad shipping prices led to the passage of this act, which forbids (1) contracts, combinations, or conspiracies in restraint of trade and (2) actual monopolies or attempts to monopolize any part of trade or commerce.

Because of vague wording and government inactivity, however, there was only one successful case against a company in the nine years after the act became law, and the Sherman Act was supplemented with the *Clayton Act* (1914). This act forbids certain actions that are likely to lessen competition, although no actual harm has yet occurred.

In the 1930s, the federal government had to act again to ensure fair competition. During that time, large chain stores appeared, such as the Great Atlantic & Pacific Tea Company (A&P). Small businesses were threatened, and they lobbied for the *Robinson-Patman Act* (1936). This act makes it unlawful to discriminate in prices charged to different purchasers of the same product, where the effect may substantially lessen competition or help to create a monopoly.

Protecting Producers and Consumers

Various federal laws are intended to protect the company while others are intended to protect the consumer. In some cases the laws are designed to protect both.

A company can protect its competitive position in new and novel products under the patent law, which gives inventors the right to exclude others from making, using, or selling products that infringe the patented invention. The federal copyright law is another way for a company to protect its competitive position in a product. The copyright law gives the author of a literary, dramatic, musical, or artistic work the exclusive right to print, perform, or otherwise copy that work. Copyright is secured automatically when the work is created. Digital technology has necessitated additional copyright legislation, called the *Digital Millennium Copyright Act* (1998), to improve protection of copyrighted digital products.[21]

consumerism
A movement started to increase the influence, power, and rights of consumers in dealing with institutions.

Federal laws also protect consumers. Various laws address each of the four elements of the marketing mix. Product requirements, for example, are specified in laws such as the *Child Protection Act* (1966), the *Nutritional Labeling and Education Act* (1990), and the *Consumer Product Safety Act* (1972), which established the Consumer Product Safety Commission. Many of these laws came about because of **consumerism**, a grassroots movement started in the 1960s to increase the influence, power, and rights of consumers in dealing with institutions.

Video 3-2
FTC
kerin.tv/cr6e/v3-2

Laws also address pricing, distribution, and promotion. The *FTC Act of 1914*, for example, established the Federal Trade Commission (FTC) to monitor unfair business practices. The FTC has the power to (1) issue cease and desist orders and (2) order corrective advertising. In issuing a cease and desist order, the FTC orders a company to stop practices the commission considers unfair. With corrective advertising, the FTC can require a company to spend money on advertising to correct previous misleading promotion. Other laws, such as the *Deceptive Mail Prevention and Enforcement*

These products are identified by protected trademarks. Are any of these trademarks in danger of becoming generic?

Companies must meet certain requirements before they can display this logo on their websites.

Better Business Bureau
 www.bbbonline.com

self-regulation
An alternative to government control, whereby an industry attempts to police itself.

Act (1999), the *Telephone Consumer Protection Act* (1991), and the *Controlling the Assault of Non-Solicited Pornography and Marketing (CAN-SPAM) Act* (2004), are designed to guide the use of direct mail, telemarketing, e-mail solicitations, and other forms of promotion.[22]

An example of a law that protects producers and consumers is the *Lanham Act* (1946), which provides for the registration of trademarks. Registration under the Lanham Act provides important advantages to a trademark owner but it does not confer ownership. A company can lose its trademark if it becomes generic, which means that it has come to be a common, descriptive word for the product. Coca-Cola, Whopper, and Xerox are registered trademarks, and competitors cannot use these names. Aspirin and escalator, however, are former trademarks that are now generic terms in the United States and can be used by anyone. Consumers benefit from trademarks because it allows them to correctly identify products they want to purchase.[23]

Control through Self-Regulation

An alternative to government regulation is **self-regulation**, where an industry attempts to police itself. The major television networks, for example, have used self-regulation to set their own guidelines for TV ads for children's toys. There are two problems with self-regulation, however: noncompliance by members and enforcement. In addition, if attempts at self-regulation are too strong, they may violate the Robinson-Patman Act. The best-known self-regulatory group is the Better Business Bureau (BBB). This agency is a voluntary alliance of companies whose goal is to help maintain fair practices. Although the BBB has no legal power, it does try to use "moral suasion" to get members to comply with its standards.

There is a distinction between laws, which are society's values that are enforceable in courts, and ethics, which deal with personal and moral principles and values. The following sections discuss ethical behavior and social responsibility in marketing.

---

learning review

3-7. The _____ Act forbids actual monopolies, whereas the _____ Act forbids actions that are likely to lessen competition.

3-8. The Federal Trade Commission (FTC) monitors _____.

3-9. How does the Better Business Bureau encourage companies to follow its standards for commerce?

UNDERSTANDING ETHICAL MARKETING BEHAVIOR

LO 3-7 Identify factors that influence ethical and unethical marketing decisions.

ethics
The moral principles and values that govern the actions and decisions of an individual or a group.

Ethics are the moral principles and values that govern the actions and decisions of an individual or group.[24] They serve as guidelines on how to act rightly and justly when faced with moral dilemmas. Researchers have identified numerous factors that influence ethical marketing behavior.[25] Figure 3–2 on the next page presents a framework that shows these factors and their relationships.

Societal Culture and Norms

As described previously, *culture* refers to the set of values, ideas, and attitudes that are learned and shared among the members of a group. Culture also serves as a socializing force that dictates what is morally right and just. This means that moral standards are relative to particular societies.[26] These standards often reflect the laws and regulations that affect social and economic behavior, which can create ethical dilemmas. Companies

FIGURE 3–2
A framework for understanding ethical behavior. Each of these influences has an effect on ethical marketing behavior, as described in the text.

that compete in the global marketplace recognize this fact. Consider UPS, the world's largest package delivery company operating in more than 200 countries and territories worldwide.[27] According to the company's global compliance and ethics coordinator, "Although languages and cultures around the world may be different, we do not change our ethical standards at UPS. Our ethics program is global in nature." Not surprisingly, UPS is consistently ranked among the world's most ethical companies.

Business Culture and Industry Practices

Societal culture provides a foundation for understanding moral behavior in business activities. *Business cultures* "comprise the effective rules of the game, the boundaries between competitive and unethical behavior, [and] the codes of conduct in business dealings."[28] Consumers have witnessed instances where business cultures in the financial (insider trading), insurance (deceptive sales practices), and defense (bribery) industries went awry. Business culture affects ethical conduct both in the exchange relationship between sellers and buyers and in the competitive behavior among sellers.

Ethics of Exchange   The exchange process is central to the marketing concept. Ethical exchanges between sellers and buyers should result in both parties being better off after a transaction.

Before the 1960s, the legal concept of *caveat emptor*—let the buyer beware—was pervasive in the American business culture. In 1962, President John F. Kennedy outlined a **Consumer Bill of Rights** that codified the ethics of exchange between buyers and sellers. These were the right (1) to safety, (2) to be informed, (3) to choose, and (4) to be heard. Consumers expect and often demand that these rights be protected, as have American businesses.

Consumer Bill of Rights
Codified the ethics of exchange between buyers and sellers, including rights to safety, to be informed, to choose, and to be heard.

Ethics of Competition   Business culture also affects ethical behavior in competition. Two kinds of unethical behavior are most common: (1) economic espionage and (2) bribery.

Economic espionage is the clandestine collection of trade secrets or proprietary information about a company's competitors. This practice is illegal and unethical and carries serious criminal penalties for the offending individual or business. Espionage activities include illegal trespassing, theft, fraud, misrepresentation, wiretapping, the search of a competitor's trash, and violations of written and implicit employment agreements with noncompete clauses. More than half of the largest firms in the United States have uncovered espionage in some form, costing them $300 billion annually in lost sales.[29] Read the Making Responsible Decisions box to learn how Pepsi-Cola responded to an offer to obtain confidential information about its archrival's marketing plans.[30]

The second form of unethical competitive behavior is giving and receiving bribes and kickbacks. Bribes and kickbacks are often disguised as gifts, consultant fees, and

Making Responsible Decisions

Corporate Conscience in the Cola War

Suppose you are a senior executive at Pepsi-Cola and that a Coca-Cola employee offers to sell you the marketing plan and sample for a new Coke product at a modest price. Would you buy it knowing Pepsi-Cola could gain a significant competitive edge in the cola war?

When this question was posed in an online survey of marketing and advertising executives, 67 percent said they would buy the plan and product sample if there were no repercussions. What did Pepsi-Cola do when this offer actually occurred? The company immediately contacted Coca-Cola, which contacted the FBI. An undercover FBI agent paid the employee $30,000 in cash stuffed in a Girl Scout cookie box as a down payment and later arrested the employee and

accomplices. When asked about the incident, a Pepsi-Cola spokesperson said: "We only did what any responsible company would do. Competition must be tough, but must always be fair and legal."

Why did the 33 percent of respondents in the online survey say they would decline the offer? Most said they would prefer competing ethically so they could sleep at night. According to a senior advertising agency executive who would decline the offer: "Repercussions go beyond potential espionage charges. As long as we have a conscience, there are repercussions."

So what happened to the Coca-Cola employee and her accomplices? She was sentenced to eight years in prison and ordered to pay $40,000 in restitution. Her accomplices were each sentenced to five years in prison.

favors. This practice is more common in business-to-business and government marketing than in consumer marketing. In general, bribery is most evident in industries experiencing intense competition and in countries in the earlier stages of economic development. According to a United Nations study, 15 percent of all companies in industrialized countries have to pay bribes to win or retain business. In Asia, this figure is 40 percent. In Eastern Europe, 60 percent of all companies must pay bribes to do business. A recent poll of senior executives engaged in global marketing revealed that Russia was the most likely country to engage in bribery to win or retain business. The Netherlands, Switzerland, and Belgium were the least likely.[31]

Corporate Culture and Expectations

A third influence on ethical practices is corporate culture. *Corporate culture* is the set of values, ideas, and attitudes that is learned and shared among the members of an organization. The culture of a company demonstrates itself in the dress ("We don't wear ties"), sayings ("The IBM Way"), and manner of work (team efforts) of employees. Culture is also apparent in the expectations for ethical behavior present in formal codes of ethics and the ethical actions of top management and co-workers.

code of ethics
A formal statement of ethical principles and rules of conduct.

Codes of Ethics   A **code of ethics** is a formal statement of ethical principles and rules of conduct. It is estimated that 86 percent of U.S. companies have some sort of ethics code and one of every four large companies has corporate ethics officers. Ethics codes typically address contributions to government officials and political parties, customer and supplier relations, conflicts of interest, and accurate recordkeeping.

Ethical Behavior of Top Management and Co-Workers   One reason for violating ethics codes rests in the perceived behavior of top management and co-workers.[32] Observing peers and top management and gauging responses to unethical behavior play an important role in individual actions. A study of business executives reported that 45 percent had witnessed ethically troubling behavior. About 22 percent of those who reported unethical behavior were penalized, through either outright

What does 3M's Scotchgard have to do with ethics, social responsibility, and a $200 million loss in annual sales? Read the text to find out.

moral idealism
A personal moral philosophy that considers certain individual rights or duties as universal, regardless of the outcome.

utilitarianism
A personal moral philosophy that focuses on the "greatest good for the greatest number."

punishment or a diminished status in the company.[33] Clearly, ethical dilemmas can bring personal and professional conflict. For this reason, numerous states have laws protecting *whistle-blowers*, employees who report unethical or illegal actions of their employers.

Your Personal Moral Philosophy and Ethical Behavior

Ultimately, ethical choices are based on the personal moral philosophy of the decision maker. Moral philosophy is learned through the process of socialization with friends and family and by formal education. It is also influenced by the societal, business, and corporate culture in which a person finds him- or herself. Two prominent personal moral philosophies have direct bearing on marketing practice: (1) moral idealism and (2) utilitarianism.

Moral Idealism   **Moral idealism** is a personal moral philosophy that considers certain individual rights or duties as universal, regardless of the outcome. This philosophy exists in the Consumer Bill of Rights and is favored by moral philosophers and consumer interest groups. For example, the right to know applies to probable defects in an automobile that relate to safety.

This philosophy also applies to ethical duties. A fundamental ethical duty is to do no harm. Adherence to this duty prompted the recent decision by 3M executives to phase out production of a chemical 3M had manufactured for nearly 40 years. The substance, used in far-ranging products from pet food bags, candy wrappers, carpeting, and 3M's popular Scotchgard fabric protector, had no known harmful health or environmental effect. However, the company discovered that the chemical appeared in minuscule amounts in humans and animals around the world and accumulated in tissue. Believing that the substance could be possibly harmful in large doses, 3M voluntarily stopped its production, resulting in a $200 million loss in annual sales.[34]

Utilitarianism   An alternative perspective on moral philosophy is **utilitarianism**, which is a personal moral philosophy that focuses on "the greatest good for the greatest number" by assessing the costs and benefits of the consequences of ethical behavior. If the benefits exceed the costs, then the behavior is ethical. If not, then the behavior is unethical. This philosophy underlies the economic tenets of capitalism and, not surprisingly, is embraced by many business executives and students.[35]

learning review

3-10. What rights are included in the Consumer Bill of Rights?

3-11. Economic espionage includes what kinds of activities?

3-12. What is meant by moral idealism?

UNDERSTANDING SOCIAL RESPONSIBILITY IN MARKETING

(LO 3-8) Describe the different concepts of social responsibility.

social responsibility
The idea that organizations are part of a larger society and are accountable to that society for their actions.

As we saw in Chapter 1, the societal marketing concept stresses marketing's social responsibility by not only satisfying the needs of consumers but also providing for society's welfare. **Social responsibility** means that organizations are part of a larger society and are accountable to that society for their actions. Like ethics, agreement on the nature and scope of social responsibility is often difficult to come by, given the diversity of values present in different societal, business, and corporate cultures.

Three Concepts of Social Responsibility

There are three concepts of social responsibility: (1) profit responsibility, (2) stakeholder responsibility, and (3) societal responsibility.

green marketing
Marketing efforts to produce, promote, and reclaim environmentally sensitive products.

cause marketing
Tying the charitable contributions of a firm directly to sales produced through the promotion of one of its products.

Video 3-3
P&G
kerin.tv/cr6e/v3-3

A cause marketing pioneer for more than three decades, Procter & Gamble focuses on supporting disadvantaged youth and disaster relief. A successful brand campaign includes the Pampers partnership with UNICEF, which has provided tetanus vaccinations to more than 100 million women and their babies since 2006.

Profit Responsibility   *Profit responsibility* holds that companies have a simple duty: to maximize profits for their owners or stockholders. This view is expressed by Nobel Laureate Milton Friedman, who said, "There is one and only one social responsibility of business—to use its resources and engage in activities designed to increase its profits so long as it stays within the rules of the game, which is to say, engages in open and free competition without deception or fraud."[36]

Stakeholder Responsibility   Criticism of the profit view has led to a broader concept of social responsibility. *Stakeholder responsibility* focuses on the obligations an organization has to those who can affect achievement of its objectives. These constituencies include consumers, employees, suppliers, and distributors. Source Perrier S.A., the supplier of Perrier bottled water, exercised this responsibility when it recalled 160 million bottles of water in 120 countries after traces of a toxic chemical were found in 13 bottles. The recall cost the company $35 million and the profit from $40 million in lost sales. Even though the chemical level was not harmful to humans, Source Perrier's president believed he acted in the best interests of the firm's consumers, distributors, and employees by removing "the least doubt, as minimal as it might be, to weigh on the image of the quality and purity of our product"—which it did.[37]

Societal Responsibility   An even broader concept of social responsibility has emerged in recent years. *Societal responsibility* refers to obligations that organizations have (1) to the preservation of the ecological environment and (2) to the general public. Today, emphasis is placed on the *triple-bottom line*—recognition of the need for organizations to improve the state of people, the planet, and profit simultaneously if they are to achieve sustainable, long-term growth.[38] Growing interest in green marketing, cause marketing, social audits, and sustainable development reflects this recognition.

   Green marketing—marketing efforts to produce, promote, and reclaim environmentally sensitive products—takes many forms.[39] At 3M, product development opportunities emanate both from consumer research and its "Pollution Prevention Pays" program. This program solicits employee suggestions on how to reduce pollution and recycle materials. Since 1975, this program has generated over 9,000 3P projects that eliminated more than 3.5 billion pounds of air, water, and solid-waste pollutants from the environment. Levi Strauss & Co. uses 8 recycled plastic bottles in each pair of Waste<Less Jeans, which are composed of at least 20 percent recycled plastic. This practice has eliminated millions of discarded plastic bottles from landfills and reduced the water consumed in the manufacturing process.

   Socially responsible efforts on behalf of the general public are becoming more common. A formal practice is **cause marketing**, which occurs when the charitable contributions of a firm are tied directly to the customer revenues produced through the promotion of one of its products.[40] This definition distinguishes cause marketing from a firm's standard charitable contributions, which are outright donations. For example, when consumers purchase selected company products, Procter & Gamble directs part of that revenue toward programs that support disadvantaged youth and provide disaster relief. MasterCard International links usage of its card with fund-raising for institutions that combat cancer, heart disease, child abuse, drug abuse, and muscular dystrophy. Barnes & Noble promotes literacy, and Coca-Cola sponsors local Boys and Girls Clubs. Avon Products, Inc., focuses on different issues in different countries, including breast cancer, domestic violence, and disaster relief, among many others.

   Cause marketing programs incorporate all three concepts of social responsibility by addressing public concerns and satisfying customer needs. They can also enhance corporate sales and profits as described in the Marketing Matters box on the next page.[41]

CHAPTER 3   Understanding the Marketing Environment, Ethical Behavior, and Social Responsibility

77

Marketing Matters

Will Consumers Switch Brands for a Cause? Yes, If . . .

American Express Company pioneered cause marketing when it sponsored the renovation of the Statue of Liberty. This effort raised $1.7 million for the renovation, increased card usage among cardholders, and attracted new cardholders. In 2001, U.S. companies raised more than $5 billion for causes they champion. It is estimated that cause marketing raised over $10 billion in 2012.

Cause marketing benefits companies as well as causes. Research indicates that 85 percent of U.S. consumers say they have a more favorable

opinion of companies that support causes they care about. Also, 85 percent of consumers say they will switch to a brand or retailer that supports a good cause if the price and quality of brands or retailers are equal. In short, cause marketing may be a valued point of difference for brands and companies, all other things being equal.

For more information, including news, links, and case studies, visit the Cause Marketing Forum website at www.causemarketingforum.com.

Sustainable Development: Doing Well by Doing Good

Sustainable development involves conducting business in a way that protects the natural environment while making economic progress. Ecologically responsible initiatives such as green marketing represent one such initiative. Recent initiatives related to working conditions at offshore manufacturing sites that produce goods for U.S. companies focus on quality-of-life issues. Public opinion surveys show that 90 percent of U.S. citizens are concerned about working conditions under which products are made in Asia and Latin America. Companies such as Reebok, Nike, Liz Claiborne, Levi Strauss, and Mattel have responded by imposing codes of conduct to reduce harsh or abusive working conditions at offshore manufacturing facilities.[42] Still, poor working conditions exist. For example, over 1,000 garment workers in Bangladesh died when their factory collapsed in 2013.

Companies that evidence societal responsibility have been rewarded for their efforts. Research has shown that these companies (1) benefit from favorable word of mouth among consumers and (2) typically outperform less responsible companies in terms of financial performance.[43]

> **learning review**
>
> 3-13. What is meant by social responsibility?
>
> 3-14. Marketing efforts to produce, promote, and reclaim environmentally sensitive products are called _____.
>
> 3-15. What is sustainable development?

LEARNING OBJECTIVES REVIEW

LO 3-1 *Explain the purpose of environmental scanning.*

Environmental scanning is the process of continually acquiring information on events occurring outside the organization to identify and interpret potential trends. Environmental trends typically arise from five sources: social, economic, technological, competitive, and regulatory forces. A firm conducting an environmental scan of the marketplace might uncover key trends such as the changing use of media, the increasing impact of new technologies, and many others.

LO 3-2 *Describe social forces such as demographics and culture.*

The social forces of the environment include the demographic characteristics and the culture of the population. Three key demographic characteristics include a population profile, a description of generational cohorts (baby boomers, Generation X, and Generation Y), and a description of racial and ethnic diversity. Culture incorporates the set of values, ideas, and attitudes that is learned and shared among the members of a group.

LO 3-3 *Discuss how economic forces affect marketing.*

Two aspects of economic forces include macroeconomic conditions related to the marketplace and microeconomic factors such as consumer income. Indicators of marketplace conditions include GDP, unemployment, and price changes (inflation or deflation). Consumer income has gross, disposable, and discretionary components. The state of the economy and changes in income can influence consumers' ability to buy products and services.

LO 3-4 *Describe how technological changes can affect marketing.*

Technological innovations can replace existing products and services. Changes in technology can also have an impact on customer value by reducing the cost of products, improving the quality of products, and providing new products that were not previously feasible. Electronic commerce is transforming how companies do business.

LO 3-5 *Discuss the forms of competition that exist in a market.*

There are four forms of competition: pure competition, monopolistic competition, oligopoly, and monopoly. While large companies are often used as examples of marketplace competitors, there are 28 million small businesses in the United States that have a significant impact on the economy.

LO 3-6 *Explain how regulatory forces ensure competition and protect producers and consumers.*

Regulation exists to protect companies and consumers. Legislation that ensures a competitive marketplace includes the Sherman Antitrust Act. Companies can protect their competitive position with patent and copyright laws. Consumers are protected by laws that address each of the four elements of the marketing mix. Laws such as the Lanham Act, which provides for the registration of trademarks, benefit both companies and consumers. Self-regulation through organizations such as the Better Business Bureau provides an alternative to federal and state regulation.

LO 3-7 *Identify factors that influence ethical and unethical marketing decisions.*

Four factors presented in Figure 3–2 influence ethical marketing behavior. They are: societal culture and norms, business culture and industry practices, corporate culture and expectations, and personal moral philosophy and ethical behavior.

LO 3-8 *Describe the different concepts of social responsibility.*

Social responsibility means that organizations are part of a larger society and are accountable to that society for their actions. There are three concepts of social responsibility: profit responsibility, stakeholder responsibility, and societal responsibility.

LEARNING REVIEW ANSWERS

3-1 Describe three generational cohorts.
Answer: (1) Baby boomers are the generation of 76 million among the U.S. population born between 1946 and 1964. These Americans are growing older and will all be 65 or older by 2030. (2) Generation X are those among the 15 percent of the U.S. population born between 1965 and 1976. These well-educated Americans, also known as the baby bust cohort because of declining birth rates, are supportive of racial and ethic diversity. (3) Generation Y, or millennials, are the 72 million Americans among the U.S. population born between 1977 and 1994. The rising birth rate of this "baby boomlet" cohort is the result of baby boomers having children.

3-2 Why are many companies developing multicultural marketing programs?
Answer: Multicultural marketing programs consist of combinations of the marketing mix that reflect the unique attitudes, ancestry, communication preferences, and lifestyles of different races and ethnic groups. The reason for developing these programs is that the racial and ethnic diversity of the U.S. is changing rapidly due to the increases in the African American, Asian, and Hispanic populations, which increases their economic impact.

3-3 How are important values such as sustainability reflected in the marketplace today?
Answer: Many Americans desire and practice sustainability to preserve the environment. Specifically, these consumers buy products such as hybrid gas-electric cars. Consumers also prefer brands that have a strong link to social action (like Ben & Jerry's—see Chapter 2). Companies are responding to this consumer trend by producing products that use renewable energy and less packaging.

3-4 What is the difference between a consumer's disposable and discretionary income?
Answer: Disposable income is the money a consumer has left after paying taxes to use for necessities such as food, housing, clothing, and transportation. Discretionary income is the money that remains after paying for taxes and necessities and is usually spent on luxury items.

3-5 How does technology impact customer value?
Answer: (1) Consumers can now assess value on the basis of dimensions such as quality, service, and relationships due to the decline in the cost of technology. (2) Technology provides value through the development of new products.

3-6 In pure competition there are a _____ number of sellers.
Answer: large

3-7 The _____ Act forbids actual monopolies, whereas the _____ Act forbids actions that are likely to lessen competition.
Answer: Sherman Antitrust; Clayton

3-8 The Federal Trade Commission (FTC) monitors _____.
Answer: unfair business practices

3-9 How does the Better Business Bureau encourage companies to follow its standards for commerce?
Answer: The Better Business Bureau (BBB) uses moral suasion to get members to comply with its standards.

3-10 What rights are included in the Consumer Bill of Rights?
Answer: The rights to safety, to be informed, to choose, and to be heard.

3-11 **Economic espionage includes what kinds of activities?**
Answer: Economic espionage is the clandestine collection of trade secrets or proprietary information about a company's competitors. This practice includes trespassing, theft, fraud, misrepresentation, wiretapping, searching competitors' trash, and violations of written and implicit employment agreements with noncompete clauses.

3-12 **What is meant by moral idealism?**
Answer: Moral idealism is a personal moral philosophy that considers certain individual rights or duties as universal, regardless of the outcome.

3-13 **What is meant by social responsibility?**
Answer: Social responsibility means that organizations are part of a larger society and are accountable to that society for their actions. It comprises three concepts: (1) profit responsibility—maximizing profits for the organization's shareholders; (2) stakeholder responsibility—the obligations an organization has to those who can affect the achievement of its objectives; and (3) societal responsibility—the obligations an organization has to preserve the ecological environment and to the general public.

3-14 **Marketing efforts to produce, promote, and reclaim environmentally sensitive products are called _____.**
Answer: green marketing

3-15 **What is sustainable development?**
Answer: Sustainable development involves conducting business in such a way that protects the natural environment while making economic progress. Green marketing is an ecological example of such an initiative.

FOCUSING ON KEY TERMS

baby boomers p. 65
cause marketing p. 77
code of ethics p. 75
competition p. 70
Consumer Bill of Rights p. 74
consumerism p. 72
culture p. 66
demographics p. 64

economy p. 67
environmental scanning p. 64
ethics p. 73
Generation X p. 65
Generation Y p. 65
green marketing p. 77
marketspace p. 70
moral idealism p. 76

multicultural marketing p. 66
regulation p. 71
self-regulation p. 73
social forces p. 64
social responsibility p. 76
technology p. 69
utilitarianism p. 76

APPLYING MARKETING KNOWLEDGE

1 For many years Gerber has manufactured baby food in small, single-sized containers. In conducting an environmental scan, identify three trends or factors that might significantly affect this company's future business, and then propose how Gerber might respond to these changes.

2 Describe the new features you would add to an automobile designed for consumers in the 55+ age group. In what magazines would you advertise to appeal to this target market?

3 New technologies are continuously improving and replacing existing products. Although technological change is often difficult to predict, suggest how the following companies and products might be affected by the Internet and digital technologies: (*a*) Kodak cameras and film, (*b*) American Airlines, and (*c*) the Metropolitan Museum of Art.

4 Why would Xerox be concerned about its name becoming generic?

5 Develop a Code of Ethics for a new online vitamin store. Does your code address advertising? Privacy? Use by children?

6 Compare and contrast moral idealism and utilitarianism as alternative personal moral philosophies.

7 How would you evaluate Milton Friedman's view of the social responsibility of a firm?

BUILDING YOUR MARKETING PLAN

Your marketing plan will include a situation analysis based on internal and external factors that are likely to affect your marketing program and an assessment of the affect of your plan on potential stakeholders.

1 To summarize information about external factors, create a table and identify three trends related to each of the five forces (social, economic, technological, competitive, and regulatory) that relate to your product or service.

2 When your table is complete, describe how each of the trends represents an opportunity or a threat for your business.

3 Identify what, if any, ethical and social responsibility issues might arise for each type of stakeholder.

VIDEO CASE 3 Toyota: Building Cleaner, Greener Cars

Video 3-4
Toyota
Video Case
kerin.tv/cr6e/v3-4

"Toyota's mission is to become the most respected and admired car company in America," explains Jana Hartline, manager of environmental communications at Toyota. To accomplish this, Jana and her colleagues at Toyota are working toward a future where a wide range of innovative vehicles, fuel technologies, and partnerships converge to create an economically vibrant, mobile society in harmony with the environment. It's a challenge Jana finds exciting and the result is cleaner, greener cars!

THE COMPANY

Kiichiro Toyoda began research on gasoline-powered engines in 1930. By 1935 he had developed passenger car prototypes, and in 1957 he introduced the "Toyopet" in the United States. The Toyopet was not successful and was discontinued. In 1965, however, the Corona was introduced, and it was followed by the Corolla in 1968. The Corolla went on to become the best-selling passenger car in the world, with 27 million purchased in more than 140 countries!

The popularity of Toyota's automobiles continued to grow in the United States and in 1975 it surpassed Volkswagen to become the number one import brand. In 1998 Toyota launched its first full-sized pickup, the Toyota Tundra. Toyota also expanded its product line by adding the Lexus brand, which has become known for its exceptional quality and customer service. By 2000, Lexus was one of the best-selling luxury brands in the United States, competing with both Mercedes-Benz and BMW. Toyota also introduced the Scion brand of moderately priced vehicles for the youth market.

The company opened a national sales headquarters in Torrance, California, and also opened manufacturing facilities so it could produce cars in the United States. By 2012 Toyota had the capacity to build 2.2 million cars and trucks and 1.45 million engines in 15 plants across North America. Toyota's sales and distribution organization includes 1,500 Toyota, Lexus, and Scion dealers. Toyota's marketing organization has led to many memorable marketing campaigns. Some of its early taglines included, "You Asked For It, You Got It!" and "Oh What a Feeling!" which included the "Toyota Jump." The Lexus tagline, "The Relentless Pursuit of Perfection," is still in use today, while Toyota's ads now exclaim, "Let's Go Places."

Today, Toyota is the world's largest automobile manufacturer. The company is ranked the tenth largest corporation by *Fortune* magazine. The company's core principle is "to contribute to society and the economy by producing high-quality products and services." Its success is often attributed to a business philosophy referred to as "The Toyota Way."

THE TOYOTA WAY

The Toyota Way is a business philosophy used to (1) improve processes and products, (2) build trust, and (3) empower individuals and teams. There are two values that act as pillars of The Toyota Way. They are continuous improvement and respect for people. These values are evident in five business practices:

- *Challenge*: To build a long-term vision and meet challenges with courage and creativity.
- *Kaizen*: To continuously improve business operations, always striving for innovation and evolution.
- *Genchi Genbutsu*: To always go to the source to find the facts and make correct decisions; to build consensus and expeditiously achieve goals.
- *Respect*: To respect others and the environment, to build trust and to take responsibility.
- *Teamwork*: To stimulate personal and professional growth, maximize individual and team performance.

In fact, according to Jana Hartline, the two values are "integrated into everything that we do on a daily basis," creating "a unique corporate environment."

As the company has grown it has also sought a larger role in society. For example, Toyota created the Toyota USA Foundation with a $10 million endowment and a mission to make Toyota a leading corporate citizen. The foundation supports programs focused on the environment, education, and safety that help strengthen communities. Since 1991 Toyota has contributed over $500 million to philanthropic programs in the United States. Combining The Toyota Way with its corporate philanthropy has been very successful. Toyota believes that the foundation of its success involves a constant spirit of challenge and enthusiasm for new ideas. For example, Toyota's environmental vision includes the concept of sustainable mobility.

ENVIRONMENTAL VISION AND THE PRIUS

To make its environmental vision actionable, Toyota developed a five-year Environmental Action Plan. The plan is structured around five key areas:

- Energy and Climate Change
- Recycling and Resource Management

- Air Quality
- Environmental Management
- Cooperation with Society

For each area Toyota creates goals and measurable targets based on a life-cycle view of vehicles: from design, to manufacturing, to sales and distribution, to use, and finally to how the vehicle is recycled at end-of-life. One of its top goals has been to develop advanced vehicle technologies to complement traditional automobile technologies. Ed LaRocque, national manager of vehicle marketing, describes how Toyota started one of these initiatives:

> *In the early 90s Toyota developed what we called the G21 vision. The goal of the G21 plan was to bring a vehicle to market that represented a great value, and had great environmental benefits, not just in Japan but globally.*

The concept was eventually introduced as the Prius, a hybrid vehicle with a gasoline engine and an electric motor combination called the Hybrid Synergy Drive. The car received an EPA-estimated mileage rating of 50 mpg. Initially the Prius was attractive to very eco-conscious consumers but met with some resistance from the press and the general population. The cars were fuel efficient, but they were not attractive. Since the first introduction, Toyota has made changes and introduced two new generations of

the Prius to help it become the world's most-popular hybrid, selling more than three million of the vehicles.

Toyota's development of new technologies such as the Hybrid Synergy Drive helped it recognize the implications for the entire mobility system. A strategy for sustainable mobility affects not only new technologies and vehicles, but also new energy sources, new transportation systems, and the many partnerships of involved stakeholders. Advertising for the Prius emphasizes this point, claiming the car provides "Harmony between man, nature, and machine." In the long-term, however, this strategy will not be successful if consumers are not aware of or knowledgeable about advanced technologies. To increase awareness and knowledge Toyota specified the development of partnerships as a goal.

STRATEGIC PARTNERSHIPS

Toyota believes that partnerships with relevant organizations help increase awareness of its technologies and products. These programs are designed to educate people so they can reduce their environmental footprint. One of these programs, for example, is *Together Green*—a $20 million, five-year alliance with Audubon to fund projects, train leaders, and offer volunteer opportunities. Similarly, Toyota has partnered with the World Wildlife Fund to establish hybrid energy systems, oil recycling programs, and renewable energy outreach campaigns. The exposure from these programs is often much more effective than other communication options. Mary Nickerson, National Manager of Advanced Technology, explains: "we [have] used partnerships with the American Lung Association, with the Electric Drive Transportation Association, Environmental Media Association, and the national parks to help touch many more millions of people than we ever could have done with a traditional advertising campaign."

Toyota recently announced a grant of $5 million and 25 Toyota vehicles in support of U.S. National Parks. Parks included in this grant and other Toyota partnerships are Yellowstone National Park, Great Smoky Mountains National Park, Everglades National Park, Yosemite National Park, the Grand Canyon, the Santa Monica National Recreation Area, and the Golden Gate Bridge Foundation. The national parks partnership offers an opportunity to enhance the experiences of visitors through education and hybrid vehicle use (park employees use the donated Toyota vehicles to reduce noise and emissions in the parks).

Generally, the goal of the national parks partnership program is to make a personal connection with park visitors about Toyota's hybrid vehicles when they are in a natural setting in which they are receptive to receiving a message about sustainable mobility. The message implies important links:

"Green" Vehicles > Cleaner Air > Preservation of Parks

In addition, Toyota believes that the programs have other benefits, including:

- Strengthening Toyota's image as an environmental leader among automakers.
- Communicating a message of environmental stewardship.
- Building awareness of the Prius and other Toyota hybrids.
- Educating park visitors on the benefits of advanced vehicle technology.

Research by Toyota indicates that the program is working. A recent corporate image study indicated that among four leading automakers (Toyota, Honda, Ford, and GM), Toyota was rated highest on dimensions such as "Leader in High MPG," "Leader in Technology Development," "Environmentally Friendly Vehicles," and "Wins Environmental Awards."

THE FUTURE

Figure 1 shows the results of a survey of consumer interests and their response to the question, "Who should take

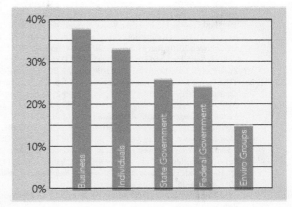

FIGURE 1

Who should take the lead in addressing environmental issues?

the lead in addressing environmental issues?" The results suggest that in the future consumers will expect businesses to be proactive about the environment and sustainability.

For Toyota, a focus on sustainability will mean considering the environmental, social, and economic consequences of the auto business and continuously working to reduce the negative and increase the positive impacts of its activities and decisions. The increasing importance of sustainability will challenge Toyota to look at these impacts from all stages of the vehicle life cycle. It will also encourage Toyota's managers to consider the opinions of many stakeholders such as consumers, regulators, local communities, and nongovernmental organizations.

The recent concerns about Toyota vehicle product quality, which led to the recall of 16 million vehicles, have hurt Toyota's reputation. In the future, all activities, including the partnership strategy and the national parks program, will determine if Toyota can become "the most respected car company in the world."

Questions

1 How does Toyota's approach to social responsibility relate to the three concepts of social responsibility described in the text (profit responsibility, stakeholder responsibility, and societal responsibility)?

2 How does Toyota's view of sustainable mobility contribute to the company's overall mission?

3 Has Toyota's National Parks project been a success? What indicators suggest that the project has had an impact?

4 What future activities would you suggest for Toyota as it strives to improve its reputation?

Chapter Notes

1. Ashlee Vance, "Facebook: The Making of 1 Billion Users," *Bloomberg Businessweek*, October 8–14, 2012, pp. 64–70; Miguel Helft and Jessi Hempel, "Inside Facebook," *Fortune*, March 19, 2012, pp. 112–22; Miguel Helft and Jessi Hempel, "Facebook vs. Google: The Battle for the Future of the Web," *Fortune*, November 21, 2011, pp. 114–24; David Kirkpatrick, *The Facebook Effect* (New York: Simon and Schuster, 2010); Barry Libert, *Social Nation* (Hoboken, NJ: John Wiley & Sons, Inc.); and Lev Grossman, "2010 Person of the Year: Mark Zuckerberg," *Time*, December 27, 2010/January 3, 2011, pp. 44–75.

2. "The Future Issue," *Fortune*, January 14, 2013, p. 49; "10 Crucial Consumer Trends for 2013," www.trendwatching.com, January 14, 2013; Brian Steinberg, "Digital Natives Are Restless–Switching Media 27 Times an Hour," *Advertising Age*, April 9, 2012, p. 1; Christine Birkner, "Marketing in 2012: The End of the Middle," *Marketing News*, January 31, 2012, p. 22; Bill Clinton, "The Case for Optimism," *Time*, October 1, 2012, p. 38; Christine Birkner and Piet Levy, "Marketing in 2011," *Marketing News*, January 30, 2011, pp. 16–21; and "Predictions 2011," *Bloomberg Businessweek*, January 3, 2011, pp. 14–36.

3. *2012 World Population Data Sheet* (Washington, DC: Population Reference Bureau, 2010), pp. 2, 5.

4. Population and Housing Unit Estimates, 2012 National Total Population Estimates, United States Census, www.census.gov, December 20, 2012; "U.S. Census Bureau Projections Show a Slower Growing, Older, More Diverse Nation a Half Century from Now," U.S. Census Bureau, December 12, 2012; and "Projections of the Population by Selected Age Groups and Sex for the United States: 2015 to 2060," U.S. Census Bureau, Table 2, December 2012.

5. Tom Sightings, "How Baby Boomers Will Change the Economy," *USNews.com*, January 15, 2013; "Lay's Unveils 2 New Kettle Cooked Potato Chip Varieties," *Entertainment Close-Up*, July 11, 2012; and Ellen Byron, "How to Market to an Aging Boomer, p. A1.

6. Leonard Klie, "Gen X: Stuck in the Middle," *destinationCRM.com*, February 1, 2012; Michele Hammond, "Gen X Pips Boomers to Lead Online Retail Spending," www.startupsmart.com.au, January 10, 2013; Chris Johns, "Hotels for Hipsters," *The Globe and Mail*, November 13, 2012, p. E1; and Piet Levy, "Segmentation by Generation," *Marketing News*, May 15, 2012, p. 20.

7. "Generations X, Y Adopt Smartphones as Media Hubs," *Business Wire*, July 31, 2012; "The Truth about Millennials—Are You Ready for These New Professionals?" *States News Service*, March 30, 2012; "The Millennials Speak, and They Want Their Packaging to Respond Boldly," *Packaging Strategies*, April 30, 2012; Elizabeth Olson, "For Millennials, It's More about Personal Style Than Luxury," *The New York Times*, November 3, 2010, p. 3; Laura Vanderkam, "Graduates, You Can Have It All," *USA Today*, May 27, 2010, p. 11A; and Carla Seaquist, "Hope for Reversing America's Decline: the Millennial Generation," *The Christian Science Monitor*, September 24, 2010.

8. "Research: Latino Purchasing Power Now Pegged at $1 Trillion, *Hispanically Speaking News*, May 3, 2011; "Black Buying Power to Reach $1.1 Trillion, Report Finds," *Huffington Post*, November 10, 2011; *State of the Asian American Consumer*, The Nielsen Company, Quarter 3, 2012, p. 14; and "The New Now: Defining the Future Together," *PR Newswire*, February 18, 2011.

9. Robin M. Williams, Jr., *American Society: A Sociological Interpretation*, 3rd ed. (New York: Knopf, 1970); L. Robert Kohls, "Why Do Americans Act Like That?" International Programs, San Francisco State University; Eric Pooley, David Welch, and Alan Ohnsman, "Charged for Battle," *Bloomberg Businessweek*, January 3, 2011, pp. 48–56; Edwin R. Stafford and Cathy L. Hartman, "Promoting the Value of Sustainably Minded Purchase Behaviors," *Marketing News*, January 2013, p. 28; and Juan Rodriguez, "Selling the Righteous Life," *The Gazette*, September 18, 2010, p. B3.

10. "Tuition and Fees and Room and Board Charges over Time in Current Dollars and 2012 Dollars," College Board, http://trends.collegeboard.org/college-pricing/figures-tables/tuition-and-fee-and-room-and-board-charges-over-time-unweighted; and Carmen DeNavas-Walt, Bernadette D. Proctor, and Jessica C. Smith, "Income, Poverty, and Health Insurance Coverage in the United States: 2011," *Current Population Reports* (Washington, DC: U.S. Census Bureau, September 2012).

11. Azhar Iqbal and Mark Vitner, "The Deeper the Recession, the Stronger the Recovery: Is It Really That Simple?" *Business Economics* (2011), pp. 22–31.

12. Carmen, DeNavas-Walt, Bernadette D. Proctor, and Jessica C. Smith, "Income, Poverty, and Health Insurance Coverage in the United States: 2012," U.S. Department of Commerce, P60-245, September 2013, p. 33, 38.

13. Betsy Bohlen, Steve Carlotti, and Liz Mihas, "How the Recession Has Changed U.S. Consumer Behavior," *McKinsey Quarterly*, Issue 1 (2010), pp. 17–20; and Mark Trumbull, "In Tough Times, U.S. Consumers Forging New Behaviors," *Christian Science Monitor*, February 3, 2009, p. 25.

14. Tiffany Hsu, "High Prices Lift Consumer Spending: But the Savings Rate Slips in August as Americans Spend More for Food and Gas," *Los Angeles Times*, September 29, 2012, p. 2; "Consumer Expenditure Survey: 2008–2011," U.S. Department of Labor, Bureau of Labor Statistics, April 2013, Table B; and Mark Trumbull, "Consumers Holding Back on Spending." *Christian Science Monitor*, August 4, 2010.

15. Kelli B. Grant, "4 Future Tech Trends," *MarketWatch*, January 15, 2013; Gillian Shaw, "Deloitte Predicts 10 Tech Trends for 2013," *The Vancouver Sun*, January 17, 2013, p. B8; "The Biggest Tech Trends Coming in 2013," *First Digital Media*, January 22, 2013; "5 Important Tech Trends of 2013," *Business2Community.com*, January 8, 2013; and "7 Engineering and Tech Trends to Watch in 2013," *Green and Clean*, January 16, 2013.

16. Eric Griffith, "The Best Free Software of 2012," *PCMag.com*, April 2, 2012; "Should Carriers End Smartphone Subsidies?" *Trefis*, January 17, 2013; and Koen Pauwels and Allen Weiss, "Moving from Free to Fee: How Online Firms Market to Change Their Business Model Successfully," *Journal of Marketing*, May 2008, pp. 14–31.

17. "CES 2013 and Amazing New Products," *CIOL*, January 15, 2013; "2013 Best New Product Awards, *Better Homes and Gardens*, www.bhg.com, January 2013; and Steven Levy, "The A.I. Revolution," *Wired*, January 2011, p. 88.

18. Marguerite Reardon, "Competitive Wireless Carriers Take on AT&T and Verizon," *CNET News*, September 10, 2012; "Market Share of Subscriptions Held by Wireless Carriers in the U.S. from 1st to 3rd Quarter 2011 and 2012," Chetan Sharma Consulting, *statista.com*, 2013; and www.fiercewireless.com/special-reports/grading-top-10-us-carriers-first-quarter-2013.

19. James Kanter, "E.U. Accuses Microsoft of Violating Antitrust Deal," *The International Herald Tribune*, October 25, 2012, p. 17; and "Google Wins an Antitrust Battle," *The New York Times*, January 6, 2013, p. 10.

20. "Frequently Asked Questions," Small Business Administration, Office of Advocacy, www.sba.gov/advocacy, September 2012; "Small Business Trends," Small Business Administration, www.sba.gov/content/small-business-trends; and Kathryn Kobe, "Small Business GDP: Update 2002–2010," Small Business Administration, Office of Advocacy, January 2012.

21. "One Year Later, SOPA Activists Reignite Copyright Conversation," *CBS News*, January 18, 2013; and "Legal Roundup," *Billboard*, January 31, 2009.

22. Cotton Delo, "You Are Big Brother (But That Isn't So Bad)," *Advertising Age*, April 23, 2012, p. 1; and Ana Radelat, "Online Privacy, Postal Hikes Top List of DMA Concerns," *Advertising Age*, April 23, 2012, p. 3.

23. Dorothy Cohen, "Trademark Strategy Revisited," *Journal of Marketing,* July 1991, pp. 46–59.

24. For a discussion of the definition of ethics, see Patrick E. Murphy, Gene R. Laezniak, Norman E. Bowie, and Thomas A. Klein, *Ethical Marketing: Basic Ethics in Action* (Upper Saddle River, NJ: Prentice Hall, 2005).

25. See, for example, Linda K. Trevino and Katherine A. Nelson, *Managing Business Ethics: Straight Talk about How to Get It Right,* 5th ed. (New York: John Wiley & Sons, 2011).

26. Thomas Donaldson, "Values in Tension: Ethics Away from Home," *Harvard Business Review,* September–October 1996, pp. 48–62.

27. Ethisphere Institute, "2012 World's Most Ethical Companies," www.ethisphere.com, accessed January 3, 2013.

28. Vern Terpstra and Kenneth David, *The Cultural Environment of International Business,* 3rd ed. (Cincinnati: South-Western Publishing, 1991), p. 12.

29. Hedich Nasheri, *Economic Espionage and Industrial Spying* (Cambridge: Cambridge University Press, 2005).

30. "Coke Employee Faces Charges in Plot to Sell Secrets," *The Wall Street Journal,* July 6, 2006, p. B6; "Do the Right Thing? Not with a Rival's Inside Info," *Advertising Age,* July 17, 2006, p. 4; and "You Can't Beat the Real Thing," *Time,* July 17, 2006, pp. 10–11.

31. www.transparency.org, downloaded January 20, 2013.

32. *The 2011 National Business Ethics Survey.*

33. *The 2011 National Business Ethics Survey;* and "Critics Blow Whistle on Law," *The Wall Street Journal,* November 1, 2010, pp. B1, B11.

34. "Scotchgard Working Out Recent Stain on Its Business," www.mercurynews.com, downloaded June 22, 2003.

35. James Q. Wilson, "Adam Smith on Business Ethics," *California Management Review,* Fall 1989, pp. 57–72.

36. Harvey S. James and Farhad Rassekh, "Smith, Friedman, and Self-Interest in Ethical Society," *Business Ethics Quarterly,* July 2000, pp. 659–74.

37. "Perrier—Overresponding to a Crisis," in Robert F. Hartley, *Marketing Mistakes and Successes,* 10th ed. (New York: John Wiley & Sons, 2006), pp. 119–30.

38. Andrew W. Savitz with Karl Weber, *The Triple Bottom Line: How Today's Best Run Companies Are Achieving Economic, Social and Environmental Success* (San Francisco, CA: Josey Bass, 2006).

39. 3M 2012 Sustainability Report, downloaded May 25, 2012; "Levi's Has a New Color for Blue Jeans: Green," *Businessweek,* October 22–October 28, 2012, pp. 26, 28; and "Walmart 2012 Global Sustainability Report," www.walmart.com downloaded January 30, 2013.

40. For a seminal discussion on this topic, see P. Rajan Varadarajan and Anil Menon, "Cause-Related Marketing: A Coalignment of Marketing Strategy and Corporate Philanthropy," *Journal of Marketing,* July 1988, pp. 58–74.

41. "Even as Cause Marketing Grows, 83 Percent of Consumers Still Want to See More," press release, Cone LLC, September 15, 2010; and Larry Chiagouris and Ipshita Ray, "Saving the World with Cause-Related Marketing," *Marketing Management,* July–August 2007, pp. 48–51.

42. Unmesh Kher, "Getting Smart at Being Good . . . Are Companies Better Off for It?" *Time,* January 2006, pp. A1–A37; and Pete Engardio, "Beyond the Green Corporation," *Businessweek,* January 29, 2007, pp. 50–64.

43. "Economics—Creating Environmental Capital," *The Wall Street Journal,* March 24, 2008, Section R; Remi Trudel and June Cotte, "Does Being Ethical Pay?" *The Wall Street Journal,* May 12, 2008, p. R4; and Pete Engardio, "Beyond the Green Corporation," *Businessweek,* January 29, 2007, pp. 50–64.

Toyota, Inc.: This case was written by Steven Hartley. Sources: "Global 500: The World's Largest Corporations," *Fortune,* July 23, 2012, p. F-1; *2010 North America Environmental Report,* Toyota Motor North America, Inc., p. 1; "Toyota's Mobile Hybrid Tour and The Power of Partnership," Presentation by Mary Nickerson, National Marketing Manager, Toyota Motor Sales, U.S.A., Inc.; Toyota website, http://www.toyota.com/sitemap.html, accessed July 6, 2013; "Lexus Seeks to Regain Luxury Crown with New Advertisement," *AutoShopper.com,* June 28, 2013; Tim Higgins, "Luxury Cars Are Neck and Neck in the U.S.," *Bloomberg Businessweek,* October 18, 2010, p. 26; Lucy Tobin, "Recall Tarnishes Toyota's Reputation," *The Evening Standard,* July 3, 2013, p. 45; and Mark Rechtin, "Toyota Reputation Starts to Recover," *Advertising Age,* January 24, 2011, p. 34.

Credits

Understanding Buyers and Markets

4 Understanding Consumer Behavior

LEARNING OBJECTIVES

After reading this chapter you should be able to:

 LO 4-1 Describe the stages in the consumer purchase decision process.

 LO 4-2 Distinguish among three variations of the consumer purchase decision process: extended, limited, and routine problem solving.

 LO 4-3 Identify the major psychological influences on consumer behavior.

 LO 4-4 Identify the major sociocultural influences on consumer behavior.

ENLIGHTENED CARMAKERS KNOW WHAT CUSTOM(H)ERS AND INFLUENC(H)ERS VALUE

Who makes 60 percent of new-car buying decisions? Who influences 80 percent of new-car buying decisions? Women. Yes, women.

Women are a driving force in the U.S. automobile industry. Enlightened carmakers have hired women designers, engineers, and marketing executives to better understand and satisfy this valuable car buyer and influencer. What have they learned? While car price and quality are important, women and men think and feel differently about car features and key elements of the new-car buying decision process and experience.

- *The sense of styling.* Women and men care about styling. For men, styling is more about a car's exterior lines and accents or "curb appeal." Women are more interested in interior design and finishes. Designs that fit their proportions, provide good visibility, offer ample storage space, and make for effortless parking are particularly important.

- *The need for speed.* Both sexes want speed, but for different reasons. Men think about how many seconds it takes to get from zero to 60 miles per hour. Women want to feel secure that the car has enough acceleration to outrun an 18-wheeler trying to pass them on a freeway entrance ramp.

- *The substance of safety.* Safety for men is about features that help avoid an accident, such as antilock brakes and responsive steering. For women, safety is about features that help to survive an accident. These features include passenger airbags and reinforced side panels.

- *The shopping experience.* The new-car-buying experience differs between men and women in important ways. Generally, men decide up front what car they want and set out alone to find it. By contrast, women approach it as an intelligence-gathering expedition. Referred to as *CROPing*, women shoppers look for *CRedible OPinions*. They actively seek information and postpone a purchase decision until all options have been evaluated. Women, more frequently than men, visit auto-buying websites, read car-comparison articles, and scan car advertisements. Still, recommendations of friends and relatives matter most to women. Women typically shop three dealerships before making a purchase decision—one more than men.

Carmakers have learned that women, more than men, dislike the car-buying experience—specifically, the experience of dealing with car salespeople. In contrast to many male car buyers, women do not typically revel in the gamesmanship of car buying. "Men get all excited about going out to buy a car and talk about how they're going to one-up the salesman and get a great deal," said Anne Fleming, president of www.women-drivers.com, a consumer ratings site. "I've never heard or seen any comments from women like that." In particular, women dread the price negotiations that are often involved in buying a new car. Not surprisingly, about half of women car buyers take a man with them to finalize the terms of sale.[1]

consumer behavior
The actions a person takes in purchasing and using products and services.

This chapter examines **consumer behavior**, the actions a person takes in purchasing and using products and services, including the mental and social processes that come before and after these actions. This chapter shows how the behavioral sciences help answer questions such as why people choose one product or brand over another, how they make these choices, and how companies use this knowledge to provide value to consumers.

CONSUMER PURCHASE DECISION PROCESS AND EXPERIENCE

LO 4-1 Describe the stages in the consumer purchase decision process.

Behind the visible act of making a purchase lies an important decision process and consumer experience that must be investigated. The stages a buyer passes through in making choices about which products and services to buy is the **purchase decision process**. This process has the five stages shown in Figure 4–1: (1) problem recognition, (2) information search, (3) alternative evaluation, (4) purchase decision, and (5) postpurchase behavior.

Problem Recognition: Perceiving a Need

purchase decision process
The stages a buyer passes through in making choices about which products or services to buy.

Problem recognition, the initial step in the purchase decision, is perceiving a difference between a person's ideal and actual situations big enough to trigger a decision.[2] This can be as simple as finding an empty milk carton in the refrigerator; noting, as a first-year college student, that your high school clothes are not in the style that other students are wearing; or realizing that your notebook computer may not be working properly.

In marketing, advertisements or salespeople can activate a consumer's decision process by showing the shortcomings of competing (or currently owned) products. For instance, an advertisement for a new generation smartphone could stimulate problem recognition because it emphasizes "maximum use from one device."

Information Search: Seeking Value

After recognizing a problem, a consumer begins to search for information, the next stage in the purchase decision process. First, you may scan your memory for previous experiences with products or brands.[3] This action is called *internal search*. For frequently purchased products such as shampoo and conditioner, this may be enough.

In other cases, a consumer may undertake an *external search* for information.[4] This is needed when past experience or knowledge is insufficient, the risk of making a wrong purchase decision is high, and the cost of gathering information is low. The primary sources of external information are (1) *personal sources*, such as relatives and friends whom the consumer trusts; (2) *public sources*, including various product-rating organizations such as *Consumer Reports*, government agencies, and TV "consumer programs"; and (3) *marketer-dominated sources*, such as information from sellers including advertising, company websites, salespeople, and point-of-purchase displays in stores.

FIGURE 4–1
The purchase decision process consists of five stages.

Suppose you are considering buying a new smartphone. You will probably tap several of these information sources: friends and relatives, advertisements, brand and

Common Selection Criteria	Brand and Model Name						
	Apple iPhone 6	Apple iPhone 5C	BlackBerry Z 30	HTC One	LG G2	Motorola Dröid Razor	Samsung Galaxy S 5
Retail Price	$200	$100	$200	$100	$100	$100	$100
Phone Display	★★★	★★★	★★★	★★★	★★★	★★★	★★★
Audio Quality	★★	★★	★	★	★	★★	★★
Text Messaging	★★	★★	★★	★★★	★★★	★★★	★★★
Web Capability	★★★	★	★★	★★★	★★★	★★★	★★★
Camera Quality	★★★	★★★	★★★	★	★★★	★★★	★★★
Battery	★★	★★	★★★	★★★	★★★	★★★	★★★

Composite Smartphone Evaluations by Testing Organization

★★★ Superior	★★ Above Average	★ Average

FIGURE 4–2
Common consumer selection criteria for the evaluation of smartphones.

company websites, and stores carrying these phones (for demonstrations). You also might study the comparative evaluation of selected smartphones from independent rating agencies in Figure 4–2.[5]

Alternative Evaluation: Assessing Value

The alternative evaluation stage clarifies the problem for the consumer by (1) suggesting criteria to use for the purchase, (2) yielding brand names that might meet the criteria, and (3) developing consumer value perceptions. Given only the information shown in Figure 4–2, which selection criteria would you use in buying a smartphone? Would you use price, phone display, audio quality, text messaging, web capability, camera image quality, battery life, or some other combination of these or other criteria?

For some of you, the information provided may be inadequate because it does not contain all the factors you might consider when evaluating smartphones. These factors are a consumer's *evaluative criteria*, which represent both the objective attributes of a brand (such as display) and the subjective ones (such as prestige) you use to compare different products and brands.[6] Firms try to identify and capitalize on both types of criteria to create the best value for the money paid by you and other consumers. These criteria are often displayed in advertisements.

Consumers often have several criteria for evaluating brands. Knowing this, companies seek to identify the most important evaluative criteria that consumers use when comparing brands. For example, among the seven criteria shown in Figure 4–2, suppose you use four in considering smartphones: (1) a retail price of $200 or less, (2) superior text messaging, (3) above average audio quality, and (4) superior battery life. These criteria establish the brands in your *consideration set*—the group of brands a consumer would consider acceptable from among all the brands in the product class of which he or she is aware.[7]

Your evaluative criteria result in one brand and model: the Samsung Galaxy S 5 in your consideration set. If other brand alternatives are equally attractive based on your

Shoppers routinely browse online and shop retail stores, often during the same shopping trip.

original criteria, you might expand your list of desirable features. For example, you might decide that camera and video image quality are also important and compare the alternatives based on those criteria as well.

Purchase Decision: Buying Value

Having examined the alternatives in the consideration set, you are almost ready to make a purchase decision. Two choices remain: (1) from whom to buy and (2) when to buy. For a product like a smartphone, the information search process probably involved visiting retail stores, seeing different brands advertised on television and newspapers, and viewing a smartphone on a seller's website. The choice of which seller to buy from will depend on such considerations as the terms of sale, your past experience buying from the seller, and the return policy. Often a purchase decision involves a simultaneous evaluation of both product attributes and seller characteristics. For example, you might choose the second-most preferred smartphone brand at a store or website with a liberal refund and return policy versus the most preferred brand from a seller with more conservative policies.

Deciding when to buy is determined by a number of factors. For instance, you might buy sooner if one of your preferred brands is on sale or its manufacturer offers a rebate. Other factors such as the store atmosphere, pleasantness or ease of the shopping experience, salesperson assistance, time pressure, and financial circumstances could also affect whether a purchase decision is made now or postponed.[8]

Use of the Internet to gather information, evaluate alternatives, and make buying decisions adds a technological dimension to the consumer purchase decision process and buying experience. For example, 45 percent of consumers with price comparison smartphone apps routinely compare prices for identical products across different sellers at the point of purchase prior to making a purchase decision.[9]

Postpurchase Behavior: Realizing Value

After buying a product, the consumer compares it with his or her expectations and is either satisfied or dissatisfied. If the consumer is dissatisfied, marketers must determine whether the product was deficient or consumer expectations were too high. Product deficiency may require a design change. If expectations are too high, a company's advertising or the salesperson may have oversold the product's features and benefits.

Sensitivity to a customer's consumption or use experience is extremely important in a consumer's value perception. For example, research on telephone services provided by Sprint and AT&T indicates that satisfaction or dissatisfaction affects consumer value perceptions.[10] Studies show that satisfaction or dissatisfaction affects consumer communications and repeat-purchase behavior. Satisfied buyers tell three other people about their experience. In contrast, about 90 percent of dissatisfied buyers will not buy a product again and will complain to nine people.[11] Satisfied buyers also tend to buy from the same seller each time a purchase occasion arises. The financial impact of repeat-purchase behavior is significant, as described in the Marketing Matters box.[12]

Firms such as General Electric (GE), Johnson & Johnson, Coca-Cola, and British Airways focus attention on postpurchase behavior to maximize customer satisfaction and retention. These firms, among many others, now provide toll-free telephone numbers, offer liberalized return and refund policies, and engage in extensive staff training to handle complaints, answer questions, record suggestions, and solve consumer problems. For example, GE has a database that stores 750,000 answers regarding about 8,500 of its models in 120 product lines to handle 3 million calls annually. Such efforts produce positive postpurchase communications among consumers and foster relationship building between sellers and buyers.

Marketing Matters

How Much Is a Satisfied Customer Worth?

Customer satisfaction and experience underlie the marketing concept. But how much is a satisfied customer worth?

This question has prompted firms to calculate the financial value of a satisfied customer over time. Frito-Lay, for example, estimates that the average loyal consumer in the southwestern United States eats 21 pounds of snack chips a year. At a price of $2.50 a pound, this customer spends $52.50 annually on the company's snacks such as Lay's and Ruffles potato chips, Doritos and Tostitos tortilla chips, and Fritos corn chips. Exxon estimates that a loyal customer will spend $500 annually for its branded gasoline, not including candy, snacks, oil, or repair services purchased at its gasoline stations. Kimberly-Clark reports that a loyal customer will buy 6.7 boxes of its Kleenex tissues each year and will spend $994 on facial tissues over 60 years, in today's dollars.

These calculations have focused marketer attention on the buying experience, customer satisfaction, and retention. Ford Motor Company set a target of increasing customer retention—the percentage of Ford owners whose next car is also a Ford—from 60 percent to 80 percent. Why? Ford executives say that each additional percentage point is worth a staggering $100 million in profits. In 2014, Ford's customer retention was 64 percent and the company remains the most profitable American automaker.

This calculation is not unique to Ford. Research shows that a 5 percent improvement in customer retention can increase a company's profits by 70 to 80 percent.

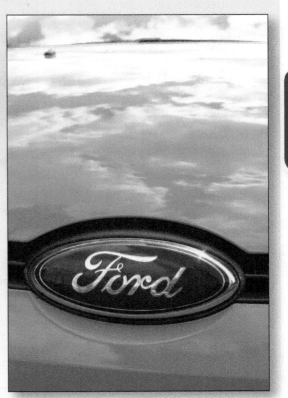

Often a consumer is faced with two or more highly attractive alternatives, such as a Samsung Galaxy S4 or Motorola Dröid Razr Maxx HD. If you choose the Galaxy S4, you might think, "Should I have purchased the Dröid Razr Maxx HD?" This feeling of postpurchase psychological tension or anxiety is called *cognitive dissonance*. To alleviate it, consumers often attempt to applaud themselves for making the right choice. So after your purchase, you may seek information to confirm your choice by asking friends questions like, "Don't you like my new phone?" or by reading ads of the brand you chose. You might even look for negative features about the brands you didn't buy and decide that the Dröid Razr Maxx HD smartphone did not feel right. Firms often use ads or follow-up calls from salespeople in this postpurchase behavior stage to comfort buyers that they made the right decision. For many years, Buick ran an advertising campaign with the message, "Aren't you really glad you bought a Buick?"

involvement
The personal, social, and economic significance of a purchase to the consumer.

Consumer Involvement Affects Problem Solving

 Distinguish among three variations of the consumer purchase decision process: extended, limited, and routine problem solving.

Sometimes consumers don't engage in the five-stage purchase decision process. Instead, they skip or minimize one or more stages depending on the level of **involvement**, the personal, social, and economic significance of the purchase to the consumer.[13] High-involvement purchase occasions typically have at least one of three characteristics: The item to be purchased (1) is expensive, (2) can have serious personal consequences,

CHARACTERISTICS OF THE CONSUMER PURCHASE DECISION PROCESS	EXTENDED PROBLEM SOLVING	LIMITED PROBLEM SOLVING	ROUTINE PROBLEM SOLVING
Number of brands examined	Many	Several	One
Number of sellers considered	Many	Several	Few
Number of product attributes evaluated	Many	Moderate	One
Number of external information sources used	Many	Few	None
Time spent searching	Considerable	Little	Minimal

FIGURE 4–3
Comparison of problem-solving variations: extended problem solving, limited problem solving, and routine problem solving.

or (3) could reflect on one's social image. For these occasions, consumers engage in extensive information searches, consider many product attributes and brands, form attitudes, and participate in word-of-mouth communication. Low-involvement purchases, such as toothpaste and soap, barely involve most of us, but audio and video systems and automobiles are very involving.

There are three general variations in the consumer purchase decision process based on consumer involvement and product knowledge. Figure 4–3 shows some of the important differences between the three problem-solving variations.

Extended Problem Solving   In extended problem solving, each of the five stages of the consumer purchase decision process is used and considerable time and effort are devoted to the search for external information and the identification and evaluation of alternatives. Several brands are in the consideration set, and these are evaluated on many attributes. Extended problem solving exists in high-involvement purchase situations for items such as automobiles and audio systems.

Limited Problem Solving   In limited problem solving, consumers typically seek some information or rely on a friend to help them evaluate alternatives. Several brands might be evaluated using a moderate number of attributes. Limited problem solving is appropriate for purchase situations that do not merit a great deal of time or effort, such as choosing a toaster or a restaurant for lunch.

Routine Problem Solving   For products such as table salt and milk, consumers recognize a problem, make a decision, and spend little effort seeking external information and evaluating alternatives. The purchase process for such items is virtually a habit and typifies low-involvement decision making. Routine problem solving is typically the case for low-priced, frequently purchased grocery products.

Consumer Involvement and Marketing Strategy   Low and high consumer involvement have important implications for marketing strategy. If a company markets a low-involvement product and its brand is a market leader, attention is placed on (1) maintaining product quality, (2) avoiding stockout situations so that buyers don't substitute a competing brand, and (3) repetitive advertising messages that reinforce

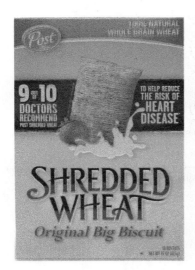

What is a behavioral explanation for why Post Cereals prominently displays heart-healthy claims on its packaging?

a consumer's knowledge or assure buyers they made the right choice. Market challengers have a different task. They must break buying habits by using free samples, coupons, and rebates to encourage trial of their brand. Advertising messages will focus on getting their brand into a consumer's consideration set. For example, Campbell's V8 vegetable juice advertising message— "Could've Had a V8"—is targeted at consumers who routinely consider only fruit juices and soft drinks for purchase. Marketers can also link their brand attributes with high-involvement issues. Post Cereals does this by linking consumption of its whole grain cereals with improved heart health and protection against major diseases.

Marketers of high-involvement products know that their consumers constantly seek and process information about objective and subjective brand attributes, form evaluative criteria, rate product attributes of various brands, and combine these ratings for an overall brand evaluation—like that described in the smartphone purchase decision. Market leaders ply consumers with product information through advertising and personal selling and use social media to create online experiences for their company or brand. Market challengers capitalize on this behavior through comparative advertising that focuses on existing product attributes and often introduce novel evaluative criteria for judging competing brands. Challengers also benefit from Internet search engines such as Microsoft Bing and Google that assist buyers of high-involvement products.

Situational Influences That Affect Purchase Decisions

Often the purchase situation will affect the purchase decision process. Five *situational influences* have an impact on the purchase decision process: (1) the purchase task, (2) social surroundings, (3) physical surroundings, (4) temporal effects, and (5) antecedent states.[14]

The purchase task is the reason for engaging in the decision. The search for information and the evaluation of alternatives may differ depending on whether the purchase is a gift, which often involves social visibility, or for the buyer's own use. Social surroundings, including the other people present when a purchase decision is made, may also affect what is purchased. Consumers accompanied by children buy about 40 percent more items than consumers shopping by themselves. Physical surroundings such as decor, music, and crowding in retail stores may alter how purchase decisions are made. Temporal effects such as time of day or the amount of time available will influence where consumers have breakfast and lunch and what is ordered. Finally, antecedent states, which include the consumer's mood or the amount of cash on hand, can influence purchase behavior and choice. For example, consumers with credit cards purchase more than those with cash or debit cards.

Figure 4–4 on the next page shows the many influences that affect the consumer purchase decision process. In addition to situational influences, the decision to buy a product also involves and is affected by important psychological and sociocultural influences. These two influences are covered in the remainder of this chapter. Marketing mix influences are described later in Part 4 of the book. Chapter 18 elaborates on consumer behavior in the context of online information search and buying.

learning review

4-1. What is the first stage in the consumer purchase decision process?

4-2. The brands a consumer considers buying out of the set of brands in a product class of which the consumer is aware are collectively called the _____.

4-3. What is the term for postpurchase anxiety?

CHAPTER 4   Understanding Consumer Behavior

93

FIGURE 4–4
Influences on the consumer purchase decision process come from both internal and external sources.

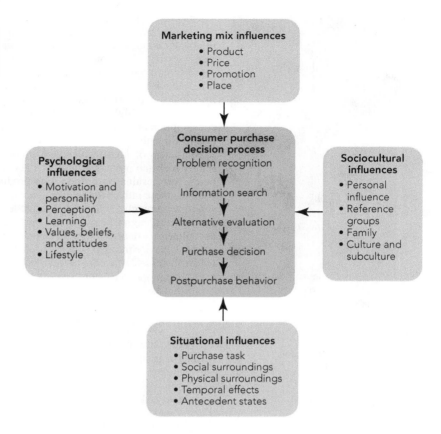

PSYCHOLOGICAL INFLUENCES ON CONSUMER BEHAVIOR

LO 4-3
Identify the major psychological influences on consumer behavior.

Psychology helps marketers understand why and how consumers behave as they do. In particular, psychological concepts such as motivation and personality; perception; learning; values, beliefs, and attitudes; and lifestyle are useful for interpreting buying processes and directing marketing efforts.

Consumer Motivation and Personality

Motivation and personality are two familiar psychological concepts that have specific meanings and marketing implications. These concepts are closely related and are used to explain why people do some things and not others.

motivation
The energizing force that stimulates behavior to satisfy a need.

Motivation   **Motivation** is the energizing force that stimulates behavior to satisfy a need. Because consumer needs are the focus of the marketing concept, marketers try to arouse these needs.

An individual's needs are boundless. People possess physiological needs for basics such as water, shelter, and food. They also have learned needs, including self-esteem, achievement, and affection. Psychologists point out that these needs may be hierarchical; that is, once physiological needs are met, people seek to satisfy their learned needs.

FIGURE 4–5

The Maslow hierarchy of needs is based on the idea that motivation comes from a need. If a need is met, it's no longer a motivator, so a higher-level need becomes the motivator. Higher-level needs demand support of lower-level needs.

Video 4-1
Match.com
kerin.tv/cr6e/v4-1

Self-actualization needs:
Self-fulfillment

Personal needs:
Status, respect, prestige

Social needs:
Friendship, belonging, love

Safety needs:
Freedom from harm, financial security

Physiological needs:
Food, water, shelter, oxygen

Figure 4–5 shows one need hierarchy and classification scheme that contains five need classes.[15] *Physiological needs* are basic to survival and must be satisfied first. A Red Lobster advertisement featuring a seafood salad attempts to activate the need for food. *Safety needs* involve self-preservation as well as physical and financial well-being. Smoke detector and burglar alarm manufacturers focus on these needs, as do insurance companies and retirement plan advisors. *Social needs* are concerned with love and friendship. Dating services, such as Match.com and eHarmony, and fragrance companies try to arouse these needs. *Personal needs* include the need for achievement, status, prestige, and self-respect. The American Express Centurian Card and Brooks Brothers Clothiers appeal to these needs. Sometimes firms try to arouse multiple needs to stimulate problem recognition. Michelin has combined safety with parental love to promote tire replacement for automobiles. *Self-actualization needs* involve personal fulfillment. For example, a long-running U.S. Army recruiting program invited enlistees to "Be all you can be."

Personality While motivation is the energizing force that makes consumer behavior purposeful, a consumer's personality guides and directs behavior. **Personality** refers to a person's consistent behaviors or responses to recurring situations.

personality
A person's consistent behaviors or responses to recurring situations.

Although many personality theories exist, most identify *key traits*—enduring characteristics within a person or in his or her relationships with others. Such traits include assertiveness, extroversion, compliance, dominance, and aggression, among others. These traits are inherited or formed at an early age and change little over the years. Research suggests that compliant people prefer known brand names and use more mouthwash and toilet soaps. Aggressive types use razors, not electric shavers, apply more cologne and aftershave lotions, and purchase signature goods such as Gucci and Yves St. Laurent as an indicator of status.[16]

These personality characteristics are often revealed in a person's *self-concept*, which is the way people see themselves and the way they believe others see them. Marketers recognize that people have an actual self-concept and an ideal self-concept. The actual self refers to how people actually see themselves. The ideal self describes how people would like to see themselves.

These two self-images—actual and ideal—are reflected in the products and brands a person buys, including automobiles, home appliances and furnishings, magazines, consumer electronics, clothing, grooming and leisure products, and frequently, the stores in which a person shops. The importance of self-concept is summed up by a senior marketing executive at Lenovo, a global supplier of notebook computers: "The notebook market is getting more like cars. The car you drive reflects you, and notebooks are becoming a form of self-expression as well."[17]

Making Responsible Decisions

The Ethics of Subliminal Messages

For over 50 years, the topic of subliminal perception and the presence of subliminal messages and images embedded in commercial communications have sparked heated debate.

The Federal Communications Commission has denounced subliminal messages as deceptive. Still, consumers spend $50 million a year for subliminal messages designed to help them raise their self-esteem, stop compulsive buying, quit smoking, or lose weight. Almost two-thirds of U.S. consumers think subliminal messages are present in commercial communications; about half are firmly convinced that this practice can cause them to buy things they don't want.

Subliminal messages are not illegal in the United States, however, and marketers are often criticized for pursuing opportunities to create these messages in both electronic and print media. A book by August Bullock, *The Secret Sales Pitch,* is devoted to this topic. Bullock identifies images and advertisements that he claims contain subliminal messages and describes techniques that can be used for conveying these messages. Do you "see" the subliminal message that is embedded in the book's cover?

Do you believe that a marketer's attempts to implant subliminal messages in electronic and print media are a deceptive practice and unethical, regardless of their intent?

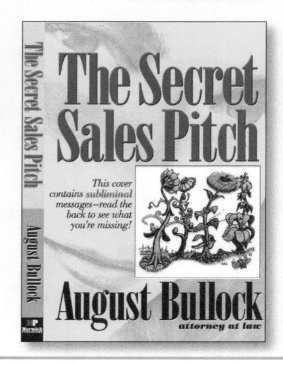

Consumer Perception

perception
The process by which a person selects, organizes, and interprets information to create a meaningful picture of the world.

One person sees a Cadillac as a mark of achievement; another sees it as ostentatious. This is the result of **perception**—the process by which an individual selects, organizes, and interprets information to create a meaningful picture of the world.

Selective Perception   Because the average consumer operates in a complex environment, the human brain attempts to organize and interpret information with a process called *selective perception*, a filtering of exposure, comprehension, and retention. *Selective exposure* occurs when people pay attention to messages that are consistent with their attitudes and beliefs and ignore messages that are inconsistent with them. Selective exposure often occurs in the postpurchase stage of the consumer decision process, when consumers read advertisements for the brand they just bought. It also occurs when a need exists—you are more likely to "see" a McDonald's advertisement when you are hungry rather than after you have eaten a pizza.

Selective comprehension involves interpreting information so that it is consistent with your attitudes and beliefs. A marketer's failure to understand this can have disastrous results. For example, Toro introduced a small, lightweight snowblower called the Snow Pup. Even though the product worked, sales failed to meet expectations. Why? Toro later found out that consumers perceived the name to mean that Snow Pup was a toy or too light to do any serious snow removal. When the product was renamed Snow Master, sales increased sharply.[18]

Selective retention means that consumers do not remember all the information they see, read, or hear, even minutes after exposure to it. This affects the internal and external information search stage of the purchase decision process. This is why furniture and automobile retailers often give consumers product brochures to take home with them when they leave the showroom.

Because perception plays an important role in consumer behavior, it is not surprising that the topic of subliminal perception is a popular item for discussion. *Subliminal perception* means that you see or hear messages without being aware of them. The presence and effect of subliminal perception on behavior is a hotly debated issue, with more popular appeal than scientific support. Indeed, evidence suggests that such messages have limited effects on behavior.[19] If these messages did influence behavior, would their use be an ethical practice? (See the Making Responsible Decisions box.)[20]

perceived risk
The anxiety felt when a consumer cannot anticipate possible negative outcomes of a purchase.

Perceived Risk   Perception plays a major role in the perceived risk in purchasing a product or service. **Perceived risk** represents the anxiety felt because the consumer cannot anticipate the outcomes of a purchase but believes there may be negative consequences. Examples of possible negative consequences are the size of the financial outlay required to buy the product (can I afford $900 for those skis?), the risk of physical harm (is bungee jumping safe?), and the performance of the product (will the whitening toothpaste work?). A more abstract form is psychosocial (what will my friends say about my tattoo?).

Perceived risk affects a consumer's information search. The greater the perceived risk, the more extensive the external search stage is likely to be. For example, the average car shopper spends more than 11 hours online researching cars and almost 4 hours visiting car dealerships when choosing a car.[21]

Recognizing the importance of perceived risk, companies develop strategies to reduce the consumer's perceived risk and encourage purchases. These strategies and examples of firms using them include the following:

* *Obtaining seals of approval:* The Good Housekeeping Seal for Fresh Step cat litter.
* *Securing endorsements from influential people:* Colgate-Palmolive secured the endorsements of dentists to make the claim that Colgate Total toothpaste is the #1 recommended toothpaste by most dentists.
* *Providing free trials of the product:* Samples of Mary Kay's Velocity fragrance.

How did Colgate-Palmolive marketers allay consumers' perceived risk and change consumers' attitudes toward Colgate Total toothpaste to create a brand with over $1 billion in sales worldwide? The answers appear in the text.

Colgate-Palmolive
www.colgate.com

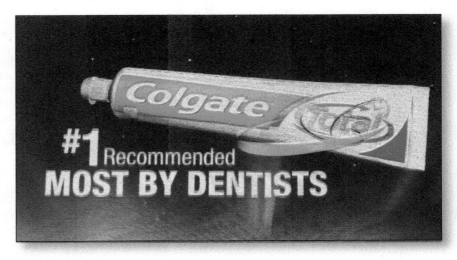

CHAPTER 4   Understanding Consumer Behavior

97

- *Giving extensive usage instructions:* Clairol hair coloring.
- *Providing warranties and guarantees:* Kia Motors's 10-year, 100,000-mile limited powertrain warranty.

Consumer Learning

Much consumer behavior is learned. Consumers learn which information sources to consult for information about products and services, which evaluative criteria to use when assessing alternatives, and, more generally, how to make purchase decisions. **Learning** refers to those behaviors that result from (1) repeated experience and (2) reasoning.

learning
Behaviors that result from repeated experience and reasoning.

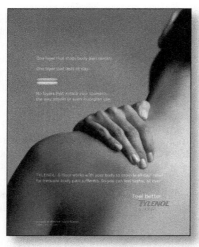

How does this advertisement for Tylenol 8-Hour apply to cognitive learning? Read the text to find out.

Tylenol
www.tylenol.com

Behavioral Learning *Behavioral learning* is the process of developing automatic responses to a situation built up through repeated exposure to it. Four variables are central to how consumers learn from repeated experience: drive, cue, response, and reinforcement. A *drive* is a need that moves an individual to action. Drives, such as hunger, might be represented by motives. A *cue* is a stimulus or symbol perceived by consumers. A *response* is the action taken by a consumer to satisfy the drive. *Reinforcement* is the reward. Being hungry (drive), a consumer sees a cue (a billboard), takes action (buys a sandwich), and receives a reward (it tastes great!).

Marketers use two concepts from behavioral learning theory. *Stimulus generalization* occurs when a response elicited by one stimulus (cue) is generalized to another stimulus. Using the same brand name for different products is an application of this concept, such as Tylenol Cold & Flu and Tylenol P.M. *Stimulus discrimination* refers to a person's ability to perceive differences in stimuli. Consumers' tendency to perceive all light beers as being alike led to Budweiser Light commercials that distinguished between many types of "light beers" and Bud Light.

Cognitive Learning Consumers also learn through thinking, reasoning, and mental problem solving without direct experience. This type of learning, called *cognitive learning*, involves making connections between two or more ideas or simply observing the outcomes of others' behaviors and adjusting your own accordingly. Firms also influence this type of learning. Through repetition in advertising, messages such as "Feel Better, Tylenol 8-Hour" link a brand (Tylenol 8-Hour) and an idea (pain reliever) by showing someone using the brand and finding relief.

Brand Loyalty Learning is also important to marketers because it relates to habit formation—the basis of routine problem solving. Furthermore, there is a close link between habits and **brand loyalty**, which is a favorable attitude toward and consistent purchase of a single brand over time. Brand loyalty results from the positive reinforcement of previous actions. A consumer reduces risk and saves time by consistently purchasing the same brand of shampoo and has favorable results—healthy, shining hair. There is evidence of brand loyalty in many commonly purchased products in the United States and the global marketplace. However, the incidence of brand loyalty appears to be declining in North America, Western Europe, and Japan.[22]

brand loyalty
A favorable attitude toward and consistent purchase of a single brand over time.

Consumer Values, Beliefs, and Attitudes

Values, beliefs, and attitudes play a central role in consumer decision making and related marketing actions.

attitude

A tendency to respond to something in a consistently favorable or unfavorable way.

beliefs

A consumer's perception of how a product or brand performs.

Attitude Formation   An **attitude** is a "learned predisposition to respond to an object or class of objects in a consistently favorable or unfavorable way."[23] Attitudes are shaped by our values and beliefs, which are learned. Values vary by level of specificity. We speak of American core values, including material well-being and humanitarianism. We also have personal values, such as thriftiness and ambition. Marketers are concerned with both but focus mostly on personal values. Personal values affect attitudes by influencing the importance assigned to specific product attributes. Suppose thriftiness is one of your personal values. When you evaluate cars, fuel economy (a product attribute) becomes important. If you believe a specific car brand has this attribute, you are likely to have a favorable attitude toward it.

Beliefs also play a part in attitude formation. **Beliefs** are a consumer's subjective perception of how a product or brand performs on different attributes. Beliefs are based on personal experience, advertising, and discussions with other people. Beliefs about product attributes are important because, along with personal values, they create the favorable or unfavorable attitude the consumer has toward certain products, services, and brands.

Attitude Change   Marketers use three approaches to try to change consumer attitudes toward products and brands, as illustrated in the following examples.[24]

1. *Changing beliefs about the extent to which a brand has certain attributes.* To allay mothers' concerns about ingredients in its mayonnaise, Hellmann's successfully communicated the product's high Omega 3 content, which is essential to human health.

2. *Changing the perceived importance of attributes.* Pepsi-Cola made freshness an important product attribute when it stamped freshness dates on its cans. Before doing so, few consumers considered cola freshness an issue. After Pepsi spent about $25 million on advertising and promotion, a consumer survey found that 61 percent of cola drinkers believed freshness dating was an important attribute.

3. *Adding new attributes to the product.* Colgate-Palmolive included a new antibacterial ingredient, triclosan, in its Colgate Total toothpaste and spent $100 million marketing the brand. The result? Colgate Total toothpaste is now a billion-dollar-plus global brand.

Consumer Lifestyle

Lifestyle is a mode of living that is identified by how people spend their time and resources, what they consider important in their environments, and what they think of themselves and the world around them. The analysis of consumer lifestyles, called *psychographics*, provides insights into consumer needs and wants. Lifestyle analysis has proven useful in segmenting and targeting consumers for new and existing products and services (see Chapter 8).

Psychographics is a catchall label used to describe a variety of segmentations such as those based on behaviors, attitudes, activities, interests, opinions, and social values. The practice of combining psychology, lifestyle, and demographics can be used to uncover consumer motivations for buying and using products and services; they are time-consuming and expensive to construct accurately and reliably. VALS™, owned and operated by Strategic Business Insights (SBI), is more than a lifestyle segmentation because VALS examines the intersection of psychology, demographics, and lifestyles.[25] VALS measures the enduring differences between people that explain and predict lifestyles meaningfully. Eight primary segments—personalities—are identified on the basis of motivations and resources.

According to SBI, consumers are motivated to buy products and services and seek life experiences that give shape, substance, and satisfaction to their lives. Consumers are

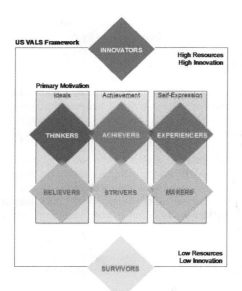

US VALS Framework

Primary Motivation

| Ideals | Achievement | Self-Expression |

INNOVATORS — High Resources High Innovation

THINKERS   ACHIEVERS   EXPERIENCERS

BELIEVERS   STRIVERS   MAKERS

Low Resources Low Innovation

SURVIVORS

The VALS survey places individuals into one of the eight groups. The VALS framework is the visualization of the consumer groups. Consumers with abundant resources—psychological, emotional, and material means and capabilities—are near the top of the framework and those with minimal resources are at the bottom. Consumer groups within a motivation can be targeted together. For instance, a marketer may target Thinkers and Believers together. Do you want to know your VALS type? If you do, respond to the questions at http://www .strategicbusinessinsights .com/vals/presurvey.shtml. Simply click on "Take the survey." You will receive your primary and secondary types in real time. In order to receive an accurate VALS type, your first language must be American English. If you are not a resident of the United States or Canada, residency should be for enough time to know the culture and its idioms.

driven by one of three motivations—ideals, achievement, and self-expression—that give meaning to their self and the world and govern their activities. The different levels of resources enhance or constrain a person's expression of his or her primary motivation.

A person's resources include psychological, emotional, demographic and material capacities such as self-confidence, curiosity, risk-taking, age and income.

VALS explains why consumers who share the same demographics and lifestyles exhibit different behaviors and why consumers who do not share the same demographics or lifestyles exhibit the same behaviors for different reasons.

- *Ideals-motivated groups.* Consumers motivated by ideals are guided by knowledge and principles. High-resource *Thinkers* are mature, reflective, and information-seeking people who value order, knowledge, and responsibility. They are practical consumers who value durability and functionality in products over styling and newness. They are not brand loyal. Low-resource *Believers* are conservative, conventional people with concrete beliefs based on established codes: family, religion, community, and the nation. They choose familiar products and brands, favor American-made products, and are generally brand loyal.
- *Achievement-motivated groups.* Consumers motivated by achievement look for products and services that demonstrate success to their peers or to a group they aspire to. High-resource *Achievers* have busy, goal-directed lifestyles and a deep commitment to career and family. Image is important to them. They favor established, prestige products and services and are interested in time-saving devices to manage hectic schedules. Low-resource *Strivers* are trend followers. They seek fun to offset frequent, self-inflicted stress-producing situations. Many believe that life is unfair but they lack the education, skills, and tenacity to change their circumstances. Money defines success for them; however, they believe that success is the result of good luck, not hard work.
- *Self-expression-motivated groups.* Consumers motivated by self-expression desire social or physical activity, variety, and risk. High-resource *Experiencers* are young, enthusiastic, and impulsive consumers who become excited about new possibilities but are equally quick to cool. They seek to make an impact on their world. Their energy finds an outlet in exercise, sports, outdoor recreation, and social activities. Much of their income is spent on technology, entertainment, and socializing. Form is more important than function because how something looks is very important to them. Low-resource *Makers* express themselves and experience the world by working on it—growing vegetables or fixing a car. They are practical people who have constructive skills, value self-sufficiency and independence, and are unimpressed by material possessions except those with a practical or functional purpose.
- *High- and low-resource groups.* Two segments stand apart from primary motivation. High-resource *Innovators* are successful, sophisticated, take-charge people. Image is important to them, not as evidence of power or status, but as an expression of cultivated tastes, independent thinking, and character. They are early adopters and change leaders. Their lives are characterized by richness and variety. Low-resource *Survivors* focus on meeting basic needs—such as food, clothing and shelter, safety and security—rather than fulfilling desires. They represent a modest market for most products and services. They are loyal to favorite brands, especially if they can be purchased at a discount.

Each segment receives and processes information differently and exhibits unique media preferences. For example, Experiencers are the most likely to visit

Facebook and to read magazines. Makers and Achievers drive the most miles each week; therefore, they are the most likely segment to view outdoor advertising. Innovators and Thinkers are the most likely to read national newspapers. Survivors watch over 50 hours of television in an average week. GeoVALS™ estimates the percentage of each VALS group by zip code.

---

learning review

4-4. The problem with the Toro Snow Pup was an example of selective
_____.

4-5. What three attitude-change approaches are most common?

4-6. What does *lifestyle* mean?

SOCIOCULTURAL INFLUENCES ON CONSUMER BEHAVIOR

 LO 4-4 Identify the major sociocultural influences on consumer behavior.

Sociocultural influences, which evolve from a consumer's formal and informal relationships with other people, also exert a significant impact on consumer behavior. These involve personal influence, reference groups, family influence, social class, culture, and subculture.

Personal Influence

opinion leaders
Individuals who have social influence over others.

A consumer's purchases are often influenced by the views, opinions, or behaviors of others. Two aspects of personal influence are very important to marketing: opinion leadership and word-of-mouth activity.

Opinion Leadership Individuals who exert direct or indirect social influence over others are called **opinion leaders**. Opinion leaders are considered to be knowledgeable about or users of particular products and services, so their opinions influence others' choices.[26] Opinion leadership is widespread in the purchase of cars and trucks, entertainment, clothing and accessories, club membership, consumer electronics, vacation destinations, food, and financial investments. A study by *Popular Mechanics* magazine identified 18 million opinion leaders who influence the purchases of some 85 million consumers for do-it-yourself products.

Companies use world-class athletes as spokespersons to represent their products, such as football player Eli Manning for Citizen watches.

Citizen Watch Company
www.citizenwatch.com

About 10 percent of U.S. adults are opinion leaders. Identifying, reaching, and influencing opinion leaders is a major challenge for companies. Some firms use actors or sports figures as spokespersons to represent their products. Others promote their products in media believed to reach opinion leaders. Still others use more direct approaches. For example, a carmaker recently invited influential community leaders and business executives to test-drive its new models. Some 6,000 accepted the offer, and 98 percent said they would recommend their tested car. The company estimated that the number of favorable recommendations totaled 32,000.

Marketing Matters

BzzAgent—The Buzz Experience

Have you recently heard about a new product, movie, website, book, or restaurant from someone you know . . . or a complete stranger? If so, you may have had a word-of-mouth experience.

Marketers recognize the power of word of mouth. The challenge has been to harness that power. Bzz-Agent Inc. does just that. Its worldwide volunteer army of one million natural-born talkers channel their chatter toward products and services they deem authentically worth talking about, either online or in person. "Our goal is to capture honest word of mouth," says David Balter, BzzAgent's founder, "and to build a network that turns passionate customers into brand evangelists."

BzzAgent's method is simple. Once a client signs on with Bzz-Agent, the company searches its "agent" database for those who match the demographic and psychographic profile of the target market for a client's offering. Agents then can sign up for a buzz campaign and receive a sample product and a training manual for buzz-creating strategies. Each time an agent completes an activity, he or she is expected to file an online report describing the nature of the buzz and its effectiveness. BzzAgent

coaches respond with encouragement and feedback on additional techniques.

Agents keep the products they promote. They also earn points redeemable for books, CDs, and other items by filing detailed reports. Who are the agents? About 65 percent are older than 25 and 70 percent are women. All are gregarious and genuinely like the product or service, otherwise they wouldn't participate in the buzz campaign.

Estée Lauder, Monster.com, Anheuser-Busch, Penguin Books, Lee, Michelin, Wrigley, Arby's, Nestlé, Hershey Foods, Procter & Gamble, Danone, and Volkswagen have used BzzAgent. But BzzAgent's buzz isn't cheap, and not everything is buzz worthy. Deploying 1,000 agents on a 12-week campaign can cost a company $95,000, exclusive of product samples. BzzAgent researches a product or service before committing to a campaign and rejects about 80 percent of the companies that seek its service. It also refuses campaigns for politicians, religious groups, and certain products, such as firearms. Interested in BzzAgent? Visit its website at www.bzzagent.com or www.facebook.com/bzzagent.

---

word of mouth
People influencing each other in personal conversations.

Video 4-2
Dove
kerin.tv/cr6e/v4-2

Word of Mouth   The influencing of people during conversations is called **word of mouth**. Word of mouth is the most powerful and authentic information source for consumers because it typically involves friends viewed as trustworthy. About 75 percent of all consumer conversations about brands happen face-to-face, 15 percent happen over the phone, and 10 percent happen online.[27] According to a recent study, 67 percent of U.S. consumer product sales are directly based on word-of-mouth activity among friends, family, and colleagues.[28]

The power of personal influence has prompted firms to promote positive and retard negative word of mouth. For instance, "teaser" advertising campaigns are run in advance of new-product introductions to stimulate conversations. Other techniques such as advertising slogans, music, and humor also heighten positive word of mouth. Many commercials shown during the Super Bowl are created expressly to initiate conversations about the advertisements and featured product or service the next day. Increasingly, companies recruit and deploy people to produce *buzz*—popularity created by consumer word of mouth. Read the Marketing Matters box to learn how this is done by BzzAgent.[29] Then scan the quick response code in the margin to see a video of Bzz-Agent's campaign for Dove hair care products.

Unfortunately, word of mouth can also be a source of negative information. For example, consider the damaging (and untrue) rumors that have plagued Kmart (snake eggs in clothing), Taco Bell (beef content in taco meat filling), Corona Extra beer (contamination), and Snickers candy bars in Russia (a cause of diabetes). Overcoming or neutralizing negative word of mouth is difficult and costly. However, supplying factual information, providing toll-free numbers for consumers to call the company, and giving appropriate product demonstrations have proven helpful.

The power of word of mouth is magnified by the Internet through online forums, blogs, social media, and websites. In fact, companies use special software to monitor online messages and find out what consumers are saying about their products, services, and brands. They have found that 30 percent of people spreading negative information have never owned or used the product, service, or brand![30]

Reference Group Influence

reference groups
People to whom an individual looks as a basis for self-appraisal or as a source of personal standards.

Reference groups are people to whom an individual looks as a basis for self-appraisal or as a source of personal standards. Reference groups affect consumer purchases because they influence the information, attitudes, and aspiration levels that help set a consumer's standards. For example, one of the first questions one asks others when planning to attend a social occasion is, "What are you going to wear?" Reference groups influence the purchase of luxury products rather than necessities—particularly when the use or consumption of a chosen brand will be highly visible to others.

Consumers have many reference groups, but three groups have clear marketing implications.[31] An *associative group* is one to which a person actually belongs, including fraternities and sororities and alumni associations. Such groups are easily identifiable and are targeted by firms selling insurance, insignia products, and charter vacations.

The Harley Owners Group (HOG) has over 1 million members and is a prototypical brand community. Read the text to learn about the characteristics of a brand community.

Associative reference groups can also form around a brand, as is the case with clubs like the HOG (Harley Owners Group), which is made up of Harley-Davidson fans. A **brand community** is a specialized group of consumers with a structured set of relationships involving a particular brand, fellow customers of that brand, and the product in use. A consumer who is a member of a brand community thinks about brand names (e.g., Harley-Davidson), the product category (e.g., motorcycles), other customers who use the brand (e.g., HOG members), and the marketer that makes and promotes the brand.

brand community
A specialized group of consumers with a structured set of relationships involving a brand, fellow customers of that brand, and the product in use.

An *aspiration group* is one that a person wishes to be a member of or wishes to be identified with, such as a professional society or sports team. Firms frequently rely on spokespeople or settings associated with their target market's aspiration group in their advertising.

A *dissociative group* is one that a person wishes to maintain a distance from because of differences in values or behaviors. Firms often avoid dissociative reference groups in their marketing. For example, retailer Abercrombie & Fitch once offered to pay cast members of the controversial TV reality show *Jersey Shore* to *not* wear its clothing. "We understand that the show is for entertainment purposes, but believe this association is contrary to the aspirational nature of our brand, and may be distressing to many of our fans," the retailer stated.[32]

Family Influence

Family influences on consumer behavior result from three sources: consumer socialization, passage through the family life cycle, and decision making within the family or household.

Consumer Socialization The process by which people acquire the skills, knowledge, and attitudes necessary to function as consumers is called *consumer* *socialization.*[33] Children learn how to purchase (1) by interacting with adults in purchase situations and (2) through their own purchasing and product usage experiences. Research shows that children evidence brand preferences at age two, and these preferences often last a lifetime. This knowledge prompted the licensing of the well-known Craftsman brand name to MGA Entertainment for its children's line of My First Craftsman toys and power tools and Time Inc.'s *Sports Illustrated Kids.*

Family Life Cycle   Consumers act and purchase differently as they go through life. The **family life cycle** concept describes the distinct phases that a family progresses through from formation to retirement, each phase bringing with it identifiable purchasing behaviors.[34] Figure 4–6 illustrates the traditional progression as well as contemporary variations of the family life cycle. Today, the *traditional family*—married couple with children younger than 18 years—constitutes just 21 percent of all U.S. households. The remaining 78 percent of U.S. households include single parents; unmarried couples; divorced, never-married, or widowed individuals; and older married couples whose children no longer live at home.

Young singles' buying preferences are for nondurable items, including prepared foods, clothing, personal care products, and entertainment. They represent a target market for recreational travel, automobile, and consumer electronics firms. Young married couples without children are typically more affluent than young singles because usually both spouses are employed. These couples exhibit preferences for furniture, housewares, and gift items for each other. Young marrieds with children are driven by the needs of their children. They make up a sizable market for life insurance, various children's products, and home furnishings. Single parents with children are the least financially secure of households with children. Their buying preferences are often affected by a limited economic status and tend toward convenience foods, child care services, and personal care items.

Middle-aged married couples with children are typically better off financially than their younger counterparts. They are a significant market for leisure products and

family life cycle
A family's progression from formation to retirement, each phase bringing with it distinct purchasing behaviors.

FIGURE 4–6
Modern family life cycle stages and flows. Can you identify people you know in different stages? Do they follow the purchase patterns described in the text?

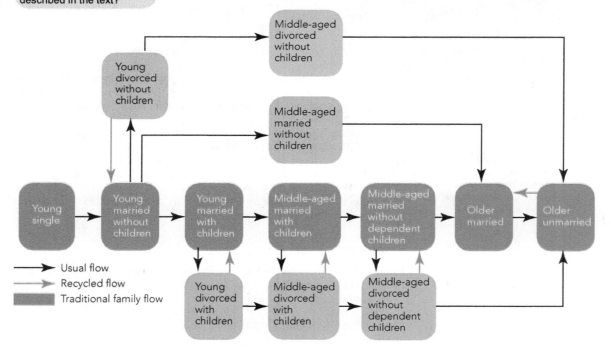

Today, 31 percent of men in the United States are the primary grocery shoppers in their households. Marketers that supply the $560 billion retail food industries are now adjusting store layouts and shelf placements to cater to men.

home improvement items. Middle-aged couples without children typically have a large amount of discretionary income. These couples buy better home furnishings, status automobiles, and financial services. Persons in the last two phases—older married and older unmarried—make up a sizable market for prescription drugs, medical services, vacation trips, and gifts for younger relatives.

Family Decision Making   A third source of family influence on consumer behavior involves the decision-making process that occurs within the family.[35] Two decision-making styles exist: spouse-dominant and joint decision making. With a joint decision-making style, most decisions are made by both husband and wife. Spouse-dominant decisions are those for which either the husband or the wife is mostly responsible. Research indicates that wives tend to have more say when purchasing groceries, children's toys, clothing, and medicines. Husbands tend to be more influential in home and car maintenance purchases. Joint decision making is common for cars, vacations, houses, home appliances and electronics, family finances, and medical care. As a rule, joint decision making increases with the education of the spouses.

Roles of individual family members in the purchase process are another element of family decision making. Five roles exist: (1) information gatherer, (2) influencer, (3) decision maker, (4) purchaser, and (5) user. Family members assume different roles for different products and services. This knowledge is important to firms. For example, 89 percent of wives either influence or make outright purchases of men's clothing. Even though women are often the grocery decision makers, they are not necessarily the purchasers. Today, 31 percent of men are the primary grocery shoppers in their households.

Increasingly, preteens and teenagers are the information gatherers, influencers, decision makers, and purchasers of products and services for the family, given the prevalence of working parents and single-parent households. The market for products bought by or for preteens and teenagers surpasses $208 billion annually. These figures help explain why, for example, Johnson & Johnson, Apple, Kellogg, P&G, Nike, Sony, and Oscar Mayer, among countless other companies, spend more than $70 billion annually in electronic and print media that reach preteens and teens.

Culture and Subculture Influences

As described in Chapter 3, *culture* refers to the set of values, ideas, and attitudes that are learned and shared among the members of a group. Thus, we often refer to the American culture, the Latin American culture, or the Japanese culture. Cultural underpinnings of American buying patterns were described in Chapter 3; Chapter 7 will explore the role of culture in global marketing.

subcultures
Subgroups within the larger, or national, culture with unique values, ideas, and attitudes.

Subgroups within the larger, or national, culture with unique values, ideas, and attitudes are referred to as **subcultures**. Various subcultures exist within the American culture. The three largest racial/ethnic subcultures in the United States are Hispanics, African Americans, and Asian Americans. Collectively, they are expected to account for one in four U.S. consumers and to spend about $2.5 trillion for goods and services in 2017, which will represent 16.4 percent of the United States' total buying power.[36] Each group exhibits sophisticated social and cultural behaviors that affect buying patterns, described next.

Hispanic Buying Patterns Hispanics represent the largest racial/ethnic subculture in the United States in terms of population and spending power. About 50 percent of Hispanics in the United States are immigrants, and the majority are under the age of 29. One-third of Hispanics are younger than 18.

Research on Hispanic buying practices has uncovered several consistent patterns:[37]

1. Hispanics are quality and brand conscious. They are willing to pay a premium price for premium quality and are often brand loyal.
2. Hispanics prefer buying American-made products, especially those offered by firms that cater to Hispanic needs.
3. Hispanic buying preferences are strongly influenced by family and peers.
4. Hispanics consider advertising a credible product information source, and U.S. firms spend about $8 billion annually on advertising to Hispanics.
5. Convenience is not an important product attribute to Hispanic homemakers with respect to food preparation or consumption, nor is low caffeine in coffee and soft drinks, low fat in dairy products, or low cholesterol in packaged foods.

Why does ACH Food Companies, Inc., advertise its Mazola Corn Oil in Spanish? Read the text for the answer.

Mazola Corn Oil
www.mazola.com

Despite some consistent buying patterns, marketing to Hispanics has proven to be a challenge for two reasons. First, the Hispanic subculture is diverse and composed of Mexicans, Puerto Ricans, Cubans, and others of Central and South American ancestry. Cultural differences among these nationalities often affect product preferences. For example, Campbell Soup Company sells its Casera line of soups, beans, and sauces using different recipes to appeal to Puerto Ricans on the East Coast and Mexicans in the Southwest. Second, a language barrier exists, and commercial messages are frequently misinterpreted when translated into Spanish. Volkswagen learned this lesson when the Spanish translation of its "Drivers Wanted" slogan suggested "chauffeurs wanted." The Spanish slogan was changed to "*Agarra Calle*," a slang expression that can be loosely translated as "let's hit the road."

Sensitivity to the unique needs of Hispanics by firms has paid huge dividends. For example, Metropolitan Life Insurance is the largest insurer of Hispanics. Goya Foods dominates the market for ethnic food products sold to Hispanics. Mazola Corn Oil captures two-thirds of the Hispanic market for this product category. Time, Inc., has more than 750,000 subscribers to its *People en Español*.

African American Buying Patterns African Americans have the second-largest spending power of the three racial/ethnic subcultures in the United States. Consumer research on African American buying patterns has focused on similarities and differences with Caucasians. When socioeconomic status differences between African Americans and Caucasians are removed, there are more similarities than points of

African American women represent a large market for health and beauty products. Cosmetics companies actively seek to serve this market.

difference. Differences in buying patterns are greater within the African American subculture, due to levels of socioeconomic status, than between African Americans and Caucasians of similar status.

Even though similarities outweigh differences, there are consumption patterns that do differ between African Americans and Caucasians.[38] For example, African Americans spend far more than Caucasians on boys' clothing, rental goods, and audio equipment. African American women spend three times more on health and beauty products than Caucasian women. Furthermore, the typical African American family is five years younger than the typical Caucasian family. This factor alone accounts for some of the observed differences in preferences for clothing, music, shelter, cars, and many other products, services, and activities. Finally, it must be emphasized that, historically, African Americans have been deprived of employment and educational opportunities in the United States. Both factors have resulted in income disparities between African Americans and Caucasians, which influence purchase behavior.

Recent research indicates that while African Americans are price conscious, they are strongly motivated by quality and choice. They respond more to products and advertising that appeal to their African American pride and heritage as well as address their ethnic features and needs regardless of socioeconomic status.

Asian American Buying Patterns   Asian Americans are the fastest growing racial/ethnic subculture in the United States. About 70 percent of Asian Americans are immigrants. Most are under the age of 30.

The Asian subculture is composed of Chinese, Japanese, Filipinos, Koreans, Asian Indians, people from Southeast Asia, and Pacific Islanders. The diversity of the Asian subculture is so great that generalizations about buying patterns of this group are difficult to make.[39] Consumer research on Asian Americans suggests that individuals and families can be divided into two groups. *Assimilated* Asian Americans are conversant in English, highly educated, hold professional and managerial positions, and exhibit buying patterns very much like the typical American consumer. *Nonassimilated* Asian Americans are recent immigrants who still cling to their native languages and customs.

The diversity of Asian Americans evident in language, customs, and tastes requires marketers to be sensitive to different Asian nationalities. For example, Anheuser-Busch's agricultural products division sells eight varieties of California-grown rice, each with a different Asian label to cover a range of nationalities and tastes. The company's advertising also addresses the preferences of Chinese, Japanese, and Koreans for different kinds of rice bowls. McDonald's actively markets to Asian Americans. According to a company executive, "We recognize diversity in this market. We try to make our messages in the language they prefer to see them."

Studies show that the Asian American subculture as a whole is characterized by hard work, strong family ties, appreciation for education, and median family incomes exceeding those of any other ethnic group. This subculture is also the most entrepreneurial in the United States, as evidenced by the number of Asian-owned businesses. These qualities led Metropolitan Life Insurance to identify Asian Americans as a target for insurance following the company's success in marketing to Hispanics.

107

CHAPTER 4   Understanding Consumer Behavior

learning review

4-7. What are the two primary forms of personal influence?

4-8. Marketers are concerned with which types of reference groups?

4-9. What two challenges must marketers overcome when marketing to Hispanic consumers?

LEARNING OBJECTIVES REVIEW

LO 4-1 *Describe the stages in the consumer purchase decision process.*

The consumer purchase decision process consists of five stages. They are problem recognition, information search, alternative evaluation, purchase decision, and postpurchase behavior. Problem recognition is perceiving a difference between a person's ideal and actual situation big enough to trigger a decision. Information search involves remembering previous purchase experiences (internal search) and external search behavior such as seeking information from other sources. Alternative evaluation clarifies the problem for the consumer by (*a*) suggesting the evaluative criteria to use for the purchase, (*b*) yielding brand names that might meet the criteria, and (*c*) developing consumer value perceptions. The purchase decision involves the choice of an alternative, including from whom to buy and when to buy. Postpurchase behavior involves the comparison of the chosen alternative with a consumer's expectations, which leads to satisfaction or dissatisfaction and subsequent purchase behavior.

LO 4-2 *Distinguish among three variations of the consumer purchase decision process: extended, limited, and routine problem solving.*

Consumers don't always engage in the five-stage purchase decision process. Instead, they skip or minimize one or more stages depending on the level of involvement—the personal, social, and economic significance of the purchase. For high-involvement purchase occasions, each of the five stages of the consumer purchase decision process is used and considerable time and effort are devoted to the search for external information and the identification and evaluation of alternatives. With limited problem solving, consumers typically seek some information or rely on a friend to help them evaluate alternatives. For low-involvement purchase occasions, consumers engage in routine problem solving. They recognize a problem, make a decision, and spend little effort seeking external information and evaluating alternatives.

LO 4-3 *Identify the major psychological influences on consumer behavior.*

Psychology helps marketers understand why and how consumers behave as they do. In particular, psychological concepts such as motivation and personality, perception, learning, values, beliefs and attitudes, and lifestyle are useful for interpreting buying processes. Motivation is the energizing force that stimulates behavior to satisfy a need. Personality refers to a person's consistent behaviors or responses to recurring situations. Perception is the process by which an individual selects, organizes, and interprets information to create a meaningful picture of the world. Consumers filter information through selective exposure, comprehension, and retention.

Much consumer behavior is learned. Learning refers to those behaviors that result from (*a*) repeated experience and (*b*) reasoning. Brand loyalty results from learning. Values, beliefs, and attitudes are also learned and influence how consumers evaluate products, services, and brands. A more general concept is lifestyle. Lifestyle, also called psychographics, combines psychology and demographics and focuses on how people spend their time and resources, what they consider important in their environment, and what they think of themselves and the world around them.

LO 4-4 *Identify the major sociocultural influences on consumer behavior.*

Sociocultural influences, which evolve from a consumer's formal and informal relationships with other people, also affect consumer behavior. These involve personal influence, reference groups, the family, culture, and subculture. Opinion leadership and word-of-mouth behavior are two major sources of personal influence on consumer behavior. Reference groups are people to whom an individual looks as a basis for self-approval or as a source of personal standards. Family influences on consumer behavior result from three sources: consumer socialization, passage through the family life cycle, and decision making within the family or household. Finally, a person's culture and subculture have been shown to influence product preferences and buying patterns.

LEARNING REVIEW ANSWERS

4-1 **What is the first stage in the consumer purchase decision process?**
Answer: problem recognition—perceiving a need

4-2 **The brands a consumer considers buying out of the set of brands in a product class of which the consumer is aware are collectively called the _____.**
Answer: consideration set

4-3 **What is the term for postpurchase anxiety?**
Answer: cognitive dissonance

4-4 **The problem with the Toro Snow Pup was an example of selective _____.**
Answer: comprehension—consumers perceived the name to mean that Snow Pup was a toy that was too light to do any serious snow removal.

4-5 **What three attitude-change approaches are most common?**
Answer: (1) Change beliefs about the extent to which a brand has certain attributes. (2) Change the perceived importance of these attributes. (3) Add new attributes to the product.

4-6 **What does *lifestyle* mean?**
Answer: Lifestyle is a mode of living that is identified by how people spend their time and resources, what they consider important in their environment, and what they think of themselves and the world around them.

4-7 **What are the two primary forms of personal influence?**
Answer: (1) Opinion leadership—persons considered to be knowledgeable about or users of particular products

and services and (2) word of mouth—the influencing of people (friends, family, and colleagues) during conversations.

4-8 **Marketers are concerned with which types of reference groups?**
Answer: Three reference groups have clear marketing implications: (1) associative groups—ones to which a person actually belongs, such as a brand community that consists of a specialized group of consumers with a structured set of relationships involving a particular

brand; (2) aspiration groups—ones that people wish to be a member of or identified with; and (3) dissociative groups—ones that people wish to maintain a distance from because of differences in values or behaviors.

4-9 **What two challenges must marketers overcome when marketing to Hispanic consumers?**
Answer: (1) The diversity of nationalities among this subculture that affect product preferences and (2) the language barrier that can lead to misinterpretation or mistranslation of commercial messages when translated into Spanish.

FOCUSING ON KEY TERMS

attitude p. 99
beliefs p. 99
brand community p. 103
brand loyalty p. 98
consumer behavior p. 88
family life cycle p. 104

involvement p. 91
learning p. 98
motivation p. 94
opinion leaders p. 101
perceived risk p. 97
perception p. 96

personality p. 95
purchase decision process p. 88
reference groups p. 103
subcultures p. 106
word of mouth p. 102

APPLYING MARKETING KNOWLEDGE

1 Review Figure 4–2, which shows common smartphone attributes. Which attributes are important to you? What other attributes might you consider? Which brand would you prefer?

2 Suppose research at Panasonic reveals that prospective buyers are anxious about buying high-definition television sets. What strategies might you recommend to the company to reduce consumer anxiety?

3 Assign one or more levels of the Maslow hierarchy of needs described in Figure 4–5 to the following products: (a) life insurance, (b) cosmetics, (c) *The Wall Street Journal*, and (d) hamburgers.

4 With which stage in the family life cycle would the purchase of the following products and services be most closely identified? (a) bedroom furniture, (b) life insurance, (c) a Caribbean cruise, (d) a house mortgage, and (e) children's toys.

BUILDING YOUR MARKETING PLAN

To conduct a consumer analysis for the product—the good, service, or idea—in your marketing plan:

1 Identify the consumers who are most likely to buy your product—the primary target market—in terms of (a) their demographic characteristics and (b) any other kind of characteristics you believe are important.

2 Describe (a) the main points of difference of your product for this group and (b) what problem they help

solve for the consumer in terms of the first stage in the consumer purchase decision process in Figure 4–1.

3 For each of the four outside boxes in Figure 4–4 (marketing mix, psychological, sociocultural, and situational influences), identify the one or two key influences with respect to your product.

This consumer analysis will provide the foundation for the marketing mix actions you develop later in your plan.

VIDEO CASE 4   Groupon: Helping Consumers with Purchase Decisions

Video 4-4
Groupon Video Case
kerin.tv/cr6e/v4-4

University of Chicago graduate student Andrew Mason was in a rut. "There's so much to do in Chicago," he explains, "but I found myself going to the same movie theaters and restaurants."

To help people like him try new places, Mason started a website that offered coupons to large groups. He reasoned that people would try something new if the price was low enough, and that businesses would offer low prices if they knew they could sell a large quantity. The result was Groupon, a company that offers "group coupons" in deal-of-the-day offerings for local or national businesses. Consumers love the concept, buying everything from restaurant certificates, to yoga lessons, to tickets to a museum exhibit. "We think the Internet has the potential to change the way people discover and buy from local businesses," says Mason.

THE COMPANY AND GROUPON CONCEPT

Mason started with a website called ThePoint.org, which was designed to organize campaigns, protests, boycotts, and fund-raising drives for important social issues. ThePoint was not successful but it provided the concept of making offers that are only carried out if enough people commit to participate in them. With that idea Mason launched Groupon in October 2008 with a two-pizzas-for-the-price-of-one offer at the Motel Bar, located in the same building where ThePoint rented space. The concept quickly grew in Chicago and Groupon expanded into other U.S. cities and then into other countries. Today Groupon is available in 375 American cities and 48 countries, and its subscriber base has grown from 400 in 2008 to 200 million today. In its fourth full year of operation, Groupon generated $5.4 billion in gross billings.

Part of Groupon's success is the simplicity of its business model—offer subscribers at least one deal in their city each day. The unique aspect of the concept is that a certain number of people need to buy into the offer before the coupon discount is valid. Approximately 95 percent of Groupon offers "tip," or reach the number of buyers required by the merchant. Once the minimum number is met, Groupon and the merchant split the revenue. For example, a yoga studio might offer a $100 membership for $50 if 200 people participate in the offer. Once 200 consumers have indicated interest, the deal "tips" and Groupon and the yoga studio each receive 50 percent of the revenue. Everyone wins. Consumers receive an exceptional value, the merchant obtains new customers without any advertising cost, and Groupon generates revenue for creating value in the marketplace.

Many of the deals have generated extraordinary demand. The Joffrey Ballet, for example, sold 2,338 season subscriptions, doubling its subscriber base in one day! Similarly, consumers purchased 445,000 Groupons offering $50 worth of merchandise for $25 at the Gap and 6,561 tickets to a King Tut exhibit in New York's Times Square for half price at $18 apiece. The most popular offering so far was a $25 ticket for an architectural boat tour in Chicago for $12. Groupon sold 19,822 tickets in eight hours! The company's attention to customer satisfaction ensures success stories like these. "We have a policy called 'The Groupon Promise' that any customer can return a Groupon, no questions asked—even if they used it—if they feel like Groupon has let them down," explains Mason. Groupon's success has attracted many more merchants than it can accommodate. In fact, only about 12 percent of all merchants that contact Groupon are selected to offer a deal.

In addition to the deal-of-the-day offerings, Groupon has several other services. GrouponLive offers deals to obtain tickets to sporting events, concerts, theatrical performances, and other forms of live entertainment. Groupon Getaways offers travel experiences in two forms—as a specific booking or as a voucher where consumers make a separate reservation. Groupon Goods features deals on new and innovative products. Finally, Groupon is testing a concept it calls "Pull," which enables customers to search among thousands of deals that they can buy and use instantly. To use the service, consumers log on to the Groupon Mobile app on their smartphone and select "Nearby." The app then determines the location of the consumer and displays a map of nearby deals. More than 40 million people have downloaded the Groupon Mobile app, and approximately 45 percent of Groupon's transactions in the United States are completed from a mobile device.

Groupon's growth is evident in some amazing numbers. The company has offered more than 400 million deals, with over 500,000 merchant partners, and employs 11,000 people around the globe. In addition, Groupon has created a market of consumer deal hunters that includes its 41.7 million active customers and an industry of approximately 500 competitive deal services. The competitors include LivingSocial, Amazon Local, Google Offers, Plum District, Tippr, Bloomspot, Scoutmob, and many others. While the industry is large and growing, the competition has been intense, leading Facebook, Yahoo!, and others to test social-buying deal services but discontinue the offerings.

USING COUPONS TO INFLUENCE CONSUMERS' BUYING BEHAVIOR

"Part of the reason that Groupon has grown as quickly as it has is because we really understand consumer behavior," explains Julie Mossler, public relations & consumer marketing manager at Groupon. Generally, Groupon consumers follow the same purchase decision process common to many consumer purchases. The first stage, problem recognition, may be triggered by an e-mail or an appointment to have lunch with friends. Groupon deal-of-the-day e-mail messages, for example, often present consumers with an opportunity to do something they wouldn't ordinarily do—take sky-diving lessons or subscribe to the ballet. Groupon Nearby presents real-time offers on smartphone apps in response to an immediate need in a specific location. While the two types of offers generate different types of purchases, they both begin the purchase process.

The second stage, information search, may simply be a review of previous experiences with the merchant making the offer, online comparisons with competitors, or discussions with friends on Facebook or Twitter. In fact, the collective buying aspect of Groupon encourages subscribers to share promotions with family and friends to increase the chances of reaching the required number of buyers.

In the alternative evaluation stage many Groupon customers focus on price as the most important evaluative criteria, although other aspects such as quantity or time restrictions may be considered. The Groupon Nearby offers, for example, may only be valid on specific days or during short windows of time. Piece Brewery & Pizzeria in Chicago, for example, used Groupon to sell a $30 coupon for $20 valid only during its slow periods—11 a.m. to 3 p.m. Tuesday through Thursday.

The fourth stage, the purchase decision, is made online and then confirmed when the deals tip. Bo Hurd, national sales manager at Groupon, believes that the purchase stage is unique for Groupon users. He explains, "the fact that [consumers] have put money on the line. . . is driving them from the online piece, to the computers. . . to do something, to try something." Finally, after the purchase consumers compare their experience with their expectations to determine if they are satisfied or dissatisfied.

Psychological, sociocultural, and situational factors also influence Groupon users' purchase behavior. The recession has increased the importance of personal values such as thriftiness, so deal-prone people who were attracted to websites such as Gilt in fashion and Woot in consumer electronics are also attracted to Groupon. The typical Groupon user is an 18- to 34-year old woman with an average income of about $70,000. This is significant because this group's affinity to social media enables the use of Groupon, which depends on e-mail and smartphone apps to reach its customers. Specific situations such as planning entertainment activities, finding a close restaurant for lunch, or buying a gift are also common to Groupon users. As Groupon has learned more about its subscribers, it has begun personalizing the deals they see. The company uses variables such as gender, location of residence or office, and buying history to match deals with the customers. This process provides offers that are more likely to be of interest to consumers and allows Groupon to serve more merchants.

GROUPON CHALLENGES

As popular as Groupon has become, it does face three challenges. The first challenge is related to the use of coupons. Some consumers buy the coupons but never use them, eventually leaving them dissatisfied and unlikely to use Groupon again. Some consumers use the coupons but do not become regular customers. Because of the deep discounts used to sell the Groupons, most of the deals are not profitable for the merchants, so they are dissatisfied if the Groupon users do not make repeat purchases. David Perlman, owner of the Essex restaurant in New York City, for example, offered deals on Groupon and Open Table, selling 1,500 and 1,000 coupons, respectively. Now he is comparing the diners each deal brought in to determine which group has generated more repeat customers. Some merchants are also concerned that frequent discounting could discourage customers from ever making purchases without a discount.

Another challenge facing Groupon is managing its growth. The company has expanded into Europe, Latin America, Asia, and Russia by acquiring local daily deal services. For example, in Europe it purchased CityDeal, in Russia it purchased Darberry, and in Japan it purchased Qpod. It also acquired sites with customer bases in Hong Kong, Singapore, Taiwan, and the Philippines. As a result, Groupon currently has more subscribers abroad than in the United States, although more deals are still sold in the United States. According to Groupon Co-CEO Eric Lefkofsky, "We're applying our North American playbook to our international business in order to standardize systems and processes." As Groupon continues to grow, it anticipates that it must also develop a comprehensive understanding of the differences in international buying behaviors.

Finally, Groupon faces an extraordinary level of competition. Part of the problem is that the daily deal technology is not very sophisticated and the model is easy to copy. Manufacturers, large retailers, and small businesses are all trying the concept. ConAgra has offered a group coupon deal for its Healthy Choice brand through a Facebook app, Walmart launched its own deal-of-the-day coupon service, and some businesses use recently developed plug-and-play software that helps build deals into their websites. Mason hopes that Groupon Nearby is one answer to this challenge because it is much more difficult to replicate. "We have always been thinking about how to solve these fundamental problems of our model. We have known since very early on that some form of real-time deal optimization is where this had to go," he explains.

Groupon's success is the result of a simple and effective business model and an insightful understanding of consumer behavior. In the future Groupon's strategies will require continued attention to understanding consumers around the globe. Mossler explains: "Groupon has been heralded as the fastest growing company of all time, and the reason for that is because we have solved this unsolvable problem, which is how do you engage with local customers. The model really works anywhere as long as you adapt for local communities."

Questions

1 How has an understanding of consumer behavior helped Groupon grow from 400 subscribers in Chicago in 2008 to 200 million subscribers in 48 countries today?

2 What is the Groupon Promise? How does the Groupon Promise affect a consumer's perceived risk and cognitive dissonance?

3 Describe the five-stage purchase decision process for a typical Groupon user.

4 What are possible psychological and sociological influences on the Groupon consumer purchase decision process?

5 What challenges does Groupon face in the future? What actions would you recommend related to each challenge?

Chapter Notes

1. "Car-Buying Tips Men Can Learn from Women," www.leasetrader.com, January 30, 2012; "New Efforts to Shorten the Car-Buying Process," *The Wall Street Journal*, February 27, 2013, p. D3; Jerry Hirsh, "Car Buying: How Men and Women Compare," www.latimes.com, April 7, 2011; "What Matters the Most When People Buy Cars," *BrandWeek*, October 11, 2010, p. 23; "Gender Wars and Car Shopping: Men Want Power, Women Want Cloth Seats," www.autos.aol.com, July 16, 2010; and Michael J. Silverstein and Kate Sayre, "The Female Economy," *Harvard Business Review*, September 2009, pp. 46–53.

2. Roger D. Blackwell, Paul W. Miniard, and James F. Engel, *Consumer Behavior*, 10th ed. (Mason, OH: South-Western Publishing, 2006).

3. For thorough descriptions of consumer expertise, see Joseph W. Alba and J. Wesley Hutchinson, "Knowledge Calibration: What Consumers Know and What They Think They Know," *Journal of Consumer Research*, September 2000, pp. 123–57.

4. For in-depth studies on external information search patterns, see Brian T. Ratchford, Debabrata Talukdar, and Myung-Soo Lee, "The Impact of the Internet on Consumers' Use of Information Sources for Automobiles: A Re-Inquiry," *Journal of Consumer Research*, June 2007, pp. 111–19; Joel E. Urbany, Peter R. Dickson, and William L. Wilkie, "Buyer Uncertainty and Information Search," *Journal of Consumer Research*, March 1992, pp. 452–63; and Sharon E. Beatty and Scott M. Smith, "External Search Effort: An Investigation across Several Product Categories," *Journal of Consumer Research*, June 1987, pp. 83–95.

5. "The 10 Best Smartphones," www.pcmag.com, September 25, 2014; "Ten Best Smartphones in the U.S.," www.techradar.com, April 16, 2014; and "Ratings: Smart Phones," *Consumer Reports*, July 2014, p. 39.

6. For an extended discussion on evaluative criteria, see Delbert I. Hawkins, David L. Mothersbaugh, and Roger Best, *Consumer Behavior: Building Marketing Strategy*, 12th ed. (Burr Ridge, IL: McGraw-Hill/Irwin, 2013).

7. John A. Howard, *Buyer Behavior in Marketing Strategy*, 2nd ed. (Englewood Cliffs, NJ: Prentice Hall, 1994). For an extended discussion on consumer choice sets, see Allan D. Shocker, Moshe Ben-Akiva, Brun Boccara, and Prakesh Nedungadi, "Consideration Set Influences on Consumer Decision Making and Choice: Issues, Models, and Suggestions," *Marketing Letters*, August 1991, pp. 181–98.

8. Robert J. Donovan, John R. Rossiter, Gillian Marcoolyn, and Andrew Nesdale, "Store Atmosphere and Purchasing Behavior," *Journal of Retailing*, Fall 1994, pp. 283–94; and Eric A. Greenleaf and Donald R. Lehmann, "Reasons for Substantial Delay in Consumer Decision Making," *Journal of Consumer Research*, September 1995, pp. 186–99.

9. "Phone-Wielding Shoppers Strike Fear into Retailers," *The Wall Street Journal*, December 16, 2010, pp. A1, A9.

10. Sunil Gupta and Valarie Zeithaml, "Customer Metrics and Their Impact on Financial Performance," *Marketing Science*, November–December 2006, pp. 718–39.

11. These estimates are given in Jagdish N. Sheth and Banwari Mitral, *Consumer Behavior*, 2nd ed. (Mason, OH: South-Western Publishing, 2003), p. 32.

12. For an in-depth examination of this topic, see "Car buyers are most loyal to these brands," cnbc.com, July 2, 2014; and Sunil Gupta and Donald R. Lehmann, *Managing Customers as Investments* (Upper Saddle River, NJ: Pearson Education, Inc., 2005).

13. For an overview of research on involvement, see Wayne D. Hoyer, Deborah J. MacInnis, and Rik Pieters, *Consumer Behavior*, 6th ed. (Florence, KY: South-Western Education Publishing, 2013).

14. Russell Belk, "Situational Variables and Consumer Behavior," *Journal of Consumer Research*, December 1975, pp. 157–63. The examples in this section are taken from Martin Lindstrom, *buy.ology: Truth and Lies about Why We Buy* (New York: Doubleday Publishing, 2008).

15. A. H. Maslow, *Motivation and Personality* (New York: Harper & Row, 1970). Also see Richard Yalch and Frederic Brunel, "Need Hierarchies in Consumer Judgments of Product Design: Is It Time to Reconsider Maslow's Hierarchy?" in Kim Corfman and John Lynch, eds., *Advances in Consumer Research* (Provo, UT: Association for Consumer Research, 1996), pp. 405–10.

16. Bernardo J. Carducci, *The Psychology of Personality*, 2nd ed. (Oxford, UK: John Wiley & Sons, 2009), pp. 182–84.

17. Jane Spencer, "Lenovo Puts Style in New Laptop," *The Wall Street Journal*, January 3, 2008, p. B5.

18. This example is provided in Michael R. Solomon, *Consumer Behavior*, 4th ed. (Upper Saddle River, NJ: Prentice Hall, 1999), p. 59.

19. For further reading on subliminal perception, see Lindstrom, *buy.ology*; B. Bahrami, N. Lavie, and G. Rees, "Attentional Load Modulates Responses of Human Primary Visual Cortex to Invisible Stimuli," *Current Biology*, March 2007, pp. 39–47; and J. Karremans, W. Stroebe, and J. Claus, "Beyond Vicary's Fantasies: The Impact of Subliminal Priming and Brand Choice," *Journal of Experimental Social Psychology* 42 (2006), pp. 792–98.

20. August Bullock, *The Secret Sales Pitch* (San Jose, CA: Norwich Publishers, 2004); and Dave Lakhani, *Subliminal Persuasion* (Hoboken, NJ: John Wiley & Sons, 2008).

21. "Say Goodbye to the Car Salesman," *The Wall Street Journal*, November 21, 2013, pp. B1, B6.

22. Steve Olenski, "Is Brand Loyalty Dying a Slow and Painful Death?" www.forbes.com, January 7, 2013; and Sholnn Freeman, "Brand Breakdown," *The Washington Post*, March 26, 2006, p. F1ff.

23. Martin Fishbein and I. Aizen, *Belief, Attitude, Intention and Behavior: An Introduction to Theory and Research* (Reading, MA: Addison-Wesley, 1975), p. 6.

24. Richard J. Lutz, "Changing Brand Attitudes through Modification of Cognitive Structure," *Journal of Consumer Research*, March 1975, pp. 49–59.

25. This discussion is based on "The VALS™ Types," www.strategic-businessinsights.com, downloaded February 1, 2014.

26. This discussion is based on Ed Keller and Jon Berry, *The Influentials* (New York: Simon and Schuster, 2003).

27. Ed Keller and Brad Fay, "Word-of-Mouth Advocacy: A New Key to Advertising Effectiveness," *Journal of Advertising Research*, December 2012, pp. 459–64.

28. Emanuel Rosen, *The Anatomy of Buzz Revisited* (New York: Crown Business, 2009).

29. www.bzzAgent.com, downloaded January 10, 2014; and Laura Burkett, "Word-of-Mouth Marketing Evolution," www.forbes.com, May 21, 2009.

30. Emanuel Rosen, "Conversation Starter," *BrandWeek*, April 12, 2010, p. 16.

31. Hoyer, MacInnis, and Pieters, *Consumer Behavior*.

32. Elizabeth Holmes, "Abercrombie and Fitch Offers to Pay 'The Situation' to Stop Wearing Its Clothes," *The Wall Street Journal*, August 16, 2011, p. B2.

33. For an extensive review on consumer socialization of children, see Deborah Roedder John, "Consumer Socialization of Children: A Retrospective Look at Twenty-Five Years of Research," *Journal of Consumer Research*, December 1999, pp. 183–213. Also see, Gwen Bachmann Achenreinver and Deborah Roedder John, "The Meaning of Brand Names to Children: A Developmental Investigation," *Journal of Consumer Psychology* 13, no. 3 (2003), pp. 205–19; and Elizabeth S. Moore, William L. Wilkie, and Richard J. Lutz, "Passing the Torch: Intergenerational Influences as a Source of Brand Equity," *Journal of Marketing*, April 2002, pp. 17–37.

34. J. Paul Peter and Jerry C. Olson, *Consumer Behavior and Marketing Strategy*, 9th ed. (Burr Ridge, IL: McGraw-Hill/Irwin, 2010); "Grocers Catering More to Men" *Dallas Morning News*, January 13, 2013, p. 3D; "Who Makes the Call at the Mall, Men or Women?" *The Wall Street Journal*, April 23–24, 2011, p. A1; and Rich Morin and D'Vera Cohn, "Women Call the Shots at Home: Public Mixed on Gender Roles in Jobs," www.pewresearch.org, downloaded February 4, 2011. Also see, Rex Y. Du and Wagner A. Kamakura, "Household Life Cycles and Lifestyles in the United States," *Journal of Marketing Research*, February 2006, pp. 121–32.

35. This discussion is based on Hawkins, Mothersbaugh, and Best, *Consumer Behavior: Building Marketing Strategy*; "Groceries Become a Guy Thing," *The Wall Street Journal*, October 17, 2013, pp. D1, D2; *The Kids and Tweens Market in the U.S.*, 9th ed. (Rockville, MD: Packaged Facts, August 1, 2008); and "How Teens Use Media" (New York: Neilsen Company, June 2009).

36. Jeffrey M. Humphreys, "The Multicultural Economy in 2013," Selig Center for Economic Growth, Terry College of Business, The University of Georgia, p. 7.

37. The remainder of this discussion is based on Hoyer, MacInnis, and Pieters, *Consumer Behavior*; "The Lust for Latino Lucre," *The Economist*, May 11, 2013, p. 71; *The State of Hispanic Consumer: Hispanic Market Imperative* (New York: The Nielsen Company, 2012); and *10th Annual Hispanic Fact Pack* (New York: Advertising Age, 2014).

38. The remainder of this discussion is based on Peter and Olson, *Consumer Behavior and Marketing Strategy;* and *The State of the African-American Consumer: Still Vital, Still Growing* (New York: The Nielsen Company, 2012).

39. The remainder of this discussion is based on *The State of the Asian American Consumer: Growing Market, Growing Impact* (New York: The Nielsen Company, 2012); Christine Birkner, "Asian-Americans in Focus," *Marketing News*, March 2013, p. 14; and Lee Siegel, "Rise of the Tiger Nation," *The Wall Street Journal*, October 27–28, 2012, pp. C1, C2.

Groupon: This case was written by Steven Hartley. Sources: Bari Weiss, "The Journal Interview with Andrew Mason: Groupon's $6 Billion Gambler," *The Wall Street Journal*, December 20, 2010, p. 12; Brad Stone and Douglas MacMillan, "Are Four Words Worth $25 Billion?" *Bloomberg Businessweek*, March 21, 2011, pp. 70–75; Brendan Coffey, "What's the Deal?" *Forbes*, April 25, 2011, pp. 20–22; Brad Stone and Douglas MacMillan, "Groupon's $6 Billion Snub," *Bloomberg Businessweek*, December 13, 2010, pp. 6–7; Christopher Steiner, "Meet the Fastest Growing Company Ever," *Forbes*, August 30, 2010; Rupal Parekh, "Groupon," *Advertising Age*, November 15, 2010, p. 20; "10 Big Stories for the Week," *Advertising Age*, December 13, 2010, pp. 12–13; Jessi Hempel, "Social Media Meets Retailing," *Fortune*, March 22, 2010, p. 30; Kunur Patel, "Suddenly, Everyone Wants to Be Groupon," *Advertising Age*, November 1, 2010, p. 1; Brad Stone, "Coupon Deathmatch, Party of Two?" *Bloomberg Businessweek*, October 4, 2010, pp. 37–38; and "Q1 2013 Fact Sheet" and "2012 Letter to Shareholders," on Groupon website, http://investor.groupon.com/, accessed July 8, 2013.

Credits

CHAPTER 4 Understanding Consumer Behavior

5 Understanding Organizations as Customers

LEARNING OBJECTIVES

After reading this chapter you should be able to:

 LO 5-1 Distinguish among industrial, reseller, and government organizational markets.

 LO 5-2 Describe the key characteristics of organizational buying that make it different from consumer buying.

 LO 5-3 Explain how buying centers and buying situations influence organizational purchasing.

 LO 5-4 Recognize the importance and nature of online buying in industrial, reseller, and government organizational markets.

BUYING IS MARKETING, TOO! PURCHASING PUBLICATION PAPER FOR JCPENNEY

Kim Nagele views paper differently than most people do. As the senior purchasing manager at JCPMedia, Inc., he and a team of purchasing professionals annually buy about 150,000 tons of publication paper.

JCPMedia, Inc., is responsible for print and paper purchasing at JCPenney, one of the largest department store retailers in the United States. Paper purchasing is a serious marketing responsibility for JCPMedia, Inc., which buys publication paper for JCPenney newspaper inserts and direct-mail pieces. Some 10 companies from around the world—including Verso Paper in the United States, Catalyst Paper, Inc., in Canada, Norske Skog in Norway, and UPM-Kymmene, Inc., in Finland—supply paper to JCPenney.

"The choice of paper and suppliers is also a significant marketing decision given the sizable revenue and expense consequences," notes Tom Cassidy, Vice President–Marketing Production at JCPMedia, Inc. JCPMedia, Inc., paper buyers work closely with senior JCPenney marketing executives and within budget constraints to assure that the right appearance, quality, and quantity of publication paper is purchased at the right price point for merchandise featured in the millions of JCPenney newspaper inserts and direct-mail pieces distributed every year in the United States.

JCPMedia, Inc., paper buyers themselves are thoroughly trained in many facets of purchasing. For example, Kim Nagele is a Certified Professional in Supply Management (CPSM). The CPSM designation is awarded to those individuals who have demonstrated competence in such areas as contracting and negotiation, cost management, forecasting, and materials and inventory management through a rigorous examination process.

In addition to paper appearance, quality, quantity, and price, JCPMedia paper buyers formally evaluate paper supplier capabilities, often by extended visits to supplier facilities in the United States, Canada, and Europe. Supplier capabilities include the capacity to deliver on-time selected grades of paper from specialty items to magazine papers, the availability of specific types of paper to meet printing deadlines, and formal programs focused on the life cycle of paper products. For example, a supplier's forestry management and sustainability practices are considered in the paper buying process.

115

In fact, paper bought by JCPMedia, Inc., is certified through the Sustainable Forestry Initiative, Forest Stewardship Council, or the Programme for the Endorsement of Forest Certification—three prominent certification programs for forest management.[1]

The next time you thumb through a JCPenney newspaper insert or direct-mail piece, take a moment to notice the paper. Considerable effort and attention was given to its selection and purchase decision by Tom Cassidy, Kim Nagele, and JCPMedia, Inc., paper buyers.

Purchasing paper for JCPMedia is one example of organizational buying. This chapter examines the different types of organizational buyers; key characteristics of organizational buying, including online buying; buying situations; unique aspects of the organizational buying process compared with the consumer purchase process; and some typical buying procedures and decisions in today's organizational markets.

THE NATURE AND SIZE OF ORGANIZATIONAL MARKETS

LO 5-1 Distinguish among industrial, reseller, and government organizational markets.

business marketing
The marketing of products and services to firms, governments, or not-for-profit organizations.

organizational buyers
Manufacturers, wholesalers, retailers, and government agencies that buy products and services for their own use or for resale.

Understanding organizational markets and buying behavior is a necessary prerequisite for effective business marketing. **Business marketing** is the marketing of products and services to companies, governments, or not-for-profit organizations for use in the creation of products and services that they can produce and market to others. Because over half of all U.S. business school graduates take jobs in firms that engage in business marketing, it is important to understand the characteristics of organizational buyers and their buying behavior.

Organizational buyers are those manufacturers, wholesalers, retailers, and government agencies that buy products and services for their own use or for resale. For example, these organizations buy computers and telephone services for their own use. However, manufacturers buy raw materials and parts that they reprocess into the finished goods they sell. Wholesalers and retailers resell the goods they buy without reprocessing them.

Organizational buyers include all buyers in a nation except ultimate consumers. These organizational buyers purchase and lease large volumes of capital equipment, raw materials, manufactured parts, supplies, and business services. In fact, because they often buy raw materials and parts, process them, and sell the upgraded product several times before it is purchased by the final organizational buyer or ultimate consumer, the total annual purchases of organizational buyers are far greater than those of ultimate consumers. IBM alone buys nearly $35 billion in products and services each year for its own use or resale.[2]

Organizational buyers are divided into three markets: (1) industrial, (2) reseller, and (3) government.[3] Each market is described next.

Industrial Markets

There are about 7.5 million firms in the industrial, or business, market. These *industrial firms* in some way reprocess a product or service they buy before selling it again to the next buyer. This is certainly true of Corning, Inc., which transforms an exotic blend of materials to create optical fiber capable of carrying much of the telephone traffic in the United States on a single strand. It is also true (if you stretch your imagination) of a firm selling services, such as a bank that takes money from its depositors, reprocesses it, and "sells" it as loans to borrowers.

The importance of services in the United States today is emphasized by the composition of industrial markets. Companies that primarily sell physical goods (manufacturers; mining; construction; and farms, timber, and fisheries) represent 25 percent of all the industrial firms. The services market sells diverse services such as legal advice, auto repair, and dry cleaning. Service companies—finance, insurance, and real estate businesses; transportation, communication, and public utility firms; and not-for-profit organizations—represent 75 percent of all industrial firms. Because of the size and importance of service companies and not-for-profit organizations (such as the American Red Cross), services marketing is discussed in detail in Chapter 10.

Reseller Markets

Wholesalers and retailers that buy physical products and resell them again without any reprocessing are *resellers*. In the United States there are about 1.1 million retailers and 435,000 wholesalers. In Chapters 12 and 13 you will see how manufacturers use wholesalers and retailers in their distribution ("place") strategies as channels through which their products reach ultimate consumers. In this chapter, we look at these resellers mainly as organizational buyers in terms of (1) how they make their own buying decisions and (2) which products they choose to carry.

The Orion spacecraft to be designed, developed, tested, and evaluated by Lockheed Martin Corp., is an example of a purchase by a government unit, namely the National Aeronautics and Space Administration (NASA). Read the text to find out how much NASA will pay for Orion's development, test flights in 2014 and 2017, and its first manned mission in 2021.

**Lockheed Martin
Corporation**

lockheedmartin.com/orion

Government Markets

Video 5-1
NASA
kerin.tv/cr6e/v5-1

Government units are the federal, state, and local agencies that buy goods and services for the constituents they serve. There are about 89,500 of these government units in the United States. These purchases include the $11.4 billion the National Aeronautics and Space Administration (NASA) intends to pay Lockheed Martin to develop and launch the Orion spacecraft scheduled for flights in 2014, 2017, and 2021.[4]

MEASURING DOMESTIC AND GLOBAL INDUSTRIAL, RESELLER, AND GOVERNMENT MARKETS

North American Industry Classification System (NAICS)
Provides common industry definitions for Canada, Mexico, and the United States.

The measurement of industrial, reseller, and government markets is an important first step for a firm interested in gauging the size of one, two, or all three of these markets in the United States and around the world. This task has been made easier with the **North American Industry Classification System (NAICS)**.[5] The NAICS provides common industry definitions for Canada, Mexico, and the United States, which makes it easier to measure economic activity in the three member countries of the North American Free Trade Agreement (NAFTA).

The NAICS replaced the Standard Industrial Classification (SIC) system, a version of which has been in place for more than 50 years in the three NAFTA member countries. The SIC neither permitted comparability across countries nor accurately measured new or emerging industries. Furthermore, the NAICS is consistent with the International Standard Industrial Classification of All Economic Activities, which is published by the United Nations and designed to facilitate the measurement of global economic activity.

The NAICS groups economic activity to permit studies of market share, demand for goods and services, import competition in domestic markets, and similar studies. It designates industries with a numerical code in a defined structure. A six-digit coding system is used. The first two digits designate a sector of the economy, the third digit designates a subsector, and the fourth digit represents an industry group. The fifth digit designates a specific industry and is the most detailed level at which comparable data are available for Canada, Mexico, and the United States. The sixth digit

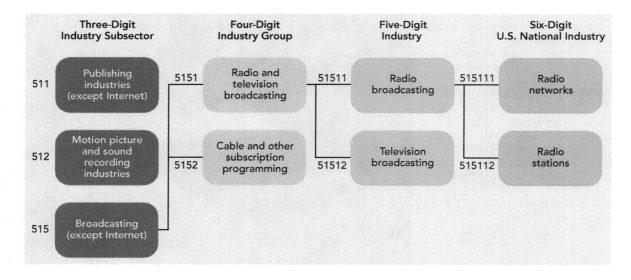

Three-Digit Industry Subsector		Four-Digit Industry Group		Five-Digit Industry		Six-Digit U.S. National Industry	
511	Publishing industries (except Internet)	5151	Radio and television broadcasting	51511	Radio broadcasting	515111	Radio networks
512	Motion picture and sound recording industries	5152	Cable and other subscription programming	51512	Television broadcasting	515112	Radio stations
515	Broadcasting (except Internet)						

FIGURE 5–1
NAICS breakdown for the information industries sector: NAICS code 51 (abbreviated).

designates individual country-level national industries. Figure 5–1 shows the breakdown within the information industries sector (code 51) to illustrate the NAICS classification scheme.

The NAICS permits a firm to find the NAICS codes of its present customers and then obtain NAICS-coded lists for similar firms. Also, it is possible to monitor NAICS categories to determine the growth in various sectors and industries to identify promising marketing opportunities. However, the NAICS has an important limitation. Five-digit national industry codes are not available for all three countries because the respective governments will not reveal data when too few organizations exist in a category.

learning review

5-1. What are the three main types of organizational buyers?

5-2. What is the North American Industry Classification System (NAICS)?

CHARACTERISTICS OF ORGANIZATIONAL BUYING

LO 5-2 Describe the key characteristics of organizational buying that make it different from consumer buying.

Organizations are different from individuals, so buying for an organization is different from buying for yourself or your family. In both cases the objective in making the purchase is to solve the buyer's problem—to satisfy a need or want. However, the unique objectives and policies of an organization put special constraints on how it makes buying decisions. Understanding the characteristics of organizational buying is essential in designing effective marketing programs to reach these buyers. Key characteristics of organizational buying are listed in Figure 5–2 and discussed next.[6]

Demand Characteristics

Consumer demand for products and services is affected by their price and availability and by consumers' personal tastes and discretionary income. By comparison,

CHARACTERISTICS   DIMENSIONS

Market characteristics
- Demand for industrial products and services is derived.
- Few customers typically exist, and their purchase orders are large.

Product or service characteristics
- Products or services are technical in nature and purchased on the basis of specifications.
- Many of the goods purchased are raw and semifinished.
- Heavy emphasis is placed on delivery time, technical assistance, and postsale service.

Buying process characteristics
- Technically qualified and professional buyers follow established purchasing policies and procedures.
- Buying objectives and criteria are typically spelled out, as are procedures for evaluating sellers and their products or services.
- There are multiple buying influences, and multiple parties participate in purchase decisions.
- There are reciprocal arrangements, and negotiation between buyers and sellers is commonplace.
- Online buying over the Internet is widespread.

Marketing mix characteristics
- Direct selling to organizational buyers is the rule, and distribution is very important.
- Advertising and other forms of promotion are technical in nature.
- Price is often negotiated, evaluated as part of broader seller and product/service qualities, and frequently affected by quantity discounts.

FIGURE 5–2
Key characteristics and dimensions of organizational buying behavior.

derived demand
The demand for industrial products and services is driven by demand for consumer products and services.

industrial demand is derived. **Derived demand** means that the demand for industrial products and services is driven by, or derived from, demand for consumer products and services. For example, the demand for Weyerhaeuser's pulp and paper products is based on consumer demand for newspapers, FedEx packages, and disposable diapers. Derived demand is based on expectations of future consumer demand. For instance, Whirlpool buys parts for its washers and dryers in anticipation of consumer demand, which is affected by the replacement cycle for these products and by consumer income.

Size of the Order or Purchase

The size of the purchase involved in organizational buying is typically much larger than that in consumer buying. The dollar value of a single purchase made by an organization often runs into thousands or millions of dollars. For example, Siemens was recently awarded a $300 million contract to build a natural-gas-fired power plant in Texas.[7]

With so much money at stake, most organizations place constraints on their buyers in the form of purchasing policies or procedures. Buyers must often get competitive bids from at least three prospective suppliers when the order is above a specific amount, such as $5,000. When the order is above an even higher amount, such as $50,000, it may require the review and approval of a vice president or even the president of the company. Knowing how order size affects buying practices is important in determining who will participate in the purchase decision, who will make the final decision, and the length of time that will be required to arrive at a purchase agreement.

Number of Potential Buyers

Firms selling consumer products or services often try to reach thousands or millions of individuals or households. For example, your local supermarket or bank probably serves thousands of people. Kellogg tries to reach 80 million North American households with its breakfast cereals and probably succeeds in selling to a third or half of these in any given year. Firms selling to organizations are often restricted to far fewer buyers. Gulfstream Aerospace Corporation can sell its business jets to a few thousand organizations throughout the world, and Goodyear sells its original equipment tires to fewer than 10 car manufacturers.

Organizational Buying Objectives

Organizations buy products and services for one main reason: to help them achieve their objectives. For business firms, the buying objective is usually to increase profits through reducing costs or increasing revenues. For example, 7-Eleven buys automated inventory systems to increase the number of products that can be sold through its convenience stores and to keep them fresh. Nissan Motor Company switched its advertising agency because it expects the new agency to devise a more effective ad campaign to help it sell more cars and increase revenues. To improve executive decision making, many firms buy advanced computer systems to process data. The objectives of nonprofit firms and government agencies are usually to meet the needs of the groups they serve.

Pitney Bowes is a leader in supplier diversity. The company has over 800 diverse suppliers that account for $63 million in annual purchases.

Many companies today have broadened their buying objectives to include an emphasis on buying from minority- and women-owned suppliers and vendors. Companies such as Pitney Bowes, PepsiCo, AT&T, Coors, and JCPenney report that sales, profits, and customer satisfaction have increased because of their minority- and women-owned supplier and vendor initiatives.

Other companies include environmental sustainability initiatives. For example, Lowe's and Home Depot no longer purchase lumber from companies that harvest timber from the world's endangered forests. Successful business marketers recognize that understanding a company's buying objectives is a necessary first step in marketing to organizations.

Organizational Buying Criteria

In making a purchase, the buying organization must weigh key buying criteria that apply to the potential supplier and what it wants to sell. *Organizational buying criteria* are the objective attributes of the supplier's products and services and the capabilities of the supplier itself. These criteria serve the same purpose as the evaluative criteria used by consumers and described in Chapter 4. The most commonly used criteria are (1) price, (2) ability to meet the quality specifications required for the item, (3) ability to meet required delivery schedules, (4) technical capability, (5) warranties and claim policies in the event of poor performance, (6) past performance on previous contracts, and (7) production facilities and capacity.[8] Suppliers that meet or exceed these criteria create customer value.

As a practical example, Figure 5–3 shows the actual buying criteria employed by organizational buyers when choosing among machine vision system products and suppliers, as well as the frequency with which these criteria are used. Interestingly, of the various selection criteria listed, a machine vision system's price is among the least frequently mentioned.[9]

FIGURE 5–3

Product and supplier selection criteria for buying machine vision equipment emphasize factors other than price.

A machine vision inspection camera is used in the automotive industry to perform a gear inspection—in this case, to check if the notches are correctly angled and sized.

Percentage of machine vision buyers citing individual selection criteria as most important when making a product or supplier decision.

Criterion	Percentage
Performance	80%
Technical support	68%
Ease of use	67%
Ease of setup	63%
Complete solution (including software)	60%
Ruggedness	56%
Customization ability	53%
Price	48%
Integration expertise	42%
Full tool set	42%
Speed	38%

Many organizational buyers today are transforming their buying criteria into specific requirements that are communicated to prospective suppliers. This practice, called *supplier development*, involves the deliberate effort by organizational buyers to build relationships that shape suppliers' products, services, and capabilities to fit a buyer's needs and those of its customers. Consider Deere & Company, the maker of John Deere farm, construction, and lawn-care equipment. Deere employs supplier-development engineers who work full-time with the company's suppliers to improve their efficiency and quality and reduce their costs. According to a Deere senior executive, "Their quality, delivery, and costs are, after all, our quality, delivery, and costs."[10]

Buyer–Seller Relationships and Supply Partnerships

Another distinction between organizational and consumer buying behavior lies in the nature of the relationship between organizational buyers and suppliers. Specifically, organizational buying is more likely to involve complex negotiations concerning delivery schedules, price, technical specifications, warranties, and claim policies. These negotiations also can last for an extended period. This was the case when the Lawrence Livermore National Laboratory acquired an IBM Sequoia supercomputer at a cost of about $250 million. In terms of processing speed, the amount of data that the Sequoia can process in one hour is equivalent to what 6.7 billion people would be able to calculate (using calculators)—if they had 320 years to do their work![11]

Reciprocal arrangements also exist in organizational buying. *Reciprocity* is an industrial buying practice in which two organizations agree to purchase each other's products and services. The U.S. Justice Department disapproves of reciprocal buying because it restricts the normal operation of the free market. However, the practice exists and can limit the flexibility of organizational buyers in choosing alternative suppliers.

Long-term contracts are also prevalent. Hewlett-Packard has a 10-year, $3 billion contract to manage Procter & Gamble's information technology in 160 countries.[12]

In some cases, buyer–seller relationships evolve into supply partnerships. A *supply partnership* exists when a buyer and its supplier adopt mutually beneficial objectives,

Marketing Matters

At Milsco Manufacturing, "Our Marketing Philosophy Is Designed to Develop Partnerships" and Deliver a Great Ride for Customers' Seats

Form, fit, and functionality are the hallmarks of a proper seating solution. Just ask the executives and engineers at Milsco Manufacturing, which produces more than 3 million seats annually in more than 200 unique variations.

Whether you are cruising the wide open spaces on your Harley-Davidson motorcycle or mowing your backyard on a John Deere lawn tractor, you're getting a comfortable ride thanks to a company you may have never heard of. Milsco is a Wisconsin-based designer and producer of seating solutions. Its customers include Harley-Davidson, John Deere, Yamaha, Caterpillar, Arctic Cat, Kubata, Toro, and Toyota, as well as numerous other well-known and respected household names in the motorcycle, power sports, agricultural, construction, marine recreation, turf care, industrial lift, golf cart, and mobility markets.

Milsco's marketing philosophy is designed to develop partnerships with its customers. The 81-year partnership between Harley-Davidson and Milsco is a case in point. Since 1934, Milsco has been the sole source of original equipment motorcycle seats and a major supplier of aftermarket parts and accessories, such as saddlebags, for Harley-Davidson. Milsco engineers and designers work closely with their Harley counterparts in the design of each year's new products.

In fact, Milsco partners with each of its customers to design and manufacture the most effective and functional seating solution. Every year, the company launches over 100 new products, many of which are crafted by hand, in response to new and changing customer requirements.

The next time you sit down on a Harley or a John Deere lawn tractor (or any other product involving a partnership with Milsco Manufacturing), notice the seat and remember that it was designed and manufactured for your form, fit, and functionality—and, of course, comfort.

policies, and procedures for the purpose of lowering the cost or increasing the value of products and services delivered to the ultimate consumer. A classic example of a supply partnership is the one between Harley-Davidson and Milsco Manufacturing. Milsco has designed and manufactured Harley-Davidson motorcycle seats for 81 years. The importance of supply partnerships for Milsco is described in the Marketing Matters box.[13]

Retailers, too, have forged partnerships with their suppliers. Walmart has such a relationship with Procter & Gamble for ordering and replenishing P&G's products in its stores. By using computerized cash register scanning equipment and direct electronic linkages to P&G, Walmart can tell P&G what merchandise is needed, along with how much, when, and to which store to deliver it on a daily basis.

Supply partnerships often include provisions for what is called *sustainable procurement*. This buying practice is described in the Making Responsible Decisions box.[14]

Video 5-2
Starbucks
Sustainability
kerin.tv/cr6e/v5-2

Making Responsible Decisions

sustainability

Sustainable Procurement for Sustainable Growth at Starbucks

Manufacturers, retailers, wholesalers, and governmental agencies are increasingly sensitive to how their buying decisions affect the environment. Concerns about the depletion of natural resources; air, water, and soil pollution; and the social consequences of economic activity have given rise to the concept of sustainable procurement. Sustainable procurement aims to integrate environmental considerations into all stages of an organization's buying process with the goal of reducing the negative impact on human health and the physical environment.

Starbucks is a pioneer and worldwide leader in sustainable procurement. The company's attention to quality coffee extends to its coffee growers located in more than 20 countries. This means that Starbucks pays coffee farmers a fair price for the beans; that the coffee is grown in an ecologically sound manner; and that Starbucks invests in

the farming communities where its coffees are produced. In this way, Starbucks focuses on the sustainable growth of its suppliers.

THE ORGANIZATIONAL BUYING PROCESS AND THE BUYING CENTER

organizational buying behavior
The process by which organizations determine the need for products and then choose among alternative suppliers.

Organizational buyers, like consumers, engage in a decision process when selecting products and services. **Organizational buying behavior** is the decision-making process that organizations use to establish the need for products and services and identify, evaluate, and choose among alternative brands and suppliers. There are important similarities and differences between the two decision-making processes. To better understand the nature of organizational buying behavior, we first compare it with consumer buying behavior. We then describe a unique feature of organizational buying—the buying center.

Stages in the Organizational Buying Process

As shown in Figure 5–4 on the next page, the five stages a student might use in buying a smartphone also apply to organizational purchases. However, comparing the two smartphone columns in Figure 5–4 reveals some key differences. For example, when a manufacturer buys an earbud headset for its units from a supplier, more individuals are involved, supplier capability becomes more important, and the postpurchase evaluation behavior is more formal. The earbud headset buying decision process is typical of the steps made by organizational buyers.

LO 5-3 Explain how buying centers and buying situations influence organizational purchasing.

The Buying Center: A Cross-Functional Group

buying center
The group of people in an organization that participates in the buying process.

For routine purchases with a small dollar value, a single buyer or purchasing manager often makes the purchase decision alone. In many instances, however, several people in the organization participate in the buying process. The individuals in this group, called a **buying center**, share common goals, risks, and knowledge important to a purchase decision. For most large multistore chain resellers, such as Sears, 7-Eleven convenience stores, Target, or Safeway, the buying center is highly formalized and is called a *buying committee*. However, most industrial firms or government units use informal groups of people or call meetings to arrive at buying decisions.

The importance of the buying center requires that a firm marketing to many industrial firms and government units understand the structure, the technical and business functions represented, and the behavior of these groups.[15] Four questions provide

STAGE IN THE BUYING DECISION PROCESS	CONSUMER PURCHASE: SMARTPHONE FOR A STUDENT	ORGANIZATIONAL PURCHASE: EARBUD HEADSET FOR A SMARTPHONE
Problem recognition	Student doesn't like the features of the smartphone now owned and desires a new one.	Marketing research and sales departments observe that competitors are improving the earbud headsets for their smartphones. The firm decides to improve the earbud headsets on its own new models, which will be purchased from an outside supplier.
Information search	Student uses personal past experience and that of friends, ads, the Internet, and *Consumer Reports* to collect information and uncover alternatives.	Design and production engineers draft specifications for earbud headsets. The purchasing department identifies suppliers of earbud headsets.
Alternative evaluation	Alternative smartphones are evaluated on the basis of important attributes desired in a phone, and several stores are visited.	Purchasing and engineering personnel visit with suppliers and assess (1) facilities, (2) capacity, (3) quality control, and (4) financial status. They drop any suppliers not satisfactory on these attributes.
Purchase decision	A specific brand of smartphone is selected, the price is paid, and the student leaves the store.	They use (1) quality, (2) price, (3) delivery, and (4) technical capability as key buying criteria to select a supplier. Then they negotiate terms and award a contract.
Postpurchase behavior	Student reevaluates the purchase decision and may return the phone to the store if it is unsatisfactory.	They evaluate suppliers using a formal vendor rating system and notify a supplier if the earbud headsets do not meet their quality standard. If the problem is not corrected, they drop the firm as a future supplier.

FIGURE 5–4
Comparing the stages in a consumer and organizational purchase decision process.

guidance in understanding the buying center in these organizations: (1) Which individuals are in the buying center for the product or service? (2) What is the relative influence of each member of the group? (3) What are the buying criteria of each member? and (4) How does each member of the group perceive our firm, our products and services, and our salespeople?

People in the Buying Center The composition of the buying center in a given organization depends on the specific item being bought. Although a buyer or purchasing manager is almost always a member of the buying center, individuals from other functional areas are included, depending on what is to be purchased. In buying a million-dollar machine tool, the president (because of the size of the purchase) and the production vice president or manager would probably be members. For key components to be included in a final manufactured product, a cross-functional group of individuals from research and development (R&D), engineering, and quality control are likely to be added. For new word-processing equipment, experienced secretaries who will use the equipment would be members. Still, a major question in penetrating the buying center is finding and reaching the people who will initiate, influence, and actually make the buying decision.

Roles in the Buying Center Researchers have identified five specific roles that an individual in a buying center can play.[16] In some purchases the same person may perform two or more of these roles.

- *Users* are the people in the organization who actually use the product or service, such as a secretary who will use a new word processor.

Effective marketing to organizations requires an understanding of buying centers and their role in purchase decisions.

- *Influencers* affect the buying decision, usually by helping define the specifications for what is bought. The information technology manager would be a key influencer in the purchase of a new mainframe computer.
- *Buyers* have formal authority and responsibility to select the supplier and negotiate the terms of the contract. Kim Nagele performs this role as senior sourcing manager at JCPMedia, as described in the chapter opening example.
- *Deciders* have the formal or informal power to select or approve the supplier that receives the contract. In routine orders the decider is usually the buyer or purchasing manager; in important technical purchases it is more likely to be someone from R&D, engineering, or quality control. The decider for a key component being incorporated in a final manufactured product might be any of these three people.
- *Gatekeepers* control the flow of information in the buying center. Purchasing personnel, technical experts, and secretaries can all keep salespeople or information from reaching people performing the other four roles.

buy classes
Three types of organizational buying situations: new buy, straight rebuy, or modified rebuy.

FIGURE 5–5
The buying situation affects buying center behavior in different ways. Understanding these differences can pay huge dividends for companies that market to organizations.

Buying Situations and the Buying Center   The number of people in the buying center largely depends on the specific buying situation. Researchers who have studied organizational buying identify three types of buying situations, called **buy classes**. These buy classes vary from the routine reorder, or *straight rebuy*, to the completely new purchase, termed *new buy*. In between these extremes is the *modified rebuy*. Figure 5–5 summarizes how buy classes affect buying center tendencies in different ways. Some examples will clarify the differences.[17]

- *New buy.* Here the organization is a first-time buyer of the product or service. This involves greater potential risks in the purchase, so the buying center is enlarged to include all those who have a stake in the new buy. Procter & Gamble's

BUYING CENTER DIMENSION	BUY-CLASS SITUATION		
	NEW BUY	STRAIGHT REBUY	MODIFIED REBUY
People involved	Many	One	Two to three
Decision time	Long	Short	Moderate
Problem definition	Uncertain	Well-defined	Minor modifications
Buying objective	Good solution	Low-priced supplier	Low-priced supplier
Suppliers considered	New/present	Present	Present
Buying influence	Technical/operating personnel	Purchasing agent	Purchasing agent and others

purchase of a multimillion-dollar fiber-optic network from Corning, Inc., for its corporate offices in Cincinnati, represented a new buy.

- *Straight rebuy.* Here the buyer or purchasing manager reorders an existing product or service from the list of acceptable suppliers, probably without even checking with users or influencers from the engineering, production, or quality control departments. Office supplies and maintenance services are usually obtained as straight rebuys.

- *Modified rebuy.* In this buying situation the users, influencers, or deciders in the buying center want to change the product specifications, price, delivery schedule, or supplier. Although the item purchased is largely the same as with the straight rebuy, the changes usually necessitate enlarging the buying center to include people outside the purchasing department.

> **learning review**
>
> 5-3. What one department is almost always represented by a person in the buying center?
>
> 5-4. What are the three types of buying situations or buy classes?

ONLINE BUYING IN ORGANIZATIONAL MARKETS

LO 5-4 Recognize the importance and nature of online buying in industrial, reseller, and government organizational markets.

Organizational buying behavior and business marketing continues to evolve with the application of Internet technology. Organizations dwarf consumers in terms of online transactions made, average transaction size, and overall purchase volume. In fact, organizational buyers account for about 80 percent of the global dollar value of all online transactions.

Prominence of Online Buying in Organizational Markets

Online buying in organizational markets is prominent for three major reasons.[18] First, organizational buyers depend heavily on timely supplier information that describes product availability, technical specifications, application uses, price, and delivery schedules. This information can be conveyed quickly via Internet technology. Second, this technology has been shown to substantially reduce buyer order processing costs. At General Electric, online buying has cut the cost of a transaction from $50 to $100 per purchase to about $5. Third, business marketers have found that Internet technology can reduce marketing costs, particularly sales and advertising expense, and broaden their potential customer base for many types of products and services.

For these reasons, online buying is popular in all three kinds of organizational markets. For example, airlines electronically order over $400 million in spare parts from the Boeing Company each year. Customers of W. W. Grainger, a large U.S. wholesaler of maintenance, repair, and operating supplies, buy more than $3 billion worth of these products annually online. Supply and service purchases totaling $650 million each year are made online by the Los Angeles County government.

E-Marketplaces: Virtual Organizational Markets

e-marketplaces
Online trading communities that bring together buyers and supplier organizations.

A significant development in organizational buying has been the creation of online trading communities, called **e-marketplaces**, that bring together buyers and supplier organizations. These online communities go by a variety of names, including *B2B exchanges* and *e-hubs*, and make possible the real-time exchange of information, money, products, and services.

E-marketplaces can be independent trading communities or private exchanges. Independent e-marketplaces act as a neutral third party and provide an Internet

Marketing Matters

eBay Means Business for Entrepreneurs

San Jose, California–based eBay Inc. is a true Internet phenomenon. By any measure, it is the predominant person-to-person trading community in the world. But there is more.

eBay offers a trading platform for millions of small businesses in the United States and even greater numbers around the world.

The eBay trading platform has proven to be a boon for small businesses. According to an eBay-commissioned survey conducted by ACNielsen, 82 percent of small businesses using eBay report that it has helped their business grow and expand, 78 percent say it has helped their business grow and expand, 78 percent say it has helped to reduce their costs, and 79 percent say it has helped their business become more profitable.

In addition, eBay promotes entrepreneurship. According to a spokesperson from the American Enterprise Institute for Public Policy Research, "The potential for entrepreneurs to realize success through eBay is significant."

technology trading platform and a centralized market that enable exchanges between buyers and sellers. They charge a fee for their service and exist in settings that have one or more of the following features: (1) thousands of geographically dispersed buyers and sellers, (2) volatile prices caused by demand and supply fluctuations, (3) time sensitivity due to perishable offerings and changing technologies, and (4) easily comparable offerings between a variety of sellers.

Examples of independent e-marketplaces include PlasticsNet (plastics), Hospital Network.com (health care supplies and equipment), and TextileWeb (garment and apparel products). Small business buyers and sellers, in particular, benefit from independent e-marketplaces. These e-marketplaces offer them an economical way to expand their customer base and reduce the cost of products and services. For example, eBay provides an electronic platform for entrepreneurs and the small business market in the United States and other countries. Read the Marketing Matters box to learn more about how eBay promotes entrepreneurship.[19]

Large companies tend to favor private exchanges that link them with their network of qualified suppliers and customers. Private exchanges focus on streamlining a company's purchase transactions with its suppliers and customers. Like independent e-marketplaces, they provide a technology trading platform and central market for buyer–seller interactions. They are not a neutral third party, however, but represent the interests of their owners. For example, NeoGrid is an international business-to-business private exchange. It connects more than 250 retail customers with 80,000 suppliers. Its members include Best Buy, Campbell Soup, Costco, RadioShack, Safeway, Target, Tesco, and Walgreens. The Global Healthcare Exchange engages in the buying and selling of health care products for over 4,000 hospitals and more than 400 health care suppliers, such as Abbott Laboratories, GE Medical Systems, Johnson & Johnson, Medtronic USA, and McKesson Corporation in North America.

Online Auctions in Organizational Markets

Online auctions have grown in popularity among organizational buyers and business marketers. Many e-marketplaces offer this service. Two general types of auctions are common: (1) a traditional auction and (2) a reverse auction.[20] Figure 5–6 on the next page shows how buyer and seller participants and price behavior differ by type of auction. Let's look at each auction type more closely to understand the implications of each for buyers and sellers.

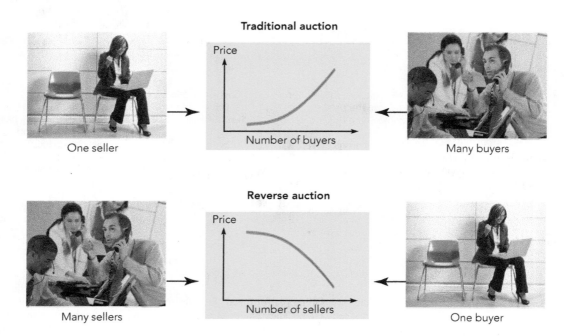

FIGURE 5–6
Buyer and seller participants and price behavior differ by type of online auction. As an organizational buyer, would you prefer to participate in a traditional auction or a reverse auction?

traditional auction
Occurs when a seller puts an item up for sale and would-be buyers bid in competition with each other.

reverse auction
Occurs when a buyer communicates a need for something and would-be suppliers bid in competition with each other.

In a **traditional auction** a seller puts an item up for sale and would-be buyers are invited to bid in competition with each other. As more would-be buyers become involved, there is an upward pressure on bid prices. Why? Bidding is sequential. Prospective buyers observe the bids of others and decide whether or not to increase the bid price. The auction ends when a single bidder remains and "wins" the item with its highest price. Traditional auctions are often used to dispose of excess merchandise. For example, Dell Inc. sells surplus, refurbished, or closeout computer merchandise at its www.dellauction.com website.

A reverse auction works in the opposite direction from a traditional auction. In a **reverse auction**, a buyer communicates a need for a product or service and would-be suppliers are invited to bid in competition with each other. As more would-be suppliers become involved, there is a downward pressure on bid prices for the buyer's business. Why? Like traditional auctions, bidding is sequential and prospective suppliers observe the bids of others and decide whether or not to decrease the bid price. The auction ends when a single bidder remains and "wins" the business with its lowest price. Reverse auctions benefit organizational buyers by reducing the cost of their purchases. As an example, United Technologies Corp. estimates that it has saved $600 million on the purchase of $6 billion in supplies using online reverse auctions.[21]

Clearly, buyers welcome the lower prices generated by reverse auctions. Suppliers often favor reverse auctions because they give them a chance to capture business that they might not have otherwise had, perhaps because of a long-standing purchase relationship between the buyer and another supplier. On the other hand, suppliers say reverse auctions put too much emphasis on prices, discourage consideration of other important buying criteria, and may threaten supply partnership opportunities.[22]

learning review

5-5. What are e-marketplaces?

5-6. In general, which type of online auction creates upward pressure on bid prices and which type creates downward pressure on bid prices?

LEARNING OBJECTIVES REVIEW

LO 5-1 *Distinguish among industrial, reseller, and government organizational markets.*

There are three different organizational markets: industrial, reseller, and government. Industrial firms in some way reprocess a product or service they buy before selling it to the next buyer. Resellers—wholesalers and retailers—buy physical products and resell them again without any reprocessing. Government agencies, at the federal, state, and local levels, buy goods and services for the constituents they serve. The North American Industry Classification System (NAICS) provides common industry definitions for Canada, Mexico, and the United States, which facilitates the measurement of economic activity for these three organizational markets.

LO 5-2 *Describe the key characteristics of organizational buying that make it different from consumer buying.*

Seven major characteristics of organizational buying make it different from consumer buying. These include demand characteristics, the size of the order or purchase, the number of potential buyers, buying objectives, buying criteria, buyer–seller relationships and supply partnerships, and multiple buying influences within organizations. The organizational buying process itself is more formalized, more individuals are involved, supplier capability is more important, and the postpurchase evaluation behavior often includes performance of the supplier and the item purchased. Figure 5–4 details how the purchase decision process differs between a consumer and an organization.

LO 5-3 *Explain how buying centers and buying situations influence organizational purchasing.*

Buying centers and buying situations have an important influence on organizational purchasing. A buying center consists of a group of individuals who share common goals, risks, and knowledge important to a purchase decision. A buyer or purchasing manager is almost always a member of a buying center. However, other individuals may affect organizational purchasing due to their unique roles in a purchase decision. Five specific roles that a person may play in a buying center include users, influencers, buyers, deciders, and gatekeepers. The specific buying situation will influence the number of people and the different roles played in a buying center. For a routine reorder of an item—a straight rebuy situation—a purchasing manager or buyer will typically act alone in making a purchasing decision. When an organization is a first-time purchaser of a product or service—a new buy situation—a buying center is enlarged and all five roles in a buying center often emerge. A modified rebuy situation lies between these two extremes. Figure 5–5 offers additional insights into how buying centers and buying situations influence organizational purchasing.

LO 5-4 *Recognize the importance and nature of online buying in industrial, reseller, and government organizational markets.*

Organizations dwarf consumers in terms of online transactions made and purchase volume. Online buying in organizational markets is popular for three reasons. First, organizational buyers depend on timely supplier information that describes product availability, technical specifications, application uses, price, and delivery schedules. This information can be conveyed quickly via Internet technology. Second, this technology substantially reduces buyer order processing costs. Third, business marketers have found that Internet technology can reduce marketing costs, particularly sales and advertising expense, and broaden their customer base. Two developments in online buying have been the creation of e-marketplaces and online auctions. E-marketplaces provide a technology trading platform and a centralized market for buyer–seller transactions and make possible the real-time exchange of information, money, products, and services. These e-marketplaces can be independent trading communities, such as PlasticsNet, or private exchanges, such as the Global Healthcare Exchange. Online traditional and reverse auctions represent a second major development. With traditional auctions, the highest-priced bidder "wins." Conversely, the lowest-priced bidder "wins" with reverse auctions.

LEARNING REVIEW ANSWERS

5-1   What are the three main types of organizational buyers?
Answer: (1) industrial firms, which in some way reprocess a product or service they buy before selling it again to the next buyer; (2) resellers, which are wholesalers and retailers that buy physical products and resell them again without any reprocessing; and (3) government units, which are the federal, state, and local agencies that buy products and services for the constituents they serve.

5-2   What is the North American Industry Classification System (NAICS)?
Answer: The NAICS provides common industry definitions for Canada, Mexico, and the United States, which makes it easier to measure economic activity in the three member countries of the North American Free Trade Agreement (NAFTA).

5-3   What one department is almost always represented by a person in the buying center?
Answer: purchasing department

5-4   What are the three types of buying situations or buy classes?
Answer: (1) new buy—the organization is a first-time buyer of the product or service; (2) straight rebuy—the organization reorders an existing product or service from a list of acceptable suppliers; and (3) modified rebuy—an organization's buying center changes the product's specifications, price, delivery schedule, or supplier.

5-5   What are e-marketplaces?
Answer: E-marketplaces are online trading communities that bring together buyers and supplier organizations to make possible the real-time exchange of information, money, products, and services.

5-6   In general, which type of online auction creates upward pressure on bid prices and which type creates downward pressure on bid prices?
Answer: traditional auction; reverse auction

FOCUSING ON KEY TERMS

business marketing p. 116
buy classes p. 125
buying center p. 123
derived demand p. 119

e-marketplaces p. 126
North American Industry
   Classification System
   (NAICS) p. 117

organizational buyers p. 116
organizational buying behavior p. 123
reverse auction p. 128
traditional auction p. 128

APPLYING MARKETING KNOWLEDGE

1 Describe the major differences among industrial firms, resellers, and government units in the United States.

2 List and discuss the key characteristics of organizational buying that make it different from consumer buying.

3 What is a buying center? Describe the roles assumed by people in a buying center and what useful questions should be raised to guide any analysis of the structure and behavior of a buying center.

4 A firm that is marketing multimillion-dollar wastewater treatment systems to cities has been unable to sell a new type of system. This setback has occurred even though the firm's systems are cheaper than competitive systems and meet U.S. Environmental Protection Agency (EPA) specifications. To date, the firm's marketing efforts have been directed to city purchasing departments and the various state EPAs to get on approved bidders' lists. Talks with city-employed personnel have indicated that the new system is very different from current systems and therefore city sanitary and sewer department engineers, directors of these two departments, and city council members are unfamiliar with the workings of the system. Consulting engineers, hired by cities to work on the engineering and design features of these systems and paid on a percentage of system cost, are also reluctant to favor the new system. (*a*) What roles do the various individuals play in the purchase process for a wastewater treatment system? (*b*) How could the firm improve the marketing effort behind its new system?

BUILDING YOUR MARKETING PLAN

Your marketing plan may need an estimate of the size of the market potential or industry potential (see Chapter 8) for a particular product market in which you compete. Use these steps:

1 Define the product market precisely, such as ice cream.

2 Visit the NAICS website at www.census.gov.

3 Click "NAICS" and enter a keyword that describes your product market (e.g., ice cream).

4 Follow the instructions to find the specific NAICS code for your product market and the economic census data that detail the dollar sales and provide the estimate of market or industry potential.

VIDEO CASE 5   Trek: Building Better Bikes through Organizational Buying

Video 5-3
Trek Video Case
kerin.tv/cr6e/v5-3

"Let me tell you a little bit about the history of Trek," says Mark Joslyn, vice president of human resources at Trek Bicycle Corporation. "It's a fantastic story," he continues proudly, "It's a story about a business that started in response to a market opportunity." That opportunity was to build bicycles with the highest-quality frames. In fact, Trek's mission was simple: "Build the best bikes in the world." To do this Trek needed to find the best raw materials from the best vendors. Michael Leighton, a Trek product manager, explains, "Our relationship with our vendors is incredibly important, and one of our recipes for success!"

THE COMPANY

Trek Bicycle was founded in 1976 by Richard Burke and Bevill Hogg. With just five employees they began manufacturing bicycles in a Wisconsin barn. From the beginning they targeted the high-quality, prestige segment of the bicycle market, using only the best materials and components for their bicycles. The first year they manufactured 900 custom-made bicycles which sold quickly. Soon, Trek exceeded its manufacturing capacity. It built a new 26,000-square-foot factory and corporate headquarters to help meet growing demand.

Trek's focus on quality meant that it was very sensitive to the materials used to manufacture the bicycles. The first models, for example, used hand-brazed steel for the frames. Then, borrowing ideas from the aerospace industry, Trek soon began making frames out of bonded aluminum. Following on the success of its aluminum bicycles, Trek began manufacturing bicycles out of carbon fiber. The idea was to be "at the front of technology," explains Joslyn.

The company also expanded its product line. Its first bikes were designed to compete directly with Japanese and Italian bicycles and included road racing models. In 1983 Trek manufactured its first mountain bike. In 1990 Trek developed a new category of bicycle—called a multitrack—that combined the speed of road bikes with the ruggedness of mountain bikes. The company also began manufacturing children's bikes, tandem bikes, BMX bikes, and models used by police departments and the U.S. Secret Service. In addition, it added a line of cycling apparel called Trek Wear and cycling accessories such as helmets. Recently, Trek also undertook an Eco Design initiative to build bicycles and parts that are "green" in terms of the environmental impact of manufacturing them, how long they last, and how they can be recycled. To accommodate these production demands, Trek expanded its facilities two more times.

As Trek's popularity increased, it began to expand outside of the United States. For example, the company acquired a Swiss bicycle company called Villiger and the oldest bicycle company in Germany, Diamant. It also expanded into China, opening two stores and signing deals with 20 Chinese distributors.

Today, Trek is one of the leading manufacturers of bicycles and cycling products, with more than $800 million in sales and 2,000 employees. Trek's products are now marketed through 1,700 dealers in North America and wholly owned subsidiaries in seven countries and through distributors in 90 other countries. Its brands include Trek, Gary Fisher, and Bontrager. As a global company, Trek's mission has evolved also, and today the mission is to "help the world use the bicycle as a simple solution to complex problems." Trek employees believe that the bicycle is the most efficient form of human transportation and that it can combat climate change, ease urban congestion, and build human fitness. Their motto: "We believe in bikes." Mark Joslyn explains:

> In the world today we are faced with a number of challenges. We are faced with congestion, issues with mobility, issues with the environment, and quite frankly, issues with health. We believe that the bicycle is a simple solution to all of those things. We are clearly an alternative to other forms of transportation and that's evident in the way that people are embracing cycling not just for recreation but also for transportation. And more and more, particularly in the United States, we are seeing people move to the bike as a way to get around and get to the places they need to ultimately get their life done.

ORGANIZATIONAL BUYING AT TREK

Trek's success at accomplishing its mission is the result of many important business practices, including its organizational buying process. The process begins when managers specify types of materials such as carbon fiber, component parts such as wheels and shifters, and finishing materials such as paint and decals needed to produce a Trek product. In addition, they specify quality requirements, sizing standards, and likely delivery schedules. According to Leighton, once the requirements are known, the next step is to "go to our buying center and say 'can you help us find this piece?'"

The buying center is the group of individuals who are responsible for finding the best suppliers and vendors for the organization's purchases. At Trek the buying center consists of a purchasing manager, buyers who identify domestic and international sources of materials and components, and representatives from research and development, production, and quality control. The communication between the product managers and the buying center is important. "I work very closely with our buying centers to ensure that we're partnering with vendors who can supply reliable quality, and they are actually the ones who, with our quality control team, go in and say 'yes this vendor is building product to the quality that meets Trek's standards,' and they also negotiate the pricing. Our buying center domestically is a relatively small team of people and they are focused on specific components."

When potential suppliers are identified, they are evaluated on four criteria—quality, delivery capabilities, price, and environmental impact of their production process. This allows Trek to compare alternative suppliers and to select the best match for Trek and its customers. Once a business is selected as a Trek supplier, it is continuously evaluated on elements of the four criteria. For example, current suppliers might receive scores on the number of defects in a large quantity of supplies, whether just-in-time orders made their deadlines, if target prices were maintained, and if recycled packaging was used. At Trek the tool that is used to record information about potential and existing suppliers is called a "white paper." Michael Leighton describes how this works: "Our buying center is tasked with developing what we call white papers. It's a sheet that managers can look at that shows issues and benefits related to working with these people." Every effort is made to develop long-term relationships with suppliers so that they become partners with Trek. These partnerships mean that Trek's success also contributes to the partner's success.

Trek's product managers and the buying center are involved in three types of organizational purchases. First, new buys are purchases that are made for the first time. Second, modified rebuys involve changing some aspect of a previously ordered product. Finally, straight rebuys are reorders of existing products from the list of acceptable suppliers. Leighton offers examples of each type of purchase at Trek:

> So, [for] a new buy, we work with our buying centers to find new products, something we've never done before whether it's a new saddle with a new material or a new technology that goes into the frame that damps vibration or gives a better ride. Another case might be electric bikes—maybe we are putting a motor in a bike, that's a new thing, so our buying center will help us go find those vendors. A modified rebuy is basically a saddle with a little bit different material but we are sharing some components of it, so the existing components of the saddle [are the same] but the cover is new, so it's a little bit different, but it's just the evolution of the product. A straight rebuy is looking at our strategic vision for the component further on down the line where we are just buying the same component and the volume goes up. We look at how can we make this a better business; can we save some money or can we make it more worth our while to keep buying the same product rather than buying something new.

While each of the types of purchases may occur frequently at Trek, the criteria that are used to select or evaluate a vendor may vary by the type of purchase and the type of product, making the buying process a dynamic challenge for managers.

ECO BUYING AND THE FUTURE AT TREK

One of Trek's criteria for evaluating existing and potential vendors is their environmental impact. Joslyn says it well: "We evaluate our vendors on many criteria including, increasingly, the elements that we would consider to be the 'green' part" of their offering. For example, Trek recently selected a supplier that (1) owned a quarry for extracting material, (2) used its own manufacturing facilities, and (3) used natural gas instead of coal in its production process. This was appealing to Trek because it suggested that the supplier had a "thorough understanding" of the impact of the product on the environment from start to finish.

Trek's organizational buying reflects the growing importance of its "Eco" perspective. Its bikes are becoming "smarter" as it adds electric-assist components to help them become a practical transportation alternative. Its bikes are also becoming "greener" as more low-impact materials and components are used and as packaging size and weight are reduced. Trek is also addressing the issue of recycling by building the bikes to last longer, using its dealers to help recycle tires and tubes, and funding a nonprofit organization called Dream Bikes to teach youth to fix and repair donated bikes.

In addition to changing bikes and the way it makes them, Trek faces several other challenges as it strives to improve its organizational buying process. For example, the growing number of suppliers and vendors necessitates constant, coordinated, and real-time communication to ensure that all components are available when they are needed. In addition, changes in consumer interests and economic conditions mean that Trek must anticipate fluctuations in demand and make appropriate changes in order sizes and delivery dates. As Mark Joslyn explains, "Everything we do all the time can and should be improved. So the search for ideas inside of our business and outside of our business, always looking for ways that we can improve and bring new technology and new solutions to the marketplace, is just a core of who we are."

Questions

1 What is the role of the buying center at Trek? Who is likely to comprise the buying center in the decision to select a new supplier at Trek?

2 What selection criteria does Trek utilize when it selects a new supplier or evaluates an existing supplier?

3 How has Trek's interest in the environmental impact of its business influenced its organizational buying process?

4 Provide an example of each of the three buying situations—straight rebuy, modified rebuy, and new buy—at Trek.

Chapter Notes

1. Interview with Kim Nagele, JCPenney, February 1, 2013.
2. International Business Machines Form 10-K, for the period ending December 31, 2011, February 17, 2012.
3. Figures reported in this discussion are found in *Statistical Abstract of the United States: 2014*, 133rd ed. (Washington, DC: U.S. Census Bureau, 2014).
4. Personal correspondence with Lockheed Martin, April 15, 2014.
5. "2012 North American Industry Classification System," www.census .gov/eos/www/naics.
6. This list of characteristics and portions of the discussion in this section are based on F. Robert Dwyer and John F. Tanner, Jr., *Business Marketing*, 4th ed. (Burr Ridge, IL: McGraw-Hill/Irwin, 2009); and Michael D. Hutt and Thomas W. Speh, *Business Marketing Management: B2B*, 11th ed. (Mason, OH: South-Western, 2012).
7. "Siemens Receives Contract for High-Efficiency Power Plant in the United States," Siemens USA press release, July 18, 2012.
8. Hutt and Speh, *Business Marketing Management: B2B*.
9. *Global Machine Vision Market 2012–2016* (Ann Arbor: Automated Imaging Association, September 2013).
10. This example is found in Sandy D. Jap and Jakki J. Mohr, "Leveraging Internet Technologies in B2B Relationships," *California Management Review*, Summer 2002, pp. 24–38.
11. "IBM's 'Sequoia' Unseats Fujitsu; Tops the List as Fastest Supercomputer," www.washingtonpost.com, June 6, 2012.
12. "HP Finalizes $3 Billion Outsourcing Agreement to Manage Procter & Gamble's IT Infrastructure," Hewlett-Packard news release, May 6, 2003.
13. "About Us," www.milsco.com, downloaded January 25, 2014; and "Milsco Manufacturing: Easy Rider," *Industry Today*, February 2010, pp. 86–87.
14. Helen Walker and Wendy Phillips, "Sustainable Procurement: Emerging Issues," *International Journal of Procurement Management* 2, no. 1 (2009), pp. 41–61.
15. Thomas V. Bonoma, "Major Sales: Who Really Does the Buying?" *Harvard Business Review*, May–June 1982, pp. 11–19. Also see, Philip L. Dawes, Don Y. Lee, and Grahame R. Dowling, "Information Control and Influence in Emerging Buying Centers," *Journal of Marketing*, July 1998, pp. 55–68; and Thomas Tellefsen, "Antecedents and Consequences of Buying Center Leadership: An Emergent Perspective," *Journal of Business-to-Business Marketing* 13, no. 1 (2006), pp. 53–59.
16. These definitions are adapted from Frederick E. Webster, Jr., and Yoram Wind, *Organizational Buying Behavior* (Englewood Cliffs, NJ: Prentice Hall, 1972), p. 6.
17. Jeffrey E. Lewin and Naveen Donthu, "The Influence of Purchase Situation on Buying Center Structure and Involvement: A Select Meta-Analysis of Organizational Buying Behavior Research," *Journal of Business Research*, October 2005, 1381–90. Representative studies on the buy-class framework that document its usefulness include Erin Anderson, Wujin Chu, and Barton Weitz, "Industrial Purchasing: An Empirical Exploration of the Buy-Class Framework," *Journal of Marketing*, July 1987, pp. 71–86; and Thomas W. Leigh and Arno J. Ethans, "A Script-Theoretic Analysis of Industrial Purchasing Behavior," *Journal of Marketing*, Fall 1984, pp. 22–32. Studies not supporting the buy-class framework include Donald W. Jackson, Janet E. Keith, and Richard K. Burdick, "Purchasing Agents' Perceptions of Industrial Buying Center Influences: A Situational Approach," *Journal of Marketing*, Fall 1984, pp. 75–83; R. Vekatesh, Ajay Kohli, and Gerald Zaltman, "Influence Strategies in Buying Centers," *Journal of Marketing*, October 1995, pp. 61–72; Gary L. Lilien and Anthony Wong, "An Exploratory Investigation of the Structure of the Buying Center in the Metal Working Industry," *Journal of Marketing Research*, February 1984, pp. 1–11; and Wesley J. Johnston and Thomas V. Bonoma, "The Buying Center: Structure and Interaction Patterns," *Journal of Marketing*, Summer 1981, pp. 143–56.
18. This discussion is based on "W. W. Grainger Surpasses $3 Billion in e-Commerce Sales," www.InternetRetailer.com, January 24, 2014; "B2B, Take 2," *Business Week Online*, November 25, 2005; and Jennifer Reinhold, "What We Learned in the New Economy," *Fast Company*, March 4, 2004, pp. 56ff.
19. "Meet the eBay Millionaires," www.huffingtonpost.com, August 4, 2011; "Former eBay CEO Urges Action on Small Business," www .washingtonpost.com, June 11, 2008; "New Study Reveals 724,000 Americans Rely on eBay Sales for Income," eBay press release, July 21, 2005; Robyn Greenspan, "Net Drives Profits to Small Biz," www .clickz.com, downloaded March 25, 2006; and "eBay Realizes Success in Small-Biz Arena," *Marketing News*, May 1, 2004, p. 11.
20. This discussion is based on Robert J. Dolan and Youngme Moon, "Pricing and Market Making on the Internet," *Journal of Interactive Marketing*, Spring 2000, pp. 56–73; and Ajit Kambil and Eric van Heck, *Making Markets: How Firms Can Benefit from Online Auctions and Exchanges* (Boston: Harvard Business School Press, 2002).
21. Susan Avery, "Supply Management Is Core of Success at UTC," *Purchasing*, September 7, 2006, pp. 36–39.
22. Shawn P. Daley and Prithwiraz Nath, "Reverse Auctions for Relationship Marketers," *Industrial Marketing Management*, February 2005, pp. 157–66; and Sandy Jap, "The Impact of Online Reverse Auction Design on Buyer–Seller Relationships," *Journal of Marketing*, January 2007, pp. 146–59.

Trek: This case was written by Steven Hartley. Sources: "Trek Bicycle Corporation," Hoovers, 2011; "Alliance Data Signs Long-Term Extension Agreement with Trek Bicycle Corporation," *PR Newswire*, November 22, 2010; Lou Massante, "Trek Bicycle Buys Villiger, a Leader in the Swiss Market," *Bicycle Retailer & Industry News*, January 1, 2003, p. 10; "Trek Bicycle Corporation," Wikipedia, accessed September 4, 2011; and Trek website, http://www.trekbikes.com/us/en/company/believe, accessed September 4, 2011.

Credits

P. 115, Courtesy J.C. Penney Corporation, Inc. P. 117, Courtesy Lockheed Martin. P. 120, Used with permission Pitney Bowes Inc. P. 121, ©Keyence Corporation of America. P. 122, Lluis Gene/AFP/Getty Images. P. 123, Jewel Samad/AFP/Getty Images. P. 125, VEER Mark Adams/Photonica/Getty Images. P. 127, PR Newswire/AP Images. P. 128, Jim Esposito/blend Images/Getty Images. P. 128, Comstock Images/Getty Images. P. 128, Comstock Images/Getty Images. P. 128, Jim Esposito/blend Images/Getty Images. P. 131, AP Photo/Keystone/Jean-Christophe Bott.

6

Understanding and Reaching Global Consumers and Markets

LEARNING OBJECTIVES

After reading this chapter you should be able to:

 LO 6-1 Identify the major trends that have influenced world trade and global marketing.

 LO 6-2 Identify the environmental forces that shape global marketing efforts.

 LO 6-3 Name and describe the alternative approaches companies use to enter global markets.

 LO 6-4 Explain the distinction between standardization and customization when companies craft worldwide marketing programs.

BUILDING A BILLION DOLLAR BUSINESS IN INDIA THE DELL INC. WAY

Why did Dell Inc. embark on a bold global growth initiative in 2007? In the words of Steve Felice, former president of Dell Asia-Pacific and Japan, "Our success was going to be largely dependent on our ability to expand globally."

Dell's global initiative focused on emerging economies in Asia, Africa, and Latin America. Compared with mature economies in North America and Western Europe, emerging economies offered significant growth potential, according to Michael Dell, Dell's founder and chief executive officer. And Dell's global strategy has proven successful. India is a major growth market for Dell Inc. and posts annual sales over $1.5 billion. In 2014, Dell employed some 25,000 people in India, which represented about one-fourth of its global workforce.

Dell's global initiative was bold in its departure from prior product development practices. Prior to its global initiative, Dell designed products for global requirements and distributed the same product globally. The company now routinely designs low-cost notebook, tablet, laptop, and desktop personal computers for customers in China, India, and other emerging economies.

Dell's global initiative also required many changes in its signature direct sales, service, and distribution strategy. The company built its U.S. business with telephone- and Internet-based sales—without retailers. However, in emerging economies and India, customers prefer to see, touch, and use a personal computer before they buy. In response, Dell uses individual sales affiliates who reach out to customers in person and give them a firsthand product experience at their doorstep.

At the same time, Dell joined hands with Indian chain retailers such as Croma and eZone for a shop-in-a-shop counter for its products. Dell backs this hybrid retail model by offering extended onsite service (technicians who visit individuals' homes) in over 650 cities to both retail and small business customers.

Dell also opened Dell exclusive stores in 2008. According to a company spokesperson, "The exclusive Dell store is a step towards enhancing the overall purchase experience for consumers in India. We have rapidly increased our presence in the consumer market here with new products and by expanding our reach. With the launch of Dell exclusive stores, we offer our customers the touch and feel for Dell branded products within a unique shopping experience."

135

Each Dell exclusive store offers the advantages of Dell's direct purchasing model with the additional benefit of retail availability—allowing customers to browse, touch, and feel the product. Dell's approach makes it possible for customers to see the products on the retail shelves and then place an order for the preferred model with the choice to customize the looks and configuration of the unit. By 2014, Dell had 200 exclusive stores in India.

Dell's global initiative also involved a new advertising campaign, with Dell opting for real-life successful entrepreneurs in India to endorse its products. The "Take Your Own Path" advertising campaign has proven to be highly effective. Dell's success in India illustrates the importance of understanding global customers and reaching them by adapting to their specific needs and preferences.[1]

This chapter describes today's complex and dynamic global marketing environment. It begins with an overview of our borderless economic world. Attention is then focused on prominent cultural, economic, and political-regulatory factors that present both an opportunity and a challenge for global marketers. Four major global market entry strategies are then detailed, including the advantages and disadvantages of each. Finally, the task of designing, implementing, and evaluating worldwide marketing programs for companies such as Dell Inc. is described.

MARKETING IN A BORDERLESS ECONOMIC WORLD

LO 6-1 Identify the major trends that have influenced world trade and global marketing.

Global marketing has been and continues to be affected by a growing borderless economic world. Five trends have significantly influenced the landscape of global marketing:

Trend 1: Gradual decline of economic protectionism by individual countries.

Trend 2: Formal economic integration and free trade among nations.

Trend 3: Global competition among global companies for global customers.

Trend 4: Emergence of a networked global marketspace.

Trend 5: Growing prevalence of economic espionage.

Decline of Economic Protectionism

protectionism
The practice of shielding one or more industries within a country's economy from foreign competition through the use of tariffs or quotas.

tariff
A government tax on goods or services entering a country, primarily serving to raise prices on imports.

Protectionism is the practice of shielding one or more industries within a country's economy from foreign competition through the use of tariffs or quotas. The argument for protectionism is that it limits the outsourcing of jobs, protects a nation's political security, discourages economic dependency on other countries, and promotes development of domestic industries. Read the Making Responsible Decisions box and decide for yourself if protectionism has an ethical dimension.[2]

Tariffs and quotas discourage world trade, as depicted in Figure 6–1. **Tariffs**, which are a government tax on products or services entering a country, primarily serve to raise prices on imports. The average tariff on manufactured products in industrialized countries is 4 percent. However, wide differences exist across nations. For example, European Union countries have a 10 percent tariff on cars imported from Japan, which is about four times higher than the tariff imposed by the United States on Japanese cars.

The effect of tariffs on consumer prices is substantial. Consider U.S. rice exports to Japan. The U.S. Rice Millers' Association claims that if the Japanese rice market were opened to imports by lowering tariffs, lower prices would save Japanese consumers $6 billion annually, and the United States would gain a large share of the Japanese rice market. Tariffs imposed on bananas by European Union countries cost consumers $2 billion a year. U.S. consumers pay $5 billion annually for tariffs on imported shoes. Incidentally, 99 percent of shoes worn in the United States are imported.

FIGURE 6–1
How does protectionism affect world trade? Protectionism hinders world trade through tariff and quota policies of individual countries. Tariffs increase prices and quotas limit supply.

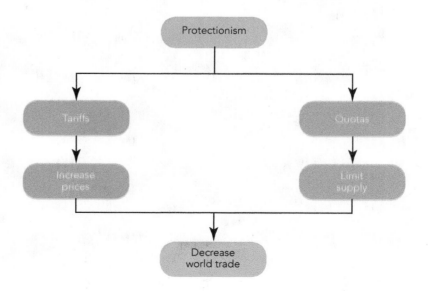

Making Responsible Decisions

Global Ethics and Global Economics— The Case of Protectionism

World trade benefits from free and fair trade among nations. Nevertheless, governments of many countries continue to use tariffs and quotas to protect their various domestic industries. Why? Protectionism earns profits for domestic producers and tariff revenue for the government. There is a cost, however. Protectionist policies cost Japanese consumers between $75 billion and $110 billion annually. U.S. consumers pay about $70 billion each year in higher prices because of tariffs and other protective restrictions.

Sugar and textile import quotas in the United States, automobile and banana import tariffs in European

countries, shoe and automobile tire import tariffs in the United States, beer import tariffs in Canada, and rice import tariffs in Japan protect domestic industries but also interfere with world trade for these products. Regional trade agreements, such as those found in the provisions of the European Union and the North American Free Trade Agreement, may also pose a situation whereby member nations can obtain preferential treatment in quotas and tariffs but nonmember nations cannot.

Protectionism, in its many forms, raises an interesting global ethical question. Is protectionism, no matter how applied, an ethical practice?

---

quota
A restriction placed on the amount of a product allowed to enter or leave a country.

A **quota** is a restriction placed on the amount of a product allowed to enter or leave a country. Quotas can be mandated or voluntary and may be legislated or negotiated by governments. Import quotas seek to guarantee domestic industries access to a certain percentage of their domestic market. For example, there is a limit on Chinese dairy products sold in India, and in Italy there is a quota on Japanese motorcycles. China has import quotas on corn, cotton, rice, and wheat.

The United States also imposes quotas. For instance, U.S. sugar import quotas have existed for more than 70 years and preserve about half of the U.S. sugar market for domestic producers. American consumers pay $3 billion annually in extra food costs because of this quota. U.S. quotas on textiles are estimated to add 50 percent to the wholesale price of clothing for American consumers—which, in turn, raises retail prices.

World Trade Organization
Institution that sets rules governing trade between its members through a panel of trade experts.

The major industrialized nations of the world formed the **World Trade Organization (WTO)** in 1995 to address an array of world trade issues.[3] There are 159 WTO member countries, including the United States, which account for more than 90 percent of world trade. The WTO is a permanent institution that sets rules governing trade between its members through panels of trade experts who decide on trade disputes between members and issue binding decisions. The WTO reviews more than 200 trade disputes annually.

Rise of Economic Integration

A number of countries with similar economic goals have formed transnational trade groups or signed trade agreements for the purpose of promoting free trade among member nations and enhancing their individual economies. Two of the best-known examples are the European Union (or simply EU) and the North American Free Trade Agreement (NAFTA). About 46 percent of all U.S. exports go to its free-trade partners.[4]

European Union The European Union consists of 28 member countries that have eliminated most barriers to the free flow of products, services, capital, and labor

FIGURE 6–2
The European Union in early 2015 consists of 28 countries with more than 500 million consumers.

European Union
www.europa.eu.int

across their borders (see Figure 6–2).[5] This single market houses more than 500 million consumers with a combined gross domestic product larger than that of the United States. In addition, 16 countries have adopted a common currency called the *euro*. Adoption of the euro has been a boon to electronic commerce in the EU by eliminating the need to continually monitor currency exchange rates.

The EU creates abundant marketing opportunities because firms do not need to market their products and services on a nation-by-nation basis. Rather, pan-European marketing strategies are possible due to greater uniformity in product and packaging standards; fewer regulatory restrictions on transportation, advertising, and promotion imposed by countries; and the removal of most tariffs that affect pricing practices. For example, Colgate-Palmolive Company now markets its Colgate toothpaste with one formula and package across EU countries at one price. Black & Decker—the maker of electrical hand tools, appliances, and other consumer products—now produces 8, not 20, motor sizes for the European market, resulting in production and marketing cost savings. These practices were previously impossible because of different government and trade regulations. Europeanwide distribution from fewer locations is also feasible given open borders. French tire maker Michelin closed 180 of its European distribution centers and now uses just 20 to serve all EU countries.

North American Free Trade Agreement The North American Free Trade Agreement (NAFTA) lifted many trade barriers between Canada, Mexico, and the United States and created a marketplace with more than 450 million consumers.

NAFTA has stimulated trade flows among member nations as well as cross-border retailing, manufacturing, and investment.[6] For example, NAFTA paved the way for Walmart to move to Mexico, Target to enter Canada, and Mexican supermarket giant Gigante to move into the United States. Whirlpool Corporation's Canadian subsidiary stopped making washing machines in Canada and moved that operation to Ohio. Whirlpool then shifted the production of kitchen ranges and compact dryers to Canada. Ford invested $60 million in its Mexico City manufacturing plant to produce smaller cars and light trucks for global sales.

In 2006, a comprehensive free trade agreement among Costa Rica, the Dominican Republic, El Salvador, Guatemala, Honduras, Nicaragua, and the United States extended many NAFTA benefits to Central American countries and the Dominican Republic. Called CAFTA-DR, this agreement is viewed as a step toward a 34-country Free Trade Area of the Americas for the Western Hemisphere.

A New Reality: Global Competition among Global Companies for Global Consumers

The emergence of a largely borderless economic world has created a new reality for marketers of all shapes and sizes. Today, world trade is driven by global competition among global companies for global consumers.

global competition
Exists when firms originate, produce, and market their products and services worldwide.

Global Competition **Global competition** exists when firms originate, produce, and market their products and services worldwide. The automobile, pharmaceutical, apparel, electronics, aerospace, and telecommunication fields represent well-known industries with sellers and buyers on every continent. Other industries that are increasingly global in scope include soft drinks, cosmetics, ready-to-eat cereals, snack chips, and retailing.

Global competition broadens the competitive landscape for marketers. The familiar "cola war" waged by Pepsi-Cola and Coca-Cola in the United States has been repeated around the world, including in India, China, and Argentina. Procter & Gamble's Pampers and Kimberly-Clark's Huggies have taken their disposable diaper rivalry from the United States to Western Europe. Boeing and Europe's Airbus vie for lucrative commercial aircraft contracts on virtually every continent.

Since opening its first international venture in Australia in 1971, Mary Kay, Inc., has expanded to more than 35 countries on five continents. This Korean ad features the company's CC Cream Sunscreen.

Mary Kay, Inc.
marykay.com

139

CHAPTER 6   Understanding and Reaching Global Consumers and Markets

Global Companies   Three types of companies populate and compete in the global marketplace: (1) international firms, (2) multinational firms, and (3) transnational firms.[7] All three employ people in different countries, and many have administrative, marketing, and manufacturing operations (often called *divisions* or *subsidiaries*) around the world. However, a firm's orientation toward and strategy for global markets and marketing defines the type of company it is or attempts to be.

An *international firm* engages in trade and marketing in different countries as an extension of the marketing strategy in its home country. Generally, these firms market their existing products and services in other countries the same way they do in their home country. Avon, for example, successfully distributes its product line through direct selling in Asia, Europe, and South America, employing virtually the same marketing strategy used in the United States.

A *multinational firm* views the world as consisting of unique parts and markets to each part differently. Multinationals use a **multidomestic marketing strategy**, which means that they have as many different product variations, brand names, and advertising programs as countries in which they do business.

For example, Lever Europe, a division of Unilever, markets its fabric softener known as Snuggle in the United States in 10 European countries under seven brand names, including Kuschelweich in Germany, Coccolino in Italy, and Mimosin in France. These products have different packages, different advertising programs, and occasionally different formulas. Procter & Gamble markets Mr. Clean, its popular multipurpose cleaner, in North America and Asia. But you won't necessarily find the Mr. Clean brand in other parts of the world. In many Latin American countries, Mr. Clean is Maestro Limpio. Mr. Clean is Mr. Proper in most parts of Europe, Africa, and the Middle East.

A *transnational firm* views the world as one market and emphasizes cultural similarities across countries or universal consumer needs and wants rather than differences. Transnational marketers employ a **global marketing strategy**—the practice of standardizing marketing activities when there are cultural similarities and adapting them when cultures differ. This approach benefits marketers by allowing them to realize economies of scale from their production and marketing activities.

Global marketing strategies are popular among many business-to-business marketers such as Caterpillar and Komatsu (heavy construction equipment) and Texas Instruments, Intel, and Hitachi (semiconductors). Consumer product marketers such as Timex, Seiko, and Swatch (watches), Coca-Cola and Pepsi-Cola (cola soft drinks), Mattel and LEGO (children's toys), Nike and Adidas (athletic shoes), Gillette (personal care products), L'Oréal and Shiseido (cosmetics), and McDonald's (quick-service restaurants) successfully execute this strategy.

Each of these companies markets a **global brand**—a brand marketed under the same name in multiple countries with similar and centrally coordinated marketing programs.[8] Global brands have the same product formulation or service concept, deliver the same benefits to consumers, and use consistent advertising across multiple countries and cultures. This isn't to say that global brands are not sometimes tailored to specific cultures or countries. However, adaptation is used only when necessary to better connect the brand to consumers in different markets.

Consider McDonald's.[9] This global marketer has adapted its proven formula of "food, fun, and families" across 100 countries on six continents. Although the Golden Arches and Ronald McDonald appear worldwide, McDonald's tailors other aspects of its marketing program. It serves beer in Germany, wine in France, and coconut, mango, and tropical mint shakes in Hong Kong. Hamburgers are made with different meat and spices in Japan, Thailand, India, and the Philippines. But McDonald's world-famous french fry is standardized. Its french fry in Beijing, China, tastes like the one in Paris, France, which tastes like the one in your hometown.

Global Consumers   Global competition among global companies often focuses on the identification and pursuit of global consumers, as described in the Marketing Matters box.[10] **Global consumers** consist of consumer groups living in many

multidomestic marketing strategy
A multinational firm's strategy of offering as many different product variations, brand names, and advertising programs as countries in which it does business.

global marketing strategy
The practice of standardizing marketing activities when there are cultural similarities and adapting them when cultures differ.

global brand
A brand marketed under the same name in multiple countries with similar and centrally coordinated marketing programs.

global consumers
Consumer groups living in many countries or regions of the world who have similar needs or seek similar benefits from products or services.

Marketing Matters

The Global Teenager—A Market of 2 Billion Voracious Consumers

The "global teenager" market consists of 2 billion 13- to 19-year-olds in Europe, North and South America, and industrialized nations of Asia and the Pacific Rim who have experienced intense exposure to television (MTV broadcasts in 169 countries in 28 languages), movies, travel, social media, and global advertising by companies such as Apple, Sony, Nike, and Coca-Cola. The similarities among teens across these countries are greater than their differences. For example, a global study of middle-class teenagers' rooms in 25 industrialized countries indicated it was difficult, if not impossible, to tell whether the rooms were in Los Angeles, Mexico City, Tokyo, Rio de Janeiro, Sydney, or Paris. Why? Teens spend $250 billion annually for a common gallery of products: Nintendo video games, Tommy Hilfiger apparel,

Levi's blue jeans, Nike and Adidas athletic shoes, Swatch watches, Apple iPhones, Benetton apparel, and Cover Girl cosmetics.

Teenagers around the world appreciate fashion and music, and they desire novelty and trendier designs and images. They also acknowledge an Americanization of fashion and culture based on another study of 6,500 teens in 26 countries. When asked what country had the most influence on their attitudes and purchase behavior, 54 percent of teens from the United States, 87 percent of those from Latin America, 80 percent of the Europeans, and 80 percent of those from Asia named the United States. This phenomenon has not gone unnoticed by parents. As one parent in India said, "Now the youngsters dress, talk, and eat like Americans."

141

countries or regions of the world who have similar needs or seek similar features and benefits from products or services. Evidence suggests the presence of a global middle-income class, a youth market, and an elite segment, each consuming or using a common assortment of products and services, regardless of geographic location.

A variety of companies have capitalized on the global consumer. Whirlpool, Sony, and IKEA have benefited from the growing global middle-income class desire for kitchen appliances, consumer electronics, and home furnishings, respectively. Levi Strauss, Nike, Adidas, Coca-Cola, and Apple have tapped the global youth market. DeBeers, Rolex, Chanel, Gucci, Rolls-Royce, and Sotheby's and Christie's, the world's largest fine art and antique auction houses, cater to the elite segment for luxury products worldwide.

Emergence of a Networked Global Marketspace

The use of Internet technology as a tool for exchanging products, services, and information on a global scale is the fourth trend affecting world trade. Over 3 billion businesses, educational institutions, government agencies, and households worldwide are expected to have Internet access by 2017. The broad reach of this technology attests to its potential for promoting world trade.

A networked global marketspace enables the exchange of products, services, and information from sellers *anywhere* to buyers *anywhere* at *any time* and at a lower cost. In particular, companies engaged in business-to-business marketing have spurred the growth of global electronic commerce.[11] Ninety percent of global electronic commerce revenue arises from business-to-business transactions among a dozen countries in North America, Western Europe, and the Asia/Pacific Rim region.

Marketers recognize that the networked global marketspace offers unprecedented access to prospective buyers on every continent. Companies that have successfully capitalized on this access manage multiple country and language websites that

Video 6-1
Nestlé Hungary Ad
kerin.tv/cr6e/v6-1

Sweden's IKEA is capitalizing on the home-improvement trend sweeping through China. The home-furnishings retailer is courting young Chinese consumers who are eagerly updating their housing with modern, colorful but inexpensive furniture. IKEA entered China in 1998. The company expects to have at least 18 stores open in China by 2015.

IKEA
www.ikea.com

economic espionage
The clandestine collection of trade secrets or proprietary information about competitors.

customize content and communicate with consumers in their native tongue. Nestlé, the world's largest packaged food manufacturer, coffee roaster, and chocolate maker, is a case in point. The company operates 65 individual country websites in more than 20 languages that span five continents.

Growing Prevalence of Economic Espionage

The borderless economic world also has a dark side—economic espionage.[12] **Economic espionage** is the clandestine collection of trade secrets or proprietary information about competitors. This practice is common in high-technology industries such as electronics, specialty chemicals, industrial equipment, aerospace, and pharmaceuticals, where technical know-how and trade secrets separate global industry leaders from followers.

It is estimated that economic espionage costs U.S. firms upwards of $250 billion a year in lost sales. The intelligence services of some 23 nations routinely target U.S. firms for information about research and development efforts, manufacturing and marketing plans, and customer lists. To counteract this threat, the *Economic Espionage Act (1996)* makes the theft of trade secrets by foreign entities a federal crime in the United States. This act prescribes prison sentences of up to 15 years and fines up to $500,000 for individuals. Agents of foreign governments found guilty of economic espionage face a 25-year prison sentence and a $10 million fine.

learning review

6-1. What is protectionism?

6-2. The North American Free Trade Agreement was designed to promote free trade among which countries?

6-3. What is the difference between a multidomestic marketing strategy and a global marketing strategy?

A GLOBAL ENVIRONMENTAL SCAN

LO 6-2 Identify the environmental forces that shape global marketing efforts.

Global companies conduct continuing environmental scans of the five sets of environmental factors described earlier in Chapter 3 in Figure 3–1 (social, economic, technological, competitive, and regulatory forces). This section focuses on three kinds of uncontrollable environmental variables—cultural, economic, and political-regulatory—that affect global marketing practices in strikingly different ways than those in domestic markets.

Cultural Diversity

cross-cultural analysis
The study of similarities and differences among consumers in two or more nations or societies.

Marketers must be sensitive to the cultural underpinnings of different societies if they are to initiate and consummate mutually beneficial exchange relationships with global consumers. A necessary step in this process is **cross-cultural analysis**, which involves the study of similarities and differences among consumers in two or more nations or societies.[13] A thorough cross-cultural analysis involves an understanding of and an appreciation for the values, customs, symbols, and language of other societies.

values
A society's personally or socially preferable modes of conduct or states of existence that tend to persist over time.

Values   A society's **values** represent personally or socially preferable modes of conduct or states of existence that tend to persist over time. Understanding and working with these aspects of a society are important factors in global marketing. For example,

You will have to visit India to sample McDonald's Maharaja Mac or the McAloo Tikki burger described in the text.

- McDonald's does not sell beef hamburgers in its restaurants in India because the cow is considered sacred by almost 85 percent of the population. Instead, McDonald's sells the Maharaja Mac: two all-chicken patties, special sauce, lettuce, cheese, pickles, onions on a sesame-seed bun. For the 40 percent of Indian consumers who eat no meat of any kind, McDonald's offers the McAloo Tikki burger, which features a spicy breaded potato patty, and the McPuff, a vegetable and cheese pastry.
- Germans have not been overly receptive to the use of credit cards such as Visa or MasterCard and installment debt to purchase products and services. Indeed, the German word for debt, *Schuld*, is the same as the German word for guilt.

Cultural values become apparent in the personal values of individuals that affect their attitudes and beliefs and the importance assigned to specific behaviors and attributes of products and services. These personal values affect consumption-specific values, such as the use of installment debt by Germans, and product-specific values, such as the importance assigned to credit card interest rates.

customs
Norms and expectations about the way people do things in a specific country.

Customs   **Customs** are what is considered normal and expected about the way people do things in a specific country. Clearly customs can vary significantly from country to country. Consider, for example, that in France, men wear more than twice the number of cosmetics than women do and that Japanese women give Japanese men chocolates on Valentine's Day.

Foreign Corrupt Practices Act (1977)
A law that makes it a crime for U.S. corporations to bribe an official of a foreign government or political party to obtain or retain business.

The custom of giving token business gifts is popular in many countries where they are expected and accepted. However, bribes, kickbacks, and payoffs offered to entice someone to commit an illegal or improper act on behalf of the giver for economic gain is considered corrupt in any culture.

The prevalence of bribery in global marketing has led to an agreement among the world's major exporting nations to make bribery of foreign government officials a criminal offense. This agreement is patterned after the **Foreign Corrupt Practices Act (1977)**, as amended by the *International Anti-Dumping and Fair Competition Act* (1998). These acts make it a crime for U.S. corporations to bribe an official of a foreign government or political party to obtain or retain business in a foreign country. For example, the German engineering company Siemens AG paid an $800 million fine for $1 billion in alleged bribes of government officials around the globe.[14]

CHAPTER 6   Understanding and Reaching Global Consumers and Markets

Cultural symbols evoke deep feelings. What cultural lesson did Coca-Cola executives learn when they used the Eiffel Tower and the Parthenon in a global advertising campaign? Read the text to find the answer.

cultural symbols
Things that represent ideas or concepts in a specific culture.

What does the Nestlé Kit Kat bar have to do with academic achievement in Japan? Read the text on the next page to find out.

Nestlé Company
www.nestle.com

Video 6-2
Nestlé Japan Ad
kerin.tv/cr6e/v6-2

Cultural Symbols   **Cultural symbols** are things that represent ideas and concepts in a specific culture. Symbols and symbolism play an important role in cross-cultural analysis because different cultures attach different meanings to things. So important is the role of symbols that a field of study, called *semiotics*, has emerged that examines the correspondence between symbols and their role in the assignment of meaning for people. By adroitly using cultural symbols, global marketers can tie positive symbolism to their products, services, and brands to enhance their attractiveness to consumers. However, improper use of symbols can spell disaster. A culturally sensitive global marketer will know that:[15]

- North Americans are superstitious about the number 13, and Japanese feel the same way about the number 4. *Shi*, the Japanese word for four, is also the word for death. Knowing this, Tiffany & Company sells its fine glassware and china in sets of five, not four, in Japan.
- "Thumbs-up" is a positive sign in the United States. However, in Russia and Poland, this gesture has an offensive meaning when the palm of the hand is shown, as AT&T learned. The company reversed the gesture depicted in ads, showing the back of the hand, not the palm.

Cultural symbols evoke deep feelings. Consider how executives at Coca-Cola Company's Italian office learned this lesson. In a series of advertisements directed at Italian vacationers, the Eiffel Tower, the Empire State Building, and the Tower of Pisa were turned into the familiar Coca-Cola bottle. However, when the white marble columns in the Parthenon that crowns the Acropolis in Athens were turned into Coca-Cola bottles, the Greeks were outraged. Greeks refer to the Acropolis as the "holy rock," and a government official said the Parthenon is an "international symbol of excellence" and that "whoever insults the Parthenon insults international culture." Coca-Cola apologized for the ad.[16]

Language   Global marketers should know not only the native tongues of countries in which they market their products and services but also the nuances and idioms of a language. Even though about 100 official languages exist in the world, anthropologists estimate that at least 3,000 different languages are spoken. There are 23 official languages spoken in the European Union, and Canada has two official languages (English and French). Seventeen major languages are spoken in India alone.

English, French, and Spanish are the principal languages used in global diplomacy and commerce. However, the best language to use to communicate with consumers is

The Mini is marketed in many countries using many languages, such as English and Italian. The Italian translation is "Stop Looking at My Rear."

back translation
Retranslating a word or phrase back into the original language using a different interpreter to catch errors.

their own, as any seasoned global marketer will attest to. Unintended meanings of brand names and messages have ranged from the absurd to the obscene:

- When the advertising agency responsible for launching Pert shampoo in Canada realized that the name means "lost" in French, it substituted the brand name Pret, which means "ready."
- The Vicks brand name common in the United States is German slang for sexual intimacy; therefore, Vicks is called Wicks in Germany.

Experienced global marketers use **back translation**, where a translated word or phrase is retranslated into the original language by a different interpreter to catch errors. For example, IBM's first Japanese translation of its "Solution for a small planet" advertising message yielded "Answers that make people smaller." The error was corrected. Nevertheless, unintended translations can produce favorable results. Consider Kit Kat bars marketed by Nestlé worldwide. Kit Kat is pronounced "kitto katsu" in Japanese, which roughly translates to "Surely win." Japanese teens eat Kit Kat bars for good luck, particularly when taking crucial school exams.[17]

Economic Considerations

Global marketing is also affected by economic considerations. Therefore, a scan of the global marketplace should include (1) an assessment of the economic infrastructure in these countries, (2) measurement of consumer income in different countries, and (3) recognition of a country's currency exchange rates.

Economic Infrastructure The *economic infrastructure*—a country's communications, transportation, financial, and distribution systems—is a critical consideration in determining whether to try to market to a country's consumers and organizations.

PepsiCo has made a huge financial investment in bottling and distribution facilities in China.

PepsiCo
pepsico.com

Parts of the infrastructure that North Americans or Western Europeans take for granted can be huge problems elsewhere—not only in developing nations but even in Eastern Europe, the Indian subcontinent, and China, where such an infrastructure is assumed to be in place. For example, PepsiCo has invested $1.5 billion in transportation and manufacturing systems in China and India since 2010.

The communication infrastructures in these countries also differ. This infrastructure includes telecommunication systems and networks in use, such as telephones, cable television, broadcast radio and television, computer, satellite, and wireless telephone. In general, the communication infrastructure in many developing countries is limited or antiquated compared with that of developed countries.

Even the financial and legal system can cause problems. Formal operating procedures among financial institutions and the notion of private property are still limited. As a consequence, it is estimated that two-thirds of the commercial transactions in Russia involve nonmonetary forms of payment. The legal red tape involved in obtaining titles to buildings and land for manufacturing, wholesaling, and retailing operations also has been a huge problem. Still, the Coca-Cola Company plans to invest $1 billion by 2015 for bottling facilities in Russia. Frito-Lay spent $60 million to build a plant outside Moscow to make Lay's potato chips.

Consumer Income and Purchasing Power   A global marketer selling consumer products must also consider what the average per capita or household income is among a country's consumers and how the income is distributed to determine a nation's purchasing power. Per capita income varies greatly between nations. Average yearly per capita income in EU countries is about $33,000 and is less than $500 in some developing countries such as Liberia. A country's income distribution is important because it gives a more reliable picture of a country's purchasing power. Generally, as the proportion of middle-income households in a country increases, the greater that nation's purchasing capability tends to be.

Seasoned global marketers recognize that people in developing countries often have government subsidies for food, housing, and health care that supplement their income. So people with seemingly low incomes are actually promising customers for a variety

Levi Strauss & Co. launched its Denizen brand jeans in China. Created for teens and young adults in emerging markets who cannot afford Levi-branded jeans, Denizen is now sold in North America.

Levi Strauss & Co.

www.levistrauss.com

Video 6-3
Denizen
kerin.tv/cr6e/v6-3

of products. For instance, a consumer in South Asia earning the equivalent of $250 per year can afford Gillette razors. When that consumer's income rises to $1,000, a Sony television becomes affordable, and a new Volkswagen or Nissan automobile can be bought with an annual income of $10,000. In developing countries of Eastern Europe, a $1,000 annual income makes a refrigerator affordable, and $2,000 brings an automatic washer within reach—good news for Whirlpool, the world's leading manufacturer and marketer of major home appliances.

Income growth in developing countries of Asia, Latin America, and Eastern Europe stimulates world trade. The number of consumers in these countries earning the equivalent of $10,000 per year is expected to surpass the number of consumers in the United States, Japan, and Western Europe combined in 2015. By one estimate, half of the world's population has now achieved "middle-class" status.[18] For this reason, developing countries represent a prominent marketing opportunity for global companies.

Currency Exchange Rates   Fluctuations in exchange rates among the world's currencies are of critical importance in global marketing. Such fluctuations affect everyone, from international tourists to global companies.

currency exchange rate
The price of one country's currency expressed in terms of another country's currency.

A **currency exchange rate** is the price of one country's currency expressed in terms of another country's currency, such as the U.S. dollar expressed in Japanese yen, euros, or Swiss francs. Failure to consider exchange rates when pricing products for global markets can have dire consequences. Mattel learned this lesson the hard way. The company was recently unable to sell its popular Holiday Barbie doll and accessories in some international markets because they were too expensive. Why? Barbie prices, expressed in U.S. dollars, were set without regard for how they would convert into foreign currencies and were too high for many buyers.[19]

Exchange rate fluctuations affect the sales and profits made by global companies. When foreign currencies can buy more U.S. dollars, for example, U.S. products are less expensive for the foreign customer. Short-term fluctuations, however, can have a significant effect on the profits of global companies.[20] Hewlett-Packard recently gained nearly a half million dollars of additional profit through exchange rate fluctuations in one year. On the other hand, Honda lost $408 million on its European operations alone in one year because of currency swings in the Japanese yen compared with the euro and British pound.

Political-Regulatory Climate

Assessing the political and regulatory climate for marketing in a country or region of the world involves not only identifying the current climate but also determining how long a favorable or unfavorable climate will last. An assessment of a country or regional political-regulatory climate includes an analysis of its political stability and trade regulations.

Political Stability   Trade among nations or regions depends on political stability. Billions of dollars in trade have been lost in the Middle East and Africa as a result of internal political strife, terrorism, and war. Losses such as these encourage careful selection of politically stable countries and regions of the world for trade.

Political stability in a country is affected by numerous factors, including a government's orientation toward foreign companies and trade with other countries. These factors combine to create a political climate that is favorable or unfavorable for marketing and financial investment in a country or region of the world. Marketing managers monitor political stability using a variety of measures and often track country risk ratings supplied by agencies such as the PRS Group, Inc. Visit the PRS Group, Inc., website at www.prsgroup.com to see political risk ratings for 140 countries. Expect to be surprised by the ranking of countries, including the United States.

Trade Regulations   Countries have a variety of rules that govern business practices within their borders. These rules often serve as trade barriers. For example, Japan has some 11,000 trade regulations. Japanese car safety rules effectively require all automobile replacement parts to be Japanese and not American or European; public health rules make it illegal to sell aspirin or cold medicine without a pharmacist present. The Malaysian government has advertising regulations stating that "advertisements must not project or promote an excessively aspirational lifestyle," Sweden outlaws all advertisements to children, and Saudi Arabia bans Mattel's Barbie dolls because they are a symbol of Western decadence.

---

learning review

6-4. Cross-cultural analysis involves the study of _____.

6-5. When foreign currencies can buy more U.S. dollars, are U.S. products more or less expensive for a foreign consumer?

COMPARING GLOBAL MARKET-ENTRY STRATEGIES

LO 6-3   Name and describe the alternative approaches companies use to enter global markets.

Once a company has decided to enter the global marketplace, it must select a means of market entry. Four general options exist: (1) exporting, (2) licensing, (3) joint venture, and (4) direct investment.[21] As Figure 6–3 demonstrates, the amount of financial commitment, risk, marketing control, and profit potential increases as the firm moves from exporting to direct investment.

Exporting

exporting
Producing goods in one country and selling them in another country.

Exporting is producing products in one country and selling them in another country. This entry option allows a company to make the least number of changes in terms of its product, its organization, and even its corporate goals. Host countries usually do not like this practice because it provides less local employment than under alternative means of entry.

Indirect exporting is when a firm sells its domestically produced products in a foreign country through an intermediary. It has the least amount of commitment and risk

Marketing Matters

Creative Cosmetics and Creative Export Marketing in Japan

How does a medium-sized U.S. cosmetics firm sell 1.5 million tubes of lipstick in Japan annually? Fran Wilson Creative Cosmetics can attribute its success to a top-quality product, effective advertising, and a novel export marketing program. The firm's Moodmatcher lip coloring comes in green, orange, silver, black, and six other hues that change to a shade of pink, coral, or red, depending on a woman's chemistry when it's applied.

The company does not sell to department stores. According to a company spokesperson, "Shiseido and Kanebo (two large Japanese cosmetics firms) keep all the other Japanese or import brands out of the major department stores." Rather, the company sells its Moodmatcher lipstick through a network of Japanese distributors that reach Japan's 40,000 beauty salons.

The result? The company, with its savvy Japanese distributors, accounted for 20 percent of the lipsticks exported annually to Japan by U.S. cosmetics companies.

but will probably return the least profit. Indirect exporting is ideal for a company that has no overseas contacts but wants to market abroad. The intermediary is often a distributer that has the marketing know-how and resources necessary for the effort to succeed. Fran Wilson Creative Cosmetics uses an indirect exporting approach to sell its products in Japan. Read the Marketing Matters box to find out how this innovative marketer and its Japanese distributors sell 20 percent of the lipsticks exported to Japan by U.S. cosmetics companies.[22]

FIGURE 6–3
A firm's profit potential and control over marketing activities increase as it moves from exporting to direct investment as a global market-entry strategy. But so does a firm's financial commitment and risk. Firms often engage in exporting, licensing, and joint ventures before pursuing a direct investment strategy.

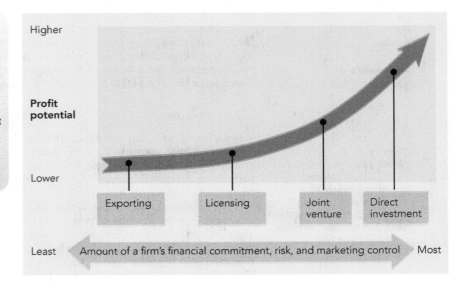

Direct exporting is when a firm sells its domestically produced products in a foreign country without intermediaries. Companies become involved in direct exporting when they believe their volume of sales will be sufficiently large and easy to obtain that they do not require intermediaries. For example, the exporter may be approached by foreign buyers that are willing to contract for a large volume of purchases. Direct exporting involves more risk than indirect exporting for the company but also opens the door to increased profits. The Boeing Company applies a direct exporting approach. Boeing is the world's largest aerospace company and the largest U.S. exporter.

Even though exporting is commonly employed by large firms, it is the prominent global market-entry strategy among small- and medium-sized companies. For example, 60 percent of U.S. firms exporting products have fewer than 500 employees. These firms account for about 34 percent of total U.S. merchandise exports.[23]

McDonald's uses franchising as a market-entry strategy, and about two-thirds of the company's sales come from non–U.S. operations. Note that the golden arches appear prominently—one aspect of its global brand promise.

McDonald's
www.mcdonalds.com

Licensing

Under licensing, a company offers the right to a trademark, patent, trade secret, or other similarly valued item of intellectual property in return for a royalty or a fee. The advantages to the company granting the license are low risk and a capital-free entry into a foreign country. The licensee gains information that allows it to start with a competitive advantage, and the foreign country gains employment by having the product manufactured locally. For instance, Yoplait yogurt is licensed from Sodima, a French cooperative, by General Mills for sales in the United States.

There are some serious drawbacks to this mode of entry, however. The licensor forgoes control of its product and reduces the potential profits gained from it. In addition, while the relationship lasts, the licensor may be creating its own competition. Some licensees are able to modify the product somehow and enter the market with product and marketing knowledge gained at the expense of the company that got them started. To offset this disadvantage, many companies strive to stay innovative so that the licensee remains dependent on them for improvements and successful operation. Finally, should the licensee prove to be a poor choice, the name or reputation of the company may be harmed.

A variation of licensing is *franchising*. Franchising is one of the fastest-growing market-entry strategies. Over 75,000 franchises of U.S. firms are located in countries throughout the world. Franchises include soft-drink, motel, retailing, fast-food, and car rental operations and a variety of business services. McDonald's is a premier global franchiser, with some 14,000 franchised units outside the United States.

Joint Venture

joint venture
When a foreign company and a local firm invest together to create a local business, sharing ownership, control, and the profits of the new company.

When a foreign company and a local firm invest together to create a local business, it is called a **joint venture**. These two companies share the ownership, control, and profits of the new company. For example, the Strauss Group has a joint venture with PepsiCo to market Frito-Lay's Cheetos, Ruffles, Doritos, and other snacks in Israel.[24]

The advantages of this option are twofold. First, one company may not have the necessary financial, physical, or managerial resources to enter a foreign market alone. The joint venture between Ericsson, a Swedish telecommunications firm, and CGCT, a French switch maker, enabled them together to beat out AT&T for a $100 million French contract. Ericsson's money and technology combined with CGCT's knowledge of the French market helped them to win the contract. Second, a government may require or strongly encourage a joint venture before it allows a foreign company to enter its market. For example, in China, international giants such as Procter & Gamble, Starbucks, and General Motors operate wholly or in part through joint ventures.

The disadvantages arise when the two companies disagree about policies or courses of action for their joint venture or when governmental bureaucracy bogs down the effort. For example, U.S. firms often prefer to reinvest earnings gained, whereas some foreign companies may want to spend those earnings. Or a U.S. firm may want to return profits earned to the United States, while the local firm or its government may oppose this—a problem faced by many potential joint ventures. The collapse of the joint venture between France's Group Danone and a local company in China is a case in point. The joint venture partners could not agree on the distribution of profits.[25]

Direct Investment

The biggest commitment a company can make when entering the global market is *direct investment*, which entails a domestic firm actually investing in and owning a foreign subsidiary or division. Examples of direct investment are Nissan's Smyrna, Tennessee, plant that produces pickup trucks and the Mercedes-Benz factory in Vance, Alabama, that makes the M-class sports utility vehicle. Many U.S.–based global companies also use this mode of entry. Reebok entered Russia by creating a subsidiary known as Reebok Russia.

For many companies, direct investment often follows one of the other three market-entry strategies.[26] For example, both FedEx and UPS entered China through joint ventures with Chinese companies. Each subsequently purchased the interests of its partner and converted the Chinese operations into a division.

The advantages to direct investment include cost savings, a better understanding of local market conditions, and fewer local restrictions. Firms entering foreign markets using direct investment believe that these advantages outweigh the financial commitments and risks involved. However, sometimes they don't. Tesco, the British supermarket giant, entered the United States in 2007 only to withdraw in 2012 after sizable operating losses and an investment of $1.6 billion.[27]

---

learning review

6-6. What mode of entry could a company follow if it has no previous experience in global marketing?

6-7. How does licensing differ from a joint venture?

CRAFTING A WORLDWIDE MARKETING PROGRAM

LO 6-4 Explain the distinction between standardization and customization when companies craft worldwide marketing programs.

The choice of a market-entry strategy is a necessary first step for a marketer when joining the community of global companies. The next step involves the challenging task of planning, implementing, and evaluating marketing programs worldwide.

Successful global marketers standardize global marketing programs whenever possible and customize them wherever necessary. The extent of standardization and customization is often rooted in a careful global environment scan supplemented with judgment based on experience and marketing research.

Product and Promotion Strategies

Global companies have five strategies for matching products and their promotion efforts to global markets. As Figure 6–4 on the next page shows, the strategies focus on whether a company extends or adapts its product and promotion message for consumers in different countries and cultures.

FIGURE 6–4

Five product and promotion strategies for global marketing exist based on whether a company extends or adapts its product and promotion message for consumers in different countries and cultures. Read the text to learn how different companies employ these strategies.

A product may be sold globally in one of three ways: (1) in the same form as in its home market, (2) with some adaptations, or (3) as a totally new product:[28]

1. *Product extension.* Selling virtually the same product in other countries is a product extension strategy. It works well for products such as Coca-Cola, Gillette razors, Sony consumer electronics, Harley-Davidson motorcycles, Nike apparel and shoes, and Nokia cell phones. As a general rule, product extension seems to work best when the consumer market target for the product is alike across countries and cultures—that is, consumers share the same desires, needs, and uses for the product.

2. *Product adaptation.* Changing a product in some way to make it more appropriate for consumer preferences or a country's climate is a product adaptation strategy. Wrigley's offers grapefruit, cucumber, and tea-flavored chewing gum in China. Frito-Lay produces and markets its potato chips in Russia, but don't expect them to taste like the chips eaten in North America. Russians prefer dairy, meat, and seafood-flavored potato chips. Gerber baby food comes in different varieties in different countries. Popular Gerber varieties outside the United States include vegetables and rabbit meat in Poland and freeze-dried sardines and rice in Japan. Maybelline's makeup is adapted to local skin types and weather across the globe, including an Asia-specific mascara that doesn't run during the rainy season.

3. *Product invention.* Alternatively, companies can invent totally new products designed to satisfy common needs across countries. Black & Decker did this with its Snake Light flexible flashlight. Created to address a global need for portable lighting, the product became a best seller in North America, Europe, Latin America, and Australia and is the most successful new product developed by Black & Decker. Similarly, Whirlpool developed a compact, automatic clothes washer specifically for households in developing countries with annual household incomes of $2,000. Called Ideale, the washer features bright colors because washers are often placed in home living areas, not hidden in laundry rooms (which don't exist in many homes in developing countries).

An identical promotion message is used for the product extension and product adaptation strategies around the world. Gillette uses the same global message for its men's toiletries: "Gillette, the Best a Man Can Get." Even though Exxon adapts its gasoline blends for different countries based on climate, the promotion message is unchanged: "Put a Tiger in Your Tank."

Global companies may also adapt their promotion message. For instance, the same product may be sold in many countries but advertised differently. As an example, L'Oréal, a French health and beauty products marketer, introduced its Golden Beauty brand of sun care products through its Helena Rubenstein subsidiary in Western Europe with a *communication adaptation strategy.* Recognizing that cultural and buying motive differences related to skin care and tanning exist, Golden Beauty advertising features dark tanning for northern Europeans, skin protection to avoid wrinkles among

Gillette delivers the same global message whenever possible, as shown in the Gillette for Women Venus ads from the United States, Mexico, and France.

The Gillette Company
www.gillette.com

Video 6-4
Nescafé China
kerin.tv/cr6e/v6-4

Latin Europeans, and beautiful skin for Europeans living along the Mediterranean Sea, even though the products are the same.

Other companies use a *dual adaptation strategy* by modifying both their products and promotion messages. Nestlé does this with Nescafé coffee. Nescafé is marketed using different coffee blends and promotional campaigns to match consumer preferences in different countries. For example, Nescafé, the world's largest brand of coffee, generally emphasizes the taste, aroma, and warmth of shared moments in its advertising around the world. However, Nescafé is advertised in Thailand as a way to relax from the pressures of daily life.

These examples illustrate the simple rule applied by global companies: Standardize product and promotion strategies whenever possible and customize them wherever necessary. This is the art of global marketing.[29]

Distribution Strategy

Distribution is of critical importance in global marketing. The availability and quality of retailers and wholesalers as well as transportation, communication, and warehousing facilities are often determined by a country's stage of economic development. Figure 6–5 outlines the channel through which a product manufactured in one country must travel to reach its destination in another country. The first step involves the seller; its headquarters is the starting point and is responsible for the successful distribution to the ultimate consumer.

The next step is the channel between two nations, moving the product from one country to another. Intermediaries that can handle this responsibility include resident buyers in a foreign country, independent merchant wholesalers who buy and sell the product, or agents who bring buyers and sellers together.

Once the product is in the foreign nation, that country's distribution channels take over. These channels can be very long or surprisingly short, depending on the product line. In Japan, fresh fish go through three intermediaries before getting to a retail outlet. Conversely, shoes only go through one intermediary. Recall that Dell has had to revise its direct-marketing channel that originally featured online and phone buying in India, as described in the chapter-opening example.

FIGURE 6–5
Channels of distribution in global marketing are often long and complex.

CHAPTER 6 Understanding and Reaching Global Consumers and Markets

Pricing Strategy

Global companies also face many challenges in determining a pricing strategy as part of their worldwide marketing effort. Individual countries, even those with free trade agreements, may impose considerable competitive, political, and legal constraints on the pricing latitude of global companies. For example, antitrust authorities in Germany limited Walmart from selling some items below cost to lure shoppers. Without this advantage, Walmart was unable to compete against German discount stores. This, and other factors, led Walmart to leave Germany following eight years without a profit.[30]

Pricing too low or too high can have dire consequences. When prices appear too low in one country, companies can be charged with dumping, a practice subject to severe penalties and fines. *Dumping* is when a firm sells a product in a foreign country below its domestic price or below its actual cost. This is often done to build a company's share of the market by pricing at a competitive level. Another reason is that the products being sold may be surplus or cannot be sold domestically and, therefore, are already a burden to the company. The firm may be glad to sell them at almost any price.

When companies price their products very high in some countries but competitively in others, they face a gray market problem. A *gray market*, also called *parallel importing*, is a situation where products are sold through unauthorized channels of distribution. A gray market comes about when individuals buy products in a lower-priced country from a manufacturer's authorized retailer, ship them to higher-priced countries, and then sell them below the manufacturer's suggested retail price through unauthorized retailers. Many well-known products have been sold through gray markets, including Seiko watches, Chanel perfume, and Mercedes-Benz cars. Parallel importing is legal in the United States. It is illegal in the European Union.

learning review

6-8. Products may be sold globally in three ways. What are they?

6-9. What is *dumping*?

LEARNING OBJECTIVES REVIEW

LO 6-1 *Identify the major trends that have influenced world trade and global marketing.*

Five major trends have influenced the landscape of global marketing in the past decade. First, there has been a gradual decline of economic protectionism by individual countries, leading to a reduction in tariffs and quotas. Second, there is growing economic integration and free trade among nations, reflected in the creation of the European Union and the North American Free Trade Agreement. Third, there exists global competition among global companies for global consumers, resulting in firms adopting global marketing strategies and promoting global brands. Fourth, a networked global marketspace has emerged using Internet technology as a tool for exchanging products, services, and information on a global scale. And finally, economic espionage has grown among countries and companies because technical know-how and trade secrets separate global industry leaders from followers.

LO 6-2 *Identify the environmental forces that shape global marketing efforts.*

Three major environmental forces shape global marketing efforts. First, there are cultural forces, including values, customs, cultural symbols, and language. Economic forces also shape global marketing efforts. These include a country's stage of economic development and economic infrastructure, consumer income and purchasing power, and currency exchange rates. Finally, political-regulatory forces in a country or region of the world create a favorable or unfavorable climate for global marketing efforts.

LO 6-3 *Name and describe the alternative approaches companies use to enter global markets.*

Companies have four alternative approaches for entering global markets. These are exporting, licensing, joint venture, and direct investment. Exporting involves producing products in one country and selling them in another country. Under licensing, a company offers the right to a trademark, patent, trade secret, or similarly valued item of intellectual property in return for a royalty or fee. In a joint venture, a foreign company and a local firm invest together to create a local business. Direct investment entails a domestic firm actually investing in and owning a foreign subsidiary or division.

LO 6-4 *Explain the distinction between standardization and customization when companies craft worldwide marketing programs.*

Companies distinguish between standardization and customization when crafting worldwide marketing programs.

Standardization means that all elements of the marketing program are the same across countries and cultures. Customization means that one or more elements of the marketing program are adapted to meet the needs or preferences of consumers in a particular country or culture. Global marketers apply a simple rule when crafting worldwide marketing programs: Standardize marketing programs whenever possible and customize them wherever necessary.

LEARNING REVIEW ANSWERS

6-1 What is protectionism?
Answer: Protectionism is the practice of shielding one or more industries within a country's economy from foreign competition through the use of tariffs or quotas.

6-2 The North American Free Trade Agreement was designed to promote free trade among which countries?
Answer: The United States, Canada, and Mexico

6-3 What is the difference between a multidomestic marketing strategy and a global marketing strategy?
Answer: Multinational firms view the world as consisting of unique markets. As a result, they use a multidomestic marketing strategy because they have as many different product variations, brand names, and advertising programs as countries in which they do business. Transnational firms view the world as one market. As a result, they use a global marketing strategy, which involves standardizing marketing activities when there are cultural similarities and adapting them it when cultures differ.

6-4 Cross-cultural analysis involves the study of _____.
Answer: similarities and differences among consumers in two or more nations or societies.

6-5 When foreign currencies can buy more U.S. dollars, are U.S. products more or less expensive for a foreign consumer?
Answer: less expensive

6-6 What mode of entry could a company follow if it has no previous experience in global marketing?
Answer: indirect exporting through intermediaries

6-7 How does licensing differ from a joint venture?
Answer: Under licensing, a company offers the right to a trademark, patent, trade secret, or other similarly valued item of intellectual property in return for a fee or royalty. In a joint venture, a foreign company and a local firm invest together to create a local business to produce some product or service. The two companies share ownership, control, and profits of the new entity.

6-8 Products may be sold globally in three ways. What are they?
Answer: Products can be sold: (1) in the same form as in their home market (product extension); (2) with some adaptations (product adaptation); and (3) as totally new products (product invention).

6-9 What is *dumping*?
Answer: *Dumping* is when a firm sells a product in a foreign country below its domestic price or below its actual cost to produce.

FOCUSING ON KEY TERMS

back translation p. 145
cross-cultural analysis p. 143
cultural symbols p. 144
currency exchange rate p. 147
customs p. 143
economic espionage p. 142
exporting p. 148

Foreign Corrupt Practices Act (1977) p. 143
global brand p. 140
global competition p. 139
global consumers p. 140
global marketing strategy p. 140
joint venture p. 150

multidomestic marketing strategy p. 140
protectionism p. 136
quota p. 137
tariffs p. 136
values p. 143
World Trade Organization (WTO) p. 137

APPLYING MARKETING KNOWLEDGE

1 Explain what is meant by this statement: "Quotas are a hidden tax on consumers, whereas tariffs are a more obvious one."

2 How successful would a television commercial in Japan be if it featured a husband surprising his wife in her dressing area on Valentine's Day with a small box of chocolates containing four candies? Explain.

3 As a novice in global marketing, which global market-entry strategy would you be likely to start with? Why? What other alternatives do you have for a global market entry?

4 Coca-Cola is sold worldwide. In some countries, Coca-Cola owns the bottling facilities; in others, it has signed contracts with licensees or relies on joint ventures. When selecting a licensee in each country, what factors should Coca-Cola consider?

BUILDING YOUR MARKETING PLAN

Does your marketing plan involve reaching global customers outside the United States? If the answer is no, read no further and do not include a global element in your plan.

If the answer is yes, try to identify the following:

1   What features of your product are especially important to potential customers?

2   In which countries do these potential customers live?

3   What special marketing issues are involved in trying to reach them?

Answers to these questions will help in developing more detailed marketing mix strategies described in later chapters.

VIDEO CASE 6   Mary Kay, Inc.: Building a Brand in India

Video 6-5
Mary Kay Video Case
kerin.tv/cr6e/v6-5

Sheryl Adkins-Green couldn't ask for a better assignment. As the newly appointed vice president of brand development at Mary Kay, Inc., she is responsible for development of the product portfolio around the world, including global initiatives and products specifically formulated for global markets. She is enthusiastic about her position, noting that, "There is tremendous opportunity for growth. Even in these economic times, women still want to pamper themselves, and to look good is to feel good."

Getting up to speed on her new company and her new position topped her short-term agenda. She was specifically interested in the company's efforts to date to build the Mary Kay brand in India.

THE MARY KAY WAY

Mary Kay Ash founded Mary Kay Cosmetics in 1963 with her life savings of $5,000 and the support of her 20-year-old son, Richard Rogers, who currently serves as executive chairman of Mary Kay, Inc. Mary Kay, Inc., is one of the largest direct sellers of skin care and color cosmetics in the world with more than $2.5 billion in annual sales. Mary Kay brand products are sold in more than 35 markets on five continents. The United States, China, Russia, and Mexico are the top four markets served by the company. The company's global independent sales force exceeds 2 million. About 65 percent of the company's independent sales representatives reside outside the United States.

Mary Kay Ash's founding principles were simple, time-tested, and remain a fundamental company business philosophy. She adopted the Golden Rule as her guiding principle, determining the best course of action in virtually any situation could be easily discerned by "doing unto others as you would have them do unto you." She also steadfastly believed that life's priorities should be kept in their proper order, which to her meant "God first, family second, and career third." Her work ethic,

approach to business, and success have resulted in numerous awards and recognitions including, but not limited to, the Horatio Alger American Citizen Award, recognition as one of "America's 25 Most Influential Women," and induction into the National Business Hall of Fame.

Mary Kay, Inc., engages in the development, manufacture, and packaging of skin care, makeup, spa and body, and fragrance products for men and women. It offers anti-aging, cleanser, moisturizer, lip and eye care, body care, and sun care products. Overall, the company produces more than 200 premium products in its state-of-the-art manufacturing facilities in Dallas, Texas, and Hangzhou, China. The company's approach to direct selling employs the "party plan," whereby independent sales representatives host parties to demonstrate or sell products to consumers.

GROWTH OPPORTUNITIES IN ASIA-PACIFIC MARKETS

Asia-Pacific markets represent major growth opportunities for Mary Kay, Inc. These markets for Mary Kay, Inc., include Australia, China, Hong Kong, India, Korea, Malaysia, New Zealand, the Philippines, Singapore, and Taiwan.

China accounts for the largest sales revenue outside the United States, representing about 25 percent of annual Mary Kay, Inc., worldwide sales. The company entered China in 1995 and currently has some 200,000 independent sales representatives or "beauty consultants" in that country.

Part of Mary Kay's success in China has been attributed to the company's message of female empowerment and femininity, which has resonated in China, a country where young women have few opportunities to start their own businesses. Speaking about the corporate philosophy at Mary Kay, Inc., KK Chua, President, Asia-Pacific, said, "Mary Kay's corporate objective is not only to create a market, selling skin care and cosmetics; it's all about enriching women's lives by helping women reach their full potential, find their inner beauty and discover how truly great they are." This view is echoed by Sheryl Adkins-Green, who notes that the

FIGURE 1
Social and economic statistics for India in 2007 and China in 1995.

	India 2007	China 1995
Population (million)	1,136	1,198
Population age distribution (0–24; 25–49; 50+)	52%, 33%, 15%	43%, 39%, 18%
Urban population	29.2%	29.0%
Population/square mile	990	332
Gross domestic product (U.S.$ billion)	3,113	728
Per capita income (U.S.$)	$950	$399
Direct selling sales percent of total cosmetics/skin care sales	3.3%	3.0%

Mary Kay brand has "transformational and aspirational" associations for users and beauty consultants alike.

Mary Kay, Inc., learned that adjustments to its product line and message for women were necessary in some Asia-Pacific markets. In China, for example, the order of life's priorities—"God first, family second, and career third"—has been modified to "Faith first, family second, and career third." Also, Chinese women aren't heavy users of makeup. Therefore, the featured products include skin cream, anti-aging cream, and whitening creams. As a generalization, whitening products are popular among women in China, India, Korea, and the Philippines, where lighter skin is associated with beauty, class, and privilege.

MARY KAY, INDIA

Mary Kay, Inc., senior management believed that India represented a growth opportunity for three reasons. First, the Indian upper and consuming classes were growing and were expected to total over 500 million individuals. Second, the population was overwhelmingly young and optimistic. This youthful population continues to push consumerism as the line between luxury and basic items continues to blur. Third, a growing number of working women have given a boost to sales of cosmetics, skin care, and fragrances in India's urban areas, where 70 percent of the country's middle-class women reside.

Senior management also believed that India's socioeconomic characteristics in 2007 were similar in many ways to China's in 1995, when the company entered that market (see Figure 1). The Mary Kay culture was viewed as a good fit with the Indian culture, which would benefit the company's venture into this market. For example, industry research has shown that continuing modernization of the country has led to changing aspirations. As a result, the need to be good looking, well-groomed, and stylish has taken on a newfound importance.

Mary Kay initiated operations in India in September 2007 with a full marketing launch in early 2008. The initial launch was in Delhi, the nation's capital and the second most populated metropolis in India, and Mumbai, the nation's most heavily populated metropolis. Delhi, with per capita income of U.S.

$1,420, and Mumbai, with per capita income of $2,850, were among the wealthiest metropolitan areas in India.

According to Rhonda Shasteen, chief marketing officer at Mary Kay, Inc., "For Mary Kay to be successful in India, the company had to build a brand, build a sales force, and build an effective supply chain to service the sales force."

Building a Brand

Mary Kay, Inc., executives believed that brand building in India needed to involve media advertising; literature describing the Mary Kay culture, the Mary Kay story, and the company's image; and educational material for Mary Kay independent sales representatives. In addition, Mary Kay, Inc., became the cosmetics partner of the Miss India Worldwide Pageant 2008. At this event, Mary Kay Miss Beautiful Skin 2008 was crowned.

Brand building in India also involved product mix and pricing. Four guidelines were followed:

1. Keep the offering simple and skin care focused for the new Indian sales force and for a new operation.
2. Open with accessibly priced basic skin care products in relation to the competition in order to establish Mary Kay product quality and value.
3. Avoid opening with products that would phase out shortly after launch.
4. Address the key product categories of Skin Care, Body Care, and Color based on current market information.

Brand pricing focused on offering accessibly priced basic skin care to the average middle-class Indian consumer between the ages of 25 and 54. This strategy, called "mass-tige pricing," resulted in product price points that were above mass but below prestige competitive product prices. Following an initial emphasis on offering high-quality, high-value products, Mary Kay introduced more technologically advanced products that commanded higher price points. For example, the company introduced the Mary Kay MelaCEP Whitening System, consisting of seven products, which was specifically formulated for Asian skin in March 2009. This system was ". . . priced on the lower price end of the prestige category with a great value for money equation," said Hina Nagarajan, country manager for Mary Kay India.

Building a Sales Force

According to Adkins-Green, "Mary Kay's most powerful marketing vehicle is the direct selling organization," which is a key component of the brand's marketing strategy. Mary Kay relied on its Global Leadership Development Program directors and National Sales directors and the Mary Kay Sales Education staff from the United States and Canada for the initial recruitment and training of independent sales representatives in India. New independent sales representatives received 2 to 3 days of intensive training and a starter kit that included not only products, but also information pertaining to product demonstrations, sales presentations, professional demeanor, the company's history and culture, and team building.

"Culture training is very important to Mary Kay (independent sales representatives) because they are going to be the messengers of Mary Kay," said Hina Nagarajan. "As a direct-selling company that offers products sold person-to-person, we recognize that there's a personal relationship between consultant and client with every sale," added Rhonda Shasteen. By late 2009, there were some 4,000 independent sales representatives in India present in some 200 cities mostly in the northern, western, and northeastern regions of the country.

Creating a Supply Chain

Mary Kay, India, imported products into India from China, Korea, and the United States. Products were shipped to regional distribution centers in Delhi and Mumbai, India, where Mary Kay Beauty Centers were located. Beauty Centers served as order pickup points for the independent sales representatives. Mary Kay beauty consultants purchased products from the company and, in turn, sold them to consumers.

LOOKING AHEAD

Mary Kay, Inc., plans to invest around $20 million in the next five years on product development, company infrastructure, and building its brand in India. "There is a tremendous opportunity for growth," says Sheryl Adkins-Green. India represents a particularly attractive opportunity. Developing the brand and brand portfolio and specifically formulating products for Indian consumers will require her attention to brand positioning and brand equity.

Questions

1   Is Mary Kay an international firm, a multinational firm, or a transnational firm based on its marketing strategy? Why?
2   What global market-entry strategy did Mary Kay use when it entered India?
3   Is Mary Kay a global brand? Why or why not?

Chapter Notes

1. "Dell India Plans to Open More Exclusive Brand Outlets in India," www.business-standard.com, December 13, 2013; "Dell's Next Big Agenda," www.crn.in, February 21, 2012; Dell India Opens Its Exclusive Store in Hyderabad, www.greatandhra.com, September 12, 2012; and "How Dell Conquered India," www.CNNMoney.com, February and 10, 2011.

2. Dennis R. Appleyard and Alfred J. Field, *International Economics,* 8th ed. (Burr Ridge, IL: McGraw-Hill/Irwin, 2013), Chapter 15; Tansa Mesa, "Africa and Carribbean Fear EU Latam Banana Tariff Cuts," *International Herald Tribune,* August 26, 2008, p. 8; Yuri Kageyama, "Selling Rice to Japan? U.S. Plans to Try," www.msnbc.com, March 7, 2004; "A Shoe Tariff with a Big Footprint," *The Wall Street Journal,* November 23, 2012, p. A13; and *Economic Report of the President* (Washington, DC: U.S. Government Printing Office, 2012).

3. This discussion is based on information provided by the World Trade Organization, www.wto.org, downloaded February 10, 2014.

4. "Time to Put Trade Above Politics," *Time,* March 7, 2014, p. 24.

5. This discussion on the European Union is based on information provided at www.europa.eu, downloaded March 5, 2014.

6. This discussion is based on "Probable Effect of Certain Modifications to the North American Free Trade Agreement Rules of Origin" (Washington, DC: U.S. International Trade Commission, 2006); and "Target Is Going Abroad to Canada," *The Wall Street Journal,* January 14, 2011, pp. B1, B2.

7. For an overview of different types of global companies and marketing strategies, see, for example, Masaaki Kotabe and Kristiaan Helsen, *Global Marketing Management,* 5th ed. (New York: Wiley, 2011), p. 221; Warren J. Keegan and Mark C. Green, *Global Marketing,* 4th ed. (Upper Saddle River, NJ: Prentice Hall, 2005); and Michael Czinkota and Ilkka A. Ronkainen, *International Marketing,* 10th ed. (Mason, OH: South-Western, 2013).

8. Johnny K. Johansson and Ilkka A. Ronkainen, "The Brand Challenge," *Marketing Management,* March–April 2004, pp. 54–55.

9. Kevin Lane Keller, *Strategic Brand Management,* 4th ed. (Upper Saddle River, NJ: Prentice Hall, 2013).

10. "Coca-Cola, Nike and Adidas Top Brands for Teens Globally, TRU Study Finds," www.teenresearch.com, March 2, 2009; "Global Habbo Youth Survey," marketinginsight@sulake.com, downloaded March 20, 2009; www.mtv.com/company, downloaded January 10, 2011; Bay Fong, "Spending Spree," *U.S. News & World Report,* May 1, 2006, pp. 42–50; and "Burgeoning Bourgeoisie," *The Economist,* February 14, 2009. Special report on the new middle classes.

11. "The Pocket World in Figures: 2014 Edition," *The Economist.*

12. "Industrial Espionage: Data Out the Door," *Financial Times,* February 1, 2011, p. 8; "FBI's New Campaign Targets Corporate Espionage," *The Wall Street Journal,* May 11, 2012, p. B4; and "The Staggering Cost of Economic Espionage Against the U.S.," www.thepochtimes.com, October 22, 2013.

13. For comprehensive references on cross-cultural aspects of marketing, see Paul A. Herbig, *Handbook of Cross-Cultural Marketing* (New York: Halworth Press, 1998); Jean Claude Usunier, *Marketing Across Cultures,* 4th ed. (London: Prentice Hall Europe, 2005); and Philip K. Cateora, Mary Gilly, and John L. Graham, *International Marketing,* 16th ed. (Burr Ridge, IL: McGraw-Hill/Irwin, 2013). Unless otherwise indicated, examples found in this section appear in these excellent sources.

14. "Bribery Law Dos and Don'ts," *The Wall Street Journal,* November 15, 2012, pp. B1, B2.

15. These examples appear in Del I. Hawkins and David L. Mothersbaugh, *Consumer Behavior,* 10th ed. (Burr Ridge, IL: McGraw-Hill/Irwin, 2010), Chapter 2.

16. "Greeks Protest Coke's Use of Parthenon," *Dallas Morning News,* August 17, 1992, p. D4.

17. "How Did Kit Kat Become King of Candy in Japan?" www.cnnmoney.com, February 2, 2012.

18. "Burgeoning Bourgeoisie," *The Economist.*

19. "Mattel Plans to Double Sales Abroad," *The Wall Street Journal,* February 11, 1998, pp. A3, A11.

20. These examples are found in Cateora, Gilly, and Graham, *International Marketing.*

21. For an extensive and recent examination of these market-entry options, see for example, Johnny K. Johansson, *Global Marketing: Foreign Entry, Local Marketing, and Global Management,* 5th ed. (Burr Ridge, IL: McGraw Hill/Irwin, 2008); A. Coskun Samli, *Entering & Succeeding in Emerging Countries: Marketing to the Forgotten Majority* (Mason, OH: South-Western, 2004); and Keegan and Green, *Global Marketing.*

22. Based on an interview with Pamela Viglielmo, Director of International Marketing, Fran Wilson Creative Cosmetics; and "Foreign Firms Think Their Way into Japan," www.successstories.com/nikkei, downloaded March 24, 2003.

23. *Small and Medium Sized Exporting Companies: Statistical Overview, 2010* (Washington, DC: International Trade Administration, April 16, 2012).

24. "About Us," www.strauss-group.com, downloaded March 15, 2011.

25. "Dannon Pulls Out of Disputed China Venture," *The Wall Street Journal,* October 1, 2009, p. B1.

26. "FedEx Expands Reach in China with Buyout of Joint Venture," *The Wall Street Journal,* January 25, 2006.

27. "After Losses at Grocery Stores, Tesco to Retreat from U.S. Operations," www.nytimes.com, December 5, 2012.

28. This discussion is based on Keller, *Strategic Brand Management,* pp. 709–10; "Gum Makers Cater to Chinese Tastes," *The Wall Street Journal,* February 26, 2014, p. B9; "Global Sales of Lay's Chips Top $10 Billion in '11," *Dallas Morning News,* March 12, 2012, pp. D1, 10D; "Machines for the Masses," *The Wall Street Journal,* December 9, 2003, pp. A19, A20; "The Color of Beauty," *Forbes,* November 22, 2000, pp. 170–76; "It's Goo, Goo, Goo, Goo Vibrations at the Gerber Lab," *The Wall Street Journal,* December 4, 1996, pp. A1, A6; Donald R. Graber, "How to Manage a Global Product Development Process," *Industrial Marketing Management,* November 1996, pp. 483–98; and Herbig, *Handbook of Cross-Cultural Marketing.*

29. Jagdish N. Sheth and Atul Parvatiyar, "The Antecedents and Consequences of Integrated Global Marketing," *International Marketing Review* 18, no. 1 (2001), pp. 16–29. Also see, D. Szymanski, S. Bharadwaj, and R. Varadarajan, "Standardization versus Adaptation of International Marketing Strategy: An Empirical Investigation," *Journal of Marketing,* October 1993, pp. 1–17.

30. "With Profits Elusive, Wal-Mart to Exit Germany," *The Wall Street Journal,* July 29, 2006, pp. A1, A6.

Mary Kay India: This case was prepared by Roger A. Kerin based on company interviews.

Credits

Targeting Marketing Opportunities

7

Marketing Research: From Customer Insights to Actions

LEARNING OBJECTIVES

After reading this chapter you should be able to:

 LO 7-1 Identify the reason for conducting marketing research.

 LO 7-2 Describe the five-step marketing research approach that leads to marketing actions.

 LO 7-3 Identify the two kinds of secondary data and give examples of each.

 LO 7-4 Describe the meanings of observational data and questionnaire data and give examples of each.

 LO 7-5 Explain how information technology and data mining lead to marketing actions.

 LO 7-6 Describe three approaches to developing a company's sales forecast.

REDUCING THE RISK OF A MOVIE'S FAILURE WITH TEST SCREENINGS AND TRACKING STUDIES

The Hunger Games, Star Trek, and *The Hobbit* are movies that rewarded their studios with huge profits.[1] Unfortunately, not every movie has such favorable results. So what can these studios do to try to reduce the costly risk that a movie will be a box-office flop?

What's in a Movie Name?

Fixing bad names for movies—like *Rope Burns*—can turn potential disasters into hugely successful blockbusters. Don't remember seeing this movie? Well, test screenings—a form of marketing research—on moviegoers like you resulted in a change in the title. *Rope Burns* became *Million Dollar Baby* because audiences didn't like the original name. The movie won the 2005 Academy Award for Best Picture and starred Hilary Swank as a woman boxer and Clint Eastwood as her trainer.

To reduce risks to the studio, filmmakers want movie titles that are concise, grab attention, capture the essence of the film, and have no legal restrictions—the same factors that make a good brand name.[2]

The Risks of Today's (and Tomorrow's) Blockbuster Movies

Bad titles, poor scripts, temperamental stars, costly special effects, and several blockbuster movies released at the same time are just a few of the nightmares studio executives face. They try to reduce their risks by developing appealing sequels, like *Iron Man 3* or *Transformers 4*. And you guessed it: *The Hunger Games* will have two more sequels in 2014 (*Mockingjay, Part 1*) and 2015 (*Mockingjay, Part 2*).

With a typical film costing over $100 million to produce and market,[3] studios also try to reduce their risks by:

- *Conducting test screenings.* In test screenings, 300 to 400 prospective moviegoers are recruited to attend a "sneak preview" of a film before its release.[4] After viewing the movie, the audience fills out an exhaustive survey to critique its title, plot, characters, music, and ending to identify improvements to make in the final edit.[5]

- *Using tracking studies.* Immediately before an upcoming film's release, studios will ask prospective moviegoers in the target audience three key questions: (1) Are you aware of the film? (2) Are you interested in seeing the film? and (3) Will you see the film this weekend?[6] Studios use these data to forecast the movie's opening weekend box office sales and, if necessary, run last-minute ads to promote the film.

Video 7-1
The Hunger Games Movie Trailer
kerin.tv/cr6e/v7-1

Converting Marketing Research Results into Actions

Director James Cameron even had to produce a short "mini" test screening of a 3D segment of *Avatar* to convince four Twentieth Century Fox executives to fund his movie. *Avatar* became #1 in all-time worldwide gross ticket sales.[7]

These examples show how marketing research leads to decisive marketing actions, the main topic of this chapter. Also, marketing research is often used to help a firm develop its sales forecasts, the final topic of this chapter.

THE ROLE OF MARKETING RESEARCH

LO 7-1 Identify the reason for conducting marketing research.

Let's (1) look at what marketing research is, (2) identify some difficulties with it, and (3) describe the five steps marketers use to conduct it.

What Is Marketing Research?

marketing research
The process of defining a marketing problem and opportunity, systematically collecting and analyzing information, and recommending actions.

Marketing research is the process of defining a marketing problem and opportunity, systematically collecting and analyzing information, and recommending actions.[8] Although imperfect, marketers conduct marketing research to reduce the risk of and thereby improve marketing decisions.

The Challenges in Doing Good Marketing Research

Whatever the marketing issue involved—whether discovering consumer tastes or setting the right price—good marketing research is challenging. For example:

- Suppose your firm is developing a new product never before seen by consumers. Will consumers really know whether they are likely to buy a product that they have never thought about before?
- Imagine if you, as a consumer, were asked about your personal hygiene habits. Even though you know the answers, will you reveal them? When personal or status questions are involved, will people give honest answers?
- Will consumers' actual purchase behavior match their stated interest or intentions? Will they buy the same brand they say they will?

Marketing research must overcome these difficulties and obtain the information needed so that marketers can assess what consumers want and will buy.

LO 7-2 Describe the five-step marketing research approach that leads to marketing actions.

Five-Step Marketing Research Approach

A *decision* is a conscious choice from among two or more alternatives. All of us make many such decisions daily. At work we choose from alternative ways to accomplish an assigned task. At college we choose from alternative courses. As consumers we choose from alternative brands. No magic formula guarantees correct decisions.

Managers and researchers have tried to improve the outcomes of decisions by using more formal, structured approaches to *decision making*, the act of consciously choosing from among alternatives. The systematic marketing research approach used to collect information to improve marketing decisions and actions described in this chapter uses five steps and is shown in Figure 7–1. Although the five-step approach described here focuses on marketing decisions, it provides a systematic checklist for making both business and personal decisions.

FIGURE 7–1
Five-step marketing research approach leading to marketing actions. Lessons learned from past research mistakes are fed back to improve each of the steps.

STEP 1: DEFINE THE PROBLEM

Every marketing problem faces its own research challenges. For example, the marketing strategy used by LEGO Group's toy designers in Denmark illustrates some key decisions involved in Step 1 of the five-step marketing research approach—defining the problem to help LEGO Group build better toys.

LEGO Group's definition of "toy" has changed dramatically in the last half century—far beyond the 600 billion LEGO Group bricks sold around the world. In 1998, LEGO Group introduced the MINDSTORMS® kit, a "toy" that integrates electronics, computers, and robots with LEGO Group bricks. The MINDSTORMS® kit appeals to a diverse market—from elementary school kids to world-class robotics experts. The latest MINDSTORMS® EV3 kits let users build 17 different robots and use "intelligent bricks" to program them. The kits can be found in homes, schools, universities, and industrial laboratories.[9]

A simplified look at the marketing research for the LEGO Group's MINDSTORMS® EV3—introduced in late 2013 at a price of $350—shows the two key elements in defining a problem: setting the research objectives and identifying possible marketing actions.

LEGO Group's MINDSTORMS® EV3 TRACK3R has an interchangeable bazooka and hammer—and can operate after only 20 minutes of assembly.

Set the Research Objectives

Research objectives are specific, measurable goals the decision maker, in this case a LEGO Group manager, seeks to achieve in conducting the marketing research. So in conducting research, marketers have to be clear on the purpose of the research—the one or more specific objectives that lead to marketing actions. For LEGO Group, let's assume the immediate research objective is to decide which of two new MINDSTORMS® designs should be selected for production and marketing.

Identify Possible Marketing Actions

measures of success
Criteria or standards used in evaluating proposed solutions to a problem.

Effective decision makers develop specific **measures of success**, which are criteria or standards used in evaluating proposed solutions to the problem. Different research outcomes, based on the measure of success, lead to different marketing actions.

So let us also assume that LEGO Group's past research shows that a team of two middle school students needs to be able to assemble a LEGO Group device and have it doing tricks within 20 minutes or they lose interest. LEGO Group can then measure if a team of two students can have a device up and elements of it working in 20 minutes, which becomes the measure of success.

To decide on a marketing action here, LEGO Group can then (1) select 10 two-person teams of middle school students, (2) let all 10 teams play with both LEGO Group designs at different times, and (3) measure how many teams have each of the devices assembled and working in 20 minutes. If all 10 teams can assemble Design B in 20 minutes but can only assemble three of Design A in that amount of time, LEGO Group would produce and market Design B.

Marketing researchers know that defining a problem is an incredibly difficult task. If the objectives are too broad, the problem may not be researchable. If they are too narrow, the value of the research results may be seriously lessened. This is why marketing researchers spend so much time defining a marketing problem precisely and writing a formal proposal that describes the research to be done.

STEP 2: DEVELOP THE RESEARCH PLAN

The second step in the marketing research process requires that the researcher (1) specify the constraints on the marketing research activity, (2) identify the data needed for marketing actions, and (3) determine how to collect the data.

163

CHAPTER 7 Marketing Research: From Customer Insights to Actions

Specify Constraints

constraints
Restrictions placed on potential solutions to a problem.

The **constraints** in a decision are the restrictions placed on potential solutions to a problem. Examples include the limitations on the time and money available to solve the problem.

What constraints might LEGO Group set in mid-2012 in developing the LEGO Group's MINDSTORMS® EV3, whose market launch is scheduled for late 2013? LEGO Group might establish the following constraints on its decision to select one of the two improved designs: The decision (1) must be made in five weeks (2) with a budget for 10 two-person teams of middle schoolers playing with the two MINDSTORMS® designs.

LEGO Group's MINDSTORMS® EV3RSTORM has infrared sensors that let it walk or skate.

Identify Data Needed for Marketing Actions

Effective marketing research studies focus on collecting data that will lead to effective marketing actions. In the MINDSTORMS® case, LEGO Group's marketers might want to know students' math skills, time spent playing video games, and so on. But that information, while nice to know, is largely irrelevant because the study should focus on collecting only those data that will help them choose between the two MINDSTORMS® designs.

Determine How to Collect Data

Determining how to collect useful marketing research data is often as important as actually collecting the data—Step 3 in the process, which is discussed later. Two key elements in collecting the data are (1) concepts and (2) methods.

Concepts   In marketing, *concepts* are ideas about products or services. To find out about consumer reactions to a potential new product, marketing researchers frequently develop a *new-product concept*, which is a picture or verbal description of a product or service the firm might offer for sale. For example, the LEGO Group designers might develop a new-product concept for an innovative MINDSTORMS® EV3 robot, like those shown, capable of walking or skating, perhaps by adding an infrared sensor.

Methods   *Methods* are the approaches that can be used to collect data to solve all or part of a problem. To collect data, the LEGO Group designers might use a combination of (1) observing the behavior of MINDSTORMS® users and (2) asking them questions about how to improve a design. Observing people and asking them questions—the two main data collection methods—are discussed in the section that follows.

How can you find and use the methods that other marketing researchers have found successful? Information on useful methods is available in tradebooks, textbooks, and handbooks that relate to marketing and marketing research. Some periodicals and technical journals, such as the *Journal of Marketing* and the *Journal of Marketing Research*, both published by the American Marketing Association, summarize methods and techniques to address marketing problems.

Special methods vital to marketing are (1) sampling and (2) statistical inference. For example, marketing researchers often use *sampling* by selecting a group of distributors, customers, or prospects, asking them questions, and treating their answers as typical of all those in whom they are interested. They may then use *statistical inference* to generalize the results from the sample to much larger groups of distributors, customers, or prospects to help decide on marketing actions.

learning review

7-1. What is marketing research?

7-2. What is the five-step marketing research approach?

7-3. What are constraints, as they apply to developing a research plan?

STEP 3: COLLECT RELEVANT INFORMATION

 LO 7-3 Identify the two kinds of secondary data and give examples of each.

Collecting enough relevant information to make an informed marketing decision sometimes simply means using your knowledge to decide quickly. At other times it entails collecting an enormous amount of information at great expense.

Technological advances enable today's companies to collect and interpret data stored in computers, smartphones, and the Internet with great sophistication. This is often termed *big data,* the art and science of amassing and combing through vast amounts of information for insights not possible on a smaller scale. The secondary and primary data in the examples below are being revolutionized by big data.[10]

Figure 7–2 shows how the different kinds of marketing information fit together. **Data**, the facts and figures related to the project, are divided into two main parts: secondary data and primary data. **Secondary data** are facts and figures that have already been recorded prior to the project at hand. As shown in Figure 7–2, secondary data are divided into two parts—internal and external secondary data—depending on whether the data come from inside or outside the organization. **Primary data** are facts and figures that are newly collected for the project. Figure 7–2 shows that primary data can be divided into observational data, questionnaire data, and other sources of data.

data
The facts and figures related to a project.

secondary data
Facts and figures that have already been recorded prior to the project at hand.

primary data
Facts and figures that are newly collected for a project.

Secondary Data: Internal

The internal records of a company generally offer the most easily accessible marketing information. These internal sources of secondary data may be divided into two related parts: (1) marketing inputs and (2) marketing outcomes.

Marketing input data relate to the effort expended to make sales. These range from sales and advertising budgets and expenditures to salespeople's call reports, which describe who was visited on sales calls and what was discussed.

Marketing outcome data relate to the results of the marketing efforts. These involve accounting records on shipments and include sales and repeat sales, often broken down by industry and geographic region. In addition, e-mails, phone calls, and letters from customers can reveal both complaints and what is working well.[11]

FIGURE 7–2
Types of marketing information. Researchers must choose carefully among these to get the best results, considering time and cost constraints.

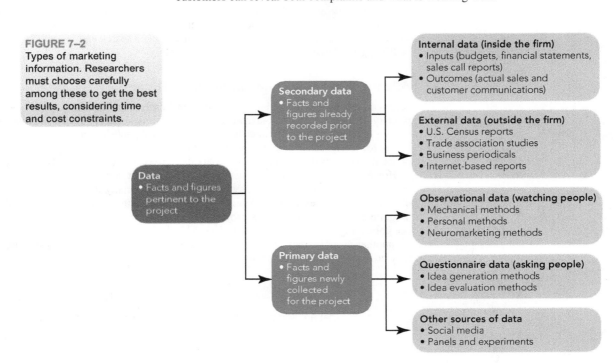

CHAPTER 7   Marketing Research: From Customer Insights to Actions

Scanner data at supermarket checkout counters provide valuable information for marketing decisions.

Video 7-2
Census 2010
kerin.tv/cr6e/v7-2

Secondary Data: External

Published data from outside the organization are external secondary data. The U.S. Census Bureau publishes a variety of useful reports. Best known is the Census 2010, which is the most recent count of the U.S. population that occurs every 10 years. This contains detailed information on American households, such as the number of people per household and the age, sex, race/ethnic background, income, occupation, and education of individuals within the household. Marketers use these data to identify characteristics and trends of ultimate consumers.

The Census Bureau also publishes the Economic Census, which is conducted every five years. These reports are vital to business firms selling products and services to organizations. The 2012 Economic Census contains data on the number and sales of establishments in the United States that produce a product or service based on each firm's geography (state, county, zip code, etc.), industry sector (manufacturing, retail trade, etc.), and North American Industry Classification System (NAICS) code.

Several market research companies pay households and businesses to record all their purchases using a paper or electronic diary. Such *syndicated panel* data answer questions that require consistent data collection over time, such as, "How many times did our customers buy our products this year compared to last year?" Examples of syndicated panels that provide a standard set of data on a regular basis are the Nielsen TV ratings and J.D. Power's automotive quality and customer satisfaction surveys.

Some data services provide comprehensive information on household demographics and lifestyle, product purchases, TV viewing behavior, and responses to coupon and free-sample promotions. Their advantage is that a single firm can collect, analyze, interrelate, and present all this information. For consumer product firms such as Procter & Gamble, sales data from various channels are critical to allocate scarce marketing resources. As a result, they use tracking services such as IRI's InfoScan to collect product sales and coupon/free-sample redemptions that have been scanned at the checkout counters of supermarket, drug, convenience, and mass merchandise retailers.

Finally, trade associations, universities, and business periodicals provide detailed data of value to market researchers and planners. These data are now available online via the Internet and can be identified and located using a search engine such as Google or Bing. The Marketing Matters box provides examples.

Advantages and Disadvantages of Secondary Data

A general rule among marketing people is to obtain secondary data first and then collect primary data. Two important advantages of secondary data are (1) the tremendous time savings because the data have already been collected and published or exist internally and (2) the low cost, such as free or inexpensive Census reports. Furthermore, a greater level of detail is often available through secondary data, especially U.S. Census Bureau data.

However, these advantages must be weighed against some significant disadvantages. First, the secondary data may be out of date, especially if they are U.S. Census data collected only every 5 or 10 years. Second, the definitions or categories might not be quite right for a researcher's project. For example, the age groupings or product categories might be wrong for the project. Also, because the data have been collected for another purpose, they may not be specific enough for the project. In such cases, it may be necessary to collect primary data.

learning review

7-4. What is the difference between secondary and primary data?

7-5. What are some advantages and disadvantages of secondary data?

Marketing Matters

technology

Online Databases and Internet Resources Useful to Marketers

Marketers today in search of secondary data can consult Internet databases. Indexes to articles in periodicals and statistical or financial data on markets, products, and organizations can be accessed either directly or via Internet search engines or portals through keyword searches. Statistical and financial data on markets, products, and organizations include:

- *The Wall Street Journal* (www.wsj.com), CNBC (www.cnbc.com), and *Fox Business* (www.foxbusiness.com), which provide up-to-the-minute business news and video clips about companies, industries, and trends that affect the marketing environment.
- The Census Bureau (www.census.gov) of the U.S. Department of Commerce provides information on U.S.

business, economic, and trade activity collected by the federal government.

Portals and search engines include:

- USA.gov (www.usa.gov), the portal to all U.S. government websites. Users can click on links to browse by topic or enter keywords for specific searches.
- Google (www.google.com), the most popular portal to the entire Internet. Users enter keywords for specific searches and then click on results of interest.

Some of these websites are accessible only if you or your educational institution have paid a subscription fee. Check with your institution's website.

167

Primary Data: Watching People

LO 7-4 Describe the meanings of observational data and questionnaire data and give examples of each.

observational data
Facts and figures obtained by watching, either mechanically or in person, how people behave.

Observing people and asking them questions are the two principal ways to collect new or primary data for a marketing study. Facts and figures obtained by watching, either mechanically or in person, how people actually behave is the way marketing researchers collect **observational data**. Observational data can be collected by mechanical (including electronic), personal, or neuromarketing methods.

Mechanical Methods   National TV ratings, such as those of Nielsen shown in Figure 7–3 on the next page, are an example of mechanical observational data collected by a "people meter." The device measures what channel and program is tuned in and who is watching. The people meter (1) is a box that is attached to TV sets, VCRs, DVRs (digital video recorders), cable boxes, and satellite dishes in about 20,000 households across the country;[12] (2) has a remote that operates the meter when a viewer begins and finishes watching a TV program; and (3) stores and then transmits the viewing information each night to Nielsen. Data are also collected on TV viewing using less sophisticated meters or TV diaries (a paper-pencil measurement system).

Nielsen recently introduced "cross-platform television ratings," which combine Nielsen's existing TV ratings with its new online ratings. These ratings include consumer viewing of TV programs seen not only on regular TV but also streamed online or wirelessly on PCs, smartphones, tablets, and video game consoles. This broader coverage is vital because research in late 2013 estimated that 18 percent of those viewing full-length TV shows are watching on tablets.[13]

What determines if *American Idol* stays on the air? For the importance of the TV "ratings game," see the text.

On the basis of all these observational data, Nielsen then calculates the rating and share of each TV program. With 115.6 million TV households in the United States, a single rating point equals 1 percent, or 1,156,000 TV households.[14] For TV viewing, a share point is the percentage of TV sets in use tuned to a particular program. Because TV and cable networks sell over $64 billion annually in advertising and set advertising rates to advertisers on the basis of those data, precision in the Nielsen data is critical.[15]

A change of 1 percentage point in a rating can mean gaining or losing millions of dollars in advertising

FIGURE 7–3
Nielsen Television Index
Ranking Report for network
TV prime-time households.
The difference of a few
share points in Nielsen TV
ratings affects the cost of a
TV ad on a show and even
whether the show remains
on the air.

Rank	Program	Network	No. of Viewers (millions)	Rating	Share
1	*NCIS*	CBS	13.5	11.8	20
2	*The Big Bang Theory*	CBS	11.0	9.6	17
3	*Dancing with the Stars*	ABC	10.1	8.8	14
4	*American Idol*—Thursday	FOX	9.9	8.7	14
5	*NCIS: Los Angeles*	CBS	9.7	8.5	13
6	*Dancing with the Stars*—Results	ABC	8.9	7.8	12
7	*American Idol*—Wednesday	FOX	8.6	7.5	13
8	*The Big Bang Theory*—Special	CBS	8.4	7.4	12
9	*Castle*	ABC	8.4	7.4	12
10	*Voice*	NBC	7.9	6.9	11

Source: Nielsen © 2013. The Nielsen Company Broadcast Ranking Report for the week ending May 19, 2013. Viewing estimates include live viewing and DVR playback on the same day, defined as 3 A.M. to 3 A.M. Rank is based on the number of U.S. viewers (in millions) from Nielsen's National People Meter Sample.

revenues because advertisers pay rates on the basis of the size of the audience for a TV program. So as shown by the green rows in Figure 7–3, we might expect to pay more for a 30-second TV ad on *NCIS* than one on *Castle*. Broadcast and cable networks may change the time slot or even cancel a TV program if its ratings are consistently poor and advertisers are unwilling to pay a rate based on a higher guaranteed rating.

But TV advertisers today have a special problem: With about three out of four TV viewers skipping ads with TiVo and DVRs, or channel surfing during commercials, how many people are actually seeing their TV ads? Now services such as Nielsen offer advertisers minute-by-minute measurement of how many viewers stay tuned during commercials. Recently, TiVo also expanded its service to allow TV advertisers to see how many and what kind of users are watching their commercials.[16] The viewership data in Figure 7–3 include not only live TV but also programs recorded on DVRs. With these more precise measures of who is likely to see a TV ad, buying TV ads is becoming more scientific.[17]

Is this *really* marketing research? A mystery shopper at work.

Personal Methods Observational data can take some strange twists. Jennifer Voitle, a laid-off investment bank employee with four advanced degrees, responded to an Internet ad and found a new career: *mystery shopper*. Companies pay mystery shoppers to check on the quality and pricing of their products and the integrity of and customer service provided by their employees. Jennifer gets paid to travel to exotic hotels, eat at restaurants, play golf, test-drive new cars, shop for clothes, and play arcade games. But her role posing as a customer gives her client unique marketing research information that can be obtained in no other way. Says Jennifer, "Can you believe they call this work?"[18]

Watching consumers in person or recording them are two other observational approaches. For example, the LEGO Group got the ideas for its new product lines by observing kids and their parents—its customers—*actually playing* with toys in the comfort of their own home. And Gillette records consumers brushing their teeth in their own bathrooms to see how they really brush—not just how they *say* they brush. The new-product result: Gillette's Oral-B CrossAction toothbrush.[19]

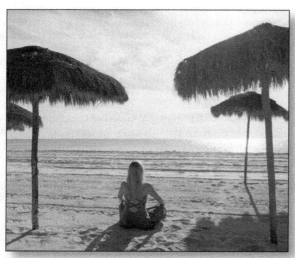

Ethnographic research is a specialized observational approach in which trained observers search for subtle behavioral and emotional reactions as consumers encounter products in their "natural use environment," such as in their home or car.[20] Recently, Kraft launched Deli Creations, which are sandwiches made with its Oscar Mayer meats, Kraft cheeses, and Grey Poupon mustard, after spending several months with consumers in their kitchens. Kraft found consumers wanted complete, ready-to-serve meals that are easy to prepare—and it had the products to create them.[21]

Personal observation is both useful and flexible, but it can be costly and unreliable when different observers report different conclusions when watching the same event. And while observation can reveal *what* people do, it cannot easily determine *why* they do it. So neuromarketing and questionnaires, our next topics, are often used.

"Neuromarketing" often uses a cap with dozens of sensors to measure brain waves to try to understand consumers better. For some changes made by Campbell Soup Company based on neuromarketing, see the text.

questionnaire data
Facts and figures obtained by asking people about their attitudes, awareness, intentions, and behaviors.

Neuromarketing Methods Global brand expert Martin Lindstrom believes that most traditional marketing research—like focus groups and surveys—is wasted because consumers' feelings toward products and brands reside deep within the subconscious part of their brains. Lindstrom used brain scanning to analyze the buying processes of more than 2,000 participants. Lindstrom merged neuroscience—the study of the brain—with marketing! His controversial findings using "neuromarketing" are summarized in his breakthrough book *Buyology*.[22]

Based on the results of neuromarketing studies, Campbell Soup Company recently changed the labels of most of its soup cans. Some of the changes: Steam now rises from more vibrant images of soup; the "unemotional spoons" have disappeared; and the script logo is smaller and has been moved to the bottom of the can.[23]

Primary Data: Asking People

How many dozens of times have you filled out some kind of a questionnaire? Maybe a short survey at school or a telephone or e-mail survey to see if you are pleased with the service you received. Asking consumers questions and recording their answers is the second principal way of gathering information.

We can divide this primary data collection task into (1) idea generation methods and (2) idea evaluation methods, although they sometimes overlap and each has a number of special techniques.[24] Each survey method results in valuable **questionnaire data**, which are facts and figures obtained by asking people about their attitudes, awareness, intentions, and behaviors.

Idea Generation Methods—Coming Up with Ideas A common way of collecting questionnaire data to generate ideas is through an *individual interview*, which involves a single researcher asking questions of one respondent. This approach has many advantages, such as being able to probe for additional ideas using follow-up questions to a respondent's initial answers. However, this method is very expensive. Later in the chapter we'll discuss some alternatives.

General Mills sought ideas about why Hamburger Helper didn't fare well when it was introduced. Initial instructions called for cooking a half-pound of hamburger separately from the noodles or potatoes, which were later mixed with the hamburger. So General Mills researchers used a special kind of individual interview, called a *depth interview*, in which researchers ask lengthy, free-flowing kinds of questions to probe for underlying ideas and feelings. These depth interviews showed consumers (1) didn't think it contained enough meat and (2) didn't want the hassle of cooking in two different pots. The Hamburger Helper product manager changed the recipe to call for a full pound of meat and to allow users to prepare it in one dish, leading to product success.

Focus groups are informal sessions of 6 to 10 past, present, or prospective customers in which a discussion leader, or moderator, asks for opinions about the firm's

Focus groups of students and instructors were used in developing this textbook. To see the specific suggestion that may help you study, read the text.

Video 7-3
Trend Hunter
kerin.tv/cr6e/v7-3

Wendy's spent over two years remaking its 42-year-old burger. The result: Dave's Hot 'N Juicy, named after Wendy's founder, Dave Thomas. See Figure 7–4 for some questions that Wendy's asked consumers in a survey to discover their fast-food preferences, behaviors, and demographics.

products and those of its competitors, including how they use these products and special needs they have that these products don't address. Often recorded and conducted in special interviewing rooms with a one-way mirror, these groups enable marketing researchers and managers to hear and watch consumer reactions.

The informality and peer support in an effective focus group help uncover ideas that are often difficult to obtain with individual interviews. For example, to improve understanding and learning by students using this textbook, focus groups were conducted among both marketing instructors and students. Both groups recommended providing answers to each chapter's set of Learning Review questions. This suggestion was followed, so you can see the answers by turning to a section at the end of each chapter or by tapping your finger on the question in the textbook's iPad version.

Finding "the next big thing" for consumers has caused marketing researchers to turn to some less traditional techniques. For example, "fuzzy front end" methods attempt early identification of elusive consumer tastes or trends. Trend Hunter is a firm that seeks to anticipate and track "the evolution of cool." Trend hunting (or watching) is the practice of identifying "emerging shifts in social behavior," which are driven by changes in pop culture that can lead to new products. Trend Hunter has identified about 200,000 "micro-trends" through its global network of 118,000 members and features several of these trends on its daily Trend Hunter TV broadcast via its YouTube channel (trendhuntertv).[25]

Idea Evaluation Methods—Testing an Idea   In idea evaluation, the marketing researcher tries to test ideas discovered earlier to help the marketing manager recommend marketing actions. Idea evaluation methods often involve conventional questionnaires using personal, mail, telephone, fax, and online (e-mail or Internet) surveys of a large sample of past, present, or prospective consumers. In choosing among them, the marketing researcher balances the cost of the particular method against the expected quality of the information and the speed with which it can be obtained.

Personal interview surveys enable the interviewer to be flexible in asking probing questions or getting reactions to visual materials but are very costly. *Mail surveys* are usually biased because those most likely to respond have had especially positive or negative experiences with the product or brand. While *telephone interviews* allow flexibility, unhappy respondents may hang up on the interviewer, even with the efficiency of computer-assisted telephone interviewing (CATI).

Increasingly, marketing researchers have begun to use *online surveys* (e-mail and Internet) to collect primary data. The reason: Most consumers have an Internet connection and an e-mail account. Marketers can embed a survey in an e-mail sent to targeted respondents. When they open the e-mail, consumers can either see the survey or click on a link to access it from a website. Marketers can also ask consumers to complete a "pop up" survey in a separate browser window when they access an organization's website. Many organizations use this method to have consumers assess their products and services or evaluate the design and usability of their websites.

The advantages of online surveys are that the cost is relatively minimal and the turnaround time from data collection to report presentation is much quicker than the traditional methods discussed earlier. However, online surveys have serious drawbacks: Some consumers may view e-mail surveys as "junk" or "spam" and may either choose to not receive them (if they have a "spam blocker") or purposely or inadvertently delete them, unopened. For Internet surveys, some consumers have a "pop-up blocker" that prohibits a browser from opening a separate window that contains the survey; thus, they may not be able to participate in the research. Research firms such as SurveyMonkey have developed technologies to prevent consumers from completing e-mail and Internet surveys multiple times.[26]

The foundation of all research using questionnaires is developing precise questions that get clear, unambiguous answers from respondents.[27] Figure 7–4 on the next pages shows a number of formats for questions taken from a Wendy's survey that assessed fast-food restaurant preferences among present and prospective consumers.

Question 1 is an example of an *open-ended question*, which allows respondents to express opinions, ideas, or behaviors in their own words without being forced to choose among alternatives that have been predetermined by a marketing researcher. This information is invaluable to marketers because it captures the "voice" of respondents, which is useful in understanding consumer behavior, identifying product benefits, or developing advertising messages.

In contrast, *closed-end* or *fixed alternative questions* require respondents to select one or more response options from a set of predetermined choices. Question 2 is an example of a *dichotomous question*, the simplest form of a fixed alternative question that allows only a "yes" or "no" response.

A fixed alternative question with three or more choices uses a *scale*. Question 5 is an example of a question that uses a *semantic differential scale*, a five-point scale in which the opposite ends have one- or two-word adjectives that have opposite meanings. For example, depending on the respondent's opinion regarding the cleanliness of Wendy's restaurants, he or she would check the left-hand space on the scale, the right-hand space, or one of the three other intervening points. Question 6 uses a *Likert scale*, in which the respondent indicates the extent to which he or she agrees or disagrees with a statement.

The questionnaire in Figure 7–4 provides valuable information to the marketing researcher at Wendy's. Questions 1 to 8 inform him or her about the respondent's likes and dislikes in eating out, frequency of eating out at fast-food restaurants generally and at Wendy's specifically, and sources of information used in making decisions about fast-food restaurants. Question 9 gives details about the respondent's personal or household characteristics, which can be used in trying to segment the fast-food market, a topic discussed in Chapter 8.

Marketing research questions must be worded precisely so that all respondents interpret the same question similarly. For example, in a question asking whether you eat at fast-food restaurants regularly, the word *regularly* is ambiguous. Two people might answer "yes" to the question, but one might mean "once a day" while the other means "once or twice a month." However, each of these interpretations suggests that dramatically different marketing actions be directed to these two prospective consumers.

The high cost of using personal interviews in homes has increased the use of *mall intercept interviews*, which are personal interviews of consumers visiting shopping centers. These face-to-face interviews reduce the cost of personal visits to consumers in their homes while providing the flexibility to show respondents visual cues such as ads or actual product samples. A disadvantage of mall intercept interviews is that the people interviewed may not be representative of the consumers targeted, giving a biased result.

Electronic technology has revolutionized traditional concepts of interviews or surveys. Today, respondents can walk up to a kiosk in a shopping center, read questions off a screen, and key their answers into a computer on a touch screen. Fully automated telephone interviews exist in which respondents key their replies on a touch-tone telephone.

Frito-Lay encourages consumers to use social media to vote on what new Lay's potato chip flavors they like. The flavors above emerged as the top four in its 2014 "Do Us a Flavor" contest.

Primary Data: Other Sources

Other methods of collecting primary data exist that overlap somewhat with the methods just discussed. These involve using (1) social media and (2) panels and experiments.

1. What things are most important to you when you decide to eat out and go to a fast-food restaurant?

_____

_____

_____

2. Have you eaten at a fast-food restaurant in the past month?

☐ Yes　　☐ No

3. If you answered yes to question 2, how often do you eat at a fast-food restaurant?

☐ Once a week or more　　☐ 2 to 3 times a month　　☐ Once a month or less

4. How important is it to you that a fast-food restaurant satisfies you on the following characteristics? [Check the box that describes your feelings for each item listed.]

Characteristic	Very Important	Somewhat Important	Important	Unimportant	Somewhat Unimportant	Very Unimportant
• Taste of food	☐	☐	☐	☐	☐	☐
• Cleanliness	☐	☐	☐	☐	☐	☐
• Price	☐	☐	☐	☐	☐	☐
• Variety of menu	☐	☐	☐	☐	☐	☐

5. For each of the characteristics listed below, check the space on the scale that describes how you feel about Wendy's. Mark an X on only **one** of the five spaces for each item listed.

Characteristic	Check the space that describes the degree to which Wendy's is . . .						
• Taste of food	Tasty	_____	_____	_____	_____	_____	Not tasty
• Cleanliness	Clean	_____	_____	_____	_____	_____	Dirty
• Price	Inexpensive	_____	_____	_____	_____	_____	Expensive
• Variety of menu	Broad	_____	_____	_____	_____	_____	Narrow

6. Check one box that describes your agreement or disagreement with each statement listed below:

Statement	Strongly Agree	Agree	Don't Know	Disagree	Strongly Disagree
• Adults like to take their families to fast-food restaurants	☐	☐	☐	☐	☐
• Our children have a say in where the family chooses to eat	☐	☐	☐	☐	☐

FIGURE 7–4
To obtain the most valuable information from consumers, this Wendy's survey utilizes four different kinds of questions discussed in the text.

Social Media Facebook, Twitter, and other social media are revolutionizing the way today's marketing research is done. Frito-Lay recently used its Lay's Facebook page to have consumers submit suggestions for new potato chip flavors. Visitors to the Lay's "Do Us A Flavor" page could also vote on their favorite flavors by clicking an "I'd Eat That" button. The winning flavor that emerged in its 2013 contest—Lay's "Cheesy Garlic Bread" flavored potato chips. The success of the 2013 "Do Us A Flavor" contest caused it to be repeated in 2014. The four favorite flavors from votes on social media: Wavy Mango Salsa, Kettle Cooked Wasabi Ginger, Cappuccino, and Cheddar Bacon Mac & Cheese. By the time you read this, the winning flavor will be on supermarket shelves and the lucky winner $1 million richer.[28]

Carma Laboratories, Inc., the maker of Carmex lip balm, is a third generation, family-owned business with a history of accessibility to customers. In fact, founder Alfred Woelbing personally responded to every letter he received from

7. How important are each of the following sources of information to you when selecting a fast-food restaurant at which to eat? [Check one box for each source listed.]

Source of information	Very Important	Somewhat Important	Not at all Important
• Television	☐	☐	☐
• Newspapers	☐	☐	☐
• Radio	☐	☐	☐
• Billboards	☐	☐	☐
• Internet	☐	☐	☐
• Social networks	☐	☐	☐

8. How often do you eat out at each of the following fast-food restaurants? [Check one box for each source listed.]

Restaurant	Once a Week or More	2 to 3 Times a Month	Once a Month or Less
• Burger King	☐	☐	☐
• McDonald's	☐	☐	☐
• Wendy's	☐	☐	☐

9. As head of the household, please answer the following questions about you and your household. [Check only one for each item.]

a. What is your gender? ☐ Male ☐ Female

b. What is your marital status? ☐ Single ☐ Married ☐ Other (widowed, divorced, etc.)

c. How many children under age 18 live in your home? ☐ 0 ☐ 1 ☐ 2 ☐ 3 or more

d. What is your age? ☐ Under 25 ☐ 25–44 ☐ 45 or older

e. What is your total annual individual or household income?
☐ Less than $15,000 ☐ $15,000–49,000 ☐ Over $49,000

FIGURE 7–4 *(continued)*

Carmex's home page topics range from its Twitter Giveaways to win Carmex products to its family history. The Using Marketing Dashboards box shows how it uses social media marketing research.

customers. Today, Carma Labs relies on social media programs to help promote its products.[29]

Carmex lip balm is meant to reduce cold sore symptoms and soothe dry and chapped lips. It is packaged in jars, sticks, and squeezable tubes. The U.S. Carmex product line includes original, strawberry, lime twist, vanilla, pomegranate, and cherry flavors. Although Carmex lip balm sales trend behind ChapStick and Blistex, Carmex consumers tend to be loyalists—true zealots.

One opportunity for Carmex (www.mycarmex.com) is to conduct marketing research using social media listening tools to understand the nature of online lip balm conversations. Lip balm is a seasonal product, with both sales and online activity peaking during the cough–cold season of November through March.

The Using Marketing Dashboards box on the next page shows how Carmex uses marketing metrics to assess its social media programs for its line of products. Data have been modified to protect proprietary information.

Carmex uses several social media metrics, such as *conversation velocity*, *share of voice*, and *sentiment*.[30] These metrics are tracked by electronic search engines that comb the Internet for consumers' behaviors and "brand mentions" to calculate share

Using Marketing Dashboards

Are the Carmex Social Media Programs Working Well?

As a marketing consultant to Carmex, you've just been asked to assess its social media activities for its lip balm product line.

Carmex has recently launched new social media programs and promotions to tell U.S. consumers more about its line of lip balm products. These include Facebook and Twitter contests that allow Carmex fans and followers to win free samples by connecting with Carmex. A creative "Carmex Kiss" widget allows users to upload their photo and to send an animated kiss to a friend.

Your Challenge To assess how the Carmex social media programs are doing, you choose these five metrics: (1) Carmex conversation velocity—total Carmex mentions on the Internet; (2) Facebook fans—the number of Facebook users in a time period who have liked Carmex's Facebook brand page; (3) Twitter followers—the number of Twitter users in a time period who follow Carmex's Twitter feed; (4) Carmex share of voice—Carmex mentions on the Internet as a percentage of mentions of all major lip balm brands; and (5) Carmex sentiment—the percentage of Internet Carmex share-of-voice mentions that are (a) positive, (b) neutral, or (c) negative.

Your Findings Analyzing the marketing dashboard here, you reach these conclusions. First, the number of both Facebook fans and Twitter followers for Carmex is up significantly for 2014 compared to 2013, which is good news. Second, the Carmex share of voice of 35 percent is good, certainly relative to the 48 percent for the #1 brand ChapStick. But especially favorable is Carmex's 12 percent increase in share of voice compared to a year ago. Third, the Carmex sentiment dashboard shows 80 percent of the mentions are positive, and only 5 percent are negative. Even more significant is that positive mentions are up 23 percent over last year.

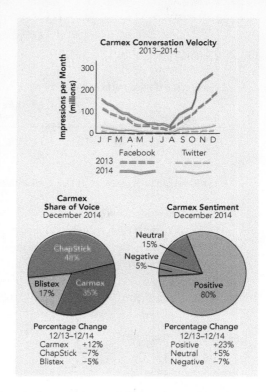

Your Actions You conclude that Carmex's social media initiatives are doing well. Your next step is to probe deeper into the data to see which ones—such as free samples or the Carmex Kiss—have been especially effective in triggering the positive results and build on these successes in the future.

of voice and determine whether these brand mentions appear to be "positive," "neutral," or "negative" in order to calculate "sentiment." A widely used Facebook metric measures the number of *likes*, which refers to the number of Facebook users opting in to a brand's messages and liking the brand.

Marketing researchers increasingly want to glean information from sites to "mine" their raw consumer-generated content in real time. However, when relying on this

To discover how Walmart used test markets to help develop its internationally successful supercenters, such as this one in China, see the text.

consumer-generated content, the sample of individuals from whom this content is gleaned may not be statistically representative of the marketplace.[31]

Panels and Experiments Two special ways that observations and questionnaires are sometimes used are panels and experiments.

Marketing researchers often want to know if consumers change their behavior over time, so they take successive measurements of the same people. A *panel* is a sample of consumers or stores from which researchers take a series of measurements. For example, the NPD Group collects data about consumer purchases such as apparel, food, and electronics from its Online Panel, which consists of nearly 2 million individuals worldwide. So a firm like General Mills can count the frequency of consumer purchases to measure switching behavior from one brand of its breakfast cereal (Wheaties) to another (Cheerios) or to a competitor's brand (Kellogg's Special K). A disadvantage of panels is that the marketing research firm needs to recruit new members continually to replace those who drop out. These new recruits must match the characteristics of those they replace to keep the panel representative of the marketplace.

An *experiment* involves obtaining data by manipulating factors under tightly controlled conditions to test cause and effect. The interest is in whether changing one of the independent variables (a cause) will change the behavior of the dependent variable that is studied (the result). In marketing experiments, the independent variables of interest—sometimes called the marketing *drivers*—are often one or more of the marketing mix elements, such as a product's features, price, or promotion (like advertising messages or coupons). The ideal dependent variable usually is a change in the purchases (incremental unit or dollar sales) of individuals, households, or organizations. For example, food companies often use *test markets*, which offer a product for sale in a small geographic area to help evaluate potential marketing actions. In 1988, Walmart opened three experimental stand-alone supercenters to gauge consumer acceptance before deciding to open others. Today, Walmart operates over 4,000 supercenters around the world.

A potential difficulty with experiments is that outside factors (such as actions of competitors) can distort the results of an experiment and affect the dependent variable (such as sales). A researcher's task is to identify the effect of the marketing variable of interest on the dependent variable when the effects of outside factors in an experiment might hide it.

Advantages and Disadvantages of Primary Data

Compared with secondary data, primary data have the advantages of being more flexible and more specific to the problem being studied. The main disadvantages are that primary data are usually far more costly and time-consuming to collect than secondary data.

---

learning review

7-6. What is the difference between observational and questionnaire data?

7-7. Which type of survey provides the greatest flexibility for asking probing questions: mail, telephone, or personal interview?

7-8. What is the difference between a panel and an experiment?

STEP 4: DEVELOP FINDINGS

 LO 7-5 Explain how information technology and data mining lead to marketing actions.

Mark Twain once observed, "Collecting data is like collecting garbage. You've got to know what you're going to do with the stuff before you collect it." So, marketing data and information have little more value than garbage unless they are (1) analyzed carefully and then (2) translated into findings, Step 4 in the marketing research approach.[32]

Analyze the Data

Analyzing marketing data today often involves very sophisticated and complex methods. Examples of this include information technology and data mining, which are discussed first below, followed by a detailed example of analyzing sales of Tony's Pizza.

information technology Involves operating computer networks that can store and process data.

Information Technology   **Information technology** involves operating computer networks that can store and process data. Today, information technology can extract hidden information from large databases, such as those containing retail sales collected through barcode scanners at checkout counters and households' product purchases and TV viewing behavior.

Figure 7–5 shows how marketers use information technology, data, models, and queries to obtain results that lead to marketing actions. Today's marketing managers can be drowned in an ocean of data; they need to adopt strategies for dealing with complex, changing views of the competition, the market, and the consumer. The Internet and PC help make sense out of this vast amount of information. The marketer's task is to convert it into useful information that will lead to marketing actions.[33]

As shown at the top of Figure 7–5, marketers use information technology that consists of computers linked together through sophisticated communication networks to access and retrieve data from internal and external sources. These data sources are stored, organized, and managed in databases. Collectively, these databases form a *data warehouse.*

FIGURE 7–5
How marketing researchers and managers use information technology to turn information into action.

As shown at the bottom of Figure 7–5, marketers use computers to query the databases in the data warehouse with marketing queries or questions. These questions go through statistical models that organize and manipulate the data to analyze and identify

Information technology: Computers and communication networks

Marketing researcher or manager at computer

Making Responsible Decisions

ethics

No More Personal Secrets: The Downside of Data Mining

eXelate, Intellidyn, Rapleaf, Google Ad Preferences, Yahoo!, BlueKai, Alliance Data, reputation.com . . . yes . . . and Facebook and Twitter, too!

The common denominator for all these is their sophisticated data mining of the Internet and social media that reveals an incredible amount of personal information about any American. *Time* journalist Joel Stein, using both online and offline sources, discovered how easily outsiders could find his social security number and then found a number of other things about himself—some correct, some not.

For example, he likes hockey, rap, rock, parenting, recipes, clothes and beauty products, and movies. He makes most of his purchases online, averaging only $25 per purchase. He uses Facebook, Friendster, LinkedIn, MySpace, Pandora, and StumbleUpon. He bought his house in November, which is when his home insurance is up for renewal. His dad's wife has a traffic ticket.

And he uses an Apple iMac and is an 18- to 19-year-old woman???!!!

OK, OK, sometimes data mining errors occur!

These data are collected in many ways from the Internet—from tracking devices (like cookies, discussed in Chapter 21) on websites to apps downloaded on a cellphone, PC, or tablet device that reveal a user's contact list and location.

These personal details have huge benefits for marketers. Data mining enables one-to-one personalization and now enables advertisers to target individual consumers. This involves using not only demographics such as age and sex but also "likes," past buying habits, social media used, brands bought, TV programs watched, and so on.

Want to do some sleuthing yourself? Download Ghostery at www.ghostery.com. It tells you all the companies grabbing your data when you visit a website.

177

---

the relationships that exist. The results are then presented using tables and graphics for easier interpretation. When querying a database, marketers can use *sensitivity analysis* to ask "what if" questions to determine how hypothetical changes in *product* or *brand drivers*—the factors that influence the buying decisions of a household or organization—can affect sales.

Traditional marketing research typically involves identifying possible drivers and then collecting data. For example, we might collect data to test the hypothesis that increasing couponing (the driver) during spring will increase trials by first-time buyers (the result).

Data Mining   In contrast, *data mining* is the extraction of hidden predictive information from large databases to find statistical links between consumer purchasing patterns and marketing actions. Some of these are common sense: Since many consumers buy peanut butter and grape jelly together, why not run a joint promotion between Skippy peanut butter and Welch's grape jelly? But would you have expected that men buying diapers in the evening sometimes buy a six-pack of beer as well? Supermarkets discovered this when they mined checkout data from scanners. So they placed diapers and beer near each other, then placed potato chips between them—and increased sales on all three items! On the near horizon is RFID (radio frequency identification) technology using "smart tags" on the diapers and beer to tell whether they wind up in the same shopping bag.

Data mining related to the Internet and social media is exploding. This increased investment in data mining is caused by a greater focus on the $50 billion spent annually on digital advertising—which includes both social media and mobile devices. And the cost to an advertiser for that one bit of special information about you? Two-fifths of a cent.[34] For how much online data mining can reveal about you personally and the ethical issues involved, see the Making Responsible Decisions box.

At 10 P.M., what is this man likely to buy besides these diapers? For the curious answer that data mining gives, see the text.

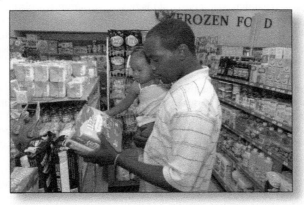

CHAPTER 7   Marketing Research: From Customer Insights to Actions

How are sales doing? To see how marketers at Tony's Pizza assessed this question and the results, read the text.

Analyzing Sales of Tony's Pizza   Schwan Food Company produces 3 million frozen pizzas a day under brand names that include Tony's and Red Baron. Let's see how Teré Carral, the marketing manager for the Tony's brand, might address a market segment question in early 2015. We will use hypothetical data to protect Tony's proprietary information.

Teré is concerned about the limited growth in the Tony's brand over the past four years. She hires a consultant to collect and analyze data to explain what's going on with her brand and to recommend ways to improve its growth. Teré asks the consultant to put together a proposal that includes the answers to two key questions:

1. How are Tony's sales doing on a household basis? For example, are fewer households buying Tony's pizzas, or is each household buying fewer Tony's pizzas? Or both?
2. What factors might be contributing to Tony's very flat sales over the past four years?

Facts uncovered by the consultant are vital. For example, is the average household consuming more or less Tony's pizza than in previous years? Is Tony's flat sales performance related to a specific factor? With answers to these questions Teré can take actions to address the issues in the coming year.

Present the Findings

Findings should be clear and understandable from the way the data are presented. Managers are responsible for *actions*. Often it means delivering the results in clear pictures and, if possible, in a single page.

The consultant gives Teré the answers to her questions using the marketing dashboards in Figure 7–6, a creative way to present findings graphically. Let's look over Teré's shoulder as she interprets these findings:

- Figure 7–6A, *Annual Sales*—This shows the annual growth of Tony's Pizza is stable but virtually flat from 2011 through 2014.
- Figure 7–6B, *Average Annual Sales per Household*—Look closely at this graph. At first glance, it seems like sales in 2014 are *half* what they were in 2011, right? But be careful to read the numbers on the vertical axis. They show that household purchases of Tony's pizzas have been steadily declining over the past four years, from an average of 3.4 pizzas per household in 2011 to 3.1 pizzas per household in 2014. (Significant, but hardly a 50 percent drop.) Now the question is, if Tony's annual sales are stable, yet the average individual household is buying fewer Tony's pizzas, what's going on? The answer is, more households are buying pizzas—it's just that each household is buying fewer Tony's pizzas. That households aren't choosing Tony's is a genuine source of concern. But again, here's a classic example of a marketing problem representing a marketing opportunity. The number of households buying pizza is *growing*, and that's good news for Tony's.
- Figure 7–6C, *Average Annual Sales per Household, by Household Size*—This chart starts to show a source of the problem: Even though average sales of pizza to households with only one or two people are stable, households with three or four people and those with five or more are declining in average annual pizza consumption. Which households tend to have more than two people? Answer: Households *with children*. Therefore, we should look more closely at the pizza-buying behavior of households with children.
- Figure 7–6D, *Average Annual Sales per Household, by Age of Children in the Household*—The real problem that emerges is the serious decline in average

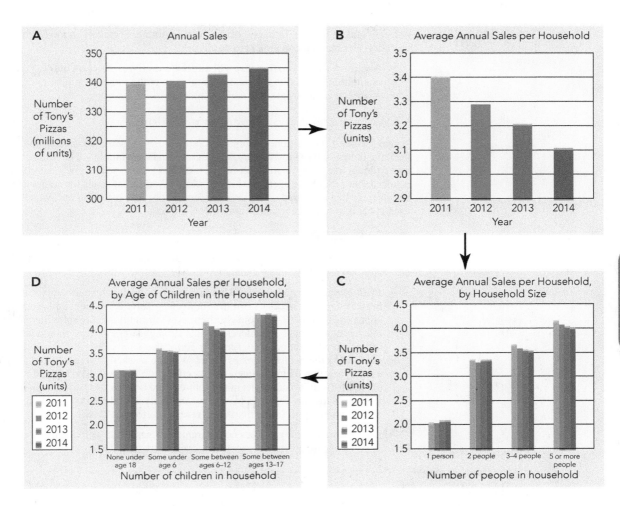

FIGURE 7–6
These marketing dashboards present findings to Tony's marketing manager that will lead to recommendations and actions.

Source: Teré Carral, Tony's Pizza.

consumption in the households with younger children, especially in households with children in the 6-to-12-year-old age group.

Identifying a sales problem in households with children 6 to 12 years old is an important discovery, as Tony's sales are declining in a market segment that is known to be one of the heaviest in buying pizzas.

STEP 5: TAKE MARKETING ACTIONS

Effective marketing research doesn't stop with findings and recommendations—someone has to identify the marketing actions, put them into effect, and monitor how the decisions turn out, which is the essence of Step 5.

Make Action Recommendations

Teré Carral, the marketing manager for Tony's Pizza, meets with her team to convert the market research findings into specific marketing recommendations with a clear objective: Target households with children ages 6 to 12 to reverse the trend among this segment and gain strength in one of the most important segments in the frozen pizza category. Her recommendation is to develop:

- An advertising campaign that will target children 6 to 12 years old.
- A monthly promotion calendar with this age group target in mind.
- A special event program reaching children 6 to 12 years old.

Implement the Action Recommendations

As her first marketing action, Teré undertakes advertising research to develop ads that appeal to children in the 6-to-12-year-old age group and their families. The research shows that children like colorful ads with funny, friendly characters. She gives these research results to her advertising agency, which develops several sample ads for her review. Teré selects three that are tested on children to identify the most appealing one, which is then used in her next advertising campaign for Tony's Pizza.

Evaluate the Results

Evaluating results is a continuing way of life for effective marketing managers. There are really two aspects of this evaluation process:

- *Evaluating the decision itself.* This involves monitoring the marketplace to determine if action is necessary in the future. For Teré, is her new ad successful in appealing to 6-to-12-year-old children and their families? Are sales increasing to this target segment? The success of this strategy suggests Teré should add more follow-up ads with colorful, funny, friendly characters.
- *Evaluating the decision process used.* Was the marketing research and analysis used to develop the recommendations effective? Was it flawed? Could it be improved for similar situations in the future? Teré and her marketing team must be vigilant in looking for ways to improve the analysis and results—to learn lessons that might apply to future marketing research efforts at Tony's.

Again, systematic analysis does not guarantee success. But, as in the case of Tony's Pizza, it can improve a firm's success rate for its marketing decisions.

---

learning review

7-9. In the marketing research for Tony's Pizza, what is an example of (*a*) a finding and (*b*) a marketing action?

7-10. In evaluating marketing actions, what are the two dimensions on which they should be evaluated?

SALES FORECASTING TECHNIQUES

LO 7-6 Describe three approaches to developing a company's sales forecast.

sales forecast
The total sales of a product that a firm expects to sell during a specified time period under specified conditions and its own marketing efforts.

Forecasting or estimating potential sales is often a key goal in a marketing research study. Good sales forecasts are important for a firm as it schedules production. The term **sales forecast** refers to the total sales of a product that a firm expects to sell during a specified time period under specified environmental conditions and its own marketing efforts. For example, Betty Crocker might develop a sales forecast of 4 million cases of cake mix for U.S. consumers in 2015, assuming consumers' dessert preferences remain constant and competitors don't change prices.

Three main sales forecasting techniques are often used: (1) judgments of the decision maker, (2) statistical methods, and (3) surveys of knowledgeable groups.

Judgments of the Decision Maker

Probably 99 percent of all sales forecasts are simply the judgment of the person who must act on the results of the forecast—the individual decision maker. *A direct forecast* involves estimating the value to be forecast without any intervening steps. Examples appear daily: How many quarts of milk should I buy? How much money should I withdraw at the ATM?

A *lost-horse forecast* involves starting with the last known value of the item being forecast, listing the factors that could affect the forecast, assessing whether they have a positive or negative impact, and making the final forecast. The technique gets its name from how you'd find a lost horse: go to where it was last seen, put yourself in its shoes, consider those factors that could affect where you might go (to the pond if you're thirsty, the hayfield if you're hungry, and so on), and go there.

For example, New Balance recently introduced its Minimus, a shoe that is 50 percent lighter than other lightweight shoes. Its unique features are designed to make running easier and limit foot injuries. Suppose a New Balance marketing manager in early 2015 needs to make a sales forecast through 2017. She would take the known value of 2014 sales and list positive factors (good acceptance of its high-tech designs, great publicity) and the negative factors (the economic recession, competition from established name brands) to arrive at the final series of sales forecasts.[35]

How might a marketing manager for the New Balance Minimus running shoe create a sales forecast through 2017? Read the text to find out.

Statistical Methods

The best-known statistical method of forecasting is *trend extrapolation*, which involves extending a pattern observed in past data into the future. When the pattern is described with a straight line, it is *linear trend extrapolation*. Suppose that in early 2000 you were a sales forecaster for the Xerox Corporation and had actual sales data running from 1988 to 1999 (see Figure 7–7). Using linear trend extrapolation, you draw a line to fit the past sales data and project it into the future to give the forecast values shown for 2000 through 2014.

If in 2013 you want to compare your forecasts with actual results, you are in for a surprise—illustrating the strength and weakness of trend extrapolation. Trend extrapolation assumes that the underlying relationships in the past will continue into the future, which is the basis of the method's key strength: simplicity. If this assumption proves correct, you have an accurate forecast. However, if this proves wrong, the forecast is likely to be wrong. In this case, your forecasts from 2000 through 2012 were too high, as shown in Figure 7–7, largely because of fierce competition in the photocopying industry. The spike in 2010 sales revenues is mainly due to new acquisitions.

Surveys of Knowledgeable Groups

If you wonder what your firm's sales will be next year, ask people who are likely to know something about future sales. Two common groups that are surveyed to develop sales forecasts are prospective buyers and the firm's salesforce.

FIGURE 7–7
Linear trend extrapolation of sales revenues at Xerox, made at the start of 2000.

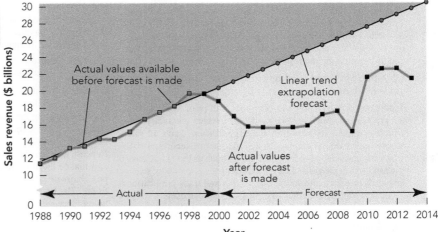

A *survey of buyers' intentions forecast* involves asking prospective customers if they are likely to buy the product during some future time period. For industrial products with few prospective buyers, this can be effective. There are only a few hundred customers in the entire world for Boeing's large airplanes, so Boeing surveys them to develop its sales forecasts and production schedules.

A *salesforce survey forecast* involves asking the firm's salespeople to estimate sales during a forthcoming period. Because these people are in contact with customers and are likely to know what customers like and dislike, there is logic to this approach. However, salespeople can be unreliable forecasters—painting too rosy a picture if they are enthusiastic about a new product or too grim a forecast if their sales quota and future compensation are based on it.

> **learning review**
>
> 7-11. What are the three kinds of sales forecasting techniques?
>
> 7-12. How do you make a lost-horse forecast?

LEARNING OBJECTIVES REVIEW

LO 7-1 *Identify the reason for conducting marketing research.*

To be successful, products must meet the wants and needs of potential customers. So marketing research reduces risk by providing the vital information to help marketing managers understand those wants and needs and translate them into marketing actions.

LO 7-2 *Describe the five-step marketing research approach that leads to marketing actions.*

Marketing researchers engage in a five-step decision-making process to collect information that will improve marketing decisions. The first step is to define the problem, which requires setting the research objectives and identifying possible marketing actions. The second step is to develop the research plan, which involves specifying the constraints, identifying data needed for marketing decisions, and determining how to collect the data. The third step is to collect the relevant information, which includes considering pertinent secondary data (both internal and external) and primary data (by observing and questioning consumers). The fourth step is to develop findings from the marketing research data collected. This involves analyzing the data and presenting the findings of the research. The fifth and last step is to take marketing actions, which involves making and implementing the action recommendations and then evaluating the results.

LO 7-3 *Identify the two kinds of secondary data and give examples of each.*

Secondary data have already been recorded prior to the start of the project and consist of two kinds: (*a*) internal secondary data, which originate from within the organization, such as sales reports and customer comments, and (*b*) external secondary data, which are created by other organizations, such as the U.S. Census Bureau (which provides data on the country's population, manufacturers, retailers, and so on) or business and trade publications (which provide data on industry trends, market size, etc.).

LO 7-4 *Describe the meanings of observational data and questionnaire data and give examples of each.*

Primary data are collected specifically for the project and are obtained by either observing or questioning people. Observational data involve obtaining facts and figures by watching how people behave—either by mechanical or personal methods. So marketing researchers can observe people (*a*) mechanically (electronically) using Nielsen people meters to measure TV viewing behavior or (*b*) personally using mystery shoppers or ethnographic techniques. A recent electronic innovation is neuromarketing—using high-tech brain scanning to record the responses of a consumer's brain to marketing stimuli like packages or TV ads. Questionnaires involve asking people questions (*a*) in person using interviews or focus groups or (*b*) via a questionnaire using a telephone, fax, print, e-mail, Internet, or social media survey.

LO 7-5 *Explain how information technology and data mining lead to marketing actions.*

Today's marketing managers are often overloaded with data—from internal sales and customer data to external data on TV viewing habits or grocery purchases from the scanner data at checkout counters. Information technology enables this massive amount of marketing data to be stored, accessed, and processed. The resulting databases can be queried using data mining to find statistical relationships useful for marketing decisions and actions.

LO 7-6 *Describe three approaches to developing a company's sales forecast.*

One approach uses the subjective judgments of the decision maker, such as direct or lost-horse forecasts. A direct forecast involves estimating the value to be forecast without any intervening steps. A lost-horse forecast starts with the last known value of the item being forecast and then lists the factors that could affect the forecast, assesses whether they have a positive or negative impact, and makes the final forecast. Statistical methods, a second approach, involve extending a pattern observed in past data into the future. The best-known statistical method is linear trend extrapolation. Surveys of knowledgeable groups are a third approach, involve obtaining information such as the intentions of potential buyers or estimates provided by the salesforce.

LEARNING REVIEW ANSWERS

7-1 What is marketing research?
Answer: Marketing research is the process of defining a marketing problem and opportunity, systematically collecting and analyzing information, and recommending actions to reduce the risk of and thereby improve marketing decisions.

7-2 What is the five-step marketing research approach?
Answer: The five-step marketing research approach provides a systematic checklist for making marketing decisions and actions. The five steps are: (1) define the problem; (2) develop the research plan; (3) collect relevant information (data); (4) develop findings; and (5) take marketing actions.

7-3 What are constraints, as they apply to developing a research plan?
Answer: Constraints in a decision are the restrictions placed on potential solutions to a problem, such as time and money. These set the parameters for the research plan—due dates, budget, etc.

7-4 What is the difference between secondary and primary data?
Answer: Secondary data are facts and figures that have already been recorded prior to the project at hand, whereas primary data are facts and figures that are newly collected for the project.

7-5 What are some advantages and disadvantages of secondary data?
Answer: Advantages of secondary data are the time savings, the low cost, and the greater level of detail that may be available. Disadvantages of secondary data are that the data may be out of date, unspecific, or have definitions, categories, or age groupings that are wrong for the project.

7-6 What is the difference between observational data and questionnaire data?
Answer: Observational data are facts and figures obtained by watching, either mechanically or in person, how people actually behave. Questionnaire data are facts and figures obtained by asking people about their attitudes, awareness, intentions, and behaviors.

7-7 Which type of survey provides the greatest flexibility for asking probing questions: mail, telephone, or personal interview?
Answer: personal interview (or individual/depth interview)

7-8 What is the difference between a panel and an experiment?
Answer: A panel is a sample of consumers or stores from which researchers take a series of measurements. An experiment involves obtaining data by manipulating factors under tightly controlled conditions to test cause and effect, such as changing a variable in a customer purchase decision (marketing drivers) and seeing what happens (increase/decrease in unit or dollar sales).

7-9 In the marketing research for Tony's Pizza, what is an example of (a) a finding and (b) a marketing action?
Answer: (a) Figure 7–6A depicts annual sales from 2011 to 2014; the finding is that annual sales are relatively flat, rising only 5 million units over the 4-year period. (b) Figure 7–6D shows a finding (the decline in pizza consumption) that leads to a recommendation to develop an ad targeting children 6 to 12 years old (the marketing action).

7-10 In evaluating marketing actions, what are the two dimensions on which they should be evaluated?
Answer: There are two aspects marketers use to evaluate the results of marketing actions: (1) evaluate the decision itself, which involves monitoring the marketplace to determine if action is necessary in the future and (2) evaluate the decision process used to determine whether (a) the marketing research and analysis used to develop the recommendations was effective or flawed in some way and (b) the process could be improved for similar situations in the future.

7-11 What are the three kinds of sales forecasting techniques?
Answer: They are: (1) judgments of the decision maker who acts on the results of a sales forecast; (2) statistical methods such as trend extrapolation, which involves extending a pattern observed in past data into the future; and (3) surveys of knowledgeable groups, those who are likely to know something about future sales.

7-12 How do you make a lost-horse forecast?
Answer: To make a lost-horse forecast, begin with the last known value of the item being forecast, list the factors that could affect the forecast, assess whether they have a positive or negative impact, and then make the final forecast.

FOCUSING ON KEY TERMS

constraints p. 164
data p. 165
information technology p. 176
marketing research p. 162

measures of success p. 163
observational data p. 167
primary data p. 165

questionnaire data p. 169
sales forecast p. 180
secondary data p. 165

APPLYING MARKETING KNOWLEDGE

1 Suppose your dean of admissions is considering surveying high school seniors about their perceptions of your school to design better informational brochures for them. What are the advantages and disadvantages of doing (a) telephone interviews and (b) an Internet survey of seniors requesting information about the school?

CHAPTER 7 Marketing Research: From Customer Insights to Actions

2 Wisk detergent decides to run a test market to see the effect of coupons and in-store advertising on sales. The index of sales is as follows:

Element in Test Market	Weeks before Coupon	Week of Coupon	Week after Coupon
Without in-store ads	100	144	108
With in-store ads	100	268	203

What are your conclusions and recommendations?

3 Nielsen obtains ratings of local TV stations in small markets by having households fill out diary question-naires. These give information on (*a*) who is watching TV and (*b*) the program being watched. What are the limitations of this questionnaire method?

4 The format in which information is presented is often vital. (*a*) If you were a harried marketing manager and queried your information system, would you rather see the results in tables or charts and graphs? (*b*) What are one or two strengths and weaknesses of each format?

5 (*a*) Why might a marketing researcher prefer to use secondary data rather than primary data in a study? (*b*) Why might the reverse be true?

6 Which of the following variables would linear trend extrapolation be more accurate for? (*a*) Annual population of the United States or (*b*) annual sales of cars produced in the United States by Ford. Why?

BUILDING YOUR MARKETING PLAN

To help you collect the most useful data for your marketing plan, develop a three-column table:

1 In column 1, list the information you would ideally like to have to fill holes in your marketing plan.

2 In column 2, identify the source for each bit of information in column 1, such as an Internet search, talking to prospective customers, looking at internal data, and so forth.

3 In column 3, set a priority on information you will have time to spend collecting by ranking each item: 1 = most important; 2 = next most important, and so forth.

VIDEO CASE 7 Carmex® (A): Leveraging Facebook for Marketing Research

Video 7-4
Carmex (A)
Video Case
kerin.tv/cr6e/v7-4

"What makes social media 'social' is its give and take," says Jeff Gerst of Bolin Marketing, who manages the Carmex® social media proper-ties. By "give" Gerst is referring to the feedback consumers send on social media; "take" is what they receive—such as news and coupons. "For Carmex, Facebook isn't just a way to share coupons or the latest product news, but it is also a marketing research resource. We have instantaneous access to the opinions of our consumers."

"While some people think of social media as 'free,' that is not true. However, almost everything in social me-dia can be faster and cheaper than in the offline world," adds Dane Hartzell, general manager of Bolin Digital. "Many platforms have been prebuilt and we marketers only need to modify them slightly."

CARMEX AND ITS PRODUCTS

Although Carmex has been making lip balm since 1937, only in the last five years has it made serious efforts to stress growth and become more competitive. For example, Carmex has:

- Extended its lip balm products into new flavors and varieties.
- Expanded into nearly 30 international markets.
- Developed the Carmex Moisture Plus line of premium lip balms for women.
- Launched a line of skin care products, its first venture outside of lip care.

Carmex has used social media tools in developing all of these initiatives, but the focus of this case is how Carmex might use Facebook marketing research to grow its lip balm varieties in the United States.

FACEBOOK MARKETING RESEARCH: TWO KEY METRICS

"We have three potential new flavors and we can only put two into quantitative testing," explains Jeff Gerst to his team. "So we have two goals in doing marketing research on this. One is to use Facebook to help us determine which two flavors we should move forward with. The second goal is to drive our Facebook metrics."

The two key Facebook metrics the Carmex marketing team has chosen to help narrow the flavor choices from three to two are "likes" and "engagement." "Likes" are the number of new "likers" to the brand's Facebook Page. This metric measures the size of the brand's Facebook audience. In contrast, "engagement" measures how active its Facebook audience is with Carmex. Any time a liker posts a comment on the Carmex Wall, likes its status, or replies to one of its posts, the engagement level increases.

The easiest way for Carmex to grow the number of "likes" on its Facebook Page is through contests and promotions. If it gives away prizes, people will be drawn to its site and its likes will increase. However, these people may not actually be fans of the Carmex product so at the end of the promotion, they may "unlike" Carmex or they may remain fans but not engage with the Carmex Page at all.

"One of the biggest challenges facing Facebook Community Managers for brands is how to grow your likes without hurting the level of engagement," says Holly Matson, director of experience planning at Bolin Marketing.

"Depending on how we go about conducting the research," Gerst adds, "we can drive engagement with our existing Facebook community, we can use this as an opportunity to grow our Facebook community or, potentially, we could do both." The benefits of this Carmex Facebook strategy are twofold: (1) narrowing the number of flavors to be researched from three to two and (2) enhancing the connections with the Carmex Facebook community.

HOW THE METRICS MIGHT BE USED

Carmex's Facebook activity can benefit (1) by using a poll to increase engagement, (2) by launching a contest to increase the number of likers, and (3) by trying to increase both engagement and likers through combining a poll with a contest.

The "Engagement" Strategy: Use a Poll

Let's look at two ways to use the engagement strategy showing actual Facebook screens. First, Carmex can post a somewhat open-ended question on its Facebook Wall, such as, "Which Carmex lip balm flavor would you most like to see next: Watermelon, Green Apple, or Peach Mango?" (Figure 1). However, consumers are less likely to respond to a question if they have to type in a response and have their name attached to it.

Alternatively, Carmex can post the same question on its Wall as a fixed-alternative poll question (Figure 2). Then consumers need only click on a flavor to vote; this is quick, anonymous, and will drive more people to vote, where more votes means more engagement. Within five minutes Carmex will have several dozen votes and, by the end of a business day, Carmex can very easily have over 500 responses.

In this scenario, the consumers are content because they are able to engage with a brand they like and have their opinions heard. Carmex is content because it has

FIGURE 1
Facebook Open-Ended Poll Question

> **CARMEX**
> Carmex
> Which Carmex lip balm flavor would you most like to see next: Watermelon, Green Apple, or Peach Mango?
> Like   Comment

FIGURE 2
Facebook Fixed-Alternative Poll Question

> **CARMEX**
> Carmex
> Which Carmex lip balm flavor would you most like to see next?
> ⊙ Watermelon
> ⊙ Green Apple
> ⊙ Peach Mango

engaged hundreds of its fans on its Facebook Page, and it gains results that are very helpful in deciding which flavors to put into testing. This scenario gets an answer quickly and drives fan engagement with existing fans but does not drive new likers to the Carmex Facebook Page.

The "Likes" Strategy: Use a Contest

If Carmex wants to grow the size of its Facebook community, which means the number of its brand page "likes," it can adopt a different strategy. Carmex can announce a contest where, if consumers "like" Carmex on Facebook and share a comment, they will be entered to win three limited-edition flavors. The chance to win limited-edition flavors is exciting to Carmex enthusiasts, and a contest like this will draw new consumers to the page. Carmex can ask the winners to review the limited-edition flavors and see if there is a consensus on which flavors should move on to quantitative testing. Setting up a contest, developing official rules, promoting the contest through Facebook ads, and fulfilling a contest can be costly and time-consuming.

The Combined Strategy: Use Poll and Contest

Carmex can also choose to layer these two strategies into a combined strategy where it runs the limited-edition flavor contest to promote new likes and meanwhile posts the poll question on its Facebook Wall to drive engagement.

REACHING A DECISION

Figure 3 on the next page shows the potential results from the three Facebook strategies being considered—the poll only, the contest only, or both strategies together. Assume the Carmex marketing team has sought your help in selecting a strategy and needs your answers to the questions below.

FIGURE 3
Potential Results from Three Possible Facebook Strategies

FACEBOOK STRATEGY	POTENTIAL IMPACT ON...		
	Increased "Engagement"	Increased "Likes"	Cost
Poll Only	High	Low	Low
Contest Only	Low	High	Moderate
Poll + Contest	High	High	Moderate to High

Favorable   Neutral   Unfavorable

MOVING FORWARD: A NEW PRODUCT LINE

This kind of Facebook marketing research has led to new Carmex products. "We have leveraged Facebook and other social media to test themes that connect best with an audience," says Patrick Hodgdon, digital strategist at Bolin Marketing. As an example he points to four "fashion-forward" designs of Carmex Moisture Plus® Glamour sticks introduced in 2013. "Good engagement with Carmex's fashion-themed Facebook posts helped validate the new product concept," says Hodgdon.

The four Moisture Plus Glamour sticks are: "Chic," a black and white hounds-tooth; "Fab," with bright purple circles; "Adventurous," a leopard print; and "Whimsical," with blue, orange, green, and pink intertwined ribbons. They are packaged in stylish, attention-getting tubes and have a slant-tip applicator (photo) that delivers the moisturizing protection. "We experienced over 25 percent annual growth for these Carmex Moisture Plus Limited Edition fashion-inspired lip balm products among key retailers from offering the new styles. We will continue rolling out new limited edition designs a few times a year to keep the line fresh, fun, and on trend for our consumers," says Alisa Allen, Bolin director of marketing.

Questions

1 What are the advantages and disadvantages for the Carmex marketing team in collecting data to narrow the flavor choices from three to two using (*a*) an online survey of a cross-section of Internet households or (*b*) an online survey of Carmex Facebook likers?

2 (*a*) On a Facebook brand page, what are "engagement" and "likes" really measuring? (*b*) For Carmex, which is more important and why?

3 (*a*) What evokes consumers' "engagement" on a brand page on Facebook? (*b*) What attracts consumers to "like" a brand page on Facebook?

4 (*a*) What are the advantages of using a fixed-alternative poll question on Facebook? (*b*) When do you think it would be better to use an open-ended question?

5 (*a*) If you had a limited budget and two weeks to decide which two flavors to put into quantitative testing, would you choose a "poll only" or a "contest only" strategy? Why? (*b*) If you had a sizable budget and two months to make the same decision, which scenario would you choose? Why?

Chapter Notes

1. Rachel Dodes, "What's in a Name?" *The Wall Street Journal,* October 19, 2012, pp. D1–D2; "'Hunger Games' One for the Record Books," *Star Tribune,* March 26, 2012, p. E8; and Michelle Tauber, "Game On," *People,* March 26, 2012, pp. 66–74.
2. John Horn, "Studios Play Name Games," *Star Tribune,* August 10, 1997, p. F11; and "Flunking Chemistry," *Star Tribune,* April 11, 2003, p. E13.
3. Tad Friend, "The Cobra," *The New Yorker,* January 19, 2009, pp. 41–49.
4. Willow Bay, "Test Audiences Have Profound Effect on Movies," *CNN Newsstand & Entertainment Weekly,* September 28, 1998. See www.cnn.com/SHOWBIZ/Movies/9809/28/screen.test.
5. Helene Diamond, "Lights, Camera . . . Research!" *Marketing News,* September 11, 1989, pp. 10–11; and "Killer!" *Time,* November 16, 1987, pp. 72–79.

6. Carl Diorio, "Tracking Projections: Box Office Calculations an Inexact Science," *Variety*, May 24, 2001.

7. Ronald Grover, Tom Lowry, and Michael White, "King of the World (Again)," *Bloomberg Businessweek*, February 1 & 8, 2010, pp. 48–56; and Richard Corliss, "Avatar Ascendant," *Time*, February 8, 2010, pp. 50–51.

8. A lengthier, expanded definition from 2004 is found on the American Marketing Association's website. See http://www.marketingpower .com/AboutAMA/Pages/DefinitionofMarketing.aspx. For a researcher's comments on this and other definitions of marketing research, see Lawrence D. Gibson, "Quo Vadis, *Marketing Research*?" *Marketing Research*, Spring 2000, pp. 36–41.

9. Felix Gillette, "Don't Mess Up," *Bloomberg Businessweek*, February 10–February 16, 2014, pp. 60–69; Franz Lidz, "Block Party," *Smithsonian*, May 2013, pp. 60–62; Harry McCracken, "Build-A-Bot," *Time*, January 21, 2013, pp. 52–53; and Warren Buckleitner, "Lego Updates Its Mindstorms Robotics Kit," *The New York Times*, January 9, 2013; see http://gadgetwise.blogs.nytimes. com/2013/01/09/lego-updates-its-mindstorms-robotics-kit·

10. Vipal Monga, "Big Data Chips Away at Cost," *The Wall Street Journal*, July 1, 2014, p. B6.

11. David A. Aaker, V. Kumar, George S. Day, and Robert P. Leone, *Marketing Research*, 10th ed. (Hoboken, NJ: John Wiley & Sons, 2010), pp. 114–16.

12. Meg James, "Nielsen 'People Meter' Changed the TV Ratings Game 25 Years Ago," *Los Angeles Times*, August 31, 2012. See http://articles.latimes.com/2012/aug/31/entertainment/ la-et-ct-nielsen-people-meter-anniversary-20120830·

13. Amol Sharma and Suzanne Vranica, "Nielson to Add Data for Mobile Viewing," *The Wall Street Journal*, September 20, 2013, p. B3.

14. "Local Television Market Universe (DMA) Estimates: 2013 TV Homes," The Nielsen Company. See http://nielsen.com/content/ dam/corporate/us/en/public%20factsheets/tv/2012-2013%20 DMA%20Ranks.pdf· p. 4.

15. "U.S. Spending Totals by Medium: ZenithOptimedia Forecast 2012," *Advertising Age*, June 25, 2012, p. 22.

16. Jessica E. Vascellaro, "On TV, New Ways to Gauge the Ads," *The Wall Street Journal*, February 4, 2011, p. B10.

17. David Kiley, "Counting the Eyeballs," *BusinessWeek*, January 16, 2006, pp. 84–85; and "The Ultimate Marketing Machine," *The Economist*, July 8, 2006, pp. 61–64.

18. Colleen Moore-Mezler, "Mystery Shoppers Are an Important Resource," *Alert! Magazine*, Marketing Research Association 46, no. 4 (April 2008), pp. 10, 12; and Robert Frank, "How to Live Large and Largely for Free, Jennifer Voitle's Way," *The Wall Street Journal*, June 9, 2003, pp. A1, A8.

19. Ryan Bradley, "How LEGO Got Hot . . . Again," *Fortune*, March 17, 2014, p. 31; Mark Maremont, "New Toothbrush Is Big-Ticket Item," *The Wall Street Journal*, October 27, 1998, pp. B1, B6.

20. Gavin Johnson and Melinda Rea-Holloway, "Ethnography: How to Know If It's Right for Your Study," *Alert! Magazine*, Marketing Research Association 47, no. 2 (February 2009), pp. 1–4. See www .mra-net.org/alert·

21. Kenneth Chang, "Enlisting Science's Lessons to Entice More Shoppers to Spend More," *The New York Times*, September 19, 2006, p. D3; and Janet Adamy, "Cooking Up Changes at Kraft Foods," *The Wall Street Journal*, February 20, 2007, p. B1.

22. Martin Lindstrom, *Buyology: Truth and Lies about Why We Buy* (New York: Doubleday, 2008), pp. 8–36; C. B. Whittemore, "Martin Lindstrom's *Buyology*," *Flooring the Consumer blogspot*, March 1, 2009; Seth Brown, "*Buyology* Offers a Peek Inside Buyers' Heads," *USA Today*, October 29, 2008; and Andrea Sachs, "Business Books," *Time*, October 23, 2008.

23. Ilan Brat, "The Emotional Quotient of Soup Shopping," *The Wall Street Journal*, February 17, 2010, p. B6.

24. For a more complete discussion of questionnaire methods, see Joseph F. Hair, Jr., Robert P. Bush, and David J. Ortinau, *Marketing Research*, 4th ed. (New York: McGraw-Hill/Irwin, 2009), Chapters 6 and 13.

25. See www.trendhunter.com/about-trend-hunter·

26. "What Is Online Research?" Marketing Research Association at http://www.marketingresearch.org/?q5node/221· See also, www.surveymonkey.com·

27. For more discussion on wording questions effectively, see Gilbert A. Churchill, Jr., Tom J. Brown, and Tracy A. Suter, *Basic Marketing Research*, 7th ed. (Mason, OH: South-Western, Cengage Learning, 2010), pp. 289–307.

28. "Lay's Potato Chips Teams Up with Eva Longoria and Iron Chef Michael Symon to Invite Consumers to Create the Next Great Potato Chip Flavor," Frito-Lay website, http://www.fritolay.com/about-us/press-release-20120720.html, accessed September 5, 2014.

29. Jeff Gerst of Bolin Marketing provided the Carmex example, with the permission of Carma Laboratories, Inc.

30. Mark Jeffery, *Data-Driven Marketing: The 15 Metrics Everyone in Marketing Should Know* (Hoboken, NJ: John Wiley & Sons, Inc., 2010), pp. 156–86.

31. Douglas D. Bates, "The Future of Qualitative Research Is Online," *Alert! Magazine*, Marketing Research Association 47, no. 2 (February 2009); Jack Neff, "The End of Consumer Surveys?" *Advertising Age*, September 15, 2008; Jack Neff, "Marketing Execs: Researchers Could Use a Softer Touch," *Advertising Age*, January 27, 2009; Bruce Mendelsohn, "Social Networking: Interactive Marketing Lets Researchers Reach Consumers Where They Are," *Alert! Magazine*, Marketing Research Association 46, no. 4 (April 2008); "Social Media Research: Interview with Joel Rubinson of ARF: Part 1," *Diva Marketing Blog*, February 16, 2009; and "Social Media Research: Interview with Joel Rubinson of ARF: Part 2," *Diva Marketing Blog*, February 23, 2009.

32. The Step 4 discussion was written by David Ford and Don Rylander of Ford Consulting Group, Inc.; the Tony's Pizza example was provided by Teré Carral of Tony's Pizza.

33. "Big Data: Before You Start Restricting It, Be Aware of All the Opportunities," *The Wall Street Journal*, November 19, 2012, p. R10; "Mining the Big Data Gold Mine," *Fortune*: Special Advertising Section, March 30, 2012; Byron Acohido, "Online Tracking Takes a Scary Turn," *USA Today*, August 4, 2011, pp. B1, B2; and "Data, Data Everywhere—A Special Report on Managing Information: A Different Game," *The Economist*, February 27, 2010, pp. 6–8.

34. Joel Stein, "Your Data, Yourself," *Time*, March 21, 2011, pp. 39–46; Suzanne Vranica, "Man vs. Bot: The Online-Ad Wars," *The Wall Street Journal*, March 24, 2014, pp. B1, B5; Elizabeth Dwoskin, "Give Me Back My Privacy," *The Wall Street Journal*, March 24, 2014, pp. R1, R2; and Ryan Flinn, "The Big Business of Sifting through Social Media Data," *Bloomberg Businessweek*, October 25–October 31, 2010, pp. 20–22.

35. See http://www.newbalance.com/NB-Minimus/minimus, default.pg.html and http://www.goodformrunning.com·

Carmex: This case was written by Jeff Gerst and Patrick Hodgdon of Bolin Marketing.

Credits

P. 161, ©Lionsgate/Photofest, Inc. P. 163, Courtesy The LEGO Group. P. 163, *See above*. P. 166, Pixtal/AGE Fotostock. P. 167, Photo by M. Caulfield/American Idol 2008/Getty Images. P. 168, Macduff Everton/The Image Bank/Getty Images. P. 169, ©iStock. P. 170, ©Spencer Grant/PhotoEdit. P. 170, AP Photo/Paul Vernon. P. 171, ©K. Rousonelos. P. 173, Altus Business Development with the permission of Carma Laboratories, Inc. P. 175, ©Imaginechina/Corbis. P. 176, Todd Warnock/Lifesize/Getty Images. P. 177, ©Brent Jones. P. 178, ©M. Hruby. P. 181, Courtesy New Balance. P. 185, *All images:* Altus Business Development with the permission of Carma Laboratories, Inc. P. 186, *See above*.

8 Market Segmentation, Targeting, and Positioning

LEARNING OBJECTIVES

After reading this chapter you should be able to:

 LO 8-1 Explain what market segmentation is and when to use it.

 LO 8-2 Identify the five steps involved in segmenting and targeting markets.

 LO 8-3 Recognize the bases used to segment consumer and organizational (business) markets.

 LO 8-4 Develop a market-product grid to identify a target market and recommend resulting marketing actions.

 LO 8-5 Explain how marketing managers position products in the marketplace.

ZAPPOS.COM'S STRATEGY: SEGMENTS + SERVICE = "WOW"

Tony Hsieh (opposite page) showed signs of being an entrepreneur early in life. For instance, in college, Hsieh sold pizzas out of his dorm room.[1] Today, he's chief executive officer (CEO) of online retailer Zappos.com, now owned by Amazon.com. The company name is derived from the Spanish word *zapatos,* which means shoes.

A Clear Market Segmentation Strategy

Nick Swinmurn founded the online shoe store when he couldn't find a pair of Airwalk desert boots at a local mall. Hsieh, Lin, and Swinmurn have given Zappos.com a clear, specific market segmentation strategy: Offer a huge selection of shoes to people who will buy them online. Recently Zappos.com has added lines of clothes, accessories, beauty aids, and housewares. This focus on the segment of online buyers generates over $1 billion in sales annually.[2]

A New Jersey customer says, "With Zappos I can try the shoes in the comfort of my own home. . . . It's fabulous."[3] Zappos.com also provides free shipping both ways and offers more than 1,000 brands to customers.

Delivering WOW Customer Service

Asked about Zappos.com, Hsieh says, "We try to spend most of our time on stuff that will improve customer-service levels."[4] This customer-service obsession for its market segment of online customers means that all new Zappos.com employees—whether the chief financial officer or the children's footwear buyer—go through four weeks of customer-loyalty training. Hsieh offers one month's salary to anyone completing the training who wants to leave Zappos.com. The theory: If you take the money and run, you're not right for Zappos.com. Few take the money!

Ten "core values" are the foundation for the Zappos.com culture, brand, and business strategies. Some examples:[5]

#1. Deliver WOW through service. This focus on exemplary customer service encompasses all 10 core values.

#3. Create fun and a little weirdness. In a Zappos.com day, cowbells ring, modified-blaster gunfights arise, and Tony Hsieh appears with Blue Man Group actors (opposite page).

#6. Build open and honest relationships with communication. Employees are told to say what they think.

The other Zappos.com core values appear on its website: www.zappos .com. Tony Hsieh's strategy concerning core values and customer service appears on Twitter, where he has more than 2.6 million followers.[6]

The Zappos.com strategy illustrates successful market segmentation and targeting, the first topics in Chapter 8. The chapter ends with the topic of positioning the organization, product, or brand.

WHY SEGMENT MARKETS?

 LO 8-1 Explain what market segmentation is and when to use it.

A business firm segments its markets so it can respond more effectively to the wants of groups of potential buyers and thus increase its sales and profits. Not-for-profit organizations also segment the clients they serve to satisfy client needs more effectively while achieving the organization's goals. Let's describe (1) what market segmentation is and (2) when to segment markets, sometimes using the Zappos.com segmentation strategy as an example.

What Market Segmentation Means

market segmentation
Aggregates prospective buyers into groups that have common needs and will respond similarly to a marketing action.

product differentiation
The strategy of using different marketing mix actions to help consumers perceive a product as being different and better than competing products.

People have different needs and wants, even though it would be easier for marketers if they didn't. **Market segmentation** involves aggregating prospective buyers into groups that (1) have common needs and (2) will respond similarly to a marketing action. As defined in Chapter 1, *market segments* are the relatively homogeneous groups of prospective buyers that result from the market segmentation process. Each market segment consists of people who are relatively similar to each other in terms of their consumption behavior.

The existence of different market segments has caused firms to use a marketing strategy of **product differentiation**. This strategy involves a firm using different marketing mix actions, such as product features and advertising, to help consumers perceive the product as being different and better than competing products. The perceived differences may involve physical features, such as size or color, or nonphysical ones, such as image or price.

Segmentation: Linking Needs to Actions The process of segmenting a market and selecting specific segments as targets is the link between the various buyers' needs and the organization's marketing program, as shown in Figure 8–1. Market segmentation is only a means to an end: It leads to tangible marketing actions that can increase sales and profitability.

Market segmentation first stresses the importance of grouping people or organizations in a market according to the similarity of their needs and the benefits they are looking for in making a purchase. Second, such needs and benefits must be related to specific marketing actions that the organization can take, such as a new product or special promotion.

Video 8-1
Zappos TV
kerin.tv/cr6e/v8-1

The Zappos.com Segmentation Strategy The Zappos.com target customer segment originally consisted of people who wanted to (1) have a wide selection of shoes, (2) shop online in the convenience of their own homes, and (3) receive quick delivery and free returns. Zappos's actions include offering a huge inventory of shoes using an online selling strategy and providing overnight delivery. These actions have enabled Zappos.com to create a positive customer experience and generate repeat purchases. Zappos's success in selling footwear has enabled it to add lines of clothing, handbags, accessories (such as sunglasses), and housewares to reach new segments of buyers.

With over 8 million customers and 5,000 calls daily to Zappos's service center, its executives believe the speed with which a customer receives an online purchase plays a big role in gaining repeat customers.[7] The company continues to stress this point of difference of providing the absolute best service among online sellers.

FIGURE 8–1
Market segmentation links market needs to an organization's marketing program—its specific marketing mix actions designed to satisfy those needs.

Identify market needs
Benefits in terms of:
- Product features
- Expense
- Quality
- Savings in time and convenience

→

Link needs to actions
Take steps to segment and target markets

→

Execute marketing program actions
A marketing mix of:
- Product
- Price
- Promotion
- Place (distribution)

Using Market Product Grids   How do you sleep—on your side, your back, or your stomach? These are really the key market segments of sleepers. Sleep researchers have discovered that you'll probably get a better night's sleep if you have the right firmness of pillow under your head. So we can develop the market-product grid shown in Figure 8–2.[8]

A **market-product grid** is a framework to relate the market segments of potential buyers to products offered or potential marketing actions. The market-product grid in Figure 8–2 shows the different market segments for bed pillows—the side, back, and stomach sleepers—in the horizontal rows. The product offerings—the pillows—appear in the vertical columns and are based on three different pillow firmnesses—firm, medium, and soft.

Market research reveals the size of each sleeper segment, as shown by both the percentages and circles in Figure 8–2. This tells pillow manufacturers the relative importance of each of the three market segments, which is critical information when scheduling production. It also emphasizes the importance of firm pillows, a product targeted at the side sleeper market segment. As Figure 8–2 shows, this segment is almost three times the size of the other two combined. Therefore, meeting the needs of this market segment with the right firmness of pillow is especially important.

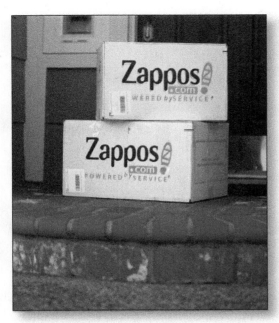

Zappos.com's emphasis on "WOW service"—like quick delivery—has enabled it to reach market segments beyond shoes.

market-product grid
A framework relating the segments of a market to products or marketing actions of the firm.

When and How to Segment Markets

One-size-fits-all mass markets—like that for Tide laundry detergent 40 years ago—no longer exist. The marketing officer at Procter & Gamble, which markets Tide, says, "Every one of our brands is targeted." Due to the recent recession, the size of the middle-income market is shrinking. In response, P&G has begun implementing a new segmentation strategy: Offer different products to reach (1) high-income and (2) low-income families.[9]

A business goes to the trouble and expense of segmenting its markets when it expects that this extra effort will increase its sales, profit, and return on investment. When expenses are greater than the potentially increased sales from segmentation, a firm should not attempt to segment its market. Three specific segmentation strategies that illustrate this point are (1) one product and multiple market segments, (2) multiple products and multiple market segments, and (3) segments of one, or mass customization.

One Product and Multiple Market Segments   When an organization produces only a single product or service and attempts to sell it to two or more market segments, it avoids the extra costs of developing and producing additional versions of the product. In this case, the incremental costs of taking the product into new market segments are typically those of a separate promotional campaign or a new channel of distribution.

FIGURE 8–2
This market-product grid shows the kind of sleeper that is targeted for each of the bed pillow products. The percentages and sizes of the circles show that side sleepers are the dominant market segment and that they prefer firm pillows.

MARKET SEGMENTS	BED PILLOW PRODUCTS		
	Firm Pillows	Medium Pillows	Soft Pillows
Side sleepers	=73%		
Back sleepers		=22%	
Stomach sleepers			=5%

Do Harry Potter books appeal only to the market segment of English-speaking kids? See the text for the answer about this amazing success story among book publishers.

Magazines and books are single products frequently directed at two or more distinct market segments. The annual *Sporting News Baseball Yearbook* uses 17 different covers featuring a baseball star from each of its regions in the United States. Yet each regional issue has the same magazine content.

Harry Potter's phenomenal seven-book success is based on both author J. K. Rowling's fiction-writing wizardry and her publisher's creativity in marketing to preteen, teen, and adult segments of readers around the world. More than 450 million Harry Potter books, audio books, and e-books have been sold in 67 languages.[10] In the United States, the books were often at the top of *The New York Times* fiction best-seller list—for adults. Although separate covers for magazines or separate advertisements for books are expensive, these expenses are minor compared with the costs of producing multiple versions of magazines or books for several different market segments.

Multiple Products and Multiple Market Segments Ford's different lines of cars, SUVs, and pickup trucks are each targeted at a different type of customer—examples of multiple products aimed at multiple market segments. Producing these different vehicles is clearly more expensive than producing only a single vehicle. But this strategy is very effective *if* it meets customers' needs better, doesn't reduce quality or increase price, and adds to Ford's sales revenues and profits.

Unfortunately, this product differentiation strategy in the auto industry has a huge potential downside: The proliferation of different models and options can reduce quality and raise prices—especially in relation to foreign imports. Perhaps the extreme was in 1982, when the Ford Thunderbird had exactly 69,120 options compared with 32 (including colors) on the 1982 Honda Accord.[11]

Three decades later Ford is relearning its models and options lessons. Its current successful turnaround is partly related to a reduction in the number of frames, engines, and brands offered. As a result, Ford has reduced its number of models from 97 to 36 and sold off the Jaguar, Land Rover, and Volvo brands. Although there are fewer choices, Ford's simplified product line provides two benefits to consumers: (1) lower prices through producing a higher volume of fewer models and (2) higher quality because of the ability to debug fewer basic designs.[12]

Segments of One: Mass Customization American marketers are rediscovering today what their ancestors running the corner general store knew a century ago: Each customer has unique needs and wants and desires special tender loving care. Economies of scale in manufacturing and marketing during the past century made

ANN INC.'s LOFT chain tries to reach younger and value-conscious women with a casual lifestyle, while its Ann Taylor chain targets more sophisticated and relatively affluent women. For the potential dangers of this two-segment strategy, see the text.

The smaller Walmart Express format makes it easier for customers to take advantage of "everyday low prices."

mass-produced products so affordable that most customers were willing to compromise their individual tastes and settle for standardized products. Today's Internet ordering and flexible manufacturing and marketing processes have made *mass customization* possible, which means tailoring products or services to the tastes of individual customers on a high-volume scale.

Mass customization is the next step beyond *build-to-order* (BTO), manufacturing a product only when there is an order from a customer. Apple uses BTO systems that trim work-in-progress inventories and shorten delivery times to customers. To do this, Apple restricts its computer manufacturing line to only a few basic models that can be assembled in four minutes. This gives customers a good choice with quick delivery. But even this system falls a bit short of total mass customization because customers do not have an unlimited number of features from which to choose.

The Segmentation Trade-Off: Synergies versus Cannibalization   The key to successful product differentiation and market segmentation strategies is finding the ideal balance between satisfying a customer's individual wants and achieving *organizational synergy*, the increased customer value achieved through performing organizational functions such as marketing or manufacturing more efficiently. The "increased customer value" can take many forms: more products, improved quality of existing products, lower prices, easier access to products through improved distribution, and so on. So the ultimate criterion for an organization's marketing success is that customers should be better off as a result of the increased synergies.

The organization should also achieve increased revenues and profits from the product differentiation and market segmentation strategies it uses. When the increased customer value involves adding new products or a new chain of stores, the product differentiation–market segmentation trade-off raises a critical issue: Are the new products or new stores simply stealing customers and sales from the older, existing ones? This is known as *cannibalization*.

Marketers increasingly emphasize a two-tier, "Tiffany/Walmart" strategy. Many firms now offer different variations of the same basic offering to high-end and low-end segments. Gap's Banana Republic chain sells blue jeans for $58, whereas Gap's Old Navy stores sell a slightly different version for $22.

Unfortunately, the lines between customer segments can often blur and lead to problems. For example, consider the competition within the ANN INC. organization between stores in its two chains—Ann Taylor and LOFT. The Ann Taylor chain targets "successful, relatively affluent, fashion-conscious women," while its sister Ann Taylor LOFT chain targets "value-conscious women who want a casual lifestyle at work and home." The LOFT stores wound up stealing sales from the Ann Taylor chain. The result: More than 100 stores from both chains were recently closed.[13] Both chains are now aggressively targeting their customers by stressing online sales and opening new factory outlet stores.

Walmart is now operating 12 stores to test the concept of "Walmart Express," stores that are one-tenth the size of its supercenters and sell groceries. These smaller stores are intended to compete with the dollar chains and bare-bones outlets (like Germany's Aldi supermarket chain), which are stealing U.S. Walmart customers and causing lagging sales. Will its own Tiffany/Walmart strategy—or perhaps "Walmart/Aldi strategy"—prove successful or simply be another case of cannibalization?[14] Time will tell.

learning review

8-1. Market segmentation involves aggregating prospective buyers into groups that have two key characteristics. What are they?

8-2. In terms of market segments and products, what are the three market segmentation strategies?

STEPS IN SEGMENTING AND TARGETING MARKETS

LO 8-2 Identify the five steps involved in segmenting and targeting markets.

Figure 8–3 identifies the five-step process used to segment a market and select the target segments on which an organization wants to focus. Segmenting a market requires both detailed analysis and large doses of common sense and managerial judgment. So market segmentation is both science and art!

For the purposes of our discussion, assume that you have just purchased a Wendy's restaurant. Your Wendy's is located next to a large urban university, one that offers both day and evening classes. Your restaurant offers the basic Wendy's fare: hamburgers, chicken and deli sandwiches, salads, french fries, and Frosty desserts. Even though you are part of a chain that has some restrictions on menu and decor, you are free to set your hours of business and to develop local advertising. How can market segmentation help? In the sections that follow, you will apply the five-step process for segmenting and targeting markets to arrive at marketing actions for your Wendy's restaurant.

A local Wendy's restaurant near a large urban university campus—like yours!

Step 1: Group Potential Buyers into Segments

It's not always a good idea to segment a market. Grouping potential buyers into meaningful segments involves meeting some specific criteria that answer the questions, "Would segmentation be worth doing?" and "Is it possible?" If so, a marketer must find specific variables that can be used to create these various segments.

Criteria to Use in Forming the Segments   A marketing manager should develop market segments that meet five essential criteria:[15]

- *Simplicity and cost-effectiveness of assigning potential buyers to segments.* A marketing manager must be able to put a market segmentation plan into effect. This means identifying the characteristics of potential buyers in a market and then cost-effectively assigning them to a segment.
- *Potential for increased profit.* The best segmentation approach is the one that maximizes the opportunity for future profit and return on investment (ROI). If this potential is maximized without segmentation, don't segment. For nonprofit organizations, the criterion is the potential for serving clients more effectively.
- *Similarity of needs of potential buyers within a segment.* Potential buyers within a segment should be similar in terms of common needs that, in turn, lead to common marketing actions, such as product features sought or advertising media used.
- *Difference of needs of buyers among segments.* If the needs of the various segments aren't very different, combine them into fewer segments. A different segment usually requires a different marketing action that, in turn, means greater costs.

FIGURE 8–3
The five key steps in segmenting and targeting markets link the market needs of customers to the organization's marketing program.

Identify market needs

Link needs to actions. The steps:
1 Group potential buyers into segments
2 Group products to be sold into categories
3 Develop a market-product grid and estimate size of markets
4 Select target markets
5 Take marketing actions to reach target markets

Execute marketing program actions

Marketing Matters

To Which "Flock" Do You Belong?

There is an old saying that "birds of a feather flock together." This also applies to the formation of market segments and gives rise to the following questions marketers must ask and answer: Who are your target customers? What are they like? Where do they live? How can you reach them?

These questions are answered in part by Nielsen, whose PRIZM® consumer segmentation system classifies every household into one of 66 demographically and behaviorally distinct neighborhood segments to identify lifestyles and purchase behavior within a defined geographic market area, such as zip code. Many organizations today use these neighborhood segments, especially with social media.

Want to know what your neighborhood is like? Go to www.claritas.com/MyBestSegments/Default.jsp and click the "ZIP Code Look-up" link or "Enter ZIP Code" button on the MyBestSegments home page. Then, type in your 5-digit zip code and security code. Last, click the "Submit" button to find out what the most common segments are in your neighborhood.

For a description of these segments, click the "Segment Explorer" tab. Is this your "flock"? What specific product or service organizations might be interested in targeting these segments?

If increased sales don't offset extra costs, combine segments and reduce the number of marketing actions.

- *Potential of a marketing action to reach a segment.* Reaching a segment requires a simple but effective marketing action. If no such action exists, don't segment.

LO 8-3 Recognize the bases used to segment consumer and organizational (business) markets.

Ways to Segment Consumer Markets Four general bases of segmentation can be used to segment U.S. consumer markets. These four segmentation bases are (1) *geographic segmentation*, which is based on where prospective customers live or work (region, city size); (2) *demographic segmentation*, which is based on some *objective* physical (gender, race), measurable (age, income), or other classification attribute (birth era, occupation) of prospective customers; (3) *psychographic segmentation*, which is based on some *subjective* mental or emotional attributes (personality), aspirations (lifestyle), or needs of prospective customers; and (4) *behavioral segmentation*, which is based on some observable actions or attitudes by prospective customers—such as where they buy, what benefits they seek, how frequently they buy, and why they buy. Some examples are:

- *Geographic segmentation: Region.* Campbell Soup Company found that its canned nacho cheese sauce, which could be heated and poured directly onto nacho chips, was too spicy for Americans in the East and not spicy enough for those in the West and Southwest. The result: Campbell's plants in Texas and California now produce a hotter nacho cheese sauce to serve their regions better.
- *Demographic segmentation: Household size.* More than half of all U.S. households are made up of only one or two persons, so Campbell packages meals with only one or two servings for this market segment.
- *Psychographic segmentation: Lifestyle.* Nielsen's lifestyle segmentation is based on the belief that "birds of a feather flock together." Thus, people of similar lifestyles tend to live near one another, have similar interests, and buy similar offerings. This is of great value to marketers. Nielsen PRIZM® classifies every household in the United States into one of 66 unique market segments. See the Marketing Matters box for a profile of where you live.
- *Behavioral segmentation: Product features.* Understanding what features are important to different customers is a useful way to segment markets because it can lead directly to specific marketing actions, such as a new product, an ad campaign, or a distribution channel. For example, college dorm residents frequently want to keep and prepare their own food to save money or have a late-night snack.

However, their dorm rooms are often woefully short of space. MicroFridge understands this and markets a combination microwave, refrigerator, freezer, and charging station appliance targeted to these students.

- *Behavioral segmentation: Usage rate.* **Usage rate** is the quantity consumed or patronage—store visits—during a specific period. It varies significantly among different customer groups. Airlines have developed frequent-flier programs to encourage passengers to use the same airline repeatedly to create loyal customers. This technique, sometimes called *frequency marketing*, focuses on usage rate. One key conclusion emerges about usage: In market segmentation studies, some measurement of usage by, or sales obtained from, various segments is central to the analysis.

usage rate
The quantity consumed or the number of store visits during a specific period.

This appliance includes everything from a small refrigerator, freezer, and microwave oven to a charging station for laptops and mobile phones. To which market segment might this appeal? The answer appears in the text.

80/20 rule
The idea that 80 percent of a firm's sales are obtained from 20 percent of its customers.

The Aberdeen Group recently analyzed which segmentation bases were used by the 20 percent most profitable organizations of the 220 surveyed. From highest to lowest, these were the segmentation bases they used:

- Geographic bases—88 percent
- Behavioral bases—65 percent
- Demographic bases—53 percent
- Psychographic bases—43 percent

The top 20 percent often use more than one of these bases in their market segmentation studies, plus measures such as purchase histories and usage rates of customers.[16]

Experian Simmons continuously surveys over 25,000 adults each year to obtain quarterly, projectable usage rate data from the U.S. national population for more than 500 consumer product categories and 8,000-plus brands. Its purpose is to discover how the products and services they buy and the media they use relate to their behavioral, psychographic, and demographic characteristics.

Usage rate is sometimes referred to in terms of the **80/20 rule**, a concept that suggests 80 percent of a firm's sales are obtained from 20 percent of its customers. The percentages in the 80/20 rule are not really fixed at exactly 80 percent and 20 percent, but they suggest that a small fraction of customers provides most of a firm's sales.

Patronage of Fast-Food Restaurants   As part of its survey, Experian Simmons asked adults which fast-food restaurant(s) was (1) the sole or only restaurant, (2) the primary one, or (3) one of several secondary ones they patronized. As a Wendy's restaurant owner, the information depicted in Figure 8–4 should give you some ideas in developing a marketing program for your local market. For example, the Wendy's bar graph in Figure 8–4 shows that the 0.7 percent of "sole restaurant" patrons of Wendy's (shaded blue) and the 12.5 percent of "primary restaurant" patrons of Wendy's (shaded yellow) are somewhat lower than the percentages for Burger King and far lower than those for McDonald's. So your challenge is to look at these two competitors and devise a marketing program to win customers from them.[17]

The green-shaded nonusers part of the Wendy's bar graph in Figure 8–4 shows that 14.6 percent of adult Americans don't go to fast-food restaurants in a typical month and are really "nonprospects"—unlikely to ever patronize any fast-food restaurant. However, the 57.0 percent of "nonusers" who do not patronize Wendy's but who are "prospects" (shaded orange) may be worth a targeted marketing program because they use the product category (fast food) but do not eat at Wendy's yet. New menu items or promotional strategies may succeed in converting these prospects into users that patronize Wendy's.

Variables to Use in Forming Segments for Wendy's   To analyze your Wendy's customers, you need to identify which variables to use to segment them. Because the restaurant is located near a large urban university, the most logical starting point for segmentation is really behavioral: Are the prospective customers students or nonstudents?

FIGURE 8–4

Comparison of various kinds of users and nonusers for Wendy's, Burger King, and McDonald's fast-food restaurants. This graphic gives Wendy's restaurants a snapshot of its customers compared to those of its major competitors.

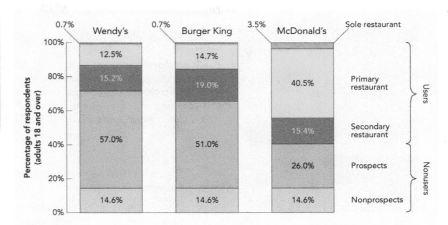

Source: Experian Marketing Services Simmons Winter 2013 NHCS Full-Year Adult Survey 12-Month OneView^SM Crosstabulation Report, Experian Marketing Services, 2013. See http://www.experian.com/marketing-services/consumer-insights.html.

What variables might Xerox use to segment organizational markets to respond to a firm's color printing needs? For the possible answer and related marketing actions, see the text.

To segment the students, you could try a variety of (1) geographic variables, such as city or zip code; (2) demographic variables, such as gender, age, year in school, or college major; or (3) psychographic variables, such as personality or needs. But none of these variables really meets the five criteria listed previously—particularly, the fifth criterion about leading to a doable marketing action to reach the various segments. The behavioral basis of segmentation for the "students" segment really combines two variables: (1) where students live and (2) when they are on campus. This results in four "student" segments:

- Students living in dormitories (residence halls, sororities, fraternities).
- Students living near the university in apartments.
- Day commuter students living outside the area.
- Night commuter students living outside the area.

The three main segments of "nonstudents" include:

- Faculty and staff members who work at the university.
- People who live in the area but aren't connected with the university.
- People who work in the area but aren't connected with the university.

People in each of these nonstudent segments aren't quite as similar as those in the student segments, which makes them harder to reach with a marketing program or action. Think about (1) whether the needs of all these segments are different and (2) how various advertising media can be used to reach these groups effectively.

Ways to Segment Organizational (Business) Markets A number of variables can be used to segment organizational (business) markets. For example, a product manager at Xerox responsible for its new line of multifunction color printers (MFPs) might use these segmentation bases and corresponding variables:

- *Geographic segmentation: Statistical area.* Firms located in a metropolitan statistical area might receive a personal sales call, whereas those in a micropolitan statistical area might be contacted by telephone.
- *Demographic segmentation: NAICS code.* Firms categorized by the North American Industry Classification System code as manufacturers that deal with customers throughout the world might have different document printing needs than retailers or lawyers serving local customers.

- *Demographic segmentation: Number of employees.* The size of the firm is related to the volume of digital documents produced, so firms with varying numbers of employees might be specific target markets for different Xerox MFPs.
- *Behavioral segmentation: Usage rate.* Similar to this segmentation variable for consumer markets, features are often of major importance in organizational markets. So Xerox can target organizations needing fast printing, copying, faxing, and scanning in color—the benefits and features emphasized in the ad for its Xerox Color WorkCentre 7755/7765/7775 Multifunction System.

---

learning review

8-3. The process of segmenting and targeting markets is a bridge between which two marketing activities?

8-4. What is the difference between the demographic and behavioral bases of market segmentation?

Step 2: Group Products to Be Sold into Categories

Video 8-2
Dave's Hot 'N Juicy Ad
kerin.tv/cr6e/v8-2

What does your Wendy's restaurant sell? Of course you are selling individual products such as Frostys, hamburgers, and fries. But for marketing purposes you're really selling combinations of individual products that become a "meal." This distinction is critical, so let's discuss both (1) individual Wendy's products and (2) groupings of Wendy's products.

Individual Wendy's Products When Dave Thomas founded Wendy's in 1969, he offered only four basic items: "Hot 'N Juicy" hamburgers, Frosty Dairy Desserts (Frostys), french fries, and soft drinks. Since then, Wendy's has introduced many new products and innovations to compete for customers' fast-food dollars. Some of these are shown in Figure 8–5. New products include salads, low trans fat chicken sandwiches, natural-cut fries with sea salt, and the "Dave's Hot 'N Juicy" hamburger. But there are also nonproduct innovations to increase consumer convenience like drive-thru services and E-Pay to enable credit card purchases.

Figure 8–5 also shows that each product or innovation is not targeted equally to all market segments based on gender, needs, or university affiliation. The cells in Figure 8–5 labeled "P" represent Wendy's primary target market segments when it introduced each product or innovation. The boxes labeled "S" represent the secondary target market segments that also bought these products or used these innovations. In some cases, Wendy's discovered that large numbers of people in a segment not originally targeted for a particular product or innovation bought or used it anyway.

Groupings of Wendy's Products: Meals Finding a means of grouping the products a firm sells into meaningful categories is as important as grouping customers into segments. If the firm has only one product or service, this isn't a problem. But when it has many, these must be grouped in some way so buyers can relate to them. This is why department stores and supermarkets are organized into product groups, with the departments or aisles containing related merchandise. Likewise, manufacturers organize products into groupings in the catalogs they send to customers.

What are the product groupings for your Wendy's restaurant? It could be the item purchased, such as hamburgers, salads, Frostys, and french fries. This is where judgment—the qualitative aspect of marketing—comes in. Customers really buy an eating experience—a meal occasion that satisfies a need at a particular time of day. So the product groupings that make the most marketing sense are the five "meals" based

MARKET SEGMENT		PRODUCT OR INNOVATION							
GENERAL	GROUP WITH NEED	HOT 'N JUICY HAMBURGER (1969)	DRIVE THRU (1970)	99¢ SUPER VALUE MEALS (1989)	SALAD SENSATIONS (2002)	E-PAY (2003)	LOW TRANS FAT CHICKEN SANDWICHES (2006)	NATURAL-CUT FRIES WITH SEA SALT (2010)	DAVE'S HOT 'N JUICY HAMBURGERS (2011)
GENDER	Male	P	P	P	S		S	P	S
	Female				S	S	S		
NEEDS	Price/Value			P	S				
	Health-Conscious				P		S		
	Convenience	S	P		S	S			S
	Meat Lovers	P		S			S	S	P
UNIVERSITY AFFILIATION	Affiliated (students, faculty, staff)	P	S	S	P	P	P		P
	Nonaffiliated (residents, workers)	S	P	S	S	S	S		S

Key: = Primary market   = Secondary market

FIGURE 8–5
Wendy's new products and other innovations target specific market segments based on a customer's gender, needs, or university affiliation.

LO 8-4 Develop a market-product grid to identify a target market and recommend resulting marketing actions.

on the time of day consumers buy them: breakfast, lunch, between-meal snack, dinner, and after-dinner snack. These groupings are more closely related to the way purchases are actually made and permit you to market the entire meal, not just your individual items such as french fries or hamburgers.

Step 3: Develop a Market-Product Grid and Estimate the Size of Markets

As noted earlier in the chapter, a market-product grid is a framework to relate the market segments of potential buyers to products offered or potential marketing actions by an organization. In a complete market-product grid analysis, each cell in the grid can show the estimated market size of a given product sold to a specific market segment. Let's first look at forming a market-product grid for your Wendy's restaurant and then estimate market sizes.

Forming a Market-Product Grid for Wendy's Developing a market-product grid means identifying and labeling the markets (or horizontal rows) and product groupings (or vertical columns), as shown in Figure 8–6 on the next page. From our earlier discussion, we've chosen to divide the market segments into students versus nonstudents, with subdivisions of each. The columns—or "products"—are really the meals (or eating occasions) customers enjoy at the restaurant.

Estimating Market Sizes for Wendy's Now the size of the market in each cell (the unique market-product combination) of the market-product grid must be estimated. For your Wendy's restaurant, this involves estimating the sales of each kind of meal expected to be sold to each student and nonstudent market segment.

The market size estimates in Figure 8–6 vary from a large market ("3") to no market at all ("0") for each cell in the market-product grid. These may be simple guesstimates if you don't have the time or money to conduct formal marketing research

FIGURE 8–6
A market-product grid for your Wendy's fast-food restaurant next to an urban university. The numbers in the grid show the estimated size of the market in each cell, which leads to selecting the shaded target market.

MARKET SEGMENTS		PRODUCT OR INNOVATION				
General	Where They Live	Break-fast	Lunch	Between-Meal Snack	Dinner	After-Dinner Snack
Student	Dormitory	0	1	3	0	3
	Apartment	1	3	3	1	1
	Day Commuter	0	3	2	1	0
	Night Commuter	0	0	1	3	2
Nonstudent	Faculty or Staff	0	3	1	1	0
	Live in Area	0	1	2	2	1
	Work in Area	1	3	0	1	0

Key: 3 = Large market; 2 = Medium market; 1 = Small market; and 0 = No market

(as discussed in Chapter 7). But even such crude estimates of the size of specific markets using a market-product grid are helpful in determining which target market segments to select and which product groupings to offer.

Step 4: Select Target Markets

A firm must take care to choose its target market segments carefully. If it picks too narrow a set of segments, it may fail to reach the volume of sales and profits it needs. If it selects too broad a set of segments, it may spread its marketing efforts so thin that the extra expense exceeds the increased sales and profits.

Criteria to Use in Selecting the Target Segments   Two kinds of criteria in the market segmentation process are those used to (1) divide the market into segments (discussed earlier) and (2) actually pick the target segments. Even experienced marketing executives often confuse them. Five criteria can be used to select the target segments for your Wendy's restaurant:

Wendy's has been aggressive in introducing new menu items to appeal to customers—such as making its classic cheeseburger thicker and offering new premium toppings.

- *Market size.* The estimated size of the market in the segment is an important factor in deciding whether it's worth going after. There is really no market for breakfasts among dormitory students with meal plans, so you should not devote any marketing effort toward reaching this tiny segment. In your market-product grid (Figure 8–6), this market segment is given a "0" to indicate there is no market.

- *Expected growth.* Although the size of the market in the segment may be small now, perhaps it is growing significantly or is expected to grow in the future. Sales of fast-food meals eaten outside the restaurants are projected to exceed those eaten inside. And Wendy's has been shown to be the fast-food leader in average time to serve a drive-thru order—faster than McDonald's. This speed and convenience is potentially very important to night commuters in adult education programs.

- *Competitive position.* Is there a lot of competition in the segment now or is there likely to be in the future? The less the competition, the more attractive the segment is. For example, if the college dormitories announce a new policy of "no meals on weekends," this segment is suddenly more promising for your restaurant. Wendy's recently introduced the E-Pay pay-by-credit-card service at its restaurants to keep up with a similar service at McDonald's.

- *Cost of reaching the segment.* A segment that is inaccessible to a firm's marketing actions should not be pursued. For example, the few nonstudents who live in the area may not be reachable with ads in newspapers or other media. As a result, you should not waste money trying to advertise to them.

- *Compatibility with the organization's objectives and resources.* If your Wendy's restaurant doesn't yet have the cooking equipment to make breakfasts and has a policy against spending more money on restaurant equipment, then don't try to reach the breakfast segment. In fact, the Wendy's strategy today involves serving breakfast at only a handful of its locations. As is often the case in marketing decisions, a particular segment may appear attractive according to some criteria and very unattractive according to others.

Choose the Wendy's Segments   Ultimately, a marketing executive has to use these criteria to choose the segments for special marketing efforts. As shown in Figure 8–6, let's assume you've written off the breakfast product grouping for two reasons: It's too small a market and it's incompatible with your objectives and resources. In terms of competitive position and cost of reaching the segment, you focus on the four student segments and *not* the three nonstudent segments (although you're certainly not going to turn their business away!). This combination of market-product segments—your target market—is shaded in Figure 8–6.

Step 5: Take Marketing Actions to Reach Target Markets

The purpose of developing a market-product grid is to trigger marketing actions to increase sales and profits. This means that someone must develop and execute an action plan in the form of a marketing program.

Your Immediate Wendy's Segmentation Strategy   For starters, you have to decide whether your Wendy's restaurant should open for breakfast and compete for the breakfast market segment. With your restaurant's location next to a college campus, your initial research shown in Figure 8–6 tells you there is probably not a significant breakfast market to try to reach. So you decide not to open for business until 10:30 A.M. In fact, Wendy's first attempt at a breakfast menu was a disaster and was discontinued in 1986. However, that strategy has changed yet again, with its new "fresh made breakfast" menu now being offered in most locations.

Another essential decision is where and what meals to advertise to reach specific market segments. An ad in the student newspaper could reach all the student segments, but it might be too expensive. If you choose three segments for special attention (Figure 8–7 on the next page), advertising actions to reach them might include:

- *Day commuters* (an entire market segment). Run ads inside commuter buses and put flyers under the windshield wipers of cars in parking lots used by day commuters. These ads and flyers promote all the meals at your restaurant to the day commuter segment of students, a horizontal orange row through the product groupings or "meals" in your market-product grid.

- *Between-meal snacks* (directed to all four student market segments). To promote eating during this downtime for your restaurant, offer "Ten percent off all purchases between 2:00 and 4:30 P.M. during winter quarter." This ad promotes a single meal to all four student segments, a vertical blue column through the market-product grid.

- *Dinners to night commuters* (selecting a unique market-product combination). The most focused of all three campaigns, this strategy promotes a single meal to the single segment of night commuter students shaded green. The campaign uses flyers placed under the windshield wipers of cars in parking lots. To encourage eating dinner at Wendy's, offer a free Frosty with the coupon when the person buys a meal between 5 and 8 P.M. using the drive-thru window.

FIGURE 8–7
Advertising actions to market various meals to a range of possible market segments of students.

MARKET SEGMENTS	PRODUCT GROUPINGS: MEAL OCCASION			
Behavioral: Where They Live	Lunch	Between-Meal Snack	Dinner	After-Dinner Snack
Dormitory Students	1	3	0	3
Apartment Students	3	3	1	1
Day Commuter Students	3	2	1	0
Night Commuter Students	0	1	3	2

Ads in buses; flyers under windshield wipers of cars in parking lots

Ad campaign: "10% off all purchases between 2:00 and 4:30 P.M." during winter quarter"

Ad on flyer under windshield wipers of cars in night parking lots: "Free Frosty with this coupon when you buy a drive-thru meal between 5:00 and 8:00 P.M."

Key: 3 = Large market; 2 = Medium market; 1 = Small market; and 0 = No market.

Depending on how your advertising actions work, you can repeat, modify, or drop them and design new campaigns for other segments you deem are worth the effort. This advertising example is just a small piece of a complete marketing program for your Wendy's restaurant.

There's always plenty of competition in the hamburger business. Five Guys Burgers and Fries has grown to more than 1,000 outlets in the past decade.

Keeping an Eye on Competition   Other competitors are not sitting still, so in running your Wendy's you must be aware of their strategies as well. McDonald's has been aggressively marketing its "garden" snack wraps, McCafe coffee beverages, oatmeal, and high-margin fruit smoothies to broaden its menu. Then in 2014 McDonald's announced its menus were getting "too complicated," which has slowed service, so McDonald's is now trying to "simplify" things.[18] Meanwhile, moving in the opposite direction, Burger King is upgrading its outlets and and broadening its Limited-Time-Only menus.[19]

Even new hamburger chains are popping up. In 1986, a Virginia husband-and-wife team started the Five Guys Burgers and Fries hamburger restaurant and 15 years later had only five restaurants in the Washington, D.C., area. But from 2003 to 2012, Five Guys exploded, with more than 1,000 locations nationwide and 1,500 new restaurants planned. Some of its points of difference: simple menu and decor, modest prices, only fresh ground beef (none frozen), and a trans-fat-free menu (cooking with peanut oil). But who's keeping track? The Big Three of McDonald's, Burger King, and Wendy's certainly are.

In addition to competition from traditional hamburger chains like Five Guys, all three are responding aggressively to reach the new "fast-casual" market segment. These customers want healthier food and lower prices in sit-down restaurants—a market segment being successfully targeted by fast-casual restaurants like Chipotle Mexican Grill and Panera Bread.[20]

Finally, a new source of competition is emerging from a variety of chains that aren't necessarily classified as restaurants at all. These include convenience store chains like 7-Eleven, coffee shops like Starbucks, smoothie outlets like Jamba Juice, and gas stations with prepared and reheatable packaged food.[21] Many of these outlets are now selling food items and trying to gain market share from the Big Three.

Future Strategies for Your Wendy's Restaurant Changing customer tastes and competition mean you must alter your strategies when necessary. This involves looking at (1) what Wendy's headquarters is doing, (2) what competitors are doing, and (3) what might be changing in the area served by your restaurant.

Wendy's recently introduced aggressive new marketing programs that include:[22]

- Refurbishing many of its restaurants and introducing new upscale, limited-time menu items like its Pretzel Bacon Cheeseburger.
- Offering coupons on higher-priced menu items to attract higher-income customers.
- Targeting 25- to 49-year-old customers, not just 18- to 24-year-old ones.
- Offering improved menu items like natural-cut fries with sea salt in 2010, the Dave's Hot 'N Juicy hamburger in 2011, and the Berry Almond Chicken Salad and Frosty Waffle Cone in 2013.

The Wendy's strategy has been remarkably successful, replacing Burger King as the #2 burger chain in terms of sales behind McDonald's. And Zagat's Fast-Food Survey recently rated Wendy's #1 on a number of key criteria among "mega" fast-food chains, including the Top Overall Chain for 2012.[23]

With these corporate Wendy's plans and new actions from competitors, maybe you'd better rethink your market segmentation decisions on hours of operation. Also, if new businesses have moved into your area, what about a new strategy to reach people that work in the area? Or you might consider a new promotion for the night owls and early birds—the 12 A.M. to 5 A.M. customers.

How has Apple moved from its 1977 Apple II to today's iMac? The Marketing Matters box provides insights.

Apple's Ever-Changing Segmentation Strategy Steve Jobs and Steve Wozniak didn't realize they were developing today's multibillion-dollar PC industry when they invented the Apple I in a garage on April Fool's Day in 1976. However, when the Apple II was displayed at a computer trade show in 1977, consumers loved it and Apple Computer was born. Typical of young companies, Apple focused on its products and had little concern for its markets. Its creative, young engineers were often likened to "Boy Scouts without adult supervision."[24] Yet in 1984 the new Apple Macintosh revolutionized computers, and its 1984 Super Bowl TV ad is generally recognized as the best TV ad in history.

In 1997, Steve Jobs detailed his vision for a reincarnated Apple by describing a new market segmentation strategy that he called the "Apple Product Matrix." This strategy consisted of developing two general types of computer products (desktops and laptops) targeted at two market segments—the consumer and professional sectors.

In most segmentation situations, a single product does not fit into an exclusive market niche. Rather, product lines and market segments overlap. So Apple's market segmentation strategy enables it to offer different products to meet the needs of different market segments, as shown in the Marketing Matters box on the next page.

Market-Product Synergies: A Balancing Act

Recognizing opportunities for key synergies—that is, efficiencies—is vital to success in selecting target market segments and making marketing decisions. Market-product grids illustrate where such synergies can be found. How? Let's consider Apple's market-product grid in the Marketing Matters box on the next page and examine the difference between marketing synergies and product synergies shown there.

- *Marketing synergies.* Running horizontally across the grid, each row represents an opportunity for efficiency in terms of a market segment. Were Apple to focus on just one group of consumers, such as the medium/large business segment,

Video 8-3
Apple's 1984 Super Bowl Ad
kerin.tv/cr6e/v8-3

203

CHAPTER 8 Market Segmentation, Targeting, and Positioning

Marketing Matters

Apple's Segmentation Strategy—Camp Runamok No Longer

Camp Runamok was the nickname given to Apple in the early 1980s because the innovative company had no coherent series of product lines directed at identifiable market segments. Today, Apple has targeted its various lines of Macintosh computers at specific market segments, as shown in the accompanying market-product grid.

Because the market-product grid shifts as a firm's strategy changes, the one here is based on Apple's product lines in mid-2013. The grid suggests the market segmentation strategy Apple is using to compete in the digital age.

MARKETS		COMPUTER PRODUCTS				
SECTOR	SEGMENT	Mac Pro	MacBook Pro	iMac	MacBook Air	Mac Mini
CONSUMER	Individuals			✓	✓	✓
	Small/home office		✓	✓	✓	
	Students			✓	✓	✓
	Teachers		✓	✓		
PROFESSIONAL	Medium/large business	✓	✓	✓	✓	✓
	Creative	✓	✓	✓		
	College faculty		✓	✓	✓	
	College staff			✓	✓	

What market-product synergies does Apple's iMac satisfy? Read the text to find out.

its marketing efforts could be streamlined. Apple would not have to spend time learning about the buying habits of students or college faculty. So it could probably create a single ad to reach the medium/large business target segment (the yellow row), highlighting the only products it would need to worry about developing: the Mac Pro, the MacBook Pro, the iMac, the MacBook Air, and the Mac mini. Although clearly not Apple's strategy today, new firms often focus only on a single customer segment.

- *Product synergies.* Running vertically down the market-product grid, each column represents an opportunity for efficiency in research and development (R&D) and production. If Apple wanted to simplify its product line, reduce R&D and production expenses, and manufacture only one computer, which might it choose? Based on the market-product grid, Apple might do well to focus on the iMac (the orange column), because every segment purchases it.

Marketing synergies often come at the expense of product synergies because a single customer segment will likely require a variety of products, each of which will have to be designed and manufactured. The company saves money on marketing but spends more on production. Conversely, if product synergies are emphasized, marketing will have to address the concerns of a wide variety of consumers, which costs more time and money. Marketing managers responsible for developing a company's product line must balance both product and marketing synergies as they try to increase the company's profits.

learning review

8-5. What factor is estimated or measured for each of the cells in a market-product grid?

8-6. What are some criteria used to decide which segments to choose for targets?

8-7. How are marketing and product synergies different in a market-product grid?

POSITIONING THE PRODUCT

LO 8-5 Explain how marketing managers position products in the marketplace.

product positioning
The place a product occupies in consumers' minds based on important attributes relative to competitive products.

product repositioning
Changing the place a product occupies in consumers' minds relative to competitive products.

When a company introduces a new product, a decision critical to its long-term success is how prospective buyers view it in relation to those products offered by its competitors. **Product positioning** refers to the place a product occupies in consumers' minds based on important attributes relative to competitive products. By understanding where consumers see a company's product or brand today, a marketing manager can seek to change its future position in their minds. This requires **product repositioning**, or *changing* the place a product occupies in a consumer's mind relative to competitive products.

Two Approaches to Product Positioning

Marketers follow two main approaches to positioning a new product in the market. *Head-to-head positioning* involves competing directly with competitors on similar product attributes in the same target market. Using this strategy, Dollar Rent A Car competes directly with Avis and Hertz.

Differentiation positioning involves seeking a less-competitive, smaller market niche in which to locate a brand. McDonald's tried to appeal to the health-conscious segment with its low-fat McLean Deluxe hamburger to avoid competing directly with Wendy's and Burger King. But this item was eventually dropped from the menu.

Crafting a Formal Positioning Statement

Marketing managers often convert their positioning ideas for the offering into a succinct written positioning statement. Ideally, the statement identifies the target market and needs satisfied, the product (service) class or category in which the organization's offering competes, and the offering's unique attributes or benefits provided. The positioning statement is used not only internally within the marketing department, but also for others outside it, such as research and development engineers or advertising agencies.[25] Here is the Volvo positioning statement for the North American market:

> For upscale American families who desire a carefree driving experience (*target market and need*), Volvo is a premium-priced automobile (*product category*) that offers the utmost in safety and dependability (*benefits*).

This positioning statement directs Volvo's North American marketing strategy and focuses its product development efforts, such as the inclusion of side door airbags in its automobiles. The statement also directs Volvo's marketing communications message. So Volvo advertising stresses safety and dependability—the two benefits that are the basis of its "Volvo for life" slogan.

Product Positioning Using Perceptual Maps

A key to positioning a product or brand effectively is discovering the perceptions in the minds of potential customers by taking four steps:

1. Identify the important attributes for a product or brand class.
2. Discover how target customers rate competing products or brands with respect to these attributes.
3. Discover where the company's product or brand is on these attributes in the minds of potential customers.
4. Reposition the company's product or brand in the minds of potential customers.

More "zip" for chocolate milk? The text and Figure 8–8 describe how American dairies have successfully repositioned chocolate milk to appeal to adults.

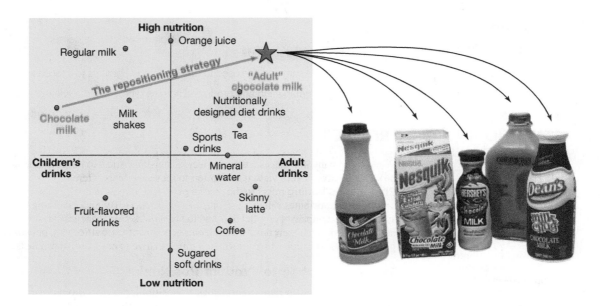

FIGURE 8–8
The strategy American dairies are using to reposition chocolate milk to reach adults: Have adults view chocolate milk as both more nutritional and more "adult."

perceptual map
A means of displaying the location of products or brands in consumers' minds.

As shown in Figure 8–8, from these data it is possible to develop a **perceptual map**, a means of displaying in two dimensions the location of products or brands in the minds of consumers. This enables a manager to see how consumers perceive competing products or brands, as well as the firm's own product or brand.

A Perceptual Map to Reposition Chocolate Milk for Adults

Recently, U.S. dairies decided to reposition chocolate milk in the minds of American adults to increase its sales. This is how dairies repositioned chocolate milk for American adults using the four steps listed above:

1. *Identify the important attributes (or scales) for adult drinks.* Research reveals the key attributes adults use to judge various drinks are (*a*) low versus high nutrition and (*b*) children's drinks versus adult drinks, as shown by the two axes in Figure 8–8.
2. *Discover how adults see various competing drinks.* Locate various adult drinks on these axes, as shown in Figure 8–8.
3. *Discover how adults see chocolate milk.* Figure 8–8 shows adults see chocolate milk as moderately nutritious (on the vertical axis) but as mainly a child's drink (on the horizontal axis).
4. *Reposition chocolate milk to make it more appealing to adults.* What actions did U.S. dairies take to increase sales? They repositioned chocolate milk to the location of the red star shown in the perceptual map in Figure 8–8.

The dairies' arguments are nutritionally powerful. For women, chocolate milk provides calcium, critically important in female diets. And dieters get a more filling, nutritious beverage than with a soft drink for about the same calories. The result: Chocolate milk sales increased dramatically, much of it because of adult consumption.[26] Part of this is due to giving chocolate milk "nutritional respectability" for adults, but another part is due to the innovative packaging that enables many new chocolate milk containers to fit in a car's cup holders.

learning review

8-8. What is the difference between product positioning and product repositioning?

8-9. Why do marketers use perceptual maps in product positioning decisions?

LEARNING OBJECTIVES REVIEW

LO 8-1 *Explain what market segmentation is and when to use it.*

Market segmentation involves aggregating prospective buyers into groups that (*a*) have common needs and (*b*) will respond similarly to a marketing action. Organizations go to the expense of segmenting their markets when it increases their sales, profits, and ability to serve customers better.

LO 8-2 *Identify the five steps involved in segmenting and targeting markets.*

Step 1 is to group potential buyers into segments. Buyers within a segment should have similar characteristics to each other and respond similarly to marketing actions like a new product or a lower price. Step 2 involves putting related products to be sold into meaningful groups. In step 3, organizations develop a market-product grid with estimated sizes of markets in each of the market-product cells of the resulting table. Step 4 involves selecting the target market segments on which the organization should focus. Finally, step 5 involves taking marketing mix actions—often in the form of a marketing program—to reach the target market segments.

LO 8-3 *Recognize the bases used to segment consumer and organizational (business) markets.*

Bases used to segment consumer markets include geographic, demographic, psychographic, and behavioral ones. Organizational markets use the same bases except for psychographic ones.

LO 8-4 *Develop a market-product grid to identify a target market and recommend resulting marketing actions.*

Organizations use five key criteria to segment markets, whose groupings appear in the rows of the market-product grid. Groups of related products appear in the columns. After estimating the size of the market in each cell in the grid, they select the target market segments on which to focus. They then identify marketing mix actions—often in a marketing program—to reach the target market most efficiently.

LO 8-5 *Explain how marketing managers position products in the marketplace.*

Marketing managers often locate competing products on two-dimensional perceptual maps to visualize the products in the minds of consumers. They then try to position new products or reposition existing products in this space to attain maximum sales and profits.

LEARNING REVIEW ANSWERS

8-1 Market segmentation involves aggregating prospective buyers into groups that have two key characteristics. What are they?
Answer: The groups (1) should have common needs and (2) will respond similarly to a marketing action.

8-2 In terms of market segments and products, what are the three market segmentation strategies?
Answer: The three market segmentation strategies are: (1) one product and multiple market segments; (2) multiple products and multiple market segments; and (3) "segments of one," or mass customization—the next step beyond build-to-order.

8-3 The process of segmenting and targeting markets is a bridge between which two marketing activities?
Answer: identifying market needs and executing the marketing program.

8-4 What is the difference between the demographic and behavioral bases of market segmentation?
Answer: Demographic segmentation is based on some objective physical (gender, race), measurable (age, income), or other classification attribute (birth era, occupation) of prospective customers. Behavioral segmentation is based on some observable actions or attitudes by prospective customers—such as where they buy, what benefits they seek, how frequently they buy, and why they buy.

8-5 What factor is estimated or measured for each of the cells in a market-product grid?
Answer: Each cell in the grid can show the estimated market size of a given product sold to a specific market segment.

8-6 What are some criteria used to decide which segments to choose for targets?
Answer: Possible criteria include market size, expected growth, competitive position, cost of reaching the segment, and compatibility with the organization's objectives and resources.

8-7 How are marketing and product synergies different in a market-product grid?
Answer: Marketing synergies run horizontally across a market-product grid. Each row represents an opportunity for efficiency in the marketing efforts to a market segment. Product synergies run vertically down the market-product grid. Each column represents an opportunity for efficiency in research and development (R&D) and production. Marketing synergies often come at the expense of product synergies because a single customer segment will likely require a variety of products, each of which will have to be designed and manufactured. The company saves money on marketing but spends more on production. Conversely, if product synergies are emphasized, marketing will have to address the concerns of a wide variety of consumers, which costs more time and money.

8-8 What is the difference between product positioning and product repositioning?
Answer: Product positioning refers to the place a product occupies in consumers' minds based on important attributes relative to competitive products. Product repositioning involves changing the place a product occupies in a consumer's mind relative to competitive products.

8-9 Why do marketers use perceptual maps in product positioning decisions?
Answer: Perceptual maps are a means of displaying in two dimensions the location of products or brands in the minds of consumers. Marketers use perceptual maps to see how consumers perceive competing products or brands as well as their own product or brand. Then they can develop marketing actions to move their product or brand to the ideal position.

FOCUSING ON KEY TERMS

80/20 rule p. 196
market segmentation p. 190
market-product grid p. 191

perceptual map p. 206
product differentiation p. 190
product positioning p. 205

product repositioning p. 205
usage rate p. 196

APPLYING MARKETING KNOWLEDGE

1 What variables might be used to segment these consumer markets? (*a*) lawn mowers, (*b*) frozen dinners, (*c*) dry breakfast cereals, and (*d*) soft drinks.

2 What variables might be used to segment these industrial markets? (*a*) industrial sweepers, (*b*) photocopiers, (*c*) computerized production control systems, and (*d*) car rental agencies.

3 In Figure 8–6, the dormitory market segment includes students living in college-owned residence halls, sororities, and fraternities. What market needs are common to these students that justify combining them into a single segment in studying the market for your Wendy's restaurant?

4 You may disagree with the estimates of market size given for the rows in the market-product grid in Figure 8–6. Estimate the market size, and give a brief justification for these market segments: (*a*) dormitory students, (*b*) day commuters, and (*c*) people who work in the area.

5 Suppose you want to increase revenues for your fast-food restaurant even further. Referring to Figure 8–7, what advertising actions might you take to increase revenues from (*a*) dormitory students, (*b*) dinners, and (*c*) after-dinner snacks consumed by night commuter students?

6 Locate these drinks on the perceptual map in Figure 8–8: (*a*) cappuccino, (*b*) beer, and (*c*) soy milk.

BUILDING YOUR MARKETING PLAN

Your marketing plan needs a market-product grid to (*a*) focus your marketing efforts and (*b*) help you create a forecast of sales for the company. Use these steps:

1 Define the market segments (the rows in your grid) using the bases of segmentation used to segment consumer and organizational markets.

2 Define the groupings of related products (the columns in your grid).

3 Form your grid and estimate the size of the market in each market-product cell.

4 Select the target market segments on which to focus your efforts with your marketing program.

5 Use the information and the lost-horse forecasting technique (discussed in Chapter 7) to make a sales forecast (company forecast).

6 Draft your positioning statement.

VIDEO CASE 8 Prince Sports, Inc.: Tennis Racquets for Every Segment

Video 8-4
Prince Sports
Video Case
kerin.tv/cr6e/v8-4

"Over the last decade we've seen a dramatic change in the media to reach consumers," says Linda Glassel, vice president of sports marketing and brand image of Prince Sports, Inc.

PRINCE SPORTS IN TODAY'S CHANGING WORLD

"Today—particularly in reaching younger consumers—we're now focusing so much more on social marketing

and social networks, be it Facebook, Twitter, or internationally with Hi5, Bebo, and Orkut," she adds.

Linda Glassel's comments are a snapshot look at what Prince Sports faces in the changing world of tennis in the 21st century.

Prince Sports is a racquet sports company whose portfolio of brands includes Prince (tennis, squash, and badminton), Ektelon (racquetball), and Viking (platform/paddle tennis). Its complete line of tennis products alone is astounding: more than 150 racquet models; more than 50 tennis strings; over 50 footwear models; and countless types of bags, apparel, and other accessories.

Prince prides itself on its history of innovation in tennis—including inventing the first "oversize" and "longbody" racquets, the first "synthetic gut" tennis string, and the first "Natural Foot Shape" tennis shoe. Its challenge today is to continue to innovate to meet the needs of all levels of tennis players.

"One favorable thing for Prince these days is the dramatic growth in tennis participation—higher than it's been in many years," says Nick Skally (center in the photo below), senior marketing manager. A recent study by the Sporting Goods Manufacturers Association confirms this point: Tennis participation in the United States was up 43 percent—the fastest-growing traditional individual sport in the country.

TAMING TECHNOLOGY TO MEET PLAYERS' NEEDS

Every tennis player wants the same thing: to play better. But they don't all have the same skills, or the same ability to swing a racquet fast. So adult tennis players fall very broadly into three groups, each with special needs:

- *Those with shorter, slower strokes.* They want maximum power in a lightweight frame.
- *Those with moderate to full strokes.* They want the perfect blend of power and control.
- *Those with longer, faster strokes.* They want greater control with less power.

To satisfy all these needs in one racquet is a big order. "When we design tennis racquets, it involves an extensive amount of market research on players at all levels," explains Tyler Herring, global business director for performance tennis racquets. Prince's research led it to introduce its breakthrough O^3 technology. "Our O^3 technology solved an inherent contradiction between racquet speed and sweet spot," he says. Never before had a racquet been designed that simultaneously delivers faster racquet speed with a

dramatically increased "sweet spot." The "sweet spot" in a racquet is the middle of the frame that gives the most power and consistency when hitting. Recently, Prince introduced its latest evolution of the O^3 platform called EXO^3. Its newly patented design suspends the string bed from the racquet frame—thereby increasing the sweet spot by up to 83 percent while reducing frame vibration up to 50 percent.

SEGMENTING THE TENNIS MARKET

"The three primary market segments for our tennis racquets are our performance line, our recreational line, and our junior line," says Herring. He explains that within each of these segments Prince makes difficult design trade-offs to balance (1) the price a player is willing to pay, (2) what playing features (speed versus spin, sweet spot versus control, and so on) they want, and (3) what technology can be built into the racquet for the price point.

Within each of these three primary market segments, there are at least two subsegments—sometimes overlapping! Figure 1 on the next page gives an overview of Prince's market segmentation strategy and identifies sample racquet models. The three right-hand columns show the design variations of length, unstrung weight, and head size. The table shows the complexities Prince faces in converting its technology into a racquet with physical features that satisfy players' needs.

DISTRIBUTION AND PROMOTION STRATEGIES

"Prince has a number of different distribution channels—from mass merchants like Walmart and Target, to sporting goods chains, to smaller specialty tennis shops," says Nick Skally. For the large chains, Prince contributes co-op advertising for its in-store circulars, point-of-purchase displays, in-store signage, consumer brochures, and even "space planograms" to help the retailer plan the layout of Prince products in its tennis area. Prince aids for small tennis specialty shops include a supply of demo racquets, detailed catalogs, posters, racquet and string guides, merchandising fixtures, and hardware, such as racquet hooks and footwear shelves, in addition to other items. Prince also provides these shops with "player standees," which are corregated life-size cutouts of professional tennis players.

Prince reaches tennis players directly through its website (www.princetennis.com), which gives product information, tennis tips, and the latest tennis news. Besides using social networks like Facebook and Twitter, Prince runs ads in regional and national tennis publications and develops advertising campaigns for online sites and broadcast outlets.

In addition to its in-store activities, advertising, and online marketing, Prince invests heavily in its Teaching Pro program. These sponsored teaching pros receive all

MARKET SEGMENTS				PRODUCT FEATURES IN RACQUET		
Main Segments	Subsegments	Segment Characteristics (Skill level, age)	Brand Name	Length (Inches)	Unstrung Weight (Ounces)	Head Size (Sq. in.)
Performance	Precision	For touring professional players wanting great feel, control, and spin	EXO³ Ignite 95	27.0	11.8	95
	Thunder	For competitive players wanting a bigger sweet spot and added power	EXO³ Red 95	27.25	9.9	105
Recreational	Small head size	For players looking for a forgiving racquet with added control	AirO Lightning MP	27.0	9.9	100
	Larger head size	For players looking for a larger sweet spot and added power	AirO Maria Lite OS	27.0	9.7	110
Junior	More experienced young players	For ages 8 to 15; somewhat shorter and lighter racquets than high school or adult players	AirO Team Maria 23	23.0	8.1	100
	Beginner	For ages 5 to 11; much shorter and lighter racquets; tennis balls with 50% to 75% less speed for young beginners	Air Team Maria 19	19.0	7.1	82

FIGURE 1
Prince targets racquets at specific market segments.

the latest product information, demo racquets, and equipment from Prince, so they can truly be Prince ambassadors in their community. Aside from their regular lessons, instructors and teaching professionals hold local "Prince Demo events" around the country to give potential customers a hands-on opportunity to see and try various Prince racquets, strings, and grips.

Prince also sponsors over 100 professional tennis players who appear in marquee events such as the four Grand Slam tournaments (Wimbledon and the Australian, French, and U.S. Opens). TV viewers can watch Russia's Maria Sharapova walk onto a tennis court carrying a Prince racquet bag or France's Gael Monfils hit a service ace using his Prince racquet.

Where is Prince headed in the 21st century? "As a marketer, one of the biggest challenges is staying ahead of the curve," says Glassel. And she stresses, "It's learning, it's studying, it's talking to people who understand where the market is going."

Questions

1 In the 21st century what trends in the environmental forces (social, economic, technological, competitive, and regulatory) (*a*) work for and (*b*) work against success for Prince Sports in the tennis industry?

2 Because sales of Prince Sports in tennis-related products depends heavily on growth of the tennis industry, what marketing activities might it use in the United States to promote tennis playing?

3 What promotional activities might Prince use to reach (*a*) recreational players and (*b*) junior players?

4 What might Prince do to gain distribution and sales in (*a*) mass merchandisers like Target and Walmart and (*b*) specialty tennis shops?

5 In reaching global markets outside the United States (*a*) what are some criteria that Prince should use to select countries in which to market aggressively, (*b*) what three or four countries meet these criteria best, and (*c*) what are some marketing actions Prince might use to reach these markets?

Chapter Notes

1. Kimberly Weisal, "A Shine in Their Shoes," *BusinessWeek*, December 5, 2005, p. 84; and information from the "Executive Biographies" section of the Zappos.com website.

2. Dinah Eng, "Zappos's Silent Founder," *Fortune*, September 3, 2012, pp. 19–22; Jeffrey M. O'Brien, "Zappos Knows How to Kick It," *Fortune*, February 2, 2009, pp. 55–60; and Max Chafkin, "Get Happy," *Inc.*, May 2009, pp. 66–71.

3. Weisal, "A Shine in Their Shoes," p. 84.

4. Duff McDonald, "Zappos.com: Success through Simplicity," *CIO-Insight*, November 10, 2006.

5. Jena McGregor, "Zappos' Secret: It's an Open Book," *Bloomberg Businessweek*, March 23 and 30, 2009, p. 62; and Jeffrey M. O'Brien, "The 10 Commandments of Zappos," *Fortune*, January 22, 2009, see http://money.cnn.com/2009/01/21/news/companies/obrien_zappos10.fortune and Zappos.com.

6. Motoko Rich, "Why Is This Man Smiling?" *The New York Times*, April 10, 2011, pp. ST1, ST10; Christopher Palmeri, "Now for Sale, the Zappos Culture," *Bloomberg Businessweek*, January 11, 2010, p. 57; and see https://twitter.com/zappos.

7. Natalie Zmuda, "Marketer of the Year: Zappos," *Advertising Age*, October 20, 2008, p. 36.

8. Eric N. Berkowitz, Roger A. Kerin, and William Rudelius, *Marketing* (St. Louis, MO: Times Mirror/Mosby College Publishing, 1986), pp. 189–91; Sleep Research Institute, the National Sleep Foundation, and the International Sleep Products Association (March 20, 2007); and Frederick G. Crane, Roger A. Kerin, Steven W. Hartley, and William Rudelius, *Marketing*, 8th Canadian ed. (Toronto, Canada: McGraw-Hill Ryerson Ltd., 2011), pp. 229–32.

9. Ellen Byron, "As Middle Class Shrinks, P&G Aims High and Low," *The Wall Street Journal*, September 12, 2011, pp. A1, A16; Ellen Byron, "P&G Puts Spotlight on Newer Products," *The Wall Street Journal*, October 21, 2010, pp. B1, B2; Anthony Bianco, "The Vanishing Mass Market," *BusinessWeek*, July 12, 2004, pp. 61–65; and Geoff Colvin, "Selling P&G," *Fortune*, September 17, 2007, pp. 163–69.

10. Jeffrey A. Trachtenberg and Ann Paul Sonne, "Rowling Casts E-Book Spell," *The Wall Street Journal*, June 24, 2011, pp. B1, B2; and Larry Neumeister, "Rowling to Testify Against Fan in Bid to Block Publication of 'Harry Potter' Encyclopedia," StarTribune.com from an Associated Press article, April 13, 2008; www.startribune.com/entertainment/17761909.html.

11. James Cook, "Where's the Niche?" *Forbes*, September 24, 1984, p. 54.

12. J. P. Donlon, "The Road Ahead," *Chief Executive*, July/August, 2011, pp. 31–37; "Epiphany in Dearborn," *The Economist*, December 11, 2010, pp. 72–74; and Bill Saporito, "How to Make Cars and Make Money Too," *Time*, August 9, 2010, pp. 36–39.

13. *2010 Ann Taylor Annual Report* and selected press releases.

14. Ann D'Innocenzio, "Wal-Mart to Accelerate Small Store Growth," *Associated Press*, October 10, 2012, see http://bigstory.ap.org/article/wal-mart-accelerate-small-store-growth; Alissa Skelton, "Wal-Mart to Test Small Store Format," *The Wall Street Journal*, June 2, 2011, see http://www.nytimes.com/2011/06/03/business/03walmart.html;

and Miguel Bastillo, "Walmart Sees Small Stores in Big Cities," *The Wall Street Journal*, October 14, 2010, pp. B1, B6.

15. The relation of these criteria to implementation is discussed in Jacqueline Dawley, "Making Connections: Enhance the Implementation of Value of Attitude-Based Segmentation," *Marketing Research*, Summer 2006, pp. 16–22.

16. Ian Michiels, "Customer Analytics: Segmentation beyond Demographics," *The Aberdeen Group*, August 2008, p. 11.

17. The discussion of fast-food trends and market share is based on Experian Simmons Fall 2012 NCS/NHCS Full-Year Adult Survey 12 OneView^{SM} Crosstabulation Report © Experian Simmons 2013. See http://www.experian.com/simmons-research/consumer-study.html.

18. Julie Jargon, "McDonald's Seeks Relevance," *The Wall Street Journal*, January 24, 2014, p. B3; and Julie Jargon, "McDonald's Picks New Chief for U.S.," *The Wall Street Journal*, August 23–24, 2014, p. B3.

19. Burt Helm, "An Expensive Face-Lift on Burger King's Menu," *Bloomberg Businessweek*, October 11–17, 2010, pp. 21–22.

20. Julie Jargon, "Millenials Lose Taste for McDonald's," *The Wall Street Journal*, August 25, 2014, pp. 81, 86; Julie Jargon, "Fast Food Aspires to Move Up the Food Chain," *The Wall Street Journal*, October 11, 2012, p. B11; Josh Sanburn, "Fast-Casual Nation," *Time*, April 23, 2012, pp. 60–61; and Don Jacobson, "Fast-Casual Restaurants Are Just What Landlords Ordered," *Star Tribune*, January 20, 2012, p. D5.

21. Keith O'Brien, "Supersize," *The New York Times Magazine*, May 6, 2012, pp. 44–48; and "A Look Ahead: 2011—Fast Food," *Advertising Age*, January 20, 2011, p. 4.

22. Julie Jargon, "Costlier Food Puts Restaurants in Bind," *The Wall Street Journal*, August 29, 2012, p. B8; and Julie Jargon, "Wendy's Stages a Palace Coup," *The Wall Street Journal*, December 21, 2011, pp. B1, B2.

23. Julie Jargon, "New Menu Helps Burger King," *The Wall Street Journal*, October 30, 2012, p. B8; and "The 2012 Zagat Fast-Food Survey," September 29, 2012. See http://blog.zagat.com/2012/09/2012-fast-food-survey-results-are-live.html.

24. The discussion of Apple's segmentation strategies through the years is based on information from its website, www.apple.com and www.apple-history.com/history.html.

25. Much of the discussion about positioning and perceptual maps is based on Roger A. Kerin and Robert A. Peterson, *Strategic Marketing Problems: Cases and Comments*, 13th ed. (Upper Saddle River, NJ: Prentice Hall, 2013), pp. 140–41; and John M. Mullins, Orville C. Walker, Jr., and Harper W. Boyd, Jr., *Marketing Management: A Strategic Decision-Marketing Approach*, 7th ed. (New York: McGraw-Hill/Irwin, 2010), p. 202.

26. Nicholas Zamiska, "How Milk Got a Major Boost by Food Panel," *The Wall Street Journal*, August 30, 2004, pp. B1, B5; and Rebecca Winter, "Chocolate Milk," *Time*, April 30, 2001, p. 20.

Prince Sports: This case was written by William Rudelius and is based on personal interviews with Linda Glassel, Tyler Herring, and Nick Skally.

Credits

Satisfying Marketing Opportunities

9 Developing New Products and Services

LEARNING OBJECTIVES

After reading this chapter you should be able to:

LO 9-1 Recognize the various terms that pertain to products and services.

LO 9-2 Identify the ways in which consumer and business products and services can be classified.

LO 9-3 Describe four unique elements of services.

LO 9-4 Explain the significance of "newness" in new products and services as it relates to the degree of consumer learning involved.

LO 9-5 Describe the factors contributing to the success or failure of a new product or service.

LO 9-6 Explain the purposes of each step of the new-product process.

APPLE: THE WORLD-CLASS NEW-PRODUCT MACHINE

The stage in front of an auditorium was empty except for a chair, a table, and a huge screen with a large white logo. Then, in walked a legend ready for his magic show in his black mock turtleneck, jeans, and gray New Balance sneakers.

Apple's Innovation Machine

The legend, of course, was Steve Jobs, co-founder and former chairman of the board of Apple Inc., who died in October 2011. *Advertising Age* anointed Steve Jobs as Marketer of the Decade. *Fortune* rated Apple as the world's most-admired company, while *Bloomberg Businessweek* has perennially identified Apple as the world's most innovative company. The magic shows Jobs orchestrated over the years introduced many to Apple's market-changing innovations, such as the:

- Apple II—the first commercial personal computer (1977).
- Macintosh—the first personal computer (PC) with a mouse and a graphical user interface (1984).
- iPod—the first and most successful MP3 music player (2001).
- iPhone—the world's best multitouch smartphone and media player with almost one million apps (2007).
- iPad (2010) and iPad mini (2012)—the thin tablet devices that allow users to read books, newspapers, magazines, and even textbooks!
- CarPlay—using your iPhone while driving to make calls, listen to music, and access messages by voice or touch (2014).

Steve Jobs's innovations revolutionized six industries: personal computing, digitally animated movies (when he was CEO of Pixar), music, smartphones, tablet computing, and digital publishing.[1] Jobs even designed and holds the patent on the staircase seen in major Apple retail stores. He said, "You want that stairway so people believe they're in someplace magical."[2]

When Steve Jobs named Tim Cook to be Apple's chief executive officer, his charge to Cook was simple: "Just do what's right." However, as this chapter reveals, developing successful new products is difficult. Tim Cook's challenge as the CEO of Apple will be to continue to market new innovations to drive the company's future growth.[3]

213

Video 9-1
**Apple CarPlay
Ad**
kerin.tv/cr6e/v9-1

CarPlay: Improving How You Use Your iPhone® in Your Car

In March 2014, Apple announced that leading car manufacturers were "rolling out CarPlay, the smarter, safer, and more fun way to use iPhone® in the car." Drivers can link CarPlay (photo above) and their iPhone to make phone calls, listen to music, and receive messages. The drivers access CarPlay from the car's interface or by punching the voice control button on the steering wheel. Once CarPlay and iPhone are interconnected, it activates Siri—a built-in "intelligent assistant" that lets Apple device users speak oral commands or ask questions to get answers. Then Siri lets the driver make calls and listen to voicemails.[4]

The life of an organization depends on how it conceives, produces, and markets *new* products (goods, services, and ideas), the topic of this chapter. Many examples involve small businesses facing the difficult task of launching a successful start-up. Chapter 10 will discuss the process of managing *existing* products, services, and brands.

product
A good, service, or idea consisting of a bundle of tangible and intangible attributes that satisfies consumers' needs and is received in exchange for money or something else of value.

WHAT ARE PRODUCTS AND SERVICES?

LO 9-1 Recognize the various terms that pertain to products and services.

The essence of marketing is in developing products and services to meet buyer needs. A **product** is a good, service, or idea consisting of a bundle of tangible and intangible attributes that satisfies consumers' needs and is received in exchange for money or something else of value. Let's clarify the meanings of goods, services, and ideas.

Nondurable goods like chewing gum are easily consumed and rely on consumer advertising.

services
Intangible activities or benefits that an organization provides to satisfy consumers' needs in exchange for money or something else of value.

A Look at Goods, Services, and Ideas

A *good* has tangible attributes that a consumer's five senses can perceive. For example, Apple's iPad can be touched and its features can be seen and heard. A good also may have intangible attributes consisting of its delivery or warranties and embody more abstract concepts, such as becoming healthier or wealthier. Goods also can be divided into nondurable goods and durable goods. A *nondurable* good is an item consumed in one or a few uses, such as food products and fuel. A *durable* good is one that usually lasts over many uses, such as appliances, cars, and smartphones. This classification method also provides direction for marketing actions. For example, nondurable goods, such as Wrigley's gum, rely heavily on consumer advertising. In contrast, costly durable goods, such as cars, generally emphasize personal selling.

Services are intangible activities or benefits that an organization provides to satisfy consumers' needs in exchange for money or something else of value. Examples of services are having a dental exam or watching a movie. In the U.S. economy today, services are an even more important part of our gross domestic product (GDP) than goods. Figure 9–1 shows that services now contribute about $7.6 trillion to the U.S. GDP, while goods provide only half that. (The three other components of GDP—business investment, government spending, and net exports are not shown in the figure.) Figure 9–1 also shows the dramatic growth in the importance of services since 1975, when their value was equal to that of goods. So today's college graduates looking for jobs must consider working in a service industry.[5]

Finally, in marketing, an *idea* is a thought that leads to a product or action, such as a concept for a new invention or getting people out to vote.

Throughout this book, *product* generally includes not only physical goods but services and ideas as well. When *product* is used in its narrower meaning of "goods," it should be clear from the example or sentence.

FIGURE 9–1
Services now contribute about twice the value to U.S. gross domestic product (GDP) that goods do.

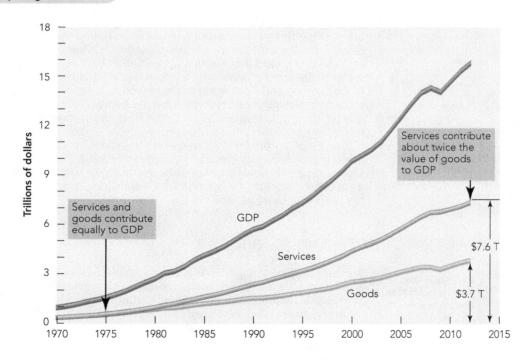

Classifying Products

LO 9-2 Identify the ways in which consumer and business products and services can be classified.

consumer products
Products purchased by the ultimate consumer.

business products
Products organizations buy that assist in providing other products for resale.

Two broad categories of products widely used in marketing relate to the type of user. **Consumer products** are products purchased by the ultimate consumer, whereas **business products** (also called *B2B products* or *industrial products*) are products organizations buy that assist in providing other products for resale. Some products can be considered both consumer and business items. For example, an Apple iMac computer can be sold to consumers for personal use or to business firms for office use. Each classification results in different marketing actions. Viewed as a consumer product, the iMac would be sold through Apple's retail stores or directly from its online store. As a business product, an Apple salesperson might contact a firm's purchasing department directly and offer discounts for large volume purchases.

Consumer Products The four types of consumer products shown in Figure 9–2 differ in terms of (1) the effort the consumer spends on the decision, (2) the attributes used in making the purchase decision, and (3) the frequency of purchase. *Convenience products* are items that the consumer purchases frequently, conveniently, and with a minimum of shopping effort. *Shopping products* are items for which the consumer compares several alternatives on criteria such as price, quality, or style. *Specialty products* are items that the consumer makes a special effort to search out and buy. *Unsought products* are items that the consumer does not know about or knows about but does not initially want.

Figure 9–2 shows how each type of consumer product stresses different marketing mix actions, degrees of brand loyalty, and shopping effort. But how a consumer product is classified depends on the individual. One woman may view a camera as a shopping

FIGURE 9–2
How a consumer product is classified significantly affects which products consumers buy and the marketing strategies used.

TYPE OF CONSUMER PRODUCT

BASIS OF COMPARISON	CONVENIENCE PRODUCT	SHOPPING PRODUCT	SPECIALTY PRODUCT	UNSOUGHT PRODUCT
Product	Toothpaste, cake mix, hand soap, ATM cash withdrawal	Cameras, TVs, briefcases, airline tickets	Rolls-Royce cars, Rolex watches, heart surgery	Burial insurance, thesaurus
Price	Relatively inexpensive	Fairly expensive	Usually very expensive	Varies
Place (distribution)	Widespread; many outlets	Large number of selective outlets	Very limited	Often limited
Promotion	Price, availability, and awareness stressed	Differentiation from competitors stressed	Uniqueness of brand and status stressed	Awareness is essential
Brand loyalty of consumers	Aware of brand but will accept substitutes	Prefer specific brands but will accept substitutes	Very brand loyal; will not accept substitutes	Will accept substitutes
Purchase behavior of consumers	Frequent purchases; little time and effort spent shopping	Infrequent purchases; needs much comparison shopping time	Infrequent purchases; needs extensive search and decision time	Very infrequent purchases; some comparison shopping

product and visit several stores before deciding on a brand, whereas her friend may view a camera as a specialty product and make a special effort to buy only a Nikon.

Business Products A major characteristic of business products is that their sales are often the result of *derived demand*; that is, sales of business products frequently result (or are derived) from the sale of consumer products. For example, as consumer demand for Ford cars (a consumer product) increases, the company may increase its demand for paint spraying equipment (a business product).

Business products may be classified as components or support products. *Components* are items that become part of the final product. These include raw materials such as lumber, as well as assemblies such as a Ford car engine. *Support products* are items used to assist in producing other products and services. These include:

- *Installations*, such as buildings and fixed equipment.
- *Accessory equipment*, such as tools and office equipment.
- *Supplies*, such as stationery, paper clips, and brooms.
- *Industrial services*, such as maintenance, repair, and legal services.

Strategies to market business products reflect both the complexities of the product involved (paper clips versus private jets) and the buy-class situations discussed in Chapter 5.

Classifying Services

Services can be classified according to whether they are delivered by (1) people or equipment, (2) business firms or nonprofit organizations, or (3) government agencies. Organizations in each of these categories often use significantly different kinds of market-mix strategies to promote their services.

Delivery by People or Equipment Figure 9–3 shows the great diversity of organizations that offer services. People-based professional services include those offered by advertising agencies or medical doctors. Sears utilizes skilled labor to offer appliance repair services. Broadview Security uses relatively unskilled labor to provide its security guard services. The quality of all these people-based services can vary significantly depending on the abilities of the person delivering the service.

Figure 9–3 also suggests that equipment-based services do not have the marketing concern of inconsistent quality because employees generally do not have direct contact when providing the service to consumers. Instead, consumers usually receive these

FIGURE 9–3
Services can be classified as people-based or equipment-based.

Southwest Airlines is an example of an equipment-based service.

automated services without interacting with any service employees, such as doing self check-in at Southwest Airlines, watching a movie at a local theater, or using Schwab's online stock trading.[6]

Delivery by Business Firms or Nonprofit Organizations As discussed in Chapter 2, privately owned firms must make profits to survive, while nonprofit organizations seek to satisfy clients and be efficient. The kinds of services each offers affect their marketing activities. Recently, many nonprofit organizations, such as The American Red Cross, have used marketing to improve their communications and better serve those in need.

Delivery by Government Agencies Governments at the federal, state, and local levels provide a broad range of services. These organizations also have adopted many marketing practices used by business firms. For example, the United States Postal Service's "Easy Come. Easy Go" marketing campaign is designed to allow it to compete better with UPS, FedEx, DHL, and foreign postal services for global package delivery business.

The Uniqueness of Services

Four unique elements distinguish services from goods. These are *intangibility, inconsistency, inseparability,* and *inventory*—referred to as the **four I's of services**.

Intangibility Being intangible, services can't be touched or seen before the purchase decision. Instead, services tend to be a performance rather than an object, which makes them much more difficult for consumers to evaluate. To help consumers assess and compare services, marketers try to make them tangible or show the benefits of using the service. For example, American Airlines attempts to make the benefits of flying on its airline more tangible by running an ad showing and emphasizing the comfort of its reclining seats.

Inconsistency Services depend on the people who provide them. As a result, their quality varies with each person's capabilities and day-to-day job performance. Inconsistency is more of a problem in services than it is with tangible goods. Tangible products can be good or bad in terms of quality, but with modern production lines, their quality will at least be consistent. On the other hand, the Philadelphia Phillies baseball team may have great hitting and pitching one day and the next day lose by 10 runs. Organizations attempt to reduce inconsistency through standardization and training.

Inseparability Inseparability means that the consumer cannot distinguish the service provider from the service itself. For example, the quality of large lectures at your university or college may be excellent, but if you don't get your questions answered, find the counseling services poor, or do not receive adequate library assistance, you may not be satisfied with the entire educational experience delivered. Therefore, you probably won't separate your perception of the "educational experience"—the service itself—from all the people delivering the educational services for that institution.

Inventory Many goods have inventory handling costs that relate to their storage, perishability, and movement. With services, these costs are more subjective and are related to **idle production capacity**, which is when the service provider is available but there is no demand for the service. For a service, inventory cost involves paying the service provider along with any needed equipment. If a physician is paid to see patients but no one schedules an appointment, the idle physician's salary must be paid regardless of whether the service was performed. In service businesses that pay employees a commission, such as a part-time clerk at Sears, the sales clerk's work hours can be reduced to lower Sears's idle production capacity.

Today, many businesses find it useful to distinguish between their core product— either a good or a service—and supplementary services. U.S. Bank has both a core service (a checking account) and supplementary services, such as deposit assistance, parking, drive-throughs, and ATMs. Supplementary services often allow service providers to differentiate their offerings from those of competitors to add value for consumers.

Assessing and Improving Service Quality

Once a consumer tries a service, how is it evaluated? Primarily by comparing expectations about a service to the actual experience a consumer has with the service. Differences between the consumer's expectations and his or her actual experiences are identified through *gap analysis*. This analysis asks consumers to assess their expectations and experiences on dimensions of service quality. For airline customers, here are three dimensions of service quality and the kinds of questions airline customers might ask to evaluate them:

- Reliability—Is my flight on time?
- Tangibility—Are the gate, the plane, and the baggage area clean?
- Responsiveness—Are the flight attendants willing to answer my questions?

Expectations are influenced by word-of-mouth communications, personal needs, past experiences, and promotional activities, while actual experiences are determined by the way an organization delivers its service.[7] What if someone is dissatisfied and complains? Recent studies suggest that customers who experience a "service failure" will increase their satisfaction if the service provider makes a sincere attempt to address the complaint.[8]

For services in which consumers are simply observers—like music concerts, zoos, or art museums—conducting marketing research to improve service quality is especially difficult. As shown in the photo, the Detroit Institute of Arts observes and interviews visitors to make its galleries more appealing. It discovered that visitors were

For how the Detroit Institute of Arts uses direct observation and interviews to measure the results of its marketing actions, see the text.

◄ The Meeting of David and Abigail by Peter Paul Rubens. It is one of the gallery's big draws.

Matt Sikora, the museum's director of evaluation, with his hand-held computer. ▼

After noticing that visitors ▲ overlooked the gallery summary panel, the museum moved it next to this Rubens.

Museum visitor from ► Youngstown, OH.

often confused by the museum's panels—the written descriptions next to the art. So it made the panels more user-friendly by:

- Moving them closer to the art.
- Reducing the maximum word count from 250 to 150.
- Increasing readability by breaking up blocks of text with bullet points, subheadings, color, and graphics.

The result: These changes have significantly increased the "readership" of these descriptive panels, some of which in the past were read by only 2 percent of gallery visitors.[9]

Product Classes, Forms, Items, Lines, and Mixes

Most organizations offer a range of products and services to consumers. Each set of offerings can be categorized according to the *product class* or industry to which they belong, like the iPad, which is classified as a tablet device. Products can exist in various *product forms* within a product class (see Chapters 2 and 10). A **product item** is a specific product that has a unique brand, size, or price. For example, Ultra Downy softener for clothes comes in different forms (liquid for the washer and sheets for the dryer) and load sizes (40, 60, etc.). Each of the different product items represents a separate *stock keeping unit* (SKU), which is a unique identification number that defines an item for ordering or inventory purposes.

A **product line** is a group of product or service items that are closely related because they satisfy a class of needs, are used together, are sold to the same customer group, are distributed through the same outlets, or fall within a given price range. Nike's product lines include shoes and clothing, whereas the Mayo Clinic's service lines consist of inpatient hospital care and outpatient physician services. Each product line has its own marketing strategy.

The "Crapola Granola" product line started as an edgy party joke from Brian and Andrea Strom, owners of tiny Brainstorm Bakery. The dried **CR**anberries and **AP**ples gran**OLA**—hence the "Crapola" name—also contains nuts and five organic grains sweetened with maple syrup and honey. Its package promises that Crapola "Makes Even Weird People Regular."

Mentioned on TV by Jay Leno, Crapola is sold in retail outlets in the Midwest, California, and Oregon as well as online at www.crapola.us. Currently, they offer two other recipes. These product line extensions enable both consumers and retailers to simplify their buying decisions. So a family liking Crapola might buy another product in the line. With a broader product line, the Stroms may obtain distribution in supermarket chains, which strive to increase efficiencies by dealing with fewer suppliers.[10]

Many firms offer a **product mix**, which consists of all of the product lines offered by an organization. For example, Cray Inc. has a small product mix of three product lines (supercomputers, storage systems, and a "data appliance") that are sold mostly to governments and large businesses. Procter & Gamble, however, has a large product mix that includes product lines such as beauty and grooming (Crest toothpaste and Gillette razors) and household care (Downy fabric softener, Tide detergent, and Pampers diapers).

Video 9-2
Crapola
kerin.tv/cr6e/v9-2

What company cheerfully tells its customers to "Have a crappy day"? Read the text to find out about this "tasty" offering!

product item
A specific product that has a unique brand, size, or price.

product line
A group of products that are closely related because they are similar in terms of consumer needs and uses, market segments, sales outlets, or prices.

product mix
All the product lines offered by a company.

learning review

9-1. What are the four main types of consumer products?

9-2. What are the four I's of services?

9-3. What is the difference between a product line and a product mix?

Marketing Matters

Feature Bloat: Geek Squad to the Rescue!

Adding more features to a product to satisfy more consumers seems like a no-brainer strategy for success. Right?

Feature Bloat

In fact, most marketing research with potential buyers of a product shows that while they *say* they want more features, in actuality they are overwhelmed with the mind-boggling complexity—or "feature bloat"—of some new products.

Computers pose a special problem for home users because there's no in-house technical assistance like that existing in large organizations. Ever call the manufacturer's toll-free "help" line? One survey showed that 29 percent of the callers swore at the customer service representative and 21 percent just screamed.

Geek Squad to the Rescue

Computer feature bloat has given rise to what TV's *60 Minutes* says is "the multibillion-dollar service industry populated by the very people who used to be shunned in the high school cafeteria: Geeks like Robert Stephens!"

More than a decade ago he turned his geekiness into the Geek Squad—a group of technically savvy people who can fix almost any computer problem.

"The biggest complaint about tech support people is rude, egotistical behavior," says Stephens. So he launched the Geek Squad to show some friendly humility by having team members work their wizardry while:

1. Showing genuine concern to customers.
2. Dressing in geeky white shirts, black clip-on ties, and white socks, a "uniform" borrowed from NASA engineers.
3. Driving to customer homes or offices in black-and-white VW "geekmobiles."

Do customers appreciate the 20,000-person Geek Squad, now owned by Best Buy? Robert Stephens answers by explaining, "People will say, 'They saved me . . . they saved my data.'" This includes countless college students working on their papers or theses with data lost somewhere in their computers—"data they promised themselves they'd back up next week."

NEW PRODUCTS AND WHY THEY SUCCEED OR FAIL

LO 9-4 Explain the significance of "newness" in new products and services as it relates to the degree of consumer learning involved.

New products are the lifeblood of a company and keep it growing, but the financial risks can be large. We'll begin by looking at *what* a new product is.

What Is a New Product?

The term *new* is difficult to define. Is Sony's PlayStation 4 *new* when there is already a PlayStation 3? Perhaps—because the PS4, Nintendo's Wii U, and Microsoft's new Xbox One will all position their consoles as entertainment "hubs" rather than just game consoles.[11] Let's look at newness from several points of view.

Newness Compared with Existing Products   If a product is functionally different from existing products, it can be defined as new. Sometimes this newness is revolutionary and creates a whole new industry, as in the case of the Apple II computer. At other times more features are added to an existing product to try to appeal to more customers. And as HDTVs, smartphones, and tablet devices become more sophisticated, consumers' lives get far more complicated. This proliferation of extra features—sometimes called "feature bloat"—overwhelms many consumers. The Marketing Matters box describes how founder Robert Stephens launched his Geek Squad to address the rise of feature bloat.[12]

Newness from the Consumer's Perspective   A second way to define new products is in terms of their effects on consumption. This approach classifies new products by the degree of learning required by the consumer, as shown in Figure 9–4.

BASIS OF COMPARISON	Degree of New Consumer Learning Needed		
	LOW — CONTINUOUS INNOVATION	DYNAMICALLY CONTINUOUS INNOVATION	HIGH — DISCONTINUOUS INNOVATION
Definition	Requires no new learning by consumers	Disrupts consumer's normal routine but does not require totally new learning	Requires new learning and consumption patterns by consumers
Examples	New improved shaver, detergent, and toothpaste	Electric toothbrush, LED HDTVs, and smartphones	Wireless router, digital video recorder, and electric car
Marketing strategy	Gain consumer awareness and wide distribution	Advertise points of difference and benefits to consumers	Educate consumers through product trial and personal selling

FIGURE 9–4
The degree of "newness" in a new product affects the amount of learning effort consumers must exert to use the product and the resulting marketing strategy.

With a *continuous innovation*, consumers don't need to learn new behaviors. Toothpaste manufacturers can add a new feature like "protects gums" when they introduce an improved product, such as Colgate Total Advanced Gum Defense toothpaste. The extra features in the new toothpaste do not require buyers to learn new tooth-brushing behaviors. So for a continuous innovation like this, effective marketing mainly depends on generating awareness, not re-educating customers.

With a *dynamically continuous innovation*, only minor changes in behavior are required. Heinz launched its EZ Squirt Ketchup with kid-friendly squeeze bottles and nozzles.[13] Encouraging kids to write their names on hot dogs as they use this new product requires only minor behavioral changes. So the marketing strategy here is to educate prospective buyers on the product's benefits, advantages, and proper use.

A *discontinuous innovation* involves making the consumer learn entirely new consumption patterns to use the product. Have you bought a wireless router for your computer? A product new to you? Recently, one-third of those bought at Best Buy were returned because they were too complicated to set up—the problem with a discontinuous innovation. So marketing efforts for discontinuous innovations involve educating consumers on both the benefits and proper use of the innovative product, costly activities that may require Geek Squad help.

Newness in Legal Terms The U.S. Federal Trade Commission (FTC) advises that the term *new* be limited to use with a product up to six months after it enters regular distribution. The difficulty with this suggestion is in the interpretation of the term *regular distribution*.

Newness from the Organization's Perspective Successful organizations view newness and innovation in their products at three levels. The lowest level, which usually involves the least risk, is a *product line extension*. This is an incremental improvement of an existing product line the company already sells. For example, Purina added its "new" line of Elegant Medleys, a "restaurant-inspired food for cats," to its existing line of 50 varieties of its Fancy Feast gourmet cat food. This has the potential benefit of adding new customers but the twin dangers of increasing expenses and cannibalizing products in its existing line.

At the next level is (1) a significant jump in innovation or technology or (2) a *brand extension* involving putting an established brand name on a new product in

For how the kind of innovation present in this ketchup bottle affects the marketing strategy, see the text.

an unfamiliar market. In the first case, the significant jump in technology might be when a manufacturer offers new smartphones or digital cameras.

The second case—using an existing brand name to introduce a new product into an unfamiliar market—looks deceptively easy for companies with a powerful, national or international brand name. *Cosmopolitan* thought so and put its brand name on a line of yogurts. The product line died quickly. *Cosmopolitan* magazine, which has 58 international editions, is distributed in more than 100 countries. *Cosmopolitan* has the magazine business down pat. One thing *Cosmo* does not do best is brand and sell yogurt. Its *Cosmopolitan* Yogurt disappeared from retail shelves in 18 months.[14]

A yogurt marketed by *Cosmopolitan* magazine? See the text for details.

The third and highest level of innovation involves a radical invention, a truly revolutionary new product. Apple's Apple II, the first commercially successful "personal computer," and its iPad and iPod are examples of radical inventions. Effective new-product development in large firms exists at all three levels.

Why Products and Services Succeed or Fail

LO 9-5 Describe the factors contributing to the success or failure of a new product or service.

We all know the giant product and service successes—such as Apple's iPad, Google, and CNN. Yet the thousands of product failures every year that slide quietly into oblivion cost American businesses billions of dollars. Ideally, a new product or service needs a precise *protocol*, a statement that, before product development begins, identifies (1) a well-defined target market; (2) specific customers' needs, wants, and preferences; and (3) what the product will be and do to satisfy consumers.

Research reveals how difficult it is to produce a single commercially successful new product, especially among consumer packaged goods (CPG) that appear on supermarket shelves one month and are gone forever a few months later. Most American families buy the same 150 items over and over again—making it difficult to gain buyers for new products. So less than 3 percent of new consumer packaged goods exceed first-year sales of $50 million—the benchmark of a successful CPG launch.[15]

New-product success or failure? Why might consumers choose *not* to buy sweetened corn flakes as a snack . . .

Marketing Reasons for New-Product Failures Both marketing and nonmarketing factors contribute to new-product failures. Using the research results from several studies on new-product success and failure, we can identify critical marketing factors—which sometimes overlap—that often separate new-product winners and losers:[16]

1. *Insignificant point of difference.* Research shows that a distinctive point of difference is the single most important factor for a new product to defeat competing ones—having superior characteristics that deliver unique benefits to the user. In the mid-1990s, General Mills launched Fingos, a sweetened cereal flake about the size of a corn chip, with a $34 million promotional budget. Consumers were supposed to snack on them dry, but they didn't.[17] The point of difference was not important enough to get consumers to stop eating competing snacks such as popcorn and potato chips.

2. *Incomplete market and product protocol before product development starts.* Without this protocol, firms try to design a vague product for a phantom market. Developed by Kimberly-Clark, Avert Virucidal tissues contained vitamin C derivatives scientifically designed to kill cold and flu germs when users sneezed,

. . . or vitamin-enriched carbonated bottled water for their dog or cat . . .

coughed, or blew their noses into them. The product failed in test marketing. People didn't believe the claims and were frightened by the "cidal" in the brand name, which they connected to words like *suicidal*. A product protocol that clearly defined how Avert would satisfy consumer needs might have prevented failure.[18]

3. *Not satisfying customer needs on critical factors.* Overlapping somewhat with point 1, this factor stresses that problems on one or two critical factors can kill the product, even though the general quality is high. For example, the Japanese, like the British, drive on the left side of the road. Until 1996, U.S. carmakers sent Japan few right-hand-drive cars—unlike German carmakers, which exported right-hand-drive models in several of their brands.

4. *Bad timing.* This results when a product is introduced too soon, too late, or when consumer tastes are shifting dramatically. Bad timing gives new-product managers nightmares. Microsoft, for example, introduced its Zune player a few years after Apple launched its iPod and other competitors offered their new MP3 players.

5. *No economical access to buyers.* Grocery products provide an example of this factor. Today's mega-supermarkets carry more than 30,000 different SKUs. With about 40,000 new consumer packaged goods (food, beverage, health and beauty aids, household, and pet items) introduced annually in the United States, the cost to gain access to retailer shelf space is huge. Because shelf space is judged in terms of sales per square foot, Thirsty Dog! (a zesty vitamin-enriched, mineral-loaded, lightly carbonated bottled water for your dog) must displace an existing product on the supermarket shelves, a difficult task with the high sales-per-square-foot demands of these stores. Thirsty Dog! and its companion product Thirsty Cat! failed to generate enough sales to meet these requirements.

6. *Poor product quality.* This factor often results when a product is not thoroughly tested. The costs to an organization for poor quality can be staggering and include the labor, materials, and other expenses to fix the problem—not to mention the lost sales, profits, and market share that usually result. In early 2007, with a $500 million promotional budget, Microsoft launched its Windows Vista to replace its successful predecessor Windows XP. But the Vista software had so many quality problems, even Microsoft's most loyal users revolted and the product failed.[19]

7. *Poor execution of the marketing mix: brand name, package, price, promotion, distribution.* Somewhere in the marketing mix there can be a showstopper that kills the product. Introduced by Gunderson & Rosario, Inc., Garlic Cake was supposed to be served as an hors d'oeuvre with sweet breads, spreads, and meats, but somehow the company forgot to tell this to potential consumers. Garlic Cake died because consumers were left to wonder just what a Garlic Cake is and when on earth a person would want to eat it.

8. *Too little market attractiveness.* The ideal is a large target market with high growth and real buyer need. But often the target market is too small or competitive to warrant the huge expenses necessary to reach it. OUT! International's Hey! There's A Monster In My Room spray was designed to rid scary creatures from a kid's bedroom and had a bubble-gum fragrance. While a creative and cute product, the brand name probably kept the kids awake at night more than their fear of the monsters because it implied the monster was still hiding in the bedroom. Also, was this a *real* market?

. . . or a spray to get rid of scary creatures from a child's bedroom? Answers appear in the text.

Simple marketing research should have revealed the problems in these new-product disasters. Developing successful new products may sometimes involve luck, but more often it involves having a product that really meets a need and has significant points of difference over competitive products.

Using Marketing Dashboards

Which States Are Underperforming?

In 2010, you started your own company to sell a nutritious, high-energy snack you developed. It is now January 2015. As a marketer, you ask yourself, "How well is my business growing?"

Your Challenge The snack is sold in all 50 states. Your goal is 10 percent annual growth. To begin 2015, you want to quickly solve any sales problems that occurred during 2014. You know that states whose sales are stagnant or in decline are offset by those with greater than 10 percent growth.

Studying a table of the sales and percent change versus a year ago in each of the 50 states would work but be very time-consuming. A good graphic is better. You choose the following marketing metric, where "sales" are measured in units:

$$\text{Annual \% sales change} = \frac{(2014\ \text{Sales} - 2013\ \text{Sales}) \times 100}{2013\ \text{Sales}}$$

You want to act quickly to improve sales. In your map, growth that is greater than 10 percent is green, 0 to 10 percent growth is orange, and decline is red. Notice that you (1) picked a metric and (2) made your own rules that green is good, orange is bad, and red is very bad.

Your Findings You see that sales growth in the northeastern states is weaker than the 10 percent target, and sales are actually declining in many of the states.

Annual Percentage Change in Unit Volume, by State

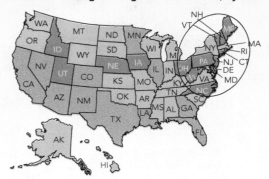

Your Action Marketing is often about grappling with sales shortfalls. You'll need to start by trying to identify and correct the problems in the largest volume states that are underperforming—in this case in the northeastern United States.

You'll want to do marketing research to see if the problem starts with (1) an external factor involving consumer tastes or (2) an internal factor such as a breakdown in your distribution system.

Organizational Inertia in New-Product Failures   Organizational problems and attitudes can also cause new-product disasters. Two key ones are:

Introduce a Life Savers soda? The text asks if "groupthink" played a part in this new-product decision.

- *Encountering "groupthink" in task force and committee meetings.* Someone in a new-product planning meeting often suspects the product concept is a dumb idea. But that person is afraid to speak for fear of being cast as a "negative thinker," "not a team player," and then ostracized from real participation in the group. Did someone on the Life Savers new-product team suspect a Life Savers soda wasn't a good idea but was afraid to speak?[20] Also, a strong public commitment to a new product in a planning meeting by its key advocate may make it difficult to kill the product even when new negative information appears.[21]
- *Avoiding the "NIH problem."* A great idea is a great idea, regardless of its source. Yet with the bureaucracy in large organizations, ideas often get rejected simply because they come from outside—what has been termed the "not-invented-here (NIH) problem." NIH was never a problem for Steve Jobs. Part of his innovation genius was being open to ideas from everywhere. Jobs got the ideas for the mouse and the graphical user interface, which led to icons and pull-down menus for the Macintosh, from visits to the Xerox Corporation's Palo Alto Research Center, known as Xerox PARC.[22]

These organizational problems also contribute to the eight marketing reasons for new-product failures described above.

How Marketing Dashboards Can Improve New-Product Performance

The Using Marketing Dashboards box shows how marketers measure actual market performance versus the goals set in new-product planning. It shows that you have set a goal of 10 percent annual growth for the new snack you developed. You have chosen a marketing metric of "annual % sales change" to measure the annual growth rate from 2013 to 2014 for each of the 50 states.

Your special concerns in the marketing dashboard are the states shown in red, where sales have actually declined. As shown in the box, having identified the northeastern United States as a problem region, you can now conduct in-depth marketing research to lead to corrective actions. For example, is the decline in sales in this region due to an external factor, such as consumer preference? Perhaps consumers in the northeastern United States prefer more regional snack tastes or think your snack is too sweet. Or perhaps the problem is due to your own internal marketing strategy, such as poor distribution, prices that are too high, or ineffective advertising.

> **learning review**
>
> 9-4. What kind of innovation would an improved electric toothbrush be?
>
> 9-5. Why can an "insignificant point of difference" lead to new-product failure?
>
> 9-6. What marketing metric might you use in a marketing dashboard to discover which states have weak sales?

THE NEW-PRODUCT PROCESS

 LO 9-6
Explain the purposes of each step of the new-product process.

new-product process
The seven stages an organization goes through to identify business opportunities and convert them into salable products or services.

To develop new products efficiently, companies such as General Electric and 3M use a specific sequence of steps to make their products ready for market. Figure 9–5 shows the **new-product process**, the seven stages an organization goes through to identify opportunities and convert them into salable products or services. Today many firms use a formal Stage-Gate® process to evaluate whether the results at each stage of the new-product development process are successful enough to warrant proceeding to the next stage. If problems in a stage can't be corrected, the project doesn't proceed to the next stage and product development is killed.[23]

Stage 1: New-Product Strategy Development

For companies, *new-product strategy development* is the stage of the new-product process that defines the role for a new product in terms of the firm's overall objectives.

FIGURE 9–5
Carefully using the seven stages in the new-product process increases the chances of new-product success.

1. New-product strategy development
2. Idea generation
3. Screening and evaluation
4. Business analysis
5. Development
6. Market testing
7. Commercialization

After inventing the digital camera in the mid-1970s, Kodak chose not to market it for fear of killing off its "cash cow" film business. Sadly, this led to a disastrous result, as the text describes.

During this stage, the firm uses both a SWOT analysis (Chapter 2) and environmental scanning (Chapter 3) to assess its strengths and weaknesses relative to the trends it identifies as opportunities or threats. The outcome not only defines the vital "protocol" for each new-product idea but also identifies the strategic role it might serve in the firm's business portfolio.

Occasionally a firm's Stage 1 activities can be blindsided by a revolutionary new product or technology that completely disrupts its business, sometimes called a "disruptive innovation." For example:

- *Wikipedia.* This free and community-edited online encyclopedia caused Encyclopedia Britannica to cease print production after 244 years.
- *Digital photography.* Even though they were invented by Kodak, digital cameras made film and film cameras obsolete by the mid-2000s and drove Kodak into bankruptcy in 2012. Kodak did not actively market its digital cameras because it wanted to protect its film business, the firm's cash cow.
- *Personal computers.* Xerox's PARC never actively marketed personal computers (whose key components were actually invented at its Palo Alto Research Center) because top management didn't envision business opportunities beyond the photocopying business; this left the market open for Steve Jobs.[24]

Clearly, a firm's new-product strategy development must be on the lookout for innovative products or technology that might disrupt its plans.

New-product development for services, such as buying a stock or airline ticket or watching a National Football League game, is often difficult. Why? Because services are intangible and performance-oriented. Nevertheless, service innovations can have a huge impact on our lives. For example, the online brokerage firm E*TRADE has revolutionized the financial services industry through its online investment trading.

Stage 2: Idea Generation

Idea generation, the second stage of the new-product process, involves developing a pool of concepts to serve as candidates for new products, building upon the previous stage's results. Many forward-looking organizations have discovered that they are not generating enough useful new-product ideas. One internal approach for getting ideas within the firm is to train employees in the art and science of asking specific, probing questions. The goal in generating new-product ideas and strategies is to move from "what is" questions that describe the present situation to "what if" questions that focus on solutions and marketing actions.[25]

Brothers John and Bert Jacobs are constantly looking for positive, upbeat messages to print on their Life Is Good T-shirts.

Many firms obtain ideas externally using *open innovation*, in which they find and execute creative new-product ideas by developing strategic relationships with outside individuals and organizations. Open innovation helps organizations overcome the not-invented-here (NIH) barriers discussed earlier. The following discussion suggests methods of generating new-product ideas both internally and externally, the latter often using open innovation relationships.[26]

Suggestions from Employees and Friends Businesses often seek new-product ideas from employees through suggestion boxes placed around their workplace. The idea for Nature Valley granola bars from General Mills came when one of its marketing managers observed co-workers bringing granola to work in plastic bags.

The breakthrough for the Life Is Good T-shirt business (introduced earlier in Chapter 1) started with a 1994 keg party the company founders, brothers Bert and John Jacobs, had with friends. At their parties the brothers often posted drawings with sayings for possible T-shirt ideas on their living room wall and asked their friends to jot down their reactions on the drawings.[27] At one party the drawing of a smiling, beret-wearing stick figure with the phrase "Life is good" got the most favorable comments. They named the character "Jake," printed 48 T-shirts with a smiling Jake and the words "Life is good," and sold them out in less than an hour at a local street fair. Today Life Is Good with its positive, upbeat messages has $100 million in annual sales and sells Life Is Good T-shirts, hats, and other items for men and women in 4,500 retail stores nationwide.[28]

Customer and Supplier Suggestions   Firms ask their salespeople to talk to customers and ask their purchasing personnel to talk to suppliers to discover new-product ideas.[29] Whirlpool gets ideas from customers on ways to standardize components so that it can cut the number of different product platforms to reduce costs.[30] Business researchers tell firms to actively involve customers and suppliers in the new-product development process. This means the focus should be on what the new product will actually do for them rather than simply what they want.[31]

A. G. Lafley, CEO of Procter & Gamble (P&G), gave his executives a *revolutionary* thought: "Look outside the company for solutions to problems rather than insisting P&G knows best." When he ran P&G's laundry detergent business, he had to redesign the laundry boxes so they were easier to open. Why? While consumers *said* P&G's laundry boxes were "easy to open," cameras they agreed to have installed in their laundry rooms showed they opened the boxes with *screwdrivers!*[32]

Procter & Gamble's new Tide Pods launch shows how it has improved both planning and implementation by involving consumers earlier in its innovation activities.

With a $150 million marketing budget, in 2012 P&G launched Tide Pods, a revolutionary three-chamber liquid dose that cleans, fights stains, and brightens. P&G describes Tide Pods as "its biggest laundry innovation in more than a quarter century." P&G says Tide Pods has produced the highest consumer-satisfaction scores the company has ever seen for a new laundry product. Following its successful new-product launch, however, P&G redesigned its packaging after discovering that some children thought the pods were candy and tried to eat them. How successful has Tide Pods been for P&G? After its first year, the product garnered a 73 percent share of the "unit dose" segment of the detergent market on estimated sales of $500 million—making it one of the most successful product launches of 2012![33]

"Crowdsourcing" is another creative idea-generation method if an R&D-marketing team wants ideas from 10,000 or 20,000 customers or suppliers. *Crowdsourcing* involves generating insights leading to actions based on ideas from massive numbers of people. It requires a precise question to focus the idea-generation process. Dell used crowdsourcing to develop an online site to generate 13,464 ideas for new products as well as website and marketing improvements, of which 402 were implemented.[34]

Research and Development Laboratories   Another source of new products is a firm's own research and development laboratories. Apple's sleek, cutting-edge designs for the iPad, iPhone, and iMac came out of its Apple Industrial Design Group, whose culture was established by the late Steve Jobs and is now guided by Senior Vice President of Design Jonathan Ive. What is the secret to Apple's world-class ability to convert vague concepts into tangible products? An action-item list from every meeting that focuses on *who* does *what* by *when!*[35]

Professional R&D and innovation laboratories that are *outside* the walls of large corporations are also sources of open innovation and can provide new-product ideas.[36] IDEO is a world-class new-product development firm that uses "design thinking," which involves incorporating human behavior as well as building upon the ideas of others in the innovation-design process. As the most prolific and influential design firm in the world, IDEO has created thousands of new products for its clients. Brainstorming sessions conducted at IDEO can generate 100 new ideas in an hour!

IDEO designs include developing the standing Crest Neat Squeeze toothpaste dispenser and improving the original Apple mouse. Recently, Fresh Express asked IDEO to design an innovative single-serve package for salads. IDEO's solution: A five-section package—one large section for the salad greens and four smaller ones for proteins, dressings, and so on—with each section sealed in plastic.[37]

Competitive Products   Analyzing the competition can lead to new-product ideas. For six months, the Marriott Corporation sent a six-person intelligence team to travel and stay at economy hotels around the country. The team assessed the competition's strengths and weaknesses on everything from the soundproof qualities of the rooms to the softness of the towels. Marriott then budgeted $500 million for a new economy hotel chain—Fairfield Inns.

Video 9-4
EPS's Whole Tree Harvester
kerin.tv/cr6e/v9-4

Smaller Firms, Universities, and Inventors   Many firms look for outside visionaries that have inventions or innovative ideas that can become products. Some sources of this open innovation strategy include:

- *Smaller, nontraditional firms.* Small technology firms and even small, nontraditional firms in adjacent industries provide creative advances. General Mills partnered with Weight Watchers to develop Progresso Light soups, the first consumer packaged product in any grocery category to carry the Weight Watchers endorsement with a 0 points value per serving.[38]
- *Universities.* Many universities have technology transfer centers that often partner with business firms to commercialize faculty inventions. The first-of-its-kind carbonated yogurt Go-Gurt Fizzix was launched by General Mills partnering with Brigham Young University to license the university's patent to put the "fizz" into the yogurt.[39]
- *Inventors.* David Ostlie, an inventor and president of Energy Performance Systems, Inc. (EPS), has spent 26 years developing machines to enhance low-pollution biomass energy production. His special focus: The 40 million acres of trees planted in rows on "tree farms" in the southeastern U.S. that are a source of wood for the lumber, paper, and biomass energy industries. EPS recently completed proof-of-concept tests on its Whole Tree Harvester™ that grabs the row trees, cuts them off at ground level, runs them up an incline, and drops them in a truck—at the mind-numbing efficiency of over 100 trees per minute.[40]

An inventor's peek at the future: The Whole Tree Harvester™ developed by Energy Performance Systems can harvest over 100 row trees per minute—enough to fill the industry's conventional 25-ton tree trailer.

Early-stage financing is almost always a problem for inventors and those starting a new business. *Crowdfunding* is a way to gather an online community of supporters to financially rally around a specific project that is unlikely to get resources from traditional sources such as banks or venture capital firms. For example, Kickstarter.com raised $1.2 million for start-up SmartThings to introduce a product that allows users to monitor their homes by remote control. But its biggest crowdfunding project was for the Pebble digital smartwatch with iPhone and Android smartphone integration: Almost 70,000 backers contributed over $10 million to develop this amazing product, which initially sold for $150! If *your* idea needs financing, here are five other crowdfunding sources and what they support:

Crowdfunder Kickstarter.com enabled Pebble to market its customizable watch that runs a variety of apps.

- *Crowdrise.* Charitable causes.
- *Crowdtilt.* Anything.
- *Fundable.* Early-stage financing for start-up businesses.
- *Rally.* Nonprofits, artists, musicians, entrepreneurs.
- *GiveForward.* Medical causes.

If you want to donate to crowdfunding projects, that's fine, too: The average Kickstarter donor gives $25.[41] Great ideas can come from almost anywhere—the challenge is recognizing and implementing them.

Stage 3: Screening and Evaluation

Screening and evaluation is the stage of the new-product process that internally and externally evaluates new-product ideas to eliminate those that warrant no further effort.

Internal Approach   In this approach to screening and evaluation, a firm's employees evaluate the technical feasibility of a proposed new-product idea to determine whether it meets the objectives defined in the new-product strategy development stage. For example, 3M scientists develop many world-class innovations in its labs. An internal assessment showed 3M's new technology with 3,000 tiny gripping "fingers" per square inch could be used to improve the gripping of both batting and work gloves.

Organizations that develop service-dominated offerings need to ensure that employees have the commitment and skills to meet customer expectations and sustain customer loyalty—an important criterion in screening a new-service idea. This is the essence of **customer experience management (CEM)**, which is the process of managing the entire customer experience within the company. Marketers must consider employees' interactions with customers so that the new services are consistently delivered and experienced.

> **customer experience management (CEM)**
> The process of managing the entire customer experience within the company.

External Approach   Firms that take an external approach to screening and evaluation use *concept tests*, external evaluations with consumers that consist of preliminary testing of a new-product idea rather than an actual product. Generally, these tests are more useful with minor modifications of existing products than with new, innovative products with which consumers are not familiar.[42] Concept tests rely on written descriptions of the product but may be augmented with sketches, mockups, or promotional literature. Key questions for concept testing include: How does the customer perceive the product? Who would use it? and How would it be used?

> **learning review**
>
> 9-7. What is the new-product strategy development stage in the new-product process?
>
> 9-8. What are the main sources of new-product ideas?
>
> 9-9. How do internal and external screening and evaluation approaches differ?

Is this what you'll be "driving" in 2020? The text describes why this Google 2014 "pod car" will have no steering wheel, gas pedal, brake, or gearshift for you.

Stage 4: Business Analysis

Business analysis specifies the features of the product and the marketing strategy needed to bring it to market and make financial projections. This is the last checkpoint before significant resources are invested to create a *prototype*—a full-scale operating model of the product. The business analysis stage assesses the total "business fit" of the proposed new product with the company's mission and objectives—from whether the product can be economically developed and manufactured to the marketing strategy needed to have it succeed in the marketplace.

This process requires not only detailed financial projections but also assessments of the marketing and product synergies related to the company's existing operations. Will the new product require a lot of new machinery to produce? Will it cannibalize sales of existing products or will it increase revenues by reaching new market segments? Can it be patented? Financial projections of expected profits require estimates of expected prices per unit and units sold, as well as detailed estimates of the costs of R&D, production, and marketing.

CHAPTER 9   Developing New Products and Services

Video 9-5
Google's Pod Car
kerin.tv/cr6e/v9-5

For services, business analysis involves using capacity management (discussed in Chapter 10) to find ways to match the availability of the service offering to when it is needed. For example, airlines and mobile phone service providers use *off-peak pricing* to charge different prices during different times of the day or during different days of the week to help match the supply and demand for their services.[43]

Stage 5: Development

Development is the stage of the new-product process that turns the idea on paper into a prototype. This results in a demonstrable, producible product that involves not only manufacturing the product efficiently but also performing laboratory and consumer tests to ensure the product meets the standards established for it in the protocol.

Google's driverless car is an extreme example of the complexity of the Stage 5 development process for a durable consumer good. In August 2012, the Google development team announced its cars had completed over 300,000 miles of accident-free driving with no one behind the wheel but with a Google engineer in the passenger seat. The only problem: Google's engineers failed to make its self-driving car return control of the steering wheel to the driver in an emergency!

Google's proposed fix: Take the "emergency driver"—the human—completely out of the picture for its driverless cars. So in mid-2014, Google started building 100 experimental, driverless electric-powered "pod cars" to seat two people. It will have a range of 100 miles at a maximum speed of 25 miles per hour—with no steering wheel, gas pedal, brake, or gearshift. The driver can only control a red "e-stop" button for emergency stops and use a separate button to start the car.

Google's self-driving "pod car" prototype won rave reviews from auto reporters. In the future, erstwhile "drivers" of Google's pod cars can be working on their laptops, e-mailing, or reading a book.[44] But it is clear Google will need to invest tens of millions of dollars into additional development and testing (see Stage 6 below) before anyone can buy a driverless car—a challenge typical of high-technology devices.

For services, improving the delivery of customer service is critical. This involves analyzing the entire sequence of steps or "service encounters" to improve the interactions between consumers and the service provider. High-contact services such as hotels, car rental agencies, and web providers use this approach to serve customers better.

Netflix is confronting changing markets, technologies, and competition. See the text for a discussion of these changes at Netflix.

The in-home movie and TV market is an example of the challenge of trying to improve customer services for consumers. So the business model for Netflix founder and chief executive officer Reed Hastings is constantly changing. It started with DVDs-by-mail in 1999, moved to movies streamed on the Internet in 2008, and then began offering original TV programming like its *House of Cards* drama in 2013 for its 44 million subscribers. But new competitors to Netflix are all around—including Amazon, a recent Verizon-Redbox venture, and Time-Warner's HBO. What is Netflix's future? Stay tuned.[45]

Stage 6: Market Testing

Market testing is a stage of the new-product process that involves exposing actual products to prospective consumers under realistic purchase conditions to see if they will buy. If the budget permits, consumer packaged goods firms do this by *test marketing*, which involves offering a product for sale on a limited basis in a defined area for a specific time period. The three main kinds of test markets are (1) standard, (2) controlled, and (3) simulated.[46] Because standard test markets are so time-consuming and expensive and can alert competitors to a firm's plans, some firms skip test markets entirely or use controlled or simulated test markets.

Consumer products, such as those from General Mills, often use controlled test markets to assess the likely success of new-product, promotional, or pricing strategies.

Standard Test Markets In a *standard test market*, a company develops a product and then attempts to sell it through normal distribution channels in a number of test-market cities. Test-market cities must be demographically representative of markets targeted for the new product, have cable TV systems that can deliver different ads to different homes, and have retailers with checkout counter scanners to measure sales. A distinguishing feature of a standard test market is that the producer sells the product to distributors, wholesalers, and retailers, just as it would do for other products.

Controlled Test Markets A *controlled test market* involves contracting the entire test program to an outside service. The service pays retailers for shelf space and can therefore guarantee a specified percentage of the test product's potential distribution volume. IRI is a leader in supplying controlled test markets to consumer packaged good firms like General Mills. Its BehaviorScan service uses five demographically representative cities to track sales made to a panel of households. In some cases the effectiveness of different TV commercials and other direct-to-consumer promotions can be measured.

Simulated Test Markets To save time and money, companies often turn to *simulated (or laboratory) test markets (STM),* a technique that somewhat replicates a full-scale test market. STMs are often run in shopping malls, to find consumers who use the product class being tested. Next, qualified participants are shown the product or the product concept and are asked about usage, reasons for purchase, and important product attributes. They then see the company's and competitors' ads for the test product. Finally, participants are given money and allowed to choose between buying the firm's product or the products of competitors from a real or simulated store environment.

When Test Markets Don't Work Not all products can use test markets. Test marketing a service is very difficult because consumers can't see what they are buying. For example, how do you test market a new building for an art museum? Similarly, test markets for expensive consumer products, such as cars or costly industrial products such as jet engines, are impractical. For these products, reactions of potential buyers to mockups or one-of-a-kind prototypes are all that is feasible.

Stage 7: Commercialization

Takeaway new-product lesson from the Boeing 787 Dreamliner: "Innovation . . . doesn't come easy." See the text for details.

Finally, the product is brought to the point of *commercialization*—the stage of the new-product process that positions and launches a new product in full-scale production and sales. This is the most expensive stage for most new products. Companies can face disasters at the commercialization stage, as shown in the Boeing 787 Dreamliner and Burger King french fries examples below.

The Boeing 787 Dreamliner Experience In 2004, Boeing announced the design for its Boeing 787 Dreamliner commercial airplane. Its technical advances would mean the plane would burn 20 percent less fuel and cost 30 percent less to maintain than present airliners. Boeing invested billions of dollars in the 787's development, and airlines had placed orders for almost 930 Dreamliners by mid-2013.

As the Dreamliner entered its commercialization stage, airlines around the world began taking deliveries. But with all the new technology in the Dreamliner, the new airplane was plagued by technical nightmares—even after extensive testing. Its wings, made with plastic-reinforced carbon fiber instead of aluminum, proved difficult to produce and attach to the fuselage. But an even more serious problem arose in early 2013: Lithium-ion batteries, which provide electrical power, caught fire on two Dreamliner aircraft, prompting regulators to ground all 50 Dreamliners in service. Perhaps *The Wall Street Journal* gave the best new-product lesson from the Boeing 787 Dreamliner example: "Innovation—for all its value—doesn't come as easily as a catchphrase. It can get messy."[47]

To discover the downs and ups of commercializing a new product, see the text discussion of Burger King's 15-year search for a french fry recipe that can compete with McDonald's.

Burger King's French Fries: The Complexities of Commercialization   McDonald's french fries are the gold standard against which all other fries in the fast-food industry are measured. In 1997, Burger King decided to take on McDonald's fries and spent millions of R&D dollars developing a whey/starch-coated fry designed to retain heat longer and add crispiness.

Burger King's thick-cut fries appeared in 2011 and have a new "coating" on the outside to create a "crispy, golden-brown deliciousness" while retaining the heat longer—for at least 10 minutes—because 75 percent of customers eat their fries "on the go" in their cars, offices, or homes. Burger King also launched the largest TV advertising campaign in its history to promote the new fries. The launch turned into a disaster. The reason: Except under ideal conditions, the new fry proved too complicated to get right day after day in Burger King restaurants.

Then in late 2013 Burger King introduced its "Satisfries" as the french fries in its kids meals. These are intended to help address concerns about nutrition for and obesity in children. Burger King reports Satisfries have about 20 percent fewer calories and 25 percent less fat than its regular fries. Burger King's latest commercialization problem: In mid-2014 Burger King discontinued its Satisfries at most of its restaurants because it couldn't communicate a meaningful point of difference to its customers and Satisfries cost more than its regular fries.

The french fries war includes Wendy's, too! Launched in 2010, Wendy's "Natural-Cut Fries with Sea Salt" have become a huge hit.[48]

The Special Risks in Commercializing Grocery Products   New grocery products pose special commercialization problems. Because shelf space is so limited, many supermarkets require a *slotting fee* for new products, a payment a manufacturer makes to place a new item on a retailer's shelf. This can run to several million dollars for a single product. But there's even another potential expense. If a new grocery product does not achieve a predetermined sales target, some retailers require a *failure fee*, a penalty payment a manufacturer makes to compensate a retailer for devoting valuable shelf space to a product that failed to sell.

These costly slotting fees and failure fees are why large grocery product manufacturers use regional rollouts. *Regional rollouts* introduce a product sequentially into geographical areas of the United States to allow production levels and marketing activities to build up gradually, to minimize the risk of new-product failure.

Speed as a Factor in New-Product Success   Companies have discovered that speed or *time to market* (TtM) is often vital in introducing a new product. Recent studies have shown that high-tech products coming to market on time are far more profitable than those arriving late. So companies like Sony, BMW, 3M, and Hewlett-Packard often overlap the sequence of stages described in this chapter.

With this approach, termed *parallel development*, cross-functional team members who conduct the simultaneous development of both the product and the production process stay with the product from conception to production. This approach enabled Hewlett-Packard to reduce the development time for notebook computers from 12 to

7 months. In software development, *fast prototyping* uses a "do it, try it, fix it" approach—encouraging continuing improvement even after the initial design. To speed up time to market, many firms insulate their new-product teams from routine administrative tasks to keep them from bogging down in red tape.[49]

> ## learning review
>
> 9-10. How does the development stage of the new-product process involve testing the product inside and outside the firm?
>
> 9-11. What is a test market, and what are the three kinds?
>
> 9-12. What is the commercialization of a new product?

LEARNING OBJECTIVES REVIEW

LO 9-1 *Recognize the various terms that pertain to products and services.*

A product is a good, service, or idea consisting of a bundle of tangible and intangible attributes that satisfies consumers and is received in exchange for money or something else of value.

A good has tangible attributes that a consumer's five senses can perceive and intangible ones such as warranties; a laptop computer is an example. Goods also can be divided into nondurable goods, which are consumed in one or a few uses, and durable goods, which usually last over many uses.

Services are intangible activities or benefits that an organization provides to satisfy consumer needs in exchange for money or something else of value, such as an airline trip. An idea is a thought that leads to a product or action, such as eating healthier foods.

LO 9-2 *Identify the ways in which consumer and business products and services can be classified.*

By type of user, the major distinctions are consumer products, which are products purchased by the ultimate consumer, and business products, which are products that assist an organization in providing other products for resale.

Consumer products can be broken down based on the effort involved in the purchase decision process, marketing mix attributes used in the purchase, and the frequency of purchase: (*a*) convenience products are items that consumers purchase frequently and with a minimum of shopping effort; (*b*) shopping products are items for which consumers compare several alternatives on selected criteria; (*c*) specialty products are items that consumers make special efforts to seek out and buy; and (*d*) unsought products are items that consumers either do not know about or do not initially want.

Business products can be broken down into (*a*) components, which are items that become part of the final product, such as raw materials or parts, and (*b*) support products, which are items used to assist in producing other goods and services and include installations, accessory equipment, supplies, and industrial services.

Services can be classified in terms of whether they are delivered by (*a*) people or equipment, (*b*) business firms or nonprofit organizations, or (*c*) government agencies.

Firms can offer a range of products, which involve decisions regarding the product item, product line, and product mix.

LO 9-3 *Describe four unique elements of services.*

The four unique elements of services—the four I's—are intangibility, inconsistency, inseparability, and inventory. Intangibility refers to the tendency of services to be a performance that cannot be held or touched, rather than an object. Inconsistency is a characteristic of services because they depend on people to deliver them, and people vary in their capabilities and in their day-to-day performance. Inseparability refers to the difficulty of separating the deliverer of the services (hair stylist) from the service itself (hair salon). Inventory refers to the need to have service production capability when there is service demand.

LO 9-4 *Explain the significance of "newness" in new products and services as it relates to the degree of consumer learning involved.*

From the important perspective of the consumer, "newness" is often seen as the degree of learning that a consumer must engage in to use the product. With a continuous innovation, no new behaviors must be learned. With a dynamically continuous innovation, only minor behavioral changes are needed. With a discontinuous innovation, consumers must learn entirely new consumption patterns.

LO 9-5 *Describe the factors contributing to the success or failure of a new product or service.*

A new product or service often fails for these marketing reasons: (*a*) insignificant points of difference, (*b*) incomplete market and product protocol before product development starts, (*c*) a failure to satisfy customer needs on critical factors, (*d*) bad timing, (*e*) no economical access to buyers, (*f*) poor product quality, (*g*) poor execution of the marketing mix, and (*h*) too little market attractiveness.

LO 9-6 *Explain the purposes of each step of the new-product process.*

The new-product process consists of seven stages a firm uses to develop salable products or services: (1) *New-product strategy development* involves defining the role for the new product within the firm's overall objectives. (2) *Idea generation* involves developing a pool of concepts from consumers, employees, basic R&D, and competitors to serve as candidates for new products. (3) *Screening and evaluation* involves evaluating new-product ideas to eliminate those that are not feasible from a technical or consumer perspective. (4) *Business analysis* involves defining the features of the new product, developing the marketing strategy and marketing program to introduce it, and making a financial forecast. (5) *Devel-* *opment* involves not only producing a prototype product but also testing it in the lab and with consumers to see that it meets the standards set for it. (6) *Market testing* involves exposing actual products to prospective consumers under realistic purchasing conditions to see if they will buy the product. (7) *Commercialization* involves positioning and launching a product in full-scale production and sales with a specific marketing program.

LEARNING REVIEW ANSWERS

9-1 **What are the four main types of consumer products?**

Answer: They are: (1) convenience products—items that the consumer purchases frequently, conveniently, and with a minimum of shopping effort; (2) shopping products—items for which the consumer compares several alternatives on criteria such as price, quality, or style; (3) specialty products—items that the consumer makes a special effort to search out and buy; and (4) unsought products—items that the consumer does not know about or knows about but does not initially want.

9-2 **What are the 4 I's of services?**

Answer: The four I's of services are: (1) intangibility, which means that they can't be held, touched, or seen; (2) inconsistency, which means that their quality varies with each person's capabilities and day-to-day job performance; (3) inseparability, which means that the consumer cannot (and does not) separate the deliverer of the service from the service itself; and (4) inventory, which means that inventory carrying costs are more subjective and are related to idle production capacity—when the service provider is available but there is no demand for the service.

9-3 **What is the difference between a product line and a product mix?**

Answer: A product line is a group of product or service items that are closely related because they satisfy a class of needs, are used together, are sold to the same customer group, are distributed through the same outlets, or fall within a given price range. The product mix consists of all the product lines offered by an organization.

9-4 **What kind of innovation would an improved electric toothbrush be?**

Answer: continuous innovation—no new learning is required by consumers

9-5 **Why can an "insignificant point of difference" lead to new-product failure?**

Answer: The product must have superior characteristics that deliver unique benefits to the user compared to those of competitors that must be sufficient enough to motivate a change in consumption behavior. Without these points of difference, the product will probably fail.

9-6 **What marketing metric might you use in a marketing dashboard to discover which states have weak sales?**

Answer: The marketing metric—annual percentage change in unit volume by state—will help identify those states that are underperforming.

9-7 **What is the new-product strategy development stage in the new-product process?**

Answer: New-product strategy development is the first stage of the new-product process that defines the role for a new product in terms of the firm's overall objectives. During this stage, the firm uses both a SWOT analysis and environmental scanning to assess its strengths and weaknesses relative to the trends it identifies as opportunities or threats. The outcome not only defines the vital "protocol" for each new-product idea but also identifies the strategic role it might serve in the firm's business portfolio.

9-8 **What are the main sources of new-product ideas?**

Answer: Many firms obtain ideas externally using open innovation, in which an organization finds and executes creative new-product ideas by developing strategic relationships with outside individuals and organizations. Some of these sources include employee and co-worker suggestions, customer and supplier suggestions (either directly, through the firm's salesforce or purchasing department or through crowd sourcing—soliciting ideas via the Internet from large numbers of people), R&D laboratories (both internal to the firm and professional innovation firms like IDEO), competitive products (analyzing their points of difference that lead to a competitive advantage for them), and smaller, nontraditional technology firms, university technology transfer centers that partner with business firms to commercialize faculty inventions, and lone inventors or entrepreneurs.

9-9 **How do internal and external screening and evaluation approaches differ?**

Answer: In internal screening, company employees evaluate the technical feasibility of new-product ideas to determine whether they meet the objectives defined in the new-product strategy development stage. For services, employees are assessed to determine whether they have the commitment and skills to meet customer expectations and sustain customer loyalty. In external screening, evaluation consists of preliminary concept testing of the new-product idea (not the actual product itself) using written descriptions, sketches, mockups, or promotional literature with consumers.

9-10 **How does the development stage of the new-product process involve testing the product inside and outside the firm?**

Answer: Development is the stage of the new-product process that turns the idea on paper into a prototype, which results in a demonstrable, producible product that can be efficiently manufactured. Internally, laboratory tests are done to see if the product achieves the physical, quality, and safety standards set for it. Externally, market testing is done to expose actual products to prospective consumers under realistic purchase conditions to see if they will buy.

9-11 What is a test market, and what are the three kinds?
Answer: Test marketing involves offering a product for sale on a limited basis in a defined area for a specific time period. The three main kinds of test markets are: (1) standard, (2) controlled, and (3) simulated. In a standard test market, a city (or cities) is selected that is viewed as being demographically representative of the markets targeted for the new product and has both cable TV systems that can deliver different ads to different homes and retailers with checkout counter scanners to measure sales results. In a controlled test market, the firm contracts the entire test program to an outside service, which pays retailers for shelf space to guarantee a specified percentage of the test product's potential distribution volume. In a simulated (or laboratory) test market (STM), the firm attempts to replicate a full-scale test market by creating a fictitious storefront in a shopping mall and exposing prospective customers to the product (or concept) and ads from both it and its competitors to see if they will buy.

9-12 What is the commercialization of a new product?
Answer: Commercialization, the most expensive stage for most new products, is the last stage of the new-product process that involves positioning and launching a new product in full-scale production and sales.

FOCUSING ON KEY TERMS

business products p. 215
consumer products p. 215
customer experience management (CEM) p. 229

four I's of services p. 217
idle production capacity p. 217
new-product process p. 225
product p. 213

product item p. 219
product line p. 219
product mix p. 219
services p. 214

APPLYING MARKETING KNOWLEDGE

1 Products can be classified as either consumer or business products. How would you classify the following products? (*a*) Johnson's baby shampoo, (*b*) a Black & Decker two-speed drill, and (*c*) an arc welder.

2 Are Nature Valley granola bars and Eddie Bauer hiking boots convenience, shopping, specialty, or unsought products?

3 Based on your answer to question 2, how would the marketing actions differ for each product and the classification to which you assigned it?

4 Explain how the four I's of services apply to a Marrriott Hotel.

5 Idle production capacity may be related to inventory or capacity management. How would the pricing component of the marketing mix reduce idle production capacity for (*a*) a car wash, (*b*) a stage theater group, and (*c*) a university?

6 In terms of the behavioral effect on consumers, how would a computer, such as an Apple iMac, be classified? In light of this classification, what actions would you suggest to the manufacturers of these products to increase their sales in the market?

7 What methods would you suggest to assess the potential commercial success for the following new products? (*a*) a new, improved ketchup; (*b*) a three-dimensional television system that took the company 10 years to develop; and (*c*) a new children's toy on which the company holds a patent.

8 Concept testing is an important step in the new-product process. Outline the concept tests for (*a*) an electrically powered car and (*b*) a new loan payment system for automobiles that is based on a variable interest rate. What are the differences in developing concept tests for products as opposed to services?

BUILDING YOUR MARKETING PLAN

In fine-tuning the product strategy for your marketing plan, do these two things:

1 Develop a simple three-column table in which (*a*) market segments of potential customers are in the first column and (*b*) the one or two key points of difference of the product to satisfy the segment's needs are in the second column.

2 In the third column of your table, write ideas for specific new products for your business in each of the rows in your table.

Video 9-6
X-1 Video Case
kerin.tv/cr6e/v9-6

X-1 started as a simple idea for a business school project and has quickly grown to become the foremost leader in waterproof, sweatproof, and weatherproof audio equipment for athletes. Many factors contribute to the success of X-1, "but new product development is the engine that drives it all," explains CEO Carl Thomas.

If you are a swimmer, runner, snowboarder, surfer, triathlete, climber, bicyclist, or any kind of sports enthusiast who enjoys music while you exercise, chances are you've seen X-1's products. The first product, a waterproof case for iPods, served as the starting point for a new-product development process that has added headphones, earbuds, cases, armbands, and accessories—an entire product line of audio solutions—to the company's offerings.

The commitment to new products has been so successful that the company now holds eight patents on its technology and was recognized by *Inc.* magazine as one of the top 500 fastest-growing companies in the United States. It is not surprising, then, to hear Thomas explain that marketing and new-product development "is a very key function for any company, but it's especially important for us."

THE COMPANY

X-1 has a fascinating history. Its founders were scuba divers who wanted to listen to music while they were diving, so they investigated how to use electronic devices and speakers underwater. The waterproof case they developed functioned to depths of 300 feet and led to a U.S. patent for a "waterproof enclosure for an audio device." At the same time, they were enrolled in a business school course that required the development of a business plan. They wrote the plan for their new technology, called their company Diver Entertainment, and began shipping products to other scuba divers.

It soon became obvious that the concept of waterproof audio equipment would appeal to many applications other than scuba diving. The company began developing waterproof headphones, changed its name to H2O Audio, and adopted the advertising tagline "Your Sport, Your Music." Swimmers, surfers, and triathletes were obvious potential customers, so Olympic swimmers Natalie Coughlin and Michael Phelps, professional surfer Laird Hamilton, and triathletes Greg and Laura Bennett were signed as official H2O Audio Ambassadors. The popularity of the brand grew rapidly as athletes in each of the sports learned about and tried the new products.

The success of H2O Audio products with aquatic athletes led the company to look for the next opportunity for growth. The obvious step was to expand to other sports and to attract athletes such as runners, kayakers, snowboarders, climbers, and weightlifters. In fact, H2O Audio soon came to realize that its market could be all athletes regardless of their sport.

The new strategy ran into an unexpected problem, however. While the H2O brand name was intuitive and descriptive and contributed to the initial success of the products, it also limited the perception of the products' uses to water sports. Applications to sports where the athletes were not actually underwater were not immediately obvious to retail store managers. Bicycle retailers and shoe stores, for example, would often decline to carry the products saying, "You're just a swim company," explains Thomas. As a result, H2O Audio undertook a six-month review of its brand.

The review process included interviews with athletes, retailers, manufacturers, and current customers. A branding agency was hired to help assess the information and to identify possible changes in the products and brand. It asked, "What characteristics are important to enable all athletes to train and perform at their peak with music?" The answer was to expand the original "waterproof" product concept to "waterproof, weatherproof, and sweatproof technology that is durable and comfortable."

According to Thomas, "We learned that every single one of the athletes out there needed the headphone to be not only durable and stable in whatever environment they were in, but they wanted it to be comfortable, they wanted it to fit, and they wanted it to not fall out." The process also identified a new brand name, X-1, which was inspired by the first aircraft to break the sound barrier—the Bell X-1. The new name led to a new advertising tag line—"Breaking the Barriers of Sound"—and immediately changed the perception of the products.

The X-1 product line was expanded to reflect the new, broader appeal to all athletes. The line included:

- *Momentum.* An in-ear ultralight headphone that is rinsable, weatherproof, and sweatproof.
- *Surge.* An in-ear headphone that is waterproof, weatherproof, and sweatproof and has bass amplified sound and sportwrap options.
- *Women's Momentum and Surge.* Headphones that are designed for petite ears.
- *Amphibx.* Armbands and cases that hold most audio devices including iPod Shuffle, iPod Touch, iPod Classic, and iPhone.
- *Interval.* A solution designed specifically for swimmers to attach to goggle straps.

All of the headphones are customizable with 3 to 5 different sizes of ear tips, and the cases all allow full function of touchscreens and buttons. The entire product line is the result of and reflects the importance of the product development process.

THE PRODUCT DEVELOPMENT PROCESS AT X-1

"Here at X-1, new-product development is essential. We are constantly monitoring and speaking with our retail buyers to make sure that we have the best product mix for the marketplace," explains Peter Dirksing, director of product development at X-1. Generally, the company follows a rigorous sequence of steps or stages.

The first stage, new-product strategy development, reflects X-1's environmental scanning efforts. They observed that while the audio industry was mature, the advent of personal or mobile audio, created by products such as the Walkman, the Discman, the iPod, and now smartphones, represents an opportunity for new products.

The second stage is idea generation. X-1 uses many sources to help generate new ideas. Employees and co-workers, for example, can make suggestions at a "blue sky" meeting where, according to Dirksing, "No idea is a bad idea." The company also uses open innovation to generate new ideas by engaging retail buyers and soliciting ideas from a group of volunteer athletes called Team X-1.

The next stage, screening and evaluation, involves an evaluation of each idea to determine if it warrants further effort. X-1 assesses the feasibility of new technical requirements, synergy with existing technology, and the magnitude of resource requirements. All the factors "mix together to determine what is the greatest priority," explains Dirksing.

The fourth step, business analysis, involves creating a "business case" for the idea. The X-1 product development team works closely with sales and marketing to create a 12-month forecast that accounts for possible cannibalization of existing products and also estimates how long the product will be on the market before it reaches the break-even point.

In the development stage of the process, X-1 actually turns the idea into a prototype. The firm uses a 3D printer to check the aesthetics and the dimensions and to see how the product will actually fit on a person. Once the dimensions are determined, a functional prototype is needed. Dirksing explains, "After we've checked the outside dimensions on a 3D printed prototype, we'll actually send the final 3D drawings to a factory and get a functional prototype made."

The initial prototypes are used to conduct safety tests and the first functionality tests. "Part of my job is also making sure that the product functions as it's intended. So one of the really cool aspects of my job is that I'm taking prototypes out and hopping in the pool in the morning before work or getting in the water on my board and catching a wave or two before I get into the office just to make sure that these products we're developing are actually functioning in a real world environment," explains Dirksing.

Once production-quality prototypes are available, X-1 begins stage six, market testing. "We have a team of a few hundred amateur athletes that will get out and test the product and provide feedback," says Dirksing. X-1 also uses its website to connect with a cross-section of consumers and to get feedback as quickly as possible. Changes from this process lead to the final stage of the new-product development process, commercialization. X-1 develops a go-to-market plan, alerts the salesforce and retail buyers of the availability of new products, and begins production. Because X-1 is an international brand, this stage also includes developing the advertising and packaging for its customers in Europe, Asia, Australia, and around the world.

The new-product development process is an ongoing activity at X-1. At any given time the company may have 10 to 15 new-product ideas at various stages of the process. X-1's use of new technologies, such as 3D printers, as well as its fast-prototyping orientation has reduced product development time to about 12 months from start to commercialization. Once the new products are ready for consumers, the marketing department adds its expertise to ensure the success of the products.

MARKETING ADVANCED AUDIO SOLUTIONS

The marketing activities at X-1 are very comprehensive. "We do everything from print advertising, digital advertising, events, trade shows, social media, pretty much anything you can think of," says Dana Swanson, X-1 director of marketing. The many activities contribute to several different objectives, including changing the name of the company, rebranding the products, introducing new products, and communicating with different segments of consumers.

Changing the name from H2O Audio to X-1, for example, required marketing that helped get the product into people's hands so they could understand the value of the product. Swanson explains, "Something that is just going to splash our logo everywhere, like sponsoring a big race or an event, isn't as important to us as something like going to an event and having a booth where we can actually interact with people, talk about our product, and get our product into people's hands." This is also one of the reasons X-1 has product ambassadors. First, X-1 has contracts with selected professional and Olympic athletes who use X-1 products. Second, X-1 created a team of amateur athletes who receive product samples to use during amateur sporting events. In both cases, the ambassadors give X-1 products exposure to the marketplace and help demonstrate how they work.

X-1 also relies on social media, particularly to develop and introduce new products. "If it's out there, we've got a page, from Facebook to Twitter to Instagram," explains Swanson. "It's really all about just being where your people are and being there for them, interacting, talking, and answering questions," she goes on. Social media also allow X-1 to ask occasional questions about satisfaction with the products, color preferences, and even how the products are being used. Many of today's customers "love

being involved," and their engagement is particularly helpful when X-1 introduces new products.

Communicating with different segments is also an important marketing objective. Currently, the three primary segments are:

- *Endurance Segment.* Includes athletes participating in all demanding athletic activities (e.g., marathons, triathalons, etc.) and training.
- *Outdoors Segment.* Includes all participants in activities that take place outside (e.g., hiking).
- *Club Segment.* Includes everyone who goes to a health club, fitness studio, or gymnasium.

One way X-1 ensures that it reaches these segments is through its sales channels. By offering its products through sporting goods stores (such as REI, Sports Chalet, and Eastern Mountain Sports), specialty retail stores, e-tailers (such as Amazon.com), and online through its own website, X-1 can reach the many potential consumers in each of the segments.

Public relations also helps provide a lot of exposure. X-1 is fortunate that it has many unique attributes such as reflective cables, customizable ear fit, ambient noise allowance, and special sizes for women to attract media interest. For example, *Fitness* magazine, *Women's Running* magazine, *MSN News, Fox News, The Wall Street Journal,* and *Travel Weekly* have all recently carried stories about X-1 products.

The combination of a great initial idea, a rigorous product development process, and excellent marketing actions all contribute to X-1's success. "I think X-1 products are successful because we actually are a solutions company," says Swanson. "We try to find a way that really works for athletes to bring their music with them while they're doing any activity."

Questions

1 What are the points of difference, or unique attributes, for X-1 products?

2 What are X-1's primary target markets?

3 Describe the new-product development process used at X-1. What are the similarities and differences to the process described in Figure 9–5?

4 Which of the eight reasons for new-product failure did X-1 avoid to ensure the success of X-1's products?

5 Identify one new-product idea you would suggest that X-1 evaluate.

Chapter Notes

1. Edward C. Baig, "On New iPad, Looks Are Everything," *USA Today*, March 16, 2012, p. B3; Walter Isaacson, "American Icon," *Time*, October 17, 2011, pp. 32–35; Brad Stone, "1997–2011: The Return," *Bloomberg Businessweek*, October 10–16, 2011, pp. 36–42; Sean Wilsey, "The Products," *Bloomberg Businessweek*, October 10–16, 2011, pp. 48–61; Beth Snyder Bulik, "Marketer of the Decade," *Advertising Age*, October 18, 2010, p. 14; and Geoff Colvin, "The World's Most Admired Companies: 2012," *Fortune*. See http://money.cnn.com /magazines/fortune/most-admired/2012/snapshots/670.html; and Adam Lashinsky, "The Decade of Steve," *Fortune*, November 23, 2009, pp. 92–100.

2. Andy Serwer, "Steve Jobs vs. Sam Walton," *Fortune*, December 3, 2012, pp. 123–30.

3. Ian Sherr, "Apple's Magic Wears Thin As Its Earnings Disappoint," *The Wall Street Journal*, January 24, 2013, pp. A1, A2; and Lev Grossman, "The Technologist: Tim Cook," *Time*, December 31, 2012–January 7, 2013, pp. 112–18.

4. Molly Wood, "Apple's CarPlay Is Almost a Step in the Right Direction," *Star Tribune*, March 12, 2014, p. D6. See http://www.apple.com/pr/library/2014/03/03apple-rolls-out-carplay.

5. "Gross Domestic Product: Fourth Quarter and Annual 2012 (Advance Estimate)," news release from the Bureau of Economic Analysis: U.S. Department of Commerce, January 30, 2013, Table 3. Gross Domestic Product and Related Measures, p. 8—calculation from data for 2012, column 1. See http://www.bea.gov/newsreleases/national/gdp/2013/pdf/gdp4q12_adv.pdf.

6. Suzanne C. Makarem, Susan M. Mudambi, and Jeffrey S. Podoshen, "Satisfaction in Technology-Enabled Service Encounters," *The Journal of Services Marketing* 3 (2009), p. 134; Peter C. Honebein and Roy F. Cammarano, "Customers at Work: Self-Service Customers Can Reduce Costs and Become Cocreators of Value," *Marketing Management*, January/February 2006, pp. 26–31; and Matthew L. Meuter, Amy L. Ostrom, Robert I. Roundtree, and Mary Jo Bitner, "Self-Service Technologies: Understanding Customer Satisfaction with Technology-Based Service Encounters," *Journal of Marketing*, July 2000, pp. 50–64.

7. Valerie A. Zeithaml, A. Parasuraman, and Leonard L. Berry, *Delivering Quality Service* (New York: Free Press, 1990); and Stephen W. Brown and Teresa Swartz, "A Gap Analysis of Professional Service Quality," *Journal of Marketing*, April 1989, pp. 92–98.

8. Anna S. Mattila, "Do Women Like Option More than Men? An Examination in the Context of Service Recovery," *Journal of Services Marketing*, 2010(7), pp. 499–508; Leslie M. Fine, "Service Marketing," *Business Horizons*, May–June 2008, pp. 163–168; and James G. Maxham III and Richard G. Netermeyer, "A Longitudinal Study of Complaining Customers' Evaluations of Multiple Service Failures and Recovery Efforts," *Journal of Marketing*, October 2002, pp. 57–71.

9. Isaac Arnsdorf, "The Museum Is Watching You," *The Wall Street Journal*, August 18, 2010, pp. D1, D2.

10. Todd Nelson, "On a Run with Crapola Granola," *Star Tribune*, January 14, 2013, p. D2; and James Norton, "Brian and Andrea Strom of Crapola Granola," *Heavy Table*, January 16, 2013. See http://heavytable.com/brian-and-andrea-strom-of-crapola-granola; Jess Fleming, "Made in Minnesota: Crapola Granola Is Better Than It Sounds," *Pioneer Press*, December 19, 2012. See http://www.twincities.com/restaurants/ci_22223106/crapola-granola-is-better-than-it-sounds; and Abe Sauer, "Minnesota's Crapola Proud to Be Number Two Brand, *Brandchannel*, December 12, 2011. See http://www.brandchannel.com/home/post/2011/12/12/Minnesota-Brand-Crapola-121211.aspx.

11. Barbara Ortutay, "Sony Likely to Unveil Next PlayStation on Feb. 20," *Associated Press*, February 1, 2013. See http://bigstory.ap.org/article/sony-likely-unveil-next-playstation-feb-20; and Daisuke Wakabayashi and Ian Sherr, "Nintendo Sticks to Its Guns," *The Wall Street Journal*, November 17–18, 2012, pp. B1, B2.

12. Interview with Geek Squad founder Robert Stephens on *60 Minutes*, January 28, 2007, www.geeksquad.com; Debora Viana Thompson, Rebecca W. Hamilton, and Roland Rust, "Feature Fatigue: When Product Capabilities Become Too Much of a Good Thing," *Journal of Marketing Research*, November 2005, pp. 431–42; and Ronald T. Rust, Debora Viana Thompson, and Rebecca W. Hamilton, "Defeating Feature Fatigue," *Harvard Business Review*, February 2006, pp. 98–107.

13. Youngme Moon, "Break Free from the Product Life Cycle," *Harvard Business Review*, May 2005, pp. 86–94.

14. See "The 25 Biggest Product Flops of All Time," www.walletpop.com/photos/top-25-biggest-product-flops-of-all-time; and Zac Frank and Tania Khadder, "The 20 Worst Product Failures," www.saleshq.monster.com/news/articles/2655-the-20-worst-product-failures.

15. Joan Schneider and Julie Hall, "Why Most Product Launches Fail," *Harvard Business Review*, April 2011, pp. 21–23.

16. Robert G. Cooper, "New Products: What Separates the Winners from the Losers?" in *The PDMA Handbook of New Product Development*, eds. M. D. Rosenau, A. Griffin, G. Castellion, and N. Anscheutz (New York: Wiley and Sons, 1996), pp. 3–18; Robert G. Cooper, "The Impact of Product Innovativeness on Performance," *Journal of Product Innovation Management*, April 1999, pp. 115–33; Thomas D. Kuczmarski, "Measuring Your Return on Innovation," *Marketing Management*, Spring 2000, pp. 25–32; and Merle Crawford and Anthony Di Benedetto, *New Products Management*, 9th ed. (New York: McGraw-Hill/Irwin, 2008), pp. 61–71.

17. Julie Fortser, "The Lucky Charm of Steve Sanger," *BusinessWeek*, March 26, 2001, pp. 75–76.

18. The Avert Virucidal tissues, Hey! There's A Monster In My Room spray, and Garlic Cake examples are adapted from Robert M. McMath and Thom Forbes, *What Were They Thinking?* (New York: Random House, 1998).

19. Schneider and Hall, "Why Most Product Launches Fail," p. 22.

20. Dan P. Lovallo and Olivier Sibony, "Distortions and Deceptions in Strategic Decisions," *The McKinsey Quarterly* 1 (2006), pp. 19–29; and Byron G. Augusto, Eric P. Harmon, and Vivek Pandit, "The Right Service Strategies for Product Companies," *The McKinsey Quarterly* 1 (2006), pp. 41–51.

21. "The 25 Biggest Product Flops of All Time"; Isabelle Royer, "Why Bad Projects Are So Hard to Kill," *Harvard Business Review*, February 2003, pp. 48–56; John T. Morn, Dan P. Lovallo, and S. Patrick Viguerie, "Beating the Odds in Market Entry," *The McKinsey Quarterly* 4 (2005), pp. 35–45; Leslie Perlow and Stephanie Williams, "Is Silence Killing Your Company?" *Harvard Business Review*, May 2003, pp. 52–58; Beverly K. Brockman and Robert M. Morgan, "The Moderating Effect of Organizational Cohesiveness in Knowledge Use and New Product Development," *Journal of Marketing Science* 3 (Summer 2006), pp. 295–306; Eyal Biyalogorsky, William Boulding, and Richard Staelin, "Stuck in the Past: Why Managers Persist with New Product Failures," *Journal of Marketing*, April 2006, pp. 108–21; and Irwin L. Janis, *Groupthink* (New York: Free Press, 1988).

22. Walter Isaacson, *Steve Jobs* (New York: Simon & Schuster, 2011), pp. 94–101.

23. Robert G. Cooper, "What Leading Companies Are Doing to Reinvent Their NPD Process," *PDMA Visions Magazine*, September 2008, pp. 6–10; Robert G. Cooper, "The Stage-Gate Idea-to-Launch Process—Update: What's New and NexGen Systems," *Journal of Product Innovation Management*, May 2008, pp. 213–32; Leland D. Shaeffer and Michael Zirkle, "Beyond 'Phase Gate'—Why Not a Tailored Solution?" *PDMA Visions Magazine*, June 2008, pp. 21–25; and Gloria Barczak, Abbie Griffin, and Kenneth B. Kahn, "Perspective: Trends and Drivers of Success in NPD Practices: Results of the 2003 PDMA Best Practices Study," *Journal of Product Innovation Management*, January 2009, pp. 3–23.

24. Walter Isaacson, *Steve Jobs*, pp. 98–101; and Malcolm Gladwell, "Creation Myth: Xerox PARC, Apple, and the Truth about Innovation," *The New Yorker*, May 16, 2011. See www.newyorker.com/reporting/2011/05/16/110516ta_fact_gladwell.

25. Hal B. Greyersen, Jeff Dyer, and Clayton M. Christensen, "Why Ask Why?" *ChiefExecutive.Net*, January/February, 2012, pp. 40–43.

26. Peter Erickson, "One Food Company's Foray into Open Innovation," *PDMA Visions Magazine*, June 2008, pp. 12–14; Benn Lawson, Kenneth J. Petersen, Paul D. Cousins, and Robert B. Handfield, "Knowledge Sharing in Interorganizational Product Development Teams: The Effect of Formal and Informal Socialization Mechanisms," *Journal of Product Innovation Management*, March 2009, pp. 156–72; and James I. Cash, Jr., Michael J. Earl, and Robert Morison, "Teaming Up to Crack Innovation and Enterprise Integration," *Harvard Business Review*, November 2008, pp. 90–100.

27. Dinah Eng, "Life Is Good in the T-Shirt Business," *Fortune*, May 19, 2014, pp. 39–42.

28. Ibid.

29. Kimberly Judson, Denise D. Schoenbachler, Geoffrey L. Gordon, Rick E. Ridnour, and Dan C. Weilbaker, "The New Product Development Process: Let the Voice of the Salesperson Be Heard," *Journal of Product & Brand Management* 15, no. 3 (2006), pp. 194–202.

30. Morgan L. Swink and Vincent A. Mabert, "Product Development Partnerships: Balancing Needs of OEMs and Suppliers," *Business Horizons*, May–June 2000, pp. 59–68.

31. C. K. Prahalad and Venkat Ramswamy, *The Future of Competition* (Boston: Harvard Business School Press, 2004); Steve Hamm, "Adding Customers to the Design Team," *BusinessWeek*, March 1, 2004, pp. 22–23; and Anthony W. Ulwick, "Turn Customer Input into Innovation," *Harvard Business Review*, January 2002, pp. 91–97.

32. Sarah Ellison, "P&G Chief's Turnaround Recipe: Find Out What Women Want," *The Wall Street Journal*, June 1, 2005, pp. A1, A16.

33. Jack Neff, "Tide Pods Winning $7 Billion Detergent Wars by Defining Value," *Advertising Age*, December 18, 2012. See http://adage.com/article/news/tide-pods-winning-7-billion-detergent-wars-redefining/23877; and Dale Buss, "P&G Awash in Success of Tide Pods Despite Wrinkles Along the Way, "*Brandchannel*, December 18, 2012. See http://www.brandchannel.com/home/post/2012/12/18/PG-Tide-Pods-121812.aspx; Emily Glazer, "Tide Rides Convenience Wave," *The Wall Street Journal*, February 23, 2012, p. 138; Jack Neff, "P&G Reinvents Laundry with $150 Million Tide Pods Launch," *Advertising Age*, April 26, 2011, downloaded April 28, 2011; and Emily Glazer, "P&G to Alter Tide Pods Packaging," *The Wall Street Journal*, May 26–27, 2012, p. B3.

34. Elisabeth A. Sullivan, "A Group Effort," *Marketing News*, February 28, 2010, pp. 22–29.

35. Adam Lashinsky, "Inside Apple," *Fortune*, May 23, 2011, p. 128; Daniel Turner, "The Secret of Apple Design," *MIT Technology Review*, May/June 2007; Leander Kahney, "Silicon Valley Loves Transparency and Cooperation. Not Steve Jobs. How Apple Got Everything Right by Doing Everything Wrong," *Wired Business Trends*, April 2008, pp. 137–43; and Karl T. Ulrich and Stephen D. Eppinger, *Product Design and Development*, 4th ed. (New York: McGraw-Hill/Irwin, 2008), Chapter 10.

36. Joseph Weber, Stanley Holmes, and Christopher Palmeri, "'Mosh Pits' of Creativity," *BusinessWeek*, November 7, 2005, pp. 98–100.

37. Charlie Rose, "How to Design Breakthrough Inventions," *CBS 60 Minutes*, air date January 6, 2013. See http://www.cbsnews.com/8301-18560_162-57562201/how-to-design-breakthrough-inventions; Bruce Nussbaum, "The Best Global Design of 2008," *BusinessWeek*, July 28, 2008, pp. 44–46; Tim Brown, "He Prizes Questions More Than Answers," *The New York Times*, October 25, 2009, p. BU2; Bruce Nussbaum, "The Power of Design," *Business-Week*, May 17, 2004, pp. 86–94; the article gives many techniques for idea and concept generation, as do Appendixes A and B in Merle Crawford and Anthony Di Benedetto, *New Products Management*, 10th ed. (New York: McGraw-Hill/Irwin, 2011).

38. Erickson, "One Food Company's Foray into Open Innovation," p. 12.

39. Ibid., p. 13.

40. L. David Ostlie, Energy Performance Systems, Inc.

41. Kristin Tillotson, "Crowdfunding Gears Up for a Fresh Kick Start," *Star Tribune*, November 6, 2012, pp. A1, A10.

42. Steve Hoeffler, "Measuring Preferences for Really New Products," *Journal of Marketing Research*, November 2003, pp. 406–20.

43. Christopher Lovelock and Jochen Wirtz, *Services Marketing* (Englewood Cliffs, NJ: Prentice Hall, 2007), pp. 260–84.

44. Alistair Barr, "Google's Bumpy Road Trip," *The Wall Street Journal*, August 25, 2014, p. B4; John Markoff, "Google's Next Phase in Driverless Cars: No Steering Wheel or Brake Pedal," *The New York Times*, May 28, 2014, p. B1; and Michal Lev-Ram, "The End of Driving (As We Know It)," *Fortune*, June 30, 2014, pp. 77–82.

45. Kyle Stock, "Briefs: HB-Whoa," *Bloomberg Businessweek*, February 10–16, 2014, p. 25; Ben Fritz and Keach Hagey, "Netflix Hires DreamWorks," *The Wall Street Journal*, June 18, 2013, p. 83; Cecilia Kang, "Netflix Takes on Hollywood with Original Programming," *The Washington Post*, February 4, 2013, p. 5B; Greg Bensinger, "Amazon, Netflix Battle Over Content," *The Wall Street Journal*, February 2, 2013, p. B3; Tom Gliatto, "*House of Cards*," *People*, February 1, 2013, p. 43; Roger Yu, "New Customers Boost Netflix," *USA Today*, January 24, 2013, p. B1; Greg Bensinger, "Netflix Shares Surge 35% on Profit," *The Wall Street Journal*, January 24, 2013, p. B1; and John Jannarone, "Netflix Signs Streaming Deal with Time Warner," *The Wall Street Journal*, January 8, 2013, p. B9.

46. Gilbert A. Churchill, Jr., Tom J. Brown, and Tracy A. Suter, *Basic Marketing Research*, 7th ed. (Mason, OH: South-Western, Cengage Learning, 2010), pp. 122–30.

47. Daniel Michaels, "Innovation Is Messy Business," *The Wall Street Journal*, January 24, 2013, pp. B1, B2; Christopher Drew, "Dreamliner Troubles Put Boeing on Edge," *The New York Times*, January 20, 2013. See http://www.nytimes.com/2013/01/21/business/battery-fire-resolution-may-weigh-on-boeing.html; Andy Pasztor and Jon Ostrower, "Probe of Boeing 787 Battery Fire Expands," *The Wall Street Journal*, January 24, 2013. See http://online.wsj.com/article/SB10001424127887324624404578253010041254492.html; and Brad Stone and Susanna Roy, "Don't Dream It's Over," *Bloomberg Businessweek*, January 28–February 3, 2013, pp. 4–16.

48. Maureen Morrison, "Burger King Adds Satisfries Meals," March 23, 2014. See http://adage.com/article/news/burger-king-adds-satisfries-kids-meals.html; and "New Fries at Burger King Restaurants," Burger King press release, November 30, 2011. See http://www.bk.com/en/us/company-info/news-press/detail/new-fries-at-burger-king-restaurants-559.html; and "Burger King Introduces Hotter, Crispier, Better-Tasting French Fries," *PRNewswire*, December 10, 2011. See http://www2.prnewswire.com/cgi-bin/stories.pl?ACCT=104&STORY=www/story/12-10-97/375783&EDATE; and Jennifer Ordonez, "How Burger King Got Burned in Quest to Make the Perfect Fry," *The Wall Street Journal*, January 16, 2001, pp. A1, A8.

49. Kerry A. Dolan, "Speed: The New X Factor," *Forbes*, December 26, 2005, pp. 74–77.

X-1: This case was written by Steven Hartley. Sources: "X-1 Breaks the Barriers of Sound with Innovative Rebranding and Website," *PR.com*, February 23, 2013; "US Patent Issued to H2O Audio on July 17 for 'Waterproof Enclosure for Audio Device,'" *US Fed News*, July 23, 2012; "NetSuite Announces Outdoor Retail Customer Wins," *ENP Newswire*, August 6, 2012; X-1 website, www.x-1.com, accessed July 18, 2013; and personal interviews with X-1 personnel.

Credits

P. 213, AFP/Getty Images. P. 214, ©M. Hruby. P. 217, ©PSL Images/ Alamy. Agency:TM Advertising; Creative Team: Bernard Park and Shep Kellam; Art Buyer: Ranelle Fowler. P. 218, ©Fabrizio Costantini. P. 219, Photo courtesy Brain Storm Bakery. P. 220, AP Photo/Dino Vournas. P. 221, ©M. Hruby. P. 222, ©M. Hruby. P. 222, © GfK Custom Research, LLC. P. 223, Courtesy of the Original Pet Drink. P. 223, ©GfK Custom Research, LLC. P. 224, ©GfK Custom Research, LLC. P. 226, Scott Olson/Getty Images. P. 226, AP Photo/Michael Dwyer. P. 227, ©M. Hruby. P. 228, Courtesy of Energy Performance Systems, Inc. P. 228, AP Photo/Mary Altaffer. P. 229, Rex Features via AP Images. P. 230, ©Francis Vachon/Alamy. P. 231, Courtesy Bolin Marketing. P. 231, Kiyoshi Ota/Bloomberg via Getty Images. P. 232, ©M. Hruby. P. 237, Courtesy X-1 Audio, Inc.

10

Managing Successful Products, Services, and Brands

LEARNING OBJECTIVES

After reading this chapter you should be able to:

 LO 10-1 Explain the product life-cycle concept.

LO 10-2 Identify ways that marketing executives manage a product's life cycle.

 LO 10-3 Recognize the importance of branding and alternative branding strategies.

 LO 10-4 Describe the role of packaging and labeling in the marketing of a product.

 LO 10-5 Recognize how the four Ps framework is expanded in the marketing of services.

GATORADE: BRINGING SCIENCE TO SWEAT TO WIN FROM WITHIN

Why is the thirst for Gatorade unquenchable? Look no further than constant product improvement and masterful brand development.

Like Kleenex in the tissue market, Jell-O among gelatin desserts, and Scotch for cellophane tape, Gatorade is synonymous with sports drinks. Concocted in 1965 at the University of Florida as a rehydration beverage for the school's football team, the drink was coined "Gatorade" by an opposing team's coach after watching his team lose to the Florida Gators in the Orange Bowl. The name stuck, and a new beverage product class was born. Stokely-Van Camp, Inc., bought the Gatorade formula in 1967 and commercialized the product.

Creating the Gatorade Brand

The Quaker Oats Company acquired Stokely-Van Camp in 1983 and quickly increased Gatorade sales through a variety of means. More flavors were added. Multiple package sizes were offered using different containers. Distribution expanded from convenience stores and supermarkets to mass merchandisers such as Walmart. Consistent advertising and promotion effectively conveyed the product's unique performance benefits and links to athletic competition. International opportunities were vigorously pursued.

Today, Gatorade is sold in more than 80 countries and is now a global brand. It is also the official sports drink of NASCAR, the National Football League, Major League Baseball, the National Basketball Association, the National Hockey League, Major League Soccer, and the Women's National Basketball Association.

Masterful brand management spurred Gatorade's success. Gatorade Frost was introduced in 1997 and aimed at expanding the brand's reach beyond organized sports to other usage occasions. Gatorade Fierce appeared in 1999. In the same year, Gatorade entered the bottled-water category with Propel Fitness Water, a lightly flavored water fortified with vitamins. The Gatorade Performance Series was introduced in 2001, featuring a Gatorade Energy Bar, Gatorade Energy Drink, and Gatorade Nutritional Shake.

Building the Gatorade Brand

Brand development accelerated after PepsiCo, Inc., purchased Quaker Oats and the Gatorade brand in 2001. Gatorade Xtremo, developed

243

with a bilingual label for Latino consumers, was launched in 2002. Gatorade X-Factor followed in 2003. In 2005, Gatorade Endurance Formula was created for serious runners, construction workers, and other people doing long, sweaty workouts. Gatorade Rain, a lighter-tasting version of regular Gatorade, arrived in 2006. In 2007, Gatorade AM, with no caffeine, debuted for the morning workout consumer. A low-calorie Gatorade called G2 appeared in 2008.

In 2009, Gatorade executives unleashed a bevy of enhanced beverages in bold new packaging. "Just like any good athlete, Gatorade is taking it to the next level," said Gatorade's chief marketing officer. "Whether you're in it for the win, for the thrill or for better health, if your body is moving, Gatorade sees you as an athlete, and we're inviting you into the brand." According to a company announcement, "The new Gatorade attitude would be most visible through a total packaging redesign." For example, Gatorade Thirst Quencher now displays the letter G front and center along with the brand's iconic bolt.

Gatorade's marketing performance is a direct result of continuous product improvement and masterful brand management as defined by the "Gatorade bath."

"For Gatorade, G represents the heart, hustle, and soul of athleticism and will become a badge of pride for anyone who sweats, no matter where they're active."

To differentiate the range of Gatorade offerings from the traditional Gatorade Thirst Quencher, newly enhanced beverages convey the attitude of a tough-love coach or personal trainer through in-your-face names on the label and nutrition benefits inside. For example, Gatorade Fierce is now Bring It and Gatorade X-Factor is now Be Tough. Continuing product development efforts guided the creation of the G Series of products in 2010 and 2011 "that [go] beyond hydration to provide fuel, fluid, and nutrients before, during, and after the game."

Gatorade Prime 01 was formulated to be consumed before a game. Gatorade Perform 02 was designed for consumption during a game. Gatorade Recover 03 was created for use after a game for rehydration and to promote muscle recovery. Starting in 2012, these products were supported with the "Win from Within" advertising campaign.[1]

The marketing of Gatorade illustrates continuous product development and masterful brand management in a dynamic marketplace. Not surprisingly, Gatorade remains a vibrant multibillion-dollar brand some 50 years after its creation. This chapter shows how the actions taken by Gatorade executives exemplify those made by successful marketers.

Video 10-1
Gatorade Ad
kerin.tv/cr6e/v10-1

CHARTING THE PRODUCT LIFE CYCLE

LO 10-1 Explain the product life-cycle concept.

product life cycle
The stages a new product goes through in the marketplace: introduction, growth, maturity, and decline.

Products, like people, are viewed as having a life cycle. The concept of the **product life cycle** describes the stages a new product goes through in the marketplace: introduction, growth, maturity, and decline (Figure 10–1).[2] The two curves shown in this figure, total industry sales revenue and total industry profit, represent the sum of sales revenue and profit of all firms producing the product. The reasons for the changes in each curve and the marketing decisions involved are detailed next.

Introduction Stage

The introduction stage of the product life cycle occurs when a product is introduced to its intended target market. During this period, sales grow slowly, and profit is minimal. The lack of profit is often the result of large investment costs in product development, such as the millions of dollars spent by Gillette to develop the Gillette Fusion razor shaving system. The marketing objective for the company at this stage is to create consumer awareness and stimulate *trial*—the initial purchase of a product by a consumer.

Companies often spend heavily on advertising and other promotion tools to build awareness and stimulate product trial among consumers in the introduction stage. For example, Gillette budgeted $200 million in advertising to introduce the Fusion shaving system to male shavers. The result? Over 60 percent of male shavers became aware of the new razor within six months and 26 percent tried the product.[3]

Advertising and promotion expenditures in the introduction stage are often made to stimulate *primary demand*, the desire for the product class rather than for a specific brand, since there are few competitors with the same product. As more competitors launch their own products and the product progresses along its life cycle, company attention is focused on creating *selective demand*, the preference for a specific brand.

The success of the Gillette Fusion shaving system can be understood using product life cycle concepts as discussed in the text.

Other marketing mix variables also are important at this stage. Gaining distribution can be a challenge because channel intermediaries may be hesitant to carry a new product. Also, a company often restricts the number of variations of the product to ensure control of product quality. As an example, the original Gatorade came in only one flavor—lemon-lime.

During introduction, pricing can be either high or low. A high initial price may be used as part of a *skimming* strategy to help the company recover the costs of development as well as capitalize on the price insensitivity of early buyers. A master of this strategy is 3M. According to a 3M manager, "We hit fast, price high, and get the heck out when the me-too products pour in."[4] High prices tend to attract competitors eager to enter the market because they see the opportunity for profit. To discourage competitive entry, a company can price low, referred to as *penetration pricing*. This pricing strategy helps build unit volume, but a company must closely monitor costs. These and other pricing techniques are covered in Chapter 11.

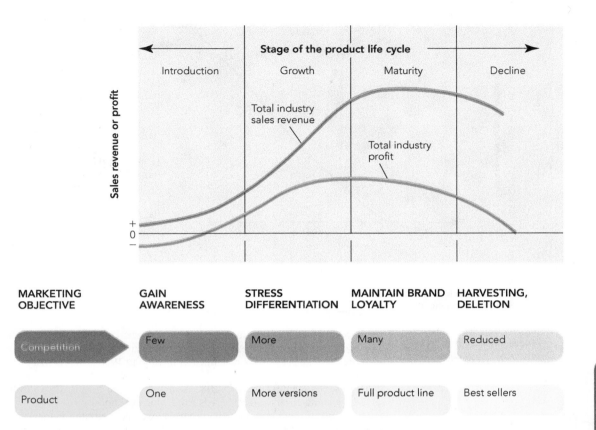

MARKETING OBJECTIVE	GAIN AWARENESS	STRESS DIFFERENTIATION	MAINTAIN BRAND LOYALTY	HARVESTING, DELETION
Competition	Few	More	Many	Reduced
Product	One	More versions	Full product line	Best sellers
Price	Skimming or penetration	Gain market share, deal	Defend market share, profit	Stay profitable
Place (distribution)	Limited	More outlets	Maximum outlets	Fewer outlets
Promotion	Inform, educate	Stress points of difference	Reminder-oriented	Minimal promotion

FIGURE 10–1
How stages of the product life cycle relate to a firm's marketing objectives and marketing mix actions.

Figure 10–2 on the next page charts the stand-alone fax machine product life cycle for business use in the United States from the early 1970s to 2016.[5] Sales grew slowly in the 1970s and early 1980s after Xerox pioneered the first portable fax machine. Fax machines were first sold direct to businesses by company salespeople and were premium priced. The average price for a fax machine in 1980 was a hefty $12,700, or almost $35,000 in today's dollars! Those fax machines were primitive by today's standards. They contained mechanical parts, not electronic circuitry, and offered few features seen in today's models.

Several product classes are in the introductory stage of the product life cycle today. These include smart TVs and all-electric-powered automobiles.

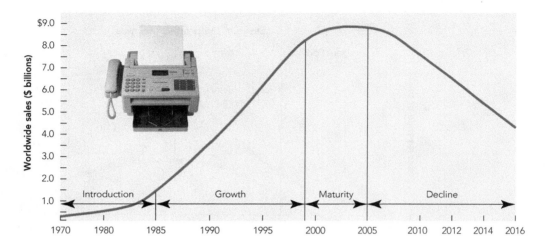

FIGURE 10–2
Product life cycle for the stand-alone fax machine for business use: 1970–2016. All four product life-cycle stages appear: introduction, growth, maturity, and decline.

Growth Stage

The growth stage of the product life cycle is characterized by rapid increases in sales. It is in this stage that competitors appear. For example, Figure 10–2 shows the dramatic increase in sales of fax machines from 1986 to 1998. The number of companies selling fax machines also increased, from one in the early 1970s to four in the late 1970s to seven manufacturers in 1983, which sold nine brands. By 1998 there were some 25 manufacturers and 60 brands from which to choose.

The result of more competitors and more aggressive pricing is that profit usually peaks during the growth stage. For instance, the average price for a fax machine plummeted from $3,300 in 1985 to $500 in 1995. At this stage, advertising shifts emphasis to stimulating selective demand; product benefits are compared with those of competitors' offerings for the purpose of gaining market share.

Product sales in the growth stage grow at an increasing rate because of new people trying or using the product and a growing proportion of *repeat purchasers*—people who tried the product, were satisfied, and bought again. For the Gillette Fusion razor, over 60 percent of men who tried the razor adopted the product permanently. For successful products, the ratio of repeat to trial purchases grows as the product moves through the life cycle. Durable fax machines meant that replacement purchases were rare. However, it became common for more than one machine to populate a business as the machine's use became more widespread.

Changes appear in the product in the growth stage. To help differentiate a company's brand from competitors, an improved version or new features are added to the original design, and product proliferation occurs. Changes in fax machines included (1) models with built-in telephones; (2) models that used plain, rather than thermal, paper for copies; and (3) models that integrated electronic mail.

In the growth stage, it is important to broaden distribution for the product. In the retail store, for example, this often means that competing companies fight for display and shelf space. Expanded distribution in the fax industry is an example. Early in the growth stage, just 11 percent of office machine dealers carried this equipment. By the mid-1990s, over 70 percent of these dealers sold fax equipment, and distribution was expanded to other stores selling electronic equipment, such as Best Buy and Office Depot.

Numerous product classes or industries are in the growth stage of the product life cycle today. Examples include smartphones, e-book readers, and other tablet devices such as the iPad.

Electric automobiles like the Chevrolet Spark made by General Motors are in the introductory stage of the product life cycle. By comparison, e-books such as Kindle offered by Amazon are in the growth stage of the product life cycle. Each product faces unique challenges based on its product life-cycle stage.

General Motors Company
www.gm.com

Amazon
www.amazon.com

Maturity Stage

The maturity stage is characterized by a slowing of total industry sales or product class revenue. Also, marginal competitors begin to leave the market. Most consumers who would buy the product are either repeat purchasers of the item or have tried and abandoned it. Sales increase at a decreasing rate in the maturity stage as fewer new buyers enter the market. Profit declines due to fierce price competition among many sellers, and the cost of gaining new buyers at this stage rises.

Marketing attention in the maturity stage is often directed toward holding market share through further product differentiation and finding new buyers. Fax machine manufacturers developed Internet-enabled multifunctional models with new features such as scanning, copying, and color reproduction. They also designed fax machines suitable for small and home businesses, which today represent a substantial portion of sales. Still, a major consideration in a company's strategy in this stage is to control overall marketing cost by improving promotional and distribution efficiency.

Fax machines entered the maturity stage in the late 1990s. At the time, about 90 percent of industry sales were captured by five producers (Hewlett-Packard, Brother, Sharp, Lexmark, and Samsung), reflecting the departure of marginal competitors. By 2004, 200 million stand-alone fax machines were installed throughout the world, sending more than 120 billion faxes annually.

Numerous product classes and industries are in the maturity stage of their product life cycle today. These include carbonated soft drinks and DVD players.

Decline Stage

The decline stage occurs when sales drop. Fax machines for business use moved to this stage in early 2005. By then, the average price for a fax machine had sunk below $100. Frequently, a product enters this stage not because of any wrong strategy on the part of companies, but because of environmental changes. For example, digital music players pushed compact discs into decline in the recorded music industry. Will Internet technology and e-mail make fax machines extinct any time soon? The Marketing Matters box on the next page offers one perspective on this question that may surprise you.[6]

Numerous product classes or industries are in the decline stage of their product life cycle. Two prominent examples include analog TVs and desktop personal computers.

Products in the decline stage tend to consume a disproportionate share of management and financial resources relative to their future worth. A company will follow one of two strategies to handle a declining product: deletion or harvesting.

Marketing Matters

Will E-mail Spell Extinction for Fax Machines?

Technological substitution that creates value for customers often causes the decline stage in the product life cycle. Will e-mail replace fax machines?

This question has been debated for years. Even though e-mail continues to grow with broadening Internet access, millions of fax machines are still sold each year. Industry analysts estimated that the number of e-mail mailboxes worldwide would be 4.3 billion in 2016. However, the phenomenal popularity of e-mail has not brought fax machines to extinction. Why? The two technologies do not directly compete for the same messaging applications.

E-mail is used for text messages, and faxing is predominately used for communicating formatted documents by business users. Fax usage is expected to increase through 2015, even though unit sales of fax machines have declined on a worldwide basis. Internet technology and e-mail may eventually replace facsimile technology and paper and make fax machines extinct, but not in the immediate future.

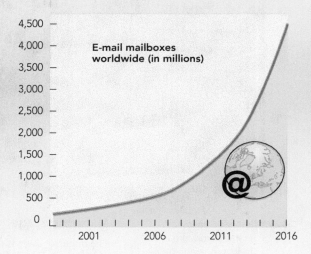

Deletion   Product *deletion*, or dropping the product from the company's product line, is the most drastic strategy. Because a residual core of consumers still consume or use a product even in the decline stage, product elimination decisions are not taken lightly. For example, Sanford Corporation continues to sell its Liquid Paper correction fluid for use with typewriters in the era of word-processing equipment.

Harvesting   A second strategy, *harvesting*, is when a company retains the product but reduces marketing costs. The product continues to be offered, but salespeople do not allocate time in selling nor are advertising dollars spent. The purpose of harvesting is to maintain the ability to meet customer requests. Coca-Cola, for instance, still sells Tab, its first diet cola, to a small group of die-hard fans. According to Coke's CEO, "It shows you care. We want to make sure those who want Tab, get Tab."[7]

Three Aspects of the Product Life Cycle

Some important aspects of product life cycles are (1) their length, (2) the shape of their sales curves, and (3) the rate at which consumers adopt products.

Length of the Product Life Cycle   There is no set time that it takes a product to move through its life cycle. As a rule, consumer products have shorter life cycles than business products. For example, many new consumer food products such as Frito-Lay's Baked Lay's potato chips move from the introduction stage to maturity in 18 months. The availability of mass communication vehicles informs consumers quickly and shortens life cycles. Technological change shortens product life cycles as new-product innovation replaces existing products. For example, smartphones have largely replaced digital cameras in the amateur photography market.

Shape of the Life-Cycle Curve   The product life-cycle sales curve shown in Figure 10–1 is the *generalized life cycle*, but not all products have the same shape to their curve. In fact, there are several life-cycle curves, each type suggesting different

FIGURE 10–3
Alternative product life-cycle curves based on product types. Note the long introduction stage for a high-learning product compared with a low-learning product. Read the text for an explanation of the different product life-cycle curves.

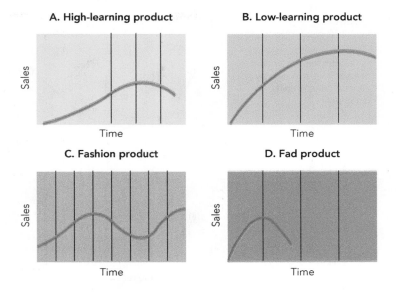

A. High-learning product

B. Low-learning product

C. Fashion product

D. Fad product

marketing strategies. Figure 10–3 shows the shape of life-cycle sales curves for four different types of products: high-learning, low-learning, fashion, and fad products.

A *high-learning product* is one for which significant customer education is required and there is an extended introductory period (Figure 10–3A). It may surprise you, but personal computers had this life-cycle curve. Consumers in the 1980s had to learn the benefits of owning the product or be educated in a new way of performing familiar tasks. Convection ovens for home use required consumers to learn a new way of cooking and alter familiar recipes used with conventional ovens. As a result, these ovens spent years in the introductory period.

In contrast, sales for a *low-learning product* begin immediately because little learning is required by the consumer and the benefits of purchase are readily understood (Figure 10–3B). This product often can be easily imitated by competitors, so the marketing strategy is to broaden distribution quickly. In this way, as competitors rapidly enter, most retail outlets already have the innovator's product. It is also important to have the manufacturing capacity to meet demand. A successful low-learning product is Gillette's Fusion razor. This product achieved $1 billion in worldwide sales in less than three years.

A *fashion product* (Figure 10–3C) is a style of the times. Life cycles for fashion products frequently appear in women's and men's apparel. Fashion products are introduced, decline, and then seem to return. The length of the cycles may be months, years, or decades. Consider women's hosiery. Product sales have been declining for years. Women consider it more fashionable to not wear hosiery—bad news for Hanes brands, the leading marketer of women's sheer hosiery. According to an authority on fashion, "Companies might as well let the fashion cycle take its course and wait for the inevitable return of pantyhose."[8]

A *fad product* experiences rapid sales on introduction and then an equally rapid decline (Figure 10–3D). These products are typically novelties and have a short life cycle. They include car tattoos, sold in southern California and described as the first removable and reusable graphics for automobiles, and vinyl dresses and fleece bikinis made by a Minnesota clothing company.

The Product Life Cycle and Consumer Behavior   The life cycle of a product depends on sales to consumers. Not all consumers rush to buy a product in the introductory stage, and the shapes of the life-cycle curves indicate that most sales occur

CHAPTER 10   Managing Successful Products, Services, and Brands

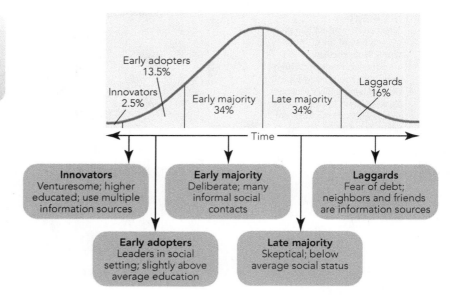

FIGURE 10–4

Five categories and profiles of product adopters. For a product to be successful, it must be purchased by innovators and early adopters.

after the product has been on the market for some time. In essence, a product diffuses, or spreads, through the population, a concept called the *diffusion of innovation*.[9]

Some people are attracted to a product early. Others buy it only after they see their friends or opinion leaders with the item. Figure 10–4 shows the consumer population divided into five categories of product adopters based on when they adopt a new product. Brief profiles accompany each category. For any product to be successful, it must be purchased by innovators and early adopters. This is why manufacturers of new pharmaceuticals try to gain adoption by respected hospitals, clinics, and physicians. Once accepted by innovators and early adopters, successful new products move on to the early majority, late majority, and laggard categories.

Several factors affect whether a consumer will adopt a new product or not. Common reasons for resisting a product in the introduction stage are *usage barriers* (the product is not compatible with existing habits), *value barriers* (the product provides no incentive to change), *risk barriers* (physical, economic, or social), and *psychological barriers* (cultural differences or image).[10]

These factors help to explain the slow adoption of all-electric-powered automobiles in the United States. About one-third of one percent of cars sold in 2014 were all-electric-powered vehicles. Industry analysts cite the usage barrier for disappointing sales. They note that prospective buyers believe these cars are not compatible with existing driving habits. Analysts also mention a value barrier. Consumers have not recognized the superiority of all-electric cars over vehicles with internal combustion engines. Thirdly, a risk barrier exists in large measure to buyer uncertainty about the actual cost of all-electric-powered car ownership. According to one auto industry analyst, "The innovators and early adopters have purchased all-electric vehicles, but mainstream consumers have not followed." Not surprisingly, all-electric-powered automobiles remain in the introductory stage of the product life cycle.[11]

Companies attempt to overcome these barriers in numerous ways. For example, manufacturers of all-electric-powered automobiles provide low-cost leasing options to overcome usage, value, and risk barriers. Other companies provide warranties, money-back guarantees, extensive usage instructions, demonstrations, and free samples to stimulate initial trial of new products. For example, software developers offer demonstrations downloaded from the Internet. Cosmetics consumers can browse through the Cover Girl ColorMatch Custom Makeup Selector on its website to find out how certain makeup products will look. Free samples are one of the most popular means to gain consumer trial. In fact, 71 percent of consumers consider a sample to be the best way to evaluate a new product.[12]

MANAGING THE PRODUCT LIFE CYCLE

 LO 10-2 Identify ways that marketing executives manage a product's life cycle.

An important task for a firm is to manage its products through the successive stages of their life cycles. This section describes the role of the product manager, who is usually responsible for this, and presents three ways to manage a product through its life cycle: modifying the product, modifying the market, and repositioning the product.

Role of a Product Manager

The product manager, sometimes called a *brand manager*, manages the marketing efforts for a close-knit family of products or brands. Introduced by Procter & Gamble in 1928, the product manager style of marketing organization is used by consumer goods firms, including General Mills and PepsiCo, and by industrial firms such as Intel and Hewlett-Packard.

All product managers are responsible for managing existing products through the stages of the life cycle. Some are also responsible for developing new products. Product managers' marketing responsibilities include developing and executing a marketing program for the product line described in an annual marketing plan and approving ad copy, media selection, and package design.

Product managers also engage in extensive data analysis related to their products and brands. Sales, market share, and profit trends are closely monitored. Managers often supplement these data with two measures: (1) a category development index (CDI) and (2) a brand development index (BDI). These indexes help to identify strong and weak market segments (usually demographic or geographic segments) for specific consumer products and brands and provide direction for marketing efforts. The calculation, visual display, and interpretation of these two indexes for Hawaiian Punch are described in the Using Marketing Dashboards box on the next page.

Harley-Davidson redesigned some of its motorcycle models to feature smaller hand grips, a lower seat, and an easier-to-pull clutch lever to create a more comfortable ride for women. According to Genevieve Schmitt, founding editor of WomenRidersNow .com, "They realize that women are an up-and-coming segment and that they need to accommodate them."

Harley-Davidson, Inc.
www.harley-davidson.com

Modifying the Product

Product modification involves altering one or more of a product's characteristics, such as its quality, performance, or appearance, to increase the product's value to customers and increase sales. Wrinkle-free and stain-resistant clothing made possible by nanotechnology revolutionized the men's and women's apparel business and stimulated industry sales of casual pants, shirts, and blouses. A common approach to product modification to increase a product's value to consumers is called *product bundling*—the sale of two or more separate products in one package. For example, Microsoft Office is sold as a bundle of computer software, including Word, Excel, and PowerPoint.

New features, packages, or scents can be used to change a product's characteristics and give the sense of a revised product. Procter & Gamble revamped Pantene shampoo and conditioner with a new vitamin formula and relaunched the brand with a multimillion-dollar advertising and promotion campaign. The result? Pantene, a brand first introduced in the 1940s, is now the top-selling shampoo and conditioner in the United States in an industry with more than 1,000 competitors.

Using Marketing Dashboards
Knowing Your CDI and BDI

Where are sales for my product category and brand strongest and weakest? Data related to this question are displayed in a marketing dashboard using two indexes: (1) a category development index and (2) a brand development index.

Your Challenge You have joined the marketing team for Hawaiian Punch, the top fruit punch drink sold in the United States. The brand has been marketed to mothers with children under 13 years old. The majority of Hawaiian Punch sales are in gallon and 2-liter bottles. Your assignment is to examine the brand's performance and identify growth opportunities for the Hawaiian Punch brand among households that consume prepared fruit drinks (the product category).

Your marketing dashboard displays a category development index and a brand development index provided by a syndicated marketing research firm. Each index is based on the calculations below:

Category Development Index (CDI) =

$$\frac{\text{Percent of a product category's total U.S. sales in a market segment}}{\text{Percent of the total U.S. population in a market segment}} \times 100$$

Brand Development Index (BDI) =

$$\frac{\text{Percent of a brand's total U.S. sales in a market segment}}{\text{Percent of the total U.S. population in a market segment}} \times 100$$

A CDI over 100 indicates above-average product category purchases by a market segment. A number under 100 indicates below-average purchases. A BDI over 100 indicates a strong brand position in a segment; a number under 100 indicates a weak brand position.

You are interested in CDI and BDI displays for four household segments that consume prepared fruit drinks: (1) households without children; (2) households with children 6 years old or under; (3) households with children aged 7 to 12; and (4) households with children aged 13 to 18.

Your Findings The BDI and CDI metrics displayed below show that Hawaiian Punch is consumed by households with children, and particularly households with children under age 12. The Hawaiian Punch BDI is over 100 for both segments—not surprising since the brand is marketed to these segments. Households with children 13 to 18 years old evidence high fruit drink consumption with a CDI over 100. But Hawaiian Punch is relatively weak in this segment with a BDI under 100.

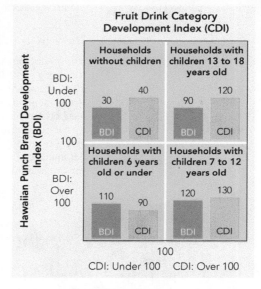

Your Action An opportunity for Hawaiian Punch exists among households with children 13 to 18 years old—teenagers. You might propose that Hawaiian Punch be repositioned for teens. In addition, you might recommend that Hawaiian Punch be packaged in single-serve cans or bottles to attract this segment, much like soft drinks. Teens might also be targeted for advertising and promotions.

Modifying the Market

With *market modification* strategies, a company tries to find new customers, increase a product's use among existing customers, or create new use situations.

Finding New Customers As part of its market modification strategy, LEGO Group is offering a new line of products to attract consumers outside of its traditional market. Known for its popular line of construction toys for young boys, LEGO Group has recently introduced a product line for young girls called LEGO Friends. Harley-Davidson has tailored a marketing program to encourage women to take up biking, thus doubling the number of potential customers for its motorcycles.

Increasing a Product's Use   Promoting more frequent usage has been a strategy of Campbell Soup Company. Because soup consumption rises in the winter and declines during the summer, the company now advertises more heavily in warm months to encourage consumers to think of soup as more than a cold-weather food. Similarly, the Florida Orange Growers Association advocates drinking orange juice throughout the day rather than for breakfast only.

Creating a New Use Situation   Finding new uses for an existing product has been the strategy behind Dockers, the U.S. market leader in casual pants. Originally intended as a single pant for every situation, Dockers now promotes different looks for different usage situations: work, weekend, dress, and golf.

Video 10-2
Dockers Ad
kerin.tv/cr6e/v10-2

Repositioning the Product

Often a company decides to reposition its product or product line in an attempt to bolster sales. *Product repositioning* changes the place a product occupies in a consumer's mind relative to competitive products. A firm can reposition a product by changing one or more of the four marketing mix elements. Four factors that trigger the need for a repositioning action are discussed next.

Reacting to a Competitor's Position   One reason to reposition a product is because a competitor's entrenched position is adversely affecting sales and market share. New Balance, Inc., successfully repositioned its athletic shoes to focus on fit, durability, and comfort rather than competing head-on against Nike and Adidas on fashion and professional sports. The company offers an expansive range of shoes and networks with podiatrists, not sports celebrities.

New Balance, Inc., effectively competes with Nike and Adidas following its repositioning to focus on fit, durability, and comfort.

New Balance, Inc.
www.newbalance.com

Reaching a New Market   When Unilever introduced iced tea in Britain, sales were disappointing. British consumers viewed it as leftover hot tea, not suitable for drinking. The company made its tea carbonated and repositioned it as a cold soft drink to compete as a carbonated beverage and sales improved. Johnson & Johnson effectively repositioned its St. Joseph aspirin from a product for infants to an adult low-strength aspirin to reduce the risk of heart problems or strokes.

Catching a Rising Trend   Changing consumer trends can also lead to product repositioning. Growing consumer interest in foods that offer health and dietary benefits is an example. Many products have been repositioned to capitalize on this trend. Quaker Oats makes the FDA-approved claim that oatmeal, as part of a low-saturated-fat, low-cholesterol diet, may reduce the risk of heart disease. Calcium-enriched products, such as Kraft American cheese and Uncle Ben's Calcium Plus rice, emphasize healthy bone structure for children and adults. Weight-conscious consumers have embraced low-fat and low-calorie diets in growing numbers. Today, most food and beverage companies offer reduced-fat and low-calorie versions of their products.

Changing the Value Offered   In repositioning a product, a company can decide to change the value it offers buyers and trade up or down. *Trading up* involves adding value to the product (or line) through additional features or higher-quality materials. Michelin, Bridgestone, and Goodyear have done this with a "run-flat" tire that can travel up to 50 miles at 55 miles per hour after suffering total air loss. Dog food manufacturers,

Making Responsible Decisions

Consumer Economics of Downsizing—Get Less, Pay More

For more than 30 years, Starkist put 6.5 ounces of tuna into its regular-sized can. Today, Starkist puts 6.125 ounces of tuna into its can but charges the same price. Frito-Lay (Doritos and Lay's snack chips), PepsiCo (Tropicana orange juice), and Nestlé (Poland Spring and Calistoga bottled waters) have whittled away at package contents 5 to 10 percent while maintaining their products' package size, dimensions, and prices.

Procter & Gamble recently kept its retail price on its jumbo pack of Pampers and Luvs diapers, but reduced the number of diapers per pack from 140 to 132. Similarly, Unilever reduced the number of Popsicles in each package from 24 to 20 without changing the package price. Georgia-Pacific reduced

the content of its Brawny paper towel six-roll pack by 20 percent without lowering the price.

Consumer advocates charge that downsizing the content of packages while maintaining prices is a subtle and unannounced way of taking advantage of consumer buying habits. They also say downsizing is a price increase in disguise and a deceptive, but legal, practice. Some manufacturers argue that this practice is a way of keeping prices from rising beyond psychological barriers for their products. Other manufacturers say prices are set by individual stores, not by them.

Is downsizing an unethical practice if manufacturers do not inform consumers that the package contents are less than they were previously?

---

such as Ralston Purina, also have traded up by offering super-premium foods based on "life-stage nutrition." Mass merchandisers, such as Target and Walmart, can trade up by adding a designer clothes section to their stores.

Trading down involves reducing a product's number of features, quality, or price. For example, airlines have added more seats, thus reducing legroom, and limited meal service by only offering snacks on most domestic flights. Trading down also exists when companies engage in *downsizing*—reducing the package content without changing package size and maintaining or increasing the package price. Companies are criticized for this practice, as described in the Making Responsible Decisions box.[13]

learning review

10-3. What does "creating a new use situation" mean in managing a product's life cycle?

10-4. Explain the difference between trading up and trading down in product repositioning.

BRANDING AND BRAND MANAGEMENT

LO 10-3 Recognize the importance of branding and alternative branding strategies.

A basic decision in marketing products is **branding**, in which an organization uses a name, phrase, design, symbols, or combination of these to identify its products and distinguish them from those of competitors. A **brand name** is any word, device (design, sound, shape, or color), or combination of these used to distinguish a seller's products or services. Some brand names can be spoken, such as Gatorade. Other brand names cannot be spoken, such as the white apple (the *logotype* or *logo*) that Apple puts on its machines and in its ads.

The strong brand equity for the Louis Vuitton brand name permits the company to charge premium prices for its products.

Louis Vuitton

www.louisvuitton.com

A single journey can change the course of a life. Cambodia, May 2011.

Follow Angelina Jolie on louisvuittonjourneys.com

LOUIS VUITTON

255

branding
An organization's use of a name, phrase, design, symbol, or combination of these to identify and distinguish its products.

brand name
Any word, device (design, shape, sound, or color), or combination of these used to distinguish a seller's products or services.

Video 10-3
Dr Pepper Ad
kerin.tv/cr6e/v10-3

brand personality
A set of human characteristics associated with a brand name.

brand equity
The added value a brand name gives to a product beyond the functional benefits provided.

Consumers may benefit most from branding. Recognizing competing products by distinct trademarks allows them to be more efficient shoppers. Consumers can recognize and avoid products with which they are dissatisfied, while becoming loyal to other, more satisfying brands. As discussed in Chapter 4, brand loyalty often eases consumers' decision making by eliminating the need for an external search.

Brand Personality and Brand Equity

Product managers recognize that brands offer more than product identification and a means to distinguish their products from those of competitors.[14] Successful and established brands take on a **brand personality**, a set of human characteristics associated with a brand name. Research shows that consumers assign personality traits to products—traditional, romantic, rugged, sophisticated, rebellious—and choose brands that are consistent with their own or desired self-image. Marketers can and do imbue a brand with a personality through advertising that depicts a certain user or usage situation and conveys emotions or feelings to be associated with the brand. For example, personality traits linked with Coca-Cola are all-American and real; with Pepsi, young and exciting; and with Dr Pepper, nonconforming and unique. The traits often linked to Harley-Davidson are masculinity, defiance, and rugged individualism.

Brand name importance to a company has led to a concept called **brand equity**, the added value a brand name gives to a product beyond the functional benefits provided. This added value has two distinct advantages. First, brand equity provides a competitive advantage. The Sunkist brand implies quality fruit. The Disney name defines children's entertainment. A second advantage is that consumers are often willing to pay a higher price for a product with brand equity. Brand equity, in this instance, is represented by the premium a consumer will pay for one brand over another when the functional benefits provided are identical. Gillette razors and blades, Bose audio systems, Duracell batteries, and Louis Vuitton luggage all enjoy a price premium arising from brand equity.

Creating Brand Equity Brand equity doesn't just happen. It is carefully crafted and nurtured by marketing programs that forge strong, favorable, and unique customer associations and experiences with a brand. Brand equity resides in the minds of consumers and results from what they have learned, felt, seen, and heard about a brand over time. Marketers recognize that brand equity is not easily or quickly achieved. Rather, it arises from a sequential building process consisting of four steps (see Figure 10–5).[15]

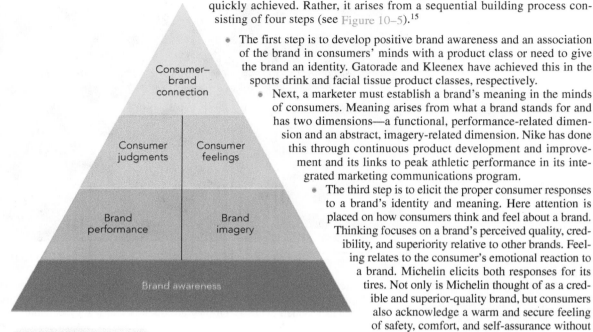

- The first step is to develop positive brand awareness and an association of the brand in consumers' minds with a product class or need to give the brand an identity. Gatorade and Kleenex have achieved this in the sports drink and facial tissue product classes, respectively.

- Next, a marketer must establish a brand's meaning in the minds of consumers. Meaning arises from what a brand stands for and has two dimensions—a functional, performance-related dimension and an abstract, imagery-related dimension. Nike has done this through continuous product development and improvement and its links to peak athletic performance in its integrated marketing communications program.

- The third step is to elicit the proper consumer responses to a brand's identity and meaning. Here attention is placed on how consumers think and feel about a brand. Thinking focuses on a brand's perceived quality, credibility, and superiority relative to other brands. Feeling relates to the consumer's emotional reaction to a brand. Michelin elicits both responses for its tires. Not only is Michelin thought of as a credible and superior-quality brand, but consumers also acknowledge a warm and secure feeling of safety, comfort, and self-assurance without worry or concern about the brand.

FIGURE 10–5
The customer-based brand equity pyramid shows the four-step building process that forges strong, favorable, and unique customer associations with a brand.

- The final, and most difficult, step is to create a consumer–brand connection evident in an intense, active loyalty relationship between consumers and the brand. A deep psychological bond characterizes a consumer–brand connection and the personal identification customers have with the brand. Brands that have achieved this status include Harley-Davidson, Apple, and eBay.

Valuing Brand Equity Brand equity also provides a financial advantage for the brand owner.[16] Successful, established brand names, such as Gillette, Louis Vuitton, Nike, Gatorade, and Apple, have an economic value in the sense that they are intangible assets. The recognition that brands are assets is apparent in the decision to buy and sell brands. For example, Triarc Companies bought the Snapple brand from Quaker Oats for $300 million and sold it three years later to Cadbury Schweppes for $900 million. This example illustrates that brands, unlike physical assets that depreciate with time and use, can appreciate in value when effectively marketed. However, brands can lose value when they are not managed properly. Consider the purchase and sale of Lender's Bagels. Kellogg bought the brand for $466 million only to sell it to Aurora Foods for $275 million three years later following deteriorating sales and profits.

Financially lucrative brand licensing opportunities arise from brand equity.[17] *Brand licensing* is a contractual agreement whereby one company (licensor) allows its brand name(s) or trademark(s) to be used with products or services offered by another company (licensee) for a royalty or fee. For example, Playboy earns more than $62 million licensing its name and logo for merchandise. Disney makes billions of dollars each year licensing its characters for children's toys, apparel, and games. Licensing fees for Winnie the Pooh alone exceed $3 billion annually.

Successful brand licensing requires careful marketing analysis to ensure a proper fit between the licensor's brand and the licensee's products. World-renowned designer Ralph Lauren earns over $140 million each year by licensing his Ralph Lauren, Polo, and Chaps brands for dozens of products, including paint by Glidden, furniture by Henredon, footwear by Rockport, eyewear by Luxottica, and fragrances by L'Oreal.[18] Kleenex diapers, Bic perfume, and Domino's fruit-flavored bubble gum are a few examples of poor matches and licensing failures.

Ralph Lauren has a long-term licensing agreement with Luxottica Group, S.p.A. of Milan for the design, production, and worldwide distribution of prescription frames and sunglasses under the Ralph Lauren brand. The agreement is an ideal fit for both companies. Ralph Lauren is a leader in the design, marketing, and distribution of premium lifestyle products. Luxottica is the global leader in the premium and luxury eyewear sector.

Luxottica Group, S.p.A.

www.luxottica.com

Ralph Lauren Corporation

www.ralphlauren.com

Picking a Good Brand Name

We take brand names such as Red Bull, iPad, Android, and Axe for granted, but it is often a difficult and expensive process to pick a good name. Companies will spend between $25,000 and $100,000 to identify and test a new brand name. Six criteria are mentioned most often when selecting a good brand name.[19]

- *The name should suggest the product benefits.* For example, Accutron (watches), Easy Off (oven cleaner), Glass Plus (glass cleaner), Cling-Free (antistatic cloth for drying clothes), Chevrolet Spark (electric car), and Tidy Bowl (toilet bowl cleaner) all clearly describe the benefits of purchasing the product.
- *The name should be memorable, distinctive, and positive.* In the auto industry, when a competitor has a memorable name, others quickly imitate. When Ford named a car the Mustang, Pinto and Bronco soon followed. The Thunderbird name led to the Phoenix, Eagle, Sunbird, and Firebird from other car companies.
- *The name should fit the company or product image.* Sharp is a name that can apply to audio and video equipment. Bufferin, Excedrin, Anacin, and Nuprin are scientific-sounding names, good for analgesics. Eveready, Duracell, and DieHard suggest reliability and longevity—two qualities consumers want in a battery.
- *The name should have no legal or regulatory restrictions.* Legal restrictions produce trademark infringement suits, and regulatory restrictions arise through the improper use of words. For example, the U.S. Food and Drug Administration discourages the use of the word *heart* in food brand names. This restriction led to changing the name of Kellogg's Heartwise cereal to Fiberwise, and Clorox's Hidden Valley Ranch Take Heart Salad Dressing had to be modified to Hidden Valley Ranch Low-Fat Salad Dressing. Increasingly, brand names need a corresponding website address on the Internet. This further complicates name selection because over 250 million domain names are already registered globally.
- *The name should be simple* (such as Bold laundry detergent, Axe deodorant and body spray, and Bic pens) *and should be emotional* (such as Joy and Obsession perfumes and Caress soap, shower gel, and lotion).

- *The name should have favorable phonetic and semantic associations in other languages.* In the development of names for international use, having a nonmeaningful brand name has been considered a benefit. A name such as Exxon does not have any prior impressions or undesirable images among a diverse world population of different languages and cultures. The 7UP name is another matter. In Shanghai, China, the phrase means "death through drinking" in the local dialect. Sales have suffered as a result.

Branding Strategies

Companies can choose from among several different branding strategies, including multiproduct branding, multibranding, private branding, and mixed branding (see Figure 10–6).

multiproduct branding
A branding strategy in which a company uses one name for all its products in a product class.

Multiproduct Branding Strategy   With **multiproduct branding**, a company uses one name for all its products in a product class. This approach is sometimes called *family branding* or *corporate branding* when the company's trade name is used. For example, Microsoft, General Electric, Samsung, Gerber, and Sony engage in corporate branding—the company's trade name and brand name are identical. Church & Dwight uses the Arm & Hammer family brand name for all its products featuring baking soda as the primary ingredient.

There are several advantages to multiproduct branding. Capitalizing again on brand equity, consumers who have a good experience with the product will transfer this favorable attitude to other items in the product class with the same name. Therefore, this brand strategy makes possible *product line extensions*, the practice of using a current brand name to enter a new market segment in its product class.

Campbell Soup Company employs a multiproduct branding strategy with soup line extensions. It offers regular Campbell's soup, home-cooking style, and chunky varieties and more than 100 soup flavors. This strategy can result in lower advertising and promotion costs because the same name is used on all products, thus raising the level of brand awareness. A risk with line extension is that sales of an extension may come at the expense of other items in the company's product line. Line extensions work best when they provide incremental company revenue by taking sales away from competing brands or attracting new buyers.

Some multiproduct branding companies employ *subbranding*, which combines a corporate or family brand with a new brand, to distinguish a part of its product line from others. Gatorade successfully used subbranding with the introduction of Gatorade G2. Similarly, Porsche successfully markets its higher-end Porsche Carrera and its lower-end Porsche Boxster.

A strong brand equity also allows for *brand extension*: the practice of using a current brand name to enter a different product class. For instance, equity in the Huggies

For how Kimberly-Clark has used a brand extension strategy to leverage its Huggies brand equity among mothers, see the text.

Kimberly-Clark Corporation
www.kimberly-clark.com

multibranding
A branding strategy that involves giving each product a distinct name.

family brand name has allowed Kimberly-Clark to successfully extend its name to a full line of baby and toddler toiletries. This brand extension strategy generates $500 million in annual sales globally for the company. Honda's established name for motor vehicles has extended easily to snowblowers, lawn mowers, marine engines, and snowmobiles.

However, there is a risk with brand extensions. Too many uses for one brand name can dilute the meaning of a brand for consumers. Some marketing experts claim this has happened to the Arm & Hammer brand given its use for toothpaste, laundry detergent, gum, cat litter, air freshener, carpet deodorizer, and antiperspirant.[20]

Multibranding Strategy   Alternatively, a company can engage in **multibranding**, which involves giving each product a distinct name. Multibranding is a useful strategy when each brand is intended for a different market segment. Procter & Gamble makes Camay soap for those concerned with soft skin and Safeguard for those who want deodorant protection. Black & Decker markets its line of tools for the household do-it-yourselfer segment with the Black & Decker name but uses the DeWalt name for its professional tool line. Disney used the Miramax and Touchstone Pictures names for films directed at adults and its Disney name for children's films.

Multibranding is applied in a variety of ways. Some companies array their brands on the basis of price-quality segments. Marriott International offers 18 hotel and resort brands, each suited for a particular traveler experience and budget. To illustrate, Marriott EDITION hotels and Vacation Clubs offer luxury amenities at a premium price. Marriott and Renaissance hotels offer medium- to high-priced accommodations. Courtyard hotels and TownePlace Suites appeal to economy-minded travelers, whereas the Fairfield Inn is for those on a very low travel budget.

Other multibrand companies introduce new product brands as defensive moves to counteract competition. Called *fighting brands*, their chief purpose is to confront competitor brands.[21] For instance, Frito-Lay introduced Santitas brand tortilla chips to go head-to-head against regional tortilla chip brands that were biting into sales of its flagship Doritos and Tostitos brand tortilla chips. Ford launched its Fusion brand to halt the defection of Ford owners who were buying competitors' midsize cars. According to Ford's car group marketing manager, "Every year we're losing around 50,000 people from our products to competitors' midsize cars. We're losing Mustang, Focus, and Taurus owners. Fusion is our interceptor."[22]

Compared with the multiproduct strategy, advertising and promotion costs tend to be higher with multibranding. The company must generate awareness among consumers and retailers for each new brand name without the benefit of any previous impressions. The advantages of this strategy are that each brand is unique to each market segment and there is no risk that a product failure will affect other products in the line. Still, some large multibrand firms have found that the complexity and expense of implementing this strategy can outweigh the benefits. For example, Procter & Gamble recently announced that it would prune 100 of its brands through product deletion and sales to other companies.[23]

Private Branding Strategy   A company uses *private branding*, often called *private labeling* or *reseller branding*, when it manufactures products but sells them under the brand name of a wholesaler or retailer. Rayovac, Paragon Trade Brands, and ConAgra Foods are major suppliers of private-label alkaline batteries, diapers, and grocery products, respectively. RadioShack, Costco, Sears, Walmart, and Kroger are large retailers that have their own brand names. Private branding is popular because it typically produces high profits for manufacturers and resellers. Consumers also buy them. It is estimated that one of every five items purchased at U.S. supermarkets, drugstores, and mass merchandisers bears a private brand.[24]

Mixed Branding Strategy   A fourth branding strategy is *mixed branding,* where a firm markets products under its own name(s) and that of a reseller because the segment attracted to the reseller is different from its own market. Beauty and fragrance marketer Elizabeth Arden is an example. The company sells its Elizabeth Arden brand through department stores, but its line of skin care products at Walmart is sold using the "skinsimple" brand name. Companies such as Del Monte, Whirlpool, and Dial produce private brands of pet foods, home appliances, and soap, respectively.

PACKAGING AND LABELING PRODUCTS

   Describe the role of packaging and labeling in the marketing of a product.

The *packaging* component of a product refers to any container in which it is offered for sale and on which label information is conveyed. A *label* is an integral part of the package and typically identifies the product or brand, who made it, where and when it was made, how it is to be used, and package contents and ingredients. To a great extent, the customer's first exposure to a product is the package and label, and both are an expensive and important part of marketing strategy. For Pez Candy, Inc., the central element of its marketing strategy is the character-head-on-a-stick plastic container that dispenses a miniature candy tablet. For more on how packaging creates customer value for Pez Candy, see the Marketing Matters box.[25]

Creating Customer Value and Competitive Advantage through Packaging and Labeling

Packaging and labeling cost U.S. companies about 15 cents of every dollar spent by consumers for products.[26] Despite their cost, packaging and labeling are essential because both provide important benefits for the manufacturer, retailer, and ultimate consumer. Packaging and labeling also can provide a competitive advantage.

Communication Benefits   A major benefit of packaging is the label information it conveys to the consumer, such as directions on how, where, and when to use the product and the source and composition of the product, which is needed to satisfy legal requirements of product disclosure. For example, the labeling system for packaged and processed foods in the United States provides a uniform format for nutritional and dietary information. Many packaged foods contain informative recipes to promote usage of the product. Campbell Soup estimates that the green bean casserole recipe on its cream of mushroom soup can accounts for $20 million in soup sales each year![27] Other information consists of seals and symbols, either government-required or commercial seals of approval (such as the Good Housekeeping Seal).

Functional Benefits   Packaging often plays a functional role—providing storage, convenience, or protection or ensuring product quality. Stackable food containers are one example of how packaging can provide functional benefits. For example, beverage companies have developed lighter and easier ways to stack products on shelves and in refrigerators. Examples include Coca-Cola beverage packs designed to fit neatly onto refrigerator shelves and Ocean Spray Cranberries's rectangular juice bottles that allow 10 units per package versus 8 of its former round bottles.

The convenience dimension of packaging is increasingly important. Kraft Miracle Whip salad dressing, Heinz ketchup, and Skippy Squeez'It peanut butter are sold in squeeze bottles; microwave popcorn has been a major market success; and Chicken of the Sea tuna and Folgers coffee are packaged in single-serving portions. Nabisco offers portion-control package sizes for the convenience of weight-conscious consumers. It offers 100-calorie packs of Oreos, Cheese Nips, and other products in individual pouches.

For the functional benefits provided by Pringles' cylindrical packaging, see the text.

Marketing Matters

Creating Customer Value through Packaging—Pez Heads Dispense More than Candy

Customer value can assume numerous forms. For Pez Candy, Inc. (www.pez.com), customer value manifests itself in some 450 Pez character candy dispensers. Each refillable dispenser ejects tasty candy tablets in a variety of flavors that delight preteens and teens alike in more than 60 countries.

Pez was formulated in 1927 by Austrian food mogul Edward Haas III and successfully sold in Europe as an adult breath mint. Pez, which comes from the German word for peppermint, *pfefferminz*, was originally packaged in a hygienic, headless plastic dispenser. Pez first appeared in the United States in 1953 with a headless dispenser, marketed to adults. After conducting extensive marketing research, Pez was repositioned with fruit flavors, repackaged with licensed character heads on top of the dispenser, and remarketed as a children's product in the mid-1950s. Since then, most top-level licensed characters and hundreds of other characters have become Pez heads. Consumers buy about 80 million Pez dispensers and 3 billion Pez tablets a year in the U.S. alone, and company sales growth exceeds that of the candy industry as a whole.

The unique Pez package dispenses a "use experience" for its customers beyond the candy itself, namely, fun.

And fun translates into a 98 percent awareness level for Pez among teenagers and an 89 percent awareness level among mothers with children. Pez has not advertised its product for years. With that kind of awareness, who needs advertising?

Consumer protection is another important function of packaging, including the development of tamper-resistant containers. Today, companies commonly use safety seals or pop-tops that reveal previous opening. Consumer protection through labeling exists in "open dating," which states the expected shelf life of the product.

Functional features of packaging also can affect product quality. Pringles, with its cylindrical packaging, offers uniform chips, minimal breakage, and for some consumers, better value for the money than chips packaged in flex-bags.

Packaging has been a major element of L'eggs hosiery positioning since its launch in 1969.

Hanes Brands, Inc.
www.leggs.com

Perceptual Benefits A third component of packaging and labeling is the perception created in the consumer's mind. Package and label shape, color, and graphics distinguish one brand from another, convey a brand's positioning, and build brand equity. According to the director of marketing for L'eggs hosiery, "Packaging is important to the positioning and equity of the L'eggs brand."[28] Why? Packaging and labeling have been shown to enhance brand recognition and facilitate the formation of strong, favorable, and unique brand associations.

Successful marketers recognize that changes in packages and labels can update and uphold a brand's image in the customer's mind. Pepsi-Cola embarked on a packaging change to uphold its image among teens and young adults. Beginning in 2013, Pepsi-Cola introduced new package graphics that change every few weeks to reflect different themes, such as sports, music, fashion, and cars.

Because labels list a product's source, brands competing in the global marketplace can benefit from "country of origin or manufacture" perceptions as described in Chapter 6. Consumers tend to hold stereotypes about country-product pairings that they judge "best"—English tea, French perfume, Italian leather, and Japanese electronics—which can affect a brand's image. Increasingly, Chinese firms are adopting the English language and Roman letters for their brand labels sold in China. This is being done because of a common perception in many Asian countries that "things Western are good."[29]

CHAPTER 10 Managing Successful Products, Services, and Brands

Packaging and Labeling Challenges and Responses

Package and label designers face four challenges. They are (1) the continuing need to connect with customers; (2) environmental concerns; (3) health, safety, and security issues; and (4) cost reduction.

Connecting with Customers   Packages and labels must be continually updated to connect with customers. The challenge lies in creating aesthetic and functional design features that attract customer attention and deliver customer value in their use. If done right, the rewards can be huge. For example, the marketing team responsible for Kleenex tissues converted its standard rectangular box into an oval shape with colorful seasonal graphics. Sales soared with this aesthetic change in packaging. After months of in-home research, Kraft product managers discovered that consumers often transferred Chips Ahoy! cookies to jars for easy access and to avoid staleness. The company solved both problems by creating a patented resealable opening on the top of the bag. The result? Sales of the new package doubled that of the old package.

Environmental Concerns   Because of widespread global concern about the growth of solid waste and the shortage of viable landfill sites, the amount, composition, and disposal of packaging material continue to receive much attention. For example, PepsiCo, Coca-Cola, and Nestlé have decreased the amount of plastic in their beverage bottles to reduce solid waste. Recycling packaging material is another major thrust. Procter & Gamble now uses recycled cardboard in over 70 percent of its paper packaging. Its Spic and Span liquid cleaner is packaged in 100 percent recycled material. Other firms, such as Walmart, are emphasizing the use of less packaging material. Since 2008, the company has worked with its 600,000 global suppliers to reduce overall packaging and shipping material by 5 percent in 2013.

Health, Safety, and Security Issues   A third challenge involves the growing health, safety, and security concerns of packaging materials. Today, most consumers believe companies should make sure products and their packages are safe and secure, regardless of the cost, and companies are responding in numerous ways. Most butane lighters sold today, like those made by Scripto, contain a child-resistant safety latch to prevent misuse and accidental fire. Childproof caps on pharmaceutical products and household cleaners and sealed lids on food packages are now common. New packaging technology and materials that extend a product's *shelf life* (the time a product can be stored) and prevent spoilage continue to be developed.

Cost Reduction   About 80 percent of packaging material used in the world consists of paper, plastics, and glass. As the cost of these materials rises, companies are constantly challenged to find innovative ways to cut packaging costs while delivering value to their customers. Many food and personal care companies have replaced bottles and cans with sealed plastic or foil pouches. Pouches cut packaging costs by 10 to 15 percent.[30]

MANAGING THE MARKETING OF SERVICES

seven Ps of services marketing
Expanding the four Ps framework to include people, physical environment, and process.

In this section we conclude the chapter with a brief discussion of the marketing mix for services. As such, it is necessary to expand the four Ps framework to include people, physical environment, and process, which is referred to as the **seven Ps of services marketing**.[31]

Recognize how the four Ps framework is expanded in the marketing of services.

Product (Service)

To a large extent, the concepts of the product component of the marketing mix apply equally well to Cheerios (a product) and to American Express (a service). Yet there are two aspects of the product/service element of the mix that warrant special attention when dealing with services: exclusivity and brand name.

Chapter 9 pointed out that one favorable dimension in a new product is its ability to be patented. However, services cannot be patented. Hence the creator of a successful quick-service restaurant chain could quickly discover the concept being copied by others. Domino's Pizza, for example, has seen competitors, such as Pizza Hut, copy the quick delivery advantage that originally propelled the company to success.

Because services are intangible and, therefore, more difficult to describe, the brand name or identifying logo of the service organization is particularly important in consumer decisions. Brand names help make the abstract nature of services more concrete. Service marketers apply branding concepts in the same way as product marketers. Consider American Express. It has applied subbranding with its American Express Green, Gold, Platinum, Optima, Blue, and Centurian charge cards, with unique service offerings for each.

American Express uses sub-branding for its charge cards and features unique service offerings for each.

American Express Company
www.americanexpress.com

Price

In the service industries, *price* is referred to in various ways. The terms used vary, depending upon whether the services are provided by hospitals (charges); consultants, lawyers, physicians, or accountants (fees); airlines (fares); or hotels (rates). Regardless of the term used, price plays two essential roles: (1) to affect consumer perceptions and (2) to be used in capacity management. Because of the intangible nature of services, price can indicate the quality of the service. Would you wonder about the quality of a $100 surgery? Studies show that when there are few cues by which to judge the quality of a product or service, consumers use price.[32]

The capacity management role of price is also important to movie theaters, airlines, restaurants, and hotels. Many service businesses use **off-peak pricing**, which consists of charging different prices during different seasons of the year and different times of the day or days of the week to reflect variations in demand for the service. Airlines offer seasonal discounts and movie theaters offer matinee prices.

off-peak pricing
Charging different prices during different seasons of the year and different times of the day or days of the week to reflect variations in demand for the service.

Place (Distribution)

Place or distribution is a major factor in developing a service marketing strategy because of the inseparability of services from the producer. Historically, little attention has been paid to distribution in services marketing. But as competition grows, the value of convenient distribution is being recognized. Hairstyling chains such as Cost Cutters Family Hair Care, tax preparation offices such as H&R Block, and accounting firms such as PricewaterhouseCoopers all use multiple locations for the distribution of services. In the banking industry, customers of participating banks using the Cirrus system can access any one of thousands of automatic teller systems throughout the United States. The availability of electronic distribution through the Internet now provides global coverage for travel services, banking, entertainment, and many other information-based services.

Promotion

The purpose of promotion for services, specifically advertising, is to show the benefits of using the service. It is valuable to stress availability, location, consistent quality, and efficient, courteous service. Also, services must be concerned with their image. Promotional efforts, such as Merrill Lynch's use of the bull in its ads, contribute to image and positioning strategies. In general, promotional concerns of services are similar to those of products.

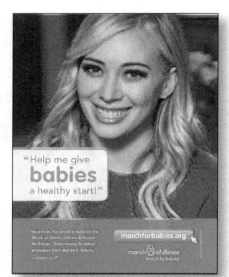

Hilary Duff volunteers her time to the March of Dimes to raise funds to give babies a healthy start in life in the March for Babies PSA. March for Babies has raised over $2.3 billion to support infant-related research, education, and vaccines.

March of Dimes

www.marchforbabies.com

Another form of promotion, *publicity,* plays a major role in the promotional strategy of nonprofit services and some professional organizations. Non-profit organizations such as public school districts, the Chicago Symphony Orchestra, religious organizations, and hospitals use publicity to dissemi-nate their messages. Because of the heavy reliance on publicity, many ser-vices use *public service announcements* (PSAs). PSAs are free and nonprofit groups tend to rely on them as the foundation of their media plan. However, the timing and location of a PSA are under the control of the medium, not the organization. Thus, the nonprofit service group cannot control who sees the message or when the message is delivered.

People

Many services depend on people for the creation and delivery of the customer service experience. The nature of the interaction between employees and customers strongly influences the customer's percep-tions of the service experience. Customers will often judge the quality of the service experience based on the performance of the people pro-viding the service.

This aspect of services marketing has led to a concept called *customer experience management* (CEM), which is the process of managing the en-tire customer experience with the firm. CEM experts suggest that the process should be intentional, planned, and consistent so that every experience is similar, differentiated from other services, relevant, and valuable to the target market. Companies such as Disney, Southwest Airlines, and Starbucks all manage the experience they offer custom-ers. They integrate their activities to connect with customers at each contact point to move beyond customer relationships to customer loyalty. Zappos.com, an online retailer, requires that all employees complete a four-week customer loyalty training program to deliver one of the company's core concepts—"Deliver WOW through service."

Physical Environment

The appearance of the environment in which the service is delivered and where the firm and customer interact can influence the customer's perception of the service. The physical evidence of the service includes all the tangibles surrounding the service: the buildings, landscaping, vehicles, furnishings, signage, brochures, and equipment. Ser-vice firms need to systematically and carefully manage physical evidence and to con-vey the proper impression of the service to the customer. This is sometimes referred to as impression, or evidence, management.[33] For many services, the physical environ-ment provides an opportunity for the firm to send consistent and strong messages about the nature of the service to be delivered.

Process

Process refers to the actual procedures, mechanisms, and flow of activities by which the service is created and delivered. The actual creation and delivery steps that the customer experiences provide customers with evidence on which to judge the service. These steps involve not only "what" gets created but also "how" it is created. Grease Monkey believes that it has the right process in the vehicle oil change and fluid ex-change service business. Customers do not need appointments, stores are open six days per week, the service is completed in 15–20 minutes, and a waiting room allows customers to read or work while the service is being completed.

Most services have a limited capacity due to the inseparability of the service from the service provider and the perishable nature of services. For example, a patient must be in the hospital at the same time as the surgeon to "buy" an appendectomy, and only one patient can be helped at that time. Similarly, no additional surgery can be

capacity management
Integrating the service component of the marketing mix with efforts to influence consumer demand.

performed tomorrow because of an unused operating room or an available surgeon today—the service capacity is lost if it is not used. So the service component of the marketing mix must be integrated with efforts to influence consumer demand. This is referred to as **capacity management**. Service organizations must manage the availability of the offering so that (1) demand matches capacity over the duration of the demand cycle (for example, one day, week, month, or year), and (2) the organization's assets are used in ways that will maximize its return on investment.

learning review

10-5. What is the difference between a line extension and a brand extension?

10-6. Explain the role of packaging in terms of perception.

10-7. How do service businesses use off-peak pricing?

LEARNING OBJECTIVES REVIEW

LO 10-1 *Explain the product life-cycle concept.*

The product life cycle describes the stages a new product goes through in the marketplace: introduction, growth, maturity, and decline. Product sales growth and profitability differ at each stage, and marketing managers have marketing objectives and marketing mix strategies unique to each stage based on consumer behavior and competitive factors. In the introductory stage, the need is to establish primary demand, whereas the growth stage requires selective demand strategies. In the maturity stage, the need is to maintain market share; the decline stage necessitates a deletion or harvesting strategy. Some important aspects of product life cycles are (*a*) their length, (*b*) the shape of the sales curves, and (*c*) the rate at which consumers adopt products.

LO 10-2 *Identify ways that marketing executives manage a product's life cycle.*

Marketing executives manage a product's life cycle in three ways. First, they can modify the product itself by altering its characteristics, such as product quality, performance, or appearance. Second, they can modify the market by finding new customers for the product, increasing a product's use among existing customers, or creating a new use situation for the product. Finally, they can reposition the product using any one or a combination of marketing mix elements. Four factors trigger a repositioning action. They include reacting to a competitor's position, reaching a new market, catching a rising trend, and changing the value offered to consumers.

LO 10-3 *Recognize the importance of branding and alternative branding strategies.*

A basic decision in marketing products is branding, in which an organization uses a name, phrase, design, symbols, or a combination of these to identify its products and distinguish them from those of its competitors. Product managers recognize that brands offer more than product identification and a means to distinguish their products from competitors. Successful and established

brands take on a brand personality and acquire brand equity—the added value a given brand name gives to a product beyond the functional benefits provided—that is crafted and nurtured by marketing programs that forge strong, favorable, and unique consumer associations with a brand. A good brand name should suggest the product benefits, be memorable, fit the company or product image, be free of legal restrictions, and be simple and emotional. Companies can and do employ several different branding strategies. With multiproduct branding, a company uses one name for all its products in a product class. A multibranding strategy involves giving each product a distinct name. A company uses private branding when it manufactures products but sells them under the brand name of a wholesaler or retailer. Finally, a company can employ mixed branding, where it markets products under its own name(s) and that of a reseller.

LO 10-4 *Describe the role of packaging and labeling in the marketing of a product.*

Packaging and labeling play numerous roles in the marketing of a product. The packaging component of a product refers to any container in which it is offered for sale and on which label information is conveyed. Manufacturers, retailers, and consumers acknowledge that packaging and labeling provide communication, functional, and perceptual benefits. Contemporary packaging and labeling challenges include (*a*) the continuing need to connect with customers, (*b*) environmental concerns, (*c*) health, safety, and security issues, and (*d*) cost reduction.

LO 10-5 *Recognize how the four Ps framework is expanded in the marketing of services.*

The four Ps framework also applies to services with some adaptations. Because services cannot be patented, unique offerings are difficult to protect. In addition, because services are intangible, brands and logos (which can be protected) are particularly important. The inseparability of production and consumption of services means that capacity management is important to services. The intangible nature of services makes price an important indication of service quality. Distribution has become an important marketing tool for services, and electronic distribution allows some services to provide global coverage. In recent years, service organizations have increased their promotional activities. Finally, the performance of people, the appearance of the physical environment, and the process involved in delivering a service are recognized as central to the customer experience.

LEARNING REVIEW ANSWERS

10-1 **Advertising plays a major role in the _____ stage of the product life cycle, and _____ plays a major role in maturity.**
Answer: introductory; product differentiation

10-2 **How do high-learning and low-learning products differ?**
Answer: A high-learning product requires significant customer education and there is an extended introductory period. A low-learning product requires little customer education because the benefits of purchase are readily understood, resulting in immediate sales.

10-3 **What does "creating a new use situation" mean in managing a product's life cycle?**
Answer: Creating a new use situation means finding new uses or applications for an existing product.

10-4 **Explain the difference between trading up and trading down in product repositioning.**
Answer: Trading up involves adding value to the product (or line) through additional features or higher-quality materials. Trading down involves reducing the number of features, quality, or price or downsizing—reducing the content of packages without changing package size and maintaining or increasing the package price.

10-5 **What is the difference between a line extension and a brand extension?**
Answer: A line extension uses a current brand name to enter a new market segment in its product class, whereas a brand extension uses a current brand name to enter a completely different product class.

10-6 **Explain the role of packaging in terms of perception.**
Answer: A package's shape, color, and graphics distinguish one brand from another, convey a brand's positioning, and build brand equity.

10-7 **How do service businesses use off-peak pricing?**
Answer: Service businesses charge different prices during different times of the day or days of the week to reflect variations in demand for the service.

FOCUSING ON KEY TERMS

brand equity p. 255
brand name p. 255
brand personality p. 255
branding p. 255

capacity management p. 265
multibranding p. 259
multiproduct branding p. 258
off-peak pricing p. 263

product life cycle p. 244
seven Ps of services marketing p. 262

APPLYING MARKETING KNOWLEDGE

1 Listed below are three different products in various stages of the product life cycle. What marketing strategies would you suggest to these companies? (*a*) Canon digital cameras—growth stage, (*b*) Hewlett Packard tablet computers—introductory stage, and (*c*) handheld manual can openers—decline stage.

2 It has often been suggested that products are intentionally made to break down or wear out. Is this strategy a planned product modification approach?

3 The product manager of GE is reviewing the penetration of trash compactors in American homes. After more than two decades in existence, this product is in relatively few homes. What problems can account for this poor acceptance? What is the shape of the trash compactor life cycle?

4 For years, Ferrari has been known as the manufacturer of expensive luxury automobiles. The company plans to attract the major segment of the car-buying market that purchases medium-priced automobiles. As Ferrari considers this trading-down strategy, what branding strategy would you recommend? What are the trade-offs to consider with your strategy?

BUILDING YOUR MARKETING PLAN

For the product offering in your marketing plan,

1 Identify (*a*) its stage in the product life cycle and (*b*) key marketing mix actions that might be appropriate, as shown in Figure 10–1.

2 Develop (*a*) branding and (*b*) packaging strategies, if appropriate for your offering.

VIDEO CASE 10   P&G's Secret Deodorant: Finding Inspiration in Perspiration

Video 10-4
Secret Video Case
kerin.tv/cr6e/v10-4

How do you revitalize a 50-plus-year-old brand? By focusing the brand's marketing efforts on its core purpose—a purpose that is both benefit-driven and inspirational—and using that purpose to build essential one-to-one personal connections with consumers.

Procter & Gamble's (P&G's) Secret brand, launched in 1956, has dominated the women's antiperspirant deodorant category for many years. Secret maintains its leadership position as one of many products in what is typically considered a low-involvement product category. Underarm deodorant isn't traditionally the type of product consumers think about engaging with in an ongoing, meaningful way. However, Secret has demonstrated that delivering the product benefit is important to establish trust and build engagement. This type of engagement often results in amplifying the brand's marketing investment, or paid media. Since 2009, Secret's purpose has been at the center of its marketing efforts, resulting in tremendous growth and brand advocacy among consumers.

PRODUCT BACKGROUND

Secret was the first deodorant marketed exclusively to women. In the 1960s and 1970s, Secret's growth was supported by a recurring series of ads featuring a husband and wife dealing with issues of the day, such as having children and

returning to work afterward. "It was all about empowering women to make the right choices for themselves and to embrace those choices fearlessly," according to Kevin Hochman, marketing director for skin and personal care at P&G North America at the time.

However, in 2004–2005, brand executives felt the theme was getting dated, so Secret backed off from that positioning. "We walked away," Hochman says. "We thought, women are empowered, and maybe this isn't so relevant. That was a mistake. Of course the idea was still relevant; we just hadn't modernized it in a contemporary way." Secret made a deliberate decision to go back to its roots.

THE ROAD TO PURPOSE

Secret started to experience slower growth in 2008 due to a down economy. The launch of a super-premium line of antiperspirant, Secret Clinical Strength, helped increase sales and market share, but competitors soon followed suit with similar products. Meanwhile, top P&G management began infusing the idea of purpose-driven marketing throughout the organization. The companywide vision focused on building brands through lifelong, one-to-one personal connections that ultimately build relationships and fulfill the company's purpose to "touch and improve more lives of more consumers more completely." With this in mind, Secret brand management realized it needed to get clear on

CHAPTER 10   Managing Successful Products, Services, and Brands

defining who Secret was, why Secret existed, and what Secret's purpose was. The brand needed a reason for its consumers to care and wanted to give them a reason to share.

Through the leadership and efforts of its senior brand management and partner agencies, including MEplusYOU (formerly imc[2]), Leo Burnett Co., SMG, Marina Maher Communications, and consultancy group BrightHouse, the Secret brand team began to establish the brand's purpose and convey it across all marketing touch points in ways that resonated with target consumers' core values and beliefs. "It becomes about more than selling deodorant, or promoting functional benefits, and more about rallying around something higher-order," says Hochman.

The Secret team started by defining the brand's core beliefs: "We believe in the equality of the genders and that all people should be able to pursue their goals without fear. We believe that by acting courageously, supporting others, empathizing with their challenges and finding innovative solutions, we can help women be more fearless." Armed with Secret's core belief, the team developed a purpose statement that is grounded in the product benefit and allowed for fearlessness when you're not sweating: "Helping women of all ages to be more fearless."

"Just a few years ago, the majority of marketers' activities and expenditures occurred across unidirectional media channels that could only talk *at* consumers. This limited the role marketing could play in developing relationships between brands and people," says Ian Wolfman, principal and chief marketing officer of MEplusYOU. "Today, new media, in combination with mature media, allows marketers to play a more sophisticated role in facilitating deep, trusting relationships between brands and people as we simultaneously drive strong transactional activity. Brands like Secret realize that taking a stand on values it shares with consumers is the key to translating a brand's purpose into meaningful relationships and profit."

The brand carefully constructed an ecosystem of tactical marketing "ignitions." Each of these ignitions focused on sparking the interest of like-minded consumers and were designed to flex and surge with the needs of the brand. The brand's purpose served as the basis for each ignition in order to engage consumers across all channels (online and offline). With Facebook as the hub, Secret brand management used the Secret.com website, print advertising, public relations, creative and social media, and appropriate paid and organic search programs to complete each ignition.

DRIVING CONSUMER ENGAGEMENT AND SALES GROWTH THROUGH IGNITIONS

Secret brand management focused on activating brand purpose around the timeless idea of being more fearless and freshened it up with contemporary topics and pop culture. This effort included several ignitions. Two of these are Let Her Jump and Mean Stinks.

Let Her Jump

The first time Secret struck gold by focusing on purpose was through Let Her Jump, an effort to sanction women's ski jumping as an official Olympic sport. The Let Her Jump ignition was a companion piece to work P&G was already doing for the 2010 Winter Olympics.

Secret launched Let Her Jump with a small online media buy and a Facebook Page that included an inspirational video, petition, and Facebook Fan Page. The inspiring video encouraged viewers to visit LetHerJump.com (a custom fan page within Facebook), where they could lead the charge to get women's ski jumping included in the 2014 Winter Olympics. In 2011, the International Olympic Committee approved women's ski jumping for the 2014 Winter Games.

Let Her Jump was one of many elements that, in the spirit of a living brand purpose, helped fuel growth over the previous year. In addition to the video being viewed more than 700,000 times, 57 percent of visitors said this initiative improved brand perception, and Secret saw a double-digit purchase intent increase among women and teens. "This [ignition] was the first time we could pinpoint that activating against purpose generated a huge sales lift," Hochman said. "We saw the Clinical Sport [stock-keeping units] up 85 percent during the [2010] Olympics. We changed the world for the better. In a small way, yes, but a deodorant brand influencing pop culture is very exciting when you can then directly attribute it to business results." As an added bonus, the Let Her Jump program won the coveted Forrester Groundswell Award in 2010. The award recognizes excellence in achieving business and organizational goals with social technology applications and is awarded to some of the best social media programs in the world.

The success of Let Her Jump helped pave the way for investment in another ignition. After proving that purpose-driven work leads to profitable growth for the brand, the team was ready to tackle one of the biggest fears young girls face—bullying. While Let Her Jump was tied to a distinct event in time, the team was excited at the prospect of rallying behind something that could live on and continue to do good in the world.

Mean Stinks

The Secret brand waged a battle for niceness through its Mean Stinks program, the next and biggest step in Secret's fearless movement. Through media monitoring and social listening, the Secret team determined that bullying was a critical issue facing many teen girls—which led to the creation of the Mean Stinks ignition. Mean Stinks, launched in early 2011, focused on ending girl-to-girl meanness, encouraging girls to grow up to be fearless, while providing a safe hub for conversation and creating brand affinity for Secret.

Through the Secret Mean Stinks movement, Secret brought a positive message to high school hallways, leading the charge to end the mean streak by showing teen girls that petty isn't pretty. Raising awareness of bullying is big, but "the need for education is tremendous—people aren't sure how to identify bullying, or what to do when it occurs," says Hochman. "And what's so compelling about the Mean Stinks program is how true it is to the brand's original essence."

The Secret team launched a Facebook media buy for Secret Mean Stinks to create awareness of the program, asking fans (primarily teen girls aged 13–24 and role models aged 25+) to share their stories. The Mean Stinks Facebook Wall was flooded with thousands of public apologies and heartfelt messages of empathy and encouragement. And as Secret continued to make a difference, women celebrities joined to take a stand, offering "nice advice" to girls through the Mean Stinks Facebook app and iAd.

In a single day, Secret gained over 200,000 Facebook fans—bringing its total number of fans to over a million, while its Mean Stinks Page gained over 20,000 new fans. Within the first two weeks, visitors accessed the Mean Stinks Facebook app more than 250,000 times and Secret became the second-fastest-growing Facebook Page globally for one week. This ignition also helped contribute to 10 percent overall sales growth for the entire fiscal year, 11.5 percent in the six-month period during which Mean Stinks was launched.

In the summer of 2011, Secret and Apple joined forces to create an iAd experience that tackled the issue for girls on the device that's most personal—their iPhone. The ignition received unusually high engagement levels and led to many "firsts" for Secret:

- First brand to create and share customized wallpapers via iPhone and iPod touch devices, which led to an "average time spent" rate that was 16 percent higher than average.
- First brand to use transition banners on the iAd Network, which resulted in exceeding benchmarks for banner "Tap through Rates" (50 percent higher than average for iAd).
- First brand to drive donations for a cause through the iAd, which resulted in donations to PACER's National Bullying Prevention Center.

In the first 10 days after launch, 23,000 consumers engaged with the Secret iAd, with more than eight page views per visit and an average of 80 seconds spent on the ad.

WHAT'S NEXT FOR SECRET

Secret executives saw success behind the purpose activation the year after it was established, but they noticed it wasn't truly part of the brand's DNA or fully integrated into every marketing element. "[At first] we had a lot of grandiose ideas, but they added layers to our existing plan. Dollars were tight, and the purpose ideas started getting cut. Old Spice was ahead of us, and I wondered what they were doing differently," says Hochman. "By [working with our agency partners], we finally were able to ensure that [the ignitions] weren't just elements of our plans; they WERE our plan," Hochman says. "The way the Secret team operates now compared with four years ago—it's like day and night."

Hochman says the brand has more ideas that include educating, generating awareness, and empowering people to take meaningful action. Secret is recognized as being best in its class, something the brand is happy to tout. "But [success] isn't a Secret-only thing ... it's a priority for all of our brands. And when people are living the brand, they're more excited to come to work. It's much more enabling and inspiring," Hochman says. And to continue in this success, Hochman suggests remembering that a brand's purpose is inextricably linked to the overall plan, it pervades everything about the business—including team culture—and it's in the company's roots.

Hochman emphasizes the importance of transparency, something he believes Secret will continue to win out on

in the future. "Today, information is free and plentiful. If there's a lack of sincerity, consumers know it."

Questions

1 What is "purpose-driven marketing" from a product and brand management perspective at Procter & Gamble?

2 How does "purpose-driven" marketing for Secret deodorant relate to the hierarchy of needs concept detailed in Chapter 4?

3 What dimensions of the consumer-based brand equity pyramid have the Secret brand team focused on with its "Let Her Jump" and "Mean Stinks" ignitions?

Chapter Notes

1. "Gatorade's New Selling Point: We're Necessary Performance Gear," www.adage.com, January 2, 2012; "The Best Goes On," *BrandWeek*, May 10, 2010, p. 22; "Gatorade: Before and After," *The Wall Street Journal*, April 23, 2010, p. B8; "Pepsi Turns to Innovation to Boost Gatorade," *The Wall Street Journal*, October 21, 2009, p. B7; "Gatorade Refreshes Look," *BrandWeek*, January 15, 2009, p. 4; Darren Rovell, *First in Thirst: How Gatorade Turned the Science of Sweat into a Cultural Phenomenon* (New York: AMACOM, 2005); and www.Gatorade.com.

2. For an extended discussion of the generalized product life cycle, see Donald R. Lehmann and Russell S. Winer, *Product Management*, 5th ed. (Burr Ridge, IL: McGraw-Hill, 2008).

3. *Gillette Fusion Case Study* (New York: Datamonitor, June 6, 2008). All subsequent references to Gillette Fusion are based on this case study.

4. Orville C. Walker, Jr., and John W. Mullins, *Marketing Management: A Strategic Decision-Making Approach*, 8th ed. (Burr Ridge, IL: McGraw-Hill/Irwin, 2014), p. 209.

5. Portions of this discussion on the fax machine product life cycle are based on Kurt Wagner, "Why the Fax Machine Refuses to Die," www.CNNMoney, May 15, 2013; Mike Elgan, "Tired Technologies That Should Die Off in 2010," www.pcworld.com, December 30, 2009; and "Atlas Electronics Corporation," in Roger A. Kerin and Robert A. Peterson, *Strategic Marketing Problems: Cases and Comments*, 8th ed. (Upper Saddle River, NJ: Prentice Hall, 1998), pp. 494–506.

6. "Email Statistics Report, 2012–2016" (Palo Alto, CA: The Radicati Group, 2012); and "Why Are Faxes Still Around?" *Wired*, January 2009, p. 47.

7. Kate MacArthur, "Coke Energizes Tab, Neville Isdell's Fave," *Advertising Age*, August 29, 2005, pp. 3, 21.

8. "Hosiery Sales Hit Major Snag," *Dallas Morning News*, December 18, 2006, p. 50.

9. Everett M. Rogers, *Diffusion of Innovations*, 5th ed. (New York: Free Press, 2003).

10. Jagdish N. Sheth and Banwasi Mitral, *Consumer Behavior: A Managerial Perspective*, 2nd ed. (Mason, OH: South-Western College Publishing, 2003).

11. "Demand Ebbs for Electric, Hybrid Cars," wsj.com, September 30, 2014.

12. "When Free Samples Become Saviors," *The Wall Street Journal*, August 14, 2001, pp. B1, B4.

13. "Pop(sicle) Quiz," *Consumer Reports*, August 2012, p. 63; "Downsized: More and More Products Lose Weight," *Consumer Reports*, February 2011, p. 32ff; "P&G Lightens the Load on Diapers," *The*

Wall Street Journal, September 9, 2013, p. B2; and Bruce Horovitz, "Shoppers Beware: Products Shrink but Prices Stay the Same," www.usatoday, June 11, 2008.

14. This discussion is based on Kevin Lane Keller, *Strategic Brand Management*, 4th ed. (Upper Saddle River, NJ: Prentice Hall, 2013). Also see, Susan Fornier, "Building Brand Community on the Harley-Davidson Posse Ride," Harvard Business School Note #5-501–502 (Boston: Harvard Business School, 2001); and Tulin Erdem, Joffre Swait, and Ana Valenzuela, "Brands as Signals: A Cross-Country Validation Study," *Journal of Marketing*, January 2006, pp. 34–49.

15. Keller, *Strategic Brand Management*.

16. This discussion is based on John Deighton, "How Snapple Got Its Juice Back," *Harvard Business Review*, January 2002, pp. 47–53; and "Breakfast King Agrees to Sell Bagel Business," *The Wall Street Journal*, September 28, 1999, pp. B1, B6. Also see, Vithala R. Rao, Manoj K. Agarwal, and Denise Dahlhoff, "How Is Manifest Branding Strategy Related to the Value of a Corporation?" *Journal of Marketing*, October 2004, pp. 125–41.

17. Keach Hagey, "Rebuilding Playboy: Less Smut, More Money," *The Wall Street Journal*, February 20, 2013, pp. B1, B2; "Judge Pooh-poohs Lawsuit over Disney Licensing Fees," USATODAY.com, March 30, 2004; and Keller, *Strategic Brand Management*.

18. John Brodie, "The Many Faces of Ralph Lauren," www.Fortune.com, August 29, 2007; and "Polo Ralph Lauren Enters into Licensing Agreement with Luxottica Group, S.p.A.," www.thebusinessedition.com, February 28, 2006.

19. Marc Fetscherin, et al., "In China? Pick Your Brand Name Carefully," *Harvard Business Review*, September 2012, p. 26; Beth Snyder Bulik, "What's in a (Good) Product Name? Sales," *Advertising Age*, February 2, 2009, p. 10; and Keller, *Strategic Brand Management*.

20. Jack Neff, "The End of the Line for Line Extensions?" *Advertising Age*, July 7, 2008, pp. 3, 28; and "When Brand Extension Becomes Brand Abuse," *BrandWeek*, October 26, 1998, pp. 20, 22.

21. Mark Ritson, "Should You Launch a Fighter Brand?" *Harvard Business Review*, October 2009, pp. 87–94.

22. "Ribbons Roll Out on Rides," *Dallas Morning News* (September 30, 2005), p. 8D.

23. "Procter & Gamble to Drop Up to 100 Brands," cnnmoney.com, September 23, 2014.

24. "Store Brand Share on the Rise," www.storebranddecisions.com, October 16, 2012.

25. www.pez.com, downloaded February 1, 2014; "So Sweet: William and Kate PEZ Dispensers," www.today.msnbc.com, March 30, 2012; David Welch, *Collecting Pez* (Murphysboro, IL: Bubba Scrubba

Publications, 1995); and "Elements Design Adds Dimension to Perennial Favorite Pez Brand," *Package Design Magazine,* May 2006, pp. 37–38.

26. "Market Statistics," www.Packaging-Gateway.com, downloaded March 25, 2008.

27. "Green Bean Casserole Turns 50," *Dallas Morning News,* November 19, 2005, p. 10D.

28. "Iconic L'eggs Sheer Energy Egg Package Returns," *Package World,* March 6, 2014, pp. 16–17.

29. "Asian Brands Are Sprouting English Logos in Pursuit of Status, International Image," *The Wall Street Journal,* August 7, 2001, p. B7C.

30. "Packaging," www.hp.com, downloaded January 17, 2007.

31. This discussion is based on Valerie A. Zeithaml, Mary Jo Bitner, and Dwayne D. Gremler, *Services Marketing: Integrating Customer Focus across the Firm,* 5th ed. (Burr Ridge, IL: McGraw-Hill/Irwin, 2009).

32. Thomas T. Nagle, John E. Hogan, and Joseph Zale, *The Strategy and Tactics of Pricing,* 5th ed. (Upper Saddle River, NJ: Prentice Hall, 2011).

33. Leonard L. Berry and Neeli Bedapudi, "Clueing in Customers," *Harvard Business Review,* February 2003, pp. 100–6.

P&G's Secret Deodorant: This case was prepared by Jana Boone. Used with permission.

Credits

11 Pricing Products and Services

LEARNING OBJECTIVES

After reading this chapter you should be able to:

LO 11-1 Describe the nature and importance of pricing and the approaches used to select an approximate price level.

LO 11-2 Explain what a demand curve is and the role of revenues in pricing decisions.

LO 11-3 Explain the role of costs in pricing decisions and describe how combinations of price, fixed cost, and unit variable cost affect a firm's break-even point.

LO 11-4 Recognize the objectives a firm has in setting prices and the constraints that restrict the range of prices a firm can charge.

LO 11-5 Describe the steps taken in setting a final price.

VIZIO, INC.—DELIVERING BEAUTIFULLY SIMPLE PRODUCTS AT A GREAT VALUE

Can you name North America's #1 Smart TV company? Stumped? It's VIZIO, Inc., an entrepreneurial, Irvine, California–based company with a bold agenda. "Our goal is to be the next Sony in 20 to 30 years," says William Wang, VIZIO's co-founder and chief executive officer, who was born in Taiwan and immigrated to the United States at age 13.

In 2002, Mr. Wang was struck by an ad for a $10,000 flat-panel HDTV set and immediately saw an opportunity. Instead of marketing these sets as luxury items, Mr. Wang thought he could make and market an HDTV that would be affordable for the average customer.

Like many entrepreneurs, he borrowed money from friends and family and mortgaged his home. Within a year, he formed a company that is now known as VIZIO, Inc., and delivered the company's first VIZIO HDTV to Costco for distribution through that company's stores. VIZIO HDTVs are now sold through Costco, Walmart, BJ's Wholesale, Best Buy, Sam's Club, and Target stores nationwide, along with authorized online partners such as Amazon. The company has sold more than 38 million HDTV units shipped since 2002.

VIZIO's ability to deliver affordable HDTVs to the average customer is based on a novel strategy. VIZIO didn't invest in expensive manufacturing facilities but instead relied on contract manufacturers to build its products. Product development and marketing specialists in the United States handle product design and marketing. "The whole goal is to ensure that we have the right product at the right time and the right price and really drive a seamless end-to-end value chain," says a company spokesperson.

"VIZIO HDTVs are more popular and in greater demand than ever," adds Laynie Newsome, VIZIO's co-founder and chief sales officer. "Consumers want to save money without sacrificing quality or technology." Matt McRae, VIZIO's chief technology officer, adds that VIZIO's strategy is to make affordable products with innovative features, saying, "We're far from the cheapest brand on the market at present. Everybody deserves the latest technology too."

VIZIO's visionary commitment to delivering high-quality technology at a great value to consumers is evident by its pioneering role in launching Smart TVs in 2010. Smart TV enables viewers to watch content from the Internet directly on their TV, for a more interactive TV watching experience. VIZIO has sold more than 3.2 million Smart TVs since 2010, making it North America's #1 Smart TV company.

TWO-SIDED REMOTE
WITH KEYBOARD

VIZIO Internet Apps Plus™

YouTube: Second-Screen Experience

Full-Screen Apps Window

VIZIO's powerful and profitable price-value position clearly resonates with consumers. VIZIO is frequently ranked "Highest in Customer Satisfaction" with HDTVs by J.D. Power and Associates. Also in 2012, VIZIO entered the personal computer market, offering desktop personal computers, home audio systems, tablet computers, and laptop computers. Not bad for a company with about 400 employees and just 12 years old![1]

Welcome to the fascinating—and intense—world of pricing, where consumer demand, company costs, and competitor actions come together in the price buyers are asked to pay. This chapter describes the important factors used by organizations to set prices for their products and services.

RECOGNIZING THE NATURE AND IMPORTANCE OF PRICE

LO 11-1 Describe the nature and importance of pricing and the approaches used to select an approximate price level.

The price paid for products and services goes by many names. You pay *tuition* for your education, *rent* for an apartment, *interest* on a bank credit card, and a *premium* for car insurance. Your dentist or physician charges you a *fee*, a professional or social organization charges *dues*, and airlines charge a *fare*. In business, an executive is given a *salary*, a salesperson receives a *commission*, and a worker is paid a *wage*. And what you pay for clothes or a haircut is termed a *price*.

Among all marketing and operations factors in a business firm, price has a unique role. It is the place where all other business decisions come together. The price must be "right"—in the sense that customers must be willing to pay it; it must generate enough sales dollars to pay for the cost of developing, producing, and marketing the product; *and* it must earn a profit for the company. Small changes in price can have big effects on both the number of units sold and company profit.

What Is a Price?

price
The money or other considerations (including other products and services) exchanged for the ownership or use of a product or service.

From a marketing viewpoint, **price** is the money or other considerations (including other products and services) exchanged for the ownership or use of a product or service. Recently, Wilkinson Sword exchanged some of its knives for advertising used to promote its razor blades. This practice of exchanging products and services for other products and services rather than for money is called *barter*. Barter transactions account for billions of dollars annually in domestic and international trade.

How would you calculate the price of a new Bugatti Veyron, the world's fastest car? Read the text to see how the price equation is used to answer this intriguing question.

Video 11-1
Bugatti Veyron
kerin.tv/cr6e/v11-1

The Price Equation   For most products, money is exchanged. However, the amount paid is not always the same as the list, or quoted, price because of discounts, allowances, and extra fees. One new 21st century pricing tactic involves using "special fees" and "surcharges." This practice is driven by consumers' zeal for low prices combined with the ease of making price comparisons on the Internet. Buyers are more willing to pay extra fees than a higher list price, so sellers use add-on charges as a way of having the consumer pay more without raising the list price.

All the factors that increase or decrease the final price of an offering help construct a "price equation," which is shown for a few products in Figure 11–1. These are key considerations if you want to buy a new Bugatti Veyron Grand Sport Vitesse (French for "speed"), the world's fastest and most expensive "open top" production car. The all-wheel car accelerates from 0 to 60 mph in just 2.5 seconds. With its 1,200 horsepower engine, top speed is 255 mph (roof on)! The aerodynamic body is made out of carbon fiber to safely handle the speed. But consider that: (1) fuel economy is a paltry 12.2 mpg, costing you about $10,000 per year; (2) every 10,000 miles, the four 20-inch Michelin tires, which cost a total of $40,000, must be replaced; and (3) maintenance will set you back about $20,000 every time the car needs servicing.[2]

Calculating a Final Price   The Bugatti Veyron Grand Sport Vitesse U.S. list price is a cool $2.5 million. But to get the special paint option seen in the photo, it will cost you an extra $430,000. An extended warranty will cost an additional $70,000. However, if you put $500,000 down and finance the balance, you will receive a $50,000 rebate off the list price. Also, the dealer has agreed to give you a trade-in allowance of $7,000 based on the trade-in value for your 2008 Honda Civic DX four-door sedan that has 75,000 miles and is in good condition. Other charges include: (1) an import duty of $50,000; (2) a gas-guzzler tax of $7,000; (3) a 7.5 percent sales tax of $229,125; (4) an

PRICE EQUATION

ITEM PURCHASED	PRICE	= LIST PRICE	− INCENTIVES AND ALLOWANCES	+ EXTRA FEES
New car bought by an individual	Final price	= List price	− Rebate Cash discount Old car trade-in	+ Financing charges Special accessories Destination charges
Term in college bought by a student	Tuition	= Published tuition	− Scholarship Other financial aid Discounts for number of credits taken	+ Special activity fees Room and meals Books, computer Student loan interest (eventually)
Merchandise bought from a wholesaler by a retailer	Invoice price	= List price	− Quantity discount Cash discount Seasonal discount Functional or trade discount	+ Late payment penalty

FIGURE 11–1
The "price" a buyer pays can take different names depending on what is purchased, and it can change depending on the price equation.

auto registration fee of $5,000 to the state; and (5) a $50,000 destination charge to ship the car to you from France. Finally, your total finance charge is $377,168 based on a five-year loan with an annual interest rate of 5 percent, compounded monthly.

Applying the price equation shown in Figure 11–1 to your Bugatti Veyron Grand Sport Vitesse purchase, your final price is:

$$\text{Final price} = [\text{List price}] - [(\text{Incentives}) + (\text{Allowances})] + [\text{Extra fees}]$$
$$= [\$2,500,000] - [(\$50,000 + \$7,000)] + [\$430,000 + \$70,000 + \$50,000 + \$7,000 + \$229,125 + \$5,000 + \$50,000 + \$377,168]$$
$$= \$2,500,000 - \$57,000 + \$1,218,293$$
$$= \$3,661,293$$

Note that your final price is $1,161,293 more than the list price! Your monthly payment for the five-year loan of $3,161,293 ($2,784,125 principal plus $377,168 total finance charge) is $52,688.21. Are you still interested in the Bugatti Veyron Grand Sport Vitesse? If so, put yourself on the waiting list.

Price as an Indicator of Value

value
The ratio of perceived benefits to price.

From a consumer's standpoint, price is often used to indicate value when it is compared with perceived benefits such as the quality or durability of a product or service. Specifically, **value** is the ratio of perceived benefits to price, or

$$\text{Value} = \frac{\text{Perceived benefits}}{\text{Price}}$$

This relationship shows that for a given price, as perceived benefits increase, value increases. For example, if you're used to paying $7.99 for a medium frozen cheese pizza, wouldn't a large one at the same price be more valuable? Conversely, for a given price, value decreases when perceived benefits decrease.

For some products, price influences consumers' perception of overall quality and ultimately its value to them.[3] In a survey of home furnishing buyers, 84 percent agreed with the statement: "The higher the price, the higher the quality."[4] For example, Kohler introduced a walk-in bathtub that is safer for children and the elderly. Although priced higher than conventional step-in bathtubs, the product is successful because buyers are willing to pay a bit more for what they perceive as the value of extra safety.

275

CHAPTER 11   Pricing Products and Services

In this context, "value" involves the judgment by a consumer of the worth of a product (walk-in bathtub) relative to substitutes (conventional bathtub) that satisfy the same need (bathing). Through the process of comparing the costs and benefits of substitute items, a "reference value" emerges.

Price in the Marketing Mix

profit equation
Profit equals total revenue minus total cost.

Pricing is a critical decision made by a marketing executive because price has a direct effect on a firm's profits. This is apparent from a firm's **profit equation**, where:

$$\text{Profit} = \text{Total revenue} - \text{Total cost}$$
$$= (\text{Unit price} \times \text{Quantity sold}) - (\text{Fixed cost} + \text{Variable cost})$$

What makes this relationship even more complicated is that price affects the quantity sold, as illustrated with demand curves later in this chapter. Furthermore, since the quantity sold usually affects a firm's costs because of efficiency of production, price also indirectly affects costs. Thus, pricing decisions influence both total revenue (sales) and total cost, which makes pricing one of the most important decisions marketing executives face.

GENERAL PRICING APPROACHES

A key for a marketing manager setting a price for a product is to find an approximate price level to use as a reasonable starting point. Four common approaches used to find this approximate price level are (1) demand-oriented, (2) cost-oriented, (3) profit-oriented, and (4) competition-oriented approaches (see Figure 11–2). Although these approaches are discussed separately below, some of them overlap, and an effective marketing manager will consider several in selecting an approximate price level.

Demand-Oriented Pricing Approaches

Demand-oriented approaches weigh factors underlying expected customer tastes and preferences more heavily than such factors as cost, profit, and competition when selecting a price level.

Skimming Pricing A firm introducing a new or innovative product can use *skimming pricing,* setting the highest initial price that customers really desiring the product are willing to pay. These customers are not very price sensitive because they weigh the new product's price, quality, and ability to satisfy their needs against the same characteristics of substitutes. As the demand of these customers is satisfied, the

FIGURE 11–2
Four approaches for selecting an approximate price level.

firm lowers the price to attract another, more price-sensitive segment. Thus, skimming pricing gets its name from skimming successive layers of "cream," or customer segments, as prices are lowered in a series of steps.

Skimming pricing is an effective strategy when (1) enough prospective customers are willing to buy the product immediately at the high initial price to make these sales profitable, (2) the high initial price will not attract competitors, (3) lowering the price has only a minor effect on increasing the sales volume and reducing the unit costs, and (4) customers interpret the high price as a signal of high quality.[5] These four conditions are most likely to exist when the new product is protected by patents or copyrights or its uniqueness is understood and valued by consumers. Gillette, for example, adopted a skimming strategy for its five-blade Fusion brand shaving system (which included no less than 70 patents!) since many of these conditions applied.

Penetration Pricing   Setting a low initial price on a new product to appeal immediately to the mass market is *penetration pricing*, the exact opposite of skimming pricing. Amazon consciously chose a penetration strategy when it introduced the Kindle Fire tablet computer at $199 when competitive models were priced at $499.

The conditions favoring penetration pricing are the reverse of those supporting skimming pricing: (1) many segments of the market are price sensitive, (2) a low initial price discourages competitors from entering the market, and (3) unit production and marketing costs fall dramatically as production volumes increase. A firm using penetration pricing may (1) maintain the initial price for a time to gain profit lost from its low introductory level or (2) lower the price further, counting on the new volume to generate the necessary profit.

Prestige Pricing   Although consumers tend to buy more of a product when the price is lower, sometimes the reverse is true. If consumers are using price as a measure of the quality of an item, a company runs the risk of appearing to offer a low-quality product if it sets the price below a certain point. *Prestige pricing* involves setting a high price so that quality- or status-conscious consumers will be attracted to the product and buy it. Rolex watches, Chanel perfume, and Cartier jewelry have an element of prestige pricing in them and may sell worse at lower prices than at higher ones.[6] As described in the Marketing Matters box on the next page, this is the pricing strategy Energizer used with its very successful e[2] high-performance AA batteries.[7]

Video 11-2
Rolex Ad
kerin.tv/cr6e/v11-2

Odd-Even Pricing   Sears offers a Craftsman radial saw for $499.99, the suggested retail price for the Gillette Fusion shaving system is $11.99, and Kmart sells Windex glass cleaner on sale for 99 cents. Why not simply price these items at $500, $12, and $1, respectively? These firms are using *odd-even pricing,* which involves setting prices a few dollars or cents under an even number. The presumption is that consumers see the Sears radial saw as priced at "something over $400" rather than "about $500." In theory, demand increases if the price drops from $500 to $499.99. There is some evidence to suggest this does happen. However, research suggests that overuse of odd-ending prices tends to mute their effect on demand.[8]

Which pricing strategy is used by DIRECTV? Read the text to find out which one and why.

Target Pricing   Manufacturers will sometimes estimate the price that the ultimate consumer will pay for a product. They then work backward through markups taken by retailers and wholesalers to determine what price they can charge wholesalers for the product. This practice, called *target pricing,* results in the manufacturer deliberately adjusting the composition and features of a product to achieve the target price to consumers. Canon uses target pricing for its digital cameras.

Bundle Pricing   A frequently used demand-oriented pricing practice is *bundle pricing*—the marketing of two or more products in a single package price. For example, Delta Air Lines offers vacation packages that include airfare, car rental, and lodging.

Marketing Matters

Energizer's Lesson in Price Perception— Value Lies in the Eye of the Beholder

Battery manufacturers are as tireless as a certain drum-thumping bunny in their efforts to create products that perform better, last longer, and, not incidentally, outsell the competition. The commercialization of new alkaline battery technology at a price that creates value for consumers is not always obvious or easy. Just ask the marketing executives at Energizer about their experience with pricing Energizer Advanced Formula and Energizer e^2 AA alkaline batteries.

When Duracell launched its high-performance Ultra brand AA alkaline battery with a 25 percent price premium over standard Duracell batteries, Energizer quickly countered with its own high-performance battery— Energizer Advanced Formula. Believing that consumers would not pay the premium price, Energizer priced its Advanced Formula brand at the same price as its standard AA alkaline battery, expecting to gain market share from Duracell. It did not happen. Why? According to industry analysts, consumers associated Energizer's low price with inferior quality in the high-performance segment. Instead of gaining market share, Energizer lost market share to Duracell and Rayovac, the No. 3 battery manufacturer.

Having learned its lesson, Energizer subsequently released its e^2 high-performance battery, this time priced 4 percent higher than Duracell Ultra and about 50 percent higher than Advanced Formula. The result? Energizer recovered lost sales and market share. The lesson learned? Value lies in the eye of the beholder.

Bundle pricing is based on the idea that consumers value the package more than the individual items. This is due to benefits received from not having to make separate purchases and enhanced satisfaction from one item given the presence of another. This is the idea behind DIRECTV's TV, phone, and Internet bundles. Moreover, bundle pricing often provides a lower total cost to buyers and lower marketing costs to sellers.

Yield Management Pricing   Have you ever been on an airplane and discovered the person next to you paid a lower price for her ticket than you paid? Annoying, isn't it? But what you observed is *yield management pricing*—the charging of different prices to maximize revenue for a set amount of capacity at any given time. Airlines, hotels, and car rental firms engage in capacity management (described in Chapter 10) by varying prices based on time, day, week, or season to match demand and supply. American Airlines estimates that yield management pricing produces an annual revenue that exceeds $500 million.[9]

Cost-Oriented Pricing Approaches

With cost-oriented approaches, a price setter stresses the cost side of the pricing problem, not the demand side. Price is set by looking at the production and marketing costs and then adding enough to cover direct expenses, overhead, and profit.

Standard Markup Pricing   Managers of supermarkets and other retail stores have such a large number of products that estimating the demand for each product as a means of setting price is impossible. Therefore, they use *standard markup pricing,* which entails adding a fixed percentage to the cost of all items in a specific product class. This percentage markup varies depending on the type of retail store (such as furniture, clothing, or grocery) and the product involved. High-volume products usually have smaller markups than do low-volume products. Supermarkets such as Kroger, Safeway, and

Jewel have different markups for staple items and discretionary items. The markup on staple items like sugar, flour, and dairy products varies from 10 percent to 23 percent, whereas markups on discretionary items like snack foods and candy range from 27 percent to 47 percent. These markups must cover all expenses of the store, pay for overhead costs, and contribute something to profits. For supermarkets these markups, which may appear very large, result in only a 1 percent profit on sales revenue.

By comparison, consider the markups on snacks and beverages purchased at your local movie theater. The markup is 87 percent on soft drinks, 65 percent on candy bars, and 90 percent on popcorn. These markups might sound high, but consider the consequences. "If we didn't charge as much for concessions as we did, the average movie ticket would cost $20," says the CEO of Regal Entertainment, the largest U.S. theater chain.[10]

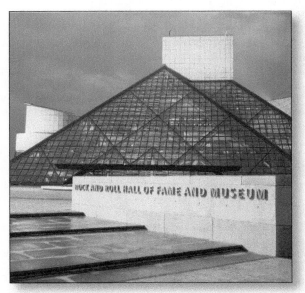

How was the price of the Rock and Roll Hall of Fame and Museum determined? Read the text to find out.

Cost-Plus Pricing   Many manufacturing, professional services, and construction firms use a variation of standard markup pricing. *Cost-plus pricing* involves summing the total unit cost of providing a product or service and adding a specific amount to the cost to arrive at a price. Cost-plus pricing is the most commonly used method to set prices for business products. For example, this pricing approach was used in setting the price for the $92 million Rock and Roll Hall of Fame and Museum in Cleveland, Ohio.

Profit-Oriented Pricing Approaches

A price setter may choose to balance both revenues and costs to set price using profit-oriented approaches. These might either involve a target of a specific dollar volume of profit or express this target profit as a percentage of sales or investment.

Target Profit Pricing   When a firm sets an annual target of a specific dollar volume of profit, this is called *target profit pricing*. For example, if you owned a picture frame store and wanted to achieve a target profit of $7,000, how much would you need to charge for each frame? Because profit depends on revenues and costs, you would have to know your costs and then estimate how many frames you would sell. Based on sales in previous years, let's assume that you expect to frame 1,000 pictures next year. The cost of your time and materials to frame an average picture is $22, while your overhead expenses (rent, manager salaries, etc.) are $26,000. Finally, your goal is to achieve a profit of $7,000. How do you calculate your price per picture?

$$\text{Profit} = \text{Total revenue} - \text{Total costs}$$
$$= (\text{Pictures sold} \times \text{Price/picture}) - [(\text{Cost/picture} \times \text{Pictures sold}) + \text{Overhead cost}]$$

Solving for price per picture, the equation becomes,

$$\text{Price/picture} = \frac{\text{Profit} + [(\text{Cost/picture} \times \text{Pictures sold}) + \text{Overhead cost}]}{\text{Pictures sold}}$$
$$= \frac{\$7,000 + [(\$22 \times 1,000) + \$26,000]}{1,000}$$
$$= \frac{\$7,000 + \$48,000}{1,000}$$
$$= \$55 \text{ per picture}$$

Clearly, this pricing method depends on an accurate estimate of demand. Because demand is often difficult to predict, this method has the potential for disaster if the estimate is too high. Generally, a target profit pricing strategy is best for firms offering new or unique products, without a lot of competition. What if other frame stores in your area were charging $40 per framed picture? As a marketing manager, you'd have to offer improved customer value with your more expensive frames, lower your costs, or settle for less profit.

Target Return-on-Sales Pricing   Firms such as supermarkets often use *target return-on-sales pricing* to set prices that will give them a profit that is a specified percentage—say, 1 percent—of the sales volume. This price method is often used because of the difficulty in establishing a benchmark of sales or investment to show how much of a firm's effort is needed to achieve the target.

Target Return-on-Investment Pricing   Firms such as General Motors and many public utilities use *target return-on-investment pricing* to set prices to achieve a return-on-investment (ROI) target such as a percentage that is mandated by its board of directors or regulators. For example, an electric utility may decide to seek a 10 percent ROI. If its investment in plant and equipment is $50 billion, it would need to set the price of electricity to its customers at a level that results in $5 billion a year in profit.

Competition-Oriented Pricing Approaches

Rather than emphasize demand, cost, or profit factors, a price setter can stress what competitors or "the market" is doing.

Has Red Bull's price premium among energy-drink brands sold in convenience stores increased or decreased? The Using Marketing Dashboards box answers this question.

Customary Pricing   For some products where tradition, a standardized channel of distribution, or other competitive factors dictate the price, *customary pricing* is used. Candy bars offered through standard vending machines have a customary price of 75 cents, and a significant departure from this price may result in a loss of sales for the manufacturer. Hershey typically has changed the amount of chocolate in its candy bars depending on the price of raw chocolate rather than vary its customary retail price so that it can continue selling through vending machines.

Above-, At-, or Below-Market Pricing   The "market price" of a product is what customers are generally willing to pay, not necessarily the price that the firm sets. For most products it is difficult to identify a specific market price for a product or product class. Still, marketing managers often have a subjective feel for the competitors' price or the market price. Using this benchmark, they then may deliberately choose a strategy of *above-*, *at-*, or *below-market pricing*.

Among watch manufacturers, Rolex takes pride in emphasizing that it makes one of the most expensive watches you can buy, a clear example of above-market pricing. Manufacturers of national brands of clothing such as Hart Schaffner & Marx and retailers such as Bloomingdale's deliberately set premium prices for their products.

Large department store chains such as JCPenney generally use at-market pricing. These chains often establish the going market price in the minds of their competitors. Similarly, Revlon cosmetics and Arrow brand shirts are generally priced "at market." They also provide a reference price for competitors that use above- and below-market pricing.

In contrast, a number of firms use below-market pricing. Manufacturers of generic products and retailers that offer their own private brands of products ranging from peanut butter to shampoo deliberately set prices for these products about 8 percent to 10 percent below the prices of nationally branded competitive products such as Skippy peanut butter or Vidal Sassoon shampoo.

Using Marketing Dashboards

Are Red Bull Prices Above, At, or Below the Market?

How would you determine whether a firm's retail prices are above, at, or below the market? You might visit retail stores and record what prices retailers are charging for products or brands. However, this laborious activity can be simplified by combining dollar market share and unit volume market share measures to create a "price premium" display on your marketing dashboard.

Your Challenge   Red Bull is the leading energy-drink brand in the United States in terms of dollar market share and unit market share (see the table below). Company marketing executives have research showing that Red Bull has a strong brand equity. What they want to know is whether the brand's price premium resulting from its brand equity has eroded due to heavy price discounting in the convenience store channel. This channel accounts for 60 percent of energy-drink sales.

A price premium is the percentage by which the actual price charged for a specific brand exceeds (or falls short of) a benchmark established for a similar product or basket of products. As such, a price premium shows whether a brand is priced above, at, or below the market. This premium is calculated as follows:

Price premium (%)

$$= \frac{\text{Dollar sales market share for a brand}}{\text{Unit volume market share for a brand}} - 1$$

Your Findings   Using 2010 energy-drink brand market share data for U.S. convenience stores, the Red Bull price premium is 1.152, or 15.2 percent, calculated as follows: (38 percent ÷ 33 percent) −1 = .152. Red Bull's average price is 15.2 percent higher than the average price for energy-drink brands sold in convenience stores. Red Bull's price premium based on 2009 brand market share data was 1.121, or 12.1 percent, calculated as follows: (37 percent ÷ 33 percent) −1 = 12.1. Red Bull's price premium has increased relative to its competitors, notably Monster Energy and Rockstar. The price premiums for Red Bull and these two competitive brands for 2009 and 2010 are displayed in the marketing dashboard shown below.

Your Action   Red Bull has increased its price premium while retaining its unit volume share, which is not only favorable news for the brand but also evidence of price discounting by other brands. Clearly, the company's brand-building effort, reflected in sponsorships and a singular focus on brand attributes valued by consumers, should be continued.

Selected Brand Price Premium Results

Brand	Dollar Sales Market Share		Unit Volume Market Share	
	2010	**2009**	**2010**	**2009**
Red Bull	38%	37%	33%	33%
Monster	18	17	19	18
Rockstar	7	8	8	9
Other brands	37	38	40	40
	100%	100%	100%	100%

Companies use a "price premium" to assess whether their products and brands are above, at, or below the market. An illustration of how the price premium measure is calculated, displayed, and interpreted appears in the Using Marketing Dashboards box.[11]

Loss-Leader Pricing   For a special promotion retail stores deliberately sell a product below its customary price to attract attention to it. The purpose of this *loss-leader pricing* is not to increase sales but to attract customers in hopes they will buy other products as well, particularly the discretionary items with large markups. For example, Best Buy, Target, and Walmart sell CDs at about half of music companies' suggested retail price to attract customers to their stores.[12]

ESTIMATING DEMAND AND REVENUE

 Explain what a demand curve is and the role of revenues in pricing decisions.

Basic to setting a product's price is the extent of customer demand for it. Marketing executives must also translate this estimate of customer demand into estimates of revenues the firm expects to receive.

Estimating Demand

How much will you pay for a frozen cheese pizza you can pop in the oven for a quick dinner while you are studying for a marketing exam? $6? $8? $10? And what are some of the factors affecting this decision? Your preference for pizza compared to other quick-service food? The ease with which you can call Domino's or your local Chinese restaurant for an already-prepared meal delivered to your residence? How much money you have available in your credit card account while you're thinking about the tuition payment that's due next month? All these factors affect demand.

To illustrate the fundamentals of estimating demand, let's assume you are a consultant to the marketing manager at Red Baron® pizza and your job is to start analyzing the demand for its Red Baron frozen cheese pizzas. In the process, you'll have to consider what the demand curve for frozen cheese pizza might look like, how it affects Red Baron's sales revenues, and the price elasticity of demand.

What key factors affect the demand for Red Baron frozen cheese pizzas? Read the text to find out.

demand curve
A graph relating the quantity sold and the price, which shows how many units will be sold at a given price.

The Demand Curve   A **demand curve** is a graph that relates the quantity sold and price, showing the maximum number of units that will be sold at a given price. Based on secondary research you conducted regarding the annual demand for Red Baron frozen cheese pizza, you are able to construct the demand curve D_1 in Figure 11–3A. Note the following relationship: As price falls, more people decide to buy Red Baron frozen cheese pizza, which increases its unit sales. But price is not the complete story when estimating demand. Economists emphasize three other key factors that influence demand for a product:

1. *Consumer tastes.* As we saw in Chapter 3, these depend on many forces such as demographics, culture, and technology. Because consumer tastes can change quickly, up-to-date marketing research is essential to estimate demand. For example, if research by nutritionists concludes that some pizzas are healthier (because they are now gluten-free or vegetarian), demand for them will probably increase.
2. *Price and availability of similar products.* If the price of a competitor's pizza that is a substitute for yours—like Tombstone® pizza—falls, more people will buy it; its demand will rise and the demand for yours will fall. Other low-priced dinners are also substitutes for pizza. For example, if you want something fast so

A: Demand curve under initial conditions

B: Shift the demand curve with more favorable conditions

FIGURE 11–3
Demand curves for Red Baron frozen cheese pizza showing the effect on annual sales (quantity demanded per year) by change in price caused by (A) a movement along the demand curve and (B) a shift of the demand curve.

you can study, you could call Domino's or a local Chinese restaurant and order a meal for home delivery. So, as the price of a substitute falls or its availability increases, the demand for your Red Baron frozen cheese pizza will fall.

3. *Consumer income.* In general, as real consumers' incomes increase (allowing for inflation), demand for a product will also increase. So, if you get a scholarship and have extra cash for discretionary spending, you might eat more Red Baron frozen cheese pizzas and fewer peanut butter and jelly sandwiches to satisfy your appetite.

The first two factors influence what consumers *want* to buy, and the third factor affects what they *can* buy. Along with price, these are often called *demand factors*, or factors that determine consumers' willingness and ability to pay for products and services. As discussed in Chapters 7 and 9, it can be challenging to estimate demand for new products, especially because consumer likes and dislikes are often so difficult to read clearly.

Movement Along versus Shift of a Demand Curve The demand curve D_1 for Red Baron frozen cheese pizzas in Figure 11–3A shows that as its price is lowered from \$8 (point 1) to \$6 (point 2), the quantity sold (demanded) increases from 2 million (Q_1) to 3 million (Q_2) units per year. This is an example of a *movement along a demand curve* and it assumes that other factors (consumer tastes, price and availability of substitutes, and consumers' incomes) remain unchanged.

What if some of these factors do change? For example, if advertising causes more people to want Red Baron frozen cheese pizzas, demand will increase. Now the initial demand curve, D_1 (the blue line in Figure 11–3B), no longer represents the demand. Instead, the new demand curve, D_2 (the red line in Figure 11–3B) represents the new demand for Red Baron frozen cheese pizzas. Economists call this a *shift in the demand curve*—in this case, a shift to the right from D_1 to D_2. This increased demand means that more Red Baron frozen cheese pizzas are wanted for a given price. At a price of \$6 (point 3), the demand is 5 million units per year (Q_3) on D_2 rather than 3 million units per year (Q_2) on D_1.

Price Elasticity of Demand

With a downward-sloping demand curve, marketing managers are especially interested in how sensitive consumer demand and the firm's revenues are to changes in the

CHAPTER 11   Pricing Products and Services

price elasticity of demand
The percentage change in the quantity demanded relative to a percentage change in price.

Price elasticity of demand =

$$E = \frac{\text{Percentage change in quantity demanded}}{\text{Percentage change in price}}$$

product's price. This can be conveniently measured by **price elasticity of demand**, or the percentage change in quantity demanded relative to a percentage change in price. Price elasticity of demand (E) is expressed as follows:

$$\text{Price elasticity of demand (E)} = \frac{\text{Percentage change in quantity demanded}}{\text{Percentage change in price}}$$

Because quantity demanded usually decreases as price increases, price elasticity of demand is usually a negative number. However, for the sake of simplicity and by convention, elasticity figures are shown as positive numbers. Finally, price elasticity of demand assumes two forms discussed here: elastic demand and inelastic demand.

Elastic demand exists when a 1 percent decrease in price produces more than a 1 percent increase in quantity demanded, thereby actually increasing total revenue. This results in a price elasticity that is greater than 1 with elastic demand. In other words, a product with elastic demand is one in which a slight decrease in price results in a relatively large increase in demand or units sold. The reverse is also true; with elastic demand, a slight increase in price results in a relatively large decrease in demand. So marketers may cut price to increase consumer demand, the units sold, and total revenue for a product with elastic demand, depending on what competitors' prices are.

Inelastic demand exists when a 1 percent decrease in price produces less than a 1 percent increase in quantity demanded, thereby actually decreasing total revenue. This results in a price elasticity that is less than 1 with inelastic demand. So a product with inelastic demand means that slight increases or decreases in price will not significantly affect the demand, or units sold, for the product. The concern for marketers is that while lowering price will increase the quantity sold, total revenue will actually fall.

Fundamentals of Estimating Revenue

total revenue
The total money received from the sale of a product; the unit price of a product multiplied by the quantity sold.

While economists may talk about "demand curves," marketing executives are more likely to speak in terms of "revenue generated." Demand curves lead directly to an essential revenue concept critical to pricing decisions: **total revenue**, or the total money received from the sale of a product. Total revenue (TR) equals the unit price (P) times the quantity sold (Q). Using this equation, let's recall our picture frame shop and assume our annual demand has improved so we can set a price of $100 per picture framed and sell 400 pictures per year. So,

$$\begin{aligned} TR &= P \times Q \\ &= \$100 \times 400 \\ &= \$40{,}000 \end{aligned}$$

This combination of price and quantity sold annually will give us a total revenue of $40,000 per year. Is that good? Are you making money, making a profit? Alas, total revenue is only part of the profit equation that we saw earlier:

Total profit = Total revenue − Total cost

The next section covers the other part of the profit equation: cost.

learning review

11-3. What three key factors are necessary when estimating consumer demand?

11-4. Price elasticity of demand is _____.

DETERMINING COST, VOLUME, AND PROFIT RELATIONSHIPS

 LO 11-3 Explain the role of costs in pricing decisions and describe how combinations of price, fixed cost, and unit variable cost affect a firm's break-even point.

total cost
The total expense incurred by a firm in producing and marketing a product; total cost is the sum of fixed costs and variable costs.

break-even analysis
A technique that examines the relationship between total revenue and total cost to determine profitability at different levels of output.

While revenues are the moneys received by the firm from selling its products or services to customers, costs or expenses are the monies the firm pays out to its employees and suppliers. Marketing managers often use break-even analysis to relate revenues and costs, topics covered in this section.

The Importance of Controlling Costs

Understanding the role and behavior of costs is critical for all marketing decisions, particularly pricing decisions. Four cost concepts are important in pricing decisions: *total cost, fixed cost, variable cost,* and *unit variable cost* (see Figure 11–4).

Many firms go bankrupt because their costs get out of control, causing their **total costs**—the sum of their fixed costs and variable costs—to exceed their total revenues over an extended period of time. So firms constantly try to control their fixed costs, like insurance and executive salaries, and reduce the variable costs in their manufactured items by having production done outside the United States. This is why sophisticated marketing managers make pricing decisions that balance both revenues and costs.

Break-Even Analysis

Break-even analysis is a technique that analyzes the relationship between total revenue and total cost to determine profitability at various levels of output. Figure 11–5 on the next page provides the data needed to conduct a break-even analysis. The *break-even point (BEP)* is the quantity at which total revenue and total cost are equal. Profit then comes from all units sold beyond the BEP. In terms of the definitions in Figure 11–4:

$$BEP_{Quantity} = \frac{\text{Fixed cost}}{\text{Unit price} - \text{Unit variable cost}} = \frac{FC}{P - UVC}$$

Calculating a Break-Even Point Suppose you are the owner of a picture frame shop and you wish to identify how many pictures you must sell to cover your fixed cost at a given price. Let's assume demand for your pictures is strong, so the average price customers are willing to pay for each picture is $120. Also, suppose your fixed cost (FC) is $32,000 (real estate taxes, interest on a bank loan, etc.) and unit variable cost (UVC) for a picture is now $40 (labor, glass, frame, and matting). Your break-even quantity (BEP) is 400 pictures, as follows:

$$BEP_{Quantity} = \frac{\$32,000}{\$120 - \$40}$$

$$BEP_{Quantity} = 400 \text{ pictures}$$

FIGURE 11–4
Fundamental concepts about "costs," which are the monies the firm pays out to its employees and suppliers.

Total cost (TC) is the total expense incurred by a firm in producing and marketing a product. Total cost is the sum of fixed cost and variable cost.

Fixed cost (FC) is the sum of the expenses of the firm that are stable and do not change with the quantity of a product that is produced and sold. Examples of fixed costs are rent on the building, executive salaries, and insurance.

Variable cost (VC) is the sum of the expenses of the firm that vary directly with the quantity of a product that is produced and sold. For example, as the quantity sold doubles, the variable cost doubles. Examples are the direct labor and direct materials used in producing the product and the sales commissions that are tied directly to the quantity sold. As mentioned above,

TC = FC + VC

Unit variable cost (UVC) is expressed on a per unit basis, or $UVC = \dfrac{VC}{Q}$

Quantity of Pictures Sold (Q)	Price per Picture (P)	Total Revenue (TR = P × Q)	Unit Variable Cost (UVC)	Total Variable Cost (VC = UVC × Q)	Fixed Cost (FC)	Total Cost (TC = FC + VC)	Profit (TR − TC)
0	$120	$0	$40	$0	$32,000	$32,000	($32,000)
400	$120	$48,000	$40	$16,000	$32,000	$48,000	$0
800	$120	$96,000	$40	$32,000	$32,000	$64,000	$32,000
1,200	$120	$144,000	$40	$48,000	$32,000	$80,000	$64,000
1,600	$120	$192,000	$40	$64,000	$32,000	$96,000	$96,000
2,000	$120	$240,000	$40	$80,000	$32,000	$112,000	$128,000

FIGURE 11–5
Calculating a break-even point for the picture frame shop in the text example shows that its profit starts at 400 pictures sold per year.

Developing a Break-Even Chart   The row shaded in orange in Figure 11–5 shows that your break-even quantity at a price of $120 per picture is 400 pictures. At less than 400 pictures, your picture frame shop incurs a loss, and at more than 400 pictures, it makes a profit. Figure 11–6 depicts a graphic presentation of the break-even analysis, called a *break-even chart*. It shows that total revenue (line DE) and total cost (line AC) intersect and are equal at a quantity of 400 pictures sold, which is the break-even point (F) at which profit is exactly $0. You want to do better? If your picture frame shop could increase the quantity sold annually to 2,000 pictures, the graph in Figure 11–6 shows you can earn an annual profit of $128,000 ($240,000 − $112,000 or line EC), shown by the row shaded in green in Figure 11–5.

FIGURE 11–6
This break-even chart for a picture frame shop shows the break-even point at 400 pictures and the annual profit at 2,000 pictures.

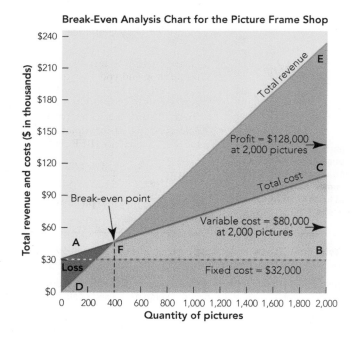

Break-Even Analysis Chart for the Picture Frame Shop

learning review

11-5. What is the difference between fixed costs and variable costs?

11-6. What is a break-even point?

PRICING OBJECTIVES AND CONSTRAINTS

LO 11-4 Recognize the objectives a firm has in setting prices and the constraints that restrict the range of prices a firm can charge.

pricing objectives
Involve specifying the role of price in an organization's marketing and strategic plans.

With such a variety of alternative pricing strategies available, a marketing manager must consider the pricing objectives and constraints that will narrow the range of choices. While pricing objectives frequently reflect corporate goals, pricing constraints often relate to conditions existing in the marketplace.

Identifying Pricing Objectives

Pricing objectives involve specifying the role of price in an organization's marketing and strategic plans. To the extent possible, these pricing objectives are carried to lower levels in the organization, such as in setting objectives for marketing managers responsible for an individual brand. These objectives may change depending on the financial position of the company as a whole, the success of its products, or the segments in which it is doing business. H. J. Heinz, for example, has specific pricing objectives for its Heinz Ketchup brand that vary by country.

Profit   Three different objectives relate to a firm's profit, which is often measured in terms of return on investment (ROI) or return on assets (ROA). These objectives have different implications for pricing strategy. One objective is *managing for long-run profits*, in which companies—such as many Japanese car or HDTV manufacturers—give up immediate profit by developing quality products to penetrate competitive markets over the long term. Products are priced relatively low compared to their cost to develop, but the firm expects to make greater profits later because of its high market share.

A *maximizing current profit* objective, such as for a quarter or year, is common in many firms because the targets can be set and performance measured quickly. American firms are sometimes criticized for this short-run orientation. A *target return* objective occurs when a firm sets a profit goal (such as 20 percent for pretax ROI), usually determined by its board of directors.

Sales   Given that a firm's profit is high enough for it to remain in business, an objective may be to increase sales revenue, which can lead to increases in market share and profit. Objectives related to dollar sales revenue or unit sales have the advantage of being translated easily into meaningful targets for marketing managers responsible for a product line or brand. However, while cutting the price on one product in a firm's line may increase its sales revenue, it may also reduce the sales revenue of related products.

Market Share   *Market share* is the ratio of the firm's sales revenues or unit sales to those of the industry (competitors plus the firm itself). Companies often pursue a market share objective when industry sales are relatively flat or declining. In the late 1990s, Boeing cut prices drastically to try to maintain its 60 percent share of the commercial airline market to compete with Airbus. As a result, it encountered huge losses. Although increased market share is a primary goal of some firms, others see it as a means to other ends: increasing sales and profits.

Unit Volume   Many firms use *unit volume*, the quantity produced or sold, as a pricing objective. These firms often sell multiple products at very different prices and need to match the unit volume demanded by customers with price and production capacity. Using unit volume as an objective can be counterproductive if a volume objective is achieved, say, by drastic price cutting that drives down profit.

Survival   In some instances, profits, sales, and market share are less important objectives of the firm than mere survival. Specialty-toy retailers increasingly are facing survival problems because they can't match the price cuts offered by big discount retailers like Walmart and Target. This was the dilemma faced by FAO Schwartz, which filed for bankruptcy and was subsequently bought by Toys "Я" Us.

Social Responsibility   A firm may forgo higher profit on sales and follow a pricing objective that recognizes its obligations to customers and society in general. For example, Gerber supplies a specially formulated product free of charge to children who cannot tolerate foods containing cow's milk.

Identifying Pricing Constraints

Factors that limit the range of prices a firm may set are **pricing constraints**. Consumer demand for the product clearly affects the price that can be charged. Other constraints on price vary from factors within the organization to competitive factors outside the organization.

Demand for the Product Class, Product, and Brand   The number of potential buyers for a product class (cars), product (sports cars), and brand (Bugatti Veyron) clearly affects the price a seller can charge. Generally, the greater the demand for a product, or brand, the higher the price that can be set. For example, the New York Mets set different ticket prices for their games based on the appeal of their opponent—prices are higher when they play the New York Yankees and lower when they play the Pittsburgh Pirates.[13]

Newness of the Product: Stage in the Product Life Cycle   The newer a product and the earlier it is in its life cycle, the higher is the price that can usually be charged. Willing to spend $9,999 for an LG 55-inch 3D OLED HD Smart TV? The high initial price is possible because of patents and limited competition early in its product life cycle. By the time you read this, the price probably will be much lower.

What is the cost of producing and marketing designer denim jeans? You might be surprised at how much a specialty retailer makes.

Cost of Producing and Marketing the Product   Another profit consideration for marketers is to ensure that firms in their channels of distribution make an adequate profit. Without profits for channel members, a marketer is cut off from its customers. Of the $200 a customer spends for a pair of designer denim jeans, 50

percent of each dollar spent by a customer goes to a specialty retailer to cover its costs and profit. The other 50 percent goes to the marketer (34 percent) and manufacturers and suppliers (16 percent).[14] So, the next time you buy a $200 pair of designer denim jeans, remember that $100 goes to the specialty retailer that stocked, displayed, and sold the jeans to you.

Competitors' Prices   When Apple introduced its iPad in 2010, it was not only unique and in the introductory stage of its product life cycle but also the first commercially successful tablet device sold. As a result, Apple had great latitude in setting a price. Now, with a wide range of competition in tablets from Samsung's Galaxy Note, Lenovo's Idea Tab, and others, Apple's pricing latitude is less broad.

Legal and Ethical Considerations   Setting a final price is clearly a complex process. The task is further complicated by legal and ethical issues. Four pricing practices that have received special scrutiny are described below:

- *Price fixing.* A conspiracy among firms to set prices for a product is termed price fixing. Price fixing is illegal under the Sherman Act. When two or more competitors collude to explicitly or implicitly set prices, this practice is called *horizontal price fixing*. For example, six foreign vitamin companies recently pled guilty to price fixing in the human and animal vitamin industry and paid the largest fine in U.S. history: $335 million.[15] *Vertical price fixing* involves controlling agreements between independent buyers and sellers (a manufacturer and a retailer) whereby sellers are required to not sell products below a minimum retail price.

- *Price discrimination.* The Clayton Act as amended by the Robinson-Patman Act prohibits price discrimination—the practice of charging different prices to different buyers for goods of like grade and quality. However, not all price differences are illegal; only those that substantially lessen competition or create a monopoly are deemed unlawful.

- *Deceptive pricing.* Price deals that mislead consumers fall into the category of deceptive pricing. Deceptive pricing is outlawed by the Federal Trade Commission. *Bait and switch* is an example of deceptive pricing. This occurs when a firm offers a very low price on a product (the bait) to attract customers to a store. Once in the store, the customer is persuaded to purchase a higher-priced item (the switch) using a variety of tricks, including (1) degrading the promoted item and (2) not having the promised item in stock or refusing to take orders for it.

- *Predatory pricing.* Predatory pricing is the practice of charging a very low price for a product with the intent of driving competitors out of business. Once competitors have been driven out, the firm raises its prices. Proving the presence of this practice has been difficult and expensive because it must be shown that the predator explicitly attempted to destroy a competitor and the predatory price was below the defendant's average cost.

---

learning review

11-7. What is the difference between pricing objectives and pricing constraints?

11-8. Explain what bait and switch is and why it is an example of deceptive pricing.

SETTING A FINAL PRICE

LO 11-5 Describe the steps taken in setting a final price.

The final price set by the marketing manager serves many functions. It must be high enough to cover the cost of providing the product or service *and* meet the objectives of the company. Yet it must be low enough that customers are willing to pay it. But not too low, or customers may think they're purchasing an inferior product. Dizzy yet? Setting price is one of the most difficult tasks the marketing manager faces, but three generalized steps are useful to follow.

Step 1: Select an Approximate Price Level

Before setting a final price, the marketing manager must understand the market environment, the features and customer benefits of the particular product, and the goals of the firm. A balance must be struck between factors that might drive a price higher (such as a profit-oriented approach) and other forces (such as increased competition from substitutes) that may drive a price down.

Marketing managers consider pricing objectives and constraints first, then choose among the general pricing approaches—demand-, cost-, profit-, or competition-oriented—to arrive at an approximate price level. This price is then analyzed in terms of cost, volume, and profit relationships. Break-even analyses may be run at this point, and finally, if this approximate price level "works," it is time to take the next step: setting a specific list or quoted price.

Making Responsible Decisions

Flexible Pricing—Is There Discrimination in Bargaining for a New Car?

What do 60 percent of prospective buyers dread when looking for a new car? That's right! They dread negotiating the price. Price bargaining demonstrates shortcomings of flexible pricing when purchasing a new car: the potential for race and gender price discrimination.

A National Bureau of Economic Research study of 750,000 car purchases indicated that African Americans, Hispanics, and women, on average, paid roughly $423, $483, and $105 more, respectively, for a new car in the $21,000 range than the typical purchaser. Smaller price premiums remained after adjusting for income, education, and other factors that may affect price negotiations.

Research shows that searching automotive and car dealer websites before buying a new car reduces price premiums paid by African Americans, Hispanics, and women.

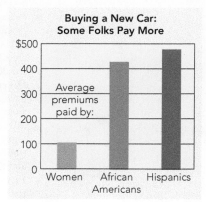

Buying a New Car: Some Folks Pay More

Step 2: Set the List or Quoted Price

Video 11-3
CarMax Ad
kerin.tv/cr6e/v11-3

A seller must decide whether to follow a one-price or flexible-price policy.

One-Price Policy   A *one-price policy*, also called *fixed pricing,* is setting one price for all buyers of a product or service. CarMax uses this approach in its stores and features a "no haggle, one price" price for cars. Some retailers have married this policy with a below-market approach. Dollar Value Stores and 99¢ Only Stores sell everything in their stores for $1 or less. Family Dollar Stores sell everything for $2.

Flexible-Price Policy   In contrast, a *flexible-price policy* involves setting different prices for products and services depending on individual buyers and purchase situations in light of demand, cost, and competitive factors. Dell Inc. uses flexible pricing as it continually adjusts prices in response to changes in its own costs, competitive pressures, and demand from its various personal computer segments (home, small business, corporate, etc.). "Our flexibility allows us to be [priced] different even within a day," says a Dell spokesperson.[16]

Flexible pricing is not without its critics because of its discriminatory potential. For example, car dealers have traditionally used flexible pricing on the basis of buyer–seller negotiations to agree on a final sales price. However, flexible pricing may result in discriminatory practices in car buying, as detailed in the Making Responsible Decisions box.[17]

Step 3: Make Special Adjustments to the List or Quoted Price

When you pay $1.00 for a bag of M&Ms in a vending machine or receive a quoted price of $50,000 from a contractor to renovate a kitchen, the pricing sequence ends with the last step just described: setting the list or quoted price. But when you are a manufacturer of M&M candies and sell your product to dozens or hundreds of wholesalers and retailers in your channel of distribution, you may need to make a variety of special adjustments to the list or quoted price. Wholesalers also must adjust the list or quoted prices they set for retailers. Two adjustments to the list or quoted price are (1) discounts and (2) allowances.

Manufacturers provide a variety of discounts to assist channel members, such as clothing retailers, offer "Buy One, Get One Free" promotions.

Discounts   *Discounts* are reductions from list price that a seller gives a buyer as a reward for some activity of the buyer that is favorable to the seller. Four kinds of discounts are especially important in marketing strategy: (1) quantity, (2) seasonal, (3) trade (functional), and (4) cash.

- *Quantity discounts.* To encourage customers to buy larger quantities of a product, firms at all levels in the channel of distribution offer quantity discounts, which are reductions in unit costs for a larger order. For example, an instant photocopying service might set a price of 10 cents a copy for 1 to 24 copies, 9 cents a copy for 25 to 99 copies, and 8 cents a copy for 100 copies or more.
- *Seasonal discounts.* To encourage buyers to stock inventory earlier than their normal demand would require, manufacturers often use seasonal discounts. A firm such as Toro that manufactures lawn mowers and snow throwers offers seasonal discounts to encourage wholesalers and retailers to stock up on lawn mowers in January and February and snow throwers in July and August—five or six months before the seasonal demand by ultimate consumers.
- *Trade (functional) discounts.* To reward wholesalers and retailers for marketing functions they will perform in the future, a manufacturer often gives trade, or functional, discounts. These reductions off the list or base price are offered to resellers in the channel of distribution on the basis of (1) where they are in the channel and (2) the marketing activities they are expected to perform in the future.
- *Cash discounts.* To encourage retailers to pay their bills quickly, manufacturers offer them cash discounts. Cash discounts are typically expressed as a percentage off the list price.

Allowances   Allowances—like discounts—are reductions from list or quoted prices to buyers for performing some activity.

- *Trade-in allowances.* A new-car dealer can offer a substantial reduction in the list price of that new Toyota Camry by offering you a trade-in allowance of $2,500 for your Chevrolet. A trade-in allowance is a price reduction given when a used product is part of the payment on a new product. Trade-ins are an effective way to lower the price a buyer has to pay without formally reducing the list price.
- *Promotional allowances.* Sellers in the channel of distribution can qualify for promotional allowances for undertaking certain advertising or selling activities to promote a product. Various types of allowances include an actual cash payment or an extra amount of "free goods" (as with a free case of pizzas to a retailer for every dozen cases purchased). Frequently, a portion of these savings is passed on to the consumer by retailers.

Some companies, such as Procter & Gamble, have chosen to reduce promotional allowances for retailers by using everyday low pricing. *Everyday low pricing*

(EDLP) is the practice of replacing promotional allowances with lower manufacturer list prices. EDLP promises to reduce the average price to consumers while minimizing promotional allowances that cost manufacturers billions of dollars every year.

learning review

11-9. What are the three steps in setting a final price?

11-10. What is the purpose of (*a*) quantity discounts and (*b*) promotional allowances?

LEARNING OBJECTIVES REVIEW

LO 11-1 *Describe the nature and importance of pricing and the approaches used to select an approximate price level.*

Price is the money or other considerations (such as barter) exchanged for the ownership or use of a product or service. Although price typically involves money, the amount exchanged is often different from the list or quoted price because of incentives (rebates, discounts, etc.), allowances (trade), and extra fees (finance charges, surcharges, etc.).

Demand, cost, profit, and competition influence the initial consideration of the approximate price level for a product or service. Demand-oriented pricing approaches stress consumer demand and revenue implications of pricing and include seven types: skimming, penetration, prestige, odd-even, target, bundle, and yield management. Cost-oriented pricing approaches emphasize the cost aspects of pricing and include two types: standard markup and cost-plus pricing. Profit-oriented pricing approaches focus on a balance between revenues and costs to set a price and include three types: target profit, target return-on-sales, and target return-on-investment pricing. And finally, competition-oriented pricing approaches stress what competitors or the marketplace are doing and include three types: customary; above-, at-, or below-market; and loss-leader pricing.

LO 11-2 *Explain what a demand curve is and the role of revenues in pricing decisions.*

A demand curve is a graph relating the quantity sold and price, which shows the maximum number of units that will be sold at a given price. Three demand factors affect price: (*a*) consumer tastes, (*b*) price and availability of substitute products, and (*c*) consumer income. These demand factors determine consumers' willingness and ability to pay for products and services. Assuming these demand factors remain unchanged, if the price of a product is lowered or raised, then the quantity demanded for it will increase or decrease, respectively. The demand curve relates to a firm's total revenue, which is the total money received from the sale of a product, or the price of one unit times the quantity of units sold.

LO 11-3 *Explain the role of costs in pricing decisions and describe how combinations of price, fixed cost, and unit variable cost affect a firm's break-even point.*

Four important costs impact a firm's pricing decisions: (*a*) total cost, or total expenses, the sum of the fixed costs and variable costs incurred by a firm in producing and marketing a product; (*b*) fixed cost, the sum of the expenses of the firm that are stable and do not change with the quantity of a product that is produced and sold; (*c*) variable cost, the sum of the expenses of the firm that vary directly with the quantity of a product that is produced and sold; and (*d*) unit variable cost, the variable cost expressed on a per unit basis.

Break-even analysis is a technique that analyzes the relationship between total revenue and total cost to determine profitability at various levels of output. The break-even point is the quantity at which total revenue and total cost are equal. Assuming no change in price, if the costs of a firm's product increase due to higher fixed costs (manufacturing or advertising) or variable costs (direct labor or materials), then its break-even point will be higher. And if total cost is unchanged, an increase in price will reduce the break-even point.

LO 11-4 *Recognize the objectives a firm has in setting prices and the constraints that restrict the range of prices a firm can charge.*

Pricing objectives specify the role of price in a firm's marketing strategy and may include profit, sales revenue, market share, unit volume, survival, or some socially responsible price level. Pricing constraints that restrict a firm's pricing flexibility include demand, product newness, production and marketing costs, prices of competitive substitutes, and legal and ethical considerations.

LO 11-5 *Describe the steps taken in setting a final price.*

Three common steps marketing managers often use in setting a final price are (1) select an approximate price level as a starting point; (2) set the list or quoted price, choosing between a one-price policy or a flexible-price policy; and (3) modify the list or quoted price by considering discounts and allowances.

LEARNING REVIEW ANSWERS

11-1 Value is _____.
Answer: the ratio of perceived benefits to price; or Value = (Perceived benefits ÷ Price)

11-2 What circumstances in pricing a new product might support skimming or penetration pricing?
Answer: Skimming pricing is an effective strategy when: (1) enough prospective customers are willing to buy the product immediately at the high initial price to make these sales profitable; (2) the high initial price will not attract competitors; (3) lowering the price has only a minor effect on increasing the sales volume and reducing the unit costs; and (4) customers interpret the high price as signifying high quality. These four conditions are most likely to exist when the new product is protected by patents or copyrights or its uniqueness is understood and valued by consumers. The conditions favoring penetration pricing are the reverse of those supporting skimming pricing: (1) many segments of the market are price sensitive; (2) a low initial price discourages competitors from entering the market; and (3) unit production and marketing costs fall dramatically as production volumes increase. A firm using penetration pricing may (1) maintain the initial price for a time to gain profit lost from its low introductory level or (2) lower the price further, counting on the new volume to generate the necessary profit.

11-3 What three key factors are necessary when estimating consumer demand?
Answer: consumer tastes, price and availability of similar products, and consumer income.

11-4 Price elasticity of demand is _____.
Answer: the percentage change in the quantity demanded relative to a percentage change in price.

11-5 What is the difference between fixed costs and variable costs?

Answer: Fixed cost is the sum of the expenses of the firm that are stable and do not change with the quantity of a product that is produced and sold. Variable cost is the sum of the expenses of the firm that vary directly with the quantity of a product that is produced and sold.

11-6 What is a break-even point?
Answer: A break-even point (BEP) is the quantity at which total revenue and total cost are equal.

11-7 What is the difference between pricing objectives and pricing constraints?
Answer: Pricing objectives specify the role of price in an organization's marketing and strategic plans. Pricing constraints are factors that limit the range of prices a firm may set.

11-8 Explain what bait and switch is and why it is an example of deceptive pricing.
Answer: Bait and switch is the practice of offering a very low price on a product (the bait) to attract customers to a store. Once in the store, the customer is persuaded to purchase a higher-priced item (the switch) using a variety of tricks, including (1) degrading the promoted item and (2) not having the promised item in stock or refusing to take orders for it.

11-9 What are the three steps in setting a final price?
Answer: They are: (1) select an appropriate price level; (2) set the list or quoted price; and (3) make special adjustments to the list or quoted price.

11-10 What is the purpose of (a) quantity discounts and (b) promotional allowances?
Answer: Quantity discounts are used to encourage customers to buy larger quantities of a product. Promotional allowances are used to encourage sellers in the channel of distribution to undertake certain advertising or selling activities to promote a product.

FOCUSING ON KEY TERMS

break-even analysis p. 285
demand curve p. 282
price p. 274
price elasticity of demand p. 284

pricing constraints p. 288
pricing objectives p. 287
profit equation p. 276
total cost p. 285

total revenue p. 284
value p. 275

APPLYING MARKETING KNOWLEDGE

1 How would the price equation apply to the purchase price of (a) gasoline, (b) an airline ticket, and (c) a checking account?

2 Under what conditions would a camera manufacturer adopt a skimming price approach for a new product? A penetration approach?

3 What are some similarities and differences between skimming pricing, prestige pricing, and above-market pricing?

4 Touché Toiletries Inc. has developed an addition to its Lizardman Cologne line tentatively branded Ode d'Toade Cologne. Unit variable costs are 45 cents for a 3-ounce bottle, and heavy advertising expenditures in the first year would result in total fixed costs of $900,000. Ode d'Toade Cologne is priced at $7.50 for a 3-ounce bottle. How many bottles of Ode d'Toade must be sold to break even?

5 What would be your response to the statement, "Profit maximization is the only legitimate pricing objective for the firm"?

BUILDING YOUR MARKETING PLAN

In starting to set a final price:

1 List two pricing objectives and three pricing constraints.

2 Think about your customers and competitors and set three possible prices.

3 Assume a fixed cost and unit variable cost and (*a*) calculate the break-even points and (*b*) plot a break-even chart for the three prices specified in step 2.

VIDEO CASE 11   Carmex (B): Setting the Price of the Number One Lip Balm

Video 11-4
Carmex (B)
Video Case
kerin.tv/cr6e/v11-4

"Carmex is dedicated to providing consumers with superior lip balm formulas —that heal, sooth and protect—while ensuring lips remain healthy and hydrated," exclaims Paul Woelbing, president of Carma Laboratories, Inc.

It's an ambitious mission, but the company has been extraordinarily successful with its 75-year-old-product. Woelbing and his management team at Carma Laboratories can attribute their success to a strong brand, a loyal customer base, a growing product line, financial strength, and an exceptional talent for setting prices that achieve company objectives and still provide value to customers. Even during the recession and periods of slow growth the company has been successful. "In a rough economy, shopping habits change," Woelbing says. "People buy smaller quantities more frequently, but they still need personal care products."

THE COMPANY

Carmex was created by Paul's grandfather, Alfred Woelbing, in his kitchen in Wauwatosa, Wisconsin, in 1937. Alfred had an entrepreneurial spirit and experimented with ingredients such as camphor, menthol, phenol, lanolin, salicylic acid, and cocoa seed butter to

make the new product. The name didn't have any meaning other than Alfred liked the sound of "Carma" and "ex" was a popular suffix for many brands at the time. He packaged the balm in small glass jars and sold the product for 25 cents from the trunk of his car by making personal sales calls to pharmacies in Wisconsin, Illinois, and Indiana. From the beginning, price and value were important to the product's success. If pharmacies weren't initially interested in Carmex, Alfred would leave a dozen jars for free. The samples would sell quickly and soon the pharmacies would place orders for more!

As the company grew, Alfred's son, Don, joined the business and helped add new products to the company's offerings. For example, in the 1980s Carmex made its first significant packaging change by also offering the balm in squeezable tubes. In the 1990s Carmex became available in stick form, which had been used by two of Carma's major competitors–ChapStick and Blistex. In the 2000s Carmex became available in mint, cherry, and strawberry flavors (see Chapter 8 for a description of the research techniques used to identify new flavors). The company also expanded into larger manufacturing facilities, added a new distribution center, and hired its first marketing experts.

Today, the company is led by Alfred's grandsons, Paul and Eric Woelbing, who continue to manage the company to new levels of success. They appeared on *The Oprah Winfrey Show* to announce the sale of their billionth jar of Carmex. The governor of Wisconsin declared a Carmex commemoration day to celebrate its 75th anniversary. NBA all-star LeBron James became a promotional partner. In addition, *Pharmacy Times* magazine recently named Carmex the number one pharmacist-recommended brand of lip balm for the 15th consecutive year. "We are honored to receive this unprecedented acknowledgement," said Woelbing.

Industry observers estimate that Carma Labs holds approximately 10 percent of the lip balm market. The company distributes its products through major drug, food, and mass merchant retailers, convenience stores, and online in more than 25 countries around the world. The company's most recent products—Carmex Healing Cream and Carmex Hydrating Lotion—represent a significant step from lip care to skin care. The expanded product line, multichannel distribution, growing volume, international trade, and direct competition make pricing decisions even more important today than when Alfred started the business many years ago.

SETTING PRICES OF CARMEX PRODUCTS

"There are many factors that go into what results in the retail price in the store," explains Kirk Hodgdon of Bolin Marketing. As one of the marketing experts who helps Carma Labs with advertising, marketing research, and pricing decisions, Hodgdon uses information about consumer demand, production and material costs, profit goals, and competition to help Woelbing and Carmex retailers arrive at specific prices. The many factors often overlap and lead to different prices for different products, channels, and target markets. "It's a challenge!" says Hodgdon.

Consumers' tastes and preferences, for example, influence the price of Carmex products. Bolin director of marketing, Alisa Allen, explains: "Consumers will tell you that they love Carmex because it's a great value. That doesn't necessarily mean that it's the absolute lowest price. It means that it does so much; they pay a dollar and they get all kinds of benefits from the product above and beyond what they would expect." A single jar of original formula Carmex may sell for $0.99 at mass retailers such as Walmart and Target, and between $1.59 and $1.79 in drug and food retailers such as Walgreens and Kroger. These prices are a good indication of how important it is to understand consumers when setting prices. "There are magic price points for consumers," says Allen, "Any time you can drop a penny off, the consumer responds to that price."

Carmex has also introduced a premium lip balm product, Carmex Moisture Plus, at a retail price between $2.49 and $2.99. Moisture Plus is a lip balm that is packaged in a sleek silver tube, offers a slant tip like lipstick, and is targeted toward women. The formula offers women a satin gloss shine and includes vitamin E and aloe for richer moisturization. The upscale package and additional product benefits help Carmex Moisture Plus command a higher price than the traditional Carmex jar and tube.

The cost of the ingredients that make up the Carmex lip balm formulas, the packaging, the manufacturing equipment, and the staffing are also factored into the price of the products. Volumes are a key driver of the cost of packaging and ingredients. For example, Carmex purchases up to 12 million yellow tubes each year for the traditional product, and 2 million sticks each year for the newer Moisture Plus product. The difference in quantities leads to a lower price for the traditional yellow tubes. Similarly, ingredient suppliers, label suppliers, and box suppliers all provide discounts for larger quantities. It is also more efficient for Carmex's manufacturing facility to make a large batch of traditional formula than it is to make a small batch of Moisture Plus. Carmex has also reduced its costs with efforts such as its new environmentally-friendly Carmex jar which holds the same amount of lip balm but uses 20 percent less plastic, eliminating 35 tons of raw material costs and the related shipping costs!

Carmex also considers retailer margins when it sets its prices. According to Allen, "We typically sell our product to two types of retailers." There are Everyday Low Price (EDLP) retailers such as Walmart, and High-Low retailers such as Walgreens. EDLP retailers offer consumers the lowest price every day without discounting through promotions. High-Low retailers charge consumers a higher price, but they occasionally discount the product through special promotions which Carmex often supports with "marketing discretionary funds." Carmex typically offers its products at different prices to EDLP and High-Low retailers to allow each retailer to achieve its profit margin goals and to account for Carmex's promotion expenditures. When the additional expenditures are considered, however, the cost to both types of retailer is similar.

Finally, Carmex considers competitors' prices when setting its prices. Burt's Bees, Chapstick, Blistex and many other brands offer lip balm products and consumers often compare their prices to the price of Carmex. "We have found through research that it is extremely important that the price gap is not too great," explains Allen. "If that gap becomes too wide consumers will leave the Carmex brand and purchase a competitor's product." When Carmex was preparing to launch its premium Moisture Plus product it conducted a thorough analysis of similar products to ensure that Moisture Plus was in an acceptable price range.

CARMEX IN THE FUTURE

The original, and now legendary, Carmex formula and packaging will continue into the future with occasional changes to its pricing practices. New products, however, are on the horizon and likely to challenge the perceptions of the traditional products and prices in the Carmex line. Carmex Moisture Plus products, for example, will be offered in limited edition designs that ask consumers "Which personality are you?" Paul Woelbing explains the new approach:

> Lip care is an important component of a daily beauty regimen and consumers need a product they can rely on that protects and serves as an important foundation. The goal of the new Carmex Moisture Plus line is to offer our consumers a hard-working lip balm line that represents and reflects their unique style.

Some of the new styles include: *Chic* in houndstooth, *Fab* in a groovy retro look, *Adventurous* in a leopard print, and *Whimsical* in an art deco design.

"We are so excited about the future of Carmex," says Hodgdon. "We are planning new products, we have new plans for retailers, and the future is nothing but bright!"

Questions

1 Which of the four approaches to setting a price does Carmex use for its products? Should one approach be used exclusively?

2 Why do many Carmex product prices end in 9? What type of pricing is this called? What should happen to demand when this approach is used?

3 Should cost be a factor in Carmex's prices? What do you think is a reasonable markup for Carmex and for its retailers?

4 What is the difference between an EDLP retailer and a High-Low retailer? Why does Carmex charge them different prices?

5 Conduct an online search of lip balm products and compare the price of a Carmex product with three similar products from competitors. How do you think the competitors are setting their prices?

Chapter Notes

1. "Vizio Wins Sales and Service Awards," *Orange County Register,* March 18, 2014, p. 8; "Vizio Takes Home Entertainment Beyond TV," hdtvmagazine.com, downloaded, January 2012; "Vizio Extends Battle Plan," *The Wall Street Journal,* January 3, 2011, p. B3; "How Vizio Beat Sony in High-Def TV," businessweek.com, April 22, 2010; and "The VIZIO Story," vizio.com, downloaded March 10, 2014.

2. Kirby Garlitos, "2014 Bugatti SuperVeyron," *TopSpeed,* November 19, 2012. See http://www.topspeed.com/cars/bugatti/2014-bugatti-superveyron-ar138038.html; "Premiere of the Bugatti Grand Sport Vitesse at the Qatar Motor Show 2013," Bugatti press release, January 28, 2013.

3. Numerous studies have examined the price-quality-value relationship. See, for example, Jacob Jacoby and Jerry C. Olsen, eds., *Perceived Quality* (Lexington, MA: Lexington Books, 1985); William D. Dodds, Kent B. Monroe, and Dhruv Grewal, "Effects of Price, Brand, and Store Information on Buyers' Product Evaluations," *Journal of Marketing Research,* August 1991, pp. 307–19; and Roger A. Kerin, Ambuj Jain, and Daniel Howard, "Store Shopping Experience and Consumer Price-Quality-Value Perceptions," *Journal of Retailing,*

Winter 1992, pp. 235–45. For a thorough review of the price-quality-value relationship, see Valerie A. Zeithaml, "Consumer Perceptions of Price, Quality, and Value," *Journal of Marketing,* July 1988, pp. 2–22.

4. Roger A. Kerin and Robert A. Peterson, "Haverwood Furniture, Inc. (A)," *Strategic Marketing Problems: Cases and Comments,* 12th ed. (Upper Saddle River, NJ: Prentice Hall, 2013), pp. 294–306.

5. The conditions favoring skimming versus penetration pricing are described in Kent B. Monroe, *Pricing: Making Profitable Decisions,* 3rd ed. (New York: McGraw-Hill/Irwin, 2003).

6. Jean-Noel Kapferer, *The New Strategic Brand Management: Advanced Insights and Strategic Thinking,* 5th ed. (London: Kogan Page Ltd, 2012).

7. "Premium AA Alkaline Batteries," *Consumer Reports,* March 21, 2002, p. 54; Kemp Powers, "Assault and Batteries," *Forbes,* September 4, 2000, pp. 54, 56; and "Razor Burn at Gillette," *BusinessWeek,* June 18, 2001, p. 37.

8. Thomas T. Nagle, John E. Hogan, and Joseph Zale, *The Strategy and Tactics of Pricing,* 5th ed. (Englewood Cliffs, NJ: Prentice Hall, 2011).

9. Robert J. Dolan and Hermann Simon, *Power Pricing: How Managing Price Transforms the Bottom Line* (New York: Free Press, 1996), p. 249; and Scott McCartney, "You Paid What for That Flight?" *The Wall Street Journal,* August 26, 2010, pp. D1, D2.

10. "What Popcorn Prices Mean for Movies," *Advertising Age,* May 19, 2008, p. 4.

11. "A New Beverage Attitude," *Convenience Store/Petroleum News,* May 2010, pp. 110–12.

12. "Is the Music Store Over?" *Business 2.0,* March 2004, pp. 115–19.

13. Ken Belson, "Mets Going for the Gold on Tickets for More Games," *The New York Times,* April 8, 2009, p. B13.

14. Christina Binkley, "How Can Jeans Cost $300?" *The Wall Street Journal,* July 7, 2011, pp. D1, D2.

15. "Six Vitamin Firms Agree to Settle Price-Fixing Suit," *The Wall Street Journal,* October 11, 2000, p. B10.

16. "How Dell Fine-Tunes Its PC Pricing to Gain Edge in a Slow Market," *The Wall Street Journal,* June 8, 2001, pp. A1, A8.

17. "Are Minority Shoppers Treated Unfairly? An Expensive Reason to Care," www.diversity.com, downloaded May 18, 2003; Florian Zettelmeyer, Fiona Scott Morton, and Jorge Silva-Risso, "How the Internet Lowers Prices: Evidence from Matched Survey and Automobile Transaction Data," *Journal of Marketing Research,* May 2006, pp. 168–81; and Fiona Scott Morton, Florian Zettelmeyer, and Jorge Silva-Risso, "Consumer Information and Discrimination: Does the Internet Affect the Pricing of New Cars to Women and Minorities?" *Quantitative Marketing and Economics* 1 (2003), pp. 65–92.

Carmex (B): This case was written by Steven Hartley and Alisa Allen. Sources: Kristen Scheuing, "The Man Behind Carmex," *Wisconsin Trails,* March/April 2011; "Carmex and Carma Laboratories: *Pharmacy Times* Names Carmex Number One Recommended Lip Balm," *India Pharma News,* June 21, 2013; "New Lip Balm Offers Sun Protection While Drenching Lips in Moisture," *Postmedia Breaking News,* May 21, 2013; Carma Laboratories website, www.mycarmex.com, accessed September 2, 2013; and interviews with Bolin Media personnel.

Credits

12

Managing Marketing Channels and Supply Chains

LEARNING OBJECTIVES

After reading this chapter you should be able to:

 LO 12-1 Explain what is meant by a marketing channel of distribution and why intermediaries are needed.

 LO 12-2 Distinguish among traditional marketing channels, electronic marketing channels, and different types of vertical marketing systems.

 LO 12-3 Describe factors that marketing executives consider when selecting and managing a marketing channel.

 LO 12-4 Explain what supply chain and logistics management are and how they relate to marketing strategy.

CALLAWAY GOLF: DESIGNING AND DELIVERING THE GOODS FOR GREAT GOLF

What do Morgan Pressel and Phil Mickelson, two world-class golf professionals, have in common? Both use Callaway Golf equipment, accessories, and apparel when playing their favorite sport.

With annual sales exceeding $800 million, Callaway Golf is one of the most recognized and highly regarded companies in the golf industry. With its commitment to continuous product innovation and broad distribution in the United States and more than 100 countries worldwide, Callaway Golf has built a strong reputation for designing and delivering the goods for golfers of all skill levels, both amateur and professional.

Callaway Golf primarily markets its products through more than 15,000 on- and off-course authorized golf retailers and sporting goods retailers, such as Golf Galaxy, Inc., Dick's Sporting Goods, Inc., and PGA Tour Superstores, which sell quality golf products and provide a level of customer service appropriate for the sale of such products. Callaway Golf considers its retailers a valuable marketing asset.

The company also has its own online store (CallawayGolf.com), which makes it a full-fledged multichannel marketer, and a successful one as well. Soon after CallawayGolf.com was launched, the chief executive of PGA of America called the store "innovative in that it combines that old legacy relationship with the retail channel with the new innovation of the Web." According to a Marketing Group spokesperson, "Callaway produces in-house a wide-ranging, high volume of original content from instructional videos, to interviews with R&D leads and Tour Pros, blog posts and even live streams of Callaway events. This commitment to creating original content helps to give consumers a better feel for the Company and its products when they go to purchase equipment online and at retail."

Today, CallawayGolf.com is a dynamic, engaging and interactive website that constantly delivers new in-depth product information and media, original social content, user-generated content, and e-commerce capabilities. All of this helps consumers become better informed during the purchasing process. Not surprisingly, CallawayGolf.com is listed among the top Internet retailers in the United States.

299

Providing Callaway's authorized golf retailers and sporting goods retailers with the right products, at the right place, at the right time, and in the right quantity and condition is the responsibility of the company's supply chain. Callaway sources raw materials for its golf equipment, accessories, and all apparel from around the world. At the same time, Callaway delivers its finished products to company retailers through external shipping companies, such as United Parcel Service (UPS).[1]

This chapter first focuses on marketing channels of distribution and why they are an important component in the marketing mix. It then shows how such channels benefit consumers and the sequence of firms that make up a marketing channel. Finally, it describes factors that influence the choice and management of marketing channels, including channel conflict and cooperation.

The discussion then turns to the significance of supply chains and logistics management. In particular, attention is placed on the necessary alignment between supply chain management and marketing strategy and the trade-offs managers make between total distribution costs and customer service.

NATURE AND IMPORTANCE OF MARKETING CHANNELS

LO 12-1 Explain what is meant by a marketing channel of distribution and why intermediaries are needed.

Reaching prospective buyers, either directly or indirectly, is a prerequisite for successful marketing. At the same time, buyers benefit from distribution systems used by companies.

What Is a Marketing Channel of Distribution?

marketing channel Individuals and firms involved in the process of making a product or service available for use or consumption by consumers or industrial users.

You see the results of distribution every day. You may have purchased Lay's potato chips at a 7-Eleven convenience store, a book online through Amazon.com, and Levi's jeans at a Kohl's department store. Each of these items was brought to you by a marketing channel of distribution, or simply a **marketing channel**, which consists of individuals and firms involved in the process of making a product or service available for use or consumption by consumers or industrial users.

Marketing channels can be compared to a pipeline through which water flows from a source to a terminus. Marketing channels make possible the flow of products and services from a producer, through intermediaries, to a buyer. Intermediaries go by various names (see Figure 12–1) and perform various functions. Some intermediaries purchase items from the seller, store them, and resell them to buyers. For example, Celestial Seasonings produces specialty teas and sells them to food wholesalers. The wholesalers then sell these teas to supermarkets and grocery stores, which, in turn, sell them to consumers. Other intermediaries such as brokers and agents represent sellers but do not actually take title to products—their role is to bring a seller and buyer together. Century 21 real estate agents are examples of this type of intermediary.

How Customer Value Is Created by Intermediaries

The importance of intermediaries is made even clearer when we consider the functions they perform and the value they create for buyers.

FIGURE 12–1 Terms used for marketing intermediaries vary in specificity and use in consumer and business markets.

Important Functions Performed by Intermediaries   Intermediaries make possible the flow of products from producers to ultimate consumers by performing three basic functions (see Figure 12–2). Intermediaries perform a *transactional function* when they buy and sell products or services. But an intermediary such as a

TERM	DESCRIPTION
Middleman	Any intermediary between the manufacturer and end-user markets
Agent or broker	Any intermediary with legal authority to act on behalf of the manufacturer
Wholesaler	An intermediary who sells to other intermediaries, usually to retailers; term usually applies to consumer markets
Retailer	An intermediary who sells to consumers
Distributor	An imprecise term, usually used to describe intermediaries who perform a variety of distribution functions, including selling, maintaining inventories, extending credit, and so on; a more common term in business markets but may also be used to refer to wholesalers
Dealer	A more imprecise term than *distributor* that can mean the same as distributor, retailer, wholesaler, and so forth

TYPE OF FUNCTION	ACTIVITIES RELATED TO FUNCTION
Transactional function	• *Buying*: Purchasing products for resale or as an agent for supply of a product • *Selling*: Contacting potential customers, promoting products, and seeking orders • *Risk taking*: Assuming business risks in the ownership of inventory that can become obsolete or deteriorate
Logistical function	• *Assorting*: Creating product assortments from several sources to serve customers • *Storing*: Assembling and protecting products at a convenient location to offer better customer service • *Sorting*: Purchasing in large quantities and breaking into smaller amounts desired by customers • *Transporting*: Physically moving a product to customers
Facilitating function	• *Financing*: Extending credit to customers • *Grading*: Inspecting, testing, or judging products and assigning them quality grades • *Marketing information and research*: Providing information to customers and suppliers, including competitive conditions and trends

FIGURE 12–2
Marketing channel intermediaries perform these fundamental functions, each of which consists of different activities.

wholesaler also performs the function of sharing risk with the producer when it stocks merchandise in anticipation of sales. If the stock is unsold for any reason, the intermediary—not the producer—suffers the loss.

The logistics of a transaction (described at length later in this chapter) involve the details of preparing and getting a product to buyers. Gathering, sorting, and dispersing products are some of the *logistical functions* of the intermediary—imagine the several books required for a literature course sitting together on one shelf at your college bookstore! Finally, intermediaries perform *facilitating functions* that, by definition, make a transaction easier for buyers. For example, Macy's issues credit cards to consumers so they can buy now and pay later.

All three functions must be performed in a marketing channel, even though each channel member may not participate in all three. Channel members often negotiate which specific functions they will perform and for what price.

Consumer Benefits Consumers also benefit from intermediaries. Having the products and services you want, when you want them, where you want them, and in the form you want them is the ideal result of marketing channels.

In more specific terms, marketing channels help create value for consumers through the four utilities described in Chapter 1: time, place, form, and possession. *Time utility* refers to having a product or service when you want it. For example, FedEx provides next-morning delivery. *Place utility* means having a product or service available where consumers want it, such as having a Chevron gas station located on a long stretch of lonely highway. *Form utility* involves enhancing a product or service to make it more appealing to buyers. Consider the importance of bottlers in the soft-drink industry. Coca-Cola and Pepsi-Cola manufacture the flavor concentrate (cola, lemon-lime) and sell it to bottlers—intermediaries—which then add sweetener and the concentrate to carbonated water and package the beverage in bottles and cans, which are then sold to retailers. *Possession utility* entails efforts by intermediaries to help buyers take possession of a product or service, such as having airline tickets delivered by a travel agency.

learning review

12-1. What is meant by a marketing channel?

12-2. What are the three basic functions performed by intermediaries?

301

CHAPTER 12   Managing Marketing Channels and Supply Chains

MARKETING CHANNEL STRUCTURE AND ORGANIZATION

 LO 12-2 Distinguish among traditional marketing channels, electronic marketing channels, and different types of vertical marketing systems.

A product can take many routes on its journey from a producer to buyers. Marketers continually search for the most efficient route from the many alternatives available. As you'll see, there are some important differences between the marketing channels used for consumer products and business products.

Marketing Channels for Consumer Products and Services

Figure 12–3 shows the four most common marketing channels for consumer products and services. It also shows the number of levels in each marketing channel, as evidenced by the number of intermediaries between a producer and ultimate buyers. As the number of intermediaries between a producer and buyer increases, the channel is viewed as increasing in length. Thus, the producer → wholesaler → retailer → consumer channel is longer than the producer → consumer channel.

Direct Channel   Channel A represents a *direct channel* because the producer and the ultimate consumers deal directly with each other. Many products and services are distributed this way. Many insurance companies sell their services using a direct channel and branch sales offices. The Schwan's Food Company of Marshall, Minnesota, the largest direct-to-home provider of frozen foods in the United States, uses route sales representatives who sell from refrigerated trucks. Because there are no intermediaries with a direct channel, the producer performs all channel functions.

Indirect Channel   The remaining three channel forms in Figure 12–3 are *indirect channels* because intermediaries are inserted between the producer and consumers and perform numerous channel functions. Channel B, with a retailer added, is most common when a retailer is large and can buy in large quantities from a producer or when the cost of inventory makes it too expensive to use a wholesaler. Automobile manufacturers such as Toyota use this channel, and a local car dealer acts as a retailer. Why is there no wholesaler? So many variations exist in the product that it would be impossible for a wholesaler to stock all the models required to satisfy buyers; in addition, the cost of maintaining an inventory would be too high. However, large retailers such as Target, 7-Eleven, Staples, Safeway, and Home Depot buy in sufficient quantities to make it cost effective for a producer to deal with only a retail intermediary.

FIGURE 12–3
Common marketing channels for consumer products and services differ by the kind and number of intermediaries involved.

What kind of marketing channel does IBM use for its Watson computer—an artificially intelligent computer system capable of answering questions in natural language? Read the text to find out.

Adding a wholesaler in Channel C is most common for low-cost, low-unit value items that are frequently purchased by consumers, such as candy, confectionary items, and magazines. For example, Mars sells case quantities of its line of candies to wholesalers, who then break down (sort) the cases so that individual retailers can order in boxes or much smaller quantities.

Channel D, the most indirect channel, is employed when there are many small manufacturers and many small retailers; in this type of channel, an agent is used to help coordinate a large supply of the product. Mansar Products, Ltd., is a Belgian producer of specialty jewelry that uses agents to sell to wholesalers in the United States, who then sell to many small independent jewelry retailers.

Marketing Channels for Business Products and Services

The four most common channels for business products and services are shown in Figure 12–4. In contrast with channels used for consumer products, business channels typically are shorter and rely on one intermediary or none at all because business users are fewer in number, tend to be more concentrated geographically, and buy in larger quantities.

Direct Channel   Channel A in Figure 12–4, represented by IBM's large, mainframe computer business, is a direct channel. Firms using this channel maintain their own salesforce and perform all channel functions. This channel is employed when buyers are large and well defined, the sales effort requires extensive negotiations, and the products are of high unit value and require hands-on expertise in terms of installation or use. Not surprisingly, IBM's Watson supercomputer, priced at $3 million, is sold and delivered directly to buyers.

Indirect Channel   Channels B, C, and D in Figure 12–4 are indirect channels with one or more intermediaries between the producer and the industrial user. In Channel B, an industrial distributor performs a variety of marketing channel functions, including selling, stocking, delivering a full product assortment, and financing. In many ways, industrial distributors are like wholesalers in consumer channels. Caterpillar

FIGURE 12–4
Common marketing channels for business products and services differ by the kind and number of intermediaries involved.

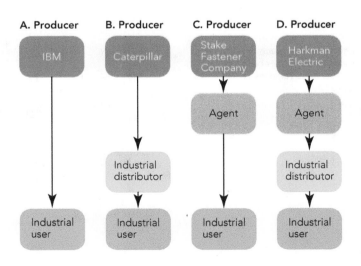

uses industrial distributors to sell its construction and mining equipment in over 180 countries. In addition to selling, Caterpillar distributors stock 40,000 to 50,000 parts and service equipment using highly trained technicians.

Channel C introduces a second intermediary, an agent, who serves primarily as the independent selling arm of producers and represents a producer to industrial users. For example, Stake Fastener Company, a producer of industrial fasteners, has an agent call on industrial users rather than employing its own salesforce.

Channel D is the longest channel and includes both agents and industrial distributors. For instance, Harkman Electric, a producer of electric products, uses agents to call on electrical distributors who sell to industrial users.

Internet Marketing Channels

These common marketing channels for consumer and business products and services are not the only routes to the marketplace. Internet commerce offers new avenues for reaching buyers and creating customer value.

Interactive electronic technology has made possible *Internet marketing channels*, which employ the Internet to make products and services available for consumption or use by consumers or organizational buyers. A unique feature of these channels is that they combine electronic and traditional intermediaries to create time, place, form, and possession utility for buyers.

Figure 12–5 shows the Internet marketing channels for books (Amazon.com), automobiles (Autobytel.com), reservation services (Orbitz.com), and personal computers (Dell.com). Are you surprised that they look a lot like common consumer product marketing channels? An important reason for the similarity resides in the channel functions detailed in Figure 12–2. Electronic intermediaries can and do perform transactional and facilitating functions effectively and at a relatively lower cost than traditional intermediaries because of efficiencies made possible by Internet technology. But electronic intermediaries are incapable of performing elements of the logistical function, particularly for products such as books and automobiles. This function remains with traditional intermediaries or with the producer, as is evident with Dell Inc. and its direct channel.

Many services can be distributed through electronic marketing channels, such as car rental reservations marketed by Alamo.com, financial securities by Schwab.com, and insurance by MetLife.com. However, many other services, such as health care and auto repair, still involve traditional intermediaries.

FIGURE 12–5
Consumer Internet marketing channels look much like those for consumer products and services. Read the text to learn why.

Eddie Bauer successfully engages in multichannel marketing through its 370 retail and outlet stores, its website, and its catalog.

Eddie Bauer
www.eddiebauer.com

multichannel marketing
The blending of different communication and delivery channels that are mutually reinforcing in attracting, retaining, and building relationships with consumers.

dual distribution
An arrangement whereby a firm reaches different buyers by using two or more different types of channels for the same basic product.

Direct and Multichannel Marketing

Many firms also use direct and multichannel marketing to reach buyers. *Direct marketing channels* allow consumers to buy products by interacting with various advertising media without a face-to-face meeting with a salesperson. Direct marketing channels include mail-order selling, direct-mail sales, catalog sales, telemarketing, interactive media, and televised home shopping (the Home Shopping Network). Some firms sell products almost entirely through direct marketing. These firms include L.L. Bean (apparel) and Newegg.com (consumer electronics). Marketers such as Nestlé, in addition to using traditional channels composed of wholesalers and retailers, also employ direct marketing through catalogs and telemarketing to reach more buyers.

Multichannel marketing sometimes called *omnichannel marketing,* is the *blending* of different communication and delivery channels that are *mutually reinforcing* in attracting, retaining, and building relationships with consumers who shop and buy in traditional intermediaries and online. Multichannel marketing seeks to integrate a firm's electronic marketing and delivery channels. At Eddie Bauer, for example, every effort is made to make the apparel shopping and purchase experience for its customers the same across its retail store, catalog, and website channels. According to an Eddie Bauer marketing manager, "We don't distinguish between channels because it's all Eddie Bauer to our customers."[2]

Multichannel marketing also can leverage the value-adding capabilities of different channels. For example, retail stores leverage their physical presence by allowing customers to pick up their online orders at a nearby store or return or exchange nonstore purchases if they wish. Catalogs can serve as shopping tools for online purchasing, as they do for store purchasing. Websites can help consumers do their homework before visiting a store. Staples has leveraged its store, catalog, and website channels with impressive results. Staples is the second largest Internet retailer in the United States.[3]

Dual Distribution and Strategic Channel Alliances

In some situations, producers use **dual distribution**, an arrangement whereby a firm reaches different buyers by employing two or more different types of channels for the same basic product. For example, GE sells its large appliances directly to home and apartment builders but uses retail stores, including Lowe's home centers, to sell to consumers. In some instances, firms pair multiple channels with a multibrand strategy (see Chapter 10). This is done to minimize cannibalization of the firm's family brand and differentiate the channels. For example, Hallmark sells its Hallmark greeting cards through Hallmark stores and select department stores and its Ambassador brand of cards through discount and drugstore chains.

Marketing Matters

Nestlé and General Mills—Cereal Partners Worldwide

Can you say Nestlé Cheerios *miel amandes*? Millions in France start their day with this European equivalent of General Mills's Honey Nut Cheerios, made possible by Cereal Partners Worldwide (CPW). CPW is a strategic alliance designed from the start to be a global business. It combines the cereal manufacturing and marketing capability of U.S.–based General Mills with the worldwide distribution clout of Swiss-based Nestlé. The photo shows Nestle's Trix cereal (not General Mills) sold in China.

From its headquarters in Switzerland, CPW first launched General Mills cereals under the Nestlé label in France, the United Kingdom, Spain, and Portugal in 1991. Today, CPW competes in more than 140 international markets.

The General Mills–Nestlé strategic channel alliance also increased the ready-to-eat cereal worldwide market share of these companies, which are already rated as the two best-managed firms in the world. CPW currently accounts for more than 10 per-

cent of the nearly $30 billion worldwide hot- and cold-cereal market, with more than $4 billion in annual revenue.

Video 12-1
**Honey Nut
Cheerios Ad**
kerin.tv/cr6e/v12-1

An innovation in marketing channels is the use of *strategic channel alliances*, whereby one firm's marketing channel is used to sell another firm's products. Strategic alliances are popular in global marketing, where the creation of marketing channel relationships is expensive and time-consuming. For example, General Mills and Nestlé have an extensive alliance that spans about 140 international markets from Mexico to China. Read the Marketing Matters box so you won't be surprised when you are served Nestlé (not General Mills) Cheerios when traveling outside North America.[4]

Vertical Marketing Systems

The traditional marketing channels described so far represent a loosely knit network of independent producers and intermediaries brought together to distribute products and services. However, other channel arrangements exist for the purpose of improving efficiency in performing channel functions and achieving greater marketing effectiveness. These arrangements are called vertical marketing systems. **Vertical marketing systems** are professionally managed and centrally coordinated marketing channels designed to achieve channel economies and maximum marketing impact.[5] Figure 12–6 depicts the three major types of vertical marketing systems: corporate, contractual, and administered.

vertical marketing systems
Professionally managed and centrally coordinated marketing channels designed to achieve channel economies and maximum marketing impact.

Corporate Systems The combination of successive stages of production and distribution under a single ownership is a *corporate vertical marketing system*. For example, a producer might own the intermediary at the next level down in the channel. This practice, called *forward integration*, is exemplified by Ralph Lauren, which manufactures clothing and also owns apparel shops. Other examples of forward integration include Goodyear, Apple, and Sherwin-Williams. Alternatively, a retailer might own a manufacturing operation, a practice called *backward integration*. For example, Kroger supermarkets operate manufacturing facilities that produce everything from aspirin to cottage cheese for sale under the Kroger label. Tiffany & Co., the exclusive jewelry retailer, manufactures about half of the fine jewelry items for sale through its over 250 specialty stores and boutiques worldwide.

Vertical marketing systems

Corporate vertical marketing system (Polo/Ralph Lauren)

Contractual vertical marketing system

Administered vertical marketing system (Procter & Gamble)

Wholesaler-sponsored voluntary chains (Ben Franklin)

Franchise program

Retailer-sponsored cooperatives (Associated Grocers)

Manufacturer-sponsored retail franchise system (Ford)

Manufacturer-sponsored wholesale franchise system (Pepsi-Cola)

Service-sponsored retail franchise system (Holiday Inn)

Service-sponsored franchise system (H&R Block)

FIGURE 12–6
There are three major types of vertical marketing systems—corporate, contractual, and administered. Contractual systems are the most popular for reasons described in the text.

Companies seeking to reduce distribution costs and gain greater control over supply sources or resale of their products pursue forward and backward integration. However, both types of integration increase a company's capital investment and fixed costs. For this reason, many companies favor contractual vertical marketing systems to achieve channel efficiencies and marketing effectiveness.

Contractual Systems   Under a *contractual vertical marketing system*, independent production and distribution firms integrate their efforts on a contractual basis to obtain greater functional economies and marketing impact than they could achieve alone. Contractual systems are the most popular among the three types of vertical marketing systems.

Three variations of contractual systems exist. *Wholesaler-sponsored voluntary chains* involve a wholesaler that develops a contractual relationship with small, independent retailers to standardize and coordinate buying practices, merchandising programs, and inventory management efforts. With the organization of a large number of independent retailers, economies of scale and volume discounts can be achieved to compete with chain stores. IGA and Ben Franklin variety and craft stores represent wholesaler-sponsored voluntary chains. *Retailer-sponsored cooperatives* exist when small, independent retailers form an organization that operates a wholesale facility cooperatively. Member retailers then concentrate their buying power through the wholesaler and plan collaborative promotional and pricing activities. Examples of retailer-sponsored cooperatives include Associated Grocers and Ace Hardware.

The most visible variation of contractual systems is franchising. *Franchising* is a contractual arrangement between a parent company (a franchisor) and an individual or firm (a franchisee) that allows the franchisee to operate a certain type of business under an established name and according to specific rules.

Four types of franchise arrangements are most popular. *Manufacturer-sponsored retail franchise systems* are prominent in the automobile industry, where a manufacturer such as Ford licenses dealers to sell its cars subject to various sales and service conditions. *Manufacturer-sponsored wholesale franchise systems* exist in the soft-drink industry. For example, Pepsi-Cola licenses wholesalers (bottlers) that purchase concentrate from Pepsi-Cola and then carbonate, bottle, promote, and distribute its products to retailers and restaurants. *Service-sponsored retail franchise systems* are

307

CHAPTER 12   Managing Marketing Channels and Supply Chains

used by firms that have designed a unique approach for performing a service and wish to profit by selling the franchise to others. Holiday Inn, Avis, and McDonald's represent this type of franchising approach. *Service-sponsored franchise systems* exist when franchisors license individuals or firms to dispense a service under a trade name and according to specific guidelines. Examples include Snelling and Snelling, Inc., employment services and H&R Block tax services.

Administered Systems   In comparison, *administered vertical marketing systems* achieve coordination at successive stages of production and distribution by the size and influence of one channel member rather than through ownership. Procter & Gamble, given its broad product assortment ranging from disposable diapers to detergents, is able to obtain cooperation from supermarkets in displaying, promoting, and pricing its products. Walmart obtains cooperation from manufacturers in terms of product specifications, price levels, and promotional support due to its position as the world's largest retailer.

> **learning review**
>
> **12-3.** What is the difference between a direct and an indirect channel?
>
> **12-4.** Why are channels for business products typically shorter than channels for consumer products?
>
> **12-5.** What is the principal distinction between a corporate vertical marketing system and an administered vertical marketing system?

MARKETING CHANNEL CHOICE AND MANAGEMENT

 LO 12-3 Describe factors that marketing executives consider when selecting and managing a marketing channel.

Marketing channels not only link a producer to its buyers but also provide the means through which a firm implements various elements of its marketing strategy. Therefore, choosing a marketing channel is a critical decision.

Factors Affecting Channel Choice and Management

Marketing executives consider three questions when choosing a marketing channel and intermediaries:

1. Which channel and intermediaries will provide the best coverage of the target market?
2. Which channel and intermediaries will best satisfy the buying requirements of the target market?
3. Which channel and intermediaries will be the most profitable?

Target Market Coverage   Achieving the best coverage of the target market requires attention to the *density*—that is, the number of stores in a geographical area—and type of intermediaries to be used at the retail level of distribution. Three degrees of distribution density exist: intensive, exclusive, and selective.

Intensive distribution means that a firm tries to place its products and services in as many outlets as possible. Intensive distribution is usually chosen for convenience products or services such as candy, fast food, newspapers, and soft drinks. For example, Coca-Cola's retail distribution objective is to place its products "within an arm's reach of desire." Cash, yes cash, is distributed intensively by Visa. It operates over 1.4 million automatic teller machines in more than 200 countries.

Exclusive distribution is the extreme opposite of intensive distribution because only one retailer in a specific geographical area carries the firm's products. Exclusive distribution is typically chosen for specialty products or services, such as some women's fragrances and men's and women's apparel and accessories. Gucci, one of the world's leading luxury products companies, uses exclusive distribution in the marketing of its Yves Saint Laurent, Sergio Rossi, Boucheron, Opium, and Gucci brands.

intensive distribution
When a firm tries to place its products or services in as many outlets as possible.

exclusive distribution
When only one retail outlet in a specific geographical area carries the firm's products.

Retailers and industrial distributors prefer exclusive distribution for two reasons. First, it limits head-to-head competition for an identical product. Second, it provides a point of difference for a retailer or distributor. For instance, luxury retailer Saks Inc. seeks exclusive product lines for its stores. According to the company CEO, "It's incumbent on us not to be just a place where you can buy the big brands. Those brands are still critical—the Chanels, the Pradas, the Guccis—but even with those brands, we need to find things unique to us."[6]

selective distribution
When a firm selects a few retail outlets in a specific geographical area to carry its products.

Selective distribution lies between these two extremes and means that a firm selects a few retailers in a specific geographical area to carry its products. Selective distribution weds some of the market coverage benefits of intensive distribution to the control over resale evident with exclusive distribution. For example, Dell Inc. chose selective distribution when it decided to sell its products through U.S. retailers along with its direct channel.[7] According to Michael Dell, the company CEO, "There were plenty of retailers who said, 'sell through us,' but we didn't want to show up everywhere." The company now sells a limited range of its products through Walmart, Sam's Club, Best Buy, and Staples. Dell's decision was consistent with current trends. Today, selective distribution is the most common form of distribution intensity.

Buyer Requirements   A second consideration in channel choice is gaining access to channels and intermediaries that satisfy at least some of the interests buyers might want fulfilled when they purchase a firm's products or services. These interests fall into four broad categories: (1) information, (2) convenience, (3) variety, and (4) pre- or postsale services. Each relates to customer experience.

Information is an important requirement when buyers have limited knowledge or desire specific data about a product or service. Properly chosen intermediaries communicate with buyers through in-store displays, demonstrations, and personal selling. Apple has opened over 400 retail outlets staffed with highly trained personnel to communicate how its products can better satisfy each customer's needs.

Convenience has multiple meanings for buyers, such as proximity or driving time to a retail outlet. For example, 7-Eleven stores, with more than 50,000 outlets worldwide, many of which are open 24 hours a day, satisfy this interest for buyers. Candy and snack-food firms benefit by gaining display space in these stores. For other consumers, convenience means a minimum of time and hassle. Jiffy Lube, which promises to change engine oil and filters quickly, appeals to this aspect of convenience. For those who shop on the Internet, convenience means that websites must be easy to locate and navigate, and image downloads must be fast. A commonly held view among website developers is the "eight second rule": Consumers will abandon their efforts to enter or navigate a website if download time exceeds eight seconds.[8]

Variety reflects buyers' interest in having numerous competing and complementary items from which to choose. Variety is evident in the breadth and depth of products and brands carried by intermediaries, which enhances their attraction to buyers. Thus, manufacturers of pet food and supplies seek distribution through pet superstores such as Petco and PetSmart, which offer a wide array of pet products and services.

Pre- or postsale services provided by intermediaries are an important buying requirement for products such as large household appliances that require delivery, installation, and credit. Therefore, Whirlpool seeks dealers that provide such services.

Profitability   The third consideration in choosing a channel is profitability, which is determined by the margins earned (revenue minus cost) for each channel member and for the channel as a whole. Channel cost is the critical dimension of profitability. These costs include distribution, advertising, and selling expenses associated with different types of marketing channels. The extent to which channel members share these costs determines the margins received by each member and by the channel as a whole.

Companies routinely monitor the performance of their marketing channels. Read the Using Marketing Dashboards box on the next page to see how Charlesburg Furniture views the sales and profit performance of its marketing channels.

Using Marketing Dashboards

Channel Sales and Profit at Charlesburg Furniture

Charlesburg Furniture is one of 1,000 wood furniture manufacturers in the United States. The company sells its furniture through furniture store chains, independent furniture stores, and department store chains, mostly in the southern United States. The company has traditionally allocated its marketing funds for cooperative advertising, in-store displays, and retail sales support on the basis of dollar sales by channel.

Your Challenge As the vice president of sales & marketing at Charlesburg Furniture, you have been asked to review the company's sales and profit in its three channels and recommend a course of action. The question: Should Charlesburg Furniture continue to allocate its marketing funds on the basis of channel dollar sales or profit?

Your Findings Charlesburg Furniture tracks the sales and profit from each channel (and individual customer) and the three-year trend of sales by channel on its marketing dashboard. This information is displayed in the marketing dashboards below.

Several findings stand out. Furniture store chains and independent furniture stores account for 85.2 percent of Charlesburg Furniture sales and 93 percent of company profit. These two channels also evidence growth as measured by annual percentage change in sales. By comparison, the annual percentage sales growth of department store chains has declined, recording negative growth in 2014. This channel accounts for 14.8 percent of company sales and 7 percent of company profit.

Your Action Charlesburg Furniture should consider abandoning the practice of allocating marketing funds solely on the basis of channel sales volume. The importance of independent furniture stores to Charlesburg's profitability warrants further spending, particularly given this channel's favorable sales trend. Doubling the percentage allocation for marketing funds for this channel may be too extreme, however. Charlesburg Furniture might also consider the longer term role of department store chains as a marketing channel.

Managing Channel Relationships: Conflict and Cooperation

Unfortunately, because channels consist of independent individuals and firms, there is always the potential for disagreements concerning who performs which channel functions, how profits are allocated, which products and services will be provided by whom, and who makes critical channel-related decisions. These channel conflicts necessitate measures for dealing with them.

channel conflict
Arises when one channel member believes another channel member is engaged in behavior that prevents it from achieving its goals.

disintermediation
A source of channel conflict that occurs when a channel member bypasses another member and sells or buys products direct.

Sources of Conflict in Marketing Channels

Channel conflict arises when one channel member believes another channel member is engaged in behavior that prevents it from achieving its goals. Two types of conflict occur in marketing channels: vertical conflict and horizontal conflict.

Vertical conflict occurs between different levels in a marketing channel—for example, between a manufacturer and a wholesaler or retailer or between a wholesaler and a retailer. Three sources of vertical conflict are most common.[9] First, conflict arises when a channel member bypasses another member and sells or buys products direct, a practice called **disintermediation**. For example, conflict occurred when American Airlines decided to terminate its relationship with Orbitz and Expedia, two online ticketing and travel sites, and sell directly through AA Direct Connect. Second, conflict occurs due to disagreements over how profit margins are distributed among channel members. This happened when the world's biggest music company, Universal Music Group, adopted a pricing policy for CDs that squeezed the profit margins for specialty music retailers. A third conflict situation arises when manufacturers believe wholesalers or retailers are not giving their products adequate attention. For example, Nike stopped shipping popular sneakers such as Nike Shox NZ to Foot Locker in retaliation for the retailer's decision to give more shelf space to shoes costing under $120.

Horizontal conflict occurs between intermediaries at the same level in a marketing channel, such as between two or more retailers (Target and Kmart) or two or more wholesalers that handle the same manufacturer's brands. Two sources of horizontal conflict are common.[10] First, horizontal conflict arises when a manufacturer increases its distribution coverage in a geographical area. For example, a franchised Cadillac dealer in Chicago might complain to General Motors that another franchised Cadillac dealer has located too close to its dealership. Second, dual distribution causes conflict when different types of retailers carry the same brands. For instance, independent Goodyear tire dealers became irate when Goodyear Tire Company decided to sell its brands through Sears, Walmart, and Sam's Club. Many switched to competing tire makers.

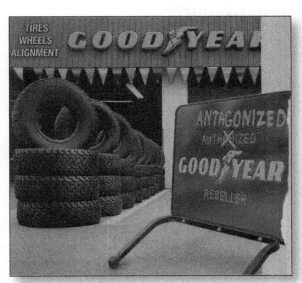

Channel conflict is sometimes visible to consumers. Read the text to learn what type of channel conflict has antagonized this independent Goodyear tire dealer.

Securing Cooperation in Marketing Channels

Conflict can have destructive effects on the workings of a marketing channel so it is necessary to secure cooperation among channel members. One means is through a *channel captain*, a channel member that coordinates, directs, and supports other channel members. Channel captains can be producers, wholesalers, or retailers. P&G assumes this role because it has a strong consumer following in brands such as Crest, Tide, and Pampers. Therefore, it can set policies or terms that supermarkets will follow. McKesson, a pharmaceutical drug wholesaler, is a channel captain because it coordinates and supports the product flow from numerous small drug manufacturers to drugstores and hospitals nationwide. Walmart is a retail channel captain because of its strong consumer image, number of outlets, and purchasing volume.

A firm becomes a channel captain because it is the channel member with the ability to influence the behavior of other members. Influence can take four forms. First, economic influence arises from the ability of a firm to *reward* other members given its strong financial position or customer franchise. Microsoft Corporation and Walmart have such influence. *Expertise* is a second source of influence. For example, American Hospital Supply helps its customers (hospitals) manage inventory and streamline order processing for hundreds of medical supplies. Third, *identification* with a particular channel member can create influence for that channel member. For instance, retailers

CHAPTER 12   Managing Marketing Channels and Supply Chains

may compete to carry the Ralph Lauren line, or clothing manufacturers may compete to be carried by Neiman Marcus, Nordstrom, or Bloomingdale's. In both instances, the desire to be identified with a channel member gives that firm influence over others. Finally, influence can arise from the *legitimate right* of one channel member to direct the behavior of other members. This situation is likely to occur in contractual vertical marketing systems where a franchisor can legitimately direct how a franchisee behaves.

learning review

12-6. What are the three questions marketing executives consider when choosing a marketing channel and intermediaries?

12-7. What are the three degrees of distribution density?

LOGISTICS AND SUPPLY CHAIN MANAGEMENT

LO 12-4 Explain what supply chain and logistics management are and how they relate to marketing strategy.

A marketing channel relies on logistics to make products available to consumers and industrial users. **Logistics** involves those activities that focus on getting the right amount of the right products to the right place at the right time at the lowest possible cost. The performance of these activities is *logistics management*, the practice of organizing the cost-effective flow of raw materials, in-process inventory, finished goods, and related information from point of origin to point of consumption to satisfy *customer requirements*.

Three elements of this definition deserve emphasis. First, logistics deals with decisions needed to move a product from the source of raw materials to consumption— that is, the *flow* of the product. Second, those decisions have to be *cost effective*. Third, while it is important to drive down logistics costs, there is a limit: A firm needs to drive down logistics costs as long as it can deliver expected *customer service*, which means satisfying customer requirements. The role of management is to see that customer needs are satisfied in the most cost-effective manner. When properly done, the results can be spectacular. Consider Procter & Gamble. The company set out to meet consumer needs more effectively by collaborating and partnering with its suppliers and retailers to ensure that the right products reached store shelves at the right time and at a lower cost. The effort was judged a success when, during an 18-month period, P&G's retail customers posted a $65 million savings in logistics costs and customer service increased.[11]

The Procter & Gamble experience is not an isolated incident. Companies now recognize that getting the right items needed for consumption or production to the right place at the right time in the right condition at the right cost is often beyond their individual capabilities and control. Instead, collaboration, coordination, and information sharing among manufacturers, suppliers, and distributors are necessary to create a seamless flow of products and services to customers. This perspective is represented in the concept of a supply chain and the practice of supply chain management.

logistics
Those activities that focus on getting the right amount of the right products to the right place at the right time at the lowest possible cost.

Supply Chains versus Marketing Channels

supply chain
The various firms involved in performing the activities required to create and deliver a product or service to consumers or industrial users.

A **supply chain** refers to the various firms involved in performing the activities required to create and deliver a product or service to consumers or industrial users. It differs from a marketing channel in terms of the firms involved. A supply chain includes suppliers that provide raw material inputs to a manufacturer as well as the wholesalers and retailers that deliver finished products to consumers. The management process is also different.

Supply chain management is the integration and organization of information and logistics activities *across firms* in a supply chain for the purpose of creating

FIGURE 12–7
Relating logistics management and supply chain management to supplier networks and marketing channels.

and delivering products and services that provide value to consumers. The relation among marketing channels, logistics management, and supply chain management is shown in Figure 12–7. An important feature of supply chain management is its application of sophisticated information technology that allows companies to share and operate systems for order processing, transportation scheduling, and inventory and facility management.

Sourcing, Assembling, and Delivering a New Car: The Automotive Supply Chain

All companies are members of one or more supply chains. A supply chain is essentially a series of linked suppliers and customers in which every customer is, in turn, a supplier to another customer until a finished product reaches the ultimate consumer. Even the simplified supply chain diagram for carmakers shown in Figure 12–8 illustrates how complex a supply chain can be.[12] A carmaker's supplier network includes thousands of firms that provide the 2,000 functional components, 30,000 parts, and 10 million lines of software code in a typical automobile. They provide items ranging from raw materials, such as steel and rubber, to components, including transmissions, tires, brakes, and seats, to complex subassemblies such as chassis and suspension systems that make for a smooth, stable ride. The process of coordinating and scheduling the flow of materials and components for their assembly into actual automobiles by carmakers is heavily dependent on logistical activities, including transportation, order processing, inventory control, materials handling, and information technology. A central link is the carmaker's supply chain manager, who is responsible for translating customer requirements into actual orders and arranging for delivery dates and financial arrangements for automobile dealers.

FIGURE 12–8
The automotive supply chain includes thousands of firms that provide the functional components, software codes, and parts in a typical car.

CHAPTER 12   Managing Marketing Channels and Supply Chains

Logistical aspects of the automobile marketing channel are also an important part of the supply chain. Major responsibilities include transportation (which involves the selection and oversight of external carriers—trucking, airline, railroad, and shipping companies—for cars and parts to dealers), the operation of distribution centers, the management of finished goods inventories, and order processing for sales. Supply chain managers also play an important role in the marketing channel. They work with car dealer networks to ensure that the right mix of automobiles is delivered to each location. In addition, they make sure that spare and service parts are available so that dealers can meet the car maintenance and repair needs of consumers. All of this is done with the help of information technology that links the entire automotive supply chain. What does all of this cost? It is estimated that logistics costs represent 25 to 30 percent of the retail price that you pay for a new car.

Supply Chain Management and Marketing Strategy

Video 12-2
IBM
kerin.tv/cr6e/v12-2

The automotive supply chain illustration shows how information and logistics activities are integrated and organized across firms to create and deliver a car to you, the consumer. What's missing from this illustration is the linkage between a specific company's supply chain and its marketing strategy. Just as companies have different marketing strategies, they also design and manage supply chains differently. The goals to be achieved by a firm's marketing strategy determine whether its supply chain needs to be more responsive or efficient in meeting customer requirements.

Aligning a Supply Chain with Marketing Strategy   There are a variety of supply chain configurations, each of which is designed to perform different tasks well. Marketers today recognize that the choice of a supply chain follows from a clearly defined marketing strategy and involves three steps:[13]

1. *Understand the customer.* To understand the customer, a company must identify the needs of the customer segment being served. These needs, such as a desire for a low price or convenience of purchase, help a company define the relative importance of efficiency and responsiveness in meeting customer requirements.
2. *Understand the supply chain.* Second, a company must understand what a supply chain is designed to do well. Supply chains range from those that emphasize being responsive to customer requirements and demand to those that emphasize efficiency with a goal of supplying products at the lowest possible delivered cost.
3. *Harmonize the supply chain with the marketing strategy.* Finally, a company needs to ensure that what the supply chain is capable of doing well is consistent with the targeted customer's needs and its marketing strategy. If a mismatch exists between what the supply chain does particularly well and a company's marketing strategy, the company will need to either redesign the supply chain to support the marketing strategy or change the marketing strategy. Read the Marketing Matters box to learn how IBM overhauled its complete supply chain to support its marketing strategy.[14]

How are these steps applied and how are efficiency and responsiveness considerations built into a supply chain? Let's look at how two well-known companies—Dell and Walmart—have harmonized their supply chain and marketing strategy.[15]

Dell: A Responsive Supply Chain   The Dell marketing strategy primarily targets customers who desire having the most up-to-date computer systems customized to their needs. These customers are also willing to (1) wait to have their customized computer system delivered in a few days, rather than picking out a model at a retail store, and (2) pay a reasonable, though not the lowest, price in the marketplace. Given Dell's customer segment, the company has the option of adopting an efficient or responsive supply chain.

An efficient supply chain may use inexpensive, but slower, modes of transportation, emphasize economies of scale in its production process by reducing the variety of

Marketing Matters

IBM's Integrated Supply Chain—Delivering a Total Solution for Its Customers

IBM is one of the world's great business success stories because of its ability to reinvent itself to satisfy shifting customer needs in a dynamic global marketplace. The company's transformation of its supply chain is a case in point.

IBM has built a single integrated supply chain that can handle raw material procurement, manufacturing, logistics, customer support, order entry, and customer fulfillment across all of IBM— something that has never been done before. Why would IBM undertake this task? According to IBM's former CEO, Samuel J. Palmisano, "You cannot hope to thrive in the IT industry if you are a high-cost, slow-moving company. Supply chain is one of the new competitive battlegrounds. We are committed to being the most efficient and productive player in our industry."

The task is not easy. IBM's supply chain management organization works out of 360 locations in 64 countries, tracking more than 1.5 million assets for both IBM and its clients. The organization also deals with about 23,000 suppliers in nearly 100 countries. Yet with surprising efficiency, IBM's supply chain is linked from raw material sourcing to postsales support.

Today, IBM is uniquely poised to configure and deliver a tailored mix of hardware, software, and service to provide a total solution for its customers. Not surprisingly, IBM's integrated supply chain is heralded as one of the best in the world!

---

system configurations offered, and limit its assembly and inventory storage facilities to a single location. If Dell opted only for efficiency in its supply chain, it would be difficult to satisfy its target customers' desire for rapid delivery and a wide variety of customizable products with its assembly and storage facilities confined to its headquarters in Austin, Texas.

Dell instead has opted for a responsive supply chain. It relies on more expensive express transportation for receipt of components from suppliers and delivery of finished products to customers. The company achieves product variety and manufacturing efficiency by designing common platforms across several products and using common components. Also, Dell has invested heavily in information technology to link itself with suppliers and customers.

Walmart: An Efficient Supply Chain Now let's consider Walmart. Walmart's marketing strategy is to be a reliable, lower-price retailer for a wide variety of mass consumption consumer goods. This strategy favors an efficient supply chain designed to deliver products to 245 million consumers each week at the lowest possible cost. Efficiency is achieved in a variety of ways. For instance, Walmart keeps relatively low inventory levels, and most of it is stocked in stores available for sale, not in warehouses gathering dust. The low inventory arises from Walmart's use of *cross-docking*—a practice that involves unloading products from suppliers, sorting products for individual stores, and quickly reloading products onto its trucks for a particular store. No warehousing or storing of products occurs, except for a few hours or, at most, a day. Cross-docking allows Walmart to operate only a small number of distribution centers to service its vast network of Walmart stores, Supercenters, Neighborhood Markets, Marketside stores, and Sam's Clubs, which contributes to efficiency.

Walmart has invested much more than its competitors in information technology to operate its supply chain. The company feeds information about customer requirements and demand from its stores back to its suppliers, which manufacture only what is being demanded. This large investment has improved the efficiency of Walmart's supply chain and made it responsive to customer needs.

Three lessons can be learned from these two examples. First, there is no one best supply chain for every company. Second, the best supply chain is the one that is consistent with the needs of the customer segment being served and complements a company's marketing strategy. And finally, supply chain managers are often called upon to make trade-offs between efficiency and responsiveness on various elements of a company's supply chain.

TWO CONCEPTS OF LOGISTICS MANAGEMENT IN A SUPPLY CHAIN

total logistics cost
Expenses associated with transportation, materials handling and warehousing, inventory, stockouts, order processing, and return products handling.

customer service
The ability of logistics management to satisfy users in terms of time, dependability, communication, and convenience.

The objective of logistics management in a supply chain is to minimize total logistics costs while delivering the appropriate level of customer service.

Total Logistics Cost Concept

For our purposes, **total logistics cost** includes expenses associated with transportation, materials handling and warehousing, inventory, stockouts (being out of inventory), order processing, and return products handling. Note that many of these costs are interrelated so that changes in one will impact the others. For example, if a firm attempts to reduce its transportation costs by shipping in larger quantities, it will increase its inventory levels. While larger inventory levels will increase inventory costs, they should also reduce stockouts. It is important, therefore, to study the impact on all of the logistics decision areas when considering a change.

Customer Service Concept

Because a supply chain is a *flow*, the end of it—or *output*—is the service delivered to customers. Within the context of a supply chain, **customer service** is the ability of logistics management to satisfy users in terms of time, dependability, communication, and convenience. As suggested by Figure 12–9, a supply chain manager's key task is to balance these four customer service factors against total logistics cost factors.

FIGURE 12–9
Supply chain managers balance total logistics cost factors against customer service factors.

Time   In a supply chain setting, time refers to *order cycle* or *replenishment* time for an item, which means the time between the ordering of an item and when it is received

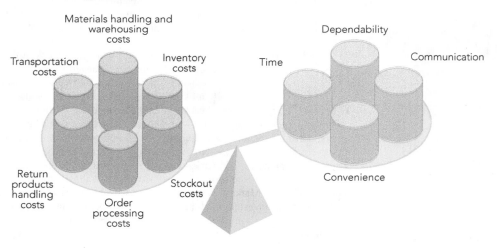

Total logistics cost factors

Materials handling and warehousing costs

Transportation costs

Inventory costs

Return products handling costs

Order processing costs

Stockout costs

Customer service factors

Dependability

Time

Communication

Convenience

and ready for use or sale. The various elements that make up the typical order cycle include recognition of the need to order, order transmittal, order processing, documentation, and transportation. A current emphasis in supply chain management is to reduce order cycle time so that the inventory levels of customers may be minimized. Another emphasis is to make the process of reordering and receiving products as simple as possible, often through inventory systems called *quick response* and *efficient consumer response* delivery systems. For example, at Saks Fifth Avenue, point-of-sale scanner technology records each day's sales. When stock falls below a minimum level, a replenishment order is automatically produced. Vendors such as Donna Karan (DKNY) receive the order, which is processed and delivered within 48 hours.[16]

Dependability   Dependability is the consistency of replenishment. This is important to all firms in a supply chain—and to consumers. How often do you return to a store if it fails to have in stock the item you want to purchase? Dependability can be broken into three elements: consistent lead time, safe delivery, and complete delivery. Consistent service allows planning (such as appropriate inventory levels), whereas inconsistencies create surprises. Intermediaries may be willing to accept longer lead times if they know about them in advance and can thus make plans.

Communication   Communication is a two-way link between the buyer and seller that helps in monitoring service and anticipating future needs. Status reports on orders are a typical example of communication between the buyer and seller.

Convenience   The concept of convenience for a supply chain manager means that there should be a minimum of effort on the part of the buyer in doing business with the seller. Is it easy for the customer to order? Are the products available from many outlets? Will the seller arrange all necessary details, such as transportation? This customer service factor has promoted the use of **vendor-managed inventory (VMI)**, whereby the *supplier* determines the product amount and assortment a customer (such as a retailer) needs and automatically delivers the appropriate items.

Campbell Soup's system illustrates how VMI works.[17] Every morning, retailers electronically inform the company of their demand for all Campbell products and the inventory levels in their distribution centers. Campbell uses that information to forecast future demand and determine which products need replenishment based on upper and lower inventory limits established with each retailer. Trucks leave the Campbell shipping plant that afternoon and arrive at the retailer's distribution centers with the required replenishments the same day.

> **vendor-managed inventory**
> An inventory management system whereby the supplier determines the product amount and assortment a customer (such as a retailer) needs and automatically delivers the appropriate items.

CLOSING THE LOOP: REVERSE LOGISTICS

The flow of products in a supply chain does not end with the ultimate consumer or industrial user. Companies today recognize that a supply chain can work in reverse. **Reverse logistics** is a process of reclaiming recyclable and reusable materials, returns, and reworks from the point of consumption or use for repair, remanufacturing, redistribution, or disposal. The effect of reverse logistics can be seen in the reduced waste in landfills and lowered operating costs for companies. The Making Responsible Decisions box on the next page describes the successful reverse logistics initiative at Hewlett-Packard.[18]

Companies such as Motorola and Nokia (return and reuse of mobile phones) and Caterpillar, Xerox, and IBM (remanufacturing and recycling) have implemented acclaimed reverse logistics programs. Other firms have enlisted third-party logistics providers such as UPS, FedEx, and Penske Logistics to handle this process along with other supply chain functions. GNB Technologies, Inc., a manufacturer of lead-acid batteries for automobiles and boats, has outsourced much of its supply chain activity to UPS Supply Chain Services.[19] The company contracts with UPS to manage its

> **reverse logistics**
> A process of reclaiming recyclable and reusable materials, returns, and reworks from the point of consumption or use for repair, remanufacturing, redistribution, or disposal.

Making Responsible Decisions

Reverse Logistics and Green Marketing Go Together at Hewlett-Packard: Recycling e-Waste

About 53 million tons of electronics and electronic equipment find their way to landfills around the world annually. Americans alone discarded over 400 million analog TV sets and computer monitors and Japanese consumers trashed more than 610 million cell phones in 2013. The result? Landfills are seeping lead, chromium, mercury, and other toxins prevalent in digital debris into the environment.

Fortunately, Hewlett-Packard has taken it upon itself to act responsibly and address this issue through its highly regarded reverse logistics program. Hewlett-Packard has recycled computer and printer hardware since 1987 and is an industry leader in this practice. The company's recycling service is available today in more than 67 countries, regions, and territories. By 2014, Hewlett-Packard will have recycled over 2 billion pounds of used electronic products and supplies to be refurbished for resale or donation or for recovery of materials.

The recycling effort at Hewlett-Packard is also part of the company's Design for Supply Chain program. Among other initiatives in this program, emphasis is placed on

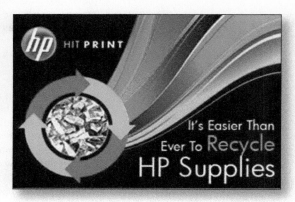

product and packaging changes to reduce reverse supply chain and environmental costs. For example, design changes have increased the recycling of its popular ink-jet supplies by 25 percent.

Video 12-3
UPS
kerin.tv/cr6e/v12-3

shipments between plants, distribution centers, recycling centers, and retailers. This includes movement of both new batteries and used products destined for recycling and covers both truck and railroad shipments. This partnership, along with the initiatives of other battery makers, has paid economic and ecological dividends. By recycling 90 percent of the lead from used batteries, manufacturers have kept the demand for new lead in check, thereby holding down costs to consumers. Also, solid waste management costs and the environmental impact of lead in landfills are reduced.

learning review

12-8. What is the principal difference between a marketing channel and a supply chain?

12-9. The choice of a supply chain involves what three steps?

12-10. A manager's key task is to balance which four customer service factors against which six logistics cost factors?

LEARNING OBJECTIVES REVIEW

LO 12-1 *Explain what is meant by a marketing channel of distribution and why intermediaries are needed.*

A marketing channel of distribution, or simply a marketing channel, consists of individuals and firms involved in the process of making a product or service available for use or consumption by consumers or industrial users. Intermediaries make possible the flow of products from producers to buyers by performing three basic functions. The transactional function involves buying, selling, and risk taking because intermediaries stock merchandise in anticipation of sales. The logistical function involves the gathering, storing, and dispensing of products. The facilitating function assists producers in making products and services more attractive to buyers. The performance of these functions by intermediaries creates time, place, form, and possession utility for consumers.

LO 12-2 *Distinguish among traditional marketing channels, electronic marketing channels, and different types of vertical marketing systems.*

Traditional marketing channels describe the route taken by products and services from producers to buyers. This route can range from a direct channel with no intermediaries, because a producer and the ultimate consumer deal directly with each other, to indirect channels where intermediaries (agents, wholesalers, distributors, or retailers) are inserted between a producer and consumer and perform numerous channel functions. Electronic marketing channels employ the Internet to make products and services available for consumption or use by consumer or business buyers. Vertical marketing systems are professionally managed and centrally coordinated marketing channels designed to achieve channel economies and maximum marketing impact. There are three major types of vertical marketing systems (VMSs). A corporate VMS combines successive stages of production and distribution under a single ownership. A contractual VMS exists when independent production and distribution firms integrate their efforts on a contractual basis to obtain greater functional economies and marketing impact than they could achieve alone. An administered VMS achieves coordination at successive stages of production and distribution by the size and influence of one channel member rather than through ownership.

LO 12-3 *Describe factors that marketing executives consider when selecting and managing a marketing channel.*

Marketing executives consider three questions when selecting and managing a marketing channel and intermediaries. (1) Which channel and intermediaries will provide the best coverage of the target market? Marketers typically choose one of three levels of market coverage: intensive, selective, or exclusive distribution.

(2) Which channel and intermediaries will best satisfy the buying requirements of the target market? These buying requirements fall into four categories: information, convenience, variety, and pre- or postsale services. (3) Which channel and intermediaries will be the most profitable? Here marketers look at the margins earned (revenues minus cost) for each channel member and for the channel as a whole.

LO 12-4 *Explain what supply chain and logistics management are and how they relate to marketing strategy.*

A supply chain refers to the various firms involved in performing the various activities required to create and deliver a product or service to consumers or industrial users. Supply chain management is the integration and organization of information and logistics across firms for the purpose of creating value for consumers. Logistics involves those activities that focus on getting the right amount of the right products to the right place at the right time at the lowest possible cost. Logistics management includes the coordination of the flows of both inbound and outbound products, an emphasis on making these flows cost effective, and customer service. A company's supply chain follows from a clearly defined marketing strategy. The alignment of a company's supply chain with its marketing strategy involves three steps. First, a supply chain must reflect the needs of the customer segment being served. Second, a company must understand what a supply chain is designed to do well. Supply chains range from those that emphasize being responsive to customer requirements and demands to those that emphasize efficiency with the goal of supplying products at the lowest possible delivered cost. Finally, a supply chain must be consistent with the targeted customer's needs and the company's marketing strategy. The Dell and Walmart examples in the chapter illustrate how this alignment is achieved by two market leaders.

LEARNING REVIEW ANSWERS

12-1 **What is meant by a marketing channel?**
Answer: A marketing channel consists of individuals and firms involved in the process of making a product or service available for use or consumption by consumers or industrial users.

12-2 **What are the three basic functions performed by intermediaries?**
Answer: Intermediaries perform transactional, logistical, and facilitating functions.

12-3 **What is the difference between a direct and an indirect channel?**
Answer: A direct channel is one in which a producer of consumer or business products and services and ultimate consumers or industrial users deal directly with each other. An indirect channel has intermediaries that are inserted between the producer and ultimate consumers or industrial users and perform numerous channel functions.

12-4 **Why are channels for business products typically shorter than channels for consumer products?**
Answer: Business channels are typically shorter than consumer channels because business users are fewer in number, tend to be more concentrated geographically, and buy in larger quantities.

12-5 **What is the principal distinction between a corporate vertical marketing system and an administered vertical marketing system?**
Answer: A corporate vertical marketing system combines successive stages of production and distribution under a single ownership. An administered vertical marketing system achieves coordination by the size and influence of one channel member rather than through ownership.

12-6 **What are the three questions marketing executives consider when choosing a marketing channel and intermediaries?**
Answer: The three questions to consider when choosing a marketing channel and intermediaries are: (1) Which will provide the best coverage of the target market? (2) Which will best satisfy the buying requirements of the target market? (3) Which will be the most profitable?

12-7 **What are the three degrees of distribution density?**
Answer: intensive; exclusive; selective

12-8 **What is the principal difference between a marketing channel and a supply chain?**

Answer: A marketing channel consists of individuals and firms involved in the process of making a product or service available for use or consumption by consumers or industrial users. A supply chain differs from a marketing channel in terms of membership. It includes suppliers who provide raw materials to a manufacturer as well as the wholesalers and retailers—the marketing channel—that deliver the finished goods to ultimate consumers.

12-9 **The choice of a supply chain involves what three steps?**

Answer: (1) Understand the customer. (2) Understand the supply chain. (3) Harmonize the supply chain with the marketing strategy.

12-10 **A manager's key task is to balance which four customer service factors against which six logistics cost factors?**

Answer: The four customer service factors are time, dependability, communication, and convenience. The logistics cost factors are transportation costs, materials handling and warehousing costs, inventory costs, stock-out costs (being out of inventory), order processing costs, and return products handling costs.

FOCUSING ON KEY TERMS

channel conflict p. 311
customer service p. 316
disintermediation p. 311
dual distribution p. 305
exclusive distribution p. 308

intensive distribution p. 308
logistics p. 312
marketing channel p. 300
multichannel marketing p. 305
reverse logistics p. 317

selective distribution p. 309
supply chain p. 312
total logistics cost p. 316
vendor-managed inventory (VMI) p. 317
vertical marketing systems p. 306

APPLYING MARKETING KNOWLEDGE

1 A distributor for Celanese Chemical Company stores large quantities of chemicals, blends these chemicals to satisfy the requests of customers, and delivers the blends to a customer's warehouse within 24 hours of receiving an order. What utilities does this distributor provide?

2 Suppose the president of a carpet manufacturing firm has asked you to look into the possibility of bypassing the firm's wholesalers (who sell to carpet, department, and furniture stores) and selling direct to these stores. What caution would you voice on this matter, and what type of information would you gather before making this decision?

3 What type of channel conflict is likely to be caused by dual distribution, and what type of conflict can be reduced by direct distribution? Why?

4 How does the channel captain idea differ among corporate, administered, and contractual vertical marketing systems with particular reference to the use of the different forms of influence available to firms?

5 List the customer service factors that would be vital to buyers in the following types of companies: (*a*) manufacturing, (*b*) retailing, (*c*) hospitals, and (*d*) construction.

BUILDING YOUR MARKETING PLAN

Does your marketing plan involve selecting channels and intermediaries? If the answer is "no," read no further and do not include this element in your plan. If the answer is "yes":

1 Identify which channel and intermediaries will provide the best coverage of the target market for your product or service.

2 Specify which channel and intermediaries will best satisfy the important buying requirements of the target market.

3 Determine which channel and intermediaries will be the most profitable.

4 Select your channel(s) and intermediary(ies).

5 If inventory is involved, (*a*) identify the three or four major kinds of inventory needed for your organization (retail stock, finished products, raw materials, supplies, and so on), and (*b*) suggest ways to reduce their costs.

6 (*a*) Rank the four customer service factors (time, dependability, communication, and convenience) from most important to least important from your customers' point of view, and (*b*) identify actions for the one or two factors that are the most important in regard to your product or service.

VIDEO CASE 12 Amazon: Delivering the Earth's Biggest Selection!

Video 12-4
Amazon
Video Case
kerin.tv/cr6e/v12-4

"The secret is we are on our seventh generation of fulfillment centers and we have gotten better every time," explains Jeff Bezos, CEO of Amazon.com, Inc. The global online retailer is a pioneer of fast, convenient, low-cost shopping that has attracted millions of consumers. Of course, while Amazon has changed the way many people shop, the company still faces the traditional and daunting task of creating a seamless flow of deliveries to its customers—often millions of times each day.

THE COMPANY

Bezos started Amazon.com with a simple idea: use the Internet to transform book buying into the fastest, easiest, and most enjoyable shopping experience possible. The company was incorporated in 1994 and launched its website in July 1995. At the forefront of a huge growth of dotcom businesses, Amazon pursued a get-big-fast business strategy. Sales grew rapidly and Amazon began adding products and services other than books. In fact, Amazon soon set its goal on being "Earth's most customer-centric company, where customers can find and discover virtually anything they might want to buy online."

Today Amazon.com continues to grow by providing low prices, vast selection, and convenience. Its selection of products covers a broad range of categories including:

Books; Movies, Music & Games; Electronics & Computers; Home, Garden & Tools; Beauty, Health & Grocery; Toys; Clothing, Shoes & Jewelry; Sports & Outdoors; and Automotive & Industrial. In addition, Amazon offers digital music, an appstore for Android, Amazon Cloud Drive, Kindle e-readers, Kindle Fire tablets, Amazon Fire TV, and the Amazon Fire phone. Other services allow customers to:

- Search for a product or brand using all or part of its name.
- Place orders with one click using the "Buy Now with 1-Click" button on the website, and the "Mobile 1-Click" button for phones.
- Receive personalized recommendations based on past purchases through opt-in e-mails.

These products and services have attracted millions of people around the globe. Further, the company's growth has made Amazon.com, along with its international sites in Australia, Brazil, Canada, China, France, Germany, India, Italy, Japan, Mexico, Spain, and the United Kingdom, the world's largest online retailer.

Amazon's e-commerce platform is also used by more than two million small businesses, retail brands, and individual sellers. For example, programs such as Selling on Amazon, Fulfillment by Amazon, Amazon Webstore, and Checkout by Amazon allow small businesses to use Amazon's e-commerce platform to facilitate sales. Online retailers store their products at Amazon's fulfillment centers and when they sell a product, Amazon ships it! Amazon.com also operates retail websites for brands such as bebe, Marks & Spencer, Lacoste, and AOL's Shop@AOL. Individual sellers use the Amazon network to reach millions of potential customers. These business partnerships all contribute to Amazon's sales, which now exceed $75 billion.

Bezos defines Amazon by its "big ideas, which are customer centricity, putting the customer at the center of everything we do, and invention—we like to pioneer, we like to explore." Amazon's success is also the result of an intense focus on cost and efficiency that leads to lower prices. More specifically, Amazon is exceptional at managing the elements of its supply chain, which make up one of the most complex and expensive aspects of the company's business.

SUPPLY CHAIN AND LOGISTICS MANAGEMENT AT AMAZON.COM

What happens after an order is submitted on Amazon's website but before it arrives at the customer's door? A lot. Amazon.com maintains huge distribution, or "fulfillment," centers where it keeps inventory of millions of products. This is one of the key differences between Amazon.com and some of its competitors—it actually stocks products. Bezos describes how they have improved: "Years ago, I drove the Amazon packages to the post office every evening in the back of my Chevy Blazer. My vision extended so far that I dreamed we might one day get a forklift. Fast-forward to today and we have 96 fulfillment centers…" So Amazon must manage the flow of products from its 15 million-plus suppliers to its U.S. and international fulfillment centers with the flow of customer orders from the fulfillment centers to individuals' homes or offices.

The process begins with the suppliers. Amazon collaborates with its suppliers to increase efficiencies and improve inventory turnover. For example, Amazon uses software to forecast purchasing patterns by region, which allows it to give its suppliers better information about delivery dates and volumes. After the products arrive at the fulfillment center they are scanned and placed on shelves in what often appear to be haphazard locations. That is, books may be on the same shelf next to toys and kitchen utensils. Dave Clark, vice president of worldwide operations and customer service at Amazon, explains: "If you look at how these items fit in the bin, they are optimized to utilize the available space, we have computers and algorithms that tell people the areas of the building that have the most space to put the product that's coming in at that time." Clark observes that one of its 1-million-square-foot fulfillment centers (the size of more than 20 football fields) represents a "physical manifestation of earth's biggest selection."

At the same time, Amazon has been improving the part of the process that sorts the products into the individual orders. Once an order is placed in the computer system, sophisticated software generates a map of the location of each product and a "pick ambassador" walks the aisles to select the products. Each item is scanned as it is selected

so that inventory levels and locations are always up-to-date. Packers ensure that all items are included in the box before it is taped and labeled. The boxes then travel along a conveyor belt and are diverted into groups based on the delivery location. A network of trucks and regional postal hubs then conclude the process with delivery of the order. Amazon actually uses more trucks than planes!

The success of Amazon's logistics and supply chain management activities may be most evident during the year-end holiday shopping season. Amazon received orders for 36.8 million items on Cyber Monday (the Monday following Thanksgiving), including orders for Xbox and PlayStation gaming consoles that reached more than 1,000 units per minute. During the entire holiday season Amazon shipped orders to 185 countries. Well over 99 percent of the orders were shipped and delivered on time.

CONTINUOUS IMPROVEMENT AT AMAZON

In a recent letter to Amazon shareholders Bezos reported that Amazon employees are "always asking how do we make this better?" He also described the Amazon Kaizen program (named for the Japanese term meaning "change for the better") and how it is used to streamline processes and reduce defects and waste. As a result there are many new changes and improvements under way at Amazon, many of which are related to its supply chain and logistics management approach.

One example of a new service at Amazon is Amazon Fresh, its online, same-day-delivery service for groceries. The service has been in trial stage in Seattle for several years and recently expanded to Los Angeles and San Francisco. The success of the service in these cities is likely to influence how quickly Amazon expands into other cities. Another new service at Amazon is based on its agreement with the United States Postal Service to offer Sunday delivery to select cities. The demand for this service in the trial cities will also influence how quickly it is rolled out to other cities. Finally Amazon received a lot of attention when it revealed that it is developing unmanned aerial drones that could fly small shipments to customers within 30 minutes. "We can carry objects up to 5 pounds which covers 86 percent of the items that we deliver," explains Bezos. Of course there are legal hurdles with the Federal Aviation Administration but it is one more example of the innovation that has characterized Amazon for years.

Amazon.com has come a long way since 1995. Its logistics and supply chain management activities have provided Amazon with a cost-effective and efficient distribution system that combines automation and communication technology with superior customer service. To continue its drive to increase future sales, profits, and customer service, Amazon continues to use its inventive spirit to encourage innovation. According to Bezos, "what we are doing is challenging and fun—we get to work in the future."

Questions

1 How do Amazon.com's logistics and supply chain management activities help the company create value for its customers?

2 What systems did Amazon develop to improve the flow of products from suppliers to Amazon fulfillment centers? What systems improved the flow of orders from the fulfillment centers to customers?

3 Why will logistics and supply chain management play an important role in the future success of Amazon.com?

Chapter Notes

1. Interview with Jeff Newton, Callaway Golf, July 3, 2014; "Callaway Golf.com: The Social Sport," *Internetretailer.com,* December 5, 2013; www.callawaygolf.com, downloaded April 15, 2014; and Stephanie Kang, "Callaway Will Use Retailers to Sell Goods Directly to Consumers Online," *The Wall Street Journal,* November 6, 2006, p. B5.

2. "Eddie Bauer's Banner Time of Year," *Advertising Age,* October 1, 2001, p. 55.

3. *Internet Retailer Top 500 Guide,* 2014 Edition. www.internetretailer .com, downloaded February 10, 2014.

4. "Cereal Marketers Race for Global Bowl Domination," *Advertising Age,* August 20, 2012, pp. 12–13; "General Mills Reports Fiscal 2014 Third-Quarter Results," General Mills press release, March 19, 2014; "Second-Largest Cereal Producer Turns 20, with Style," General Mills Press Release, September 13, 2010.

5. For an overview of vertical marketing systems, see Lou Pelton, Martha Cooper, David Strutton, and James R. Lumpkin, *Marketing Channels,* 3rd ed. (Burr Ridge, IL: McGraw-Hill/Irwin, 2005).

6. "Saks to Add Exclusive Lines," *The Wall Street Journal,* February 25, 2010, p. B2.

7. "Dell Treads Carefully into Selling PCs in Stores," *The Wall Street Journal,* January 3, 2008, p. B1.

8. Rafi A. Mohammed, Robert J. Fisher, Bernard J. Jaworski, and Gordon J. Paddison, *Internet Marketing: Building Advantage in a Networked Economy,* 2nd ed. (Burr Ridge, IL: McGraw-Hill/Irwin, 2004).

9. "American Airlines Yanks Its Flights off Travel Sites," www .USAtoday.com, December 23, 2010; Ethan Smith, "Why a Grand Plan to Cut CD Prices Went off the Track," *The Wall Street Journal,* June 4, 2004, pp. A1, A6; and "Feud with Seller Hurts Nike Sales, Shares," *Dallas Morning News,* June 28, 2003, p. 30.

10. For an extensive discussion on channel influence and power, see Robert W. Palmatier, Louis W. Stern, and Adel I. El-Ansary, *Marketing Channel Strategy,* 8th ed. (Upper Saddle River, NJ: Prentice Hall, 2015), Chapter 10 and 11.

11. David Simchi-Levi, Philip Kaminsky, and Edith Simchi-Levi, *Designing and Managing the Supply Chain,* 4th ed. (Burr Ridge, IL: McGraw-Hill/Irwin, 2011).

12. *The Smarter Supply Chain of the Future: Industry Edition* (Somer, NY: IBM Corporation, 2009); and John Paul MacDuffie and Takahiro Fujimoto, "Why Dinosaurs Will Keep Ruling the Automobile Industry," *Harvard Business Review,* June 2010, pp. 23–25.

13. Major portions of this discussion are based on Sunil Chopra and Peter Meindl, *Supply Chain Management: Strategy, Planning, and Operations,* 5th ed. (Upper Saddle River, NJ: Prentice Hall, 2013), Chapters 1–3; and Hau L. Lee, "The Triple-A Supply Chain," *Harvard Business Review* (October 2004), pp. 102–12.

14. Jessi Hempel, "IBM's Super Second Act," *Fortune,* March 21, 2011, pp. 115 ff; Kevin O'Marah, "The AMR Supply Chain Top 25 for 2010," Gartner, Inc., June 2010; and Thomas A. Foster, "World's Best-Run Supply Chains Stay on Top Regardless of the Competition," *Global Logistics & Supply Chain Strategies,* February 2006, pp. 27–41.

15. This discussion is based on "The 2014 Supply Chain Top 25: Leading the Decade," *Supply Chain Management Review,* September-October, 2014, pp. 8–17. "*Harvard Business Review,* on Managing Supply Chains," *Harvard Business Review,* June, 2011; "The Lessons from Dell's Supply Chain Transformation," www.supplychaindigest .com, March 18, 2011; Brett Booen, "Walmart's Supply Chain Acts as If Every Day Is Black Friday," *Supply Chain Digital,* November 19, 2010; and Chopra and Meindl, *Supply Chain Management.*

16. "Retailers Aim to Turn Minutes into Millions," *The Wall Street Journal,* December 19, 2012, pp. B1, B2; Christina Passariello, "Logistics Are in Vogue with Designers," *The Wall Street Journal,* June 27, 2008, p. B1; and Bill Mongelluzzo, "Logistics Makeover at Saks: Retailer Says Changes in Supply Chain Practices Have Reduced Inventory and Costs," *The Journal of Commerce,* October 24, 2005.

17. Jean Murphy, "Better Forecasting, S&OP Support Transformation at Campbell's Soup Co.," *Global Logistics & Supply Chain Strategies,* June 2004, pp. 28–30.

18. *Second Annual Report of the eCycling Leadership Initiative* (Consumer Electronics Association, April 2013); "Rewriting the Rules for E-Cycling," *Fortune,* March 22, 2010, Special Section; Steve Miller, "Recycling Becomes Electric for CE Brands," *BrandWeek,* May 13, 2008, p. 4; "Don't Toss Out That Old Gadget," *Newsweek,* November 3, 2008, p. E8; and Lorraine Woellert, "HP Wants Your Old PCs Back," *BusinessWeek,* April 10, 2006, pp. 82–83.

19. Doug Bartholomew, "IT Delivers for UPS," *Industry Week,* August 2002, pp. 35–36.

This case was written by Steven Hartley. Sources: Tim Worstall, "Both Amazon and WalMart Are Really Logistics Companies, Not Retailers," *forbes.com,* April 11, 2014; Dan Mitchell, "Next Up for Disruption: The Grocery Business," *fortune.com,* April 4, 2014; Mae Anderson, "Amazon's Bezos Outlines Grocery, Drone Plans," *businessweek.com,* April 10, 2014; Jeff Bercovici, "The Same-Day War: Amazon, Google and Walmart Race to Bring Your Groceries," *Forbes,* May 5, 2014; Brad Stone, "Why Amazon's Going Up In the Air," *Bloomberg Businessweek,* December 9–15, 2013, pp.12–13; "Record-Setting Holiday Season for Amazon Prime," Amazon Press Release, December 26, 2013; "Company Info: Overview," http://phx.corporate-ir.net/phoenix.zhtml?c=176060&p=irol-mediaKit; Jeff Bezos, "2013 Letter to Shareholders," http://phx.corporate-ir.net/phoenix.zhtml?c=97664&p=irol-reportsannual; "Amazon's Jeff Bezos Looks to the Future," 60 Minutes episode, December 1, 2013; and Mark Veverka, "The World's Best Retailer," *Barron's,* March 30, 2009.

Credits

13   Retailing and Wholesaling

LEARNING OBJECTIVES

After reading this chapter you should be able to:

 LO 13-1 Identify retailers in terms of the utilities they provide.

LO 13-2 Explain the alternative ways to classify retail outlets.

 LO 13-3 Describe the many methods of nonstore retailing.

 LO 13-4 Specify the retailing mix actions used to implement a retailing strategy.

LO 13-5 Explain changes in retailing with the wheel of retailing and the retail life cycle concepts.

 LO 13-6 Describe the types of firms that perform wholesaling activities and their functions.

IF YOU LIKE TO SHOP, YOU WILL LOVE GOOGLE GLASS(ES)!

You've shopped in a store. You've also shopped online. Now you can enjoy the benefits of both thanks to new technologies such as Google Glass!

Google Glass products resemble a pair of eyeglasses with a small display screen visible to the wearer. Image and voice recognition capabilities identify relevant information to display on the screen. The sound, video, and graphics accessed through the glasses create an *augmented reality* that overlays the physical, real-world environment being viewed at the same time. When used by shoppers, this technology adds rich content to the shopping experience, improving the purchase decision process. It's a perfect way to combine the fast, personalized, and customized information consumers enjoy when they shop online with the traditional brick-and-mortar in-store shopping experience!

In addition to the head-worn displays being developed by Google, other companies are developing augmented reality software and apps for smartphones, tablet devices, and 3D projectors. IBM, for example, is developing a mobile app that uses the camera in a smartphone to identify a product and then display information about the product (e.g., price, nutritional value, etc.) based on preferences specified by the consumer. Similarly, a company called Aurasma is developing image and pattern recognition technology to identify real-world objects and then activate interactive animations for consumers to view.

Retailers are excited about the opportunity to enhance the customer experience. IKEA's new catalog allows consumers to access information, videos, and 3D models through a tablet image recognition app. A Japanese furniture manufacturer is developing an app that allows customers to take a picture of a room in their house and then overlay digital images of furniture items in the photo to simulate the appearance of furniture arrangements before making a purchase. Toshiba offers a similar app that allows customers to see what a television will look like in their home. In addition, clothing retailers are developing augmented reality technology that allows consumers to take pictures of themselves and then superimpose images of clothing in the photo. The convenience of the technology encourages customers to try styles, combinations, and colors they might not take time to actually put on in a brick-and-mortar store.

Augmented reality has the potential to significantly change the way consumers shop by making the experience faster, more effective, and

Video 13-1
Google Glass
kerin.tv/cr6e/v13-1

more enjoyable. According to industry expert Stuart Nugent, "The future of augmented reality lies in offering potential customers much more valuable information about the products they're viewing."[1]

These are just a few examples of the many exciting changes occurring in retailing today. This chapter examines the critical role of retailing in the marketplace and the challenging decisions retailers face as they strive to create value for customers.

What types of products will consumers buy through catalogs, television, the Internet, or by telephone? In what type of store will consumers look for products they don't buy directly? How important is the location of the store? Will customers expect services such as alterations, delivery, installation, or repair? What price should be charged for each product? These are difficult and important questions that are an integral part of retailing. In the channel of distribution, retailing is where the customer meets the product. It is through retailing that exchange (a central aspect of marketing) occurs. **Retailing** includes all activities involved in selling, renting, and providing products and services to ultimate consumers for personal, family, or household use.

retailing
All activities involved in selling, renting, and providing products and services to ultimate consumers for personal, family, or household use.

THE VALUE OF RETAILING

 LO 13-1 Identify retailers in terms of the utilities they provide.

Retailing is an important marketing activity. Not only do producers and consumers meet through retailing actions, but retailing also creates customer value and has a significant impact on the economy. To consumers, the value of retailing is in the form of utilities provided (see Figure 13–1). Retailing's economic value is represented by the people employed in retailing as well as by the total amount of money exchanged in retail sales.

Consumer Utilities Offered by Retailing

The utilities provided by retailers create value for consumers. Time, place, form, and possession utilities are offered by most retailers in varying degrees, but one utility is often emphasized more than others. Look at Figure 13–1 to see how well you can match the retailer with the utility being emphasized in the description.

FIGURE 13–1
Which retailer best provides which utilities?

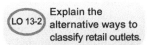

Video 13-2
CarMax
kerin.tv/cr6e/v13-2

Providing mini banks in supermarkets, as Wells Fargo does, puts the bank's products and services close to the consumer, providing place utility. By providing financing or leasing and taking used cars as trade-ins, CarMax makes the purchase easier and provides possession utility. Form utility—production or alteration of a product—is offered by Ralph Lauren through its online *Create Your Own* program, which offers shirts that meet each customer's specifications. Finding the right sporting equipment during the off-season is the time utility provided by Sports Authority. Many retailers offer a combination of the four basic utilities. Some supermarkets, for example, offer convenient locations (place utility); are open 24 hours a day (time utility); customize purchases in the bakery, deli, and florist (form utility); and allow several payment and credit options (possession utility).

Carrefour is one of the largest retailers outside the United States.

The Global Economic Impact of Retailing

Retailing is important to the U.S. and global economies. Four of the 40 largest businesses in the United States are retailers (Walmart, Costco, Home Depot, and Target). Walmart's $469 billion in annual sales in 2012 surpassed the gross domestic product of all but 29 countries for that same year. Walmart, Costco, Home Depot, and Target together have more than 3 million employees—more than the combined populations of Jacksonville, Florida; El Paso, Texas; and Stockton, California.[2] Many types of retailers, including food stores, automobile dealers, and general merchandise outlets, are also significant contributors to the U.S. economy.[3]

Outside the United States large retailers include Aeon in Japan, Carrefour in France, Metro Group in Germany, and Tesco in Britain.[4] In emerging economies such as China and Mexico, a combination of local and global retailers is evolving. Walmart, for example, has more than 6,200 stores outside the United States, including stores in Argentina, Brazil, China, India, Japan, Mexico, and the United Kingdom. Despite the presence of these large retailers, however, most international markets are dominated by local retailers.[5]

> **learning review**
>
> **13-1.** When Ralph Lauren makes shirts to a customer's exact preferences, what utility is provided?
>
> **13-2.** Two measures of the impact of retailing in the global economy are _____ and _____.

CLASSIFYING RETAIL OUTLETS

LO 13-2 Explain the alternative ways to classify retail outlets.

For manufacturers, consumers, and the economy, retailing is an important component of marketing that has several variations. Because of the large number of alternative forms of retailing, it is easier to understand the differences among retail institutions by recognizing that outlets can be classified in several ways. First, *form of ownership* distinguishes retail outlets based on whether independent retailers, corporate chains, or contractual systems own the outlet. Second, *level of service* is used to describe the degree of service provided to the customer. Three levels of service are provided by self-, limited-, and full-service retailers. Finally, the type of *merchandise line* describes how many different types of products a store carries and in what assortment. The alternative types of outlets are discussed in greater detail in the following pages. For many consumers today, retail outlets are also evaluated in terms of their environmentally friendly, or green, activities, in addition to their level of service and merchandise line. The Making Responsible Decisions box on the next page gives examples of the green activities of several retailers.[6]

Making Responsible Decisions

What Color Is Your Retailer? Is It Green?

You might remember when "going green" was an expression used by consumers to describe their purchase and use of environmentally friendly products. Initially, retailers responded by offering products that matched consumers' new environmental interests. Over time, however, retailers have come to realize that consumers also want to purchase those products from like-minded retailers. Today, many retailers are developing comprehensive and sophisticated business practices that reflect a new focus on social and environmental responsibility.

The U.S. Green Retail Association offers guidance for retailers implementing new practices, and it also provides a third-party certification that recognizes a commitment to "green" values. Some practices are intuitive and simple, such as encouraging the use of reusable shopping bags, installing LED lighting, and using nontoxic cleaning products. Many retailers are even using recyclable materials for credit and gift cards, rather than plastic. Other practices, such as using more economical delivery vehicles to reduce CO_2 emissions, using rainwater

for landscape maintenance, or finding alternative uses for landfill waste, require a more concerted effort. Very often, however, these environmental initiatives also have financial benefits. When Home Depot switched light displays to CFL and LED light bulbs, painted the roofs of stores white, and installed solar panels, it reduced its energy use by 20 percent.

Many retailers are also requiring that their suppliers make similar efforts and meet the same standards. When Walmart noticed that some packaging led to waste, it required its toy suppliers to trim one square inch of packaging from their lines and reduce packaging by 3,500 tons. In addition, Walmart is taking these green initiatives overseas.

Do sustainability practices such as these influence your purchase decisions? The issue is becoming so important that *Newsweek* now publishes rankings of retailers with the best green practices. Office Depot, Staples, Best Buy, Home Depot, and Walmart were at the top of the most recent list. Are your favorite retailers "green"?

Form of Ownership

There are three general forms of retail ownership—independent retailer, corporate chain, and contractual systems.

Independent Retailer One of the most common forms of retail ownership is the independent business owned by an individual. Independent retailers account for most of the 1.1 million retail establishments in the United States and include hardware stores, convenience stores, clothing stores, and computer and software stores. In addition, there are 26,700 jewelry stores, 18,500 florists, and 22,100 sporting goods and hobby stores. For the independent retailer, the advantage of this form of ownership is simple: The owner is the boss. For customers, the independent store can offer convenience, personal service, and lifestyle compatibility.[7]

Corporate Chain A second form of ownership, the corporate chain, involves multiple outlets under common ownership. Macy's, Inc., for example, operates 810 Macy's department stores in 45 states. Macy's also owns 37 Bloomingdale's, which compete with other chain stores such as Saks Fifth Avenue and Neiman Marcus.

In a chain operation, centralization in decision making and purchasing is common. Chain stores have advantages in dealing with manufacturers, particularly as the size of the chain grows. A large chain can bargain with a manufacturer to obtain good service or volume discounts on orders. Target's large volume makes it a strong negotiator with manufacturers of most products. For consumers, the buying power of chains translates into lower prices compared with other types of stores. Consumers also benefit in dealing with chains because there are multiple outlets with similar merchandise and consistent management policies.

Retailing has become a high-tech business for many large chains. Walmart, for example, has developed a sophisticated inventory management and cost control system that allows rapid price changes for each product in every store. In addition, stores such as Walmart and Target are implementing pioneering new technologies such as radio frequency identification (RFID) tags to improve the quality of information available about products.

Subway is a popular business-format franchisor.

Contractual Systems Contractual systems involve independently owned stores that band together to act like a chain. Recall that in Chapter 12, we discussed three kinds of contractual vertical marketing systems: retailer-sponsored cooperatives, wholesaler-sponsored voluntary chains, and franchises. One retailer-sponsored cooperative is Associated Grocers, which consists of neighborhood grocers that all agree with several other independent grocers to buy their goods directly from food manufacturers. In this way, members can take advantage of volume discounts commonly available to chains and also give the impression of being a large chain, which may be viewed more favorably by some consumers. Wholesaler-sponsored voluntary chains such as Independent Grocers Alliance (IGA) try to achieve similar benefits.

In a franchise system, an individual or firm (the franchisee) contracts with a parent company (the franchisor) to set up a business or retail outlet. The franchisor usually assists in selecting the location, setting up the store or facility, advertising, and training personnel. The franchisee usually pays a one-time franchise fee and an annual royalty, usually tied to the franchise's sales. There are two general types of franchises: *business-format franchises*, such as McDonald's, RadioShack, and Subway, and *product-distribution franchises*, such as a Ford dealership or a Coca-Cola distributor. In business-format franchising, the franchisor provides step-by-step procedures for most aspects of the business and guidelines for the most likely decisions a franchisee will face. In product-distribution franchising, the franchisor provides a few general guidelines and the franchisee is much more independent.

Franchise fees paid to the franchisor can range from $15,000 for a Subway franchise to $45,000 for a McDonald's restaurant franchise. When the fees are combined with other costs such as real estate and equipment, however, the total investment can be much higher. Franchisees also pay an ongoing royalty fee that ranges from 5 percent for a Papa John's pizza franchise to 30 percent for an H&R Block tax preparation franchise. By selling franchises, an organization reduces the cost of expansion but loses some control. A good franchisor, however, will maintain strong control of the outlets in terms of delivery and presentation of merchandise and try to enhance recognition of the franchise name.[8]

Redbox provides a service without clerks.

Level of Service

Although most customers have little reason to notice form of ownership differences among retailers, they are typically aware of differences in terms of level of service. In some department stores, such as Loehmann's, very few services are provided. Some grocery stores, such as the Cub Foods chain, encourage customers to bag their groceries themselves. In contrast, outlets such as Neiman Marcus provide a wide range of customer services, from gift wrapping to wardrobe consultation.

Self-Service Self-service requires that customers perform many functions during the purchase process. Warehouse clubs such as Costco, for example, are usually self-service, with all nonessential customer services eliminated. Many gas stations, supermarkets, and airlines today also have self-service lanes and terminals. Video retailer Redbox has 35,500 kiosks throughout the United States—and operates without a single clerk. New forms of self-service are being developed at convenience stores, fast-food restaurants, and even coffee shops! Shop24 is building self-service, automated convenience stores in 15 countries, including the United States. At Pizza Hut, you can place an order through an iPhone app or on the website. Similarly, there will be more than 2,000 Marley Coffee Automated Cafes in the next two years. In general, the trend is toward retailing experiences that make customers co-creators of the value they receive. Experts estimate that automated sales will reach $1.1 trillion by 2015.[9]

Limited Service   Limited-service outlets provide some services, such as credit and merchandise return, but not others, such as clothing alterations. General merchandise stores such as Walmart, Kmart, and Target are usually considered limited service outlets. Customers are responsible for most shopping activities, although salespeople are available in departments such as consumer electronics, jewelry, and lawn and garden.

Full Service   Full-service retailers, which include most specialty stores and department stores, provide many services to their customers. Neiman Marcus, Nordstrom, and Saks Fifth Avenue, for example, all rely on better service to sell more distinctive, higher-margin goods and to retain their customers. Nordstrom offers a wide variety of services, including on-site alterations and tailoring; free exchanges and easy returns; gift cards; credit cards through Nordstrom Bank; a 7-days-a-week customer service line; a live chat line with beauty, design, and wedding specialists; online shopping with in-store pickup; catalogs; and a four-level loyalty program called Nordstrom Fashion Rewards. Some Nordstrom stores also offer a "Personal Stylist" department, which provides shopping assistants for consumers who need help with style, color, and size selection, as well as a concierge service for assistance with anything else. Nordstrom stores typically have 50 percent more salespeople on the floor than similarly sized stores, and the salespeople are renowned for their professional and personalized attention to customers. Nordstrom also offers e-mail, an RSS (rich site summary) feed, Twitter messages, a blog, a website, and mobile apps to notify customers about fashion trends, new merchandise, and sales.[10]

Type of Merchandise Line

Retail outlets also vary by their merchandise lines, the key distinction being the breadth and depth of the items offered to customers (see Figure 13–2). *Depth of product line* means the store carries a large assortment of each item, such as a shoe store that offers running shoes, dress shoes, and children's shoes. *Breadth of product line* refers to the variety of different items a store carries, such as appliances and books.

Depth of Line   Stores that carry a considerable assortment (depth) of a related line of items are limited-line stores. Sports Authority sporting goods stores carry considerable depth in sports equipment ranging from weight-lifting accessories to running shoes. Stores that carry tremendous depth in one primary line of merchandise

FIGURE 13–2
Stores vary in terms of the breadth and depth of their merchandise lines.

Breadth: Number of different product lines

| Shoes | Appliances | Books | Men's clothing |

Depth: Number of items within each product line

Shoes	Appliances	Books	Men's clothing
• Nike running shoes • Florsheim dress shoes • Sperry boat shoes • Adidas tennis shoes	• General Electric dishwashers • Panasonic microwave ovens • Whirlpool washers	• Mystery • Romance • Science fiction • History • Poetry • Entertainment	• Suits • Ties • Jackets • Overcoats • Socks • Shirts

Staples is the category killer in office supplies because it dominates the market in that category.

scrambled merchandising
Offering several unrelated product lines in a single store.

are single-line stores. Victoria's Secret, a nationwide chain, carries great depth in women's lingerie. Both limited- and single-line stores are often referred to as *specialty outlets*.

Specialty discount outlets focus on one type of product, such as electronics (Best Buy), office supplies (Staples), or books (Barnes & Noble), at very competitive prices. These outlets are referred to in the trade as *category killers* because they often dominate the market. Best Buy, for example, is the largest consumer electronics retailer with more than 1,400 stores.

Breadth of Line   Stores that carry a broad product line, with limited depth, are referred to as *general merchandise stores*. For example, large department stores such as Dillard's, Macy's, and Neiman Marcus carry a wide range of different types of products but not unusual sizes. The breadth and depth of merchandise lines are important decisions for a retailer. Traditionally, outlets carried related lines of goods. Today, however, **scrambled merchandising**, offering several unrelated product lines in a single store, is common. For example, the modern drugstore carries food, camera equipment, magazines, paper products, toys, small hardware items, and pharmaceuticals. Supermarkets sell flowers and videos and print photos, in addition to selling groceries.

learning review

13-3. Centralized decision making and purchasing are an advantage of _____ ownership.

13-4. What are some examples of new forms of self-service retailers?

13-5. A shop for big men's clothes carries pants in sizes 40 to 60. Would this be considered a broad or a deep product line?

NONSTORE RETAILING

LO 13-3 Describe the many methods of nonstore retailing.

Most of the retailing examples discussed thus far in the chapter, such as corporate chains, department stores, and limited- and single-line specialty stores, involve store retailing. Many retailing activities today, however, are not limited to sales in a store. Nonstore retailing occurs outside a retail outlet through activities that involve varying levels of customer and retailer involvement. The six forms of nonstore retailing are automatic vending, direct mail and catalogs, television home shopping, online retailing, telemarketing, and direct selling.

Automatic Vending

Nonstore retailing includes vending machines, or *v-commerce*, which make it possible to serve customers when and where stores cannot. Machine maintenance, operating costs, and location leases can add to the cost of the products, so prices in vending machines are often higher than those in stores. About 31 percent of the products sold from vending machines are cold beverages, another 21 percent are candy and snacks, and 5 percent are food. Many new types of products are quickly becoming available in vending machines. Best Buy now uses vending machines to sell mobile phone and computer accessories, digital cameras, flash drives, and other consumer electronics products in airports, hospitals, and businesses. Similarly, HealthyYou Vending manufactures machines designed to distribute healthy drinks, snacks, and entrées in offices, health clubs, hospitals, schools, and colleges. The 5.4 million vending machines currently in use in the United States generate more than $19 billion in annual sales.[11]

Vending machines offer a variety of products. How does technology make vending machines easier to use? For the answer, see the text.

Video 13-3
IKEA
kerin.tv/cr6e/v13-3

Specialty catalogs appeal to market niches. They create value by providing a fast and convenient way to shop.

Improved technology is making vending easier to use. Many vending machines now have touchscreens and credit card readers. In addition, some vending machine companies are testing wireless technology to allow consumers to make vending machine purchases using their mobile phones. Wireless technology is also being used by companies to monitor sales; this information is used to schedule trips to restock machines when items are sold out. Another improvement in vending machines is the trend toward "green" machines, which consume less energy by using more efficient compressors, more efficient lighting, and better insulation. For today's consumers, vending machines represent an extension of brands that are already available in stores, through catalogs, and online.[12]

Direct Mail and Catalogs

Direct-mail and catalog retailing has been called "the store that comes to the door." It is attractive for several reasons. First, it can eliminate the cost of a store and clerks. Dell, for example, is one of the largest computer and information technology retailers, and it does not have any stores. Second, direct mail and catalogs improve marketing efficiency through segmentation and targeting, and they create customer value by providing a fast and convenient means of making a purchase. Finally, many catalogs now serve as a tool to encourage consumers to visit a website, a social media page, or even a store. Online retailers such as Zappos, Amazon, and eBay, for example, now offer catalogs. The average U.S. household today receives 24 direct-mail items or catalogs each week. The Direct Marketing Association estimates that direct-mail and catalog retailing creates $642 billion in sales. Direct-mail and catalog retailing is popular outside the United States, also. Furniture retailer IKEA delivered 212 million copies of its catalog in 17 languages to 28 countries last year.[13]

Several factors have had an impact on direct-mail and catalog retailing in recent years. The influence of large retailers such as IKEA, Crate and Barrel, L.L. Bean, and others has been positive as their marketing activities have increased the number and variety of products consumers purchase through direct mail and catalogs. Higher paper costs and increases in postage rates, the growing interest in do-not-mail legislation, the concern for "green" mailings and catalogs, and the possibility of the U.S. Postal Service reducing delivery to five days, however, have caused direct-mail and catalog retailers to search for ways to provide additional customer value. One approach has been to send specialty catalogs to market niches identified in their databases. L.L. Bean, for example, has developed an individual catalog for fly-fishing enthusiasts.[14]

Television home shopping programs serve millions of customers each year. See the text to learn how they are attracting new customers.

Television Home Shopping

Television home shopping is possible when consumers watch a shopping channel on which products are displayed; orders are then placed over the telephone or the Internet. Currently, the three largest programs are QVC, HSN, and ShopNBC. QVC ("quality, value, convenience") broadcasts live 24 hours each day, 364 days a year, and reaches more than 300 million homes in the United States, United Kingdom, Germany, Japan, Italy, and China. The company generates sales of $8.6 billion from its 60 million customers by offering more than 1,150 products each week.[15]

In the past, television home shopping programs attracted mostly 40- to 60-year-old women. To attract a younger audience, QVC has invited celebrities onto the show. For example, Heidi Klum has been on the show promoting her jewelry collection, and Kim, Khloe, and Kourtney Kardashian have been hosts selling their apparel line. Singer Dolly Parton recently appeared on the show to promote her newest album. Broadcasting events such as the Red Carpet Style show at the Four Seasons Hotel in Beverly Hills also helps attract new customers. In addition, QVC supports its television program with retail stores, a website, mobile apps, text alerts, and online chats during programming. Similarly, Home Shopping Network now offers a multiplatform shopping experience. Some experts suggest that television shopping programs are becoming a modern version of door-to-door retailing by combining elements of reality TV programs, talk shows, and infomercials.[16]

Online Retailing

Online retailing allows consumers to search for, evaluate, and order products through the Internet. For many consumers, the advantages of this form of retailing are the 24-hour access, the ability to comparison shop, in-home privacy, and variety. Traditional and online retailers—"bricks and clicks"—are melding, using experiences from both approaches to create better value and experiences for customers. For example, Walmart (www.walmart.com) offers its Site-to-Store service that allows customers to place an order online and pick it up at a Walmart store or a FedEx location. In addition, Walmart now offers its HomeFree option, which provides free shipping to customers' homes when they order $45 or more of selected items. The Walmart Mobile app allows shoppers to order products using their smartphones and tablets. Two of the biggest days for online retailing are the Friday after Thanksgiving—Black Friday—and the Monday after Thanksgiving—Cyber Monday—which generated $11.2 billion in total sales and $1.4 billion in online sales, respectively. Online sales account for approximately 5 percent of all retail sales and are expected to reach $327 billion in 2016.[17]

Shopping "bots" like mysimon.com find the best prices for products specified by consumers. Read the text to learn more!

Online retail purchases can be the result of several very different approaches. First, consumers can pay dues to become a member of an online discount service such as www.netmarket.com. The service offers thousands of products and hundreds of brand names at very low prices to its subscribers. Another approach to online retailing is to use a shopping "bot" such as www.mysimon.com. This site searches the Internet for a product specified by the consumer and provides a report listing retailers with the best prices. Consumers can also use the Internet to go directly to online malls (www.fashionmall.com), apparel retailers (www.gap.com), bookstores (www.amazon.com),

CHAPTER 13   Retailing and Wholesaling

computer manufacturers (www.dell.com), grocery stores (www.peapod.com), music and video stores (www.tower.com), and travel agencies (www.travelocity.com). A final approach to online retailing is the online auction, such as www.ebay.com, where 112 million users "trade practically anything."[18]

One of the biggest problems online retailers face is that nearly two-thirds of online shoppers make it to "checkout" and then leave the website to compare shipping costs and prices on other sites. Of the shoppers who leave, 70 percent do not return. One way online retailers are addressing this issue is to offer consumers a comparison of competitors' offerings. Experts also suggest that online retailers should think of their websites as dynamic billboards that should be easy to use and customizable, and that facilitate interaction.[19] For example, BMW, Mercedes, and Jaguar encourage website visitors to "build" a vehicle by selecting interior and exterior colors, packages, and options; view the customized virtual car; and then use Facebook, Twitter, or e-mail to share the configuration. Online retailing is also evolving to include social shopping options, including: *intermediaries*, such as Groupon and LivingSocial, that match consumers with merchants; *marketplaces*, such as Google Offer and Storenvy, that provide a self-service advertising site; and *aggregators*, such as Yipit, that crawl the Web to find deals to list on their own site.

Telemarketing

telemarketing
Using the telephone to interact with and sell directly to consumers.

Another form of nonstore retailing, called **telemarketing**, involves using the telephone to interact with and sell directly to consumers. Compared with direct mail, telemarketing is often viewed as a more efficient means of targeting consumers. Insurance companies, brokerage firms, and newspapers have often used this form of retailing as a way to cut costs but still maintain access to their customers. According to the Direct Marketing Association, annual telemarketing sales exceed $332 billion.[20]

The telemarketing industry has recently gone through dramatic changes as a result of new legislation related to telephone solicitations. Issues such as consumer privacy, industry standards, and ethical guidelines have encouraged discussion among consumers, Congress, the Federal Trade Commission, and businesses. As a result, legislation created the National Do Not Call Registry (www.donotcall.gov) for consumers who do not want to receive telephone calls related to company sales efforts. Currently, there are more than 221 million phone numbers on the registry. Companies that use telemarketing have already adapted by adding compliance software to ensure that numbers on the list are not called.[21]

Direct Selling

MARY KAY

Direct selling, sometimes called door-to-door retailing, involves direct sales of products and services to consumers through personal interactions and demonstrations in their home or office. A variety of companies, including familiar names such as Avon, Fuller Brush, Mary Kay Cosmetics, and World Book, have created an industry with more than $29 billion in U.S. sales by providing consumers with personalized service and convenience. In the United States, there are more than 15 million direct salespeople working full-time and part-time in a variety of product categories, including wellness, home durables, and personal care.[22]

Growth in the direct-selling industry is the result of two trends. First, many direct selling retailers are expanding into markets outside of the United States. Avon, for example, has 6 million sales representatives in 100 countries. More than one-third of Amway's $11 billion in sales now comes from China.[23] The second trend is the growing number of companies that are using direct selling to reach consumers who prefer one-on-one customer service and a social shopping experience rather than online shopping or big discount stores. The Direct Selling Association reports that the number of companies using direct selling is increasing. Pampered Chef, for example, has

60,000 independent sales reps who sell the company's products at in-home kitchen parties. Interest among potential sales representatives has grown during the recent economic downturn as people seek independence and control of their work activities.[24]

learning review

13-6. Successful catalog retailers often send _____ catalogs to _____ markets identified in their databases.

13-7. How are retailers increasing the number of online shoppers who make it through "checkout"?

13-8. Where are direct selling retail sales growing? Why?

RETAILING STRATEGY

 LO 13-4 Specify the retailing mix actions used to implement a retailing strategy.

This section describes how a retailer develops and implements a retailing strategy. In developing a retailing strategy, managers work with the **retailing mix**, which includes activities related to managing the store and the merchandise in the store. The retailing mix is similar to the marketing mix and includes retail pricing, store location, retail communication, and merchandise (see Figure 13–3).

retailing mix
The activities related to managing the store and the merchandise in the store, which includes retail pricing, store location, retail communication, and merchandise.

Retail Pricing

In setting prices for merchandise, retailers must decide on the markup, markdown, and timing for markdowns. The *markup* refers to how much should be added to the cost the retailer paid for a product to reach the final selling price. Retailers decide on the *original markup*, but by the time the product is sold, they end up with a *maintained markup*. The original markup is the difference between retailer cost and initial selling price. When products do not sell as quickly as anticipated, their price is reduced. The difference between the final selling price and retailer cost is the maintained markup, which is also called the *gross margin*.

Discounting a product, or taking a *markdown*, occurs when the product does not sell at the original price and an adjustment is necessary. Often new models or styles force the price of existing models to be marked down. Discounts may also be used to increase demand for complementary products.[25] For example, retailers might take a markdown on the price of cake mix to generate frosting purchases. The *timing* of a markdown can be important. Many retailers take a markdown as soon as sales fall off to free up valuable selling space and cash. However, other stores delay markdowns to discourage bargain hunters and maintain an image of quality. There is no clear answer,

FIGURE 13–3
Retailing strategy is related to the retailing mix. Note the similarity between the retailing mix and the marketing mix.

At off-price retail stores like T.J. Maxx, prices are low but selection may be unpredictable.

but retailers must consider how the timing might affect future sales. Research indicates that frequent promotions increase consumers' ability to remember regular prices.[26]

Although most retailers plan markdowns, many retailers use price discounts as part of their regular merchandising policy. Walmart and Home Depot, for example, emphasize consistently low prices and eliminate most markdowns with a strategy often called *everyday low pricing* (EDLP).[27] Because consumers often use price as an indicator of product quality, however, the brand name of the product and the image of the store become important decision factors in these situations.[28] Another strategy, *everyday fair pricing*, is advocated by retailers that may not offer the lowest price but try to create value for customers through service and the total buying experience.[29] Consumers often use the prices of *benchmark* or *signpost* items, such as a can of Coke, to form an overall impression of a store's prices.[30] In addition, price is the most likely factor to influence consumers' assessment of merchandise value.[31] When store prices are based on rebates, retailers must be careful to avoid negative consumer perceptions if the rebate processing time is long (e.g., six weeks).[32]

Off-price retailing is a retail pricing practice that is used by retailers such as T.J. Maxx, Burlington Coat Factory, and Ross Stores. *Off-price retailing* involves selling brand-name merchandise at lower than regular prices. The difference between the off-price retailer and a discount store is that off-price merchandise is bought by the retailer from manufacturers with excess inventory at prices below wholesale prices. The discounter, however, buys at full wholesale prices but takes less of a markup than traditional department stores. Because of this difference in the way merchandise is purchased by the retailer, selection at an off-price retailer is unpredictable, and searching for bargains has become a popular activity for many consumers. "It's more like a sport than it is like ordinary shopping," says Christopher Boring of Columbus, Ohio's Retail Planning Associates.[33] Savings to the consumer at off-price retailers are reportedly as high as 70 percent off the prices of a traditional department store. A variation of off-price retailing includes outlet stores such as Nordstrom Rack and Off 5th (an outlet for Saks Fifth Avenue) which allow retailers to sell excess merchandise and still maintain an image of offering merchandise at full price in their primary store.

Off 5th provides an outlet for excess merchandise from Saks Fifth Avenue.

Store Location

A second aspect of the retailing mix involves choosing a location and deciding how many stores to operate. Department stores, which started downtown in most cities, have followed customers to the suburbs, and in recent years more stores have been opened in large regional malls. Most stores today are near several others in one of four settings: the central business district, the regional center, the strip mall, or the power center.

The *central business district* is the oldest retail setting, the community's downtown area. Until the regional outflow to suburbs, it was the major shopping area, but the suburban population has grown at the expense of the downtown shopping area. Consumers often view central business district shopping as less convenient because of lack of parking, higher crime rates, and exposure to the weather. Many cities such as Louisville, Denver, and San Antonio have implemented plans to revitalize shopping in central business districts by attracting new offices, entertainment, and residents to downtown locations.

Regional shopping centers consist of 50 to 150 stores that typically attract customers who live or work within a 5- to 10-mile range. These large shopping areas often contain two or three *anchor stores*, which are well-known national or regional stores such as Sears, Saks Fifth Avenue, and Bloomingdale's. The largest variation of a regional center in North America is the West Edmonton Mall in Alberta, Canada. This shopping center is a conglomerate of more than 800 stores, the world's largest indoor amusement park, more than 100 restaurants, a movie complex, and two hotels, all of which attract 30 million visitors each year.[34]

Not every suburban store is located in a shopping mall. Many neighborhoods have clusters of stores, referred to as a *strip mall*, to serve people who are within a 5- to 10-minute drive. Gas station, hardware, laundry, grocery, and pharmacy outlets are commonly found in a strip mall. Unlike the larger shopping centers, the composition of these stores is usually unplanned. A variation of the strip mall is called the *power center*, which is a huge shopping strip with multiple anchor (or national) stores such as Home Depot, Best Buy, or JCPenney. Power centers combine the convenience of location provided by strip malls with the power of national stores. These large strip malls often have two to five anchor stores and contain a supermarket, which brings the shopper to the power center on a weekly basis.[35]

The many retailing formats described in this chapter represent an exciting menu of choices for creating customer value in the marketplace. Each format allows retailers to offer unique benefits and meet the particular needs of various customer groups. While each format has many successful applications, retailers in the future are likely to combine many of the formats to offer a broader spectrum of benefits and experiences and to appeal to different segments of consumers.[36] These **multichannel retailers** will utilize and integrate a combination of traditional store formats and nonstore formats such as catalogs, television, home shopping, and online retailing.[37] Barnes & Noble, for example, created <u>Barnesandnoble.com</u> to compete with <u>Amazon.com</u>. Similarly, Office Depot has integrated its store, catalog, and Internet operations.

multichannel retailers
Retailers that use a combination of traditional store formats and nonstore formats, such as catalogs, television, and online retailing.

Retail Communication

A retailer's communication activities can play an important role in positioning a store and creating its image. While the typical elements of communication and promotion are discussed in Chapter 15 on advertising, sales promotion, and public relations, Chapter 16 on social media, and Chapter 17 on personal selling, the message communicated by the many other elements of the retailing mix is also important.

Deciding on the image of a retail outlet is an important retailing mix factor that has been widely recognized and studied since the late 1950s. Pierre Martineau described image as "the way in which the store is defined in the shopper's mind," partly by its functional qualities and partly by an aura of psychological attributes.[38] In this definition, *functional* refers to mix elements such as price ranges, store layouts, and breadth and depth of merchandise lines. The psychological attributes are the intangibles such as a sense of belonging, excitement, style, or warmth. Image has been found to include impressions of the corporation that operates the store, the category or type of store, the product categories in the store, the brands in each category, merchandise and service quality, and the marketing activities of the store.[39]

Closely related to the concept of image is the store's atmosphere, or ambience. Many retailers believe that sales are affected by layout, color, lighting, music, scent,[40] and other elements of the retail environment. This concept leads many retailers to use **shopper marketing**—the use of displays, coupons, product samples, and other brand communications to influence shopping behavior in a store. Shopper marketing can also influence behavior in an online shopping environment and when shoppers use smartphone apps to identify shopping needs or make purchase decisions.[41] In creating the right image and atmosphere, a retail store tries to attract a target audience and fortify beliefs about the store, its products, and the shopping experience in the store. While store image perceptions can exist independently of shopping experiences, consumers' shopping experiences influence their perceptions of a store.[42] In addition, the physical surroundings of the retail environment influence a store's employees.[43]

shopper marketing
The use of displays, coupons, product samples, and other brand communications to influence shopping behavior in a store.

Merchandise

The final element of the retailing mix is the merchandise offering. Managing the breadth and depth of the product line requires retail buyers who are familiar with both the needs of the target market and the alternative products available from the many

CHAPTER 13   Retailing and Wholesaling

Using Marketing Dashboards

Why Apple Stores May Be the Best in the United States!

How effective is my retail format compared to other stores? How are my stores performing this year compared to last year? Information related to these questions is often displayed in a marketing dashboard using two measures: (1) sales per square foot and (2) same-store sales growth.

Your Challenge   You have been assigned to evaluate the Apple Store retail format. The store's simple, inviting, and open atmosphere has been the topic of discussion among many retailers. Apple, however, is relatively new to the retailing business, and many experts have been skeptical of the format. To allow an assessment of Apple Stores, use *sales per square foot* as an indicator of how effectively retail space is used to generate revenue and *same-store sales growth* to compare the increase in sales of stores that have been open for the same period of time. The calculations for these two indicators are:

$$\text{Sales per square foot} = \frac{\text{Total sales}}{\text{Selling area in square feet}}$$

Same-store sales growth

$$= \frac{\text{Store sales in year 2} - \text{Store sales in year 1}}{\text{Store sales in year 1}}$$

Your Findings   You decide to collect sales information for Target, Neiman Marcus, Best Buy, Tiffany, and Apple Stores to allow comparisons with other successful retailers. The information you collect allows the calculation of *sales per square foot* and *same-store growth* for each store. The results are then easy to compare in the graphs below.

Your Action   The results of your investigation indicate that Apple Stores' sales per square foot are higher than any of the comparison stores at $5,647. In addition, Apple's same-store growth rate of 41.9 percent is higher than all of the other retailers. You conclude that the elements of Apple's format are very effective and even indicate that Apple may currently be the best retailer in the United States.

---

category management
An approach to managing the assortment of merchandise to maximize sales and profits in the category.

manufacturers that might be interested in having a product available in the store. A popular approach to managing the assortment of merchandise today is called **category management**. This approach assigns a manager the responsibility for selecting all products that consumers in a market segment might view as substitutes for each other, with the objective of maximizing sales and profits in the category. For example, a category manager might be responsible for shoes in a department store or paper products in a grocery store. As such, he or she would consider trade deals, order costs, and the between-brand effects of price range changes to determine brand assortment, order quantities, and prices.[44]

Retailers have a variety of marketing metrics that can be used to assess the effectiveness of a store or retail format. First, there are measures related to customers such as the number of transactions per customer, the average transaction size per customer, the number of customers per day or per hour, and the average length of a store visit. Second, there are measures related to the stores and the products such as level of inventory, number of returns, inventory turnover, inventory carrying cost, and average number of items per transaction. Finally, there are financial measures, such as gross margin, sales per employee, return on sales, and markdown percentage.[45] The two most popular measures for retailers are *sales per square foot* and *same-store sales growth*. The Using Marketing Dashboards box on the previous page describes the calculation of these measures for Apple Stores.[46]

learning review

13-9. How does original markup differ from maintained markup?

13-10. A huge shopping strip mall with multiple anchor stores is a _____ center.

13-11. What is a popular approach to managing the assortment of merchandise in a store?

THE CHANGING NATURE OF RETAILING

LO 13-5 Explain changes in retailing with the wheel of retailing and the retail life cycle concepts.

Retailing is the most dynamic aspect of a channel of distribution. New types of retailers are always entering the market, searching for a new position that will attract customers. The reason for this continual change is explained by two concepts: the wheel of retailing and the retail life cycle.

The Wheel of Retailing

wheel of retailing
A concept that describes how new forms of retail outlets enter the market.

The **wheel of retailing** describes how new forms of retail outlets enter the market.[47] Usually they enter as low-status, low-margin stores such as a drive-in hamburger stand with no indoor seating and a limited menu (Figure 13–4, box 1). Gradually these outlets add fixtures and more embellishments to their stores (in-store seating, plants, and chicken sandwiches as well as hamburgers) to increase the attractiveness for customers.

FIGURE 13–4
The wheel of retailing describes how retail outlets change over time. Read the text to find out the position of McDonald's and In-N-Out Burgers on the wheel of retailing.

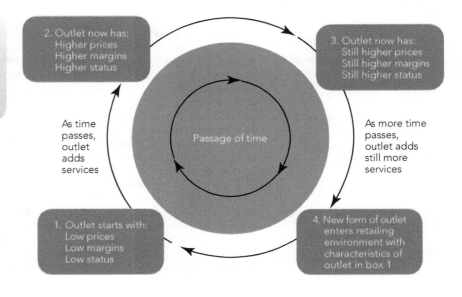

2. Outlet now has:
Higher prices
Higher margins
Higher status

3. Outlet now has:
Still higher prices
Still higher margins
Still higher status

As time passes, outlet adds services

Passage of time

As more time passes, outlet adds still more services

1. Outlet starts with:
Low prices
Low margins
Low status

4. New form of outlet enters retailing environment with characteristics of outlet in box 1

With these additions, prices and status rise (box 2). As time passes, these outlets add still more services and their prices and status increase even further (box 3). These retail outlets now face some new form of retail outlet that again appears as a low-status, low-margin operator (box 4), and the wheel of retailing turns as the cycle starts to repeat itself.

When Ray Kroc bought McDonald's in 1955, it opened shortly before lunch and closed just after dinner, and it offered a limited menu for the two meals without any inside seating for customers. Over time, the wheel of retailing has led to new products and services. In 1975, McDonald's introduced the Egg McMuffin and turned breakfast into a fast-food meal. Today, McDonald's offers an extensive menu, including oatmeal and premium coffee, and it provides seating and services such as wireless Internet connections and kid-friendly PlayPlaces. For the future, McDonald's is testing new food products, including a double-sausage McMuffin, a barbecued pork sandwich, and Spicy Chicken McBites, and new formats, such as in-car touchscreen ordering and table service![48]

Video 13-4
McDonald's
kerin.tv/cr6e/v13-4

These changes are leaving room for other forms of outlets, such as In-N-Out Burgers. The In-N-Out Burger chain offers a limited menu consisting of burgers, french fries, shakes, and fountain drinks—and now has 290 locations throughout the southwest United States. The wheel is turning for other outlets, too—Boston Market has added pickup, delivery, and full-service catering to its original restaurant format, and it also provides Boston Market meal solutions through supermarket delis and Boston Market frozen meals in the frozen food sections of groceries. For still others, the wheel has come full circle. Taco Bell is now opening small, limited-offering outlets in gas stations, discount stores, or "wherever a burrito and a mouth might possibly intersect."[49]

Outlets such as In-N-Out Burgers enter the wheel of retailing with limited menus and services.

The wheel of retailing is also evident in retail outlets outside the restaurant industry. Discount stores were a major new retailing form in the 1960s and priced their products below those of department stores. As prices in discount stores rose in the 1980s, they found themselves overpriced compared with a new form of retail outlet—the warehouse club. Today, off-price retailers and factory outlets are offering prices even lower than warehouse clubs.

The Retail Life Cycle

retail life cycle
The process of growth and decline that retail outlets experience over time.

The process of growth and decline that retail outlets, like products, experience is described by the **retail life cycle**.[50] Figure 13–5 shows the stages of the retail life cycle and where various forms of retail outlets are currently positioned along its spectrum. *Early growth* is the stage of emergence of a retail outlet, with a sharp departure from existing competition. Market share rises gradually, although profits may be low because of start-up costs. In the next stage, *accelerated development*, both market share and profit achieve their greatest growth rates. Usually multiple outlets are established as companies focus on the distribution element of the retailing mix. In this stage, some later competitors may enter. Wendy's, for example, appeared on the hamburger chain scene almost 20 years after McDonald's had begun operation. The key goal for the retailer in this stage is to establish a dominant position in the fight for market share.

The battle for market share is usually fought before the *maturity stage*, and some competitors drop out of the market. In the war among hamburger chains, Jack in the Box, Gino's Hamburgers, and Burger Chef used to be more dominant outlets. In the maturity stage, new retail forms enter the market (such as Fatburger and In-N-Out Burger in the hamburger chain industry), stores try to maintain their market share, and price discounting occurs. A challenge facing many retailers today is to delay entering the *decline stage*, in which market share and profit fall rapidly.

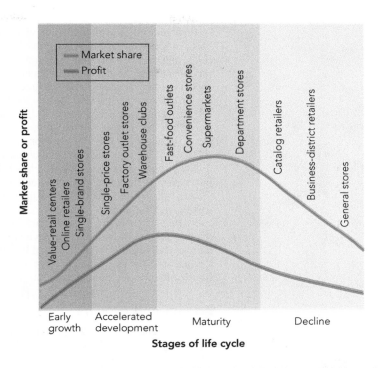

FIGURE 13–5
The retail life cycle describes stages of growth and decline for retail outlets.

> **learning review**
>
> 13-12. Using the wheel of retailing, describe the characteristics of a new retail form that has just entered the market.
>
> 13-13. Market share is usually fought out before the _____ stage of the retail life cycle.

WHOLESALING

LO 13-6 Describe the types of firms that perform wholesaling activities and their functions.

Many retailers depend on intermediaries that engage in wholesaling activities—selling products and services for the purposes of resale or business use. There are several types of intermediaries, including wholesalers and agents (described briefly in Chapter 12), as well as manufacturers' sales offices, which are important to understand as part of the retailing process.

Merchant Wholesalers

merchant wholesalers
Independently owned firms that take title to the merchandise they handle.

Merchant wholesalers are independently owned firms that take title to the merchandise they handle. They go by various names, including *industrial distributor.* Most firms engaged in wholesaling activities are merchant wholesalers.

Merchant wholesalers are classified as either full-service or limited-service wholesalers, depending on the number of functions performed. Two major types of full-service wholesalers exist. *General merchandise* (or *full-line*) *wholesalers* carry a broad assortment of merchandise and perform all channel functions. This type of wholesaler is most prevalent in the hardware, drug, and clothing industries. However, these wholesalers do not maintain much depth of assortment within specific product lines. *Specialty merchandise* (or *limited-line*) *wholesalers* offer a relatively narrow range of products but have an extensive assortment within the product lines carried. They perform all channel functions and are found in the health foods, automotive parts, and seafood industries.

Four major types of limited-service wholesalers exist. *Rack jobbers* furnish the racks or shelves that display merchandise in retail stores, perform all channel functions, and sell on consignment to retailers, which means they retain the title to the products displayed and bill retailers only for the merchandise sold. Familiar products such as hosiery, toys, housewares, and health and beauty items are sold by rack jobbers. *Cash and carry wholesalers* take title to merchandise but sell only to buyers who call on them, pay cash for merchandise, and furnish their own transportation for merchandise. They carry a limited product assortment and do not make deliveries, extend credit, or supply market information. This type of wholesaler is common in electric supplies, office supplies, hardware products, and groceries.

Drop shippers, or *desk jobbers*, are wholesalers that own the merchandise they sell but do not physically handle, stock, or deliver it. They simply solicit orders from retailers and other wholesalers and have the merchandise shipped directly from a producer to a buyer. Drop shippers are used for bulky products such as coal, lumber, and chemicals, which are sold in extremely large quantities. *Truck jobbers* are small wholesalers that have a small warehouse from which they stock their trucks for distribution to retailers. They usually handle limited assortments of fast-moving or perishable items that are sold for cash directly from trucks in their original packages. Truck jobbers handle products such as bakery items, dairy products, and meat.

Agents and Brokers

manufacturer's agents
Agents who work for several producers and carry noncompetitive, complementary merchandise in an exclusive territory.

brokers
Independent firms or individuals whose principal function is to bring buyers and sellers together to make sales.

Unlike merchant wholesalers, agents and brokers do not take title to merchandise and typically perform fewer channel functions. They make their profit from commissions or fees paid for their services, whereas merchant wholesalers make their profit from the sale of the merchandise they own.

Manufacturer's agents and selling agents are the two major types of agents used by producers. **Manufacturer's agents**, or *manufacturer's representatives*, work for several producers and carry noncompetitive, complementary merchandise in an exclusive territory. Manufacturer's agents act as a producer's sales arm in a territory and are principally responsible for the transactional channel functions, primarily selling. They are used extensively in the automotive supply, footwear, and fabricated steel industries. The Manufacturers' Agents National Association (MANA) facilitates the process of matching manufacturer's representatives with logical products and companies.

By comparison, *selling agents* represent a single producer and are responsible for the entire marketing function of that producer. They design promotional plans, set prices, determine distribution policies, and make recommendations on product strategy. Selling agents are used by small producers in the textile, apparel, food, and home furnishing industries.

Brokers are independent firms or individuals whose principal function is to bring buyers and sellers together to make sales. Brokers, unlike agents, usually have no continuous relationship with the buyer or seller but negotiate a contract between two parties and then move on to another task. Brokers are used extensively by producers of seasonal products (such as fruits and vegetables) and in the real estate industry.

A unique broker that acts in many ways like a manufacturer's agent is a food broker, representing buyers and sellers in the grocery industry. Food brokers differ from conventional brokers because they act on behalf of producers on a permanent basis and receive a commission for their services. For example, Nabisco uses food brokers to sell its candies, margarine, and Planters peanuts, but it sells its line of cookies and crackers directly to retail stores.

Manufacturer's Branches and Offices

Unlike merchant wholesalers, agents, and brokers, manufacturer's branches and sales offices are wholly owned extensions of the producer that perform wholesaling activities. Producers assume wholesaling functions when there are no intermediaries to perform these activities, customers are few in number and geographically concentrated, or orders are large or require significant attention. A *manufacturer's branch office* carries a producer's inventory and performs the functions of a full-service wholesaler. A *manufacturer's sales office* does not carry inventory, typically performs only a sales function, and serves as an alternative to agents and brokers.

learning review

13-14. What is the difference between merchant wholesalers and agents?

13-15. Under what circumstances do producers assume wholesaling functions?

LEARNING OBJECTIVES REVIEW

LO 13-1 *Identify retailers in terms of the utilities they provide.*

Retailers provide time, place, form, and possession utilities. Time utility is provided by stores with convenient time-of-day (e.g., open 24 hours) or time-of-year (e.g., seasonal sports equipment available all year) availability. Place utility is provided by the number and location of the stores. Possession utility is provided by making a purchase possible (e.g., financing) or easier (e.g., delivery). Form utility is provided by producing or altering a product to meet the customer's specifications (e.g., custom-made shirts).

LO 13-2 *Explain the alternative ways to classify retail outlets.*

Retail outlets can be classified by their form of ownership, level of service, and type of merchandise line. The forms of ownership include independent retailers, corporate chains, and contractual systems that include retailer-sponsored cooperatives, wholesaler-sponsored voluntary chains, and franchises. The levels of service include self-service, limited-service, and full-service outlets. Stores classified by their merchandise line include stores with depth, such as sporting goods specialty stores, and stores with breadth, such as large department stores.

LO 13-3 *Describe the many methods of nonstore retailing.*

Nonstore retailing includes automatic vending, direct mail and catalogs, television home shopping, online retailing, telemarketing, and direct selling. The methods of nonstore retailing vary by the level of involvement of the retailer and the level of involvement of the customer. Vending, for example, has low involvement, whereas both the consumer and the retailer have high involvement in direct selling.

LO 13-4 *Specify the retailing mix actions used to implement a retailing strategy.*

Retailing mix actions are used to manage a retail store and the merchandise in a store. The mix variables include pricing, store location, communication activities, and merchandise. Two common forms of assessment for retailers are sales per square foot and same-store growth.

LO 13-5 *Explain changes in retailing with the wheel of retailing and the retail life cycle concepts.*

The wheel of retailing concept explains how retail outlets typically enter the market as low-status, low-margin stores. Over time, stores gradually add new products and services, increasing their prices, status, and margins, and leaving an opening for new low-status, low-margin stores. The retail life cycle describes the process of growth and decline for retail outlets through four stages: early growth, accelerated development, maturity, and decline.

LO 13-6 *Describe the types of firms that perform wholesaling activities and their functions.*

There are three types of firms that perform wholesaling functions. First, merchant wholesalers are independently owned and take title to merchandise. They include general merchandise wholesalers, specialty merchandise wholesalers, rack jobbers, cash and carry wholesalers, drop shippers, and truck jobbers. Merchant wholesalers can perform a variety of channel functions. Second, agents and brokers do not take title to merchandise and primarily perform marketing functions. Finally, manufacturer's branches, which may carry inventory, and sales offices, which perform sales functions, are wholly owned by the producer.

LEARNING REVIEW ANSWERS

13-1 **When Ralph Lauren makes shirts to a customer's exact preferences, what utility is provided?**
Answer: form utility—involves the production or alteration of a product

13-2 **Two measures of the impact of retailing in the global economy are _____ and _____.**
Answer: the total annual sales—four of the 40 largest businesses in the United States are retailers; the number of employees working at large retailers

13-3 **Centralized decision making and purchasing are an advantage of _____ ownership.**
Answer: corporate chain

13-4 **What are some examples of new forms of self-service retailers?**
Answer: New forms of self-service are being developed at convenience stores, fast-food restaurants, and even coffee shops.

13-5 **A shop for big men's clothes carries pants in sizes 40 to 60. Would this be considered a broad or deep product line?**
Answer: deep product line; the range of sizes relates to the assortment of a product item (pants) rather than the variety of product lines (pants, shirts, shoes, etc.)

13-6 **Successful catalog retailers often send _____ catalogs to _____ markets identified in their databases.**
Answer: specialty; niche

13-7 **How are retailers increasing the number of online shoppers who make it through "checkout"?**
Answer: Some retailers now offer the ability to compare competitors' offerings. In addition, retailers are building websites that are easy to use, customizable, and facilitate interaction.

13-8 **Where are direct selling retail sales growing? Why?**
Answer: Direct-selling retailers are (1) expanding into global markets outside the United States and (2) reaching consumers who prefer one-on-one customer service and a social shopping experience rather than shopping online or at big discount stores.

13-9 **How does original markup differ from maintained markup?**
Answer: The original markup is the difference between retailer cost and initial selling price, whereas maintained markup is the difference between the final selling price and retailer cost, which is also called the gross margin.

13-10 **A huge shopping strip mall with multiple anchor stores is a _____ center.**
Answer: power

13-11 **What is a popular approach to managing the assortment of merchandise in a store?**
Answer: category management

13-12 **Using the wheel of retailing, describe the characteristics of a new retail form that has just entered the market.**
Answer: a low-status, low-margin, low-price outlet

13-13 **Market share is usually fought out before the _____ stage of the retail life cycle.**
Answer: maturity

13-14 **What is the difference between merchant wholesalers and agents?**
Answer: Merchant wholesalers are independently owned firms that take title to the merchandise they handle and make their profit from the sale of merchandise they own. Agents do not take title to merchandise, typically perform fewer channel functions, and make their profit from commissions or fees paid for their services.

13-15 **Under what circumstances do producers assume wholesaling functions?**
Answer: Producers assume wholesaling functions when there are no intermediaries to perform these activities, customers are few in number and geographically concentrated, or orders are large or require significant attention.

FOCUSING ON KEY TERMS

brokers p. 342
category management p. 338
manufacturer's agents p. 342
merchant wholesalers p. 341

multichannel retailers p. 337
retail life cycle p. 340
retailing p. 326
retailing mix p. 335

scrambled merchandising p. 331
shopper marketing p. 337
telemarketing p. 334
wheel of retailing p. 339

APPLYING MARKETING KNOWLEDGE

1 Discuss the impact of the growing number of dual-income households on (*a*) nonstore retailing and (*b*) the retail mix.

2 In retail pricing, retailers often have a maintained markup. Explain how this maintained markup differs from original markup and why it is so important.

3 What are the similarities and differences between the product and retail life cycles?

4 How would you classify Walmart in terms of its position on the wheel of retailing versus that of an off-price retailer?

5 Develop a chart to highlight the role of each of the four main elements of the retailing mix across the four stages of the retail life cycle.

6 Breadth and depth are two important components in distinguishing among types of retailers. Discuss the breadth and depth implications of the following retailers discussed in this chapter: (*a*) Nordstrom, (*b*) Walmart, (*c*) L.L. Bean, and (*d*) Best Buy.

7 According to the wheel of retailing and the retail life cycle, what will happen to factory outlet stores?

8 The text discusses the development of online retailing in the United States. How does the development of this retailing form agree with the implications of the retail life cycle?

9 Comment on this statement: "The only distinction among merchant wholesalers and agents and brokers is that merchant wholesalers take title to the products they sell."

BUILDING YOUR MARKETING PLAN

Does your marketing plan involve using retailers? If the answer is "no," read no further and do not include a retailing element in your plan. If the answer is "yes":

1 Use Figure 13–3 to develop your retailing strategy by specifying the details of the retailing mix.

2 Develop a positioning statement describing the breadth of the product line (broad versus narrow) and value added (low versus high).

3 Describe an appropriate combination of retail pricing, store location, retail communication, and merchandise assortment.

4 Confirm that the wholesalers needed to support your retailing strategy are consistent with the channels and intermediaries you selected in Chapter 12.

VIDEO CASE 13 — Mall of America®: Shopping and a Whole Lot More

Video 13-5
**Mall of America
Video Case**
kerin.tv/cr6e/v13-5

"If you build it, they will come" not only worked in the movie *Field of Dreams* but also applies—big time—to Mall of America®.

Located in a suburb of Minneapolis, Mall of America (www.mall ofamerica.com) is the largest completely enclosed retail and family-entertainment complex in the United States. "We're more than a mall, we're a destination," explains Maureen Cahill, executive vice president at Mall of America. More than 109,000 people each day—40 million visitors each year—visit the one-stop complex offering retail shopping, guest services, convenience, a huge variety of entertainment, and fun for all. "Guest services" include everything from a mobile concierge to a wedding chapel.

THE CONCEPT AND CHALLENGE

The idea for Mall of America came from the West Edmonton Mall in Alberta, Canada. The Ghermezian Brothers, who developed that mall, sought to create a unique mall that would attract not only local families but also tourists from the Upper Midwest, the nation, and even from abroad.

The two challenges for Mall of America: How can it (1) attract and keep the large number of retail establishments needed to (2) continue to attract even more millions of visitors than today? A big part of the answer is in Mall of America's positioning—"Always New!"

THE STAGGERING SIZE AND OFFERINGS

Opened August 1992 amid tremendous worldwide publicity, Mall of America faced skeptics who had their doubts because of its size, its unique retail-entertainment mix, and the nationwide recession. Despite these concerns, the mall opened with more than 80 percent of its space leased and attracted more than 1 million visitors its first week.

Mall of America is 4.2 million square feet, the equivalent of 88 football fields. This makes it three to four times the size of most other regional malls. It includes four anchor department stores: Nordstrom, Macy's, Bloomingdale's, and Sears. It also includes more than 520 specialty stores, from Armani Exchange to DSW (Designer Shoe Warehouse). Approximately 36 percent of Mall of America's space is devoted to anchors and 64 percent to specialty stores and attractions. This makes the space allocation the reverse of most regional malls.

The retail-entertainment mix of Mall of America is incredibly diverse. For example, there are more than 165 apparel and accessory stores, 14 jewelry stores, and 26 shoe stores. Two food courts with 27 restaurants, plus more than 20 other restaurants scattered throughout the building, meet most food preferences of visitors. Another surprise: Mall of America is home to many "concept stores," where retailers introduce a new type of store or design. In addition, it has an entrepreneurial program for people with an innovative retail idea and limited resources. They can open a kiosk, wall unit, or small store for a specified time period or as a temporary seasonal tenant.

Unique features of Mall of America include:

- Nickelodeon Universe®, a 7-acre theme park with more than 30 attractions and rides, including a roller coaster, a ropes course, a zip line, and games in a glass-enclosed, skylighted area with more than 400 trees and 30,000 plants.
- SEA LIFE® Minnesota Aquarium, where visitors are surrounded by stingrays, jellyfish, and sea turtles; can adventure among fish native to the north woods; and swim with sharks!
- Entertainment choices include a 14-screen theater featuring D-Box seating, A.C.E.S. Flight Simulation, the Amazing Mirror Maze, and Moose Mountain Adventure Golf.

- Rick Bronson's House of Comedy, featuring comedians from *Last Comic Standing*, *Saturday Night Live*, and *Just for Laughs*.
- Radison Blu hotel, featuring 500 rooms and world-class dining attached directly to the mall.

As a host to corporate events and private parties, Mall of America has a rotunda that opens to all four floors, facilitating presentations, demonstrations, and exhibits. Organizations such as PepsiCo, Visa USA, and Ford have used the facilities to gain shopper awareness. Mall of America is a rectangle with the anchor department stores at the corners and an amusement park in the skylighted central area, making it easy for shoppers to understand and navigate. It has 12,850 free parking ramp spaces on-site and another 7,000 spaces nearby during peak times.

THE MARKET

The Minneapolis–St. Paul metropolitan area is a market with more than 3 million people. A total of 30 million people live within a day's drive of Mall of America. A survey of its shoppers showed that 32 percent of the shoppers travel 150 miles or more and account for more than 50 percent of the sales revenues. Located three miles from the Minneapolis/St. Paul International Airport, Mall of America has a light-rail service from the airport and downtown Minneapolis available.

Tourism accounts for 4 out of 10 visits to Mall of America. About 6 percent of visitors come from outside the United States. Some come just to see and experience Mall of America, while others take advantage of the cost savings available on goods (Japan) or taxes (Canada and states with sales taxes on clothing).

THE FUTURE: FACING THE CHALLENGES

Where is Mall of America headed in the future? "Mall of America is one of the most recognized brands in the world," Cahill says. "They might not know where we are sometimes, but they've heard of Mall of America and they know they want to come.

"What we've learned since 1992 is to keep Mall of America fresh and exciting," she explains. "We're constantly looking at what attracts people and adding to that. We're adding new stores, new attractions, and new events." For example, the mall holds more than 425 events each year, including celebrity appearances and performances, book signings, fashion shows, and live Cirque du Soleil performances.

Mall of America announced a plan for a 5.6 million-square-foot expansion, the area of another 117 football fields, connected by pedestrian skyway to the present building. "The second phase will not be a duplicate of what we have," Cahill says. "We have plans for boutique, family, and business hotels, 20,000 square feet of event space, an ice rink, a spa and wellness center, museum-quality exhibit space, a performing arts theater, and new restaurants and retail offerings."

The expansion is expected to attract an additional 20 million visitors annually. In addition, the development is designed to exceed environmental certification standards. All of these new additions and the many offerings of the current mall reinforce that Mall of America is a shopping destination and a whole lot more!

Questions

1 Why has Mall of America been such a marketing success so far?

2 What (*a*) retail and (*b*) consumer trends have occurred since Mall of America was opened in 1992 that it should consider when making future plans?

3 What criteria should Mall of America use in adding new facilities to its complex? Evaluate (*a*) retail stores, (*b*) entertainment offerings, and (*c*) hotels on these criteria.

4 What specific marketing actions would you propose that Mall of America managers take to ensure its continuing success in attracting visitors (*a*) from the local metropolitan area and (*b*) from outside of it?

Chapter Notes

1. "Augmented Reality's Real Implications for Hardware, Software and Advertising: A Roadmap for Success," *PR Newswire,* February 5, 2013; Yomiuri, "Will Augmented Reality Technology Replace Fitting Rooms with Apps, Tablets?" *The Daily Yomiuri,* February 19, 2013, p. 6; Chris Ciaccia, "Google Glass Edges Closer to Reality," *The Street,* February 20, 2013; "Virtual Shopping: What Augmented Reality Means for Retailers," *Marketing Thought Leaders,* February 2013; "How Augmented Reality Is Changing the Consumer Experience," *Business 2 Community.com,* December 11, 2012; "Augmented Reality: A Growing Force in Retail," *Retailcustomerexperience.com,* October 5, 2012; and "Augmented Reality Makes Shopping More Personal," www.research.ibm.com, accessed February 20, 2013.

2. "The Fortune 500," *Fortune,* May 20, 2013, p. F-1; *The World Factbook* (Washington, DC: Central Intelligence Agency). www.cia.gov, accessed April 7, 2011; *Statistical Abstract of the United States: 2009,* 128th ed. (Washington, DC: U.S. Department of Commerce, Bureau of the Census, 2008), Table 19, Large Metropolitan Statistical Areas.

3. "Monthly and Annual Retail Trade," United States Census Bureau, http://www.census.gov/retail/, February 13, 2013.

4. "The Global 2000," *Forbes,* May 7, 2012, p. 99; and http://www.forbes.com/global2000.

5. "Where in the World Is Walmart?" Walmart website, http://corporate.walmart.com/our-story/locations, accessed February 22, 2013; and Marcel Corstjens and Rajiv Lal, "Retail Doesn't Cross Borders," *Harvard Business Review,* April 2012, pp. 104–11.

6. "Some Actions Last a Lifetime," *Home Depot 2012 Sustainability Report;* Edwin R. Stafford and Cathy L. Hartman, "Promoting the Value of Sustainably Minded Purchase Behaviors," *Marketing News,* January 2013, p. 28; "Neenah Paper Gives Retailers a 'Green' Option with Environmental Retail Card," *Product News Network,* December 10, 2012; "Green Rankings 2012: U.S. Companies," *Newsweek,* October 22, 2012; "Can Green Marketing Work?" *Advertising Age,* November 8, 2010, p. 19; Nathalie Atkinson, "Green Army, Sure Companies Are Jumping on the Eco-Bandwagon but It's This Sort of Retailing We Should Encourage," *National Post,* April 17, 2010, p. TO4; and "The Company of the Future: Fact Sheet," Wal-Mart, Inc., www.walmartfacts.com, accessed April 8, 2011.

7. "Retail Trade—Establishments, Employees, and Payroll," *County Business Patterns,* U.S. Census Bureau, July 2010, Table 1048.

8. "2013 Franchise 500," *Entrepreneur,* http://www.entrepreneur.com/franchise500/index.html#.

9. "The Next Generation of Retailing Driven by Automated, Self-Service Solutions," *Market News Publishing,*" February 4, 2013; "Apartment Complex Readies for Automated C-Store," *States News Service,* September 10, 2012; "Marley Coffee and AVT Bet Big on the Future of Automated Cafes," *Market News Publishing,* February 6, 2013; "Automated Retailing Industry Expected to Grow to More Than $1.1 Trillion in 2015," *PR Newswire,* January 24, 2013; Alana Semuels, "Self-Service Machines Replacing Retail Workers," *The Star-Ledger,* March 13, 2011, p. 1; and Bridget Carey, "You Can Get Most Anything at a Kiosk," *The Miami Herald,* August 20, 2010.

10. "Wealthy Customers Sing Praises of Shopping Experiences at Bergdorf, Nordstrom and Barneys," *Marketwire,* February 5, 2013; Megan Conniff, "Customer Service Is Changing, and So Is Nordstrom," www.Shop.org, September 12, 2012; and Michael A. Wiles, "The Effect of Customer Service on Retailers' Shareholder Wealth: The Role of Availability and Reputation Cues," *Journal of Retailing,* 2007, pp. 19–31.

11. "No Time to Shop for Your Valentine? From Flowers to Caviar, a Vending Machine Can Save the Day," *Targeted News Service,* February 11, 2013; Jill Becker, "Vending Machines for All Your Needs,"

www.CNN.com, August 15, 2012; Jackie Crosby, "Vending Machine Variety Goes beyond Snack Food Offerings," *Los Angeles Times,* January 18, 2011, p. B2; Carlie Kollath, "Veggies in Vending Machines?" *Biz Buzz,* April 6, 2011; "2012 State of the Vending Industry Report," *Automatic Merchandiser,* June/July 2012, pp. 8–19; and http://www.vendingmarketwatch.com/document/10756834/2012-state-of-the-vending-industry-report-pdf.

12. Yukihiro Omoto, "Coca-Cola Setting Up More Green Vending Machines," *The Nikkei Weekly,* February 18, 2013; Ilan Brat, "Business Technology: Restocking the Snack Machine—Sales Pinched, Vending-Machine Operators Add Touch Screen, Card Readers," *The Wall Street Journal,* August 3, 2010, p. B5.

13. *Statistical Fact Book* (New York: Direct Marketing Association, 2010), pp. 4, 33; David Kaplan, "Catalogs Thinner but Still Carry Weight, Retailers Use Them to Draw Consumers to Stores, Web or Social Media Sites," *The Houston Chronicle,* November 28, 2010, p. 1; Mercedes Cardona, "Catalog Role Is Communications, Not Sales," *DM News,* November 1, 2010; and IKEA website, http://www.ikea.com/ms/en_CA/customer_service/faq/ faq.html#/0100, accessed February 25, 2013.

14. "How Much Will Postal Cuts Hurt?" *Advertising Age,* February 11, 2013, p. 3; and Ira Teinowitz and Nat Ives, "No Day Is a Good Day for No Mail," *Advertising Age,* February 9, 2009, p. 8.

15. "Fact Sheet" from the QVC website, http://www.qvc.com/AboutQVCFacts.content.html, accessed February 26, 2013.

16. Bianca Carneiro, "Mum Camila McConaughey Outshines Supermodels Miranda Kerr and Heidi Klum at QVC's Red Carpet Style Event," *Mail Online,* February 23, 2013; Jordan Zakarin, "Inside QVC: The Semi-Scripted Reality of the $8 Billion Business Next Door," *The Hollywood Reporter,* December 17, 2012; and Elizabeth Holmes, "The Golden Age of TV Shopping," *The Wall Street Journal,* November 11, 2010, p. D1.

17. Ian Thomas, William Davie, and Deanna Weidenhamer, "Quarterly Retail e-Commerce Sales," *U.S. Census Bureau News,* February 15, 2013; Brad Tuttle, "Cyber Monday Was a Monster—But We Still Love Shopping in Stores," www.Time.com, November 28, 2012; and "Black Friday 2012 Retail Foot Traffic Rises 3.5%," *International Business Times News,* November 25, 2012.

18. "eBay Marketplaces Fast Facts At-a-Glance," eBay website, http://www.ebayinc.com/assets/pdf/fact_sheet/eBay_Marketplaces_Fact_Sheet_Q42012.pdf, accessed February 26, 2013.

19. Susan Rose, Moira Clark, Phillip Samouel, and Neil Hair, "Online Customer Experience in e-Retailing: An Empirical Model of Antecedents and Outcomes," *Journal of Retailing* 2 (2012), pp. 308–22; and Feng Zhu and Xiaoquan (Michael) Zhang, "Impact of Online Consumer Reviews on Sales: The Moderating Role of Product and Consumer Characteristics," *Journal of Marketing* 74 (March 2010), pp. 133–48.

20. "DM-Driven Sales by Medium and Market," *Statistical Fact Book* (New York: Direct Marketing Association, 2010), p. 5.

21. "FTC Issues FY 2012 National Do Not Call Registry Data Book," *Federal Trade Commission Documents and Publications,* October 16, 2012; and Nate Anderson, "Do Not Call List Tops 200 Million, Some Scammers Still Ignore It," www.Wired.com, July 31, 2010.

22. "Direct Selling USA—Pinpoint Growth Sectors and Identify Factors Driving Change," *M2 Presswire,* April 12, 2011; and *Fact Sheet,* Direct Selling Association, http://www.dsa.org/research/industry-statistics/11gofactsheet.pdf, accessed February 27, 2013.

23. "Amway Says China Sales Increase to 27.1b Yuan," *China Daily,* February 21, 2013; and "Avon Announces Management Realignments," *PR Newswire,* February 24, 2011.

24. Virginia Bridges, "In a Slow Economy, Some Try the Direct Approach," *The Virginian-Pilot,* February 17, 2013, p. K1; Maria Croce, "Recession Sparks a Massive Boom in Direct Selling Parties but Gone Are the Days of Selling Tupperware," *Daily Record,* June 2,

CHAPTER 13　Retailing and Wholesaling

2012, pp. 34–35; Olivera Perkins, "Direct Sales Proves Attractive to Long-Term Jobless Workers; Companies Selling Retail Goods at Home Parties See Profits Climbing," *Plain Dealer,* February 6, 2011, p. D1; and "Company Facts," The Pampered Chef website, http://www.pamperedchef.com/company-facts.jsp, accessed February 27, 2013.

25. Francis J. Mulhern and Robert P. Leon, "Implicit Price Bundling of Retail Products: A Multiproduct Approach to Maximizing Store Profitability," *Journal of Marketing,* October 1991, pp. 63–76.

26. Marc Vanhuele and Xavier Dreze, "Measuring the Price Knowledge Shoppers Bring to the Store," *Journal of Marketing,* October 2002, p. 72–85.

27. "Are Sales a Thing of the Past?" *Newstex,* www.jennstrathman .com, January 10, 2013; and Gwen Ortmeyer, John A. Quelch, and Walter Salmon, "Restoring Credibility to Retail Pricing," *Sloan Management Review,* Fall 1991, pp. 55–66.

28. "On Sale! But Does Inexpensive Mean Cheap?" www.Futurity.org, November 27, 2012; Rajneesh Suri, Jane Zhen Cai, Kent B. Monroe, and Mrugank V. Thakor, "Retailers' Merchandise Organization and Price Perceptions," *Journal of Retailing* 1 (2012), pp. 168–79; and William Dodds, "In Search of Value: How Price and Store Name Information Influence Buyers' Product Perceptions," *Journal of Consumer Marketing,* Spring 1991, pp. 15–24.

29. Stephanie Clifford, "Stores Bend to Cost-Savvy Shoppers: Experiments in Pricing Move Away from Usual Markups and Discounts," *The International Herald Tribune,* March 29, 2012, p. 18; and Leonard L. Berry, "Old Pillars of New Retailing," *Harvard Business Review,* April 2001, pp. 131–37.

30. Eric Anderson and Duncan Simester, "Mind Your Pricing Cues," *Harvard Business Review,* September 2003, pp. 96–103.

31. Julie Baker, A. Parasuraman, Dhruv Grewal, and Glenn B. Voss, "The Influence of Multiple Store Environment Cues on Perceived Merchandise Value and Patronage Intentions," *Journal of Marketing,* April 2002, pp. 120–41.

32. Hyeong Min Kim, "Consumers' Responses to Price Presentation Formats in Rebate Advertisements," *Journal of Retailing* 4 (2006), pp. 309–17.

33. Rita Koselka, "The Schottenstein Factor," *Forbes,* September 28, 1992, pp. 104, 106.

34. "About WEM," West Edmonton Mall website, http://www.wem .ca/#/about-wem/overview, accessed February 27, 2013.

35. Ernesto Portillo, "Home Depot Part of Center Plan," *McClatchy-Tribune Business News,* November 20, 2008; and Lisa A. Bernard, "Anchor ID'd for 'Big Box' Power Center," *Dayton Daily News,* July 19, 2007.

36. "A Business Survival Guide to Multi-Channel Retail," www.Business2Community.com, December 3, 2012; Umut Konus, Peter C. Verhoef, and Scott A. Neslin, "Multichannel Shopper Segments and Their Covariates," *Journal of Retailing,* December 2008, p. 398; and Robert A. Peterson and Sridhar Balasubramanian, "Retailing in the 21st Century: Reflections and Prologue to Research," *Journal of Retailing,* Spring 2002, pp. 9–16.

37. "PWC's Annual Survey of Online Shoppers Debunks 10 Myths of Multichannel Retailing," *PR Newswire,* February 6, 2013; Lawrence A. Crosby, "Multi-Channel Relationships," *Marketing Management,* Summer 2011, pp. 12–13; and Jim Carter and Norman Sheehan, "From Competition to Cooperation: E-Tailing's Integration with Retailing." *Business Horizons,* March–April 2004, pp. 71–78.

38. Pierre Martineau, "The Personality of the Retail Store," *Harvard Business Review,* January–February 1958, p. 47.

39. Julie Baker, Dhruv Grewal, and A. Parasuraman, "The Influence of Store Environment on Quality Inferences and Store Image," *Journal of the Academy of Marketing Science,* Fall 1994, pp. 328–39;

Howard Barich and Philip Kotler, "A Framework for Marketing Image Management," *Sloan Management Review,* Winter 1991, pp. 94–104; Susan M. Keaveney and Kenneth A. Hunt, "Conceptualization and Operationalization of Retail Store Image: A Case of Rival Middle-Level Theories," *Journal of the Academy of Marketing Science,* Spring 1992, pp. 165–75; James C. Ward, Mary Jo Bitner, and John Barnes, "Measuring the Prototypicality and Meaning of Retail Environments," *Journal of Retailing,* Summer 1992, p. 194; and Dhruv Grewal, R. Krishnan, Julie Baker, and Norm Burin, "The Effect of Store Name, Brand Name and Price Discounts on Consumers' Evaluations and Purchase Intentions," *Journal of Retailing,* Fall 1998, pp. 331–52. For a review of the store image literature, see Mary R. Zimmer and Linda L. Golden, "Impressions of Retail Stores: A Content Analysis of Consumer Images," *Journal of Retailing,* Fall 1988, pp. 265–93.

40. Andreas Herrmann, Manja Zidansek, David E. Sprott, and Eric R. Spangenberg, "The Power of Simplicity: Processing Fluency and the Effects of Olfactory Cues on Retail Sales," *Journal of Retailing* 1 (2013), pp. 30–43.

41. Jack Neff, "Shopper Marketing's New Frontier: e-Commerce," *Advertising Age,* March 14, 2011, p. 14; Andrew Adam Newman, "Taking Pickles Out of the Afterthought Aisle," *The New York Times,* April 26, 2011, p. 3; Piet Levy, "Snack Attack," *Marketing News,* February 28, 2011, p. 12; Yong Jian Wang, Michael S. Minor, and Jie Wei, "Aesthetics and the Online Shopping Environment: Understanding Consumer Responses," *Journal of Retailing* 87, no. 1 (2011), pp. 46–58; and Els Breugelmans and Katia Campo, "Effectiveness of In-Store Displays in a Virtual Store Environment," *Journal of Retailing* 87, no. 1 (2011), pp. 75–89.

42. Jans-Benedict Steenkamp and Michel Wedel, "Segmenting Retail Markets on Store Image Using a Consumer-Based Methodology," *Journal of Retailing,* Fall 1991, p. 300; Philip Kotler, "Atmospherics as a Marketing Tool," *Journal of Retailing* 49 (Winter 1973–74), p. 61; and Roger A. Kerin, Ambuj Jain, and Daniel L. Howard, "Store Shopping Experience and Consumer Price-Quality-Value Perceptions," *Journal of Retailing,* Winter 1992, pp. 376–97.

43. Mary Jo Bitner, "Servicescapes: The Impact of Physical Surroundings on Customers and Employees," *Journal of Marketing,* April 1992, pp. 57–71.

44. Joseph M. Hall, Praveen K. Kopale, and Aradhna Krishna, "Retailer Dynamic Pricing and Ordering Decisions: Category Management versus Brand-by-Brand Approaches," *Journal of Retailing* 86, no. 2 (2010), pp. 172–83; and "Category Management Professionals Can Benefit from Integration of Leading Category and Space Management Suite with Comprehensive and Accurate Product Information," *Business Wire,* April 28, 2011.

45. Kevin Peters, "How I Did It: Office Depot's President on How 'Mystery Shopping' Helped Spark a Turnaround," *Harvard Business Review,* November 2011, pp. 47–50; and John Davis, *Measuring Marketing* (Singapore: Wiley and Sons, 2007), p. 46.

46. Tom Webb, "Retail Ramifications: Best Buy and Apple Seem a Perfect Pair—Except for Apple's Store Ambitions," *St. Paul Pioneer Press,* February 19, 2011; Paul W. Farris, Neil T. Bendle, Phillip E. Pfeifer, and David J. Reibstein, *Marketing Metrics* (Philadelphia: Wharton School Publishing, 2006), p. 106; Jerry Useem, "Simply Irresistible," *Fortune,* March 19, 2007, pp. 107–12; "Apple 2.0," blogs.business2.com/apple/the_evil_empire/index.html; Steve Lohr, "Apple, a Success at Stores, Bets Big on Fifth Avenue," *The New York Times,* May 19, 2006; Jim Dalrymple, "Inside the Apple Stores," *MacWorld,* June 2007, pp. 16–17; John Davis, *Measuring Marketing,* pp. 280–81; and Retailsails 2011 Chain Store Productivity Report, September 23, 2011, http://retailsails.files.wordpress .com/2011/09/rs_spsf.pdf, accessed October 7, 2011.

47. The wheel of retailing theory was originally proposed by Malcolm P. McNair, "Significant Trends and Developments in the Postwar Period," in *Competitive Distribution in a Free, High-Level Economy and Its Implications for the University,* ed. A. B. Smith, (Pittsburgh: University of Pittsburgh Press, 1958), pp. 1–25; also see Stephen Brown, "The Wheel of Retailing—Past and Future," *Journal of Retailing,* Summer 1990, pp. 143–49; and Malcolm P. McNair and Eleanor May, "The Next Revolution of the Retailing Wheel," *Harvard Business Review,* September–October 1978, pp. 81–91.

48. Lorene Yue, "Putting More on the Menu: McDonald's Promises New Products to Drive Revenue Growth," *Crain's Chicago Business,* February 18, 2013, p. 1; "The Special Tonight: Big Mac Served with Style," *The New York Times,* February 13, 2013; and Ashley Lutz, "Starbucks Could Be Laying the Groundwork for the Next Generation of Ordering," *Business Insider,* January 29, 2013.

49. "Our Story," Checkers website, http://checkerscompany.com/our_story, accessed February 28, 2013; and "Company Milestones," Boston Market website, http://www.bostonmarket.com/newsroom/index.jsp?page=milestones, accessed February 29, 2013.

50. William R. Davidson, Albert D. Bates, and Stephen J. Bass, "Retail Life Cycle," *Harvard Business Review,* November–December 1976, pp. 89–96.

Mall of America: This case was written by David P. Brennan and is based on an interview with Maureen Cahill and materials provided by Mall of America.

Credits

P. 325, *All images:* AP Photo/Google. P. 327, ©TAO Images Limited/Alamy. P. 328, ©M. Hruby. P. 328, ©Kristofer Tripplaar/Alamy. P. 329, ©PRNewsFoto/AP Images. P. 329, Ross Dettman/AP Images for Redbox. P. 331, ©K. Rousonelos. P. 332, Courtesy Healthy You Vending. P. 332, ©M. Hruby. P. 332, ©M. Hruby. P. 332, Courtesy of L. L. Bean. P. 333, Photo by Rick Diamond/Getty Images for Webster PR. P. 333, ©NetPhotos2/Alamy. P. 334, Courtesy Mary Kay, Inc. P. 336, ©Ian Dagnall/Alamy. P. 336, ©M. Hruby. P. 336, AP Photo/Paul Sakuma. P. 336, ©Stars and Stripes/Alamy. P. 340, ©John Crowe/Alamy. P. 346, ©Steve Skjold/Alamy. P. 346, ©Alvis Upitis/Alamy.

14 Integrated Marketing Communications and Direct Marketing

LEARNING OBJECTIVES

After reading this chapter you should be able to:

 LO 14-1 Discuss integrated marketing communication and the communication process.

 LO 14-2 Describe the promotional mix and the uniqueness of each component.

 LO 14-3 Select the promotional approach appropriate to a product's target audience, life-cycle stage, and channel strategies.

 LO 14-4 Describe the elements of the promotion decision process.

 LO 14-5 Explain the value of direct marketing for consumers and sellers.

WHAT ARE THEY SAYING ON THE TWITTERSPHERE? YO QUIERO TACO BELL!

What company recently implemented its largest integrated marketing campaign ever? What company has mastered consumer engagement and interaction? What's the hottest brand on Twitter today? If you've ever had a late-night snack, you may have guessed—it's Taco Bell!

Taco Bell has been wildly successful with its Cool Ranch Doritos Locos Tacos campaign. It began three weeks before the new taco was launched with password-only social media events. Taco Bell listened to real-time conversations on Twitter (@TacoBell) and rewarded fans with "epic deliveries." A woman who asked Taco Bell to be her Valentine, a student who promised to gather enough friends to eat 1,000 tacos, and a fan who posted a message about tacos on YouTube all received early tastes of the new product.

The campaign then used television, radio, outdoor, and cinema ads, as well as public relations support. The television ads included two 15-second spots titled "Wow" and "Duh" that were supported by a contest (printed on taco wrappers) inviting customers to post photos to Instagram or Twitter using the #wow and #duh hashtags for a chance to have their entry appear on a billboard in Times Square. The most unique element of the campaign was a 3D ad showing a Dorito chip exploding and then morphing into a Cool Ranch Doritos Locos Taco chip. The ad appeared in more than 8,000 movie theaters nationwide, and the new product quickly became the company's most liked, shared, retweeted, and talked-about product on Facebook, Twitter, and Vine.

One reason for Taco Bell's success is that all of the elements of its Doritos Locos Tacos campaign are integrated to have the same message and tone, and they focus on engaging consumers. Some marketers have observed that our marketplace is in the midst of a shift from traditional branding to an "age of engagement" and that social media promotions are the best way to accommodate this shift. In addition, they suggest several aspects of social media promotions are essential to engage today's customers. They are:

1. Post relevant content about the benefits and uses of the product.

2. Supplement text with photos and videos.

3. Create sweepstakes, contests, and deals that reward current and new customers.

351

4. Encourage and respond to comments and feedback, both positive and negative.

5. Be current and timely with all interactions.

In addition to a presence on the Twittersphere, many brands are using other new forms of engagement, such as Facebook Pages, RSS (rich site summary) feeds, mobile apps, blogs, websites, and QR (quick response) codes. Even traditional media are engaging customers—for example, TV reality shows like *Dancing with the Stars* and *American Idol* encourage online and telephone voting. In the future, successful integrated marketing communications campaigns will certainly be engaging you![1]

Taco Bell's successful Doritos Locos Tacos campaign demonstrates the opportunity for engaging potential customers and the importance of integrating the various elements of a marketing communication program. Promotion represents the fourth element in the marketing mix. The promotional element consists of five communication tools, including advertising, personal selling, sales promotion, public relations, and direct marketing. The combination of one or more of these communication tools is called the **promotional mix**. All

promotional mix
The combination of one or more of the communication tools used to inform, persuade, or remind prospective buyers.

of these tools can be used to (1) inform prospective buyers about the benefits of the product, (2) persuade them to try it, and (3) remind them later about the benefits they enjoyed by using the product. In the past, marketers often viewed these communication tools as separate and independent. The advertising department, for example, often designed and managed its activities without consulting departments or agencies that had responsibility for sales promotion or public relations. The result was often an overall communication effort that was uncoordinated and, in some cases, inconsistent. Today, the concept of designing marketing communications programs that coordinate all promotional activities—advertising, personal selling, sales promotion, public relations, and direct marketing—to provide a consistent message across all audiences is referred to as **integrated marketing communications (IMC)**. By taking consumer expectations into consideration, IMC is a key element in a company's customer experience management strategy.[2]

This chapter provides an overview of the communication process, a description of the promotional mix elements, several tools for integrating the promotional mix, and a process for developing a comprehensive promotion program. One of the promotional mix elements, direct marketing, is also discussed in this chapter. Chapter 15 covers advertising, sales promotion, and public relations, Chapter 16 covers social media, and Chapter 17 discusses personal selling.

integrated marketing communications
The concept of designing marketing communications programs that coordinate all promotional activities to provide a consistent message across all audiences.

THE COMMUNICATION PROCESS

 LO 14-1 Discuss integrated marketing communication and the communication process.

communication
The process of conveying a message to others; it requires six elements: a source, a message, a channel of communication, a receiver, and the processes of encoding and decoding.

Communication is the process of conveying a message to others, and it requires six elements: a source, a message, a channel of communication, a receiver, and the processes of encoding and decoding[3] (see Figure 14–1). The *source* may be a company or person who has information to convey. The information sent by a source, such as a description of a new smartphone, forms the *message*. The message is conveyed by means of a *channel of communication* such as a salesperson, advertising media, or public relations tools. Consumers who read, hear, or see the message are the *receivers*.

FIGURE 14–1
The communication process consists of six key elements. See the text to learn about factors that influence the effectiveness of the process.

UNSTILL LIFE.

INTRODUCING MINI PACEMAN.

How would you decode this ad? What message is MINI trying to send?

MINI

www.miniusa.com

Video 14-1
MINI Ad
kerin.tv/cr6e/v14-1

Encoding and Decoding

Encoding and decoding are essential to communication. *Encoding* is the process of having the sender transform an idea into a set of symbols. *Decoding* is the reverse, or the process of having the receiver take a set of symbols, the message, and transform the symbols into an idea. Look at the accompanying MINI USA advertisement: Who is the source, and what is the message?

Decoding is performed by the receivers according to their own frame of reference: their attitudes, values, and beliefs.[4] MINI USA is the source and the advertisement is the message, which appeared in *Wired* magazine (the channel). How would you interpret (decode) this advertisement? The picture and text in the advertisement show that the source's intention is to generate interest in its product with the headline "Unstill Life"—a statement the source believes will appeal to the readers of the magazine.

The process of communication is not always a successful one. Errors in communication can happen in several ways. The source may not adequately transform the abstract idea into an effective set of symbols, a properly encoded message may be sent through the wrong channel and never make it to the intended receiver, the receiver may not properly transform the set of symbols into the correct abstract idea, or finally, feedback may be so delayed or distorted that it is of no use to the sender. Although communication appears easy to perform, truly effective communication can be very difficult.

For the message to be communicated effectively, the sender and receiver must have a mutually shared *field of experience*—a similar understanding and knowledge they apply to the message. Figure 14–1 shows two circles representing the fields of experience of the sender and receiver, which overlap in the message. Some of the better-known message problems have occurred when U.S. companies have taken their messages to cultures with different fields of experience. Many misinterpretations are merely the result of bad translations. For example, KFC made a mistake when its "finger-lickin' good" slogan was translated into Mandarin Chinese as "eat your fingers off"![5]

Feedback

Figure 14–1 shows a line labeled *feedback loop*, which consists of a response and feedback. A *response* is the impact the message had on the receiver's knowledge, attitudes, or behaviors. *Feedback* is the sender's interpretation of the response and indicates whether the message was decoded and understood as intended. Chapter 15 reviews approaches called *pretesting*, which ensure that messages are decoded properly.

Noise

Noise includes extraneous factors that can work against effective communication by distorting a message or the feedback received (Figure 14–1). Noise can be a simple error, such as a printing mistake that affects the meaning of a newspaper advertisement or the use of words or pictures that fail to communicate the message clearly. Noise can also occur when a salesperson's message is misunderstood by a prospective buyer, such as when a salesperson's accent, use of slang terms, or communication style make hearing and understanding the message difficult.

> **learning review**
>
> **14-1.** What six elements are required for communication to occur?
>
> **14-2.** A difficulty for U.S. companies advertising in international markets is that the audience does not share the same _____.
>
> **14-3.** A misprint in a newspaper ad is an example of _____.

THE PROMOTIONAL ELEMENTS

LO 14-2 Describe the promotional mix and the uniqueness of each component.

advertising
Any paid form of nonpersonal communication about an organization, product, service, or idea by an identified sponsor.

Magazines are a mass media outlet for advertising.

To communicate with consumers, a company can use one or more of five promotional alternatives: advertising, personal selling, public relations, sales promotion, and direct marketing. Figure 14–2 summarizes the distinctions among these five elements. Three of these elements—advertising, sales promotion, and public relations—are often said to use *mass selling* because they are used with groups of prospective buyers. In contrast, personal selling uses *customized interaction* between a seller and a prospective buyer. Personal selling activities include face-to-face, telephone, and interactive electronic communication. Direct marketing also uses messages customized for specific customers.

Advertising

Advertising is any paid form of nonpersonal communication about an organization, product, service, or idea by an identified sponsor. The *paid* aspect of this definition is important because the space for the advertising message normally must be bought. An occasional exception is the public service announcement, where the advertising time or space is donated. A full-page, four-color ad in *Time* magazine, for example, costs $339,400. The *nonpersonal* component of advertising is also important. Advertising involves mass media (such as TV, radio, and magazines), which are nonpersonal and do not have an immediate feedback loop as does personal selling. So before the message is sent, marketing research plays a valuable role; for example, it determines that the target market will actually see the medium chosen and that the message will be understood.

There are several advantages to a firm using advertising in its promotional mix. It can be attention-getting—as with the Columbia ad shown on page 356—and also communicate specific product benefits to prospective buyers. By paying for the

PROMOTIONAL ELEMENT	MASS OR CUSTOMIZED	COST	STRENGTHS	WEAKNESSES
Advertising	Mass	Fees paid for space or time	• Efficient means for reaching large numbers of people	• High absolute costs • Difficult to receive good feedback
Personal selling	Customized	Fees paid to salespeople as either salaries or commissions	• Immediate feedback • Very persuasive • Can select audience • Can give complex information	• Extremely expensive per exposure • Messages may differ between salespeople
Public relations	Mass	No direct payment to media	• Often most credible source in the consumer's mind	• Difficult to get media cooperation
Sales promotion	Mass	Wide range of fees paid, depending on promotion selected	• Effective at changing behavior in short run • Very flexible	• Easily abused • Can lead to promotion wars • Easily duplicated
Direct marketing	Customized	Cost of communication through mail, telephone, or computer	• Messages can be prepared quickly • Facilitates relationship with customer	• Declining customer response • Database management is expensive

FIGURE 14–2
Each of the five elements of the promotional mix has strengths and weaknesses.

advertising space, a company can control *what* it wants to say and, to some extent, to *whom* the message is sent. Advertising also allows the company to decide *when* to send its message (which includes how often). The nonpersonal aspect of advertising also has its advantages. Once the message is created, the same message is sent to all receivers in a market segment. If the pictorial, text, and brand elements of an advertisement are properly pretested, an advertiser can ensure the ad's ability to capture consumers' attention and trust that the same message will be decoded by all receivers in the market segment.[6]

Advertising has some disadvantages. As shown in Figure 14–2 and discussed in depth in Chapter 15, the costs to produce and place a message are significant, and the lack of direct feedback makes it difficult to know how well the message was received.

Personal Selling

personal selling
The two-way flow of communication between a buyer and seller, often in a face-to-face encounter, designed to influence a person's or group's purchase decision.

The second major promotional alternative is **personal selling**, which is the two-way flow of communication between a buyer and seller designed to influence a person's or group's purchase decision. Unlike advertising, personal selling is usually face-to-face communication between the sender and receiver. Why do companies use personal selling?

There are important advantages to personal selling, as summarized in Figure 14–2. A salesperson can control to *whom* the presentation is made, reducing the amount of *wasted coverage*, or communication with consumers who are not in the target audience. The

CHAPTER 14 Integrated Marketing Communications and Direct Marketing personal component of selling has another advantage in that the seller can see or hear the potential buyer's reaction to the message. If the feedback is unfavorable, the salesperson can modify the message.

The flexibility of personal selling can also be a disadvantage. Different salespeople can change the message so that no consistent communication is given to all customers. The high cost of personal selling is probably its major disadvantage. On a cost-per-contact basis, it is generally the most expensive of the five promotional elements.

Public Relations

public relations
A form of communication management that seeks to influence the feelings, opinions, or beliefs held by customers, potential customers, stockholders, suppliers, employees, and others about a company and its products or services.

publicity
A nonpersonal, indirectly paid presentation of an organization, product, or service.

Public relations is a form of communication management that seeks to influence the feelings, opinions, or beliefs held by customers, prospective customers, stockholders, suppliers, employees, and other publics about a company and its products or services.[7] Many tools such as special events, lobbying efforts, annual reports, press conferences, social media (including Facebook and Twitter), and image management may be used by a public relations department, although publicity often plays the most important role.[8] **Publicity** is a nonpersonal, indirectly paid presentation of an organization, product, or service. It can take the form of a news story, editorial, or product announcement. A difference between publicity and both advertising and personal selling is the "indirectly paid" dimension. With publicity a company does not pay for space in a mass medium (such as television or radio) but attempts to get the medium to run a favorable story on the company. In this sense, there is an indirect payment for publicity in that a company must support a public relations staff.

An advantage of publicity is credibility. When you read a favorable story about a company's product (such as a glowing restaurant review), there is a tendency to believe it. Travelers throughout the world have relied on Frommer's guides such as *Frommer's France.* These books describe out-of-the-way, inexpensive restaurants and hotels, giving invaluable publicity to these establishments. Such businesses do not (nor can they) buy a mention in the guide.

The disadvantage of publicity relates to the lack of the user's control over it. A company can invite media to cover an interesting event such as a store opening or a new-product release, but there is no guarantee that a story will result, that it will be positive, or that the target audience will receive the message. Social media, such as blogs, have grown dramatically and allow uncontrollable public discussions of almost any company activity. Many public relations departments now focus on facilitating and responding to online discussions. McDonald's, for example, responds to comments about McDonald's

The Columbia ad, Frommer's travel guide, and M&M's sweepstakes are examples of three elements of the promotional mix—advertising, public relations, and sales promotion.

Video 14-2
McDonald's
kerin.tv/cr6e/v14-2

products and promotions on its corporate social responsibility blog, *Let's Talk*.[9] Generally, publicity is an important element of most promotional campaigns, although the lack of control means that it is rarely the primary element. Research related to the sequence of IMC elements, however, indicates that publicity followed by advertising with the same message increases the positive response to the message.[10]

Sales Promotion

sales promotion
A short-term inducement of value offered to arouse interest in buying a product or service.

A fourth promotional element is **sales promotion**, a short-term inducement of value offered to arouse interest in buying a product or service. Used in conjunction with advertising or personal selling, sales promotions are offered to intermediaries as well as to ultimate consumers. Coupons, rebates, samples, contests, and sweepstakes such as the M&M's promotion featured on the previous page are just a few examples of sales promotions discussed later in this chapter.

The advantage of sales promotion is that the short-term nature of these programs (such as a coupon or sweepstakes with an expiration date) often stimulates sales for their duration. Offering value to the consumer in terms of a cents-off coupon or rebate may increase store traffic from consumers who are not store-loyal.[11]

Sales promotions cannot be the sole basis for a campaign because gains are often temporary and sales drop off when the deal ends. Advertising support is needed to convert the customer who tried the product because of a sales promotion into a long-term buyer. If sales promotions are conducted continuously, they lose their effectiveness. Customers begin to delay purchase until a coupon is offered, or they question the product's value. Some aspects of sales promotions also are regulated by the federal government.[12] These issues are reviewed in detail in Chapter 15.

Direct Marketing

direct marketing
Promotional alternative that uses direct communication with consumers to generate a response in the form of an order, a request for further information, or a visit to a retail outlet.

Another promotional alternative, **direct marketing**, uses direct communication with consumers to generate a response in the form of an order, a request for further information, or a visit to a retail outlet. The communication can take many forms, including face-to-face selling, direct mail, catalogs, telephone solicitations, direct response advertising (on television and radio and in print), and online marketing.[13] Like personal selling, direct marketing often consists of interactive communication. It also has the advantage of being customized to match the needs of specific target markets. Messages can be developed and adapted quickly to facilitate one-to-one relationships with customers.

While direct marketing has been one of the fastest-growing forms of promotion, it has several disadvantages. First, most forms of direct marketing require a comprehensive and up-to-date database with information about the target market. Developing and maintaining the database can be expensive and time-consuming. In addition, growing concern about privacy has led to a decline in response rates among some customer groups. Companies with successful direct marketing programs are sensitive to these issues and often use a combination of direct marketing alternatives together, or direct marketing combined with other promotional tools, to increase value for customers.

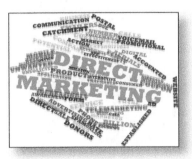

learning review

14-4. Explain the difference between advertising and publicity when both appear on television.

14-5. Cost per contact is high with the _____ element of the promotional mix.

14-6. Which promotional element should be offered only on a short-term basis?

INTEGRATED MARKETING COMMUNICATIONS— DEVELOPING THE PROMOTIONAL MIX

 LO 14-3 Select the promotional approach appropriate to a product's target audience, life-cycle stage, and channel strategies.

A firm's promotional mix is the combination of one or more of the promotional tools it chooses to use. In putting together the promotional mix, a marketer must consider two issues. First, the balance of the elements must be determined. Should advertising be emphasized more than personal selling? Should a promotional rebate be offered? Would public relations activities be effective? Several factors affect such decisions: the target audience for the promotion, the stage of the product's life cycle, the characteristics of the product, the decision stage of the buyer, and even the channel of distribution. Second, because the various promotional elements are often the responsibility of different departments, coordinating a consistent promotional effort is necessary. A promotional planning process designed to ensure integrated marketing communications (IMC) can facilitate this goal.

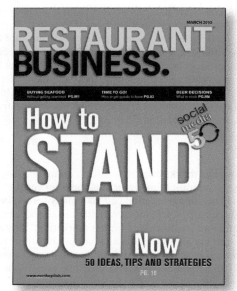

Publications such as *Restaurant Business* reach business buyers.

The Target Audience

Promotional programs are directed to the ultimate consumer, to an intermediary (retailer, wholesaler, or industrial distributor), or to both. Promotional programs directed to buyers of consumer products often use mass media because the number of potential buyers is large. Personal selling is used at the place of purchase, generally the retail store. Direct marketing may be used to encourage first-time or repeat purchases. Combinations of many media alternatives are a necessity for some target audiences today. The Marketing Matters box describes how today's college students can be reached through mobile marketing programs.[14]

Advertising directed to business buyers is used selectively in trade publications such as *Restaurant Business* magazine for buyers of restaurant equipment and supplies. Because business buyers often have specialized needs or technical questions, personal selling is particularly important. The salesperson can provide information and the necessary support after the sale.

Intermediaries are often the focus of promotional efforts. As with business buyers, personal selling is the major promotional ingredient. The salespeople assist intermediaries in making a profit by coordinating promotional campaigns sponsored by the manufacturer and by providing marketing advice and expertise. Intermediaries' questions often pertain to the allowed markup, merchandising support, and return policies.

The Product Life Cycle

All products have a product life cycle (see Chapter 10), and the composition of the promotional mix changes over the four life-cycle stages, as shown in Figure 14–3.

- *Introduction stage.* Providing information to consumers in an effort to increase their level of awareness is the primary promotional objective in the introduction stage of the product life cycle. In general, all the promotional mix elements are used at this time.
- *Growth stage.* The primary promotional objective of the growth stage is to persuade the consumer to buy the product. Advertising is used to communicate brand differences, and personal selling is used to solidify the channel of distribution.

Marketing Matters

technology

How Can You Reach Today's College Students? With Mobile Marketing!

Today's college students include the tail end of Generation Y and the new generation of young consumers often called Millennials. Nationwide Bank estimates that college students spend more than $400 billion each year, making them an attractive market for many businesses. In an effort to reach students with their offerings, marketers are tailoring their activities to match the segment's unique characteristics.

College students consist of "digital natives" who have grown up with technology. They have and use laptop computers, high-definition televisions, video game consoles, tablet devices, and smartphones. In fact, a recent study of university and college students found that 82 percent of new college students own a smartphone. They access Facebook, Twitter, YouTube, and Instagram; they download apps, coupons, and information 24/7; and they communicate with e-mail, text messages, and blogs. For many businesses, these facts suggest that marketing through smartphones, or mobile marketing, will be an essential element in integrated marketing communications campaigns in the future.

Several guidelines can help ensure the success of mobile marketing. First, it is important to create a mobile-ready app that is flashy, fun, and has the potential to "go viral." In addition, because the recession has created financial hardships for Millennials, successful mobile apps should help shoppers make price comparisons and match product characteristics to their needs, preferences, and lifestyles. Communication must be short (140 characters on Twitter!), honest, authentic, and transparent about the purpose and value of the brand. Finally, mobile marketing campaigns should facilitate multitasking. According to one expert, marketers "should picture students looking at text and images while traveling on a bus, rushing to a lecture, or out socializing."

Examples of successful mobile marketing campaigns include MTV's use of a Twitter jockey to provide messages to its viewers and the Starbucks Mobile Card application to make payments easier.

Watch for other brands that use mobile marketing as part of their campaigns to reach college students in the future.

- *Maturity stage.* In the maturity stage the need is to maintain exiting buyers. Advertising's role is to remind buyers of the product's existence. Sales promotion, in the form of discounts, coupons, and events, is important in maintaining loyal buyers.
- *Decline stage.* The decline stage of the product life cycle is usually a period of phase-out for the product, and little money is spent in the promotional mix.

FIGURE 14–3
The product life cycle illustrates how promotional objectives and activities change over the four stages.

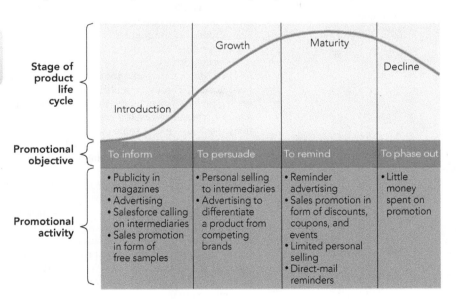

FIGURE 14-4
Push and pull strategies
direct the promotional mix
to different points in the
channel of distribution.

Channel Strategies

Chapter 12 discussed the channel flow from a producer to intermediaries to consumers. Achieving control of the channel is often difficult for the manufacturer, and promotional strategies can assist in moving a product through the channel of distribution. This is where a manufacturer has to make an important decision about whether to use a push strategy, pull strategy, or both in its channel of distribution.[15]

push strategy
Directing the promotional
mix to channel members
to gain their cooperation
in ordering and stocking
a product.

Push Strategy   Figure 14-4A shows how a manufacturer uses a **push strategy**, directing the promotional mix to channel members to gain their cooperation in ordering and stocking the product. In this approach, personal selling and sales promotions play major roles. Salespeople call on wholesalers to encourage orders and provide sales assistance. Sales promotions, such as case discount allowances (20 percent off the regular case price), are offered to stimulate demand. By pushing the product through the channel, the goal is to get channel members to push it to their customers.

Ford Motor Company, for example, provides support and incentives for its 3,290 Ford dealers. Through a multilevel program, Ford provides incentives to reward dealers for meeting sales goals. Dealers receive an incentive when they are near a goal, another when they reach a goal, and an even larger one if they exceed sales projections. Ford also offers some dealers special incentives for maintaining superior facilities or improving customer service. All of these actions are intended to encourage Ford dealers to "push" the Ford products through the channel to consumers.[16]

pull strategy
Directing the promotional
mix at ultimate consumers
to encourage them to ask
the retailer for a product.

Pull Strategy   In some instances, manufacturers face resistance from channel members who do not want to order a new product or increase inventory levels of an existing brand. As shown in Figure 14-4B, a manufacturer may then elect to implement a **pull strategy** by directing its promotional mix at ultimate consumers to encourage them to ask the retailer for a product. Seeing demand from ultimate consumers, retailers order the product from wholesalers and thus the item is pulled through the intermediaries. Pharmaceutical companies, for example, now spend more than $3.4 billion annually on *direct-to-consumer* prescription drug advertising, to complement traditional personal selling and free samples directed only at doctors.[17]

The strategy is designed to encourage consumers to ask their doctor for a specific drug by name—pulling it through the channel. Successful campaigns such as Merck's print ads, which say, "Ask your doctor if Zetia is right for you," can have dramatic effects on the sales of a product.

learning review

14-7. Promotional programs can be directed to _____, _____, or both.

14-8. Describe the promotional objective for each stage of the product life cycle.

14-9. Explain the differences between a push strategy and a pull strategy.

DEVELOPING AN IMC PROGRAM

LO 14-4 Describe the elements of the promotion decision process.

Because media costs are high, promotion decisions must be made carefully, using a systematic approach. Paralleling the planning, implementation, and evaluation steps described in the strategic marketing process (Chapter 2), the promotion decision process is divided into (1) developing, (2) executing, and (3) assessing the promotion program (see Figure 14–5).

Identifying the Target Audience

The first step in developing the promotion program involves identifying the *target audience*, the group of prospective buyers toward which a promotion program will be directed. To the extent that time and money permit, the target audience for the promotion program is the target market for the firm's product, which is identified from primary and secondary sources of marketing information. The more a firm knows about its target audience—including demographics, interests, preferences, media use, and purchase behaviors—the easier it is to develop a promotional program. A firm might use a profile based on gender, age, and income, for example, to place ads during specific TV programs or in particular magazines. Similarly, a firm might use *behavioral targeting*—collecting information about your web-browsing behavior to determine the banner and display ads that you will see as you surf the Web. Behavioral targeting is discussed in more detail in Chapter 18.[18]

FIGURE 14–5
The promotion decision process includes planning, implementation, and evaluation.

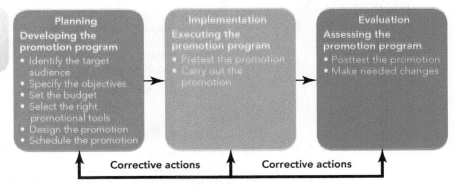

Specifying Promotion Objectives

After the target audience has been identified, a decision must be reached on what the promotion should accomplish. Consumers can be said to respond in terms of a **hierarchy of effects**, which is the sequence of stages a prospective buyer goes through from initial awareness of a product to eventual action (either trial or adoption of the product).[19] The five stages are:

* *Awareness*—the consumer's ability to recognize and remember the product or brand name.
* *Interest*—an increase in the consumer's desire to learn about some of the features of the product or brand.
* *Evaluation*—the consumer's appraisal of the product or brand on important attributes.
* *Trial*—the consumer's actual first purchase and use of the product or brand.
* *Adoption*—through a favorable experience on the first trial, the consumer's repeated purchase and use of the product or brand.

For a totally new product, the sequence applies to the entire product category, but for a new brand competing in an established product category, it applies to the brand itself. These steps can serve as guidelines for developing promotion objectives.

Although sometimes an objective for a promotion program involves several steps in the hierarchy of effects, it often focuses on a single stage. Regardless of what the specific objective might be, from building awareness to increasing repeat purchases, promotion objectives should possess three important qualities. They should (1) be designed for a well-defined target audience, (2) be measurable, and (3) cover a specified time period.

Setting the Promotion Budget

After setting the promotion objectives, a company must decide how much to spend. The promotion expenditures needed to reach U.S. households are enormous. Ten companies—including P&G, GM, Comcast, AT&T and Verizon—each spend a total of more than $2 billion annually on promotion.[20] Determining the ideal amount for the budget is difficult because there is no precise way to measure the exact results of spending promotion dollars.[21] However, several methods can be used to set the promotion budget.[21]

* *Percentage of sales*. In the percentage of sales budgeting approach, the amount of money spent on promotion is a percentage of past or anticipated sales. A common budgeting method,[22] this approach is often staged in terms such as "our promotion budget for this year is 3 percent of last year's gross sales." See the Using Marketing Dashboards box for an application of the promotion-to-sales ratio to the soft-drink industry.[23]
* *Competitive parity*. Competitive parity budgeting matches the competitor's absolute level of spending or the proportion per point of market share.[24]
* *All you can afford*. Common to many businesses, the all-you-can-afford budgeting method allows money to be spent on promotion only after all other budget items—such as manufacturing costs—are covered.[25]
* *Objective and task*. The best approach to budgeting is objective and task budgeting, whereby the company (1) determines the promotion objectives, (2) outlines the tasks to accomplish those objectives, and (3) determines the promotion cost of performing those tasks.[26]

Of the various methods, only the objective and task method takes into account what the company wants to accomplish and requires that the objectives be specified.[27]

Selecting the Right Promotional Tools

Once a budget has been determined, the combination of the five basic IMC tools—advertising, personal selling, sales promotion, public relations, and direct marketing—can be specified. While many factors provide direction for selection of the appropriate mix,

Using Marketing Dashboards

How Much Should You Spend on IMC?

Integrated marketing communications (IMC) programs coordinate a variety of promotion alternatives to provide a consistent message across audiences. The amount spent on the various promotional elements, or on the total campaign, may vary depending on the target audience, the type of product, where the product is in the product life cycle, and the channel strategy selected. Managers often use the promotion-to-sales ratio on their marketing dashboard to assess how effective the IMC program expenditures are at generating sales.

Your Challenge   As a manager at PepsiCo, you've been asked to assess the effectiveness of all promotion expenditures during the past year. The promotion-to-sales ratio can be used to make year-to-year comparisons of a company's promotional programs, to compare the effectiveness of a company's program with competitors' programs, or to make comparisons with industry averages. You decide to calculate the promotion-to-sales ratio for PepsiCo. In addition, to allow a comparison, you decide to make the same calculation for one of your competitors, Coca-Cola, and for the entire nonalcoholic beverage industry. The ratio is calculated as follows:

Promotion-to-sales ratio =
Total promotion expenditures ÷ Total sales

Your Findings   The information needed for these calculations is readily available from trade publications and annual reports. The following graph shows the promotion-to-sales ratio for PepsiCo, Coca-Cola, and the entire nonalcoholic beverage industry. PepsiCo spent $196 million on its promotion program to generate $2.3 billion in sales for a ratio of 8.5 (percent). In comparison, Coca-Cola's ratio was 5.3, and the industry average was 5.5.

Your Action   PepsiCo's promotion-to-sales ratio is higher than Coca-Cola's and higher than the industry average. This suggests that the current mix of promotional activities and the level of expenditures may not be creating an effective IMC program. In the future, you will want to monitor the factors that may influence the ratio.

Video 14-3
Olympics
kerin.tv/cr6e/v14-3

This logo for the 2016 Summer Olympics in Rio de Janeiro, Brazil, is part of a comprehensive IMC program.

the large number of possible combinations of the promotional tools means that many combinations can achieve the same objective. Therefore, an analytical approach and experience are particularly important in this step of the promotion decision process. The specific mix can vary from a simple program using a single tool to a comprehensive program using all forms of promotion.

The Olympics have become a very visible example of a comprehensive integrated communications program. Because the Games are repeated every two years, the promotion is continuous during "on" and "off" years. Included in the program are advertising campaigns, personal selling efforts by the Olympic committee and organizers, sales promotion activities such as product tie-ins and sponsorships, public relations programs managed by the host cities, online and social media communication, and direct marketing efforts targeted at a variety of audiences, including governments, organizations, firms, athletes, and individuals.[28] At this stage, it is also important to assess the relative importance of the various tools. While it may be desirable to utilize and integrate several forms of promotion, one may deserve emphasis. The Olympics, for example, place primary importance on public relations and publicity.

Designing the Promotion

The central element of a promotion program is the promotion itself. Advertising consists of advertising copy and the artwork that the target audience is intended to see or hear. Personal selling efforts depend on the characteristics and skills of the salesperson.

Sales promotion activities consist of the specific details of inducements such as coupons, samples, and sweepstakes. Public relations efforts are readily seen in tangible elements such as news releases, and direct marketing actions depend on written, verbal, and electronic forms of delivery. The design of the promotion will play a primary role in determining the message that is communicated to the audience. This design activity is frequently viewed as the step requiring the most creativity. In addition, successful designs are often the result of insight regarding consumers' interests and purchasing behavior. All of the promotion tools have many design alternatives. Advertising, for example, can utilize fear, humor, attractiveness, or other themes in its appeal. Similarly, direct marketing can be designed for varying levels of personal or customized appeals. One of the challenges of IMC is to design each promotional activity to communicate the same message.[29]

Scheduling the Promotion

Once the design of each of the promotional program elements is complete, it is important to determine the most effective timing of their use. The promotion schedule describes the order in which each promotional tool is introduced and the frequency of its use during the campaign.

Walt Disney Pictures movie studio, for example, uses a schedule of several promotional tools for its movies. To generate interest in a movie such as *Oz: The Great and Powerful*, the studio first invited the television program *Entertainment Tonight* to visit the set to film a behind-the-scenes story about the movie. The trailer for the movie was then released in regular format and in 3D format. In addition, a television commercial for the movie debuted during the Super Bowl, and the studio created a website with movie information, links to Twitter and Facebook, and games such as "Journey to Oz." An app called "Temple Run: Oz" was also created for the iPhone, iPad, and Android phones. As the premiere of the movie approached, Disney began a hot air balloon tour of the United States, added an Oz garden at Epcot Center, and sent the lead actor from the movie, James Franco, to serve as the grand marshal of the Daytona 500. Disney also launched a sweepstakes with partner World Market and collaborated with Home Shopping Network to create an exclusive collection of fashions, jewelry, and accessories based on the movie. After the movie was released, Disney used online promotions to encourage fans to purchase the DVD.[30]

What promotional tools did Disney use to support the release of *Oz: The Great and Powerful*?

Overall, the scheduling of the various promotions was designed to generate interest, bring consumers into theaters, and then encourage additional purchases after seeing the movie. Several factors such as seasonality and competitive promotion activity can also influence the promotion schedule. Businesses such as ski resorts, airlines, and professional sports teams are likely to reduce their promotional activity during the off-season. Similarly, restaurants, retail stores, and health clubs are likely to increase their promotional activity when new competitors enter the market.

EXECUTING AND ASSESSING THE PROMOTION PROGRAM

As shown earlier in Figure 14–5, the ideal execution of a promotion program involves pretesting each design before it is actually used to allow for changes and modifications that improve its effectiveness. Similarly, posttests are recommended to evaluate the impact of each promotion and the contribution of the promotion toward achieving the program objectives. The most sophisticated pretest and posttest procedures have been developed for advertising and are discussed in Chapter 15. Testing procedures for sales promotion and direct marketing efforts currently focus on comparisons of different designs or responses of different segments. To fully

The San Diego Padres baseball team uses database information to assess the impact of its IMC program.

Video 14-4
Carat
kerin.tv/cr6e/v14-4

benefit from IMC programs, companies must create and maintain a test-result database that allows comparisons of the relative impact of the promotional tools and their execution options in varying situations. Information from the database will allow informed design and execution decisions and provide support for IMC activities during internal reviews by financial or administrative personnel. The San Diego Padres baseball team, for example, developed a database of information relating attendance to its integrated campaign, which included a new logo, special events, merchandise sales, and a loyalty program.

Carrying out the promotion program can be expensive and time-consuming. One researcher estimates that "an organization with sales less than $10 million can successfully implement an IMC program in one year, one with sales between $200 million and $500 million will need about three years, and one with sales between $2 billion and $5 billion will need five years." In addition, firms with a market orientation are more likely to implement an IMC program, and firms with support from top management have more effective IMC programs.[31] To facilitate the transition, approximately 200 integrated marketing communications agencies are in operation. In addition, some of the largest agencies are adopting approaches that embrace "total communications solutions."

Media agency Carat, which recently won *Advertising Age* magazine's Media Agency of the Year award, for example, is part of a global network of 5,000 people in 70 countries who "help clients get the most from the new era of media." In fact, the agency website proclaims that it is "Redefining Media." The agency's services include sponsorship; product placement; direct marketing; strategy and planning; and digital, social, mobile, search, and out-of-home media buying. One of its integrated campaigns for Nokia included television and print advertising, banner ads, and online video ads. The campaign resulted in 5.1 million video views and a 61 percent increase in purchase intent. Other Carat clients include Home Depot, Disney, General Motors, Macy's, and GoPro. CEO Doug Ray explains that "clients are trying to globalize their brands," so Carat helps them "go to market faster, in a consistent way, across markets." While many agencies may still be specialists, the trend today is clearly toward an integrated perspective that includes all forms of promotion. Agencies can accomplish this by including account managers, channel experts, media specialists, and planning personnel in their campaign design efforts.[32]

An important factor in developing successful IMC programs is to create a process that facilitates their design and use. A tool used to evaluate a company's current process is the IMC audit. The audit analyzes the internal communication network of the company; identifies key audiences; evaluates customer databases; assesses messages in recent advertising, public relations releases, packaging, websites, e-mail and social media communication, signage, sales promotions, and direct mail; and determines the IMC expertise of company and agency personnel.[33] This process is becoming increasingly important as consumer-generated media such as blogs, RSS, podcasts, and social networks become more popular and as the use of search engines increases. Now, in addition to ensuring that traditional forms of communication are integrated, companies must be able to monitor consumer content, respond to inconsistent messages, and even answer questions from individual customers.

learning review

14-10. What are the stages of the hierarchy of effects?

14-11. What are the four approaches to setting the promotion budget?

14-12. How have advertising agencies changed to facilitate the use of IMC programs?

DIRECT MARKETING

LO 14-5 Explain the value of direct marketing for consumers and sellers.

Direct marketing takes many forms and utilizes a variety of media. Several forms of direct marketing—direct mail and catalogs, television home shopping, telemarketing, and direct selling—were discussed as methods of nonstore retailing in Chapter 13. In addition, although advertising is discussed in Chapter 15, a form of advertising—direct response advertising—is an important form of direct marketing. Finally, interactive marketing is discussed in detail in Chapter 18. In this section, the growth of direct marketing, its value for consumers and sellers, and key global, technological, and ethical issues are discussed.

The Growth of Direct Marketing

The increasing interest in customer relationship management is reflected in the dramatic growth of direct marketing. The ability to customize communication efforts and create one-to-one interactions is appealing to most marketers, particularly those with IMC programs, because it leads to more favorable attitudes from the recipients. While many direct marketing methods are not new, the ability to design and use them has increased with the availability of customer information databases and new printing technologies. In recent years, direct marketing growth has outpaced total economic growth. Direct marketing expenditures exceed $168 billion and are growing at a rate of 3.4 percent. Similarly, revenues are expected to grow to $2.4 trillion by 2016. Direct marketing currently accounts for 8.7 percent of the total U.S. gross domestic product.[34]

While telemarketing receives the highest level of expenditures, most campaigns use several methods. Many companies also integrate their direct marketing with other forms of promotion. Porsche, for example, recently launched television ads to change consumer perceptions of its cars and supported the campaign with direct-mail brochures, a mobile application, and an online video contest. Mobile direct marketing sales and social network direct marketing sales are growing at 33 percent and 20 percent, respectively—the fastest of all direct marketing tools.[35]

The Value of Direct Marketing

One of the most visible indicators of the value of direct marketing for consumers is its increasing level of use in its various forms. For example, in the past year, 52 percent of the U.S. population ordered merchandise or services by mail; more than 110 million people made purchases online; and consumers spent more than $147 billion on products available through television offers. In addition, 57 percent of social media users say that they are more likely to purchase a product after seeing a positive post.

For consumers, direct marketing offers a variety of benefits, including: They don't have to go to a store; they can usually shop 24 hours a day; buying direct saves time; they avoid hassles with salespeople; they can save money; it's fun and entertaining; and it offers more privacy than in-store shopping. Many consumers also believe that direct marketing provides excellent customer service. Toll-free telephone numbers, customer service representatives with access to information regarding purchasing preferences, overnight delivery services, and unconditional guarantees all help create value for direct marketing customers. At Landsend.com, when customers need assistance they can click the "Live Help" icon to receive help from a sales representative on the phone or through online chat or online video until the correct product is found. "It's like we were walking down the aisle in a store!" says one Lands' End customer.[36]

The value of direct marketing for sellers can be described in terms of the responses it generates. **Direct orders** are the result of offers that contain all the information necessary for a prospective buyer to make a decision to purchase and complete the transaction. Priceline.com, for example, will send *PriceBreaker* RSS

Video 14-5
Priceline Ad
kerin.tv/cr6e/v14-5

direct orders
The result of direct marketing offers that contain all the information necessary for a potential buyer to make a decision to purchase and complete the transaction.

lead generation
The result of a direct marketing offer designed to generate interest in a product or a service and a request for additional information.

traffic generation
The outcome of a direct marketing offer designed to motivate people to visit a business.

Direct mail can be used to obtain orders, generate leads, or motivate people to visit a store.

Video 14-6
Ad Choices
kerin.tv/cr6e/v14-6

alerts to people in its database. The messages offer discounted fares and rates to customers who can travel on very short notice. **Lead generation** is the result of an offer designed to generate interest in a product or service and a request for additional information. Four Seasons Hotels now sell private residences in several of their properties and send direct mail to prospective residents asking them to request additional information on the telephone or through a website. Finally, **traffic generation** is the outcome of an offer designed to motivate people to visit a business. Home Depot, for example, uses an opt-in e-mail alert to announce special sales that attract consumers to the store. Similarly, Target uses direct mail to generate traffic in new and remodeled stores.[37]

Technological, Global, and Ethical Issues in Direct Marketing

The information technology and databases described in Chapter 8 are key elements in any direct marketing program. Databases are the result of organizations' efforts to create profiles of customers so that direct marketing tools, such as e-mail and catalogs, can be directed at specific customers. While most companies try to keep records of their customers' past purchases, many other types of data are needed to use direct marketing to develop one-to-one relationships with customers. Some data, such as lifestyles, media use, and demographics, are best collected from the consumer. Other types of data, such as price, quantity, and brand, are best collected from the businesses where purchases are made. New integrated marketing databases match consumers' postal addresses, telephone numbers, and e-mail addresses. In addition, many businesses are beginning to match their customer records with Facebook profiles, Twitter following behavior, and Google search activity.[38]

Direct marketing faces several challenges and opportunities in global markets today. Many countries, including the United Kingdom, Australia, the European Union, and Japan, have requirements for a mandatory "opt-in"—that is, potential customers must give permission to be included on a list for direct marketing solicitations. In addition, the mail, telephone, and Internet systems in many countries are not as well developed as they are in the United States. The need for improved reliability and security in these countries has slowed the growth of direct mail, while the dramatic growth of mobile phone penetration has created an opportunity for direct mobile marketing campaigns.[39]

Global and domestic direct marketers both face challenging ethical issues today. Concerns about privacy, for example, have led to various attempts to provide guidelines that balance consumer and business interests. The European Union passed a consumer privacy law, called the *Data Protection Directive*, after several years of discussion with the Federation of European Direct Marketing and the U.K.'s Direct Marketing Association. A new version of the law, called the *General Data Protection Regulation*, will address new developments such as social networks and cloud computing and is scheduled to take effect in 2016. In the United States several bills that call for a do-not-mail registry similar to the Do Not Call Registry are being discussed. Similarly, there are growing concerns about the web "tracking" tools used by direct marketers to segment consumers and match them with advertising. The Making Responsible Decisions box on the next page describes some of the issues under consideration.[40]

learning review

14-13. The ability to design and use direct marketing programs has increased with the availability of _____ and _____.

14-14. What are the three types of responses generated by direct marketing activities?

CHAPTER 14 Integrated Marketing Communications and Direct Marketing

Making Responsible Decisions

What Is the Future of Your Privacy?

In 2003, the Federal Trade Commission opened the National Do Not Call Registry to give Americans a tool for maintaining their privacy on home and cellular telephone lines. More than 70 percent of all Americans registered. Since then, several state legislatures have also passed laws to create do-not-call lists for automated (robo) telephone calls. In addition, new discussions about privacy related to mail and computer use are now taking place.

Generally, the question being debated is, "What information is private?" Are telephone numbers, addresses of residences, and online activities private or public information? Proponents of a do-not-mail registry argue that, like telephone calls, citizens should be able to stop unsolicited mail. Proponents of do-not-track regulations suggest that website owners who use cookies to collect information about consumers' shopping habits should only do so with a consumer's consent. Marketers counter that consumers who

share this information are more likely to receive messages and advertising that better match their interests.

The Direct Marketing Association currently advocates several solutions. First, it has created DMAchoice, an online tool to help consumers manage the types of mail and e-mail they receive. Second, the organization endorses a self-regulatory program for online behavioral advertising (OBA) that encourages advertisers to include an "Ad Choices" icon in the corner of online ads to allow consumers to opt out of having data collected about their online activities. Moving beyond self-regulation, the European Union recently passed the *E-Privacy Directive* to provide explicit laws for website owners. And in the United States, the Senate is evaluating the "Do Not Track Online Act." These guidelines and regulations, of course, have huge implications for advertisers, portals such as Facebook and Google, and consumers.

What is your opinion? What types of information should be private? Can we find a balance between self-regulation and legislation?

LEARNING OBJECTIVES REVIEW

LO 14-1 *Discuss integrated marketing communication and the communication process.*

Integrated marketing communication is the concept of designing marketing communications programs that coordinate all promotional activities—advertising, personal selling, sales promotion, public relations, and direct marketing—to provide a consistent message across all audiences. The communication process conveys messages with six elements: a source, a message, a channel of communication, a receiver, and encoding and decoding. The communication process also includes a feedback loop and can be distorted by noise.

LO 14-2 *Describe the promotional mix and the uniqueness of each component.*

There are five promotional alternatives. Advertising, sales promotion, and public relations are mass selling approaches, whereas personal selling and direct marketing use customized messages. Advertising can have high absolute costs but reaches large numbers of people. Personal selling has a high cost per contact but provides immediate feedback. Public relations is often difficult to obtain but is very credible. Sales promotion influences short-term consumer behavior. Direct marketing can help develop customer relationships, although maintaining a database can be very expensive.

LO 14-3 *Select the promotional approach appropriate to a product's target audience, life-cycle stage, and channel strategies.*

The promotional mix depends on the target audience. Programs for consumers, business buyers, and intermediaries might

emphasize advertising, personal selling, and sales promotion, respectively. The promotional mix also changes over the product life-cycle stages. During the introduction stage, all promotional mix elements are used. During the growth stage advertising is emphasized, while the maturity stage utilizes sales promotion and direct marketing. Little promotion is used during the decline stage. Finally, the promotional mix can depend on the channel strategy. Push strategies require personal selling and sales promotions directed at channel members, while pull strategies depend on advertising and sales promotion directed at consumers.

LO 14-4 *Describe the elements of the promotion decision process.*

The promotional decision process consists of three steps: planning, implementation, and evaluation. The planning step consists of six elements: identify the target audience, specify the objectives, set the budget, select the right promotional elements, design the promotion, and schedule the promotion. The implementation step includes pretesting. The evaluation step includes posttesting.

LO 14-5 *Explain the value of direct marketing for consumers and sellers.*

The value of direct marketing for consumers is indicated by its increasing level of use. For example, during the past year, 52 percent of the U.S. population made a purchase by mail and more than 110 million people shopped online. The value of direct marketing for sellers can be measured in terms of three types of responses: direct orders, lead generation, and traffic generation.

LEARNING REVIEW ANSWERS

14-1   **What six elements are required for communication to occur?**
Answer: The six elements required for communication to occur are: a source, a message, a channel of communication, a receiver, and the processes of encoding and decoding.

14-2   **A difficulty for U.S. companies advertising in international markets is that the audience does not share the same _____.**
Answer: field of experience

14-3   **A misprint in a newspaper ad is an example of _____.**
Answer: noise

14-4   **Explain the difference between advertising and publicity when both appear on television.**
Answer: Since advertising space on TV is paid for, a firm can control what it wants to say and to whom and how often the message is sent. Since publicity is an indirectly paid presentation of a message, the firm has little control over what is said to whom or when. Instead, it can only suggest to the TV medium that it run a favorable story on the firm or its offerings.

14-5   **Cost per contact is high with the _____ element of the promotional mix.**
Answer: personal selling

14-6   **Which promotional element should be offered only on a short-term basis?**
Answer: sales promotion

14-7   **Promotional programs can be directed to _____, _____, or both.**
Answer: the ultimate consumer; an intermediary (retailer, wholesaler, or industrial distributor)

14-8   **Describe the promotional objective for each stage of the product life cycle.**
Answer: Introduction—to inform; Growth—to persuade; Maturity—to remind; and Decline—to phase out.

14-9   **Explain the differences between a push strategy and a pull strategy.**
Answer: In a push strategy, a firm directs the promotional mix to channel members to gain their cooperation in ordering and stocking the product. In a pull strategy, a firm directs the promotional mix at ultimate consumers to encourage them to ask retailers for the product, who then order it from wholesalers or the firm itself.

14-10   **What are the stages of the hierarchy of effects?**
Answer: The five stages of the hierarchy of effects are awareness, interest, evaluation, trial, and adoption.

14-11   **What are the four approaches to setting the promotion budget?**
Answer: The four approaches to setting the promotion budget are percentage of sales, competitive parity, all you can afford, and objective and task.

14-12   **How have advertising agencies changed to facilitate the use of IMC programs?**
Answer: Some agencies have adopted: (1) a total communications solutions approach that includes all forms of promotion; (2) an IMC audit to analyze the internal communication network of their clients; and (3) the use of both pretesting and posttesting to improve the effectiveness of IMC programs.

14-13   **The ability to design and use direct marketing programs has increased with the availability of _____ and _____.**
Answer: customer information databases; new printing technologies

14-14   **What are the three types of responses generated by direct marketing activities?**
Answer: They are direct orders, lead generation, and traffic generation.

FOCUSING ON KEY TERMS

advertising p. 354
communication p. 352
direct marketing p. 357
direct orders p. 366
hierarchy of effects p. 362
integrated marketing communications
   (IMC) p. 352

lead generation p. 367
personal selling p. 355
promotional mix p. 351
public relations p. 356
publicity p. 356
pull strategy p. 360

push strategy p. 360
sales promotion p. 357
traffic generation p. 367

APPLYING MARKETING KNOWLEDGE

1   After listening to a recent sales presentation, Mary Smith signed up for membership at the local health club. On arriving at the facility, she learned there was an additional fee for racquetball court rentals. "I don't remember that in the sales talk; I thought they said all facilities were included with the membership fee," complained Mary. Describe the problem in terms of the communication process.

2   Develop a matrix to compare the five elements of the promotional mix on three criteria—to *whom* you deliver the message, *what* you say, and *when* you say it.

3 Explain how the promotional tools used by an airline would differ if the target audience were (*a*) consumers who travel for pleasure and (*b*) corporate travel departments that select the airlines to be used by company employees.

4 Suppose you introduced a new consumer food product and invested heavily both in national advertising (pull strategy) and in training and motivating your field sales-force to sell the product to food stores (push strategy). What kinds of feedback would you receive from both the advertising and your salesforce? How could you increase both the quality and quantity of each?

5 Fisher-Price Company, long known as a manufacturer of children's toys, has introduced a line of clothing for children. Outline a promotional plan to get this product introduced in the marketplace.

6 Many insurance companies sell health insurance plans to companies. In these companies the employees pick the plan, but the set of offered plans is determined by the company.

Recently, Blue Cross–Blue Shield, a health insurance company, ran a television ad stating, "If your employer doesn't offer you Blue Cross–Blue Shield coverage, ask why." Explain the promotional strategy behind the advertisement.

7 Identify the sales promotion tools that might be useful for (*a*) Tastee Yogurt, a new brand introduction, (*b*) 3M self-sticking Post-it® Notes, and (*c*) Wrigley's Spearmint gum.

8 Design an integrated marketing communications program—using each of the five promotional elements—for Rhapsody, the online music service.

9 BMW recently introduced its first sport activity vehicle, the X6, to compete with other popular crossover vehicles such as the Mercedes-Benz R-Class. Design a direct marketing program to generate (*a*) leads, (*b*) traffic in dealerships, and (*c*) direct orders.

10 Develop a privacy policy for database managers that provides a balance of consumer and seller perspectives. How would you encourage voluntary compliance with your policy? What methods of enforcement would you recommend?

BUILDING YOUR MARKETING PLAN

To develop the promotion strategy for your marketing plan, follow the steps suggested in the planning phase of the promotion decision process described in Figure 14–5.

1 You should (*a*) identify the target audience, (*b*) specify the promotion objectives, (*c*) set the promotion budget, (*d*) select the right promotion tools, (*e*) design the promotion, and (*f*) schedule the promotion.

2 Also specify the pretesting and posttesting procedures needed in the implementation and evaluation phases.

3 Finally, describe how each of your promotion tools is integrated to provide a consistent message.

VIDEO CASE 14   Taco Bell: Using IMC to Help Customers Live Más!

Video 14-7
Taco Bell
Video Case
kerin.tv/cr6e/v14-7

"Every touch point is considered," explains Stephanie Perdue, Taco Bell's senior director of marketing, "from the posters in the restaurants down to the packaging, and all of the different media channels." Stephanie is describing the integrated marketing communications approach used by Taco Bell, the nation's leading Mexican-style quick service restaurant. IMC is one of the key factors that has contributed to the extraordinary success of the food chain, which serves more than 36 million customers each week!

THE COMPANY

The story behind Taco Bell and its success is fascinating. After World War II, a young marine named Glen Bell returned to his home state of California with an entrepreneurial spirit and an observation that people were hungry for fast, good food. He opened his first restaurant, Bell's Burgers, based on the simple concept that customers might want to walk up and get their food from a service window. Not far away, two brothers named McDonald were operating their new restaurant using a "drive-in" concept. For several years, Bell and the McDonald brothers enjoyed friendly competition as pioneers of the growing fast-food industry. However, when the burger restaurant market became crowded with competitors, Bell decided to try something new—tacos!

Tacos were new to most Americans so Bell experimented with many concepts. First he developed a crunchy taco shell and opened a restaurant called Taco Tia. His marketing activities consisted of handing out sombreros and having Mariachis play outside the restaurant. Next, Bell started another restaurant, El Taco, with a group of celebrity partners. Finally, after a friend suggested that Glen should use his name in his business, the first Taco Bell was opened in Downey, California.

Taco Bell grew quickly and as Bell began opening additional locations he decided that the restaurants should resemble the appearance of California's historic missions. With the help of an architect he created an inviting design based on an adobe-like exterior with a red clay-tile roof. The name and logo utilized a mission-style bell, a version of which is still in use today. Through franchises and additional corporate locations Taco Bell soon reached from coast to coast.

Today Taco Bell is a subsidiary of Yum! Brands, which also owns and operates KFC, Pizza Hut, and WingStreet. Taco Bell now has more than 6,500 locations and $7 billion in sales. Many locations are cobranded with KFC, Pizza Hut, and Long John Silver stores. Taco Bell also operates Taco Bell Express locations in convenience stores, truck stops, shopping malls, and airports.

INTEGRATED MARKETING COMMUNICATIONS AT TACO BELL

From its beginning, Taco Bell has used very creative promotional activities. For example, when the Mir space station was about to reenter the Earth's atmosphere, Taco Bell placed a target in the Pacific Ocean and announced that every person in the United States would receive a free taco if any piece of the falling space station hit the target. Similarly, in its "Steal a Base, Steal a Taco" promotion, Taco Bell promised to give everyone a free taco if any player steals a base in the World Series. While the space station did not hit the target, several players have stolen bases in the World Series, leading to free tacos for everyone! Taco Bell has also offered special promotions with Mountain Dew, partnered with the NBA as its official fast food, and created videos for movie-theater advertising.

You might remember some of Taco Bell's advertising campaigns such as "Yo quiero Taco Bell," "Grand Taste. Loco Value," or "Get it at The Bell." The more recent "Think Outside the Bun" campaign was designed for Millennials. Then as that group changed, Taco Bell executives recognized that they had an opportunity to reposition the chain. Tracee Larocca, brand creative director at Taco Bell, explains, "We realized there was a big opportunity as the culture shifted from 'food as fuel' to 'food as experience'." Taco Bell considered many new taglines, such as "Keep Life Spicy" and "Hunger for Más," and eventually developed the "Live Más" campaign. As campaigns and positioning changes, integrated marketing becomes increasingly important. According to Larocca, "as the brand's creative director, my job is to make sure that all of our communications have the same look, tone, and feel across all platforms, making sure we maintain consistency in our brand voice no matter what we're doing internally or externally."

Advertising Age magazine recently named Taco Bell the winner of its Marketer of the Year award for its extraordinary use of integrated marketing in the launch of its Doritos Locos Tacos. The new product went through three years of development and 45 prototypes before its launch, which led to sales of 100 million units in its first 10 weeks. Taco Bell allocates approximately 70 percent of its budget to traditional media, 20 percent to digital media, and 10 percent to new media where it can "explore." The traditional media budget included a Super Bowl ad utilizing the "Live Más" theme. "It was all about a mindset and not necessarily an age range or a demographic," explains Larocca. The ad, called "Forever Young," showed "a group of old people breaking out of a retirement home and having a great night on the town," she adds.

The social media component of the campaign included Facebook, Twitter, Vine, Snapchat, and Instagram. The Twitter campaign, for example, included a Hometown Tweet-off where anyone could send a tweet saying why a Taco Bell truck should visit their hometown. Similarly, Taco Bell posted pictures to Facebook and watched the responses in the comments and the "likes." Some of the new media budget was used to try things such as Taco Bell's own video channels for Web and mobile, and a live stream to a billboard in Times Square. As Rob Poetsch, director of public affairs and engagement, observed about the Doritos Locos Tacos launch, "for the first time, we had a fully integrated plan that engaged all of our constituents."

THE FUTURE AT TACO BELL

Taco Bell continues to develop new products, brand concepts, and promotions. For example, waffle tacos, Cinnabon Delights, and the A.M. Crunchwrap are new additions to the menu. In addition, a new brand concept called U.S. Taco Co., which is testing its first locations in California, will offer "designer" tacos to segments that are willing to spend more for higher quality. Finally, a new breakfast menu campaign used 25 men named Ronald McDonald to help suggest that a new generation of fast-food breakfast items is now available at Taco Bell. All of these activities are contributing to the company's continued growth. Yum! Brands expects Taco Bell's domestic sales to double by 2021!

Questions

1 What factors contributed to Taco Bell's early success?
2 Which of the promotional elements described in Figure 14–2 were used by Taco Bell in its Doritos Locos Tacos campaign?
3 How does Taco Bell ensure the continued success of the food chain?

Chapter Notes

1. Jenni Romaniuk, "Are You Ready for the Next Big Thing?" *Journal of Advertising Research*, December 2012, pp. 397–99; "Taco Bell Implements Its Largest Marketing Campaign Ever," *QSRweb*, March 7, 2013; "Highly Anticipated, Most Socially Requested Taco Bell Product Launch to Be Largest Marketing Campaign in Brand's History," *Business Wire*, March 7, 2013; "Yo Quiero Engagement? Taco Bell Charms the Twittersphere," www.Business2Community.com, February 4, 2013; and Lynne D. Johnson, "Customer Engagement Is the New Marketing," *Journal of Advertising Research*, June 2010, pp. 118–19.

2. Sita Mishra and Sushma Muralie, "Managing Dynamism of IMC—Anarchy to Order," *Journal of Marketing and Communication*, September 2010, pp. 29–37; and Philip J. Kitchen, Ilchul Kim, and Don E. Schultz. "Integrated Marketing Communications: Practice Leads Theory," *Journal of Advertising Research*, December 2008, pp. 531–46.

3. Wilbur Schramm, "How Communication Works," in *The Process and Effects of Mass Communication*, Wilbur Schramm, ed., (Urbana, IL: University of Illinois Press, 1955), pp. 3–26.

4. E. Cooper and M. Jahoda, "The Evasion of Propaganda," *Journal of Psychology* 22 (1947), pp. 15–25; H. Hyman and P. Sheatsley, "Some Reasons Why Information Campaigns Fail," *Public Opinion Quarterly* 11 (1947), pp. 412–23; and J. T. Klapper, *The Effects of Mass Communication* (New York: Free Press, 1960), Chapter VII.

5. "Mistakes in Advertising," on the Learn English website, http://www.learnenglish.de/mistakes/HorrorMistakes.htm, accessed March 18, 2013; and Bianca Bartz, "International Ads Lost in Translation," TrendHunter Marketing website, http://www.trendhunter.com/trends/advertising-bloopers-international-ads-lost-in-translation, accessed March 18, 2013.

6. Rik Pieters and Michel Wedel, "Attention Capture and Transfer in Advertising: Brand, Pictorial, and Text-Size Effects," *Journal of Marketing*, April 2004, pp. 36–50.

7. Adapted from American Marketing Association, Resource Library Dictionary, http://www.marketingpower.com/layouts/Dictionary.aspx?dLetter=P, accessed March 18, 2013.

8. Dave Folkens, "3 Ways Social Media Is Changing Public Relations," *Online Marketing Blog*, February 17, 2011; and Michael Bush, "How Social Media Is Helping the Public-Relations Sector Not Just Survive, but Thrive," *Advertising Age*, August 23, 2010, p. 1.

9. Piet Levy, "CSR Take Responsibility," *Marketing News*, May 30, 2010, p. 20; and *Let's Talk*. McDonald's corporate blog. http://community.aboutmcdonalds.com/t5/Let-s-Talk/bg-p/blog1, accessed March 18, 2013.

10. Jooyoung Kim, Hye Jin Yoon, and Sun Young Lee, "Integrating Advertising and Publicity: A Theoretical Examination of the Effects of Exposure Sequence, Publicity Valence, and Product Attribute Consistency," *Journal of Advertising*, Spring 2010, p. 97; and Marsha D. Loda and Barbara Carrick Coleman, "Sequence Matters: A More Effective Way to Use Advertising and Publicity," *Journal of Advertising Research* 45 (December 2005), pp. 362–71.

11. Kusum L. Ailawadi, Scott A. Neslin, and Karen Gedenk, "Pursuing the Value-Conscious Consumer: Store Brands versus National Brand Promotions," *Journal of Marketing*, January 2001, pp. 71–89.

12. Nikki Hopewell, "The Rules of Engagement: A Bevy of Rules and Best Practices Govern Promotions and Contests," *Marketing News*, June 1, 2008, p. 6; and Gerard Prendergast, Yi-Zheng Shi, and Ka-Man Cheung, "Behavioural Response to Sales Promotion Tools," *International Journal of Advertising* 24 (2005), pp. 467–86.

13. Adapted from American Marketing Association, Resource Library Dictionary, http://www.marketingpower.com/layouts/Dictionary.aspx?dLetter=D, accessed March 18, 2013.

14. "Top 5 Brands Using Mobile Marketing Successfully," www.Business2Community.com, March 11, 2013; "Eight Out of Ten Freshers Have Smartphones, According to New UCAS Media Survey," *M2 Presswire*, March 13, 2013; "Mysteries and Myths of Millennials in Social Media," www.Business2Community.com,

July 21, 2012; Stuart Elliott, "In an Upgrade, Google Adds to Its Model for Mobile Marketing," *The New York Times*, March 7, 2013, p. 3; "Tailoring Your Mobile Strategy to the New Millennials," *VentureBeat*, July 18, 2012; Nationwide Bank website, http://www.nationwide.com/cps/college-student-spending-habits-infographic.htm, accessed March 19, 2013; and "5 Tips for Marketing to Millennials," *Advertising Age*, October 11, 2010, p. 17.

15. "Push vs. Pull Strategies," *Daily News*, May 3, 2011; "Question: Should B2B Be Focusing All Its Efforts on 'Pull' Marketing Therefore Turning Its Back on 'Push' Marketing Techniques?" *B2B Marketing Magazine*, September 2009; and Michael Levy, John Webster, and Roger Kerin, "Formulating Push Marketing Strategies: A Method and Application," *Journal of Marketing*, Winter 1983, pp. 25–34.

16. Bradford Wernle, "Quality, Market Share, Leasing Top Ford Dealers' Agenda," *Automotive News*, February 10, 2013; Jamie LaReau, "Ford Dealers Revamp Pay Plans; Some Efforts Resemble Stair-Step Programs," *Automotive News*, February 14, 2011, p. 10; and *Ford Motor Company Annual Report, 2012*, p. 14.

17. Tracy Staton, "Pharma DTC Ad Spending Sinks 11.5%," *FiercePharma*, April 2, 2013, www.fiercepharma.com; John Mack, "DTC Not as Dead as We Thought," *Pharma Marketing Blog*, April 2, 2013, www.pharmamkting.blogspot.com; and Beth Snyder Bulik, "Ad Spending: 15 Years of DTC," *Advertising Age Insights White Paper*, October 17, 2011.

18. Don E. Shultz, Martin P. Block, and Kaylan Raman, "Understanding Consumer-Created Media Synergy," *Journal of Marketing Communications*," July 2012, pp. 173–87; "Why Behavioral Targeting Is Effective," www.Business2Community.com, January 15, 2013; and Lauren Drell, "4 Ways Behavioral Targeting Is Changing the Web," *Mashable*, April 26, 2011.

19. Robert J. Lavidge and Gary A. Steiner, "A Model for Predictive Measurement of Advertising Effectiveness," *Journal of Marketing*, October 1961, p. 61.

20. "100 Leading National Advertisers," *Advertising Age*, June 24, 2013, p. 16.

21. George S. Low and Jakki J. Mohr, "Setting Advertising and Promotion Budgets in Multi-Brand Companies," *Journal of Advertising Research*, January/February 1999, pp. 67–78; Don E. Schultz and Anders Gronstedt, "Making Marcom an Investment," *Marketing Management*, Fall 1997, pp. 41–49; and J. Enrique Bigne, "Advertising Budget Practices: A Review," *Journal of Current Issues and Research in Advertising*, Fall 1995, pp. 17–31.

22. John Philip Jones, "Ad Spending: Maintaining Market Share," *Harvard Business Review*, January–February 1990, pp. 38–42; and Charles H. Patti and Vincent Blasko, "Budgeting Practices of Big Advertisers," *Journal of Advertising Research* 21 (December 1981), pp. 23–30.

23. "U.S. Market Leaders," *Advertising Age*, June 25, 2012, pp. 24–25.

24. Brenda Marlin, "Adding It Up: You Can Save Time by Trying One of Three Short-Cut Approaches to an Annual Budget," *ABA Banking*, October 1, 2007, p. 36; James A. Shroer, "Ad Spending: Growing Market Share," *Harvard Business Review*, January–February 1990, pp. 44–48; and Jeffrey A. Lowenhar and John L. Stanton, "Forecasting Competitive Advertising Expenditures," *Journal of Advertising Research* 16, no. 2 (April 1976), pp. 37–44.

25. Daniel Seligman, "How Much for Advertising?" *Fortune*, December 1956, p. 123.

26. James E. Lynch and Graham J. Hooley, "Increasing Sophistication in Advertising Budget Setting," *Journal of Advertising Research* 30 (February–March 1990), pp. 67–75.

27. Jimmy D. Barnes, Brenda J. Muscove, and Javad Rassouli, "An Objective and Task Media Selection Decision Model and Advertising Cost Formula to Determine International Advertising Budgets," *Journal of Advertising* 11, no. 4 (1982), pp. 68–75.

28. "The Olympic Brand Maintains Its Global Strength and Recognition," *States News Service*, February 12, 2013; Graham Ruddock, "London Olympics Sponsors Are Already into Their Stride," *The Daily Telegraph*,

May 6, 2011, p. 8; "The Olympics Come But Once Every Two Years," *Marketing News*, November 1, 2008, p. 12; "Olympics Will Bring Online Opportunities for Many Brands," *Revolution*, July 14, 2008, p. 13; and Don E. Schultz, "Olympics Get the Gold Medal in Integrating Marketing Event," *Marketing News*, April 27, 1998, pp. 5, 10.

29. "It's Time to Take an Integrated Marketing Approach," www.Business2Community.com, January 22, 2013; "Integrated Marketing: One Message, Many Media," *Marketing Week*, September 18, 2008, p. 31; and Cornelia Pechman, Guangzhi Zhao, Marvin E. Goldberg, and Ellen Thomas Reibling, "What to Convey in Anti-smoking Advertisements for Adolescents: The Use of Protection Motivation Theory to Identify Effective Message Themes," *Journal of Marketing*, April 2003, pp. 1–18.

30. Brooks Barnes, "Great and Powerful Opening for New 'Oz' Movie," *The New York Times*, March 11, 2013, p. 3; "Small Bits of First Look Footage Unveiled from Sam Raimi's 'Oz: The Great and Powerful,'" *indieWire*, July 11, 2012; "Cost Plus World Market Collaborates with Disney for the Release of "'Oz the Great and Powerful,'" *Business Wire*, February 19, 2013; and "HSN and Disney Collaborate for Oz the Great and Powerful Retail Experience," www.chipandco.com, January 23, 2013.

31. Sabine A. Einwiller and Michael Boenigk, "Examining the Link between Integrated Communication Management and Communication Effectiveness in Medium-Sized Enterprises," *Journal of Marketing Communications*, December 2012, pp. 335–61; and Mike Reid, "Performance Auditing of Integrated Marketing Communication (IMC) Actions and Outcomes," *Journal of Advertising* 34 (Winter 2005), p. 41.

32. Alexandra Bruell, "Agency A-List: Media Agency of the Year Carat," *Advertising Age*, January 28, 2013, p. 26; "Nokia Connects with South East Asia," *Microsoft Advertising*, http://advertising.microsoft.com/asia/WWDocs/User/Asia/ResearchLibrary/CaseStudy/MSA_Nokia%20Case%20Study.pdf; and the Carat website, http://www.carat.com, accessed April 5, 2013.

33. "Integrated Marketing: The Benefits of Integrated Marketing," *Marketing Week*, September 18, 2008, p. 33; and Tom Duncan, "Is Your Marketing Communications Integrated?" *Advertising Age*, January 24, 1994, p. 26.

34. Tae Hyun Baek and Mariko Morimoto, "Stay Away from Me," *Journal of Advertising*, Spring 2012, pp. 59–76; and *Statistical Fact Book 2012* (New York: Direct Marketing Association, 2012), pp. 5, 16.

35. Tim Peterson, "Porsche Launches Integrated Campaign to Shift Consumer Perception," *DMNews*, March 25, 2011; and *Statistical Fact Book 2012* (New York: Direct Marketing Association, 2012), p. 5.

36. *Statistical Fact Book 2012* (New York: Direct Marketing Association, 2012), pp. 24, 67; and "Six Ways Lands' End Makes Online Shopping a Joy," *PR Newswire*, November 21, 2007.

37. Theresa Howard, "E-mail Grows as Direct-Marketing Tool: They're Quicker to Make, Cheap to Send," *USA Today*, November 28, 2008, p. 5B.

38. Cotton Delo, "Facebook Testing Effort to Match Offline Purchases to Online Profiles," *Advertising Age*, February 25, 2013, p. 6; Michael Learmonth, "Facebook Goes the Route of Direct Marketing, While Twitter Plays It Safe with Focus on User Interests," *Advertising Age*, September 10, 2012, p. 20; and "Infogroup Targeting Solution Launches Sapphire™, a New Integrated Marketing Database," *GlobeNewswire*, August 7, 2012.

39. "Companies Opposing Anti-Spam Laws," *The Toronto Star*, February 9, 2013, p. B5; Beth Negus Viveiros, "New Bill Takes Permission Beyond Opt-In in EU," *Chief Marketer*, April 19, 2011; "China: New Media Blossoming as Business Models Revamp," BBC Monitoring World Media, December 9, 2008; "The Data Dilemma," *Marketing Direct*, February 6, 2007, p. 37; and Marc Nohr, "South Africa—A Worthy Contender," *Marketing Direct*, March 5, 2007, p. 20.

40. "Protecting Your Identity and Your Privacy," *Targeted News Service*, March 1, 2013; "The Do Not Track Online Act Was Reintroduced in Congress," *The Business Insider*, March 1, 2013; "Online Behavioral Advertising," in the DMA OBA Guidelines, Direct Marketing Association website, http://thedma.org/issues/dma-oba-guidelines, accessed April 6, 2013; Don E. Shultz, "The Bugaboo of Behaviors," *Marketing Management*, Summer 2011, pp. 10–11; "Cell Phones Now Protected by the Do Not Call List," *States News Service*, May 16, 2011; Jonathan Brunt, "'Do Not Mail' Can't Gain Traction," *Spokesman Review*, May 5, 2010, p. 7; "DMA: 'Do Not Track Online Act' Is Unnecessary," *States News Service*, May 9, 2011; "DMA Updates Its 'Guidelines for Ethical Business Practice,'" *States News Service*, May 25, 2011; Martin Courtney and Tony Lock, "Keep It Safe, Keep It Legal," *Computing*, May 26, 2011; Siobhain Butterworth, "Cookie Law Shambles Really Takes the Biscuit," *Guardian Unlimited*, May 27, 2011; and Lara O'Reilly, "New Cookie Law: What You Need to Know," *Marketing Week*, May 26, 2011.

Taco Bell: This case was written by Steven Hartley. Sources: Maureen Morrison, "In Breakfast Wars, Taco Bell's Bold Marketing Pays Off with Big Sales," *Advertising Age*, July 28, 2014, p. 6; Maureen Morrison, "Taco Bell's New Concept: Designer Tacos in California," *Advertising Age*, April 28, 2014, p. 4; Vanessa Wong, "Taco Bell's Secret Recipe for New Products," *Bloomberg Businessweek*, June 2–8, 2014, pp. 18–20; Maureen Morrison, "Marketer of the Year 2013," *Advertising Age*, September 2, 2013, p. 15; Mark Brandau, "Yum Plans to Double U.S. Taco Bell Sales," *Restaurant News*, May 22, 2013; "The Glen Bell Legacy," www.tacobell.com/static_files/TacoBell/StaticAssets/documents/GlenBellLegacy.pdf; "Taco Bell," http://www.yum.com/brands/tb.asp; and interviews with Taco Bell executives.

Credits

15 Advertising, Sales Promotion, and Public Relations

LEARNING OBJECTIVES

After reading this chapter you should be able to:

 LO 15-1 Explain the differences between product advertising and institutional advertising and the variations within each type.

 LO 15-2 Describe the steps used to develop, execute, and evaluate an advertising program.

 LO 15-3 Explain the advantages and disadvantages of alternative advertising media.

 LO 15-4 Discuss the strengths and weaknesses of consumer-oriented and trade-oriented sales promotions.

 LO 15-5 Recognize public relations as an important form of communication.

WHAT IS THE KILLER APP OF ADVERTISING? TELEVISION!

By every measure, television represents the single largest medium for advertisers. The combination of broadcast TV and cable/satellite TV has a powerful grip on consumers. Watch closely, though, and in the next few years you will see the newest version of television—online TV—become a key third element to television advertising!

Television has been a dominant part of the advertising landscape for decades. Over the years there have been many changes to the technology, including the invention of remote controls, VCRs, DVRs, pay-per-view, videotape and DVD rental, and high-definition transmission. The changing technology has also led to changes in television advertising. For example, the potential for skipping ads encouraged a shift from traditional 60-second ads to 30-, 15-, 5-, and even 1-second ads. As viewers increased their use of rentals, advertisers increased their focus on live events and reality programming that was more likely to be viewed in real time. As technology improved, advertisers experimented with 3D formats. All of these changes were attempts to adjust to the behaviors and preferences of consumers. None of them, however, are likely to compare to the changes coming during the next few years.

What's the next big thing in TV? In addition to traditional broadcast, cable, and satellite television, programming will be available through the Internet. OTV, or online TV, is the growing capability to view streaming video that is available online. This new capability makes it possible to view programming on desktop computers, laptops, tablets, and smartphones—anywhere and anytime. In fact, the availability of programming on these devices has prompted some households to stop using cable and satellite services and to view all of their programming through the Internet. Television rating company Nielsen has labeled this group "Zero TV" households. They watch television programming, just not on televisions!

You may already be familiar with some versions of OTV. Hulu, for example, is an ad-supported subscription service offering streaming video of TV shows, movies, and other content from NBC, Fox, ABC, and other networks. Similarly, Machinima is a YouTube channel that offers how-to clips, user-generated video, and original series such as *Mortal Kombat: Legacy* and *Bite Me.* The channel currently has more than 8 million subscribers. Netflix, Apple, and Amazon also offer video-on-demand services.

Many companies are preparing to participate in this transformation. Microsoft is talking to TV networks about providing a package of channels to its 76 million Xbox users and 46 million Xbox Live subscribers. In addition, the company recently opened the Xbox Entertainment Studio to create original programming. Verizon is setting up a new business unit, Verizon Digital Media Services, to deliver live TV on the Web to any network-connected device. In addition, YouTube is developing premium-content offerings in categories ranging from sports, to cooking, to video games. "It's going to be the Wild West for a while until it settles down and matures and the economics settle out," explains David Rips, president of Verizon's TV service.

Advertisers are excited because OTV will offer targeted audiences who are engaged in the programming. According to Allen DeBevoise, CEO of Machinima, "People are not only watching these videos, they're also embedding, ranking, and replying to them." Early evidence suggests that OTV will provide many challenges and opportunities for advertisers. There is no question that television is becoming advertising's killer app![1]

The growth of OTV is just one of the many exciting changes occurring in the field of advertising today. They illustrate the importance of advertising as one of the five promotional mix elements in marketing communications programs. This chapter describes three of the promotional mix elements—advertising, sales promotion, and public relations. Direct marketing was covered in Chapter 14, and personal selling is covered in Chapter 17.

TYPES OF ADVERTISEMENTS

LO 15-1 Explain the differences between product advertising and institutional advertising and the variations within each type.

Chapter 14 described **advertising** as any paid form of nonpersonal communication about an organization, a product, a service, or an idea by an identified sponsor. As you look through any magazine, watch television, listen to the radio, or browse the Internet, the variety of advertisements you see or hear may give you the impression that they have few similarities. Advertisements are prepared for different purposes, but they basically consist of two types: product advertisements and institutional advertisements.

Product Advertisements

advertising
Any paid form of nonpersonal communication about an organization, product, service, or idea by an identified sponsor.

product advertisements
Advertisements that focus on selling a product or service; forms include pioneering (informational), competitive (persuasive), and reminder.

Focused on selling a product or service, **product advertisements** take three forms: (1) pioneering (or informational), (2) competitive (or persuasive), and (3) reminder. Look at the ads for Welch's, Fidelity Investments, and Dove Chocolate to determine the type and objective of each ad.

Used in the introductory stage of the product life cycle, *pioneering* advertisements tell people what a product is, what it can do, and where it can be found. The key objective of a pioneering advertisement (such as the ad for Farmer's Pick by Welch's) is to inform the target market. Informational ads, particularly those with specific message content, have been found to be interesting, convincing, and effective.[2]

Advertising that promotes a specific brand's features and benefits is *competitive*. The objective of these messages is to persuade the target market to select the firm's brand rather than that of a competitor. An increasingly common form of competitive advertising is *comparative* advertising, which shows one brand's strengths relative to those of competitors.[3] The Fidelity ad, for example, highlights the competitive advantages of Fidelity's online trading service compared to Schwab, E*TRADE, and TD Ameritrade. Studies indicate that comparative ads attract more attention and increase the perceived quality of the advertiser's brand although their impact may vary by product type, message content, and audience gender.[4] Firms that use comparative advertising need market research to provide legal support for their claims.[5]

Product advertisements take three forms—pioneering, competitive, or reminder—depending on their objective. See if you can correctly identify the ads shown here.

Reminder advertising is used to reinforce previous knowledge of a product. The Dove Promises® ad reminds consumers about a special event, in this case, Valentine's Day. Reminder advertising is good for products that have achieved a well-recognized position and are in the mature phase of their product life cycle. Another type of reminder ad, *reinforcement*, is used to assure current users they made the right choice. For example, consider the tag line used in Dial soap advertisements: "Aren't you glad you use Dial? Don't you wish everybody did?"

Institutional Advertisements

institutional advertisements
Advertisements designed to build goodwill or an image for an organization, rather than promote a specific product or service.

Video 15-1
Chevron
kerin.tv/cr6e/v15-1

The objective of **institutional advertisements** is to build goodwill or an image for an organization rather than promote a specific product or service. Institutional advertising has been used by companies such as Texaco, Pfizer, and IBM to build confidence in the company name.[6] Often this form of advertising is used to support the public relations plan or counter adverse publicity. Four alternative forms of institutional advertisements are often used:

1. *Advocacy* advertisements state the position of a company on an issue. Chevron's "We Agree" campaign places ads stating its position on issues such as renewable energy, protecting the planet, and community development. Another form of advocacy advertisement is used when organizations make a request related to a particular action or behavior, such as a request by the American Red Cross for blood donations.

2. *Pioneering institutional* advertisements, like the pioneering ads for products discussed earlier, are used for announcements about what a company is, what it can do, or where it is located. Recent Bayer ads stating, "We cure more headaches than you think," are intended to inform consumers that the company produces many products in addition to aspirin. Bridgestone uses pioneering institutional ads in its "One Team. One Planet." campaign to inform people about its rubber tree farms, tire recycling, and environmentally friendly factories.

3. *Competitive institutional* advertisements promote the advantages of one product class over another and are used in markets where different product classes compete for the same buyers. America's milk processors and dairy farmers use their "Got Milk?" campaign to increase demand for milk as it competes against other beverages.

4. *Reminder institutional* advertisements, like reminder ads for products, simply bring the company's name to the attention of the target market again. The Army branch of the U.S. military sponsors a campaign to remind potential recruits of the opportunities available in the Army.

got milk?

A competitive institutional ad by dairy farmers tries to increase demand for milk.

377

learning review

15-1. What is the difference between pioneering and competitive ads?

15-2. What is the purpose of an institutional advertisement?

CHAPTER 15 Advertising, Sales Promotion, and Public Relations

DEVELOPING THE ADVERTISING PROGRAM

 LO 15-2 Describe the steps used to develop, execute, and evaluate an advertising program.

The promotion decision process described in Chapter 14 can be applied to each of the promotional elements. Advertising, for example, can be managed by following the three steps (developing, executing, and evaluating) of the process.

Identifying the Target Audience

To develop an effective advertising program, advertisers must identify the target audience. All aspects of an advertising program are likely to be influenced by the characteristics of the prospective consumer. Understanding the lifestyles, attitudes, and demographics of the target market is essential. Diet Mountain Dew, for example, is targeted at Generation X males, while Kraft's Crystal Light Liquid is targeted at calorie-conscious women. Both campaigns emphasize advertising

Under Armour places its ads to reach competitive women.

techniques that match their target audiences. Similarly, the placement of the advertising depends on the audience. When Under Armour introduced its recent "What's Beautiful" campaign featuring women's apparel, it ran ads with the tag line, "No matter what, sweat every day. I will." on ESPNW, DailyCandy, and Gilt Groupe to reach competitive women. Even scheduling can depend on the audience. Nike schedules advertising, sponsorships, deals, and endorsements to correspond with the Olympics to appeal to amateur, college, and professional athletes.[7]

Specifying Advertising Objectives

The guidelines for setting promotion objectives described in Chapter 14 also apply to setting advertising objectives. This step helps advertisers with other choices in the promotion decision process, such as selecting media and evaluating a campaign. Advertising with an objective of creating awareness, for example, would be better matched with a magazine than a directory such as the Yellow Pages. The Association of Magazine Media believes objectives are so important that it is developing an awards program to recognize magazine advertising campaigns that demonstrate both creative excellence and effectiveness in meeting campaign objectives. Similarly, the Advertising Research Foundation sponsors research forums to advance the practice of measuring and evaluating the effectiveness of advertising and marketing communication.[8]

Setting the Advertising Budget

Video 15-2
Doritos
kerin.tv/cr6e/v15-2

In 1990, advertisers paid $700,000 to place a 30-second ad during the Super Bowl. By 2014, the cost of placing a 30-second ad during Super Bowl XLVIII was

$4 million. The escalating cost is related to the growing number of viewers: 111 million people watch the game. In addition, the audience is attractive to advertisers because research indicates it is equally split between men and women and many viewers look forward to watching the ads. The ads are effective too: GoDaddy reported that the day following its Super Bowl ad was the "biggest sales day in company history", Coca-Cola generated 11 million visits to its website; and Mercedes-Benz reported that its number of inquiries increased by 122 percent after running four ads during the Super Bowl. As a result, the Super Bowl attracts many advertisers such as Anheuser-Busch, Doritos, and Coca-

Do you remember this GoDaddy ad from the Super Bowl?

Cola. Recently, an Anheuser-Busch ad about the bond between a Clydesdale horse and a puppy received the highest rating.[9]

Designing the Advertisement

An advertising message usually focuses on the key benefits of the product that are important to a prospective buyer in making trial and adoption decisions. The message depends on the general form or appeal used in the ad and the actual words included in the ad.

Message Content   Most advertising messages are made up of both informational and persuasive elements. Information and persuasive content can be combined in the form of an appeal to provide a basic reason for the consumer to act. Although the marketer can use many different types of appeals, common advertising appeals include fear, sex, and humor.

Fear appeals suggest to the consumer that he or she can avoid some negative experience through the purchase and use of a product or service, a change in behavior, or a reduction in the use of a product. Examples with which you may be familiar include

Read the text to learn why Karl Lagerfeld uses sex appeal in its advertising.

automobile safety ads that depict an accident or injury; political candidate endorsements that warn against the rise of other, unpopular ideologies; or social cause ads warning of the serious consequences of drug and alcohol use. When using fear appeals, the advertiser must be sure that the appeal is strong enough to get the audience's attention and concern but not so strong that it will lead them to tune out the message. In fact, research on antismoking ads indicates that stressing the severity of long-term health risks may actually enhance smoking's allure among youth.[10]

In contrast, *sex appeals* suggest to the audience that the product will increase the attractiveness of the user. Sex appeals can be found in almost any product category, from automobiles to toothpaste. The contemporary women's clothing store Bebe, for example, designs its advertising to "attract customers who are intrigued by the playfully sensual and evocative imagery of the Bebe lifestyle." Studies indicate that sex appeals increase attention by helping advertising stand out in today's cluttered media environment. Unfortunately, sexual content does not always lead to changes in recall, recognition, or purchase intent. Experts suggest that sexual content is most effective when there is a strong fit between the use of a sex appeal in the ad and the image and positioning of the brand, as seen in the Karl Lagerfeld ad.[11]

Humorous appeals imply either directly or subtly that the product is more fun or exciting than competitors' offerings. As with fear and sex appeals, the use of humor is widespread in advertising and can be found in many product categories. You may have smiled at the popular Geico ads that use a talking pig, cavemen, a gecko, a stack of money with eyes named Kash, and a Rod Serling look-alike actor. These ads use humor to differentiate the company from its competitors. Geico has also created viral videos and posted them on video-sharing websites such as YouTube, where millions of viewers watch them within days.[12] You may have a favorite humorous ad character, such as the Energizer battery bunny, the AFLAC duck, or Travelocity's gnome. Advertisers believe that humor improves the effectiveness of their ads, although some studies suggest that humor wears out quickly, losing the interest of consumers. Another problem with humorous appeals is that their effectiveness may vary across cultures if used in a global campaign.[13]

Creating the Actual Message   Copywriters are responsible for creating the text portion of the messages in advertisements. Translating the copywriter's ideas into an actual advertisement is a complex process. Designing quality artwork, layout, and production for advertisements is costly and time-consuming. The American Association of Advertising Agencies reports that a high-quality, 30-second TV commercial typically costs about $354,000 to produce. One reason for the high cost is that as companies have developed global campaigns, the need to shoot commercials in several locations has increased. Actors are also expensive: Compensation for a typical TV ad is $19,000.[14]

Advertising agency 72andSunny was recently designated *Advertising Age* magazine's U.S. Agency of the Year for using an optimistic and collaborative style to help shape its clients' voices for consumers. Examples of the agency's approach include its "The Next Big Thing Is Already Here" campaign for Samsung Galaxy smartphones, its "The Eat Like You Mean It" campaign for Carl's Jr. burgers, and its "Unleash Your Music" campaign for Sonos wireless HiFi systems. 72andSunny was also recognized at the Cannes Lions International Festival for its use of online media. Its K-Swiss athletic shoe campaign, for example, generated millions of views of online videos, a 1,256 percent increase in Facebook fans, designation on the "biggest buzz" list in trade publication *Footwear News*, and a 250 percent increase in online sales![15]

learning review

15-3. Describe three common forms of advertising appeals.

15-4. _____ are responsible for creating the text portion of the messages in advertisements.

Selecting the Right Media

Every advertiser must decide where to place its advertisements. The alternatives are the *advertising media*, the means by which the message is communicated to the target audience. Newspapers, magazines, radio, and TV are examples of advertising media. Media selection is related to the target audience, type of product, nature of the message, campaign objectives, available budget, and the costs of the alternative media. Figure 15–1 shows the distribution of the $214 billion spent on advertising by medium.[16]

In deciding where to place advertisements, a company has several media to choose from and a number of alternatives, or vehicles, within each medium. Often advertisers use a mix of media forms and vehicles to maximize the exposure of the message to the target audience while at the same time minimizing costs. These two conflicting goals are of central importance to media planning.

Because advertisers try to maximize the number of individuals in the target market exposed to the message, they must be concerned with reach. *Reach* is the number of different people or households exposed to an advertisement. The exact definition of reach sometimes varies among alternative media. Newspapers often use reach to

FIGURE 15–1
Television, direct mail, and newspapers account for more than 60 percent of all advertising expenditures ($ in millions).

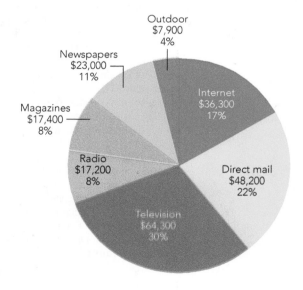

Outdoor
$7,900
4%

Newspapers
$23,000
11%

Magazines
$17,400
8%

Radio
$17,200
8%

Internet
$36,300
17%

Direct mail
$48,200
22%

Television
$64,300
30%

Using Marketing Dashboards

What Is the Best Way to Reach 1,000 Customers?

Marketing managers must choose from many advertising options as they design a campaign to reach potential customers. Because there are so many media alternatives (television, radio, magazines, etc.) and multiple options within each medium, it is important to monitor the efficiency of advertising expenditures on your marketing dashboard.

Your Challenge   As the marketing manager for a company about to introduce a new soft drink into the U.S. market, you are preparing a presentation in which you must make recommendations for the advertising campaign. You have observed that competitors use magazine ads, newspaper ads, and even Super Bowl ads! To compare the cost of some of the alternatives you decide to use one of the most common measures in advertising: cost per thousand impressions (CPM). The CPM is calculated as follows:

$$CPM = \left(\frac{Cost\ of\ ad}{Audience\ size} \right) \times 1000$$

Your challenge is to determine the most efficient use of your advertising budget.

Your Findings   Your research department helps you collect cost and audience size information for three options: full-page color ads in *Bloomberg Businessweek* magazine and *USA Today* newspaper, and a 30-second television ad during the Super Bowl. With this information you are able

Media Alternative	Cost of Ad	Audience Size	Cost per Thousand Impressions
Bloomberg Businessweek (magazine)	$161,600	980,000	$165
USA Today (newspaper)	$199,000	1,662,766	$120
Super Bowl (television)	$3,800,000	108,400,000	$35

to calculate the cost per thousand impressions for each alternative.

Your Action   Based on the calculations for these options, you see that there is a large variation in the cost of reaching 1,000 potential customers (CPM) and also in the absolute cost of the advertising. Although advertising during the Super Bowl has the lowest CPM, $35 for each 1,000 impressions, it also has the largest absolute cost! Your next step will be to consider other factors such as your total available budget, the profiles of the audiences each alternative reaches, and whether the type of message you want to deliver is better communicated in print or on television.

describe their total circulation or the number of different households that buy the paper. Television and radio stations, in contrast, describe their reach using the term *rating*—the percentage of households in a market that are tuned to a particular TV show or radio station. In general, advertisers try to maximize reach in their target market at the lowest cost.

Although reach is important, advertisers are also interested in exposing their target audience to a message more than once. This is because consumers often do not pay close attention to advertising messages, some of which contain large amounts of relatively complex information. When advertisers want to reach the same audience more than once, they are concerned with *frequency*, the average number of times a person in the target audience is exposed to a message or advertisement. Like reach, greater frequency is generally viewed as desirable. Studies indicate that with repeated exposure to advertisements consumers respond more favorably to brand extensions.[17]

When reach (expressed as a percentage of the total market) is multiplied by frequency, an advertiser will obtain a commonly used reference number called *gross rating points (GRPs)*. To obtain the appropriate number of GRPs to achieve an advertising campaign's objectives, the media planner must balance reach and frequency. The balance will also be influenced by cost. *Cost per thousand (CPM)* refers to the cost of reaching 1,000 individuals or households with the advertising message in a given medium (*M* is the Roman numeral for 1,000). See the Using Marketing Dashboards box for an example of the use of CPM in media selection.

Different Media Alternatives

LO 15-3 Explain the advantages and disadvantages of alternative advertising media.

Figure 15–2 summarizes the advantages and disadvantages of the major advertising media, which are described in more detail below. Direct mail was discussed in Chapter 14.

Television Television is a valuable medium because it communicates with sight, sound, and motion. Print advertisements alone could never give you the sense of a sports car accelerating from a stop or cornering at high speed. In addition, television reaches more than 96 percent of all households—115.6 million, including 5 million "Zero TV" households that watch only through a broadband connection. There are also many opportunities for out-of-home TV viewing, as televisions are present in many bars, hotels, offices, airports, and college campuses.[18]

Television's major disadvantage is cost: The price of a prime-time, 30-second ad can range from $593,694 to run on *Sunday Night Football,* to $316,912 to run on *Big Bang Theory,* to $63,129 to run on *America's Funniest Home Videos.* Because of these high charges, many advertisers choose less expensive "spot" ads, which run between programs, or 15-second ads, rather than investing in ads that run the more traditional length of 30 or 60 seconds. Approximately 34 percent of all TV ads are now 15 seconds long. In addition, there is some indication that advertisers are shifting their interest to live events rather than programs that might be watched on a DVR days later.[19]

FIGURE 15–2

Advertisers must consider the advantages and disadvantages of the many media alternatives.

MEDIUM	ADVANTAGES	DISADVANTAGES
Television	Reaches extremely large audience; uses picture, print, sound, and motion for effect; can target specific audiences	High cost to prepare and run ads; short exposure time and perishable message; difficult to convey complex information
Radio	Low cost; can target specific local audiences; ads can be placed quickly; can use sound, humor, and intimacy effectively	No visual element; short exposure time and perishable message; difficult to convey complex information
Magazines	Can target specific audiences; high-quality color; long life of ad; ads can be clipped and saved; can convey complex information	Long time needed to place ad; relatively high cost; competes for attention with other magazine features
Newspapers	Excellent coverage of local markets; ads can be placed and changed quickly; ads can be saved; quick consumer response; low cost	Ads compete for attention with other newspaper features; short life span; poor color
Yellow Pages	Excellent coverage of geographic segments; long use period; available 24 hours/365 days	Proliferation of competitive directories in many markets; difficult to keep up to date
Internet	Video and audio capabilities; animation can capture attention; ads can be interactive and link to advertiser	Animation and interactivity require large files and more time to load; effectiveness is still uncertain
Outdoor	Low cost; local market focus; high visibility; opportunity for repeat exposures	Message must be short and simple; low selectivity of audience; criticized as a traffic hazard
Direct mail	High selectivity of audience; can contain complex information and personalized messages; high-quality graphics	High cost per contact; poor image (junk mail)

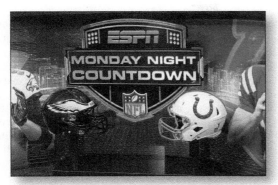

ESPN is one of many specialized channels available to advertisers on cable networks.

Another problem with television advertising is the likelihood of *wasted coverage*—having people outside the market for the product see the advertisement. The cost and wasted coverage problems of TV advertising can be reduced through the specialized cable and satellite channels. Advertising time is often less expensive on cable and satellite channels than on the broadcast networks. According to the National Cable and Telecommunication Association, there are 900 cable channels such as Disney, ESPN, History, MTV, Oxygen, and Lifetime. Cable channels are also "tagging" their programs to allow advertisers to place ads in scenes with particular themes. Advertisements for golf equipment, for example, might be placed after a program scene that shows characters playing golf.[20]

Another popular form of television advertising is the infomercial. **Infomercials** are program-length (30-minute) advertisements that take an educational approach to communication with potential customers. You may remember seeing infomercials for the Magic Bullet, ThighMaster, and OxiClean products, using Ron Popeil, Suzanne Somers, and Anthony Sullivan, respectively, as the spokesperson. Infomercials are increasingly popular because they can be both informative and entertaining, and because the average cost of a 30-minute block of television time is only $425.

infomercials
Program-length (30-minute) advertisements that take an educational approach to communication with potential customers.

Radio   The United States has more than 27,800 radio stations. These stations consist of approximately 4,700 AM, 10,600 FM, and 12,800 HD and Internet stations. The major advantage of radio is that it is a segmented medium. For example, the Farm Radio Network, the Family Life Network, Business Talk Radio, and the Performance Racing Network are all listened to by different market segments. Satellite radio service SiriusXM offers more than 165 commercial-free, digital, coast-to-coast channels to consumers for a monthly fee, and Internet radio service Pandora offers up to 100 personalized channels to each listener. The large number of media options today has reduced the amount of time spent listening to radio, although radio still reaches 77 percent of all adults daily. The average 18- to 34-year-old listens to radio an average of 13.7 hours each week, making radio an important medium for businesses with college students and recent graduates as a target market.[21]

Magazines such as *Runner's World* appeal to narrowly defined segments such as athletes who are interested in running.

A disadvantage of radio is that it has limited use for products that must be seen. Another problem is the ease with which consumers can tune out a commercial by switching stations. Radio is also a medium that competes for people's attention as they do other activities, such as driving, working, or relaxing. Radio listening time reaches its peak during the morning drive time (7 to 8 A.M.), remains high during the day, and then begins to decline in the afternoon (after 4 P.M.) as people return home and start evening activities.[22]

Magazines   Magazines have become a very specialized medium. In fact, there are currently more than 7,179 consumer magazines. Some 213 new magazines were introduced last year, including *As If*, a large-format quarterly magazine focusing on creative visionaries; *Ink and Hustle*, a magazine about tattoos and tattoo artists; *Modern Farmer*, a magazine for people who want to be part of the "new food culture"; and *Click*, a bimonthly magazine designed and written for female photographers. Many publishers are also adding digital versions of existing magazines. *Skateboarder*, for example, can now also be read on the magazine's website, an iPad, or a smartphone. Some magazines, such as *Auto Trader* and *Computer Weekly*, are dropping their print format to offer only an online version.[23]

The marketing advantage of this medium is the great number of special-interest publications that appeal to narrowly defined segments. Runners read *Runner's World*, sailors buy *Yachting*, gardeners subscribe to *Garden*

Metro offers a global audience of daily readers.

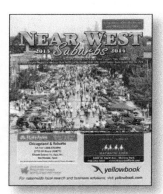

Print yellow pages are used more than 11 billion times each year. See the text for advantages and disadvantages of this media alternative.

Design, and children peruse *Sports Illustrated for Kids*. More than 675 publications focus on travel, 146 are dedicated to interior design and decoration, and 98 are related to golf. Each magazine's readers often represent a unique profile. Take the *Rolling Stone* reader, who tends to listen to music more than most people. SiriusXM Satellite Radio knows an ad in *Rolling Stone* is reaching the desired target audience. In addition, recent studies comparing advertising in different media suggest that magazine advertising is perceived to be more "inspirational" than other media.[24]

The cost of advertising in national magazines is a disadvantage, but many national publications publish regional and even metro editions, which reduces the absolute cost and wasted coverage. *Time* publishes well over 400 editions, including Latin American, Canadian, Asian, South Pacific, European, and U.S. editions.

Newspapers   Newspapers are an important local medium with excellent reach potential. Daily publication allows advertisements to focus on specific current events, such as a 24-hour sale. Local retailers often use newspapers as their sole advertising medium. Newspapers are rarely saved by the purchaser, however, so companies are generally limited to ads that call for an immediate customer response (although customers can clip and save ads they select). Companies also cannot expect newspapers to offer the same quality color reproduction available in most magazines.

National advertising campaigns rarely include this medium except in conjunction with local distributors of their products. In these instances, both parties often share the advertising costs using a cooperative advertising program, which is described later in this chapter. Another exception is the use of newspapers such as *The Wall Street Journal* and *USA Today*, which have national distribution of more than 2.4 and 1.7 million readers, respectively. One newspaper, *Metro*, offers a global audience of 18 million daily readers in Boston, New York, Philadelphia, and 100 cities in Europe, North and South America, and Asia.[25]

Yellow Pages   Yellow pages represent an advertising media alternative comparable to outdoor advertising in terms of expenditures—about $8 billion in the United States. According to the Local Search Association, consumers turn to print yellow pages approximately 11 billion times annually and online yellow pages (desktop, tablet, and mobile) an additional 5.6 billion times per year. One reason for this high level of use is that the 6,500 yellow pages directories reach almost all households. Yellow pages are a "directional" medium because they direct consumers to where purchases can be made after other media have created awareness and demand. The yellow pages face several disadvantages. One disadvantage faced by yellow pages today is the proliferation of directories. AT&T (*Real Yellow Pages*), Dex Media (*Dex One* and *Superpages*), and Hibu (*Yellowbook*) now produce competing directories for many cities, neighborhoods, and ethnic groups.[26]

Internet   The Internet represents a relatively new medium for many advertisers, although it has already attracted a wide variety of industries. Online advertising is similar to print advertising in that it offers a visual message. It has additional advantages, however, because it can also use the audio and video capabilities of the Internet. Sound and movement may simply attract more attention from viewers, or they may provide an element of entertainment to the message. Online advertising also has the unique feature of being interactive. Called *rich media*, these interactive ads have drop-down menus, built-in games, or search engines to engage viewers. Although online advertising is relatively small compared to other traditional media, it offers an opportunity to reach younger consumers who have developed a preference for online communication.

Another disadvantage to online advertising is the difficulty of measuring impact. Several companies are testing methods of tracking where viewers go on their computer in the days and weeks after seeing an ad. Nielsen's online rating service, for

Making Responsible Decisions

Who Is Responsible for Click Fraud?

Spending on Internet advertising is expected to exceed $20 billion in 2014 as many advertisers shift their budgets from print and TV to the Internet. For most advertisers one advantage of online advertising is that they pay only when someone clicks on their ad. Unfortunately, the growth of the medium has led to "click fraud," which is the deceptive clicking of ads solely to increase the amount advertisers must pay. There are several forms of click fraud. One method is the result of Paid-to-Read (PTR) websites that recruit and pay members to simply click on ads. Another method is the result of "clickbots," which are software programs that produce automatic clicks on ads, sometimes through mobile devices. The activity is difficult to detect and stop. Experts estimate that up to 20 percent of clicks may be the result of fraud and may be costing advertisers as much as $800 million each year!

Two of the largest portals for Internet advertising are Google and Yahoo! Both firms try to filter out illegitimate clicks, although some advertisers claim that they are still being charged for PTR and clickbot traffic. Although the laws that govern click fraud are not very clear, Google and Yahoo! have each settled class action lawsuits and agreed to provide rebates or credits to advertisers who were charged for fraudulent clicks.

Investigations of the online advertising industry have discovered a related form of click fraud that occurs when legitimate website visitors click on ads without any intention of looking at the site. As one consumer explains, "I always try and remember to click on the ad banners once in a while to try and keep the sites free." Stephen Dubner calls this "webtipping"!

As the Internet advertising industry grows it will become increasingly important to resolve the issue of click fraud. Consumers, advertisers, websites that carry paid advertising, and the large web portals are all involved in a complicated technical, legal, and social situation. Who do you think is responsible for click fraud? Who should lead the way in the effort to find a solution?

example, measures actual Internet use through meters installed on the computers of 500,000 individuals in 20 countries. Measuring the relationship between online and offline behavior is also important. Research by comScore, which studied 139 online ad campaigns, revealed that online ads didn't always result in a "click," but they increased the likelihood of a purchase by 17 percent and they increased visits to the advertiser's website by 40 percent.[27] The Making Responsible Decisions box describes how click fraud is increasing the necessity of assessing online advertising effectiveness.[28]

Outdoor advertising can be an effective medium for reminding consumers about a product.

Outdoor A very effective medium for reminding consumers about your product is outdoor advertising, such as the scoreboard at New York's Yankee Stadium. The most common form of outdoor advertising, called *billboards*, often results in good reach and frequency and has been shown to increase purchase rates.[29] The visibility of this medium is good supplemental reinforcement for well-known products, and it is a relatively low-cost, flexible alternative. Also, a company can buy space in a specific, targeted geographical market. A disadvantage to billboards, however, is that no opportunity exists for lengthy advertising copy. Also, a good billboard site depends on traffic patterns and sight lines.

If you have ever lived in a metropolitan area, chances are you might have seen another form of outdoor advertising, *transit advertising.* This medium includes messages on the interior and exterior of buses, subway and light-rail cars, and taxis. As the use of mass transit grows, transit advertising may become increasingly important. Selectivity is available to advertisers, who can buy space by neighborhood or bus route. One disadvantage to this medium is that the heavy travel times, when the audiences are the largest, are not conducive to reading advertising copy. People are standing shoulder to shoulder on the subway, hoping not to miss their stop, and little attention is paid to the advertising.

Other Media   As traditional media have become more expensive and cluttered, advertisers have been attracted to a variety of nontraditional advertising options called out-of-home advertising, or *place-based media*. Messages are placed in locations that attract a specific target audience such as airports, doctors' offices, health clubs, theaters (where ads are played on the screen before the movies are shown), grocery stores, storefronts, and even the bathrooms of bars, restaurants, and nightclubs. Soon there will be advertising on video screens on gas pumps, ATMs, and in elevators, and increasingly it will be interactive.

The $2.5 billion industry has attracted advertisers such as AT&T and JCPenney, which use in-store campaigns, and Geico, Sprint, and FedEx, which use out-of-home advertising to reach mobile professionals in health clubs, airports, and hotels. Research suggests that creative use of out-of-home advertising, such as preshow theater ads, enhances consumer recall of the ads.[30]

Out-of-home advertising such as this outdoor display is becoming interactive to engage consumers.

Scheduling the Advertising

There is no correct schedule to advertise a product, but three factors must be considered. First is the issue of *buyer turnover*, which is how often new buyers enter the market to buy the product. The higher the buyer turnover, the greater the amount of advertising required. A second issue in scheduling is the *purchase frequency*; the more frequently the product is purchased, the less repetition is required. Finally, companies must consider the *forgetting rate*, the speed with which buyers forget the brand if advertising is not seen.

Setting schedules requires an understanding of how the market behaves. Most companies tend to follow one of three basic approaches:

1. *Continuous (steady) schedule.* When seasonal factors are unimportant, advertising is run at a continuous or steady schedule throughout the year.
2. *Flighting (intermittent) schedule.* Periods of advertising are scheduled between periods of no advertising to reflect seasonal demand.
3. *Pulse (burst) schedule.* A flighting schedule is combined with a continuous schedule because of increases in demand, heavy periods of promotion, or introduction of a new product.

For example, products such as breakfast cereals have a stable demand throughout the year and would typically use a continuous schedule of advertising. In contrast, products such as snow skis and suntan lotions have seasonal demands and receive flighting-schedule advertising during the seasonal demand period. Some products such as toys or automobiles require pulse-schedule advertising to facilitate sales throughout the year and during special periods of increased demand (such as holidays or new car introductions). Some evidence suggests that pulsing schedules are superior to other advertising strategies.[31] In addition, research indicates the effectiveness of a particular ad wears out quickly and, therefore, many alternative forms of a commercial may be more effective.[32]

learning review

15-5. You see the same ad in *Time* and *Fortune* magazines and on billboards and TV. Is this an example of reach or frequency?

15-6. Why has the Internet become a popular advertising medium?

15-7. Describe three approaches to scheduling advertising.

EXECUTING THE ADVERTISING PROGRAM

Executing the advertising program involves pretesting the advertising copy and actually carrying out the advertising program. John Wanamaker, the founder of Wanamaker's Department Store in Philadelphia, remarked, "I know half my advertising is wasted, but I don't know what half." By evaluating advertising efforts, marketers can try to ensure that their advertising expenditures are not wasted.[33] Evaluation is done usually at two separate times: before and after the advertisements are run in the actual campaign. Several methods used in the evaluation process at the stages of idea formulation and copy development are discussed below.

Pretesting the Advertising

pretests
Tests conducted before an advertisement is placed in any medium to determine whether it communicates the intended message or to select among alternative versions of the advertisement.

To determine whether the advertisement communicates the intended message or to select among alternative versions of the advertisement, **pretests** are conducted before the advertisements are placed in any medium.

Portfolio Tests   Portfolio tests are used to test copy alternatives. The test ad is placed in a portfolio with several other ads and stories, and consumers are asked to read through the portfolio. Afterward, subjects are asked for their impressions of the ads on several evaluative scales, such as from "very informative" to "not very informative."

Jury Tests   Jury tests involve showing the ad copy to a panel of consumers and having them rate how they liked it, how much it drew their attention, and how attractive they thought it was. This approach is similar to the portfolio test in that consumer reactions are obtained. However, unlike the portfolio test, a test advertisement is not hidden within other ads.

Theater Tests   Theater testing is the most sophisticated form of pretesting. Consumers are invited to view new television shows or movies in which test commercials are also shown. Viewers register their feelings about the advertisements either on handheld electronic recording devices used during the viewing or on questionnaires afterward.

Carrying Out the Advertising Program

The responsibility for actually carrying out the advertising program can be handled by one of three types of agencies. The *full-service agency* provides the most complete range of services, including market research, media selection, copy development, artwork, and production. In the past, agencies that assisted a client by both developing and placing advertisements often charged a commission of 15 percent of the media costs. As corporations introduced integrated marketing communication approaches, however, many advertisers switched from paying commissions to incentive plans based on performance. These plans typically pay for agency costs and a 5 to 10 percent profit, plus bonuses if specific performance goals related to brand preference, lead generation, sales, and market share are met. The Association of National Advertisers estimates that 46 percent of all agency clients currently use this approach.

Limited-service agencies specialize in one aspect of the advertising process, such as providing creative services to develop the advertising copy, buying previously unpurchased media (media agencies), or providing Internet services (Internet agencies). Limited-service agencies that deal in creative work are compensated by a contractual agreement for the services performed. Finally, *in-house agencies* made up of the company's own advertising staff may provide full services or a limited range of services.

CHAPTER 15   Advertising, Sales Promotion, and Public Relations

ASSESSING THE ADVERTISING PROGRAM

The advertising decision process does not stop with executing the advertising program. The advertisements must be evaluated to determine whether they are achieving their intended objectives, and results may indicate that changes must be made in the advertising program.

Posttesting the Advertising

posttests
Tests conducted after an advertisement has been shown to the target audience to determine whether it has accomplished its intended purpose.

An advertisement may go through **posttests** after it has been shown to the target audience to determine whether it accomplished its intended purpose. Five approaches common in posttesting are discussed here.[34]

Aided Recall After being shown an ad, respondents are asked whether their previous exposure to it was through reading, viewing, or listening. The Starch test shown in the accompanying photo uses aided recall to determine the percentage of those who (1) remember seeing a specific ad (*noted*), (2) saw or read any part of the ad identifying the product or brand (*seen-associated*), (3) read any part of the ad's copy (*read some*), and (4) read at least half of the ad (*read most*). Elements of the ad are then tagged with the results, as shown in the photo.[35]

Unaided Recall The unaided recall approach involves asking respondents a question such as, "What ads do you remember seeing yesterday?" without any prompting to determine whether they saw or heard advertising messages.

The Starch test uses aided recall to evaluate an ad on four dimensions. See the text to learn more.

Attitude Tests Attitude tests involve asking respondents questions to measure changes in their attitudes after an advertising campaign. For example, they might be asked whether they now have a more favorable attitude toward the product advertised. Recent research suggests that attitudes can be influenced by many factors, including the increasingly popular use of co-creation to develop consumer-generated ads.[36]

Inquiry Tests Inquiry tests involve offering additional product information, product samples, or premiums to an ad's readers or viewers. Ads generating the most inquiries are presumed to be the most effective.

Sales Tests Sales tests involve studies such as controlled experiments (e.g., using radio ads in one market and newspaper ads in another and comparing the results) and consumer purchase tests (measuring retail sales that result from a given advertising campaign). The most sophisticated experimental methods today allow a manufacturer, a distributor, or an advertising agency to manipulate an advertising variable (such as schedule or copy) through cable systems and observe subsequent sales effects by monitoring data collected from checkout scanners in supermarkets.[37]

Making Needed Changes

Results of posttesting the advertising copy are used to reach decisions about changes in the advertising program. If the posttest results show that an advertisement is doing poorly in terms of awareness, cost efficiency, or sales, it may be dropped and other ads run in its place in the future. On the other hand, sometimes an advertisement may be so successful it is run repeatedly or used as the basis of a larger advertising program.

> **learning review**
>
> 15-8. Explain the difference between pretesting and posttesting advertising copy.
>
> 15-9. What is the difference between aided and unaided recall posttests?

SALES PROMOTION

LO 15-4 Discuss the strengths and weaknesses of consumer-oriented and trade-oriented sales promotions.

Sales promotion is a key element of the promotional mix today; it now accounts for more than $70 billion in annual expenditures. In a recent forecast by ZenithOptimedia, sales promotion expenditures accounted for 19 percent of all promotional spending.[38] The large allocation of marketing expenditures to sales promotion reflects the trend toward integrated marketing communications programs, which often include a variety of sales promotion elements. Selection and integration of the many promotion techniques require a good understanding of the advantages and disadvantages of each kind of sales promotion.[39] The two major kinds of sales promotions, consumer-oriented and trade-oriented, are discussed below.

Consumer-Oriented Sales Promotions

consumer-oriented sales promotions
Sales tools, such as coupons, sweepstakes, and samples, used to support a company's advertising and personal selling directed to ultimate consumers.

Directed to ultimate consumers, **consumer-oriented sales promotions**, or simply *consumer promotions*, are sales tools used to support a company's advertising and personal selling. A variety of consumer-oriented sales promotion tools may be used, including coupons, deals, premiums, contests, sweepstakes, samples, loyalty programs, point-of-purchase displays, rebates, and product placements.

Coupons   Coupons are sales promotions that usually offer a discounted price to the consumer, which encourages trial. Approximately 305 billion coupons worth $467 billion are distributed in the United States each year. More than 90 percent of all coupons are distributed as freestanding inserts in newspapers. Research indicates that consumer use of coupons rose during the recession and has remained at 79 percent in subsequent years. Consumers redeemed 2.8 billion of the coupons last year, for a savings of approximately $3.7 billion. Companies that have increased their use of coupons include Procter & Gamble, Nestlé, and Kraft, while the top retailers for coupon redemption were Walmart, Kroger, and Target. The number of coupons generated at Internet sites (e.g., www.valpak.com and www.coupon.com) and on mobile phones has been increasing as well, although they account for less than 2 percent of all coupons. The redemption rate for online coupons—approximately 14 percent—however, is substantially higher than other forms of coupons. The TV show *Extreme Couponing: All Stars* and "daily deal" sites like Groupon and LivingSocial have helped fuel the growth in couponing. Today, coupons are available in almost every product category and they are used by men and women of all ages.[40]

Coupons are often far more expensive than the face value of the coupon; a 25-cent coupon can cost three times that after paying for the advertisement to deliver it, dealer handling, clearinghouse costs, and redemption. In addition, misredemption, or attempting to redeem a counterfeit coupon or a valid coupon when the product was not purchased, should be added to the cost of the coupon. The Coupon Information Corporation estimates that companies pay out refunds worth hundreds of millions of dollars each year as a result of coupon fraud. Recent growth in coupon fraud has marketers considering adding holograms and visual aids to help cashiers identify valid coupons.[41]

Coupons encourage trial by offering a discounted price. See the text to learn if coupons increase sales.

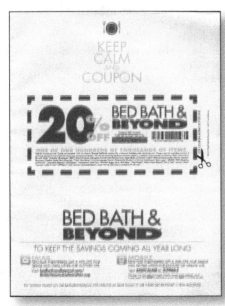

Deals   Deals are short-term price reductions, commonly used to increase trial among potential customers or to retaliate against a competitor's actions. For example, if a rival manufacturer introduces a new cake mix, the company responds with a "two packages for the price of one" deal. This short-term price reduction builds up the stock on the kitchen shelves of cake mix buyers and makes the competitor's introduction more difficult.

Premiums   A promotional tool often used with consumers is the premium, which consists of merchandise offered free or at a significant savings over its retail price. This latter type of premium is called self-liquidating because the cost charged to the consumer covers the cost of the item. McDonald's, for example, used a free premium in a promotional partnership with 20th Century Fox during the release of the movie *Epic*. Collectible toys that portrayed movie characters were given away free with the purchase of a Happy Meal. What are the most popular premiums? According to the Promotional Products Association International, the top premiums are apparel, writing instruments, shopping bags, cups and mugs, and desk accessories. By offering a premium, companies encourage customers to return frequently or to use more of the product. Research suggests that deal-prone consumers and value seekers are attracted to premiums.[42]

Contests   Contests represent a fourth sales promotion tool in which consumers apply their skill or analytical or creative thinking to try to win a prize. This form of promotion has been growing as requests for videos, photos, and essays are a good match with the trend toward consumer-generated content. For example, Doritos sponsors the "Crash the Super Bowl" ad contest, asking people to create their own 30-second ad about Doritos. A panel of judges then selects five finalists, posts the submissions on the Doritos Facebook Page, and opens up voting by the public. The two winners are aired during the Super Bowl, and if one of the ads is ranked No. 1 on *USA Today's* Super Bowl Ad Meter, the winner is awarded a $1 million prize! If you like contests, you can enter online now at websites such as www.contests.about.com.[43]

McDonald's Monopoly sweepstakes offers a grand prize of $1 million.

Sweepstakes   Sweepstakes are sales promotions that require participants to submit some kind of entry but are purely games of chance requiring no analytical or creative effort by the consumer. Popular sweepstakes include the HGTV "Dream Home Giveaway," which receives more than 76 million entries each year, and McDonald's Monopoly, which offers a grand prize of $1 million.[44]

Two variations of sweepstakes are popular now. First are sweepstakes that offer products that consumers value as prizes. Mars Chocolate, for example, created a sweepstakes where consumers enter a UPC code from M&M's products for a chance to win one of five Toyota automobiles. Coca-Cola has a similar sweepstakes called "My Coke Rewards" that allows consumers to use codes from bottle caps to enter to win prizes or to collect points to be redeemed for rewards. The second type of sweepstakes offers an "experience" as the prize. For example, one of television's most popular series, *American Idol*, and AT&T sponsor a sweepstakes for a chance to win a trip for two to the season finale of *American Idol* in Los Angeles. Similarly, StumbleUpon and the Academy of Motion Picture Arts and Sciences created a sweepstakes where consumers entered for a chance to win a trip to the Oscars in Hollywood.

Federal laws, the Federal Trade Commission, and state legislatures have issued rules covering sweepstakes, contests, and games to regulate fairness, ensure that the chance for winning is represented honestly, and guarantee that the prizes are actually awarded. Several well-known sweepstakes created by Publishers Clearing House and *Reader's Digest* have paid fines and agreed to new sweepstakes guidelines in response to regulatory scrutiny.[45]

Samples   Another common consumer sales promotion is sampling, which is offering the product free or at a greatly reduced price. Often used for new products, sampling puts the product in the consumer's hands. A trial size is generally offered that is smaller than the regular package size. If consumers like the sample, it is hoped they will remember and buy the product. Taco Bell has offered free tacos nationwide six times in the past to encourage customers to try new products. Most recently, Taco Bell gave a free Doritos Locos Taco to each guest on the day of the promotion. The taco has become the company's most successful new product. Some consumers watch for free samples online at sites such as www.startsampling.com. According to Stacy Fisher, who started trying free samples in college and now blogs about them, free samples are "a great way to try new things and save money."[46]

Loyalty programs encourage and reward repeat purchases.

Loyalty Programs Loyalty programs are a sales promotion tool used to encourage and reward repeat purchases by acknowledging each purchase made by a consumer and offering a premium as purchases accumulate. The most popular loyalty programs today are credit card reward programs. More than 75 percent of all cards offer incentives for use of their card. Citibank, for example, offers "Thank You" points for using Citi credit or debit cards. The points can be redeemed for books, music, gift cards, cash, travel, and special limited time rewards. Airlines, retailers, hotels, and grocery stores also offer popular loyalty programs. Specialty retailers such as Toys 'Я' Us and Best Buy have enhanced their reward programs to add value to their offerings as they compete with low-cost merchandise. There are now more than 2 billion loyalty program memberships, for an average of 18 for each household in the United States, with point balances close to $50 billion.[47]

Point-of-Purchase Displays In a store aisle, you often encounter a sales promotion called a point-of-purchase display. These product displays take the form of advertising signs, which sometimes actually hold or display the product, and are often located in high-traffic areas near the cash register or the end of an aisle. Point-of-purchase displays are designed to maximize consumers' attention and provide storage for the products. Annual expenditures on point-of-purchase promotions now exceed $20.3 billion and are expected to grow as point-of-purchase becomes integrated with all forms of promotion.

Rebates Another consumer sales promotion tool, the cash rebate, offers the return of money based on proof of purchase. For example, Virgin Mobile recently offered a $100 rebate to T-Mobile subscribers who switched their service during a seven-week period. When a rebate is offered on lower-priced items, the time and trouble of mailing in a proof of purchase to get the rebate check often means that many buyers never take advantage of it. However, this "slippage" is less likely to occur with frequent users of rebate promotions. In addition, online consumers are more likely to take advantage of rebates.[48]

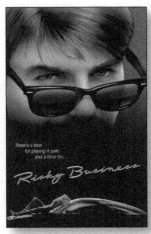

Product placement can take many forms today. Are you familiar with this example?

product placement
A consumer sales promotion that uses a brand-name product in a movie, television show, video, or commercial for another product.

trade-oriented sales promotions
Sales tools used to support a company's advertising and personal selling directed to wholesalers, distributors, or retailers.

Product Placements A final consumer promotion tool, **product placement**, uses a brand-name product in a movie, television show, video game, or commercial for another product. It was Steven Spielberg's placement of Hershey's Reese's Pieces in *E.T. the Extra Terrestrial* that first brought a lot of interest to the candy. Similarly, when Tom Cruise wore Bausch and Lomb's Ray-Ban sunglasses in *Risky Business* and its Aviator glasses in *Top Gun*, sales skyrocketed from 100,000 pairs to 7,000,000 pairs in five years. More recently, you might remember seeing Sony laptops, phones, and TVs in *The Amazing Spider-Man 2*.

Product placement has also grown in television programs. *American Idol* ranks No. 1 with Coca-Cola, Ford, and AT&T product appearances, followed by *The Biggest Loser*. Companies are usually eager to gain exposure for their products, and studios believe that product placements can add authenticity to the film or program.

The annual value of all product placements is estimated to be $8.3 billion. Complaints that product placement has become excessive have led the Federal Communications Commission to begin developing guidelines for TV product placements. Meanwhile, the British government recently passed a law allowing product placement only if a bold "P" logo is shown before and after the program.[49]

Trade-Oriented Sales Promotions

Trade-oriented sales promotions, or simply *trade promotions*, are sales tools used to support a company's advertising and personal selling directed to wholesalers, distributors, or retailers. Some of the sales promotions just reviewed are used for this purpose, but three other common approaches are targeted uniquely to these

391

CHAPTER 15 Advertising, Sales Promotion, and Public Relations

intermediaries: (1) allowances and discounts, (2) cooperative advertising, and (3) training of distributors' salesforces.

Allowances and Discounts   Trade promotions often focus on maintaining or increasing inventory levels in the channel of distribution. An effective method for encouraging such increased purchases by intermediaries is the use of allowances and discounts. However, overuse of these price reductions can lead to retailers changing their ordering patterns in the expectation of such offerings. Although there are many variations that manufacturers can use with discounts and allowances, three common approaches are the merchandise allowance, the case allowance, and the finance allowance.[50]

Reimbursing a retailer for extra in-store support or special featuring of the brand is a *merchandise allowance*. Performance contracts between the manufacturer and trade member usually specify the activity to be performed, such as a picture of the product in a newspaper with a coupon good at only one store. The merchandise allowance then consists of a percentage deduction from the list case price ordered during the promotional period. Allowances are not paid by the manufacturer until it sees proof of performance (such as a copy of the ad placed by the retailer in the local newspaper).

A second common trade promotion, a *case allowance*, is a discount on each case ordered during a specific time period. These allowances are usually deducted from the invoice. A variation of the case allowance is the "free goods" approach, whereby retailers receive some amount of the product free based on the amount ordered, such as 1 case free for every 10 cases ordered.[51]

A final trade promotion, the *finance allowance*, involves paying retailers for financing costs or financial losses associated with consumer sales promotions. This trade promotion is regularly used and has several variations. One type is the floor stock protection program—manufacturers give retailers a case allowance price for products in their warehouse, which prevents shelf stock from running down during the promotional period. Also common are freight allowances, which compensate retailers that transport orders from the manufacturer's warehouse.

Cooperative Advertising   Resellers often perform the important function of promoting the manufacturer's products at the local level. One common sales promotional activity is to encourage both better quality and greater quantity in the local advertising efforts of resellers through **cooperative advertising**. These are programs by which a manufacturer pays a percentage of the retailer's local advertising expense for advertising the manufacturer's products.

Usually, the manufacturer pays a percentage, often 50 percent, of the cost of advertising up to a certain dollar limit, which is based on the amount of the manufacturer's products purchased by the retailer. In addition to paying for the advertising, the manufacturer often furnishes the retailer with a selection of different ad executions, sometimes suited for several different media. A manufacturer may provide, for example, several different print layouts as well as a few broadcast ads for the retailer to adapt and use.[52]

cooperative advertising Advertising programs by which a manufacturer pays a percentage of the retailer's local advertising expense for advertising the manufacturer's products.

Training of Distributors' Salesforces   One of the many functions the intermediaries perform is customer contact and selling for the producers they represent. Both retailers and wholesalers employ and manage their own sales personnel. A manufacturer's success often rests on the ability of the reseller's salesforce to represent its products. Thus, it is in the best interest of the manufacturer to help train the reseller's salesforce.

Because the reseller's salesforce is often less sophisticated and knowledgeable about the products than the manufacturer might like, training can increase their sales performance. Training activities include producing manuals and brochures to educate the reseller's salesforce. The salesforce then uses these aids in selling situations. Other activities include national sales meetings sponsored by the manufacturer and field visits to the reseller's location to inform and motivate the salesperson to sell the products. Manufacturers also develop incentive and recognition programs to motivate a reseller's salespeople to sell their products.

learning review

15-10. What is the difference between a coupon and a deal?

15-11. Which trade promotion is used to encourage the local advertising efforts of resellers?

PUBLIC RELATIONS

LO 15-5 Recognize public relations as an important form of communication.

publicity tools
Methods of obtaining nonpersonal presentation of an organization, product, or service without direct cost.

As noted in Chapter 14, public relations is a form of communications management that seeks to influence the image of an organization and its products and services. In developing a public relations campaign, several methods of obtaining nonpersonal presentation of an organization, product, or service without direct cost—**publicity tools**—are available to the public relations director. Many companies frequently use the *news release*, consisting of an announcement regarding changes in the company or the product line. The objective of a news release is to inform a newspaper, radio station, or other medium of an idea for a story.

A second common publicity tool is the *news conference*. Representatives of the media are all invited to an informational meeting, and advance materials regarding the content are sent. This tool is often used when new products are introduced or significant changes in corporate structure and leadership are being made.

Nonprofit organizations rely heavily on *public service announcements* (PSAs), which are free space or time donated by the media. For example, the charter of the American Red Cross prohibits any local chapter from advertising, so to solicit blood donations local chapters often depend on PSAs on radio or television to announce their needs.

Hillary Clinton receives publicity for her book by visiting programs such as *The Daily Show with Jon Stewart.*

learning review

15-12. What is a news release?

15-13. What type of publicity tool is used most often by nonprofit organizations?

LEARNING OBJECTIVES REVIEW

LO 15-1 *Explain the differences between product advertising and institutional advertising and the variations within each type.*

Product advertisements focus on selling a good or service and take three forms: Pioneering advertisements tell people what a product is, what it can do, and where it can be found; competitive advertisements persuade the target market to select the firm's brand rather than a competitor's; and reminder advertisements reinforce previous knowledge of a product. Institutional advertisements are used to build goodwill or an image for an organization. They include advocacy advertisements, which state the position of a company on an issue, and pioneering, competitive, and reminder advertisements, which are similar to the product ads but focused on the institution.

LO 15-2 *Describe the steps used to develop, execute, and evaluate an advertising program.*

The promotion decision process can be applied to each of the promotional elements. The steps to develop an advertising program include the following: identify the target audience, specify the advertising objectives, set the advertising budget, design the advertisement, create the message, select the media, and schedule the advertising. Executing the program requires pretesting, and evaluating the program requires posttesting.

LO 15-3 *Explain the advantages and disadvantages of alternative advertising media.*

Television advertising reaches large audiences and uses picture, print, sound, and motion; its disadvantages, however, are that it is expensive and perishable. Radio advertising is inexpensive and can be placed quickly, but it has no visual element and is perishable. Magazine advertising can target specific audiences and can convey complex information, but it takes a long time to place the ad and is relatively expensive. Newspapers provide excellent coverage of local markets and can be changed quickly, but they have a short life span and poor color. Yellow pages advertising has a long use period and is available 24 hours per day; its disadvantages, however, are that there is a proliferation of directories and they cannot be updated frequently. Internet advertising can be interactive, but its effectiveness is difficult to measure. Outdoor advertising provides repeat exposures, but its message must be very short and simple. Direct mail can be targeted at very selective audiences, but its cost per contact is high.

LO 15-4 *Discuss the strengths and weaknesses of consumer-oriented and trade-oriented sales promotions.*

Coupons encourage retailer support but may delay consumer purchases. Deals reduce consumer risk but also reduce perceived value. Premiums offer consumers additional merchandise they want, but they may be purchasing only for the premium. Contests create involvement but require creative thinking. Sweepstakes encourage repeat purchases, but sales drop after the sweepstakes. Samples encourage product trial but are expensive. Loyalty programs help create loyalty but are expensive to run. Displays provide visibility but are difficult to place in retail space. Rebates stimulate demand but are easily copied. Product placements provide a positive message in a noncommercial setting that is difficult to control. Trade-oriented sales promotions include (*a*) allowances and discounts, which increase purchases but may change retailer ordering patterns, (*b*) cooperative advertising, which encourages local advertising, and (*c*) salesforce training, which helps increase sales by providing the salespeople with product information and selling skills.

LO 15-5 *Recognize public relations as an important form of communication.*

Public relations activities usually focus on communicating positive aspects of the business. A frequently used public relations tool is publicity. Publicity tools include news releases and news conferences. Nonprofit organizations often use public service announcements.

LEARNING REVIEW ANSWERS

15-1 **What is the difference between pioneering and competitive ads?**
Answer: Pioneering (or informational) ads, used in the introductory stage of the product life cycle, tell people what a product is, what it can do, and where it can be found. The key objective of a pioneering ad is to inform the target market. Competitive (or persuasive) ads promote a specific brand's features and benefits to persuade the target market to select the firm's brand rather than that of a competitor.

15-2 **What is the purpose of an institutional advertisement?**
Answer: The purpose of an institutional advertisement is to build goodwill or an image for an organization rather than a specific offering.

15-3 **Describe three common forms of advertising appeals.**
Answer: The three common forms of advertising appeals are: (1) fear appeals, which suggest to the consumer that he or she can avoid some negative experience through the purchase and use of a product or service, a change in behavior, or a reduction in the use of a product; (2) sex appeals, which suggest to the audience that the product will increase the attractiveness of the user; and (3) humorous appeals, which imply either directly or subtly that the product is more fun or exciting than competitors' offerings.

15-4 _____ **are responsible for creating the text portion of the messages in advertisements.**
Answer: Copywriters

15-5 **You see the same ad in *Time* and *Fortune* magazines and on billboards and TV. Is this an example of reach or frequency?**

Answer: Reach—using more of the same media type (magazines) as well as using more of different types of media (magazines, billboards, and TV)—is an attempt to maximize the number of individuals in a target market that are exposed to the advertisement. Frequency uses the same medium/media more than once to present the advertising message.

15-6 **Why has the Internet become a popular advertising medium?**

Answer: The Internet offers a visual message, can use both audio and video, is interactive through rich media, and tends to reach younger consumers.

15-7 **Describe three approaches to scheduling advertising.**

Answer: The three approaches to scheduling advertising are: (1) a continuous (steady) schedule, which is when advertising is run at a continuous or steady schedule throughout the year because seasonal factors are unimportant; (2) a flighting (intermittent) schedule, which is when periods of advertising are scheduled between periods of no advertising to reflect seasonal demand; and (3) a pulse (burst) schedule, which is when a flighting schedule is combined with a continuous schedule because of increase in demand, heavy periods of promotion, or introduction of a new product.

15-8 **Explain the difference between pretesting and posttesting advertising copy.**

Answer: Pretests are conducted before ads are placed in any medium to determine whether they communicate the intended message or to select among alternative versions of the ad. Posttests are conducted after the ads are shown to the target audience to determine whether they accomplished their intended purpose.

15-9 **What is the difference between aided and unaided recall posttests?**

Answer: Aided recall involves showing an ad to respondents who then are asked if their previous exposure to it was through reading, viewing, or listening. Aided recall is used to determine the percentage of those (1) who remember seeing a specific magazine ad (*noted*), (2) who saw or read any part of the ad identifying the product or brand (*seen-associated*), (3) who read any part of the ad's copy (*read some*), and (4) who read at least half of the ad (*read most*). Unaided recall involves specifically asking respondents if they remember an ad without any prompting to determine if they saw or heard its message.

15-10 **What is the difference between a coupon and a deal?**

Answer: A coupon provides a reduced price for an item based on redemption to encourage the trial of an offering. A deal is a short-term price reduction used to increase trial among potential customers or to retaliate against a competitor's actions.

15-11 **Which trade promotion is used to encourage the local advertising efforts of resellers?**

Answer: Cooperative advertising, a promotion program by which a manufacturer pays a percentage of a retailer's advertising expense, is used to encourage both better quality and greater quantity in the local advertising efforts of resellers.

15-12 **What is a news release?**

Answer: A news release is a publicity tool that consists of an announcement regarding changes in the company or the product line.

15-13 **What type of publicity tool is used most often by nonprofit organizations?**

Answer: public service announcements (PSAs)

FOCUSING ON KEY TERMS

advertising p. 376
**consumer-oriented sales
    promotions** p. 389
cooperative advertising p. 392

infomercials p. 383
institutional advertisements p. 377
posttests p. 388
pretests p. 387

product advertisements p. 376
product placement p. 391
publicity tools p. 393
trade-oriented sales promotions p. 391

APPLYING MARKETING KNOWLEDGE

1 How does competitive product advertising differ from competitive institutional advertising?

2 Suppose you are the advertising manager for a new line of children's fragrances. Which form of media would you use for this new product?

3 You have recently been promoted to be director of advertising for the Timkin Tool Company. In your first meeting with Mr. Timkin, he says, "Advertising is a waste! We've been advertising for six months now and

sales haven't increased. Tell me why we should continue." Give your answer to Mr. Timkin.

4 A large life insurance company has decided to switch from using a strong fear appeal to a humorous approach. What are the strengths and weaknesses of such a change in message strategy?

5 Some national advertisers have found that they can have more impact with their advertising by running a large number of ads for a period and then running no ads at all for a period. Why might such a flighting schedule be more effective than a continuous schedule?

6　Which medium has the lowest cost per thousand (CPM)?

Medium	Cost of Ad	Audience Size
TV show	$5,000	25,000
Magazine	2,200	6,000
Newspaper	4,800	7,200
FM radio	420	1,600

7　Each year, managers at Bausch and Lomb evaluate the many advertising media alternatives available to them as they develop their advertising program for contact lenses. What advantages and disadvantages of each alternative should they consider? Which media would you recommend to them?

8　What are two advantages and two disadvantages of the advertising posttests described in the chapter?

9　Federated Banks is interested in consumer-oriented sales promotions that would encourage senior citizens to direct deposit their Social Security checks with the bank. Evaluate the sales promotion options, and recommend two of them to the bank.

10　How can public relations be used by GM following investigations into complaints about ignition switch failures?

BUILDING YOUR MARKETING PLAN

To augment your promotion strategy from Chapter 14:

1　Use Figure 15–2 to select the advertising media you will include in your plan by analyzing how combinations of media (e.g., television and Internet advertising, radio and yellow pages advertising) can complement each other.

2　Select your consumer-oriented sales promotion activities.

3　Specify which trade-oriented sales promotions and public relations tools you will use.

VIDEO CASE 15　Google, Inc.: The Right Ads at the Right Time

Video 15-5
**Google
Video Case**
kerin.tv/cr6e/v15-5

"So what we did, in essence, is we said advertising should be useful to a consumer just as much as the organic search results, and we don't want people just to buy advertising and be able to show an ad if it's irrelevant to the consumer's need," says Richard Holden, director of product management at Google. To accomplish this, Google developed a "Quality Score" model to predict how effective an ad will be. The model uses many factors such as click-through rates, advertiser history, and keyword performance to develop a score for each advertisement. "Essentially, what we're trying to do is predict ahead, before we actually show an ad, how a consumer will react to that ad, and our interest is in showing fewer ads, not more ads; just the right ads at the right time," Holden continues. The Google advertising model has revolutionized the advertising industry, and it continues to improve every day!

THE COMPANY

Google began in 1996 as a research project for Stanford computer science students Larry Page and Sergey Brin. They started with a simple idea—that a search engine based on the relationships between websites would provide a better ranking than a search engine based only on the number of times a key term appeared on a website. The success of their model led to rapid growth, and the founders moved the company from their dorm room, to a friend's garage, to offices in Palo Alto, California, and eventually to its current location, known as the Googleplex, in Mountain View, California. In 2000, Google began selling advertising as a means of generating revenue. Its advertising model allowed advertisers to bid on search words and pay for each "click" by a search-engine user. The ads were required to be simple and text-based so that the search result pages remained uncluttered and the search time was as fast as possible.

Page and Brin's first search engine was called "BackRub" because their technique was based on relationships, or backlinks, between websites. The name quickly changed, however. The name "Google" is a misspelling of the word "googol," which is a mathematical term for a 1 followed by 100 zeros. Page and Brin used the name in the original domain, www.google .stanford.edu, to reflect their interest in organizing the immense amount of information available on the Web. The domain name, of course, became www.google .com and eventually Webster's dictionary added the verb "google" with the definition "to use the Google search engine to obtain information on the Internet." The name has become so familiar that *Advertising Age* recently reported that Google is "the world's most powerful brand"!

Today, Google receives several hundred million inquiries each day as it pursues its mission: to organize the world's information and make it universally accessible and useful. The company generates more than $21 billion in annual revenue and has more than 20,000 employees. As Google has grown, it has developed 10 guidelines that represent the corporate philosophy. They are:

1. Focus on the user and all else will follow.
2. It's best to do one thing really, really well.
3. Fast is better than slow.
4. Democracy on the Web works.
5. You don't need to be at your desk to need an answer.
6. You can make money without doing evil.
7. There's always more information out there.
8. The need for information crosses all borders.
9. You can be serious without a suit.
10. Great just isn't good enough.

Using these guidelines, Google strives to continually improve its search engine. "The perfect search engine," explains Google co-founder Larry Page, "would understand exactly what you mean and give back exactly what you want."

ONLINE ADVERTISING

Google generates revenue by offering online advertising opportunities—next to search results or on specific web pages. The company always distinguishes ads from the search results or the content of a web page and it never sells placement in the search results. This approach ensures that Google website visitors always know when someone has paid to put a message in front of them. The advantage of online advertising is that it is measurable and allows immediate assessment of its effectiveness. As Gopi Kallayil, product marketing manager, explains: "There is a very high degree of measurability and trackability that you get through online advertising." In addition, he says, "With online advertising you can actually track the value of every single dollar that you spend, understand which

particular customers the ad reached, and what they did after they received the advertising message."

The online advertising market has grown from its initial focus on simple text ads to a much larger set of options. There are five key categories of online advertising. They are:

- Search: 47%
- Display: 35%
- Classified: 10%
- Referral: 7%
- E-mail: 1%

Google is the dominant provider of online search requests and receives more than 60 percent of the search advertising revenue. The fastest-growing advertising category, however, is display advertising, where Yahoo! and Microsoft are established providers. Google believes that there is an opportunity to grow its display advertising sales by making the ads useful information instead of visual clutter. According to Google co-founder Sergey Brin, "It's like search—matching people with information they want. It just happens to be promotional."

Several improvements in technology and business practice tools contributed to Google's success. First, Google developed its patented PageRank™ algorithm, which evaluates the entire link structure of the Web and uses the link structure to determine which pages are most important. Then the process uses hypertext-matching analysis to determine which pages are relevant to a specific search. A combination of the importance and the relevance of web pages provides the search results—in just a fraction of a second. Second, Google developed two business practice tools—AdWords and AdSense—to help (1) advertisers create ads and (2) content providers generate advertising revenue. Both tools have become essential elements of Google's advertising model.

AdWords

To help advertisers place ads on their search-engine results, Google developed an online tool called AdWords. Advertisers can use AdWords to create ad text, select target keywords, and manage their account. The process allows advertisers to reach targeted audiences. Frederick Vallaeys, AdWords evangelist, explains: "One of my favorite things about AdWords is the fact that it really helps you find the right customer at the right time and show them the right message. With AdWords you can very specifically target your market because you're targeting them at a time when they do a search on Google. At that time they've told you a keyword, you know exactly what they're looking for, and here is your opportunity as a marketer to give them the exact answer to what they've just told you they wanted to find." Google has found that text ads that are relevant to the person reading them have much higher response ("click-through") rates than ads that are not targeted.

AdWords is also easy for any advertiser to use. Large or small businesses can simply open an account with a credit card and have ads appear within minutes. "When AdWords rolled out their self-service product, it really was one of the first times when it was very easy for a small business to put their ad up on the Internet on a search engine and compete on a level playing field alongside *Fortune* 1000 companies," says Vallaeys. Google has an experienced sales and service team available to help any advertiser select appropriate keywords, generate ad copy, and monitor campaign performance. The team is dedicated to helping its advertisers improve click-through rates because high click-through rates are an indication that ads are relevant to a user's interests. Methods of improving advertising performance include changing the keywords and rewriting copy. Because there is no limit to the number of keywords that an advertiser can select and each keyword can be matched with different ad copy, the potential for many very customer-specific options is high.

Another advantage of Google's AdWords program is that it allows advertisers to easily control costs. The ads appear as a "Sponsored Link" next to search results each time the Google search engine matches the search request with the ad's keywords and Quality Score, although the advertiser is not charged unless someone "clicks" on the link. In a traditional advertising model, advertisers were charged using a CPM (cost-per-thousand) approach, which charged for the impressions made by an ad. According to Holden, the Google model "transformed that to what we call a CPC, or a cost-per-click model, and this is a model that an advertiser, instead of paying for an impression, only pays when somebody actually clicks on that ad and is delivered to their website. So, in effect, they may be getting the benefit from impressions being shown, but we're not actually charging them anything unless there's a definite lead being delivered to their website." Google also offers advertisers real-time analytical services to allow assessment of and changes to any component of an advertising campaign.

AdSense

The AdSense program was designed for website owners as a tool for placing ads next to their web page content rather than next to search results. Currently, thousands of website managers use AdSense to place ads on their sites and generate revenue. Google applies the same general philosophy to matching ads with websites as it does to matching ads to search requests. By delivering ads that precisely target the content on the site's pages, Google believes the advertising enhances the experience for visitors to the website. In this way advertisers, website publishers, and information seekers all benefit.

AdSense is one of the tools Google is using to pursue its goal of increasing its display advertising business. Yahoo! and Microsoft's Bing are leaders in display advertising because they can put ads on their own websites such as Yahoo! Finance and MSN Money. To provide additional outlets for display ads, Google recently purchased YouTube. In addition, Google purchased DoubleClick, an advertising exchange where websites put space up for auction and ad agencies bid to place ads for their clients. Google is also trying to make it easy for anyone to create a display ad by introducing a new tool called Display Ad Builder. Some experts observe that because Google is so dominant at search advertising, its future growth will depend on success in display advertising.

GOOGLE'S FUTURE STRATEGY

How will Google continue its success? One possibility is that it will begin to try to win advertising away from the U.S. TV industry. While this is a new type of advertising requiring creative capabilities and relationships with large advertising agencies, Google has dedicated many of its resources to becoming competitive for television advertising expenditures. For example, Google recently helped Volvo develop a campaign that included a YouTube ad and Twitter updates. Google is also likely to develop new websites, establish blogs, and build relationships with existing sites.

Another opportunity for Google will be mobile telephone advertising. There are currently more than 5.4 billion mobile phones in use, and 1 billion of those are Internet-capable. Just as Google's search engine provides a means to match relevant information with consumers, phones offer a chance to provide real-time and location-specific information. Some of the challenges in mobile advertising will be that the networks are not fast and that the ad formats are not standardized. Google believes its new phone and its Android operating system will also help.

Finally, as Google pursues its mission it will continue to expand throughout the world. Search results are already available in 35 languages, and volunteers are helping with many others. It is obvious that Google is determined to "organize the world's information" and make it "accessible and useful."

Questions

1 Describe several unique characteristics about Google and its business practices.

2 What is Google's philosophy about advertising? How can less advertising be preferred to more advertising?

3 Describe the types of online advertising available today. Which type of advertising does Google currently dominate? Why?

4 How can Google be successful in the display advertising business? What other areas of growth are likely to be pursued by Google in the future?

Chapter Notes

1. Geoffrey Precourt, "What We Know about TV Today (and Tomorrow)," *Journal of Advertising Research*, March 2013, pp. 3–4; "Television Advertising: Destined for Eternity?" *Branding Strategy Insider*, May 3, 2013; Verne Gay, "Small Screen, Big Troubles: Television Networks Finding It Harder to Draw Conventional Audiences," *Spokesman Review*, March 8, 2013; Ryan Nakashima, "'Zero TV' Viewers Are Pulling the Plug on Traditional Television," *The Washington Post*, April 8, 2013, p. A14; "More U.S. Consumers Shun Traditional Television," *Multichannel News*, March 18, 2013; Dan Farber, "Microsoft's Xbox Entertainment Studio Working on Interactive TV," *CNET News*, February 11, 2013; Brian Steinberg, "12 Minutes, 10 Ideas That Tried to Change TV Ad Time Forever," *Advertising Age*, April 18, 2011, p. 12; Michael Learmonth, "Web TV? Xbox, Verizon and Others Appear to Be Up for the Challenge," *Advertising Age*, April 18, 2011, p. 6; and Andrew Hampp, "The Next Big Thing in TV? Well, It's Not on TV," *Advertising Age*, May 16, 2011, p. 4.

2. Karen V. Fernandez and Dennis L. Rosen, "The Effectiveness of Information and Color in Yellow Pages Advertising," *Journal of Advertising*, Summer 2000, p. 61; David A. Aaker and Donald Norris, "Characteristics of TV Commercials Perceived as Informative," *Journal of Advertising Research* 22, no. 2 (April–May 1982), pp. 61–70.

3. Larry D. Compeau and Dhruv Grewal, "Comparative Price Advertising: An Integrative Review," *Journal of Public Policy & Marketing*, Fall 1998, pp. 257–73; and William Wilkie and Paul W. Farris, "Comparison Advertising: Problems and Potentials," *Journal of Marketing*, October 1975, pp. 7–15.

4. Chingching Chang, "The Relative Effectiveness of Comparative and Noncomparative Advertising: Evidence for Gender Differences in Information-Processing Strategies," *Journal of Advertising*, Spring 2007, p. 21; Jerry Gotlieb and Dan Sarel, "The Influence of Type of Advertisement, Price, and Source Credibility on Perceived Quality," *Journal of the Academy of Marketing Science*, Summer 1992, pp. 253–60; and Cornelia Pechmann and David Stewart, "The Effects of Comparative Advertising on Attention, Memory, and Purchase Intentions," *Journal of Consumer Research*, September 1990, pp. 180–92.

5. Kathy L. O'Malley, Jeffrey J. Bailey, Chong Leng Tan, and Carl S. Bozman, "Effects of Varying Web-Based Advertising-Substantiation Information on Attribute Beliefs and Perceived Product Quality," *Academy of Marketing Studies Journal*, 2007, p. 19; Bruce Buchanan and Doron Goldman, "Us vs. Them: The Minefield of Comparative Ads," *Harvard Business Review*, May–June 1989, pp. 38–50; Dorothy Cohen, "The FTC's Advertising Substantiation Program," *Journal of Marketing*, Winter 1980, pp. 26–35; and Michael Etgar and Stephen A. Goodwin, "Planning for Comparative Advertising Requires Special Attention," *Journal of Advertising* 8, no. 1 (Winter 1979), pp. 26–32.

6. David W. Schumann, Jan M. Hathcote, and Susan West, "Corporate Advertising in America: A Review of Published Studies on Use, Measurement, and Effectiveness," *Journal of Advertising*, September 1991, p. 35; Lewis C. Winters, "Does It Pay to Advertise in Hostile Audiences with Corporate Advertising?" *Journal of Advertising Research*, June–July 1988, pp. 11–18; and Robert Selwitz, "The Selling of an Image," *Madison Avenue*, February 1985, pp. 61–69.

7. "New Crystal Light Liquid Drink Mix Frees You from the Choice between Taste or Calories," *PR Newswire*, February 11, 2013; Natalie Zmuda, "Diet Mtn Dew Steps Out from Shadow of Flagship Brand," *Advertising Age*, March 5, 2012, p. 4; E. J. Schultz and Natalie Zmuda, "No Solo Mio: Kraft's Smash Product Attracts Rival in Coke's Dasani," *Advertising Age*, November 5, 2012, p. 10; Natalie Zmuda, "No More 'Shrinking It and Pinking It' at Under Armour," *Advertising Age*, September 24, 2012, p. 46; Molly Soat, "Moving Beyond Shrink IT & Pink IT," *Marketing News*, February 2013, p. 32; Katie Smith, "US: Nike in Uniform Deal with International

Olympic Committee," *Just-Style Global News*, October 17, 2012; and Shareen Pthak, "How Nike Ambushed the Olympics with This Neon Shoe," *Advertising Age*, August 20, 2012, p. 1.

8. See the Advertising Research Foundation website, http://thearf .org/advancing-marketing-forum.php, accessed May 4, 2013.

9. "Who Bought What in Super Bowl XLVIII," *Advertising Age*, adage .com, February 3, 2014; "Super Bowl XLVIII Set a New Record for TV Viewers," *Advertising Age*, adage.com, February 3, 2014; Chris Sorensen, "Tackling the Super Bowl," *MacLean's*, February 11, 2013, p. 47; Stuart Elliott, "Replaying Super Bowl Ads' Effectiveness," *The New York Times Blogs*, February 6, 2013; "The Complete 2013 USA Today Ad Meter Results," February 3, 2013, http://admeter .usatoday.com/articles/view/the-results; and Rama Ylkur, Chuck Tomkovick, and Patty Traczyk, "Super Bowl Effectiveness: Hollywood Finds the Games Golden," *Journal of Advertising Research*, March 2004, pp. 143–59.

10. Cornelia Pechmann, Guangzhi Zhao, Marvin E. Goldberg, and Ellen Thomas Reibling, "What to Convey in Antismoking Advertisements for Adolescents: The Use of Protection Motivation Theory to Identify Effective Message Themes," *Journal of Marketing*, April 2003, pp. 1–18; Jeffrey D. Zbar, "Fear!" *Advertising Age*, November 14, 1994, pp. 18–19; and John F. Tanner, Jr., James B. Hunt, and David R. Eppright, "The Protection Motivation Model: A Normative Model of Fear Appeals," *Journal of Marketing*, July 1991, pp. 36–45.

11. "About Bebe," Bebe website, www.bebe.com, accessed June 16, 2011; and Sanjay Putrevu, "Consumer Responses toward Sexual and Nonsexual Appeals: The Influence of Involvement, Need for Cognition (NFC), and Gender," *Journal of Advertising*, Summer 2008, p. 57.

12. Rupal Parekh, "With Strong Work for Walmart and Geico, Martin Agency Is Creating a New Specialty: Making Marketers Recession-Proof," *Advertising Age*, January 19, 2009, p. 30; and Louis Llovio, "Geico Gecko's Viral Videos," *Richmond Times Dispatch*, March 28, 2009, p. B-9.

13. Thomas W. Cline and James J. Kellaris, "The Influence of Humor Strength and Humor-Message Relatedness on Ad Memorability: A Dual Process Model," *Journal of Advertising*, Spring 2007, p. 55; Yong Zhang and George M. Zinkham, "Responses to Humorous Ads," *Journal of Advertising*, Winter 2006, p. 113; and Yih Hwai Lee and Elison Ai Ching Lim, "What's Funny and What's Not: The Moderating Role of Cultural Orientation in Ad Humor," *Journal of Advertising*, Summer 2008, p. 71.

14. "Results of 4A's 2011 Television Production Cost Survey," *4A's Bulletin*, January 22, 2013 (New York: American Association of Advertising Agencies); and "Washington: Results of 4A's 2011 Television Production Cost Survey," *Plus Media Solutions*, January 23, 2013.

15. Rupal Parekh, "Agency of the Year," *Advertising Age*, January 28, 2013, p. 15; and Teressa Iezzi, "Kenny Powers Returns for Second K-Swiss Campaign," posted on 72andSunny website, www.72andsunny/work/k-swiss/mfceo.com, no date.

16. "U.S. Ad Spending Totals by Medium," *Advertising Age*, December 31, 2012, p. 13.

17. Vicki R. Lane, "The Impact of Ad Repetition and Ad Content on Consumer Perceptions of Incongruent Extensions," *Journal of Marketing*, April 2000, pp. 80–91.

18. "Nielsen Includes Internet Viewers for the First Time, Estimates That There Are Now 115.6 Million TV Homes in the U.S.," *Engadget HD*, May 8, 2013; "Rise of the 'Zero TV' Home: Ratings Altered to Take into Account the People Who Only Watch Online," *Mail Online*, April 8, 2013; and "Nielsen Estimates 115.6 Million TV Homes in the U.S., Up 1.2%," Nielsen website, www.nielsen.com/us/en/ newswire, May 7, 2013.

19. Jeanine Poggi, "Broadcast TV's Most Expensive Show: 'Sunday Night Football,'" *Advertising Age*, October 21, 2013, p. 12; Emily Fredrix, "TV Commercials Shrink to Match Attention Spans," *USA Today*, October 30, 2010; Kate Newstead and Jenni Romaniuk,

CHAPTER 15   Advertising, Sales Promotion, and Public Relations

"Cost per Second: The Relative Effectiveness of 15- and 30-Second Television Advertisements," *Journal of Advertising Research,* 2009, pp. 68–76; and Srinivasan Swaminathan and Robert Kent, "Second-by-Second Analysis of Advertising Exposure in TV Pods," *Journal of Advertising Research,* March 2013, pp. 91–100.

20. "Michael Powell Testimony to House Energy & Commerce Subcommittee on Communications & Technology," press release, National Cable & Telecommunications Association, www.ncta.com, June 25, 2012; and Brian Steinberg, "Turner Experiments with Building a Smarter Ad for Its Cable Networks," *Advertising Age,* April 11, 2011, p. 3.

21. "National Radio Format Shares and Station Counts," *Radio Today 2013: How America Listens to Radio,* Arbitron, 2013; "Radio Today by the Numbers," Arbitron, Spring 2013; "Radio's Weekly Reach: Hours per Week Spent Listening," "Daily Media Reach," and "Radio Listeners Listen," *Why Radio Fact Sheet,* Radio Advertising Bureau, April 2012; and Anthony Ha, "Pandora Resurrects Its 40-Hour Limit on Free Music," www.techcrunch.com, February 27, 2013.

22. "Hour-by-Hour Listening," in *Radio Today,* 2010 Edition, Arbitron, p. 89.

23. "A Magazine for Everyone," *Magazine Media Factbook 2012/13* (New York: The Association of Magazine Media), p. 85; "April Arrives: Brings 74 New Titles to the Nation's Newsstands," mr.magazine website, www.mrmagazine.com, May 2, 2013; "Skateboarder Magazine Changes the Game with Innovative Digital-First Platform," *States News Service,* April 16, 2013; and Rebecca Clancy, "*Auto Trader* Print Edition to Stop as Focus Shifts to Digital," *The Telegraph,* May 7, 2013.

24. "Number of Magazines by Category," The Association of Magazine Media, http://www.magazine.org/insights-resources/research-publications/trends-data/magazine-industry-facts-data/1998-2010-number, accessed May 13, 2013; and "Magazines Mean Engagement," *Magazine Media Factbook 2012/13* (New York: The Association of Magazine Media), p. 14.

25. "Top 25 U.S. Newspapers for March 2013," Research and Data, Alliance for Audited Media, http://www.auditedmedia.com/news/research-and-data/top-25-us-newspapers-for-march-2013.aspx; "About Us," *Metro* website, http://www.metro.us/newyork/about-us/; and "Metro Newspaper Is the #1 Free Daily Newspaper in Boston," *Business Wire,* June 13, 2011.

26. "U.S. Ad Spending Forecast from ZenithOptimedia," *Advertising Age,* December 31, 2012, p. 13; "Can Yellow Pages Make a Come Back?" *Zacks Investment Research,* March 21, 2013; Chris Silver Smith, "Are Yellow Pages Toast?" www.searchengineland.com, March 26, 2012; "Mobile Searches for Local Business Info Replacing Desktop and Yellow Pages," *SBWire,* April 10, 2013; "Yellow Page Group Reminds Winnipeg Residents of Directory Opt-Out Program," *Marketwire,* March 18, 2013; Heather Knight, "Yellow Pages Ruling Endangers SF Ban," *SFGate,* October 15, 2012; and "As Media Habits Evolve, Yellow Pages and Search Engines Firmly Established as Go-To Sources for Consumer Shopping Locally," *PR Newswire,* June 13, 2011.

27. See "Guidelines, Standards & Best Practices," at the Interactive Advertising Bureau website, http://www.iab.net/guidelines; "IAB Releases New Standard Ad Unit Portfolio," press release, International Advertising Bureau, February 26, 2012; "Online Measurement," Nielsen website, http://www.nielsen.com/us/en/nielsen-solutions/nielsen-measurement/nielsen-online-measurement.html, accessed May 16, 2013; and Abbey Klaassen, "Why the Click Is the Wrong Metric for Online Ads," *Advertising Age,* February 23, 2009, p. 4.

28. "Why We Need to Pivot in the Fight against Ad Fraud," *VentureBeat,* April 18, 2013; "Three Ways Advertisers Can Avoid Click Fraud," *ReadWriteWeb,* September 6, 2012; "Click Fraud Rate Drops to 19.1 Percent in Q4 2010," *Business Wire,* January 26, 2011; Sara Yin, "Click Fraud Skyrockets," *PC Magazine,* October 21, 2010; Alex Mindlin, "Click Fraud Climbs with Mobile Gear," *The New York*

Times, November 1, 2010, p. 2; and Gareth Jones, "Briefing—Paid Search—Advertisers Stung by Rising Click Fraud," *Revolution,* May 1, 2009, p. 18.

29. Arch G. Woodside, "Outdoor Advertising as Experiments," *Journal of the Academy of Marketing Science* 18 (Summer 1990), pp. 229–37.

30. "Clear Channel Outdoor Holdings Releases 'Out-of-Home Advertising and the Retail Industry' Report," *Professional Services Close-Up,* January 25, 2011; Andrew Hampp, "What's New with Outdoor Ads, and What's This Digital Out-of-Home I Keep Hearing About?" *Advertising Age,* September 27, 2010, p. 48; "The Year Ahead for … Outdoor," *Campaign,* January 9, 2009, p. 28; Andrew Hampp, "Digital Out of Home. That's Those Pixilated Billboards, Right?" *Advertising Age,* March 30, 2009; Andrew Hampp, "Out of Home That Stood Out," *Advertising Age,* December 15, 2008, p. 22; and Daniel W. Baack, Rick T. Wilson, and Brian D. Till, "Creativity and Memory Effects," *Journal of Advertising,* Winter 2008, p. 85.

31. Sehoon Park and Minhi Hahn, "Pulsing in a Discrete Model of Advertising Competition," *Journal of Marketing Research,* November 1991, pp. 397–405.

32. Peggy Masterson, "The Wearout Phenomenon," *Marketing Research,* Fall 1999, pp. 27–31; and Lawrence D. Gibson, "What Can One TV Exposure Do?" *Journal of Advertising Research,* March–April 1996, pp. 9–18.

33. Rik Pieters, Michel Wedel, and Rajeev Batra, "The Stopping Power of Advertising: Measure and Effects of Visual Complexity," *Journal of Marketing,* September 2010, pp. 48–60; Rob Norton, "How Uninformative Advertising Tells Consumers Quite a Bit," *Fortune,* December 26, 1994, p. 37; and "Professor Claims Corporations Waste Billions on Advertising," *Marketing News,* July 6, 1992, p. 5.

34. The discussion of posttesting is based on William F. Arens, Michael F. Weigold, and Christian Arens, *Contemporary Advertising,* 12th ed. (New York: McGraw-Hill Irwin, 2009), pp. 228–30.

35. "ROI Metric Available in MRI Starch Syndicated," Mediamark Research & Intelligence, www.mediamark.com, accessed April 23, 2009.

36. Debora V. Thompson and Prashant Malaviya, "Consumer-Generated Ads: Does Awareness of Advertising Co-Creation Help or Hurt Persuasion?" *Journal of Marketing,* May 2013, pp. 33–47; David A. Aaker and Douglas M. Stayman, "Measuring Audience Perceptions of Commercials and Relating Them to Ad Impact," *Journal of Advertising Research* 30 (August–September 1990), pp. 7–17; and Ernest Dichter, "A Psychological View of Advertising Effectiveness," *Marketing Management* 1, no. 3 (1992), pp. 60–62.

37. David Krugel, "Television Advertising Effectiveness and Research Innovation," *Journal of Consumer Marketing,* Summer 1988, pp. 43–51; and Laurence N. Gold, "The Evolution of Television Advertising Sales Measurement: Past, Present, and Future," *Journal of Advertising Research,* June–July 1988, pp. 19–24.

38. "U.S. Ad Spending Forecast from ZenithOptimedia," *Advertising Age,* June 24, 2013, p. 22.

39. Tom Hansen, "Media Mash," *Promo,* February 1, 2007, p. 66; Magid M. Abraham and Leonard M. Lodish, "Getting the Most Out of Advertising and Promotion," *Harvard Business Review,* May–June 1990, pp. 50–60; Steven W. Hartley and James Cross, "How Sales Promotion Can Work For and against You," *Journal of Consumer Marketing,* Summer 1988, pp. 35–42; Robert D. Buzzell, John A. Quelch, and Walter J. Salmon, "The Costly Bargain of Trade Promotion," *Harvard Business Review,* March–April 1990, pp. 141–49; and Mary L. Nicastro, "Break-Even Analysis Determines Success of Sales Promotions," *Marketing News,* March 5, 1990, p. 11.

40. "Annual Coupon Facts," NCH Marketing Services, 2013; "NCH Annual Topline U.S. CPG Coupon Facts Report for Year-End 2012," NCH Marketing Services, January 2013; "2012 NCH Consumer Survey: Demographic Profile of Coupon Users," NCH Marketing Services, 2012; Claudia Buck, "Coupon Industry: No Scissors Required," *The State Journal-Register,* February 24, 2013, p. 40; "Coupons.com Report Shows Upward Trend among Digital Coupon

Users," *Wireless News,* May 19, 2013; and "How Mobile Coupons Are Driving an Explosion in Mobile Commerce," *The Business Insider,* May 22, 2013.

41. "What Is Coupon Fraud?" The Coupon Information Corporation, http://www.couponinformationcenter.com, accessed May 26, 2013; Josh Elledge, "Coupon Fraud Hurts Us All," *Grand Rapids Press,* April 19, 2011, p. B1; and Amy Johannes, "Flying the Coup," *Promo,* July 1, 2008, p. 28.

42. *Epic* website, http://www.epicthemovie.com, accessed May 27, 2013; "The Influence of Promotional Products on Consumer Behavior," Promotional Product Association International, November 2012; Amy Johannes, "Premium Connections," *Promo,* October 2008, p. 34; and Gerard P. Prendergast, Alex S. L. Tsang, Derek T. Y. Poon, "Predicting Premium Proneness," *Journal of Advertising Research,* June 2008, p. 287.

43. "Two Consumer-Created Doritos Ads Crash the Super Bowl Advertising Stage, Now Compete for $1 Million Bonus Prize," *PR Newswire,* February 3, 2013; "Official Rules," Doritos Crash the Super Bowl Ad Contest, Frito-Lay Inc., https://ctsb.grindnetworks.com/voting_finalists_winners_phase/officialrules.php; and "User Content Offers a New Perspective," *PR Week,* February 23, 2009, p. 21.

44. Sarah Firshein, "HGTV Dream Home Winner Revealed!: Here's a Warm 'n' Fuzzy Story … " *Curbed NY,* March 11, 2011; and Charlotte McEleny, "Social Media and Mobile Boost Participation for McDonald's Monopoly," *New Media Age Online,* April 18, 2011.

45. "Mars Chocolate North America Launches 5 Characters, 5 Cars Promotion," *Travel & Leisure Close-Up,* June 20, 2011; "Buy a Large Coke at Carl's Jr. and Win—Guaranteed; Guests Can Win Big with My Coke Rewards Point and Food Prizes," *Business Wire,* May 27, 2011; and "StumbleUpon Partners with the Academy of Motion Picture Arts and Sciences for Sweepstakes," *Marketwire,* January 17, 2013.

46. Tiffany Hsu, "Taco Bell Gives Away Free Doritos Locos Tacos after World Series," *Money and Company,* October 30, 2012; "Free Doritos Locos Tacos Available at Taco Bell If Bases Stolen in World Series," *Huff Post,* October 19, 2012; Elana Ashanti Jefferson, "Sample Hunters Offer Advice for Trying—Before You Buy," *Denver Post,* July 16, 2012, p. 3C; and Schuyler Velasco, "Ben & Jerry's Free Cone Day," *The Christian Science Monitor,* April 9, 2013.

47. "Who Says Loyalty Is Dead? Americans Have More Than 2B Loyalty Memberships," *PandoDaily on Facebook,* February 22, 2013; Kelly Hlavinka and Jim Sullivan, *The Billion Member March: The 2011 Colloquy Loyalty Census,* LoyaltyOne Colloquy, http://www.colloquy.com/files/2011-COLLOQUY-Census-Talk-White-Paper.pdf, 2011; Kara McGuire, "Retailers Work to Make Shopping Its Own Reward," *Star Tribune,* December 19, 2010, p. 1A; and "Loyalty Rewards Membership on the Rise," *Brandweek.com,* April 17, 2009.

48. "Virgin Mobile Offers $100 Rebate to T-Mobile Turncoats," *Engadget HD,* April 9, 2013; Nathalia Dens, Patrick De Pelsmacker, Marijke Wouters, and Nathalia Purnawirawan, "Do You Like What You Recognize?" *Journal of Advertising,* Fall 2012, pp. 35–53; "The Case for Rebates," *Chief Marketer,* July 1, 2011; and Marvin A. Jolson, Joshua L. Wiener, and Richard B. Rosecky, "Correlates of Rebate Proneness," *Journal of Advertising Research,* February–March 1987, pp. 33–43.

49. Kirstan Acuna, "The Amount of Sony Product Placement in 'The Amazing Spider-Man' Sequel Is Ridiculous," *The Business Insider,* May 1, 2014; "Primetime Shows with the Most Product Placement," www.CNBC.com, http://www.cnbc.com/id/45884892/page/1, accessed May 27, 2013; "Celebrity Product Brands … Now Showing!" www.Business2Community.com, May 8, 2013; "FCC Examines Product Placement Rules," *Marketing News,* July 15, 2008, p. 8; Josh Halliday, "Product Placement: P Logo Stands for Puzzled Public," *Guardian Unlimited,* June 20, 2011; Brandchannel.com website, http://www.brandchannel.com/brandcameo_films.asp?movie_year=2011#movie_list, accessed May 27, 2013; and Ekaterina V. Karniouchina, Can Uslay, and Grigori Erenburg, "Do Marketing Media Have Life Cycles? The Case of Product Placement in Movies," *Journal of Marketing,* May 2011, pp. 27–49.

50. This discussion is drawn particularly from John A. Quelch, *Trade Promotions by Grocery Manufacturers: A Management Perspective* (Cambridge, MA: Marketing Science Institute, August 1982).

51. Michael Chevalier and Ronald C. Curhan, "Retail Promotions as a Function of Trade Promotions: A Descriptive Analysis," *Sloan Management Review* 18 (Fall 1976), pp. 19–32.

52. G. A. Marken, "Firms Can Maintain Control over Creative Co-op Programs," *Marketing News,* September 28, 1992, pp. 7, 9.

Google, Inc.: This case was written by Steven Hartley. Sources: "Mobile Cellular Subscriptions: 2000–2010," International Telecommunication Union, accessed October 15, 2011, http://www.itu.int/ITU-D/ict/material/FactsFigures2010.pdf; Jessica E. Vascellaro, "Google Decides to Find Its Creative Side," *The Wall Street Journal,* October 7, 2009; Robert D. Hof, "Google's New Ad Weapon," *BusinessWeek,* June 22, 2009, p. 52; Maria Bartiromo, "Eric Schmidt on Where Google Is Headed," *BusinessWeek,* August 17, 2009, p. 11; "Why Microsoft-Yahoo Deal Could Be Good for Google," *Advertising Age,* August 10, 2009, p. 10; Peter Burrow, "Apple and Google: Another Step Apart," *BusinessWeek,* August 17, 2009, p. 24; Jeff Jarvis, "How The Google Model Could Help," *BusinessWeek,* February 9, 2009, p. 32; Abbey Klaassen, "Google Says Print Ads Isn't the Answer for Newspapers," *Advertising Age,* January 26, 2009, p. 17; Matthew Creamer, "Recession Doesn't Dent Total Value of Top 100 Brands," *Advertising Age,* April 27, 2009; "The 500 Largest U.S. Corporations," *Fortune,* May 4, 2009, F-1; "ComScore Releases August 2009 U.S. Search Engine Rankings," www.comscore.com, October 10, 2009; interviews with Google personnel; and information contained on the Google website (www.google.com).

Credits

CHAPTER 15   Advertising, Sales Promotion, and Public Relations

16 Using Social Media to Connect with Consumers

LEARNING OBJECTIVES

After reading this chapter you should be able to:

 Define social media and describe how they differ from traditional advertising media.

 Identify the four major social networks and how brand managers integrate them into marketing actions.

 Describe the differing roles of those receiving messages through traditional versus social media and how brand managers select a social network.

 Compare the performance measures of social media linked to costs (inputs) versus revenues (outputs).

 Identify the cause of the convergence of the real and digital worlds and how this will affect the future of social media.

HOW TO CONNECT WITH TODAY'S COLLEGE STUDENT? TRY FACEBOOK AND TWITTER!

Like Kimmy Summers at the University of North Carolina (wearing cap in the photo), thousands of "brand ambassadors" at U.S. colleges and universities face a special challenge right before freshman week.[1]

Finding Volunteers for Freshman Move-In Day

The challenge: How can she recruit student volunteers to help incoming freshmen during campus move-in day? Use the campus newspaper?

The answer is a no-brainer for most upperclassmen working as brand ambassadors for firms like American Eagle Outfitters (AE), Target, and Apple: Use Facebook and Twitter! Here's a somewhat generic marketing plan they use for freshman week, with AE as an example:

- Use the college Facebook Page and Twitter messages to recruit about 40 volunteers to assist freshmen on move-in day.

- Tell incoming freshmen about the volunteers on the college Facebook Page with teasers like: "Need help moving in? No worries. AE will be there."

- Have these volunteers help freshmen move into their college dorms.

- Give each freshman who was helped a coupon for a free pair of AE flip-flops.

The volunteers often get a free American Eagle T-shirt (photo).

College Students and Social Media

"College students are wary of old-school marketing," says Paul Himmelfarb, managing director of Youth Marketing Connection, which links marketers with college students. "You have to take a brand and incorporate it into the college lifestyle by peer-to-peer marketing."[2]

In the past decade, college students have more than doubled their use of the Internet and social media to collect information and buy products. College marketers increasingly use social media to reach students because they work better than traditional print and TV ads.[3] More than 10,000 student brand ambassadors on the 4,000 U.S. college campuses use social media to connect with other students.

This chapter defines social media, describes four widely used social networks, explains how organizations use them in developing marketing strategies, and considers where social media are headed in the future.

UNDERSTANDING SOCIAL MEDIA

LO 16-1 Define social media and describe how they differ from traditional advertising media.

Defining *social media* is challenging, but it's necessary to help a brand or marketing manager select the right one. This section defines social media, positions a number of social networks, and compares social and traditional media. As you read this, consider how you might choose a social network if *you*—like college students around the globe—were using one to launch a start-up business or expand a small business.

What Are Social Media?

This section describes how social media came about, defines social media, and provides a means of classifying the countless social media networks available to assist marketing managers in choosing among them.

social media
Online media where users submit comments, photos, and videos—often accompanied by a feedback process to identify "popular" topics.

Defining Social Media   Social media represent a unique blending of technology and social interaction to create personal value for users. **Social media** are online media where users submit comments, photos, and videos—often accompanied by a feedback process to identify "popular" topics.[4] Most social media involve a genuine online conversation among people about a subject of mutual interest, one built on their personal thoughts and experiences. However, other social media sites involve games and virtual worlds, in which the online interaction includes playing a game, completing a quest, controlling an avatar, and so on. Business firms also refer to social media as "consumer-generated media." A single social media site with millions of users interacting with each other, like Facebook, Twitter, LinkedIn, and YouTube, is referred to as a *social network*.

The text describes how Web 2.0 and user-generated content are the foundations of today's social media.

blog
A contraction of "web log," a web page that serves as a publicly accessible personal journal and online forum for an individual or organization.

user-generated content (UGC)
The various forms of online media content that are publicly available and created by end users.

How do marketing managers choose the best social media sites to reach their target markets? As a first step, the text describes how social media can be classified and how they differ from traditional media.

How Social Media Came About   The term "social media" is sometimes used interchangeably with the terms "Web 2.0" and "user-generated content"—two concepts that are the foundations of today's social media.[5] Web 2.0 does not refer to any technical update of the World Wide Web, but identifies functionalities that make possible today's high degree of interactivity among users. So with Web 2.0, content is no longer seen as being created and published in final form exclusively by one author. Instead, the content can be modified continuously by all users in a participatory fashion, such as with blogs and wikis.

A **blog**—a contraction of "web log"—is a web page that serves as a publicly accessible personal journal and online forum for an individual or organization. Companies like Hewlett-Packard and Frito-Lay routinely monitor blogs to gain insights into customer complaints and suggestions. A *wiki* is a website whose content is created and edited by the ongoing collaboration of end users—such as generating and improving new-product ideas. They differ in that a blog is a diary that shows a sequential journey while a wiki shows the end result as a single entry.[6]

User-generated content (UGC) refers to the various forms of online media content that are publicly available and created by end users. The term "user-generated content" (also referred to as *consumer-generated content*) was in common use by 2005 and covers all the ways people can use social media. UGC satisfies three basic criteria:[7]

1. It is published either on a publicly accessible website or on a social networking site, so it is not simply an e-mail.
2. It shows a significant degree of creative effort, so it is more than simply posting a newspaper article on a personal blog without editing or comments.
3. It is consumer-generated by an individual outside of a professional organization, without a commercial market in mind.

Classifying Social Media   Most of us would probably say that Facebook, Twitter, LinkedIn, and YouTube are well-known social networks. But marketing managers trying to reach potential customers need a system to classify the more than 400 specialized and diverse social networks to select the best among them. Kaplan and Haenlein have proposed a classification system for marketers based on two factors:[8]

1. *Media richness.* This involves the degree of acoustic, visual, and personal contact between two communication partners—face-to-face communications, say, being higher in media richness than telephone or e-mail communications. The higher the media richness and quality of presentation, the greater the social influence that communication partners have on each other's behavior.
2. *Self-disclosure.* In any type of social interaction, individuals want to make a positive impression to achieve a favorable image with others. This favorable image is affected by the degree of self-disclosure about a person's thoughts, feelings, likes, and dislikes—where greater self-disclosure is likely to increase one's influence on those reached.

Figure 16–1 uses these two factors of media richness and self-disclosure to position a number of social media sites in two-dimensional space. For example, Wikipedia is a collaborative project that is low on both self-disclosure and media richness.[9] LinkedIn, on the other hand, contains detailed career and résumé information for business networking and is high in self-disclosure but only moderate in media richness.

Marketing managers look carefully at the positioning of the social networks shown in Figure 16–1 when selecting those to use in their plans. For example, World of Warcraft (WoW), positioned in the Virtual Game Worlds segment in Figure 16–1, is a multiplayer, online role-playing game in the fantasy Warcraft universe. Toyota recently

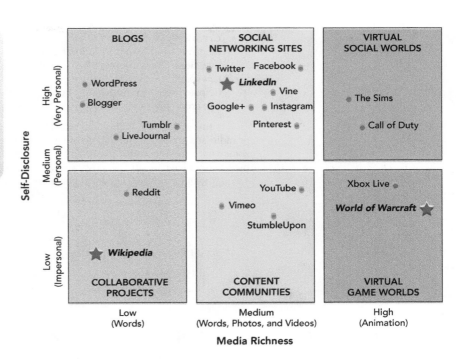

FIGURE 16–1
A sample of social media, classified by media richness and self-disclosure. Note that in moving from words to photos, videos, and animation, media richness increases. Also, in moving from very impersonal messages to highly personal ones, self-disclosure increases.

used mechanics and pictures from World of Warcraft in a commercial to promote its cars to the millions of people who play the game in the United States.

Comparing Social and Traditional Media

World of Warcraft (WoW) is a multiplayer, online role-playing game where players control a character avatar within a fantasy world. For how Toyota promoted its cars to WoW players, see the text.

Consumers receive information, news, and education from print (newspapers, magazines) and electronic (radio, television) media. But marketing managers know that social media are very different from traditional media like newspapers or even radio or television. Social media and traditional media have both similarities and differences that impact marketing strategies, as described below:[10]

- *Ability to reach both large and niche audiences.* Both kinds of media can be designed to reach either a mass market or specialized segments; however, good execution is critical, and audience size is not guaranteed.
- *Expense and access.* Messages and ads in traditional media like newspapers or television generally are expensive to produce and have restricted access by individuals. Also, traditional media are typically owned privately or by the government. In contrast, messages on social media networks are generally accessible everywhere to those with smartphones, computers, and tablet devices and can be produced cheaply.
- *Training and number of people involved.* Producing traditional media typically requires specialized skills and training and often involves teams of people. In contrast, sending messages on social media requires only limited skills, so practically anyone can post a message that includes words and images.
- *Time to delivery.* Traditional media can involve days or even months of continuing effort to deliver the communication, and time lags can be extensive. In contrast, individuals using social media can post virtually instantaneous content.
- *Permanence.* Traditional media, once created, cannot be altered. For example, once a magazine article is printed and distributed, it cannot be changed. But social media message content can be altered almost instantaneously by comments or editing.

- *Credibility and social authority.* Individuals and organizations can establish themselves as "experts" in their given field, thereby becoming "influencers" in that field. For example, *The New York Times* has immense credibility among newspaper media. But with social media, a sender often simply begins to participate in the "conversation," hoping that the quality of the message will establish credibility with the receivers, thereby enhancing the sender's influence.

In terms of privacy, with minor exceptions, recipients of traditional media like TV or radio ads are completely anonymous. Subscribers to newspapers or magazines are somewhat less so because publishers can sell subscription lists to advertisers. Social media users have much less privacy and anonymity. When social media sites breach expectations for privacy, unethical outsiders can access users' names.

> **learning review**
>
> 16-1. What are social media?
>
> 16-2. In classifying social media, what do we mean by (*a*) media richness and (*b*) self-disclosure?
>
> 16-3. Compare traditional media and social media in terms of time required to deliver the communication.

A LOOK AT FOUR IMPORTANT SOCIAL NETWORKS

 LO 16-2 Identify the four major social networks and how brand managers integrate them into marketing actions.

Facebook, Twitter, LinkedIn, and YouTube are four widely used networks in the world of social media. So marketing managers need a special understanding of these four platforms as they integrate social media into their marketing strategies to supplement the traditional media they already use. This section briefly compares, defines, and explains each of these four major social media and shows how brand managers can use them. Because of its importance, Facebook merits more detailed coverage.

Comparing Four Social Networks

Figure 16–2 compares four major social networks (Facebook, Twitter, LinkedIn, and YouTube) from the point of view of a brand manager.[11] Facebook can increase brand exposure by enabling convenient user posting of links, photos, and videos. Twitter makes it easy to place brand messages and gain online customer support. While primarily a powerful network in helping users find jobs, LinkedIn has also found a niche in helping small businesses network to reach potential customers, as well as filling its traditional role of connecting job seekers and jobs. YouTube's videos make it especially useful in explaining a complex product.

Facebook

Facebook is the first choice among people seeking to create and maintain online connections with others by using photos, videos, and short text entries. Facebook enhanced its photo-sharing capability with its 2012 acquisition of Instagram. With over 1 billion active users—1 in every 7 people on the planet—Facebook is truly the 900-pound gorilla among all social media.

Facebook
A website where users may create a personal profile, add other users as friends, and exchange comments, photos, videos, and "likes" with them.

Facebook: An Overview **Facebook** is a website where users may create a personal profile, add other users as friends, and exchange comments, photos, videos, and "likes" with them. Facebook users today can keep friends and family updated on what they are thinking, doing, and feeling. In addition, users may chat with friends and create and join common-interest groups organized by workplace, high school, college, and Pages—some of the latter maintained by organizations as a means of advertising. Facebook is open to anyone age 13 and older.

BASIS OF COMPARISON	SOCIAL NETWORKS			
	facebook	**twitter**	**Linked in**	**You Tube**
Male-Female Breakdown (U.S.)	46% male, 54% female	54% male, 46% female	62% male, 38% female	58% male, 42% female
Brand Exposure	Powerful for gaining brand exposure through convenient user posting of links, photos, and videos.	Consistent placement of brand messages is easy with applications like HootSuite and TweetCastor. Sponsored tweets promote brands.	Free opportunities exist, like Business Pages and LinkedIn Influencer posts. Paid Sponsored Updates provide added reach.	Powerful in gaining attention and explaining a complex product, and branding. Channels unite users on content and heighten viewership.
Customer Communication	Great for people who like your brand and want to share their opinions. Leads all social networks for this.	Twitter is powerful for gaining online customer support. Engaging one-on-one is simple and easy to track.	Half of those using social media for customer service use a LinkedIn Company Page while 40% do so with LinkedIn Groups.	YouTube gains user's ready attention in attracting customer support. Easy to allow responses to user comments and ratings.
Traffic to Website	Is the traffic leader through rewording engaging content with better news feed placement. But its share of referred visits is falling.	Referral traffic from Twitter is growing faster than any other social network. Photos and videos make tweets even more clickable.	LinkedIn generates referrals—though less than many other social networks—but can be valuable for B2B and business development.	YouTube is an important source of traffic. Get traffic back to user's site by adding a hyperlink in the video description.

Source: The 2014 Male-Female Breakdowns are provided by Compete, Inc.; the other information is adapted from "The CMO's Guide to the 2014 Social Landscape."

FIGURE 16–2
How brand managers can use four social networks in developing their marketing strategies.

Time magazine's selection of Mark Zuckerberg as its "Person of the Year" reflects the staggering impact of Facebook today.[12] Consider that Facebook:

- Processes 350 million photos, 4.5 billion "likes," and 10 billion messages a day.[13]
- Has 86 percent of its users living outside the U.S.[14]
- Now reaches 680 million users on smartphones and mobile devices.[15]

The average American Facebook user has 130 friends, and 48 percent of 18- to 34-year-olds check Facebook when they wake up.[16]

Mark Zuckerberg, a *Time* magazine "Person of the Year," is the creator of Facebook, a social network that now connects over a billion users.

Facebook in a Brand Manager's Strategy   Facebook Pages were created as a method for brand managers to generate awareness for their product, service, or brand within Facebook. They allow brand managers to promote their business on Facebook, separate from their private and personal profiles. Done well, these are magnets for feedback. Additionally, Facebook Page information is generally public and cataloged by search engines so brand managers can identify influencers within their customer base.

To generate new customers and increase traffic to their Facebook Pages, brand managers can use paid ads and sponsored stories within the Facebook advertising platform. An advantage of these Facebook ads is that the content can migrate into Facebook conversations among friends—to the delight of advertisers.

The marketing challenge for an organization's Facebook Page is to post content that will generate the best response. Brand managers using Facebook seek to maintain a conversation with their fans. Research suggests the following guidelines to engage fans on Facebook:[17]

- *Be creative* in using links, photos, and videos.
- *Make it familiar, but with a twist.* Focus content strategy on imagery and messaging that is familiar to fans—punctuated with something unique. Aflac uses its

Aflac Duck—the well-known "spokes-duck"—to treat fans to Aflac Duck commercials, virtual Duck gifts, and supplemental insurance offers.

- *Keep it fresh.* Redbox uses frequent posts to keep fans informed about its latest film releases.
- *Learn users' passions and let them guide content.* Taco Bell polls users to see which menu item they'd like featured in the following week's menu profile photo.

Gaining meaningful user loyalty enables a company to target promotional offers to its best customers. A recent study found that "Likes" or "Followers" on a brand's Facebook Page are worth an astounding $174 in terms of product spending, brand loyalty, and "propensity to recommend" the site to others.[18]

Launching a New Social Network Using Facebook   Want to launch your own social network? For example, StuffDOT—"Share, Shop, Earn!"—is a place for people to post the things they like and earn rewards for their recommendations and online purchases. It differs from other social-sharing websites because users "dot" their favorite things to StuffDOT and *receive financial rewards* when someone purchases that item. Reward money can be redeemed for gift cards with many major retailers, such as Amazon and Target.[19]

Figure 16–3 shows the Facebook Page for StuffDOT, a new start-up that targets college-aged women. The notes in the margins in Figure 16–3 show how elements on the StuffDOT Facebook Page seek to connect with fans, generate conversations, and help measure the success of the Facebook Page:

- *Profile and Cover Image.* Show StuffDOT's attention-getting logo.
- *People Like This.* Tells the number of people clicking the "Like" button.
- *Facebook Page Posts.* Pictures items like clothes and travel information shared with users.

Facebook offers its business customers a variety of ad templates that help measure the results of an ad, such as "Page Likes" (chosen by StuffDOT) or "Clicks to Website." StuffDOT also uses Facebook's "App Install" template to inform and encourage people to download the StuffDOT app.

StuffDOT's challenge is to break through the social media clutter and attract loyal users. So the StuffDOT marketing team works continuously to present an attention-getting, user-friendly Facebook Page.

As a start-up, StuffDOT finds new users and website testers by recruiting college Campus Ambassadors. StuffDOT Campus Ambassadors actively promote the site nationally through workshops, social media marketing, word-of-mouth, and promotional partnerships with events and businesses on college campuses. To learn more about what StuffDOT is up to now, go to http://www.stuffdot.com/.

Updating Facebook   Keeping a billion user "customers" happy is a tall order— even for Facebook. To achieve this goal, Facebook continually refreshes elements of its social network site. Some recent updates include:

- *Ads on mobile devices.* These didn't exist until early 2012. But as more Facebook users access their friends with mobile devices, Facebook sought ways to generate revenues by placing ads there. By early 2014, more than half of Facebook's sales revenues came from ads on mobile devices.[20]
- *Customizing Facebook's News Feed.* In March 2013, Facebook announced that a version of its News Feed was being tailored for images to appear on mobile devices. This is important because about half of the average Facebook user's News Feed consists of photos and videos.[21]
- *Hashtag roll-out.* In June 2013, Facebook introduced hashtags in its network "to help people more easily discover what others are saying about a specific topic and participate in public conversations."[22]

Profile and Cover Image
Brand identifying image; usually includes a logo or promotional image

People Like This
The number of people who have clicked the Like button

People Likes
The number of people who Like a specific post

Post Views
The number of people who saw a specific post

Facebook Page Posts
Messages that appear in the News Feed of people who Like the Page

FIGURE 16–3
StuffDOT's Facebook Page shows elements of interest to both its marketing team and potential users who will respond to its "Share, Shop, Earn!" appeal.

- *Recent purchase of the WhatsApp and Oculus companies for over $20 Billion.* For this money, Facebook gets WhatApp's messaging app that reaches 450 million users who can send text messages and share photos with contacts one-on-one or in very small groups without incurring charges from telecom firms. With Oculus, Facebook buys its virtual reality headset that may have applications in video games.[23]

Where is Facebook headed with these new acquisitions? Perhaps only Mark Zuckerberg knows!

Twitter

Now that "tweets" have become part of our everyday language, it's apparent that Twitter has entered the mainstream of American life. Twitter now has over 240 million active monthly users worldwide, who post 500 million tweets per day.[24]

Twitter
A website that enables users to send and receive "tweets," messages up to 140 characters long.

Twitter: An Overview   **Twitter** is a website that enables users to send and receive *tweets*, messages up to 140 characters long. Twitter is based on the principle of "followers." So when you choose to follow another Twitter user, that user's tweets appear in reverse chronological order on your Twitter page.

Because of its short message length, the ease of posting and receiving tweets, and its convenience on a smartphone, Twitter can be a good source of information about a

CHAPTER 16 Using Social Media to Connect with Consumers

409

Carmex (@Carmex) used Twitter to partner with members of TeamLeBron to give away a jar of Carmex lip balm with a 14 karat gold cap.

brand or product. Carma Laboratories, the maker of Carmex lip balm and skin care products, uses Twitter as an important tool in its social media program to communicate brand messages to its followers. As part of Carmex's social media outreach, the brand is active on Twitter with daily messages, retweets, and replies.

The immediacy of Twitter messaging allows brands like Carmex to operate promotions in real time. For example, Carmex partnered with LeBronJames.com to conduct a scavenger hunt on Twitter where members of TeamLeBron tweeted clues to their location. The first person to arrive at the destination won a jar of Carmex with a 14 karat gold cap.

Beyond sending out messages, Carmex relies on Twitter as a listening device. Carmex's social media team monitors mentions of Carmex on Twitter to see what people are saying. If there are product concerns, Carmex can reach out to consumers to make sure their concerns are quickly addressed. For more on Carmex and how it uses social media to conduct marketing research, see Chapter 7.

Twitter in a Brand Manager's Strategy   With the 140-character limit on tweets, brand managers cannot expect extensive comments on their brands. But they can use social media management tools like TweetDeck or HootSuite to see what Twitter users are saying—good and bad—about both their own brands and competitive ones. They can then respond to the negative comments and retweet the positive ones.

Brand managers have various other strategies for listening to and interacting with current and potential consumers using Twitter. For example, they can:[25]

- Generate brand buzz by developing an official Twitter profile, recruiting followers, and showing photos of their products.
- Follow the Twitter profiles that mention their product and monitor what is being said, responding to user criticisms to develop happier customers.
- Tweet on topics that provide information of value to their consumers.

As with Facebook, Twitter can actively engage customers if done creatively. To further enhance this engagement, in 2014 Twitter introduced new features to make the site more appealing and acquired Grip to analyze tweets for businesses hungry for user insights.[26]

LinkedIn

Unlike Facebook and Twitter, the LinkedIn site's main purpose is professional networking and job searching.

LinkedIn
A business-oriented website that lets users post their professional profiles to connect to a network of businesspeople.

LinkedIn: An Overview   LinkedIn is a business-oriented website that lets users post their professional profiles to connect to a network of businesspeople. These businesspeople are also called *connections*. This social network has over 275 million registered members who conduct 6 billion professionally oriented searches annually. Because of its popularity, over 3 million companies have LinkedIn Company Pages to post news and job openings. LinkedIn's international presence, too, is staggering, used in over 200 countries and 20 languages.[27]

LinkedIn in a Brand Manager's Strategy   Marketing managers can use LinkedIn to promote their brand in subtle ways. This is done mainly for business-to-business (B2B) image building and networking with industry-related groups. Using

College students—like the one shown here—use LinkedIn to search for summer internships and permanent jobs after graduation.

LinkedIn, brand managers can demonstrate the organization's expertise and create and moderate discussion groups.

According to a 2013 survey of small business owners, 41 percent see LinkedIn as potentially beneficial to their company—more than twice that for Facebook, Twitter, or YouTube.[28] LinkedIn recently streamlined its research process for finding qualified employees so that an employer can type its needs into the LinkedIn "search box," which results in a summary that includes people, jobs, groups, and companies. Brand managers also use LinkedIn for business development to identify sales leads and locate vendors.[29] Sales representatives often use LinkedIn to see the profiles of purchasing personnel or managers with whom they are meeting.

LinkedIn in a College Senior's Job Search   Of growing importance, LinkedIn has over 30 million students and recent college graduates as members. College career centers and the LinkedIn student link (http://university.linkedin.com/linked-for-students.html) give key ideas for building an attention-getting LinkedIn profile for students looking for jobs:[30]

- Write an informative short, memorable profile headline.
- Include an appropriate photo of you, nicely dressed, with a plain background that isn't a goofy Instagram "selfie." And smile.
- Create a professional summary—concisely giving your education, qualifications, goals, relevant work experience, and extracurriculars.
- Fill the Skills & Expertise section with keywords and phrases the recruiters use in their searches.
- Include recommendations from people who know you well—supervisors, colleagues, instructors, advisors.
- Set your LinkedIn profile to "public" and create a unique URL (www.linkedin.com/in/JohnSmith) that you also include in your résumé.

Finally, in your LinkedIn profile avoid these 10 most overused 2013 buzzwords: responsible, strategic, creative, effective, patient, expert, organizational, driven, innovative, analytical.[31]

YouTube

The ability of YouTube to reach its audience stretches the imagination. Think about this: In 2014, YouTube's 1-billion-plus users: (1) watched over 6 billion hours of video each month; (2) uploaded 100 hours of video each minute; and (3) reached more 18- to 34-year-old U.S. adults than any cable network.[32]

YouTube
A video-sharing website in which users can upload, view, and comment on videos.

YouTube: An Overview   **YouTube** is a video-sharing website in which users can upload, view, and comment on videos. YouTube uses streaming video technology to display user-generated video content that includes movie and TV clips, music videos, and original videos developed by amateurs. While most of the content is uploaded by amateurs, many companies offer material on the site through a YouTube channel.

YouTube redesigns its home page periodically to provide a more organized structure to steer users to "channels," rather than simply encourage them to browse like in the past. This probably helped Rebecca Black's "Friday" YouTube video (over 50 million views), which went viral."[33] Recently, YouTube also redesigned the format for its YouTube channels. These channels serve as home pages for organizations and individuals and allow them to upload their own videos, as well as post and share videos created by others. For example, Rebecca Black now has a YouTube channel that aggregates all her music and other videos she has uploaded for fans and other users to view.

411

CHAPTER 16   Using Social Media to Connect with Consumers

Marketing Matters

What Are Some of Your Other Favorite Social Networks?

Other social networks that are popular among college students with diverse interests include the following:

reddit—An entertainment and sharing network where members submit content users can vote "up" or "down."

Google+—A social-sharing network from Google that allows you to organize friends in "circles" for easy sharing, host "hangouts," and more.

StumbleUpon—A discovery engine for finding and sharing the best content on the Web.

Pinterest—A content sharing network where members "pin" images, videos, and more to "boards" they create, which are categorized into different themes.

Tumblr—A feature-rich, micro-blogging platform that allows users to share text, photos, music, links, videos, and more.

Instagram—A fast and fun way to share photos; users simply snap a photo, choose a specialized filter to alter the look and feel of the image, and share the image with family and friends.

YouTube in a Brand Manager's Strategy   YouTube offers great opportunity for a brand manager to produce and show a video that explains the benefits of a complex product. Since YouTube is owned by Google, it incorporates a search engine, so users interested in a specific topic can find it easily. In terms of cost advantages, while a brand manager must pay the cost of creating a video, launching a new channel on YouTube is free.

YouTube offers a program to help small businesses create video ads on its social network. Small businesses can now buy and manage key words for their video ads on YouTube. So, a baker who runs a YouTube video ad for her bakery can buy words like "baking," "cookies," and "cake," and her video will appear when someone searches for those terms on YouTube.[34] For the hundreds of social networks in the secondary tier, the ones discussed in the Marketing Matters box are among the most widely used by college students today.

OK Go, a music group, watched downloaded songs from the Internet cause a meltdown in its CD sales and experienced difficulty in getting its own record label. So it used YouTube to win fans, licensees, and sponsors for its *very* offbeat music creations. OK Go's YouTube music videos—what it calls "treadmill videos"—are the foundation for its success. Examples include: an animation with 2,300 pieces of toast, the first-ever Rube Goldberg machine that operates in time to music, and paintball guns. OK Go is an example of unknown musicians using YouTube to achieve music success, a route far different than trying to attract attention from a music label company.[35]

Guidelines for marketing and promoting a brand using YouTube videos include:[36]

- Exploit visual aspects of your message, perhaps sacrificing product messages to tell a more entertaining story.
- Create a branded channel rich in key words to improve the odds of the video showing up in user searches.
- Target viewers by using YouTube's insights and analytics research to reveal the number of views, the number of visits to your website, and what key words are driving user visits.

Video 16-1
OK Go Music
kerin.tv/cr6e/v16-1

For how OK Go has used "This Too Shall Pass" (40 million views) on YouTube to gain fans, licensees, live shows, and sponsors, see the text.

Of special interest to brand managers: In 2014, YouTube started guaranteeing its audience size to advertisers—airing additional ads across its channels until they reach a specified percentage of the target audience.[37]

INTEGRATING SOCIAL MEDIA INTO TODAY'S MARKETING STRATEGIES

LO 16-3 Describe the differing roles of those receiving messages through traditional versus social media and how brand managers select a social network.

Thousands of marketing managers around the globe understand how to use traditional media to generate sales for their brand. Some are successful, and others are not. But many of these same managers will admit that social networks are so complex they are not sure how best to use them.

This section looks at (1) how social media tie to the strategic marketing process, (2) how to select a social network, (3) how social media can be used to generate sales, and (4) how to measure the results of social media programs. The section closes by describing Carmex's "Shot Seen 'Round the World" promotion. The ultimate dream for a brand manager, this Carmex–LeBronJames.com promotion went viral on YouTube!

Social Media and the Strategic Marketing Process

The strategic marketing process described in Chapter 2 and the communication process from sender to receiver in Chapter 14 apply to both traditional and social media. But note these important differences in the communication process:

- Traditional media like magazine or TV ads generally use one-way communication from sender to receiver, those whom the marketer hopes will buy the product advertised. A little word-of-mouth chatting may occur among the "passive receivers," but communications generally end with the receiver.
- Social media deliberately seek to ensure that the message *does not end* with an individual receiver. Instead, the goal is to reach "active receivers," those who will become "influentials" and be "delighted" with the brand advertised. These customers will then become "evangelists," who will send messages to their online friends and then back to the advertiser about the joys of using the brand.

Success in social media marketing relies heavily on the ability of a marketing program to convert passive "receivers" of the message to active "evangelists" who will spread favorable messages about the brand.

Selecting the Social Network

In using social media, a brand manager tries to select and use one or more social networks from the hundreds that exist. This often entails assessing (1) the characteristics of these visitors and (2) the number of users or unique visitors to the website.

Audience Data Available for Social Networks Both marketing research organizations and the social networks themselves provide user profile data for the social media to help brand managers choose among them. As presented earlier, the top row of Figure 16–2 shows a recent profile of the U.S. male–female audience breakdown for four major social networks. As shown in the figure, Facebook users are 54 percent female and 46 percent male, while Twitter users are the reverse, important differences to brand managers allocating promotion budgets.[38]

FIGURE 16–4

FIGURE 16–4
The number of U.S. unique visitors and visits for four social network sites: YouTube, Facebook, Twitter, and LinkedIn.

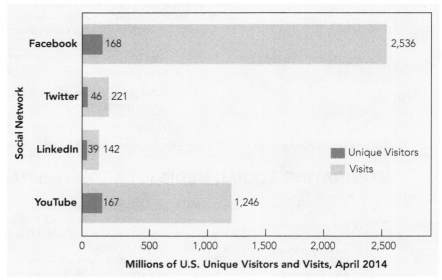

Source: Data provided by Compete, Inc.

Recent Activity on the Four Social Networks   Figure 16–4 compares the unique visitors and visits in the U.S. to the Facebook, Twitter, LinkedIn, and YouTube websites in early 2014. *Unique visitors* is a measure of popularity, each visitor being counted only once. *Visits* is a measure of loyalty, multiple visits by the same visitor being included in the count. In terms of millions of unique visitors to their U.S. websites, Facebook and YouTube are the leaders—both having slightly under 170 million unique visitors per month. For U.S. monthly visits, Facebook leads with almost 1.25 billion visits.[39]

How Social Media Produce Sales

An example shows how a PepsiCo brand manager can use social media to produce sales and profits for her product or brand. Consider the roles of both the PepsiCo brand manager and social media in the following example.[40]

Role of the PepsiCo Brand Manager   The PepsiCo brand manager composes title, copy, and images or photos for the social network ad. She often specifies the web address to which its ad should link based on the brand's social media marketing goals. To increase awareness and build up a fan base, she might link the ad to the PepsiCo website or its Facebook, Twitter, or Pinterest sites. Ideally, to encourage and produce new sales that can be tracked, she must link the ad to a coupon code, a specific product on the PepsiCo website, or other promotional offer.

The brand manager then defines the characteristics of the one or more market segments she wants to reach on the social media she has selected. This starts with demographic characteristics like geographic region, sex, age range, and education. She then adds factors like relationship status and user interests.

Video 16-2
Pepsi MAX
kerin.tv/cr6e/v16-2

Role of Social Media   Ads and videos on social media like YouTube and Facebook are less likely than traditional print ads to have a marketing objective of immediate sales. This is because social network images are often on the screen for only seconds. A more likely goal is to have viewers go to the advertiser's website and post it on their Facebook Pages or forward it to friends. The key for a brand manager using social media is to gain viewers' attention for a few extra seconds.

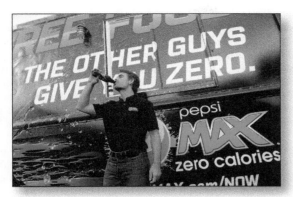

In choosing to run a social media ad campaign like this Pepsi MAX video on YouTube, brand managers must assess the potential sales likely to result compared to a campaign using traditional media.

PepsiCo's 2013 "Test Drive" YouTube video is an example of this strategy. Building on its highly successful "Uncle Drew" videos and TV ads, PepsiCo used its entertaining "Test Drive" video to promote its Pepsi MAX beverages—a zero-calorie cola. In the video, NASCAR driver Jeff Gordon is disguised as "Mike," an average guy taking a test drive at a local dealership. The unsuspecting car salesman riding along will never forget it!

"Test Drive" was a huge hit for Pepsi MAX, with over 35 million views in its first two months. Even better, the video reinforces the product's tag line of "a great-tasting, zero-calorie cola in disguise." As a product in the mature stage of its product life cycle, Pepsi MAX uses an entertaining message to make its diet beverages relevant to a younger target audience. The video captures the viewer's attention by replacing some product messaging with entertainment.[41]

Measuring the Results of Social Media Programs

Performance measures for social media can be divided into (1) those linked to inputs or costs (Figure 16–5) and (2) those tied to the outputs or revenues resulting from social media. Clearly, the ideal performance measure for both conventional and social media is one that ties actual sales revenues to the cost of the ad or other promotion. With the explosion in the growth of social media, marketing and brand managers are being challenged to connect the cost of these new social network promotions to the sales they generate. The result has been an emergence of many new performance measures, often requiring a whole new language.

Compare the performance measures of social media linked to costs (inputs) versus revenues (outputs).

Performance Measures Linked to Inputs or Costs   Figure 16–5 shows three performance measures for social networks linked mainly to inputs or costs. Moving down the list of measures shown in Figure 16–5, one starts with a measure tied only to costs (the cost per thousand measure) and then moves to a measure linked more closely to the sales revenues generated from the social media ad or action (cost per action, or CPA).

FIGURE 16–5
Performance measures for social networks linked mainly to inputs or costs, as seen by a brand manager.

Performance Measure	Costs to Advertisers	Who Provides It	Who Uses It	An Assessment	
				Advantages	Disadvantages
Cost per thousand (CPM)	"I will pay $0.50 for every 1,000 times this ad loads, up to $100 per month."	Small websites that sell ads directly (may be using a third-party service)	Advertisers who simply want to build "awareness"	Simple to use	Impressions don't always lead to sales
Cost per click (CPC)	"I will pay $1.00 for every visitor who clicks on this ad and goes from your website to mine."	Most websites use this method— executed by a third party like Google/AdWords	Advertisers who want to pay for success, but may not be able to track sales from advertisement to purchase	I only pay for a visitor who has expressed an interest in my ad.	Ads may not display if they are a poor fit for the viewing audience
Cost per action (CPA)	"I will pay $5 for every purchase that originates from an ad on your site."	Usually executed through third parties; Google AdSense offers this feature	Sophisticated advertisers who want to pay for success	I only pay for what works.	Similar to CPC but harder to track and more expensive per action

The cost per thousand (CPM) measure ties to the number of times the ad loads and a user might see it—but not whether the user has actually reacted to it. This measure is roughly equivalent to the CPM for traditional media discussed in Chapter 15. The cost per click (CPC) measure gives the rate the advertiser pays, say to Facebook, every time a visitor clicks on the ad and jumps from that page to the advertiser's website. Finally, the cost per action (CPA) measure ties loosely to actual sales—for example, paying $5 for every purchase that originates from an ad, say, on the Facebook site. By summing up the revenues from all these purchases, a difficult task, this CPA measure most closely ties the cost of the social media ad to the sales revenues the ad generates.

Performance Measures Linked to Outputs or Revenues Many of the measures for evaluating how a brand manager's social network promotion is doing reflect the two-way communications present in social media. These measures often tie to output results in terms of "fans," "friends," "followers," or "visitors" to a social network site, which can be a first step to estimating the sales revenue generated. From a brand manager's viewpoint, here are some of the frequently used Facebook measures, moving from the more general to the more specific:

- *Users/members.* Individuals who have registered on a social networking site by completing the process involved, such as providing their name, user ID (usually an e-mail address), and password, as well as answering a few questions (date of birth, gender, etc.).
- *Fans.* The number of people who have opted in to a brand's messages through a social media platform at a given time.
- *Share of voice.* The brand's share or percentage of all the online social media chatter related to, say, its product category or a topic.
- *Page views.* The number of times a Facebook Page is loaded in a given time period.
- *Visitors.* The total number of visitors to a Facebook Page in a given time period; if someone visits three times in one day, she is counted three times.
- *Unique visitors.* The total number of unique visitors to a Facebook Page in a given time period; if someone visits three times in one day, he is counted only once.
- *Average Page views per visitor.* Page views divided by visitors in a given time period.
- *Interaction rate.* The number of people who interact with a Post ("like," make a comment, and so on) divided by the total number of people seeing the Post.
- *Click-through rate (CTR).* Percentage of recipients who have clicked on a link on the Page to visit a specific site.
- *Fan source.* Where a social network following comes from—with fans coming from a friend being more valuable than those coming from an ad.

Pinterest allows users to "pin" or share images of favorite interests on its site, which is useful for brand managers promoting their company's products.

Note that while sales revenues resulting from social media do not appear in these measures, as we move down the list, the measures are often more specific than comparable ones used in traditional media. This is because it is far simpler to electronically track the social network users who click on a website or ad than it is to track consumers who watch, listen to, or read traditional media.

Specialized Focus for Other Social Networks One of the advantages of social media is that communities can form around ideas and commonalities, regardless of the physical location of their members. While major social networks such as Facebook or YouTube may garner the majority of the traffic, smaller networks like Pinterest may be more successful for some products and services.

Pinterest, a virtual pinboard and content-sharing social network, allows people to "pin" or share images of their favorite things such as clothing, craft ideas, home décor, and recipes. Pinterest members

The Shot	Nothing but Net!	LeBron's Bear Hug

Achieving a brand manager's wildest dream! The text describes how the Carmex "shot seen 'round the world" achieved this dream—including 30 million YouTube viewers.

create customized, themed "pinboards" to categorize their images such as "Odds & Ends," "Food," and "Knitting" shown on the Pinterest screen. These images are shared with other members of the Pinterest community. Members can also share their pinned images on Facebook and Twitter.[42]

Pinterest has over 70 million users, 80 percent of whom are women—with 75 percent of daily traffic coming through mobile applications.[43] So it has become a major sales driver for retailers and manufacturers that target women. In using Pinterest, brand managers can post images of their company's products on their Pinterest board and link them back to their websites.

Carmex Goes Viral with Luck and a LeBron James Bear Hug

Brand managers dream about their stars aligning—having their promotions go viral and reaping millions of dollars worth of free brand exposure. Carmex lip balm had this experience!

Video 16-3
Carmex
kerin.tv/cr6e/v16-3

The Background   As noted earlier in the chapter, Carmex has a partnership with LeBronJames.com. It started when the firm found out that LeBron James of the NBA's Miami Heat professional basketball team uses Carmex in his pre-game routine.

The Half-Court Hero Contest   As part of their partnership, Carmex created the "Carmex and LeBronJames.com Half-Court Hero" promotion in 2012. The promotion featured an online entry form and weekly prizes leading up to a grand prize drawing for one lucky winner to travel to Miami and have the chance to take a half-court shot worth $75,000. The "Hero" part meant that if the winner hit the shot—made the basket—Carmex would also donate $75,000 to the LeBron James Family Foundation and the Boys and Girls Clubs of America.

On January 25, 2013, Michael Drysch walked to center court at American Airlines Arena between the third and fourth quarters of the Miami Heat–Detroit Pistons game in front of a sold-out crowd of 20,000 fans. Michael carefully aligned himself just left of center court, took two steps, and launched a one-handed hook shot.

Nothing but net!! And $75,000 richer!

The crowd erupted as Michael turned and pumped his fist. But before he could celebrate any further, LeBron himself came running out of his Miami Heat huddle to bearhug Michael to the ground in a moment of pure jubilation.

The "Shot Seen 'Round the World" Goes Viral   Instantly, the footage of Half-Court Hero winner Michael Drysch's incredible hook shot and the celebratory bear hug from LeBron James went viral online. NBATV interviewed him side-by-side with James after the game. It was the #1 Play of the Day on ESPN's SportsCenter. The Carmex brand team immediately arranged a public relations tour for Michael Drysch that included a trip to New York City for appearances on *Good Morning America*, *Inside Edition*, *CNN Early Start*, and dozens of local radio shows.

Meanwhile, the Carmex marketing team kept Carmex's social media accounts and website updated throughout the weekend with Twitter and Facebook Posts from the

417

CHAPTER 16   Using Social Media to Connect with Consumers

Michael Drysch receives his reward for sinking his unlikely hook shot in the "Carmex and LeBronJames.com 'Half-Court Hero'" promotion. Also benefiting were the LeBron James Family Foundation and the Boys and Girls Clubs of America!

public relations tour. Within three months, Carmex's Half-Court Hero shot had been seen by over 30 million YouTube viewers and became the most-watched video of all time on the National Basketball Association's YouTube page. In all, the promotion earned Carmex over 500 million media impressions across TV, print, online, and social media.[44]

Later, Michael and "The Shot" were featured in an ESPN commercial as part of their "I was on Sports Center" campaign. In January 2014, the Miami Heat visited President Barack Obama to recognize their 2013 National Basketball Association Championship. President Obama, a big basketball fan himself, even referred to Michael and the Carmex Half-Court Hero shot by saying:

Now, one of the cool things about this job is welcoming championship sports teams from across the sporting world to the White House. And usually people enjoy coming to the White House. I have to say, I've never seen folks more excited than the Heat when they came last year. (Laughter.) I mean, LeBron was so pumped up I thought he was going to give me a hug and knock me over like the guy on SportsCenter who hit the half-court shot.[45]

Social Media Lessons for Brand Managers   "The lesson for brand managers is this: Watch for opportunities to manage luck," says Patrick Hudgdon, digital strategist who managed the promotion for Carmex. "Small, smart investments can pay off in big ways when your brand gets lucky. Find ways to use *both* social and traditional media—as we did for Carmex—to help the campaign go viral and to maximize the opportunity to achieve even greater success. Be ready!"

> **learning review**
>
> 16-7. What is the difference between and marketing significance of a "passive receiver" for conventional media and an "active receiver" for social media?
>
> 16-8. Stated simply, how can an advertiser on Facebook expect to generate sales?
>
> 16-9. What did the Carmex team do to exploit its incredible good fortune after seeing Michael Drysch make his "Half-Court Hero" shot?

THE FUTURE: SOCIAL MEDIA + SMARTPHONES + EXOTIC APPS

 LO 16-5 Identify the cause of the convergence of the real and digital worlds and how this will affect the future of social media.

Trends in marketing's use of social media reflect what scientists call "mirror worlds" or "smart systems" that are really the convergence of the real and digital worlds. A *smart system* is a computer-based network that triggers actions by sensing changes in the real or digital world. This section discusses: (1) the convergence of real and digital worlds; (2) how this convergence links social media to marketing actions; and (3) where all this *may* be headed in *your* future.

The Convergence of Real and Digital Worlds

Saying that our physical and virtual worlds are converging sounds like science fiction. This convergence of real and digital worlds is the result of a proliferation of inter-linked smartphones, tablet devices, sensors, special identification tags, databases, algorithms, apps, and other elements. A look at several of these elements helps explain this real world–digital world convergence and what it means for marketing.

Smartphones   Seeing today's smartphones, users often forget how far they've come in 15 years and how they've changed marketing. In 1998, the RIM 950 revolutionized mobile e-mail. The device had a screen and a keyboard—but *no phone*. The revolution was completed in 2007 with Apple's legendary iPhone. It had all three basics—screen, multitouch keyboard, and phone. Today's GPS-enabled smartphones give mobile consumers access to online ads, local restaurant promotions, and time-sensitive discounts at retailers.[46]

Databases and Algorithms   As discussed in Chapters 7 and 8, finding prospective customers often involves market segmentation that requires databases searched with exotic algorithms—models used to query, organize, manipulate, and present data. The owners of these databases, among them Google and Facebook, must make them as useful as possible to potential advertisers in order to succeed.

The product life cycle of even very successful video game apps can reach the decline stage quickly—as shown by the Angry Birds game.

Among databases, Google is the hands-down winner—indexing 30 trillion unique web pages across 230 million sites. Its search engine now gives results in answers to research queries in photos, facts, and "direct answers," and not just the "blue links" of website addresses. Google now offers its own social networking service, Google+, to obtain data about individuals by name, personal interests, and identities of friends.[47]

In 2013, Facebook entered Google's territory by announcing Graph Search, its own search engine algorithm. Facebook users can conduct their own queries about people, places, photos, and interests. An example is "restaurants recommended by friends." This lets Facebook give advertisers real value in the "likes" found on its site. For example, a small chocolate retail shop in New York City can target (1) young parents (2) who buy lots of organic food products.[48] So it's not difficult to see how a casual "like" for a brand by a user in a database's "digital world" can converge into an actual "real world" purchase by the user through a very targeted promotion planned by a brand manager.

apps
Small, downloadable software programs that run on smartphones and tablet devices.

Video 16-4
Clash of Clans
kerin.tv/cr6e/v16-4

Apps   The apps for smartphones are accelerating the convergence of the real and digital worlds. **Apps** (or *mobile apps* or *applications*) are small, downloadable software programs that run on smartphones and tablet devices. When Apple launched its iPhone, it didn't expect smartphone apps to be very important. Wrong! By 2013, Apple's App Store offered over 900,000 apps either free or for sale. Google Play has over 800,000 apps for users of Android devices. With the wide array of apps to choose from, today's consumers typically spend two hours a day using about eight apps.[49]

Many apps are video games. Angry Birds is an example of a video game app in the declining stage of its product life cycle (PLC). Although downloaded more than 2 billion times since its 2009 release, this app was in decline stage by 2013, a reason the Angry Birds–themed products now range from mascara to toys and entertainment parks.[50] The video games Farmville, Temple Run, QuizUp, 4Pics1Word, and Fruit Ninja show the short PLC for these apps in today's tough competition.

Enter Clash of Clans and Candy Crush Saga video games that exploit the real world–digital world convergence. Today's successful new video games (1) build on a huge personal-rewards psychology for players; (2) can be played on the small smartphone screens; (3) top the most-downloaded charts of Apple iOS, Google, Android, and Facebook; and (4) often use a "freemium strategy"— where the download is free but users pay for extra features, such as for ways to speed up the game.

419

CHAPTER 16   Using Social Media to Connect with Consumers

Time magazine analyzes how designers of the Candy Crush video game (Figure 16–6) use its key elements to link the *digital world* of Candy Crush to the personal *real-world* satisfactions and rewards of its players:[51]

* *It's better with friends.* Users can give—and get—extra lives using Facebook.
* *It never ends.* There are over 500 levels, and designers add more almost every week.
* *It makes the player feel special.* The game gives positive feedback for nearly every click and tap.
* *It lets a player—sort of—cheat.* Players can pay for power-ups to skip past wait times.
* *It's challenging.* Increasingly varied puzzles often take multiple attempts to complete.

By 2014 the Candy Crush app had been installed over 500 million times across Facebook, iOS, and Android devices.

Even Angry Birds has changed its strategy from charging a download cost to a freemium strategy with its recently launched "Angry Birds Go." Sound easy to build an app? Maybe. But hundreds of creative apps die a quiet death each year!

FIGURE 16–6
The text describes the strategy Candy Crush Saga uses to link the technical power of the *digital world* to the human psychology of its players in the *real world*.

Mobile Marketing: Tightening Links to Marketing Actions

This convergence of the real and digital worlds has resulted in increasing use of *mobile marketing*, or any marketing activity conducted through several Internet networks to which consumers are continuously connected using a personal mobile device.[52] This continuous connection present in mobile marketing has led to important smartphone apps, such as:

* *Price-comparison searches.* Scan product bar codes or QR codes and research 500,000 stores, synchronizing searches between your computer and your smartphone.
* *Location-based promotions.* Use your GPS-enabled smartphone for location check-ins to receive discounts at stores such as JCPenney.
* *Loyalty programs.* Win loyalty points for walking into stores like Target or Macy's and receive discounts from them.

The number of smartphone shopping searches and purchases has exploded in recent years, causing huge challenges (such as showrooming) for conventional brick-and-mortar retailers.

Where to Now?

The clear point of difference in mobile marketing is its unique ability to empower users by connecting with them individually and continuously—learning about their likes and personal characteristics and sharing this information with online friends and (often) marketers selling products. This socially networked world will lead to connected users having more direct interactions with sellers.

The convergence of social media, smartphones, tablet devices, and new apps will lead to companies having a more dynamic interaction with their customers. But is this an unqualified success for buyers? Consider the following perspectives.

A Consumer Purchase Where Sensors Have Some Control A vending machine scans your face to identify your age and sex and changes its display and—in the future—may give you a quantity discount for buying two of your favorite candy bars (it knows about your Facebook "likes") while showing an electronic dinner coupon for a nearby restaurant if you appear between 7:00 and 9:00 P.M. this evening. The results of the candy and dinner offer are directly measurable for marketers. While it offers unusual convenience, does this buying situation start to interfere with your personal privacy?

Too busy to visit your grocery store this week? If you are in South Korea or China, you can shop on the wall of your subway station with your smartphone—and have your purchases delivered to your door!

A Consumer Purchase Where the Buyer Controls All Some cities in South Korea and China are on the leading edge of virtual supermarket shopping. Tesco Home Plus, a South Korean supermarket chain, provides a quick spur-of-the-moment opportunity for grocery shopping. Shoppers use their smartphones to scan images on the wall of a subway station to buy Tesco's grocery products while waiting for their train. They use the smartphone app to pay for the groceries, which are delivered to their door right after they get home.[53] In this example, buyers achieve great convenience—probably an unqualified success.

On Privacy: How Much "Convergence" Is Too Much? Smart systems are fine up to a point. For example, most of us are comfortable letting convergence find us a timely deal at a local restaurant using a location-based app on our smartphone. It may even be all right if Google's latest database breakthrough automatically proposes an "ideal vacation plan" for us based on our normal preferences, weather conditions, and available hotel and airline prices.

But we may be concerned if retailers now place sensors in several hundred locations to track us following the signals emitted from our Wi-Fi-enabled smartphone. Here are some other numbers that may frighten you:

- 2000-plus. Estimated number of times the online activity of an average Internet user is tracked every day.
- 3000-plus. Number of "shopping tendencies" Acxiom says it can measure for nearly every U.S. household.
- 700 million. Approximate number of adult consumers in the global database of Acxiom Corp., a leading data broker.

About 68 percent of Internet users today feel that privacy laws don't protect them adequately. So 86 percent of them have used privacy technologies to take online steps to remove or mask their digital data.[54]

The future? Concerned about Internet privacy, the White House in 2014 announced it would seek legislation to define the rights of consumers in the use of data involving their personal characteristics and activities.

learning review

16-10. What is an example of how the real (physical) and digital (virtual) worlds are converging?

16-11. What are apps and why are they important?

16-12. Can personal privacy become a problem as the real and digital worlds converge with smart systems?

LEARNING OBJECTIVES REVIEW

LO 16-1 *Define social media and describe how they differ from traditional advertising media.*

Social media are online media where users submit comments, photos, and videos, often accompanied by a feedback process to identify "popular" topics. Social media differ from traditional advertising media (newspapers, magazines, radio, and television) in that user-generated content (1) is relatively inexpensive to create, publish, and access, (2) requires little training to develop, (3) can

deliver virtually instantaneous responses, (4) can quickly alter and repost, and (5) may not be as private or anonymous as users expect.

LO 16-2 *Identify the four major social networks and how brand managers integrate them into marketing actions.*

Four major social networks are Facebook, Twitter, LinkedIn, and YouTube. Facebook is a social network where users create a personal profile, add other users as "friends," and exchange comments, photos, videos, and "likes" with them. To increase traffic to a Facebook Page, brand managers can use paid ads and sponsored stories. Twitter enables users to send and receive "tweets," messages up to 140 characters long. For Twitter, brand managers can use monitoring programs to track what people are saying about their organization's brand. LinkedIn lets users post their personal profiles to a network of business-people. LinkedIn can be used to create a company profile to share brand information and career opportunities with LinkedIn users and to demonstrate the company's expertise and professionalism. YouTube is a video-sharing website where users can upload, view, and comment on videos. YouTube also allows marketers to create a brand channel to promote a product, show ads for it, and have viewers comment on it.

LO 16-3 *Describe the differing roles of those receiving messages through traditional versus social media and how brand managers select a social network.*

With promotional messages received through traditional media, recipients are generally "passive receivers" and the communication ends with them. In contrast, recipients of social media messages are "active receivers," and the company sending them messages hopes they will become "evangelists" and send positive messages back to the company and to online friends. The factors a marketer uses to select a specific social network involve assessing (1) the number of registered users and unique visitors to the company's website, (2) the characteristics (or profile) of those visitors, and (3) the focus of the social network. Also, because each social network has a unique focus (videos, short text messaging, and so on), marketers

can modify their marketing programs to take advantage of these differences.

LO 16-4 *Compare the performance measures of social media linked to costs (inputs) versus revenues (outputs).*

Performance measures linked to costs (inputs) include (1) cost per thousand (similar to the CPM for a print ad), which is the number of times an ad is displayed to a user; (2) cost per click (CPC), which gives the rate the advertiser pays each time a visitor clicks on the ad and then jumps to the advertiser's web page; and (3) cost per action (CPA), which is the amount paid for every purchase that originates from an ad on a social media network site. Examples of performance measures linked to revenues (outputs) include (1) users/members that have registered on social media websites; (2) the number of unique monthly users viewing the website at a given time; (3) page views, or the number of times a specific web page is loaded; and (4) visitors, or the total number of users viewing a particular web page during a specified time period.

LO 16-5 *Identify the cause of the convergence of the real and digital worlds and how this will affect the future of social media.*

The convergence of the real and digital worlds in social networking is the result of the proliferation of interlinked smartphones, tablet devices, sensors, RFIDs, databases, algorithms, apps, and other elements. This convergence will allow consumers and marketers to increase the exchange of personal and product-related information with each other. For consumers, however, this could lead to a loss of privacy and possible exploitation by unscrupulous marketers.

LEARNING REVIEW ANSWERS

16-1 **What are social media?**
Answer: Social media are online media where users submit comments, photos, and videos—often accompanied by a feedback process to identify "popular" topics. Business firms also refer to social media as "consumer-generated media." A single social media site is a social network.

16-2 **In classifying social media, what do we mean by (a) media richness and (b) self-disclosure?**
Answer: Social media can be classified based on two factors: (a) Media richness involves the degree of acoustic, visual, and personal contact between two communication partners. For example, face-to-face communication is higher in media richness than telephone or e-mail communication. The higher the media richness and quality of presentation, the greater the social influence that these communication partners have on each other's behavior. (b) Self-disclosure involves the degree to which an individual shares his or her thoughts, feelings, likes, and dislikes when engaged in a social interaction. The greater the self-disclosure, the greater the likelihood that the person will increase his or her influence on those reached.

16-3 **Compare traditional media and social media in terms of time required to deliver the communication.**
Answer: Traditional media can involve days or even months of continuing effort to deliver the communication,

and time lags can be extensive. In contrast, individuals using social media can post virtually instantaneous content.

16-4 **How is user-generated content presented by someone using Facebook?**
Answer: User-generated content (UGC) refers to the various forms of online media content that are publicly available and created by end users. Facebook users create a personal profile, add other users as friends, and exchange comments, photos, videos, and "likes" with them. Additionally, users may chat with friends and create and join common-interest groups.

16-5 **What are some ways brand managers use Facebook to converse with a brand's fans?**
Answer: A brand manager can create awareness for a product, service, or brand by creating a Facebook Page for it. So Facebook allows brand managers to request a range of user data like addresses and phone numbers—with the users' permission (an "opt-in" approach). To generate new customers and increase traffic to their Facebook Pages, brand managers can use paid ads and sponsored stories within the Facebook advertising platform. The marketing challenge for a Facebook Page is to post and create the content that will generate the best response. An advantage of a Facebook ad for a brand is

that it can migrate into Facebook conversations among friends—to the delight of advertisers.

16-6 **How can brand managers use YouTube to converse with customers?**

YouTube allows brand managers to create an actual brand channel to host its advertisements and other video clips that can explain or demonstrate complex products. YouTube can also link to a brand's website. YouTube, because it is a visual medium, allows a brand manager to entertain as well as inform users about the brand. YouTube traffic goes directly to the video; a hyperlink is needed to get users back to the brand's website.

16-7 **What is the difference between and marketing significance of a "passive receiver" for conventional media and an "active receiver" for social media?**

Answer: Traditional media, like magazine or TV ads, generally use one-way communication from the sender to the receiver, whom the marketer hopes will buy the product advertised. A little word-of-mouth chatting may occur among the consumer "passive receivers," but communications generally end with the receiver. Social media deliberately seek to ensure that the message does not end with an individual receiver. Instead, the goal is to reach "active receivers," those who will become "influentials" and be "delighted" with the brand advertised. These will then become "evangelists," who will send messages—user-generated content—to their online friends and then back to the advertiser about the joys of using the brand. So success in social media marketing relies heavily on the ability of a marketing program to convert passive "receivers" of the message to active "evangelists" who will spread favorable messages about the brand.

16-8 **Stated simply, how can an advertiser on Facebook expect to generate sales?**

Answer: The brand manager composes title, copy, and images or photos for an ad to be placed on Facebook. A website address links the ad to the brand's website or its Facebook Page. To encourage and produce new sales that can be tracked, the brand manager might also link the ad to a coupon code or some other promotional offer.

16-9 **What did the Carmex team do to exploit its incredible good fortune after seeing Michael Drysch make his "Half-Court Hero" shot?**

Answer: On January 25, 2013, at a Miami Heat–Detroit Pistons game, Michael Drysch did the impossible and made Carmex's Half-Court Hero basketball shot. LeBron James came running out of his Miami Heat huddle—congratulating Michael with a bear hug. Instantly, the footage of Half-Court Hero winner Michael Drysch's incredible hook shot and the celebratory bear hug from LeBron James went viral online. The Carmex brand team immediately arranged a public relations tour for Drysch that included four Miami area news stations and a trip to New York City for appearances on several TV and radio shows. Meanwhile, the Carmex marketing team kept Carmex's social media accounts and website updated throughout the weekend with Twitter and Facebook posts from the public relations tour. Within three months, Carmex's Half-Court Hero shot had been seen by over 20 million YouTube viewers.

16-10 **What is an example of how the real (physical) and digital (virtual) worlds are converging?**

Answer: The convergence of real and digital worlds is the result of a proliferation of interlinked smartphones, tablet devices, sensors, special identification tags, databases, algorithms, apps, and other elements. For example, GPS-enabled smartphones give mobile consumers access to online ads, local restaurant promotions, and time-sensitive discounts at retailers. In addition, apps for smartphones are accelerating the convergence of the real and digital worlds as they make the devices more productive and provide users with entertainment. Finally, marketers can tailor specific messages to targeted users by using their personal data and preferences so that they can order products and services as a result of receiving these offers.

16-11 **What are apps and why are they important?**

Answer: Apps are small, downloadable software programs that run on smartphones and tablet devices. They are speeding up the convergence of the real (physical) and digital (virtual) worlds. Many apps are related to social media, such as programs for (1) price-comparison searches, (2) loyalty programs, (3) location-based promotions, and (4) entertainment, such as video games, music, and others.

16-12 **Can personal privacy become a problem as the real and digital worlds converge with smart systems?**

Answer: The convergence of social media, smartphones, tablet devices, and new apps will lead to companies having a more dynamic interaction with their customers. This convergence allows for the collection of users' personal data, preferences, and behaviors, which allows marketers to tailor offerings based on these data. A recent analysis of Facebook users revealed that the "likes" they posted can reveal their political and religious views, drug use, and marital status. The issue is, do we want others to know all this information about us?

FOCUSING ON KEY TERMS

apps p. 419
blog p. 404
Facebook p. 406

LinkedIn p. 410
social media p. 403
Twitter p. 409

user-generated content (UGC) p. 404
YouTube p. 411

APPLYING MARKETING KNOWLEDGE

1 In the chapter opener, why was Kimmy Summers more successful using Facebook and Twitter to get volunteers and promote freshman move-in day at her university than she might have been using more conventional print media?

2 You and three college friends have decided to launch an online business selling clothes college students wear—T-shirts, shorts, sweats, and so on. You plan to use Facebook ads. What "likes" or interests do (*a*) college men and (*b*) college women have that might help you in planning your Facebook strategy?

3 You are about to graduate from college and want a job in marketing research or sales. Go to the LinkedIn site, register, and determine what information you would put on your LinkedIn profile to help you find a new job.

4 What is the significance of user-generated content when contrasted with social media and traditional media?

5 You are a brand manager for a sneaker manufacturer like Nike or New Balance and are trying to use Facebook to reach (*a*) college-age women and (*b*) men over 55 years of age. What three or four "likes" or interests would you expect each segment to have when you try to reach it with Facebook?

6 In measuring the results of a social network, what are the (*a*) advantages and (*b*) disadvantages of performance measures linked directly to revenues versus costs?

BUILDING YOUR MARKETING PLAN

Remembering the target market segments you identified in Chapter 8 for your marketing plan:

1 (*a*) Identify which one of the four social networks described in the chapter would be most useful and (*b*) give your reasons. Would you consider other social networks like Pinterest? Why or why not?

2 Briefly describe (*a*) how you would use this social network to try to increase sales of your products and (*b*) why you expect target market customers to respond to it.

VIDEO CASE 16 | StuffDOT™, Inc.: Rewarding Users for Actively Shopping and Sharing!

> Video 16-5
> **StuffDOT**
> **Video Case**
> kerin.tv/cr6e/v16-5

"Coming from a rewards and loyalty background, I often wondered how to combine the best of rewards with the expanding universe of social media," says Jennifer Katz, founder and chief executive officer of StuffDOT, Inc.

"Further, it seemed really unfair that only a few people were benefiting from all the content millions of people were providing for free online. I believe the individuals creating all this online content deserve to benefit from their efforts," says Katz.

"Thinking about this, one day our marketing director came into a meeting and explained how a really cute anchor bracelet that she posted on a social sharing site went viral. But now she faced a six-week backlog to purchase it. So we all said, if she made a commission on every anchor bracelet that was sold because of that one post, she could have bought five. Right then and there, StuffDOT was born," explains Katz.

While the young social network is constantly changing, its beginnings in 2013 offer a valuable case study.

StuffDOT's VISION, BRAND NAME, AND LOGO

StuffDot is designed to be the all-in-one site for online shopping and sharing. StuffDOT's vision is to reward users for what they are already doing online. Most other sites tend to keep all the affiliate fees and commissions for themselves. StuffDOT, however, enables users to benefit from all this online shopping and sharing. This is the first time, to StuffDOT's knowledge, that a firm has developed a platform where the people posting to social media are the same people who are rewarded for it. In addition, the StuffDOT team has added coupons and loyalty elements that broaden its reach, as well as its value to merchants.

"We chose the brand name StuffDOT because it was catchy and [we] felt we could really build on it," says Katz. "With the name StuffDOT, we could use Stuff, DOT, and StuffDOT, which also gives flexibility. The name also is great for campaigns like 'CareDot,' 'Spot the Dot,' or 'Stuff I Like.' The team tried other names, but they just didn't have that fun stickiness that the name StuffDOT does," says Jennifer Katz.

The StuffDOT team tried and tested several different logos before coming up with its memorable, attention-getting logo shown here. "People see the orange dot as friendly, familiar, and eye-catching. It has proven to be an easy logo to build on," says Amanda Axvig, StuffDOT's marketing director.

HOW StuffDOT WORKS

Kelsey Fisher, StuffDOT's creative director, explains to a group of student interns what a "Dot" is and the steps in "Dotting"—keys to understanding how StuffDOT users earn and redeem their resulting rewards.

What Is a "Dot"?

"Dots are posts ranging all the way from products, Do-It-Yourself projects, recipes, and news stories to funny videos to random photos," Fisher explains. "A dot is something posted to view, to share, or to track for a future purchase. A dot is simply a post of anything you want to display on the StuffDOT site," she says.

How to "Dot"

Kelsey Fisher walks the interns through the three steps to dot:

1. "Use the simple drag-and-drop process to add the 'Dot It' button to your toolbar in your web browser.
2. "Dot or post items you 'like' online by clicking on that button on your toolbar. For example, if you are browsing Macy's online store and see something you like, you can click on the 'Dot It' button in your toolbar and it will show up on your StuffDOT page.
3. "Watch your rewards grow as people share, buy, or click on the stuff you've 'dotted.' You can also earn rewards on your own purchases!" Fisher says.

Earning and Redeeming StuffDOT Rewards

So how does an online user actually earn rewards? "When you find things you want to share or purchase online, you dot or post the item to StuffDOT," says Amanda Axvig. "If the item appears with a red border around it, this means it is from one of our over 20,000 retail sites and is rewards eligible."

"When your dot leads to a purchase or a click-through view or share by you or someone else, you will see your rewards increase," Axvig says. "You can also earn rewards by posting and purchasing your own items. Once your balance reaches $15, you can start redeeming gift cards from a variety of popular retailers."

ENHANCING StuffDOT's USER-FRIENDLINESS

A challenge for the StuffDOT team is keeping it simple, yet having features that make StuffDOT fun and rewarding.

"I work closely with the StuffDOT team to turn the concepts they create into user-friendly features on StuffDOT," says Sudipta Tripathy, StuffDOT's chief technology officer. "For example, we want to ensure that all new features have the same look and feel across all parts of the StuffDOT platform—website, Android app, or iOS app," he says.

Recent updates and features now enable StuffDOT users more ways to earn rewards. By moving many features to its mobile apps (photo), StuffDOT has added the flexibility to share, shop, and earn anywhere at any time.

Some other examples of user-friendly features:

- Retailer List. Adding a list of retailers and their reward percentages lets StuffDOT shoppers know the exact rewards from each store. Also, users can discover reward-eligible shops they did not even know about.
- Search Shops & Deals. Users now can search for products and deals from StuffDOT's retailers without leaving the site. StuffDOT members can then find, dot, and buy reward-eligible items in one easy-to-use platform.
- Rewards Status. The redesigned rewards section shows users the values of their lifetime, current, and pending rewards. So they can track their purchase rewards and confirm their purchases are reward-eligible.

CHAPTER 16   Using Social Media to Connect with Consumers

MARKETING StuffDOT

StuffDOT has focused its initial marketing efforts on three areas: (1) partnerships, (2) the StuffDOT Internship and Campus Ambassador Program, and (3) social sharing.

StuffDOT's partnership works with online affiliate aggregators that give users access to over 20,000 online retailers that share affiliate fees and rewards. In addition, StuffDOT has been working with select retailers to create unique promotional programs that benefit users and make the partner brand more prominent. For example, a recent promotion featured a free pair of running shoes for signing up, referring friends, and dotting. This not only built awareness for the brand of running shoes, but it also created a new user base for StuffDOT.

The StuffDOT Internship and campus ambassador program (photo) not only gives students a rich experience working in new social media, but it has greatly enhanced the benefits of the StuffDOT platform. Student interns work both at the home office and on campus to create StuffDOT promotions. Depending on their interests, students may focus on organizing new-user workshops and street-team promotions or finding new partners and users through social networks. StuffDOT is looking continuously for new

Campus Ambassadors. Applications are submitted through the orange star in the upper left corner of the StuffDot home page.

Major social-sharing features throughout the StuffDOT site make it very convenient for users to share items with friends or family. For example, a student who wants a new laptop for her birthday can share that item with friends on Facebook, and she can also e-mail that item with an embedded link to her parents as a reminder. That student can also earn a StuffDOT reward on the purchase— a "double" birthday present.

Questions

1 What recent StuffDOT actions have added to its user-friendliness?

2 (*a*) Who are StuffDOT's major competitors and (*b*) what point(s) of difference should StuffDOT use to distinguish itself from them?

3 How should StuffDOT be marketed so that it becomes an integral part of everyday life?

4 How can the team create "buzz" for StuffDOT and grow its user base most effectively (*a*) using social media platforms (like Facebook and Twitter) and (*b*) using its own website?

Chapter Notes

1. Natasha Singer, "On Campus, It's One Big Commercial," *The New York Times,* September 11, 2011, pp. BU1, BU4; Natalie Zmuda, "Marketers Hitting Campus Harder Than Ever," *Advertising Age,* October 17, 2011, pp. 26, 28; and Bruce Horovitz, "Marketers Pull an Inside Job on College Campuses," *USA Today,* October 4, 2010, pp. 2A, 2B.

2. Ibid.

3. Ibid.

4. Dave Evans, *Social Media Marketing: An Hour a Day* (Indianapolis, IN: Wiley Publishing, Inc., 2009), pp. 57–59.

5. Andreas M. Kaplan and Michael Haenlein, "Users of the World, Unite! The Challenges and Opportunities of Social Media," *Business Horizons* 53, no. 1 (2010), pp. 59–68.

6. Dave Evans, *Social Media Marketing: An Hour a Day,* pp. 57–59; Jason Miletsky, *Principles of Internet Marketing* (Boston, MA: Course Technology, Cengage Learning, 2010), pp. 75–76; Kristin Tillotson, "Blogging's Getting Old These Days," *Star Tribune,* December 22, 2010, p. E1; and Soumitra Dutta and Matthew Fraser, "Web 2.0: The ROI Case," *CEO Magazine,* May/June 2009, pp. 42–44.

7. "Participative Web and User-Created Content: Web 2.0, Wikis, and Social Networking" (Paris: Organization for Economic Co-operation and Development, 2007); and Jason Daley, "Tearing Down the Walls," *Entrepreneur,* December 2010, pp. 57–60.

8. Kaplan and Haenlein, "Users of the World, Unite!" pp. 62–64.

9. Drake Bennett, "Ten Years of Inaccuracy and Remarkable Detail," *Bloomberg Businessweek,* January 10–January 16, 2011, pp. 57–61.

10. Starr Hall and Chadd Rosenberg, *Get Connected: The Social Networking Toolkit for Business* (Madison, WI: Entrepreneur Press, 2009), pp. 17–20.

11. Figure 16–2 is adapted from "The CMO's Guide to the 2014 Social Landscape." See http://visual.ly/cmos-guide-2014-social-landscape.

12. Lev Grossman, "2010 Person of the Year: Mark Zuckerberg," *Time,* December 27, 2010–January 3, 2011, pp. 44–75.

13. Ashlee Vance, "Your Facebook Data Are Here," *Bloomberg Businessweek,* October 7–October 13, 2013, pp. 42–44.

14. Cooper Smith, "7 Statistics about Facebook Users That Reveal Why It's Such a Powerful Marketing Platform," *Business Insider,* November 16, 2013. See http://www.businessinsider.com/a-primer-on-facebook-demographics.

15. Facebook Statistics. See http://www.statisticbrain.com/facebook-statistics/.

16. Ibid.

17. "Top 10 Ways to Engage Fans on Facebook," Buddy Media, Inc., 2010.

18. Ned Smith, "How Much Is a Facebook Friend Worth? $174.17," *BusinessNewsDaily,* April 26, 2013. See http://www.businessnewsdaily.com/4402-value-facebook-friend-marketing.html.

19. The discussion of StuffDOT was provided by Kelsey Fisher, Jenny Caffoe, Lexi Diederich, and Malyn Mueller of StuffDOT, Inc.

20. Vindu Goel, "Rise in Mobile Ads Pushes Up Facebook Results," *Star Tribune,* January 30, 2014, p. D3; and Evelyn M. Rusli, "For Mark

Zuckerberg, Tumult and Turnaround," *The Wall Street Journal*, January 6, 2014, pp. A1, A10.

21. Rachael Metz, "Facebook Gets More Visual to Keep Its Users Engaged," *MIT Technology Review*, March 7, 2013.

22. Evelyn M. Rusli, "Facebook Unveils Hashtags," *The Wall Street Journal*, June 13, 2013, p. B7.

23. "Getting the Messages: Facebook and Whatsapp," *Star Tribune*, February 24, 2014, p. D4; and Barbara Ortutay, "Facebook Gets into Virtual Reality," *Star Tribune*, March 26, 2014, p. D3.

24. https://about.twitter.com/company.

25. Thomas Lee, "Social-Media Bees Create Target Buzz," *Star Tribune*, April 13, 2013, pp. A1, A6; and Jeff Herring and Maritza Parra, "Make the Most of Tweeting," *Star Tribune*, January 6, 2011, p. E4.

26. Elizabeth Dwoskin and Yoree Koh, "Twitter Pushes Deeper into Data," *The Wall Street Journal*, April 16, 2014, p. B2.

27. Craig Smith, "(March 2014) By the Numbers: 80 Amazing LinkedIn Statistics," *DMR Digital Marketing Ramblings*, February 9, 2014. See http://expandedramblings.com/index.php/by-the-numbers-a-few-import.

28. "LinkedIn Is Trying to Quicken Its Pulse," *Bloomberg Businessweek*, April 22–April 28, 2013, pp. 32–33; Emily Moltby and Shira Ovide, "Which Social Media Work?" *The Wall Street Journal*, January 31, 2013, p. B8; and Brandon Bailey, "Who Needs Friends? LinkedIn Has Success with Members," *Star Tribune*, April 25, 2013, pp. D1, D3.

29. Johnathon Podensky, "LinkedIn Search Just Got Smarter," *LinkedIn Official Blog*, March 25, 2013. See http://blog.linkedIn .com/2013/03/25/linkedin-search-just-got-smarter/.

30. "Building a Great Student Profile," *LinkedIn for Students*. See http://university.linkedin.com/linkedin-for-students.html.

31. Kolby Goodman, "Stand Above the Rest," *Dairy of Alpha Kappa Psi*, Spring, 2014, pp.12–14.

32. YouTube Statistics. See http://www.youtube.com/yt/press/ statistics.html; and Amanda Axvig, Vice President of Marketing, AOI Marketing, Inc.

33. Alex Perry, "The Warlord vs. the Hipsters," *Time*, March 26, 2012, pp. 36–41; and Solomon Moore, "U.S. Plays a Bigger Part in Hunt for Kony," *The Wall Street Journal*, April 30, 2012, p. A16.

34. Brad Stone and Andy Fixmar, "MustSee YouTube," *Bloomberg Businessweek*, May 7–May 13, 2012, pp. 42–44; and Tanzina Vega, "Your Ad, as Seen on YouTube," *Media Decoder: The New York Times*, April 23, 2012.

35. Jonah Weiner, "Video Makes the Radio Star," *Bloomberg Businessweek*, April 1–April 7, 2013, pp. 75–77; Damian Kulash, Jr., "The New Rock Star Paradigm," *The Wall Street Journal*, December 17, 2010, p. D1; and "YouTube Press Room: Statistics." See http://www.youtube.com/t/press_statistics.

36. Christa Toole, "Ten Tips for Those Who Still Aren't Using YouTube," *Advertising Age* (www.adage.com), October 19, 2010; and Felix Gillette, "On YouTube, Seven-Figure Views, Six-Figure Paychecks," *Bloomberg Businessweek*, September 27–October 3, 2010, pp. 35–36.

37. Suzanne Vranica, "YouTube to Offer Guarantees to Advertisers," *The Wall Street Journal*, March 31, 2014, p. B5.

38. Social network male–female breakdown data were provided by Compete, Inc. See https://www.compete.com.

39. Social network unique visitors and visits data for Facebook, Twitter, LinkedIn, and YouTube were provided by Compete, Inc. See https://www.compete.com.

40. This example and the section on measuring results were provided by Brian Stuckey and Amanda Axvig of StuffDOT, Inc.

41. The Jeff Gordon–Pepsi Max example was provided by Nancy Harrower, Concordia University–St. Paul; and Sheila Shayon, "Pepsi Continues to Bask in Branded Content Glory with Top YouTube Views," *Brand Channel*, April 8, 2013. See http://www.brandchannel.com/home/ post/2013/04/08/Pepsi-Tops-YouTube-Leaderboard-040813.aspx.

42. Mae Anderson. "A Look at Why Social Media Site Pinterest Is Catnip to Retailers and Shoppers Alike," *Star Tribune*, April 25, 2014. See startribune.com.

43. Craig Smith, "(April 2014) By the Numbers: 65 Amazing Pinterest Stats," *DMR Digital Marketing Ramblings*, March 4, 2014. See http://expandedramblings.com/index.php/pinterest-stats/.

44. The Carmex "Half-Court Hero" example was written by Patrick Hodgdon, Digital Strategist, Bolin Marketing.

45. See http://www.whitehouse.gov/photos-and-video/video/ 2014/01/14/president-obama-honors-2013-nba-champion-miami-heat#transcript.

46. Sam Grobart, "Think Colossal," *Bloomberg Businessweek*, April 1, 2013, pp. 58–64.

47. Evelyn M. Rusli and Amir Efrati, "Facebook on Collision Course with Google on Web Searches," *The Wall Street Journal*, January 16, 2013, pp. A1, A10.

48. Evelyn M. Rusli, "Buy Signal: Facebook Widens Data Targeting," *The Wall Street Journal*, April 10, 2013, p. B4; and Hayley Tsukayama, "Facebook's Big Reveal: Social Search," *Star Tribune*, January 16, 2013, p. D6.

49. Jessi Hempel, "Smartphones: The War to Be No. 3," *Fortune*, February 4, 2013, pp. 35–36.

50. Juhana Rossi, "Rovio's 'Angry Birds' Fly Free," *The Wall Street Journal*, January 3, 2014, p. B5; Juhana Rossi, "Angry Birds' Maker Perches for Global Growth Takeoff," *The Wall Street Journal*, April 4, 2013, p. B4; Spencer E. Ante, "Rovio Mines Video with 'Angry Birds Toons,'" and *The Wall Street Journal*, March 12, 2013, p. B6.

51. Telis Demos, " 'Candy Crush' Maker Targets $7.6 Billion Value," *The Wall Street Journal*, March 13, 2014, p. B7; and "Tech, Mobile Games: Sweet! Delicious!" *Time*, December 2, 2013, pp. 51–54.

52. Andreas M. Kaplan, "If You Love Something, Let It Go Mobile: Mobile Marketing and Mobile Social Media 4x4," *Business Horizons* 55, no. 2 (2012), pp. 129–39.

53. Kara McGuire, "Shoppers Hunt Bargains via Their Smart Phones," *Star Tribune*, November 28, 2010, pp. D1, D10; Michelle Higgins, "Smart Phone Apps Can Help You Avoid Holiday Travel Headaches," *Star Tribune*, December 19, 2010, p. 63; and Sue Stock, "Code Alert for Smart Phones," *Star Tribune*, November 17, 2010, p. D8.

54. Elizabeth Dwoskin, "Give Me Back My Privacy," *The Wall Street Journal*, March 24, 2014, pp. R1, R2; Georgia Wells, "Real-Time Marketing in a Real-Time World," *The Wall Street Journal*, March 24, 2014, p. R3; Elizabeth Dwoskin, "What Your Phone Is Sharing about Your Secrets," *The Wall Street Journal*, January 14, 2014, pp. B1, B4.

StuffDOT, Inc.: This case was written by Jennifer Katz, Amanda Axvig, and William Rudelius.

Credits

17 Personal Selling and Sales Management

LEARNING OBJECTIVES

After reading this chapter you should be able to:

LO 17-1 Discuss the nature and scope of personal selling and sales management in marketing.

LO 17-2 Identify the different types of personal selling.

LO 17-3 Explain the stages in the personal selling process.

LO 17-4 Describe the major functions of sales management.

MEET TODAY'S SUCCESSFUL SALES PROFESSIONAL

Have you been considering sales as a career opportunity? If so, then consider Lindsey Smith as a role model (see opposite page).

Ms. Smith began her career representing Molecular Imaging Products within the Medical Diagnostics Division of GE Healthcare Americas. She joined the company eleven years ago right out of college with a BBA degree. The epitome of today's sales professional, she lists integrity, motivation, trust and relationship building, and a team orientation as just a few of the ingredients necessary for a successful sales career today.

As a sales professional, she recognizes the importance of constantly updating and refining her product knowledge, analytical and communication skills, and strategic thinking about opportunities to more fully satisfy each customer's clinical, economic, and technical requirements. And for good reason. Her customer contacts include physicians (radiologists, neurologists, and cardiologists), medical technologists, nurses, and health care provider CEOs, CFOs, and other administrators.

Lindsey Smith's selling orientation and customer relationship philosophy rest on four pillars:

1. *A commitment to creating value for clients*. Lindsey believes "every sales call and client interaction should create value for both the customer and the company."

2. *Seek to serve clients as a trusted consultant*. Lindsey emphasizes "being a resource for my customers by providing novel solutions for them."

3. *Reinforce the company's competitive advantage*. Lindsey continually reinforces GE Healthcare Americas' competitive advantage: "I emphasize my company's value proposition and showcase the company's product innovation, solutions, and service."

4. *Regard challenges as opportunities*. Lindsey says, "I consider challenges as opportunities to provide innovative solutions and resources to customers and to build client trust and long-term relationships."

Lindsey Smith's approach to selling and customer relationships has served her customers and her well. She is among the company's top revenue producers and has a long list of loyal customers. Not surprisingly, Ms. Smith has been a recipient of the company's Commercial Excellence Award in six of the last eight years.

In 2011, Lindsey Smith was promoted to her current position as Client Director at GE Healthcare Americas. In this capacity, she represents and manages the entire GE Healthcare Americas company portfolio, including medical technology, health care consulting, information technology, and finance solutions for one of GE's largest strategic health care systems.[1]

This chapter describes the scope and significance of personal selling and sales management in marketing and creating value for customers. It first highlights the many forms of personal selling. Next, the major steps in the selling process are outlined with an emphasis on building buyer–seller relationships.

The chapter then focuses on salesforce management and its critical role in achieving a company's broader marketing objectives. Three major salesforce management functions are then detailed. They are sales plan formulation, sales plan implementation, and salesforce evaluation. Finally, technology's pervasive influence on how selling is done and how salespeople are managed is described.

SCOPE AND SIGNIFICANCE OF PERSONAL SELLING AND SALES MANAGEMENT

 LO 17-1

Discuss the nature and scope of personal selling and sales management in marketing.

personal selling
The two-way flow of communication between a buyer and seller, often in a face-to-face encounter, designed to influence a person's or group's purchase decision.

sales management
Planning the selling program and implementing and evaluating the personal selling effort of the firm.

Chapter 14 described personal selling and management of the sales effort as being part of the firm's promotional mix. Although it is important to recognize that personal selling is a useful vehicle for communicating with present and potential buyers, it is much more.

Nature of Personal Selling and Sales Management

Personal selling involves the two-way flow of communication between a buyer and seller, often in a face-to-face encounter, designed to influence a person's or group's purchase decision. However, with advances in telecommunications, personal selling also takes place over the telephone and through video teleconferencing and Internet-enabled links between buyers and sellers.

Personal selling remains a highly human-intensive activity despite the use of technology. Accordingly, the people involved must be managed. **Sales management** involves planning the selling program and implementing and evaluating the personal selling effort of the firm. The tasks involved in managing personal selling include setting objectives; organizing the salesforce; recruiting, selecting, training, and compensating salespeople; and evaluating the performance of individual salespeople.

Selling Happens Almost Everywhere

"Everyone lives by selling something," wrote author Robert Louis Stevenson a century ago. His observation still holds true today. The U.S. Bureau of Labor Statistics reports that about 14 million people are employed in sales positions in the United States. Included in this number are manufacturing sales personnel, real estate brokers, stockbrokers, and salesclerks who work in retail stores. In reality, however, virtually every occupation that involves customer contact has an element of personal selling. For example, attorneys, accountants, bankers, and company personnel recruiters perform sales-related activities, whether or not they acknowledge it.

Could this be a salesperson in the operating room? Read the text to find out why Medtronic salespeople visit hospital operating rooms.

Medtronic
www.medtronic.com

Personal Selling in Marketing

Video 17-1
Cambridge Sales
kerin.tv/cr6e/v17-1

Personal selling serves three major roles in a firm's overall marketing effort. First, salespeople are the critical link between the firm and its customers. This role requires that salespeople match company interests with customer needs to satisfy both parties in the exchange process. Second, salespeople *are* the company in a consumer's eyes. They represent what a company is or attempts to be and are often the only personal contact a customer has with the company. For example, as acknowledged by IBM's former chief executive officer, the company's 40,000-strong salesforce is "our face to the client."[2] Third, personal selling may play a dominant role in a firm's marketing program. This situation typically arises when a firm uses a push marketing strategy, described in Chapter 14. Avon, for example, pays almost 40 percent of its total sales dollars for selling expenses. Pharmaceutical firms and office and educational equipment manufacturers also rely heavily on personal selling in the marketing of their products.

Creating Customer Solutions and Value through Salespeople: Relationship Selling

As the critical link between the firm and its customers, salespeople can create customer value in many ways. For instance, by being close to the customer, salespeople can identify creative solutions to customer problems. Salespeople at Medtronic, Inc., the world leader in the heart pacemaker market, are in the operating room for more than 90 percent of the procedures performed with their product and are on call 24 hours a day. "It reflects the willingness to be there in every situation, just in case a problem arises—even though nine times out of ten the procedure goes just fine," notes a satisfied customer.[3]

Salespeople can create value by easing the customer buying process. This happened at TE Connectivity, a producer of electrical products. Salespeople and customers had a difficult time getting product specifications and performance data on the company's 70,000 products quickly and accurately. The company now has all of its information on its website, which can be downloaded instantly by salespeople and customers.

Customer value is also created by salespeople who follow through after the sale. At Jefferson Smurfit Corporation, a multibillion-dollar supplier of packaging products, one of its salespeople juggled production from three of the company's plants to satisfy an unexpected demand for boxes from General Electric. This person's action led to the company being given GE's Distinguished Supplier Award.

relationship selling
The practice of building ties to customers based on a salesperson's attention and commitment to customer needs over time.

Customer value creation is made possible by **relationship selling**, the practice of building ties to customers based on a salesperson's attention and commitment to customer needs over time. Relationship selling involves mutual respect and trust among buyers and sellers. It focuses on creating long-term customers, not a one-time sale. A survey of 300 senior sales executives revealed that 96 percent consider "building long-term relationships with customers" to be the most important activity affecting sales performance. Companies such as Xerox, American Express, and Owens Corning have made relationship building a core focus of their sales effort.[4]

Relationship selling represents another dimension of customer relationship management. It emphasizes the importance of first learning about customer needs and wants and then tailoring solutions to customer problems as a means to customer value creation. Recent research suggests that a salesperson may have a genetic predisposition to create customer value. See the Marketing Matters box on the next page for details.[5]

> **learning review**
>
> 17-1. What is personal selling?
>
> 17-2. What is involved in sales management?

Marketing Matters

Science and Selling: Is Customer Value Creation in Your Genes?

Is a predisposition to create customer value in your genes? Are you a born salesperson? Recent research by University of Michigan Marketing Professor Richard P. Bagozzi and his colleagues offers a novel insight into this question that may or may not surprise you.

Their research identifies a genetic marker, the 7R variant of the DRD_4 gene, that is correlated with a salesperson's predisposition or willingness to interact with customers and learn about their problems in order to meet their needs. The researchers also found that the presence of the A1 variant of the DRD_2 gene is correlated with a predisposition or tendency to try to persuade customers to buy a given product rather than listen to their needs.

These two different genetic markers help explain the difference between a salesperson's customer orientation versus sales orientation. A customer orientation is guided by such ideas as, "I try to align customers who have problems with products that will help them solve their problems," where the aim is to satisfy mutual needs and the hope is to build a long-term relationship.

In contrast, a sales orientation is driven by notions such as, "I try to sell customers all I can convince them to buy, even if I think it is more than a wise customer should buy." In this case, the motivation is to satisfy one's own short-term interests and not necessarily the needs of the customer.

Faced with a selling situation, do you have a sales orientation or a customer orientation? Customer value creation may be in your genes!

THE MANY FORMS OF PERSONAL SELLING

LO 17-2 Identify the different types of personal selling.

Personal selling assumes many forms based on the amount of selling done and the amount of creativity required to perform the sales task. Broadly speaking, three types of personal selling exist: order taking, order getting, and customer sales support activities. While some firms use only one of these types of personal selling, others use a combination of all three.

Order-Taking Salespeople

order taker
A salesperson who processes routine orders or reorders for products that were already sold by the company.

Typically, an **order taker** processes routine orders or reorders for products that were already sold by the company. The primary responsibility of order takers is to preserve an ongoing relationship with existing customers and maintain sales.

Two types of order takers exist. *Outside order takers* visit customers and replenish inventory stocks of resellers, such as retailers or wholesalers. For example, Frito-Lay salespeople call on supermarkets, convenience stores, and other establishments to ensure that the company's line of snack products (such as Lay's potato chips and Doritos and Tostitos tortilla chips) is in adequate supply. In addition, outside order takers often provide assistance in arranging displays.

Inside order takers, also called *order clerks* or *salesclerks*, typically answer simple questions, take orders, and complete transactions with customers. Many retail clerks are inside order takers. Inside order takers are often employed by companies that use *inbound telemarketing*, the use of toll-free telephone numbers that customers can call to obtain information about products or services and make purchases. In business-to-business settings, order taking arises in straight rebuy situations as described in Chapter 5.

Order takers generally do little selling in a conventional sense. They engage in modest problem solving with customers. They often represent products that have few options, such as magazine subscriptions and highly standardized industrial products. Inbound telemarketing is also an essential selling activity for more "customer service" driven firms, such as Dell. At these companies, order takers undergo extensive training so that they can better assist callers with their purchase decisions.

Order-Getting Salespeople

order getter

A salesperson who sells in a conventional sense and identifies prospective customers, provides customers with information, persuades customers to buy, closes sales, and follows up on customers' use of a product or service.

An **order getter** sells in a conventional sense and identifies prospective customers, provides customers with information, persuades customers to buy, closes sales, and follows up on customers' use of a product or service. Like order takers, order getters can be inside (an automobile salesperson) or outside (a Xerox salesperson).

Order getting involves a high degree of creativity and customer empathy and is typically required for selling complex or technical products with many options, so considerable product knowledge and sales training are necessary. In modified rebuy or new-buy purchase situations in business-to-business selling, an order getter acts as a problem solver who identifies how a particular product may satisfy a customer's need. Similarly, in the purchase of a service, such as insurance, an insurance agent can provide a mix of plans to satisfy a buyer's needs depending on income, stage of the family's life cycle, and investment objectives.

Order getting is not a 40-hour-per-week job. Industry research shows that outside order getters, or field service representatives, often work over 50 hours per week. As shown in Figure 17–1 on the next page, 41 percent of an average field sales representative's time is actually spent selling by phone or face-to-face. Another 24 percent is devoted to generating leads and researching customer accounts. The remainder of a sales representative's workweek is occupied by administrative tasks, meetings, service calls, travel, training, and customer follow-up.[6]

Order getting by outside salespeople is also expensive. It is estimated that the average cost of a single field sales call on a business customer is about $350, factoring in the salesperson's compensation, benefits, and travel-and-entertainment expenses. This cost illustrates why outbound telemarketing is popular. *Outbound telemarketing* is the practice of using the telephone rather than personal visits to contact current and prospective customers. A much lower cost per sales call (from $20 to $25) and little or no field expense accounts for its widespread appeal.[7]

learning review

17-3. What is the principal difference between an order taker and an order getter?

17-4. What percentage of an order-getting salesperson's time is spent selling?

CHAPTER 17   Personal Selling and Sales Management

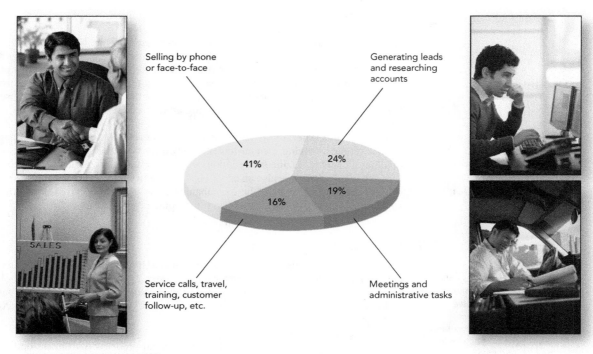

Selling by phone or face-to-face

Generating leads and researching accounts

41%

24%

19%

16%

Service calls, travel, training, customer follow-up, etc.

Meetings and administrative tasks

FIGURE 17–1
How do outside order-getting salespeople spend their time each week? You might be surprised after reading the text.

THE PERSONAL SELLING PROCESS: BUILDING RELATIONSHIPS

LO 17-3 Explain the stages in the personal selling process.

Selling, and particularly order getting, is a complicated activity that involves building buyer–seller relationships. Although the salesperson–customer interaction is essential to personal selling, much of a salesperson's work occurs before this meeting and continues after the sale itself. The **personal selling process** consists of six stages: (1) prospecting, (2) preapproach, (3) approach, (4) presentation, (5) close, and (6) follow-up (see Figure 17–2).

Prospecting: Identifying and Qualifying Prospective Customers

personal selling process
Sales activities occurring before and after the sale itself, consisting of six stages: (1) prospecting, (2) preapproach, (3) approach, (4) presentation, (5) close, and (6) follow-up.

Personal selling begins with the *prospecting* stage—the search for and qualification of potential customers. There are three types of prospects. A *lead* is the name of a person who may be a possible customer. A *prospect* is a customer who wants or needs the product. If an individual wants the product, can afford to buy it, and is the decision maker, this individual is a *qualified prospect*.

Leads and prospects are generated using several sources. For example, advertising may contain a coupon or a toll-free number to generate leads. Some companies use exhibits at trade shows, professional meetings, and conferences to generate leads or prospects. Staffed by salespeople, these exhibits are used to attract the attention of prospective buyers and share information. Others utilize the Internet for generating leads and prospects. Today, salespeople are using websites, e-mail, and social networks, such as LinkedIn, to connect to individuals and companies that may be interested in their products or services.

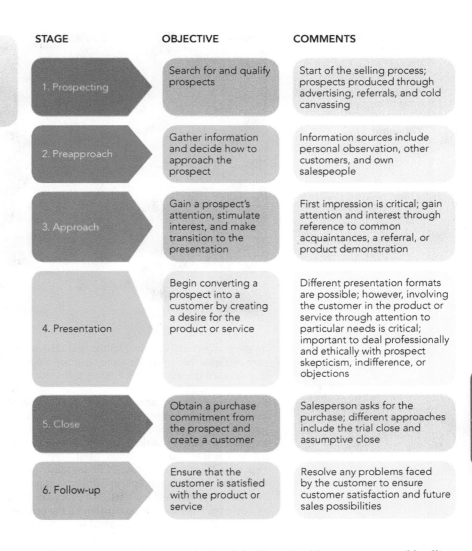

FIGURE 17–2
Stages and objectives
of the personal selling
process. Each stage is
critical for successful
selling and building a
customer relationship.

STAGE	OBJECTIVE	COMMENTS
1. Prospecting	Search for and qualify prospects	Start of the selling process; prospects produced through advertising, referrals, and cold canvassing
2. Preapproach	Gather information and decide how to approach the prospect	Information sources include personal observation, other customers, and own salespeople
3. Approach	Gain a prospect's attention, stimulate interest, and make transition to the presentation	First impression is critical; gain attention and interest through reference to common acquaintances, a referral, or product demonstration
4. Presentation	Begin converting a prospect into a customer by creating a desire for the product or service	Different presentation formats are possible; however, involving the customer in the product or service through attention to particular needs is critical; important to deal professionally and ethically with prospect skepticism, indifference, or objections
5. Close	Obtain a purchase commitment from the prospect and create a customer	Salesperson asks for the purchase; different approaches include the trial close and assumptive close
6. Follow-up	Ensure that the customer is satisfied with the product or service	Resolve any problems faced by the customer to ensure customer satisfaction and future sales possibilities

Another approach for generating leads is through *cold canvassing* or *cold calling*, either in person or by telephone. This approach simply means that a salesperson may open a directory, pick a name, and contact that individual or business. Despite its high refusal rate, cold canvassing can be successful.[8]

Cold canvassing is often criticized by U.S. consumers and is now regulated. Research shows that 75 percent of U.S. consumers consider this practice an intrusion on their privacy, and 72 percent find it distasteful.[9] The *Telephone Consumer Protection Act* (1991) contains provisions to curb abuses such as early morning or late night calling. Additional federal regulations require more complete disclosure regarding solicitations, include provisions that allow consumers to avoid being called at any time through the Do Not Call Registry, and impose fines for violations. For example, satellite television provider DirecTV was fined $5.3 million for making thousands of calls to consumers who had put their telephone numbers on the Do Not Call Registry.[10]

Preapproach: Preparing for the Sales Call

Once a salesperson has identified a qualified prospect, preparation for the sale begins with the preapproach. The *preapproach* stage involves obtaining further information

Trade shows are a popular source for leads and prospects. Companies like TSCentral provide comprehensive trade show information.

TSCentral

www.tscentral.com

on the prospect and deciding on the best method of approach. Knowing how the prospect prefers to be approached and what the prospect is looking for in a product or service is essential, regardless of industry or cultural setting.

For instance, a Merrill Lynch stockbroker will need information on a prospect's discretionary income, investment objectives, and preference for discussing brokerage services over the telephone or in person. For business product companies such as Texas Instruments, the preapproach involves identifying the buying role of a prospect (for example, influencer or decision maker), important buying criteria, and the prospect's receptivity to a formal or informal presentation. Identifying the best time to contact a prospect is also important. Northwestern Mutual Life Insurance Company suggests that the following are the best times to call on people in different occupations: dentists before 9:30 A.M., lawyers between 11:00 A.M. and 2:00 P.M., and college professors between 7:00 and 8:00 P.M.

Successful salespeople recognize that the preapproach stage should never be short-changed. Their experience coupled with research on customer complaints indicates that failure to learn as much as possible about the prospect is unprofessional and the ruin of a sales call.

Approach: Making the First Impression

The *approach* stage involves the initial meeting between the salesperson and the prospect, where the objectives are to gain the prospect's attention, stimulate interest, and build the foundation for the sales presentation itself and the basis for a working relationship. The first impression is critical at this stage, and it is common for salespeople to begin the conversation with a reference to common acquaintances, a referral, or even the product or service itself. Which tactic is taken will depend on the information obtained in the prospecting and preapproach stages.

The approach stage is very important in international settings.[11] In many societies outside the United States, considerable time is devoted to nonbusiness talk designed to establish a rapport between buyers and sellers. For instance, it is common for two or three meetings to occur before business matters are discussed in the Middle East and Asia. Gestures are also very important. The initial meeting between a salesperson and a prospect in the United States customarily begins with a firm handshake. Handshakes also apply in France, but they are gentle, not firm. Forget the handshake in Japan. An

How business cards are exchanged with Asian customers is very important. Read the text to learn the appropriate protocol in the approach stage of the personal selling process.

appropriate bow is expected. What about business cards? Business cards should be printed in English on one side and the language of the prospective customer on the other. Knowledgeable U.S. salespeople know that their business cards should be handed to Asian customers using both hands, with the name facing the receiver. In Asia, anything involving a person's name demands respect.

Presentation: Tailoring a Solution for a Customer's Needs

The *presentation* stage is at the core of the order-getting selling process, and its objective is to convert a prospect into a customer by creating a desire for the product or service. Three major presentation formats exist: (1) stimulus-response format, (2) formula selling format, and (3) need-satisfaction format.

Stimulus-Response Format   The *stimulus-response presentation* format assumes that given the appropriate stimulus by a salesperson, the prospect will buy. With this format the salesperson tries one appeal after another, hoping to hit the right button. A counter clerk at McDonald's is using this approach when he or she asks whether you'd like an order of french fries or a dessert with your meal. The counter clerk is engaging in what is called *suggestive selling*. Although useful in this setting, the stimulus-response format is not always appropriate, and for many products a more formalized format is necessary.

Formula Selling Format   The *formula selling presentation* format is based on the view that a presentation consists of information that must be provided in an accurate, thorough, and step-by-step manner to inform the prospect. A popular version of this format is the *canned sales presentation*, which is a memorized, standardized message conveyed to every prospect. Used frequently by firms in telephone and door-to-door selling of consumer products (for example, Kirby vacuum cleaners), this approach treats every prospect the same, regardless of differences in needs or preferences for certain kinds of information.

Canned sales presentations can be advantageous when the differences between prospects are unknown or with novice salespeople who are less knowledgeable about the product and selling process than experienced salespeople. Although it guarantees a thorough presentation, it often lacks flexibility and spontaneity. More important, it does not provide for feedback from the prospective buyer—a critical component in the communication process and the start of a relationship.

Need-Satisfaction Format   The stimulus-response and formula selling formats share a common characteristic: The salesperson dominates the conversation. By comparison, the *need-satisfaction presentation* format emphasizes probing and listening by the salesperson to identify the needs and interests of prospective buyers. Once these are identified, the salesperson tailors the presentation to the prospect and highlights product benefits that may be valued by the prospect. The need-satisfaction format, which emphasizes problem solving and customer solutions, is the most consistent with the marketing concept and relationship building.

adaptive selling
A need-satisfaction sales presentation style that involves adjusting the presentation to fit the selling situation.

Two selling styles are common with this format.[12] **Adaptive selling** involves adjusting the presentation to fit the selling situation, such as knowing when to offer solutions and when to ask for more information. Sales research and practice show that knowledge of the customer and sales situation are key ingredients for adaptive selling. Many consumer service firms such as brokerage and insurance firms and consumer product firms like Rockport, AT&T, and Gillette effectively apply this selling style.

437

CHAPTER 17   Personal Selling and Sales Management

Marketing Matters

Imagine This . . . Putting the Customer into Customer Solutions!

Solutions for problems are what companies are looking for from suppliers. At the same time, suppliers focus on customer solutions to differentiate themselves from competitors. So what is a customer solution and what does it have to do with selling?

Sellers view a solution as a customized and integrated combination of products and services for meeting a customer's business needs. But what do buyers think? From a buyer's perspective, a solution is one that (1) meets their requirements, (2) is designed to uniquely solve their problem, (3) can be implemented, and (4) ensures follow-up.

This insight arose from a field study conducted by three researchers at Emory University. Their in-depth study also yielded insight into

what an effective customer solution offers. According to one buyer interviewed in their study:

> They (the supplier) make sure that their sales and marketing guys know what's going on. The sales and technical folks know what's going on, and the technical and support guys know what's going on with me. All these guys are in the loop, and it's not a puzzle for them.

So what does putting the customer into customer solutions have to do with selling? Three things stand out. First, considerable time and effort is necessary to fully understand a specific customer's requirements. Second, effective customer solutions are based on relationships among sellers and buyers. And finally, consultative selling is central to providing novel solutions for customers, thereby creating value for them.

---

consultative selling
A need-satisfaction sales presentation style that focuses on problem identification, where the salesperson serves as an expert on problem recognition and resolution.

Consultative selling focuses on problem identification, where the salesperson serves as an expert on problem recognition and resolution. With consultative selling, problem solution options are not simply a matter of choosing from an array of existing products or services. Rather, novel solutions often arise, thereby creating unique value for the customer.

Consultative selling is prominent in business-to-business marketing. Johnson Controls's Automotive Systems Group, IBM's Global Services, DHL Worldwide Express, GE Healthcare Americas, and Xerox offer customer solutions through their consultative selling style. According to a senior Xerox sales executive, "Our business is no longer about selling boxes. It's about selling digital, network-based information management solutions, and this requires a highly customized and consultative selling process. So we look for consultative and business-savvy salespeople." But what does a customer solution really mean? The Marketing Matters box offers a unique answer.[13]

IBM is a leader in consultative selling with its focus on developing novel solutions that create customer value.

Handling Objections A critical concern in the presentation stage is handling objections. *Objections* are excuses for not making a purchase commitment or decision. Some objections are valid and are based on the characteristics of the product or service or price. However, many objections reflect prospect skepticism or indifference. Whether valid or not, experienced salespeople know that objections do not put an end to the presentation. Rather, techniques can be used to deal with objections in a courteous, ethical, and professional manner. The following six techniques are the most common:[14]

1. *Acknowledge and convert the objection.* This technique involves using the objection as a reason for buying. For example, a prospect might say, "The price is too high." The reply: "Yes, the price is high because we use the finest materials. Let me show you. . . . "

2. *Postpone.* The postpone technique is used when the objection will be dealt with later in the presentation: "I'm going to address that point shortly. I think my answer would make better sense then."

3. *Agree and neutralize.* Here a salesperson agrees with the objection, then shows that it is unimportant. A salesperson would say, "That's true. Others have said the same. But, they thought that issue was outweighed by other benefits."

4. *Accept the objection.* Sometimes the objection is valid. Let the prospect express such views, probe for the reason behind it, and attempt to stimulate further discussion on the objection.

5. *Denial.* When a prospect's objection is based on misinformation and clearly untrue, it is wise to meet the objection head on with a firm denial.

6. *Ignore the objection.* This technique is used when it appears that the objection is a stalling mechanism or is clearly not important to the prospect.

Each of these techniques requires a calm, professional interaction with the prospect and is most effective when objections are anticipated in the preapproach stage. Handling objections is a skill requiring a sense of timing, appreciation for the prospect's state of mind, and adeptness in communication. Objections also should be handled ethically. Lying or misrepresenting product or service features are grossly unethical practices.

Close: Asking for the Customer's Order or Business

The *closing* stage in the selling process involves obtaining a purchase commitment from the prospect. This stage is the most important and the most difficult because the

The closing stage involves obtaining a purchase commitment from the prospect. Read the text to learn how the close itself can take several forms.

salesperson must determine when the prospect is ready to buy. Telltale signals indicating a readiness to buy include body language (prospect reexamines the product or contract closely), statements ("This equipment should reduce our maintenance costs"), and questions ("When could we expect delivery?").

The close itself can take several forms. Three closing techniques are used when a salesperson believes a buyer is about ready to make a purchase: (1) trial close, (2) assumptive close, and (3) urgency close. A *trial close* involves asking the prospect to make a decision on some aspect of the purchase: "Would you prefer the blue or gray model?" An *assumptive close* entails asking the prospect to consider choices concerning delivery, warranty, or financing terms under the assumption that a sale has been finalized. An *urgency close* is used to commit the prospect quickly by making reference to the timeliness of the purchase: "The low interest financing ends next week," or "That is the last model we have in stock." Of course, these statements should be used only if they accurately reflect the situation; otherwise, such claims would be unethical. When a prospect is clearly ready to buy, the final close is used, and a salesperson asks for the order.

Follow-up: Solidifying the Relationship

The selling process does not end with the closing of a sale; rather, professional selling requires customer follow-up. One marketing authority equated the follow-up with courtship and marriage by observing, "The sale merely consummates the courtship. Then the marriage begins. How good the marriage is depends on how well the relationship is managed."[15] The *follow-up* stage includes making certain the customer's purchase has been properly delivered and installed and addressing any difficulties experienced with the use of the item. Attention to this stage of the selling process

439

CHAPTER 17   Personal Selling and Sales Management

solidifies the buyer–seller relationship. Research shows that the cost and effort to obtain repeat sales from a satisfied customer is roughly half of that necessary to gain a sale from a new customer.[16] In short, today's satisfied customers become tomorrow's qualified prospects or referrals.

learning review

17-5. What are the six stages in the personal selling process?

17-6. Which presentation format is most consistent with the marketing concept? Why?

THE SALES MANAGEMENT PROCESS

 LO 17-4 Describe the major functions of sales management.

Selling must be managed if it is going to contribute to a firm's marketing objectives. Although firms differ in the specifics of how salespeople and the selling effort are managed, the sales management process is similar across firms. Sales management consists of three interrelated functions: (1) sales plan formulation, (2) sales plan implementation, and (3) salesforce evaluation (see Figure 17–3).

Sales Plan Formulation: Setting Direction

Formulating the sales plan is the most basic of the three sales management functions. According to the vice president of the Harris Corporation, a global communications company, "If a company hopes to implement its marketing strategy, it really needs a detailed sales planning process."[17] The **sales plan** is a statement describing what is to be achieved and where and how the selling effort of salespeople is to be deployed. Sales plan formulation involves three tasks: (1) setting objectives, (2) organizing the salesforce, and (3) developing account management policies.

sales plan
A statement describing what is to be achieved and where and how the selling effort of salespeople is to be deployed.

Setting Objectives Setting objectives is central to sales management because this task specifies what is to be achieved. In practice, objectives are set for the total salesforce and for each salesperson.

Selling objectives can be output related and focus on dollar or unit sales volume, number of new customers added, or profit. Alternatively, they can be input related and emphasize the number of sales calls and selling expenses. Output- and input-related objectives are used for the salesforce as a whole and for each salesperson. A third type of objective that is behaviorally related is typically specific for each salesperson and includes his or her product knowledge, customer service satisfaction ratings, and selling and communication skills.

Whatever objectives are set, they should be precise and measurable and specify the time period over which they are to be achieved. Once established, these objectives serve as performance standards for the evaluation of the salesforce, the third function of sales management.

FIGURE 17–3
The sales management process involves sales plan formulation, sales plan implementation, and salesforce evaluation.

Sales plan formulation	Sales plan implementation	Salesforce evaluation
• Setting objectives	• Salesforce recruitment and selection	• Quantitative assessment
• Organizing the salesforce	• Salesforce training	• Behavioral evaluation
• Developing account management policies	• Salesforce motivation and compensation	

Organizing the Salesforce   Organizing a selling organization is the second task in formulating the sales plan. Companies organize their salesforce on the basis of (1) geography, (2) type of customer, or (3) specific products or services.

A *geographical sales organization* is the simplest structure, where the United States, or indeed the globe, is first divided into regions and each region is divided into districts or territories. Salespeople are assigned to each district with defined geographical boundaries and call on all customers and represent all products sold by the company. An advantage of this structure is that it can minimize travel time, expenses, and duplication of selling effort. However, if a firm's products or customers require specialized knowledge, then a geographical structure is unsuitable.

When different types of buyers have different needs, a *customer sales organization* is used. In practice this means that a different salesforce calls on each separate type of buyer or marketing channel. For example, Konica switched from a geographical to a marketing channel structure with different sales teams serving specific retail channels: mass merchandisers, photo specialty outlets, and food and drug stores. The rationale for this approach is that more effective, specialized customer support and knowledge are provided to buyers. However, this structure often leads to higher administrative costs and some duplication of selling effort, because several salesforces are used to represent the same products.

An important variation of the customer organizational structure is **major account management** or *key account management*—the practice of using team selling to focus on important customers so as to build mutually beneficial, long-term, cooperative relationships. Key account management involves teams of sales, service, and often technical personnel who work with purchasing, manufacturing, engineering, logistics, and financial executives in customer organizations. This approach, which often assigns company personnel to a customer account, results in "customer specialists" who can provide exceptional service. Procter & Gamble uses this approach with Walmart, as does Black & Decker with Home Depot.

When specific knowledge is required to sell certain types of products or services, then a *product or service sales organization* is used. For example, Maxim Steel has a salesforce that sells drilling pipe to oil companies and another that sells specialty steel products to manufacturers. The advantage of this structure is that salespeople can develop expertise with technical characteristics, applications, and selling methods associated with a particular product or family of products. However, this structure produces high administrative costs and duplication of selling effort, because two company salespeople may call on the same customer.

In short, there is no one best sales organization for all companies in all situations.[18] Rather, the organization of the salesforce should reflect the marketing strategy of the firm. Each year about 10 percent of U.S. firms change their sales organizations to implement new marketing strategies.

Developing Account Management Policies   The third task in formulating a sales plan involves developing **account management policies** specifying whom salespeople should contact, what kinds of selling and customer service activities should be engaged in, and how these activities should be carried out. These policies might state which individuals in a buying organization should be contacted, the amount of sales and service effort that different customers should receive, and the kinds of information salespeople should collect before or during a sales call.

An example of an account management policy in Figure 17–4 on the next page shows how different accounts or customers can be grouped according to level of opportunity and the firm's competitive sales position.[19] When specific account names are placed in each cell, salespeople clearly see which accounts should be contacted, with what level of selling and service activity, and how to deal with them. Accounts in cells 1 and 2 might have high frequencies of personal sales calls and increased time spent on a call. Cell 3 accounts will have lower call frequencies, and cell 4 accounts might be contacted through telemarketing or direct mail rather than in person. For example, Union Pacific Railroad

---

major account management
The practice of using team selling to focus on important customers so as to build mutually beneficial, long-term, cooperative relationships; also called *key account management.*

account management policies
Policies that specify who salespeople should contact, what kinds of selling and customer service activities should be engaged in, and how these activities should be carried out.

CHAPTER 17   Personal Selling and Sales Management

Competitive position of sales organization

High

Low

Account opportunity level

High

1
Attractiveness: Accounts offer a good opportunity because they have high potential and the sales organization has a strong position.

Account management policy: Accounts should receive a high level of sales calls and service to retain and possibly build accounts.

3
Attractiveness: Accounts may offer a good opportunity if the sales organization can overcome its weak position.

Account management policy: Emphasize a heavy sales organization position or shift resources to other accounts if a stronger sales organization position is impossible.

Low

2
Attractiveness: Accounts are somewhat attractive because the sales organization has a strong position, but future opportunity is limited.

Account management policy: Accounts should receive a moderate level of sales and service to maintain the current position of the sales organization.

4
Attractiveness: Accounts offer little opportunity, and the sales organization position is weak.

Account management policy: Consider replacing personal calls with telephone sales or direct mail to service accounts. Consider dropping the account if unprofitable.

FIGURE 17–4
An account management policy grid grouping customers according to level of opportunity and the firm's competitive sales position.

put its 20,000 smallest accounts on a telemarketing program. A subsequent survey of these accounts indicated that 84 percent rated Union Pacific's sales effort "very effective" compared with 67 percent before the switch.

Sales Plan Implementation: Putting the Plan into Action

The sales plan is put into practice through the tasks associated with sales plan implementation. Whereas sales plan formulation focuses on "doing the right things," implementation emphasizes "doing things right." The three major tasks involved in implementing a sales plan are (1) salesforce recruitment and selection, (2) salesforce training, and (3) salesforce motivation and compensation.

Salesforce Recruitment and Selection   Effective recruitment and selection of salespeople is one of the most crucial tasks of sales management. It entails finding people who match the type of sales position required by a firm. Recruitment and selection practices will differ greatly between order-taking and order-getting sales positions, given the differences in the demands of these two jobs. Therefore, recruitment and selection begin with a carefully crafted job analysis and job description followed by a statement of job qualifications.

A *job analysis* is a study of a particular sales position, including how the job is to be performed and the tasks that make up the job. Information from a job analysis is used to write a *job description*, a written document that describes job relationships and requirements that characterize each sales position. It explains (1) to whom a salesperson reports, (2) how a salesperson interacts with other company personnel, (3) the customers to be called on, (4) the specific activities to be carried out, (5) the physical and mental demands of the job, and (6) the types of products and services to be sold.

The job description is then translated into a statement of job qualifications, including the aptitudes, knowledge, skills, and a variety of behavioral characteristics considered necessary to perform the job successfully. Qualifications for order-getting sales positions often mirror the expectations of buyers: (1) imagination and problem-solving ability, (2) strong work ethic, (3) honesty, (4) intimate product knowledge, (5) effective

Marketing Matters

What Is Your Emotional Intelligence? Test Yourself and See.

A person's success at work depends on many talents, including intelligence and technical skills. Recent research indicates that an individual's emotional intelligence or EI is also important, if not more important!

Evidence suggests that emotional intelligence is two times more important in contributing to performance than intellect and expertise alone. Emotional intelligence has five dimensions: (1) self-motivation skills; (2) self-awareness, or knowing one's own emotions; (3) the ability to manage one's emotions and impulses; (4) empathy, or the ability to sense how others are feeling; and (5) social skills, or the ability to handle the emotions of other people. These qualities are important in selling.

What is your emotional intelligence? Visit the website at www.ihhp.com/quiz.php and answer the 24 questions to learn what your emotional intelligence is and obtain additional insights.

communication and listening skills, and (6) attentiveness reflected in responsiveness to buyer needs and customer loyalty and follow-up. Firms use a variety of methods for evaluating prospective salespeople. Personal interviews, reference checks, and background information provided on application forms are the most frequently used methods.[20]

Successful selling also requires a high degree of emotional intelligence. *Emotional intelligence* is the ability to understand one's own emotions and the emotions of people with whom one interacts on a daily basis. These qualities are important for adaptive selling and may spell the difference between effective and ineffective order-getting salespeople.[21] Are you interested in what emotional intelligence is and how it is measured? Read the Marketing Matters box and test yourself.

Salesforce Training   Whereas the recruitment and selection of salespeople is a one-time event, salesforce training is an ongoing process that affects both new and seasoned salespeople.[22] Sales training covers much more than selling practices. For example, IBM Global Services salespeople, who sell consulting and various information technology services, take at least two weeks of in-class and Internet-based training on both consultative selling and the technical aspects of business.

Training new salespeople is an expensive process. Salespeople in the United States receive employer-sponsored training annually at a cost of over $7 billion per year. On-the-job training is the most popular type of training, followed by individual instruction taught by experienced salespeople. Formal classes, seminars taught by professional sales trainers, and computer-based training are also popular.

Salesforce Motivation and Compensation   A sales plan cannot be successfully implemented without motivated salespeople. Research on salesperson motivation suggests that (1) a clear job description, (2) effective sales management practices, (3) a personal need for achievement, and (4) proper compensation, incentives, or rewards will produce a motivated salesperson.[23]

The importance of compensation as a motivating factor means that close attention must be given to how salespeople are financially rewarded for their efforts. Salespeople are paid using one of three plans: (1) straight salary, (2) straight commission, or (3) a combination of salary and commission. Under a *straight salary compensation plan*, a salesperson is paid a fixed fee per week, month, or year. With a *straight commission compensation plan*, a salesperson's earnings are directly tied to the sales or profit generated. For example, an insurance agent might receive a 2 percent commission of $2,000 for selling a $100,000 life insurance policy. A *combination compensation plan* contains a specified salary plus a commission on sales or profit generated.

Each compensation plan has its advantages and disadvantages.[24] A straight salary plan is easy to administer and gives management a large measure of control over how salespeople allocate their efforts. However, it provides little incentive to expand sales volume. This plan is used when salespeople engage in many nonselling activities, such as account or customer servicing. A straight commission plan provides the maximum amount of selling incentive but can discourage salespeople from providing customer service. This plan is common when nonselling activities are minimal. Combination plans are most preferred by salespeople and attempt to build on the advantages of salary and commission plans while reducing the potential shortcomings of each. A majority of companies use combination plans today.

Nonmonetary rewards are also given to salespeople for meeting or exceeding objectives. These rewards include trips, honor societies, distinguished salesperson awards, and letters of commendation. Some unconventional rewards include the new pink Cadillacs and Buicks and jewelry given by Mary Kay Cosmetics to outstanding salespeople. Mary Kay, with 12,000 cars, has the largest fleet of General Motors cars in the world.[25]

Effective recruitment, selection, training, motivation, and compensation programs combine to create a productive salesforce. Ineffective practices often lead to costly salesforce turnover. The expense of replacing and training a new salesperson, including the cost of lost sales, can be high. Also, new recruits are often less productive than seasoned salespeople.[26]

Salesforce Evaluation: Measuring Results

The final function in the sales management process involves evaluating the salesforce. It is at this point that salespeople are assessed as to whether sales objectives were met and account management policies were followed. Both quantitative and behavioral measures are used to tap different selling dimensions.

Quantitative Assessments   Quantitative assessments are based on input- and output-related objectives set forth in the sales plan. Input-related measures focus on the actual activities performed by salespeople such as those involving sales calls, selling expenses, and account management policies. The number of sales calls made, selling expense related to sales made, and the number of reports submitted to superiors are frequently used input measures.

sales quota
Specific goals assigned to a salesperson, sales team, branch sales office, or sales district for a stated time period.

Output measures often appear in a sales quota. A **sales quota** contains specific goals assigned to a salesperson, sales team, branch sales office, or sales district for a stated time period. Dollar or unit sales volume, last year/current year sales ratio, sales of specific products, new accounts generated, and profit achieved are typical goals. The time period can range from one month to one year.

Behavioral Evaluation   Behavioral measures are also used to evaluate salespeople. These include assessments of a salesperson's attitude, attention to customers, product knowledge, selling and communication skills, appearance, and professional demeanor. Even though these assessments are sometimes subjective, they are frequently considered and, in fact, inevitable, in salesperson evaluation. Why? These factors are often important determinants of quantitative outcomes.

Using Marketing Dashboards

Tracking Salesperson Performance at Moore Chemical & Sanitation Supply, Inc.

Moore Chemical & Sanitation Supply, Inc. (MooreChem) is a large midwestern supplier of cleaning chemicals and sanitary products. MooreChem sells to janitorial companies that clean corporate and professional office buildings.

MooreChem recently installed a sales and account management planning software package that included a dashboard for each of its sales representatives. Salespeople had access to their dashboards as well. These dashboards included seven metrics—sales revenue, gross margin, selling expense, profit, average order size, new customers, and customer satisfaction. Each metric was gauged to show actual salesperson performance relative to target goals.

Your Challenge As a newly promoted district sales manager at MooreChem, your responsibilities include tracking each salesperson's performance in your district. You are also responsible for directing the sales activities and practices of district salespeople.

In anticipation of a performance review with one of your salespeople, Brady Boyle, you review his dashboard for the previous quarter. This information can be used to provide a constructive review of his performance.

Your Findings Brady Boyle's quarterly performance is displayed below. Boyle has exceeded targeted goals for sales revenue, selling expenses, and customer satisfaction. All of these metrics show an upward trend. He has met his target for gaining new customers and average order size. But, Boyle's gross margin and profit are below targeted goals. These metrics evidence a downward trend as well. Brady Boyle's mixed performance requires a constructive and positive correction.

Your Action Brady Boyle should already know how his performance compares with targeted goals. Remember, Boyle has access to his dashboard. Recall that he has exceeded his sales target, but is considerably under his profit target. Boyle's sales trend is up, but his profit trend is down.

You will need to focus attention on Boyle's gross margin and selling expense results and trend. Boyle, it seems, is spending time and money selling lower-margin products that produce a targeted average order size. It may very well be that Boyle is actually expending effort selling more products to his customers. Unfortunately, the product mix yields lower gross margins, resulting in a lower profit.

Metric	Actual as % of Target	Trend	Actual
Sales Revenue		↗	$913,394
Gross Margin		↘	$356,212
Selling Expense		↗	$162,356
Profit		↘	$193,856
Average Order Size		→	$5,766
New Customers		→	10
Customer Satisfaction		↗	4.73 / 5.00

About 60 percent of U.S. companies now include customer satisfaction as a behavioral measure of salesperson performance. The relentless focus on customer satisfaction by Eastman Chemical Company salespeople contributed to the company being named a recipient of the prestigious Malcolm Baldrige National Quality Award.[27] Eastman surveys its customers with multiple versions of its customer satisfaction questionnaire delivered in nine languages. Some 25 performance items are studied, including on-time and correct delivery, product quality, pricing practice, and sharing of market information. Salespeople review the results with customers. Eastman salespeople know that "the second most important thing they have to do is get their customer satisfaction surveys out to and back from customers," says Eastman's sales training director. "Number one, of course, is getting orders."

Increasingly, companies are using marketing dashboards to track salesperson performance for evaluation purposes. An illustration appears in the Using Marketing Dashboards box.

CHAPTER 17 Personal Selling and Sales Management

Toshiba America Medical
Systems salespeople have
found computer technology
to be an effective sales
presentation tool and
training device.

**Toshiba America Medical
Systems**
www.toshiba.com

Salesforce Automation and Customer Relationship Management

Personal selling and sales management have undergone a technological revolution with the integration of salesforce automation into customer relationship management processes. In fact, the convergence of computer, information, communication, and Internet technologies has transformed the sales function in many companies and made the promise of customer relationship management a reality. **Salesforce automation (SFA)** is the use of these technologies to make the sales function more effective and efficient. SFA applies to a wide range of activities, including each stage in the personal selling process and management of the salesforce itself.

salesforce automation (SFA)
The use of technology to make the sales function more effective and efficient.

Salesforce automation exists in many forms. Examples of SFA applications include computer hardware and software for account analysis, time management, order processing and follow-up, sales presentations, proposal generation, and product and sales training.[28] Each application is designed to ease administrative tasks and free time for salespeople to be with customers building relationships, designing solutions, and providing service.

Salesforce Technology   Technology has become an integral part of field selling. Today, most companies supply their field salespeople with laptop computers. For example, salespeople for Godiva Chocolates use their laptop computers to process orders, plan time allocations, forecast sales, and communicate with Godiva personnel and customers. While in a department store candy buyer's office, such as Neiman Marcus, a salesperson can calculate the order cost (and discount), transmit the order, and obtain a delivery date within minutes from Godiva's order processing department.

Toshiba America Medical Systems salespeople use laptop computers with built-in DVD capabilities to provide interactive presentations for their computerized tomography (CT) and magnetic resonance imaging (MRI) scanners. The computer technology allows the customer to see elaborate three-dimensional animations, high-resolution scans, and video clips of the company's products in operation as well as narrated testimonials from satisfied customers. Toshiba has found this application to be effective both for sales presentations and for training its salespeople.

Salesforce Communication   Technology has changed the way salespeople communicate with customers, other salespeople and sales support personnel, and management. Facsimile, electronic mail, and voice mail are common communication technologies used by salespeople today. Mobile phone and tablet device technologies now allow salespeople to exchange data, text, and voice transmissions. Whether traveling or in a customer's office, these technologies provide information at the salesperson's fingertips to answer customer questions and solve problems.

Perhaps the greatest impact on salesforce communication is the application of Internet technology. Today, salespeople are using their company's intranet for a variety of purposes. At HP Enterprise Services, a professional services firm, salespeople access its intranet to download client material, marketing content, account information, technical papers, and competitive profiles. In addition, HP Enterprise Services offers 7,000 training classes that salespeople can take anytime and anywhere.

Salesforce automation is clearly changing how selling is done and how salespeople are managed. Its numerous applications promise to boost selling productivity, improve customer relationships, and decrease selling cost.

> **learning review**
>
> 17-7. What are the three types of selling objectives?
>
> 17-8. What three factors are used to structure sales organizations?

LEARNING OBJECTIVES REVIEW

LO 17-1 *Discuss the nature and scope of personal selling and sales management in marketing.*

Personal selling involves the two-way flow of communication between a buyer and seller, often in a face-to-face encounter, designed to influence a person's or group's purchase decision. Sales management involves planning the selling program and implementing and controlling the personal selling effort of the firm. The scope of selling and sales management is apparent in three ways. First, virtually every occupation that involves customer contact has an element of personal selling. Second, selling plays a significant role in a company's overall marketing effort. Salespeople occupy a boundary position between buyers and sellers; they *are* the company to many buyers and account for a major cost of marketing in a variety of industries; and they can create value for customers. Finally, through relationship selling, salespeople play a central role in tailoring solutions to customer problems as a means to customer value creation.

LO 17-2 *Identify the different types of personal selling.*

Three types of personal selling exist: (*a*) order taking, (*b*) order getting, and (*c*) customer sales support activities. Each type differs from the others in terms of actual selling done and the amount of creativity required to perform the sales task. Order takers process routine orders or reorders for products that were already sold by the company. They generally do little selling in a conventional sense and engage in only modest problem solving with customers. Order getters sell in a conventional sense and identify prospective customers, provide customers with information, persuade customers to buy, close sales, and follow up on customers' use of a

product or service. Order getting involves a high degree of creativity and customer empathy and is typically required for selling complex or technical products with many options.

LO 17-3 *Explain the stages in the personal selling process.*

The personal selling process consists of six stages: (*a*) prospecting, (*b*) preapproach, (*c*) approach, (*d*) presentation, (*e*) close, and (*f*) follow-up. Prospecting involves the search for and qualification of potential customers. The preapproach stage involves obtaining further information on the prospect and deciding on the best method of approach. The approach stage involves the initial meeting between the salesperson and prospect. The presentation stage involves converting a prospect into a customer by creating a desire for the product or service. The close involves obtaining a purchase commitment from the prospect. The follow-up stage involves making certain that the customer's purchase has been properly delivered and installed and addressing any difficulties experienced with the use of the item.

LO 17-4 *Describe the major functions of sales management.*

Sales management consists of three interrelated functions: (*a*) sales plan formulation, (*b*) sales plan implementation, and (*c*) salesforce evaluation. Sales plan formulation involves setting objectives, organizing the salesforce, and developing account management policies. Sales plan implementation involves salesforce recruitment, selection, training, motivation, and compensation. Finally, salesforce evaluation focuses on quantitative assessments of sales performance and behavioral measures such as customer satisfaction that are linked to selling objectives and account management policies.

LEARNING REVIEW ANSWERS

17-1 **What is personal selling?**
Answer: Personal selling involves the two-way flow of communication between a buyer and seller, often in a face-to-face encounter, designed to influence a person's or group's purchase decision.

17-2 **What is involved in sales management?**
Answer: Sales management involves planning the selling program and implementing and evaluating the personal selling effort of the firm.

17-3 **What is the principal difference between an order taker and an order getter?**
Answer: An order taker processes routine orders or reorders for products that were already sold by the company. An order getter sells in a conventional sense and identifies prospective customers, provides customers with information, persuades customers to buy, closes sales, and follows up on customers' use of a product or service.

17-4 What percentage of an order-getting salesperson's time is spent selling?
Answer: 41 percent

17-5 What are the six stages in the personal selling process?
Answer: The six stages in the personal selling process are: (1) prospecting, (2) preapproach, (3) approach, (4) presentation, (5) close, and (6) follow-up.

17-6 Which presentation format is most consistent with the marketing concept? Why?
Answer: The need-satisfaction presentation format emphasizes probing and listening by the salesperson to identify the needs and interests of prospective buyers and then tailors the presentation to the prospect and highlights product benefits, which is consistent with the marketing concept and its focus on relationship building.

17-7 What are the three types of selling objectives?
Answer: The three types of selling objectives are: (1) output-related (dollars or unit sales, new customers, profit); (2) input-related (sales calls, selling expenses); and (3) behavioral-related (product knowledge, customer service, selling and communication skills).

17-8 What three factors are used to structure sales organizations?
Answer: geography; customer; product/service

FOCUSING ON KEY TERMS

account management policies p. 441
adaptive selling p. 437
consultative selling p. 438
major account management p. 441
order getter p. 433

order taker p. 432
personal selling p. 430
personal selling process p. 434
relationship selling p. 431
sales management p. 430

sales plan p. 440
sales quota p. 444
salesforce automation (SFA) p. 446

APPLYING MARKETING KNOWLEDGE

1 Jane Dawson is a new sales representative for the Charles Schwab brokerage firm. In searching for clients, Jane purchased a mailing list of subscribers to *The Wall Street Journal* and called them all regarding their interest in discount brokerage services. She asked if they have any stocks and if they have a regular broker. Those people without a regular broker were asked their investment needs. Two days later, Jane called back with investment advice and asked if they would like to open an account. Identify each of Jane Dawson's actions in terms of the personal selling process.

2 Where would you place each of the following sales jobs on the order-taker/order-getter continuum shown below? (*a*) Burger King counter clerk, (*b*) automobile insurance salesperson, (*c*) Hewlett-Packard computer salesperson, (*d*) life insurance salesperson, and (*e*) shoe salesperson.

Order taker	Order getter

3 Listed here are two different firms. Which compensation plan would you recommend for each firm, and what reasons would you give for your recommendations? (*a*) A newly formed company that sells lawn care equipment on a door-to-door basis directly to consumers; and (*b*) the Nabisco Company, which sells heavily advertised products in supermarkets by having the salesforce call on these stores and arrange shelves, set up displays, and make presentations to store buying committees.

4 Suppose someone said to you, "The only real measure of a salesperson is the amount of sales produced." How might you respond?

BUILDING YOUR MARKETING PLAN

Does your marketing plan involve a personal selling activity? If the answer is "no," read no further and do not include a personal selling element in your plan. If the answer is "yes":

1 Identify the likely prospects for your product or service.
2 Determine what information you should obtain about the prospect.

3 Describe how you would approach the prospect.
4 Outline the presentation you would make to the prospect for your product or service.
5 Develop a sales plan, focusing on the organizational structure you would use for your salesforce (geographic, product/service, or customer).

VIDEO CASE 17 Xerox: Building Customer Relationships through Personal Selling

Video 17-2
Xerox Video Case
kerin.tv/cr6e/v17-2

"I'm like the quarterback of the team. I manage 250 accounts, and anything from billing issues, to service issues, to selling the products. I'm really the face to the customer," says Alison Capossela, a Washington, DC–based Xerox sales representative.

As the primary company contact for Xerox customers, Alison is responsible for developing and maintaining customer relationships. To accomplish this she uses a sophisticated selling process that requires many activities from making presentations, to attending training sessions, to managing a team of Xerox personnel, to monitoring competitors' activities. The face-to-face interactions with customers, however, are the most rewarding for Capossela. "It's an amazing feeling; the more they challenge me the more I fight back. It's fun!" she explains.

THE COMPANY

Xerox Corporation's mission is to "help people find better ways to do great work by constantly leading in document technologies, products, and services that improve customers' work processes and business results." To accomplish this mission Xerox employs 130,000 people in 160 countries. Xerox is the world's leading document management enterprise and a *Fortune* 500 company.

Xerox offers a wide range of products and services. These include printers, copiers and fax machines, multifunction and network devices, high-speed color presses, digital imaging and archiving products and services, and supplies such as toner, paper, and ink. The entire company is guided by customer-focused and employee-centered core values (e.g., "We succeed through satisfied customers") and a passion for innovation, speed, and adaptability.

THE SELLING PROCESS AT XEROX

In 2001, Xerox began a shift to a consultative selling model that focused on helping customers solve their business problems rather than just placing more equipment in their office. The shift meant that sales reps needed to be less product-oriented and more relationship- and value-oriented. Xerox wanted to be a provider of total solutions.

Today, Xerox has more than 8,000 sales professionals throughout the world who spend a large amount of their day developing customer relationships. Capossela explains: "Fifty percent of my day is spent with my customers, 25 percent is following up with phone calls or e-mails, and another 25 percent involves preparing proposals." The approach has helped Xerox attract new customers and keep existing customers.

The sales process at Xerox typically follows the six stages of the personal selling process identified in Figure 20–3: (1) Xerox identifies potential clients through responses to advertising, referrals, and telephone calls; (2) the salesforce prepares for a presentation by familiarizing themselves with the potential client and its document needs; (3) a Xerox sales representative approaches the prospect and suggests a meeting and presentation; (4) as the presentation begins, the salesperson summarizes relevant information about potential solutions Xerox can offer, states what he or she hopes to get out of the meeting, explains how the products and services work, and reinforces the benefits of working with Xerox; (5) the salesperson engages in an action close (gets a signed document or a firm confirmation of the sale); and then (6) continues to meet and communicate with the client to provide assistance and monitor the effectiveness of the installed solution.

Xerox sales representatives also use the selling process to maintain relationships with existing customers. In today's competitive environment it is not unusual to have customers who have been approached by competitors or who are required to obtain more than one bid before renewing a contract. Xerox has teams of people who collect and analyze information about competitors and their products. The information is sent out to sales reps or offered to them through workshops and seminars. The most difficult competitors are the ones that have also invested in customer relationships. The selling process allows Xerox to continually react and respond to new information and take advantage of opportunities in the marketplace.

THE SALES MANAGEMENT PROCESS AT XEROX

The Xerox salesforce is divided into four geographic organizations: North America, which includes the United States and Canada; Europe, which includes 17 countries; Global Accounts, which manages large accounts that operate in multiple locations; and Developing Markets, which includes all other geographic territories that may require Xerox products and services. Within each geographic area, the majority of Xerox products and services are typically sold through its direct salesforce. Xerox also utilizes a variety of other channels, including value-added resellers, independent agents, dealers, systems integrators, telephone, and Internet sales channels.

Motivation and compensation are important aspects of any salesforce. At Xerox there is a passion for winning that provides a key incentive for sales reps. Compensation also plays an important role. In addition, Xerox has a recognition program called the President's Club where the top performers are awarded a five-day trip to one of the top resorts in the world. The program has been a huge success and has now been offered for more than 30 years.

Perhaps the most well-known component of Xerox's sales management process is its sales representative recruitment and training program. "For recruitment, Xerox looks for seasoned businesspeople who can talk to customers," says Kevin Warren, president of United States customer operations at Xerox. "Our value proposition is that we take care of document management to help run your business," Warren explains. "So we look for consultative and business-savvy salespeople."

On the training front, Xerox developed the "Create and Win" program to help sales reps learn the consultative selling approach. The components of the program consist of interactive training sessions and distance-learning webinars. Every new sales representative at Xerox receives eight weeks of training development in the field and at the Xerox Corporate University in Virginia. "The training program is phenomenal!" according to Capossela. The training and its focus on the customer is part of the Xerox culture outside of the sales organization also. Every senior executive at Xerox is responsible for working with at least one customer. They also spend a full day every month responding to incoming customer calls and inquiries.

WHAT IS IN THE FUTURE FOR THE XEROX SALESFORCE?

The recent growth and success at Xerox is creating many opportunities for the company and its sales representatives. For example, Xerox is accelerating the development of its top salespeople. Mentors are used to provide advice for day-to-day issues and long-term career planning. In addition, globalization has become such an important initiative at Xerox that experienced and successful sales representatives are quickly given opportunities to manage large global accounts.

Xerox is also moving toward an approach that empowers sales representatives to make decisions about how to handle accounts. The large number of Xerox customers means there are a variety of different corporate styles, and the sales reps are increasingly the best qualified to manage the relationship. This approach is just one more example of Xerox's commitment to customers and creating customer value.

Questions

1 How does Xerox create customer value through its personal selling process?
2 How does Alison Capossela provide solutions for Xerox customers?
3 Why is the Xerox training program so important to the company's success?

Chapter Notes

1. Interview with Lindsey Smith, GE Healthcare Americas, April 17, 2013.
2. Jessi Hempel, "IBM's All-Star Salesman," www.cnnmoney.com, September 26, 2008.
3. "Surgical Visits," *Business 2.0*, April 2006, p. 94.
4. Mark W. Johnston and Greg W. Marshall, *Contempory Selling; Building Relationships, Creating Value* (Burr Ridge, IL: McGraw-Hill/Irwin, 2014).
5. Richard P. Bagozzi, et al., "Genetic and Neurological Foundations of Customer Orientation: Field and Experimental Evidence," *Journal of the Academy of Marketing Science*, September 2012, pp. 639–58; and "Does Your Salesperson Have the Right Genes?" *Harvard Business Review*, April 2013, p. 24.
6. Gerhard Gschwandtner, "How Much Time Do Your Salespeople Spend Selling?" *Selling Power*, March/April 2011, p. 8.
7. "The New Willy Loman Survives by Staying Home," *Bloomberg Businessweek*, January 14–January 20, 2013, pp. 16–17.
8. Scott Sterns, "Cold Calls Have Yet to Breathe Their Last Gasp," *The Wall Street Journal*, December 14, 2006, p. D2.
9. Jim Edwards, "Dinner, Interrupted," *BrandWeek*, May 26, 2003, pp. 28–32.
10. Christopher Conkey, "Record Fine Levied for Telemarketing," *The Wall Street Journal*, December 14, 2005, pp. D1, D4.

11. Philip R. Cateora, Mary C. Gilly, and John L. Graham, *International Marketing*, 16th ed. (Burr Ridge, IL: McGraw-Hill/Irwin, 2013).
12. This discussion is based on Johnston and Marshall, *Contemporary Selling*; and "In Transition—Xerox," www.sellingpower.com, June 15, 2011.
13. Kapil R. Tuli, Ajay K. Kohli, and Sundar G. Bharadwaj, "Rethinking Customer Solutions: From Product Bundles to Relational Processes," *Journal of Marketing*, July 2007, pp. 1–17.
14. For an extensive discussion of objections, see Charles M. Futrell, *Fundamentals of Selling*, 13th ed. (Burr Ridge, IL: McGraw-Hill/Irwin, 2014), chapter 12.
15. Theodore Levitt, *The Marketing Imagination* (New York: Free Press, 1983), p. 111.
16. Barton A. Weitz, Stephen B. Castleberry, and John F. Tanner, Jr., *Selling: Building Partnerships*, 8th ed. (Burr Ridge, IL: McGraw-Hill/Irwin, 2012).
17. *Management Briefing: Sales and Marketing* (New York: Conference Board, October 1996), pp. 3–4.
18. William L. Cron and David W. Cravens, "Sales Force Strategy," in Robert A. Peterson and Roger A. Kerin, eds., *Wiley International Encyclopedia of Marketing: Volume 1—Marketing Strategy* (West Sussex, UK: John Wiley & Sons, Ltd., 2011), pp. 197–207.

19. This discussion is based on William L. Cron and Thomas E. DeCarlo, *Dalrymple's Sales Management*, 10th ed. (Hoboken, NJ: John Wiley & Sons, Inc., 2009).

20. René Y. Darmon, *Leading the Sales Force* (New York: Cambridge University Press, 2007).

21. Blair Kidwell, David M. Hardesty, Brian R. Murtha, and Shibin Sheng, "Emotional Intelligence in Marketing Exchanges," *Journal of Marketing*, January 2011, pp. 78–93; and Elizabeth J. Rozell, Charles E. Pettijohn, and R. Stephen Parker, "Customer-Oriented Selling: Exploring the Roles of Emotional Intelligence and Organizational Commitment," *Psychology & Marketing*, June 2004, pp. 405–24.

22. Thomas L. Powers, Thomas E. DeCarlo, and Gouri Gupte, "An Update on the Status of Sales Management Training," *Journal of Personal Selling & Sales Management*, Fall 2010, pp. 319–26.

23. Julia Chang, "Wholly Motivated," *Sales & Marketing Management*, March 2007, pp. 24ff.

24. This discussion is based on Johnston and Marshall, *Sales Force Management*, 11th ed. (Burr Ridge, IL: McGraw & Hill, 2014), chapter 11; and Andris Zoltners, Prabhakant Sinha, and Sally E. Lorimer, *The Complete Guide to Sales Force Incentive Compensation* (New York: AMACOM, 2006).

25. www.MaryKay.com, downloaded April 10, 2014.

26. Jeffrey E. Lewin and Jeffrey K. Sager, "The Influence of Personal Characteristics and Coping Strategies on Salespersons' Turnover Intentions," *Journal of Personal Selling & Sales Management*, Fall 2010, pp. 355–70; and René Y. Darmon, "The Concept of Salesperson Replacement Value: A Sales Force Turnover Management Tool," *Journal of Personal Selling & Sales Management*, Summer 2008, pp. 211–32.

27. Gary Hallen and Robert Latino, "Eastman Chemical's Success Story," *Quality Progress*, June 2003, pp. 50–54.

28. Ronald Jelinek, "All Pain, No Gain? Why Adapting Sales Force Automation Tools Is Insufficient for Performance Improvement," *Business Horizon* 56, 2013, pp. 635–42; and Mark Cotteleer, Edward Inderrieden, and Felissa Lee, "Selling the Sales Force on Automation," *Harvard Business Review*, July–August 2006, pp. 18–22.

Xerox: This case was written by Steven Hartley and Roger Kerin. Sources: "In Transition—Xerox," www.sellingpower.com, June 15, 2011; Joseph Kornik, "Table Talk: A Sales Leaders Roundtable," *Sales & Marketing Management*, February 2007; Philip Chadwick, "Xerox Global Service," *Printweek*, October 11, 2007, p. 32; Sarah Campbell, "What It's Like Working for Xerox," *The Times*, September 14, 2006, p. 9; Simon Avery, "CEO's HR Skills Turn Xerox Fortunes," *The Globe and Mail*, June 2, 2006, p. B3; Julia Chang, "Ultimate Motivation Guide: Happy Sales Force, Happy Returns," *Sales & Marketing Management*, March 2006; and resources available on the Xerox website, www.xerox.com.

Credits

18

Implementing Interactive and Multichannel Marketing

LEARNING OBJECTIVES

After reading this chapter you should be able to:

 LO 18-1 Describe what interactive marketing is and how it creates customer value, customer relationships, and customer experiences.

 LO 18-2 Explain why certain types of products and services are particularly suited for interactive marketing.

 LO 18-3 Describe why consumers shop and buy online and how marketers influence online purchasing behavior.

 LO 18-4 Define cross-channel shoppers and the role of transactional and promotional websites in reaching these shoppers.

SEVEN CYCLES DELIVERS JUST ONE BIKE. YOURS.

"One Bike. Yours." is the company tagline for Seven Cycles, Inc., located in Watertown, Massachusetts. And for good reason.

Seven Cycles is the world's largest custom bicycle frame builder. The company produces a broad range of road, mountain, cyclocross, tandem, touring, single-speed, and commuter bikes annually, and no two bikes are exactly alike.

At Seven Cycles, attention is focused on each customer's unique cycling experience through the optimum fit, function, performance, and comfort of his or her very own bike. According to one satisfied customer, "Getting a Seven is more of a creation than a purchase."

While Seven Cycles does offer stock frames in more than 200 sizes, each is still built-to-order and a full 95 percent of the bicycle frames that Seven ships are completely custom made. Customized elements include frame size, frame geometry, tubing diameters, and wall thickness, as well as countless options such as cable routing, water bottle mounts, paint color, and decal color. Every custom option is available at no additional charge and the number of combinations is virtually infinite.

The marketing success of Seven Cycles is due to its state-of-the-art bicycle frames. But as Rob Vandermark, company founder and president, says, "Part of our success is that we are tied to a business model that includes the Internet."

Seven uses its multilanguage (English, German, Chinese, Japanese, Korean, and Flemish) website (www.sevencycles.com) to let customers get deeply involved in the frame-building process and the selection of components to outfit their complete bike. It enables customers to collaborate on the design of their own bike using the company's Custom Kit fitting system, which considers the rider's size, aspirations, and riding habits. Then customers can monitor their bike's progress through the development and production process by clicking "Where's My Frame?" on the Seven Cycles website.

This customization process and continuous feedback make for a collaborative relationship between Seven Cycles, its nearly 200 authorized retailers in the United States, some 30 international distributors, and customers in 40 countries. "Our whole process is designed to keep the focus on the rider the bike is being built for, so it ends up being a very different and more interactive experience than most people are used to. That experience is a large part of the value we sell, above and beyond the bike," explains Jennifer Miller, operations manager at Seven Cycles.

In addition to the order process, website visitors can peruse weekly news stories and learn about new product introductions to get a unique perspective on the business. They can read employee biographies online to learn more about the people who build the bikes. The website also offers a retailer-specific section as a 24/7 repository of updated information for the company's channel partners.

Beyond the website, current Seven owners can interact with the company on the Seven Cycles blog to learn about its activities and products. Seven Cycles also uses its company Facebook Page and Twitter account to post brief and timely updates and build a stronger sense of community around the brand.[1]

This chapter describes how companies design and implement interactive marketing programs. It begins by explaining how Internet technology can create customer value, build customer relationships, and produce customer experiences in novel ways. Next, it describes how Internet technology affects and is affected by consumer behavior and marketing practice. Finally, the chapter shows how marketers integrate and leverage their communication and delivery channels using Internet technology to implement multichannel marketing programs to better serve cross-channel shoppers.

CREATING CUSTOMER VALUE, RELATIONSHIPS, AND EXPERIENCES IN MARKETSPACE

LO 18-1 Describe what interactive marketing is and how it creates customer value, customer relationships, and customer experiences.

Consumers and companies populate two market environments today. One is the traditional *marketplace*. Here buyers and sellers engage in face-to-face exchange relationships in a material environment characterized by physical facilities (stores and offices) and mostly tangible objects. The other is the *marketspace*, an Internet-enabled digital environment characterized by face-to-screen exchange relationships and electronic images and offerings.

The existence of two market environments has been a boon for consumers. Today, consumers can shop for and purchase a wide variety of products and services in either market environment. Actually, many consumers now browse and buy in both market environments. More are expected to do so in the future as mobile devices, notably smartphones, expand their capabilities.

Figure 18–1 shows the growth in online retail sales in the United States since 2012. About 90 percent of Internet users ages 15 and older shop online in the United States. They are expected to buy $370 billion worth of products and services in 2017 (excluding travel, automobile, and prescription drugs).[2]

Marketing in two market environments poses significant challenges and opportunities for companies. Companies with origins in the traditional marketplace, such as Procter & Gamble, Walmart, and General Motors, are continually challenged to define the nature and scope of their marketspace presence. These and other companies consistently refine the role of Internet technology in attracting, retaining, and building consumer relationships to improve their competitive positions in the traditional marketplace while also bolstering their marketspace presence.

On the other hand, companies with marketspace origins, including Amazon.com, Google, eBay, E*TRADE, and others, are challenged to continually refine, broaden, and deepen their marketspace presence. At the same time, these companies must consider what role, if any, the traditional marketplace with a physical presence will play in their future. Regardless of origin, a company's success in achieving a meaningful marketspace presence hinges largely on its ability to design and execute a marketing program that capitalizes on the unique value-creation and relationship-building capabilities of Internet technology in delivering a favorable customer experience.[3]

Creating Customer Value in Marketspace

Why has the marketspace captured the eye and imagination of marketers worldwide? Recall from Chapter 1 that marketing creates time, place, form, and possession

FIGURE 18–1
Online retail sales will grow at a compound annual rate of 10% from 2012 to 2017. By 2017, online retail sales will account for 10% of total U.S retail sales.

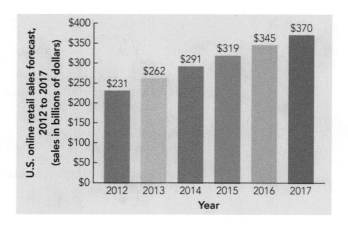

utilities, thereby providing value. Marketers believe that the possibilities for customer value creation are greater in the digital marketspace than in the physical marketplace.

Consider place and time utility. In marketspace, the provision of direct, on-demand information is possible from marketers *anywhere* to customers *anywhere, at any time*. Why? Operating hours and geographical constraints do not exist in marketspace. For example, Recreational Equipment, Inc. (www.rei.com), an outdoor gear marketer, reports that 35 percent of its orders are placed between 10:00 P.M. and 7:00 A.M., long after and before retail stores are open for business. Similarly, a U.S. consumer from Chicago can access Marks & Spencer (www.marks-and-spencer.co.uk), the well-known British department store, to shop for clothing as easily as a person living near London's Piccadilly Square.

Possession utility—getting a product or service to consumers so they can own or use it—is accelerated. Airline, car rental, and lodging electronic reservation systems such as Orbitz (www.orbitz.com) allow comparison shopping for the lowest fares, rents, and rates and almost immediate access to and confirmation of travel arrangements and accommodations.

The greatest marketspace opportunity for marketers, however, lies in its potential for creating form utility. Interactive two-way Internet-enabled communication capabilities in marketspace invite consumers to tell marketers specifically what their requirements are, making customization of a product or service to fit their exact needs possible. Today, 35 percent of online consumers are interested in customizing product features or in purchasing build-to-order products that use their specifications.[4] At Seven Cycles, customers can arrange for a custom-made mountain bike to fit their specifications, as described in the chapter-opening example.

Seven Cycles offers form utility by creating customized bikes for customers in 40 countries.

Seven Cycles, Inc.
www.sevencycles.com

Mars, Inc., uses choiceboard technology to decorate M&M's® candies with personal photos and messages.

Mars, Inc.

www.mymms.com

Video 18-1
My M&M's®
kerin.tv/cr6e/v18-1

interactive marketing
Two-way buyer–seller electronic communication in a computer-mediated environment in which the buyer controls the kind and amount of information received from the seller.

choiceboard
An interactive, Internet-enabled system that allows individual customers to design their own products and services.

collaborative filtering
A process that automatically groups people with similar buying intentions, preferences, and behaviors and predicts future purchases.

personalization
The consumer-initiated practice of generating content on a marketer's website that is custom tailored to an individual's specific needs and preferences.

Creating Interactivity, Individuality, and Customer Relationships in Marketspace

Marketers also benefit from two unique capabilities of Internet technology that promote and sustain customer relationships. One is *interactivity*; the other is *individuality*.[5] Both capabilities are important building blocks for buyer–seller relationships. For these relationships to occur, companies need to interact with their customers by listening and responding to their needs. Marketers must also treat customers as individuals and empower them to (1) influence the timing and extent of the buyer–seller interaction and (2) have a say in the kind of products and services they buy, the information they receive, and in some cases, the prices they pay.

Internet technology allows for interaction, individualization, and customer relationship building to be carried out on a scale never before available and makes interactive marketing possible. **Interactive marketing** involves two-way buyer–seller electronic communication in a computer-mediated environment in which the buyer controls the kind and amount of information received from the seller. Interactive marketing is characterized by sophisticated choiceboard and personalization systems that transform information supplied by customers into customized responses to their individual needs.

Choiceboards   A **choiceboard** is an interactive, Internet-enabled system that allows individual customers to design their own products and services by answering a few questions and choosing from a menu of product or service attributes (or components), prices, and delivery options. Customers today can design their own computers with Dell's online configurator, style their own athletic shoe at www.reebok.com, assemble their own investment portfolios with Schwab's mutual fund evaluator, build their own bicycle at www.sevencycles.com, create a diet and fitness program to fit their lifestyle at www.ediet.com, and decorate M&M's® with photos of themselves and unique messages at www.mymms.com. Because choiceboards collect precise information about the preferences and behavior of individual buyers, a company becomes more knowledgeable about a customer and better able to anticipate and fulfill that customer's needs.

Most choiceboards are essentially transaction devices. However, companies have expanded the functionality of choiceboards using collaborative filtering technology. **Collaborative filtering** is a process that automatically groups people with similar buying intentions, preferences, and behaviors and predicts future purchases. For example, say two people who have never met buy a few of the same books over time. Collaborative filtering software is programmed to reason that these two buyers might have similar tastes: If one buyer likes a particular book, then the other will like it as well. The outcome? Collaborative filtering gives marketers the ability to make a dead-on sales recommendation to a buyer in *real time*. You see collaborative filtering applied each time you view a selection at Amazon.com and see "Customers who bought this (item) also bought. . . ."

Personalization   Choiceboards and collaborative filtering are marketer-initiated efforts to provide customized responses to the needs of individual buyers. Personalization systems are typically buyer-initiated efforts. **Personalization** is the consumer-initiated practice of generating content on a marketer's website that is custom tailored to an individual's specific needs and preferences.

Today, one-half of the largest online retailers in the United States use personalization techniques.[6] For example, Yahoo! (www.yahoo.com) allows users to create personalized MyYahoo! pages. Users can add or delete a variety of types of information

Reebok uses choiceboard technology to create customized athletic shoes for its customers.

Reebok

www.reebok.com

from their personal pages, including specific stock quotes, weather conditions in any city in the world, and local television schedules. In turn, Yahoo! uses the buyer profile data entered when users register at the site to tailor e-mail messages, advertising, and content to the individual—and post a happy birthday greeting on the user's special day.

An important aspect of personalization is a buyer's willingness to have tailored communications brought to his or her attention. Obtaining this approval is called **permission marketing**—the solicitation of a consumer's consent (called *opt-in*) to receive e-mail and advertising based on personal data supplied by the consumer. Permission marketing is a proven vehicle for building and maintaining customer relationships, provided it is properly used.

Companies that successfully employ permission marketing adhere to three rules. First, they make sure opt-in customers receive only information that is relevant and meaningful to them. Second, their customers are given the option to *opt-out*, or change the kind, amount, or timing of information sent to them. Finally, their customers are assured that their name or buyer profile data will not be sold or shared with others. This assurance is important because 86 percent of adult Internet users are so concerned about the privacy of their personal information that they have taken steps to remove or mask their digital footprints.[7]

> **permission marketing**
> The solicitation of a consumer's consent (called *opt-in*) to receive e-mail and advertising based on personal data supplied by the consumer.

Creating an Online Customer Experience

A continuing challenge for companies is the design and execution of marketing programs that capitalize on the unique customer value-creation capabilities of Internet technology. Companies realize that applying Internet technology to create time, place, form, and possession utility is just a starting point for creating a meaningful marketspace presence. Today, the quality of the customer experience produced by a company is the standard by which a meaningful marketspace presence is measured.

From an interactive marketing perspective, *customer experience* is defined as the sum total of the interactions that a customer has with a company's website, from the initial look at a home page through the entire purchase decision process.[8] Companies

Context Site's layout and visual design		**Commerce** Site's capabilities to enable commercial transactions
Content Text, pictures, sound, and video that the site contains		**Community** The ways that the site enables user-to-user communication
Customization Site's ability to tailor itself to different users or to allow users to personalize the site	**Connection** Degree that site is linked to other sites	**Communication** The ways the site enables site-to-user, user-to-site, or two-way communication

FIGURE 18–2
Seven website design elements that drive customer experience.

produce a customer experience through seven website design elements. These elements are context, content, community, customization, communication, connection, and commerce. Each is summarized in Figure 18–2. A closer look at these elements illustrates how each contributes to customer experience.

Context   *Context* refers to a website's aesthetic appeal and the functional look and feel of the site's layout and visual design. A functionally oriented website focuses largely on the company's offering, be it products, services, or information. Deal-oriented travel websites, such as Priceline.com, tend to be functionally oriented with an emphasis on destinations, scheduling, and prices. In contrast, beauty websites, such as Revlon.com, are more aesthetically oriented. As these examples suggest, context attempts to convey the core consumer benefit provided by the company's offerings.

Content   *Content* applies to all digital information on a website, including the presentation form—text, video, audio, and graphics. Content quality and presentation along with context dimensions combine to engage a website visitor and provide a platform for the five remaining design elements.

Customization   Website *customization* is the ability of a site to modify itself to, or be modified by and for, each individual user. This design element is prominent in websites that offer personalized content, such as My eBay and MyYahoo!

Connection   The *connection* element is the network of linkages between a company's site and other sites. These links are embedded in the website; appear as highlighted words, a picture, or graphic; and allow a user to effortlessly visit other sites with a mouse click. Connection is a major design element for informational websites such as *The New York Times*. Users of NYTimes.com can access the book review

Travelocity pays close attention to creating a favorable customer experience by employing all seven website design elements.

Travelocity
www.travelocity.com

section and link to Barnes & Noble to order a book or browse related titles without ever visiting a store.

Communication   *Communication* refers to the dialogue that unfolds between the website and its users. Consumers—particularly those who have registered at a site—now expect that communication to be interactive and individualized in real time much like a personal conversation. In fact, some websites now enable a user to talk directly with a customer representative while shopping the site. For example, two-thirds of the sales through Dell.com involve human sales representatives.

Community   In addition, many company websites encourage user-to-user communications hosted by the company to create virtual communities, or simply, *community*. This design element is popular because it has been shown to enhance customer experience and build favorable buyer–seller relationships. Examples of communities range from the Pampers Village hosted by Procter & Gamble (www .pampers.com) to the Harley Owners Group (HOG) sponsored by Harley-Davidson (www.harley-davidson.com).

Commerce   The seventh design element is *commerce*—the website's ability to conduct sales transactions for products and services. Online transactions are quick and simple in well-designed websites. Amazon.com has mastered this design element with "one-click shopping," a patented feature that allows users to order products with a single mouse click.

   Most websites do not include every design element. Although every website has context and content, they differ in the use of the remaining five elements. Why? Websites have different purposes. For example, only websites that emphasize the actual sale of products and services include the commerce element. Websites that are used primarily for advertising and promotion purposes emphasize the communication element. The difference between these two types of websites is discussed later in the chapter in the description of multichannel marketing.

   Companies use a broad array of measures to assess website performance. For example, the amount of time per month visitors spend on their website, or "stickiness," is used to gauge customer experience.[9] Read the Using Marketing Dashboards box on the next page to learn how stickiness is measured and interpreted at one of the largest automobile dealerships in the United States.

learning review

18-1.   The consumer-initiated practice of generating content on a marketer's website that is custom tailored to an individual's specific needs and preferences is called _____.

18-2.   What are the seven website design elements that companies use to produce a customer experience?

CHAPTER 18   Implementing Interactive and Multichannel Marketing

Using Marketing Dashboards

Sizing Up Site Stickiness at Sewell Automotive Companies

Automobile dealerships have invested significant time, effort, and money in their websites. Why? Car browsing and shopping on the Internet is now commonplace.

Dealerships commonly measure website performance by tracking visits, visitor traffic, and "stickiness"—the amount of time per month visitors spend on their website. Website design, easy navigation, involving content, and visual appeal combine to enhance the interactive customer experience and website stickiness.

To gauge stickiness, companies monitor the average time spent per unique monthly visitor (in minutes) on their websites. This is done by tracking and displaying the average visits per unique monthly visitor and the average time spent per visit, in minutes, in their marketing dashboards. The relationship is as follows:

Average Time Spent per Unique Monthly Visitor (minutes) =

$$\begin{pmatrix} \text{Average Visits per} \\ \text{Unique Monthly Visitor} \end{pmatrix} \times \begin{pmatrix} \text{Average Time Spent} \\ \text{per Visit (minutes)} \end{pmatrix}$$

Your Challenge As the manager responsible for Sewell .com, the Sewell Automotive Companies's website, you have been asked to report on the effect that recent improvements in the company's website have had on the amount of time per month visitors spend on the website. Sewell ranks

among the largest U.S. automotive dealerships and is a recognized customer service leader in the automotive industry. Its website reflects the company's commitment to an unparalleled customer experience at its family of dealerships.

Your Findings Examples of monthly marketing dashboard traffic and time measures are displayed below for June 2008, three months before the website improvements (green arrow), and June 2009, three months after the improvements were made (red arrow).

The average time spent per unique monthly visitor increased from 8.5 minutes in June 2008 to 11.9 minutes in June 2009—a sizable jump. The increase is due primarily to the upturn in the average time spent per visit from 7.1 minutes to 8.5 minutes. The average number of visits also increased, but the percentage change was much less.

Your Action Improvements in the website have noticeably "moved the needle" on average time spent per unique monthly visitor. Still, additional action may be required to increase average visits per unique monthly visitor. These actions might include an analysis of Sewell's web advertising program, search engine initiatives with Google, links to automobile manufacturer corporate websites, and broader print and electronic media advertising.

Average Time Spent per Unique Monthly Visitor (minutes)

=

Average Visits per Unique Monthly Visitor

×

Average Time Spent per Visit (minutes)

ONLINE CONSUMER BEHAVIOR AND MARKETING PRACTICE IN MARKETSPACE

Who are online consumers, and what do they buy? Why do they choose to shop and purchase products and services in the digital marketspace rather than (or in addition to) the traditional marketplace? Answers to these questions have a direct bearing on marketspace marketing practices.

Who Is the Online Consumer?

Online consumers are the subsegment of all Internet users who employ this technology to research products and services and make purchases. As a group, online consumers are equally likely to be women and men and tend to be better educated, younger, and

Marketing Matters

Meet Today's Internet Mom on a Mission

Do you have fond childhood memories of surfing the Internet with your mother?

Research indicates that 95 percent of mothers with children under 18 years old will be online regularly by 2015. Internet moms are typically 38 years old. They tend to be married, college educated, and work outside the home.

Results from a recent Disney Online M.O.M.—Mom on a Mission—study show how today's mother uses the Internet. Consider that:

1. Internet moms spend the most time online between the hours of 5 A.M. and noon.
2. Seventy-five percent of moms go online with a specific task or goal in mind. They are not surfers.
3. Moms spend an average of 6.9 hours per week online connecting with family and friends: 84 percent stay connected through e-mail and 69 percent through social networks.
4. For subjects other than their child's health, moms turn to the Internet as their primary source of information about: (a) shopping deals or discounts; (b) cooking/baking recipes and nutrition/dieting; (c) family activities, entertainment, and travel; (d) holiday planning and activities; (e) beauty/style suggestions; and (f) financial planning.

According to a Disney Online spokesperson, "Moms juggle so many roles, from being the caregiver and household CEO, to coordinating the family's activities. Our study results showed that the Internet is helping to make moms' lives more manageable, so they can spend more quality time with their families."

more affluent than the general U.S. population.[10] This makes them an attractive market. Even though online shopping and buying is popular, a small percentage of online consumers still account for a disproportionate share of online retail sales in the United States. It is estimated that 20 percent of online consumers who spend $1,000-plus per year online account for 87 percent of total consumer online sales. Also, women tend to purchase more products and services online than men.

Numerous marketing research firms have studied the lifestyles and shopping habits of online consumers. A recurrent insight is that online consumers are diverse and represent different kinds of people seeking different kinds of online experiences. As an illustration, the Marketing Matters box provides an in-depth look at the lifestyle and shopping habits of today's "Internet mom."[11]

What Online Consumers Buy

 LO 18-2 Explain why certain types of products and services are particularly suited for interactive marketing.

Much still needs to be learned about online consumer purchase behavior. Although research has documented the most frequently purchased products and services bought online, marketers also need to know *why* these items are popular in the digital marketspace.

Five general product and service categories account for about two-thirds of online consumer buying today and for the foreseeable future. One category consists of items for which product information is an important part of the purchase decision, but prepurchase trial is not necessarily critical. Items such as computers, computer accessories, and consumer electronics fall into this category. So do books. Booksellers like Barnes & Noble publish short reviews of new books that visitors to their websites can read before making a purchase decision.

A second category includes items for which audio or video demonstration is important. The third category contains items that can be delivered digitally, including computer software, music, and video.

Unique items, such as specialty products, foods, beverages, and gifts, represent a fourth category. A fifth category includes items that are regularly purchased and where convenience is very important. Many consumer packaged goods, such as grocery products, personal care items, and office products, fall into this category. A final category of items consists of highly standardized products and services for which information about price is important. Certain kinds of home and automotive products, casual apparel, and toys make up this category.

Why Consumers Shop and Buy Online

LO 18-3 Describe why consumers shop and buy online and how marketers influence online purchasing behavior.

Why do consumers shop and buy online? Marketers emphasize the customer value-creation possibilities, the importance of interactivity, individuality, and relationship building, and their ability to produce a positive customer experience in the new marketspace. However, consumers typically refer to six reasons they shop and buy online: convenience, choice, customization, communication, cost, and control (Figure 18–3).

bots
Electronic shopping agents or robots that comb websites to compare prices and product or service features.

Convenience Online shopping and buying is *convenient*. Consumers can visit Walmart at www.walmart.com to scan and order from among thousands of displayed products without fighting traffic, finding a parking space, walking through long aisles, and standing in store checkout lines. Alternatively, online consumers can use **bots**, electronic shopping agents or robots that comb websites to compare prices and product or service features. In either instance, an online consumer has never ventured into a store. However, for convenience to remain a source of customer value creation, websites must be easy to locate and navigate, and image downloads must be fast.

eight-second rule
A view that customers will abandon their efforts to enter and navigate a website if download time exceeds eight seconds.

A commonly held view among online marketers is the **eight-second rule**: Customers will abandon their efforts to enter and navigate a website if download time exceeds eight seconds. Furthermore, the more clicks and pauses between clicks required to access information or make a purchase, the more likely it is a customer will exit a website.

Choice *Choice*, the second reason consumers shop and buy online, has two dimensions. First, choice exists in the product or service selection offered to consumers. Buyers desiring selection can avail themselves of numerous websites for almost anything they want. For instance, online buyers of consumer electronics can shop individual manufacturers such as Bose (www.bose.com) and QVC.com, a general merchant that offers more than 100,000 products.

FIGURE 18–3
Why do consumers shop and buy online? Read the text to learn how convenience, choice, customization, communication, cost, and control result in a favorable customer experience.

Zappos.com is successful because it meets all the requirements necessary for consumers to shop and buy online. In less than 10 years, the company has posted significant annual sales of shoes, apparel, bags, accessories, housewares, and jewelry.

Zappos.com
www.zappos.com

web communities
Websites that allow people to meet online and exchange views on topics of common interest.

spam
Electronic junk mail or unsolicited e-mail.

Choice assistance is the second dimension. Here, the interactive capabilities of Internet-enabled technologies invite customers to engage in an electronic dialogue with marketers for the purpose of making informed choices. Choice assistance is one of the reasons for the continued success of Zappos.com. The company offers an online chat room that enables prospective buyers to ask questions and receive answers in real time. In addition, carefully designed search capabilities permit consumers to review products by brand and particular items.

Customization Even with a broad selection and choice assistance, some customers prefer one-of-a-kind items that fit their specific needs. *Customization* arises from Internet-enabled capabilities that make possible a highly interactive and individualized information and exchange environment for shoppers and buyers. Remember the earlier Reebok, Schwab, Dell, and Seven Cycles examples? To varying degrees, online consumers also benefit from *customerization*—the growing practice of not only customizing a product or service but also personalizing the marketing and overall shopping and buying interaction for each customer.

Customerization seeks to do more than offer consumers the right product, at the right time, and at the right price. It combines choiceboard and personalization systems to expand the exchange environment beyond a transaction and makes shopping and buying an enjoyable, personal experience.

Communication Online consumers particularly welcome the *communication* capabilities of Internet-enabled technologies. This communication can take three forms: (1) marketer-to-consumer e-mail notification, (2) consumer-to-marketer buying and service requests, and (3) consumer-to-consumer chat rooms and instant messaging, in addition to social networking websites such as Twitter and Facebook.

Communication has proven to be a double-edged sword for online consumers. On the one hand, the interactive communication capabilities of Internet-enabled technologies increase consumer convenience, reduce information search costs, and make choice assistance and customization possible. Communication also promotes the development of company-hosted and independent **web communities**—websites that allow people to congregate online and exchange views on topics of common interest. For instance, Coca-Cola hosts MyCoke.com, and iVillage.com is an independent web community for women and includes topics such as career management, personal finances, parenting, relationships, beauty, and health.

Web logs, or blogs, are another form of communication. A *blog* is a web page that serves as a publicly accessible personal journal for an individual or organization. Blogs are popular because they provide online forums on a wide variety of subjects ranging from politics to car repair. Companies such as Hewlett-Packard, PepsiCo, and Harley-Davidson routinely monitor blogs and social media posts to gather customer insights.[12]

On the other hand, communications can take the form of electronic junk mail or unsolicited e-mail, called **spam**. In fact, 67 percent of e-mail messages in the world are spam.[13] The prevalence of spam has prompted many online services to institute policies and procedures to prevent spammers from spamming their subscribers, and several states have antispamming laws. The 2004 *CAN-SPAM (Controlling the Assault of Non-Solicited Pornography and Marketing) Act* restricts information collection and unsolicited e-mail promotions on the Internet.

463

CHAPTER 18 Implementing Interactive and Multichannel Marketing

Staffers in Gatorade's "Mission Control" room in Chicago, Illinois, monitor Internet and social media outlets, such as Facebook and Twitter, 24 hours a day. Whenever someone uses Twitter to say they are drinking a Gatorade or mentions the brand on Facebook or in a blog, it pops up on-screen at Mission Control. In this way, conversations featuring Gatorade provide useful consumer insights into how the brand is viewed and used.

Gatorade
www.gatorade.com

viral marketing
An Internet-enabled promotional strategy that encourages users to forward marketer-initiated messages to others via e-mail, social networking websites, and blogs.

Internet-enabled communication capabilities also make possible *buzz*, a popular term for word-of-mouth behavior in marketspace. Chapter 4 described the importance of word of mouth in consumer behavior. Internet technology has magnified its significance. According to Jeff Bezos, president of Amazon.com, "If you have an unhappy customer on the Internet, he doesn't tell his six friends, he tells his 6,000 friends!"[14] Buzz is particularly influential for toys, cars, sporting goods, motion pictures, apparel, consumer electronics, pharmaceuticals, health and beauty products, and health care services. Some marketers have capitalized on this phenomenon by creating buzz through viral marketing.

Viral marketing is an Internet-enabled promotional strategy that encourages individuals to forward marketer-initiated messages to others via e-mail, social networking websites, and blogs. There are three approaches to viral marketing. First, marketers can embed a message in the product or service so that customers hardly realize they are passing it along. The classic example is Hotmail, which was one of the first companies to provide free, Internet-based e-mail. Each outgoing e-mail message had the tagline: "Get Your Private, Free Email from MSN Hotmail." This effort produced more than 350 million users.

Second, marketers can make the website content so compelling that viewers want to share it with others. Careerbuilder.com has done this with its Monk-e-mail site, which allows users to send personalized, private-themed e-cards for all occasions. More than 100 million Monk-e-mails have been sent since 2006. Finally, marketers can offer incentives (discounts, sweepstakes, or free merchandise). For example, Burger King asked, "What do you love more, your friend or the Whopper?" in its Whopper Sacrifice campaign. Facebook users were asked to "unfriend" 10 people from their Facebook friends list in exchange for a free burger.[15]

Video 18-2
Frito-Lay
kerin.tv/cr6e/v18-2

Cost   Consumer *cost* is a fifth reason for online shopping and buying. Many popular items bought online can be purchased at the same price or cheaper than in retail

Careerbuilder.com, an online career placement company, has produced a great viral marketing success with its Monk-e-mail featuring talking monkeys. People can stylize their monkeys by choosing headgear, clothes, glasses, backgrounds, and other features. They can also record a message using one of four monkey voices, or their own voice. Monk-e-mail can be sent to friends or posted on Twitter.

CareerBuilder

www.careerbuilder.com

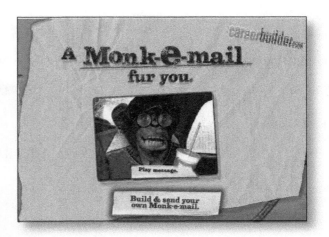

showrooming
Occurs when a shopper visits a retail store to inspect merchandise but then goes online to compare prices from other retail and online sellers to attempt to make the best purchase.

dynamic pricing
The practice of changing prices for products and services in real time in response to supply and demand conditions.

stores. The likelihood of lower online prices has given rise to a consumer practice called **showrooming**. Showrooming occurs when a shopper visits a retail store to inspect merchandise but then purchases the merchandise online. While obtaining a lower price is the primary motivator for showrooming, shoppers also engage in this practice to gather additional merchandise information, look for online promotions or deals, and check merchandise reviews and ratings. About half of U.S. online shoppers engage in showrooming. Consumer electronics, apparel, books, and home appliances are the most popular showrooming product categories.[16]

Lower prices also result from Internet-enabled software that permits **dynamic pricing**, the practice of changing prices for products and services in real time in response to supply and demand conditions. As described in Chapter 11, dynamic pricing is a form of flexible pricing and can often result in lower prices. It is typically used for pricing time-sensitive items such as airline seats, scarce items found at art or collectible auctions, and out-of-date items such as last year's models of computer equipment and accessories. Ticketmaster has recently experimented with dynamic pricing to adjust the price of sports and concert tickets in response to demand.

A consumer's cost of external information search, including time spent and often the hassle of shopping, is also reduced. Greater shopping convenience and lower external search costs are two major reasons for the popularity of online shopping and buying among women—particularly those who work outside the home.

cookies
Computer files that a marketer can download onto the computer and mobile phone of an online shopper who visits the marketer's website.

behavioral targeting
Uses information provided by cookies for directing online advertising from marketers to those online shoppers whose behavioral profiles suggest they would be interested in such advertising.

Control   The sixth reason consumers prefer to buy online is the *control* it gives them over their shopping and purchase decision process. Online shoppers and buyers are empowered consumers. They deftly use Internet technology to seek information, evaluate alternatives, and make purchase decisions on their own time, terms, and conditions. For example, studies show that shoppers spend an average of eleven hours researching cars online before setting foot in a showroom.[17] The result of these activities is a more informed and discerning shopper.

Even though consumers have many reasons for shopping and buying online, a segment of Internet users refrains from making purchases for privacy and security reasons. These consumers are concerned about a rarely mentioned seventh C—cookies.

Cookies are computer files that a marketer can download onto the computer and mobile phone of an online shopper who visits the marketer's website. Cookies allow the marketer's website to record a user's visit, track visits to other websites, and store and retrieve this information in the future. Cookies also contain visitor information such as expressed product preferences, personal data, passwords, and credit card numbers.

Cookies make possible customized and personal content for online shoppers. They also make possible the practice of behavioral targeting for marketers. **Behavioral targeting** uses information provided by cookies for directing online advertising from

Making Responsible Decisions

Who Is Responsible for Internet Privacy and Security?

Privacy and security are two key reasons consumers are leery of online shopping and buying. A recent Pew Internet & American Life Project poll reported that 86 percent of online consumers have privacy and security concerns about the Internet. And, 73 percent of online consumers considered it an invasion of privacy if a search engine tracked their activity to personalize future search results. Even more telling, many have stopped shopping a website or forgone an online purchase because of these concerns. Industry analysts estimate that over $30 million in e-commerce sales are lost annually because of privacy and security concerns among online shoppers.

Consumer concerns are not without merit. According to the Federal Trade Commission, 46 percent of fraud complaints are Internet related, costing consumers $560 million. In addition, consumers lose millions of dollars each year due to identity theft resulting from breaches in company security systems.

A percolating issue is whether the U.S. government should pass more stringent Internet privacy and security laws. About 70 percent of online consumers favor such action. Companies, however, favor self-regulation. For example, TRUSTe (www.truste.com) awards its trademark to company websites that comply with standards of privacy protection and disclosure. Still, consumers are ultimately responsible for using care and caution when engaging in online behavior, including e-commerce. Consumers have a choice of

whether or not to divulge personal information and are responsible for monitoring how their information is being used.

What role should the U.S. government, company self-regulation, and consumer vigilance play in dealing with privacy and security issues in the digital marketspace?

---

marketers to those online shoppers whose behavioral profiles suggest they would be interested in such advertising. A controversy surrounding cookies is summed up by an authority on the technology: "At best cookies make for a user-friendly web world: like a salesclerk who knows who you are. At worst, cookies represent a potential loss of privacy."[18] Read the Making Responsible Decisions box to learn more about privacy and security issues in the digital marketspace.[19]

When and Where Online Consumers Shop and Buy

Shopping and buying also happen at different times in marketspace than in the traditional marketplace.[20] About 80 percent of online retail sales occur Monday through Friday. The busiest shopping day is Wednesday. By comparison, 35 percent of retail store sales are registered on the weekend. Saturday is the most popular shopping day. Monday through Friday online shopping and buying often occur during normal work hours—some 30 percent of online consumers say they visit websites from their place of work, which partially accounts for the sales level during the workweek.

Favorite websites for workday shopping and buying include those featuring event tickets, auctions, online periodical subscriptions, flowers and gifts, consumer electronics, and travel. Websites offering health and beauty items, apparel and accessories, and music and video tend to be browsed and bought from a consumer's home.

learning review

18-3. What is viral marketing?

18-4. What are the six reasons consumers prefer to shop and buy online?

CROSS-CHANNEL SHOPPERS AND MULTICHANNEL MARKETING

 LO 18-4 Define cross-channel shoppers and the role of transactional and promotional websites in reaching these shoppers.

cross-channel shopper
An online consumer who researches products online and then purchases them at a retail store.

Consumers are more likely to browse than buy online. Consumer marketspace browsing and buying in the traditional marketplace has given rise to the cross-channel shopper and the importance of multichannel marketing.

Who Is the Cross-Channel Shopper?

The opposite of showrooming, a **cross-channel shopper** is an online consumer who researches products online and then purchases them at a retail store.[21] Recent research shows that 95 percent of U.S. online consumers are cross-channel shoppers. These shoppers represent both genders equally and are only slightly younger, on average, than online consumers. They tend to have a higher education, earn significantly more money, and are more likely to embrace technology in their lives than online consumers who don't cross-channel shop.

Cross-channel shoppers want the right product at the best price, and they don't want to wait several days for delivery. The top reasons these shoppers research items online before buying in stores include (1) the desire to compare products among different retailers; (2) the need for more information than is available in stores; and (3) the ease of comparing their options without having to trek to multiple retail locations.

Research shows that sales arising from cross-channel shoppers dwarf exclusive online retail sales. Retail sales revenue from cross-channel shoppers is estimated to be about five times greater than online retail sales.

Implementing Multichannel Marketing

The prominence of cross-channel shoppers has focused increased attention on multichannel marketing. Recall from Chapter 12 that *multichannel marketing* is the blending of different communication and delivery channels that are mutually reinforcing in attracting, retaining, and building relationships with consumers who shop and buy in the traditional marketplace and online—the cross-channel shopper.

The most common cross-channel shopping and buying path is to browse one or more websites and then purchase an item at a retail store. In fact, 63 percent of adult smartphone users go online while shopping in-store.[22] This shopping path might suggest that company websites for cross-channel shoppers should be similar. But they are not. Websites play a multifaceted role in multichannel marketing because they can serve as either a communication or delivery channel. Two general applications of websites exist based on their intended purpose: (1) transactional websites and (2) promotional websites.

Multichannel Marketing with Transactional Websites *Transactional websites* are essentially electronic storefronts. They focus principally on converting an online browser into an online, catalog, or in-store buyer using the website design elements described earlier. Transactional websites are most common among store and catalog retailers and direct selling companies, such as Tupperware. Retailers and direct selling firms have found that their websites, while cannibalizing sales volume from stores, catalogs, and sales representatives, attract new customers and influence sales. Consider Victoria's Secret, the well-known specialty retailer of intimate apparel for women ages 18 to 45. It reports that almost 60 percent of its website customers are men, most of whom generate new sales volume for the company.[23]

Transactional websites are used less frequently by manufacturers of consumer products. A recurring issue for manufacturers is the threat of *channel conflict*, described in Chapter 12, and the potential harm to trade relationships with their retailing intermediaries. Still, manufacturers do use transactional websites, often cooperating with retailers. For example, Callaway Golf Company markets its golf merchandise at www.callawaygolf.com but relies on a retailer close to the buyer to fill the order. The

Promotional websites seek to engage the visitor in an interactive experience involving games, contests, and quizzes with electronic coupons and other gifts as prizes.

Video 18-3
Pampers
kerin.tv/cr6e/v18-3

retailer ships the order to the buyer within 24 hours and is credited with the sale. The majority of retailers that sell Callaway merchandise participate in this relationship, including retail chains Golf Galaxy and Dick's Sporting Goods. According to Callaway's chief executive officer, "This arrangement allows us to satisfy the consumer but to do so in a way that didn't violate our relationship with our loyal trade partners—those 15,000 outlets that sell Callaway products."[24] For more on the unique arrangement between Callaway Golf and its marketing channel partners, see the opening example in Chapter 12.

In addition, Callaway, like other manufacturers, lists stores on its website where its merchandise can be shopped and bought. More often than not, however, manufacturers using multichannel marketing channels employ websites for advertising and promotion purposes.

Multichannel Marketing with Promotional Websites *Promotional websites* have a very different purpose than transactional sites. They advertise and promote a company's products and services and provide information on how items can be used and where they can be purchased. They often engage the visitor in an interactive experience involving games, contests, and quizzes with electronic coupons and other gifts as prizes. Procter & Gamble maintains separate websites for many of its leading brands, including Scope mouthwash (www.scopemouthwash.com) and Pampers diapers (www.pampers.com). Promotional sites are effective in generating interest in and trial of a company's products (see Figure 18–4).[25] Hyundai Motor America reports that 80 percent of the people visiting a Hyundai store first visited the brand's website (www.hyundaiusa.com) and 70 percent of Hyundai leads come from its website.

Promotional websites also can be used to support a company's traditional marketing channel and build customer relationships. This is the objective of the Clinique Division of Estée Lauder, Inc., which markets cosmetics through department stores. Clinique reports that 80 percent of current customers who visit its website (www.clinique.com) later purchase a Clinique product at a department store, while 37 percent of non-Clinique buyers make a Clinique purchase after visiting the company's website.

FIGURE 18–4
Implementing multichannel marketing with promotional websites is common today. Two successes are found at Hyundai Motor America and the Clinique Division of Estée Lauder, Inc.

- 70% of Hyundai leads come from its website.
- 80% of people visiting a Hyundai dealer first visited its website.

- 80% of current Clinique buyers who visit its website later purchase a Clinique product at a store.
- 37% of non-Clinique buyers make a Clinique purchase after visiting its website.

The popularity of multichannel marketing is apparent in its growing impact on online retail sales. Fully 75 percent of U.S. online retail sales are made by companies that practice multichannel marketing. Multichannel marketers are expected to register over 90 percent of U.S. online retail sales in 2017.

> **learning review**
>
> 18-5. A cross-channel shopper is _____.
>
> 18-6. Channel conflict between manufacturers and retailers is likely to arise when manufacturers use _____ websites.

LEARNING OBJECTIVES REVIEW

LO 18-1 *Describe what interactive marketing is and how it creates customer value, customer relationships, and customer experiences.*

Interactive marketing involves two-way buyer–seller electronic communication in a computer-mediated environment in which the buyer controls the kind and amount of information received from the seller. It creates customer value by providing time, place, form, and possession utility for consumers. Customer relationships are created and sustained through two unique capabilities of Internet technology: interactivity and individuality. From an interactive marketing perspective, customer experience represents the sum total of the interactions that a customer has with a company's website, from the initial look at a home page through the entire purchase decision process. Companies produce a customer experience through seven website design elements. These elements are context, content, community, customization, communication, connection, and commerce.

LO 18-2 *Explain why certain types of products and services are particularly suited for interactive marketing.*

Certain types of products and services seem to be particularly suited for interactive marketing. One category consists of items for which product information is an important part of the purchase decision, but prepurchase trial is not necessarily critical. A second category involves items for which audio or video demonstration is important. A third category contains items that can be digitally delivered. Unique items represent a fourth category. A fifth category includes items that are regularly purchased and where convenience is very important. A final category consists of highly standardized items for which information about price is important.

LO 18-3 *Describe why consumers shop and buy online and how marketers influence online purchasing behavior.*

There are six reasons consumers shop and buy online. They are convenience, choice, customization, communication, cost, and control. Marketers have capitalized on these reasons through a variety of means. For example, they provide choice assistance using choiceboard and collaborative filtering technology, which also provides opportunities for customization. Company-hosted web communities and viral marketing practices capitalize on the communications dimensions of Internet-enabled technologies. Dynamic pricing provides real-time responses to supply and demand conditions, often resulting in lower prices for consumers. Permission marketing is popular given consumer interest in control.

LO 18-4 *Define cross-channel shoppers and the role of transactional and promotional websites in reaching these shoppers.*

A cross-channel shopper is an online consumer who researches products online and then purchases them at a retail store. These shoppers are reached through multichannel marketing. Websites play a multifaceted role in multichannel marketing because they can serve as either a delivery or communication channel. In this regard, transactional websites are essentially electronic storefronts. They focus principally on converting an online browser into an online, catalog, or in-store buyer using the website design elements described earlier. On the other hand, promotional websites serve to advertise and promote a company's products and services and provide information on how items can be used and where they can be purchased.

LEARNING REVIEW ANSWERS

18-1 **The consumer-initiated practice of generating content on a marketer's website that is custom tailored to an individual's specific needs and preferences is called _____.**
Answer: personalization

18-2 **What are the seven website design elements that companies use to produce a customer experience?**
Answer: The seven website design elements are: context, content, community, customization, communication, connection, and commerce.

469

18-3 **What is viral marketing?**

Answer: Viral marketing is an Internet-enabled promotional strategy that encourages individuals to forward marketer-initiated messages to others via e-mail.

18-4 **What are the six reasons consumers prefer to shop and buy online?**

Answer: The six reasons why consumers prefer to shop and buy online are: convenience, choice, customization, communication, cost, and control.

18-5 **A cross-channel shopper is** _____.

Answer: an online consumer who researches products online and then purchases them at a retail store.

18-6 **Channel conflict between manufacturers and retailers is likely to arise when manufacturers use** _____ **websites.**

Answer: transactional

FOCUSING ON KEY TERMS

behavorial targeting p. 465
bots p. 462
choiceboard p. 456
collaborative filtering p. 456
cookies p. 465

cross-channel shopper p. 467
dynamic pricing p. 465
eight-second rule p. 462
interactive marketing p. 456
permission marketing p. 457

personalization p. 456
showrooming p. 465
spam p. 463
viral marketing p. 464
web communities p. 463

APPLYING MARKETING KNOWLEDGE

1 Have you made an online purchase? If so, why do you think so many people who have access to the Internet are not also online buyers? If not, why are you reluctant to do so? Do you think that electronic commerce benefits consumers even if they don't make a purchase?

2 Like the traditional marketplace, the digital marketspace offers marketers opportunities to create time, place, form, and possession utility. How do you think Internet-enabled technology rates in terms of creating these values? Take a shopping trip at a virtual retailer of your choice (don't buy anything unless you really want to). Then compare the time, place, form, and possession utility provided by the virtual retailer to that provided by a traditional retailer in the same product category.

3 Visit Amazon.com (www.amazon.com) or Barnes & Noble (www.barnesandnoble.com). As you tour the website, think about how shopping for books online compares with a trip to your university bookstore to buy books. Specifically, compare and contrast your shopping experiences with respect to convenience, choice, customization, communication, cost, and control.

4 Visit the website for your university or college. Based on your visit, would you conclude that the site is a transactional site or a promotional site? Why? How would you rate the site in terms of the six website design elements that affect customer experience?

BUILDING YOUR MARKETING PLAN

Does your marketing plan involve a marketspace presence for your product or service? If the answer is "no," read no further and do not include this element in your plan. If the answer is "yes," then attention must be given to developing a website in your marketing plan. A useful starting point is to:

1 Describe how each website element—context, content, community, customization, communication, connection, and commerce—will be used to create a customer experience.

2 Identify a company's website that best reflects your website conceptualization.

Video 18-4
Pizza Hut
Video Case
kerin.tv/cr6e/v18-4

It's no surprise that Pizza Hut is the world's largest pizza chain with more than 10,000 restaurants in 100 countries. But did you know that Pizza Hut became one of the top 35 U.S. Internet retailers in 2009?

According to Brian Niccol, Pizza Hut's chief marketing officer (CMO), "We've done what many would say is impossible. We successfully built an online business in three years that produces hundreds of millions of dollars in annual revenue. Today, Pizza Hut is a category leader in the interactive and emerging marketplace." So how did they do it? Pizza Hut simply revolutionized the quick serve restaurant (QSR) world through a multichannel marketing approach that created a customer experience and a customer engagement platform that was second to none.

THE RETAIL PIZZA BUSINESS

With three national competitors dominating the marketplace, the pizza business is very competitive. Even customers who could be considered heavy users of a particular brand regularly purchase from competitors on the basis of timing, pricing, and convenience.

In general, Pizza Hut's most frequent customers (and likely those of the other two major competitors) divide into two categories: (1) families, primarily time-starved mothers, looking for a quick and simple mealtime solution; and (2) young adult males who fuel their active lifestyle with one of the world's most versatile and convenient foods (no cooking, no utensils, no cleanup, and leftovers are perfect for breakfast). While these two groups could not be more dissimilar on the surface, value and convenience are important for both groups. Cost-conscious mothers look for a good quality product and a hassle-free eating experience. Deal-seeking young adult males seek more of the food they love with less time and cash invested in the process.

The importance of the take-home and delivery segment of the U.S. pizza market is illustrated by the fact that Pizza Hut's principal national competitors focus exclusively on this aspect of the business. Most take-home and delivery sales are ordered before a customer enters the restaurant. By 2006, a growing number of retail pizza customers had become comfortable ordering pizza online. Pizza ordering, as it turned out, was an ideal product for the digital world. People understood the basic menu, generally knew that they could customize their order in a variety of ways, and were accustomed to not being in the store when ordering. Brand retail presence and established customer delivery

networks also made the shift to online ordering easier for national pizza chains than other national quick serve restaurants. But, as Pizza Hut understood, there is still an incredible level of complexity in making something truly sophisticated simple and easy for the customer.

CREATING A PLAN OF ACTION

For the most part, the intent of online ordering for the pizza business was to make transactions with the customer easier and cheaper for the brand. Pizza Hut recognized the opportunity to engage people with its brand and with other people directly and do something special; namely, build sustainable relationships with its customers and enable Pizza Hut to engage people in a more meaningful and profitable way. In short, Pizza Hut set about to reinvent the retail pizza business by breaking away from a transactional platform to an efficient and powerful customer engagement platform by reaching out to customers' kitchens and couches to offer a better mealtime ordering, delivery, and dining experience.

Pizza Hut selected imc² (www.imc2.com) as one of its lead agencies to plan a comprehensive interactive strategy that focused first on the redesign of the Pizza Hut corporate website (including redefining the customer experience online and across all of the brand's touchpoints) and then on a series of progressively sophisticated and industry-leading customer engagement strategies. imc² brought 15 years of experience in interactive marketing and brand engagement to the assignment. Its clients have included Coca-Cola, Johnson & Johnson, Pfizer, Omni Hotels, Hasbro, Procter & Gamble, and Samsung, among a host of other companies, large and small.

PIZZAHUT.COM, CUSTOMER EXPERIENCE, AND BRAND ENGAGEMENT

Pizza Hut and imc² executives agreed that the strategy for reinventing the retail pizza business would involve developing opportunities for customers to engage with the brand by using the right technologies to enable and encourage interaction. A new website was necessary to better address all major design elements. How Pizza Hut and imc² executed these design elements not only created value for its customers, but also served as a basis for differentiation in the retail pizza business. Let's look at these design elements and PizzaHut.com's performance.

Context and Content

The Pizza Hut website was completely redesigned to support nationwide online ordering in 2007 (including all franchise locations for the first time) and is updated frequently to keep up with the company's fast-paced marketing strategy and ambitious product innovation rollout schedule. Since promotions are an important expectation in pizza purchasing and speak to the brand's consumers in a language that clearly connects with their desire for value, the website *context* and *content* balance the ability to shop for a deal with quick and easy ordering access for people who arrive at PizzaHut.com ready to purchase. The site presents a number of Pizza Hut's current offers in the central viewing window as well as through the rolling navigation directly underneath the main content. Primary navigation for information, such as the menu, locations, and nutrition facts, are displayed horizontally across the top of the rotating content.

Customization

Website *customization* is achieved in several ways, but the primary utility is to simplify ordering. For customers who have already registered, there are several personalization options, including rapid ordering called *Express Checkout*—a feature that's based on saved preferences similar to a "playlist." For example, if you have a group of friends that likes to watch movies together, you might create an order named *Movie Night* that has your group's favorite pizzas. Using the *Express Checkout* option

accessible directly on the home page, you can select *Movie Night*, quickly review the order, click the "submit" button, and the pizzas are on their way, relying on saved delivery and payment options through a stored *cookie* (a piece of digital code that is used to identify previous visitors) to speed the transaction. With this type of functionality, you can think of convenience as an investment that creates loyalty and somewhat insulates the brand against switching down the line when customers would have to register with and learn a competitor's system, and where access to their favorite features might not be available.

Communication

Website *communications* are integrated with the company's overall communications programs—including traditional media—with product innovations, promotions, and special events shared across platforms. True to the brand, communications are fun and energetic, matching bold images and vibrant color with a smart, clever, and light-hearted voice.

One noteworthy example includes the 2008 April Fools' Day rebranding of the company as "Pasta Hut" to coincide with the launch of the brand's innovative line of Tuscani Pastas. This campaign included online support in the form of display media (banner ads) and the temporary rebranding of PizzaHut.com as PastaHut.com with special imagery and copy supporting the name change. Not only did the brand get plenty of coverage in the press, but it deepened the connection with customers by showing their willingness to be spontaneous and fun, inviting people to play along with the joke.

Pizza Hut's integrated marketing communications approach enables the company to easily test and incorporate other items and brands under the larger corporate umbrella, such as the WingStreet operation and the pasta extension. This demonstrates the brand's ability to stretch the QSR concept way beyond its pizza roots and suggests the kind of direction the company may pursue in the future.

Commerce

PizzaHut.com and the brand's other online assets are all about getting the world's favorite pizza and signature products into the hands and stomachs of customers. Since *commerce* is a huge consideration on the site, there are multiple pathways for ordering, including several onsite methods, a Facebook app (the first national pizza chain to produce an ordering application for the world's leading social networking site), a branded desktop widget, mobile ordering (also known as Total Mobile Access, added in 2008, that includes both a WAP [wireless application protocol] site and text ordering), and a sophisticated and simple iPhone app released in 2009 that lets customers build and submit their order visually. Additional revenue streams can also be quickly built online, as demonstrated by the eGift Card program conceived and implemented by imc^2 over a weekend during the 2008 holiday season.

Community

Realizing that it did not make sense for the company or its customers to create a *community* on the site, Pizza Hut tapped into Facebook to achieve results in a very cost-effective manner. With approximately 1 million fans and the first of its kind Facebook ordering application, the brand can efficiently engage a huge group of people in a very natural way without disrupting their daily routine. Again, the brand understands that if you make something convenient, you can increase trust while securing greater transactional loyalty. Pizza Hut's 2009 program to identify a summer intern, or *Twintern*, responsible for monitoring and encouraging dialogue on Twitter and other social media networks is another example of how the brand is building on existing platforms and making effective use of the massive social marketing infrastructure.

Connection

PizzaHut.com connects mobile, desktop, social networks, and other digital gateways to complement traditional media and its retail presence. So when Pizza Hut thinks about the *connection* design element, it includes more than just linking to other websites online. Rather, it provides a comprehensive approach to creating a seamless customer experience wherever and whenever people want to engage with the brand.

PERFORMANCE MEASUREMENT AND OUTCOMES

Pizza Hut diligently measures the performance of PizzaHut.com. The company created a customized marketing dashboard that allows the Pizza Hut management team to monitor various aspects of the brand's marketing program and provides an almost constant stream of fresh information that it can use to optimize engagement with people or tweak various aspects of performance.

The results have been remarkable, but understand that due to the highly competitive nature of the industry, they are fluid and only represent a moment in time. Consider, for example:

1. PizzaHut.com dominates the pizza category with number one rankings in website traffic and search volume. According to comScore, a global leader in digital analytics and measurement, the Pizza Hut site achieves the most traffic per online dollars spent in the pizza category.
2. PizzaHut.com became one of the top 35 Internet retailers in the United States in 2009, up from 45th in 2008.
3. Pizza Hut's iPhone app had more than 100,000 downloads in the first two weeks after release.

WHAT'S NEXT

So what's next for PizzaHut.com? While the brand has made huge gains in a very short time period, staying on top in the rapidly evolving digital marketplace requires constant attention. Pizza Hut envisions that its online business will surpass the $1 billion mark within the next five years, and that digital transactions will lead all revenue within a decade.

While understandably protective of the company's future strategy, Pizza Hut CMO Niccol has ambitious goals and he's not joking when he deadpans, "I want Pizza Hut to become the Amazon of food service and be pioneers for the digital space. I do not want us to be a brick-and-mortar company that just dabbles in the space." The transition to something along the lines of the Amazon model suggests that the brand might further evolve its identity as a pizza business and stretch or completely redefine the QSR model.

Most brands that want to grow in the evolving economy will have to think and plan long-term and be able to act swiftly as marketplace conditions change. imc^2 Chief Marketing Officer Ian Wolfman, when assessing the future of marketing, sums up the opportunity neatly. "Our agency believes that marketing's current transformation will result in a complete reorientation of how brands and companies engage with their consumers and other stakeholders. Brands that thrive will be those, like Pizza Hut, that can efficiently build sustainable relationships with people—relationships that have both high trust and high transactions". He goes on to explain that "brands taking a longer view have an unexpected advantage over traditional models that often focus too tightly on hitting near-term quarterly targets." Referring to research his agency

CHAPTER 18   Implementing Interactive and Multichannel Marketing

has done on the subject, Wolfman points out that the most successful brands in the future will likely be those that resonate with people on a deeply emotional level and operate with a clearly defined sense of purpose.

Pizza Hut, with its focus on digitally enabled customer convenience and category innovation, is ideally positioned to connect with people on a level that builds trust and increases transactions. Referring to the initial time investment, however modest, that customers have to make in registering with the system and enabling various devices, Niccol sees the landscape as very promising for brands that put their customers' interests and preferences first. "If we do our job right—creating authentic engagement and making it convenient and valuable for people to interact with the brand—the numbers follow."

Questions

1 What kind of website is PizzaHut.com?

2 How does PizzaHut.com incorporate the seven website design elements?

3 How are choiceboard and personalization systems used in the PizzaHut.com website?

Chapter Notes

1. Interview with John Lewis, account executive at Seven Cycles, Inc., April 19, 2013; and www.sevencycles.com, April 20, 2013.
2. "U.S. Online Retail Forecast: 2012–2017," www.forrester.com, March 5, 2014.
3. "Amazon Experiments with First Physical Store," *The Wall Street Journal*, October 10, 2014, pp. A1, A2; "Mixing Bricks with Clicks," www.economist.com, March 23, 2013; "When Clicks Turn to Bricks: Online Retailers Dabble in Physical Stores," *Advertising Age*, May 27, 2013, p.13.
4. Rupal Parekh, "Personalized Products Please but Can They Create Profit?" *Advertising Age*, May 21, 2013, p. 4.
5. Rafi A. Mohammed, Robert J. Fisher, Bernard J. Jaworski, and Gordon J. Paddison, *Internet Marketing: Building Advantage in a Networked Economy*, 2nd ed. (Burr Ridge, IL: McGraw-Hill/Irwin, 2004).
6. Natasha Singer, "E-Tailer Customization: Convenient or Creepy?" www.nytimes.com, June 23, 2012.
7. "Give Me Back My Privacy," *The Wall Street Journal*, March 24, 2014, pp. R1, R2.
8. This discussion is drawn from Jeffrey F. Rayport and Bernard J. Jaworski, *e-Commerce*, 2nd ed. (Burr Ridge, IL: McGraw-Hill/Irwin, 2004); and *The Essential Guide to Best Practices in eCommerce* (Portland, OR: Webtrends, Inc., 2006).
9. Mylene Mangalindan, "Web Sites Want You to Stick Around," *The Wall Street Journal*, April 15, 2008, p. B5.
10. "Demographics of Internet Users," www.pewinternet.org, downloaded March 1, 2014.
11. "Infographic: The Digital Lives of American Moms," www.nielson.com, May 11, 2012; Beth Bulik, "Technology No Longer Just Kid Stuff," *Advertising Age*, February 2, 2009, p. 12; "Internet Moms," www.newmediatrend.com, April 28, 2011; "Today's New Mom Is Never Disconnected, Says a New Survey," www.internetretailer.com, June 30, 2009; and "New Study Reveals Internet Is the Medium Moms Rely on Most," Disney Online news release, March 25, 2008.
12. Valerie Bauerkin, "Gatorade's Mission: Sell More Drinks," *The Wall Street Journal*, September 14, 2010, p. B6; Tom Hayes and Michael S. Malone, "Marketing in the World of the Web," *The Wall Street Journal*, November 29–30, 2008, p. A13. Also see, Kate Fitzgerald, "Blogs Fascinate, Frighten Marketers Eager to Tap Loyalists," *Advertising Age*, March 5, 2007, p. S-4.
13. "Read This and Win Million$!!!" *The Economist*, January 26, 2013, p. 60.
14. Quoted in Judy Strauss, Adel El-Ansary, and Raymond Frost, *E-Marketing*, 5th ed. (Upper Saddle River, NJ: Prentice Hall, 2009), p. 357.
15. Victoria Taylor, "The Best-Ever Social Media Campaigns," www.forbes.com, August 17, 2010.
16. "Showrooming Hits Luxury Fashion," *The Wall Street Journal*, April 10, 2014, p. B10.
17. "Say Goodbye to the Car Salesman," *The Wall Street Journal*, November 21, 2013, pp. B1, B2.
18. "Cookies Cause Bitter Backlash," *The Wall Street Journal*, September 20, 2010, pp. B1, B2.
19. Joseph Turow, "Behavior Aside, Consumers Do Want Control of Their Privacy," *Advertising Age*, January 28, 2013, p. 32; "Are Digital Foxes Guarding the Web's Privacy Hen House?" *The Wall Street Journal*, December 14, 2012, p. B1; "Ad Industry Takes Another Look at 'Do Not Track' in Browsers," *The Wall Street Journal*, March 31, 2011, p. B5; Edmund Lee, "Online Self-Regulation May Not Satisfy Administration," *Advertising Age*, March 21, 2011, p. 3; *2013 Internet Crime Report*, www.ic3.gov; and Joel Stein, "Your Data, Yourself," *Time*, March 21, 2011, pp. 40–46.
20. Kathleen Kim, "More Employers Letting Employees Shop Online at Work," www.inc.com, November 14, 2012; and "Survey: Many Admit to Online Shopping at Work," www.moneycentral.msn.com, December 2, 2008.
21. This discussion is based on "Consumers Want It All: Omni-Channel Shopping Activity Is Virtually Everywhere," *PR Newswire*, April 22, 2014.
22. "Brands Recognize the 'I' in Influences in Social Media," *Direct Marketing News*, December 12, 2012, p. 4.
23. "Retailers' Panty Raid on Victoria's Secret," *The Wall Street Journal*, June 20, 2007, pp. B1, B12.
24. www.Callaway.com, May 5, 2012; and Stephanie Kang, "Callaway Will Use Retailers to Sell Goods Directly to Consumers Online," *The Wall Street Journal*, November 6, 2006, p. B5.
25. Erik Hauser and Max Lenderman, "Experiential Marketing," *Brandweek*, September 20, 2008.

Pizza Hut: This case was prepared by Pizza Hut and imc² executives for exclusive use in this text.

Credits

P. 453, *Both images:* Seven Cycles, Inc.; www.sevencycles.com. P. 455, Seven Cycles Inc., www.sevencycles.com. P. 456, ©Ira Roberts. P. 457, Photo courtesy of Reebok. P. 458, ©NetPhotos/Alamy. P. 459, ©Ira Roberts. P. 461, ©Paul Barton/Corbis. P. 462, ©Tom Grill/Corbis. P. 463, ©Ira Roberts. P. 464, ©Clayton Hauck Photography. P. 465, ©Ira Roberts. P. 466, ©Fotosearch/Publitek, Inc. P. 468, ©Inmagine LLC. P. 472, Courtesy Pizza Hut, Inc.

GETTING A JOB: THE PROCESS OF MARKETING YOURSELF

Getting a job is usually a lengthy process, and it is exactly that—a *process* that involves careful planning, implementation, and evaluation. You may have everything going for you: a respectable grade point average (GPA), relevant work experience, several extracurricular activities, superior communication skills, and demonstrated leadership qualities. Despite these, you still need to market yourself systematically and aggressively; after all, even the best products lie dormant on retailers' shelves unless marketed effectively.

The process of getting a job involves the same activities marketing managers use to develop and introduce products and brands into the marketplace.[1] The only difference is that you are marketing yourself, not a product. You need to conduct marketing research by analyzing your personal qualities (performing a self-audit) and by identifying job opportunities.

Based on your research results, select a target market—those job opportunities that are compatible with your interests, goals, skills, and abilities—and design a marketing mix around that target market. *You* are the "product"; you must decide how to "position" and "brand" yourself in the job market.[2]

The price component of the marketing mix is the salary range and job benefits (such as health and life insurance, vacation time, and retirement benefits) that you hope to receive. Promotion involves communicating with prospective employers through written and electronic correspondence (advertising) and job interviews (personal selling). The place element focuses on how to reach prospective employers—at the career services office, job fairs, or online, for example.

This appendix will assist you in career planning by (1) providing information about careers in marketing and (2) outlining a job search process.

CAREERS IN MARKETING

The diversity of marketing opportunities is reflected in the many types of marketing jobs, including product management, marketing research, and public relations. While many of these jobs are found at traditional employers such as manufacturers, retailers, and advertising agencies, there are also many opportunities in a variety of other types of organizations.

The diversity of marketing jobs is also changing because of changes in the marketing discipline. The growth of interactive marketing and social media has created a variety of new jobs such as data miners and social media managers. The growth of multichannel marketing has led to the need for communication channel managers and integration specialists. The increasing involvement and control by consumers has required public relations personnel to become social networking experts and consumer-generated content managers. Specialties in demand now include digital marketing, multicultural marketing, and viral marketing.[3]

Recent studies of career paths and salaries suggest that marketing careers can also provide excellent opportunities for advancement and substantial pay. For example, one of every eight chief executive officers (CEOs) of the nation's 500 most valuable publicly held companies held positions in marketing before becoming CEO.[4] Similarly, reports of average starting salaries of college graduates indicate that salaries in marketing compare favorably with those in many other fields. The average starting salary

Video B-1
Careers
kerin.tv/cr6e/vB-1

of new marketing undergraduates in 2014 was $57,500, compared with $42,400 for journalism majors and $47,100 for advertising majors.[5] The future is likely to be even better. The U.S. Department of Labor reports that employment of advertising, marketing, promotion, public relations, and sales managers is expected to grow at a rate of 14 percent through 2020. This growth is being spurred by the introduction of new products to the marketplace and the growing need to "manage digital media campaigns which often target customers through the use of websites, social media, and live chats."[6]

Figure B–1 describes marketing occupations in seven major categories: product management and physical distribution, advertising and promotion, retailing, sales,

FIGURE B–1
Seven major categories of marketing occupations.

PRODUCT MANAGEMENT AND PHYSICAL DISTRIBUTION

Product development manager creates a road map for new products by working with customers to determine their needs and with designers to create the product.
Product or brand manager is responsible for integrating all aspects of a product's marketing program including research, sales, sales promotion, advertising, and pricing.
Supply chain manager oversees the part of a company that transports products to consumers and handles customer service.
Operations manager supervises warehousing and other physical distribution functions and often is directly involved in moving products on the warehouse floor.
Inventory control manager forecasts demand for products, coordinates production with plant managers, and tracks shipments to keep customers supplied.
Physical distribution specialist is an expert in the transportation and distribution of products and also evaluates the costs and benefits of different types of transportation.

SALES

Direct or retail salesperson sells directly to consumers in the salesperson's office, the consumer's home, or a retailer's store.
Trade salesperson calls on retailers or wholesalers to sell products for manufacturers.
Industrial or semitechnical salesperson sells supplies and services to businesses.
Complex or professional salesperson sells complicated or custom-designed products to businesses. This requires understanding of the product technology.
Customer service manager maintains good relations with customers by coordinating the sales staff, marketing management, and physical distribution management.

NONPROFIT MARKETING

Marketing manager develops and directs marketing campaigns, fund-raising, and public relations.

GLOBAL MARKETING

Global marketing manager is an expert in world-trade agreements, international competition, cross-cultural analysis, and global market-entry strategies.

ADVERTISING AND PROMOTION

Account executive maintains contact with clients while coordinating the creative work among artists and copywriters. Account executives work as partners with the client to develop marketing strategy.
Media buyer deals with media sales representatives in selecting advertising media and analyzes the value of media being purchased.
Copywriter works with art director in conceptualizing advertisements and writes the text of print or radio ads or the storyboards of television ads.
Art director handles the visual component of advertisements.
Sales promotion manager designs promotions for consumer products and works at an ad agency or a sales promotion agency.
Public relations manager develops written or video messages for the public and handles contacts with the press.
Online marketing manager develops and executes the e-business marketing plan and manages all aspects of the advertising, promotion, and content for the online business.
Social media marketing manager plans and manages the delivery of marketing messages through all social media and monitors and responds to the feedback received.

RETAILING

Buyer selects products a store sells, surveys consumer trends, and evaluates the past performance of products and suppliers.
Store manager oversees the staff and services at a store.

MARKETING RESEARCH

Project manager for the supplier coordinates and oversees the market studies for a client.
Account executive for the supplier serves as a liaison between client and market research firm, like an advertising agency account executive.
In-house project director acts as project manager (see above) for the market studies conducted by the firm for which he or she works.
Competitive intelligence researcher uses new information technologies to monitor the competitive environment.
Marketing database manager compiles and analyzes consumer data to identify behavior patterns, preferences, and user profiles for personalized marketing programs.

Source: Adapted from Lila B. Stair and Leslie Stair, *Careers in Marketing* (New York: McGraw-Hill, 2008); and David W. Rosenthal and Michael A. Powell, *Careers in Marketing*, ©1984, pp. 352–54.

marketing research, global marketing, and nonprofit marketing. One of these may be right for you. Additional sources of marketing career information are provided at the end of this appendix.

Product Management and Physical Distribution

Product or brand managers are involved in all aspects of a product's marketing program.

Many organizations assign one manager the responsibility for a particular product. For example, Procter & Gamble (P&G) has separate managers for Tide, Cheer, Gain, and Bold. Product or brand managers are involved in all aspects of a product's marketing program, such as marketing research, sales, sales promotion, advertising, and pricing, as well as manufacturing. Managers of similar products typically report to a category manager, or marketing director, and may be part of a *product management team* to encourage interbrand cooperation.[7]

Several other jobs related to product management (see Figure B–1) deal with physical distribution issues such as storing the manufactured product (inventory), moving the product from the firm to the customers (transportation), and engaging in many other aspects of the manufacture and sale of goods. Prospects for these jobs are likely to increase as a wider range of products and technologies lead to increased demand. In addition, as manufacturers cut costs, they are increasingly shifting more responsibilities to wholesalers.[8]

Advertising and Promotion

Advertising positions are available in three kinds of organizations: advertisers, media companies, and agencies. Advertisers include manufacturers, retail stores, service firms, and many other types of companies. Often they have an advertising department responsible for preparing and placing their own ads. Advertising careers are also possible with the media: television, radio stations, magazines, and newspapers. Finally, advertising agencies offer job opportunities through their use of account management, research, media, and creative services.

Starting positions with advertisers and advertising agencies are often as assistants to employees with several years of experience. An assistant copywriter facilitates the development of the message, or copy, in an advertisement. An assistant art director participates in the design of visual components of advertisements. Entry-level media positions involve buying the media that will carry the ad or selling airtime on radio or television or page space in print media. Some agencies are encouraging employees to develop skills in multiple roles. Advancement to supervisory positions requires planning skills, a broad vision, and an affinity for spotting an effective advertising idea. Students interested in advertising should develop good communication skills and try to gain advertising experience through summer employment opportunities or internships.[9]

Retailers such as Macy's offer careers in merchandise management and store management.

Retailing

There are two separate career paths in retailing: merchandise management and store management. The key position in merchandising is that of a buyer, who is responsible for selecting merchandise, guiding the promotion of the merchandise, setting prices, bargaining with wholesalers, training the salesforce, and monitoring the competitive environment. The buyer must also be able to organize and coordinate many critical activities under severe time constraints. In contrast, store management involves the supervision of personnel in all departments and the general management of all facilities, equipment, and merchandise displays. In addition, store managers are responsible for the financial performance of each department and for the store as a whole. Typical positions beyond the store manager level include district manager, regional manager, and divisional vice president.[10]

Most starting jobs in retailing are trainee positions. A trainee is usually placed in a management training program and then given a position as an assistant buyer or assistant department manager. Advancement and responsibility can be achieved quickly because there is a shortage of qualified personnel in retailing and because superior performance of an individual is quickly reflected in sales and profits—two visible measures of success. In addition, the growth of multichannel retailing has created new opportunities such as website management and online merchandise procurement.[11]

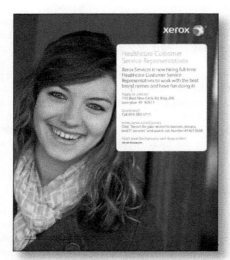

Xerox is well known for its sales career opportunities.

Sales

College graduates from many disciplines are attracted to sales positions because of the increasingly professional nature of selling jobs and the many opportunities they can provide. A selling career offers benefits that are hard to match in any other field: (1) the opportunity for rapid advancement (into management or to new territories and accounts); (2) the potential for extremely attractive compensation; (3) the development of personal satisfaction, feelings of accomplishment, and increased self-confidence; and (4) independence— salespeople often have almost complete control over their time and activities.

Employment opportunities in sales occupations are found in a wide variety of organizations, including insurance agencies, retailers, and financial services firms. In addition, many salespeople work as manufacturers' representatives for organizations that have selling responsibilities for several manufacturers.[12] Activities in sales jobs include *selling duties*, such as prospecting for customers, demonstrating the product, or quoting prices; *sales-support duties*, such as handling complaints and helping solve technical problems; and *nonselling duties*, such as preparing reports, attending sales meetings, and monitoring competitive activities. Salespeople who can deal with these varying activities and have empathy for customers are critical to a company's success. According to *Bloomberg Businessweek*, "Great salespeople feel for their customers. They understand their needs and pressures; they get the challenges of their business. They see every deal through the customer's eyes."[13]

Marketing Research

Marketing researchers play important roles in many organizations today. They are responsible for obtaining, analyzing, and interpreting data to facilitate making marketing decisions. This means marketing researchers are basically problem solvers. Success in the area requires not only an understanding of statistical analysis, research methods, and programming, but also a broad base of marketing knowledge, writing and verbal presentation skills, and an ability to communicate with colleagues and clients. According to Stan Sthanunathan, vice president of marketing strategy and insights at Coca-Cola, a researcher's job "is to bring out opportunities."[14] Individuals who are inquisitive, methodical, analytical, and solution-oriented find the field particularly rewarding.

The responsibilities of the men and women currently working in the market research industry include defining the marketing problem, designing the questions, selecting the sample, collecting and analyzing the data, and, finally, reporting the results of the research. These jobs are available in three kinds of organizations. *Marketing research consulting firms* contract with large companies to provide research about their products or services.[15] *Advertising agencies* may provide research services to help clients with questions related to advertising and promotional problems. Finally, some companies have an *in-house research staff* to design and

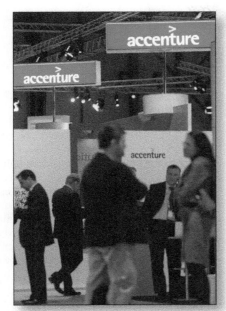

Accenture places thousands of consultants throughout the world.

execute their research projects. Online marketing research, which is likely to become the most common form of marketing research in the near future, requires an understanding of new tools such as dynamic scripting, response validation, intercept sampling, instant messaging surveys, and online consumer panels.[16]

International Careers

Many of the careers just described can be found in international settings—in large multinational U.S. corporations, small- to medium-size firms with export business, and franchises. The international consulting firm Accenture, for example, has thousands of consultants around the world. Similarly, many franchises such as 7-Eleven, which has 42,316 foreign locations, are rapidly expanding outside of the United States.[17] The changes in the European Union, Brazil, Russia, India, China, and other growing markets are likely to provide many opportunities for international careers.

Several methods of gaining international experience are possible. For example, some companies may alternate periods of work at domestic locations with assignments outside of the United States. In addition, working for a firm with headquarters outside of the United States at one of its local offices may be appealing. In many organizations, international experience has become a necessity for promotion and career advancement. "If you are going to succeed, an expatriate assignment is essential," says Eric Kraus of Gillette Co. in Boston.[18]

THE JOB SEARCH PROCESS

Activities you should consider during your job search process include assessing yourself, identifying job opportunities, preparing your résumé and related correspondence, and going on job interviews.

Assessing Yourself

You must know your product—you—so that you can market yourself effectively to prospective employers. Consequently, a critical first step in your job search is conducting a self-inquiry or self-assessment. This activity involves understanding your interests, abilities, personality, preferences, and individual style. You must be confident that you know what work environment is best for you, what makes you happy, the balance you seek between personal and professional activities, and how you can be most effective at reaching your goals. This process helps ensure that you are matching your profile to the right job, or as business consultant and author Jim Collins explains, "Finding the right seat on the bus."[19]

A self-analysis, in part, entails identifying your strengths and weaknesses. To do so, draw a vertical line down the middle of a sheet of paper and label one side of the paper "strengths" and the other side "weaknesses." Based on your answers to the questions, record your strong and weak points in their respective columns. Ideally, this cataloging should be done over a few days to give you adequate time to reflect on your attributes. In addition, you might seek input from others who know you well (such as parents, close relatives, friends, professors, or employers) and can offer more objective viewpoints. A hypothetical list of strengths and weaknesses is shown in Figure B–2 on the next page.

FIGURE B–2
Hypothetical list of a job candidate's strengths and weaknesses.

Strengths	Weaknesses
I have good communication skills.	I have minimal work experience.
I work well with others.	I have a mediocre GPA.
I am honest and dependable.	I will not relocate.
I am willing to travel in the job.	I procrastinate unless there is a deadline.
I am a good problem solver.	I have poor technical skills.

Personality and vocational interest tests, provided by many colleges and universities, can give you other ideas about yourself. After tests have been administered and scored, test takers meet with testing service counselors to discuss the results. Test results generally suggest jobs for which students have an inclination. The most common tests at the college level are the Strong Interest Inventory and the Campbell Interest and Skill Survey. Some counseling centers and career coaches also use the Myers-Briggs® Type Indicator personality inventory and the Peoplemap™ assessments to help identify professions you may enjoy.[20] If you have not already done so, you may wish to see whether your school offers such testing services.

Identifying Your Job Opportunities

To identify and analyze the job market, you must conduct some marketing research to determine what industries *and* companies offer promising job opportunities that relate to the results of your self-analysis. Several sources that can help in your search are discussed next.

Career Services Office   Your campus career services office is an excellent source of job information. Personnel in that office can (1) inform you about which companies will be recruiting on campus; (2) alert you to unexpected job openings; (3) advise you about short-term and long-term career prospects; (4) offer advice on résumé construction; (5) assess your interviewing strengths and weaknesses; and (6) help you evaluate a job offer. In addition, the office usually contains a variety of written materials focusing on different industries and companies and tips on job hunting.

Online Career and Employment Services   Many companies no longer make frequent on-campus visits. Instead, they may use the many online services available to advertise an employment opportunity or to search for candidate information. The National Association of Colleges and Employers, for example, maintains a site on the Internet called JobWeb (www.jobweb.org). Similarly, Monster.com and Careerbuilder.com are online databases of employment ads, candidate résumés, and other career-related information. Some of the information resources include career guidance, a cover letter library, occupational profiles, résumé templates, and networking services.[21] Employers may contact students directly when the candidate's qualifications meet their specific job requirements.

Campus career centers and online databases such as Monster.com are excellent sources for job information.

Library   The public or college library can provide you with reference material that, among other things, describes successful firms and their operations, defines the content of various jobs, and forecasts job opportunities. For example, *Fortune* publishes a list of the 1,000 largest U.S. and global companies and their respective sales and profits, and Dun & Bradstreet publishes directories of more than 26 million companies in the United States. The *Occupational Outlook Handbook* is an annual publication of the

U.S. Department of Labor that provides projections for specific job prospects, as well as information pertaining to those jobs. A librarian can indicate reference materials that will be most pertinent to *your* job search.

Advertisements   Help-wanted advertisements provide an overview of what is happening in the job market. Local (particularly Sunday editions) and college newspapers, trade press (such as *Marketing News* or *Advertising Age*), and business magazines (such as *Sales & Marketing Management*) contain classified advertisement sections that generally have job opening announcements, often for entry-level positions. Reviewing the want ads can help you identify what kinds of positions are available and their requirements and job titles, which firms offer certain kinds of jobs, and levels of compensation.

Employment Agencies   An employment agency can make you aware of several job opportunities very quickly because of its large number of job listings available through computer databases. Many agencies specialize in a particular field (such as sales and marketing). The advantages of using an agency include that it (1) reduces the cost of a job search by bringing applicants and employers together, (2) often has exclusive job listings available only by working through the agency, (3) performs much of the job search for you, and (4) tries to find a job that is compatible with your qualifications and interests.[22]

Video B-2
LinkedIn
kerin.tv/cr6e/vB-2

Personal Contacts and Networking   An important source of job information that students often overlook is their personal contacts. People you know often may know of job opportunities, so you should advise them that you're looking for a job. Relatives and friends might aid your job search. Instructors you know well and business contacts can provide a wealth of information about potential jobs and even help arrange an interview with a prospective employer. They may also help arrange *informational interviews* with employers that do not have immediate openings. These interviews allow you to collect information about an industry or an employer and give you an advantage if a position does become available. Creating and maintaining a network of professional contacts is one of the most important career-building activities you can undertake.[23] There are many popular social networking sites available to job seekers. LinkedIn, for example, has 225 million users, including recruiters. Other sites include Plaxo, Twitter, Jobster, Facebook, Craigslist, MyWorkster, VisualCV, and JobFox.[24]

State Employment Office   State employment offices have listings of job opportunities in their state and counselors to help arrange a job interview for you. Although state employment offices perform functions similar to employment agencies, they differ in listing only job opportunities in their state and providing their services free of charge.

Direct Contact   Another means of obtaining job information is direct contact—personally communicating to prospective employers (either by mail, e-mail, or in person) that you would be interested in pursuing job opportunities with them. Often you may not even know whether jobs are available in these firms. If you correspond with the companies in writing, a letter of introduction and an attached résumé should serve as your initial form of communication. Your goals in direct contact are to create a positive impression and, ultimately, to arrange a job interview.

Preparing Your Résumé

A résumé is a document that communicates to prospective employers who you are. An employer reading a résumé is looking for a snapshot of your qualifications to decide if you should be invited to a job interview. It is imperative that you design a résumé that presents you in a favorable light and allows you to get to that next important step.[25] Personnel in your career services office can provide assistance in designing résumés.

The Résumé Itself A well-constructed résumé generally contains up to nine major sections: (1) identification (name, address, telephone number, and e-mail address); (2) job or career objective; (3) educational background; (4) honors and awards; (5) work experience or history; (6) skills or capabilities (that pertain to a particular kind of job for which you may be interviewing); (7) extracurricular activities; (8) personal interests; and (9) personal references.[26] If possible, you should include quantitative information about your accomplishments and experience, such as "increased sales revenue by 20 percent" for the year you managed a retail clothing store.[27]

Technology has created a need for a new type of résumé—the digital résumé. Although traditional versions of résumés may be visually appealing, today most career experts suggest that résumés accommodate delivery through mail, e-mail, and fax machines. In addition, résumés must accommodate employers who use scanning technology to enter résumés into their own databases or who search commercial online databases.

To fully utilize online opportunities, an electronic résumé with a popular font (e.g., Times New Roman) and relatively large font size (e.g., 10–14 pt.)—and without italic text, graphics, shading, underlining, or vertical lines—must be available. In addition, because online recruiting starts with a keyword search, it is important to include keywords, focus on nouns rather than verbs, and avoid abbreviations. Related to this use of technology—don't forget that many employers may visit social networking sites such as Facebook, or may simply "Google" your name, to see what comes up. Review your online profiles before you start your job search to provide a positive and accurate image![28]

The Cover Letter The letter accompanying a résumé, or cover letter, serves as the job candidate's introduction. As a result, it must gain the attention and interest of the reader or it will fail to give the incentive to examine the résumé carefully. In designing a letter to accompany your résumé, address the following issues:

- Address the letter to a specific person.
- Identify the position for which you are applying and how you heard of it.
- Indicate why you are applying for the position.
- Summarize your most significant credentials and qualifications.
- Refer the reader to the enclosed résumé.
- Request a personal interview, and advise the reader when and where you can be reached.

As a general rule, nothing works better than an impressive cover letter and good academic credentials.[29]

Interviewing for Your Job

The job interview is a conversation between a prospective employer and a job candidate that focuses on determining whether the employer's needs can be satisfied by the candidate's qualifications. The interview is a "make or break" situation: If the interview goes well, you have increased your chances of receiving a job offer; if it goes poorly, you probably will be eliminated from further consideration.

Preparing for a Job Interview To be successful in a job interview, you must prepare for it so you can exhibit professionalism and indicate to a prospective employer that you are serious about the job. When preparing for the interview, several critical activities need to be performed.

Before the interview, gather facts about the industry, the prospective employer, and the job. Relevant information might include the general description for the occupation; the firm's products or services; the firm's size, number of employees, and financial and

FIGURE B–3
Anticipate questions
frequently asked by
interviewers and practice
how you might respond.

Interviewer Questions
1. What do you consider to be your greatest strengths and weaknesses?
2. What do you see yourself doing in 5 years? In 10 years?
3. What are three important leadership qualities that you have demonstrated?
4. What jobs have you enjoyed the most? The least? Why?
5. Why do you want to work for our company?

competitive position; the requirements of the position; and the name and personality of the interviewer. Obtaining this information will provide you with additional insight into the firm and help you formulate questions to ask the interviewer. This information might be gleaned, for example, from corporate annual reports, *The Wall Street Journal*, Moody's manuals, Standard & Poor's *Register of Corporations, Directors, and Executives, The Directory of Corporate Affiliations*, selected issues of *Bloomberg Businessweek*, or trade publications. You should also study the LinkedIn profiles, Twitter feeds, and blogs of the people you'll be meeting. If information is not readily available, you could call the company and indicate that you wish to obtain some information about the firm before your interview.[30]

Preparation for the job interview should also involve role playing, or pretending that you are in the "hot seat" being interviewed. Before role playing, anticipate questions interviewers may pose and how you might address them (see Figure B–3). Do not memorize your answers, though, because you want to appear spontaneous, yet logical and intelligent. Nonetheless, it is helpful to practice how you might respond to the questions. In addition, develop questions you might ask the interviewer that are important and of concern to you (see Figure B–4). "It's an opportunity to show the recruiter how smart you are," comments one recruiter.[31]

Before the job interview you should attend to several details. Know the exact time and place of the interview; write them down—do not rely on your memory. Get the full company name straight. Find out what the interviewer's name is and how to pronounce it. Bring a notepad and pen along to the interview in case you need to record anything. Make certain that your appearance is clean, neat, professional, and conservative. And be punctual; arriving tardy to a job interview gives you an appearance of being unreliable.

Succeeding in Your Job Interview   You have done your homework, and at last the moment arrives and it is time for the interview. Although you may experience some apprehension, view the interview as a conversation between the prospective employer and you. Both of you are in the interview to look over the other party, to see whether there might be a good match. When you meet the interviewer, greet him or her by name, be cheerful, smile, and maintain good eye contact. Take your lead from the interviewer at the outset. Sit down after the interviewer has offered you a seat. Sit up straight in your chair, and look alert and interested at all times. Appear relaxed, not tense. Be enthusiastic.

FIGURE B–4
Interviewees should develop
questions about topics that
are important to them.

Interviewee Questions
1. What is the company's promotion policy?
2. Describe the typical first-year assignment for this job.
3. How is an employee evaluated?
4. Why do you enjoy working for your firm?
5. How much responsibility would I have in this job?

During the interview, be yourself. If you try to behave in a manner that is different from the real you, your attempt may be transparent to the interviewer or you may ultimately get the job but discover that you aren't suited for it. However, remember that the interview is not the time to tweet, text, or take a telephone call.[32] In addition to assessing how well your skills match those of the job, the interviewer will probably try to assess your long-term interest in the firm.

As the interview comes to a close, leave it on a positive note. Thank the interviewer for his or her time and the opportunity to discuss employment opportunities. If you are still interested in the job, express this to the interviewer. The interviewer will normally tell you what the employer's next step is—probably a visit to the company.[33] Rarely will a job offer be made at the end of the initial interview. If it is and you want the job, accept the offer; if there is any doubt in your mind about the job, however, ask for time to consider the offer.

View the interview as a conversation between the prospective employer and you.

Following Up on Your Job Interview   After your interview, send a thank-you note to the interviewer and indicate whether you are still interested in the job. If you want to continue pursuing the job, polite persistence may help you get it. The thank-you note is a gesture of appreciation and a way of maintaining visibility with the interviewer. (Remember the adage, "Out of sight, out of mind.") Even if the interview did not go well, the thank-you note may impress the interviewer so much that his or her opinion of you changes.

As you conduct your follow-up, be persistent but polite. If you are too eager, one of two things could happen to prevent you from getting the job: The employer might feel that you are a nuisance and would exhibit such behavior on the job, or the employer may perceive that you are desperate for the job and thus are not a viable candidate.

Handling Rejection   You have put your best efforts into your job search. You developed a well-designed résumé and prepared carefully for the job interview. Even the interview appears to have gone well. Nevertheless, a prospective employer may send you a rejection letter. ("We are sorry that our needs and your superb qualifications don't match.") Although you will probably be disappointed, not all interviews lead to a job offer because there normally are more candidates than there are positions available.

If you receive a rejection letter, you should think back through the interview. What appeared to go right? What went wrong? Perhaps personnel from your career services office can shed light on the problem, particularly if they are accustomed to having interviewers rate each interviewee. Try to learn lessons to apply in future interviews. Keep interviewing and gaining interview experience; your persistence will eventually pay off.

SELECTED SOURCES OF MARKETING CAREER INFORMATION

The following is a selected list of marketing information sources that you should find useful during your academic studies and professional career.

Business and Marketing Publications

Scott Dacko, *The Advanced Dictionary of Marketing: Putting Theory to Use* (Oxford University Press, 2008). This dictionary focuses on leading-edge terminology for individuals who are serious about the theory and practice of marketing. Each term includes six elements: description, key insights, key words, implications, applications, and a bibliography.

Paul Hague, Nick Hague, and Carol-Ann Morgan, *Market Research in Practice: How to Get Greater Insight from Your Market* (Sterling, VA: Kogan Page, 2013). This practical book offers a clear, step-by-step guide to the market research process and explains how to use research tools and methods effectively to obtain reliable results.

Hoover's Handbook of World Business (Austin, TX: Hoover's Business Press, 2013). A detailed source of information about companies outside of the United States, including firms from Canada, Europe, Japan, China, India, and Taiwan.

Jagdish Sheth and Naresh Malhotra, eds., *Wiley International Encyclopedia of Marketing* (West Sussex: John Wiley & Sons Ltd., 2011). This six-volume reference contains 360 entries from over 500 global experts. Entries are arranged alphabetically within each subject volume, and each volume carries an index.

Ray Poynter, *The Handbook of Online and Social Media Research: Tools and Techniques for Market Researchers* (West Sussex: John Wiley & Sons Ltd., 2010). This reference book covers new innovations in the fields of online and social media research, including community panels, blog mining, social networks, mobile research, and e-ethnography.

Career Planning Publications

Richard N. Bolles, *What Color Is Your Parachute? 2015: A Practical Manual for Job-Hunters and Career-Changers* (Berkeley, CA: Ten Speed Press, 2014). A companion workbook is also available. See www.jobhuntersbible.com.

Dennis V. Damp, *The Book of U.S. Government Jobs: Where They Are, What's Available & How to Complete a Federal Résumé*, 11th ed. (McKees Rocks, PA: Bookhaven Press, 2011).

Alison Doyle, *Internet Your Way to a New Job*, 3rd ed. (Cupertino, CA: Happy About, 2011).

Jay Conrad Levinson and David E. Perry, *Guerrilla Marketing for Job Hunters 3.0: How to Stand Out from the Crowd and Tap Into the Hidden Job Market Using Social Media and 999 Other Tactics Today* (Hoboken, NJ: John Wiley & Sons, Inc., 2011).

Miriam Salpeter, *Social Networking for Career Success: Using Online Tools to Create a Personal Brand* (New York: Learning Express, 2013).

Martin Yate, *Knock'em Dead 2014: The Ultimate Job Search Guide* (Avon, MA: Adams Media Corporation, 2013). See www.adamsmedia.com.

Selected Periodicals

Advertising Age, Crain Communications, Inc. (bi-weekly). See www.adage.com. (Subscription rate: $109 per year)

Bloomberg Businessweek, McGraw-Hill Companies (weekly). See www.businessweek.com. (Subscription rate: $40 per year)

Journal of International Marketing, American Marketing Association (quarterly). See www.ama.org. (Subscription rates: $125 print; $150 print + online)

Journal of Marketing, American Marketing Association (bi-monthly). See www.ama.org. (Subscription rates: $140 print; $170 print + online)

Journal of Marketing Education, Sage Publications (3 times per year). See www.sagepub.com. (Subscription rate: $122)

Journal of Personal Selling and Sales Management, Pi Sigma Epsilon National Educational Foundation (quarterly). See www.jpssm.org. (Subscription rate: $255)

Journal of Public Policy and Marketing, American Marketing Association (semiannually). See www.ama.org. (Subscription rates: $85 print; $105 print + online)

Journal of Retailing, Elsevier Science Publishing (quarterly). See www.elsevier.com. (Subscription rate: $203)

Marketing Insights, American Marketing Association (bi-monthly). See www.ama.org. (Subscription rate: $105)

Marketing News, American Marketing Association (monthly). See www.ama.org. (Subscription rate: $105)

The Wall Street Journal Interactive, Dow Jones & Company, Inc. (daily). See www.wsj.com. (Subscription rate: $12 for 12 weeks and then $28.99 monthly online + print)

Professional and Trade Associations

American Advertising Federation
1101 Vermont Ave. N.W., Suite 500
Washington, DC 20005-6306
(202)898-0089
www.aaf.org

American e-Commerce Association
2346 Camp St.
New Orleans, LA 70130
(504)495-1748
www.aeaus.com

American Marketing Association
311 S. Wacker Dr., Suite 5800
Chicago, IL 60606
(800)AMA-1150
www.ama.org

American Society of Transportation and Logistics
8430 W. Bryn Mawr Ave., Suite 1000
Chicago, Il 60631
(773)355-4900
www.astl.org

Business Marketing Association
1833 Centre Point Circle, Suite 123
Naperville, IL 60563
(630)544-5054
www.marketing.org

Direct Marketing Association
1120 Avenue of the Americas
New York, NY 10036-6700
(212)768-7277
www.thedma.org
International Franchise Association
1900 K Street, N.W., Suite 700
Washington, DC 20006
(202)628-8000
www.franchise.org
Marketing Science Institute
1000 Massachusetts Ave.
Cambridge, MA 02138-5396
(617)491-2060
www.msi.org
National Retail Federation
1101 New York Ave NW
Washington, DC 20005
(800)673-4692
www.nrf.com
Public Relations Society of America
33 Maiden Lane
New York, NY 10038-5150
(212)460-1400
www.prsa.org
Sales and Marketing Executives International
P.O. Box 1390
Sumas, WA 98295-1390
(312)893-0751
www.smei.org

Appendix B Notes

1. Catherine Kaputa, *You Are a Brand!: How Smart People Brand Themselves for Business Success* (Nicholas Brealey Publishing, Boston: MA, 2010); Diane Brady, "Creating Brand You," *Bloomberg Businessweek,* August 22, 2007, pp. 72–73; and Denny E. McCorkle, Joe F. Alexander, and Memo F. Diriker, "Developing Self-Marketing Skills for Student Career Success," *Journal of Marketing Education,* Spring 1992, pp. 57–67.

2. Morag Cuddeford-Jones, "Managing a Marketing Career Is Academic," *Marketing Week,* January 16, 2013; Linda J. Popky, *Marketing Your Career: Positioning, Packaging and Promoting Yourself for Success,* Woodside Business Press, 2009; Marianne E. Green, "Marketing Yourself: From Student to Professional," *Job Choices for Business & Liberal Arts Students,* 50th ed., 2007, pp. 30–31; and Joanne Cleaver, "Find a Job through Self-Promotion," *Marketing News,* January 31, 2000, pp. 12, 16.

3. Kevin Cochrane, "The 21st Century Marketer," *Marketing News,* March 30, 2011, p. 22; and John N. Frank, "Stand Out from the Crowd, Landing a Marketing Job Today Means Touting Your Specialty and Staying Positive," *Marketing News,* January 30, 2009, p. 22.

4. Anjali Bansal, David S. Daniel, John T. Mitchell, and Patrick B. Walsh, "The CEO Today: Sharing Leadership at the Top," *Research & Insight,* SpencerStuart, March 2013, http://www.spencerstuart.com/research/articles/1642/; Jonathan Harper and Frank Birkel, "From CMO to CEO: The Route to the Top," *Research & Insight,* SpencerStuart, December 2009, http://www.spencerstuart.com/research/articles/1329/; and "Leading CEOs: A Statistical Snapshot of S&P 500 Leaders," *Research & Insight,* SpencerStuart, December 2008, http://www.spencerstuart.com/research/ceo/975/.

5. Salary Survey (Bethlehem, PA: National Association of Colleges and Employers, September 2014), p. 10.

6. "Advertising, Promotions, and Marketing Managers," *Occupational Outlook Handbook,* 2012–13 Edition (Washington, DC: US Department of Labor), http://www.bls.gov/ooh/management/advertising-promotions-and-marketing-managers.htm#tab-6, accessed June 4, 2013.

7. Matthew Creamer, "P&G Primes Its Pinpoint Marketing," *Advertising Age,* May 7, 2007.

8. "Wholesale and Manufacturing Sales Representatives," *Occupational Outlook Handbook,* 2012–13 Edition (Washington, DC: US Department of Labor), http://www.bls.gov/ooh/sales/wholesale-and-manufacturing-sales-representatives.htm#tab-6, accessed June 4, 2013.

9. "Freedom to Explore Different Career Paths Makes for a More Well-Rounded, Dedicated Staff," *Advertising Age,* March 26, 2012, p. 14; and S. William Pattis, *Careers in Advertising* (New York: McGraw-Hill, 2004).

10. Roslyn Dolber, *Opportunities in Retailing Careers* (New York: McGraw-Hill, 2008).

11. Peter Coy, "Help Wanted," *Bloomberg Businessweek,* May 11, 2009, pp. 40–46; and "The Way We'll Work," *Time,* May 25, 2009, pp. 39–50.

12. "Wholesale and Manufacturing Sales Representatives," *Occupational Outlook Handbook,* 2012–13 Edition (Washington, DC: U.S. Department of Labor), http://www.bls.gov/ooh/sales/wholesale-and-manufacturing-sales-representatives.htm#tab-6, accessed June 4, 2013.

13. Jack and Suzy Welch, "Dear Graduate . . . To Stand Out among Your Peers, You Have to Overdeliver," *Bloomberg Businessweek,* June 19, 2006, p. 100.

14. Piet Levy, "10 Minutes with Stan Sthanunathan, Vice President of Marketing Strategy and Insights, The Coca-Cola Co.," *Marketing News,* February 28, 2011, p. 34; and Edmund Hershberger and Madhav N. Segal, "Ads for MR Positions Reveal Desired Skills," *Marketing News,* February 1, 2007, p. 28.

15. "Market Research Analyst," in Les Krantz, ed., *Jobs Rated Almanac,* 6th ed. (New York: St. Martin's Press, 2002).

16. Deborah L. Vence, "In an Instant, More Researchers Use IM for Fast, Reliable Results," *Marketing News,* March 1, 2006, p. 53; and Joshua Grossnickle and Oliver Raskin, "What's Ahead on the Internet," *Marketing Research,* Summer 2001, pp. 9–13.

17. "2014 Franchise 500," *Entrepreneur* website, at www.entrepreneur.com, accessed May 12, 2014.

18. Lisa Bertagnoli, "Marketing Overseas Excellent for Career," *Marketing News,* June 4, 2001, p. 4.

19. Barbara Flood, "Turbo Charge Your Job Search, Job Searching and Career Development Tips," *Information Outlook,* May 1, 2007, p. 40.

20. Ibid.

21. Barbara Kiviat, "The New Rules of Web Hiring," *Time,* November 24, 2003, p. 57; Karen Epper Hoffman, "Recruitment Sites Changing Their Focus," *Internet World,* March 15, 1999; Pamela Mendels, "Now That's Casting a Wide Net," *Bloomberg Businessweek,* May 25, 1998; and James C. Gonyea, *The Online Job Search Companion* (New York: McGraw-Hill, 1995).

22. Ronald B. Marks, *Personal Selling: A Relationship Approach,* 6th ed. (New York: Pearson, 1996).

23. Chris Farrell, "It's Not What Grads Know, It's Who They Know," *Bloomberg Businessweek,* June 18, 2012, pp. 9–10; Sima Dahl, "A New Job Is No Excuse to Ease Up on Networking," *Marketing News,* February 28, 2011, p. 4; Leonard Felson, "Undergrad Marketers Must Get Jump on Networking Skills," *Marketing News,* April 8, 2001, p. 14; Wayne E. Baker, *Networking Smart* (New York: McGraw-Hill, 1994); and Piet Levy, "AMA Chapters across the Country Are Increasingly Using Job Boards, Networking Events and Other Techniques to Help Members in This Economy," *Marketing News,* March 15, 2009, p. 14.

24. "Careers in Marketing: Utilizing Social Networking to Improve Your Job Prospects," *CareerAlley*, July 22, 2012; "Finding Job Candidates Who Aren't Looking," *Bloomberg Businessweek*, December 17, 2012, pp. 41–42; Sima Dahl, "Pinning Your Career Hopes on Pinterest," *Marketing News*, May 15, 2012, p. 5; Tim Post, "New Graduates Use Social Media to Look for Jobs," *St. Paul Pioneer Press*, June 3, 2011; Susan Berfield, "Dueling Your Facebook Friends for a New Job," *Bloomberg Businessweek*, March 7, 2011, p. 35; and Dan Schawbel, "Top 10 Social Sites for Finding a Job," *Mashable*, February 24, 2009.

25. Amy Diepenbrock, "Will Your Résumé Open the Door to an Interview?" *Job Choices for Business & Liberal Arts Students, 2011*, National Association of Colleges and Employers, p. 31; and Marianne E. Green, "Marketing Yourself: From Student to Professional," *Job Choices for Business & Liberal Arts Students: 2009* (Bethlehem, PA: National Association of Colleges and Employers, 2008), pp. 28–29.

26. Marianne E. Green, "Résumé Writing: Sell Your Skills to Get the Interview!" *Job Choices for Business & Liberal Arts Students*, 50th ed., 2007, pp. 39–47.

27. C. Randall Powell, "Secrets of Selling a Résumé," in Peggy Schmidt, ed., *The Honda How to Get a Job Guide* (New York: McGraw-Hill, 1984), pp. 4–9.

28. Sima Dahl, "Social Media and Your Job Search: How the Age of the Referral May Impact Your Career," *Marketing News*, September 30, 2012, p. 6; "Post with Caution: Your Online Profile and Our Job Search," *Job Choices for Business & Liberal Arts Students: 2009*

(Bethlehem, PA: National Association of Colleges and Employers, 2008), p. 30; "If I 'Google' You, What Will I Find?" *Job Choices for Business and Liberal Arts Students*, 50th ed., 2007, p. 16; Joyce Lain Kennedy, "Computer-Friendly Résumé Tips," *Planning Job Choices: 1999*, 42nd ed. (Bethlehem, PA: National Association of Colleges and Employers, 1998), p. 49; and Joyce Lain Kennedy and Thomas J. Morrow, *Electronic Résumé Revolution* (New York: Wiley and Sons, 1994).

29. William J. Banis, "The Art of Writing Job-Search Letters," *Job Choices for Business and Liberal Arts Students*, 50th ed., 2007, pp. 32–38; and Arthur G. Sharp, "The Art of the Cover Letter," *Career Futures* 4, no. 1 (1992), pp. 50–51.

30. Lindsey Pollak, "The 10 Commandments of Social Media Job Seeking," *Job Choices for Business & Liberal Arts Students, 2011*, National Association of Colleges and Employers, p. 20; Alison Damast, "Recruiters' Top 10 Complaints," *Bloomberg Businessweek*, April 26, 2007; and Marilyn Moats Kennedy, "'Don't List' Offers Important Tips for Job Interviews," *Marketing News*, March 15, 2007, p. 26.

31. Sima Dahl, "Where Do You See Yourself in Five Years?" *Marketing News*, November 15, 2010, p. 4; and Dana James, "A Day in the Life of a Corporate Recruiter," *Marketing News*, April 10, 2000, pp. 1, 11.

32. Paul Davidson, "Managers to Millennials: Job Interview No Time to Text," *USA Today*, April 29, 2013.

33. Robert M. Greenberg, "The Company Visit—Revisited," *NACE Journal*, Winter 2003, pp. 21–27.

Credits

COMPANY/PRODUCT INDEX

A

A. M. Crunchwrap, 371
AA Direct Connect, 311
Abbott Laboratories, 127
ABC network, 374
Abercrombie & Fitch, 103
Aberdeen Group, 196
Accenture, 479
Accutron, 256
Ace Hardware, 307
A.C.E.S. Flight Simulation, 346
ACH Food Companies, 106
Acxiom Corporation, 421
Adidas, 140, 141, 253, 330
Aeon, 327
Aflac, 407–408
AFLAC duck, 379, 408
Airbus, 139, 287
AirO Lightning MP, 210
AirO Team Maria 23, 219
Air Team Maria 19, 210
Alamo.com, 304
Aldi, 193
Alliance Data, 177
Amazing Spider-Man 2, 391
Amazon.com, 230, 247, 300, 304,
        332, 333, 374, 408, 464
   continuous improvement, 322
   international expansion, 321
   logistics, 322
   offerings, 321–322
   supply chain management, 322
Amazon Fresh, 322
Amazon Kindle, 28, 34, 247, 277
Amazon Local, 111
Ambassador cards, 305
American Advertising
        Federation, 485
American Airlines, 217, 276, 311
American Eagle Outfitters, 402
American e-Commerce
        Association, 485
American Express Blue Card, 263
American Express Centurion Card,
        95, 263
American Express Company,
        78, 263, 431
American Express Gold Card, 263
American Express Green Card, 263
American Express Optima
        Card, 263
American Express Platinum
        Card, 263
American Hospital Supply, 311
American Idol, 167, 168, 351,
        390, 391
American Lung Association, 83
American Marketing Association, 485
American Red Cross, 29, 116, 217,
        377, 393
American Society of
        Transportation and
        Logistics, 485

America Online, 322
*America's Funniest Home
        Videos*, 382
Amway, 334
Anacin, 257
Android smartphone, 228, 256,
        364, 398, 419
Angry Birds video games, 28, 29,
        419, 420
Anheuser-Busch, 102,
        107, 378
ANN INC., 193
Ann Taylor LOFT, 193
Apple App Store, 419
Apple CarPlay, 212, 213
Apple II computer, 7, 203, 212,
        220, 222
Apple iMac, 11, 32–33, 34, 204,
        215, 227
Apple Inc., 4, 7, 41, 105, 141, 193,
        254, 256, 269, 306, 309,
        374, 402
   business portfolio analysis,
        32–34
   market-product grid, 204
   new-product process, 212–213
   segmentation strategy, 203–204
Apple Industrial Design
        Group, 227
Apple iPad, 28, 33, 41, 212, 214,
        219, 222, 227, 246, 256,
        269, 288, 364, 383
Apple iPhone, 10, 34, 41, 141,
        212, 213, 227, 228, 269,
        364, 473
Apple iPhone 5C, 89
Apple iPhone 5S, 89
Apple iPod, 34, 212, 222, 223
Apple Mac, 177
Apple MacBook, 33, 34
Apple MacBook Air, 204
Apple MacBook Pro, 204
Apple Macintosh, 203, 212, 224
Apple Mac mini, 204
Apple Mac Pro, 33, 34, 41, 204
Apple mouse, 228
Apple Stores, 339
   retail format, 338
Arby's, 102
Arctic Cat, 122
Arm & Hammer, 258, 259
Armani Exchange, 345
Arrow shirts, 280
As If, 383
Associated Grocers, 307, 329
AT&T, 71, 90, 120, 144, 150, 362,
        384, 386, 391, 437
Audi, 70
Audubon Society, 82
Aurasma, 324
Aurora Foods, 256
Autobytel.com, 304
Auto Trader, 383
Avatar, 161
Avert Virucidal, 222, 223

Aviator glasses, 391
Avis, 205, 308
Avon Products, Inc., 77, 140,
        334, 431
Axe, 256, 257

B

Baked Lay's potato chips, 248
Banana Republic, 193
Barbie dolls, 147, 148
Barnes & Noble, 28, 77, 331, 337,
        459, 461
Bausch and Lomb, 391
Bayer, 377
Bebe, 379
Bed Bath & Beyond, 389
Bell's burgers, 370
Ben & Jerry's, 22–23, 26, 27, 32
   marketing dashboard, 31
   market-product strategies, 34–35
   SWOT analysis, 36–37
Ben Franklin, 307
Best Buy, 127, 220, 221, 246, 272,
        282, 309, 328, 331, 337,
        338, 391
Be Tough, 243
Betty Crocker, 180
Bic pens, 257
Bic perfume, 256
Big Bang Theory, 168, 382
Bite Me, 374
BJ's Wholesale, 272
Black & Decker, 138, 152,
        259, 441
Blackberry Z 30, 89
Blistex, 173, 296
Bloomingdale's, 69, 280, 312, 328,
        336, 345, 477
Bloomspot, 111
BlueKai, 177
BMW, 232, 334
Boeing Company, 71, 126, 139,
        150, 287
   787 Dreamliner experience,
        231–232
Bold detergent, 257
Bolin Digital, 184
Bolin Marketing, 184, 185,
        186, 295
Bose, 255, 462
Boston Consulting Group, 39, 41
   business portfolio analysis,
        32–34
Boston Market, 340
Boucheron, 308
Boys and Girls Clubs of America,
        77, 417, 418
Brainstorm Bakery, 219
Brawny paper towels, 254
Bridgestone, 253, 377
BrightHouse, 268
British Airways, 90
Broadview Security, 216

Brooks Brothers Clothiers, 95
Brother, 247
Budweiser Light, 98
Bufferin, 257
Bugatti Veyron Grand Sport
        Vitesse, 274–275, 288
Buick, 91, 444
Burger Chef, 340
Burger King, 196, 202, 205,
        231–232, 464
   complexities of
        commercialization, 232
Burlington Coat Factory, 336
Burt's Bees, 296
Business Marketing
        Association, 485
Business Talk Radio, 383
BzzAgent Inc., 102

C

Cadbury Schweppes, 256
Cadillac, 311, 313, 444
Calistoga, 254
CallawayGolf.com, 298
Callaway Golf Company, 467–468
   marketing channels, 298–299
Call of Duty, 405
Camay soap, 259
Campbell Soup Company, 106,
        127, 169, 195, 253, 258,
        260, 317
Campbell's V8, 93
Campus Ambassadors, 408
Candy Crush Saga, 419–420
Carat, 365
CareerBuilder, 464, 480
   viral marketing success, 465
Caress soap, 257
Carl's Jr., 380
Carma Laboratories, Inc., 172–174,
        294, 410
   marketing research, 184–186
CarMax, 290, 326–327
Carmex, 47
   Healing Cream, 295
   Hydrating Lotion, 295
   Kiss, 174
   LeBron James partnership,
        417–418
   lip balm, 172–174
   Moisture Plus, 184, 295
   Moisture Plus Glamour, 186
   price-setting for, 295–296
   social media use, 410
Carmex-LeBronJames.com, 413
Carrefour, 327
Cartier, 277
Casera, 106
Castle, 168
Catalyst Paper, 114
Caterpillar, Inc., 122, 140,
        303–304, 317
Cause Marketing Forum, 78

CC Cream Sunscreen, 139
Celestial Seasonings, 300
Century 21, 300
Cereal Partners Worldwide, 306
CGCT, 150
Champion pacemaker, 37–38
Chanel, 141, 154, 277, 309
Chaps, 256
Chapstick, 173, 174, 296
Charlesburg Furniture, 309
    marketing dashboard, 310
Checkers Drive-In Restaurants, 340
Cheerios, 175, 231, 263
Cheese Nips, 260
Cheetos, 150
Chevrolet, 291, 313
Chevrolet Spark, 247, 256
Chevron, 301, 377
Chevy Volt, 66, 69
Chicago Symphony Orchestra, 264
Chicken of the Sea, 260
Chipotle Mexican Grill, 202
Chips Ahoy!, 262
Chobani Greek Yogurt, 8, 10
    company background, 2–3
    idea origin, 18
    place strategy, 19
    price strategy, 19
    product strategy, 18–19
    promotion strategy, 19–20
Christie's, 141
Church & Dwight, 258
Cinnabon Delights, 371
Cirrus system, 263
Citibank, 391
Citizen Eco-Drive watch, 101
Citizen Watch Company, 101
CityDeal, 111
Clairol, 98
Claritas.com, 195
Clash of Clans, 419
Click, 383
Cling-Free, 256
Clinique, 468
Clorox, 257
CNBC, 167
CNN, 222
CNN Early Start, 417
Coca-Cola Company, 67, 73, 77,
    90, 139, 140, 141, 146, 152,
    248, 255, 260, 262, 301,
    308, 329, 363, 378, 390,
    391, 463, 471, 478
    advertising mistake, 144
Coccolino, 140
Colgate-Palmolive, 97, 99
Colgate toothpaste, 138
Colgate Total Advanced Gum
    Defense toothpaste, 221
Colgate Total toothpaste, 97, 99
Columbia, 354, 356
Computer Weekly, 383
comScore, 385
ConAgra Foods, 112, 259
Cool Ranch Doritos Locos Tacos,
    350, 351, 371
Coors Brewery, 120
Corning, Inc., 116, 126
Corona Extra, 102
Cosmopolitan, 222

Costco Wholesale, 54, 127, 259,
    272, 327, 329
Cost Cutters Family Hair Care, 263
Coupon Information
    Corporation, 389
Courtyard hotels, 259
Cover Girl, 107
Cover Girl ColorMatch Custom
    Makeup Selector, 250
Craftsman tools, 104, 277
Craigslist, 481
Crapola Granola, 219
Crate and Barrel, 332
Cray Inc., 219
Cree, 23, 24
Crest Neat Squeeze
    toothpaste, 228
Crest toothpaste, 219, 311
Croma, 134
Crowdrise, 228
Crowdtilt, 228
Cub Foods, 329
Cunard Cruise Line, 68

DailyCandy, 378
Dancing with the Stars, 168, 351
Dannon, 3
Danone, 102
DeBeers, 141
Deere & Company, 121
Deli Creations, 169
Dell Asia Pacific and Japan, 134
Dell.com, 304, 459
Dell Inc., 128, 153, 227, 260,
    290, 304, 309, 332, 433,
    456, 463
    marketing in India, 134–135
    supply chain, 314–315
Del Monte, 260
Delta Air Lines, 277
Detroit Institute of Arts, 218–219
DeWalt, 259
Dex Media, 384
Dex One, 384
DHL Worldwide Express, 438
Dial soap, 377
Diamant, 131
Dick's Sporting Goods, Inc.,
    298, 468
DieHard, 257
Diet Mountain Dew, 378
Dillard's, 331
Direct Marketing, United
    Kingdom, 367
Direct Marketing Association,
    332, 334, 368, 486
DIRECTV, 276, 277
Discman, 237
Disney; *see* Walt Disney Company
Disney channel, 383
Disney Online, 461
Diver Entertainment, 236
DKNY, 317
DMAchoice, 368
Dockers, 253
Dollar Rent-A-Car, 205
Dollar Value Stores, 290

Domino's fruit-flavored bubble
    gum, 256
Domino's Homemade Pan Pizza, 6
Domino's pizza, 6, 263, 282–283
Don Miguel, 56
Donna Karen, 317
Doritos, 91, 150, 259, 378,
    390, 432
Doritos Locos Tacos, 390
DoubleClick, 398
Dove Chocolate, 376
Downy fabric softener, 219
Dr. Care Toothpaste, 7, 8
Dr Pepper, 255
DSW (Designer Shoe
    Warehouse), 345
Dun & Bradstreet, 480
Duracell, 255, 257
Duracell Ultra AA alkaline
    batteries, 276

Eagle, 256
Eastern Mountain Sports, 238
Eastman Chemical Company, 445
Eastman Kodak, 226
Easy Off, 256
eBay, 256, 332, 334, 454
    and entrepreneurs, 127
Eddie Bauer, 305
Ediet.com, 456
eHarmony, 95
Ektelon, 208
Electric Drive Transportation
    Association, 83
Elegant Medleys, 221
Elizabeth Arden, 260
Encyclopedia Britannica, 226
Energizer, 277, 379
    pricing strategy, 276
Energizer Advanced Formula, 276
Energizer e² AA alkaline
    batteries, 276
Energy Performance Systems,
    Inc., 228
Entertainment Tonight, 364
Environmental Media
    Association, 83
E-Pay, 198, 201
Epcot Center, 364
Epic, 389
Ericsson, 150
ESPN, 383, 417
ESPNW, 378
Essex restaurant, NY, 111
Estée Lauder, 102, 468
E*TRADE, 226, 376, 454
E.T. the Extra Terrestrial, 391
Eveready, 257
Excedrin, 257
Excel, 251
eXelate, 177
EXO Ignite 95, 210
EXO Red 95, 210
Expedia, 311
Experian Simmons, 196
Extreme Couponing: All Stars, 389
Exxon, 152, 258

eZone, 134
EZ Squirt Ketchup, 221

F

Facebook, 3, 4, 13–14, 22, 30, 67,
    100, 111, 112, 172, 174,
    177, 238, 268, 269, 334,
    351, 356, 359, 364, 367,
    371, 380, 390, 402, 403,
    404, 405, 410, 411, 413,
    416, 419, 453, 463, 464,
    473, 481, 482
in brand manager's strategy,
    407–408
compared to other social
    networks, 407
and environmental forces, 62–63
for launch of StuffDOT, 408
origin and use, 406–407
responding to future changes, 63
unique visitors, 414
updating, 408–409
use by Carmex, 184–186
Fairfield Inns, 228, 259
Family Dollar Stores, 290
Family Life Network, 383
Fancy Feast, 221
FAO Schwartz, 288
Farmer's Pick by Welch, 376
Farm Radio Network, 383
Farmville, 419
Fashionmall.com, 333
Fatburger, 340
Federal Express, 119, 151, 217,
    301, 317, 333, 386
Federation of European
    Marketing, 367
Fiber One, 231
Fiberwise, 257
Fidelity Investments, 376
Fingos, 222
Firebird, 257
Fitbit, 69
Five Guys Burgers and Fries, 202
Florida Orange Growers
    Association, 253
Florsheim, 330
Folgers, 260
Foot Locker, 311
Ford Bronco, 256
Ford C-MAX, 67
Ford Focus, 259
Ford Fusion, 259
Ford Motor Company, 4, 83, 91,
    139, 192, 259, 307,
    313, 329, 360, 391
Ford Mustang, 256, 259
Ford Pinto, 256
Ford Taurus, 259
Ford Thunderbird, 192, 256
4pics1Word, 419
Four Seasons Hotel, Beverly
    Hills, 333
Four Seasons Hotels, 367
Fox Business, 167
Fox network, 374
Fran Wilson Creative Cosmetics,
    marketing in Japan, 149

Fresh Express, 228
Friendster, 177
Frito-Lay, 91, 146, 150, 152,
  171, 172, 248, 254, 259,
  404, 432
Frommer's France, 356
Fuller Brush, 334
Fundable, 228

G

Gap, Inc., 110, 193
Gap.com, 333
Garden Design, 383–384
Garlic Cake, 223
Gatorade, 254, 256
  brand management, 242–244
  mission room, 464
Gatorade AM, 243
Gatorade Endurance Formula, 243
Gatorade Energy Bar, 242
Gatorade Energy Drink, 242
Gatorade Fierce, 242
Gatorade Frost, 242
Gatorade G2, 243, 258
Gatorade Nutritional Shake, 242
Gatorade Perform 02, 244
Gatorade Performance Series, 242
Gatorade Prime 01, 244
Gatorade Rain, 243
Gatorade Recover 03, 244
Gatorade Thirst Quencher, 243
Gatorade X-Factor, 243
Gatorade Xtremo, 242–243
Geek Squad, 221
  and feature bloat, 220
Geico, 379, 386
General Electric, 13, 90, 126, 225,
  258, 305, 330, 431
General Electric Healthcare
  Americas, 438
  personal selling, 428–429
General Electric Medical
  Systems, 127
General Foods, 50
General Mills, 4, 37, 150, 169, 175,
  222, 226, 228, 231, 251
  and Cereal Partners
  Worldwide, 306
General Motors, 83, 151, 247,
  280, 311, 313, 362, 365,
  444, 454
Georgia-Pacific, 254
Gerber, 152, 258, 288
Ghostery, 177
Gigante, 139
Gillette Company, 140, 153, 168,
  256, 437, 479
Gillette Fusion razor, 244, 246, 249
Gillette razors, 147, 152, 219, 255
Gilt, 111
Gilt Groupe, 378
Gino's Hamburgers, 340
Girl Scout cookies, 75
GiveForward, 228
Glass Plus, 256
Glidden paint, 256
Global Healthcare Exchange, 127
GNB Technologies, Inc., 317

GoDaddy, 378
Godiva Chocolates, 445
Go-Gurt Fizzix, 228
GoldenBeauty, 152
Golf Galaxy, Inc., 298, 468
Good Morning America, 417
Goodyear Tire & Rubber
  Company, 120, 253,
  306, 311
Google, Inc., 62–63, 71, 93, 166,
  167, 222, 324, 367, 368,
  385, 405, 412, 415, 419,
  421, 454, 460
  online advertising, 397–398
  ownership of YouTube, 412
Google Ad Preferences, 177
Google Glass, aid for retailing,
  324–325
Google Offer, 111, 334
Google Play, 419
Google pod car, 229–230
GoPro, 365
Goya Foods, 106
Grease Monkey, 264
Great Atlantic & Pacific Tea
  Company, 72
Grey Poupon mustard, 169
Group Danone, 151
Groupon, 334, 389
  challenges, 111–112
  company and concept, 110–111
  influencing consumer
  behavior, 111
Groupon Mobile app, 111
Gucci, 95, 141, 308, 309
Gulfstream Aerospace
  Corporation, 120
Gunderson & Rosario, Inc., 223

H

H. J. Heinz Company, 15, 221, 287
Hallmark Cards, 305
Hamburger Helper, 169, 231
H&R Block, 263, 308, 329
Hanes Brands, Inc., 249, 261
Harkman Electric, 303–304
Harley-Davidson, Inc., 103, 152,
  251, 253, 255, 256, 459, 463
  partnership with Milsco
  Manufacturing, 122
Harris Corporation, 440
Harry Potter books, 192
Hart Schaffner & Marx, 280
Hasbro, 471
Hawaiian Punch, 251, 252
HBO, 230
Healthy Choice, 112
Healthy You Vending, 331
Heinz Ketchup, 260, 287
Helena Rubinstein, 152
Hellman's, 99
Henredon, furniture, 256
Hershey Foods, 102, 280, 391
Hertz, 205
Hewlett-Packard, 121, 147,
  232–233, 247, 251, 317,
  404, 463
  recycling e-waste, 318

Hey! There's A Monster In My
  Room, 223
Hibu, 384
Hidden Valley Ranch Low-Fat
  Salad Dressing, 257
Hidden Valley Ranch Take Heart
  Salad Dressing, 257
Hisense, 70
History channel, 383
Hobbit, The, 160
Holiday Barbie, 147
Holiday Inn, 308
Home Depot, 120, 302, 327, 328,
  336, 337, 365, 367, 441
Home Shopping Network,
  305, 333, 364
Honda Accord, 192
Honda Civic, 274
Honda Motors, 83, 147, 259
Honey Nut Cheerios, 306
HootSuite, 410
Hospital Network.com, 127
Hot Pockets Bacon Cheddar
  Cheese Melt, 8
House of Cards, 230
House of Comedy, 346
Howlin' Coyote Chili, 51–61
HPEnterprise Services, 446–447
HTC One, 89
H2O Audio, 236, 238
Huggies, 139, 258–259
Hulu, 374
Hunger Games, 160
Hyundai Motor America, 468

I

IBM, 15, 16, 75, 116, 145, 303,
  314, 317, 377, 431, 438
  company background, 44
  integrated supply chain, 315
  Smarter Planet initiative,
  45–46
  values, mission, and strategy,
  44–45
IBM Global Services, 438, 443
IBM Sequoia supercomputer, 121
IBM Watson computer, 303
Ideale clothes washer, 152
IDEO, 227–228
IGA; *see* Independent Grocers
  Alliance
Ihhp.com/quiz.php, 443
IKEA, 141, 142, 324, 332
imc², 268, 471
Independent Grocers Alliance,
  307, 329
Ink and Hustle, 383
In-N-Out Burger, 340
Inside Edition, 417
Instagram, 3, 359, 371, 405, 412
Intel Corporation, 140, 251
Intellidyn, 177
International Franchise
  Association, 486
IRI, 231
Iron Man 3, 160
ISI InfoScan, 166
iVillage.com, 463

J

J. D. Power & Associates,
  166, 273
Jack in the Box, 340
Jaguar, 192, 334
JCPenney, 114, 115, 120, 280,
  337, 386
JCPMedia, Inc., 125
  as organizational buyer, 114–115
Jefferson Smurfit Corporation, 431
Jell-O, 232
Jewel supermarkets, 279
Jiffy Lube, 309
JobFox, 481
Jobster, 481
JobWeb, 480
Joffrey Ballet, 110
John Deere equipment, 121, 122
Johnson & Johnson, 25, 90, 105,
  127, 253, 471
Johnson Control's Automotive
  Systems Group, 438
José Olé, 56
Joy perfume, 257

K

Kanebo, 149
Karl Lagerfeld, 379
Kellogg, 105, 120, 175, 256
Kellogg's Heartwise cereal, 257
Kentucky Fried Chicken, 353, 371
Kia Motors, 98
Kickstarter, 48, 228
Kimberly-Clark Corporation,
  91, 139, 222–223, 259
Kirby vacuum cleaners, 437
Kit Kat bars, 144, 145
Kleenex, 10, 91, 242, 256, 262
Kleenex diapers, 256
Kmart, 102, 311, 330
Kohler, 274
Kohl's, 300
Komatsu, 140
Konica, 441
Kraft American cheese, 253
Kraft Foods, 169, 262, 389
Kraft Miracle Whip, 260
Kraft's Crystal Light Liquid, 378
Kroger, 259, 276, 295, 306, 389
K-Swiss athletic shoes, 380
Kuschelweich, 140

L

L. L. Bean, 305, 332
Land Rover, 192
Lands' End, 32, 366
Landsend.com, 366
Lay's potato chips, 91, 146, 171,
  172, 300, 432
Lay's snack chips, 254
LeBron James Family Foundation,
  417, 418
Lee, 102
L'eggs, 261
LEGO Friends, 253

LEGO Group, 140, 168
  marketing research, 163–164
Lender's Bagels, 256
Lenovo, 95
Lenovo Tab, 288
Leo Burnett Company, 268
Lever Europe, 140
Levi's jeans, 141, 300
Levi Strauss & Company, 77, 78,
    141, 147
Lexmark, 247
Lexus, 70, 81, 313
LG Corporation, 4
LG 55-inch 3D OLED HD Smart
    TV, 288
LG G2, 89
Life Is Good T-shirts, 8, 226–227
Life Savers soda, 224
Lifetime channel, 383
Lincoln, 313
LinkedIn, 177, 403, 404, 405, 406,
    434, 481
  in brand manager's strategy,
    410–411
  compared to other social
    networks, 407
  for job search, 411
  overview, 410
  unique visitors, 414
Liquid Paper, 248
LiveJournal, 405
LivingSocial, 111, 334, 389
Liz Claiborne, 32, 78
Lockheed Martin Corporation,
    39, 71, 117
Loehmann's, 329
Long John Silver, 371
L'Oréal, 140, 152, 256
Louis Vuitton, 255, 256
Lowe's, 120, 305
Lufthansa, 65
Luvs, 254
Luxottica Group, S.p.A., 256, 257

M

Machinima, 374, 375
Macy's, Inc., 301, 328, 331, 345,
    365, 420, 477
Maestro Limpio, 140
Magic Bullet, 383
Major League Baseball, 232
Major League Soccer, 232
Mall of America
  concept and challenge, 345
  market for, 346
  size and offerings, 345–346
M&Ms, 8, 290, 356, 357, 390, 456
Mansar Products, Ltd., 302, 303
Manufacturers' Agents National
    Association, 342
March of Dimes, 264
Marina Maher Communications, 268
Marketing Group, 298
Marketing Science Institute, 486
Marketside stores, 315
Marks & Spencer, 322, 455
Marley Coffee Automated
    Cafes, 330

Marriott Corporation, 13, 15, 228
Marriott EDITION hotels, 259
Marriott International, 259
Marriott Vacation clubs, 259
Mars, Inc., 302, 303, 456
Mars Chocolate, 390
Mary Kay, India, 157–158
Mary Kay Beauty Centers, 158
Mary Kay Cosmetics, 139,
    334, 444
  brand-building in India, 156–158
Mary Kay MelaCEP Whitening
    System, 157
Mary Kay's Velocity, 97
MasterCard International, 77, 143
Match.com, 95
Mattel, 78, 140, 147, 148
Maxim Steel, 441
Maybelline, 152
Mayo Clinic, 219
Mazola Corn Oil, 106
McDonald's, 96, 107, 140,
    143, 150, 196, 200, 201,
    202, 203, 205, 308, 329,
    340, 390
McKesson, 311
McKesson Corporation, 127
Medtronic, 27, 28, 29, 32, 48, 430
  in Asia, 37–38
Medtronic USA, 127
MEplusYOU, 268
Mercedes-Benz, 81, 151, 154,
    334, 378
Merck, 479
Mercury, 313
Merrill Lynch, 263, 436
MetLife.com, 304
Metro Group, 327
Metropolitan Life Insurance,
    106, 107
MGA Entertainment, 104
Michelin, 9, 95, 102, 138, 253,
    256, 274
Microsoft Bing, 93, 166, 398
Microsoft Corporation, 71, 258,
    311, 397
Microsoft Office, 251
Microsoft Project, 40
Microsoft Word, 251
Microsoft Xbox, 220, 322, 375
Microsoft Zune, 223
Million Dollar Baby, 160
Milsco Manufacturing, Harley-
    Davidson partnership, 122
Mimosin, 140
MindMeld, 69
MINDSTORMS kit, 163, 164
Mini, 145, 353
MINI USA, 353
Miramax, 259
Mission Foods, 56
Mockingjay, 160, 161
Modern Farmer, 383
Monk-e-mail, 464, 465
Monster.com, 102, 480
Monster Energy, 281
Moodmatcher, 149
Moody's Investor Services, 483
Moore Chemical & Sanitation
    Supply, Inc., 445

Mortal Kombat, 374
Motorola, 317
Motorola Dröid Razr Maxx, 89
Motorola Dröid Razr Maxx HD, 91
Mountain Dew, 371
Mr. Clean, 140
Mr. Proper, 140
MSN Hotmail, 464
MSN Money, 398
MTV, 383
MyCoke.com, 463
My eBay, 458
My First Craftsman toys, 104
Mymms.com, 456
MySimon.com, 333
MySpace, 62–63, 177
MyWorkster, 481
My Yahoo!, 456, 458

N

Nabisco, 260, 342
NASCAR, 232, 415
National Basketball Association,
    232, 371, 418
National Football League, 226, 232
National Hockey League, 232
National Retail Federation, 486
Nationwide Bank, 359
Nature Conservancy, 15
Nature Valley, 231
Nature Valley granola bars, 226
NBATV, 417
NBC, 374
NCIS: Los Angeles, 168
Neiman Marcus, 312, 328, 329,
    330, 331, 338
NeoGrid, 127
Nescafé, 153
Nestlé Company, 37, 102, 144,
    153, 254, 262, 389
  and Cereal Partners
    Worldwide, 306
Nestlé Crunch Girl Scout Thin
    Mint, 70
Netflix, 230, 374
Net Impact, 66
Netmarket.com, 333
New Balance, Inc., 212, 253
New Balance Minimus running
    shoe, 181
Newegg.com, 305
New York Mets, 288
New York Yankees, 288
Nickelodeon Universe, 345
Nielsen PRIZM, 195
Nielsen's online rating service,
    384–385
Nielsen Television Index Ranking
    Report, 168
Nielsen TV ratings, 166, 167, 374
Nike, Inc., 23, 78, 105, 140,
    141, 152, 253, 256, 311,
    330, 378
Nike Shox NZ, 311
Nikon, 216
99 cents Only Stores, 290
Nintendo Wii, 220
Nissan Motor Company, 120, 147

Nissan Smyrna, 151
Nokia, 152, 317, 365
Nokia Lumia Icon, 89
Nordstrom, 312, 330, 345
Nordstrom Bank, 330
Nordstrom Rack, 336
Norkse Skog, 114
Northrup Grumman, 71
Northwestern Mutual Life
    Insurance Company, 436
NPD Group, 54, 175
Nuprin, 257
NYTimes.com, 458

O

Obsession perfume, 257
Ocean Spray Cranberries, 260
Oculus, 409
Off 5th, 336
Office Depot, 246, 328, 337
Old Navy, 193
Old Spice, 26
Omni Hotels, 471
Opium, 308
Oral-B Cross Action toothbrush, 168
Orbitz.com, 304, 311, 455
Oreos, 260
Orion spacecraft, 117
Oscar Mayer, 105, 169
OUT! International, 223
Owens Corning, 431
OxiClean, 383
Oxygen channel, 383
Oz: The Great and Powerful, 364

P

Paid-to-Read, 385
Pampered Chef, 334–335
Pampers, 77, 139, 219, 254, 311,
    459, 468
Panasonic microwave ovens, 330
Pandora, 177, 383
Panera Bread, 202
Pantene, 251
Papa John's pizza, 329
Paradise Kitchens, Inc., marketing
    plan, 50–61
Paragon Trade Brands, 259
Peace Corps, 15, 66
Peapod.com, 334
Pebble digital smartwatch, 228
Penguin Books, 102
Penske Logistics, 317
People en Español, 107
PepsiCo, Inc., 3, 99, 120, 139,
    140, 146, 150, 251, 254,
    255, 261, 262, 301, 307,
    363, 463
  acquisition of Quaker Oats,
    242–243
  social media use, 414–415
Pepsi MAX, 415
Performance Racing Network, 383
Perrier, 77
Pert, 145
Petco, 309

Pets.com, 16
PetSmart, 309
Pez Candy, Inc., 260
   packaging for customer
     value, 261
Pfizer, Inc., 377, 471
PGA Tour Superstores, 298
Philadelphia Phillies, 217
Phoenix, 256
Piece Brewery & Pizzeria, 111
Pillsbury Company, 50, 55
Pinterest, 405, 412
   description, 416–417
Pitney Bowes, 120
Pittsburgh Pirates, 288
Pixar Animation Studios, 212
Pizza Hut, 263, 330, 371
   action plan, 471
   commerce, 473
   communication, 472–473
   customer experience, 471–472
   customization, 472
   multichannel marketing,
     471–474
   performance measurement, 473
   web communities, 473
PizzaHut.com, 473
Planters peanuts, 342
PlasticsNet, 127
Plaxo, 481
Playboy, 256
Plum District, 111
Poland Spring, 254
Polo, 256
Porsche, 258, 366
Porsche Boxter, 258
Porsche Carrera, 258
Post Cereals, 93
Post-it Flag, 11
Post-it Flag + Gel Pen, 13
Post-it Flag Highlighter, 7, 10,
   12–13
Post-it Flag Pen, 12–13
Post-it Flag + Permanent Marker, 13
Post-it Note, 11
PowerPoint, 251
Prada, 25, 26, 309
Pret, 145
Priceline.com, 366–367, 458
PricewaterhouseCoopers, 263
Prince, 208
Prince Sports, Inc. market
   segmentation strategy,
     208–210
Pringles, 260, 261
Procter & Gamble, 77, 102,
   105, 121, 122, 125–126,
   139, 140, 151, 166, 191,
   219, 227, 251, 254, 259,
   262, 291, 308, 311, 312,
   362, 389, 441, 454, 459,
   468, 471
   brand management, 267–270
Progresso Light soups, 228
Promotional Products Association
   International, 390
Propel Fitness Water, 242
PRS Group, Inc., 148
Prudential Insurance, 65
Public Relations Society of
   America, 486

Publishers Clearing House, 390
Purina, 221

Q

Qpod, 111
Quaker Oats Company, 232, 253, 256
QuizUp, 419
QVC, 333
QVC.com, 462

R

Race for the Cure, 15
RadioShack, 127, 259, 329
Rally, 228
Ralph Lauren Corporation, 256,
   306, 312, 326–327
Ralston Purina, 254
Rapleaf, 177
Ray-Ban, 391
Rayovac, 259
Reader's Digest, 390
Real Yellow Pages, 384
Recreational Equipment, Inc.,
   238, 455
Red Baron pizza, 178, 282–283
Redbox, 329, 408
Red Bull, 256, 280
   pricing strategy, 281
Reddit, 405, 412
Red Lobster, 95
Reebok, 78, 151, 457, 463
Reebok Russia, 151
Reece's Pieces, 391
Regal Entertainment, 279
REI; *see* Recreational Equipment,
   Inc.
Renaissance Hotels, 259
Reputation.com, 177
Restaurant Business, 358
Revlon, 280
Risky Business, 391
Rock and Roll Hall of Fame and
   Museum, 279
Rockport, 256, 437
Rockstar, 281
Rolex, 141, 277, 280
Rolling Stone, 384
Rolls-Royce, 141
Ross Stores, 336
Rovio Entertainment, Ltd.,
   28, 29
Ruffles, 150
Ruiz Foods, 56
Runner's World, 383

S

Safeguard, 259
Safeway, 123, 127, 276, 302
Saks Fifth Avenue, 317, 328,
   330, 336
Saks Inc., 309
Sales and Marketing Executives
   International, 486
Sam's Club, 272, 309, 311, 315
Samsung Electronics, 34, 70, 247,
   258, 471

Samsung Galaxy, 65, 380
Samsung Galaxy Note, 288
Samsung Galaxy S5, 89
Samsung Galaxy S4, 91
San Diego Padres, 365
Sanford Corporation, 248
Santitas, 259
Schwab, 304, 376, 456, 463
Schwan's Food Company, 302
Scion, 81
Scope, 463
Scotchbrite Greener Clean, 15
Scotchgard, 76
Scoutmob, 111
Scripto, 262
Sea Life, 345
Sears, 123, 216, 217, 259, 277,
   311, 336, 345
Secret Clinical Strength, 267
Secret deodorant, 267–270
Seiko, 140, 154
Sergio Rossi, 308
Seven Cycles, Inc., 463
   customization, 452–453, 455
   interactive marketing,
     452–453
Sevencycles.com, 456
7-Eleven, 120, 123, 300, 302,
   309, 479
72andSunny, 380
7UP, 258
Sewell Automotive
   Companies, 460
Sharp, 247, 257
Shepherd's Gift Foundation, 20
Sherwin-Williams, 306
Shiseido, 140, 149
Shop@AOL, 322
ShopNBC, 333
Shop24, 330
Shredded Wheat, 93
Siemens AG, 119, 143
SightLife, social entrepreneurship
   by, 24
Sirius XM Satellite Radio,
   383, 384
Skateboarder, 383
Skippy peanut butter, 280
Skippy Squeez'It, 260
Skype, 69
SmartThings, 228
SMG, 268
Snapchat, 371
Snapple, 256
Snelling & Snelling, Inc., 308
Snickers, 102
Snow Master, 96
Snow Pup, 96
Snuggle, 140
Sodima, 150
Sonatica, 29, 30
Sonos, 380
Sony Corporation, 105, 141,
   152, 258
Sony laptops, 391
Sony PlayStation, 322
Sony PlayStation 4, 220
Sony PlayStation 3, 220
Sotheby's, 141
Source Perrier S.A., 77
Southwest Airlines, 29, 217, 264

Special K, 175
Sperry boat shoes, 330
Spic and Span, 262
Sporting Goods Manufacturers
   Association, 209
Sports Authority, 326–327, 330
Sports Chalet, 238
Sports Illustrated for Kids,
   104, 384
Sprint, 71, 90, 386
St. Joseph Aspirin, 253
Stake Fastener Company,
   303–304
Standard and Poor's, 483
Staples, 302, 305, 309, 328
Starbucks, 10, 264
   sustainable procurement, 123
Starbucks Mobile, 359
Starkist, 254
Star Trek, 160
Startsampling.com, 390
Stokely-Van Camp, Inc., 232
Storenvy, 334
Strategic Business Insights, 99
Strauss Group, 150
StuffDOT, Inc., 7–8, 409
   functions, 425
   marketing, 426
   new social network, 408
   user-friendliness, 425
   vision, brand name, and logo,
     424–425
StumbleUpon, 177, 390, 405, 412
Subway, 329
Summer Olympics of 2016, 363
Sunbird, 257
Sunday Night Football, 382
Sunkist, 255
Superpages, 384
SurveyMonkey, 171
Swatch, 140, 141

T

T. J. Maxx, 336
Tab, 248
Taco Bell, 102, 340, 390, 408
   integrated marketing
     communications,
     350–351, 371
Taco Bell Express, 371
Taco Tia, 370
Target stores, 10, 16, 23, 54, 123,
   127, 139, 254, 272, 282,
   288, 295, 302, 311, 327,
   328, 329, 330, 367, 389,
   402, 408, 420
Taste Nirvana, 70
TD Ameritrade, 376
Teach for America, social
   entrepreneurship by, 24
TE Connectivity, 431
Temple Run, 419
Tesco, 127, 151, 327, 420
Tesco Home Plus, 420
Texaco, 377
Texas Instruments, 140, 436
TextileWeb, 127
ThePoint.org, 110
The Sims, 405

ThighMaster, 383
Thirsty Cat, 223
Thirsty Dog, 223
3M Corporation, 7, 15, 76, 77, 225, 229, 232, 244
    marketing program, 11–13
Ticketmaster, 465
Tide, 70, 191, 219, 311
Tide Pods, 227
Tidy Bowl, 256
Tiffany & Company, 144, 306, 338
Time, 177, 384
Time, Inc., 104, 106
Time-Warner, 71, 230
Timex, 140
T-Mobile, 71, 391
Tombstone pizza, 282
Tommy Hilfiger, 141
Tony's Pizza
    action recommendations, 179–180
    sales analysis, 178–179
Top Gun, 391
Toro, 96, 122, 291
Toshiba, 324
Toshiba America Medical Systems, 445
Tostitos, 91, 259, 433
Touchstone Pictures, 259
TownePlace Suites, 259
Toyopet, 81
Toyota Camry, 291
Toyota Corolla, 81
Toyota Corona, 81
Toyota Motor Corporation, 122, 302, 313, 390, 405–405
    environmental concerns, 81–83
Toyota Prius, 66, 82
Toyota Tundra, 81
Toyota USA Foundation, 81
Toys "R" Us, 288, 391
Trader Joe's, 14, 15
Transformers 4, 160
Travelocity, 379
Travelocity.com, 334
Trek Bicycle Corporation
    company history, 130–131
    organizational buying, 131–132
Trend Hunter, 170
Triarc Companies, 256
Tropicana, 254
TRUSTe, 466
TSCentral, 436
Tumblr, 405, 412
Tupperware, 467
TweetDeck, 410
Twentieth Century Fox, 161
Twilight Saga movies, 391
Twitter, 3, 14, 111, 172, 174, 177, 238, 330, 334, 350, 356, 359, 364, 371, 402, 403,

404, 405, 406, 411, 413, 453, 463, 481
    in brand manager's strategy, 410
    compared to other social networks, 407
    overview, 409–410
    unique visitors, 414
Tylenol Cold & Flu, 98
Tylenol 8-Hour, 98
Tylenol P.M., 98

U

Ultra Downy, 219
Uncle Ben's Calcium Plus rice, 253
Under Armour, 378
Unilever, 22, 37, 140, 253, 254, 259
Union Pacific Railroad, 441–442
United Parcel Service, 74, 151, 217, 299, 317–318
United Parcel Service Supply Chain Services, 317–318
United States Postal Service, 217, 322, 332
United States Rice Millers' Association, 136
United Technologies Corporation, 128
Universal Music Group, 311
UPM-Kymmene, Inc., 114
U.S. Bank, 10, 218
U.S. Green Retail Association, 328
U.S. Taco Company, 371
USA Today, 390

V

Verizon, 362
Verizon Digital Media Services, 375
Verizon-Redbox venture, 230
Verizon Wireless, 71, 89
Verso Paper, 114
Viacom, 71
Vicks, 145
Victoria's Secret, 331, 467
Vidal Sassoon shampoo, 280
Viking, 208
Villager, 131
Vimeo, 405
Vine, 371, 405
Virgin Mobile, 391
Virtual Game Worlds, 405
Visa International, 143, 308
VisualCV, 481
Vizio, Inc.
    distribution, 272
    pricing strategy, 272–273
    quality assurance, 272–273

Voice, 168
Volkswagen, 81, 102, 106, 147
Volvo, 192

W

W. W. Grainger, 126
Walgreens, 127, 295
Walkman, 237
Wall Street Journal, 167
Walmart.com, 462
Walmart Express, 193
Walmart Mobile, 333
Walmart Neighborhood Markets, 315
Walmart Stores, Inc., 9, 54, 67, 112, 122, 139, 175, 254, 259, 260, 262, 272, 282, 288, 295, 308, 309, 311, 314, 327, 328, 329, 330, 333, 336, 389, 441, 454
    failure in Germany, 154
    supply chain, 315–316
Walmart Supercenters, 315
Walt Disney Company, 71, 255, 256, 259, 264, 365
Walt Disney Pictures, 364
Wanamaker's Department Store, 387
Weight Watchers, 228
Welch's grape jelly, 177
Wells Fargo, 326–327
Wendy's, 170, 171, 194, 196, 205, 232, 340
    market-product grid, 199–200
    product groupings, 198–199
    segmentation strategy, 201–203
    target segment selection, 200–201
West Edmonton Mall, 336
Weyerhaeuser, 119
WhatsApp, 409
Wheaties, 175
Whirlpool Corporation, 119, 139, 141, 147, 152, 227, 260, 309
Whirlpool washers, 330
Whole Tree Harvester, 228
Whopper, 73
Wicks, 145
Wikipedia, 226, 404, 405
Wilkinson Sword, 274
Windex, 277
Windows Vista, 223
Windows XP, 223
WingStreet, 371
Winnie the Pooh, 256
WomenRidersNow.com, 251
Women's National Basketball Association, 232

Woot, 111
WordPress, 405
World Book, 334
World Market, 364
World of Warcraft, 404, 405
World Wildlife Fund, 83
Wrigley's gum, 102, 152, 214

X

Xbox Entertainment Studio, 375
Xbox Live, 405
Xerox Color WorkCentre 7755/7765/7775 Multifunction system, 198
Xerox Corporation, 181, 197, 245, 317, 431, 433, 438, 478
    Palo Alto Research Center, 224, 226
    sales management process, 449–450
    selling process, 449
X-1, new-product process, 236–238

Y

Yachting, 383
Yahoo!, 111, 177, 385, 397, 398, 456
Yahoo! Finance, 398
Yamaha, 122
Yellowbook, 384
Yellow Pages, 378
Yoplait, 3, 150
Youth Marketing Connection, 402
YouTube, 3, 14, 170, 359, 375, 379, 398, 403, 404, 405, 406, 416, 418
    in brand manager's strategy, 412–413
    compared to other social networks, 407
    overview, 411
    unique visitors, 414
Yum! Brands, 371
Yves Saint Laurent, 95, 308

Z

Zagat's Fast-Food Survey, 203
Zappos.com, 264, 332, 463
    core values, 188–189
    customer service, 188
    market segmentation strategy, 188–189, 190–191
ZenithOptimedia, 389

SUBJECT INDEX

A

Above-, at-, or below-market pricing, 280–281
Abu Dhabi satellite museum, 15
Accelerated development, retail life cycle, 341
Access, of media, 405
Accessory equipment, 216
Account executive, 476
Account management policies, 441
  policy grid, 442
  at Union Pacific, 441–442
Achievement-motivated groups, 100
Achievers, 100
Acquisitions
  by Facebook of Instagram, 406
  by Facebook of Oculus and Whatsapp, 409
  Quaker Oats by PepsiCo, 242
  Stokely-Van Camp by Quaker Oats, 242
  by Trek Bicycle Company, 131
  Zappos.com by Amazon, 188
Action item list, 39–40
Adaptive selling, 437
Administered vertical marketing systems, 308
Adoption, 362
Advertisements
  design of
    message content, 379
    message creation, 379–380
  institutional, 377
  potential for ad-skipping, 374
  for products, 376–377
Advertising, 354, 376
  advantages for firms, 354–355
  careers in, 477
  Chobani Greek Yogurt, 2–3
  cooperative, 392
  costs, 355
  directed to business buyers, 358
  direct-to-consumer, 360–361
  dominance of TV, 374
  focus on consideration set, 93
  and Internet TV, 375
  lack of feedback, 355
  and mass selling, 354
  mistakes with cultural symbols, 144
  nonpersonal component, 354
  occupations, 476
  online, 397–398
  paid aspect, 354
  posttests, 388

  pretests, 387
  as promotional tool, 364
  regulation in Malaysia, 148
  regulation in Sweden, 148
  scheduling
    and buyer turnover, 386
    continuous schedule, 386
    flighting schedule, 386
    and forgetting rate, 386
    pulse schedule, 386
    and purchase frequency, 386
  strengths and weaknesses, 355
  subliminal messages, 96
  to support sales promotions, 357
  target audience, 354
  trade promotions for, 391–392
  and TV viewing, 168
Advertising Age, 365, 380, 481
Advertising agencies
  aid in marketing research, 478
  Carat, 365
  creation of ads, 379–380
  full-service, 387
  in-house, 387
  limited-service, 387
  72andSunny, 380
  used by Procter & Gamble, 268
Advertising budget, 378
Advertising campaign
  by Dell Inc. in India, 135
  by Taco Bell, 350–351
Advertising department, 352
Advertising expenditures
  cost per thousand, 381
  in growth stage, 246
  for Internet advertising, 385
  in introduction stage, 244
  with multibranding, 259
  in multiproduct branding, 258
  percent by media types, 380
  for television ads, 382
Advertising media; *see* Social media; Social networks
  advantages and disadvantages of each, 382
  Internet, 384–385
  magazine, 383–384
  media buyers, 476
  newspapers, 384
  outdoor, 385–386
  place-based, 386
  radio, 383
  selection criteria
    alternatives, 380
    cost per thousand, 381

  expenditures for each type, 380
  frequency, 381
  gross ratings points, 381
  reach, 380–381
  target audience, 380
social *vs.* traditional, 405–406
television, 382–383
Yellow Pages, 384
Advertising program
  advantages and disadvantages of media, 382
  assessing
    making needed changes, 388
    posttests, 388
  designing advertisements, 379–380
  executing
    carrying out, 387
    pretests, 387
  identifying target audience, 378
  media alternatives, 382–386
  media selection, 380–381
  scheduling, 386
  setting budget, 378
  specifying objectives, 378
Advertising Research Foundation, 378
Advocacy advertisements, 377
African Americans
  buying patterns, 106–107
  price discrimination in car buying, 290
  projected spending by, 66
Agents, 342
  as intermediaries, 300
Aided recall, 388
Airline industry, frequent-flyer programs, 196
Algorithms, 419
Allowances
  case, 392
  finance, 392
  merchandise, 392
  promotional, 291–292
  trade-in, 291
All-you-can-afford budgeting, 362
Alternative evaluation
  by consumers, 89–90
  in organizational buying, 124
American Association of Advertising Agencies, 379
Americanization of fashion and culture, 141
American Marketing Association, 4
Anchor stores, 336, 337
Antecedent states, 93, 94

Antitrust law
  Clayton Act, 72
  on pricing, 288–289
  Robinson-Patman Act, 72
  Sherman Act, 71
  and Walmart in Germany, 154
Applications, 419
Approach stage
  business cards, 437
  first impression, 436
  in international settings,
    436–437
  objectives, 435
Approximate price level, 289
Apps, 419
  video games, 419–420
Art director, 476
Asian Americans
  assimilated, 107
  buying patterns, 107
  composition of subculture, 107
  nonassimilated, 107
  projected spending by, 66
Asia-Pacific markets, 156–157
Aspiration groups, 103
Assimilated Asian Americans, 107
Association of Magazine Media, 378
Association of National Advertisers, 387
Associative groups, 103
Assumptive close, 439
At-market pricing, 280–281
Attitude, 99
Attitude change, 99
Attitude tests, 388
Auctions
  reverse, 127–128
  traditional, 127–128
Audience data for social media, 413
Automated telephone calls, 368
Automatic vending, 331–332
Automobile industry
  failing to meet customer needs, 223
  price discrimination by dealers, 290
  product differentiation downside, 192
  resistance to electric cars, 250
  supply chain management, 313–314
  trade-in allowances, 291
  women car buyers, 86–87
Awareness, 362

B

Baby boomers, 65
Baby boomlet, 65
Back translation, 144
Backward integration, 307
Bad timing, 223
Bait-and-switch pricing, 289
Barter transactions, 274
Behavioral advertising, online, 368

Behavioral evaluation
  composition of, 444
  and customer satisfaction, 445
Behavioral learning, 98
Behavioral segmentation
  business markets by usage rate, 198
  consumer markets
    by product features, 195–196
    by usage rate, 196
Behavioral targeting, 361, 465–466
Beliefs, 99
  and attitude change, 99
Believers, 100
Below-market pricing, 280–281, 290
Benchmark items, 336
Better Business Bureau, 73
Better Homes and Gardens, 70
Big data, 165
Billboards, 385
Black Friday, 333
Blockbuster movies, risks of, 160
Blogs, 404, 463
Bloomberg Businessweek, 32, 212,
    381, 478
Board of directors, 25
Borderless economic world
  decline of protectionism, 136–137
  economic espionage, 142
  economic integration, 137–139
  global competition, 139–140
  global customers, 140–141
  networked global marketspace, 141–142
Bots, 462
Brain scanning, 169
Brand awareness, 256
Brand-building by Mary Kay Cosmetics
    in India, 156–158
Brand community, 103
Brand development index, 251
  marketing dashboard, 252
Brand drivers, 177
Brand engagement, Pizza Hut, 471–472
Brand equity, 255
  advantages, 255
  and brand extension, 258–259
  creating, 255–256
    consumer-brand connection, 256
    develop brand awareness, 256
    elicit proper response, 256
    establish brand meaning, 256
  valuing
    brand licensing, 256
    financial advantages, 256
Brand extension
  definition, 221–222
  nature of, 258–259
  risks, 259
Branding, 254–255
  benefits to consumers, 255
  corporate, 258
  family, 258

  multiproduct, 258
  and subbranding, 258
Branding strategies
  mixed branding, 260
  multibranding, 259
  multiproduct branding, 258–259
  private branding, 259
Brand licensing, 256
Brand loyalty, 98
  in ideals-motivated groups, 100
  and type of product, 215
Brand management
  brand equity, 255–256
  brand personality, 255
  Gatorade, 242–244
  logotype/logo, 254–255
  mixed branding, 260
  multibranding, 259
  multiproduct branding, 258–259
  nature of brands, 254
  picking brand names, 257–258
  private branding, 259
  Procter & Gamble, 267–268
Brand managers, 39
  functions, 476
  lessons from social media, 418
  at PepsiCo, 414
  role in product life cycle, 251
  use of Facebook, 407–408
  use of LinkedIn, 410–411
  use of Twitter, 410
  use of YouTube, 412–413
Brand names, 254–255
  and brand equity, 255
  criteria for choosing
    fir for company and product
      image, 257
    memorable, distinctive, and
      positive, 257
    no legal or regulatory
      restrictions, 257
    phonetic and semantic
      associations, 258
    product benefits, 257
    simple and emotional, 257
  in services marketing, 263
  unintended meanings, 145
Brand personality, 255
Brand preferences of children, 104
Brands
  attributes and attribute change, 99
  consideration set, 89
  establishing meaning of, 256
  evaluative criteria, 89–90
  fighting, 259
  global, 140
  Trek Bicycle Company, 131
Breadth of product line, 330, 331
Break-even analysis, 285
  break-even chart, 286
  break-even point, 285

Break-even chart, 286
Break-even point, 285
Bribes, 74–75
    and Foreign Corrupt Practices
        Act, 143
Brigham Young University, 228
Brokers, 342
    as intermediaries, 300
Built-to-order, 193
Bullet graphs, 30
Bundle pricing, 277–278
Bureau of Labor Statistics
    on employment in sales, 430
    on savings rate, 68
Business, 28
Business analysis of new products
    business fit, 229
    for services, 230
Business cards, 437
Business culture
    components, 74
    ethics of competition
        bribes and kickbacks, 74–75
        economic espionage, 74
    ethics of exchange, 74
Business firms, 23
    advantages of advertising, 354–355
    and behavioral learning, 98
    and brand loyalty, 98
    and cognitive learning, 98
    costs of packaging and
        labeling, 261
    costs of salesforce training, 443
    focus on postpurchase behavior, 91
    in-house research staff, 478–479
    marketing in two environments, 454
    and opinion leaders, 101
    with origins in marketspace, 454
    overcoming resistance to products,
        250–251
    reasons for market segmentation, 190
    reasons for personal selling, 355–356
    role of salespeople, 431
    services delivered by, 217
    types of goals, 28
    underperforming states, 224
    unique role of prices, 274
    and word of mouth advertising, 102
Business-format franchises, 329
Business marketing, 116
Business markets
    behavioral segmentation, 198
    demographic segmentation
        by NAICS codes, 197
        by number of employees, 198
    geographic segmentation, 197
Business model, 28
Business philosophy, Toyota, 81–82
Business plan, 48
    compared to marketing plan, 48–49
    elements of, 49

most asked questions, 49
    writing and style suggestions, 49–50
Business portfolio analysis, 32
    at Apple Inc., 34
    growth share matrix, 33
    market growth rate, 33
    relative market share, 33
Business products and services, **215**
    components, 216
    derived demand for, 216
    Internet marketing channels, 304
    marketing channels, 303–304
    support products, 216
Business publications, 485
Business-to-business exchanges, 126
Business-to-business marketers, 140
Business-to-business
        networks, 410–411
Business-to-business products, 215
Buy classes, 125
    modified rebuy, 126
    new buy, 125–126
    straight rebuy, 126
Buyer, 16
    in buying centers, 125
    control in mobile marketing, 420
    grouped into segments, 194–197
    no economical access to, 223
    in retailing, 476
Buyer requirements, and
        channel choice
    convenience, 309
    information, 309
    pre- and postsale
        services, 309
    variety, 309
Buyer-seller relationships, 121–122
Buyer turnover, 386
Buying center, 123
    buy classes
        modified rebuy, 126
        new buy, 125–126
        straight rebuy, 126
    buying committee, 123
    composition of, 124
    questions for guidance,
        123–124
    roles in
        buyers, 125
        deciders, 125
        gatekeepers, 125
        influencers, 124
        users, 124
Buying experience, 91
Buying patterns
    African Americans, 106–107
    Asian Americans, 107
    Hispanics, 106
Buyology (Lindstrom), 169
Buzz, 102
    Internet-enabled, 464

C

CAFTA-DR trade agreement, 139
Campbell Interest and Skills Survey, 480
Canada
    and NAFTA, 138–139
    number of languages, 144
Canned sales presentation, 437
Cannes Lions International
        Festival, 380
Cannibalization *vs.* synergies, 193
CAN-SPAM Act, 73, 462
Capacity management, 265
Career planning publications, 485
Career service office, 480
Careers in marketing, 4
    advertising, 477
    advertising occupations, 476
    average starting salary, 475–476
    changing nature of, 475
    diversity of opportunities, 475
    global marketing manager, 476
    information sources
        business and marketing
            publications, 485
        career planning
            publications, 485
        periodicals, 485
        professional and trade
            associations, 485–486
    international careers, 479
    job interview, 482–484
    job search process, 479–482
    marketing research, 478–479
    marketing research
        occupations, 476
    nonprofit marketing, 476
    opportunities for advancement, 475
    physical distribution, 477
    product management, 477
    product management
        occupations, 476
    promotion, 477
    promotion occupations, 476
    retailing, 477–478
    retailing occupations, 476
    sales, 4
        functions, 478
        occupations, 476
Case allowances, 392
Cash and carry wholesalers, 342
Cash cows, 33, 41
Cash discounts, 291
Catalogs
    for online purchases, 305
    for retailing, 332
Category development
        index, 251
    marketing dashboard, 252
Category killers, 331
Category management, 338

Cause marketing, 77
and American Express, 78
benefits to companies, 78
examples, 77
Caveat emptor concept, 74
Census Bureau; *see* United States
Census Bureau
Central business district, 336
CEOs, 25, 475
Certified Professional in Supply
Management, 114
Channel captain
economic influence, 311
expertise, 311
identification, 311–312
legitimate right, 312
Channel conflict, 310–311, 311
from disintermediation, 311
horizontal, 311
reduced by channel captain, 311–312
threat in transactional
websites, 467
vertical, 311
Channel cost, 309
Channel of communication, 352
Channels of distribution; *see*
Distribution *entries;* Marketing
channels
in global market, 153
promotion allowances, 291
Channel strategies, in promotional mix,
360–361
Chief marketing officer, 39
definition, 25
Child Protection Act of 1966, 72
Children
brand preferences, 104
consumer socialization, 103–104
China
IKEA in, 142
social and economic statistics, 157
Choice, in online shopping, 462–463
Choice assistance, 463
Choiceboard, 456
collaborative filtering, 456
Clayton Act, 72
on price discrimination, 298
Clickbots, 385
Click fraud, 385
Closed-end questions, 171
Closing stage
assumptive close, 439
objectives, 435
trial close, 439
urgency close, 439
Code of ethics, 75
Cognitive dissonance, 90
Cognitive learning, 98
Cola war, 75
repetition of, 139
Cold calling, 435

Cold canvassing, 435
Collaborative filtering, 456
College Board, 67
College students
digital natives, 359
job search on LinkedIn, 411
social media use, 402–403
College tuition increases, 67
Combination compensation plan, 444
Commerce
Pizza Hut website, 473
in websites, 459
Commercialization
Boeing's experience, 231–232
complexities, 232
definition, 231
parallel development, 232–233
risks in grocery products
failure fees, 232
regional rollouts, 232
slotting fees, 232
speed factor, 232–233
time to market, 232–233
Commission, 274
Communication, 352
in advertising, 354–355
channel of, 352
decoding, 353
in direct marketing, 357
encoding, 353
errors in, 353
feedback, 354
feedback loop, 354
fields of experience, 353
in logistics management, 317
in marketing, 6
message, 352
mobile marketing, 359
noise, 354
in online retailing
buzz, 464
spam, 463
viral marketing, 464
web communities, 463
from packaging and labeling, 261
in personal selling, 355–356
Pizza Hut website, 473
in public relations, 356–357
receivers, 352
in retailing, 337
salesforce, 446–447
source, 352
in websites, 459
Communication adaptation strategy, 152
Communications infrastructure, 146
Community
Pizza Hut website, 473
in websites, 459
Companies; *see* Business firms
Company analysis, Paradise Kitchens, 55
Comparative advertisements, 376

Compensation
of salesforce
combination plan, 444
straight commission
plan, 444
straight salary plan, 444
starting salary in marketing, 475–476
at Xerox, 450
Competition, 70
created from licensing, 150
dot-com failures, 16
ethics of, 74–75
forms of
monopolistic competition, 70
oligopoly, 70–71
pure competition, 70
pure monopoly, 71
and penetration pricing, 244
protecting
Clayton Act, 72
Robinson-Patman Act, 72
Sherman Antitrust Act, 71
in target markets, 202–203
Competition-oriented pricing
above-, at-, or below-market
pricing, 281
customary pricing, 280
loss-leader pricing, 282
Competitive advantage
from competitors, 32
created from licensing, 150
reinforcing, 428
Competitive bids in organizational
buying, 119
Competitive forces
and Facebook, 62
forms of competition, 70–71
small businesses, 71
Competitive institutional
advertisements, 377
Competitive intelligence researcher, 476
Competitive parity budgeting, 362
Competitive product advertisements, 376
Competitive products, new product ideas
from, 228
Competitor analysis, Paradise Kitchens,
54–55
Competitors, 32
and predatory pricing, 289
prices of, as constraint, 288
reacting to, 253
Complete delivery, 317
Complex salesperson, 476
Components, 216
Concept tests, 229
Connection
Pizza Hut website, 473
in websites, 458–459
Connectivity, 69
Consideration set, 89
advertising focus on, 93

Consistent lead times, 317
Constraints, 164
Consultant to clients, 428
Consultative selling, 438
Consumer behavior, 88; *see also*
    Online consumer behavior
  learning
    behavioral, 98
    cognitive, 98
  and product life cycle, 249–251
    early adopters, 250
    early majority, 250
    laggards, 250
    late majority, 250
    reasons for resistance, 250
  psychological influences, 94–98
  purchase decision process
    alternative evaluation, 89–90
    information search, 88
    level of involvement, 91–93
    postpurchase behavior, 90–91
    price comparisons, 90
    problem recognition, 88
    purchase decision, 90
    situational influences, 93
  sociocultural influences, 101–107
  and type of product, 215
  values, beliefs, and attitudes, 98–99
  women car buyers, 86–87
Consumer Bill of Rights, 74, 76
Consumer-brand connection, 256
Consumer Electronics Show, 70
Consumer Expenditure Survey, 68
Consumer income
  discretionary income, 68
  disposable income, 68
  gross income, 67
  influence on demand, 283
Consumer involvement
  high-involvement purchases, 91
  low-involvement purchases, 92
  variations
    extended problem solving, 92
    limited problem solving, 92
    routine problem solving, 92
Consumerism, 72
Consumer learning
  behavioral, 98
  and brand loyalty, 98
  cognitive, 98
Consumer lifestyle, VALS
  survey results, 100
Consumer markets
  behavioral segmentation
    by product features, 195–196
    by usage rate, 196
  demographic segmentation, 195
  geographic segmentation, 195
  psychographic segmentation, 195
Consumer needs, 4–5; *see also* Needs
  boundless, 94

discovering, 7
met with new products, 7–8
satisfying, 9
unmet by auto industry, 223
versus wants, 8
Consumer-oriented sales
    promotions, 389
  contests, 390
  coupons, 389
  deals, 389
  loyalty programs, 391
  point-of-purchase displays, 391
  premiums, 389–390
  product placement, 391
  rebates, 391
  samples, 390
  sweepstakes, 390
Consumer products, 215
  convenience products, 215
  shopping products, 215
  specialty products, 215
  unsought products, 215
Consumer Product Safety Act
  of 1972, 72
Consumer Product Safety
  Commission, 72
Consumer products and services
  Internet marketing channels, 304
  marketing channels, 302–303
Consumer promotions, 389
Consumer protection, 8
  Child Protection Act, 72
  Consumer Bill of Rights, 74, 76
  Consumer Product Safety Act, 72
  Controlling the Assault of Non-
    Solicited Pornography and
    Marketing Act, 73
  Deceptive Mail Prevention
    Enforcement Act, 72–73
  Federal Trade Commission Act, 72
  Lanham Act, 73
  Nutritional Labeling and Education
    Act, 72
  from packaging, 261
  Telephone Consumer Protection
    Act, 73
Consumer purchase tests, 388
Consumer Reports, 88, 89
Consumers; *see* Global consumers
  advertising and characteristics of, 378
  advertising posttests, 388
  advertising pretests, 387
  benefits from intermediaries, 301
  benefits of branding, 255
  buying experience, 91
  costs of Internet fraud, 466
  and gap analysis, 218
  global, 140–141
  hierarchy of effects, 362
  Internet privacy and security, 466
  motivation, 94–95

newness from perspective of, 220–221
personality, 95
prices of benchmark items, 336
proper response to brand identity, 256
status conscious, 277
ultimate, 16
utilities offered by retailing, 326–327
Consumer socialization, 103–104
Consumer spending, by global
  teenagers, 141
Consumer tastes, influence on
  demand, 282
Consumer trends, 253
Consumer wants, 8
Content
  Pizza Hut website, 472
  of websites, 458
Contests, 390
Context
  Pizza Hut website, 472
  of websites, 458
Continuous innovation, 221
  Callaway Golf, 298
Continuous (steady) schedule, 386
Contract manufacturing, 272
Contractual retail systems
  franchise systems, 329
  retailer-sponsored cooperatives, 329
  wholesaler-sponsored voluntary
    chains, 329
Contractual vertical marketing systems
  manufacturer-sponsored retail
    franchise systems, 307
  manufacturer-sponsored wholesale
    franchise systems, 307
  retailer-sponsored cooperatives, 307
  service-sponsored franchise
    systems, 308
  service-sponsored retail franchise
    systems, 307–308
  wholesaler-sponsored voluntary
    chains, 307
Control, reason for online shopping,
  465–466
Controllable forces, 9
Controlling the Assault of Non-Solicited
  Pornography and Marketing Act
  of 2004, 73, 462
Convenience
  buyer requirement, 309
  in logistics management, 317
  in online shopping, 462
Convenience products
  definition and basis of comparison, 215
  intensive distribution, 308
Convergence of real and digital worlds,
  418–421
Cookies, 465
  information provided by, 465–466
Cooperative advertising, 392
Copywriter, 379, 476

Core competencies, 32
　Paradise Kitchens, 52
Core values, 26
　Zappos.com, 188–189
Corporate branding, 258
Corporate chains
　dealing with manufacturers, 328
　high-tech business, 329
Corporate culture
　behavior of management and
　　co-workers, 75–76
　code of ethics, 75
　definition, 75
Corporate level, 25
Corporate vertical marketing systems
　and backward integration, 306–307
　definition, 306
　and forward integration, 306–307
Cost(s)
　of economic espionage, 142
　of integrated marketing
　　communications, 365
　of marketing channels, 309
　of packaging and labeling, 261
　performance measures linked to,
　　415–416
　of personal selling, 356
　of promotional elements, 355
　reason for online shopping, 464–465
　of salesforce training, 443
　total logistics cost, 316
Cost control, 285
Cost of marketing, pricing constraint, 288
Cost of production, pricing constraint, 288
Cost-oriented pricing
　cost-plus pricing, 279
　standard markup pricing, 278–279
Cost per action, social media, 415–416
Cost per click, social media, 415–416
Cost per thousand, 381
　social media, 415–416
Cost-plus pricing, 279
Cost reduction in packaging, 262
Country of origin or manufacture
　perception, 261
Coupon Information Corporation, 389
Coupons, 389
Cover letter, 482
Co-workers, ethical behavior, 75–76
Credibility of media, 406
Credit cards, unpopular in Germany, 143
Cross-channel shoppers, 90, 467
　most common buying path, 467
　sales from, 467
Cross-cultural analysis, 143
　cultural symbols, 144
　customs, 143
　languages, 144–145
　values, 143
Cross-docking, 315
Cross-functional teams, 26, 232–233

Cross-platform television ratings, 167
Crowdfunding, 228
Crowdsourcing, 227
Cultural diversity
　in approach stage, 436–437
　cultural symbols, 144
　customs, 143
　languages, 144–145
　values, 143
　on values, 66
Cultural symbols, 144
Cultural values, 143
Culture, 66
　Americanization of, 141
　components, 66
　and environmental concerns, 66–67
　influence on consumers, 106
　as socializing force, 73–74
Currency exchange rate, 147
Customary pricing, 280
Customer analysis, Paradise Kitchens,
　55–56
Customer dissatisfaction, 90
Customer experience
　definition, 457
　direct contacts, 14
　indirect contacts, 14
　nature of, 14
　online, 457–459
　Pizza Hut, 471–472
　problem of disconnect, 14
　Seven Cycles, Inc., 452
**Customer experience management,
　229, 264**
Customerization, 463
Customer loyalty, and frequency
　marketing, 196
Customer relationship management, 14
　relationship selling, 431
Customer relationship philosophy, 428
Customer relationships, at Xerox, 449
Customer requirements, and logistics
　management, 312
Customer retention, 91
Customers, 16
　cross-channel shoppers, 467
　finding new, 252–253
　new product ideas from, 227
　packaging and labeling to connect
　　with, 262
　prospects, 434–435
　and supply chain management, 314
Customer sales organization, 441
Customer satisfaction, 4–5, 90
　financial value of, 91
　in marketing concept, 91
　organizational goal, 28
　and salesperson performance, 445
Customer service, 316
　in logistics management
　　communication, 317

　convenience, 317
　dependability, 317
　order cycle time reduction, 316–317
　at Nordstrom, 330
Customer service manager, 476
Customer solutions, 438
　from personal selling, 431
Customer value, 10
　created in marketspace, 454–455
　impact of technology, 70
　means of increasing, 193
　from personal selling, 431
　from relationship selling, 431
Customer value proposition, 9
Customization
　benefit of marketspace, 455
　with choiceboards, 456
　Pizza Hut website, 472–473
　reason for online shopping, 463
　Seven Cycles, Inc., 452–453
　in websites, 458
Customized interaction, 354
Customs, 143
　cultural differences, 143
Cyber Monday, 333

D

Data, 165
　collection method, 164
　needed for marketing actions, 164
　observational, 167
　primary, 165, 167–175
　questionnaire, 169
　secondary, 165–166
Data analysis
　by data mining, 177–178
　with information technology, 176–177
　by product managers, 251
Databases
　in direct marketing, 357, 367
　Google and Facebook, 419
Data mining
　for data analysis, 177–178
　downside, 177
Data Protection Directive, European
　Union, 367
Data warehouses, 177
Deadlines, 39–40
Dealers, as intermediaries, 300
Deals, 389
Deceptive Mail Prevention and
　Enforcement Act, 72–73
Deceptive pricing
　bait-and-switch pricing, 289
　and Federal Trade Commission, 289
Deciders, in buying center, 125
Decision
　evaluation of, 180
　in marketing research, 162

Decision making, in marketing research, 162
Decision process, evaluation of, 180
Decline stage; *see* Product life cycle; Retail life cycle
Decoding, 353
Deletion, 248
Demand
  and demand curve, 282–283
  estimating, 282
  factor in target profit pricing, 280
  factors influencing
    availability of substitutes, 282–283
    consumer income, 283
    consumer tastes, 282
  inelastic, 284
  in organizational buying, 118–119
  pricing constraint, 288
Demand curve, 282
  movement along *vs.* shift in, 283
  and revenue estimation, 284
Demand factors, 283
Demand-oriented pricing
  bundle pricing, 277–278
  odd-even pricing, 277
  penetration pricing, 277
  prestige pricing, 277
  skimming pricing, 276–277
  target pricing, 277
  yield management pricing, 278
Demographics, 64
  China and India, 157
  generational cohorts, 65
  household, 166
  and population explosion, 64–65
  population profile, 64–56
  racial and ethnic diversity, 65–66
Demographic segmentation
  business markets
    by NAICS codes, 197
    by number of employees, 198
  consumer markets, 195
Density, and distribution
  exclusive, 308–309
  intensive, 308
  selective, 309
Department of Commerce, 24
Department of Energy, 45
Department of Justice
  and monopolies, 71
  on reciprocal buying, 121
Department of Labor
  Consumer Expenditure Survey, 68
  Occupational Outlook Handbook, 480–481
Departments, 26
Department stores, 331, 336
Dependability, in logistics management, 317
Dependent variables, in experiments, 175

Depth interviews, 169
Depth of product line, 330–331
Derived demand, 119
  for business products, 216
Desk jobbers, 342
Detroit Institute of Art, 218–219
Developing countries
  income growth, 147
  per capita income, 146
  population explosion, 64–65
Deviations
  acting on
    correcting negative aspects, 41
    exploiting positive aspects, 41
  identifying, 41
Dex One, 384
Dichotomous questions, 171
Differentiation positioning, 205
Diffusion of innovation, 250
Digital Millennium Copyright Act of 1998, 72
Direct channels
  for business products and services, 303
  for consumer products and services, 302
Direct contacts, 14
Direct exporting, 150
Direct forecast, 181
Direct investment
  advantages and risks, 151
  characteristics, 151
Direct-mail retailing, 332
  advantages and disadvantages, 382
Direct marketing, 357, 358
challenges in global markets, 367
  consumer benefits, 366
  costs, 355
  databases, 367
  disadvantages, 357
  expenditures, 366
  forms of, 366
  growth of, 366
  lead generation, 367
  legislation on, 367
  mobile, 366
  opt-in requirement, 367
  percent of GDP, 366
  percent of population using, 366
  privacy issue, 367, 368
  sales volume, 366
  strengths and weaknesses, 355
  tracking tools, 367
  traffic generation, 367
  value for sellers, 366–367
Direct Marketing Association, 368
Direct Marketing Association, United Kingdom, 367
Direct marketing channels, 305
Direct orders, 366
Direct salesperson, 476

Direct selling
  companies involved in, 334
  reasons for growth, 334–335
Direct-to-consumer drug advertising, 360–361
Discontinuous innovation, 221
Discounts, 335, 392
  cash, 291
  quantity, 291
  seasonal, 291
  trade, 291
Discount stores, 340
Discretionary income, 68
Disintermediation, 311
Disposable income, 68
Disruptive innovation, 226
Dissociative groups, 103
Distribution
  Chobani Greek Yogurt, 2–3
  in growth stage, 246
  in introduction stage, 244
  regular, 221
  in services marketing, 263
  and type of product, 215
  by Vizio, Inc., 272
Distribution density, 309
Distribution strategy
  by Dell Inc., 134
  in global market, 153
  Prince Sports, Inc., 209–210
  worldwide marketing program, 153
Distributors
  as intermediaries, 300
  trade promotions directed at, 391–392
Diversification analysis, 34
  diversification potential, 35
  market development, 35
  market penetration, 34–35
  product development, 35
Diversification potential, 35
Divestitures, by Ford Motor Company, 192
Dogs, 33
Do Not Track Online Act, proposed, 368
Dot-com business failures, 16
Downsizing package contents, 254
Drivers
  brand, 177
  marketing, 175
  product, 177
Drives, 98
Drop shippers, 342
Dual adaptation strategy, 153
Dual distribution, 305
Dues, 274
Dumping, 154
Durable goods, 214
Dynamically continuous innovation, 221
Dynamic pricing, 465

E

Early adopters, 250
Early growth stage, retail life
cycle, 340–341
Early majority, 250
Early-stage financing, 228
by Vizio, Inc., 272
Economic Census, 166
Economic espionage, 74, **142**
costs to U.S. firms, 142
Economic Espionage Act of
1996, 142
Economic forces
consumer income, 67–68
and Facebook, 62
in global market
currency exchange rates, 147
income and purchasing power,
146–147
infrastructure, 145–146
macroeconomic conditions, 67
Economic infrastructure, 145–146
Economic integration
CAFTA-DR, 139
European Union, 137–138
North American Free Trade
Agreement, 138–139
Economies of scale, 192–193
Economy, 67
impact of retailing, 327
Efficient customer response delivery
systems, 317
Efficient supply chain, 315–316
E-hubs, 126
Eight-second rule, 309, **462**
80/20 rule, 196
Elastic demand, 284
Electric vehicles, resistance to, 250
Electronic commerce, 70
benefit of euro for, 138
networked global marketspace,
141–142
Electronic intermediaries, 304
E-mail
consent to receive, 457
versus fax machines, 248
number of boxes worldwide, 248
E-mail survey, 170–171
E-marketplaces
independent, 126–127
private exchanges, 127
Emory University, 438
Emotional intelligence, 443
Employees, new product ideas from,
226–227
Employee welfare, organizational
goal, 28
Employment agencies, 481
Encoding, 353
Endorsements, 97

Entrepreneurs, and eBay, 127
Entrepreneurship, by Vizio, Inc., 272
Environmental forces, 5, 10
competitive, 70–71
diagram, 64
economic, 67–68
for Facebook, 52
regulatory, 71–73
social, 64–67
technological, 69–70
Environmental protection
and culture, 66–67
and Generation Y, 66
and packaging, 262
Toyota, 81–82
Trek Bicycle Company, 132
Environmental scanning, 64
competitive forces, 70–71
economic forces, 67–68
global, 143–148
regulatory forces, 71–73
social forces, 64–67
technological forces, 69–70
Environmental sustainability,
in organizational buying, 120
E-Privacy Directive, European
Union, 368
Equipment-based services, 216
Espionage activities, 74
Ethical considerations in pricing
deceptive pricing, 289
predatory pricing, 289
price discrimination, 289
price fixing, 288–289
Ethical marketing behavior
business culture and industry
practices, 74–75
cola war, 75
corporate culture, 75–76
personal moral philosophy, 76
societal culture and norms,
73–74
Ethics of competition
bribes and kickbacks, 74–75
economic espionage, 74
Ethics of downsizing, 254
Ethics of exchange, 74
Ethnic subcultures, 106–107
Ethnographic research, 169
Euro, 138
European Union
common currency, 138
Data Protection Directive, 367
E-Privacy Directive, 368
*General Data Protection
Regulation,* 367
map, 138
and monopolies, 71
number of languages, 144
number of member countries, 137
pan-European market strategies, 138

per capita income, 146
as single market, 137–138
tariffs, 137
Evaluation, 362
Evaluative criteria, 89–90
Everyday fair pricing, 336
Everyday low pricing, 291–292, 336
Exchange, 5
by barter, 274
ethics of, 74
transaction, 6
Exchange rate fluctuations, 147
Exclusive distribution, 308
Expense of media, 405
Experiencers, 100
Experiments
sales tests, 388
source of primary data, 175
Expertise, 311
Exporting, 148
direct, 150
indirect, 148–149
Extended problem solving, 92
External sources of information, 88

F

Facebook, 406
acquisition of Instagram, 406
acquisition of Oculus and
WhatsApp, 409
in brand manager's strategy, 407–408
guidelines to engage fans, 407–408
impact of, 407
launch of new social network, 408
number of unique visitors, 414
number of users, 406
overview, 406
updating, 408–409
Facilitating function, 301
Fad products, 249
Failure fees, 232
Family branding, 258
Family decision making
joint, 105
roles, 105
spouse-dominant, 105
Family influences
consumer socialization, 103–104
decision making, 105
family life cycle, 104–105
Family life cycle, 104
middle-aged married couples,
104–105
older married or unmarried, 105
single parents, 104
traditional family, 104
young married couples, 104
young singles, 104
Fares, 274

Fashion, Americanization of, 141
Fashion products, 249
Fast-food restaurant patronage, 196
Fast prototyping
    parallel development, 232–233
    time to market, 232
Fax machines, product life cycle,
    245–248
Fear appeals, 379
Federal Bureau of Investigation, 75
Federal Communications Commission
    on product placement, 391
    on subliminal messages, 96
Federal Trade Commission
    on Internet fraud
        complaints, 466
    and monopolies, 71
    National Do Not Call Registry, 368
    on newness of products, 221
    powers of, 72
    on sweepstakes, 390
    and telemarketing, 334
Federal Trade Commission Act
    of 1914, 72
Federation of European Direct
    Marketing, 367
Feedback
    lacking in advertising, 355
    to Seven Cycles, Inc., 452–453
Feedback loop, 352, 354
Fees, 274
Field of Dreams, 345
Fields of experience, 352
Fighting brands, 259
Final price, setting
    adjustments to list price, 290–292
    allowances, 291–292
    discounts, 291
    necessary conditions, 289
    select approximate price
        level, 289
    set list or quoted price
    flexible-price policy, 290
    one-price policy, 290
Finance allowances, 392
Financial performance, Paradise
    Kitchens, 59–61
Financial systems, 146
Financing, early-stage, 229
Fitness magazine, 238
Fixed-alternative questions, 171
Fixed costs, 285
Fixed pricing, 290
Flexible price policy, 290
Flighting (intermittent) schedule, 386
Floor stock protection program, 392
Florida Gators, 242
Focus groups, 167–170
Follow-up, 439–440
    in job interview, 484
    objectives, 435

Food and Drug Administration, and
    brand names, 257
Food brokers, 342
Footwear News, 380
Forbes, 44
Foreign Corrupt Practices Act, 143
Forest Stewardship Council, 115
Forgetting rate, 386
Forms of retail ownership, 327–328
Formula selling presentation, 437
Form utility, 301
    created in marketspace, 454–455
    definition, 16
    offered by retailing, 326–327
For-profit organizations, 23
Fortune, 14, 212, 480
Fortune 500, 449–450
Forward integration, 306–307
Four I's of services, 217
    inconsistency, 217
    inseparability, 217
    intangibility, 217
    inventory, 217–218
Four Ps of marketing, 9
Fox News, 238
Franchise system
    business-format, 329
    product-distribution, 329
Franchising, 150
    definition, 307
    manufacturer-sponsored retail
        franchise systems, 307
    manufacturer-sponsored wholesale
        franchise systems, 307
    service-sponsored franchise
        systems, 308
    service-sponsored retail franchise
        systems, 307–308
Free Trade Area of the Americas, 139
Free trials of products, 97
Frequency marketing, 196
Frequency of advertising, 381
Frequent-flyer programs, 196
Full-line wholesalers, 341
Full-service agency, 387
Full-service retailers, 330
Full-service wholesalers, 342
Functional benefits of packaging and
    labeling, 261
Functional discounts, 291
Functional level, 26
Fuzzy front end methods, 170

G

Gantt chart, 40
Gap analysis, 218
Gatekeepers, in buying centers, 125
General Data Protection Regulation,
    European Union, 367
Generalized life cycle, 248–249

General merchandise stores, 331
General merchandise
    wholesalers, 341
Generational cohorts
    baby boomers, 65
    Generation X, 65
    Generation Y, 65
Generation X, 65
Generation Y, 65
    environmental concerns, 66
Geographical sales organization, 441
Geographic segmentation
    business markets, 197
    consumer markets, 195
GeoVALS, 100
Germany
    opposition to credit cards, 143
    Walmart's failure in, 154
Global brand, 140
Global companies
    distribution strategy, 153
    international firms, 140
    multinational firms, 140
    pricing strategy, 154
    product and promotion, 151–153
    transnational firms, 140
Global competition, 139
    among global companies, 140
    cola war repeated, 139
    and global consumers, 140–141
Global consumers, 140–141
    income and purchasing power,
        146–147
Global environmental scan
    cultural diversity, 143–145
    economic conditions, 145–147
    political stability, 148
    trade regulations, 148
Global impact of retailing, 327
Global market entry strategies; *see*
    Market-entry strategies, global
Global marketing, 476
Global marketing manager, 476
Global marketing strategy, 140
    Dell Inc., 134–135
Global markets, direct
    marketing in, 367
Global teenagers, 141
Goal-directed lifestyle, 100
Goals, 28; *see also* Objectives
    Paradise Kitchens, 52
Good Housekeeping Seal, 97
Goods
    contribution to GDP, 214
    durable, 214
    marketing of, 15
    nondurable, 214
Government
    consumer protection, 8
    revenues from tariffs, 137
    stimulus checks, 68

Government agencies, 23
  functions, 24
  goals, 28
  number of, 117
  services delivered by, 217
Government markets
  in NAICS, 117–118
  organizational buying by, 117
Gray market, 154
Green machines, 332
Green marketing, 77
  and reverse logistics, 318
Green technologies, 69
Grocery products, commercialization
  risks, 232
Gross domestic product, 67
  contribution of goods
    to, 214
  contribution of services
    to, 214
Gross ratings points, 381
Groupthink, 224
Growth share matrix, 33
Growth stage; *see* Product life cycle
Growth strategies
  business portfolio analysis, 32–34
  diversification analysis, 34–35
Guarantees, 98

H

Harley Owners Group, 103, 459
Harvesting strategy, 248
Head-to-head positioning, 205
Health issues in packaging, 262
Help-wanted ads, 481
Hierarchy of effects, 362
Hierarchy of needs, 94–95
High- and low-resource groups, 100
High-involvement purchases
  decision, 91–92
  information search, 93
High-learning products, 249
High-resource achievers, 100
High-resource experiencers, 100
High-resource innovators, 100
High-resource thinkers, 100
Hispanics
  buying patterns, 106
  makeup of subculture, 106
  price discrimination in car
    buying, 290
  projected spending by, 66
Home price decline, 68
Horizontal channel conflict, 311
Horizontal price fixing, 289
Households
  demographics, 166
  income, 67–68
  segmentation by, 195
Humorous appeals, 379

I

Idea evaluation methods, 170–171
Idea generation
  competitive products, 228
  crowdsourcing, 227
  customer suggestions, 226–227
  employees and friends, 226
  inventors, 228
  methods, 169–170
  open innovation, 226
  research and development labs,
    227–228
  smaller firms, 228
  supplier suggestions, 227
  universities, 228
Ideals-motivated groups, 100
Ideas, 214
  marketing of, 15
Identification, 311–312
Idle production capacity, 217
Image, 100
IMC; see Integrated marketing
  communications
Inbound telemarketing, 433
Income
  of consumers, 67–68
  of global consumers, 146–147
  growth in developing
    countries, 147
Income distribution, 146
Inconsistency of services, 217
Independent e-marketplaces,
  126–127
Independent retailers, 307, 328
Independent variables in
  experiments, 175
India
  Dell Inc. in, 134–135
  Mary Kay Cosmetics in, 156–158
  number of languages, 144
  social and economic statistics, 157
Indirect channels
  for business products and
    services, 303–304
  for consumer products and
    services, 302–303
Indirect contacts, 14
Indirect exporting, 148–149
Individual interviews, 169
Individuality, Internet capability,
  457–457
Industrial distributors, 304, 341
  preference for exclusive
    distribution, 309
Industrial markets
  in NAICS, 117–118
  organizational buyers, 116
Industrial products, 215
Industrial salesperson, 476
Industrial services, 216

Industries
  definition, 24
  in marketing plan, 48
  number of firms, 116
  revolutionized by Steve
    Jobs, 212
Industry analysis, Paradise
  Kitchens, 54
Industry practices
  ethics of competition, 74–75
  ethics of exchange, 74
Inelastic demand, 284
Inflation-adjusted income, 67–68
Inflationary economy, 67
Influencers, in buying centers, 124
Infomercials, 383
Information, buyer requirement, 309
Informational interviews, 481
Information search
  by consumers, 88
  high-involvement purchases, 93
  in organizational buying, 124
  and perceived risk, 97
Information sources
  external, 88
  internal, 88
  Internet, 90
  market-dominated, 88
  personal, 88
  public, 88
Information technology, 178
  components, 176
  for data analysis, 176–177
  in direct marketing, 367
  to operate supply chain, 315–316
Infrastructure, 145–146
In-house agencies, 387
In-house project manager, 476
In-house research staff, 478–479
Innovation
  at Apple Inc., 212–213
  continuous, 221
  diffusion of, 250
  discontinuous, 221
  disruptive, 226
  dynamically continuous, 221
  open, 226
Innovators, 100, 250
Input-related objectives, 440
Inputs, performance measures linked
    to, 415–416
Inquiry tests, 388
Inseparability of services, 217
Inside order takers, 432–433
Installations, 216
Institutional advertisements, 377
  advocacy, 377
  competitive, 377
  pioneering, 377
  reminder, 377
Intangibility of services, 217

Integrated marketing communications, 352; *see also* Promotion program
to develop promotional mix
    channel strategies, 360–361
    product life cycle stages, 358–359
    target audience, 358
Olympic Games and, 363
program development, 361–364
program execution and assessment, 364–365
quick response (QE) codes, 351
rich site summary, 351
Taco Bell, 350–351, 371
Integrated supply chain, 315
Intensive distribution, 308
Interactive marketing, 456
customer value creation, 454–455
individuality and customer relationships, 455–456
online customer experience, 457–459
Seven Cycles, Inc., 452–453
Interactivity, Internet capability, 457–457
Interest, 274, 362
Intermediaries
for business products and services, 303–304
consumer benefits, 301
for consumer products and services, 302–303
customer value created by, 300–301
electronic, 304
focus of promotion, 368
functions
    facilitating, 301
    logistical, 301
    transactional, 300–301
terms for, 300
trade promotions directed at, 392–393
Internal sources of information, 88
International Anti-Dumping and Fair Competition Act of 1998, 143
International careers in marketing, 479
International firms, marketing strategy, 140
International marketing, Dell Inc., 134–135
International Standard Classification of All Economic Activities, 117
International trade
barter transactions, 274
benefits of European Union, 137–138
benefits of NAFTA, 138–139
dumping, 154
effect of exchange rate fluctuations, 147
effect of tariffs and quotas, 136–137
exporting, 148–150
parallel importing, 154
and political stability, 148
regulations, 148

Internet; *see* Online advertising; Online consumer behavior; Online retailing
choiceboards, 456
coupons generated by, 389
networked global marketspace, 141–142
for online TV, 374–375
organizational buying, 126
and privacy laws, 421
product information source, 90
for salesforce communication, 446–447
word of mouth magnified by, 103
Internet-enabled technologies
for communication, 463–464
for individuality, 457–457
for interactivity, 457–457
for viral marketing, 464
for web communities, 463
Internet marketing channels, 304
Internet moms, 461
Internet search engines, 93
Interviews
depth, 169
individual, 169
mall-intercept, 171
personal, 170–171
telephone, 170
Introduction stage; *see* Product life cycle
Inventors, new product ideas from, 228
Inventory control manager, 476
Inventory handling costs, 217
Inventory management
efficient customer response, 317
quick response, 317
vendor-managed inventory, 317
at Walmart, 315
Involvement, 91

J

Japan
Fran Wilson Cosmetics in, 149
tariffs, 136
trade regulations, 148
Jeopardy, 44
Jersey Shore, 103
Job analysis, 442
Job description, 442
Job interview
follow-up, 483–484
handling rejection, 484
information sources for, 483
preparing for, 482–483
role playing, 483
succeeding in, 483
Job opportunities, identifying
career service office, 480
direct contact, 481

employment agencies, 481
help-wanted ads, 481
informational interviews, 481
library reference materials, 480–481
networking, 481
online career and employment services, 480
personal contacts, 481
state employment office, 481
Job qualifications, 442–443
Job search
identifying opportunities, 480–481
job interview, 482–484
on LinkedIn, 411
marketing mix, 475
marketing oneself, 475
résumé preparation, 481–482
self-analysis, 479–480
target market, 475
Joint decision making, 105
Joint ventures, 150
advantages, 150–151
disadvantages, 151
Journal of Marketing, 164
Journal of Marketing Research, 164
Judgment of decision makers, 180–181
Jury tests, 387

K

Key account management, 441
Kickbacks, 74–75
and Foreign Corrupt Practices Act, 143

L

Labeling
challenges and responses
    connecting with customers, 262
    cost reduction, 262
    environmental concerns, 262
    health, safety, and security issues, 262
communication benefits, 260
costs to companies, 261
creating customer value, 260–261
functional benefits, 260–261
perceptual benefits, 261
private, 259
Labels
definition, 260
list product sources, 261
to update brand image, 261
Laboratory test markets, 231
Laggards, 250
Language(s)
back translation, 145
for diplomacy and commerce, 144–145
number of
    in Canada, 144

in European Union, 144
in India, 144
unintended brand name meanings, 145
Lanham Act of 1946, 73
Late majority, 250
Lawrence Livermore Laboratory, 121
Lead, 434
Leadership in Energy and Environmental
Design, 66
Lead generation, 367
Lead times, 317
Learning, 98
LEED; *see* Leadership in Energy and
Environmental Design
Legal considerations in pricing
deceptive pricing, 289
predatory pricing, 289
price discrimination, 289
price fixing, 288–289
Legal forces, and Facebook, 62
Legal systems, 146
Legitimate right, 312
Library reference materials, 480–481
Licensing, 150
Life-cycle curve
fad products, 249
fashion products, 249
generalized life cycle, 248–249
high-learning products, 249
low-learning products, 249
shape of, 248
Lifestyle analysis, 99–100
Lifestyle segmentation, 195
Limited-line wholesalers, 341
Limited problem solving, 92
Limited-service agencies, 387
Limited-service retailers, 330
Limited-service wholesalers, 342
Linear trend extrapolation, 181
LinkedIn, 410–411
in brand manager's strategy, 410–411
business orientation, 410
for job search, 411
number of members, 410
number of unique visitors, 414
List or quoted price
flexible price policy, 290
one-price policy, 290
special adjustments to, 290–292
allowances, 291–292
discounts, 291
Local Search Association, 384
Location-based promotions, 420
Logistical function, 301
not done by electronic
intermediaries, 304
Logistics, 312
decisions needed
cost effectiveness, 312
customer service, 312
flow of product, 312

reverse, 317–318
in supply chain management, 312–313
of transactions, 301
Logistics management
Amazon.com, 322
definition, 312
at Procter & Gamble, 312
in supply chain
customer service, 316–317
total logistics cost, 316
vendor-managed inventory, 317
and supply chain management, 313
Logotype/logo, 254
Loss-leader pricing, 282
Lost-horse forecast, 181
Louvre, 15
Low-involvement purchase decision, 92
Low-learning products, 249
Low-resource believers, 100
Low-resource makers, 100
Low-resource strivers, 100
Low-resource survivors, 100
Loyalty programs, 391
in mobile marketing, 420
Luxury goods
exclusive distribution, 308–309
prestige pricing, 277
and reference groups, 103

M

Macroeconomic conditions, 67
Magazine advertising
advantages and disadvantages, 382
cost disadvantage, 384
marketing advantages, 383–384
number of magazines, 383
specialty publications, 383–384
Mail surveys, 170
Maintained markup, 335
Major account management, 441
Makers, 100
Malcolm Baldrige National Quality
Award, 445
Mall intercept interviews, **171**
Management of product life cycle
market modification, 252–253
product manager role, 251
product modification, 251
product repositioning, 253–254
Managing for the long-run profits, 287
Manufacturers
cash discounts, 291
cooperative advertising, 392
cost-plus pricing, 279
dealing with corporate chains, 328
performance contracts, 392
promotional strategies
pull strategy, 360–361
push strategy, 360

target pricing by, 277
trade discounts, 291
training of distributors' salesforce,
392–393
use of transactional websites, 467–468
Manufacturer's agents, 342
Manufacturer's branch office, 342–343
Manufacturer-sponsored retail franchise
systems, 307
Manufacturer-sponsored wholesale
franchise systems, 307
Manufacturer's representative, 342
Manufacturer's sales office, 342–343
Markdown, 336
Market, 8
for Mall of America, 346
reaching new, 253
two environments, 454
Market attractiveness, too little, 223
Market development, 35
Market-dominated information
sources, 88
Market-entry strategies, global
direct investment, 151
exporting, 148–150
franchising, 150
joint ventures, 150–151
licensing, 150
Market growth rate, 33
Marketing, 4; *see also* Careers in
marketing
breadth and depth of
beneficiaries, 16
organizational buyers, 16
ultimate consumers, 16
utilities created, 16
what is marketed, 15
who markets, 15
concepts in, 164
controllable marketing mix, 9
customer value proposition, 9
discovering consumer needs, 7
diversity of jobs in, 475
effect of technological advances, 70
elements influencing
environmental forces, 5
organizational goals, 5
and ethics, 14
evolution of market orientation, 13–14
factors required for
ability to satisfy needs, 6
communication, 6
exchange, 6
unsatisfied needs, 6
four Ps of, 9
of Gatorade, 242–244
nature of markets, 8–9
needs *vs.* wants, 8
objectives, 4–5
personal selling in, 431
satisfying consumer needs, 9

Marketing, *continued*
　satisfying needs with new
　　products, 7–8
　and social responsibility, 15
　target market, 9
　Tiffany/Walmart strategy, 193
　in two environments, 454
　uncontrollable environmental
　　forces, 10
Marketing actions
　evaluation of results, 180
　identifying, 163
　identifying data needed for, 164
　implementation, 180
　in market segmentation, 190
　measures of success, 163
　Pizza Hut plan, 471
　potential to reach segments, 195
　to reach target markets
　　and changing consumer tastes, 203
　　ever-changing segmentation
　　　strategies, 203
　　immediate segmentation strategy,
　　　201–202
　　and market-product synergies,
　　　203–204
　　watching competition, 202–203
　recommendations, 179–180
Marketing channels, 300; *see also*
　　Channel *entries;* Distribution;
　　Wholesalers
　Amazon.com, 321–323
　automobile industry, 313–314
　for business products and services
　　direct, 303
　　indirect, 303–304
　Callaway Golf, 298–299
　Cereal Partners Worldwide, 306
　channel captains, 311–312
　channel conflict, 310–311
　Charlesburg Furniture, 310
　for consumer products and services
　　direct, 302
　　indirect, 302–303
　direct, 305
　dual distribution, 305
　factors in choice and management
　　buyer requirements, 309
　　profitability, 309
　　target market coverage, 308–309
　functions of intermediaries, 300–301
　Internet, 305
　multichannel marketing, 305
　reliance on logistics, 312
　strategic channel alliances, 306
　strategies in IMC, 360–361
　versus supply chain, 312–313
　vertical marketing systems,
　　306–308
Marketing communication
　　programs, 352

Marketing concept, 13
　customer satisfaction, 91
Marketing dashboards, 29
　advertising media selection, 381
　Apple Stores, 338
　Ben & Jerry's, 31
　brand development index, 252
　bullet graphs, 30
　Carma Laboratories, 174
　category development index, 252
　to improve new-product
　　performance, 225
　IMC spending, 363
　marketing metrics, 30
　Red Bull pricing, 281
　sales and profit in marketing
　　channels, 310
　site stickiness, 460
　for Sonatica, 30
　spark lines, 30
　tracking salesperson
　　performance, 445
　underperforming states, 224
Marketing database manager, 476
Marketing decisions, 5
Marketing department
　diagram, 9
　key role of, 26
Marketing drivers, 175
Marketing goals, 37
Marketing information, 165
Marketing input data, 165
Marketing manager, 476
Marketing metric, 29, 338–339
　sales per square foot, 339
　same-store sales growth, 339
Marketing mix, 9
　in introduction stage, 244
　in job search, 475
　in marketing careers, 475
　in market segmentation, 190
　place strategy, 12
　poor execution of, 223
　prices in, 276
　price strategy, 12
　product strategy, 12
　promotion strategy, 12
　in services marketing, 263
Marketing News, 481
Marketing objectives
　Paradise Kitchens
　　current market, 56
　　food services, 56
　　new markets, 56
　　new products, 56–57
　　points of difference, 57
　　positioning, 57
　　target market, 57
　in product life cycle, 245
Marketing organization, 39
Marketing outcome data, 165

Marketing plan, 29
　compared to business plan, 48–49
　elements of, 49
　industry, 48
　kind and complexity of organization, 48
　most-asked questions, 49
　Paradise Kitchens
　　core competencies, 52
　　evaluation, 61
　　financial data, 59–61
　　goals, 52
　　implementation plan, 61
　　interpreting, 50
　　marketing and product
　　　objectives, 56–57
　　marketing program, 58–59
　　mission, 51
　　place strategy, 59
　　points of difference, 57
　　positioning, 57
　　price strategy, 58
　　product strategy, 58
　　promotion strategy, 58–59
　　situation analysis, 53–57
　　strategic focus and plan, 51–52
　　sustainable competitive advantage, 52
　　target markets, 57
　Smarter Planet, 45–46
　target audience and purpose, 48
　writing and style suggestions, 49–50
Marketing program, 11
　actions, 12
　cross-functional teams for, 26
　execution of, 40
　and market segments, 11
　for Medtronic, 38
　Paradise Kitchens
　　place strategy, 59
　　price strategy, 58
　　product strategy, 58
　　promotion strategy, 58–59
　rationale for actions, 12
　relationship marketing, 10–11
　at 3M Corporation, 11–13
　worldwide
　　distribution strategy, 153
　　pricing strategy, 154
　　product strategy, 151–153
　　promotion strategy, 151–153
Marketing publications, 485
Marketing research, 162
　challenges, 162
　data collection
　　primary data, 166–175
　　secondary data, 165–166
　data collection methods
　　sampling, 164
　　statistical inference, 164
　decision making, 162
　developing findings, 176–178
　feedback to learn lessons, 162

five-step approach, 162
functions, 478–479
by LEGO Group, 163–164
marketing actions based on, 179–180
by movie industry, 160–161
occupations, 476
online, 479
plan development, 163–164
problem definition, 163
sales forecasting techniques, 180–182
types of data, 165
use of social media by Carmex,
    184–186
Marketing research consulting
    firms, 478
Marketing strategy, 40
Ben & Jerry's, 22
and consumer involvement, 92–93
diversification
    market development, 35
    market penetration, 34–35
    product development, 35
global, 140
at IBM, 45–46
integrating social media into
    Carmex example, 417–418
    measuring results, 415–417
    sales production, 414–415
    selecting social network, 413–414
pan-European, 138
supply chain aligned with
    harmonization, 314
    understanding customers, 314
    understanding supply chain, 314
Marketing synergies, 203–204
Marketing tactics, 40
Market modification
    creating new product situations, 253
    finding new customers, 252–253
    increasing product use, 253
Market orientation, 14
    and customer experience, 14
    customer relationship management, 14
    evolution of, 13–14
Market penetration, 34–35
Marketplace
    compared to marketspace, 454
    impact of racial and ethnic diversity,
        65–66
Market price, 280
Market-product focus, Paradise
    Kitchens, 56–57
Market-product grid, 191
Apple Inc., 203, 204
example, 191
Wendy's, 199–200, 202
Market segmentation, 37, 190
analysis of bases for, 196
Apple Inc., 203–204
business markets, 197–200
consumer markets, 195–197

cost-benefit analysis, 191
criteria for forming segments, 194–195
databases for, 419
grouping buyers into segments, 194–198
and marketing actions, 190
marketing actions to reach, 201–204
    changing consumer tastes, 203
    ever-changing strategy, 203
    market-product synergies, 203–204
    watching competition, 202–203
with market-product grids, 191, 199,
    200, 202, 204
by Prince Sports, Inc., 208–210
and product differentiation, 190
reasons for, 190
strategy at Zappos.com, 188–191
target market selection, 200–201
timing and means of
    mass customization, 192–193
    multiple products in multiple
        segments, 192
    one product in multiple segments,
        191–192
    synergies *vs.* cannibalization, 193
at Wendy's, 196–197, 198–203
Market segments, 11
blurred lines between, 193
criteria for forming
    differences in needs, 194–195
    marketing actions potential, 195
    profit potential, 194
    similarity of needs, 194
    simplicity and cost-effectiveness, 194
definition, 190
and mass customization, 192–193
with multiple products, 192
with one product, 191–192
Prince Sports, Inc., 210
variables for forming, 196–197
Market share, 28
organizational goal, 28
pricing objective, 287
relative, 33
Market size estimation, 199–200
Marketspace, 70
choiceboards, 456
collaborative filtering, 456
companies with origin in, 454
creating customer value, 454–455
customer relationships, 456–457
definition, 454
global, 141–142
individuality, 456–457
interactivity, 456–457
online customer experience, 457–459
permission marketing, 457
personalization, 456–457
Market testing
definition, 230
types of test markets, 231
when not feasible, 231

Markup, 278–279, 335
Mass customization, 192–193
Mass selling, 354
Maturity stage; *see* Product life cycle;
    Retail life cycle
Maximizing current profit, 287
Measures of success, 163
Media; *see* Advertising media
Media buyer, 476
Media richness, 404
Men as grocery shoppers, 105
Merchandise, in retailing mix
    category management, 338
    marketing metrics, 338–339
Merchandise allowances, 392
Merchandise line
    breadth of, 330, 331
    depth of, 330–331
Merchandise management, 477
Merchant wholesalers, 341
full-service
    general merchandise
        wholesalers, 341
    specialty merchandise
        wholesalers, 341
limited-service
    cash and carry wholesalers, 342
    drop shippers, 342
    rack jobbers, 342
    truck jobbers, 342
Message, 352
content
    fear appeals, 379
    humorous appeals, 379
    sex appeals, 379
creation of
    by ad agencies, 379–380
    artwork, layout, and
        production, 379
    copywriters, 379
problems with, 353
Methods, 164
Metro, 384
Mexico, and NAFTA, 138–139
Middle-aged married
    couples, 104–105
Middle-class status, 147
Middleman, 300
Millennials, 65
    environmental concerns, 66
    mobile marketing, 359
Minority-owned firms, 120
Mission, 27
of IBM, 44–45
Paradise Kitchens, 51
Mission statement
    characteristics, 27
    social element of, 27
    Zappos.com, 189
Mixed branding, 260
Mobile apps, 419

Mobile marketing, 359
  buyer control, 420
  location-based promotions, 420
  loyalty programs, 420
  price comparisons, 420
  privacy issue, 421
  sensor control, 421
  smartphone apps, 420
Modified rebuy, 126
  definition, 126
  Trek Bicycle Company, 132
Money, as defining success, 100
Monopolistic competition, 70
Monopoly, 71
Moral idealism, 76
Motivation, 94
  from lifestyle differences, 99–100
  of salesforce, 443–444
    compensation plans, 444
    nonmonetary rewards, 444
  at Xerox, 450
Movement along a demand curve, 283
Movie industry
  marketing research, 160–161
  product placement in, 391
  test screenings, 160
  tracking studies, 160
MSN News, 238
Multibranding, 259
Multichannel marketing, 305
  and careers, 475
  characteristics, 467
  cross-channel shoppers, 467
  implementing, 467
  percent of online sales, 469
  by Pizza Hut, 471–474
  with promotional websites, 468–469
  with transactional websites, 467–468
  value-adding capabilities, 305
Multichannel retailers, 337
Multicultural marketing, 66
  by PepsiCo, 242–243
Multidomestic marketing
  strategy, 140
Multilanguage website, 452–453
Multinational firms, marketing
  strategy, 140
Multiproduct firms, strategic business
  units, 25–26
Multiproduct branding, 258
Myers-Brigg Type Indicator, 480
Mystery shopper, 168

N

NAICS; *see* North American Industry
  Classification System
National Aeronautics and Space
  Administration, 117
National Association of Colleges and
  Employers, 480

National Association of PET Container
  Resources, 70
National Bureau of Economic Research, 290
National Cable and Telecommunication
  Association, 383
National Do Not Call Registry, 334, 367,
  368, 435
Needs; *see* Consumer needs
  ability to satisfy, 6
  boundless, 94
  hierarchy of, 94–95
  in market segments
    differences, 104–195
    similarity, 194
  perception of, 88
  unmet, 6
  versus wants, 8
Need-satisfaction presentation
  adaptive selling, 437
  consultative selling, 438
Networked global marketspace, 141–142
Networking, 481
Neuromarketing data collection, 169
New buy
  definition, 125–126
  Trek Bicycle Company, 132
Newness of product, pricing
  constraint, 288
New-product concepts, 164
New product development, 35, 70
  Chobani Greek Yogurt, 2, 15
  Dell Inc., 134
  at Google Inc.
    home movies, 230
    for services, 230
  idea generation, 12
  production, 12
  product line extension, 12–13
New-product failure
  examples, 222–223
  marketing reasons for
    bad timing, 223
    incomplete protocol, 222–223
    insignificant points of difference, 222
    no economical access to buyers, 223
    not satisfying customer needs, 223
    poor execution of marketing mix, 223
    poor quality, 223
    too little attractiveness, 223
  from organizational inertia, 224
New product launch
  Chobani Greek Yogurt, 2
  Paradise Kitchens, 61
  penetration pricing, 277
  product positioning, 205
  regional rollouts, 232
  skimming pricing, 276–277
New-product process, 225
  at Apple Inc., 212–213
  business analysis, 229–230
  commercialization, 231–233

  concept tests, 229
  crowdfunding, 228
  development, 230
  early-stage financing, 228
  idea generation, 226–228
  market testing, 230–231
  prototype creation, 229
  screening and evaluation, 229
  strategy development for, 225–226
  at X-1, 237–238
New products
  hierarchy of effects, 362
  marketing dashboards to improve
    performance, 225
  meeting consumers with, 7–8
  newness of
    compared to existing products, 220
    from consumers' perspective,
      220–221
    Federal Trade Commission
      perspective, 221
    from organizational perspective,
      220–221
  success of
    brand extension, 221–222
    product line extension, 221
New-product strategy development,
  225–226
News conference, 393
New-service ideas, and customer
  experience management, 229
Newspaper advertising
  advantages and disadvantages, 382
  coupons, 389
  local medium, 384
  in national newspapers, 384
  reach of, 380–381
News release, 393
New York Times, 192, 406, 458–459
Noise, 354
Nonassimilated Asian Americans, 107
Nondurable goods, 214
Nonpersonal component of advertising, 354
Nonprofit marketing, 476
Nonprofit organizations, 23
  functions, 24
  goals, 28
  services delivered by, 217
Nonselling duties, 478
Nonstore retailing. *see* Retailing
Norms, 73–74, 143
North American Free Trade Agreement,
  117, 138
  size of marketplace, 139
  trade benefits, 139
North American Industry
  Classification System, 117, 166
  breakdown for industries, 118
Not-invented-here problem, 224, 226
Nutritional Labeling and Education
  Act of 1990, 72

O

Objections, handling
accept, 439
acknowledge and convert, 438
agree and neutralize, 439
denial, 439
ignore, 439
postpone, 439
Objective and task budgeting, 362
Objectives, 28
for advertising, 378
of marketing for Paradise Kitchens, 56–57
in marketing research, 163
of organizational buying
environmental sustainability, 120
increase profits, 120
minority- and women-owned firms, 120
in personal selling, 435
of pricing, 287–288
of promotion program, 362
of sales plan, 440
Observational data, 167
ethnographic research, 169
mechanical methods, 167–168
mystery shopper, 168
neuromarketing methods, 169
personal methods, 168–169
Occupational Outlook Handbook, 480–481
Odd-even pricing, 277
Offering, 23
Off-peak pricing, 230, 263
Off-retail pricing, 336
Older married or unmarried, 105
Oligopoly, 70–71
Olympic Games, 363
One-price policy, 290
Online advertising
advantages and disadvantages, 382
and click fraud, 385
difficulty of measuring impact, 384–385
by Google, Inc., 397–398
rich media, 384
Online auctions, 127–128
Online behavioral advertising, 368
Online buyers
e-marketplaces, 126–127
online auctions, 127–128
in organizational markets, 126
Online career and employment services, 480
Online consumer behavior
annual spending, 461
characteristics of online consumers, 460–461
cross-channel shoppers, 467
eight-second rule, 462

favorite websites, 466
privacy and security issues, 466
purchases, 461–462
reasons for online shopping
choice, 462–463
choice assistance, 463
communication, 463–464
control, 465–466
convenience, 462
cost, 464–465
customization, 463
and showrooming, 465
timing of shopping, 466
Online customer experience, 457–459
commerce, 459
communication, 459
community, 459
connection, 458–459
content, 458
context, 458
Online malls, 333–334
Online marketing manager, 476
Online marketing research, 479
Online retailing; *see* Marketspace
advantages for consumers, 333
approaches to, 333–334
biggest days of the year, 333
Callaway Golf, 298
choice assistance, 463
choiceboards, 456
dynamic pricing, 465
eight-second rule, 309
growth of, 454
main product categories, 461–462
permission marketing, 457
personalization, 456–457
problems in, 334
and showrooming, 465
social shopping options
aggregators, 334
intermediaries, 334
marketplaces, 334
by traditional retailers, 333
Online surveys, 170–171
Online TV, 374–375
Open-ended questions, 171
Open innovation, 226
Operations manager, 476
Opinion leaders, 101
Opportunities; *see* SWOT analysis
challenges as, 428
examples, 37
Opt-in, 367, 457
Opt-out, 457
Order clerks, 43
Order cycle time, 316–316
Order getter, 433
job qualifications, 442–443
Order size in organizational buying, 119
Order taker, 432

and inbound telemarketing, 433
inside, 433
outside, 432–433
Organizational buyers, 16, 116
advertising directed to, 358
competitive bids, 119
government markets, 117
industrial markets, 116
number of potential, 120
reseller markets, 116
service market, 116
Organizational buying
buyer-seller relationships, 121–122
buying center, 123–126
complex negotiations, 121
criteria, 120–121
demand characteristics, 118–119
derived demand, 118–119
e-marketplaces, 126–127
at Harley-Davidson, 122
Internet applications, 126
by JCPMedia, Inc., 114–115
key characteristics, 119
long-term contracts, 121
number of potential buyers, 120
objectives, 120
online auctions, 127–128
prominence of online buying, 126
purchase decision process
alternative evaluation, 124
information search, 124
postpurchase behavior, 124
problem recognition, 124
purchase decision, 124
reciprocity, 121
by service companies, 116
size of order or purchase, 119
stages in, 123, 124
supply partnerships, 121–122
sustainable procurement, 123
training for, 114
by Trek Bicycle Company, 131–132
Organizational buying behavior, 123
Organizational buying criteria
commonly used, 120
supplier development, 121
Organizational chart, 5, 39
Organizational culture, 27
Organizational direction, 27–28
business, 28
goals and objectives, 28
Organizational foundation
core values, 26–27
mission, 27
Organizational goals, 5
Organizational inertia
from groupthink, 224
from not-invented-here problem, 224

Organizational markets; *see*
    Business markets
  business marketing in, 116
  buying in, 118–126
  government markets, 117
  industrial markets, 116
  measuring, 117–118
  organizational buyers, 116
  prominence of online buying, 16–128
  reseller markets, 116
Organizational strategy
  Ben & Jerry's, 22
  variation by level, 29
  variation by product, 29
Organizational structure
  corporate level, 25
  functional level, 26
  Paradise Kitchens, 60–61
  strategic business unit level, 25–26
Organizational synergy, 193
Organizations; *see* Business firms
  business model, 28
  complexity and type, 48
  definition and types, 23
  newness from perspective of, 221–222
Outbound telemarketing, 433
Outdoor advertising
  advantages and disadvantages, 382
  billboards, 385
  transit advertising, 385–386
Output-related objectives, 440
Outputs, performance measures
  linked to, 416
Outside order takers, 432–433
Outsourcing, by Dell Inc., 134

P

Packaging
  challenges and responses
    connecting with customers, 262
    cost reduction, 262
    environmental concerns, 262
    health, safety, and security issues, 262
  communication benefits, 260
  consumer protection from, 261
  costs to companies, 261
  creating customer value, 261
  definition, 260
  downsizing contents of, 254
  functional benefits, 260–261
  Paradise Kitchens, 58
  perceptual benefits, 261
Paid aspect of advertising, 354
Panels
  jury tests, 387
  source of primary data, 175
Parallel development, 232–233
Parallel importing, 154
PC Magazine, 70

Penetration pricing, 244
  for new products, 277
People-based services, 216, 264
Peoplemaps, 480
People meter, 167
Per capita income
  China and India, 157
  national variations, 146
Perceived risk, 97
  strategies to reduce
    endorsements, 97
    extensive usage instructions, 98
    providing free trials, 97
    seals of approval, 97
    warranties and guarantees, 98
Percentage of sales budgeting, 362
Perception, 96
  selective, 96–97
  subliminal, 96, 97
Perceptual benefits of packaging and
  labeling, 261
Perceptual maps, 206
  for product positioning, 205–206
  for repositioning, 206
Performance, tracked with marketing
  dashboards, 29–31
Performance contracts, 392
Performance measures
  Pizza Hut, 473
  for social media
    cost per action, 415–416
    cost per click, 415–416
    cost per thousand, 415–416
    linked to inputs or costs, 415–416
    linked to outputs or revenues, 416
Periodicals related to marketing, 485
Permanence, traditional *vs.* social
  media, 405
Permission marketing, 457
  rules, 457
Personal collection of observational
  data, 168–169
Personal computer industry, feature
  bloat, 220
Personal contacts, 481
Personal influences on consumers
  opinion leaders, 101
  reference groups, 103
  word of mouth, 102–103
Personal interview surveys, 170
Personality, 95
Personality tests, 480
Personality traits, 95
Personalization, 456
Personal moral philosophy
  moral idealism, 76
  utilitarianism, 76
Personal needs, 95
Personal selling, 355, 358, **430**
  creating customer solutions and
    value, 431

customized interaction, 354
disadvantages
  flexibility, 356
  high costs, 356
emotional intelligence, 443
at GE Healthcare Americas, 428
in marketing, 431
number of employees in, 430
order getters, 433
order takers, 432–433
personal element, 355–356
pervasiveness of, 430
as promotional tool, 363
and push strategy, 360
reduced wasted coverage, 355
relationship selling, 431
strengths and weaknesses, 355
technological revolution, 446
trade promotions for, 391–392
Personal selling process, 434
approach, 436–437
close, 439
follow-up, 439–440
objectives of stages in, 435
preapproach, 435–436
presentation stage
  formula selling format, 437
  handling objections, 438–439
  need-satisfaction format, 437–438
  stimulus-response format, 437
prospecting, 434–435
at Xerox, 449
Personal sources of information, 88
Pharmaceutical companies, direct-to-
  consumer drug advertising, 360–361
Physical distribution, 477
  occupations, 476
Physical distribution specialist, 476
Physical environment of services, 264
Physical surroundings, 93, 94
Physiological needs, 95
Pinterest, 412
  description, 416–417
Pioneering institutional advertisements, 377
Pioneering product advertisements, 376
Place, 9
Place-based media, 386
Place strategy
  Chobani Greek Yogurt, 19
  definition, 12
  Medtronic, 38
  Paradise Kitchens, 59
Place utility, 301
  created in marketspace, 454–455
  definition, 16
  offered by retailing, 326–327
Point-of-purchase displays, 391
Points of difference, 37
  insignificant, 222
  Paradise Kitchens, 57
Political stability, 148

Popular Mechanics, 101
Population
  China and India, 157
  world, 64–67
Population explosion, 64–65
Pop-up blocker, 170
Portfolio tests, 387
Positioning statement, Volvo, 205
Possession utility, 301
  created in marketspace, 454–455
  definition, 16
  offered by retailing, 326–327
Postpurchase behavior
  by consumers
    cognitive dissonance, 91
    repeat purchases, 90
    satisfaction or dissatisfaction, 90
    selective exposure, 96
  in organizational buying, 124
Postpurchase evaluation, organizational
    buying, 124
Postsale services, buyer requirement, 309
Posttests, 364–365, **388**
  aided recall, 388
  attitude tests, 388
  inquiry tests, 388
  jury tests, 387
  portfolio tests, 387
  sales tests, 388
  theater tests, 387
  unaided recall, 388
Power centers, 337
Preapproach
  information about prospect, 435–436
  objectives, 435
Predatory pricing, 289
Premium, 274, 389–390
Pre-sale services, buyer requirement, 309
Presentation
  canned sales presentation, 437
  formula selling format, 437
  need-satisfaction format
    adaptive selling, 437
    consultative selling, 438
  objectives, 435
  stimulus-response format, 437
  suggestive selling, 437
Prestige pricing, 277
  by Energizer, 278
Preteens, in family decision making, 105
Pretests, 364–365, **387**
  jury tests, 387
  portfolio tests, 387
  theater tests, 387
Price(s), 274
  alternative terms for, 274
  based on rebates, 336
  of benchmark items, 336
  of competitors as constraint, 288
  definition, 9
  effects of income changes, 68

final, 274–275, 290–292
indicator of value, 275–276
in marketing mix, 276
in services marketing, 263
and type of product, 215
unique role in business, 274
Price comparisons, 90
Price-comparison searches, 420
Price discrimination
  in car buying, 290
  legal *vs.* illegal, 298
Price elasticity of demand, 284
  elastic demand, 284
  inelastic demand, 284
Price equation, 274
  diagram, 275
Price fixing
  horizontal, 289
  and Sherman Act, 288
  vertical, 289
Price premium, 281
Price-value position of Vizio, Inc., 273
Pricing approaches/strategy
  Carmex, 295–296
  Chobani Greek Yogurt, 19
  competition-oriented, 280–281
  cost, volume, and profit relationships,
      285–286
  cost-oriented, 278–279
  definition, 12
  and demand estimation, 282–284
  demand-oriented, 276–278
  and dumping, 154
  dynamic pricing, 465
  in global market, 154
  Medtronic, 38
  off-peak, 263
  Paradise Kitchens, 58
  and parallel importing, 154
  penetration pricing, 244
  profit-oriented, 279–280
  in retailing, 335–336
  and revenue estimation, 284
  skimming strategy, 244
  by Vizio, Inc., 272–273
  worldwide marketing
      program, 154
Pricing constraints, 286
  costs of production and marketing, 288
  demand, 288
  legal and ethical considerations
    deceptive pricing, 289
    predatory pricing, 289
    price discrimination, 289
    price fixing, 288–289
  newness of product, 288
  prices of competitors, 288
Pricing objectives, 287
  market share, 287
  profit, 287
  sales, 287

social responsibility, 288
survival, 287–288
unit volume, 287
Primary data, 165
  advantages and disadvantages, 175
  from experiments, 175
  observational data, 167–169
  from panels, 175
  questionnaire data
    idea evaluation, 170–171
    idea generation, 168–170
  from social media, 172–175
Primary demand, in introduction stage, 244
Privacy
  and data mining, 177
  and direct marketing, 357
  in direct marketing, 367, 368
  in mobile marketing, 421
  in online shopping, 466
  traditional *vs.* social media, 406
Private branding, 259
Private exchanges, 127
Private labeling, 259
Problem definition, in marketing
    research, 163
Problem recognition
  by consumers, 88
  in organizational buying, 124
Problem solving, 92
Process, in services marketing, 264–265
Producer protection
  Digital Millennium Copyright Act, 72
  Lanham Act, 73
Product(s), 9, **15**, **213**
  brand development index, 251, 252
  business products, 215, 216
  categories in online retailing, 461–462
  category development index, 251, 252
  competitive, 228
  consumer products, 215–216
  effects of income changes, 68
  evaluative criteria, 89–90
  feature bloat, 220
  free trials, 97
  grouped into categories, 198–199
  increasing use of, 253
  meaning of, 214
  multiple, for multiple segments, 192
  multiple markets with one, 191–192
  newness compared to existing, 220
  new situations for, 253
  overcoming resistance to, 250–251
  protocol, 222
  reasons for failure, 222–224
  reasons for resistance to
    psychological barriers, 250
    risk barriers, 250
    usage barriers, 250
    value barriers, 250
  stock keeping units, 219
  tangibility, 217

Product adaptation, in global
  market, 152
Product advertisements, 376
  comparative, 376
  competitive, 376
  pioneering, 376
  reinforcement, 377
  reminder, 376–377
Product bundling, 251
Product classes, 219
Product deletion, 248
Product development manager, 476
Product differentiation, 190
  in auto industry, 192
  in growth stage, 246
  in maturity stage, 247
  synergies *vs.* cannibalization, 193
Product-distribution franchises, 329
Product drivers, 177
Product extension, in global market, 152
Product feature, segmentation by,
  195–196
Product forms, 219
Product goals, 37
Product invention, in global market, 152
Product item, 219
  benchmark items, 336
Product life cycle, 244; *see also* Retail
    life cycle
  and consumer behavior, 249–251
    resistance to new products, 250
    types of buyers, 250
  decline stage
    drop in sales, 247
    harvesting strategy, 248
    product deletion, 248
  diagram, 245
  fax machines, 245–248
  generalized, 248–249
  growth stage
    broadened distribution, 246
    differentiation, 246
    increased sales, 246
    repeat purchasers, 246
  introduction stage
    advertising and promotion, 244
    gaining distribution, 244
    penetration pricing, 244
    primary demand, 244
    selective demand, 244
    skimming strategy, 244
    trials, 244
  length of, 248
  lifestyle curve, 248–249
  management of
    market modification, 252–253
    product manager role, 251
    product modification, 252
    product repositioning, 253–254
  marketing objectives, 245
  maturity stage

further differentiation, 247
  profit decline, 247
  reminder advertising, 376–377
  slow sales, 247
paper products, 114
and promotional elements
  decline stage, 359
  growth stage, 358
  introduction stage, *358*
  maturity stage, 359
Product line, 219
  Paradise Kitchens, 58
  simplified at Ford, 192
  Trek Bicycle Company, 131
  Zappos.com, 189
Product line extension, 13
  and branding strategy, 258
  definition, 221
Product management
  functions, 477
  occupations, 476
Product managers, 39, 476
  role in product life cycle, 251
Product mix, 219
Product modification, 251
Product objectives, Paradise Kitchens,
  56–57
Product placement, 391
Product positioning, 38, 205
  differentiation, 205
  head-to-head, 205
  Paradise Kitchens, 57
  using perceptual maps, 205–206
Product repositioning, 205
  with perceptual maps, 206
  in product life cycle
    catch rising trends, 253
    changing value offered, 253–254
    reaching new markets, 253
    reacting to competitors, 253
Product-service sales organization, 441
Product strategy
  Chobani Greek Yogurt, 18–19
  definition, 12
  Medtronic, 38
  Paradise Kitchens, 58
  worldwide marketing program,
    151–153
Product synergies, 204
Product trial, 362
  in introduction stage, 244
  promotional websites for, 468
Professional organizations, 485–486
Professional salesperson, 476
Profit, 23
  criterion for forming segments, 194
  decline in maturity stage, 247
  effect of exchange rate
    fluctuations, 147
  objective of organizational
    buying, 120

organizational goal, 28
  potential of market-entry strategies, 149
  pricing objective, 287
Profitability
  break-even analysis, 285–286
  and channel choice, 309
Profit equation, 276
Profit maximization, 287
Profit-oriented pricing
  target profit pricing, 279–280
  target return-on-investment pricing, 280
  target return-on-sales pricing, 280
Profit responsibility, 77
Programme for the Endorsement of
    Forest Certification, 115
Project manager, 476
Promotion
  careers in, 477
  communication adaptation strategy, 152
  definition, 9
  design of, 363–364
  dual adaptation strategy, 153
  in job search, 475
  loss-leader pricing, 282
  in marketing mix, 351–352
  occupations, 476
  publicity, 264
  public service announcements, 264
  in services marketing, 263–264
  and type of product, 215
Promotional elements
  advertising, 354–355, 374–388
  costs, 355
  direct marketing, 357, 366–368
  personal selling, 355–356,
    430–440
  public relations, 356–357, 383
  sales promotion, 357
  sales promotions, 389–393
  strengths and weaknesses, 355
  uses of, 351–352
Promotion allowances
  in channels of distribution, 291
  everyday low pricing, 291–292
Promotional mix, 351–352
  and integrated marketing
      communications
    channel strategies, 360–361
    product life cycle stages, 358–359
    target audience, 358
Promotional tools, selecting, 362–363
Promotional websites, 468–469
  for product trials, 468
  purpose, 468
  as support for traditional marketing
      channels, 468
Promotion budget, 362
Promotion costs
  in introduction stage, 244
  with multibranding, 259
  in multiproduct branding, 258

Promotion program
  designing program, 363–364
  executing and assessing
    expenses, 365
    IMC audit, 365
    media agency, 365
    pretests and posttests, 364–365
  identifying target audience, 361
  scheduling, 364
  selecting right tools, 362–363
  setting budget, 362
  specifying objectives, 362
  using marketing dashboard, 363
Promotion strategy
  Chobani Greek Yogurt, 19–20
  definition, 12
  Medtronic, 38
  Paradise Kitchens, 58–59
  Prince Sports, Inc., 209–210
  worldwide marketing program,
    151–153
Prospect, 434
  information about, 435–436
Prospecting
  cold canvassing, 435
  leads, 434
  objectives, 435
  qualified prospect, 434
Protectionism, 136
  costs to consumers, 136, 137
  versus free trade, 137
  with tariffs and quotas, 136–137
Protocol
  defining, 226
  definition, 222
  incomplete, 222–223
Prototype, 229
Psychographic analysis, 99–100
Psychographic segmentation, consumer
  markets, 195
Psychological barriers, 250
Psychological influences on consumers
  learning, 98
  lifestyle analysis, 99–101
  motivation, 94–95
  perceived risk, 97–98
  perception, 96–97
  personality, 95
  values, beliefs, and attitudes, 98–99
Publicity, 264, 356
  blogs, 357
  credibility advantage, 356
  lack of user's control, 356
Publicity tools, 393
  news conference, 393
  news release, 393
  public service announcements, 393
Public relations, 356
  costs, 355
  and mass selling, 354
  as promotional tool, 364

publicity, 356–357
publicity tools, 393
strengths and weaknesses, 355
tools of, 356
Public relations manager, 476
Public service announcements, 264, 393
Public sources of information, 88
Pull strategy, 360
Pulse (burst) schedule, 386
Purchase decision
  by consumers
    when to buy, 90
    from whom to buy, 90
  online consumers, 461–462
  organizational buying, 124
Purchase decision process, 88
  aided by Groupon, 110–112
  for consumers
    alternative evaluation, 89–90
    information search, 88
    level of involvement, 91–93
    postpurchase behavior, 90–91
    problem recognition, 88
    purchase decision, 90
    situational influences, 93
    women car buyers, 86–87
  organizational buying
    alternative evaluation, 124
    information search, 124
    postpurchase behavior, 124
    problem recognition, 124
    purchase decision, 124
Purchase size in organizational
  buying, 119
Purchase task, 93, 94
Purchasing, training for, 114
Purchasing power of global consumers,
  146–147
Pure competition, 70
Pure monopoly, 71
Push strategy, 360

Qualified prospect, 434
Quality
  organizational goal, 28
  Paradise Kitchens, 58
  poor, 223
  and price, 275
  of services, 218–219
  Trek Bicycle Company, 131
Quantitative assessments, 444
Quantity discounts, 291
Question marks, 33
Questionnaire data, 169
  depth interviews, 169
  focus groups, 169–170
  fuzzy front end methods, 170
  idea evaluation, 170–171

idea generation, 169–170
individual interviews, 169
mail surveys, 170
mall-intercept interviews, 171
online surveys, 170–171
personal interview
  surveys, 170–171
telephone interviews, 170
types of questions, 171
Quick response (QR) codes, 351, 420
Quick serve restaurants, 471
Quotas, 136, 137
  in Italy on motorcycles, 137
  in U.S. on sugar, 137
Quoted price; *see* List or quoted price

R

Racial and ethnic diversity
  multicultural marketing, 66
  in United States, 65–66
Racial subcultures, 106–107
Rack jobbers, 342
Radio advertising
  advantages, 382
  disadvantages, 382, 383
  number of stations, 383
  segmented medium, 383
Radio frequency identification
  tags, 177, 329
Reach
  of advertising, 380–381
  traditional *vs.* social
    media, 405
Real Yellow Pages, 384
Rebates, 336, 391
Receivers, 352
  decoding by, 353
Recessions, 67
Reciprocity, 121
Recycling of e-waste, 318
Red Carpet Style show, 333
Red tape, 146
Reference groups, 103
  aspiration, 103
  associative, 103
  dissociative, 103
Region, segmentation by, 195
Regional rollouts, 232
Regional shopping centers, 336
Regular distribution, 221
Regulation, 71
Regulatory forces
  and Facebook, 62
  protecting competition, 71–72
  protecting producers and
    consumers, 72–73
  self-regulation, 73
Reinforcement, 98
Reinforcement advertisements, 377

Relationship marketing, 11
customer value, 10
difficult to achieve, 11
examples, 10
Relationship selling, 431
Relative market share, 33
Reminder institutional
    advertisements, 377
Reminder product
    advertisements, 376–377
Rent, 274
Repeat purchase behavior, 90
Repeat purchasers, 247
Replenishment time, 316–317
Research and development laboratories,
    227–228
Reseller branding, 259
Reseller markets
    in NAICS, 117–118
    organizational buyers, 116
Resources, obtaining, 39
Response supply chain, 314–315
Responsibilities, defining, 39–40
Restaurant Business magazine, 358
Restaurant industry, 339–340
Résumé
    construction, 482
    cover letter, 482
    preparation, 481–482
Retail communication
    atmosphere and ambiance, 337
    elements of, 337
    outlet image, 337
    shopper marketing, 337
Retailers
    for Callaway Golf, 298
    consumer-oriented sales promotions,
        389–391
    cooperative advertising, 392
    as intermediaries, 300
    number of, 116
    preference for exclusive
        distribution, 309
    supplier partnerships, 122
    trade discounts for, 291
    trade promotions directed at, 391–392
    transactional websites, 468
Retailer-sponsored cooperatives,
    307, 329
Retailing, 326
    aided by Google Glasses, 324–325
    career paths, 477–478
    changing nature of
        retail life cycle, 340–341
        wheel of retailing, 339–340
    consumer utilities offered by, 326–327
    by Dell Inc. in India, 134–135
    global impact, 327
    nonstore
        automatic vending, 331–332
        catalogs, 332

direct-mail, 332
direct selling, 334–335
online retailing, 333–334
telemarketing, 334
TV home shopping, 333
occupations, 476
Retailing mix, 335
    communication, 337
    merchandise offering, 338–339
    pricing, 335–336
    store location, 336–337
Retailing strategy
    communication, 337
    merchandise offerings, 337–338
    pricing, 335–336
    store location, 336–337
Retail life cycle, 340; *see also* Product
        life cycle
    accelerated development stage, 340–341
    decline stage, 341
    early growth stage, 340–341
    maturity stage, 340–341
Retail outlets
    category killers, 331
    forms of ownership
        contractual systems, 329
        corporate chains, 328–329
        independent, 328
    image of, 337
    level of service
        full service, 330
        limited service, 330
        self-service, 329–330
    at Mall of America, 345–346
    merchandise line, 330–331
    number of, in U.S., 328
    retailing mix in, 335–339
    store location
        central business district, 336
        and multichannel retailers, 337
        power centers, 337
        regional shopping centers, 336
        strip malls, 337
Retail Planning Associates, Columbus,
        Ohio, 336
Retail pricing; *see* Pricing approaches/
        strategy
    everyday fair pricing, 336
    everyday low pricing, 336
    maintained markup, 335
    markdown, 335–336
    markup, 335
    off-retail pricing, 336
Retail salesperson, 476
Return on assets, 287
Return on investment, 194, 280, 287
Revenue estimation, 284
Revenues
    from cross-channel shoppers, 467
    Paradise Kitchens, 49–60
    performance measures linked to, 416

Reverse auction, 128
Reverse logistics, 317
    company examples, 317–318
    and green marketing, 318
Rich media, 384
Rich site summary, 330, 351, 365
Risk, perceived, 97–98
Risk barriers, 250
Robinson-Patman Act, 72
    on price discrimination, 298
Routine problem solving, 92
RSS. *see* Rich site summary
Rube Goldberg machine, 412
Russia, Hermitage Museum, 15

S

Safe delivery, 317
Safety, in packaging, 262
Safety needs, 95
Salary, 274
Sales
    activities, 478
    based on word of mouth, 102
    Callaway Golf, 298
    careers in, 4
    from cross-channel shoppers, 467
    by Dell Inc., 134
    drop in decline stage, 247
    effect of exchange rate
        fluctuations, 147
    increase in growth stage, 246
    in introduction stage, 244
    low in maturity stage, 247
    occupations, 476
    in online retailing, 333
    organizational goal, 28
    pricing objective, 287
    produced by social media, 414–415
    Tiffany/Walmart strategy, 193
    types of organizations, 478
Sales & Marketing Management, 481
Sales call, preparing for, 435–436
Sales clerks, 43
Salesforce
    compensation at Xerox, 450
    Mary Kay Cosmetics in India, 158
    motivation and compensation,
        443–444
    organizing
        customer sales organization, 441
        geographical organization, 441
        major account management, 441
        product-service organization, 441
    recruitment and selection
        emotional intelligence, 443
        job analysis, 442
        job description, 442
        job qualifications, 442–443
    training by manufacturers, 392–393

Salesforce automation, 446
   communication, 446–447
   technology, 446
Salesforce communication, 446–447
Salesforce evaluation
   behavioral evaluation, 444–445
   quantitative assessments, 444
Salesforce survey forecast, 182
Salesforce technology, 446
Salesforce training, 443
   at Xerox, 450
Sales forecast, 180
   direct forecast, 180–181
   by linear trend extrapolation, 181
   lost-horse forecast, 181
   salesforce survey, 182
   survey of buyers' intentions, 182
Sales forecasting techniques
   judgment of decision makers, 180–181
   statistical methods, 181
   surveys of knowledgeable groups,
      181–182
      buyers' intentions, 182
      salesforce survey, 182
   trend extrapolation, 181
Sales management, 430
   customer relationship management,
      446–447
   salesforce automation, 444–447
   salesforce communication, 446–447
   salesforce evaluation, 444–445
   salesforce technology, 446
   sales plan formulation, 440–442
   sales plan implementation, 442–444
   at Xerox, 449–450
Salespeople
   creating customer solutions and
      value, 431
   genetic markers, 431
   relationship selling, 431
   role in marketing, 431
Sales plan, 440
   formulation
      account management policies,
         441–442
      organizing salesforce, 441
      setting objectives, 40
   implementation
      motivation and compensation,
         443–444
      recruitment and selection, 442–443
      training, 443
Sales promotion, 357
   advantages, 357
   advertising support, 357
   consumer-oriented, 389–391
   costs, 355
   expenditures
      on loyalty programs, 391
      on point-of-purchase
         displays, 391

   on product placement, 391
   and mass selling, 354
   as promotional tool, 364
   and push strategy, 360
   strengths and weaknesses, 355
   tools of, 357
   trade-oriented, 391–392
Sales promotion manager, 476
Sales quota, 444
Sales-support duties, 478
Sales tests, 388
Samples, 390
Sampling, 164
Saudi Arabia, ban on Barbie dolls, 148
Savings rate, 68
Scanning data, 166
Scheduling promotions, 364
Scrambled merchandising, 331
Screening and evaluation of new products
   external approach, 229
   internal approach, 229
Seals of approval, 97
Seasonal discounts, 291
Secondary data, 165
   advantages and disadvantages, 166
   external
      Census Bureau, 166
      syndicated panel data, 166
   household demographics, 166
   internal
      marketing input data, 165
      marketing outcome data, 165
   online databases, 167
   online sources, 166
Secret Sales Pitch (Bullock), 96
Securities and Exchange Commission, 62
Security
   in online shopping, 466
   in packaging, 262
Selective comprehension, 96
Selective demand, in introduction
   stage, 244
Selective distribution, 308
Selective exposure, 96
Selective perception, 96–97
Selective retention, 97
Self-actualization needs, 95
Self-analysis, 479–480
Self-concept, 95
Self-disclosure, 404
Self-expression-motivated groups, 100
Self-image, 95, 100
Self-liquidating premium, 389–390
Self-regulation, 73
Self-service retailers, 329–330
Selling agents, 342
Selling duties, 478
Semantic differential scale, 171
Semiotics, 144
Semitechnical salesperson, 476
Sensitivity analysis, 177

Sensor control, in mobile marketing, 421
Service companies, 116
Service level in retailing
   full service, 330
   limited service, 330
   self-service, 329–330
Services, 214
   assessing and improving quality,
      218–219
   contribution to gross domestic
      product, 214
   cost-plus pricing, 279
   delivery method
      by business firms, 217
      by government agencies, 217
      by nonprofit organizations, 217
      by people or equipment, 216–217
   by Dell Inc., 134
   electronic distribution, 263
   gap analysis, 218
   inconsistency, 217
   inseparability, 217
   intangibility of, 217
   inventory, 217–218
   marketing mix, 263
   marketing of, 15
   protocol, 222
   reasons for failure, 222–224
   supplementary, 218
Services market, 116
Services marketing
   capacity management, 265
   customer experience
      management, 264
   and customer experience
      management, 229
   process, 264–265
Service-sponsored franchise
   systems, 308
Service-sponsored retail franchise
   systems, 307–308
**Seven Ps of services
   marketing, 262**
   people, 264
   physical environment, 264
   place, 263
   price, 263
   process, 264–265
   product/service, 263
   promotion, 263–264
Sex appeals, 379
Shelf life, 262
Sherman Antitrust Act, 71
   on price fixing, 288
Shift in the demand curve, 283
Shopper marketing, 337
Shopping bots, 333
Shopping products, 215
Showrooming, 465
Signpost items, 336
Single parents, 104

Situational influences on consumers
  antecedent states, 93, 94
  physical surroundings, 93, 94
  purchase task, 93, 94
  social surroundings, 93, 94
  temporal effects, 93, 94
Situation analysis, 36
  Paradise Kitchens
    company analysis, 55
    competitor analysis, 54–55
    customer analysis, 55–56
    industry analysis, 54
    SWOT analysis, 53–54
  SWOT analysis steps, 36
60 Minutes, 220
Skimming pricing, 244
  effectiveness factors, 277
  for new products, 276–277
Slotting fees, 232
Small businesses
  marketing careers, 4
  new product ideas from, 228
Smarter Planet initiative, IBM, 44, 45–46
Smartphones, 419
  for mobile marketing, 420–421
  ratings of, 89
Smart systems, 418
  and privacy, 421
Social authority of media, 406
Social entrepreneurship, 24
Social forces, 64
  culture, 66–67
  demographics, 64–66
  and Facebook, 62
Social media, 403
  blogs, 404
  classifying
    media richness, 404–405
    self-disclosure, 404–405
  compared to traditional media
    credibility and social authority, 406
    expense and access, 405
    number of people
      involved, 405
    permanence, 405
    reach, 405
    time to delivery, 405
    training, 405
  to connect with college students,
    402–403
  convergence of real and digital
    worlds, 418–421
  apps, 419–420
  buyer control, 420
  databases and algorithms, 419
  mobile marketing, 420–421
  and privacy, 421
  sensor control, 421
  smartphones, 419
  for integrated marketing
    communications, 350–351

lessons for brand managers, 418
marketing research by Carmex,
    184–186
in marketing strategy
    Carmex example, 417–418
    measure results, 415–417
    sales production, 414–415
    selecting social network, 413–414
origins, 404
to reach college students, 359
source of primary data, 172–175
and strategic marketing process, 413
use by X-1, 238
user-generated content, 404
Social media marketing manager, 476
Social media metrics, 173–174
Social needs, 95
Social networks, 403
  comparisons, 406, 407
  Facebook, 406–409
  Google, 412
  Instagram, 412
  for job search, 481
  launched by Facebook, 408–409
  LinkedIn, 410–411
  Pinterest, 412, 416–417
  reddit, 412
  selecting
    audience data, 413
    recent activity, 414
  smart systems, 418
  stuffDOT, Inc., 424–426
  StumbleUpon, 412
  Tumblr, 412
  Twitter, 409–410
  unique visitors, 414
  use by Seven Cycles, Inc., 453
  YouTube, 411–413
Social responsibility, 15, 76
  cause marketing, 77–78
  concepts of
    profit responsibility, 77
    societal responsibility, 77–78
    stakeholder responsibility, 77
  definition, 77
  green marketing, 77
  organizational goal, 28
  pricing objective, 288
Social shopping option, 334
Social surroundings, 93, 94
Societal culture, 73–74
Societal marketing concept, 15
Sociocultural influences on consumers
  culture and subcultures, 106–107
  family, 103–105
  opinion leaders, 101
  reference groups, 103
  word of mouth, 102–103
Source of communication, 352, 353
Spam, 463
Spam blocker, 170

Spark lines, 30
Special fees, 274
Specialty catalogs, 332
Specialty merchandise wholesalers, 341
Specialty products
  definition and basis of comparison, 215
  exclusive distribution, 308–309
Sporting News Baseball Yearbook, 192
Sports Illustrated Kids, 104
Sports marketing
  by Prince Sports, Inc., 208–210
  by X-1, 236–238
Spouse-dominant decision making, 105
Stakeholder responsibility, 77
Stakeholders, 26–27, 77
Standard Industrial Classification
    system, 117
Standard markup pricing, 278–279
Starch test, 388
Stars, 33, 41
State employment agencies, 481
State Hermitage Museum, Russia, 15
Statistical forecasting techniques, 181
Statistical inference, 164
Status conscious consumers, 277
Stimulus discrimination, 98
Stimulus generalization, 98
Stimulus-response presentation, 437
Stock keeping units, 219
  in supermarkets, 223
Store location. *see* Retail outlets
Store management, 477
Store manager, 476
Straight commission compensation
    plan, 444
Straight rebuy, 126
  definition, 125
  Trek Bicycle Company, 132
Straight salary compensation plan, 444
Strategic alliances, by Dell Inc. in India, 134
Strategic business units
  business portfolio analysis, 32–34
  cash cows, 33
  dogs, 33
  question marks, 33
  stars, 33
Strategic channel alliances, 306
Strategic direction/focus
  growth strategies
    business portfolio analysis, 32–34
    diversification analysis, 34–35
  Paradise Kitchens
    core competencies, 52
    goals, 52
    mission, 51
    sustainable competitive advantage, 52
  present status
    competencies, 31–32
    competitors, 32
    customers, 32
    questions for, 35

Strategic marketing process, 35
evaluation phase
acting on deviations, 41
comparing results to identify
deviations, 41
implementation phase
defining tasks, responsibilities, and
deadlines, 39–40
designing marketing organization, 39
obtaining resources, 39
program execution, 40
planning phase
goal-setting, 37–38
marketing program, 38
market-product focus, 37–38
SWOT analysis, 36–37
Strategic partnerships, Toyota, 82–83
Strategy, 25
to accomplish goals, 24
at Facebook, 62
at IBM, 45–46
Strengths; *see* SWOT analysis
examples, 37
of promotional elements, 355
Strip malls, 337
Strivers, 100
Subbranding, 258
Subcultures, 106
African Americans, 106–107
Asian Americans, 106–107
Hispanics, 106
Subliminal messages, 96
Subliminal perception, 97
Substitutes, effect on demand, 282–283
Sugar import quotas, 137
Suggestive selling, 437
Super Bowl, 381
and advertising budget, 378
Chobani Greek Yogurt commercial, 3
and word of mouth advertising, 102
Super Bowl Ad Meter, 390
Supermarkets
number of stock keeping units, 223
scanning data, 166
standard markup pricing, 278–279
target return-on-sales pricing, 280
Superpages, 384
Supplier development, 121
Suppliers
choice of, as marketing decision, 114
evaluation by Trek Bicycle
Company, 132
evaluation of capabilities, 114
to JCPMedia, Inc., 114
new product ideas from, 227
vendor-managed inventory, 317
Supplier/Supply partnerships
definition, 121–122
at Harley-Davidson, 122
retailers, 122
sustainable procurement, 123

Supplies, 216
Supply chain, 312
Callaway Golf, 298–299
company understanding of, 314
efficient, 315–316
integrated at IBM, 315
response, 314–315
Supply chain management
aligned with marketing strategy, 314
Amazon.com, 322
in auto industry, 313–314
cross-docking, 315
at Dell Inc., 314–315
information technology for, 315–316
logistics in, 312–313
to reduce order cycle time, 317
at Walmart, 315–316
Support products, 216
Surcharges, 274
Survey of buyers' intentions, 182
Survival, pricing objective, 287–288
Survivors, 100
Sustainable competitive advantage,
Paradise Kitchens, 52
Sustainable development, 78
Sustainable Forestry Institution, 115
Sustainable procurement, 123
Sweden, ban on advertising to children, 148
Sweepstakes, 390
SWOT analysis, 36
Paradise Kitchens, 51–54
steps, 36–37
Syndicated panel data, 166
Synergies
versus cannibalization, 193
marketing, 203–204
product, 204

T

Tangible products, 217
Target audience
for advertising, 378
identifying, 361
for marketing plan, 48
and media selection, 380
in promotional mix, 358
Target market, 8
for advertising, 354
choosing, 201
in job search, 475
marketing actions to reach, 201–204
Paradise Kitchens, 57
selection criteria
compatibility with objectives and
resources, 201
competitive position, 200–201
cost, 201
expected growth, 200
market size, 200

and strategic business units, 25
Target market coverage
attention to density, 308
exclusive distribution, 308–309
intensive distribution, 308
selective distribution, 309
Target pricing, 277
Target profit pricing, 279–280
Target return-on-investment pricing,
280, 287
Tariffs, 136
in European Union, 136
in Japan, 136
Tasks, defining, 39–40
Team selling, 441
Teaser advertising campaign, 102
Technological advances/changes
and big data, 165
impact on product life
cycle, 248
projected trends, 69
in television, 374–375
in vending machines, 332
Technological forces
and Facebook, 62
impact on consumer value, 70
technology of tomorrow, 69
Technological substitution, 248
Technology, 69
salesforce, 446
Teenagers
in family decision making, 105
global, 141
Telemarketing, 334
inbound, 433
National Do Not Call Registry, 367,
368, 435
outbound, 433
Telephone Consumer Protection Act of
1991, 73, 435
Telephone interviews, 170
Television
consumer programs, 88
number of cable channels, 383
online, 374–375
product placement in, 391
zero TV households, 374
Television advertising
actors' compensation, 379
advantages and disadvantages, 382
Chobani Greek Yogurt, 3
cost disadvantage, 382
dominance of, 374
infomercials, 383
number of households, 382
potential for ad-skipping, 374
reach of, 381
Super Bowl, 378
and technology changes, 374
and viewing habits, 168
wasted coverage, 383

Television home shopping, 333
Television ratings, 167–168
Temporal effects, 93, 94
Test markets, 175
  controlled, 231
  simulated, 231
  standard, 231
Theater tests, 387
Thinkers, 100
Threats; *see* SWOT analysis
  examples, 37
3D technologies, 69
Tiffany/Walmart strategy, 193
Time, 354, 384, 407
Time to delivery, 405
Time to market, 232–233
Time utility, 301
  created in marketspace, 454–455
  definition, 16
  offered by retailing, 326–327
Timing of online shopping, 466
TiVo, 168
Top management, ethical behavior,
  75–76
Total cost, 284, **285**
  break-even analysis, 285–286
Total logistics cost, 316
Total profit, 284
Total revenue, 284
  break-even analysis, 285–286
Tracking tools, 367
Trade barriers, 148
Trade discounts, 291
Trade-in allowances, 291
Trademark protection, 73
Trade organizations, 485–486
Trade-oriented sales promotions,
  391–392
  allowances and discounts, 392
  cooperative advertising, 392
  training distributors' salesforce,
    392–393
Trade promotions, 391
Trade regulations, 148
Trade salesperson, 476
Trading down, 254
Trading up, 253–254
Traditional auction, 128
Traditional family, 104
Traffic generation, 367
Training
  costs of, for salesforce, 443
  for media, 405
  for retailing, 478
  of salesforce, 392–393
  at Xerox, 450
Transactional function, 300–301
Transactional websites
  channel conflict threat, 467
  electronic storefronts, 467
  use by manufacturers, 467–468

Transit advertising, 385–386
Transnational firms, marketing
  strategy, 140
Travel Weekly, 238
Trend extrapolation, 181
Trial. *see* Product trial
Trial close, 439
Truck jobbers, 342
Tuition, 274
Twitter, 409
  in brand manager's strategy, 410
  number of unique visitors, 414
  overview, 409–410
  use by Carmex, 410

U

Ultimate customers, 16
Unaided recall, 388
Uncontrollable forces, 10
Unethical behavior
  bribes and kickbacks, 74–75
  economic espionage, 74
Unique visitors, 414
United Kingdom, Direct Marketing
  Association, 367
United States
  costs of economic espionage, 142
  and NAFTA, 138–139
  number of employees in sales, 430
  number of industrial firms, 116
  number of retailers, 116
  number of retail outlets, 328
  number of wholesalers, 116
  population projections, 65
  racial and ethnic diversity, 65–66
  recessions since 1970, 67
  sugar import quotas, 137
United States Army, 95, 377
United States Census Bureau, 24, 65, 67
  Economic Census, 166
  for secondary data, 166
  website, 167
United States government website, 167
United States National Parks, 83
United States, subcultures in, 106–107
Unit variable costs, 285
Unit volume, pricing objective, 287
Universal Product Code, 44
Universities, new product ideas
  from, 228
University of Florida, 242
Unsought products, 215
Urgency close, 439
Usage barriers, 250
Usage instructions, 98
Usage rate, 196
  80/20 rule, 196
  segmentation by, 196
  and segmentation of business
    markets, 198

USA Today, 381, 384, 390
User-generated content, 404
Users, in buying centers, 124
Utilitarianism, 76
Utility, 16
  created in marketspace, 454–455
  offered by retailing, 326–327
  provided by intermediaries, 301

V

VALS consumer survey
  achievement-motivated groups, 100
  high- and low-resource groups, 100
  ideals-motivated groups, 100
  information processing, 100
  purpose, 99
  self-expression-motivated groups, 100
Value, 275
  buying, 90
  price as indicator of, 275
  in product repositioning
    trading down, 254
    trading up, 253–254
  seeking, 88
Value barriers, 250
Value creation, 428
Values, 143
  and attitude change, 99
  cultural differences, 66
  of IBM, 44–45
Variable costs, 285
Variables, for forming market segments,
  196–197
Variety, buyer requirement, 309
V-commerce, 331–332
Vending machines
  green machines, 332
  and privacy, 421
  products and prices, 331
  technological advances, 332
Vendor-managed inventory, 317
Vertical channel conflict, 311
Vertical marketing systems, 306
  administered, 308
  contractual, 307–308
  corporate, 306–307
  diagram, 307
Vertical price fixing, 289
Video games, 419–420
  product placement in, 391
Viral marketing, 464
Virtual organizational markets, 126–127
Vocational interest tests, 480

W

Wages, 274
Wall Street Journal, 232, 238, 384
Wants *vs.* needs, 8

Warranties, 98
Wasted coverage, 355
  in TV advertising, 383
Watson supercomputer, 44
Weaknesses; *see* SWOT analysis
  examples, 37
  of promotional elements, 355
Web communities, 459, **463**
Websites
  blogs, 463
  cookies, 465
  and customer experience
    commerce, 459
    communication, 459
    community, 459
    connection, 458–459
    content, 458
    context, 458
    customization, 458
  eight-second rule, 462
  favorite, 466
  multiple purposes, 459
  Pizza Hut, 472–473
  promotional, 468–469
  spam, 463
  stickiness, 459–460
  transactional, 467–468

Web 2.0, 404
Wheel of retailing, 339
  discount stores, 340
  restaurant industry, 339–340
Wholesalers
  agents and brokers, 342
  food brokers, 342
  intermediaries, 300–301
  manufacturer's branches and offices,
    342–343
  merchant wholesalers, 341–342
  number of, 116
  trade discounts for, 291
  trade promotions directed at, 391–392
Wholesaler-sponsored voluntary chains,
    307, 329
Wiki, 404
Women
  car-buying criteria, 86–87
  price discrimination in car buying, 290
Women-owned firms, 120
Women's Running magazine, 238
Word of mouth, 102
  buzz, 102, 464
  magnified by Internet, 103
  source of negative information, 102–103
  teaser advertising campaign, 102

Working conditions overseas, 78
World population
  current and projected, 64–65
  middle-class status in, 147
World Trade Organization, 127
Worldwide marketing program; *see*
    Marketing program
World Wide Web, 404

Y

Yellow Pages
  advantages and disadvantages, 382
  expenditures on, 384
  proliferation disadvantage, 384
Yield management pricing, 278
Young marrieds, 104
Young singles, 104
YouTube, 411
  in brand manager's strategy, 412–413
  number of unique visitors, 414
  overview, 411

Z

Zero TV households, 374

LEARN WITHOUT LIMITS

Continually evolving, McGraw-Hill Connect® has been redesigned to provide the only true adaptive learning experience delivered within a simple and easy-to-navigate environment, placing students at the very center.

* **Performance Analytics** – Now available for both instructors and students, easy-to-decipher data illuminates course performance. Students always know how they're doing in class, while instructors can view student and section performance at-a-glance.

* **Mobile** – Available on tablets, students can now access assignments, quizzes, and results on-the-go, while instructors can assess student and section performance anytime, anywhere.

* **Personalized Learning** – Squeezing the most out of study time, the adaptive engine within Connect creates a highly personalized learning path for each student by identifying areas of weakness and providing learning resources to assist in the moment of need. This seamless integration of reading, practice, and assessment ensures that the focus is on the most important content for that individual.

connect.mheducation.com

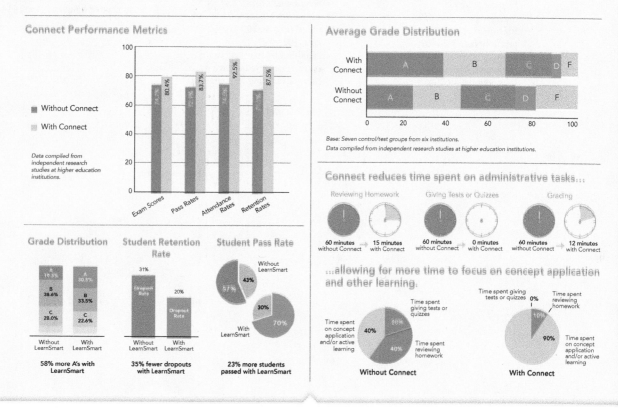

LEARNSMART ADVANTAGE

LearnSmart®

LearnSmart, the most widely used adaptive learning resource, is proven to improve grades. By focusing each student on the most important information they need to learn, LearnSmart personalizes the learning experience so they can study as efficiently as possible.

SmartBook®

SmartBook—an extension of LearnSmart—is an adaptive eBook that helps students focus their study time more effectively. As students read, SmartBook assesses comprehension and dynamically highlights where they need to study more.

CONNECT FEATURES

Interactive Applications

Interactive Applications offer a variety of automatically graded exercises that require students to **apply** key concepts. Whether the assignment includes a *click and drag*, *video case*, or *decision generator*, these applications provide instant feedback and progress tracking for students and detailed results for the instructor.

eBook

Connect includes a media-rich eBook that allows you to share your notes with your students. Your students can insert and review their own notes, highlight the text, search for specific information, and interact with media resources. Using an eBook with Connect Plus gives your students a complete digital solution that allows them to access their materials from any computer.

Connect Insight

The first and only analytics tool of its kind, Connect Insight is a series of visual data displays, each of which is framed by an intuitive question and provides at-a-glance information regarding how an instructor's class is performing. Connect Insight is available through Connect titles.

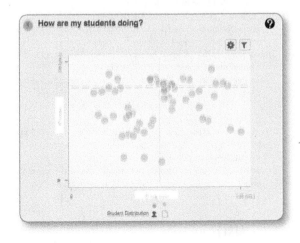

GLOSSARY

80/20 rule A concept that suggests 80 percent of a firm's sales are obtained from 20 percent of its customers. p. 196

account management policies Policies that specify who salespeople should contact, what kinds of selling and customer service activities should be engaged in, and how these activities should be carried out. p. 441

adaptive selling A need-satisfaction sales presentation style that involves adjusting the presentation to fit the selling situation, such as knowing when to offer solutions and when to ask for more information. p. 437

advertising Any paid form of nonpersonal communication about an organization, product, service, or idea by an identified sponsor. pp. 354, 376

apps Small, downloadable software programs that can run on smartphones and tablet devices. p. 419

attitude A learned predisposition to respond to an object or class of objects in a consistently favorable or unfavorable way. p. 99

baby boomers Includes the generation of 76 million children born between 1946 and 1964. p. 65

back translation The practice where a translated word or phrase is retranslated into the original language by a different interpreter to catch errors. p. 145

behavioral targeting Uses information provided by cookies for directing online advertising from marketers to those online shoppers whose behavioral profiles suggest they would be interested in such advertising. p. 465

beliefs A consumer's subjective perception of how a product or brand performs on different attributes based on personal experience, advertising, and discussions with other people. p. 99

blog A contraction of "web log," a web page that serves as a publicly accessible personal journal and online forum for an individual or organization. p. 404

bots Electronic shopping agents or robots that comb websites to compare prices and product or service features. p. 462

brand community A specialized group of consumers with a structured set of relationships involving a particular brand, fellow customers of that brand, and the product in use. p. 103

brand equity The added value a brand name gives to a product beyond the functional benefits provided. p. 255

brand loyalty A favorable attitude toward and consistent purchase of a single brand over time. p. 98

brand name Any word, device (design, sound, shape, or color), or combination of these used to distinguish a seller's products or services. p. 255

brand personality A set of human characteristics associated with a brand name. p. 255

branding A marketing decision in which an organization uses a name, phrase, design, symbols, or combination of these to identify its products and distinguish them from those of competitors. p. 255

break-even analysis A technique that analyzes the relationship between total revenue and total cost to determine profitability at various levels of output. p. 285

brokers Independent firms or individuals whose principal function is to bring buyers and sellers together to make sales. p. 342

business The clear, broad, underlying industry or market sector of an organization's offering. p. 28

business marketing The marketing of products and services to companies, governments, or not-for-profit organizations for use in the creation of products and services that they can produce and market to others. p. 116

business portfolio analysis A technique that managers use to quantify performance measures and growth targets to analyze their firms' strategic business units (SBUs) as though they were a collection of separate investments. p. 32

business products Products organizations buy that assist in providing other products for resale. Also called *B2B products* or *industrial products*. p. 215

buy classes Consist of three types of organizational buying situations: straight rebuy, new buy, and modified rebuy. p. 125

buying center The group of people in an organization who participate in the buying process and share common goals, risks, and knowledge important to a purchase decision. p. 123

capacity management Integrating the service component of the marketing mix with efforts to influence consumer demand. p. 265

category management An approach to managing the assortment of merchandise in which a manager is assigned the responsibility for selecting all products that consumers in a market segment might view as substitutes for each other, with the objective of maximizing sales and profits in the category. p. 338

cause marketing Occurs when the charitable contributions of a firm are tied directly to the customer revenues produced through the promotion of one of its products. p. 77

channel conflict Arises when one channel member believes another channel member is engaged in behavior that prevents it from achieving its goals. p. 311

choiceboard An interactive, Internet-enabled system that allows individual customers to design their own products and services by answering a few questions and choosing from a menu of product or service attributes (or components), prices, and delivery options. p. 456

code of ethics A formal statement of ethical principles and rules of conduct. p. 75

collaborative filtering A process that automatically groups people with similar buying intentions, preferences, and behaviors and predicts future purchases. p. 456

communication The process of conveying a message to others that requires six elements: a source, a message, a channel of communication, a receiver, and the processes of encoding and decoding. p. 352

competition The alternative firms that could provide a product to satisfy a specific market's needs. p. 70

constraints In a decision, the restrictions placed on potential solutions to a problem. p. 164

consultative selling A need-satisfaction sales presentation style that focuses on problem identification, where the salesperson serves as an expert on problem recognition and resolution. p. 438

consumer behavior The actions a person takes in purchasing and using products and services, including the mental and social processes that come before and after these actions. p. 88

Consumer Bill of Rights **(1962)** A law that codified the ethics of exchange between buyers and sellers, including the rights to safety, to be informed, to choose, and to be heard. p. 74

consumer products Products purchased by the ultimate consumer. p. 215

consumerism A grassroots movement started in the 1960s to increase the influence, power, and rights of consumers in dealing with institutions. p. 72

consumer-oriented sales promotion Sales tools used to support a company's advertising and personal selling directed to ultimate consumers. Also called *consumer promotions*. p. 389

cookies Computer files that a marketer can download onto the computer and mobile phone of an online shopper who visits the marketer's website. p. 465

cooperative advertising Advertising programs by which a manufacturer pays a percentage of the retailer's local advertising expense for advertising the manufacturer's products. p. 392

core values The fundamental, passionate, and enduring principles of an organization that guide its conduct over time. p. 26

cross-channel shopper An online consumer who researches products online and then purchases them at a retail store. p. 467

cross-cultural analysis The study of similarities and differences among consumers in two or more nations or societies. p. 143

cultural symbols Things that represent ideas and concepts. p. 144

culture The set of values, ideas, and attitudes that are learned and shared among the members of a group. p. 66

currency exchange rate The price of one country's currency expressed in terms of another country's currency. p. 147

customer experience management (CEM) The process of managing the entire customer experience within the company. p. 229

customer service The ability of logistics management to satisfy users in terms of time, dependability, communication, and convenience. p. 316

customer value The unique combination of benefits received by targeted buyers that includes quality, convenience, on-time delivery, and both before-sale and after-sale service at a specific price. p. 10

customer value proposition The cluster of benefits that an organization promises customers to satisfy their needs. p. 9

customs What is considered normal and expected about the way people do things in a specific country. p. 143

data The facts and figures related to the project that are divided into two main parts: secondary data and primary data. p. 165

demand curve A graph that relates the quantity sold and price, showing the maximum number of units that will be sold at a given price. p. 282

demographics Describing a population according to selected characteristics such as age, gender, ethnicity, income, and occupation. p. 64

derived demand The demand for industrial products and services that is driven by, or derived from, the demand for consumer products and services. p. 119

direct marketing A promotion alternative that uses direct communication with consumers to generate a response in the form of an order, a request for further information, or a visit to a retail outlet. p. 357

direct orders The result of direct marketing offers that contain all the information necessary for a prospective buyer to make a decision to purchase and complete the transaction. p. 366

disintermediation A source of channel conflict that occurs when a channel member bypasses another member and sells or buys products direct. p. 311

diversification analysis A technique that helps a firm search for growth opportunities from among current and new markets as well as current and new products. p. 34

dual distribution An arrangement whereby a firm reaches different buyers by employing two or more different types of channels for the same basic product. p. 305

dynamic pricing The practice of changing prices for products and services in real time in response to supply and demand conditions. p. 465

economic espionage The clandestine collection of trade secrets or proprietary information about competitors. p. 142

economy Pertains to the income, expenditures, and resources that affect the cost of running a business and household. p. 67

eight-second rule A view that customers will abandon their efforts to enter and navigate a website if download time exceeds eight seconds. p. 462

e-marketplaces Online trading communities that bring together buyers and supplier organizations to make possible the real time exchange of information, money, products, and services. Also called *B2B exchanges* or *e-hubs*. p. 126

environmental forces The uncontrollable forces that affect a marketing decision and consist of social, economic, technological, competitive, and regulatory forces. p. 10

environmental scanning The process of continually acquiring information on events occurring outside the organization to identify and interpret potential trends. p. 64

ethics The moral principles and values that govern the actions and decisions of an individual or group. p. 73

exchange The trade of things of value between buyer and seller so that each is better off after the trade. p. 5

exclusive distribution A level of distribution density whereby only one retailer in a specific geographical area carries the firm's products. p. 308

exporting A global market-entry strategy in which a company produces products in one country and sells them in another country. p. 148

Facebook A website where users may create a personal profile, add other users as friends, and exchange comments, photos, videos, and "likes" with them. p. 406

family life cycle The distinct phases that a family progresses through from formation to retirement, each phase bringing with it identifiable purchasing behaviors. p. 104

Foreign Corrupt Practices Act **(1977)** A law, amended by the *International Anti-Dumping and Fair Competition Act* (1998), that makes it a crime for U.S. corporations to bribe an official of a foreign government or political party to obtain or retain business in a foreign country. p. 143

four I's of services The four unique elements that distinguish services from goods: intangibility, inconsistency, inseparability, and inventory. p. 217

Generation X Includes the 50 million people born between 1965 and 1976. Also called the *baby bust.* p. 65

Generation Y Includes the 72 million Americans born between 1977 and 1994. Also called the *echo-boom* or the *baby boomlet.* p. 65

global brand A brand marketed under the same name in multiple countries with similar and centrally coordinated marketing programs. p. 140

global competition Exists when firms originate, produce, and market their products and services worldwide. p. 139

global consumers Consumer groups living in many countries or regions of the world who have similar needs or seek similar features and benefits from products or services. p. 140

global marketing strategy A strategy used by transnational firms that employ the practice of standardizing marketing activities when there are cultural similarities and adapting them when cultures differ. p. 140

goals Statements of an accomplishment of a task to be achieved, often by a specific time. Also called *objectives.* p. 28

green marketing Marketing efforts to produce, promote, and reclaim environmentally sensitive products. p. 77

hierarchy of effects The sequence of stages a prospective buyer goes through from initial awareness of a product to eventual action that includes awareness, interest, evaluation, trial, and adoption of the product. p. 362

idle production capacity Occurs when the service provider is available but there is no demand for the service. p. 217

infomercials Program-length (30-minute) advertisements that take an educational approach to communication with potential customers. p. 383

information technology Involves operating computer networks that can store and process data. p. 176

institutional advertisements Advertisements designed to build goodwill or an image for an organization rather than promote a specific product or service. p. 377

integrated marketing communications (IMC) The concept of designing marketing communications programs that coordinate all promotional activities—advertising, personal selling, sales promotion, public relations, and direct marketing—to provide a consistent message across all audiences. p. 352

intensive distribution A level of distribution density whereby a firm tries to place its products and services in as many outlets as possible. p. 308

interactive marketing Two-way buyer–seller electronic communication in a computer-mediated environment in which the buyer controls the kind and amount of information received from the seller. p. 456

involvement The personal, social, and economic significance of the purchase to the consumer. p. 91

joint venture A global market-entry strategy in which a foreign company and a local firm invest together to create a local business in order to share ownership, control, and profits of the new company. p. 150

lead generation The result of a direct marketing offer designed to generate interest in a product or service and a request for additional information. p. 367

learning Those behaviors that result from (1) repeated experience and (2) reasoning. p. 98

LinkedIn A business-oriented website that lets users post their professional profiles to connect to a network of businesspeople, who are also called *connections.* p. 410

logistics Those activities that focus on getting the right amount of the right products to the right place at the right time at the lowest possible cost. p. 312

major account management The practice of using team selling to focus on important customers so as to build mutually beneficial, long-term, cooperative relationships; also called *key account management.* p. 441

manufacturer's agents Agents who work for several producers and carry noncompetitive, complementary merchandise in an exclusive territory. Also called *manufacturer's representatives.* p. 342

market People with both the desire and the ability to buy a specific offering. p. 8

market orientation Focusing organizational efforts on (1) continuously collecting information about customers' needs, (2) sharing this information across departments, and (3) using it to create customer value. p. 14

market segmentation Involves aggregating prospective buyers into groups, or segments, that (1) have common needs and (2) will respond similarly to a marketing action. pp. 37, 190

market segments The relatively homogeneous groups of prospective buyers that (1) have common needs and (2) will respond similarly to a marketing action. p. 11

market share The ratio of sales revenue of the firm to the total sales revenue of all firms in the industry, including the firm itself. p. 28

marketing The activity for creating, communicating, delivering, and exchanging offerings that benefit customers, the organization, its stakeholders, and society at large. p. 4

marketing channel Consists of individuals and firms involved in the process of making a product or service available for use or consumption by consumers or industrial users. p. 300

marketing concept The idea that an organization should (1) strive to satisfy the needs of consumers while also (2) trying to achieve the organization's goals. p. 13

marketing dashboard The visual computer display of the essential information related to achieving a marketing objective. p. 29

marketing metric A measure of the quantitative value or trend of a marketing action or result. p. 29

marketing mix The marketing manager's controllable factors—product, price, promotion, and place—that can be used to solve a marketing problem. p. 9

marketing plan A road map for the marketing actions of an organization for a specified future time period, such as one year or five years. p. 29

marketing program A plan that integrates the marketing mix to provide a good, service, or idea to prospective buyers. p. 11

marketing research The process of defining a marketing problem and opportunity, systematically collecting and analyzing information, and recommending actions. p. 162

marketing strategy The means by which a marketing goal is to be achieved, usually characterized by a specified target market and a marketing program to reach it. p. 40

marketing tactics The detailed day-to-day operational marketing actions for each element of the marketing mix that contribute to the overall success of marketing strategies. p. 40

market-product grid A framework to relate the market segments of potential buyers to products offered or potential marketing actions. p. 191

marketspace An information- and communication-based electronic exchange environment mostly occupied by sophisticated computer and telecommunication technologies and digitized offerings. p. 70

measures of success Criteria or standards used in evaluating proposed solutions to the problem. p. 163

merchant wholesalers Independently owned firms that take title to the merchandise they handle. p. 341

mission A statement of the organization's function in society that often identifies its customers, markets, products, and technologies. Often used interchangeably with *vision*. p. 27

moral idealism A personal moral philosophy that considers certain individual rights or duties as universal, regardless of the outcome. p. 76

motivation The energizing force that stimulates behavior to satisfy a need. p. 94

multibranding A branding strategy that involves giving each product a distinct name when each brand is intended for a different market segment. p. 259

multichannel marketing The blending of different communication and delivery channels that are mutually reinforcing in attracting, retaining, and building relationships with consumers who shop and buy in traditional intermediaries and online. p. 305

multichannel retailers Retailers that utilize and integrate a combination of traditional store formats and nonstore formats such as catalogs, television home shopping, and online retailing. p. 337

multicultural marketing Combinations of the marketing mix that reflect the unique attitudes, ancestry, communication preferences, and lifestyles of different races and ethnic groups. p. 66

multidomestic marketing strategy A strategy used by multinational firms that have as many different product variations, brand names, and advertising programs as countries in which they do business. p. 140

multiproduct branding A branding strategy in which a company uses one name for all its products in a product class. p. 258

new-product process The seven stages an organization goes through to identify opportunities and convert them into salable products or services. p. 255

North American Industry Classification System (NAICS) Provides common industry definitions for Canada, Mexico, and the United States, which makes it easier to measure economic activity in the three member countries of the *North American Free Trade Agreement* (NAFTA). p. 117

objectives Statements of an accomplishment of a task to be achieved, often by a specific time. Also called *goals*. p. 28

observational data Facts and figures obtained by watching, either mechanically or in person, how people actually behave. p. 167

off-peak pricing Charging different prices during different seasons of the year and different times of the day or during different days of the week to reflect variations in demand for the service. p. 263

opinion leaders Individuals who exert direct or indirect social influence over others. p. 101

order getter A salesperson who sells in a conventional sense and identifies prospective customers, provides customers with information, persuades customers to buy, closes sales, and follows up on customers' use of a product or service. p. 433

order taker A salesperson who processes routine orders or reorders for products that were already sold by the company. p. 432

organizational buyers Those manufacturers, wholesalers, retailers, and government agencies that buy products and services for their own use or for resale. pp. 16, 116

organizational buying behavior The decision-making process that organizations use to establish the need for products and services and identify, evaluate, and choose among alternative brands and suppliers. p. 123

organizational culture The set of values, ideas, attitudes, and norms of behavior that is learned and shared among the members of an organization. p. 27

perceived risk The anxiety felt because the consumer cannot anticipate the outcomes of a purchase but believes there may be negative consequences. p. 97

perception The process by which an individual selects, organizes, and interprets information to create a meaningful picture of the world. p. 96

perceptual map A means of displaying in two dimensions the location of products or brands in the minds of consumers to enable a manager to see how they perceive competing products or brands, as well as the firm's own product or brand. p. 206

permission marketing The solicitation of a consumer's consent (called "opt-in") to receive e-mail and advertising based on personal data supplied by the consumer. p. 457

personal selling The two-way flow of communication between a buyer and seller, often in a face-to-face encounter, designed to influence a person's or group's purchase decision. pp. 355, 430

personal selling process Sales activities occurring before, during, and after the sale itself, consisting of six stages: (1) prospecting, (2) preapproach, (3) approach, (4) presentation, (5) close, and (6) follow-up. p. 434

personality A person's consistent behaviors or responses to recurring situations. p. 95

personalization The consumer-initiated practice of generating content on a marketer's website that is custom tailored to an individual's specific needs and preferences. p. 456

points of difference Those characteristics of a product that make it superior to competitive substitutes. p. 37

posttests Tests conducted after an advertisement has been shown to the target audience to determine whether it accomplished its intended purpose. p. 388

pretests Tests conducted before an advertisement is placed in any medium to determine whether it communicates the intended message or to select among alternative versions of the advertisement. p. 387

price (P) The money or other considerations (including other products and services) exchanged for the ownership or use of a product or service. p. 274

price elasticity of demand The percentage change in quantity demanded relative to a percentage change in price. p. 284

pricing constraints Factors that limit the range of prices a firm may set. p. 288

pricing objectives Specifying the role of price in an organization's marketing and strategic plans. p. 287

primary data Facts and figures that are newly collected for the project. p. 165

product A good, service, or idea consisting of a bundle of tangible and intangible attributes that satisfies consumers' needs and is received in exchange for money or something else of value. pp. 15, 213

product advertisements Advertisements that focus on selling a product or service and which take three forms: (1) pioneering (or informational), (2) competitive (or persuasive), and (3) reminder. p. 376

product differentiation A marketing strategy that involves a firm using different marketing mix actions to help consumers perceive the product as being different and better than competing products. p. 190

product item A specific product that has a unique brand, size, or price. p. 219

product life cycle Describes the stages a new product goes through in the marketplace: introduction, growth, maturity, and decline. p. 244

product line A group of product or service items that are closely related because they satisfy a class of needs, are used together, are sold to the same customer group, are distributed through the same outlets, or fall within a given price range. p. 219

product mix Consists of all of the product lines offered by an organization. p. 219

product placement A consumer sales promotion tool that uses a brand-name product in a movie, television show, video game, or a commercial for another product. p. 391

product positioning The place a product occupies in consumers' minds based on important attributes relative to competitive products. p. 205

product repositioning Changing the place a product occupies in a consumer's mind relative to competitive products. p. 205

profit The money left after a for-profit organization subtracts its total expenses from its total revenues and is the reward for the risk it undertakes in marketing its offerings. p. 23

profit equation Profit = Total revenue − Total cost; or Profit = (Unit price × Quantity sold) − (Fixed cost + Variable cost). p. 276

promotional mix The combination of one or more communication tools used to: (1) inform prospective buyers about the benefits of the product, (2) persuade them to try it, and (3) remind them later about the benefits they enjoyed by using the product. p. 351

protectionism The practice of shielding one or more industries within a country's economy from foreign competition through the use of tariffs or quotas. p. 136

public relations A form of communication management that seeks to influence the feelings, opinions, or beliefs held by customers, prospective customers, stockholders, suppliers, employees, and other publics about a company and its products or services. p. 356

publicity A nonpersonal, indirectly paid presentation of an organization, product, or service. p. 356

publicity tools Methods of obtaining nonpersonal presentation of an organization, product, or service without direct cost, such as news releases, news conferences, and public service announcements (PSAs). p. 393

pull strategy Directing the promotional mix at ultimate consumers to encourage them to ask the retailer for a product. p. 360

purchase decision process The five stages a buyer passes through in making choices about which products and services to buy: (1) problem recognition, (2) information search, (3) alternative evaluation, (4) purchase decision, and (5) postpurchase behavior. p. 88

push strategy Directing the promotional mix to channel members to gain their cooperation in ordering and stocking the product. p. 360

questionnaire data Facts and figures obtained by asking people about their attitudes, awareness, intentions, and behaviors. p. 169

quota A restriction placed on the amount of a product allowed to enter or leave a country. p. 137

reference groups People to whom an individual looks as a basis for self-appraisal or as a source of personal standards. p. 103

regulation Restrictions state and federal laws place on a business with regard to the conduct of its activities. p. 71

relationship marketing Links the organization to its individual customers, employees, suppliers, and other partners for their mutual long-term benefit. p. 11

relationship selling The practice of building ties to customers based on a salesperson's attention and commitment to customer needs over time. p. 431

retail life cycle The process of growth and decline that retail outlets, like products, experience, consisting of the early growth, accelerated development, maturity, and decline stages. p. 340

retailing All activities involved in selling, renting, and providing products and services to ultimate consumers for personal, family, or household use. p. 326

retailing mix The activities related to managing the store and the merchandise in the store, which includes retail pricing, store location, retail communication, and merchandise. p. 335

reverse auction In an e-marketplace, an online auction in which a buyer communicates a need for a product or service and would-be suppliers are invited to bid in competition with each other. p. 128

reverse logistics A process of reclaiming recyclable and reusable materials, returns, and reworks from the point of consumption or use for repair, remanufacturing, redistribution, or disposal. p. 317

sales forecast The total sales of a product that a firm expects to sell during a specified time period under specified environmental conditions and its own marketing efforts. p. 180

sales management Planning the selling program and implementing and evaluating the personal selling effort of the firm. p. 430

sales plan A statement describing what is to be achieved and where and how the selling effort of salespeople is to be deployed. p. 440

sales promotion A short-term inducement of value offered to arouse interest in buying a product or service. p. 357

sales quota Specific goals assigned to a salesperson, sales team, branch sales office, or sales district for a stated time period. p. 444

salesforce automation (SFA) The use of computer, information, communication, and Internet technologies to make the sales function more effective and efficient. p. 446

scrambled merchandising Offering several unrelated product lines in a single store. p. 331

secondary data Facts and figures that have already been recorded prior to the project at hand. p. 165

selective distribution A level of distribution density whereby a firm selects a few retailers in a specific geographical area to carry its products. p. 309

self-regulation An alternative to government control whereby an industry attempts to police itself. p. 73

services Intangible activities or benefits that an organization provides to satisfy consumers' needs in exchange for money or something else of value. p. 214

seven Ps of services marketing An expanded marketing mix concept for services that includes the four Ps (product, price, promotion, and place or distribution) as well as people, physical environment, and process. p. 262

shopper marketing The use of displays, coupons, product samples, and other brand communications to influence shopping behavior in a store. p. 337

showrooming Occurs when a shopper visits a retail store to inspect merchandise but then goes online to compare prices from other retail and online sellers to attempt to make the best purchase. p. 465

situation analysis Taking stock of where the firm or product has been recently, where it is now, and where it is headed in terms of the organization's marketing plans and the external forces and trends affecting it. p. 36

social forces The demographic characteristics of the population and its culture. p. 64

social media Online media where users submit comments, photos, and videos—often accompanied by a feedback process to identify "popular" topics. p. 403

social responsibility The idea that organizations are part of a larger society and are accountable to that society for their actions. p. 76

societal marketing concept The view that organizations should discover and satisfy the needs of consumers in a way that provides for society's well-being. p. 15

spam Communications that take the form of electronic junk mail or unsolicited e-mail. p. 463

strategic marketing process The approach whereby an organization allocates its marketing mix resources to reach its target markets. p. 35

strategy An organization's long-term course of action designed to deliver a unique customer experience while achieving its goals. p. 25

subcultures Subgroups within the larger, or national, culture with unique values, ideas, and attitudes. p. 106

supply chain The various firms involved in performing the activities required to create and deliver a product or service to consumers or industrial users. p. 312

SWOT analysis An acronym describing an organization's appraisal of its internal Strengths and Weaknesses and its external Opportunities and Threats. p. 36

target market One or more specific groups of potential consumers toward which an organization directs its marketing program. p. 9

tariffs Government taxes on products or services entering a country that primarily serve to raise prices on imports. p. 136

technology Inventions or innovations from applied science or engineering research. p. 69

telemarketing Using the telephone to interact with and sell directly to consumers. p. 334

total cost (TC) The total expense incurred by a firm in producing and marketing a product. Total cost is the sum of fixed cost and variable cost. p. 285

total logistics cost The expenses associated with transportation, materials handling and warehousing, inventory, stockouts (being out of inventory), order processing, and return products handling. p. 316

total revenue (TR) The total money received from the sales of a product. p. 284

trade-oriented sales promotions Sales tools used to support a company's advertising and personal selling directed to wholesalers, distributors, or retailers. Also called *trade promotions*. p. 391

traditional auction In an e-marketplace, an online auction in which a seller puts an item up for sale and would-be buyers are invited to bid in competition with each other. p. 128

traffic generation The outcome of a direct marketing offer designed to motivate people to visit a business. p. 367

Twitter A website that enables users to send and receive "tweets," messages up to 140 characters long. p. 409

ultimate consumers The people who use the products and services purchased for a household. Also called *consumers, buyers,* or *customers.* p. 16

usage rate The quantity consumed or patronage (store visits) during a specific period. Also called *frequency marketing.* p. 196

user-generated content (UGC) The various forms of online media content that are publicly available and created by end users. Also called *consumer-generated content.* p. 404

utilitarianism A personal moral philosophy that focuses on "the greatest good for the greatest number" by assessing the costs and benefits of the consequences of ethical behavior. p. 76

utility The benefits or customer value received by users of the product. p. 16

value The ratio of perceived benefits to price; or Value = (Perceived benefits ÷ Price). p. 275

values A society's personally or socially preferable modes of conduct or states of existence that tend to persist over time. p. 143

vendor-managed inventory (VMI) An inventory management system whereby the supplier determines the product amount and assortment a customer (such as a retailer) needs and automatically delivers the appropriate items. p. 317

vertical marketing systems Professionally managed and centrally coordinated marketing channels designed to achieve channel economies and maximum marketing impact. p. 306

viral marketing An Internet-enabled promotional strategy that encourages individuals to forward marketer-initiated messages to others via e-mail, social networking websites, and blogs. p. 464

web communities Websites that allow people to congregate online and exchange views on topics of common interest. p. 463

wheel of retailing A concept that describes how new forms of retail outlets enter the market. p. 339

word of mouth The influencing of people during conversations. p. 102

World Trade Organization (WTO) A permanent institution that sets rules governing trade between its members through panels of trade experts who decide on trade disputes between members and issue binding decisions. p. 137

YouTube A video-sharing website in which users can upload, view, and comment on videos. p. 411

NAME INDEX

A

Aaker, David A., 187, 399, 400
Abell, Derek F., 47
Abraham, Magid M., 400
Abrams, Rhonda, 49, 50
Acohido, Byron, 187
Adamy, Janet, 187
Adkins-Green, Sheryl, 156, 158
Agarwal, Manoj K., 270
Ailawadi, Kusum L., 372
Aizen, I., 113
Alba, Joseph W., 112
Alexander, Joe F., 486
Allen, Alissa, 186, 295, 296, 297
Amsdorf, Isaac, 239
Anderson, Eric, 133, 348
Anderson, Mae, 323, 427
Anderson, Nate, 347
Anscheutz, N., 239
Ansoff, H. Igor, 47
Ante, Spencer E., 427
Appleyard, Dennis R., 159
Arens, Christian, 400
Arens, William F., 400
Armstrong, J.Scott, 47
Arndt, Michael, 47
Ash, Mary Kay, 156
Atkinson, Nathalie, 347
Augusto, Byron G., 239
Avery, Simon, 451
Avery, Susan, 133
Axvig, Amanda, 425, 427

B

Baack, Daniel W., 400
Bachmann, Gwen, 113
Badenhausen, Kurt, 47
Baek, Tae Hyun, 373
Bagozzi, Richard P., 20, 412, 450
Bahrami, B., 113
Baig, Edward C., 239
Bailey, Brandon, 427
Bailey, Jeffrey J., 399
Baker, Julie, 348
Baker, Wayne E., 486
Bakken, Earl, 27
Balasubramanian, Sridhar, 348
Balter, David, 102
Banis, William J., 487
Bansal, Anjali, 486
Barczak, Gloria, 239
Barich, Howard, 348
Barnes, Brooks, 373
Barnes, Jimmy D., 372
Barnes, John, 348
Barr, Alistair, 240
Bartholomew, Doug, 323
Bartiromo, Maria, 401
Barton, Paul, 474
Bartz, Bianca, 372
Bass, Stephen J., 349

Bastillo, Miguel, 211
Bates, Albert D., 349
Bates, Douglas D., 187
Batra, Rajeev, 400
Bauerkin, Valerie, 474
Bay, Willow, 186
Beatty, Sharon E., 112
Becker, David, 211
Becker, Jill, 347
Bedapudi, Neeli, 271
Belk, Russell, 113
Bell, Glen, 370
Belson, Ken, 297
Ben-Akiva, Moshe, 112
Bendle, Neil T., 47, 348
Bennett, Drake, 426
Bennett, Greg, 236
Bennett, Laura, 236
Bensinger, Ben, 240
Bercovici, Jeff, 323
Berfield, Susan, 487
Berkowitz, Eric N., 211
Bernard, Lisa A., 348
Berry, Jon, 113
Berry, Leonard L., 239, 271, 348
Bertagnoli, Lisa, 486
Best, Roger, 112, 113
Bezos, Jeff, 321, 322, 464
Bharadwaj, Sundar G., 159, 450
Bianco, Anthony, 211
Bigne, Enrique, 372
Binkley, Christina, 297
Birkel, Frank, 486
Birkner, Christine, 84, 113
Bitner, Mary Jo, 239, 271, 348
Biyalogorsky, Eyal, 239
Björk, Ingvar, 401, 427
Black, Rebecca, 411
Blackler, Jeffrey, 427
Blackwell, Roger D., 112
Blanco, Brian, 427
Blasko, Vincent, 372
Block, Martin P., 372
Boccara, Brun, 112
Boenigk, Michael, 373
Bohlen, Betsy, 84
Bolles, Richard N., 485
Bonoma, Thomas V., 133
Booen, Brett, 323
Boring, Christopher, 336
Boulding, William, 239
Bowie, Norman E., 85
Boyd, Harper W., Jr., 211
Bozman, Carl S., 399
Bradley, Ryan, 187
Brady, Diane, 486
Brandau, Mark, 373
Brat, Ilan, 187, 347
Brennan, David P., 349
Breugelmans, Els, 348
Bridges, Virginia, 347
Brin, Sergey, 396–397
Brockman, Beverly K., 239
Brodie, John, 270
Brodie, Roderick J., 47

Brown, Seth, 187
Brown, Stephen W., 239, 349
Brown, Tim, 240
Brown, Tom J., 187, 240
Bruel, Alexandra, 373
Brunel, Frederic, 113
Brunt, Jonathan, 373
Buchanan, Bruce, 399
Buck, Claudia, 400
Buckleitner, Warren, 187
Bulik, Beth Snyder, 239, 270, 372, 474
Bullock, August, 96, 113
Buorrow, Peter, 401
Burdick, Richard K., 133
Burin, Norm, 348
Burke, Richard, 130
Burkett, Laura, 113
Bush, Michael, 372
Bush, Robert P., 187
Buss, Dale, 240
Butterworth, Siobhain, 373
Buzzell, Robert D., 400
Byron, Ellen, 84, 211

C

Caffoe, Jenny, 426, 427
Cahill, Maureen, 345, 346, 349
Cai, Jane Zhen, 348
Callahan, Kristin, 271
Cameron, James, 161
Cammarano, Roy F., 239
Campbell, Sarah, 451
Campo, Katia, 348
Caposacola, Alison, 449, 450
Cardona, Mercedes, 347
Carducci, Bernardo J., 113
Carey, Bridget, 347
Carlotti, Steve, 84
Carneiro, Bianca, 347
Carpenter, Gregory S., 21
Carral, Teré, 178, 179–180, 187
Carson, Niall, 373
Carter, Jim, 348
Cash, James J., 240
Cassidy, Tom, 114, 115
Castellion, G., 239
Castleberry, Stephen B., 450
Cateora, Philip K., 159, 450
Caulfeld, M., 187
Chadwick, Philip, 451
Chafkin, Max, 211
Chang, Chingching, 399
Chang, Julia, 451
Chang, Kenneth, 187
Chevalier, Michael, 401
Chiagouris, Larry, 85
Chiang, Alexander, 47
Chopra, Sunil, 323
Christiansen, Clayton M., 240
Chu, Wujin, 133
Chua, K. K., 156
Churchill, Gilbert A., Jr., 187, 240

Ciaccia, Chris, 347
Clancy, Rebecca, 400
Clark, Dave, 322
Clark, Moira, 347
Claus, J., 113
Cleaver, Joanne, 486
Clifford, Stephanie, 348, 474
Cline, Thomas W., 399
Clinton, Bill, 84
Cochrane, Kevin, 486
Coffey, Brendan, 113
Cohen, Ben, 22
Cohen, Dorothy, 85, 399
Cohen, William A., 50
Cohn, D'Vera, 113
Coleman, Barbara Carrick, 372
Collins, Jim, 46, 47
Colvin, Geoff, 47, 211, 239
Compeau, Larry D., 399
Conkey, Christopher, 450
Cook, James, 211
Cook, Tim, 32, 34, 212
Cooper, E., 372
Cooper, Martha, 323
Cooper, Robert G., 239
Corfman, Kim, 113
Corliss, Richard, 187
Corstjens, Marcel, 347
Cotte, June, 85
Cotteleer, Mark, 451
Coughlin, Natalie, 236
Cousins, Paul D., 240
Couttney, Martin, 373
Covello, Joseph A., 50
Coy, Peter, 486
Crane, Frederick G., 211
Cravens, David W., 450
Crawford, Merle, 239, 240
Creamer, Matthew, 401, 486
Croce, Maria, 347
Cron, William L., 450, 451
Crosby, Jackie, 347
Crosby, Lawrence A., 348
Cross, James, 400
Crowe, John, 349
Cruise,Tom, 391
Cuddleford-Jones, Morag, 486
Curhan, Ronald C., 401
Czinkota, Michael, 159

D

D'Innocenzio, Ann, 211
Dacko, Scott, 485
Dagnall, Ian, 349
Dahl, Sima, 486, 487
Dahlhoff, Denise, 270
Daley, Jason, 426
Daley, Shawn P., 133
Dalrymple, Jim, 348
Dalton, Catherine M., 46
Damast, Alison, 487
Damp, Dennis V., 485
Daniel, David S., 486

Dant, Rajiv P., 21
Darmon, René Y., 451
David, Kenneth, 85
Davidson, Paul, 487
Davidson, William R., 349
Davie, William, 347
Davis, John, 348
Dawes, Philip L., 133
Dawley, Jacqueline, 211
Day, George S., 46, 187
De Pelsmacker, Patrick, 401
Dean, Francis, 487
Dean, Joshua, 21
DeBevoise, Allen, 375
DeCarlo, Thomas E., 451
Deighton, John, 270
Dell, Michael, 134, 309
Delo, Cotton, 84, 373
Demos, Telis, 20, 427
DeNavas-Walt, Carmen, 84
Dens, Nathalia, 401
DePass, Dee, 21
Dettman, Ross, 349
Di Benedetto, Anthony, 239, 240
Diamond, Helene, 186
Diamond, Rick, 349
Dichter, Ernest, 400
Dickson, Peter R., 112
Diederich, Lexi, 426
Diepenbrock, Amy, 487
Diorio, Carl, 187
Diriker, Memo F., 486
Dirksing, Peter, 237
Djansezian, Kevork, 271
Dodds, William D., 296, 348
Dodes, Rachel, 186
Dolan, Kerry A., 240
Dolan, Robert J., 133, 297
Dolber, Roslyn, 486
Donaldson, Thomas, 85
Donlon, J. P., 211
Donovan, Robert J., 112
Donthu, Naveen, 133
Dorfman, Elena, 21
Dowling, Grahame R., 133
Doyle, Alison, 485
Drell, Lauren, 372
Drew, Christopher, 240
Dreze, Xavier, 348
Drysch, Michael, 417–418
Du, Rex Y., 113
Dubner, Stephen, 385
Duff, Hilary, 264
Duncan, Tom, 373
Durisin, Megan, 21
Dutta, Soumitra, 426
Dwoskin, Elizabeth, 187, 427
Dwyer, F. Robert, 133
Dwyer, Michael, 241
Dyer, Jeff, 240

E

Earl, Michael J., 240
Eastwood, Clint, 160
Edwards, Jim, 450
Efrati, Amir, 427
Eighmie, Bob, 271
Einwiller, Sabine A., 373
El-Ansary, Adel I., 323, 474

Elgan, Mike, 270
Elledge, Josh, 401
Elliott, Stuart, 372, 399
Ellison, Sarah, 240
Endig, Peter, 47
Eng, Dinah, 21, 211, 240
Engardio, Pete, 85
Engel, James F., 112
Eppinger, Stephen D., 240
Eppright, David R., 399
Erdem, Tulin, 270
Erenberg, Grigori, 401
Erickson, Peter, 240
Etgar, Michael, 399
Ethans, Arno J., 133
Evans, Dave, 426

F

Fahey, Liam, 21
Farber, Dan, 399
Farrell, Chris, 486
Farris, Paul W., 47,
    348, 399
Favre, Jerome, 47
Fay, Brad, 113
Felice, Steve, 134
Felson, Leonard, 486
Feng Zhu, 347
Fernandez, Karen V., 399
Ferrari, Cesare, 47
Fetscherin, Marc, 270
Few, Stephen, 47
Field, Alfred J., 159
Fine, Leslie M., 239
Firshein, Sarah, 401
Fishbein, Martin, 113
Fisher, Kelsey, 425, 426
Fisher, Robert J.,
    323, 474
Fisher, Stacy, 390
Fitzgerald, Kate, 474
Fixmar, Andy, 427
Fleming, Anne, 87
Fleming, Jess, 239
Flinn, Ryan, 187
Flood, Barbara, 486
Folkens, Dave, 372
Fong, Bay, 159
Forbes, Thom, 21, 239
Ford, David, 187
Fornier, Susan, 270
Forster, Julie, 239
Foster, Thomas A., 323
Fowler, Ranelle, 241
Franco, James, 364
Frank, John N., 486
Frank, Robert, 187
Frank, Zac, 239
Franklin, Frank, II, 401
Fraser, Matthew, 426
Fredrix, Emily, 399
Freeman, Sholnn, 113
Friedman, Milton, 77
Friend, Tad, 186
Fritz, Ben, 240
Frost, Raymond, 474
Fujimoto, Takahiro, 323
Fusaro, Dave, 20
Futrell, Charles M., 450

G

Galdwell, Malcolm, 240
Gans, Keri, 20
Gantt, Henry L., 40
Garlitos, Kirby, 296
Gasparo, Anne, 20
Gay, Verne, 399
Gebhardt, Gary F., 21
Gedenk, Karen, 372
Gerst, Jeff, 184, 185, 187
Ghermezian Brothers, 345
Gibson, Lawrence D., 187, 400
Gillette, Felix, 187, 427
Gilly, Mary C., 159, 450
Glassel, Linda, 208, 210, 211
Glazer, Emily, 240
Gliatto, Tom, 240
Goel, Vindu, 426
Gold, Laurence N., 400
Goldberg, Marvin E., 373, 399
Golden, Linda L., 348
Golden, Richard, 396, 398
Goldman, Doron, 399
Gonyea, James C., 486
Goodman, Kolby, 427
Goodpaster, Kenneth E., 47
Goodwin, Stephen A., 399
Gordon, Geoffrey L., 240
Gordon, Jeff, 415
Gotlieb, Jerry, 399
Graber, Donald R., 159
Graham, John L., 159, 450
Grant, Kelli B., 84
Green, Marianne E., 486, 487
Green, Mark C., 159
Greenberg, Robert M., 487
Greenfield, Jerry, 22
Greenleaf, Eric A., 112
Greenspan, Robyn, 133
Gremler, Dwayne D., 271
Grewal, Dhruv, 21, 296,
    348, 399
Greyersen, Hal B., 240
Griffin, Abie, 239
Griffith, Eric, 84
Grobart, Sam, 427
Gronstedt, Anders, 372
Grossman, Lev, 20, 84, 239, 426
Grossnickle, Joshua, 486
Grover, Ronald, 187
Gruley, Bryan, 20
Gschwandtner, Gerhard, 450
Gumbel, Peter, 21
Gupta, Sunil, 112
Gupte, Gouri, 451

H

Ha, Anthony, 400
Haenlein, Michael, 404, 426
Hagey, Keach, 240, 270
Hague, Nick, 485
Hague, Paul, 485
Hahn, Minhi, 400
Hair, Joseph F., Jr., 187
Hair, Neil, 347
Hall, Joseph M., 348
Hall, Julie, 239

Hall, Starr, 426
Hallen, Gary, 451
Halliday, Josh, 401
Hamilton, Laird, 236
Hamilton, Rebecca W., 239
Hamm, Steve, 240
Hammond, John S., 47
Hammond, Michele, 84
Hampp, Andrew, 399, 400
Handfield, Robert B., 240
Hansen, Tom, 400
Hardesty, David M., 451
Harmon, Eric P., 239
Harper, Jonathan, 486
Harris, Jerod, 271
Harrower, Nancy, 427
Hartley, Robert F., 85
Hartley, Steven W., 47, 85, 113,
    133, 211, 240, 297, 323,
    373, 400, 401, 451
Hartline, Jana, 81
Hartman, Cathy L., 84, 347
Hartzell, Dane, 184
Hastings, Reed, 230
Hathcote, Jan M., 399
Hauser, Erik, 474
Hawkins, Delbert I., 112, 113, 159
Hayes, Tom, 474
Hazelgren, Brian J., 50
Helft, Miguel, 84
Helm, Burt, 211
Helsen, Kristiaan, 159
Hempel, Jessi, 47, 84, 113, 323,
    427, 450
Henn, Brian, 21
Henning, Marc F., 211
Herbig, Paul A., 159
Herholdt, Frank, 451
Hermann, Andreas, 348
Herring, Jeff, 427
Herring, Tyler, 209, 211
Hershberger, Edmund, 486
Higgins, Michelle, 427
Higgins, Tim, 85
Himmelfarb, Paul, 402
Hirsh, Jerry, 112
Hlavinka, Kelly, 401
Hochman, Kevin, 267, 269, 270
Hochman, Sara, 66
Hodgdon, Kirk, 295, 296
Hodgdon, Patrick, 186, 187,
    418, 427
Hoeffler, Steve, 240
Hof, Robert D., 401
Hoffman, Karen Epper, 486
Hogan, John E., 271, 296
Hogg, Bevill, 130
Holloran, Tom, 46
Holmes, Elizabeth, 113, 347
Holmes, Stanley, 240
Honebein, Peter C., 239
Hooley, Graham J., 372
Hopewell, Nikki, 372
Horn, John, 186
Horovitz, Bruce, 270, 426
Howard, Daniel L., 296, 348
Howard, John A., 112
Howard, Theresa, 373
Hoyer, Wayne D., 112, 113
Hruby, M., 21
Hsieh, Tony, 188–189

Hsu, Tiffany, 84, 401
Humphreys, Jeffrey M., 113
Hunt, James B., 399
Hunt, Kenneth A., 348
Hurd, Bo, 111
Hutchinson, J. Wesley, 112
Hutt, Michael D., 133
Hyman, H., 372

I

Iezzi, Teressa, 399
Inderrieden, Edward, 451
Iqbal, Azhar, 84
Isaacson, Walter, 239, 240
Islam, Zak, 47
Ive, Jonathan, 227
Ives, Nat, 347

J

Jackson, Donald W., 133
Jacobson, Don, 211
Jacoby, Jacob, 296
Jahoda, M., 372
Jain, Ambuj, 296, 348
James, Dana, 487
James, Harvey S., 85
James, LeBron, 295, 410, 417–418
James, Meg, 187
Janis, Irwin L., 239
Jannarone, John, 240
Jap, Sandy D., 133
Jargon, Julie, 211
Jarrell, Phillip, 451
Jarvis, Jeff, 401
Jaworski, Bernard J., 323, 474
Jefferson, Elana Ashanti, 401
Jeffery, Mark, 47, 187
Jelinek, Ronald, 451
Jobs, Steve, 203, 212, 224, 226, 227
Jobst, Peter, 271
Johannes, Amy, 401
Johansson, Johnny K., 159
John, Deborah Roedder, 113
Johns, Chris, 84
Johnson, Gavin, 187
Johnson, Gerry, 46
Johnson, Lynne D., 372
Johnston, Mark W., 450, 451
Johnston, Wesley J., 133
Jolson, Marvin A., 401
Jones, Brent, 401
Jones, Gareth, 400
Jones, John Philip, 372
Joslyn, Mark, 130, 131, 132
Judson, Kimberly, 240

K

Ka-Man Cheung, 372
Kador, John, 46
Kageyama, Yuri, 159
Kahn, Kenneth B., 239
Kahney, Leander, 240
Kalker, Daniel, 323
Kallayil, Gopi, 397
Kamakura, Wagner A., 113

Kambil, Ajit, 133
Kamin, Bonnie, 323
Kaminsky, Philip, 323
Kanemans, J., 113
Kang, Cecilia, 240
Kang, Stephanie, 323, 474
Kanter, James, 84
Kapferer, Jean-Noel, 296
Kaplan, Andreas M., 404, 426, 427
Kaplan, David, 347
Kaputa, Catherine, 486
Kardashian, Khloe, 333
Kardashian, Kim, 333
Kardashian, Kourtney, 333
Karniouchina, Ekaterina V., 401
Katz, Jennifer, 424, 425, 427
Kava, Juho, 47
Keaveney, Susan M., 348
Keefe, Lisa M., 20
Keegan, Warren J., 159
Keith, Jane E., 133
Kellam, Shep, 241
Kellaris, James J., 399
Keller, Ed, 113
Keller, Kevin Lane, 159, 270
Kennedy, John, 45
Kennedy, John F., 74
Kennedy, Joyce Lain, 487
Kennedy, Marilyn Moats, 487
Kent, Robert, 400
Keribar, Izzet, 21
Kerin, Roger A., 21, 46, 47, 159, 211, 270, 296, 348, 372, 450, 451
Khadder, Tania, 239
Kher, Unmesh, 85
Kidwell, Blair, 451
Kiley, David, 187
Kim, Hyeong Min, 348
Kim, Ilchul, 372
Kim, Jooyoung, 372
Kim, Kathleen, 474
Kim, W. Chan, 46
Kimball, Brian, 297
Kirkpatrick, David, 84
Kitchen, Philip J., 372
Kiviat, Barbara, 486
Klaassen, Abbey, 400, 401
Klapper, J. T., 372
Klein, Thomas A., 85
Klie, Leonard, 84
Klum, Heidi, 333
Knight, Heather, 400
Kobe, Kathryn, 84
Koh, Yoree, 427
Kohis, L. Robert, 84
Kohli, Ajay K., 133, 450
Kollath, Carlie, 347
Konus, Umut, 348
Kopale, Praveen K., 348
Kornik, Joseph, 451
Koselka, Rita, 348
Kotabe, Masaaki, 159
Kotler, Philip, 21, 348
Kowalski, Jeff, 85
Kowitt, Beth, 21
Krattenmaker, Tom, 46
Kraus, Eric, 479
Krishna, Aradhna, 348
Krishnan, R., 348

Kroc, Ray, 340
Krugel, David, 400
Kuczmarski, Thomas D., 239
Kulsah, Damian, Jr., 427
Kumar, V., 21, 187
Kydd, Arthur R., 48, 50

L

Laezniak, Gene R., 85
Lafley, A. G., 227
Lakhani, Dave, 113
Lal, Rajiv, 347
Lane, Vicki R., 399
Lange, Jeremy M., 427
LaReau, Jamie, 372
Larocca, Tracee, 371
LaRocque, Ed, 82
Lashinsky, Adam, 239, 240
Latino, Robert, 451
Lauren, Ralph, 256, 257
Lavidge, Robert J., 372
Lavie, N., 113
Law, Stella Wai-Art, 21
Learmonth, Michael, 373, 399
Lee, Don Y., 133
Lee, Edmund, 474
Lee, Felissa, 451
Lee, Hau L., 323
Lee, Myung-Soo, 112
Lee, Sujean, 19, 21
Lee, Sun Young, 372
Lee, Thomas, 427
Lee, Yih Hwai, 399
Lee-Jac Won, 21
Lefkofsky, Eric, 111
Lehmann, Donald R., 112, 270
Leigh, Thomas W., 133
Leighton, Michael, 130, 131, 132
Lencioni, Patrick M., 46
Lenderman, Max, 474
Leno, Jay, 219
Leone, Robert P., 187, 348
Lev-Ram, Michal, 240
Levinson, Jay Conrad, 485
Levitt, Theodore, 28, 47, 450
Levy, Michael, 372
Levy, Piet, 84, 348, 372, 486
Levy, Sidney J., 21
Levy, Steven, 84
Lewin, Jeffrey E., 133, 451
Leyden, Peter, 66
Libert, Barry, 84
Lidz, Franz, 187
Lilien, Gary L., 133
Lim, Elison Ai Ching, 399
Lindstrom, Martin, 113, 169, 187
Llovio, Louis, 399
Lock, Tony, 373
Loda, Marsha D., 372
Lodish, Leonard M., 400
Lohr, Steve, 348
Lorimer, Sally E., 451
Lovallo, Dan P., 239
Lovelock, Christopher, 240
Low, George S., 372
Lowenhar, Jeffrey A., 372
Lowry, Tom, 187
Lumpkin, James R., 323

Lunden, Ingrid, 47
Lutz, Ashley, 349
Lutz, Richard J., 113
Lynch, James E., 372
Lynch, John, 113

M

Mabert, Vincent A., 240
MacArthur, Kate, 270
MacDuffie, John Paul, 323
MacInnis, Deborah J., 112, 113
Mack, John, 372
MacMillan, Douglas, 113
Mafford, Spike, 401
Magid, Larry, 47
Mahajan, Vijay, 47
Mainchillo, John, 21
Makarem, Suzanne C., 239
Malaviya, Prashant, 400
Malcolm, Robert, 46
Malhotra, Naresh, 485
Malone, Michael S., 474
Mangalindan, Mylene, 474
Manning, Eli, 101
Marcoolyn, Gillian, 112
Maremont, Mark, 187
Marken, G. A., 401
Markoff, John, 240
Marks, Ronald B., 486
Marlin, Brenda, 372
Marshall, Greg W., 450, 451
Martineau, Pierre, 337, 348
Maslow, Abraham H., 95, 113
Mason, Andrew, 110, 112
Massante, Lou, 133
Masterson, Peggy, 400
Matson, Holly, 185
Mattila, Anna S., 239
Mauborgne, Renée, 46
Maxham, James G., III, 239
May, Eleanor, 349
McCarthy, E. Jerome, 9, 21
McCartney, Scott, 297
McCorkle, Denny E., 486
McCracken, Harry, 187
McDermott, John, 47
McDonald brothers, 370
McDonald, Duff, 211
McEleny, Charlotte, 401
McElroy, Terry, 297
McGregor, Jena, 211
McGuire, Kara, 401, 427
McIsaac, Jim, 401
McMath, Robert M., 7, 21, 239
McNair, Malcolm P., 349
McRae, Matt, 272
Meindl, Peter, 323
Mendels, Pamela, 486
Mendelsohn, Bruce, 187
Menon, Anil, 85
Meric, J., 271
Mesa, Tansa, 159
Metz, Rachael, 427
Meuter, Matthew L., 239
Meyer, Christopher, 21
Mezrich, Ben, 20
Michaels, Daniel, 240
Michaels, Ian, 211
Mickelson, Phil, 298, 299
Mihas, Liz, 84
Miles, Stuart, 487

Miletsky, Jason, 426
Miller, Jennifer, 453
Miller, Steve, 323
Mindlin, Alex, 400
Miniard, Paul W., 112
Minor, Michael S., 348
Mishra, Sita, 372
Mitchell, Dan, 323
Mitchell, John T., 486
Mitral, Banwari, 112, 270
Mohammed, Rafi A., 323, 474
Mohr, Jakki J., 133, 372
Moltby, Emily, 427
Monfils, Gael, 210
Monga, Vipal, 187
Mongelluzzo, Bill, 323
Monroe, Kent B., 296, 348
Montgomery, Henrik, 401
Moon, Youngme, 133, 239
Moore, Elizabeth S., 21, 113
Moore, Janet, 46
Moore, Solomon, 427
Moore-Mezler, Colleen, 187
Moorman, Christine, 46
Morgan, Carol-Ann, 485
Morgan, Robert M., 239
Morimoto, Mariko, 373
Morin, Rich, 113
Morison, Robert, 240
Morn, John T., 239
Morris, David Paul, 373
Morrison, Maureen, 240, 373
Morrow, Thomas J., 487
Morton, Fiona Scott, 297
Mossler, Julie, 111, 112
Mothersbaugh, David L., 112, 113, 159
Mudambi, Susan M., 239
Mulhern, Francis J., 348
Mullins, John M., 211, 270
Muralie, Sushma, 372
Murphy, Jean, 323
Murphy, Patrick E., 85
Murtha, Brian R., 451
Muscove, Brenda J., 372

N

Nagarajan, Hina, 158
Nagele, Kim, 114, 115, 125, 133
Nagle, Thomas T., 271, 296
Nakashima, Ryan, 399
Narver, John C., 21
Nasheri, Hedich, 85
Nassauer, Sarah, 20
Nath, Prithwiraz, 133
Navarrete, Angel, 487
Nedungadi, Prakesh, 112
Needleman, Sarah E., 21
Neff, Jack, 187, 240, 270, 348
Nelson, Katherine A., 85
Nelson, Todd, 239
Nesdale, Andrew, 112
Neslin, Scott A., 348, 372
Netermeyer, Richard G., 239
Neumeister, Larry, 211
Newman, Andrew Adam, 348
Newsome, Layne, 272
Newstead, Kate, 399
Nicastro, Mary L., 400
Niccol, Brian, 471, 473, 474
Nickerson, Mary, 83, 85
Nohr, Marc, 373

Norris, Donald, 399
Norton, James, 239
Norton, Rob, 400
Nugent, Stuart, 325
Nussbaum, Bruce, 240

O

O'Brien, Jeffrey M., 47, 211
O'Brien, Keith, 211
O'Brien, Kyle, 19, 21
O'Malley, Kathy L., 399
O'Marah, Kevin, 323
O'Reilly, Lara, 373
Obama, Barack, 418
Ohnsman, Alan, 84
Olenski, Steve, 113
Olson, Elizabeth, 84
Olson, Jerry C., 113, 296
Olson, Scott, 241
Omoto, Yukihiro, 347
Ordonez, Jennifer, 240
Ortinau, David J., 187
Ortmeyer, Gwen, 348
Ortulay, Barbara, 239, 427
Ostlie, L. David, 228, 240
Ostrom, Amy L., 239
Ostrower, Jon, 240
Ota, Kiyoshi, 241
Ovide, Shira, 427

P

Paddison, Gordon J., 474
Page, Larry, 396–397
Palmatier, Robert W., 21, 323
Palmeri, Christopher, 211, 240
Palmisano, Samuel J., 45, 46, 47, 315
Pandit, Vivek, 239
Parasuraman, A., 239, 348
Parekh, Rupal, 113, 399, 474
Park, Bernard, 241
Park, Sehoon, 400
Parker, R. Stephen, 451
Parra, Maritza, 427
Parvatiyar, Atul, 159
Passariello, Christina, 323
Pasztor, Andy, 240
Patel, Kunur, 113
Patti, Charles G., 372
Pauwels, Koen, 47, 84
Pawson, Benn, 240
Pechman, Cornelia, 373, 399
Pelton, Lou, 323
Perdue, Stephanie, 370
Perkins, Olivera, 348
Perlman, David, 111
Perlow, Leslie, 239
Perry, Alex, 427
Perry, David E., 485
Peter, J. Paul, 113
Peters, Kevin, 348
Peters, Leah E., 50, 51
Peters, Randall F., 50, 51
Petersen, Kenneth J., 240
Peterson, Robert A., 21, 46, 47, 211, 270, 296, 348, 450
Peterson, Tim, 373
Pettijohn, Charles E., 451

Pfeifer, Phillip E., 47, 348
Pfleger, Mickey, 47
Phelps, Michael, 236
Phillips, Wendy, 133
Pieters, Rik, 112, 113, 372, 400
Podensky, Jonathan, 427
Podoshen, Jeffrey S., 239
Poetsch, Rob, 371
Poggi, Jeanine, 399
Pollak, Lindsey, 487
Pooley, Eric, 84
Poon, Derek T. Y., 401
Popeil, Ron, 383
Popky, Linda J., 486
Poroy, Denis, 373
Porras, Jerry I., 46, 47
Porter, Michael E., 46
Portillo, Ernesto, 348
Post, Tim, 487
Powell, C. Randall, 487
Powell, Michael A., 400, 476
Powers, Kemp, 296
Powers, Thomas L., 451
Poynter, Ray, 485
Prahalad, C. K., 240
Precourt, Geoffrey, 399
Prendergast, Gerard P., 372, 401
Pressel, Morgan, 298
Probst, Peter, 373
Proctor, Bernadette D., 84
Pthak, Shareen, 399
Purnawirawan, Nathalia, 401
Putrevu, Sanjay, 399

Q

Quelch, John A., 348, 400, 401

R

Radelat, Ana, 84
Raimi, Sam, 373
Raman, Kaylan, 372
Ramswamy, Venkat, 240
Rao, Vithala R., 270
Rapaport, Lisa, 47
Raskin, Oliver, 486
Rassekh, Farhad, 85
Rassouli, Javad, 372
Ratchford, Brian T., 112
Ray, Doug, 365
Ray, Ipshita, 85
Rayport, Jeffrey F., 474
Rea-Holloway, Melinda, 187
Reardon, Marguerite, 84
Rechtin, Mark, 85
Rees, G., 113
Reibling, Ellen Thomas, 373, 399
Reibstein, David J., 47, 348
Reid, Mike, 373
Reinhold, Jennifer, 133
Rendon, Jim, 21
Reinhold, Jennifer, 399
Selwitz, Robert, 399
Rich, Motoko, 211
Ridnour, Rick E., 240
Rips, David, 375
Ritson, Mark, 270
Roberts, Ira, 474
Robinson, J., 85
Rodriguez, Juan, 84
Rogers, Everett M., 270

Romaniuk, Jenni, 372, 399
Rometty, Virginia, 44
Ronkainen, Ilkka A., 159
Rosario, Antonio M., 159
Rose, Charlie, 240
Rose, Susan, 347
Rosecky, Richard B., 401
Rosen, Dennis L., 399
Rosen, Emanuel, 113
Rosenau, M. D., 239
Rosenberg, Chad, 426
Rosenthal, David W., 476
Rossi, Juhanna, 427
Rossiter, John R., 112
Roundtree, Robert I., 239
Rovell, Darren, 270
Rowling, J. K., 192
Roy, Susanna, 240
Royer, Isabelle, 239
Rozell, Elizabeth J., 451
Rubin, Ann, 46
Rubinson, Joel, 187
Ruddock, Graham, 372
Rudelius, William, 21, 50, 211, 427
Rusli, Evelyn M., 426, 427
Rust, Ronald T., 239
Ruttle, Craig, 427, 487
Rylander, Don, 187

S

Sachs, Andrea, 187
Sager, Jeffrey K., 451
Sakuma, Paul, 349
Salmon, Walter J., 348, 400
Salpeter, Miriam, 485
Samli, A. Coskun, 159
Samouel, Phillip, 347
Sanburn, Josh, 211
Saporito, Bill, 211
Sapp, Rebecca, 271
Sarel, Dan, 399
Sarkar, Dibyangshu, 487
Sauer, Abe, 239
Savita, Andrew W., 85
Sayre, Kate, 112
Schawbel, Dan, 487
Scheuing, Kristen, 297
Schmidt, Peggy, 487
Schmitt, Gnevieve, 251
Schneider, Joan, 239
Schoenbachler, Denise D., 240
Scholes, Kevan, 46
Schramm, Wilbur, 372
Schultz, Don E., 372, 373
Schultz, E. J., 399
Schumann, David W., 399
Schwager, Andre, 21
Seaquist, Carla, 84
Segal, Madhav N., 486
Seligman, Daniel, 372
Selwitz, Robert, 399
Semuels, Alana, 347
Serling, Rod, 379
Serwer, Andy, 239
Shaeffer, Leland D., 239
Shambora, Jessica, 46
Sharma, Amol, 187
Sharp, Arthur G., 487
Shasteen, Rhonda, 157, 158
Shaw, Gillian, 84

Shayon, Sheila, 427
Sheatsley, P., 372
Sheehan, Norman, 348
Sheng, Shibin, 451
Sherr, Ian, 239
Sherry, John F., Jr., 21
Shervani, Tasadduq A., 21
Shesol, Jeff, 487
Sheth, Jagdish N., 112, 159, 270, 485
Shicker, Allan D., 112
Shroer, James A., 372
Sibonu, Olivier, 239
Siegel, Lee, 113
Sightings, Tom, 84
Silva-Risso, Jorge, 297
Silverstein, Michael J., 112
Simchi-Levy, David, 323
Simchi-Levy, Edith, 323
Simester, Duncan, 348
Simon, Hermann, 297
Singer, Natasha, 426, 474
Skally, Nick, 209, 211
Skelton, Alisa, 211
Skjold, Steve, 349
Smith, A. B., 349
Smith, Cooper, 426
Smith, Craig, 427
Smith, Ethan, 323
Smith, Jessica C., 84
Smith, Katie, 399
Smith, Lindsey, 428, 429, 450
Smith, Ned, 426
Smith, Scott M., 112
Smith, Shane, 47
Soat, Molly, 399
Solomon, Michael R., 113
Somers, Suzanne, 383
Sonne, Ann Paul, 211
Sorensen, Chris, 399
Spangenberg, Eric R., 348
Speh, Thomas W., 133
Spencer, Jane, 113
Spielberg, Steven, 391
Sprott, David E., 348
Srivastava, Rajendra K., 21
Staelin, Richard, 239
Stafford, Edwin R., 84, 347
Stair, Leslie, 476
Stair, Lisa B., 476
Stanton, John L., 372
Staton, Tracy, 372
Stayman, Douglas M., 400
Steenkamp, Jans-Benedict, 348
Stein, Joel, 177, 187, 474
Steinberg, Brian, 84, 399, 400
Steiner, Christopher, 113
Steiner, Gary A., 372
Stephens, Robert, 220, 239
Stern, Louis W., 323
Sterns, Scott, 348
Stevenson, Robert Louis, 430
Stewart, David, 399
Sthanunathan, Stan, 478
Stock, Kyle, 240
Stock, Sue, 427
Stone, Brad, 113, 240, 323, 427
Strauss, Judy, 474
Stroebe, W., 113
Strom, Andrea, 219
Strom, Brian, 219
Strunk, William, Jr., 50
Strutton, David, 323
Stuckey, Brian, 427

Sullivan, Anthony, 383
Sullivan, Elisabeth A., 240
Sullivan, Jim, 401
Summers, Kimmy, 402
Suri, Rajneesh, 348
Suter, Tracy A., 187, 240
Swait, Joffre, 270
Swaminathan, Srinivasan, 400
Swank, Hilary, 160
Swanson, Dana, 238
Swartz, Teresa, 239
Swenson, Linda, 47
Swink, Morgan L., 240
Swinmurn, Nick, 188
Swire, Donald, 47
Szymanski, D., 159

Talukdar, Debabrata, 112
Tan, Chong Leng, 399
Tan, Gillian, 20
Tanner, John F., Jr., 133, 399, 450
Tauber, Michelle, 186
Taylor, Victoria, 474
Teinowitz, Ira, 347
Teixeira, Ruy, 66
Tellefsen, Thomas, 133
Terpstra, Vern, 85
Tesfaye, Bizuayehu, 211
Tew, C., 85
Thakor, Mrugank V., 348
Thomas, Carl, 236
Thomas, Dave, 170, 198
Thomas, Ian, 347
Thompson, Debora Viana, 239, 400
Till, Brian D., 400
Tillotson, Kristin, 240, 426
Tobin, Lucy, 85
Tomkovick, Chuck, 399
Toole, Christa, 427
Toyli, Jukka, 47
Toyoda, Kiichiro, 81
Trachtenberg, Jeffrey A., 211
Traczyk, Patty, 399
Treacy, Michael, 21
Trevino, Linda K., 85
Tripathy, Sudipta, 425
Tripplaar, Kristofer, 323, 349
Trudel, Remi, 85
Trumbull, Mark, 84
Tsang, Alex S. L., 401
Tsukayama, Hayley, 427
Tsuno, Yoshikazu, 85
Tufte, Edward R., 47
Tuli, Kapil R., 450
Turner, Daniel, 240
Turow, Joseph, 474
Tuttle, Brad, 347
Twain, Mark, 176

Ulrich, Karl T., 240
Ulukaya, Hamdi, 2, 3, 18, 19
Ulwick, Anthony W., 240
Urbany, Joel E., 112

Useem, Jerry, 348
Usunier, Jean Claude, 159

V

Vachon, Francis, 241
Valenzuela, Ana, 270
Vallaeys, Frederick, 397–398
Van Brussel, Joe, 46
Van Heck, Eric, 133
Vance, Ashley, 84, 426
Vanderkam, Laura, 84
Vandermark, Rob, 452
Vanhuele, Marc, 348
Varadarajan, P. Rajan, 47, 85, 159
Vascellaro, Jessica E., 187, 401
Vega, Tanzina, 427
Vekatesh, R., 133
Velsaco, Schuyler, 401
Vence, Deborah L., 486
Verhoef, Peter C., 348
Vernon, Paul, 187
Veverka, Mark, 323
Viglielmo, Pamela, 159
Viguerie, S. Patrick, 239
Vitner, Mark, 84
Viveiros, Beth Negus, 373
Voitle, Jenifer, 168
Von Jutrczenka, Bernd, 401
Voss, Glenn B., 348
Vournas, Dino, 241
Vranica, Suzanne, 187, 427

W

Wagner, Kurt, 270
Wakabayashi, Daisuke, 239
Walker, Helen, 133
Walker, Orville C., Jr., 211, 270
Walsh, James, 46
Walsh, Meghan, 20
Walsh, Patrick B., 486
Wanamaker, John, 387
Wang, William, 272
Wang, Yong Jian, 348
Ward, James C., 348
Warren, Kevin, 450
Webb, Tom, 348
Weber, Joseph, 240
Weber, Karl, 85
Webster, Frederick E., Jr., 133
Webster, John, 372
Wedel, Michel, 348, 372, 400
Wei, Jie, 348
Weidenhamer, Deanna, 347
Weigold, Michael F., 400
Weilbaker, Dan C., 240
Weiner, Jonah, 427
Weinstein, Art, 47
Weisal, Kimberly, 211
Weiss, Allen, 84
Weiss, Bari, 113
Weitz, Barton A., 21, 133, 450
Welch, David, 84, 270
Welch, Jack, 486
Welch, Suzy, 486
Wells, Georgia, 427
Wensley, Robin, 21

Wernle, Bradford, 372
West, Susan, 399
White, E. B., 50
White, Michael, 187
Whittemore, C. B., 187
Wiener, Joshua L., 401
Wiersema, Fred, 21
Wiles, Michael A., 347
Wilkie, William L., 21, 112, 113, 399
Williams, Robin M., Jr., 84
Williams, Stephanie, 239
Wilsey, Sean, 239
Wilson, James Q., 85
Wilson, Rick T., 400
Wind, Yoram, 47, 133
Windorski, David, 11–13
Winer, Russell S., 270
Winfrey, Oprah, 13
Winter, Rebecca, 211
Winters, Lewis C., 399
Wirtz, Jochen, 240
Wittington, Richard, 46
Woelbing, Alfred, 172, 294
Woelbing, Don, 294
Woelbing, Eric, 294–295
Woelbing, Paul, 294, 296
Woellert, Lorraine, 323
Wolfman, Ian, 268, 473–474
Wong, Anthony, 133
Wong, Vanessa, 373
Wood, Molly, 239
Woodside, Arch G., 400
Worstall, Tim, 323
Wouters, Marijke, 401

Y

Yalch, Richard, 113
Yate, Martin
Yi-Zheng Shi, 372
Yikur, Rama, 399
Yin, Sara, 400
Yong Zhang, 399
Yoon, Hye Jin, 372
Yu, Roger, 240
Yue, Lorene, 349

Z

Zakarin, Jordan, 347
Zale, Joseph, 271, 296
Zaltman, Gerald, 133
Zamiska, Nicholas, 211
Zbar, Jeffrey D., 399
Zeithaml, Valerie A., 112, 239, 271, 296
Zettelemeyer, Florian, 297
Zhang, Xiaoquan (Michael), 347
Zhao, Guangzhi, 373, 399
Zidansek, Manja, 348
Zimmer, Mary R., 348
Zinkham, George M., 399
Zirkle, Michael, 239
Zmuda, Natalie, 211, 399, 426
Zoltners, Andris, 451
Zuckerberg, Mark, 4, 62, 63, 407, 409

Online Supplements

Connect Online Access for Marketing: The Core, Sixth Edition

McGraw-Hill Connect is a digital teaching and learning environment that improves performance over a variety of critical outcomes. With Connect, instructors can deliver assignments, quizzes and tests easily online. Students can practice important skills at their own pace and on their own schedule.

HOW TO REGISTER

Using a <u>Print Book</u>?
To register and activate your Connect account, simply follow these easy steps:
1. **Go to the Connect course web address provided by your instructor or visit the Connect link set up on your instructor's course within your campus learning management system.**
2. **Click on the link to register.**
3. **When prompted, enter the Connect code found on the inside back cover of your book and click Submit. Complete the brief registration form that follows to begin using Connect.**

Using an <u>eBook</u>?
To register and activate your Connect account, simply follow these easy steps:
1. **Upon purchase of your eBook, you will be granted automatic access to Connect.**
2. **Go to the Connect course web address provided by your instructor or visit the Connect link set up on your instructor's course within your campus learning management system.**
3. **Sign in using the same email address and password you used to register on the eBookstore. Complete your registration and begin using Connect.**

Note: Access Code is for one use only. If you did not purchase this book new, the access code included in this book is no longer valid.

Need help? Visit mhhe.com/support

Online Supplements

Connect Online Access for Marketing: The Core, Sixth Edition

McGraw-Hill Connect is a digital teaching and learning environment that improves performance over a variety of critical outcomes. With Connect, instructors can deliver assignments, quizzes and tests easily online. Students can practice important skills at their own pace and on their own schedule.

HOW TO REGISTER

Using a <u>Print Book</u>?
To register and activate your Connect account, simply follow these easy steps:
1. **Go to the Connect course web address provided by your instructor or visit the Connect link set up on your instructor's course within your campus learning management system.**
2. **Click on the link to register.**
3. **When prompted, enter the Connect code found on the inside back cover of your book and click Submit. Complete the brief registration form that follows to begin using Connect.**

Using an <u>eBook</u>?
To register and activate your Connect account, simply follow these easy steps:
1. **Upon purchase of your eBook, you will be granted automatic access to Connect.**
2. **Go to the Connect course web address provided by your instructor or visit the Connect link set up on your instructor's course within your campus learning management system.**
3. **Sign in using the same email address and password you used to register on the eBookstore. Complete your registration and begin using Connect.**

Note: Access Code is for one use only. If you did not purchase this book new, the access code included in this book is no longer valid.

Need help? Visit mhhe.com/support